FORENSIC AND INVESTIGATIVE ACCOUNTING

D. Larry Crumbley, CPA, CFF, MAFF, Cr.FA

KPMG Endowed Professor
Department of Accounting
Louisiana State University

Lester E. Heitger, CPA

BKD Distinguished Professor of Forensic Accounting
School of Accountancy
Missouri State University

G. Stevenson Smith, CPA, CMA

John Massey Endowed Professor of Accounting
Department of Accounting and Finance
Southeastern Oklahoma State University

Wolters Kluwer
CCH

Chapter 17 includes material adapted from *CCH Business Valuation Guide* by George B. Hawkins, ASA, CFA and Michael A. Paschall, ASA, CFA, J.D.

Editorial Staff

Technical Reviewers .... Bill Sipes, CPA/ABV, BVAL,
David L. Gibberman, J.D.,
Michael Elia, J.D.,
Robert J. Collins, CPA
Editor .... Lynn Kopon, J.D., LL.M.
Production........................... Don Torres, Lou Dagostino
Cover Design .... Laila Gaidulis

ISBN 978-0-8080-3487-2

Printed in the United States of America

Certified Chain of Custody
Promoting Sustainable Forestry
www.sfiprogram.org
SFI-00712

The SFI logo applies to the text and cover stock.

PREFACE

Forensic and Investigative Accounting fills a void in accounting education literature by providing the first broad-based text covering all the important topics that have come to be identified with modern forensic accounting. Certainly, there are books on fraud auditing, litigation support, valuation (both damages and businesses), cybercrime and other key forensic topics, but no other text is specifically written to cover the forensic accounting waterfront. The authors hope that teachers will find *Forensic and Investigative Accounting 6th Edition* a particularly powerful teaching tool. The twin towers of forensic accounting—litigation support and investigative auditing—are covered in detail. The 6th Edition includes the 2011 Forensic and Valuation Services Trend Survey, Foreign Corrupt Practices Act, more information about the AICPA's Certified in Financial Forensics, Financial Fraud Enforcement Task Force, Transparency International Index 2012, Financial Secrecy Index, Center for Audit Quality suggestions, well designed hotline programs, unfunded pension plans, interview room arrangements, Up-John warnings, Clawback provisions, fraud prevention using narrative disclosures, 2012 Wells Report, five disbursement fraud tests, KPMG's Who Is the Typical Fraudster Survey, IIA Practice Guide, social engineering, Ernst & Young 12th Global Fraud Survey, piercing the corporate veil, different types of witnesses, more eyewitnesses and spotlight stories, and new problems and cases. This edition brings the reader up to date with the latest cybercrime activity and cases, and it documents the latest corruption schemes and explains how to find and prevent them.

Please visit *http://www.cchgroup.com/Resources* for any periodic updates or clarifications that may become available related to the 6th Edition of *Forensic and Investigative Accounting* as well CCH's Daily Tax Day News, Tax Briefings and other items of interest.

Today's forensic accounting teachers and students have a difficult task in studying this developing topic, but they are compensated by the fact that forensic accounting is red hot and relevant. In 2002, Congress took up the financial markets reform mantle and passed the Sarbanes-Oxley Act, which was in part designed to restore financial accountability by preventing and punishing fraud. The Act created a new independent accounting oversight group called the Public Company Accounting Oversight Board (PCAOB), subject to Securities and Exchange Commission review. Sarbanes-Oxley, recent SEC actions, initiatives starting to take shape from the PCAOB, aggressive pronouncements by the Institute of Internal Auditors and the AICPA, and new rules promulgated by the various stock exchanges have all worked to change the perception of who is responsible for detecting and fighting fraud in financial statements and throughout the corporation and other entities. External auditors, internal auditors, company management, and audit committees are all charged in one way or another with fighting fraud under new initiatives. Yet, the task of fraud detection has proven so difficult (e.g., Bernard Madoff, Sir Robert Allen Stanford, Satyam Computer Services) that the continued growth in forensic accounting specialists seems assured along with the development of the forensic accounting discipline to match wits with new advanced technological and fraud schemes. The federal government's economic stimulus and bailout programs and the shortfalls in many states' budgets should provide much work for forensic accountants.

Students and teachers alike will find that forensic accounting also is extremely interesting, and the authors of *Forensic and Investigative Accounting 6th Edition* worked hard to build a sense of interest and yes, even excitement into the text. Some would argue that forensic accountants are more like "Quincy" (a once popular TV show about a crime-solving coroner) or the CSI characters than the traditional starch-collared, numbers-cruncher. Forensic accountants work on books and records, but often in the context of legal conflicts and even criminal activities.

Forensic and Investigative Accounting 6th Edition demonstrates that this developing discipline is challenging. As the text demonstrates, an effective forensic accountant needs an understanding of accounting, investigative auditing techniques, computers, criminology, and courtroom procedures. Many forensic accountants will further specialize and have varying concentrations of these five sets of knowledge and skills.

All three authors are teachers, forensic accountants, and perhaps most of all, forensic accounting fans. While there are many complex forensic issues explained in this book, the authors worked hard to try to convey to students the contemporaneous nature of forensic accounting—forensic accounting is constantly developing in the news, in the legal and regulatory system, and as part of the accounting industry.

The authors believe that forensic accounting should be fun to teach and with the many internet-related assignments in the chapter exercises, students are encouraged to continue to seek out new stories and developments as they occur. Of course, studying a discipline that is experiencing such dramatic change will be challenging. However, there are plenty of fundamental concepts and topics that require a good deal of earnest attention and concentration that will help keep both students and teachers anchored to reality.

In today's climate all accountants—external, internal, corporate accountants and yes, the forensic-accounting specialist—must develop forensic competencies. The authors believe it will only be a matter of time before all accounting majors will take one or more forensic-type courses. The authors agree with James Gordon Brown, Prime Minister of England, that "what the use of finger prints was to the 19th century and DNA analysis was to the 20th, forensic accounting will be to the 21st century."

June 2013

D. Larry Crumbley
Lester E. Heitger
G. Stevenson Smith

About the Authors

Professor D. Larry Crumbley, CPA, MAFF, Cr.FA, CFF, is the KPMG Endowed Professor in the Department of Accounting, Louisiana State University. He has published more than 350 articles in accounting journals and authored more than 60 books, including 13 educational novels, including *The Big R: A Forensic Accounting Action Adventure*. He is the long-time editor of the *Oil, Gas & Energy Quarterly* and founding editor of the *Journal of Forensic Accounting: Auditing, Fraud & Risk*. Professor Crumbley was a member of the AICPA's Litigation and Dispute Resolution Services Subcommittee Fraud Task Force and is on the Fraud Deterrence Board of National Association of Certified Valuation Analysts. He has served on the Executive Board of the American Board of Forensic Accounting (ACFEI). He was the organizer of and first president of the Forensic & Investigative Accounting section in the AAA. He is the editor of the *Journal of Forensic and Investigative Accounting*.

Professor Lester E. Heitger, CPA, taught for many years in the Accounting Department at Indiana University in Bloomington, Indiana. While there, he created and taught a graduate level course in Forensic and Investigative Accounting. In the fall of 2008, he accepted the position as the BKD Distinguished Professor of Forensic Accounting in the School of Accountancy at Missouri State University. There he has developed and teaches several forensic accounting courses, and he has helped develop a Certificate in Forensic Accounting in the graduate accounting program. He served as a member of the task force funded by the United State Justice Department, White Collar Crimes Division that created the "Model Curriculum in Forensic Accounting." Professor Heitger has been very active in litigation support and expert witnessing over the past 25 years. He has worked as a forensic accountant on over 50 cases testifying as an expert witness in state and federal courts and in the United State Tax Court. He has also testified in alternative dispute resolution environments such as arbitrations and mediations. He continues to be very active as an expert witness and as a litigation support specialist. In May 2013, Professor Heitger was elected national Vice President/President Elect of the Forensic and Investigative Accounting (FIA) section of the American Accounting Association. In 2014, Professor Heitger also will become the Chair of the Higher Education Initiative Committee of the ACFE.

G. Stevenson Smith is the John Massey Endowed Professor of Accounting and Head of the Department of Accounting and Finance in the John Massey School of Business at Southeastern Oklahoma State University. He is a CMA and a CPA. Professor Smith received his Ph.D. from the University of Arkansas and his M.B.A. from Michigan State University. Dr. Smith has authored three books dealing with financial management for the American Library Association. His most recent title is , *Cost Control for Nonprofits in Crisis* (ALA 2011) He has authored numerous articles on forensic accounting that have been published in *Journal of Forensic Accounting, Journal of Financial Fraud, Fraud Magazine, Digital Investigation, and the Journal of Digital Forensics, Security and Law*. His HTCIA White Paper on RFID received the Best Paper Award at the HTCIA's International Conference in 2007. His professional experience includes working for the Securities and Exchange Commission in Washington, D.C., as a financial analyst. He has been a Visiting Professor at the University of Victoria in Wellington, New Zealand and a Visiting Fellow at the University of New England in Armdale, Australia. In 2011, he was a Fulbright Scholar at the University of Pula in Croatia, where he lectured and developed research on forensic issues in Eastern Europe.

ACKNOWLEDGMENTS

CaseWare IDEA Inc. provided students with access to the demo version of IDEA® – Data Analysis Software and support resources. Audimation Services, Inc., a CaseWare partner and the U.S. distributor of CaseWare IDEA® contributed a case study and corresponding data sets. Additional information is available at *www.audimation.com/academic*.

IDEA companion for the Tallahassee Bean Counter problem provided by Audimation Services, Inc., a CaseWare partner and the U.S. distributor of IDEA®.

Data sets and accompanying documentation for the HR Project in Chapter 13 provided by Audimation Services, Inc., a CaseWare partner and the U.S. distributor of IDEA®.

Chapter 18 project is adapted from the case article by Brian Ballou, Associate Professor, Miami University; Jennifer Mueller, Assistant Professor, Auburn University; and Paul Zikmund, Director Forensic Audit, Tyco International (US) Inc. and is included here with permission of the authors and the Journal Of Forensic Accounting, Vol. V (September 2004), pp. 433-456.

Chapter 18 project is adapted from, Carol Callaway Dee and Cindy Durtschi, "Return of the Tallahassee BeanCounters: A Case in Forensic Accounting," Issues In Accounting Education, Vol. 25, No. 2., pp. 279-321, and is included here with permission from The American Accounting Association. The full text of many AAA articles are available online at *http://aaapubs.org/*.

Finally, we'd like to thank our fellow instructors who adopt this book and the students who support our efforts.

D. Larry Crumbley
Lester E. Heitger
G. Stevenson Smith

HOW TO USE THIS BOOK

Forensic and Investigative Accounting is organized to engage students in the study of forensic accounting. Special features, end-of-chapter exercises, appendices, and a forensic glossary are provided to further assist students in the learning process.

Chapter Openings

All chapters begin with the same elements: a list of the learning objectives and an overview. This information provides a framework for understanding the material that will be studied in the chapter.

Special Features

Hundreds of forensic stories, featured factoids, and illustrations are interjected throughout the chapters.

 Eyewitness features are typically descriptive short snippets expressing a forensic event, action, or slant on an issue.

 Spotlight features are used to interject a longer story in the forensic news or a statement on a forensic concept.

 Ethics features are used when a forensic related standard or ethics-related authority is reproduced.

 Law and Order features identify a legal case or regulatory ruling.

 Examples are used when a specific situation is used to illustrate an important point.

End-of-Chapter Materials

Every chapter ends with a conclusion that ties together the ideas presented in the chapter and with the chapter opening and overview help to give students a point of reference for additional study. End of chapter exercises are used to help the student assess his or her understanding of the chapter's salient points. Some will help direct the student to additional research. The exercises also provide the instructor with a ready means to evaluate student understanding of the material.

End-of-Book Materials

A special forensic glossary is offered at the end of the book that can be referenced throughout the student's reading. Appendices offer additional source materials for extended reading and research.

Website

Please visit *http://www.cchgroup.com/Resources* for any periodic updates or clarifications that may become available related to the 6th Edition of *Forensic and Investigative Accounting* as well as CCH's Daily Tax Day News, Tax Briefings and other items of interest.

CONTENTS

A detailed Table of Contents for each chapter begins on page xi.

Page

Part 1: The Field and Practice of Forensic Accounting

Chapter 1   Introduction to Forensic and Investigative Accounting 1-1

Chapter 2   Forensic Accounting Education, Institutions, and Specialties 2-1

Part 2: Uncovering Accounting Crime

Chapter 3   Fraudulent Financial Reporting 3-1

Chapter 4   Detecting Fraud in Financial Reporting 4-1

Chapter 5   Employee Fraud: The Misappropriation of Assets 5-1

Chapter 6   Indirect Methods of Reconstructing Income....................................6-1

Chapter 7   Money Laundering and Transnational Financial Flows.................7-1

Part 3: Courtroom Procedures and Litigation Support

Chapter 8   Litigation Services Provided by Accountants 8-1

Chapter 9   Proper Evidence Management 9-1

Chapter 10   Commercial Damages 10-1

Chapter 11   Litigation Support in Special Situations 11-1

Chapter 12   Computing Economic Damages 12-1

Part 4: Cybercrime

Chapter 13   Investigation of Electronic Data: A Brief Introduction 13-1

Chapter 14   Digital Forensics Analysis..14-1

Chapter 15   Cybercrime Management: Legal Issues 15-1

Chapter 16   Cybercrime Loss Valuations 16-1

Part 5: Business Valuations

Chapter 17   Business Valuations 17-1

Part 6: Forensic Capstone Illustration

Chapter 18   Forensic Accounting in Action..18-1

  Appendices A-1

  Glossary of Terms G-1

  Topical Index I-1

TABLE OF CONTENTS

CHAPTER 3   **FRAUDULENT FINANCIAL REPORTING**

CHAPTER 4   **DETECTING FRAUD IN FINANCIAL REPORTING**

CHAPTER 5

EMPLOYEE FRAUD: THE MISAPPROPRIATION OF ASSETS

CHAPTER 6　　　INDIRECT METHODS OF RECONSTRUCTING INCOME

CHAPTER 7　　　MONEY LAUNDERING AND TRANSNATIONAL FINANCIAL FLOWS

CHAPTER 8   LITIGATION SERVICES PROVIDED BY ACCOUNTANTS

CHAPTER 9 **PROPER EVIDENCE MANAGEMENT**

CHAPTER 10 **COMMERCIAL DAMAGES**

CHAPTER 11   LITIGATION SUPPORT IN SPECIAL SITUATIONS

CHAPTER 12   COMPUTING ECONOMIC DAMAGES

CHAPTER 16   CYBERCRIME LOSS VALUATIONS

CHAPTER 17   BUSINESS VALUATIONS

CHAPTER 18 — FORENSIC ACCOUNTING IN ACTION

APPENDICES

GLOSSARY
OF TERMS

TOPICAL INDEX

Please visit *http://www.cchgroup.Com/resources* for any periodic updates or clarifications that may become available related to the 6th edition of *Forensic and Investigative Accounting* as well CCH's *Daily Tax Day* news, tax briefings and other items of interest.

PART 1

THE FIELD AND PRACTICE OF FORENSIC ACCOUNTING

1

INTRODUCTION TO FORENSIC AND INVESTIGATIVE ACCOUNTING

With the virtual media cottage industry blooming on the corpse of bankrupt Enron and its complicated array of alleged financial shenanigans, could it be just a matter of time before some television executive plots a new drama starring…forensic accountants?

—Catherine Valenti, ABCnews.com[1]

OBJECTIVES

After completing Chapter 1, you should be able to:
1. Distinguish forensic accounting from fraud auditing.
2. Understand the definition of forensic accounting.
3. Understand the threads of accounting history and other commercial developments that led to the creation of today's forensic accounting.
4. Understand how public auditing trends may have led to accounting scandals.
5. View the parallel developments of formal accounting practice, accounting literature, and forensic and investigative accounting.

OVERVIEW

Although forensic accounting is not a new discipline, it is one that is rapidly developing and gaining status in the accounting and legal communities. The media have been energetically covering accounting scandals and intrigues, which are often characterized as the forensic accountant's "beat." If the number of articles written on the topic is any indication, readers of such esteemed newspapers as *The Wall Street Journal* and *The New York Times* are captivated by the forensic accounting topic. The good news for accounting students is that if current trends persist, forensic accounting and its many subspecialties will provide some very interesting and lucrative career opportunities.

Accountants, long the butt of bean-counter jokes, are viewed a bit differently these days. Major scandals certainly have tarnished the image of the accountant, but the "forensic accountant" is getting a lot of respect. Gordon Brown, then the British Chancellor of the Exchequer, on October 10, 2006, said that "what the use of finger prints was to the 19th century and DNA analysis was to the 20th, forensic accounting will be to the 21st century."

His partner in the movie, *The Other Guys*, asks Allen Gamble (played by Will Ferrell) a detective/forensic accountant this question:

> Terry: So you think he is dealing in drugs?
>
> Allen: No! It's not drugs! It's not murder! It's economies influx, shadow banking, and offshore accounts. We're going to have to do paperwork, due diligence, and financial ledgers.

After the terrorist attacks of September 11, 2001, it was determined that a number of the perpetrators used debit cards that had been set up by cash—largely untraceable—brought into the country. There were even some transactions with no moving money, possibly using offsetting receivables and payables, that were still traceable.[2] The FBI agents employed forensic-type techniques when looking at credit cards, phone records, and interviews with terrorists' neighbors and friends. Shutting down the cash flowing into the terrorists' network was accomplished using financial sleuths.

Accounting also made the big screen, and its new notoriety has been satirized in the popular media. A short film entitled *The Accountant* won an Academy Award in March 2002. The hard-drinking, chain-smoking backwoods movie accountant cynically states that "numbers and facts are already fudged here and there; it's called accounting." Leon Martel (played by Tracy Howe), a forensic accountant, has been a recurring character in three "Law and Order" series: the original, "Law and Order: Criminal Intent," and "Law and Order: SVU." A Jack Ziegler cartoon in the March 10, 2002, *New Yorker* magazine shows a couple of women at a bar with one telling the other that "being an accountant gives him that extra aura of danger."[3]

These may be unwelcome visions of accounting, but they point out that accounting—and forensic accounting in particular—is not only noteworthy, but newsworthy. In light of the notoriety and scandal, one movie analogy does seem appropriate: Similar to the agents in the film *Men in Black*, the forensic accountant's armory must be equipped with talent to suit every purpose, from detecting cooked books, to kiting, to money laundering. As Al Pacino said in the movie *The Recruit*, "Things are not what you think they are." Is your business losing money to fraud like pop flies in the baseball stands?

This chapter provides a broad definition of forensic accounting and creates a frame of reference for students to read and understand the rest of the book. Upon tracing the threads of forensic accounting through its history and development, students will understand forensic accounting to be a challenging discipline that substantially interacts with economics, finance, information systems, and the law. Terry McCarthy, audit partner with Green & Seifter, "liken[s] it to 'CSI' or 'Law & Order,' but instead of figuring out the trajectory of a bullet, you're trying to find out how a transaction occurred."[5]

After reading and studying our textbook, we hope people cannot say the following about forensic accountants and auditors:

"The bad guys are a lot slicker today," I said.

"They ain't no slicker, son. The good guys are just dumber."[6]

Remember, there are only three things certain in life: death, taxes, and fraud.

Definition and Development of Forensic Accounting

¶ 1001   ## DEFINING FORENSIC ACCOUNTING

Many people believe forensic accounting and fraud auditing are synonymous. They are not. A fraud auditor is an accountant specially skilled in auditing who is generally engaged in auditing with a view toward fraud discovery, documentation, and prevention. A forensic accountant may take on fraud auditing engagements and may in fact be a fraud auditor, but he or she will also use other accounting, consulting, and legal skills in broader engagements. In addition to the accounting and investigative skills that should certainly be present in the fraud auditor, the forensic accountant needs a working knowledge of the legal system and excellent quantitative analysis and communication skills to carry out expert testimony in the courtroom and to aid in other litigation support engagements.

Bruce Dubinsky, a partner in Klausner, Dubinsky & Associates, stresses their broad approach by emphasizing that there are plenty of accountants getting involved who should not be involved in the niche. "'The only limit to our size is finding competent professionals.' He explains that just being an accountant is no longer enough to do this work—the person has to understand the legal system, and what the law says. How to interrogate and interview people are musts. Tracking leads and obtaining legally usable intelligence is also crucial. 'Many accountants think it is simply fraud investigation and it's not. It really is much more than dealing with the numbers. It's no longer just basic fraud work.'"[7]

Robert Overbaugh, a partner at Pittsburgh-based Sisterson & Co., is more blunt. He asserts that "forensic accounting is often thought of, in somewhat narrow terms, as dealing with the investigations of fraud or financial misconduct." His firm thinks in broad terms and performs engagements in most areas in which attorneys use financial experts in litigation and disputes.[8] To put it another way, a forensic accountant reduces the complexity by distilling information and slicing away deceptions to help a judge or jury to see the essence of a financial dispute.[9]

In a 2011 Forensic and Valuation Services Trend Survey the practitioners were involved in these main niches:[10]

Valuation	21%
Fraud prevention, detection, and response	20%
Economic damages	19%
Family Law	14%
Financial statement misrepresentations	13%
Bankruptcy and insolvency	8%
Computer forensic analysis	4%
Others	1%

Of the respondents, 42 percent had spent up to 24 percent of their time on forensic services. A total of 47 percent had spent more time on forensic work during the past year with an average increase of 20 percent.

Forensic accountants provide perspective in situations evaluating whether accounting information is presented fairly without GAAP-based constraints, such as:

- Identification of financial issues.
- Knowledge of investigating techniques.
- Knowledge of evidence.
- Interpretation of financial information.
- Presentation of finding.[11]

James Edwards, the former publisher of the *Journal of Forensic Accounting*, championed this broad definition rather than the narrow fraud examination definition. He believes that forensic accountants are employed to seek, interpret, and communicate transactional and reporting event evidence in an objective, legally sustainable fashion, not only in situations in which there are specific allegations of wrongdoing, but also in situations in which interested parties judge that the risk of loss from wrongdoing is such that proper prudence requires legally sustainable evidence to support the conclusion that no wrongdoing is occurring.

Concisely defined, *forensic accounting* is the use of accounting for legal purposes. Hal Rosenthal gives the modern definition of forensic accounting as "the use of intelligence-gathering techniques and accounting/business skills to develop information and opinion for use by attorneys involved in civil litigation and give trial testimony if called upon."[12] But in order to establish a context for understanding all the various forensic activities that are associated with forensic accounting today, this book uses a more expansive definition.

FORENSIC ACCOUNTING SERVICES DEFINED. An AICPA committee says that "forensic accounting services generally involve the application of special skills in accounting, auditing, finance, quantitative methods, certain areas of the law and research, and investigative skills to collect, analyze, and evaluate evidential matter and to interpret and communicate findings, and may involve either an attest or consulting engagement."[13]

Forensic

First, to many readers *forensic* may bring to mind a popular academic activity called "forensics" where students from different schools face off in various contests of argumentative and oratorical skill. In fact the term "forensic" refers to items that are used in debate or argument, such as items used in public debate or forum. In commerce or business, things forensic are generally those things that relate to a legal forum or court.

Accounting

Accounting students know that there are many definitions of accounting. For some it is the language of business; for others it is quantifying data for financial purposes—setting up accounts for things. Taken in a broad sense, accounting refers to many activities that relate to financial accounts. Although not all-inclusive, these include identifying, recording, settling, extracting, sorting, reporting, and verifying financial data.

When the terms *accounting* and *forensic* are placed together, however, the sum is greater than its parts. Implicitly, there are a few other factors to incorporate in the definition: time, purpose, and peremptory.

Time

Most students are familiar with the term *forensic medicine*. Forensic medicine focuses on events that have happened—the cause of illness or death—an analysis of the evidence surrounding trauma that has occurred in the past. Forensic accounting also looks at things past, but it should be noted that some of its most challenging tasks require projections into the future.

Forensic accountants who value a business, for example, may examine past history, but they often project out in time to look at future cash flows. When a forensic accountant is engaged to determine the monetary loss to a family for harm done to a working mother, he or she may look at past earnings but projects future earnings lost. Forensic accounting focuses on the past, although it may do so in order to look forward.

Purpose

Purpose also is important. Forensic accounting is accounting performed in some circumstances for a specific legal forum; in other circumstances it is accounting performed in anticipation of presentation before a formal forum. One could argue that all accounting work might presuppose that work performed may be destined for review or argument in a legal forum, but the forensic purpose is more explicit.

Peremptory

Forensic accountants also are engaged in preventing fraud. Just as a physician may recommend certain preventative health measures for healthy patients, the forensic accountant might be called in as a preemptive strike to manage fraud risk. Forensic accountants may be employed in a wide variety of risk management engagements within business enterprises as a matter of right, without the necessity of allegations (e.g., proactive). For example, a forensic accountant may take a preventive approach as a result of normal operations (e.g., review of internal controls or identify areas of fraud exposure). There is no reason to suspect fraud. Second, a forensic accountant may be used to detect indicia of fraud.[14]

Thus, it's possible to construct a good broad working definition for forensic accounting that reflects real-world use of the term.

Forensic Accounting Defined

Forensic accounting is the action of identifying, recording, settling, extracting, sorting, reporting, and verifying past financial data or other accounting activities for settling current or prospective legal disputes or using such past financial data for projecting future financial data to settle legal disputes.

A CLOSER LOOK AT FORENSIC TEAMS. In 2006, Ernst & Young's forensic team was comprised of 350 practitioners in the United States alone and focused on strategies to mitigate and manage conflict in bankruptcy disputes, financial and economic damages, fraud and investigations, government contracts and grants, insurance claims, intellectual assets, and legal technology.[15] Today Ernst & Young has more than 1,700 team members and 100 partners in fraud investigations and dispute professionals around the world.

According to Frank Piantidosi, chairman and chief executive of Deloitte Financial Advisory Services (FAS), their "forensic accounting expertise includes anti-money laundering, the Foreign Corrupt Practices Act, purchase price disputes, arbitrations, construction fraud, health care fraud, construction oversight, intellectual property theft, and misdirected royalty revenues, to name just a few."

"'We have forensic labs in nine major cities across the U.S. and an additional 18 cities around the world, including Hong Kong, London, Amsterdam, Frankfurt, Cape Town and Melbourne,' he said, adding that all FAS labs meet the FBI's chain of custody requirements. 'They are secure, state-of-the-art, and house advanced systems for storing and accessing data, including dedicated servers and fire-resistant safes.'"[16]

Distinction Between Forensic Audit and Financial Audit

A forensic audit is often different than a typical financial audit. A financial audit is generally a sampling activity that does not look at every transaction. Thus, the system can be exploited by someone, such as an executive, who knows how to "cook the books."

A forensic audit looks at the detail of a specific aspect of the records, trying to determine why everything does not or should not add up. Thus, a forensic audit is much more time-consuming and can be significantly more expensive than a regular financial audit.[17] Doug Carmichael, former Chief Auditor for PCAOB, faults auditors for not adopting forensic techniques. He prefers more tests of detail rather than relying on tests of controls.[18]

Ronald L. Durkin suggests the following differences in a forensic audit versus a traditional audit:

- Not limiting the scope of the engagement based upon materiality.
- Not accepting sampling as evidence.
- Not assuming management has integrity.
- Seeking the best legal evidence.
- Melding the requirements of the evidential matter standard with the rules of evidence.[19]

Two practitioners have suggested these additional procedures may be used in a forensic audit:[20]

- Extensive use of *interviews* and leveraging techniques designed to elicit sufficient information to prove or disprove a hypothesis.
- Document *inspection* that may extend to authentication procedures and handwriting analysis.
- Significant *public records* search to uncover, for example, unexpected title or ownership, other known addresses, and prior records of individuals.
- Legal knowledge regarding *rules of evidence* including chain of custody and preservation of evidence integrity.

Table 1.0 contrasts auditing, forensic accounting, and fraud examination.[21]

Table 1.0. Contrast Auditing, Forensic Accounting, and Fraud Examination

Characteristic:	Audit	Fraud Examination	Forensic Accounting
Time Perspective:	Historical	Historical	Future and Historical
Primary Focus:	Periodic	Reactive	Proactive and Ongoing
Investigation Scope:	Narrow	Narrow	Broad Ranging
Main Work Product is:	Audit Opinion	Fraud Case Report	Forensic Audit Report
Main Responsibility to:	Company and Public	Defrauded party	Concerned principal or third party
Guidelines are:	Rules-based	Principles-based; under audit rules, it is rules-based	Principles-based
Purpose of Report:	Ensure GAAP is followed	Identify perpetrator of fraud	Fraud Risk Assessment and Strategic Services
Professional Stance:	Non-adversarial	Adversarial	Adversarial and non-adversarial

A fictional example of a FBI agent illustrates the difference between a financial audit and a forensic audit and how a successful forensic accountant should be perceived.[22]

> That was where Holly Johnson's arrival had made things easier. She had the talent. She could look at a balance sheet and just know if anything was wrong with it. It was like she could smell it. She'd sit at her desk and look at the papers, and cock her head slightly to one side, and think. Sometimes, she'd think for hours, but when she stopped thinking, she'd know what the hell was going on. Then she'd explain it all in the case conference. She'd make it all sound easy and logical, like there was no way anybody could be in any kind of doubt about it.

¶ 1011   HISTORICAL ROOTS OF ACCOUNTING

Professor Gary Giroux believes that 10,000 years ago temple priests in Jericho took inventory of the village livestock by using tokens to keep track of the herd size and to count the grain harvest. By 3,000 B.C., the first accountants appeared in the form of scribes scribbling figures that recorded the ruler's wealth, which encompassed stashes of grain, livestock, gold, foodstocks, and jewelry.[23]

In ancient Egypt, scribes inventoried the pharaohs' grain, gold, and other assets—probably to prevent and detect theft. This type of accounting activity continued to be the accountant's main area of responsibility until the turn of the 20th century, when accrual basis accounting became common and reporting issues became a top priority.[24]

A more formal, modern approach to accounting started to take root in the United States in the late 1800s. The American Association of Public Accountants (eventually becoming the AICPA in 1957) was formed with 31 members in 1887. In 1896, New York State legislated the first CPA law, followed by the opening of a School of Commerce, Accounts, and Finance at New York University in 1900. Congress called for audit reports for large corporations in a 1902 Act.[25] In the early 1900s the United States business regulatory system started to take more formal shape. The Federal Reserve Board was created in 1913, the same year the Federal income tax law was passed. The Federal Trade Commission was created in 1914, and by 1921, all states had passed laws requiring examination for the CPA certificate.

¶ 1021   HISTORY OF FINANCIAL REPORTS AND LEGAL CHALLENGES

Financial reports on business operations and performance were created by accountants in the United States, Canada, and Europe for a long time before actual independent audits were mandated. Although financial reports and documents could often be challenged in court, outside auditors were not part and parcel of the process until the mid-1800s in England and early 1900s in English-speaking North America. The current system of accounting checks and balances—financial reporting coupled with both internal and external auditing—is relatively recent. In theory, the outside independent audit helps ensure the fairness and accuracy of reports for all intended audiences. Before financials were audited by independent outside experts, the courts were often the place where challenges were made and accounting experts were brought in to give testimony on the disputes in question. So even before independent accountants were asked to certify financial statements in auditing engagements, the practice of forensic accounting (i.e., accounting discipline applied to a legal forum) was common.

FRAUD IS AN INTERNATIONAL PROBLEM. Surely an outsourcing company that does business with 200 of the Fortune 500 companies has accurate financial statements. The fourth-largest Indian IT outsourcing company, Satyam Computer Services, was audited by PricewaterhouseCoopers, registered with the SEC, and both their CEO and CFO certified to their financial statements. Of course, Satyam means truth.

Surprise, $1.04 billion in cash and bank loans listed as assets for its second quarter in 2008 were nonexistent. What started as a marginal gap between actually operating profits and the real amount on the books ballooned into the $1 billion of systematically falsified accounts. There is a need for forensic accountants around the world.[26]

¶ 1031   THREADS OF FORENSIC ACCOUNTING

Hercules De Cordes, a schoolmaster and bookkeeper in Antwerp, was an early expert witness on at least three occasions. Apparently, in a November 8, 1554, dispute regarding merchants, he had to be qualified as an expert witness in the modern sense rather than as a fact witness. He stated to the magistrate that "he had kept merchants'" accounts for some twenty years while in Italy. Again on January 15, 1570, De Cordes testified as an expert witness since he had kept the merchant's books. Seven years later in April 1559, he stated in his deposition that, "he had compiled four 'states' of accounts kept in debit and credit from the ledger of Otto Uher."[27]

In North America, forensic accounting can be traced as far back as 1817 to a Canadian court decision:

> *Meyer* v. *Sefton* was *inter alia,* an inquiry to determine the value of a bankrupt's estate. Here a witness who had examined the bankrupt's accounts was allowed to testify, since from the nature of the case such an inquiry could not be made in court.[28]

Thus, the website of the Association of Certified Forensic Investigators of Canada maintains that the field of forensic and investigative accounting had its genesis in Canada.[29] Seven years after the Canadian case, on March 12, 1824, a young accountant by the name of James McClelland started his business in Glasgow, Scotland, and issued a circular that advertised the various classes of work he was prepared to undertake. These classes included "the making up of Statements, Reports, and Memorials on Account Books, on disputed Accounts, and Claims for the purpose of laying before Arbiters, Courts, or Counsel."[30]

As accounting evolved in more formal ways, accountants grew in stature and their expertise was more in demand in the courtroom. In 1856 in England, the audit of corporations became required.

PUMPKIN PILFERING. A forerunner of the forensic investigative accountant is found in Spanish 19th century literature penned by Pedro Antonio de Alarcon. He relates a tale of a pumpkin and tomato farmer, Buscabeatas, whose most prized pumpkins are stolen one night, so he rushes to the market town of Cadiz. The farmer discovers his own products in one of the stalls, but the merchant says, "If you don't prove your accusation, and I know you can't, you will go to jail." Buscabeatas then took the green stems from his stolen pumpkins and fitted them to the pumpkins, one by one. "The spectators were amazed to see that the stems really fit the pumpkins exactly, and delighted by such strange proof, they all began to help Buscabeatas."[31]

CCH® Study MATE™

Your Personal Online Tax "Tutor"—24/7!

Forensic Accounting can be puzzling, but now you have CCH® Study MATE™, a personal online tutor, to help you understand many of the complexities. With Study MATE you can plug into online learning any time of day or night. Study MATE walks you through the most important concepts covered in your textbook using individual learning sessions designed to make learning as easy as possible.

Study MATE is easy to use, and since you've bought our book, you have free access to our Forensic Accounting Topics Library for a full year! Study MATE courses are designed with web learning in mind, so you can navigate your way through them independently. They are relatively short, but each course covers a substantial amount of material—including the top concepts covered in your textbook. These are student-centered courses with presentations that are different than those found in the text, so they give you another voice— another opportunity for concepts to sink in.

CCH® Study MATE™
Mentor for Accounting and Tax Education

Home | Log In | Register

HOME >

Technical Support
866 798-5897 • support@learning.net

Welcome to Study MATE.

Study MATE provides a new and exciting way to expand your knowledge of taxes, auditing, and accounting. The courses provide examples, observations, and study questions to help you further develop your knowledge in these areas. Think of Study MATE as your own personal study partner.

Already enrolled?
Member Login

User Name: _____
Password: _____

Forget Password? | Login

New Users:

If you have an *access code* (provided with your CCH textbook)...
1. Whether you are a professor or student, register for an account by clicking on the appropriate sign up box.
2. Click on a library title or course name to enroll in a library and use your access code as payment.
3. Complete the courses in the library.

If you want to *purchase* a topic or entire library...
1. Whether you are a professor, student, or practitioner, register for an account by clicking on the appropriate sign up box.
2. Click on a library title to view the courses available, and then click on a library title or course name to enroll and pay by credit card.
3. Complete the courses you purchased.

» **Students** Sign up here if you are a student
» **Professors** Sign up here if you are a professor

» **Students** Sign up here if you are a student
» **Professors** Sign up here if you are a professor
» **Practitioners** Other members may sign up here.

How Many Courses Do I Take?

Your instructor may want you to access all the courses in the series, you may be asked to take selective courses on certain topics, or your instructor may leave it up to you to use Study MATE as you choose.

So, How Do I Get In?

Getting started is easy.

1 Go to www.cchstudymate.com and follow the instructions for New Users with an **access code** to sign up for a free account. Fill in the information on the registration page including a user ID and password of your choice.

2 Continue following the online instructions to enter your access code (provided below).

3 Click on MY COURSES to view the list of online courses, then click on the course title to begin.

ACCESS CODE:

CCHSM_13_FIA6ED_2_034304

Technical Support: 866-798-5897 • support@learning.net

Over for course features ▶ ▶ ▶

Access CCH Study MATE at www.cchstudymate.com

For your records, print your User ID and Password below:

User ID: _____

Password: _____

CCH® StudyMATE™

Features of each course:

Learning Objectives
A list of what you will learn in the course.

Introduction
A brief introduction to the course.

Discussions and Illustrations of the Concepts
Each course is designed to cover only the most important concepts. Your teacher may expect you to understand more than the concepts covered in Study MATE, but here you will see the core concepts.

Paced Learning
After some concepts are presented, the "Test Your Knowledge" feature helps you think back on what you've just read so you retain it.

Helpful Tools
On the right side of your screen, you will see clickable features such as additional reading materials, a tax term glossary, a special PDF print feature that allows you to print the entire course for offline reading and more.

CCH® StudyMATE™ — Cybercrime Loss Valuations — Course Outline | Glossary | Help

Learning Objectives

2 of 53
Course Progress:

After completing this course, you should be able to:

- Understand variance among federal and state statutes that provide computer loss descriptions.
- Identify the types of tangible and intangible losses that can occur during a cyber attack.
- Place a dollar valuation on losses from cyber attacks.
- Discern types of insurance coverage for protection against cybercrime losses best suited to your situation.

Print This Page
Notebook
Ask an Expert
Course PDF

Introduction

Welcome to the Cybercrime Loss Valuations cybercrime specialist, G. Stevenson Smith, e traditional loss valuations and those for cyber loss valuations, factors shown as remediabl of tangible and intangible losses that figure i intricacies of insurance against cybercrime.

This course is one of a series of courses dev accounting. Each course takes one aspect o concepts, and concisely explains those conc

To help you understand a particular aspect o included special learning aids:

- Examples - clarify what you have read
- Observations - give you greater insigh
- Test of Knowledge - help you remem

At the end of each course, there are questio demonstrate mastery of the subject.

Attacks on Tangibles and Intangibles

Today no online business or organization can assume it is safe from a cyber attack or a criminal act against its network. When these cyber attacks occur, businesses need to assess their losses.

Losses can occur from the removal or destruction of proprietary information, unauthorized access, access above clearance levels by either employees or others, and lessening a company's reputation or loss of shareholder confidence with trauma to the company's stock price.

These losses are usually considered tangible if they can be correlated with direct costs such as material and labor charges. However, the most significant damage from a cyber attack is from th

Intangible losses may b this typifies loss determ to have misused the rig

When an intangible los personal data over the l attack, the question is n

Observation: **Tiger Teams.** Tiger teams are groups of IT professionals who are hired to determine why network security has been broken. In addition, the team can be hired proactively to test network security in facilities prone to attack. The product of their work is a vulnerability report and recommendations for corrections and security enhancements.

Another cost that is also easily determined is the cost of hiring a private high-tech security firm and its team of forensic specialists to collect evidence about the intrusion and bring the system back online. Security firms are likely to send a group of security specialists specifically trained to bring a network back online quickly. Private security costs related to such engagements are easily quantifiable from the billings sent by the security service firm.

CCH® StudyMATE™ — Cybercrime Loss Valuations

- Reasons to Conduct a Loss Valuation Following Cyber Attacks
- Extent of the Problem
- Test Your Knowledge

Test Your Knowledge

1. Which of the following is not a reason to conduct a loss valuation after a cyber attack?

- a. To report the crime to law enforcement officials
- b. To set the value for an insurance claim
- c. To determine the cause of the attack
- d. To use the information internally

Check Answers

Examples and Observations
Presented to illustrate ideas and principles using colors and graphics to make your experience more memorable.

Testing—One, Two, Three
At the end of each course, a 15-question quiz is presented. The quiz questions are not easily answered—they really test whether you understand the concepts! You can take the quiz up to three times if you like and after successfully completing the quiz, you can print a certificate for your records and e-mail the certificate to your instructor to show you've successfully completed the course.

Get started! ▶ ▶ ▶

¶ 1041 ACCOUNTING LITERATURE PARALLELS ACCOUNTING PRACTICE

Concurrent with the practice developments described above were developments in accounting literature. In this literature the role of the accountant as an expert witness was gaining attention. In the first volume of the *Accountants' Index*, forensic-type articles are found under two categories: (1) Evidence and (2) Arbitration and Awards. Arbitration articles began as early as 1883,[32] and fraud-type articles began the next year.[33] Investigation-type articles started in 1889,[34] and the first expert witness article, by William H. Shawcross entitled "How to Receive and Give Evidence," appeared in 1898.[35]

In the inaugural year of *The Journal of Accountancy* (1905), a lawyer named Cleveland Bacon penned the article "The Accountant as an Expert Witness."[36] Bacon stated that "judges all over the country recognize that experts are alone able to arrive at the true meaning of complicated accounts,"[37] and he asserted "that the certificate of certified public accountants is the most essential single element of" qualifying as an accounting expert witness.

Two years later a Glasgow accountant, Alex Moore, stated that an accountant as an expert witness is required from time to time in criminal cases and more often in civil cases and arbitrations.[38] Moore also helped to mold the prototype accountant expert witness by describing Wyllie Guild, who Moore believed to be one of the best professional witnesses:

> He expounded his own views with a wealth of imagery and illustration which often affected the obdurate hearts of a British jury, and woe to the counsel who rashly attempted to cross-examine him. He was not severe upon any counsel who cross-examined him. He just overwhelmed him with a bland cloud-like mass, against which no ill nature on the part of the counsel could prevail, which no incisive questions could penetrate. Mr. Wyllie Guild was left standing in the box, leading everybody who heard him to think that he was absolutely right, that he alone of anybody in the Court knew anything about the case, and those who differed from him were exceedingly to be pitied.[39]

In 1925, the Chairman of the U.S. Board of Tax Appeal (the current U.S. Tax Court) said that CPAs were disproving the saying "you cannot teach a new dog old tricks" because of their mastery of the rules of evidence.[40] In the next issue the *Journal* proposed that educational institutions should start including in their curricula the study of the law of evidence, particularly as it applies to practice before the U.S. Board of Tax Appeal (now the U.S. Tax Court).[41]

EYEWITNESS

This expansion of accounting into areas such as forensic accounting and other perhaps broader business considerations was addressed in a 1924 speech given by Arthur Andersen, then senior partner in the CPA firm he founded, before the National Association of Cost Accountants Western Regional Conference on Industrial and Financial Investigations. Andersen said, "Some ten years ago I had the idea that accounting was not in itself an end, and that the sooner public accountants developed that bigger and broader viewpoint, the sooner they would place their services on a professional level."[42] Unfortunately, the vision of this proud accounting pioneer could not have foreseen his firm's demise in 2002 from several highly public lawsuits—Sunbeam, Waste Management, Baptist Foundation of Arizona, and Global Crossing. The subsequent bankruptcy of Enron, shredding of documents by Andersen personnel, and indictment of the entire firm essentially destroyed the company. Some have suggested that the broad vision of the firm's founder was replaced by a myopic view that mortgaged the firm's reputation and resources for pure profit motive.

Internal Revenue Service

In May 1927, the Supreme Court held that a bootlegger, Manny Sullivan, had to pay income tax on his illegal income,[43] opening the door for Elmer Ivey to work with FBI agent Elliot Ness. Al Capone had been quoted as saying, "the income tax law is a lot of bunk. The government cannot collect legal taxes from illegal money." Of course, Capone was wrong, because he did not understand investigative and auditing techniques like those used by Frank J. Wilson.

One can argue that the Internal Revenue Service ushered forensic accounting into the modern age in the United States when they went after Al Capone. Elmer Ivey, who headed the IRS's SIU, went to Chicago and met with Arthur Madden to collect evidence to arrest Al Capone on tax evasion charges. Two agents posed as gangsters and infiltrated Capone's inner circle. Frank Wilson was assigned from the Special Intelligence Unit (SIU) Baltimore office to investigate Al Capone. Forty-two years old, balding, with wire-rim glasses, Wilson feared "nothing that walks." Wilson could "pore over a set of books, eighteen hours a day, seven days a week, forever. He sweats ice water,"[44] said an associate. Wilson and his agents utilized the usual methods: they developed informers, tapped phones, seized books, and looked for weak points in Capone's empire.[45] Wilson found a "smoking gun" in the form of an accountant's cash receipts ledger showing net profits from a gambling house, with Al Capone's name on it.[46]

Although Federal tax agents estimated his annual income to be $50 million,[47] Al Capone dealt only in cash, owned nothing in his name, had never filed an income tax return, nor ever made a declaration of any assets or income.[48] In an early indictment the government charged that Al Capone had enjoyed an income of $1,038,660.84 from 1924 through 1929, and had not paid taxes in the amount of $215,080.48.[49] At trial, "Wilson provided a list of Capone's nondeductible expenses: $8,000 worth of diamond belt buckles, a $6,500 meat bill, $27 shirts, furnishings bought on a spending spree for his home—all told, '$116,000 that is not deductible from his income,' Wilson said. 'And yet counsel comes here and argues to you that the man has no income!'"[50]

Al Capone eventually received an eleven year sentence for income tax evasion.

The then-chairman of the House Ways and Means Committee, which writes the tax code and oversees the budget, was Representative Charles Rangel. He admitted in September 2008 that his own records were in such disarray that he had to hire a forensic accountant.

Rangel failed to pay taxes for 17 years on rental income from a Caribbean vacation villa. Eventually, he received a 45-second slap on the wrist by Nancy Pelosi as a result of his 333-79 censure for failing to pay these taxes, filing misleading financial statements, improperly seeking contributions from corporate interests for a college center bearing his own name, and establishing a campaign office in a subsidized, New York apartment designated for residential use.

What has been overlooked by most stories is that Rangel illegally used at least $393,000 in PAC funds to pay his legal defense team (which is taxable). Since legal expenditures are not deductible for the alternative minimum tax, Rangel owes taxes on this amount. But the IRS ignored this tax fraud violation.

Rangel is following in the footsteps of previous chairmen, such as Wilbur Mills' escapades with stripper Fannie Foxe. Fannie Foxe jumped out of his car while being pulled over by the D.C. police early in the morning. The "Argentine Firecracker" jumped into The Tidal Basin trying to escape, and Mr. Mills was found to be intoxicated, bleeding from his nose, and with scratches on his face. Dan Rostenkowski served federal prison time for embezzling public money in a cash-for-stamp scheme and other corruption charges, but he received a $125,000 pension while in prison

¶ 1051   THE PHRASE "FORENSIC ACCOUNTING" IS BORN

A major benchmark in forensic accounting was the use of the term *forensic accounting* in accounting literature. The first person to coin the phrase in print was probably Maurice E. Peloubet in 1946.[51] At that time Mr. Peloubet was a prolific writer and partner in the public accounting firm of Pogson, Peloubet & Co. in New York. Peloubet stated that "during the war both the public accountant and industrial accountant have been" and are now "engaged in the practice of forensic accounting."[52] Peloubet suggested that until recently forensic accounting had been only practiced in the courtroom, and that the preparation of financial statements had some but not all of the characteristics of forensic accounting. As the number and power of administrative and regulatory agencies increase, the accountant increasingly becomes "more involved in what is essentially a type of forensic practice." The preparation of data for, and the appearance before, such agencies "as a witness to facts, to accounting principles, or to the application of accounting principles is essentially forensic accounting practice rather than advocacy."[53] Peloubet's quote is really the essence of today's forensic accounting. In this way, Peloubet was not only witnessing the use of the term but was also chronicling the expansion of forensic practice from testimony to investigation.

By the late 1940s and early 1950s more expert witness articles began to appear in the literature. The entire Winter 1951 issue of the *Iowa Law Review* was devoted to the interrelationship of law and accounting.[54] Kenneth W. Robinson suggested that there is teamwork to be done by lawyers and accountants.[55] In the following year, George B. Pearson, Jr., a former judge, gave 10 warnings to the accountant who wished to do a good job on the witness stand.[56]

Max Lourie, a lawyer employed in the New York Supreme Court, published an article in 1953, which was awarded Second Prize in the N.Y. Society's 1953 Prize Essay Contest.[57] In this otherwise very informative article Lourie suggests that he probably invented the term forensic accounting. Although his article appeared seven years after Maurice E. Peloubet had apparently coined the term, Lourie presented an excellent history and overview of forensic accounting. Max Lourie also voiced three positions of importance:

- An accountant should not have to attend a law school to learn the art of expert testimony.
- Colleges and universities should deliver forensic accounting training.
- Forensic accounting reference books and textbooks should be developed for students. (However, the first textbook was not published until almost 30 years later.[58])

In 1964, as the U.S. accounting profession grew to more than 80,000 CPAs, Philip J. Gallagher in the *Journal of Accountancy* suggested that an accounting expert witness must be able to define the basic concepts of the profession and be able to explain accounting terminology.[59] Gallagher then asked: "If the *trained* mind of a lawyer finds the complexities of modern day accounting somewhat of a puzzle, what then might we expect the *untrained* mind of a layman to comprehend?"[60]

Forensic Accounting and Investigative Accounting Come of Age

¶ 1061   THE FORENSIC ACCOUNTANT BECOMES AN INVESTIGATOR

Once accrual accounting took hold and the role of external auditor became much more broad based and control-oriented than transaction-oriented, there developed a need for a fraud auditor—a specialist who would ferret out deception in financial statements and reporting. Gradually the definition of forensic accounting expanded from the accountant who testifies in court to the investigative accountant as Maurice Peloubet chronicled. The forensic accountant learned to detect fraud itself, not merely to testify about it. Perhaps nowhere is this more evident than in the use of accountants and forensic accounting skills by the FBI.

¶ 1071   FBI AND FORENSICS

In 1948 a related article entitled "Investigative Accounting" highlighted the growth of accounting and the FBI's use of accountants during World War II.[61] According to Lee R. Pennington, during the period of hostilities the FBI employed a total of 500 agents who were accountants. During the period from December 6, 1940, to June 24, 1941, Special Agent Accountants monitored and examined financial transactions totaling $538 million. Many of the war accounting investigations involved the Surplus Property Act, Contract Settlement Act, and War Fraud Claims, but nonwartime investigations involved violations of the National Bankruptcy Act, mail fraud violations, antitrust cases, and Court of Claims cases.[62] In 1960, J. Edgar Hoover began to emphasize fraud detection. At this time the FBI had 6,000 agents, with 700 designated as Special Agent Accountants. These agents investigated violations of the Federal Reserve Act, check kiting, embezzlements, fraud in government contracts, criminal investigations under the National Bankruptcy Act, and various civil investigations.[63] Five years later Hoover again spoke of the fraud that FBI Agents encounter: fraudulent check schemes, securities frauds, confidence game swindles, embezzlements, false bills of lading, fraudulent bankruptcies, false claims, and various frauds perpetrated against the government. He suggested that "many employee frauds are made possible either because the company lacks an adequate system of internal control, or it does not follow reasonable precautions in using the services of internal auditors and/or public accountants."[64]

Today there are more than 600 FBI agents with an accounting background, and many are CPAs. The FBI Internet site says that FBI special agents work closely with investigators from the Securities and Exchange Commission, the Internal Revenue Service, the U.S. Postal Inspection Service, the Commodity Futures Trading Commission, and Treasury's Financial Crimes Enforcement Network, among others. Together, they target sophisticated, multi-layered fraud cases that injure the marketplace and threaten our economy.

White-collar crime is one of the FBI's eight national security priorities. Their investigations include:

- Antitrust.
- Bankruptcy fraud.
- Corporate/ securities fraud.
- Health care fraud.
- Insurance fraud.
- Mass marketing fraud.
- Money laundering.
- Mortgage fraud.[65]

They define white-collar crime as lying, cheating, and stealing. In late December 2013, they listed 39 white-collar criminals with photos wanted by the FBI.[66]

¶ 1081   FIRST FORENSIC ACCOUNTING BOOKS IN UNITED STATES

Forensic accounting articles surfaced many years before the first forensic accounting book. The first forensic accounting book appeared in 1982, written by Francis C. Dykeman, a retired partner of Price Waterhouse. His book included no footnotes or history of forensic accounting. Both a CPA and attorney, Dykeman's 12 chapters include an overview of the judicial process, trial attorney's cases, court systems, administrative agencies, working in an ambiguous environment, developing and managing information, preparing and presenting direct testimony, cross-examination, the trial, and others.[67]

Four years later in 1986, Kalman A. Barson published a second forensic book entitled *Investigative Accounting*.[68] He stated that the following areas were ripe for investigative work:

- Matrimonial cases;
- Partnerships dissolutions;
- Minority stockholder suits;
- Insurance claims;
- Audits or inspections by corporate internal audit staffs, of various branches or divisions; and
- Acquisitions or mergers.

Mr. Barson has since written books on investigative accounting techniques, investigative accounting in divorce, and ways to discover unreported income.

In 1987, a third book was published entitled *Fraud Auditing and Forensic Accounting: New Tools and Techniques*.[69] As the title indicates, authors Jack Bologna and Robert Lindquist emphasized fraud, with three chapters dealing with expert witnessing. They said that the structural and behavioral considerations of fraud were like an iceberg: many of the behavioral considerations lurk beneath the surface, posing a danger to the unsuspecting auditor.[70]

A series of fictional novels involving the financial and investigative intrigue of fraud portrays a forensic accountant as the hero. Author Iris Weil Collett (pen name of Larry Crumbley) and various co-authors place Professor Lenny Cramer in exotic locations with colorful characters and surround him with murders and crime. Some of the plots include "track[ing] foreign receipts to uncover a plot to steal Burmese religion treasures...conducting an audit at Coca-Cola [and] uncovering a scheme to steal the company's secret formula...[and using] his forensic accounting skills to solve a series of murders in the New York art world."[71]

A more recent novel teaching forensic accounting entitled *The Big R: A Forensic Accounting Action Adventure* provides a description of the forensic accountant character called Fred Campbell:[72]

> Now he did more than just disputed divorce-settlement work. His areas included antitrust analysis, general consulting, and cost allocation. Anytime someone had to dig into the books and records, he was available. Super Accountant Campbell! Maybe he should get a special cape to wear like Superman. Or was that Batman? He packed a HP 12-X pocket calculator and a notebook computer. He thought of himself like the forensic anthropologist in a Patricia Cornwell or Kathy Reichs novel.

¶ 1091   AICPA PRACTICE AID

In 1986, the AICPA broke forensic accounting into two broad areas: investigative accounting and litigation support. The Institute issued Practice Aid 7, which outlined the six areas of litigation services shown in Table 1.1.[73]

Table 1.1. Types of Litigation Services

Damages	Valuation
Lost profits	Business and professional practices
Lost value	Pension
Lost cash flow	Intangibles
Lost revenue	Property
Extra cost	

Antitrust Analyses	General Consulting
Price-fixing	Actuarial analyses
Market share, market definition	Statistical analyses
Pricing below cost	Projections
Dumping and other price discrimination	Industrial engineering
Anticompetition actions	Market analyses
Monopolization	Computer consulting

Accounting	Analyses
Bankruptcy	Tax bases
Tracing	Cost allocations
Contract cost and claims	Tax treatment of specific transactions
Regulated industries	
Frauds (civil and criminal)	
Historical analyses	
Family law	

PricewaterhouseCoopers' web site indicates that their 800 full-time forensic specialists can deal with the following areas:

- Dispute analysis.
- Forensic technology solutions.
- Fraud risk management.
- Investigations and forensic accounting.
- Insurance claims.
- Licensing management and contract compliance.
- Regulatory compliance reviews.

¶ 1101　AMERICAN MANAGEMENT ASSOCIATION COURSE

The American Management Association has offered a self-study course, "Forensic Accounting and Financial Fraud," which breaks forensic accounting into four broad areas: pretrial support, trial support, expert witnessing, and settlement support.[74] Wayne Bremser suggests that forensic accountants can help in the following situations: antitrust, commercial contracts, patent infringement, trademark and copyright infringement, product liability, mergers and acquisitions, insurance claims, shareholder suits, reorganization and bankruptcy, taxation, malpractice, and corporate fraud.[75] He covers various fraudulent financial reporting schemes, methods of computing lost profits, damages, and damage calculations.[76]

¶ 1111　THE PANEL ON AUDIT EFFECTIVENESS

Even before Enron, the Public Oversight Board (an independent private sector body created in 1977) appointed the Panel on Audit Effectiveness in 1998 at the request of then SEC Chairman Arthur Levitt to review and evaluate how independent audits of the financial statements of public companies are performed and to assess whether recent trends in audit practices serve the public interest. The Panel conducted the most exhaustive study ever undertaken of the audit model and on September 6, 2000, released a report of more than 200 pages entitled *Report and Recommendations*.

The report's goal is to foster more effective audits that improve the reliability of financial statements, enhance their credibility, contribute to investors' confidence in the profession, and improve the efficiency of the capital markets. Among its most important recommendations is that auditors should perform some "forensic-type" procedures during every audit to enhance the prospects of detecting material financial statement fraud. This new forensic-type phase should become an integral part of the audit, with careful thought given to how and when to carry out the audit. A forensic-type fieldwork phase does not mean converting a traditional audit to a "fraud audit." Rather, the characterization of this phase of an audit as a forensic-type phase seeks to convey an attitudinal shift in the auditor's degree of skepticism.

¶ 1121   AICPA FRAUD TASK FORCE REPORT

In 2003, the AICPA's Litigation and Dispute Resolution Services Subcommittee issued a report of its Fraud Task Force entitled "Incorporating Forensic Procedures in an Audit Environment." The task force paper provides guidance to practitioners in applying procedures in an audit environment in light of the Sarbanes-Oxley Act and newly issued AICPA Statement on Auditing Standards (SAS) No. 99, Consideration of Financial Fraud in Financial Statement Audit.

The Fraud Task Force report covers the professional standards that apply when forensic procedures are employed in an audit and explains the various means of gathering evidence through the use of forensic procedures and investigative techniques.[77] As a traditional audit moves toward an investigation or an investigation moves toward an audit, the report covers the professional standards that apply to both an auditor and a forensic accountant.[78]

If forensic accountants are brought into an audit for purposes of complying with SAS No. 99 (AU 316), they are required to follow auditing standards. When forensic accountants are brought into an audit engagement for the purpose of conducting a separate investigation (and not an adjunct to an audit), because it is a litigation services engagement, consulting standards apply (rather than auditing standards).[79]

On July 15, 2004, the Committee itself issued a Discussion Memorandum entitled Forensic Services, Audits, and Corporate Governance: Bridging the Gap, "to explore ways in which forensic accounting professionals can provide assistance to an audit committee, financial statement audit teams, and others."[80] The memorandum gave nine questions in which the task force requested input from practitioners. Professor Edward Ketz provided a critical response to this memorandum and gave his answers to the nine questions. He believes that the "guidance in SAS No. 99 is sufficient to improve the quality of the audit process" as long as there is "an active court to punish audit failures."[81]

The results from the questionnaires provide the AICPA's position:[82]

- The AICPA does not require auditors to carry out specific forensic procedures, but rather provides guidance on how to include forensic techniques within processes outlined in SAS 99. This combination will enhance the detection and prevention of fraudulent financial statement reporting and misappropriation of assets, thus protecting investors and financial statement users.

- Public accounting firms could use forensic accountants to help revise their approach to planning and fieldwork on all audits, while requiring forensic accountants only on high risk audit clients to aid in the interpretation of forensic testing results and preventive control enhancements.

- The inclusion of audit procedures focused towards detecting misappropriation of corporate assets may lead to the identification of weaknesses within corporate governance or control weaknesses. Frauds that are identified which represent a material misappropriation of assets could significantly impact public perception.

- Professional forensic accountants can best be used by ensuring such procedures are properly developed and executed in-line with internal audit and audit committee concerns. Forensic accountants could then be engaged in high-risk situations, or when a fraud is suspected.

- Companies should not use the forensic services of their outside audit firm, unless it pertains to the annual audit.

- Putting a price on a substantive test or forensic auditing procedure may be smart for business; however, the inherent risk is that short-cuts geared towards reducing audit costs may eventually cause investors to question the companies' true financial position.

¶ 1131   CONTROVERSY SURROUNDING THE ACCOUNTANT'S ROLE IN FRAUD DETECTION

In the early 1980s there was a subtle shift in the way external auditors reviewed clients' records. Companies began to use computers to perform their record keeping, and intense competition caused the auditing fees to fall as much as 50 percent from the mid-1980s to the mid-1990s. Thus, auditors had to cut costs by reducing the labor-intensive process of reviewing hundreds of corporate accounts. They grew more reliant on internal controls and worked less with account balances and entries. Because top executives can circumvent internal controls, they could manipulate the records and cook the books. Eventually the results were what happened to Enron, WorldCom, Xerox, Adelphia Communications, and the fall of Arthur Andersen in the early 2000s. Thus, the pendulum will swing back to more forensic techniques in audits and higher fees.[83]

Much of the disputed line costs in the WorldCom debacle were initially expensed properly, but later entries were made to turn these costs into capitalized assets. Arthur Andersen was given limited access to the general ledger. The backup or support for the following $771 million entry was a yellow post-it note:

Property, Plant, and Equipment	$629,000,000
Construction in Progress	$142,000,000
Operating Expenses	$771,000,000

However, accounting experts debate the role of auditors in uncovering fraud and hold many different views. Some believe that every audit engagement should include much more skepticism and detailed review of transactions. Others suggest that only special engagements specifically targeting fraud can adequately and effectively root out the problem. Whether forensic accounting skills will be a necessary competency of every accountant or if those skills will be the domain of an elite specialty remains to be seen.

The American Institute of Certified Public Accountants (AICPA) has recognized the need for accounting professionals to change their attitudes toward fraud detection. The organization has produced Statement on Auditing Standards No. 99 (AU 316) to feature brainstorming risks of fraud, increased professional skepticism, discussions with management, responding to management override of controls, and use of unpredictable audit tests. But the AICPA notes that of the two essentials of this attitudinal change, only one is the purview of accountants—greater professional skepticism. The other defense is the job of corporate America, which should raise awareness of financial crime in order to prevent it, coupled with encouraging employees to identify fraud.[84]

The AICPA had an Internet game called "Catch Me Game" which says "numbers don't lie; criminals are another story." Students and professors were to use their skills and smarts to track the money trail back to the crooks. "When shady characters are up to no good, they often leave a trail of questionable financial transactions."[85]

The accounting profession may be making a strategic shift as they see that SAS No. 99 and the other rules are not protecting them from being the insurer of last resort. The Big Four along with Grant Thornton and BDO International released a report entitled "Serving Global Capital Markets and the Global Economy." They suggest that a forensic audit is akin to a police investigation.

In the report, one of the things they are suggesting is for companies to have a forensic audit. Companies would be required to have such an audit every three or five years or face these audits on a random basis. Forensic auditors would scrutinize all records of companies, including e-mails, and would be able, if not required, to question all company employees and to require statements under oath. It might be necessary for an audit network or a specialized forensic auditor to complete a forensic audit with the aid of independent attorneys (not those who have represented the audit client in the other engagements).[86]

This November 2006 report indicated another possibility is to let shareholders decide on the intensity of the fraud detection effort they want auditors to perform. Shareholders could be assisted in making this decision by disclosure in the proxy materials of the costs of the different levels of audits, as well as the historical experience of the company with fraud. A different choice model would be to rely upon boards, or audit committees, to decide on the level of fraud detection intensity.[87] A Standing Advisory Committee of the PCAOB was not enthusiastic about the ideas indicating that they were not cost-effective or effective at all.[88]

The AICPA, along with the Institute of Internal Auditors, and Association of Certified Fraud Examiners sponsored Managing the Business Risk of Fraud: A Practical Guide. This guide recommends ways in which those responsible for dealing with fraud, such as boards of directors, audit committees, senior management, shareholders, and internal and external auditors can fight fraud and abuse in their organization. The document includes creditable guidance from leading professional organizations that defines principles and theories for fraud risk management and describes how organizations of various sizes and types establish their own fraud risk management program. The guide provides examples of key program components and resources that entities can use as a starting place to develop a fraud risk management program effectively and efficiently.[89] This advice is provided in subsequent chapters.

FORENSIC ACCOUNTING IN THE CLASSROOM. The scandals of the past ten years and their resultant cost to society, to the business community, and to the reputation of the accounting profession are evidence enough for many accounting educators to make forensic accounting part of their curriculum. Accounting students don't find it easy to acquire a solid understanding of financial accounting and auditing, *plus* a good sense of how the American legal system works. However, a forensic accounting course complements rather than replaces foundational accounting and auditing courses. This text focuses on the forensic discipline itself and the context in which the forensic accountant operates, but the text does not replace the detail provided in financial accounting, financial statement analysis, and auditing courses. To be a good forensic accountant, one must have a solid background in accounting and auditing.

A form of forensic accounting is corporate investigation or corporate espionage. For example, Diligence, Inc. is a Washington private intelligence firm that has former director of CIA and FBI, William Webster on its advisory board. Corporate intelligence firms "essentially help businesses deal with the risks of operating in challenging markets," but "we always respect the jurisdictions in which we operate,"[90] according to Nick Day, founder of Diligence, Inc.

On their Internet site Diligence indicates that they specialize in all types of business litigation on behalf of plaintiffs and defendants. Major litigation services include:[91]
- Standards and practices of financial institutions
- Lender liability and bank operations
- Bankruptcy
- Business and real estate valuation
- Lost profits and damages calculation
- Accounting malpractice
- Fidelity bond claims
- Directors and officers claims
- Business judgment
- Breach of contract
- Product liability

PONZI SCHEMES STILL OPERATE. Sir Allen Stanford is not as well known as Bernard Madoff, who stole as much as $64 billion from investors. Both, however, are accused of operating a 1921-type ponzi scheme. A ponzi investing scam promises high returns with little risk, and the fraudster pays off older investors with money from new investors. The scam usually collapses when new investments dry up.

Mr. Stanford, a Texas banking billionaire, was accused by the SEC of operating a multi-billion-dollar ponzi scheme, defrauding about 30,000 investors of $7 billion. His company had 200 different accounting systems. Mr. Stanford also was making a series of bribe payments to Leroy King, the top banking regulator in Antigua. Apparently, Mr. King would conduct fake audits aimed at assuring American regulators and investors that Mr. Stanford's bank was sound.

SEC Robert Khuzami said that "instead of buying the safe and sound investments he promised his clients, Stanford bought Antigua's top securities cop. While Stanford quarterbacked his massive CD ponzi scheme, he paid the Antigua referee to spy on the huddles and provide an insider's play-by-play of the SEC investigation." Apparently, Mr. King showed Mr. Stanford the SEC's inquiries as they came in so Mr. Stanford and his lieutenants could dictate the substance, and even the contents of responses, which Mr. King then returned to the SEC on the Antiguan banking regulators' letterhead.[92]

Financier and cricket mogul, Mr. Stanford was sentenced to a 100-year prison sentence.

Client lists, customer lists, trade secrets, personnel records, research documents, and new products and services are only some of the items that a business may seek through various means. Theft of trade secrets is estimated to be around $100 billion a year.[93]

Spies can be both inside and outside a business. Insiders can be executives, IT experts, and janitors, and outsiders can be hackers or physical break-in specialists. Tools and methods of these investigators include walking in the door, hacking, tricking personnel into revealing information, dumpster diving, wireless hacking, and eavesdropping on phone lines. The purpose, of course, is to obtain needed information.[94]

Hewlett-Packard Chairwoman Patricia Dunn used investigators to find the source of Board of Directors leaks. Nick Day, founder of Diligence, Inc., needed to obtain advance KPMG audit information about a client's rival, IPOC, an investment fund based in Bermuda. Posing as a British intelligence officer, Day befriended, Guy Enright, a British-born accountant at KPMG. Under the cloak of top secret national security, the accountant began to hand over confidential audit documents, including transcripts of KPMG's interviews dealing with IPOC.[95]

Under the cover name Project Yucca, Guy Enright would place documents in a plastic container at a certain rock along his 20-minute daily commute. Nick Day and Diligence used their own employees to follow Mr. Enright to make sure he was not a plant or corporate spy. Diligence was apparently paid handsomely.[96]

However, once discovered by an unknown whistleblower, the dispute was settled on June 20, 2006, with an approximately $1.7 million settlement.[97]

There are ways for businesses to protect themselves from corporate spies. Personnel must be made aware of the damage from financial spies, and the normal closed-circuit cameras and security guards patrolling premises are important. Other preventive measures include:
- An eavesdropping protection kit that releases a soft noise that blocks out voices, making it impossible for eavesdroppers to hear.
- A vanishing e-mail, called VaporStream, lets people send e-mails that leave no trail. The e-mails cannot be tracked, copied, or printed. The cost is $40 a year.
- A wiretap-detection device that alerts you if a phone is being tapped, or if there is any interruption in the phone line.
- FiberGuard Net 800 uses fiber optics that send an alert if a fence or gate is cut or if someone climbs over the fence.[98]

Committee on Sponsoring Organizations

The Committee on Sponsoring Organizations (COSO) was formed in 1985. Sometimes called the Treadway Commission, COSO is dedicated to providing thought leadership through the development of comprehensive frameworks and guidance on enterprise risk management, internal controls, and fraud deterrence designed to improve organizational performance and governance and to reduce the extent of fraud in private organizations. COSO is a private sector initiative, jointly sponsored by the American Accounting Association, American Institute of CPAs, Financial Executives International, Institute of Management Accountants, and the Institute of Internal Auditors. The Committee's internal control framework first promulgated in 1992 is used by more than 80 percent of companies (i.e., the COSO framework).[99] The COSO Cube is discussed in Chapter 4.

Sarbanes–Oxley Legislation

The Sarbanes-Oxley Act (SOX) contains 11 titles having a direct impact on forensic accounting and fraud. Some of the more important subjects are outlined here and discussed in subsequent chapters:

1. Title 1 establishes the Public Company Accounting Oversight Board (PCAOB) under the SEC to regulate auditing and to discipline auditors.
2. Title 2 contains a series of rules to ensure that auditors are independent from their clients. For example, neither the primary nor reviewing partner may audit the same client for more than five consecutive years, and the auditor must report all material written communication to the audit committee.
3. Title 3 requires publicly traded companies to have an audit committee, states that the CEO and CFO must certify their company's financial statements, and provides rules for the conduct of officers and their attorneys.
4. Title 4 prohibits personal loans and requires certain financial disclosures.
5. Title 5 mandates rules for financial security analysts (i.e., research analysts) to avoid conflicts of interest.
6. Titles 6, among other provisions, allows federal courts the power to bar individuals who violate security laws from participating in penny stocks.
7. Title 7 requires reports and studies on consolidation of accounting firms, credit rating agencies, enforcement actions, and investment banks.
8. Title 8 provides protection for whistleblowers and mandates penalties and fines for certain acts not dischargeable by bankruptcy. For example, failure of an auditor to keep working papers for 5 years is subject to fines and 10 years in prison, and fine or imprisonment of up to 25 years for anyone knowingly defrauding shareholders of publicly traded companies. A person can receive 20 years in prison and fines for altering, destroying, mutilating, concealing, covering up, falsifying or making a false entry in any record, document, or tangible object.
9. Title 9 increases maximum prison sentences for mail and wire fraud from 5 to 20 years. Willfully and knowingly certifying financial reports not in compliance with the Act is now a criminal offense.
10. Title 10 says that it is the "Sense of the Senate" to require the CEO to sign the corporate tax return.
11. Title 11 provides a possible 20-year prison sentence for anyone altering, destroying, mutilating, or concealing a record, document, or other object (or otherwise impeding) for an official proceeding.

Some Fraud and Forensic Accounting Sources[100]

There are various sources of forensic accounting information available to practitioners, educators, executives, and students.

Digital Forensic Investigator is a multi-media resource for digital forensic professionals working in academic, government, law enforcement, and corporate settings. www.dfinews.com

The Forensic Examiner is the official peer-reviewed journal of the American College of Forensic Examiners International that contains periodic forensic accounting articles. *www.theforensicexaminer.com*

Fraud Magazine is a bi-monthly publication by the Association of Certified Fraud Examiners that gives readers practical "down-in-the-trenches" information. *www.fraud-magazine.com*

Journal of Forensic Accounting (2000-2008) was an independent international forum for the publication of research dealing with the models and methodologies of investigative and forensic accounting, seeking to establish a balance between theoretical and empirical studies, and striving to foster practitioner-academic dialogue and collaboration. *www.rtedwards.com/journals/JFA/students.html*

Journal of Forensic and Investigative Accounting is a bi-yearly electronic magazine started in 2009 that publishes original creative and innovative academic studies with some practical articles. Published by Larry Crumbley at Louisiana State University. *http://www.bus.lsu.edu/accounting/faculty/lcrumbley/jfia/Default.htm*

Journal of Forensic Studies in Accounting and Business provides an outlet for communication and research collaboration among fraud and forensic accounting practitioners and education programs. Published by Georgia Southern University. *www.fraudforensicacct.org*

The Forensic and Valuation Services Center (AICPA) provides members with up-to-date sources of professional guidance and tools available. *http://www.aicpa.org/InterestAreas/ForensicAndValuation/Resources/Pages/default.aspx*

The Value Examiner is an independent, professional development journal published bi-monthly by the National Association of Certified Valuation Analysts, containing substantive, peer-reviewed articles in business valuation, forensic accounting, fraud risk management, and other topics. *http://www.nacva.com/examiner/examiner.asp*

¶ 1135   AMERICAN ACCOUNTING ASSOCIATION FORENSIC ACCOUNTING SECTION

After a struggle over a number of years, Larry Crumbley was able to obtain 500 signatures, and the American Accounting Association agreed to allow a new section called Forensic and Investigative Accounting (FIA). The FIA section is dedicated to the continual improvement of forensic accounting research and education, through the encouragement, development, and sharing of:

- The promotion and dissemination of forensic and investigative academic and practitioner research.
- The relevant and innovative curricula with an emphasis on effective and efficient instruction.
- The exploration of knowledge-organization issues related to forensic accounting programs.
- The creation and presentation of CPE courses to members and professionals.

Forensic and investigative accounting often intersects with other professions including those of the law, criminology, sociology, psychology, intelligence, information technology (open sourcing, cyber-crime, digital evidence, data mining, and IT systems and control), computer forensics, and other forensic sciences. Graduate students may wish to be associate members, and practitioners could become full-time members.

¶ 1141   FOREIGN CORRUPT PRACTICES ACT

Following investigations by the SEC as a result of the Watergate scandal, over 400 businesses were found to have paid over $300 million in bribes coming from slush funds to foreign governmental officials and politicians. As a result of these discoveries by the SEC, the Foreign Corrupt Practices Act (FCPA) was enacted as a federal law in 1977. The FCPA prohibits companies from paying corrupt bribes to foreign government officials and political figures for the purpose of obtaining or retaining business.

The purpose of the FCPA is to combat corrupt business practices such as bribes and kickbacks. Thus, for more than 35 years these foreign bribery laws in the United States have restricted all U.S. employees, regardless of where the business is conducted.

FCPA prohibits corrupt payments to foreign officials for the purpose of obtaining or keeping business, or directing business to anyone. These laws apply to foreign firms and persons who take any act in furtherance of such a corrupt payment while in the United States. Companies whose securities are listed in the United States must meet FCPA. Also, FCPA prohibits corrupt payments through intermediaries.

There are two provisions to the Foreign Corrupt Practices Act. First, the anti-bribery provision, which is enforced by the Department of Justice and second, the accounting provisions, which are enforced by the Securities and Exchange Commission (SEC). The FCPA prohibits any U.S. citizen, U.S. business, foreign corporations trading securities in the U.S., or foreign persons or entities currently in the U.S. to make corrupt payments to foreign governmental officials directly or through an agent in an effort to obtain or retain business.

A government official can be any government employee and may even extend to employees of state owned businesses. A payment can consist of anything of value, but such payment must have corrupt intent to improperly influence the governmental official.

Under the books and records provision, issuers of U.S. securities are required to make and keep books, records, and accounts that accurately reflect the issuer's transactions and disposition of assets. Under the internal controls provision, issuers must devise and maintain a system of internal controls sufficient to assure managements control and responsibility of the firm's assets. These two provisions do not only apply to bribe-related violations.

Often bribes are concealed under accounts such as consulting fees or traveling expenses. In instances in which all the elements of the anti-bribery provision cannot be proven, often the companies are still liable under the accounting provisions.

The FCPA covers both issuers and domestic concerns. Issuers includes any U.S. or foreign corporation that has a class of securities registered in the U.S, or that is required to file reports under the Securities and Exchange Act of 1934.

Domestic concerns refers to any individual who is a citizen, national, or resident of the United States and any corporation and other business entity organized under the laws of the United States or of any individual U.S. State, or having its principal place of business in the United States.

During 2010 alone, the Securities and Exchange Commission and Justice Department reached settlements with 23 companies for alleged violations of the law, collecting a total of $1.8 billion in financial penalties. For more detail, see A Resource Guide to the U.S. Foreign Corrupt Practices Act, by the Criminal Division of the U.S. Department of Justice and the Enforcement Division of the U.S. Securities and Exchange Commission. Listen to http://www.justice.gov/criminal/fraud/fcpa/guide.pdf

EYEWITNESS 101

Oracle Corporation was charged by the SEC with violating the FCPA by failing to prevent their Indian subsidiary firm from secretly setting aside money off their books that was then used to make unauthorized payments to phony Indian vendors.

An Oracle Corporation subsidiary, Oracle India, sold software licenses and services to the government of India through local distributors. Over a dozen times between the years of 2005 and 2007, Oracle India structured payments with the Indian government in a way that allowed Oracle India's distributors to keep approximately $2.2 million in unauthorized funds off Oracle India's books. The distributors were told to keep excess funds for "marketing development purposes." The distributors were then instructed to make payments ranging from $110,000 to $396,000 to various third party vendors that provided no actual service to Oracle India and were not on Oracle's approved vendor list. The third party payments created the risk that the money could be used for illicit purposes such as bribery or embezzlement.

Oracle agreed to pay $2 million in order to settle the charges with the SEC. The settlement took into account the fact that Oracle voluntarily disclosed the conduct in India and co-operated fully with the SEC investigation. Oracle also fired all employees associated with the misconduct and made significant enhancements to its FCPA compliance program.

Organization for Economic Cooperation and Development (OECD)

The OECD began in 1948 as the Organization for European Economic Cooperation (OEEC) with the goal to help administer the Marshall Plan during the reconstruction of Europe through American financial aid after World War Two. Eventually non-European countries were admitted, and the OEEC became the OECD in 1961 The OECD's primary goal is to improve the social and economic well-being of people around the world.

In 1997, the United States and 31 other countries signed the OECD Convention on Combating Bribery of Foreign Public Officials in International Business Transactions. Both civil and criminal sanctions may be imposed for violation of the FCPA. The OECD provides a forum for its 34 member countries to meet and share common problems, seek solutions, compare policy experiences, identify which new policies and laws are effective, and coordinate international policies between members.

The OECD compares and measures data on a wide variety of topics including school systems, pension systems, taxes, average leisure time, the global flows of trade and investments, and many others. The OECD also works with businesses, trade unions, labor unions, and with other representatives of civil society to help develop policies that benefit the citizens and the economies of its member countries. The organization also attempts to implement policies to make life harder for terrorists, tax dodgers, crooked businessmen, and others who undermine a fair and open society.

The OECD uses peer pressure to implement and improve policies and set standards which member countries can adopt.

Member Countries

AUSTRALIA	GREECE	NEW ZEALAND
AUSTRIA	HUNGARY	NORWAY
BELGIUM	ICELAND	POLAND
CANADA	IRELAND	PORTUGAL
CHILE	ISRAEL	SLOVAK REPUBLIC
CZECH REPUBLIC	ITALY	SLOVENIA
DENMARK	JAPAN	SPAIN
ESTONIA	KOREA	SWEDEN
FINLAND	LUXEMBOURG	SWITZERLAND
FRANCE	MEXICO	TURKEY
GERMANY	NETHERLANDS	UNITED KINGDOM
		UNITED STATES

¶ 1146   CONCLUSION

Why is forensic accounting such a hot issue today? Why do many people think of it as a new and exciting field? Automation changed the business landscape to the point where in the 1980s the number and speed of business transactions required a faster means to create financial statements and audit them. The computer helped direct a revolution in accounting because business transaction volume grew to such an extent that it was impossible for accountants to examine each transaction. Internal controls, sizing risks, and sampling became the focus. Business got hooked on cheaper "automated" auditing engagements. Unfortunately, unethical managers learned to skirt the modern controls; thus, weaknesses in the modern risk control and sampling approach grew during the 1990s and became even more apparent in the first few years of the 21st century.

There are many views about forensic accounting practice today. After all the recent accounting scandals, some industry experts suggest that the task of fighting accounting fraud is like Sisyphus, condemned to roll a rock up a hill each day only to watch it roll back down again. Others suggest it may simply require more vigilant external and internal accountants who can make great strides in eliminating fraud. "During one investigation, we found in the auditing working papers a statement written in the margin of the internal audit working papers by the internal audit manager: 'Conceal from bankers,'" says Nicholas L. Feakins, CPA, partner at San Mataeo, California-based forensic accounting firm Feakings & Feakins. "It sounds amazing, but the [third party] auditors had put B-level staff on the project who simply didn't read the documents and missed it."[102]

For broad-based, system-wide relief from today's financial scandals, many suggest the weaknesses can be attacked successfully in repositioning the auditing engagement and mandating more stringent ethical and independence requirements to start. Both external and internal auditors should make forensic accounting their steering wheel and not just their spare tire.

ENDNOTES

1. Catherine Valenti, "Fraud Squad As Financial Scandals Mount, Forensic Accounting Becomes Hot Area," ABCnews.com (April 10, 2002).
2. NJSCPA.org, "Accounting Makes the Headlines as Forensic CPAs Trace Terrorists' Funding," (December 7, 2001) www.njscpa.org/story.cfm?m.
3. Cassell Bryan-Low, "A Sullied Profession Discovers It's Hip to Be Calculating," The Wall Street Journal (March 26, 2002), pp. A-1 and 8.
4. www.CatchMeGame.com/college.
5. Jeff Stimpson, "Forensic Accounting: Exponential Growth," WebCPA (February 1, 2007), p. 1.
6. James Lee Burke, Bitterroot, New York: Pocket Books, 2001, p. 171.
7. Stuart Kahan, "Sherlock Holmes Enters Accounting," WebCPA (May 1, 2006).
8. Jeff Stimpson, "Forensic Accounting: Exponential Growth," WebCPA (February 1, 2007), p. 2.
9. Ibid.
10. The 2011 Forensic and Valuation Services Trend Survey, AICPA, 2011-2012, p.5
11. G. Bologna and R. Lindquist, Fraud Auditing and Forensic Accounting (New York: John Wiley, 1995). F.T. DeZoort and J.D. Stanley, "Fair Presentation in the SOX Era: An Assessment Framework and Opportunities for Forensic Accountants," Journal of Forensic Accounting 7 (2006), p. 289.
12. Ask Hal home page, www.askhal.com.
13. Definition adopted by the AICPA Business Valuation/Forensic Litigation Services Executive Committee, January 2006. A similar definition has been adopted by the AICPA's CFF certification.
14. H.R. Davia, "Fraud Specific Auditing," Journal of Forensic Accounting 3 (2002), pp. 111-120.
15. Jeff Stimpson, "Forensic Accounting: Exponential Growth," WebCPA (February 1, 2007), p. 3.
16. Stuart Kahan, "Sherlock Holmes Enters Accounting," WebCPA (May 1, 2006).
17. Jake Poinier, "Fraud Finder," Future Magazine, Fall 2004 http://www.phoenix.edu/students/future/oldissue/winter2004.fraud.htm.
18. Kris Frieswick, "How Audit Must Change," CFO (July 2003), p. 48.
19. R.L. Durkin, "Defining the Practice of Forensic Accounting," CPA Expert (Special Edition, 1999).
20. Annett Stalker and M.G. Ueltzen, "An Audit Versus A Fraud Examination," CPA Expert (Winter 2009), p. 4.
21. G.S. Smith and D.L. Crumbley, "Defining a Forensic Audit," Journal of Digital Forensics, Security, and Law, 2009, Vol. 4, No. 1, p. 69.
22. Lee Child, Die Trying, New York: Jove Books, 1999, p.29.
23. See http://acct.tamu.edu/giroux/acctride.html.
24. J.T. Wells, "So That's Why It's Called a Pyramid Scheme," Journal of Accountancy 190 (October 2000), pp. 91–95.
25. Anita Dennis, "Taking Account: Key Dates for the Profession," Journal of Accountancy 190 (October 2000), pp. 97–105.
26. Heather Timmons and Bettina Wassener, "Satyam Chief Admits Huge Fraud," New York Times (January 7, 2009), http://www.nytimes.com/2009/01/08/business/worldbusiness/08satyam.html.
27. Phillip McClelland and Patricia Stantov, "Forensic Accounting: It's Positively Ancient," Journal of Forensic Accounting 5 (2004), pp. 554-555.
28. Meyer v. Sefton, 2 Stark. 274 (1817); see Clarence V. McArthur, "Evidence—Accountants as Experts," Canadian Bar Review XXVI (5) (May 1948), p. 873.
29. See www.homewoodave.com/LifetimeAchievementAward.htm.
30. Alex Moore, "The Accountant as an Expert Witness," The Accountant (June 29, 1907), pp. 879–886. See also Leopold Frankel, "Court Testimony of Accountants," Certified Public Accountant XIII (5) (May 1933), p. 263.
31. Richard Mattessich, "A Tale of Forensic Accounting Before Forensic Accounting," Journal of Forensic Accounting 10 (2001), pp. 293–296.
32. Astrup Cariss, "On Arbitration; and on Forms of Balance Sheets," Accountant (April 14, 1883); Joshua Slater, "Arbitration and Awards," Accountant (November 10, 17, 1883).
33. Arnold T. Watson, "Falsified Accounts," Accountant (October 10, 18, 1884).
34. Frank Creke, "Investigation of Public Companies' Accounts and Reports Thereof," Accountant (January 5, 1889), pp. 7–11.
35. William H. Shawcross, "How to Receive and Give Evidence," Accountant XXIV, New Series, No. 1206 (January 15, 1898), p. 73. See also William N. Ashman, "Preparation of Accounts for the Court," Business (June 1895), pp. 234–239.
36. Cleveland F. Bacon, "The Accountant as an Expert Witness," Journal of Accountancy 1: 2 (December 1905), pp. 99–105.
37. Ibid.
38. Alex Moore, "The Accountant as an Expert Witness," Accountant (June 29, 1907), p. 880.
39. Ibid., p. 886.
40. J.G. Korner, Jr., "Practice Before the U.S. Board of Tax Appeals," Journal of Accountancy 40 (1) (July 1925), pp. 1–14.
41. Editorial, Journal of Accountancy (August 1925), pp. 104–115.
42. "Industrial and Financial Investigations," paper presented to the National Association of Cost Accountants, First Western Regional Conference, Chicago, February 7, 1924.
43. M.S. Sullivan, SCt, 1 ustc ¶236, 274 US 259, 47 SCt 607 (1927). See also R. Capone, CA-7, 2 ustc ¶786, 51 F2d 609 (1931).
44. R.J. Schoenberg, Mr. Capone: The Real and Complete Story of Al Capone (Great Britain: St. Edmundsbury Press, 1992), p. 247.
45. Thomas Reppetto, American Mafia (New York: Henry Holt, 2004), p. 123.

[46] "Road to Perdition, a Smoking Gun," *http://www.awesomestories. com/movies/nav_top.html*.

[47] Thomas Reppetto, AMERICAN MAFIA (New York: Henry Holt, 2004), p. 114.

[48] R.J. Schoenberg, MR. CAPONE: THE REAL AND COMPLETE STORY OF AL CAPONE (Great Britain: St. Edmundsbury Press, 1992), p. 233.

[49] Schoenberg, op. cit. p. 309.

[50] Amy Hamilton, "IRS: Setting the Stage for a Sequel," TAX NOTES (January 6, 2003), p. 34.

[51] Maurice E. Peloubet, "Forensic Accounting: Its Place in Today's Economy," JOURNAL OF ACCOUNTANCY 81 (6) (June 1946), pp. 458–462.

[52] *Ibid.*, p. 459.

[53] *Ibid.*, p. 460.

[54] Editorial, "Interrelationship of Law and Accounting," JOURNAL OF ACCOUNTING 92 (1) (July 1951), pp. 36–37.

[55] Kenneth W. Robinson, "Accountants' Usefulness as Expert Witness Grows as Business Gets More Complex," JOURNAL OF ACCOUNTANCY 91 (5) (May 1951), p. 689.

[56] George B. Pearson, Jr., "Ten Warnings for the Accountant Who Wants to Do a Good Job on the Witness Stand," JOURNAL OF ACCOUNTANCY 94 (1) (July 1952), pp. 78–81.

[57] Max Lourie, "Forensic Accounting," NEW YORK CPA (November 1953), pp. 696–705.

[58] Francis C. Dykeman, FORENSIC ACCOUNTING: THE ACCOUNTANT AS EXPERT WITNESS (New York: John Wiley & Sons, 1982).

[59] Philip J. Gallagher, "Are You An Expert Witness?" JOURNAL OF ACCOUNTANCY (June 1964), pp. 73–74.

[60] *Ibid.*

[61] Lee R. Pennington, "Investigative Accounting," NEW YORK CPA, Vol. XVII (April 1948), pp. 288–293.

[62] *Ibid.*, p. 288.

[63] J. Edgar Hoover, "The Accountant's Role in the FBI," JOURNAL OF ACCOUNTANCY (May 1960), pp. 36–40.

[64] J. Edgar Hoover, "FBI Investigation of Fraud," JOURNAL OF ACCOUNTANCY (July 1965), pp. 34–39.

[65] FBI.gov.

[66] FBI.gov.

[67] Francis C. Dykeman, FORENSIC ACCOUNTING: THE ACCOUNTANT AS EXPERT WITNESS (New York: John Wiley & Sons, 1982). *See also* Joseph Belogna, GUIDELINES ON FORENSIC ACCOUNTING (Computer Systems, Inc., 1984).

[68] Kalman A. Barson, INVESTIGATIVE ACCOUNTING (New York: Van Nostrand Reinhold, 1986).

[69] G. Jack Bologna and Robert L. Lindquist, FRAUD AUDITING AND FORENSIC ACCOUNTING: NEW TOOLS AND TECHNIQUES (New York: John Wiley & Sons, 1987).

[70] G. Jack Bologna and Robert L. Lindquist, FRAUD AUDITING AND FORENSIC ACCOUNTING: NEW TOOLS AND TECHNIQUES (2d ed.) (New York: John Wiley & Sons, 1995), p. 37.

[71] "Book 'em! Forensic Accounting in History and Literature," The Kessler Report Vol. 1, No. 2. I.W. Collett is the pen name of Larry Crumbley. See FORENSIC ACCOUNTANTS APPEARING IN THE LITERATURE, *www.bus.lsu.edu/accounting/faculty/lcrumbley/forensic.html*.

[72] D.L. Crumbley, THE BIG R: A FORENSIC ACCOUNTING ACTION ADVENTURE (Durham, N.C: Carolina Academic Press, 2009).

[73] M.J. Wagner and P.B. Frank, MANAGEMENT ADVISORY SERVICES TECHNICAL CONSULTING PRACTICE AID 7: LITIGATION SERVICES (New York: AICPA, 1986).

[74] Wayne G. Bremser, FORENSIC ACCOUNTING AND FINANCIAL FRAUD (Watertown, Mass.: American Management Association, 1995).

[75] *Ibid.*, p. 2.

[76] *Ibid.*, pp. 17–32.

[77] R.L. Durkins, et al., "Incorporating Forensic Procedures in an Audit Environment," LITIGATION AND DISPUTE RESOLUTION SERVICES SUBCOMMITTEE FRAUD TASK FORCE (New York: AICPA), p. 3.

[78] *Ibid.*, p. 10.

[79] *Ibid.*

[80] *http://www/aicpa.org/members/div/mcs/exec_summ_forensics_svcs.htm*.

[81] J. Edward Ketz, "Comments of the Forensic Services Discussion Memorandum: An Open Letter to the AICPA," JOURNAL OF FORENSIC ACCOUNTING 5 (2004), p. 489.

[82] AICPA, Discussion Memo Question Responses, *www.theiia.org*.

[83] Ken Brown, "Auditors' Methods Make It Hard to Catch Fraud By Executives," THE WALL STREET JOURNAL (July 8, 2002), pp. C-1 and C-3.

[84] AICPA website, *www.aicpa.org/pubs/cpaltr/nov2002/fraud.htm*. Accessed April 16, 2003.

[85] *www.CatchMeGame.com/college*.

[86] NYSSCPA.org News Staff, "Auditing Firms Urge New Ways to Detect Fraud," (November 11, 2006), p. 13, *NYSSCPA.org*. Big Audit Firms Release, "Serving Global Markets and the Global Economy: A Vision From the CEOs of the International Audit Networks," (November 2006), p. 13, *www.globalpublicsymposium.com*.

[87] Big Audit Firm Release, "Serving Global Markets and the Global Economy: A View from the CEO's of the International Audit Network" (November 2006), p. 13.

[88] *See* Tammy Whitehouse, "Add Forensic Checks to Routine Audits," COMPLIANCE WEEK (March 5, 2007), pp. 1-4.

[89] IIA, AICPA, ACFE, MANAGING THE BUSINESS RISK OF FRAUD: A PRACTICAL GUIDE (2008). Locate on the internet site of the three groups (e.g., *http://www.acfe.com/documents/managing-business-risk.pdf*).

[90] Eamo Javers, "Spies, Lies & KPMG," BUSINESS WEEK (February 26, 2007), pp. 86-87.

[91] *http://www.diligenceinc.com*.

[92] Clifford Krauss, "Texas Financier and Antiguan Official Charged with Fraud," *New York Times*, June 20, 2009, *http://www.nytimes. com/2009/06/20/business/20stanford.html?em*.

[93] Corporate Espionage 101, *www.sans.org/reading_room/whitepaper/ engineering/512.php*.

[94] *Ibid.*

[95] Eamo Javers, "Spies, Lies & KPMG," BUSINESS WEEK (February 26, 2007), pp. 86-87.

[96] *Ibid.*

[97] *Ibid.*

[98] Joseph Pisani, "Spy v. Spy: Corporate Espionage," BUSINESS WEEK ONLINE (October 2, 2006).

[99] Helen Shaw, "The Trouble with COSO," The CFO, March 15, 2006.

[100] For an excellent list of the available legal resources relating to white collar crime, see J.D. Gill and M. Scott, "The Legal Environment and White Collar Crime," White Paper, Institute of Fraud Prevention, December 4, 2008.

[101] www.sec.gov./litigation.litreleases/2012/lr22450.htm

[102] Jake Poinier, "Fraud Finder," FUTURE MAGAZINE (Fall 2004), *http://www.phoneix.edu/students/future/oldissues/winter2004.fraud.htm*.

EXERCISES

1. What does *forensic* mean?
2. Define forensic accounting.
3. What are the key components of the definition of forensic accounting?
4. How does a forensic audit differ from a regular audit?
5. Who may have been the earliest expert witness?
6. What impact did the IRS have on forensic accounting in the United States?
7. Who was Frank Wilson?

8. What country claims the genesis of the discipline of forensic and investigative accounting?

9. What early accountant issued a circular advertising his desire to engage in forensic-type accounting activities?

10. What may be the forerunner of forensic and investigative accounting?

11. Which state legislated the first CPA law?

12. What was the forerunner of the American Institute of CPAs?

13. The first volume of the *Accountant's Index* listed forensic-type articles under which categories?

14. Which country was the first to require the audit of corporations, England or the United States?

15. In the 1920s, what senior partner began giving speeches encouraging financial and industrial investigations?

16. What huge bankruptcy in 2001–2002 caused forensic accountants to become rising stars within the accounting profession?

17. When an accountant testifies in court, the testimony may fall into two broad classes. Discuss them.

18. Who was probably the first person to coin the phrase *forensic accounting* in print?

19. Which type of auditor ferrets out deception in financial statements?

20. Investigative accounting activities in the FBI grew dramatically during what 20th century conflict?

21. In the 1960s, what legendary U.S. crime-fighter began to emphasize fraud detection in his federal government bureau?

22. What was the title and who was the author of the first forensic book?

23. Forensic accounting also may be known by another phrase, as indicated by the second forensic book published. What is the phrase and who published the book?

24. What book introduced the structural and behavioral consideration of fraud? What is the iceberg theory?

25. The modern role of forensic accounting has been defined by Wayne Bremser to include four elements. Which of the following is *not* one of the four:
    a. Pretrial support
    b. Trial support
    c. Expert witnessing
    d. Settlement support
    e. Decisions on the case

26. What situations did Wayne Bremser suggest are active areas for forensic accountants?

27. What unpredicted audit steps did the Panel on Audit Effectiveness suggest in 1998?

28. What is meant by the forensic-type fieldwork phase of an audit?

29. Common litigation services provided by CPAs while serving as expert witnesses would include all *except* which of the following:
    a. Economic analysis.
    b. Computation based on market share of each participant based on sales.
    c. Rendering an audit opinion.
    d. Macro and micro economic analysis.
    e. All of the above.

30. An AICPA Fraud Task Force suggests that if a forensic accountant is brought into an audit to conduct a separate investigation (and not an adjunct to an audit), what standards apply?

31. What subtle shift in external auditing occurred in the early 1980s?

32. Using the Internet, learn how Xerox pumped up its earnings.

33. Using the Internet, examine how WorldCom cooked its books.

34. Using the Internet, search for the terms *"litigation support"* and *"litigation services"* and visit five or six sites that involve forensic accounting services. Also explore several sites involving divorce situations.

35. Using the Internet, visit the Kessler International website and read some of the stories in "Kessler in the News." Who was the first "forensic auditor"?

36. Using the Internet, find several definitions of forensic accounting.

37. Using an advanced Google search (e.g., Larry Crumbley, forensic), learn about these forensic accountants:
    a. Jack Burke
    b. Craig L. Greene
    c. Susan Henry
    d. Bruce Dubinsky
    e. Howard Davia
    f. Gerry Lagerberg

38. Using the Internet, find some universities that offer forensic accounting courses.

39. On the Internet find the *KPMG India Fraud Survey Report*, 2010.
    a. How many chief executive officers received the questionnaire?

b. How many of the respondents do not have a written fraud policy?

c. Maximum losses in monetary terms involved what account?

d. Where is the blame for fraud placed by the organizations?

e. What is the profile of the typical fraudster in India?

40. Using the Internet, locate and review these sites:

a. National Fraud Center

b. The Fraud Detectives Consultant Network

c. Milberg Weiss Bershad Hynes & Lerach

d. Mark R. Simmons

e. Communications Fraud Control Association

f. Securities Exchange Commission, Litigation Release

41. Using Google, determine the number of hits for these terms:

a. Forensic accounting.

b. Fraud auditing.

c. Forensic auditing.

d. Fraud examination.

42. Go to the Internet site titled White Collar Fraud by Sam Antar and check out his White Collar Fraud Blog.

43. Search the Internet for the company MAXIMA Group. List the main consequences of corporate fraud.

44. Search the Internet and learn about the AICPA's site on Business Valuation and Forensic/Litigation Services.

45. Search the Internet: Is plagiarism fraud?

46. On the Internet, compare the forensic accounting programs at Florida Atlantic University and West Virginia University. What is your opinion with respect to getting a degree over the Internet? Does one need to have an accounting degree to be a forensic accountant?

47. On the Internet, locate the U.S. Dept. of Justice, "Education and Training in Fraud and Forensic Accounting: A Guide for Educational Institutions, Stakeholder Organizations, Faculty, and Students," March 2007. Does this report take the "narrow approach" or "broad approach" with respect to the definition of forensic accounting? Why? What is your opinion?

48. Go to the *Journal of Forensic Accounting* Internet site. What approach does the publisher, James Edwards, take with respect to the definition of forensic accounting? Is the narrow or broad approach best?

49. Who says a forensic audit is akin to a police investigation?

50. What is the AICPA's position with respect to a forensic audit?

51. Forensic accounting always involves which one of the following?

a. Business valuation

b. Investigating suspected fraud

c. Testifying in the courtroom as an expert

d. Using accounting techniques and financial expertise in a legal environment

e. All of the above

52. Who said "what the use of finger prints was to the 19th century, and DNA analysis was to the 20th, forensic accounting will be to the 21st century"?

a. Joe Wells

b. Gordon Brown

c. Gary Giroux

d. Wyllie Guild

e. Alex Moore

53. Who is the father of the term forensic accounting?

a. Max Lourie

b. James McCleland

c. Maurice E. Peloubet

d. Robert Lindquist

e. Someone else

54. The authors give whom the credit for being the first forensic accountant?

a. James McCleland

b. Doug Carmichael

c. Maurice E. Peloubet

d. Joe Wells

e. Robert Lindquist

55. Which is not one of the six main categories of the 1986 types of litigation services?

a. Antitrust analysis

b. Valuation

c. Damages

d. Analyses

e. Fraud

56. What was WorldCom's main fraud strategy?

a. Moving expenses into asset accounts

b. Bill-and-hold strategy

c. Big bath

d. Channel stuffing

e. Cookie-jar reserves

57. Which was one of the first groups/laws to encourage auditors to incorporate forensic techniques into audit programs?
    a. Sarbanes-Oxley Act
    b. PCAOB
    c. SAS No. 99 (AU 316)
    d. Panel on Audit Effectiveness
    e. COSO
58. Which statement is false?
    a. The AICPA does *not* require auditors to carry out specific forensic techniques.
    b. The AICPA states that companies should *not* use the forensic services of their external auditors, unless it pertains to the annual audit.
    c. Doug Carmichael faults auditors for *not* adopting forensic techniques.
    d. WorldCom's external auditors missed about $21 billion of improperly booked items.
    e. The threat of a future investigation reduces the occurrence of fraudulent behavior from about 75 percent to 43 percent.
59. Search the Internet and determine what happened to these individuals.
    a. Robert Pfaff (KPMG).
    b. Adrian Dicker (BDO Seidman).
60. Using the Internet, write a paper about Bernard Madoff's ponzi scheme. Include Shawn Merriman and Andrew Hamilton Williams, Jr. in your discussion.

61. Search for the latest about Robert Allen Stanfords' alleged ponzi scheme.
62. Go to the Internet and search for the Harvard University student Adam Wheeler and determine what he did.
63. Go to the Securities and Exchange Commission Internet site and diagram the structure of the SEC.
64. From the Internet, determine what is a 10K Report. A 10Q Report.
65. Go to the Internet and list some of the major Ponzi schemes and their possible amounts scammed.
66. Go to the Deloitte Forensic Center Videos and listen to these videos:
    a. Applying Six Degrees of Separation to Preventing Fraud.
    b. Understanding The Foreign Corrupt Practices Act.
67. Go to Youtube.com and listen to Frank W. Abagnale Jr. – "Catch Me If You Can," Part 2 (19:08). Or rent the movie and watch "Catch Me If You Can."
68. What is the purpose of the FCPA, and what does the FCPA prohibit?
69. How did Oracle India try to get around the FCPA?
70. How does the OECD try to improve the social and well-being of people around the world.

2

FORENSIC ACCOUNTING EDUCATION, INSTITUTIONS, AND SPECIALTIES

It's tedious. It's very difficult. You have to group difficult concepts. A forensic accountant is like someone eating a bowl of spaghetti. When you start pulling at each strand of spaghetti, you don't know where it will lead, and you have to follow it. Being a forensic accountant is like eating spaghetti one strand at a time.

—Danny Heitman[1]

OBJECTIVES

After completing Chapter 2, you should be able to:

1. Chart a plan for coursework that prepares you to become a forensic accountant.
2. Describe career opportunities in forensic and investigative accounting.
3. Know the main professional organizations and credentials of importance to practicing forensic accountants.

OVERVIEW

Forensic accountant qualifications work together and support each other like a three-layered wedding cake. The largest, bottom layer is a strong accounting background. A middle, smaller layer is a thorough knowledge of auditing, risk assessment and control, and fraud detection. The smallest, top layer of the cake is a basic understanding of the legal environment. The icing on the cake is a strong set of communication skills, both written and oral. A forensic accountant is often engaged in a combination of fraud detection and litigation support, both requiring an inquisitive mind and attention to details.[2]

Forensic accounting is a growing and exciting career that reduces the complexity by distilling information and slicing away deceptions to help a judge or jury to see the essence of a financial scam.[3] According to Andrew Bernstein, with Miami-based Berkowitz, Dick, Pollak & Brant, "you're trying to piece together a puzzle where you do not have the picture on the box to know what it's going to look like. The facts are not settled, and actually it's the facts that are in dispute."[4]

As forensic accountant Michael G. Kessler suggests, forensic accountants should follow the attributes of Columbo, the television detective who wore a crumpled raincoat in the 1970s. "Peter Falk could quickly solicit the cooperation of defendants and solve cases using a gentle approach and the use of 'forensic evidence.'"[5]

However, the main difference between fiction and reality is that instead of using mask and gun, today's villains use mouse and keyboard. Instead of hiding behind a lamppost in a trench coat and fedora, today's forensic accountants are more likely to be hiding behind their own computers, searching for clues amid mountains of data.[6]

The field is broader than fraud auditing because it involves accounting, auditing, psychology, criminology, computer forensics, and litigation support. In addition to the broader perspective, forensic accounting also requires a different mindset. Many accountants are trained that numbers do not lie. Auditing is about following the rules. Forensic accountants take the opposite tack because they cannot assume books and financial statements are correct. Books may be cooked; financial statements may be deceptively constructed; records may be false; and invoices may be fake. Forensic accountants look beyond the records and invoices. Forensic accountants follow the motto: "Nothing is as it seems."[7] What kind of knowledge, skills, and abilities does the forensic accountant need? What specific courses help ensure the competencies of the financial sleuth who unearths fraud by delving into the Form 10Ks, Form 10Qs, and all the other records and documents?

This chapter explores how coursework in multiple disciplines prepares students to enter the forensic accounting field and what professional associations serve the specialists in this rapidly growing profession. As Lorraine Horton, a forensic accountant, says, "Forensic accounting is very different from auditing in that there is no template to use. There are no set rules. You don't know when you go into a job how it is going to be."[8]

Hopefully, however, forensic accountants are not like the analogy of the difference between external auditors and forensic accountants. "External auditors come down the hill after the battle and bayonet the wounded. Forensic accountants are the guys who follow behind them, going through the soldiers' pockets looking for money."

Preparing to Become a Forensic Accountant

¶ 2001   COLLEGE AND UNIVERSITY PROGRAMS

As long ago as 1953, Max Lourie advised colleges and universities to launch forensic accounting courses. Lourie suggested that accounting programs should offer forensic accounting courses and recommended that such programs be developed in conjunction with law schools where practicable.[9]

Lourie was somewhat ahead of his time; the growth in forensic curriculum has only begun in earnest in the wake of accounting scandals and the call for accounting reforms. A study by Buckoff and Schrader found "that adding a forensic accounting course to the accounting curriculum can greatly benefit the three major stakeholders in accounting education: (1) academic institutions, (2) students, and (3) employers of accounting graduates."[10]

The number of universities and colleges that offer courses or programs in forensic and fraud auditing is growing, and many more are being planned.[11] Regretably, however, many of these courses are very narrowly focused on fraud examination and not the more exciting forensic accounting.

A number of the current programs focus primarily on fraud auditing and not necessarily forensic accounting. A forensic accountant needs knowledge of the courtroom and the legal system. Knowledge of both statute law and case law may be relevant to the goals or objectives of a forensic accountant. According to Robert J. DiPasquale, a forensic accountant, forensic accounting is an extremely competitive field. "What is interesting is that you may be a good accountant, but not a good forensic accountant. The training and the way you look at transactions are different."[12]

In forensic accounting there are few rules; "anything is possible."[13] Forensic accountants need an understanding of accounting, criminology, law, and investigative auditing techniques, as indicated by the four overlapping content areas in Figure 2.1's Venn diagram. The large circle refers to a need for computer knowledge in all four areas. Forensic accountants having different specialties will create different balances of the four inside sets of knowledge.

Figure 2.1. Forensic Accountant's Knowledge Base

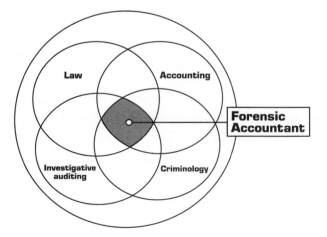

Superimposed upon these four categories is the need for a forensic accountant to have excellent computer skills and excellent oral and written communication skills. As Joe Anastasi, a forensic accountant, suggests, "today's Sergeant Joe Friday does not write in a small notebook in the course of solving crimes; he now reconstructs the data from imaged hard drives."[14]

Using a survey, two professors found that the following were the most important skills of a forensic accountant:[15]

		Mean
1.	Analytical Skills	6.51
2.	Basic Accounting Skills	6.31
3.	Problem Solving Skills	6.30
4.	Data Analysis Skills	6.27
5.	Interviewing Skills	6.25
6.	Verbal Communication Skills	6.11
7.	Basic Computer Skills	6.05

This same academic and practitioner survey found the following ranking of characteristics of a forensic accountant:[16]

		Mean
1.	Persistence	6.12
2.	Skepticism	6.12
3.	Puzzle Skills	6.08
4.	People Skills	6.04
5.	Flexibility	5.91
6.	Works Well in Teams	5.84
7.	Experience in Auditing	5.80

Other research sponsored by the AICPA found the following essential traits and characteristics of a forensic accountant:[17]

	Attorney	Rank	Academic	Rank	CPA	Rank
Analytical	78%	1	90%	1	86%	1
Detail-oriented	64%	2	35%		49%	3
Ethical	60%	3	65%	2	49%	3
Responsive	41%	4	2%		10%	
Insightful	39%	5	29%		24%	
Inquisitive	22%		48%	4	52%	2
Intuitive	26%		40%		38%	5
Persistent	19%		46%	5	30%	
Skepticism	12%		54%	3	43%	4
Evaluative	30%		15%		16%	
Function well under pressure	28%		23%		35%	

The same AICPA research found the following core skills of a forensic accountant:[18]

	Attorney	Rank	Academic	Rank	CPA	Rank
Effective oral communicator	61%	1	28%		43%	3
Simplify the information	57%	2	11%		30%	
Critical/strategic thinker	49%	3	62%	1	50%	1
Identify key issues	38%	4	30%		32%	
Auditing skills	37%	5	53%	2	31%	
Investigative ability	37%	5	45%	3	41%	4
Effective written communicator	21%		34%		43%	2
Investigative intuitiveness	24%		36%		39%	5
Synthesize results of discovery and analysis	37%		43%	4	36%	
Think like the wrongdoer	4%		38%	5	14%	
Understand the goals of a case	33%		9%		19%	
Tell the story	30%		9%		16%	
See the big picture	30%		21%		30%	

¶ 2011 KEYSTONES OF FORENSIC ACCOUNTING CURRICULA

A survey of professors in 2003 ranked 49 curriculum content items for forensic accounting, as shown in Table 2.1.[19] Although many of these topics, such as statistical sampling and analytical review procedures, may be covered in core accounting courses, the forensic accounting student may find some needs are not met by current course offerings. A good forensic accounting course can cover many of the topics not typically offered by core courses, but institutions may need to develop creative ways to fill voids by working with other departments and resources at their schools.

Practitioners took a broader approach and ranked litigation support and expert witnessing much higher than did professors responding to the same survey. Likewise, practitioners ranked "Effective report writing" number two and "Shareholder litigation" number three. Forensic accounting is much broader than some of the narrowly focused university programs and courses devoted solely to fraud investigation and fraud examination.

Table 2.1. Forensic Accounting Curricula Topics Ranked by Importance

Rank	Curriculum Content Items	Rank	Curriculum Content Items
1	Fundamentals of Fraud		
2	Financial statement fraud		programs
3	Types of fraud (e.g., employees, management)	11	Anti-fraud auditing standards
		12	Analytical review procedures
4	Cooking the books and problems in accounting	13	Environmental and business red flags
		14	Antifraud criteria
5	Elements of fraud: pressure, opportunity and rationalization	15	Cyber and computer fraud
		16	Antifraud education
6	Antifraud controls	17	Antifraud training
7	Internal control evaluation	18	Professional standards pertaining to forensic accounting
8	Theory and methodology of fraud examination		
		19	Manipulation of related party transactions
9	Principles of ethics and corporate code of conduct	20	Earnings management
10	Fraud detection and deterrence	21	Effective report writing

Rank	Curriculum Content Items	Rank	Curriculum Content Items
			of interviews
22	Financial reporting process and analysis	36	Intellectual property fraud
23	Criminology and white-collar and economic crimes	37	Conflicts of interest investigating techniques
24	Financial reporting standards and principles	38	Compliance with applicable laws and regulations
25	Techniques in locating hidden assets	39	Crime control techniques
26	Legal elements of fraud	40	Shareholder litigation
27	Corporate governance	41	Professional organizations sponsoring forensic accounting
28	Conducting internal investigations	42	Resolution of allegations of misconduct
29	Security and privacy	43	Rules of evidence
30	Knowledge of the legal system	44	Business valuations and cost estimates
31	Statistical sampling	45	Expert testimony and expert witness techniques
32	Occupational fraud	46	Litigation consulting techniques
33	Careers in forensic accounting	47	Modeling and discounting future damages
34	Bribery and corruption investigation	48	Trial and cross-examination
35	Interview skills and legal aspects	49	Valuation expert in divorce

Another survey in 2009 found these to be the most important topics for a fraud/forensic accounting course:[20]

- Fraudulent financial reporting analysis.
- The psychology of criminology.
- Examination of changes in records.
- Corporate culture reviews.
- Investigating electronic evidence.
- Net worth analysis.
- Damage/loss valuation analysis.
- Litigation consulting.
- Flowcharting internal controls.
- Applying Benford's Law.

The conclusion of this 2009 survey was as follows:[21]

Course developers need to know that there are conceptual differences between fraud examination and forensic accounting. Forensic investigations are broad and far-ranging. Accounting curriculum developers need to determine whether they should base their program revisions on a fraud model [narrow approach], a more wide-ranging forensics model [broad approach], or a combination of the two approaches. Such decisions affect the direction of learning and topic coverage in the accounting curriculum. Just as accounting practitioners are reconsidering their professional roles in providing future client services, accounting academics should also consider the implications their revisions will have on meeting the future needs of our profession.

¶ 2021   KSAs AND EDUCATION OF THE FORENSIC ACCOUNTANT

How does one get an education that will provide the knowledge, skills, and abilities (KSAs) one needs for a forensic accounting career? Accounting majors are already well on their way. The fundamentals provided in such programs—accounting courses, auditing, risk assessment, and controls—must be part of the curriculum. However, there is a need for legal and investigative skills (to say nothing of communication, writing, and even a bit of psychology training) that are needed.

Table 2.2 outlines a number of courses that would be valuable to a student preparing for a career in forensic accounting. Other than the basic accounting and auditing courses, a basic understanding of investigative techniques and courtroom procedures are quite helpful. Table 2.2 addresses areas that build on the accounting foundation and in a perfect world would be easily accessible to accounting students.

Table 2.2. Forensic Accounting KSAs and Courses

KSA Description	Courses	Academic Program Area
Knowledge of law, legal system, courts, and courtroom procedure.	A forensic accounting course ought to cover these topics, but not in great detail. A tax research course could help fill this need.	Taxation and Business Law
Financial statement fraud. It is imperative for the forensic accountant to have an excellent working knowledge of financial statement analysis. A forensic accountant needs expertise to view such statements critically, use ratio analysis, and employ other tools to scour for inconsistencies and red flags.	A solid financial statement analysis course should be taken. A fraud auditing course would also be helpful.	Accounting or Finance
Corporate governance, shareholder rights and litigation, securities laws, and protections. The forensic accountant needs to understand at a high level the rules governing corporations and securities.	A course on securities law and/or corporate governance would be helpful.	Accounting or Finance
Report writing and communication. Not only must the forensic accountant be a good report writer but also needs advanced oral communication skills.	A financial or legal report-writing course is ideal to take. Otherwise, a good writing course through the English or communication department would be helpful. Speech is also a helpful course.	Business, English, and Communications
Crime. Many aspects of criminal law and procedure are helpful. Criminology, fraud, white collar crime, etc.	An introductory course on criminal law and a course on criminal procedure are helpful.	Law Enforcement, Sociology

Computer fraud and cyber-crime. Students should understand how computers, computer networks and the Internet work. They also need to know how cybercrime is perpetrated and how it is detected.	Courses on information systems are important and helpful. Courses on auditing that cover computer auditing essentials are excellent. A specific course on computer crime would be especially helpful.	Business, Information Systems
Human factors involved in intelligence gathering, interview techniques, and understanding the motivations for fraud and other criminal activities. The forensic accountant will need a grounding in psychology to be able to deal effectively with people, understand their motives, and gather intelligence.	A psychology course is important. If the school has a criminal law program, a course on interviewing and gathering intelligence is recommended.	Psychology, Criminal Law, Law
Ethical issues in business.	A business ethics course will raise contemporary situations that give rise to fraudulent acts and legal dilemmas.	Business
Valuation. One of the more technical pursuits of forensic accountants is business valuations. In most cases a forensic accountant who works substantially with business valuations will specialize in the area because of its complexity.	Business valuation is a curriculum in and of itself, but there may be a finance course the accounting student can take to help. Accounting students with a penchant for finance who want to double major in accounting and finance may want to consider this specialty, although information systems is extremely important also.	Business and Finance

Career Tracks in Forensic Accounting

Parade magazine on April 15, 2007, indicated that the hottest jobs for college graduates were forensic accountants. A forensic accountant was described as combining accounting, auditing, and investigative skills with a salary ranging from $30,000 to $150,000.[22]

Economic recessions often increase fraud, since executives may engage in more "cooking the books" techniques to improve financial results, and financially strapped employees will steal business funds or commit other types of fraud and abuse. Robert Half 2013 Salary Guide indicates that there is still a strong demand for forensic accountants.[23] A 2012 AICPA survey says forensic accountants "are seeing a noticeable increase in demand for their services. Forty-seven percent of respondents saw an increase in the hours spent working on forensic accounting, compared with 14 percent who said their hours decreased."[24] In 2012, Ken Tysiac predicted that forensic accounting revenues will grow 6.8 percent annually over the next five years.[25]

A 2011 Forensic and Valuation Services Trend Survey found that about one-half of the participants said they devoted more time to forensic work during the past year, with an average increase of 20 percent. One-quarter had added more professionals to their practice.[26]

The Federal Government's $787 billion economic stimulus and bailout programs are breeding grounds for fraud, waste, and abuse. Dan Weil estimated that up to $50 billion of the total (or 5 to 10 percent) will be susceptible to fraud. FBI Director Robert Mueller warns of fraud stemming from the stimulus packages.[27] There should be much work for forensic accountants.

In the late 1980s, there were the collapse and scandals in the savings and loan (S&L) industry. Forensic accountant Fred Smolen unraveled a $200 million mortgage-loan Ponzi scheme by Virginia-based Landbank Equity Corporation inside the company's densely layered structure. Smolen discovered that the company had used spin-off companies to inflate property appraisals and hide foreclosure losses, sold to other S&Ls bad loan portfolios that included notes on nonexistent property, charged points that sometimes were as high as 40 percent of the loan value, and covered old losses with new loans. The company's founder and wife received 40 and 31 years, respectively, in prison for conspiracy, racketeering, tax fraud, and obstruction of justice.[28]

¶ 2031   INCOME EXPECTATIONS FOR FORENSIC ACCOUNTANTS

Salaries for forensic accountants range from $50,000 to more than $190,000. Gumshoe gumption can lead to high-level careers at law firms, corporations, and government agencies such as the FBI. These employers look for candidates with bachelor's of science degrees in accounting, plus two to four years of accounting experience. A Certified Public Accounting license is almost always required, along with a CFF, CFE, Cr.FA, MAFF, or FCPA certificate. AICPA research indicates that CPAs represent 94 percent of forensic experts hired over two years.[29]

Government Employees

According to the U.S. Office of Personnel Management, a senior agent (GS 12 or 13) with 10 or more years of experience can earn between $75,000 and $90,000 annually. In the private sector, a good forensic investigator can make a base salary of between $125,000 and $190,000, charging as much as $500 an hour.[30]

Consulting Fees for Independent Contractors

Forensic accountants work with attorneys, private investigators, law enforcement officers, corporate security specialists, the IRS, and the FBI. Kessler International charges about $300 per hour for forensic consultations, one-third more than the firm does for audit work. Forensic accounting services are a meaningful part of many CPA firms' practices.[31] Two professors found that the hiring potential of students is enhanced by the completion of a forensic accounting course.[32]

The Board of Directors at Fannie Mae hired the Huron Consulting Group to perform a forensic accounting probe. The final report cleared the current management of knowingly participating in any wrongdoing.

The report took 17 months and was 616 pages plus 2,000 pages of supporting documents. The fraud was estimated to be $11 billion, and the cost of the forensic probe was $60 million to $70 million.

¶ 2041 SPECIALTIES WITHIN FORENSIC AND INVESTIGATIVE ACCOUNTING

After the corporate scandals in 2001 and 2002, one reporter said that "Former cops are being hired by auditors to try to spot fraud." These new green eyeshades are looking for inflated profits, hidden assets, questionable payments, and other corporate shenanigans. Forensic accountants are hunting for what Fed Chairman Alan Greenspan termed "infectious greed."[33]

Much of this text focuses on the specialties in forensic accounting, with chapters focusing on skills that forensic accountants need to uncover fraudulent financial reporting, employee fraud related to the misappropriation of assets, money laundering, litigation support and expert witnessing, cybercrime, and business valuations. A forensic accounting background is helpful in these professional specialties:

- Accountants
- Consultants
- Internal auditors
- IRS auditors
- Government auditors
- FBI agents [Of the 12,000 agents worldwide, about 15 percent have accounting backgrounds.]
- SEC accountants
- Bankruptcy specialists
- Professors
- Bank examiners
- Chief financial officers
- Valuators of closely held businesses

Employee Crime Specialist

Employees steal more than shoplifters. A survey by Kessler International found that 79 percent of employees steal from their employers at an annual loss of more than $120 billion. Almost 87 percent of the respondents admitted to stealing office supplies, falsifying expense reports, and were paid for hours they did not work. Motivation includes greed (49 percent), vindictiveness (43 percent), and need (8 percent). An astonishing 92 percent of the employees said they lied on their job applications that asked whether they stole from a previous employer. Sixty-eight percent did not disclose that they were discharged from a previous job due to theft.[34] More than 25 percent of 1,000 resumes sent to technology companies contained phony information or false credentials.[35] One can easily purchase a fake degree and fake set of transcripts.

Defining Employee Fraud

What is employee fraud? Professor Jack Robertson defines *employee fraud* (or crime) as the "use of fraudulent means to take money or other property from an employer," usually involving some kind of falsification (e.g., false documents, lying, exceeding authority, or violating employer policies).[36]

White-collar crimes according to the FBI are categorized by deceit, concealment, or violation of trust and are not dependent on the application or threat of physical force or violence. Such acts are committed by individuals and organizations to obtain money, property, or services; to avoid the payment or loss of money or services; or to secure a personal or business advantage.[37]

To be sure, like termites, fraud never sleeps. Fraud can destroy the foundations of a for-profit, governmental, or not-for-profit entity. So fighting fraud is a marathon, not a sprint. And even PCAOB believes that internal controls "can not provide absolute assurance of achieving financial reporting objectives because of inherent limitations." "A process that involves human diligence and compliance can be intentionally circumvented."[38]

There are many instances that don't qualify as employee fraud. As Nan DeMass concludes, "We all know that we take pens. We use the telephones for personal calls and the fax machines and the copy machines. I go down to two words: 'reasonable use,'" she said. "I think most companies are putting in their (employee) handbooks the simple statement that all of these things can be used by personnel if it is 'reasonable use.'"[39]

However, an employee at the Australian mint stole $100,145 over ten months by hiding bills and coins in his lunch box and boots. He carried away on an average 150 coins in each boot every day.

Bologna and Lindquist state that forensic accountants investigating employee crimes typically look for transactions that are odd as to:
- Time (of day, week, month, year, or season)
- Frequency (too many, too few)
- Places (too far, too near, and too "far out")
- Amount (too high, too low, too consistent, too alike, too difficult)
- Parties or personalities (related parties, strange and estranged relationships between parties, management performing clerical functions).

An alert Canadian Mountie illustrates the benefit of finding that small clue. When two men tried to pass off $25 million worth of bonds in Toronto in 2001, the Mountie noticed the bonds bore the word "**dollar**" rather "**dollars**."

A former Scotland Yard scientist had tried to create the world's biggest fraud by authenticating $2.5 trillion worth of fake U.S. Treasury bonds. Police later raided a London bank vault and discovered that the bonds had been printed with an ink jet printer that had not been invented when the bonds were allegedly produced. Zip codes were used even though they were not introduced until 1963.[40] Thus, with a single clue a forensic accountant can solve a fraudulent mystery.

However, "economic crimes and fraud often do not involve obvious evidence like the smoking gun. Forensic accountants look behind the deals and handshakes and probe beyond the numbers to uncover the reality of financial situations."[41] As Tom Carlucci suggests, "every investigation I did as a prosecutor, you have a particular target, but it always branches off because something else gets your attention. And that's what is going to happen with a forensic accountant."[42]

Finding fraud is not easy. A British publication suggests that prosecutors think that accountants have x-ray vision. "It is assumed that if an accountant stares really hard at a set of accounts, then somehow, magically, information will appear before his/her eyes that are invisible to lesser mortals."[43]

A small-time Miami hood settled a domestic argument by hitting his wife with a left hook. A bad move because the woman's father beat the guy senseless. At the hospital an attendant cut away a strange bandage around the hood's ankle. The gold coin found inside the bandage was the stolen famed 1787 Brasher doubloon, part of an $8.5 million-7,000 coin heist from Willis H. DuPont. These coins may never have been discovered if the hood had settled the dispute differently or the attendant had not been inquisitive.[44]

Additionally, forensic accountants should be alerted by:
- Internal controls that are unenforced or too often compromised by higher authorities.
- Employee motivations, morale, and job satisfaction levels that are chronically low.
- A corporate culture and reward system that supports unethical behavior toward employees, customers, competitors, lenders, and shareholders.[45]

A SHELL CORPORATION. The Securities and Exchange Commission filed a civil injunction against a Cypress corporation, ACLN, that was a vehicle for an exceptionally bold and elaborate financial fraud that resulted in losses of hundreds of millions of dollars to investors in the U.S. and abroad.

The commission alleged the following about ACLN:

ACLN significantly overstated the volume of its used car transactions, and claimed substantial revenue from a purported new car sales operation that, in fact, never existed.

ACLN claimed to have bank deposits of more than $117 million. The actual balance at that time was less than $2 million. This deception was furthered through the creation of forged bank documents that ACLN provided to its auditors.

ACLN did not own the largest physical asset on its balance sheet, the car-carrier vessel the Sea Atef, and, in any event, significantly inflated the vessel's value.[46]

Criminal Acts at the Top

Forensic accountants have to look for suspicious behavioral clues in conducting investigations. A lavish lifestyle could indicate that a manager or owner of a business is skimming money from the corporate till. Based upon enforcement actions by the SEC between 1987 and 1999, of the 276 frauds that took place, the company's chief executive was involved about 70 percent of the time.[47]

For someone who earned a salary of just $1,000 a month, Rana Koleilat managed to live a pretty nice life. She traveled by private jet, took along her servant and hairdresser, and stayed at the poshest locality in London and Paris. Back home in Beirut, Lebanon, she lived in a three-story penthouse. To anyone who asked how she lived so well, she replied that she had a "rich uncle."

Actually, Koleilat helped manage a private bank in Beirut, and therein lies the truth: the chairman of the bank said he lost $1.2 billion, and depositors lost another several hundred million dollars.[48]

Even when internal controls exist, top management can circumvent them. The founder and his two sons were charged with looting billions of dollars from Adelphia Communication under the eyes of auditors of the auditing firm Deloitte & Touche.

Auditing firms can become too enmeshed with the companies being audited. Sherron Watkins said that by the mid-1990s Arthur Andersen "needed Enron more than Enron needed Andersen, both for the prestige and for the billings, which were closing in on $1 million a week."[49] Is it any wonder that Andersen approved many aggressive accounting techniques?

Before the fraud was found at HealthSouth, Ernst & Young collected $2.6 million from HealthSouth (as audit-related fees) to check the cleanliness and physical appearances of 1,800 facilities. A 50-point checklist was used by dozens of junior-level accountants in unannounced visits. For 2000, the Ernst & Young audit fee was $1.03 million; other fees were $2.65 million.

Data-driven approaches do not detect all fraud schemes such as bribery and kickbacks. Often corruption and collusion involve circumvention of controls by top executives. So searching the relevant transactions data for patterns, red flags, and unexplained relationships may not yield positive results because the information may not be recorded within the system. Thus, "behavioral concepts and qualitative factors frequently allow the auditor to look beyond the data, both with respect to data that is there and data that isn't."[50]

Thus, employee crime specialists meld expertise from internal and external auditing, financial auditing, psychological training, and criminology studies to their practice of uncovering or preventing employee misdeeds.

Fraudulent Financial Reporting

Related to the underworld of employee and management fraud is the manipulation of financial statements to misrepresent losses, expenses, and other bad news to investors and customers. Corporations given to dubious business practices employed dubious financial reporting methods, as exemplified by Enron's special purpose entities and other, now famous (or infamous) financial reporting schemes.

SOFTWARE SCAM. The Securities and Exchange Commission (SEC) brought action against the CEO and CFO of a software company alleging fraudulent accounting practices. The two officers caused their company to misstate its financial results during its fiscal years 1994 through 1996 by improperly reporting revenues on sales of a development-stage Unix-language software product.

Those customers who purchased SSA's Unix product during the relevant period experienced severe and continuing difficulties with its functionality and performance and in many instances rejected the product. Since there existed significant uncertainties about customer acceptance of the product and collectibility of the contract price and significant vendor obligations remained, the earnings process was not complete and recognition of revenues on sales of the product was improper under applicable accounting standards.

The SEC also alleged that, during 1995 and 1996, in addition to the above fraudulent practice, the company recognized approximately $52 million in revenue from sales of its Unix product that were subject to side letters or other material contingencies.[51]

Asset Tracing Specialist

Aside from fraud, shrinking gross margins, employees going to work for competitors, and loss of customers may be warning signs that a forensic accountant is needed.

Forensic accountants may be hired to trace missing or undervalued assets. In a divorce situation one spouse may try to disguise or undervalue marital assets. Alternatively, in a partnership setting a forensic accountant may trace properties, evaluate financial reports, and assess the value of a business or investments.

In the Parmalat scandal, three Italian lawyers stated in a bankruptcy court filing that they had traced $ 7.7 billion in missing Parmalat funds. They claimed that the money was stolen, not lost. Lawyer Carlo Zauli told Reuters that "it would be an illusion to believe proof of electronic transfer of the funds could be found."[52] Lawyers representing the Parmalat Creditors Committee had not said where this money was being held or if it was recoverable.

Craig L. Greene unraveled a corporate kickback scheme in a manufacturing company. There was an anonymous tip that an executive of the company was receiving kickbacks from a vendor in Florida. Greene felt that the vendor's address looked wrong, like a street in a residential neighborhood. Checking maps and satellite images of Florida on the Internet, he determined that the address was in a complex of townhouses. He flew to Florida, found the vendor's mother living in the townhouse, and sweet-talked her into showing him the books and the cancelled kickback checks. Case closed.[53]

Mark Kohn gives this advice when searching for unreported income or hidden assets:[54]
1. Look at the lifestyles of the individuals (behavioral aspects).
2. Look at the expenses of the business.
3. Compare the cash flow with income.
4. Know the business operations.
5. Look at the industry ratios (see Chapters 5 and 6).
6. Consider using private investigators.
7. Use the net worth method (see Chapter 6).

Many of these techniques are covered in subsequent chapters.

Financial sleuths have to deal with complex corporate entities. Knowledge of advanced accounting and consolidated returns, accounting and tax aspects of reorganizations, and the various types of business entities (including controlled groups, parent/subsidiary, and brother/sister corporations) is helpful to fraud detectives.

John O'Connor says the conviction on racketeering and other charges of businessman W. James E Oelsner III in the U.S. Virgin Islands was his most complicated case. "[Oelsner] took great pains to make his ownership of these assets bulletproof." Oelsner had a complex web of financial holding companies.[55]

After accounting problems surfaced at Xerox when $2 billion in revenues disappeared in 2002, PricewaterhouseCoopers (PWC) replaced KPMG as auditor. The new auditors charged Xerox $20.4 million in accounting fees, with about one-half for forensic accounting services to help identify the alleged fraud. PWC charged about half that amount for the normal audit.[56] Another report stated that Xerox paid PWC a total of $71.6 million in 2001. In January 2013, PWC had some 1,450 forensic professionals.

Rush jobs are common because time is of the essence in recovering sensitive data. Thus, forensic accountants may scour hard drives, retrieve long-lost e-mails, and confront suspected wrongdoers in the course of recovering valuable assets.[57]

A Deloitte & Touche forensic team was called into a computer company when an entire research unit departed suddenly for jobs with a competitor. With planes grounded following the September 11, 2001, terrorist attacks, the Deloitte group drove 13 hours to the client, imaged hard drives, and brought secret company data back to their super-secure clean-room at Deloitte's Boston office.

The investigators found 50 company secret documents printed by an engineer the night before his departure. The client used this evidence to obtain an injunction that kept the competitor from using the pirated information. The job took three weeks from start to finish.

Michael Kessler was hired by Monsanto Company to track down a sweetener-counterfeiting ring. Fake Equal packages were showing up in stores from Minnesota to South Carolina. Stores were complaining to Monsanto that scanners could not read the bar codes on some Equal boxes.

Kessler found bogus boxes of the Monsanto sugar substitute buried among packing crates and cardboard in a trash bin outside of Brooklyn's Haskel Trading Company.[58] From a database that links people to product counterfeiting, Kessler decided to stake out Haskel, where he obtained numerous photographs to substantiate counterfeiting charges. Monsanto obtained a court order and seized Haskel's books. Kessler found that Haskel was buying Equal in 2,000-pack boxes and repackaging the sweetener into 50-pack counterfeit boxes. Monsanto sued Haskel, and the suit was settled out of court.

Litigation Services Specialist and Expert Witness

The Litigation and Dispute Resolution Subcommittee of the AICPA defines *litigation services* as "services that involve pending or potential formal legal or regulatory proceedings before a trier of fact in connection with the resolution of a dispute between two or more parties. A *trier of fact* is a court, regulatory body, or government authority; their agents; a grand jury; or an arbitrator or mediator of a dispute."[59]

This subcommittee believes that a litigation service practitioner can be an expert witness or consultant in these broad areas:

- Computation
- Consulting
- Business valuations
- Proactive and reactive fraud investigation
- Pre- and post-bankruptcy restructuring, solvency analysis, and liquidation consulting
- Special accountings, tracings, reconstructions, and cash flow analysis
- Tax issues assessment and analysis
- Martial dissolution's assessment and analysis
- Contract costs and claims assessment and analysis
- Antitrust and other business combinations assessment and analysis
- Construction and environmental disputes assessment and analysis
- Business interruption and other insurance claims assessment and analysis[60]

The subcommittee outlines the following tasks of a litigation services practitioner:
- Issue identification
- Locating other experts
- Fact-finding
- Analysis
- Discovery assistance
- Document management
- Settlement assistance
- Expert testimony
- Trial and deposition assistance
- Post-trial support (for example, accounting services and funds administration)
- Negotiations
- Arbitration
- Mediation
- Training[61]

The 2011 AICPA Forensic and Valuation Services Trend Survey found a strong demand for forensic and valuation services across the board. An overwhelming majority expected continued robust demand during the coming two to five years, coincident with an increase in litigation and regulatory enforcement. At least 25 percent reported that they had hired more professionals. The majority of business and industry professionals studied said they used outside valuation experts, underscoring the demand for litigation services.

EYEWITNESS

In a divorce dispute, a small business owner claimed to have only about $75,000 of annual business income. He said that he had borrowed and not paid back huge sums of money. His wife said that he was spending about $400,000 per year more than his salary.

During trial the expert witness for the wife presented four schedules:
1. What was known and alleged about the husband's expenditures.
2. A schedule comparing income with expenditures.
3. Amounts the husband claimed he had borrowed.
4. The company's income statements side-by-side:

	His	New Gross Profit Per Industry
	—	—
	—	—
	$75,000	$475,000

The divorce expert used the gross profit percentage for that industry to show that the business owner, in reality, had $475,000 of business income. The husband had overstated the cost of goods sold by numerous checks issued to vendors. Some of the vendors cashed the checks and returned the money to the husband.[62]

Forensic Groups and Credentials

With such a diverse and complex list of topics to master in preparing to practice, several factors have slowed the growth of forensic accounting as a profession: the CPA profession is attempting to control it with a new CFF certificate; internal auditors created their own certificate (CIA); Joseph Wells created the certified fraud examiner (CFE); and the economic profession and various certificate groups (i.e., certified valuation analyst, accreditation in business valuation, and accreditation member of the American Society for Appraisers for Business Valuation) have fought to retain valuation issues. Also, none of the current certification groups have been able to control forensic accountants (i.e., Cr.FA, MAFF, FASNA, CA-IFA). To an extent, forensic accounting is business's orphan, being pushed and pulled by the accounting, economics, finance, and valuation professions.

The AICPA has an "Antifraud & Corporate Responsibility Resource Center" on their website at *www.aicpa.org/antifraud/homepage.htm*. This resource center gives practitioners some articles and sites needed to help combat fraud. The home page states that "some of the biggest challenges facing businesses today are...establishing clarity in reporting procedures." Most of the sites deal with fraud rather than forensic or litigation support. The AICPA also offers fraud courses and holds an annual Litigation Service conference.

¶ 2045   SUMMARY OF FORENSIC CERTIFICATIONS

Below is a table summarizing the forensic certifications and requirements. Following the table is a more detailed description of these certifications.

Table 2.3. Professional Groups and Credentials

Organization	Certification	Description	Prerequisites	Education/Experience	Course/Exam	Continuing Requirements
American Institute of CPAs. http://www.aicpa.org/	Certified in Financial Forensics	The objectives of the CFF credential program: - Achieve public recognition of the CFF as the preferred forensic accounting professional. - Enhance the quality of forensic services CFFs provide. - Increase practice development and career opportunities for CFFs. - Promote members' services through the Forensic and Valuation Services (FVS) website.	- Be a CPA member in good standing of the AICPA. - Hold a valid and unrevoked CPA certificate issued by a legally constitued state authority. - Have at least five years of experience in practicing accounting. - Complete a CFF application and meet the 100-point requirement. - Sign a Declaration of Intent to comply with the requirements of CFF recertification.	Be a CPA member in good standing of the AICPA.	Examination is now required.	40 hours of continuting education credit.
American College of Forensic Examiners International (ACFEI) www.acfei.com	Certified Forensic Accountant (Cr.FA)	The Cr.FA credential recognizes the expertise in forensic accounting for accountants who have achieved additional training, experience, education, knowledge or skill in forensic accounting and have met all of their State Board of Accountancy requirements.	The applicant must: - Be registered with his/her State Board of Accountancy, if required by state law. - Have no record of disciplinary action during the past 10 years. - Have no felony convictions within the past 10 years. - Agree to uphold the ACFEI Principles of Professional Practice.	An applicant with a bachelor's degree in business or 10 years of accounting-related experience who does not hold an accounting-related certificate (CPA, CMA, CFFA, CVA, CBA, etc.) must pass Exam 1 and Exam 2. Hold an accounting related certificate and pass an examination.	Exam covers an introduction and overview of forensic accounting, the engagement, fraud investigations and fraudulent financial reporting, additional services of the forensic accountant, and valuation.	- 15 hours of continuing education credit each year. - Membership with the ACFEI.
	Certified Forensic Consultant (CFC)	The CFC credential certifies the forensic professional's understanding of ethics, jurisprudence and knowledge of the field of law that leads to successful consulting roles in the adversarial system of American jurisprudence.	The applicant must: - Be a member of the ACFEI. - Have no records of disciplinary action for any ethical, criminal or other offense by any disciplinary body or court of law within the past 10 years. - Hold degrees exclusively from accredited universities (domestic or foreign). - Comply with all applicable local ordinances, state laws and federal regulations for his/her professions.	If a candidate already possesses adequate knowledge of forensic consultations and the legal system, as demonstrated by sufficient previous experience or documentation from a recognized education source, he/she may request an exemption from the requirement of the CFC course and sit for the proctored examination.	The course begins with classroom instruction, followed by interactive role-playing scenarios, including a mock trial, and adversarial confrontations related to such issues as giving deposition testimony, testifying at trial, and assisting counsel and clients during the opposing expert's testimony.	- 15 hours of continuing education credits each year.

Organization	Certification	Description	Prerequisites	Education/ Experience	Course/Exam	Continuing Requirements
Association of Certified Fraud Examiners (ACFE) www.CFEnet.com	Certified Fraud Examiner (CFE)	The CFE designation certifies proven expertise in fraud prevention, detection and investigation.	The applicant must: - Be an Associate Member of the ACFE. - Be of high moral character: - Agree to abide by the Bylaws and Code of Professional Ethics of the ACFE.	The applicant must have either: - A bachelor's degree and two years of professional experience in a field either directly or indirectly related to the detection or deterrence of fraud; or - Ten years of fraud-related professional experience.	The CFE Exam covers four areas critical to the fight against fraud: Criminology & Ethics, Financial Transactions, Fraud Investigation, and Legal Elements of Fraud. The exam takes approximately 10 hours and consists of 500 questions.	- 20 hours of continuing professional education each year, with at least 10 hours fraud-related. - ACFE member in good standing.
Forensic CPA Society www.fcpa.org	Forensic CPA (FCPA)	The purpose is to promote excellence in the forensic accounting profession.	The applicant must: - Be a CPA or CA. - The CPA has a number of requirements.	n/a	The applicant must: - Pass a 5-part exam which is based upon five books. Each test covers one book. - Have CPA and CFE certificates.	- 20 hours of continuing professional education each year.
Association of Certified Fraud Specialists (ACFS) www.acfsnet.org	Certified Fraud Specialist (CFS)	The CFS designation denotes Candidates found to have complied with the education, knowledge and skill level requirements established by a 16-member Board of Regents and who possess significant expertise in the investigation of white-collar crime and fraud issues.	The applicant must: - Be an Associate Member of the ACFS. - Be of good character: - Agree to abide by the ACFS Bylaws, and; - Agree to abide by the ACFS Code of Ethics.	To apply for Membership, a Candidate must work in a fraud-related field and demonstrate 25 points on the application. To apply for Certification, a Candidate must be an Associate Member and: - Pass the written examination process as part of the Entrance Examination or as part of the ACFS Academy, or; - Apply under the Grandfathering provision and demonstrate a minimum of 8 years of practical experience and a minimum of 100 points on the application.	The applicants must do one of the following: - Pass the Certified Fraud Specialist Entrance Examination. - Complete each required Core Course in the ACFS Academy and achieve a passing score on each course's proctored exam. - Fall under the Grandfathering provision, which is only available to Associate Members with substantial experience.	- Obtain 48 hours of continuing professional education (CPE) every two years with 32 CPE hours required to be in a fraud-related field. - Training must be by/from an accredited or nationally recognized CPE provider. - Maintain status as a Member in good standing.

Organization	Certification	Description	Prerequisites	Education/ Experience	Course/Exam	Continuing Requirements
Institute of Business Appraisers (IBA) www.go-iba.org	Certified Business Appraiser (CBA)	The CBA denotes a level of competence attained only by the most accomplished business appraisers, grants its recipients special recognition and prestige among fellow appraisers, the courts and throughout the business appraisal community.	The applicant must: - Be a member in good standing of the IBA. - Provide four satisfactory references for character and fitness. - Submit two demonstration reports demonstrating a high degree of skill, knowledge and judgment as a business appraiser for juried peer review.	The applicant must: - Possess a four-year college degree or equivalent. - Have completed at least 90 classroom hours of upper level course work in BV, 24 hours of which must be courses offered by IBA. In lieu of the 90-hour requirement, the applicant may demonstrate 10,000 hours active experience as a business appraiser:	- Four-hour written CBA exam. (Applicants may be exempt from the exam if they hold an ASA, ABV, CVA or AVA.) - Complete IBA's 16-hour course 1010, Report Writing.	- 24 hours of continuing professional education credit every two years. - Continued membership in IBA.
	Accredited by IBA (AIBA)	Candidates study fundamentals of the business valuation body of knowledge and submit work for peer review.	The applicant must: - Be a member in good standing of IBA. - Provide two satisfactory references for character and fitness. - Submit one demonstration report demonstrating a high degree of skill, knowledge and judgment as a business appraiser for juried peer review.	The applicant must: - Possess a four-year college degree or equivalent.	- Complete IBA's 64-hour course 8001, Valuing Closely Held Businesses, or hold an ASA, ABV, CVA or AVA - Four-hour written AIBA exam. (Applicants may be exempt from the exam if they hold an ASA, ABV, CVA or AVA.) - Complete IBA's 16-hour course 1010, Report Writing.	- 24 hours of continuing professional education credit every two years. - Continued membership in IBA.
	Business Valuator Accredited for Litigation (BVAL)	BVAL was designed to recognize experienced business appraisers who demonstrate their ability to competently present expert testimony which supports their objective conclusion of value.	The applicant must: - Be a member in good standing of the IBA. - Provide two satisfactory references from attorneys who have witnessed applicant's formal testimony on BV or provide 16 hours of Continuing Legal Education (CLE). - Submit one demonstration report demonstrating a high degree of skill, knowledge and judgment as a business appraiser for juried peer review.	The applicant must: - Possess a four-year college degree or equivalent. - Demonstrate a high level of proficiency in Business Appraisal. - Hold either a CVA, ASA or ABV designation or pass the CBA exam.	- Complete IBA's 56-hour course 7001, Excellence in Expert Witnessing Skills. - Four-hour written BVAL exam.	- 24 hours of continuing professional education credit every two years. - Continued membership in IBA.

Organization	Certification	Description	Prerequisites	Education/ Experience	Course/Exam	Continuing Requirements
	Master Certified Business Appraiser (MCBA)	The MCBA is the highest professional designation awarded in the business valuation industry, and recognizes the extraordinary competence of a few highly skilled and experienced individuals whose work has been widely accepted by clients and acknowledged by their most senior professional colleagues.	The applicant must: - Be a member in good standing of the IBA. - Have held the CBA designation not less than 10 years. - Also hold either an ASA-BV, ABV, or CVA. - Provide three satisfactory references of others who hold the MCBA designation.	The applicant must: - Posses a post-graduate degree or equivalent. - Have 15 years full-time BV experience.	n/a	- 24 hours of continuing professional education credit every two years. - Continued membership in IBA.
National Association of Certified Valuation Analysts (NACVA) www.nacva.com	Certified Valuation Analyst (CVA)	The CVA is an accreditation in business valuation for certified public accountants (CPAs).	The applicant must: - Be a CPA. - Be a member of NACVA.	The applicant must have education and experience required for certification as a CPA.	A five-day training program as prescribed by NACVA. A comprehensive two-part examination. Part 1 is a five-hour proctored exam, and Part 2 is a take-home/in-office exam that incorporates a standardized case study that requires performing a complete business valuation. Part 2 of the exam takes 40-60 hours to complete.	Every three years: - 36 hours of continuing professional education (CPE) credit; - Attend NACVA's Current Update in Valuations course; - Participate in NACVA's Quality Enhancement program; or - Meet certain other professional requirements.

Organization	Certification	Description	Prerequisites	Education/Experience	Course/Exam	Continuing Requirements
	Accredited Valuation Analyst (AVA)	The AVA is an accreditation in business valuation. It differs from the CVA in that applicants are not required to be CPAs.	The applicant must be a member of NACVA.	The applicant must: - Hold a business degree and/or an MBA or higher business degree. - Have two years or more full-time or equivalent experience in business valuation and related disciplines; or - Have performed 10 or more business valuations where the applicant's role was significant; or be able to demonstrate substantial knowledge of business valuation concepts having published works on the subject, completed graduate work in the field, or obtained accreditation from another recognized business valuation accrediting organization.	A five-day training program as prescribed by NACVA. A comprehensive two-part examination. Part 1 is a five-hour proctored exam, and Part 2 is a take-home/in-office exam that incorporates a standardized case study that requires performing a complete business valuation. Part 2 of the exam takes 40-60 hours to complete.	Every three years: - 36 hours of continuing professional education (CPE) credit; - Attend NACVA's Current Update in Valuations course; - Participate in NACVA's Quality Enhancement program; or - Meet certain other professional requirements.
	Certified Forensic Financial Analyst (CFFA)	The CFFA certifies a level of experience and knowledge to provide competent and professional forensic financial support services.	The applicant must be a Practitioner member of NACVA.	The applicant must possess one of the following: - CVA, AVA, ABV, ASA, AM, CBA, CBV, CFA, CMA, CPA, or CA; - An advanced degree in economics, accounting or finance; or - An undergraduate degree in a business field combined with an MBA. The applicant must show proof of substantial experience providing litigation consulting, defined as having rendered services in 10 different litigation matters, in at least 5 of which the applicant gave depositions and/or testified in court.	Eight days of training offered in NACVA's Forensic Institute. A two-part exam. Part 1 is an eight-hour proctored exam, and Part 2 is a take-home/in-office case study that requires drafting a report for federal court under Federal Rule 26. The second part of the exam takes approximately 4-16 hours based on one's prior experience.	- Maintain active membership status with NACVA. Every three years: - 36 hours of continuing professional education credit. - Participate in six litigation matters.

¶ 2051   AMERICAN COLLEGE OF FORENSIC EXAMINERS

The American College of Forensic Examiners International (ACFEi)[63] is located in Springfield, Missouri. ACFEi is a not-for-profit educational body that provides advanced training to its members, composed of twelve boards. One board is the American Board of Forensic Accounting.

Membership

The AFCEi is a multiassociation organization having some 15,000 members worldwide.

Certified Forensic Accountant (Cr.FA)

ACFEi introduced the Certified Forensic Accountant (Cr.FA) designation in 2001. Certified forensic accountants are needed for litigation support, corporate investigations, criminal matters, assisting governments, and preparing and assessing insurance claims.

The certified forensic accountant, Cr.FA, is an advanced credential that recognizes the expertise in forensic accounting for accountants who have achieved additional training, experience, education, knowledge, or skill in forensic accounting and have met all of their State Board of Accountancy requirements. A person with an accounting-related certificate (CPA, CMA, MAFF, CVA, CBA, etc.) must pass an examination.

According to ACFEi, this Cr.FA program fills a vital niche for accountants, because it is unlike any other accounting credential. Whereas most accountants have credentials verifying their accounting expertise, such as CPA, CMA, CFFE, CVA, or CBA, few have credentials verifying their forensic accounting expertise. With the Cr.FA credential, accountants show they have not only the ability to work with numbers but also the ability to use their accounting experience professionally and accurately in a legal setting.

Cr.FA Expertise. Accountants holding the Cr.FA credential have expertise beyond the narrow realm of their peers in accounting, auditing, and fraud. As James DiGabriel, CPA, Cr.FA, points out, "Unlike other accounting designations, it distinguishes me from other accountants who do not have my experience or knowledge in forensic accounting."[64]

With the rigid qualifications and high standards of achievement required for this credential, the Cr.FA helps to distinguish designees in terms of experience, knowledge, competence, and prestige. Finding expert accountants knowledgeable about legal procedures and competent on the witness stand is made easier when such designations help identify those who have undergone rigorous training and testing in forensic accounting.

Because applicants are required to be registered with their State Boards of Accountancy and possess accounting credentials, the exam specifically assesses the candidates' accounting expertise as it applies to the courtroom and forensic accounting. Questions cover expert evidence admissibility, causes of action, varieties of fraud, expert report writing procedures, valuation approaches, and much more. Since most Cr.FAs have another certification, they must follow the Code of Ethics for the companion professional group.

¶ 2061   ASSOCIATION OF CERTIFIED FRAUD EXAMINERS

The mission of the Association of Certified Fraud Examiners (ACFE) is to reduce the incidence of fraud and white-collar crime and to assist the members in its detection and deterrence. To accomplish this mission, the ACFE:
- Provides bona fide qualifications for certified fraud examiners through administration of the Uniform CFE Examination.
- Sets high standards for admission, including demonstrated competence through mandatory continuing professional education.

- Requires certified fraud examiners to adhere to a strict code of professional conduct and ethics.
- Serves as the international representative for certified fraud examiners to business and government.
- Provides leadership to inspire public confidence in the integrity, objectivity, and professionalism of certified fraud examiners.[65]

Membership

Established in 1988, the ACFE is headquartered in Austin, Texas, and has around 55,000 members in 106 countries. Its website says the ACFE is continually researching and developing new publications, self-study products, and cutting-edge fraud training conferences designed to educate and prepare fraud examiners for the challenges they face. Typical members of the association include accounting and auditing professionals, special investigators, law enforcement personnel, loss prevention specialists, attorneys and prosecutors, managers and executives, academicians and students, and anti-fraud consultants. Thus, some of the members may have little or no accounting or auditing background and may not fit within the typical definition of a forensic accountant.

There are two classes of members: associate (noncertified) and certified fraud examiner (CFE). Associate members are not required to demonstrate experience or educational history. A professional interest in fraud examination is all that is needed. Educators and college students may consider the educator and student associate memberships, respectively.[66]

Certified Fraud Examiner (CFE)

The Certified Fraud Examiner (CFE) designation is held by many forensic accountants. The CFE examination is administrated by the ACFE. The Association has an unpublished number of CFEs who were grandfathered without sitting for and passing an examination. Today, new CFEs must sit for and pass a 500 question exam designed to measure academic as well as practical knowledge in four main areas: criminology and ethics, financial transactions, legal elements of fraud, and fraud examination and investigation. Like other tests, the difficulty can vary widely, based upon individual circumstances such as experience and preparation. Each section of the computerized exam consists of 125 questions in a Windows format, in two computer disks, with a maximum completion time of 2.5 hours for each section and can be taken any time during the year. A person is allowed three attempts to pass all four parts of the exam before losing credit for previously completed sections. A score of 75 percent is required on each part to pass the exam.[67]

To be eligible to take the Uniform CFE examination an applicant must meet a set of educational and experience requirements based on a point system. A minimum score of 40 points is required to take the exam and 50 points to obtain certification by examination. A bachelor's degree counts for 60 points and two years of related experience for 10 points. Different combinations of points for education and experience can be determined in meeting the minimum requirements. The computerized Uniform CFE examination is currently offered in the United States and Canada and residents of these countries must pass the exam to obtain the CFE certificate.

Aside from the examination, a person must show proof of education and experience in a fraud-related field. Once certified, the person is required to maintain his or her certification with continuing professional education (CPE). CFEs gather evidence, take statements, write reports, and assist in investigating fraud in its varied forms. Some CFEs are employed by most major corporations and government agencies; others provide consulting and investigative services.

ACFE CODE OF PROFESSIONAL ETHICS

A Certified Fraud Examiner shall, at all times, demonstrate a commitment to professionalism and diligence in the performance of his or her duties.

A Certified Fraud Examiner shall not engage in any illegal or unethical conduct, or any activity which would constitute a conflict of interest.

A Certified Fraud Examiner shall, at all times, exhibit the highest level of integrity in the performance of all professional assignments and will accept only assignments for which there is reasonable expectation that the assignment will be completed with professional competence.

A Certified Fraud Examiner will comply with lawful orders of the courts and will testify to matters truthfully and without bias or prejudice.

A Certified Fraud Examiner, in conducting examinations, will obtain evidence or other documentation to establish a reasonable basis for any opinion rendered. No opinion shall be expressed regarding the guilt or innocence of any person or party.

A Certified Fraud Examiner shall not reveal any confidential information obtained during a professional engagement without proper authorization.

A Certified Fraud Examiner will reveal all material matters discovered during the course of an examination which, if omitted, could cause a distortion of the facts.

A Certified Fraud Examiner shall continually strive to increase the competence and effectiveness of professional services performed under his or her direction. [68]

¶ 2071　ASSOCIATION OF CERTIFIED FRAUD SPECIALISTS

The Association of Certified Fraud Specialists (ACFS) is an educational, nonprofit corporation headquartered in Sacramento, California. As a professional organization, part of the association's mandate is to administer the Certified Fraud Specialist program in the United States. As an educational entity, the association provides various services such as conferences, specialized training, and research in addition to the networking opportunities afforded its members. ACFS also believes in service to the members' communities. The pro bono work provided where chapters operate is considered key to the organization as a contributing member of the local community.[69]

Membership

ACFS applications for membership come from four primary disciplines:
- Accounting/auditing;
- Law enforcement/investigation;
- Law (both for the prosecution and defense); and
- Academics (professors of accounting, sociology, criminology, etc.)

In just six years (2000–2006), ACFS has grown rapidly to include members in nearly all states, Washington, D.C., and Puerto Rico as well as in Canada, the West Indies, Hong Kong, Pakistan, and Saudi Arabia. However, many of their members are from California and other western states, which have an interest in white collar crime, fraud, and abuse. The ACFS has associate members (seeking access to association membership), regular members, and fellow members (sustained and superior contribution to the organization). Regular and fellow members must hold the Certified Fraud Specialist designation.[70]

Certified Fraud Specialist Certification (CFS)

The entrance examination to be certified as a CFS consists of a written examination covering all core areas of training (CAT) in which a candidate must demonstrate proficiency. Test questions consist of information considered critical from the various disciplines contending with the detection, deterrence, investigation, and prosecution of white collar crime, fraud, and abuse. The Certified Fraud Specialist Entrance Examination is a multipart, multiple choice examination designed to require approximately three to four hours to complete. As of February 2011, the exam had not been completed.

Completion of the Association Academy for CFS certification consists of attending various courses offered by the association. Members participating in the academy are granted priority registration in, and must submit to a proctored examination given at the conclusion of, each core course. Certification is awarded after the member has successfully completed all academy requirements. As of February 2011, the core courses had not been identified.

The grandfathering mechanism for CFS certification consists of experienced members completing various informational forms and submitting various documentation, designed to establish that the members' education and work experience exceed the level of competency established by the Certified Fraud Specialist Entrance Examination or the Association Academy. In general, an individual must get 100 points, with only 60 points attainable through formal education.

¶ 2081 FORENSIC ACCOUNTING SOCIETY OF NORTH AMERICA

The Forensic Accounting Society of North America (FASNA) is a member-driven and self-governed network of CPA firms who adhere to high standards of quality and services.[71] The firms commit their time, dollars, and human hours to ensure their success in developing forensic accounting opportunities, especially with insurance situations.

The goal of FASNA is to help member firms reap tangible benefits through various marketing and business development strategies, including:

- Newsletter production
- Attendance and booth hosting at industry trade shows
- Contact research for member special requests
- Relationship building on behalf of members
- Web site presence
- Acting as a referral agent for inquiries

Membership

The FASNA website indicates that new members receive market cultivation, training, support, and business development. Each new member firm is required to complete two days of technical training in forensic accounting, preferably conducted onsite of the new member firm to encourage participation.

FASNA member firms meet twice each year to discuss trends and issues in forensic accounting, business development, and membership development. These meetings enable members to have face-to-face conversations with other professionals involved in forensic accounting, and develop relationships helpful to the ongoing success of the members. The group does not appear to have a Code of Ethics, and there were 4 member firms listed on the organization's website as of February 2013, 5 as of February 2011, and 6 in April 2005.

¶ 2091 NATIONAL ASSOCIATION OF CERTIFIED VALUATION ANALYSTS

The National Association of Certified Valuation Analysts (NACVA)[67] was formed in 1990 with the mission of providing resources to members and enhance their status, credentials, and esteem in the field of performing valuations and other advisory services. To further this purpose, NACVA advances these services as an art and science; establishes standards for admission; provides professional education and research; fosters practice development; advances standards of ethical and professional practice; enhances public awareness of the NACVA and its members; and promotes working relationships with other professional organizations.[73]

Along with this training and certification programs, NACVA offers a range of support services, marketing tools, software programs, reference materials, and customized databases to enhance the professional capabilities and capacities of its members.

Membership

NACVA is a global association of more than 6,000 CPAs, government valuation analysts, and other professionals who perform valuation and litigation services.

Valuation and Financial Analyst Credential

This group offers three certifications:
- Certified Valuation Analyst (CVA)
- Master Analyst Financial Analyst (MAFF)
- Certified Fraud Deterrence (CFD) (to be merged with the MAFF)

These certifications are described as follows:
- An accreditation program for certified public accountants (CPAs) leading to the designation of "certified valuation analyst" (CVA), upon completion of training and a comprehensive examination;
- An accreditation program for litigation consultants leading to the designation of "certified forensic financial analyst" (MAFF), upon completion of training and a comprehensive examination;[74] and
- An accreditation program for practitioners leading to the designation of "certified fraud deterrence" (CFD), upon completion of training and a comprehensive examination. Passing the CFD certificate "ensures that the individual has the skills and the knowledge to serve business owners in the deterrence of fraud in the workplace." This credential was merged with the MAFF in early 2007.

NACVA's original business valuation certificate was the certified valuation analyst, and a primary requirement for becoming a CVA is to hold a valid CPA license. Certification involves completion of a five-day training program and a 60-hour take-home examination, which includes one case study and report writing requirement. Practitioner members of the association may apply for certification as a certified forensic financial analyst, which was established in 2000. Certified members are required to obtain 36 hours of continuing professional education (CPE) every three years.

Most recently, the Master Analyst Forensic Financial (MAFF) designation offered practitioners seven different pathways to acquire the specialized training and concomitant credibility necessary for practice development. Today many CPAs, forensic accountants, valuation experts, and other financial professionals are called upon to render professional services and formulate opinions in legal matters involving bankruptcy and insolvency and in legal matters involving business valuation opinions. Each of these areas has its own set of dynamics, including legal code sections, case law, and other variables, which sets it apart from other areas of forensics and litigation. Thus, the Financial Forensics Institute and the Consultants' Training Institute have partnered to create educational programs to serve the needs of experts in these seven important areas.

The seven areas are
- Financial Litigation Specialization
- Forensic Accounting Specialization
- Business and Intellectual Property Damages Specialization
- Matrimonial Litigation Support Specialization
- Business Valuation in Litigation Specialization

- Bankruptcy/Insolvency Specialization
- Fraud Risk Management Specialization

A description of these areas can be found on their website (http://www.nacva.com/cti/cffa/asp).

¶ 2101   NATIONAL LITIGATION SUPPORT SERVICES ASSOCIATION

The National Litigation Support Services Association (NLSSA) is a nationwide not-for-profit association of CPA firms specifically selected for their experience in and commitment to providing litigation support services to the legal and business communities.[75] The NLSSA Internet site[76] states that the association is an excellent technical resource for the media looking for source information on financial and technical issues.

Membership

NLSSA membership can provide one with cutting-edge information on:
- Fact finding during the discovery process
- Investigatory accounting
- Business valuations
- Intangible asset valuations
- Casualty and damage calculations - business interruption
- Cost estimation
- Lost profits
- Lost earnings
- Contract cost overruns/disputes
- Divorce
- Bankruptcy debtor/creditor
- Governmental claims and audits
- Insurance claims defense/plaintiff counsel
- Fraud
- Securities fraud
- Professional malpractice for CPAs/attorneys
- Investment portfolio analysis
- Personal injury
- Anti-trust
- Statistical and economical analysis
- Estate planning
- Mergers and acquisitions

¶ 2111   NETWORK OF INDEPENDENT FORENSIC ACCOUNTANTS

In England a group of 16 specialist accountancy practices banded together to create the Network of Independent Forensic Accountants (NIFA) in 1999, claiming to be the first network of independent forensic accountants. Andrew Knight, the Chairman, said that "the founding members spent 12 months developing the service, standardizing procedures, and getting NIFA and its panelists ready for the launch." They appointed their own external, independent auditor to ensure that the members consistently deliver the high standards they have set.

Membership

By employing NIFA members in an advisory role, a party should reduce costs, speed up settlement and thereby get through an increased volume of cases. Time spent on quantum does not delay you in getting to the next case.[77]

In addition to acting in the expert role either as a party appointed expert or as Single Joint Expert, NIFA members provide advisory services to solicitors and insurers. In England,

April 1999 saw a huge change in the conduct of litigation and resulted in a reduction in the number of experts being retained by solicitors, particularly in cases involving personal injury. Since April 1999, to have an expert give oral evidence in court, generally a solicitor first needs the leave of the court to present evidence from that expert. By employing accountants in an advisory capacity within a team, clients gain the use of the accountant's expertise without the complication of seeking the court's approval.

NIFA members can present findings either by way of formal letter of comment or advice, a mini-report, or a schedule of special damages prepared on a subcontract basis.

There is no rule that prevents solicitors (or insurance companies) from appointing accountants in an advisory role to assist in the preparation of the claimant's (or defendant's) case, even doing work on a sub-contract basis for the solicitor such as preparing the special damages calculations to be used in the schedule of special damages.

NIFA members will work as advisors only under conditional fee agreements on some types of cases, such as personal injuries.

Members offer the following services, whether as advisor or as expert:
- Preliminary advice/review of documents
- Preparation of expert (party appointed or Single Joint Expert) or advisory report on quantum
- Review of expert (or advisor) report for the other side
- Attending conference with counsel
- Attending meetings of experts
- Advising on Part 36 offers and payments into court
- Giving evidence at court
- Advising counsel and instructing solicitors/insurers at trial

¶ 2121   INSTITUTE OF BUSINESS APPRAISERS

The Institute of Business Appraisers (IBA) is the oldest not-for-profit professional organization devoted solely to the appraisal of closely held businesses.[78] There are more than 20 million small companies in the American economy, employing two out of every three taxpayers, producing 39 percent of the Gross National Product, and providing more than half of the nation's technical innovations. At least 90 percent of all U.S. businesses are closely-held. The IBA's goal is to provide a supportive and nurturing environment for more than 3,000 members through their resources including technical support, market data, professional certification and practical education in all aspects of appraisal of small and mid-size businesses. In fulfilling this mission, the headquarters staff is assisted by many volunteers who provide professional mentoring, report review, instruction and technical publications for the enhancement of the profession.[79]

The IBA has the following goals:
- To increase awareness of business valuation as a specialized profession.
- To ensure that the services of qualified, ethical appraisers are widely available.
- To expand the available body of knowledge regarding the theory and practice of business valuation.
- To develop and provide essential industry information, programs and services for members.
- To impact national policy and law affecting the business valuation community.[80]

Certified Business Appraiser

A member who has five years of full-time active experience as a business appraiser or meets an education requirement may take a comprehensive written examination on current business valuation theory and practice.

The written examination requirement may be waived by holders of journeyman level designations in business valuation from compeer organizations recognized by the Institute of Business Appraisers, upon application to the IBA. The person must submit two Demonstration Reports demonstrating a high degree of skill, knowledge, and judgment as a business appraiser.

Successful completion of the exam or Demonstration Reports results in the designation of certified business appraiser (CBA).[81]

¶2126 AICPA CERTIFIED IN FINANCIAL FORENSICS CREDENTIAL

The Certified in Financial Forensics (CFF) credential is a certification that recognizes the combined specialized forensic accounting expertise and core knowledge and skills. The American Institute of Certified Public Accountants (AICPA) established the Certified in Financial Forensics (CFF) credential in 2008 for CPAs who specialize in forensic accounting. The CFF credential is granted to CPAs who demonstrate an expertise in forensic accounting through their extensive knowledge, skills, and experience in the field. The CFF includes fundamental and specialized forensic accounting skills that CPAs use in a variety of service areas including; bankruptcy and insolvency; computer forensic analysis; family law; valuations; fraud prevention, detection, and response; financial statement misrepresentation; and economic damages calculations.

The CFF credential program is designed to achieve the following objectives:
- Increase exposure for CPAs who have obtained the CFF credential.
- Enhance the quality of the forensic services CFFs provide.
- Provide CPAs with continuous access to support and resources in order to maintain their competitiveness over other forensic accounting services.
- Increase career opportunities for CFFs.
- Promote members' services.
- Achieve public recognition of the CPA/CFF as the preferred forensic accounting professional.

Once becoming a CFF, an individual is entitled to a number of benefits, including:
- Networking opportunities at the AICPA National Forensic Accounting Conference and the AICPA National Business Valuation Conference.
- Professional discounts, including vendor discounts and special offers on selected products and publications used in their forensic practices.
- Ongoing media-relations campaign to heighten the awareness of the CFF credential among clients, the business and legal communities, and various media outlets.

The CFF Credential is exclusively granted by the AICPA only to qualified CPAs. To qualify, new CFF applicants must:
- Hold a valid and unrevoked CPA license or certificate issued by a legally constituted state authority.
- Pass the CFF examination.
  - Upon successfully passing the CFF Examination, complete the CFF Credential Application. Applicants must attest to meeting the minimum Business Experience and Education requirements and pay the appropriate credential fee.
  - Business Experience Requirement
    A CFF candidate must have a minimum of 1,000 hours of business experience in forensic accounting within the 5-year period preceding the date of the CFF application. A potential applicant should refer to the CFF Application Kit for examples of business experience.
  - Education Requirement
    A CFF candidate must have 75 hours of forensic accounting related continuing professional education (CPE). All hours must have been obtained within the 5-year period preceding the date of the CFF application. Their CFF Application Kit provides further details.
- Sign a Declaration of Intent to comply with the requirements of CFF Recertification.

The AICPA has recognized forensic accounting services to generally involve:

- The application of specialized knowledge and investigative skills possessed by CPAs.
- Collecting, analyzing, and evaluating evidential matter.
- Interpreting and communicating findings in the courtroom, boardroom, or other legal/administrative venues.

Fundamental forensic knowledge of a CFF includes:

- Professional responsibilities and practice management.
- Laws, courts, and dispute resolution.
- Planning and preparation.
- Information gathering and preservation (documents, interviews/interrogations, and electronic data).
- Discovery.
- Reporting, experts, and testimony.

The AICPA website suggests these essential traits and characteristics of a forensic accountant:

Essential Traits and Characteristics

	Attorney	Rank	Academic	Rank	CPA	Rank
Analytical	78%	1	90%	1	86%	1
Detail-oriented	64%	2	35%		49%	3
Ethical	60%	3	65%	2	49%	3
Responsive	41%	4	2%		10%	
Insightful	39%	5	29%		24%	
Inquisitive	22%		48%	4	52%	2
Intuitive	26%		40%		38%	5
Persistent	19%		46%	5	30%	
Skepticism	12%		54%	3	43%	4
Evaluative	30%		15%		16%	
Function well under pressure	28%		23%		35%	
Generate new ideas and scenarios	27%		10%		16%	
Confident	24%		10%		20%	
Makes people feel at ease	13%		17%		9%	
Team player	10%		4%		5%	
Adaptive	8%		13%		20%	
Other (please specify)	8%		2%		6%	

Figure 3

¶ 2131   OTHER ORGANIZATIONS SERVING FORENSIC PRACTITIONERS

The American Society of Appraisers (ASA) is a multidisciplinary professional organization offering courses and examinations leading to designations in the appraisal businesses and business interests, real estate, machinery and equipment, and others.[82] The Canadian Institute of Chartered Accountants (CICA) established in 1998 an Alliance for Excellence in Investigative Accounting with the CA.IFA designation. As of August 2002, more than 200 chartered accountants (CAs) have chosen to obtain a CA.IFA designation. The key to the process of becoming a CA.IFA is a specially designed two-year, part-time graduate program, the Diploma in Investigative and Forensic Accounting (DIFA) from the Joseph L. Rotman School of

Management at the University of Toronto and the Ecole des hautes Commerciales in Montreal. The CA.IFA designation informs lawyers, law enforcement professionals, the courts, those in government and in business that the holder brings thousands of hours of experience, graduate-level education, and ongoing training to the job of uncovering, investigating and analyzing financial evidence and fraud, testifying as an expert witness, risk management and fraud prevention, damage qualification, litigation support, and dispute resolution."[83]

Another related Canadian group is the Certified Forensic Investigator (CFI). This association is responsible for administering the Certified Forensic Investigators' program in Canada. CFIs are professional fraud investigators who have by experience, education and examination satisfied the requirements of the Association of Certified Forensic Investigators of Canada (ACFI) and have been admitted as regular members of the Association.[84]

Its website indicates that "The services provided by a CFI relate to the prevention, detection and investigation of fraud. This may involve, but not be limited to, providing a thorough and complete investigation to sustain or refute allegations of impropriety and subsequently providing testimony related. Another service provided might be the audit of business systems to determine the adequacy of controls to detect, prevent and investigate fraud."[85]

Further, the CFI also promotes and fosters a national forum and governing body for the affiliation of professionals who offer to the public, governments, and employers, their expertise in the area of fraud prevention, detection, and investigation, as well as liaison with other nonprofit associations for the purpose of promulgating fraud awareness.

The High Technology Crime Investigation Association (HTCIA)[86] is designed to encourage, promote, aid, and effect the voluntary interchange of data, information, experience, ideas, and knowledge about methods, processes, and techniques relating to investigations and security in advanced technologies. Membership is composed of peace officers, investigators, prosecuting attorneys, and security professionals in private business or industry.

Established in 1973, the Society for Financial Examiners is a professional organization for examiners of insurance companies, banks savings and loans, and credit unions. SOFE offers three professional designations which are earned by completing extensive requirements and a series of examinations.[87]

The International Association of Asset Recovery (IAAR) has a new certification called the Certified Specialist in Asset Recovery (CSAR). The IAAR mission is to help practitioners to win back assets that rightfully belong to victims, government agencies, other organizations, or individuals who have been victimized by criminal or wrongful conduct.[88]

The American Anti-Corruption Manager provides a Certified Anti-Corruption Manager (CACM) for an annual fee of $150. The exam consists of 100 multiple choice questions with a grandfathering path (theaaci.com).

The Corporate Crime Reporter is a legal print newsletter published and mailed 48 times a year (corporatecrimereporter.com). Some articles are posted on their website, but they are only highlights from the print newsletter.

¶ 2141   CONCLUSION

As long ago as 1953, experts have called for universities and colleges to develop forensic accounting courses. Recently, educational organizations answered this call as forensic accounting grew in popularity as a response to public revulsion to the corporate accounting scandals of the early 21st century.

Forensic accounting has evolved into both forensic investigation and litigation support, but no single certification group has captured the hearts and minds of all the various types of forensic accountants.[89]

In fact, one author questions the holders of forensic accounting credentials themselves. Dennis Huber found in his online survey that forensic accountants' failure to investigate the companies that issue forensic certificates reflects on either their ability to exercise due diligence or their dedication to exercising due diligence.[90]

Huber states that "forensic accountants' failure to exercise due diligence, coupled with the failure of forensic accounting corporations to disclose important information concerning their legal status and qualifications of officers and board of directors, suggests that the market is not functioning and the profession is unable to regulate itself. If the profession is unable to regulate itself, the potential for state or even federal intervention is significantly increased.[91]

ENDNOTES

1   Danny Heitman, "Tracking Money," BATON ROUGE ADVOCATE (February 17, 2002), p. 1-H.

2   As of June 2003, the phrase "litigation support" on the Google search engine retrieved 1,250,000 entries, and the phrase "forensic accounting" found 122,000 items.

3   Terry Carter, "Accounting Gumshoes," ABA JOURNAL (September 1997), p. 36.

4   Jeff Stimpson, "Forensic Accounting: Exponential Growth," WEBCPA (February 1, 2007), p. 1.

5   "Michael G. Kessler Cited as First 'Forensic Auditor,'" press release January 15, 2001, *http://www.investigation.com/press/press14.htm*.

6   "Book 'EM! Forensic Accounting in History and Literature," THE KESSLER REPORT, Vol. 1, No. 2.

7   Motto used by Al Pacino's character in the movie, *The Recruit*, Touchstone Pictures, 2003.

8   H.W. Wolosky, "Forensic Accounting to the Forefront," PRACTICAL ACCOUNTANT (February 2004), pp. 23-28.

9   Max Lourie, "Forensic Accounting," NEW YORK CPA (November 1953), pp. 696–705.

10 T.A. Buckoff and R.W. Schrader, "The Teaching of Forensic Accounting," JOURNAL OF FORENSIC ACCOUNTING 1 (1) (2000), pp. 135–146.

11 B.K. Peterson and B.P. Reider, "An Examination of Forensic Accounting Courses: Content and Learning Activities," JOURNAL OF FORENSIC ACCOUNTING 2 (January 2001), p. 29.

12 H.W. Wolosky, " Forensic Accounting to the Forefront," PRACTICAL ACCOUNTANT (February 2004), pp. 23-28.

13 "Bean Counters As Gumshoes," BLOOMBERG, November, 1999, *www.investigation.com/articles/library/1999/articles6.htm*.

14 Joe Anastasi, THE NEW FORENSICS (John Wiley & Sons, 2003).

15 D.A. McMullen and M.H. Sanchez, "A Preliminary Investigation of the Necessary Skills, Education Requirements, and Training Requirements for Forensic Accountants," JOURNAL OF FORENSIC AND INVESTIGATIVE ACCOUNTING, Vol. 2, Issue 2, July-December, 2010, p.43.

16 *Ibid.*, p.43.

17 C. Davis, R. Farrell, and S. Ogilby, "Characteristics and Skills of the Forensic Accountant," AICPA/FVS section, p. 11 http://www.bus.lsu.edu/accounting/faculty/lcrumbley/oilgas.html.

18 *Ibid.*, p. 12.

19 Z. Rezaee, D.L. Crumbley, and R. Elmore, "Forensic Accounting Education: A Survey of Academicians and Practitioners," ADVANCES IN ACCOUNTING TEACHING AND CURRICULUM INNOVATIONS (November 6, 2005).

20 G.S. Smith and D.L. Crumbley, "How Divergent Are Pedagogical Views Toward the Fraud/Forensic Accounting Curriculum," *Global Perspectives on Accounting Education*, Vol. 6, 2009, pp. 1-24.

21 Ibid, p.19.

22 Lynn Brenner, "How Did You Do?" PARADE, THE ADVOCATE (April 15, 2007), p. 4.

23 Robert Half, 2013. Robert Half 2013 Salary Guide, Accounting and Finance. P.R. Newswire, 2013.

24 James Schiavone, "And the Survey Says….Increasing Demand for Forensic Accounting," AICPA Insights, May 21, 2012.

25 Ken Tysiac, "Demand Strong for Forensic Accountants in Wake of Financial Crisis," CPA Insider, September 24, 2012.

26 "The 2011 Forensic and Valuation Services (FVS) Trend Survey," 2011-2012 members of CFF Committee.

27 Dan Weil, "Expert Stimulus Fraud May Hit $50 Billion," *Newsmax.com,* June 16, 2009, *http://mmoneynews.newsmax.com/printTemplate.html*.

28 Terry Carter, "Accounting Gumshoes," ABA JOURNAL (September 1997), p. 37.

29 "Field of Forensic Service Remains Hot," A.E. Feldman Blog, *http://blogaefeldman.com/2009/04/13/field-of-forensic-services-rem*.

30 Ron Scherer, "When Audits Get Tough, Firms Call the Cops," CHRISTIAN SCIENCE MONITOR (July 25, 2002).

31 M. Watters, K.M. Casey and D. Flaherty, "Survey Evidence Regarding CPA Firms' Forensic Accounting Services," JOURNAL OF FORENSIC ACCOUNTING 3 (1) (2002), pp. 17–26.

32 P.H. Mouce and J.J. Frazier, "The Effect of Forensic Accounting Education on an Accountant's Employment Potential," JOURNAL OF FORENSIC ACCOUNTING 3 (1) (2002), pp. 91–102.

33 Ron Scherer, "When Audits Get Tough, Firms Call the Cops," CHRISTIAN SCIENCE MONITOR (July 25, 2002).

34 "Employee Theft," KESSLER INTERNATIONAL, April 1, 2000, *www.investigation.com/articles/library/2000articles/articles29.htm*.

35 "Background Checks Crucial," PC MAGAZINE (October 1, 2001), *www.investigation.com*.

36 J.C. Robertson, FRAUD EXAMINATION FOR MANAGERS AND AUDITORS (Austin, Tex.: Viesca Books, 2000), p. 73.

37 *FBI.gov*.

38 PCAOB Release 2004-001, March 9, 2004.

39 *Ibid*.

40 Sue Clough, "Bungling Scientist Is Jailed for Plotting World's Biggest Fraud," *News.telegraph.co.uk,* January 11, 2003.

41 D.W. Squires, "Problem Solved with Forensic Accounting: A Legal Perspective," JOURNAL OF FORENSIC ACCOUNTING 4 (2003), p. 131.

42 Tom Carlucci, E-library Reuters Library, September 20, 2002.

43 NIFA NEWS, No. 10, p. 1.

44 Les Staniford, "The Great Coin Heist," READER'S DIGEST (April 2005), p. 124.

45 J. Bologna and R.J. Lindquist, FRAUD AUDITING AND FORENSIC ACCOUNTING: TOOLS AND TECHNIQUES, 2d ed. (New York: John Wiley & Sons, 1995), pp. 134–135.

46 Litigation Release No. 17,776, November 18, 2002.

47 Ken Brown, "Auditor's Methods Make It Hard to Catch Fraud by Executives," THE WALL STREET JOURNAL (July 8, 2002), p. C-3.

48 E.T. Pound, "Following the Old Money Trail," U.S. NEWS & WORLD REPORT (April 4, 2005), p. 30.

49 Mimi Swartz and Sherron Watkins, POWER FAILURE (New York: Doubleday, 2003), p. 96.

50 S. Ramamoorti and S. Curtis, "Procurement Fraud & Data Analytics," JOURNAL OF GOVERNMENT FINANCIAL MANAGEMENT (Winter 2003), Vol. 52, No. 4, pp. 16-24.

51 SEC Litigation Release 16627, November 18, 2002.

52 Emilio Parodi and Stefano Bernabei, "Wrap-up 2: Pamalat Fraud Probe Widens to Auditors, Ex- Banker," *forbes.com* (January 8, 2004).

53 "Accounting's Bloodhounds in Demand: Number Crunching Now Appears Sexy," CHICAGO TRIBUNE (March 10, 2002), *www.investigation.com/articles*.

54 Mark Kohn, "Unreported Income and Hidden Assets," FORENSIC ACCOUNTING IN MATRIMONIAL DIVORCE (Philadelphia: R.T. Edwards, 2005), pp. 49-57.

55 Justin Pope, "Forensic Accountants In Demand," CHICAGO SUN-TIMES *(July 5, 2002), www.suntimes.com/output/business/cst*.

56 Ken Brown, "Auditor's Methods Make It Hard to Catch Fraud by Executives," THE WALL STREET JOURNAL (July 8, 2002), p. C-3.

57 Justin Pope, "Forensic Accountants Back in Vogue," Daytona Beach NEWS-JOURNAL *(July 5, 2002), p. 20*.

58 "Bean Counters As Gumshoes," BLOOMBERG, November 1999, *www.investigation.com/articles/library/1999articles/articles6.htm*.

59 AICPA Proposed Statement on Responsibilities for Litigation Services No. 1, December 1, 2001.

60 *Ibid.*

61 AICPA Proposed Statement on Responsibilities for Litigation Services No. 1, December 1, 2001.

62 Mark Kohn, "Unreported Income and Hidden Assets," FORENSIC ACCOUNTING IN MATRIMONIAL DIVORCE (Philadelphia: R.T. Edwards, 2005), pp. 49-57.

63 American College of Forensic Examiners, Attn: Certified Forensic Accountant, Cr.FA Program, 2750 E. Sunshine, Springfield, MO 65804, 800-423-9737, *www.acfei.com*.

64 "New Certified Forensic Accountant, Cr.FA Designation a Success," THE FORENSIC EXAMINER (January/February 2002), p. 19.

65 See *http://www.cfenet.com/about/mission.asp*.

66 See *http://www.cfenet.com/member*.

67 Zabihollah Rezaee, "Forensic Accounting Practices, Education, and Certifications," JOURNAL OF FORENSIC ACCOUNTING 3 (2002), pp. 207–224.

68 See *http://www.cfenet.com/about/codeethics.asp*.

69 Association of Certified Fraud Specialists, P.O. Box 13070, Sacramento, CA 95813, 916-681-5991, *http://acfsnet.org*.

70 *Ibid.*

71 FASNA National Offices, 4248 Park Glen Road, Minneapolis, MN 60060, 952-928-4668, *www.fasna.org*.

72 NACVA, 1245 East Brickyard Road, Suite 110, Salt Lake City, Utah 84106, 801-486-0600.

73 See *http://www.nacva.com/association/A_mission.html*.

74 See *www.nacva.com/association/Abenefit.html*.

75 NLSSA–60 Bristol Road East, Suite 248, Mississauga, ON L423K8 Canada, 905-502-7890, *www.NLSSA.com*.

76 See *http://nlssa.qa3.net/default.asp?section=262*.

77 "Forensic Accounting Specialists Band Together," ACCOUNTANCY AGE.COM (November 11, 1999).

78 IBA, P.O. Box 17410, Plantation, FL 33318; 954-584-1144.

79 See *www.go-iba.org/who.asp*.

80 *Ibid.*

81 See *www.go-iba.org/certify.asp*.

82 ASA, 555 Herndon Parkway, Suite 125, Herndon, VA 20170.

83 enews, "Student Investigative and Forensic Accountants Training in One of the Most Rigorous Programs of Its Kind in the World," (August 20, 2002), *www.aacsb.edu/publications/enewsline/VIIssue9/prgm-toronto.asp*. See also Real Labelle, "Investigative and Forensic Accounting Accredited as a Specialization of Public Accounting," JOURNAL OF FORENSIC ACCOUNTING 5 (2004), pp. 491-499.

84 See *www.acfi.ca*.

85 See *www.homewoodave.com*.

86 HTCIA, Inc., 1474 Freeman Drive, Amissville, VA 20106.

87 www.sofe.org/about.

88 www.iaaronline.org.

89 Professor Edmund Fenton has an internet site to keep up with the numerous accounting related professional certifications: *http://www.accounting.eku.edu/FentonE/Certifications.htm*.

90 Dennis Huber, "Forensic Accountants, Forensic Accounting Certifications, and Due Diligence," J. of Forensic & Investigative Accounting, Vol.5, Issue 1, January – June, 2013, pp. 182-203.

91 Ibid., p.195

EXERCISES

1. Explain why forensic accounting is like a three-layered wedding cake.
2. Consult your university course catalog(s) and put together a list of courses outside the accounting curriculum that you believe would help create a well-rounded forensic education.
3. In the Kessler International survey, what percentage of employees steal from their employers?
   a. 42%
   b. 51%
   c. 56%
   d. 79%
   e. None of the above
4. In the Kessler International Survey, what was the major motivation for employee fraud?
   a. Greed
   b. Need
   c. Vindictiveness
   d. Lack of internal controls
   e. None of the above
5. In the Kessler International Survey, what percentage of the employees said they lied on their job application?
   a. 43%
   b. 49%
   c. 79%
   d. 92%
   e. None of the above
6. Explain why the FBI would need forensic accountants. What other government agencies might need forensic accounting skills?
7. Of the 49 topics listed by a group of educators, what five topics are more important?
8. As an expert witness, the forensic accountant should have an understanding of:
   a. Business valuations
   b. Commercial litigation
   c. Bankruptcy
   d. Courtroom terminology
   e. All of the above
9. A forensic accountant may:
   a. Perform fraud audits
   b. Provide litigation support
   c. Investigate an embezzlement
   d. Trace missing funds
   e. All of the above
10. Should a forensic accountant have a CPA certificate? What other certificates are appropriate?
11. What four disciplines make up the knowledge base of forensic accounting?
12. Why may behavioral forensic techniques catch some fraud schemes that data driven techniques miss?
13. Why is fraud like termites and rust?
14. What forensic certificate does the American College of Forensic Examiners International offer? How many tests are required? What city is the organization located?
15. May a forensic accountant have a monetary interest in the outcome of a court decision?
16. Where is the home office of the Association of Certified Fraud Examiners? Would all of its members have an accounting and auditing background? Does the group have a Code of Ethics?
17. Should a forensic accountant express an opinion in a report regarding the guilt or innocence of any person or party?
18. What certificate does the FASNA group issue?
19. What three certifications does the National Association of Certified Valuation Analysts offer?
20. What is the primary requirement of a CVA certificate?
21. Which is the oldest appraisal organization? What certificate does it issue? Where is its home office?
22. To what certificates do these abbreviations relate:
   a. CPA
   b. Cr.FA
   c. CFI
   d. CFE
   e. CA.IFA
   f. CVA
   g. MAFF
   h. CFD
   i. FCPA
   j. CFF
   k. CSAR
23. Find the Internet site "Forensic Accounting Demystified" and determine what types of assignments forensic accountants perform.
24. Find the Internet site of Zysman Forensic Accounting, Inc. Where is the company located?

25. Using the Internet, find five or six websites of the many forensic accounting firms.

26. On the Internet, locate "Corruption and Related Matters: An Annotated Bibliography" by the Independent Commission Against Corruption, especially the Chapters on White Collar Crime and Workplace Crime. Review three articles in three different countries.

27. Go to the Association of Certified Fraud Examiners web site and locate the 2012 *Report to the Nation on Occupational Fraud and Abuse* (The 2012 Wells Report).
    a. The estimates in this report are based upon how many questionnaires?
    b. The average organization loses about what percentage of revenue to occupational fraud?
    c. The median loss from these cases was what amount?
    d. The average duration of a fraud scheme is how many months?
    e. Employees provide how many of the tips of fraud?
    f. Which industry had the highest percentage of fraud cases? Which industry was in second place?
    g. Which control weakness results in the most fraud?

28. Go to the AICPA's Antifraud Resource Center and search for forensic accounting topics. Read some of the material listed. Search for material dealing with litigation support. What type of forensic program do they have?

29. Using the Internet, learn about the SEC's Financial Fraud Task Force.

30. Interview a forensic accountant and get answers to the following questions:
    a. What education did the accountant seek to qualify as a forensic accountant?
    b. What special certification did the accountant seek to qualify as a forensic accountant?
    c. What advice does the accountant have for you and your classmates about a forensic career?

31. Interview someone in law enforcement or the legal field who has worked with forensic accountants and discuss the following:
    a. Describe your experiences with forensic accountants.
    b. What qualifications do you want in a forensic accountant?

32. A employee comes to your office and opens a can of motor oil with your company's label on it. The oil is unrefined (e.g., unrefined oil in a supposedly refined can of motor oil). Outline the steps you would take to solve this mystery. What problems may your company have?

33. How valuable is computer knowledge to a forensic accountant?

34. Using the Internet, determine the goals of the National White Collar Crime Center?

35. Using the Internet, determine some universities offering a forensic accounting major or minor.

36. Sketch an outline of a pitch for a television series about a forensic accountant?

37. Using the Internet, list some novels starring a forensic accountant.

38. What would be a forensic accounting certification of the NACVA?
    a. CFE
    b. Cr.FA
    c. MAFF
    d. FCPA
    e. CFF

39. Which would be the youngest forensic accounting certification?
    a. CFE
    b. Cr.FA
    c. MAFF
    d. FCPA
    e. CFF

40. Who was the auditor for HealthSouth during their fraudulent period?
    a. Ernst & Young
    b. Arthur Andersen
    c. PwC
    d. Deloitte & Touche
    e. KPMG

41. What would be a forensic accounting certificate from the AICPA?
    a. Cr. FA
    b. CFF
    c. MAFF
    d. CFS
    e. CVA

42 What does CFF stand for? What organization provides this certificate?

43. How does the FBI define white-collar crimes?

44. Which certificate holder represented more than 90 percent of Forensic Experts over two years?
    a. CFE
    b. Cr. FA
    c. CFF
    d. MAFF
    e. None of above

45. Find on the Internet "Managing the Business Risk of Fraud: A Practical Guide". Who sponsored this guide?

46. Sketch a pitch for a movie with the main character as a forensic accountant.

47. Rent and view one of these movies. What do they have to do with forensic accounting?
    a. My Cousin Vinny
    b. Breach
    c. Catch Me if You Can
    d. Boiler Room
    e. Caller
    f. Untouchables
    g. The Other Guys
    h. Arbitrage

48. Go to the website (stateintegrity.com) and determine the rankings of the most corrupt states in the U.S. (as of March 22, 2012). Why may the ranking be wrong?

49. Check the websites of some of the organizations that offer forensic accounting certifications and determine if you can obtain a certificate.

PART 2

UNCOVERING ACCOUNTING CRIME

3

FRAUDULENT FINANCIAL REPORTING

The task before us is to restore the confidence of the American people and others around the world that the accounting statements issued by public companies registered in our country and certified by public accounting firms present a complete, true and timely report that can be relied on. Confidence in the accuracy of accounting statements is the bedrock of investors being willing to invest, in lenders to lend, and for employees knowing that their firm's obligations to them can be trusted.

—William McDonough[1]

OBJECTIVES

After completing Chapter 3, you should be able to:
1. List ways financial statements are manipulated with fraudulent intent.
2. Describe types of financial statement fraud schemes.
3. Identify several financial fraud risk factors.
4. Identify characteristics of white-collar criminals who conduct fraudulent financial accounting.
5. Explain the role of AICPA's guidance on fraud detection in financial statement audits.

OVERVIEW

The first few years of the 21st century may well be known as a time when the United States and other capitalist countries decided business as usual was in need of a substantial make-over. Financial scandals and their resultant fallout in the United States drew comparisons with activities surrounding the stock market crash of 1929. Superstar companies such as Enron and WorldCom were caught in fraudulent behaviors that seemed untenable for most investors and unfathomable for most Americans at large. The stock market shook. One of the most respected, storied, and successful accounting firms, Arthur Andersen, also became a casualty of the major scandals. Investors, employees, and taxpayers suffered billions of dollars in losses, and Congress took action to jump-start reform in the regulatory structure that many suggested had been relatively static for decades.

President George W. Bush signed into law the Sarbanes-Oxley Act on July 30, 2002. This landmark legislation should fundamentally change the way public companies do business and how the accounting profession performs its statutorily required audit function. The President, by means of Executive Order 13271, also established the Corporate Fraud Task Force within the Department of Justice. This task force includes membership of top federal government officials from the executive branch, such as the Secretary of the Treasury and Chairman of the Securities and Exchange Commission.

White-collar crime has been called a type of crime by the advantaged. According to Herbert Stern, "crime is the most flourishing and lucrative business in America... I speak now not only of the crime in the streets, the burglaries and the robberies, which represent tens of billions of dollars each year; I speak of the crime which we call 'white collar'—the crimes committed by the advantaged, not the disadvantaged; the crimes committed with pen and pencil, not with gun or 'jimmy'; under the bright lights of the executive offices, not by stealth in the dark."[2]

Sam Antar of Crazy Eddie fame, says that white collar crime is one involving persuasion and deceit, gentle and subtle intimidation, and the art of spinning. He would pair "cute, hot female" employees with male auditors as part of his distraction strategy. My goal was to have the auditors leave 80 percent of their work until the last week. "It's like David Cooperfield; it's an illusion. I want them to look over here so you don't see what I'm doing over there."[3]

Ongoing regulatory efforts are underway to systematically prevent and root out financial reporting fraud. These efforts are changing the processes of checks and balances that are charged with ensuring open and honest disclosures and reporting. The term *transparency* is the descriptor being used generously in position papers and articles on how financial reporting needs to be reformed. However, PwC in their 2009 Global Economic Crime survey states that accounting fraud has more than tripled since 2003.

Regulatory, auditing and accounting, legal and other institutional changes will certainly help to reduce fraud. However, the role of individual forensic accountants and other fraud fighters cannot be ignored. Catching fraud is like the old story about the Gingerbread man: "Run, run as fast as you can. You can't catch me. I'm the Gingerbread man [fraudster]." The objectives of this chapter are to promote an understanding of reporting fraud, the types that exist, how it comes about, and the motives and personalities of those who perpetrate such fraud.

Fraud can happen anywhere. Europol believes that match-fixing threatens the integrity of European football (soccer). The European crime fighters are probing as many as 68 soccer games for match-fixing by an organized crime syndicate based in Asia. More than 300 matches outside of Europe are under suspicion. An estimated $21.7 million have been bet on matches by criminals, yielding $10.8 million profit. Lifetime bans have been handed to 41 South Korean players found guilty of prearranging soccer matches.[4]

¶ 3001   FINANCIAL FRAUD ENFORCEMENT TASK FORCE

On November 17, 2009, by executive order President Barack Obama replaced the Corporate Fraud Task Force with the interagency Financial Fraud Enforcement Task Force. The purpose of the new task force is to build upon efforts already underway to combat mortgage, securities, and corporate fraud by increasing coordination and fully utilizing the resources and expertise of the government's law enforcement and regulatory apparatus.

The then SEC Chairman, Mary Schapiro, said that "many financial frauds are complicated puzzles that require painstaking efforts to piece together. By formally coordinating our efforts, we will be better able to identify the pieces, assemble the puzzle, and put an end to the fraud."[5]

The task force is composed of senior-level officials from the following departments, agencies, and offices: The Department of Justice; The Department of the Treasury; The Department of Commerce; The Department of Labor; The Department of Housing and Urban Development; The Department of Education; The Department of Homeland Security; The Securities and Exchange Commission; The Commodity Futures Trading Commission; The Federal Trade Commission; The Federal Deposit Insurance Corporation; The Board of Governors of the Federal Reserve System; The Federal Housing Finance Agency; The Office of Thrift Supervision; The Office of the Comptroller of the Currency; The Small Business Administration; The Federal Bureau of Investigation; The Social Security Administration; The Internal Revenue Service, Criminal Investigations; The Financial Crimes Enforcement Network; The United States Postal Inspection Service; The United States Secret Service; The United States Immigration and Customs Enforcement.

Importance of Transparent Financial Information

¶ 3003   AN INTERNATIONAL PROBLEM

Fraud is an international phenomenon touching all countries. Transparency International (TI) is a global network including more than 90 locally established national chapters and chapters-in-formation, whose goal is to fight corruption in the national arena. They bring together relevant players from government, civil society, business, and the media to promote transparency in elections, in public administration, in procurement, and in business. TI's global network of chapters and contacts also uses advocacy campaigns to lobby governments to implement anti-corruption reforms.

TI produces a Transparency International Corruption Perception Index (CPI), which ranks more than 175 countries by their perceived levels of corruption, as determined by expert assessments and opinion surveys. For example, the 2012 Index ranks the United States 24th, after Japan and United Kingdom. Denmark, New Zealand, and Finland were tied for first. TI defines corruption as the abuse of entrusted power for private gain. It hurts everyone whose life, livelihood, or happiness depends on the integrity of people in a position of authority.[6] Certainly financial statement fraud falls under this definition of corruption.

Table 3.1. Transparency International Corruption Perceptions Index 2012

Rank	Country	Score
1	New Zealand	9.5
2	Denmark	9.4
2	Finland	9.4
4	Sweden	9.3
5	Singapore	9.2
6	Norway	9
7	Netherlands	8.9
8	Australia	8.8
8	Switzerland	8.8
10	Canada	8.7
12	Hong Kong	8.4
14	Japan	8
16	United Kingdom	7.8
24	United States	7.1
32	Portugal	6.1
60	Malaysia	4.3
69	Italy	3.9
73	Brazil	3.8
75	China	3.6
80	Thailand	3.4
95	India	3.1
100	Indonesia	3
112	Vietnam	2.9
143	Russia	2.4
172	Burundi	1.9
182	Somalia (Lowest)	1

Even foreign companies are being forced to be more transparent with shareholders. Foreign stock exchanges and regulators are beginning to force disclosure requirements more in line with those in the West. *The Wall Street Journal* prepared this chart comparing the U.S. with Asia:[7]

Disclosure and Governance | How rules in the U.S. and Asia compare

	U.S.	CHINA	HONG KONG	TAIWAN	INDIA
Filing earnings	Quarterly	Quarterly	Main board companies, every six months; other companies*, including those also on mainland exchanges, quarterly	Quarterly	Quarterly
Board independence	A majority of members must be independent.	At least a third must be independent.	At least a third must be independent.	For financial companies and large** nonfinancial companies, at least two directors, representing at least a fifth of board, must be independent.	At least a third must be independent (or half in certain cases, such as if the board has an executive chairman).
Compensation disclosure	Top five executives, breaking down components such as salary, bonus and stock options	No individuals; top executives and executive directors in aggregate	Individual compensation for executive directors; lump sum for other top executives	Top executives in aggregate	Executive directors

* Listed on the Growth Enterprise Market   ** With paid-in capital of more than 50 billion New Taiwan dollars (US$1.72 billion)

Sources: Hong Kong Exchanges & Clearing (Hong Kong); Institutional Shareholder Services (other markets)   The Wall Street Journal

There is a Financial Secrecy Index which ranks the U.S. at 5. Notice that Switzerland is ranked number 1 (e.g., the worst).

1. Switzerland
2. Cayman Islands
3. Luxembourg
4. Hong Kong
5. USA
6. Singapore
7. Isle of Jersey
8. Japan
9. Germany
10. Bahrain
11. British Virgin Island
12. Bermuda
13. United Kingdom
18. United Arab Emirates
24. Canada
25. India
27. Malaysia
31. Ireland
48. Denmark
50. Portugal

The U.S. does rank high on the 2011 Global Integrity Report.

Country	Score
United States	85
Japan (2008)	83
Indonesia	81
Columbia	80
Ireland	80
Germany	78
Macedonia	78
Brazil (2009)	76
Serbia	73
India	70
Mexico	68
China	64
Malaysia (2010)	50
Vietnam	44

¶ 3005 STATEMENT OF FINANCIAL ACCOUNTING CONCEPTS NO. 2

In May 2000, then SEC Chairman Arthur Levitt stated that:

Too many CFOs are being judged today not by how effectively they manage operations, but by how they manage (Wall) Street. Too many analysts are being judged not by how well they analyze a particular company, but by how well they assist in selling the latest deal. And too many auditors are being judged not just by how well they manage an audit, but by how well they cross-market their firm's non-audit services.[8]

Statement of Financial Accounting Concepts No. 2 provides nine qualities and characteristics that make financial information useful for investors, creditors, analysts, and other users of financial information:

- Relevance
- Timeliness
- Reliability
- Verifiability
- Representational faithfulness
- Neutrality
- Comparability and consistency
- Materiality
- Feasibility or costs and benefits[9]

Along with a whole host of accounting reporters, authors, legal and financial experts, Zabihollah Razaee suggests a more important quality: transparency.[10] Razaee believes that reliable financial statements can be achieved with a well-functioning system of corporate governance composed of six groups: the board of directors, the audit committee, the top management team, internal auditors, external auditors, and certain governing bodies (e.g., SEC, AICPA, NYSE, and NASD). He calls this function the six-legged stool of the financial reporting process.[11]

Means and Schemes of Financial Reporting Fraud

¶ 3011   THREE M'S OF FINANCIAL REPORTING FRAUD

At the highest level, there are three types of fraud that are present in fraudulent financial reporting situations. These types of fraud can be thought of as the three M's of financial reporting fraud.

The three M's of financial reporting fraud are as follows:

1. *Manipulation,* falsification, or alteration of accounting records or supporting documents from which financial statements are prepared;
2. *Misrepresentation* in or intentional omission from the financial statements of events, transactions, or other significant information; and
3. Intentional *misapplication* of accounting principles relating to amounts, classification, manner of presentation, or disclosure.[12]

Most fraudulent schemes touching financial reporting should fit into one of these three categories.

EYEWITNESS

Miniscribe Corp. in the mid-1980s was able to increase sales and profits, improving their financial results, leading to a successful $98 million bond issuance. Regrettably, most of the improved financial results were fabricated by manipulation of reserves to reduce expenses and fictitious shipments of inventory. The disk-drive maker shipped bricks rather than disk drives to the Far East and fake customer warehouses and received credit from the bank for the amount of the shipments.

At the end of 1993, Bausch & Lomb oversupplied distributors with contact lenses and sunglasses. Eventually the company said that it had "inappropriately recorded as sales" some of its inventory sent to distributors.

In 1997, Waste Management took $3.54 billion in pretax charges and write-downs. The company said that "incorrect vehicle and container salvage values had been used, and errors had been made in the expense calculations."

Financial Statement Fraud, Bankruptcy, Shareholder Losses, and Executive Penalties

A 2010 COSO study covering a 10-year period (1998-2007)[13] found that fraudulent financial reporting results in significant negative consequences for investors and executives. The nearly 350 alleged accounting fraud cases investigated by the SEC found the following facts:[14]

- Financial fraud affects companies of all sizes, with the median company having assets and revenues just under $100 million.
- The median fraud was $12.1 million. More than 30 of the fraud cases each involved misstatements/misappropriations of $500 million or more.
- The SEC names the CEO and/or CFO for involvement in 89 percent of the fraud cases. Within two years of the completion of the SEC investigation, about 20 percent of the CEOs/CFOs had been indicted. Over 60 percent of those indicted were convicted.
- Motivations include meeting expectations, concealing deteriorating financial conditions, and preparing for debt/equity offerings.
- Revenue frauds accounted for over 60 percent of the cases. Overstated assets, 51 percent. Understatement of expenses/liabilities, 31 percent. Misappropriation of assets, 14 percent.
- Many of the commonly observed board of directors and audit committee characteristics such as size, meeting frequency, composition, and experience do not differ meaningfully between fraud and no-fraud companies. Recent corporate governance regulatory efforts appear to have reduced variation in observable board-related governance characteristics.
- Twenty-six percent of the firms engaged in fraud changed auditors during the period examined compared to a 12 percent rate for no-fraud firms.
- Initial news in the press of an alleged fraud resulted in an average 16.7 percent abnormal stock price decline for the fraud company in the two days surrounding the announcement.
- News of an SEC or Department of Justice investigation resulted in an average 7.3 percent abnormal stock price decline.
- Companies engaged in fraud often experienced bankruptcy, delisting from a stock exchange, or material asset sales at rates much higher than those experienced by no-fraud firms.
- Fifty percent of the stock traded on NASDAQ over a variety of industries.
- Twenty percent of the fraud companies were in the computer hardware/software industry and 20 percent were in financial service providers. Eleven percent were in health care and health products.
- Forty-five percent of the Section 404 opinions indicated effective controls and 45 percent indicated ineffective controls.

EYEWITNESS

JP Morgan executives were told of Bernard Madoff's fraud concerns, but they ignored the warnings. E-mails and other documents allegedly show that executives at JP Morgan were complicit in Madoff's massive fraud. Lawyers working for the court-appointed trustee Irving Picard filed a $6.4 billion complaint in 2010 against JP Morgan, the disgraced primary bank for two decades.

Attorney Deborah Renner said that "the bank's top executives were warned in blunt terms about speculation that Madoff was running a Ponzi scheme. Yet the bank appears to have been more concerned only with protecting its own investments in (the Madoff firm's) feeder funds."[15]

¶ 3021   ABUSIVE SCHEMES INVOLVING FRAUDULENT FINANCIAL REPORTING

Fraudulent financial statements compose a small percentage of fraud schemes but pack a major economic wallop for investors and employees. Typically, fraudulent statement schemes are perpetrated with the knowledge of—if not the support of—top corporate executives. Because the Enron Corporation committed so many types of fraudulent financial reporting (as well as its other misdeeds), its financial and earnings management offer classic examples of abuse toward investors and employees that earmark fraud in SEC filings.

In the late 1990s, Professors Bonner, Palmrose, and Young analyzed SEC enforcement releases to determine common types of fraud involving accounting and auditing schemes.[16] The types of rule-bending and -breaking the professors gleaned from the releases reveal creatively devious ways to mask bad news and fool investors and authorities about the real state of company finances. Major fraud types are described here.

The fact that "cooking the books" is an international phenomenon is illustrated by the sentencing of Takafumi Horie, one of Japan's highest-profile Internet entrepreneurs, to 2½ years in prison for securities fraud. In Japan white-collar crimes rarely result in a jail term; white-collar criminals often receive suspended prison terms if they express remorse.

Horie adamantly maintained his innocence, placing the blame on his colleagues. He "publicly flaunted his disdain for the 'jealous elite of old Japan,' which rankled prosecutors and judges." The judge said that "though the value of accounting fraud was not great, he [Horie] has never indicated remorse."[17]

Fictitious or Overstated Revenues and Assets

What Is This Method?

Fraudsters use any of multiple methods to create *fictitious revenues or assets* in order to inflate income on financial statements. A slightly different approach is simply to *overstate* income—either by omitting elements that would lower actual revenues (such as returns of purchases) or by using mark-to-market accounting to make records of (future) income more "flexible."

One type of overstated-income scheme is the bill-and-hold transaction. The customer agrees to purchase goods and the seller invoices the customer but retains physical possession of the products until a later delivery date. Not all such transactions involve fraud, but the practice must be closely examined in light of accounting rules because it is open to abuse. Fraudsters may use this approach to count both sales and inventory on hand as revenue-producers.

How Do Perpetrators Use This Scheme?

In a well-publicized case, Sunbeam created revenues in 1997 by using a bill and hold practice. The company sold products to customers but held on to the shipments with an agreement to deliver the goods later.

Enron's 10-Q quarterly SEC filing dated October 16, 2001, described a $618 million third-quarter loss. However, in its November 19, 2001, restatement, the loss was revised (for the second time that quarter) to be $664 million.

Because the government had not established rules for reporting derivatives, and Enron depended in large part on revenues from derivatives, anytime the company needed to show revenue increases on its financial statements it could change assumptions about the value of derivatives contracts (such as raising anticipated interest earnings or lowering interest charges the company would owe). Then Enron could record adjusted income on its books. By the end of 2000, Enron showed $21 billion in assets from derivatives on its statements.

Mark-to-market accounting was a useful tool for Enron in its deceptive earnings management. Enron was the first nonfinancial company to obtain SEC approval to use mark-to-market accounting, and the energy company even applied it retroactively to deals made before the commission's approval. The financial executives and special-purpose entity (SPE) directors used this tool to value items in manipulating prices and boosting revenues/decreasing liabilities as needed. Using mark-to-market accounting rather than the more conventional accrual accounting, Enron's Jeff Skilling pulled future revenues into the current quarter to improve his business unit's statements of revenues.

Coca-Cola created income by loading up syrup trucks near the end of the year and driving the trucks outside the warehouse and parking them. After the end of the year, the trucks with spoiled syrup came back inside the warehouse and the inventory was written-off.

Cendant Corporation created at least $500 million in fictitious revenues, and Barry Minkow created a $200 million corporation based upon fictitious sales revenues. Equity Funding sold a large number of fake insurance policies and misreported them on their financial statements.

A company may engage in channel stuffing by offering large discounts or other inducements to a distributor/retailer to receive large orders late in the reporting quarter to increase their revenue. If the distributor has a side agreement that gives them the right to return any unsold inventory, these sales do not meet the revenue recognition in SAB No. 104.

Symbol Technology, Inc. improperly recognized at least $16 million in revenue from 1999 through the first quarter of 2001. Under a fraudulent warehousing arrangement with Symbol and a distributor located in South America, the distributor placed multimillion dollar orders for whatever products Symbol had available at the time, even though the distributor did not need the products. There was a side agreement that the distributor did not have to pay for the products. Symbol did not ship the products, but instead they moved the inventory to a warehouse in New York and retained the risk of loss and other indicia of ownership. The sole purpose of the warehouse scheme was to enable Symbol to inflate revenue figures.

Symbol also engaged in channel stuffing by stuffing the distribution channel by granting resellers return rights and contingent payment terms in side agreements. The company instructed employees to refrain from scanning new components and returned goods into the automatic accounting system.

Fictitious Reductions of Expenses and Liabilities

What Is This Method?
Perpetrators improve the bottom line on financial statements using unscrupulous approaches—fictitious reductions of expenses and liabilities—to mask a corporation's true losses or debt. Common approaches to such reductions include the burial of deals likely to generate losses in derivative instruments whose creation does not require an initial cash outflow so their creation does not appear on the books.

Despite rules for futures contracts in FASB Statement No. 80, which requires recognition of market value changes in futures contracts when the effects for the hedged items are recognized, unscrupulous officers have used these instruments to report deferred losses as assets.

How Do Perpetrators Use This Scheme?
FASB No. 133 was to change reporting requirements to prevent abuses possible under FASB No. 80, so Enron used its SPEs to transact (and hide) derivative activities.

WorldCom shifted almost $11 billion of line-cost expenses into capital accounts, thereby increasing income by a like amount.

Lehman Brothers used a so-called Repo 105 accounting gimmick to move $50 billion off of its balance sheet in the second quarter of 2008. Lehman borrows money from cash cow companies, and Lehman then "sold" the large companies bonds. Thus, if Lehman went bankrupt before repaying the loan, the large companies could sell the bonds. Lehman also agreed to buy back the bonds at the end of the loan period, less an amount that the large companies kept as interest.

Lehman apparently often bought back the bonds a few days after the "sale." Since Lehman was not really selling the bonds of the cash cow companies (but really borrowing money), the bonds used by Lehman in the repo stayed on their balance sheet. Lehman then sold the bonds and paid off some of its debts. After its quarterly reports were issued, Lehman borrowed more money to repurchase the bonds.

In late December 2010, the New York attorney general brought a civil fraud lawsuit against Ernst & Young, accusing them of helping Lehman.

Premature Revenue Recognition

What Is This Method?

Premature revenue recognition is a means of recording income as actual in order to inflate earnings totals when sales have not been completed, the products delivered, or invoices paid. In general, revenue from product sales should not be recognized on financial statements until it has been realized or realizable and earned. Based on the provisions of SAB 101, income should not be recognized under these circumstances because delivery has not actually occurred.

Customers on the other side of early delivery schemes often return the unfinished product or demand more completion before payment is rendered.

Many abusers record and recognize revenue whose receipt is contingent on the completion of a contract. Too many side agreements may indicate premature revenue recognition, bill-and-hold schemes, and channel stuffing.

Premature revenue recognition is a key ingredient when fraudsters cook the books. It is the number one reason that corporations must restate financial statements.

How Do Perpetrators Use This Scheme?

Companies commit this fraud by *holding books open*. In 2003 the SEC reported that financial executives of Minuteman International, Inc., were being sanctioned for holding Minuteman's quarterly books open and filing false periodic reports to the SEC. The executives repeatedly held books open for one or more days in the first three quarters of a year to improperly capture and reflect sales that should have been recorded in the subsequent quarter. Invoices for sales that were shipped after the end of the quarter were backdated to the last business day of the prior quarter. Daily sales register records were also backdated to aide in inflating revenues for the first three quarters each year. Minuteman was forced to restate its quarterly information to 1998.

Xerox overstated revenue for more than four years by accelerating the recognition of $3 billion in revenue and inflating earnings by about $1.5 billion. In this scheme perpetrators allegedly included the recognition of revenue on Xerox office copier leases too early in their cycles.

Enron also played with the timing of revenue recognition. In December 1997, the JEDI SPE entered into an agreement to pay Enron an annual management fee. Under GAAP, the fee should be recognized when the services are rendered. However, in March 1998, Enron and JEDI amended the agreement to convert 80 percent of the annual management fee to a "required payment" to Enron. Enron then recorded a $28 million asset—the discounted NPV of the "required payment"—and immediately recognized its revenue in Q1 of 1998 rather than waiting to perform the services.

Misclassified Revenues and Assets

What Is This Method?

Securities investments have been widely misclassified by fraudulent corporate chiefs. GAAP requires investments of debt securities (such as bonds) to be classified as trading, held to maturity, or available for sale. Investments may be classified as held to maturity only if the holder intends to and is able to hold those securities to maturity. Held to maturity securities are reported at *amortized cost*, with no adjustment made for unrealized holdings gains or losses unless the value has declined below cost. If the value will not increase, the security is written down to *fair value* and a loss recorded in earnings.

Under GAAP, investments must be classified as trading if they are bought and held principally for sale in the near term. Securities classified neither as trading or as held-to-maturity are classified as available-for-sale securities.

Trading and available for sale securities are reported at *fair market value* and must be periodically adjusted for unrealized gains and losses to bring them to fair market value. Unrealized gains or losses from trading securities are included in income for the period. Unrealized gains or losses from changes held as available for sale are reported as a component of other comprehensive income. Common or preferred stock can be classified only as trading or available for sale.

The transfer of a security between categories of investments is required to be accounted for at fair value. Securities transferred from the trading category will already have had any unrealized holding gain or loss reflected in earnings. For securities transferred into the trading category, the unrealized holding gain or loss at the date of the transfer must be recognized in earnings immediately. For a debt security transferred into the available-for-sale category from the held-to-maturity category, the unrealized holding gain or loss at the date of the transfer must be reported in other comprehensive income. Securities transferred from available for sale to held to maturity report unrealized holding gain or loss at the date of the transfer as a separate component of other comprehensive income and amortized to interest income over the remaining life of the security.

Fraudsters manipulate financial statements by intentionally misclassifying securities or transferring securities to a different class that would trigger the recognition of gain or conversely postpone the recognition of a loss. A corporation might misclassify a debt security as held to maturity so as to avoid recognizing a decline of value in the current quarter. Conversely, transferring a security from held to maturity to either trading or available for sale may allow the recognition of gains that had not been previously recognized.

Inventory is another area ripe for earnings management and misclassification. GAAP requires that inventory be reported at the lower of replacement cost or market value (i.e., current replacement cost.) Inflating inventory value achieves the same impact on earnings as manipulating the physical count. Fraudulent managers can accomplish this simply by creating false journal entries that increase the balance in the inventory account. Another common way to inflate inventory value is to delay the writedown of obsolete or slow moving inventory, since a write down would require a charge against earnings.

How Do Perpetrators Use This Scheme?

In 2002, Microsoft Corp. settled SEC allegations that it had misstated earnings by maintaining unsupported reserves regarding accruals, allowances, and liability accounts relating to marketing expenses, sales to original equipment manufacturers, accelerated depreciation, inventory obsolescence, valuation of financial assets, interest income, and impairment of manufacturing facilities. These reserves totaled $200 million to $900 million during fiscal years ending June 30, 1995–June 30, 1998. These corporate reserves did not have properly substantiated bases but were partially based on judgment regarding the likelihood of future business events.

Overvalued Assets or Undervalued Expenses and Liabilities

What Is This Method?

Overvalued assets comprise property for which fraudsters set prices that are unsupportable using standard business valuation approaches. These assets might be bought to essentially pay off parties to which the fraudsters are beholden, sold to artificially boost income, or simply held and recorded on statements at far more than their actual worth.

Gain-on-sale accounting is a technique enabling fraudulent executives to use SPEs to purchase or sell overvalued ventures at unsupportable values, which are recorded by the corporation as massive losses/revenues.

Accounts receivable offers myriad opportunities for valuation schemes. GAAP requires accounts receivable to be reported at net realizable value—the gross value of the receivable minus an estimated allowance for uncollectible accounts. Companies circumvent GAAP rules by *underestimating* the uncollectible portion of a receivable. Underestimating the value of the provision (the amount deemed uncollectible) artificially *inflates* the receivable's value and records it at an amount greater than net realizable value. A related fraud is failing or delaying to write off receivables that have become uncollectible.

How Do Perpetrators Use This Scheme?

In 1998, General Electronic Company underaccrued warranty obligations by $100 million for a series of gas-fired turbines used in power plants. The turbines had a design flaw.

Pension funds lend themselves to undervaluing of liabilities. In the 2002–2003 stock market decline, many companies understated their pension expenses.

Finally, Enron committed this type of reporting fraud as well. Its Braveheart SPE was designed to book a gain-on-sale income on an abortive deal between Enron and Blockbuster Inc. The video giant was to develop and market an on-demand movie product through an Enron-supplied broadband fiber system. Six months after the project was signed, the system still had no paying customers and was only in the testing phase. Although traditional accounting rules would allow no profits to be shown, Enron "sold" the joint venture to Braveheart, thereby recognizing $111 million net gain, reported in Q4 2000 and Q1 2001. The venture never came to fruition, dying a swift death in its test markets.

Although GAAP requires expenses to be recognized in the period in which they are incurred, Symbol Technologies, Inc. deferred $3.5 million of FICA expenses to a later year in order to boost its net income.

Omitted Liabilities

What Is This Method?

Omitted liabilities are the mirror image of fictitious revenues and assets: fraudsters hide debt or employ other off-balance sheet financing to avoid having to include the negative picture on corporate financial statements. SPEs may be used to bury poorly performing assets because their transactions are not part of the corporate financial statements.

How Do Perpetrators Use This Scheme?

By the time Enron declared bankruptcy in December 2001, it was reported to have hidden billions of dollars of off-balance sheet debt using SPEs. Also, Enron entered into futures contracts with financing organizations such as J.P. Morgan that were thinly disguised loans not actually based on delivery of energy commodities.

Enron also used *prepaid swaps* through its Delta subsidiary wherein CitiGroup paid the fair value of its portion of the swaps but Enron was allowed repayments spread over five years—in effect, obtaining loans. Enron never disclosed these transactions as such on its financial statements, accounting for the deals as "assets from price risk management" and as "accounts receivable."

Omitted or Improper Disclosures

What Is This Method?

Disclosure, one of the categories of management assertions in financial statements, requires that certain information, such as assets held as collateral and preferred stock dividends in arrears, be included in the notes to financial statements. Fraudsters use *omitted or improper disclosures* to avoid listing questionable or bad news on the balance sheet. For example, contingent liabilities may be underestimated and their likelihood of loss may be understated to minimize their financial statement effect.

Improper disclosures can take the form of misrepresentations, intentional inaccuracies, or deliberate omissions in: descriptions of the corporate or its products, in media reports and interviews, as well as in financial statements/annual reports. Omissions may also occur in management discussions and other nonfinancial statement sections of annual reports, 10-Ks, 10-Qs, and other reports; as well as in footnotes to the financial statements.

How Do Perpetrators Use This Scheme?

Enron used subsidiaries and SPEs as a "parking lot" for assets and losses the corporation's managers wished not to reveal on Enron's financial statements. Andrew Fastow, Enron's CFO, managed the LJM1 and LJM2 SPEs to hide charges in Enron's accounting treatment of gas supply contracts and to inflate accounting income. Enron thus began transacting derivatives deals with companies that were inside Enron. The derivatives were even based on the value of Enron's own stock.

Equity Fraud

What Is This Method?

Equity fraud, also known as *investment* or *securities fraud*, basically involves the promotion and sale of nonexistent or illegal securities investments as well as intentional misrepresentation or concealment of investment and financial related information. Equity fraud causes third parties to suffer financial loss. Equity fraud is usually perpetrated to deceive or mislead and is illegal. The many forms of investment fraud range from boiler rooms, shady stock promotions, real estate transactions, and corporate financial fraud, all of which dupe investors in public companies.

How Do Perpetrators Use This Scheme?

Enron's most publicized equity fraud involved issuing $1.2 billion in stock to a related special-purpose entity and recording a $1.2 billion note receivable for the transaction, rather than a contra account to shareholder equity.

Related-party Transactions

What Is This Method?

According to AccountingBuzz.com, a *related party transaction* is an interaction between two parties, one of whom can exercise control or significant influence over the operating policies of the other. A special relationship may (and often does) exist between the parties, e.g., a corporation and a major shareholder or parent and subsidiary.

How Do Perpetrators Use This Scheme?

Enron became infamous for engaging in many related-party transactions through its special-purpose entities. Through Andrew Fastow's LJM2 SPE, Enron pledged millions of shares of Enron's stock to the four Raptors off-balance-sheet entities. Enron's finance group recorded the Raptors' promissory note as an addition (rather than the correct reduction) to Enron's shareholder equity. The Raptors SPEs absorbed financial results the executives did not wish to reveal on Enron statements, and the corporation wound up taking massive loans to prop up the SPEs' financial status before Enron's eventual bankruptcy.

REFCO used a related third party controlled by REFCO's CEO Phillip Bennett to conceal as much as $545 million in bad debts. Engaging in a series of circular transactions, REFCO would shift debt each quarter to REFCO Group Holdings, which was not a subsidiary and did not have to be consolidated with REFCO under GAAP. REFCO was able to favorably inflate its financial position, but in 2004 after the scheme was discovered, REFCO filed for bankruptcy.

Baptist Foundation of Arizona (BFA) set up subsidiary companies owned by insiders to buy real estate from BFA. Although the real estate had fallen greatly as a result of the real estate bubble crash, BFA sold the property to the subsidiaries at book value and recorded notes receivables at book value on their books. According to the State Board of Accountancy, their auditor, Arthur Andersen, should have reported qualified or adverse opinions from 1991-1994 and adverse opinions from 1995-1997. Andersen reported unqualified opinions.[18]

Alter Ego

What Is This Method?

Alter ego, or second self, is an equitable remedy which permits a person to win a dispute against a corporation that a plaintiff does not have standing to sue under regular law. Under this *alter ego* doctrine, the owners of a corporation are held responsible for corporate acts by "piercing the corporate veil" and disregarding the corporate entity.

How Do Perpetrators Use This Scheme?

The *Litigation Services Handbook* indicates that a two-prong test must be satisfied: (1) such unity of interest and ownership exists that the corporation and shareholders no longer have separate personalities, and (2) viewing the acts of the corporation alone will result in inequity.[19] Forensic accountants are sometimes used in the courtroom to discuss the indicators of *alter ego*, such as:

- Financial dependence behaviors.
- Confusion about corporate identity.
- Lack of separateness.
- Dominance and control.[20]

Piercing the corporate veil is discussed in more detail in Chapter 6.

Minimizing Income or Inflating Expenses to Reduce Tax Liabilities

What Is This Method?

Although tax evasion is a strong term, less ethical corporations often stretch available deductions or *overstate expenses to reduce their tax liabilities*.

All corporations seek to minimize—and even avoid—tax liabilities. The difference between *avoidance* and *evasion* is key. Tax evasion is illegal: it is the willful attempt to circumvent the tax laws through misrepresentation or deceit. By minimizing income in these ways, fraudsters hide the true nature or misrepresent the facts to take advantage of a tax exemption or exclusion that does not actually apply.

How Do Perpetrators Use This Scheme?

The Louisiana Department of Revenue website lists common ploys used by businesses that manipulate income and expenses in an attempt to dodge tax liabilities:

- Making false or fraudulent claims for refunds.
- Deliberately omitting sales tax transactions on state returns for which sales tax was collected.
- Failing to maintain records that show the true income and expenses of a business.
- Preparing documents, books, and records that understate the true income or overstate the expenses of a business.

- Sales of imported cigarettes and other tobacco products without payment of the excise tax on these products.
- Sales of imported beer, liquor, or wine without the payment of the excise tax on these products.
- Operating a business without registering with the Louisiana Department of Revenue.
- Payment of cash wages to employees for the purpose of avoiding Louisiana withholding tax.
- Avoiding the excise tax on diesel fuel by using "off road diesel" in the fuel supply tanks of a motor vehicle for use on highways.
- Ignoring the requirements to report and pay use taxes on goods imported into the state.
- Opening and closing of new businesses to evade taxes.
- Operating a business using someone else's name to avoid business and income taxes.

Of course, as this list indicates, income tax is not the only form of tax liability avoided. Fraudsters attempt to avoid sales, excise, and withholding taxes.

In 2002, Warren Buffett noted that the most flagrant financial statement deceptions occurred in stock-option accounting and in assumptions about pension fund returns.[21] With respect to pension plan deceptions, firms assume rates of returns with great latitude, resulting in questionable assumptions. An analysis of 50 large U.S. companies revealed that they reported more than $54 billion in pension-fund profits when in fact their plans had lost almost $36 billion.[22] Accounting firms attested to this discrepancy of $90 billion, stating that financial statements "present fairly, in all material respect, the financial position" of the company. This ability for a company to select its assumed rate of return gives CEOs an enormous discretion to manipulate pension earnings charges annually either downwardly or upwardly.

Many of these fraud schemes occur because of management's ability to override controls. SAS No. 99 gives three major ways that management overrides controls:

- Recording *fictitious* journal entries (especially near the end of a quarter or year).
- Intentionally *biasing* assumptions and judgments used to estimate accounts (e.g., pension plan assumptions or bad debt allowances).
- *Altering* records and terms related to important and unusual transactions.

The same SAS No. 99 gives three ways to overcome the risk of management overriding controls:

- Examining journal entries and other adjustments.
- Reviewing accounting estimates for bias, including a retrospective review of significant management estimates.
- Evaluating the business rationale for significant unusual transactions.

Ernst & Young's 11th Global Survey provides these mechanisms to detect fraud involving management overrides:

- Stronger internal audit   71%
- More robust segregation of duties   59%
- Stronger compliance   52%
- Additional board/ audit committee oversight   40%
- Stronger legal function   30%
- Better use of outside advisors to test fraud risks   29%
- Additional regulatory oversight   25%

An example of bias assumptions involved the oil and gas reserve estimates of the Royal Dutch/Shell Group. "During the first week of January 2004, Shell slashed its estimates of oil reserve by 20 percent or about 3.9 billion barrels of oil. Its stock fell by nine percent,[23] and Chairman Sir Philip was ousted in March 2002."[24] By the end of 2002, a total of 4.47 billion barrels were cut, and another 1.4 million barrels were slashed in 2003. There are almost as many oil and gas reserve definitions as there are countries.[25]

Another area of assumption is in the retirement plan area. Though companies have made greater contributions, pension plans at the Fortune 1,000 companies were still underfunded in early 2013. The turmoil in the financial markets in 2008 and 2009 caused a number of pension funds to be underwater, and the stock market increase in 2012 has not erased the unfunded plans. Public pension plans are even in worse shape.

In late 2003, the SEC asked six companies to provide them with information about how they calculate their retirement benefit obligations. The SEC was looking to see if companies are reverse-engineering their rates to get certain financial results. Kenneth Lench at the SEC said that "even a small change in rates can have a huge impact on income." In this area he sees "potentially significant risks, and that's why we are taking a look at it."[26]

The SEC has adopted the proactive strategy of "wildcatting," where investigations into entire industries and business sectors are begun after evidence emerges from only one company in the group regarding financial reporting problems (e.g., oil and gas industry).

Over time, the PCAOB will probably be able to identify peculiarities within existing or evolving industries that require either standard setting or regulatory attention or both.[27]

Management's control policy is important in determining the risk of management fraud. Financial fraud is more likely to occur if a company has:

- A poor management control philosophy;
- Weak control structure;
- Strong motive for engaging in financial statement fraud.

Paul Dunn[28] believes that these red flags point to a poor management philosophy:

- Large number of unrelated transactions;
- Continuing presence of the firm's founders;
- Absence of a long-term institutional investor.

A Starwood Hotels poll of executives gives a glimpse of the dishonesty of 401 top executives who golf. The poll results are surprising:[29]

Consider themselves to be honest in business	99%
Played with someone who cheats at golf	87%
Cheated themselves at golf	82%
Hated others who cheated at golf	82%
Believe that business and golf behaviors are parallel	72%

Little may have changed as a result of the passage of Sarbanes-Oxley according to a 2004 survey of CFOs. Almost one-half (47 percent) of the CFOs in the survey reported they still feel pressure from their superiors to use aggressive accounting to improve results. Of those who have felt pressure in the past, only 38 percent think there is less pressure than three years ago, and 20 percent say there is more pressure today.

There is also little confidence in the financial numbers of their colleagues. Only 27 percent assert that if they were investing their own money, they would feel very confident about the financial information from public companies.[30]

¶3025   SHENANIGANS TO BOOST EARNINGS

Howard M. Schilit explains, "financial shenanigans are acts or omissions intended to hide or distort the real financial performance or financial condition of an entity."31 He uses the term "stock detective." Schilit describes seven shenanigans; the first five boost current-year earnings, and the last two shift current-year earnings to the future: 1. Recording revenue before it is earned (sales on consignment, e.g., Cendant and Sunbeam). In 1997, Sunbeam offered deep discounts on gas grills in the fourth quarter under a classic "bill and hold" strategy. They booked the income and held the grills in their warehouses. For 1997, Sunbeam restated earnings by about $93 million. In another example, Qwest had 19 transactions where they booked income before receiving payments. The SEC calls this practice "channel stuffing."

2. Creating fictitious revenue (false journal entries; almost 40 percent of earnings misstatements from 1995 to 1999 had to do with revenue recognition, and one-half of these involved complete fabrication, as with Kroger).

3. Boosting profits with nonrecurring transactions (selling stock for a gain).

4. Shifting current expenses to a later period (debit an asset account rather than expensing, e.g., Waste Management). In 1999, AMR changed the depreciation schedule from 20 to 25 years on some planes which reduced depreciation expense in 2000 by $158 million. WorldCom shifted at least $3.8 billion of line-cost expenses to its capital accounts over at least five quarters starting in 2001. So rather than $1.4 billion of reported profits in 2001, the company actually had a loss.

5. Failing to record or disclose liabilities (Adelphia omitted at least $1.8 billion of debt from its balance sheet).

6. Shifting current income to a later period (recognizing current revenues as deferred revenues).

7. Shifting future expenses to an earlier period (expensing items that should be debited to an asset account, e.g., software costs).

Sources of Fraudulent Financial Reporting

¶ 3031   INTERNAL VERSUS EXTERNAL FRAUD

It is important to understand the sources of financial report fraud. One traditional way to view fraud sources is to distinguish management fraud from employee fraud. A 1995 KPMG survey provides an excellent illustration by categorizing the sources by internal fraud and external fraud with a further breakdown of management and employee fraud under internal fraud. Table 3.2 shows the various types of fraud in these categories.

Table 3.2. Internal and External Fraud

Types of Internal Fraud

Employee Fraud	Management Fraud	Types of External Fraud
Stock theft	Lapping	Check forgery
Misappropriation of cash/assets	Expense accounts	False insurance claims
Lapping	False financial statements	Credit card fraud
Check forgery	Misappropriation of cash/assets	False invoices
Expense account	Unnecessary purchase	Product substitution
Petty cash	Check forgery	Bribes/secret commission
Kickbacks	Kickbacks	Bid rigging/price fixing
Loans/investments	Ghost vendors	False representation of funds
	Diversion of sales	

Source: KPMG, Fraud Awareness Survey, Dublin: KPMG, 1995, pp. 10–12.

Each source is associated with particular types of fraud, although there is overlap. For example, both management and employees can submit fraudulent expense accounts, misappropriate assets and accept kickbacks. External sources of fraud can also be significant.

Centuri, Inc. boosted earnings by not accruing employee vacation expenses, employee payroll taxes and medical expenses, and real estate taxes. The total internal fraud comprised an understatement of $912,679.[32]

HealthSouth committed external fraud against Medicare. The SEC alleged in April 2003, that HealthSouth overstated profits by at least $1.4 billion by billing Medicare for physical-therapy services the company never performed. The company submitted falsified documents to Medicare to verify the claims.

Motivation and Contributing Factors

¶ 3041   ## CONTRIBUTING FACTOR MODEL

Students are familiar no doubt with the often-used sleuth's model for analyzing crime: motive, opportunity, and means. Something akin to this has been adopted for fraud. Donald L. Cressey, a student of Edwin H. Sutherland, described three factors contributing to business fraud: motive, opportunity, and lack of integrity (or rationalization). See the fraud pyramid in Figure 3.1. If the three factors are present in an organization, fraud will probably occur. However, there is no requirement for the three elements to be in the same amounts.

Figure 3.1. The Fraud Pyramid

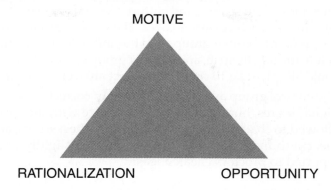

A 2007 KPMG "Profile of a Fraudster" survey found that 89 percent of fraud was committed by employees against an employer, and two-thirds were members of top management. "Need" was the primary motive behind the fraud in 47 percent of the cases KPMG investigated, and opportunity explained 26 percent of the cases.

COSO suggests these major motives for financial statement fraud:

1. Cover up assets misappropriated for personal gain.
2. Increase the stock price to increase the benefits of insider traders and to receive higher cash proceeds when issuing new securities.
3. Obtain national stock exchange listing status or maintain minimum exchange listing requirements to avoid de-listing.
4. Avoiding a pretax loss and bolstering other financial results.

Rationalization reduces the offender's inhibitions. As Jerry Lee Lewis in his cheatin' song entitled *Home Away from Home* sings "It all began the day my conscience died." Fraudsters may rationalize as follows:

- "Borrowing" money temporarily.
- Justifying the theft out of a sense of being underpaid. "I only took what is mine."
- Depersonalizing the victim of the theft. "I'm not stealing from my boss; I'm stealing from the company."
- "Everyone is doing it."
- "I deserve it."

Behavorial psychologists call this rationalization "reframing," where someone who is about to cheat will adjust the definition of cheating to exclude his or her actions. Dan Ariely says "people who would never take $5 from petty cash have no problem paying for a drink for a stranger and putting it on a company tab."[33]

Three professors tempted 2,000 Ivy League students to cheat with little to gain. Ten questions about science and culture were posed to the students, and they were paid 10 cents for each correct answer. The control group gave their answers directly to the proctor, but other groups had the ability to cheat. One group could alter answers before turning them in, and another group could self-report their score. A third group could simply take 10 cents per correct answer from a jar without reporting results.

The control group averaged 32.6 percent correct answers, but the other groups had higher scores, but not in strict accordance with increased opportunity. The group allowed to change its answers had the highest scores, at 36.2 percent correct, while the group that paid itself directly cheated slightly less, and the group that self-reported to proctors cheated least.[34]

What is the price of committing a white collar crime? President Abraham Lincoln is supposed to have thrown a man out of his office after being offered a bribe. The bribe involved a substantial sum, and Lincoln was very angry. His anger was directed at the man in question, but also at himself. He is reputed to have said, "Every man has his price, and he was getting too close to mine."[35]

Two professors argue that the fraud diamond is a better view of the factors leading to fraud. See Figure 3.2. They add a fourth variable, capacity. The person must have the necessary traits, abilities, or positional authority to pull off the crime.[36]

Figure 3.2. The Fraud Diamond

Incentive / Pressures

Capacity

Opportunity

Rationalization / Integrity

P. D. Goldmann has suggested the fraud pentagon[37] as shown in Figure 3.3:

Figure 3.3 The Fraud Pentagon

Pressure

Personal Greed

Opportunity

Employee Disenfranchisement

Rationalization

The personal greed part of the fraud pentagon may or may not explain the actions of Thomas M. Coughlin, a vice-chairman of WalMart, who periodically created false invoices over a five-year period to pay for his personal living expenses. He invoiced at least $100,000 to $500,000 of questionable items, such as a $2,590 dog pen and a $1,359 pair of alligator boots. Coughlin's total annual compensation was more than $6 million.[38]

Looking at fraud from a psychological perspective, there are other motivations for a fraudster: fraudster's emotions (e.g., revenge, social status comparisons, crimes of passion), mastery of a situation or technique (e.g., "catch-me-if-you-can game"), self-interest or group interest, and noble cause corruption.[39] Do these other reasons explain why some executives with huge salaries and high positions participate in fraudulent activities (e.g., Thomas Coughlin, Jeffrey Skilling, Martha Stewart, Allen Stanford)?

Some characteristics of many of the executive fraudsters include hypercompetitiveness, perfectionism, and excessive pride (narcissism). Some have even suggested that senior executives should be given mental health exams. Executives are given annual physical examinations, yet they do more work with their minds than their hands.[40]

Three other authors agree that a corporate psychopath "is often intelligent, charming, confident, decisive, and a risk taker." These traits are beneficial to an organization if directed toward their legal goals. But when "turned egocentric and combined with deceptive skills and sometimes often cruelty, they become a major threat."[41]

As a general rule, a forensic accountant should be careful of the trusted employees in a business. As Dick Francis said in *To The Hilt*, "the greater the trust, the safer the opportunity."[42]

A business owner had a successful business with a trusted employee who helped him over a 15-year period. One year she had to go to the hospital, and the business owner felt guilty because his employee worked long hours and was extremely efficient.

The bank statement and cancelled checks came to him while she was in the hospital. He decided to reconcile the bank statement and discovered that there were four unauthorized checks of $200, $325, $410, and $625 made out to his trusted employee. The checks had been signed by him.

Since he signed all the checks and did not sign blank checks, he did not know how the trusted employee had cheated.

How did the trusted employee pull off this theft? Answer in the footnote.[43]

Forensic accountants and auditors should follow an old Malaysian proverb: "Don't think that there are no crocodiles because the water is calm." Here are some hints for auditors to follow:

- SAS No. 99 does not require auditors to make inquiries of "others," as opposed to management. Auditors must talk to and interview others below management level. If asked, employees may be willing to report suspicious activities.
- Use independent sources for evaluating management (e.g., financial analysts). Surf the Internet.
- Auditors need to follow the performance history of managers and directors.
- If a company has an anonymous reporting system, obtain information about the incidents reported and consider them when assessing fraud risk.
- Be sure to perform analytical procedures, and the work should be reviewed by senior members of the audit team.
- Auditors should select sample items below their normal testing scope (e.g., HealthSouth).
- Fraud procedures should be more than checklists. Audits should focus on finding and detecting fraud.
- Ask for and review all "top drawer" entries.

- Ask for and review all side agreements.
- Look for hockey stick revenue patterns (e.g., increase in revenue at the end of a quarter or at the end of the year).
- Do not accept photocopies of confirmations (which occurred at Satyam computers) and follow-up with faxes or phone calls.

There can be a different side to the trusted employee theory. Annette Bongiorno was Bernie Madoff's trusted executive assistant (e.g., secretary) for 40 years. This high school graduate allegedly pocketed at least $14 million or around $350,000 per year.

She recruited investors, falsified documents, and prepared statements peppered with false stock trades for executives, Madoff's family accounts, and hundreds of other investors. Prosecutors believe that she prepared the documentation for the Madoff's family accounts and moved cash to them.

With no stock market knowledge, after WorldCom stock dropped 87 percent, she fabricated a "short trade" in the stock in her account and allegedly produced a $1.037 million profit.[44]

The Australian Institute of Criminology asserts that fraud can be explained by three factors:

- Supply of motivated offenders.
- Availability of suitable targets.
- Absence of capable guardians (e.g., internal controls).

They argue that some fraudsters wish to make fools of their victims. They take delight in the act itself. Also, risk of fraud is a product of both personality and environmental (or situational) variables.[45]

Willie Sutton, a famous bank robber, explained his motivation as follows:[46]

> Because I enjoyed it. I loved it. I was more alive when I was inside a bank robbing it, than any other time in my life. I enjoyed everything about it so much that one or two weeks later I'd be out looking for the next job. But to me the money was the chips, that's all.

In general, Alan Oliphant says he does not "see many ways to eliminate greed; it is an inherent part of the human character. So anti-fraud measures must be aimed at educating people on the risks and the type of technical controls that they can implement."[47]

Fraudsters test the waters to see if anyone is watching. If no one is watching, the fraud occurs. "If you have the right controls in place and someone says stop, you quell the urge. Stamping down that desire [to steal] is the number-one way to prevent fraud," says Ken Yormark.[48] When the cat is away, the mice will play. When the controls are absent, the fraudsters will play.

Three Duke Energy employees were charged in April 2004, for allegedly ginning up "phony electricity and material-gas trades to boost trading volumes" and inflating "profits in a trading book that was the basis of their annual profits." "The trading schemes are alleged to have inflated their bonuses by at least $7 million" between March 2001 and May 2002. There were 400 rigged trades that produced a $50 million profit in the trade books.

Duke used mark-to-market accounting to record profit and loss contracts that might not be settled for years. So called round-trips trades (or wash sales) were used to jack up reported trading volumes.[49]

Sherron Watkins provided an excellent comment about rationalizing fraud with respect to Enron's Jeff Skilling and Andrew Fastow: "But there is not a defining point where they became corrupt. It was one small step after another, with more and more rationalizations. There was a slow erosion of values over time."[50]

Another view of factors leading to fraud is provided by Zabihollah Razaee in his book *Financial Statement Fraud*. Razaee uses a 3-C model to explain the fraud triangle. He suggests that financial statement fraud is possible when these three factors are present in a company: conditions, corporate structure, and choice.

- *Conditions* refer to economic pressure resulting from a continuous deterioration of earnings, a downturn in organizational performance, a continuous decline in industry performance, or a general economic recession.
- *Corporate structure* refers to an environment characterized by irresponsible and ineffective corporate governance.
- *Choice* means that management can use its discretion to choose between illegal or legal earnings management or ethical or unethical accounting strategies.

The right combination of these variables is a perfect recipe for financial statement fraud.[51]

Both Sutherland's and Razaee's models play on the theme that financial fraud has been associated with certain maladies found in unhealthy business environments. By expanding on the means, motive, and opportunity criminal model, these researchers point to particular maladies that are associated with fraud such as declining earnings, ineffective corporate governance, and lack of integrity. Also, as Hal Holbrook says, "the lack of money is the root of all evil [fraud]." Thus, these are included in the "symptoms for diagnosis" that the forensic accountant should note.

The Center for Audit Quality suggests these perceived root causes of misconduct:[52]

Perceived Root Causes of Misconduct (a survey of 5,065 working adults)	
Pressure to do "whatever it takes" to meet business targets	59%
Believe will be rewarded for results, not means	52%
Believe code of conduct not taken seriously	51%
Lack familiarity with standards for their jobs	51%
Lack resources to get job done without cutting corners	50%
Fear losing job if miss targets	49%
Believe policies easy to bypass or override	47%
Seek to bend rules for personal gain	34%

KPMG LLP (U.S.) *Integrity Survey 2008–2009*

¶ 3051   SURVEYS SHOW GLOBAL FRAUD PERSISTS

Two fraud surveys by PricewaterhouseCoopers (PwC) also show the increased costs to organizations from fraud. Using the fraud triangle, PwC found in their 2009 survey that 68 percent of fraud was caused by incentives and pressures, 18 percent by opportunity, and 14 percent by attitude/rationalization. PwC found that large corporations have more fraud.

Their Global Economic Crime Survey (2009) found these major factors that contributed toward increased incentive/pressure to commit fraud:

Financial targets more difficult to achieve.	47%
Fear of losing job.	37%
Desire to earn personal performance bonuses.	27%
For senior executives to achieve desired financial results.	25%
Bonuses not paid this year.	23%
Maintain financial performance to avoid debt cancelation.	18%

The opportunity factor included these items:

Staff reductions resulting in fewer resources being deployed on internal controls	62%
Shift of management's focus towards survival of business.	49%
Increased workload of internal audit staff.	34%
Weakening of IT controls resulting in increased vulnerability of external penetration.	22%
Transfer of operations to new territories.	22%
Diversification of product portfolio.	15%
Reduced regulatory oversight.	12%
Other factors.	6%

In their 2011 survey PwC found that internal fraudsters (56%) stole more than external fraudsters (40%). The main sectors with external fraudsters were financial services (60%) and insurance (59%).

PwC found that 34% of the 3,377 respondents experienced economic crimes in the last 12 months (an increase of 13% from 2009). Almost one in ten reported a fraud loss of more than $5 million. Cybercrime is increasing, ranking as one of the top four economic crimes [asset misappropriation (72%), accounting fraud (24%), bribery and corruption (24%), and cybercrime (23%)]. Fifty-six percent of the respondents said the fraud was an inside job.

A 2011 Deloitte survey also illustrates the international problem of fraud. A summary of their findings are as follows:[53]

- 35% of executives reported that their entity had experienced at least one fraudulent incident during the year, 14% of which were valued at over $1 million, and 7% over $10 million.
- Respondents indicated that theft of physical assets and theft or misuse of information was the most common types of fraud. Respondents also indicated that fraud was more likely to take place within the operations of the business, information technology department, and the procurement function.
- 56% of respondents described internal processes and controls as the most effective methods to detect fraud related incidents.
- More than one-third of respondents reported that the global financial crisis had directly resulted in an increase in the likelihood of fraud.
- 73% of establishments surveyed confirmed that they have some form of framework in place to prevent and detect fraud and minimize fraud related losses.
- Most respondents identified the existence of multiple anti-fraud controls within the organization, although they expressed concern over the effectiveness of these controls.
- 40% of respondents had spent less than $50,000 in response efforts when they had experienced fraud.
- Participants disclosed that a whistleblowing policy setting out the procedures for reporting fraud exists in only half of the organizations surveyed. Yet those who had a policy in place identified it as one of the most effective means of fraud prevention and detection.

KPMG's 2011 Who is the Typical Fraudster survey found that the typical fraudster is between the age of 36 to 45 (41%), followed closely by the 46 to 55 year old employee (35%). Men were more likely the fraudster, 87 percent in 2011 and 85 percent in 2007. Senior level personnel remain the most likely fraudster, falling to 35 percent from 49 percent in 2007. But board level perpetrators increased from 11 percent to 18 percent from 2007 to 2009.

Most perpetrators worked in the finance function, 36 percent in the 2007 and 32 percent in 2011. The CFO was in second place (26 percent), and operations/sales were in third place, moving to 25 percent in 2011 from 32 percent in 2007. Employees in the legal department were the least likely fraudsters. The average loss was $1.1 million in the U.S. The duration of the loss in the U.S. was 4.2 years.

There was an increase in the detection of fraud among long-term employees (60 percent worked for more than 5 years). There was a significant increase in the collusion – doubling from 32 percent in 2007 to 66 percent in 2009 in the U.S. Perpetrator groups were typically all-male or mixed gender.

KPMG found a significant increase in cases involving weak internal control exploitation, 74 percent in 2011 versus only 49 percent in 2007. Reckless dishonesty regardless of controls fell from 36 percent in 2007 to 15 percent in 2011. Collusion to circumvent good controls moved downward from 15 percent in 2007 to 11 percent in 2011.

¶ 3061   INTERNAL CONTROLS

Internal controls are perhaps the most essential element in managing risk. The absence or lapse of internal controls in an organization is a tempting open door or opportunity for fraud. When linked with the lack of integrity or with the ability to rationalize criminal behavior, this absence or lapse completes the fraud pyramid and allows an individual to engage in fraudulent activities, without admitting to being a criminal.

Internal controls were defined in the *COSO Report* as "a process, effected by an entity's board of directors, management and other personnel, designed to provide reasonable assurance regarding the achievement of objectives in the following categories:

- Effectiveness and efficiency of operations,
- Reliability of financial reporting, and
- Compliance with applicable laws and regulations."[54]

There are five interrelated components of internal controls:

- Control environment (e.g., tone at the top)
- Risk assessment
- Control activities or control procedures
- Information and communication systems support
- Monitoring.[55]

NOW THAT'S SECURE! The TIAA-CREF's Charlotte building is covered with green faux windows and comes with security features such as a revolving door that weighs visitors when they go in and out, cameras that track them throughout the building, and security badges that won't let them leave if they stay longer than expected.

The James Bond technology protects a financial service entity's most precious commodity: cartridges containing customer data. "These are our crown jewels," CTO Sue Kozik said. The data center could be guarded better only if it was buried underground.[56]

These are discussed in detail in Chapter 4.

PCAOB and the SEC define internal control over financial reporting as "a process designed by, or under the supervision of, the company's principal executive and principal financial officers, or persons performing similar functions, and effected by the company's board of directors, management, and other personnel, to provide reasonable assurances regarding the reliability of financial reporting and the preparation of financial statements for external purpose in accordance with generally accepted accounting principles and includes those policies and procedures that:

1. Pertain to the maintenance of records that, in reasonable detail, accurately and fairly reflect the transactions and dispositions of the assets of the company;

2. Provide reasonable assurance that transactions are recorded as necessary to permit preparation of financial statements in accordance with generally accepted accounting principles, and that receipts and expenditures of the company are being made only in accordance with authorizations of management and directors of the company; and

3. Provide reasonable assurance regarding prevention or timely detection of unauthorized acquisition, use or disposition of the company's assets that could have a material effect on the financial statements."[57]

There are generally three major types of controls: preventive, detective, and corrective controls. Preventive controls are first in line to prevent errors, omissions, or misappropriation of assets from occurring. This type of controls is more efficient (e.g., passwords, safes, fences, locks).

Detective controls find errors or fraudulent incidents that escape the preventive controls. These controls are important when preventive controls are weak. For example, there are situations in which transactions are obtained from third parties, such as sales reports from franchisees or baggage claims reported by passengers at airports.

Corrective controls are the actions taken to minimize further losses. They are there to correct errors, omissions, and frauds after detection. But internal controls can be broken, often by top executives.

Figure 3.3. Types of Controls

Preventive controls
- Segregating duties
- Requiring approvals
- Securing assets
- Password protection
- Using document control numbers
- Testing for drugs
- Positive pay system
- Rotating jobs and duties
- Backing up computers
- Lockbox system
- Pre-employment testing
- Pre-employment background checks

Detective controls
- Written confirmations
- Reconciliations
- Management reviews
- Event notifications
- Surprise cash counts

- Counting inventory
- Hot lines

Corrective controls
- Training personnel
- Redesigning processes
- Improving controls
- Budget variance reports
- Insurance
- Civil or criminal action

Companies must balance risks and controls. Exessive controls creates problems, but absence of controls creates other problems:

Excessive Risks
- Loss of Assets and Goodwill
- Poor Business Decisions
- Noncompliance with Regulations
- Public Scandals and Embarrassment
- Increased Regulations

Excessive Controls
- Increased Bureaucracy
- Reduced Productivity
- Increased Complexity
- Increased Cycle Time
- Reduction in Morale

The ACFE has categorized the risks of fraud within an organization:[58]
1. Intentional manipulation of financial statements, which can lead to:
    a. Inappropriately reported revenues.
    b. Inappropriately reported expenses.
    c. Inappropriately reflected balance sheet amounts, including reserves.
    d. Inappropriately improved and/or masked disclosures.
    e. Concealing misappropriation of assets.
    f. Concealing unauthorized receipts and expenditures.
    g. Concealing unauthorized acquisition, disposition, and use of assets.
2. Misappropriation of:
    a. Tangible assets by:
        i. Employees.
        ii. Customers.
        iii. Vendors.
        iv. Former employees and others outside the organization.
    b. Intangible assets.
    c. Proprietary business opportunities.
3. Corruption including:
    a. Bribery and gratuities to:
        i. Companies.
        ii. Private individuals.
        iii. Public officials.
    b. Receipt of bribes, kickbacks, and gratuities.
    c. Aiding and abetting fraud by other parties (e.g., customers, vendors).

These categories are discussed in Chapters 3, 4, and 5.

Incidence of Crime and Characteristics of Perpetrators

¶ 3071   STUDIES OF THE PREVALENCE OF FRAUD IN BUSINESS

The following two sections look at fraud in business and at white-collar crime, not at financial report fraud itself. Nonetheless, they present useful information that needs to be considered by the forensic accountant when investigating both financial reporting fraud and broader fraud topics.

An Ernst & Young study of leading companies and public bodies in 32 countries found that more than 50 percent have been victims of fraud in the past year, with 84 percent of total losses attributable to staff and 50 percent of the most serious fraud being committed by the organization's own management. Theft of cash and purchasing schemes (i.e., employee kickbacks) constituted the majority of frauds reported in the study. Reasons respondents cited were poor internal controls and limited knowledge of internal controls by finance directors.

In a 1999 report on fraudulent financial reporting, Beasley, Carcello and Hemanson indicated that the CEO was involved in 72 percent of the cases, the CFO in 43 percent of the cases, and the CEO/CFO 83 percent of the time.[59] Michelle Perry of the UK says that "the biggest frauds are committed with the aid of either an accountant or lawyer, or perhaps both."[60]

¶ 3081   CHARACTERISTICS OF THE WHITE-COLLAR CRIMINAL

Typical white-collar criminals have these characteristics:

- Likely to be married
- Member of a church
- Educated beyond high school
- No arrest record
- Age range from teens to older than 60
- Socially conforming
- Employment tenure from 1 to 20 years
- Acts alone 70 percent of the time.[61]

G.E. Moulton enumerates certain fraud identifiers: large ego, substance abuse problems or gambling addiction, living beyond apparent means, self-absorption, hardworking/taking few vacations, under financial pressure (e.g., heavy borrowings), and sudden mood changes.[62]

A 2007 study discovered that the primary reasons for fraud are "pressures to do whatever it takes to meet goals" (81 percent of respondents) and "to seek personal gain" (72 percent). Many respondents indicated that "they do not consider their actions fraudulent" (40 percent) as a reason for wrongful behavior.[63]

EYEWITNESS

An economic motive for fraud may be the simple need for money to pay hospital bills, for drugs, for gambling debts, or for alimony payments. A gambling addiction caused former mayor of San Diego Maureen O'Connor to steal more than $2 million from her late husband's charitable foundation. Ms. O'Connor was a teacher at a catholic school before serving as mayor from 1986 to 1992.[64]

She had between $40 million to $50 million before her brief gambling problem. O'Connor made more than one billion dollars at video poker, but she lost more than one billion dollars over 9 years. Her net losses were around $13 million. But to lose over a billion dollars over 9 years would have required losing more than $300,000 a day, seven days a week.[65]

The bottom line is that given the right pressures, opportunities, and rationalizations, many employees are capable of committing fraud. Senior level management fraudsters tend to be overly ambitious people, obsessed with enhancing power and control, narcissistic personality, with an over-inflated sense of superiority. They are surrounded by "yes employees," and believe they are above the rules.

KPMG's three studies in 1994, 1998, and 2003 compared conditions conducive to fraud, as shown in Figure 3.4.

Figure 3.4. Conditions Conducive to Fraud

Condition	2003	1998	1994
Collusion between Employees and Third Parties	48	31	33
Inadequate Internal Controls	39	58	59
Management Override of Internal Controls	31	36	36
Collusion between Employees and Management	15	19	23
Lack of Control over Management by Directors	12	11	6
Ineffective or Nonexistent Ethics or Compliance Program	10	8	7

■ 2003   ■ 1998   ▢ 1994

Source: KPMG Fraud Study.

Lantham, Jacobs, and Kotchetova[66] found that companies experiencing resource scarcity and/or financial difficulty might be more prone to engage in fraudulent behavior. Also, fraudulent companies were more likely to have management teams with a high concentration of individuals with no military experience and peripheral background (law and finance).

Sherron Watkins, Enron's whistle-blower, advises job-hunting employees to avoid companies that have flawed values. She recalled Enron's effort to steer employees to a travel agency owned by the sister of Ken Lay, Enron's former chairman.[67] In other words, employees should realize the importance of an ethical "tone at the top" in deterring white-collar crime.

An argument for forensic audits was illustrated by the merger of CUC International, Inc. with HFS, Inc., becoming Cendant Corporation. Arthur Andersen was hired to perform a forensic audit on CUC; the previous auditor, Ernst & Young had given CUC a clean bill of financial health. The forensic audit found that CUC had inflated its operating income by 50 percent over a number of years (e.g., at least $500 million). Andersen's report said that irregularities were pervasive; operating income had been inflated in 17 of 21 company units. More than 20 employees said that they merely followed instructions from CUC headquarters to "cook the books."[68]

MANAGEMENT OVERRIDE/SKEPTICISM DESCRIBED IN THE AUDIT.[69] "And second, I want to tell you that you and your people did nothing short of uncovering a quarter-of-a-million–dollar embezzling scheme that Loomis [the controller of the entity who had a gambling problem] was involved in."

Looking around the room, he explained to the other partners how Pat [an auditor] investigated the mysterious check made out to Richard Loomis and how he used the bank and Nationwide Express to get the statement back to the unsuspecting controller.

He told them that Pat had talked privately to Gordon Banks [Executive Director], explaining to him how Loomis had switched the checks before giving the statement back to Pat.

"After Pat left Banks' office, Gordon called me personally and told me that he needed my help. He wanted a fresh pair of eyes to look over what Pat showed him.

"So Russell and I drove down there the same day to meet Gordon. He showed us the check made payable to the post office, and it appeared to have cleared the bank. And sure enough, it was for the same amount and had the same check number as the check that did, in fact, clear the bank with Loomis as the payee. Fortunately, Pat made a copy of the check before Loomis had a chance to destroy it."

"What did you do next?" Bob Ramsey asked. He and the others were mesmerized.

"I asked Gordon to get a few old bank statements for us, and Russell and I pulled out every check payable to the post office, and the three of us went to the bank."

"And?"

"We asked the bank to pull their photocopy of each check that we had payable to the U.S. Postal Service. There was the proof. The bank's copies of several of the checks had the same number and were for the same amount, but had Loomis as the payee."

"But you said that the checks had the same check numbers, and appeared to have cleared the bank. How did he manage to do that?" Ramsey asked again, astonished.

"Actually, it was very simple once it was uncovered. As it turned out, Loomis ordered two sets of identically numbered checks from two different check-printing companies. They looked exactly the same."

"And?"

"He ran checks routinely on his office computer. Every week or so, he would make one check out to the U.S. Postal Service and, of course not mail it because the post office had nothing to do with it. He'd go home with a copy of the diskette he used to make out the checks in the office. There he used his name as the payee on that particular check, printed the check on his printer, forged a signature, and cashed the check at a different bank, of course. Because he got the bank statements, he only had to pull out the check he cashed, destroy it, and replace it with the original check from the bank statement, payable to the post office."

"But you said that it looked like the check had been cashed and it had a receipt. How did he manage that?" one of the other partners asked.

"Simple. He had a friend who worked at the post office in on the scheme. His friend endorsed the check with the post office's actual endorsement stamp and then gave him a real post office receipt."

"But how about the bank's encoding information on the bottom right front of the check and their clearinghouse stamps on the back. How did he fake that?" Bob Ramsey asked, incredulous.

"That wasn't hard," Autry continued, "He had duplicates of clearinghouse stamps made at a rubber stamp company. They'll make just about anything you need. He stamped them himself, and they looked authentic enough to fool anyone."

Earnings Management and GAAP

¶ 3091 FLEXIBILITY OF GAAP

Financial statement fraud or fraudulent earnings management has become of increasing concern to accounting regulators in recent years, especially in the post-Enron era. The flexibility in generally accepted accounting principles (GAAP) gives management discretion to use its professional opinion to choose from a range of guidelines and standards in selecting those that suit the needs of a company (e.g., FIFO or LIFO inventory methods). Different accounting methods result in different earnings and earnings per share, and often management prefers to smooth earnings. *Earnings management* may be defined as the "purposeful intervention in the external financial reporting process, with the intent of obtaining some private gain."[70]

Nonfraudulent earnings management is accomplished within the GAAP framework; whereas fraudulent earnings management does not follow GAAP (e.g., recording fictitious sales). The National Center for Continuing Education even offers a seminar on "How to Manage Earnings in Conformance with GAAP. Yet nothing gives greater fear to a corporate officer or investor than when there is a rumor about "an accounting problem."

A 2006 survey of CFOs is not encouraging.[71] They say:
- More than one-half of CFOs say they can legally influence reported earnings by three percent or more.
- Operational levers: delaying operational spending, accelerating order processing, and driving sales force more.
- Accounting steps: changing the timing of an accounting change and adjusting estimates.
- One-third of CFOs would try to influence results: 24 percent upward or eight percent would try to cut them.
- Few CFOs think their auditors would catch them.
- If the auditors caught it, they probably would not bring it up to management.

Some examples of nonfraudulent earnings management would include:
- Careful timing of capital gains and losses.
- Use of conferencing technology to reduce travel costs.
- Postponement of repair and maintenance activities when faced with unexpected cash flow declines.[72]

Abusive earnings management would include:
- Improper revenue recognition (e.g., bill and hold sales).
- Improper expense recognition.
- Using reserves to inflate earnings in years with falling revenues (cookie jar accounting).
- Shifting debt to special purpose entity (SPE).
- Channel stuffing.
- Capitalizing marketing costs rather than expensing.
- Extending useful lives and inflating salvage values.
- Accelerating revenue from leasing equipment.
- SPEs that are not consolidated.

Early warning signs of earnings management include:

- Cash flows that are not correlated with earnings.
- Receivables that are not correlated with revenues.
- Allowances for uncollectible accounts that are not correlated with receivables.
- Reserves that are not correlated with balance sheet items.
- Acquisitions with no apparent business purpose.
- Earnings that consistently and precisely meet analysts' expectations.[73]

There is some research on earnings management. Of the twenty-seven firms accused by the SEC of earnings management, researchers estimate that the firms sacrificed on the average eight cents in additional income taxes per dollar of inflated pretax earnings. In total, they estimate that the firms in the sample paid $320 million in taxes on overstated earnings of about $3.36 billion. These results indicate how far managers are willing to go when allegedly inflating earnings.[74]

EYEWITNESS

In his 2001 memoir, former General Electric CEO Jack Welch bragged about his GE managers volunteering to help plug an unexpected $350 million write-off *after* the quarter's book closed. "Some said they could find an extra $10 million, $20 million, and even $30 million from their businesses to offset the surprise."

Companies that consist solely of independent directors and meet at least four times a year are likely to have lower non-audit service fees.[75] An auditor who is also an industry specialist further enhances the credibility of accounting information (e.g., less earnings management).[76]

Lower perceptions of earnings quality lead investors to **more thoroughly** examine a firm's audited financial statements. A more thorough analysis of a firm's financial statements lead investors to lower their assessment of the firm's earnings quality.[77] Scott Richardson found no evidence that short sellers trade on the basis of information contained in accruals.[78] Small companies tend to more frequently manage earnings to avoid losses than large companies.[79]

There are some red flags or patterns to help guide forensic accountants:[80]

- Look for aggressive revenue recognition policies (Qwest Communication, $1.1 billion in 1999-2001).
- Beware of hockey stick pattern near the end of a quarter.
- Beware of the ever-present nonrecurring charges (e.g., Kodak for at least 12 years).
- Check for regular changes to reserves, depreciation, amortization, or comprehensive income policy.
- Related-party transactions (e.g., Enron).
- Complex financial products (e.g., derivatives).
- Unsupported top-side entries (e.g., WorldCom).
- Under-funded defined pension plans.
- Unreasonable management compensation.

SPOTLIGHT

ACCOUNTING'S ERIN BROCKOVICH? Sherron Watkins, the so-called whistle-blower inside Enron, grew up in Tomball, Texas, graduated from the University of Texas with two accounting degrees, went to work with Arthur Andersen in Houston and eventually the New York office. Later she came back to Houston with a job from the company with a "crooked E logo," eventually becoming a vice president.

Depicted as a feminist icon, Watkins was compared by Hollywood to Erin Brockovich. The Guardian Unlimited called her the "woman who took on a giant."[81] Time. com named her the "Person of the Week" for putting her suspicions about accounting practices at Enron in writing and marking the investigative trail.[82] At the end of 2002, *Time* magazine named her one of three persons of the year. Sherron Watkins wrote a one-page anonymous letter to Enron Chairman Kenneth Lay raising "suspicions of accounting improprieties" and later a seven-page "smoking-gun" letter to Lay (with a copy to her mother) that his company was essentially a Ponzi scheme. "I am incredibly nervous that we will implode in a wave of accounting scandals," she told a friend at Arthur Andersen who alerted that firm's Enron auditors.

When Enron's attorneys talked to Watkins for more than three hours about the Raptors (one of Enron's special purpose entities) structure, they had been told by David Duncan that the special-purpose entities were properly disclosed, meeting all of the technical requirements. Andrew Fastow had told the attorneys that Sherron Watkins was conspiring with Jeff McMahon "to take out Andy Fastow." The lawyers' final report found no real problems at Enron.[83]

Was Watkins the whistle-blower extraordinaire? Did she pen her notice to Lay to protect herself? The Institute of Internal Auditors' Internet site indicated that Enron's management (including Watkins), the board of directors, audit committee, internal and external auditors were aware of off-balance sheet transactions, special-purpose entities created to hide related-party transactions and absorb investment losses, loans using Enron stock as collateral, and statements with inaccurate, incomplete or misleading footnotes.[84]

Critics charge that Watkins simply wrote a memo "to the bank robber suggesting he stop robbing the bank and offering ways to avoid getting caught. Then she met with the robber, who said he didn't believe he was robbing the bank, but said he'd investigate to find out for sure."[85]

Whatever her intentions, Watkins started a chain reaction leading to executive sackings, a suicide, testimony before Congress, the demise of Arthur Andersen, casting doubt on the entire accounting industry, and her company's bankruptcy. The whole debacle was a key factor in the steep decline in the stock market during 2000. She became the "corporate high-flyer recast as a heroine who stood up to the corrupt, greedy men who had cashed in their shares to make millions of dollars while their deceived employees were trapped in a 'stock-lock', which prevented them from doing the same."[86] Hollywood's response was to feature Watkins in a made-for-TV movie.

¶ 3101   RESTATEMENTS OF EARNINGS

During the past decade—even before Enron's demise—several major instances of misstated earnings generated headlines reporting huge declines in market capitalization. An example is Cendant, a marketing and franchising firm that owns franchising rights to such brands as Days Inn and Ramada hotels, Century 21 real-estate brokerage, and Avis car rental. The disclosure of Cendant's accounting irregularities in April of 1998 caused the collapse of the stock by 46.5 percent in a single day. This decline represented a decrease in Cendant's market capitalization (price per share times the number of shares outstanding) of approximately $14 billion.

Glass Lewis indicates that 200 to 500 publicly traded companies (or about 5 to 12 percent of the total) listed in the U.S. restate their earnings each year, but restatements are declining.[87] The SEC estimates that about one percent of all company accounts submissions are subject to retrospective restatement. Lynn Turner, former chief accountant of the SEC suggests that investors have lost more than $100 billion because of financial fraud and the resulting earnings restatements since 1995.[88] The SEC defines *abusive earnings management* as an intentional and material misrepresentation of results. The difference between nonfraudulent earnings management and abusive earnings management may be the thickness of a prison cell.

These restatements may trigger class-action lawsuits and may cause drops in the company's stock. For example, Krispy Kreme restated its 2004 earnings and saw its stock price fall 22 percent.

William S. Larach, the "poster boy" for securities law actions, said that his law firm "saw case after case of deliberate falsification of financial results. When people have the opportunity to pocket millions and millions of dollars—in some cases, hundreds of millions—without risk, what do you think they are going to do?"[89]

Table 3.6. Class Action Securities Fraud Actions[90]

Year		Year	
2012	152	2003	228
2011	188	2002	266
2010	176	2001	497
2009	167	2000	216
2008	223	1999	208
2007	177	1998	240
2006	120	1997	175
2005	182	1996	112
2004	239	1995	188

The percentage of S&P index financial firms named as defendants in securities class action dropped from 32.6 percent in 2008 to 11.5 percent in 2009, but they still represent 39.1 percent of the sector's total market capitalization.[91]

Federal securities fraud action filing activity decreased sharply in 2012, with 152 class actions in 2012 versus 188 in 2011. This number was the second-lowest number of filings in 16 years. Fewer filings targeted large corporations, and filings were more prevalent in the consumer non-cyclical sector.[92]

Stock Option Backdating

The abuse *du jour* during the past several years has been stock option backdating by as many as 160 companies. This practice is illustrated by an SEC action against Symbol Technology, Inc. The SEC stated that Symbol's general counsel manipulated stock option exercise dates without regard to the stated terms of the stock option plans to allow senior executives (including himself) to profit unfairly at the company's expense.[93]

The general counsel "cherry picked" the exercise date during the year so as to reduce the cost of the exercise to the executive. Rather than use the actual exercise date as defined by the option plans, he would institute (without board of directors approval or public disclosure) a fraudulent practice of using a more advantageous date chosen from a 30-day "look-back" period to calculate the cost of the exercise.[94]

By picking a *grant* date on which the stock price is lower, an executive pays the corporation less when the executive buys the stock (e.g., exercises the option). Further, the company's deduction for options exercised by executives is increased because it is based on the difference between the amount paid by the executive on the exercise and its market value.

There is a resulting tax savings to the company, which partially offsets the lower amount it received from the stock. Conversely, manipulating a stock option's *exercise* date to a lower price will *decrease* the corporation's deduction and reduce the amount taxed to the executive as ordinary income.[95]

Interactive Software, Inc. pleaded guilty to a state felony charge in connection with a backdating stock option scheme.

The former general counsel of Monster Worldwide pleaded guilty to a security fraud in a secret stock option backdating scheme. The backdating scheme allowed Monster to falsely inflate its net income from 1997 to 2005 by $340 million.

Research in Motion, maker of the Blackberry, restated $250 million in earnings, and Jim Balsille, its co-chief executive, stepped down as chairman after a seven-month study into its backdating of stock option grants.

Should Steve Jobs, CEO of Apple, go to jail? No, says Al Gore, an Apple Director and member of the special two-person committee that investigated and exonerated Steve Jobs.

Yet Mr. Jobs was aware of or recommended some backdating of options that were awarded to others. Also, Mr. Jobs received a grant of 7.5 million of options that was finalized on December 18, 2001, but was backdated to October. Further, the grant was recorded as having been approved at a special board meeting that never happened. In reality, the Apple Board had provisionally approved Jobs' option grant in August.[96]

¶ 3111   CONCLUSION

There are many ways for financial statements to be manipulated with fraudulent intent, such as premature revenue recognition or fictitious assets. For example, in mid-2003, Tyco International announced $1.2 billion more accounting problems, on top of $590 million of restatements in March 2003. A number of critics had asserted that Tyco "puffed up earnings through all manner of accounting legerdemain" over the years.[97]

"Rather than combing torn clothing," forensic accountants "comb through corporate books, looking for oddities that could signal swindles,"[98] says Bruce Dubinsky. Investigations can be extremely complex, with crate upon crate of documents and thousands of computer files. Investigators typically uncover financial statement fraud by looking for unusual flags or patterns.[99]

There certainly is a thin line between legal earnings management and abusive earnings management. Where does a company cross the line between criminal behavior and merely conduct that is beneficial to the organization?

Fraud is not necessarily only stealing assets or falsifying financial statements. There are pressures in many areas that cause people to fudge data. Five colleges misreported data in one year to *U.S. News and World Report* in order to increase their annual graduate school rankings. Tulane University, Emory University, Claremont McKenna College, Bucknell University, and George Washington University recently acknowledged they had submitted incorrect test scores or overstated the high school ranking of their freshmen class. One survey found that 91 percent of the participants felt that other universities had falsely reported standardized test scores and other admission data.[100]

Almost $19 billion in state unemployment benefits were paid in error during a three year period ending June 2011. These improper payments occur when recipients claim benefits even after they return to work, employers or their administrators do not submit timely or accurate information about worker separations, and the recipients do not correctly file with a state's employment-service organization.[101]

Former Rep. Jesse Jackson, Jr. pleaded guilty to conspiracy to commit fraud and false statements over his misuse of campaign funds for personal expenses. Prosecutors said he misused about $750,000 of campaign donations on Michael Jackson memorabilia, furniture, and $60,000 to pay bills at nightclubs.[102]

ENDNOTES

1   Statement upon being nominated as Chairman of the Public Company Accounting Oversight Board (PCAOB). At the time of the statement, McDonough was serving as Chairman of the Federal Reserve Bank of New York. *http://www.sec.gov/news/extra/mcdonough41503.htm.*

2   Herbert Stern, from his discussion of prosecutorial philosophy in the 1973 book TIGER IN THE COURT, by Paul Hoffman.

3   *http://www.whitecollarfraud.com/1583432.html*; K. Voigt, "Sex, Lies and Accounting Fraud," July 6, 2010, *http://www.accountingweb.com/topic/watchdog/sex-lies-and-accounting-fraud.*

4   "Match-fixing threatens 'integrity of football in Europe,'" CNN.com, February 4, 2013, *http://www.cnn.com/2013/02/04/sport/football/match-fixing-championships.*

5   President Obama Establishes Interagency Financial Fraud Enforcement Task Force, *http://www.sec.gov/news/press/2009/2009-249.htm*

6   See *http://www.transparency.org/layout/set/print/about_us.*

7   *Kathy Chu, "Pressures Increase in Asia for Firms to Come Clean" Wall Street Journal, January 24, 2013, p. B-3*

8   Sam Ames, "SEC Targets Financial Accounting Fraud," *CNET News.com* (May 25, 2000).

9   Financial Accounting Standards Board, Statement of Financial Accounting Concepts No. 2, Norwalk, Conn.

10 Z. Razaee, FINANCIAL STATEMENT FRAUD (New York: John Wiley & Sons, 2002), p. 26.

11 *Ibid.*, pp. 26–7.

12 D.S. Hilzenrath, "Forensic Auditors Find What Some Companies Try to Hide," THE WASHINGTON POST (November 23, 2002), p. 19.

13 M.S. Beasley, *et al.*, "Fraudulent Financial Reporting: 1998-2007 — An Analysis of U.S. Public Companies (2010)," COSO, May 2010.

14 COSO News Release, Alamonte Springs, May 20, 2010, *http://www.coso.org/documents/COSOReleaseonFraudulentReporting2010PDF_001.pdf.*

15 Tom Hays, "Madoff Trustee: JP Morgan Executives Warned of Fraud," Yahoo! Finance, February 3, 2011, *http://finance.yahoo.com/news/Madoff-trustee-JP-Morgan-apf-1265049826.html?x=0.*

16 S.E. Bonner, Z. Palmrose, and S.M. Young, "Fraud Type and Auditor Litigation: An Analysis of SEC Accounting and Auditing Enforcement Releases," THE ACCOUNTING REVIEW (October 1998), pp. 503–532.

17 Mariko Sanchanta, "Japan Internet Upstart Receives Jail Term," FINANCIAL TIMES (March 17/18, 2007), p. 5.

18 Lawrence Mohrweis, "Lessons from the Baptist Foundation Fraud," CPA JOURNAL (July 2003).

19 M.J. Wagner and B.J. Goldsmith, "Alter Ego," LITIGATION SERVICES HANDBOOK (New York: John Wiley & Sons, 2001), p. 38-2.

20 For more detail see D.D. Dorrell and G.A. Gadawski, FINANCIAL FORENSIC, II, 53 (3) (May 2005), p. 20.

21 Warren Buffett, "Who Really Cooks the Books?" *http://www.nytimes.com* (July 24, 2002).

22 Floyd Norris, "Pension Folly: How Losses Become Profits," THE NEW YORK TIMES (April 26, 2002), p. C-1.

23 Susan Warren and P.A. McKay, "Methods for Citing Oil Reserves Prove Unrefined," WALL STREET JOURNAL (January 14, 2004, p. C-4.

24 Stephen Labaton and Jeff Gerth, "At Shell, New Accounting and Rosier Oil Outlook," NEW YORK TIMES (March 12, 2004), pp. A-1 and C-4.

25 Chip Cummins, "Shell Slashes Oil Reserve Again; News Overshadows Profit Surge," WALL STREET JOURNAL (February 4, 2005), p. A-3.

26 Alix Nyberg, "Death to Smoothing," CFO MAGAZINE (February 22, 2005), pp. 24-25.

27 Berton, L., "U.S. Accounting Watchdogs Try to Shut Barn Door," Bloomberg.com, April 2, 2004: J.H. Edwards, "Audit Committees: The Last Best Hope," JOURNAL OF FORENSIC ACCOUNTING 4 (2004), pp. 1-20.

28 Paul Dunn "Aspect of Management Control Philosophy That Contribute to Fraudulent Financial Reporting," JOURNAL OF FORENSIC ACCOUNTING 4 (2003), pp. 35-60.

29 Del Jones, "Many CEOs Bend the Rules (of Golf)," USA TODAY (June 26, 2002), p. A-1.

30 Don Durfee, " It's Better (and Worse) Than You Think," CFO MAGAZINE (May 3, 2004).

31 H.M. Schilit, FINANCIAL SHENANIGANS (New York: McGraw-Hill, Inc., 1993).

32 Accounting and Auditing Enforcement Release No. 774, IN THE MATTER OF CHARLES W. WALLIN, CPA (Washington, D.C.: Securities and Exchange Commission, April 19, 1996).

33 S.L. Mintz, "The Gauge of Innocence," CFO (April 2009), p. 56.

34 *Ibid.*, p. 56.

35 From a speech by Lynn Turner, former chief accountant of U.S. Securities and Exchange Commission, given at the 39th Annual Corporate Counsel Institute, Northwestern University School of Law, October 12, 2000.

36 D.T. Wolfe and D.R. Hermanson, "The Fraud Diamond: Considering The Four Elements of Fraud," THE CPA J. (December 2004), pp. 38-42.

37 P.D. Goldmann, *Fraud in the Markets*, John Wiley & Sons, 2010, pp.24-25

38 J. Bandler and A. Zimmerman, "A WalMart Legend's Trail of Deceit," *Wall Street Journal*, April 5, 2005.

39 S. Ramamoorti, D. Morrison, and J.W. Koletar, "Bringing Freud to Fraud," December 22, 2009, IFP White Paper. p. 2.

40 *Ibid.*, p. 18.

41 T. Brytting, R. Minogue, and V. Morino, *The Anatomy of Fraud and Corruption*, Burlington, Vt.: Ashgate Publishing Company, 2011, p. 89.

42 Dick Francis, *To the Hilt*, New York: Berkeley Books, 1996.

43 She had used disappearing ink. Real vendor's name was initially written on the check when the owner signed the check. That name disappeared, and the trusted employee wrote her name on the check. Erasable ballpoint pens also can be used for this scheme.

44 Allan D. Frank, "Madoff's Millionaire Secretary," Yahoo! News, December 20, 2010, *http://www.thedailybeast.com/articles/2010/12/20/bernie-madoffs-millionaire-secretary-annette-bongiorno.html.*

45 Grace Duffield and Peter Grabosky, "The Psychology of Fraud," Australian Institute of Criminology, No. 19.

46 W. Sutton and E. Linn, *Where the Money Was: The Memoirs of a Bank Robber.* New York: Ballantine Books, 1977.

47 David G. Banks, "The Fight Against Fraud," INTERNAL AUDITOR (April 2004), pp. 36-37.

48 S.L. Mintz, "The Gauge of Innocence," CFO (April 2009), p. 56.

49 Rebecca Smith, "Former Employees of Duke Charged Over Wash Trades," WALL STREET JOURNAL (April 22, 2004), p. A-15.

50 Pamela Colloff, "The Whistle-Blower," TEXAS MONTHLY (April 2003), p. 141.

51 Z. Razaee, FINANCIAL STATEMENT FRAUD (New York: John Wiley & Sons, 2002), pp. 68–69.

52 Center for Audit Quality, Deterring and Detecting Financial Reporting Fraud: A Platform for Action, October 2010, p. 4.

53 Deloitte's Gulf Cooperation Council Fraud Survey 2011

54 Committee of Sponsoring Organization of the Treadway Commission, INTERNAL CONTROL: INTEGRATED FRAMEWORK, (New York: COSO, 1999), p. 9.

55 SAS No. 94, The Effect of Information Technology on the Auditor's Consideration of Internal Control in a Financial Statement Audit *(*New York: AICPA).

56 Rick Rothacker, "Charlotte Site Has Quickly Become the Firm's Largest," CHARLOTTE OBSERVER (December 28, 2006), p. 2D.

57 PCAOB Release 2004-001, par. 7.

58 IIA, AICPA, ACFE, MANAGING THE BUSINESS RISK OF FRAUD: A PRACTICAL GUIDE (2008), *http://www.acfe.com/documents/managing-business-risk.pdf.*

59 M.S. Beasley, J.V. Carcello, and D.R. Hermanson, FRAUDULENT FINANCIAL REPORTING: 1987–1997, AN ANALYSIS OF U.S. PUBLIC COMPANIES, 1999, COSO.

60 Michelle Perry, "Corporate Fraud-Unusual Suspects," MANAGEMENT CONSULTANCY (January 3, 2002), *www.managementconsultancy.co.uk.*

61 Jack Robertson, FRAUD EXAMINATION FOR MANAGERS AND AUDITORS, (Austin, Tex.: Viesca Books, 1997).

62 G.E. Moulton, "Profile of a Fraudster," Deloitte Touche Tohatsu, *www.deloitte.com,* 1994.

63 Oversight Systems Report on Corporate Fraud (2007), *www. oversightsystems.com*; IIA, AICPA, ACFE, MANAGING THE BUSINESS RISK OF FRAUD: A PRACTICAL GUIDE (2008), *http://www.acfe.com/documents/managing-business-risk.pdf,* p. 6.

64 Jennifer Medina, "Ex-Mayor of San Diego Confronts $1 Billion Gambling Problem," New York Times, February 15, 2013, pp.A1 and A18.

65 Ibid.

66 C.K. Latham, F.A. Jacobs, and N. Kotchetova, "The Impact of Agency Structure and Management Team Characteristics on Disclosure Fraud," JOURNAL OF FORENSIC ACCOUNTING 1 (2000), pp. 147–180.

67 Dale Lezon, "Watkins Calls Action a Step Toward Truth," HOUSTON CHRONICLE (May 2, 2003), p. 17-A.

68 David Hilzenrath, "Forensic Auditors Find What Some Companies Try to Hide," THE WASHINGTON POST (November 23, 2002), p. E-1.

69 E.J. McMillan, THE AUDIT (Churchton, Md.: Harwood Publishing, 2000), pp. 36–39.

70 Katherine Schipper, "Commentary on Earnings Management," ACCOUNTING HORIZON (December 1989), p. 92.

71 Don Durfee, "Management of Manipulation?" CFO (December 2006), p. 28.

72 L.G. Weld et. al, "Anatomy of a Financial Fraud," THE CPA JOURNAL (October 2004).

73 Magrath and Weld, "Abusive Earnings Management and Early Warning Signs," THE CPA JOURNAL (August 2002).

74 M. Erickson et. al., "How Much Will Firms Pay for Earnings That Do Not Exist? Evidence of Taxes Paid on Allegedly Fraudulent Earnings," ACCOUNTING REVIEW 79 (2) (2004), pp. 387.

75 L.J. Abbott et al, "An Empirical Investigation of Audit Fees, Non-Audit Fees, and Audit Committees," CONTEMPORARY ACCOUNTING RESEARCH (Summer 2003), p. 230.

76 G.V. Krishnan, "Does Big 6 Auditor Industry Expertise Constrain Earnings Management?" ACCOUNTING HORIZONS 17 (Supplement 2003), p. 15.

77 F.D. Dodge, "Investors Perceptions of Earnings Quality, Auditor Independence, and the Usefulness of Audited Financial Information,"ACCOUNTING HORIZONS 17 (Supplement 2003), p. 46.

78 Scott Richardson, "Earnings Quality and Short Sellers," ACCOUNTING HORIZONS 17 (Supplement 2003), p. 49.

79 Brian Lee and Ben Choi, "Company Size, Auditor Type, and Earnings Management," JOURNAL OF FORENSIC ACCOUNTING 3 (2002), pp. 27-50.

80 Scott Green, "Fighting Financial Reporting Fraud," INTERNAL AUDITOR (December 2003), pp. 58-63.

81 Ed Vulliamy, "The Woman Who Took on a Giant," GUARDIAN UNLIMITED (January 27, 2002).

82 Frank Pellegrini, "Person of the Week: Enron Whistleblower' Sherron Watkins," *Time.com* (August 18, 2002).

83 Mimi Swartz and Sherron Watkins, POWER FAILURE (New York: Doubleday, 2003), pp. 303–304.

84 "Enron-related Initiatives Continue," *www.theiia.org/ecm/guide-ia.cfm?doc_id=3114* (June 17, 2002).

85 Dan Ackman, "Sherron Watkins Had Whistle, But Blew It," *Forbes.com* (February 14, 2002).

86 Ed Vulliamy, "The Woman Who Took on a Giant," GUARDIAN UNLIMITED (January 27, 2002).

[87] Glass Lewis & Co., "Trend Report: Restatements," March 19, 2009.

[88] Jeremy Kahn, "One Plus One Makes What?" FORTUNE, (January 7, 2002), p. 89.

[89] "I Told You So," CFO, September 2002, pp. 63–64.

[90] Stanford Law School Securities Class Action Clearinghouse, *http://securities.stanford.edu/index.html.*

[91] Stanford's Securities Class Action Clearinghouse, *http://securities.stanford.edu/litigation_activity.html*

[92] in book.

[93] SEC Complaint, *SEC v. Symbol Technologies, Inc.*, DC N.Y., No. 04 CV 2267 (June 3, 2004).

[94] *Ibid.*

[95] Greig Geisler, "Comment on Stock Option Exercise Date Manipulation," TAX NOTES (January 15, 2007), p. 215.

[96] "The Nasty Taste Left by Apple's Options," FINANCIAL TIMES (December 30/31, 2006), p. 8; H.W. Jenkins, Jr.,

"Apple's Gore," WALL STREET JOURNAL (January 10, 2007), p. A-16.

[97] Mark Maremont, "Tyco Is Likely to Report New Woes," THE WALL STREET JOURNAL (April 30, 2003), p. C-1.

[98] *Ibid.*

[99] *Ibid.*

[100] Nick Anderson, "Five Colleges Misreported Data to U.S. News, Raising Concerns About Rankings, Reputation, "The Washington Post", February 6, 2012.

[101] "Sara Murray, "Billions in Unemployment Benefits Paid in Error, The Wall Street Journal, September 14, 2011. http://blogs.wsj.com/economics/2011/09/14/billions-in-unemployment-...

[102] Devlin Barrett, "Illinois Democrat Jackson Guilty in Misuse of Funds, "The Wall Street Journal," February 21, 2013, p. A-6.

EXERCISES

1. The Sarbanes-Oxley Act will fundamentally change the way public companies do business and how the accounting profession performs its statutorily required audit functions. True/False?

2. When was the Sarbanes-Oxley Act signed into law by President George W. Bush?

3. Explain the six-legged stool of the financial reporting process.

4. What are the three M's of financial reporting fraud?

5. How did Sunbeam create revenues?

6. Break financial statement fraud schemes into 10 types.

7. What are the three ways managers override internal controls? How can a forensic accountant overcome managers overriding internal controls?

8. Give some examples where companies use biased assumption? What is meant by "wildcatting?"

9. Where might financial statement fraud occur in a company (e.g., what are some red flags)?

10. Is check forgery generally an internal or external fraud? How about credit card fraud?

11. What are major motives of fraud according to COSO?

12. How did the three Duke employees allegedly commit fraud in 2001 and 2002? Why?

13. Give some examples of internal fraud.

14. Give some examples of external fraud.

15. What are the three factors of the fraud pyramid?

16. What did Sherron Watkins say about rationalization and Jeff Skilling and Andy Fastow?

17. What is the 3-C model of Professor Zab Razaee?

18. What superseded SAS No. 82?

19. Define internal controls.

20. In SAS No. 82, what are some industry condition risk factors? Some operating and financial stability risk characteristics?

21. What is PCAOB's definition of internal controls?

22. Do you fit within the profile or characteristics of a white collar criminal? Explain.

23. What are G.E. Moulton's fraud identifiers?

24. Give the percentages when CEOs and CFOs are involved in fraudulent financial fraud cases.

25. Give Professor Robertson's typical white-collar criminal characteristics.

26. What was the pressure on Tracey Henderson, an executive of the Australia Football League, to steal?

27. Describe senior level management fraudsters.

28. What are the number one and two conditions conducive for fraud according to KPMG surveys?

29. What companies are more prone to engage in fraudulent behavior?

30. Why is it difficult to develop an accurate profile of a fraudster?

31. What is a definition of earnings management? What is fraudulent earnings management?

32. How many restatements of earnings occurred in 2012?
33. How does the SEC define abusive earnings management?
34. Here is the letter written by Sherron Watkins, CPA. Is she a whistle-blower? Did she commit a discreditable act under AICPA Rule 501?

Dear Mr. Lay,

Has Enron become a risky place to work? For those of us who didn't get rich over the last few years, can we afford to stay?

Skilling's abrupt departure will raise suspicions of accounting improprieties and valuation issues. Enron has been very aggressive in its accounting—most notably the Raptor transactions and the Condor vehicle. We do have valuation issues with our international assets and possibly some of our EES MTM positions.

The spotlight will be on us, the market just can't accept that Skilling is leaving his dream job. I think that the valuation issues can be fixed and reported with other goodwill write-downs to occur in 2002. How do we fix the Raptor and Condor deals? They unwind in 2002 and 2003, we will have to pony up Enron stock and that won't go unnoticed.

To the layman on the street, it will look like we recognized funds flow of $800 mm from merchant asset sales in 1999 by selling to a vehicle (Condor) that we capitalized with a promise of Enron stock in later years. Is that really funds flow or is it cash from equity issuance?

We have recognized over $550 million of fair value gains on stocks via our swaps with Raptor, much of that stock has declined significantly—Avici by 98 percent, from $178 mm to $5 mm, The New Power Co by 70 percent, from $20/share to $6/share. The value in the swaps won't be there for Raptor, so once again Enron will issue stock to offset these losses. Raptor is an LJM entity. It sure looks to the layman on the street that we are hiding losses in a related company and will compensate that company with Enron stock in the future.

I am incredibly nervous that we will implode in a wave of accounting scandals. My 8 years of Enron work history will be worth nothing on my resume, the business world will consider the past successes as nothing but an elaborate accounting hoax. Skilling is resigning for 'personal reasons' but I think he wasn't having fun, looked down the road and knew this stuff was unfixable and would rather abandon ship now than resign in shame in 2 years.

Is there a way our accounting guru's [sic] can unwind these deals now? I have thought and thought about how to do this, but I keep bumping into one big problem—we booked the Condor and Raptor deals in 1999 and 2000, we enjoyed a wonderfully high stock price, many executives sold stock, we then try and reverse or fix the deals in 2001 and it's a bit like robbing the bank in one year and trying to pay it back 2 years later. Nice try, but investors were hurt, they bought at $70 and $80/share looking for $120/share and now they're at $38 or worse. We are under too much scrutiny and there are probably one or two disgruntled 'redeployed' employees who know enough about the 'funny' accounting to get us in trouble.

35. Using the Internet, find descriptions of recent fraud schemes based on SEC releases.
36. On the Internet, locate some current examples of external fraud.
37. Follow-up the careers of Sherron Watkins and Kenneth Lay using Internet and book resources.
38. Research on the Internet how many restatements of earnings occurred during 2006.
39. Check Internet descriptions about the $18 million McKesson Robbins fraud. Summarize the fraud scheme and describe how it was uncovered.
40. Read about the $100 million Equity Funding reinsurance fraud using the Internet. Summarize the fraud scheme.
41. What are Howard M. Schilit's seven financial shenanigans?
42. Research the Sarbanes-Oxley Act and read about the debate that led up to its passage. Based on your research:
    a. Is there consensus on whether Sarbanes is good law?
    b. What did you read about those who have influenced accounting regulation in the past?
    c. Can you name the important players in accounting regulation before Sarbanes? After Sarbanes? What has changed?
43. The amount of financial reporting fraud in business seems staggering. What do you believe has contributed to financial statement fraud's growth?
44. If you were going to research financial reporting fraud what questions would you like to address?
45. Find the SEC's press release with respect to Rite Aid in 2002 and list the bag of tricks that the company used to cook the books. *www.sec.gov/news/press/2002-92.htm.*

46. When Krispy Kreme restated its 2004 earnings, what impact did the restatement have on the price of the stock?

47. Give some patterns or red flags of financial statement fraud.

48. How much are firms willing to sacrifice in income taxes in order to smooth earnings?

49. Do smaller firms tend to manage earnings when compared to larger firms?

50. On the Internet, find the SEC Staff Accounting Bulletin No. 101. What are the criteria for determining if revenue is realized or realizable and earned?

51. What is meant by *alter ego*?

52. Find the Internet site "The Fraud Farm." Prepare your own "Gallery of Weasels."

53. Find the Internet site "Bob Jensen's Enron Quiz Questions." Take the Quiz.

54. Explain why backdating the grant date of a stock option to a lower price cheats the corporation.

55. Search the Internet about the Apple stock option backdating scandal and decide whether CEO Steve Jobs should have gone to jail. Why did other executives go to jail and not Steve? Is politics sometimes involved with who is prosecuted?

56. On the Internet find the 2012 Transparency International Corruption Perception Index and determine the ranking of these countries.
    a. United States
    b. Japan
    c. Chad
    d. Iceland
    e. Denmark

57. Which is not a factor, according to the Australian Institute of Criminology, that can explain fraud?
    a. Rationalization or lack of integrity
    b. Supply of motivated offenders
    c. Availability of suitable targets
    d. Absence of capable guardians
    e. All of the above are factors

58. Which factor is in the fraud diamond that is not in the fraud pyramid?
    a. Motive
    b. Capacity
    c. Attitude
    d. Opportunity
    e. None of the above

59. What is generally the most difficult thing to prove in a fraud court case?
    a. A false representation or willful omission regarding a material fact
    b. The fraudster knew the representation was false
    c. The target relied on this misappropriation
    d. The victim suffered damages or incurred a loss
    e. None of the above

60. Which would *not* be a preventive control?
    a. Guards
    b. Swipe cards
    c. Fences
    d. Data mining software
    e. Background checks

61. Which would *not* be a detective control?
    a. Drug testing
    b. Reconciliations
    c. Surprise cash counts
    d. Counting inventory
    e. Management reviews

62. Which would be a corrective control?
    a. Process redesign
    b. Drug testing
    c. Using document control numbers
    d. Job rotation
    e. Event notifications

63. Which fraud scheme did Sunbeam *not* do?
    a. Cookie-jar reserves
    b. Accelerated revenues from leasing equipment
    c. Channel stuffing
    d. Guaranteed sales
    e. Improper bill and hold

64. Which is *not* one of the three B's of fraud?
    a. Bucks
    b. Babes
    c. Booze
    d. Bets
    e. B and C above

65. Which statement is false?
    a. A growing "days sales outstanding" figure is often a sign that receivables are impaired by channel stuffing.
    b. Backdating stock option exercise dates is not abusive earnings management.
    c. Receivables that are not correlated with revenue is a sign of earnings management.
    d. Cash flow not correlated to revenues is a sign of earnings management.
    e. None of the above.

66. Motive to commit fraud usually will include all of the following except:
    a. Feelings of resentment
    b. Alcohol, drug, or gambling addiction
    c. Financial pressures and personal habits
    d. Inadequate separation of duties
    e. None of the above

67. Which statement is false with respect to backdating of stock options?
    a. Steve Jobs, CEO of Apple, was involved with backdating.
    b. Manipulating a stock option exercise date to a lower price will decrease the corporation's tax deduction.
    c. By picking a grant date on which the stock price is lower, an executive pays the corporation less when she exercises the stock.
    d. By picking a grant date on which the stock price is lower, the company's deduction for options exercised by executives is increased.
    e. None of the above is false.

68. Which would *not* be an indicator of *alter ego*?
    a. Financial dependence behaviors
    b. Confusion about corporate identity
    c. Risk assessment
    d. Dominance and control
    e. None of the above

69. Is the Internal Revenue Code responsible for the backdating problem? Did Code Sec. 162(m), which restricts the deductibility of nonperformance-based executive compensation to $1 million, cause the stock option explosion and the resulting backdating scandal? Prepare a working paper on this subject.

70. Determine whether the following are preventive (P), detective (D), or corrective (C) controls.
    a. Employee training
    b. Bank reconciliations
    c. Password controls
    d. Surprise cash count
    e. Insurance
    f. Job rotation
    g. Counting inventory

71. Go to the FBI internet site or search other sources and prepare a report as to the fraudulent activities in these companies. How did the people pull off the fraud?
    a. Quest Communication.
    b. AmeriFunding.

72. Go to the Securities and Exchange Commission's Internet site (sec.gov) and find a Litigation Release number that deals with each of the following issues. Give the Litigation Release number and write a short paragraph about the issue(s) involved.
    a. Company pushing income into the future.
    b. Company inflating revenues.
    c. Company decreasing expenses.
    d. A Ponzi scheme.
    e. A shell company.
    f. Company increasing assets.
    g. Pump and dump scheme.
    h. An oil and gas promoter.
    i. Bernard Madoff (LR no. 20834 / 12-19-2008).
    j. Foreign Corrupt Practices Act (bribery).
    k. Kickbacks.
    l. Mark Cuban (LR no. 20810 / 11-17-08).
    m. Backdating stock options.
    n. Misappropriation of assets.
    o. An external accountant.

73. Which variable is not an element of the Fraud Pentagon?
    a. Pressure.
    b. Motive.
    c. Opportunity.
    d. Rationalization.
    e. Personal greed.

74. What characteristic would probably not be a motive for a highly paid executive/fraudster?
    a. Hypercompetitiveness.
    b. Opportunity.
    c. Perfectionism.
    d. Excessive pride.
    e. All of the above could be motivation.

75. Write a report about the two companies that absorbed many of the employees from Arthur Andersen when they went bankrupt: Huron Consulting and Protiviti.

76. Go to the "White Collar Crime Professor Blog" edited by Ellen S. Podgor and summarize the last three Recent Posts. To what does "The Collar" refer?

77. The following are questions about Lee B. Farkas. You are to fill in the missing information or answer the questions in the scavenger hunt.

a. When was I born?
b. I was born in what state?
c. What is my middle name?
d. What are the last four digits of my social security number?
e. What is my passport number?
f. What does my last name mean in Hungarian?
g. What is my religion?
h. Am I married and how many children do I have?
i. Where do I live?
j. What is my last phone number?
k. How tall I am and how much do I weigh?
l. What color is my hair and my eyes?
m. Do I have any brothers or sisters? What are their names if so?
n. Which relative wrote a letter to The Vile Plutocrat?
o. What are my college degrees?
p. What theater did I help restore in Florida?
q. What Human Society did I support in Florida?
r. Are my mother and father alive? If not, when did they die?
s. What is my occupation?
t. What mortgage company do I (did I) own?
u. Provide some of my sources of income from assets?
v. I was the CEO of what company until 2003?
w. I became the Chairman of what company until 2003?
x. How much did I steal from my company?
y. In a "preliminary forfeiture order," what assets were forfeited?
z. In a "preliminary forfeiture order," what cars or trucks was I forced to forfeit?

4

DETECTING FRAUD IN FINANCIAL REPORTING

Qwest's brand-new CFO, Oren Shaffer—part of the present management, which is supposed to be turning the company around—delivered a rambling speech in which he explained that Qwest was erasing $1.5 billion of revenue from [Joe] Nacchio's tenure because the company had not found the ledger justifying Qwest's accounting for more than a billion dollars in deals.

—Mark Gimein[1]

OBJECTIVES

After completing Chapter 4, you should be able to:

1. Identify the different roles and responsibilities of those involved in financial reporting.
2. Describe how responsibilities are evolving in light of financial reporting reform.
3. Describe the major types of financial statement fraud.
4. Explain the forensic accountant's role in fighting financial statement fraud.

OVERVIEW

Chapter 1 discusses the subtle shift in the way external auditors reviewed clients' records in the '80s and '90s. As auditing competition increased and companies began to use computers to perform their recordkeeping, auditors had to cut costs by reducing the labor-intensive process of reviewing millions of transactions and hundreds of corporate accounts. They placed more reliance on internal controls and worked less with account balances and entries.

Because top executives can circumvent internal controls, they could manipulate the records and cook the books.[2] Eventually the results were scandals at Enron, WorldCom, Xerox, Adelphia Communications, and the fall of Arthur Andersen in the early 2000s. SEC officials and many other financial and accounting experts also voiced concerns over what Arthur Levitt called "a gradual, but perceptible, erosion in the quality of financial reporting."[3] If the pendulum does swing back, there will be more forensic techniques in financial audits, coupled with higher audit fees.

A summary statement from a forensic accounting report about the HealthSouth fraud is instructive:[4]

> The accounting fraud at HealthSouth was by any standard both enormous and complex. Its concealment over the course of nearly seven years required considerable effort and, in some cases, luck. For all its size and complexity, however, the fraud shared much in common with other highly publicized earnings overstatement cases, a fact that provided a measure of confidence that significant accounting or reporting misstatements did not escape the Committee's attention.
>
> Stated most simply, the fraud was accomplished by making over $2.7 billion in false or unsupported entries in the Company's accounting systems. These improper accounting entries, made for the purpose of inflating HealthSouth's earnings, took two principal forms: (1) exaggeration of reported revenue, primarily through reductions to contractual adjustment accounts, and (2) failure to properly characterize and record operating expenses.

Accounting experts continue to debate the role of auditors in uncovering fraud. In the following sections, the current role of the independent auditor, the role of the internal auditor, the audit committee and management, and the role of the forensic accountant are outlined. The last sections of the chapter describe in more detail the forensic accountant's role and describe fraud detection guidance from authoritative sources.

Definitions of Fraud

¶ 4001 WHAT IS FRAUD?

There are numerous definitions of fraud. The Securities and Exchange Commission defines fraud as follows:[5]

> It shall be unlawful for any person, directly or indirectly, by the use of any means or instrumentality of interstate commerce, or the mails, or of any facility of any national securities exchange,
>
> a. To employ any device, scheme, or artifice to defraud,
> b. To make any untrue statement of a material fact or to omit to state a material fact necessary in order to make the statements made, in the light of the circumstances under which they were made, *not* misleading, or
> c. To engage in any act, practice, or course of business which operates or would operate as a fraud or deceit upon any person, in connection with the purchase or sale of any security.

The AICPA in SAS No. 99 and PCAOB follow this definition:

> The primary factor that distinguishes fraud from error is whether the underlying action is intentional or unintentional. Fraud is an intentional act that results in a material misstatement in financial statements that are the subject of an audit. Two types of misstatements are relevant to the auditor's consideration of fraud—misstatements arising from financial reporting and misstatements arising from misappropriation of assets.[6]

The Institute of Internal Auditors suggests this definition:[7]

> Any illegal acts characterized by deceit, concealment, or violation of trust. These acts are not dependent upon the applications to obtain money, property, or services; to avoid payment or loss of services; or to secure personal or business advantage.

A fraud definition of the AICPA, IIA, and ACFE is as follows:[8]

> Fraud is any intentional act or omission designed to deceive others, resulting in the victim suffering a loss and/or the perpetrator achieving a gain.

Black's Law Dictionary defines fraud as:

> All multifarious means which human ingenuity can devise, and which are resorted to by one individual to get an advantage over another by false suggestions or suppression of the truth, and includes all surprise, trick, cunning or dissembling, and any unfair way by which another is cheated.

Thus, four major legal elements of fraud would be:

- A false representation or willful omission regarding a material fact.
- The fraudster knew the representation was false.
- The target relied on this misappropriation.
- The victim suffered damages or incurred a loss.

The SEC in securities fraud cases generally uses the term "scienter"; the SEC or a plaintiff must prove that "scienter" or fraudulent intent is present. For example, if someone commits a fraud against a government agency, knowing full well that such fraud may result in injury or loss of life (e.g., selling defective fire hoses to fire departments), this criminal intent would be scienter. Generally, a less stringent "knowingly" is often required in the prosecution of financial crime.

PricewaterhouseCooper's 2009 Global Economic Crime survey lists these types of economic crimes with percentage.

- Asset misappropriation   67%
- Accounting fraud   38%
- Bribery and corruption   27%
- IP infringement   15%
- Money laundering   12%
- Tax fraud   5%
- Illegal insider trading   4%
- Market fraud involving cartels colluding to fix prices   3%
- Espionage   3%

Responsibilities and Roles in Financial Reporting

¶ 4005   INDEPENDENT AUDIT PROCEDURES AND THE AUDITOR'S ROLE

Today's independent auditor acquires a knowledge of the client's business and competitive environment.[9] Analytical procedures are used to get a better idea of the client's business and to identify areas of audit risk. The auditor must understand the implications of various risk factors to plan the financial audit and must also determine whether any specialists are needed to assist with the audit. Audit evidence is gathered in two fieldwork stages: (1) the internal control testing phase, and (2) the account balance testing phase. Auditors apply audit procedures to obtain reasonable assurance that the financial statements are free of material misstatement. Auditing procedures also must include procedures to detect fraud. The primary objective of the auditor's examination of financial statements is to express an opinion about whether the financial statements present fairly, in all material respects, values of assets and liabilities in terms of GAAP. Proper application of GAAP should support management assertions. Management assertions can serve as guidelines for the audit objectives.

Because auditing decisions are based on the significance of accounts and transactions, *materiality* (the measure of whether something is significant enough to change an investor's investment decision) is a prime consideration in how the audit is conducted. *Control risk* (risk that a material error in the balance or transaction class will not be prevented or detected) rises with weaknesses in the internal controls. *Inherent risk,* which also must be assessed, is the risk that an account or transactions contain material misstatements before the effects of the controls. *Detection risk* (risk that audit procedures will not turn up material error when it exists) rises with smaller quantities and less competence of audit evidence. When control or inherent risk is high, the auditor must plan on gathering more and better evidence because the auditor is less willing to accept a high level of detection risk.

Substantive tests are performed in which auditors seek account balance misstatements. These tests are time-consuming and expensive tests of details of account balances—they also include analytical procedures. The auditor satisfies auditing objectives by gathering evidence provided by the underlying accounting data and all other available corroborating information.

Auditing generally is governed by the materiality concept, but investigating auditing is the opposite. A forensic accountant is "looking for the one transaction that will be the key. The one transaction that is a little different, no matter how small is the difference, and that will open the door," says Lorraine Horton.[10] Lorraine Horton also says that "unlike auditing, lower-level staff often can't be used for an engagement. They normally will not spot anything out of the ordinary, and an experienced person should be the one testifying as well as doing the investigative work."[11]

EYEWITNESS

There is a story told by a controller who was writing checks to a related entity owned by the controller. The external auditor asked for a sample of checks from the controller, but one of the requested checks given by the controller to the auditor was missing. So the auditor asked for the missing check.

The missing one was a red flag related entity check; so overnight the controller "created" a new cancelled check and gave it to the auditor the next day.

But when the auditor took the check, he said, "Oh, we found the check yesterday. But I can see how there can be two checks. No problem. We'll use this one." The auditor did nothing.

External Auditors and Fraud Detection

The external auditor's responsibility for detecting financial statement fraud has evolved over time. As a result of a number of high-profile financial statement frauds (e.g., McKesson & Robbins), the independent Cohen Commission was established by the AICPA in 1974. In 1985, this commission became known as the Treadway Commission, which in 1992 issued a report entitled *Internal Controls—Integrated Framework*, which stressed the need for enhancing controls.

A highly publicized statement on financial red flags was published in early February of 1997 by the AICPA. Statement on Auditing Standards No. 82, *Consideration of Fraud in a Financial Statement Audit,* provided guidance to the auditor in the detection of financial statement fraud. This statement also clarified the auditor's responsibility to detect fraud. The statement is rather lengthy, and, although it was eventually superceded by SAS No. 99, the earlier statement clearly specifies that the detection of *material misstatement* in financial statements is central to an audit. Nevertheless, paragraph 10 of SAS No. 82 states the difficulties of detecting fraud in financial records when management collusion and/ or falsified documents are present:

> An auditor cannot obtain absolute assurance that material misstatements in the financial statements will be detected. Because of (a) the concealment aspects of fraudulent activity, including the fact that fraud often involves collusion or falsified documentation, and (b) the need to apply professional judgment in the identification and evaluation of fraud risk factors and other conditions, even a properly planned and performed audit may not detect a material misstatement resulting from fraud. Accordingly because of the above characteristics of fraud and the nature of fraud evidence…the auditor is able to obtain only reasonable assurance that material misstatements in the financial statements, including misstatements resulting from fraud, are detected.[12]

Although auditors have previously had the responsibility to detect material misstatement caused by fraud, SAS No. 82 details much more precisely what is required to fulfill those responsibilities. Now, auditors must specifically assess and respond to the risk of material misstatement due to fraud and must assess that risk from the perspective of the broad categories listed in the SAS. In addition, the external auditor has to satisfy new documentation and communication requirements.

Lee Seidler says that external auditors have a poor record of uncovering fraud: "No major fraud has ever been discovered by auditors." He believes that auditors will continue to miss fraud because much of their work is predicated on the assumption that separation of duties prevents fraud. The Equity Funding decision "shakes the foundation of auditing, in that so much is based on the assumption that people don't collude, or they wouldn't collude very long."[13] In Equity Funding at least 20 individuals colluded for nine years. This multibillion dollar insurance scandal involved thousands of fictitious transactions that should have been caught by the company's auditors. The fraudsters created false insurance policy files and actually killed off fictitious people. By the time the scandal was discovered, at least one-half of the policies were fake. The many disclosures of cooked books in the early 2000s proved Seidler correct.

DO NOT BE A RUBBER STAMP. In November 2008, Bernard Madoff told his investors that they had $65 billion, but investigators found only about $1 billion. Prosecutors said that Madoff's accountant, David Friehling, operating from a 13 by 18 feet office, rubber-stamped Madoff's books for 17 years.

The government said Friehling did not meaningfully audit Madoff's books or confirm that securities supposedly held by Madoff on behalf of his customers even existed. The SEC said Friehling pretended to conduct minimal audit procedures of certain accounts to make it appear that he was conducting an audit, but he failed to document his purported findings. He failed to examine a bank account through which billions of dollars flowed. The FBI said he did little or no testing or verification.

The SEC said the 49-year-old accountant lied to the AICPA for years, denying that he conducted any auditing. He was afraid that his audit work would be peer reviewed.[14] Do not be a David Friehling.

Limitations of Audits and Auditing Standards

Basically, generally accepted audit standards (GAAS) are not designed to catch fraud other than financial statement fraud. Independent auditors are not charged professionally with finding asset fraud, merely material misstatement of financial statements. "Current standards purposely give CPAs wiggle room to avoid responsibility when financial statements turn out to be fraudulent."[15] Clearly there is a gap between the public's expectations and the product that independent auditors deliver. The typical audit client is probably unwilling to pay for an audit that would catch most fraud, so the expectation gap will not disappear. After Enron, the auditing environment changed. But the typical juror will still believe that the purpose of an audit is to uncover any type of fraud or wrongdoing. Even internal auditors do not wish to take the responsibility of finding fraud, and they are most often concerned with employee fraud rather than management and external fraud.

The two attorneys in the lawsuit between the United Companies and Deloitte & Touche illustrates this expectation gap. The plaintiff's attorney said to the jury that the role of the auditor is to act as the watchdog for a company. "A good watchdog barks when somebody comes into the yard. D & T is supposed to bark when there is a problem." But the defendant's attorney said, "the problem was much larger than a watchdog could handle. Can a watchdog stop your house from being hit by a hurricane? Of course not."[16] As is often the case in an accountant's malpractice dispute, there was a mid-court settlement.

But as Robert J. DiPasquale says, "if there is fraud and you don't detect it, you are going to be sued, and you will likely lose, as the public perception is that the accountant is the watchdog."[17]

Panel on Audit Effectiveness Recommendations

In October 1998 the Public Oversight Board (POB), at the request of the then SEC Chairman Arthur Levitt, appointed the Panel on Audit Effectiveness. Its challenge was to review and evaluate how independent audits of the financial statements of public companies are performed and to assess whether recent trends in audit practices serve the public interest.

After undertaking the most thorough review ever of the audit model, the Panel issued a 255-page report on September 6, 2000, entitled "The Panel on Audit Effectiveness Report and Recommendations." The Panel made more than 200 recommendations for improvements in the conduct of audits and the governance of the profession, and called for the POB to monitor their implementation. Of particular interest to forensic accountants is the recommendation that auditors should perform some "forensic-type" procedures on every audit to enhance the prospects of detecting material financial statement fraud.[18] This new forensic-type phase would become an integral part of the audit, with careful thought directed to how and when to carry out the audit. The Panel characterizes this phase as an attitudinal shift in the auditor's degree of skepticism. During this phase, auditors would presume the possibility of dishonesty at various levels of management, including collusion, override of internal controls, and falsification of documents. The Panel defines the key question the auditor should ask as "Where is the entity vulnerable to financial statement fraud if management were inclined to perpetuate it?"[19]

AICPA's SAS No. 99 Reflects Panel of Audit Effectiveness Recommendations

In response to the research and recommendations made by the Public Oversight Board's Panel on Audit Effectiveness, in 2002 the AICPA issued *Statement on Auditing Standards (SAS) 99: Consideration of Fraud in a Financial Statement Audit.* The main points of the standard are as follows:

- *Increased Emphasis on Professional Skepticism*—Members of the audit team must exchange ideas or brainstorm how fraud could occur so that they might design audit tests responsive to the risks of fraud.
- *Discussions with Management*—Auditors must ask the client's management and other employees about the risk of fraud and whether they know of its existence in the organization.
- *Unpredictable Audit Tests*—Auditors should design tests that would be unpredictable and unexpected and should test areas, locations, and accounts that otherwise might not be tested.
- *Responding to Management Override of Controls*—The engagement team must test for management override of controls.
- *Brainstorming*—Audit teams are now required to hold a session to generate ideas about how fraud might be committed and concealed in an entity.

THOUGHTS ON SAS No. 99. Thoughts on SAS No. 99 from AccountingMalpractice.com, a leading web page that tracks accounting liability issues: "From a legal liability standpoint, the adoption of this standard represents a significant step in closing the ever-widening expectation gap between professional standards and the beliefs of investors, judges and juries about the role auditors play in the maintenance of financial statement integrity. For years, nonauditors have been asking '*if they are not there to detect fraud, then what are they there for*?' Auditors will now have to comply with an obligation factfinders believed they already had. Management integrity simply cannot be assumed anymore. It must be tested and then retested."

Maintaining Objectivity

SAS No. 1 states that auditors must plan and perform an audit to obtain "reasonable assurance" that the financial statements are free of material misstatements caused by errors or fraud. In the planning stage the audit team must discuss the potential for material misstatement due to fraud. Such discussions should involve key members of the audit team from the significant locations. These discussions should consider the pyramid of external and internal variables affecting the entity that might (a) create incentives/pressures for management and others to commit fraud, (b) provide the opportunity for fraud to be perpetrated, and (c) indicate a culture or environment that enables management to rationalize committing fraud.

SEC and Public Company Accounting Oversight Board

Creation of PCAOB

The Sarbanes-Oxley Act of 2002 created a new, five-member oversight group called the Public Company Accounting Oversight Board (PCAOB).[20] This group is a strong, independent, and full-time oversight board with broad authority to regulate auditors of public companies, set auditing standards, and investigate violations. Only two of its members can be or have been CPAs. The Board is subject to the SEC review and will establish auditing, quality control, ethics, and independence standards for public company auditors. PCAOB's mission is to protect investors in U.S. securities markets and to further the public interest by ensuring that public company financial statements are audited according to the highest standards of quality, independence, and ethics. The Board will be funded by fees from public companies.

PCAOB is empowered to set accounting standards that establish auditing, quality control, and ethical standards for accountants. The Board also is empowered to adopt or amend standards issued or recommended by private accounting industry groups or to adopt its own standards independent of such private industry standards or recommendations. Auditing Standards have been historically created by the AICPA and many had thought that the PCAOB would delegate its authority to set standards to the AICPA. However, the Board has indicated its intention to set standards itself.[21]

Former SEC Chairman Harvey Pitt, however, complained that historically it takes more than five years for the SEC to investigate a problem and bring an action.[22] Does this slow process explain the Bernard Madoff and Robert Allen Stanford's scandals?

¶ 4011   INTERNAL AUDITOR'S PROCEDURES AND ROLE

The Institute of Internal Auditors (IIA) offers the following definition of *internal auditing:*

> Internal auditing is an independent, objective assurance and consulting activity designed to add value and improve an organization's operations. It helps an organization accomplish its objectives by bringing a systematic, disciplined approach to evaluate and improve the effectiveness of risk management, control and governance processes.[23]

Like the role of the independent external auditor, the role of the internal auditor also has changed significantly in the past several decades. As this definition states, today's internal auditor offers various consulting services within an organization and works to add value and improve operations. The focus is on evaluating and improving the effectiveness of risk management, control, and governance processes. In the past, internal auditing groups may have concentrated on performing financial and compliance audits with a focus on lowering the cost of the annual financial audit by the organization's external auditors.

CHANGING ROLES. Can one draw a parallel between the additional consulting services offered by the internal auditing department and the expanded services offered by public accounting firms? Have they gone too far? Both the AICPA and IIA have really asked accountants to think well outside auditing and feature consulting as a big part of their services—yet it has backfired to some extent in both cases.

Although the external independent auditor will assess internal controls, corporate governance, and many types of risk, it is the internal auditor who has already examined and identified such controls and directs improvements and the reduction of such risks.

Internal auditors review the reliability and integrity of financial and operating information and the means used to identify, measure, classify, and report such information. Internal auditors review the systems established to ensure compliance with those policies, plans, procedures, laws, and regulations that could have a significant impact on operations and reports, and determine whether the organization is in compliance. Internal auditors review the means of safeguarding assets from various types of losses, such as those resulting from theft, fire, improper or illegal activities, and exposure to the elements and as appropriate, verifying the existence of such assets. Internal auditors appraise the economy and efficiency with which resources are employed. Internal auditors review operations or program to ascertain whether results are consistent with established objectives and goals and whether the operations or programs are being carried out as planned.

The internal auditing function may or may not be carried out by an internal auditing department. Sometimes the function is outsourced. Enron had outsourced much of its internal auditing work to Arthur Andersen. WorldCom kept its internal auditors away from financial-type auditing.

Yet internal audit departments that report to senior management are perceived as less likely to prevent financial statement fraud than outsourced internal auditing functions (even when outsourced to the financial statement auditor).[24] If a department exists it may have a charter that identifies its responsibilities. Often the charter will explicitly address the internal auditing department's responsibility with respect to fraud.

Internal Auditors and Fraud Detection

Internal auditors are potential auditing combatants of fraud and abuse, but the internal auditing profession suggests that internal auditors are not responsible for finding fraud on the job. The Institute of Internal Auditors' (IIA's) Due Professional Care Standard (Section 280) assigns the internal auditor the task of assisting in the control of fraud by examining and evaluating the adequacy and effectiveness of the internal control system. However, Section 280 says that management has the primary responsibility for the deterrence of fraud, and management is responsible for establishing and maintaining the control systems. In general, internal auditors are more concerned with employee fraud than with management and other external fraud.[25]

A leading internal auditing textbook describes a fraud audit as "atypical, as fraud is an unusual occurrence."[26] But the textbook does say that "internal auditors are likely to face [a] higher expectation [of catching fraud] than are external auditors."[27] The internal auditing department is responsible for examining and evaluating the adequacy and the effectiveness of management's actions to fulfill this fraud finding obligation. Internal auditors should be familiar with fraud indicators and if control weaknesses are detected, additional tests should be conducted by internal audits including those directed towards the identification of other indicators of fraud. Internal auditors are not expected to have knowledge equivalent to that of a person whose primary responsibility is to detect and investigate fraud. The internal auditors' Competency Framework for Internal Auditing (CFIA) lists the knowledge, skills, and abilities that future auditors will need to perform internal auditing services. The competencies include a broad range of topics, but *technical accounting* knowledge is not stressed. Auditing procedures alone do not guarantee that fraud will be detected. Internal auditors will assist in the investigation of fraud in order to determine whether controls need to be implemented or strengthened or design audit tests to help disclose the existence of similar fraud.

The Center for Audit Quality makes these suggestions with respect to tone at the top in an organization:[28]

1. Work productively with the audit committee to develop a clear, shared vision of the internal audit function in order to reinforce the integrity and importance of the function throughout the company.
2. Require basic fraud detection training, including the detection of financial reporting fraud, for all internal auditors.
3. If warranted, consider allocating one internal audit position for a fraud specialist, ideally someone with appropriate experience and certifications.
4. Take an active and visible role in supporting the ethical culture, including evaluating hotline results, conducting ethics surveys of employees, and collaborating with other

departments to address results and remediate applicable findings. Analyze year-over-year changes in key metrics.

5. Evaluate soft controls and the corporate culture, including assessment of the company's fraud risk management program, and involve appropriate departments in addressing the results.

6. Establish or otherwise ensure there is a formal process to educate the board and audit committee on the risk and red flags of financial reporting fraud, with a particular focus on the risk of management override of controls.

An internal auditor was the one who discovered the shift of at least $3.8 billion of line-cost expenses to capital accounts at WorldCom (eventually totaling about $11 billion).

At least 40 people knew about the fraud, but they were apparently afraid to talk. CFO Scott Sullivan handed out $10,000 checks to at least seven involved individuals. Employees altered key documents and denied Arthur Andersen access to the database where most of the sensitive numbers were stored, and Andersen apparently did not complain. In the words of Rudyard Kipling, "but I'd shut my eyes in the sentry box, so I didn't see nothing wrong."

David Schneedan, CFO at a division, refused to release reserves twice. An e-mail from David Myers, WorldCom comptroller, to Schneedan: "I guess the only way I am going to get this booked is to fly to DC and book it myself. Book it right now; I cannot wait another minute." Buddy Gates [director of general accounting] said to an employee complaining about a large accounting discrepancy: "Show those numbers to the damn auditors, and I'll throw you out the window."[29]

Often managers perceive that internal audits are of sufficient scope and depth to detect irregularities. Further, because internal auditors' primary focus is on controls, these controls are expected to deter fraud.[30] Susan Henry says that accounting is the language of business, and internal controls set the ethical standards that govern business activities.[31]

The internal auditors' standards state that the auditor must consider the possibility of material irregularities or noncompliance during an internal audit. The internal auditor's responsibility for detecting fraud includes having sufficient knowledge of fraud to be able to identify indicators that fraud has been committed. He or she should be alert to opportunities that could allow fraud, and if found, the auditor should notify the appropriate authorities in the organization if there are sufficient indicators to recommend an investigation. If the internal auditor recommends an investigation, he or she must follow up to determine that the internal auditing department has fulfilled its responsibilities.

Recently, the IIA has suggested a more expansive role of the internal auditor with respect to fraud controls. Internal auditors "should provide objective assurance to the board and management that fraud controls are sufficient for identifying fraud risks and ensure that the controls are functioning effectively. Internal auditors may review the comprehensiveness and adequacy of the risks identified by management—especially with regard to management override risks."[32]

Likewise, the IIA is asking internal auditors to be more active in the risk assessment process.

Internal auditors should consider the organization's assessment of fraud risk when developing their annual audit plan and review management's fraud management capabilities periodically. They should interview and communicate regularly with those conducting the organization's risk assessments, as well as others in key positions throughout the organization, to help them ensure that all fraud risks have been considered appropriately. When performing engagements, internal auditors should spend adequate time and attention to evaluating the design and operation of internal controls related to fraud risk management. They should exercise professional skepticism when reviewing activities and be on guard for the signs of fraud. Potential frauds uncovered during an engagement should be treated in accordance with a well-defined response plan consistent with professional and legal standards. Internal auditing should also take an active role in support of the organization's ethical culture.[33]

Institute of Internal Auditors

The Institute of Internal Auditors (IIA) is the leading voice of authority and educator of internal auditors in the United States. The IIA follows the various accounting reform developments and acknowledges that the role of boards of directors, audit committees, corporate management, and external and internal auditors is changing. The IIA Research Foundation is a separate nonprofit research organization arm of the IIA conducting an ongoing research project called Internal Auditor's Role in Corporate Governance. According to the IIA, the primary focus of the research is to examine what internal auditors are doing to help their companies meet the new U.S. listing requirements. The study addresses broader issues, such as balancing the conflicting needs of audit committees and management, finding the resources to do more with governance, and expanding into meaningful evaluations of the heart of corporate governance (e.g., the corporate culture) rather than retreating into a narrow scope of financial audit testwork.

Internal Auditor's Action When Management Fraud Is Discovered

But suppose management is perpetrating the fraud. In 1999, the Committee of Sponsoring Organizations of the Treadway Commission (COSO) released its report, *Fraudulent Financial Reporting: 1987–1997, An Analysis of U.S. Public Companies*. This study analyzed approximately 200 companies that were alleged to have been involved in fraudulent financial reporting and investigated by the SEC from 1987–1997. According to this report, the chief executive officer (CEO) was involved in 72 percent of fraudulent financial reporting cases, whereas the chief financial officer (CFO) was involved in 43 percent of these cases. The frequent involvement of top executives confirms management's ability to override controls that might otherwise prevent fraudulent financial statements. Thus, the internal audit director should report directly to the audit committee of the board of directors, and not to senior management.

COSO lists these as the most common financial statement fraud methods:

1. Overstatement of earnings.
2. Fictitious earnings.
3. Understatement of expenses.
4. Overstatement of assets.
5. Understatement of allowances for accounts receivables.
6. Overstatements of the value of inventories by *not* writing down the value of obsolete goods.
7. Overstatement of property values and creation of fictitious assets.

Standards for the Professional Practice of Internal Auditing No. 2 outlines the steps that an internal auditor should take in communicating the results of a fraud investigation:

1. Notify management or the board when the incidence of significant fraud has been established to a reasonable certainty.
2. If the results of a fraud investigation indicate that previously undiscovered fraud materially adversely affected previous financial statements, for one or more years, the internal auditor should inform appropriate management and the audit committee of the board of directors of the discovery.
3. A written report should include all findings, conclusions, recommendations, and corrective actions taken.
4. A draft of the written report should be submitted to legal counsel for review, especially where the internal auditor chooses to invoke client privilege.

The AICPA, IIA, and ACFE suggest these possible actions:[34]

- **Criminal referral**—The organization may refer the problem to law enforcement voluntarily, and, in some situations, it may be required to do so. Law enforcement has access to additional information and resources that may aid the case. Additionally, referrals for criminal prosecution may increase the deterrent effect of the organization's fraud prevention policy. An appropriate member of senior management, such as the chief legal counsel, should be authorized to make the decision as to whether pursuing criminal prosecution is appropriate.
- **Civil action**—An organization may wish to pursue its own civil action against the perpetrators to recover funds.
- **Disciplinary action**—Internal disciplinary action against a fraudster may include termination, suspension (with or without pay), demotion, or warnings.
- **Insurance claim**—The organization may be able to pursue an insurance claim for some or all of its losses.

SPOTLIGHT

WHERE WERE WORLDCOM'S INTERNAL AUDITORS? Cynthia Cooper, an internal auditor at WorldCom, became head of the internal auditing department at LDDS (former name of WorldCom) in the mid-1990s. She was apparently motivated and dedicated, saying that "I want to be a vice president some day." She became a vice president and became famous (or at least infamous).[35] *Time* magazine named her one of the three persons of the year in 2002.

Cooper grew up in Clinton, Mississippi, the home base of WorldCom. She graduated from Mississippi State University and earned a master's degree from the University of Alabama. She passed the CIA (Certified Internal Auditor) exam.[36] At WorldCom, she uncovered the biggest accounting scam in U.S. history—at least $3.8 billion (eventually $11 billion).

Did Cooper initiate the audit on her own, or was the audit the result of John Sidgmore, the company's new chief executive, asking her to check spending records? Sidgmore took over from WorldCom's cowboy boot-wearing founder, Bernie Ebbers.[37] (Some reports said that the new external auditors suggested that the capital accounts should be audited.) A SEC document filed by World-Com on June 30, 2002, states that "during May 2002, Cynthia Cooper, Vice President—Internal Audit, began an investigation of certain of the company's capital expenditures and capital accounts. Cooper determined that a number of questionable transfers had been made into the company's capital accounts during 2001 and the first quarter of 2002." Even reports favorable to Cooper indicate that she was asked to check spending records.[38]

Another version has her uncovering the shifting of connection cost to capital accounts. Cooper's position is that she discovered the massive fraud on her own initiative. She met resistance from Scott Sullivan, CFO, when she confronted him with evidence of the questionable accounting procedures. She reported her findings to the head of the audit committee, who delayed taking action.[39]

Still another report stated that Scott Sullivan tried to persuade Cooper to postpone her internal audit of the capital account. Cooper apparently had already begun the audit before Sullivan intervened.[40] "When Cooper confronted Sullivan with the questionable accounting practices, he [Sullivan] told her to delay the audit for another quarter. By that time, the second quarter would have been over and the charge would have already washed the $3.8 billion through the company's books." Sullivan was fired, and in July 2002 was charged by the Justice Department with securities fraud and making false filings.

The version of Cooper's discovery is important. If she found the fraud *after* being instructed to audit the capital accounts, one can question why she did not find the $3.8 billion fraud on her own. She was in charge of the internal auditing department. Is she a whistle-blower if she found the fraud as instructed? Was she really trying to protect herself? Apparently her 24-person auditing department did only a small amount of financial auditing. They were confined to performing operational audits, consisting of measuring the performance of the company's units. Their job was to make sure proper spending controls were in place, and the external auditors, Arthur Andersen, did the financial auditing.

She can argue, of course, that the book cooking occurred in 2001 and the early part of 2002; thus, she did not have time to audit for the fraud. Or, according to a leading internal auditing textbook, a fraud audit "is atypical, as fraud is an unusual occurrence."[41] But this textbook goes on to state that "internal auditors are likely to face higher expectation [of catching fraud] than are the external auditors."[42] External auditors actually disclaim responsibility for looking for fraud, unless there is a material misstatement in the financial statements.

A favorable report in *The Wall Street Journal* said three "unlikely sleuths" were credited with discovering the fraud at WorldCom: Gene Morse, Glyn Smith, and Cynthia Cooper.[43] Morse and Smith were internal auditors working under Cooper. But why *unlikely* sleuths? Internal auditors are the most *likely* to find fraud; that should be their job.

A series of obscure tips had led Cooper and Morse to believe someone was cooking the books. "Often working late at night to avoid detection by their bosses, they combed through hundreds of thousands of accounting entries, nearly crashing the company's computer in the process."[44] Morse first found a questionable $500 million accounting entry on May 28 for computer expenses, took the discovery to Cooper, who told him to keep going.[45]

On June 11, CFO Sullivan asked Cooper to delay any audit. She did not, and by June 23, auditors had uncovered $3.8 billion in misallocated expenses and phony accounting entries. Morse was afraid that others in the company would discover what he had uncovered and would try to destroy the evidence. So, with his own money, he bought a CD burner and copied all of the incriminating data onto a CD-ROM.[46]

Glyn Smith, a manager under Cooper, entered the picture when he received an employee's e-mail with an attached local newspaper article about a Texas World-Com employee who had been fired after he had raised questions about a minor accounting matter involving capital expenditures. Eventually the group would find that some executives were keeping two sets of books for the $36 billion company—one fraudulent. They found a $2 billion entry that was supposedly spent on capital expenditures, but no money had been authorized for capital spending. The executives were shifting operating costs into capital expenditure accounts.[47]

In early August a bankrupt WorldCom disclosed another $3.3 billion restatement, for 1999 through 2001. These new accounting irregularities involved reserve reversal of taxes, litigation, uncollectible receivables, and acquisition-related expenses. In October 2002, the SEC disclosed that the fraud was closer to $9 billion. The company also had loaned CEO Bernie Ebbers $415 million, and he personally guaranteed or pledged WorldCom stock to receive $1 billion of loans. So WorldCom's external auditing firm, Arthur Andersen, missed almost $11 billion in improperly booked items. Andersen's audit gave WorldCom an unqualified opinion on the company's 2001 financial statements.

¶ 4021   AUDIT COMMITTEE'S ROLE

The audit committee is the subcommittee of an organization's board of directors charged with overseeing the organization's financial reporting and internal control processes. The audit committee's biggest responsibility is monitoring the component parts of the audit process. It is imperative that audit committee members are both diligent in carrying out their duties and knowledgeable. The audit committee must have candid and open communications with internal auditors, external auditors, and company management.

The Sarbanes-Oxley Act of 2002 set out to help reform financial reporting, and specific provisions address weaknesses in audit committees. As directed by the Sarbanes-Oxley Act, the SEC adopted a new rule that directs the national securities exchanges and national securities associations to prohibit the listing of any security of an issuer that is not in compliance with the audit committee requirements mandated by the Act.[48] These requirements can be summarized as follows:

- Each member of the audit committee of the issuer must be independent according to specified criteria and at least one member should have an accounting background;
- The audit committee of each issuer must be directly responsible for the appointment, compensation, retention, and oversight of the work of any registered public accounting firm engaged for an audit report and such accounting firm must report directly to the audit committee;
- Each audit committee must establish procedures for complaints on accounting, internal accounting controls, or auditing matters (e.g., a hotline);
- Each audit committee must have the authority to engage independent counsel and other advisors, as it determines necessary to carry out its duties;
- Each issuer must provide appropriate funding for the audit committee; and
- With a few exceptions, listed issuers must be in compliance with the new listing rules by the earlier of (1) their first annual shareholders meeting after January 15, 2004, or (2) October 31, 2004.

PCAOB suggests a number of factors or red flags which an auditor or accountant should consider when determining the reliability of an audit committee in a company:

- Amount of independence of audit committee from the management—the audit committee should report to the board of directors, not the CEO;
- The clarity with which the audit committee's responsibilities are articulated, such as in the charter, and how well the audit committee and management understand those responsibilities;
- Audit committee's interaction and involvement with the independent and internal auditor; and
- Whether the audit committee raises and pursues with management and the independent auditor the appropriate questions, including questions that indicate an understanding of the critical accounting policies and judgmental accounting estimates.

PCAOB requires the external auditor to communicate various matters to the audit committee, including, but not limited to, the following:[49]

- Significant accounting policies, management judgments and accounting estimates.
- The auditor's judgment about the quality, not just the acceptability, of the company's accounting principles.
- Significant difficulties, if any, encountered during the audit.
- Uncorrected misstatements that were determined by management to be immaterial and in the aggregate.
- Audit adjustments arising from the audit, either individually or in the aggregate, that in the auditor's judgment could have a significant effect on the entity's financial reporting process.
- Significant internal control deficiencies or material weaknesses and disagreements with management.

A forensic accountant, likewise, should consider these factors. Furthermore, "misstating companies are more likely to have CEOs who sit on the nominating committees, less independent BODs and audit committees, and more CFO turnover."[50]

Further, senior officers may try to bypass or force the process to go too fast for the audit committee to perform a proper job. They may use their power to turn the entire organization against the audit committee.[51]

¶ 4026 BOARD OF DIRECTORS' ROLE

The board of directors (BOD) and its representative audit committee should oversee (1) the integrity, quality, transparency, and reliability of the financial reporting process; (2) the adequacy and effectiveness of the internal control structure in preventing, detecting, and correcting material misstatements in the financial statements; and (3) the effectiveness, efficacy, and objectivity of audit functions.

The SEC gives these signs of a possible fraudulent company:[52]
- Insiders having greater than 50 percent control of the BOD.
- CEO also being chairman of the BOD.
- CEO being the company's founder.
- Lack of an audit committee.

The AICPA, IIA, and ACFE maintain that the BOD should:[53]
- Understand fraud risks.
- Maintain oversight of the fraud risk assessment by ensuring that fraud risk has been considered as part of the organization's risk assessment and strategic plans. This responsibility should be addressed under a periodic agenda item at board meetings when general risks to the organization are considered.
- Monitor management's reports on fraud risks, policies, and control activities, which include obtaining assurance that the controls are effective. The board also should establish mechanisms to ensure it is receiving accurate and timely information from management, employees, internal and external auditors, and other stakeholders regarding potential fraud occurrences.
- Oversee the internal controls established by management.
- Set the appropriate tone at the top through the CEO job description, hiring, evaluation, and succession-planning processes.
- Have the ability to retain and pay outside experts when needed.
- Provide external auditors with evidence regarding the board's active involvement and concern about fraud risk management.

The interaction of the audit committee with the internal and external auditors is described by the AICPA, IIA, and ACFE.[54]

> The audit committee should be aware that the organization's external auditors have a responsibility to plan and perform the audit of the organization's financial statements to obtain reasonable assurance about whether the financial statements are free of material misstatement, whether caused by error or fraud. The extent and limitations of an external audit are generally governed by the applicable audit standards in place. The audit committee should insist on openness and honesty with the external auditors. The external auditors should also have commitment and cooperation from the audit committee. This cooperation includes open and candid dialogue between audit committee members and the external auditors regarding the audit committee's knowledge of any fraud or suspected fraud affecting the organization as well as how the audit committee exercises oversight activities with respect

to the organization's assessment of the risks of fraud and the programs and controls the organization has established to mitigate these risks.

¶ 4031   MANAGEMENT ROLE

Certainly Congress believes that management ought to be held responsible for the financial representations of their companies. The Sarbanes-Oxley Act (SOX) mandates that CEOs and CFOs certify in periodic reports containing financial statements filed with the SEC the appropriateness of financial statements and disclosures.

Specifically, the Act requires that the CEO and CFO must certify in each annual or quarterly report the following:[55]

- Signing officer has reviewed the report;
- Based on the officer's knowledge, the report does not contain any untrue statement of a material fact or omit to state a material fact necessary in order to make the statements made, in light of the circumstances under which such statements were made, not misleading;
- Based on the officer's knowledge, the financial statements and other financial information included in the report fairly present in all material respects, the financial condition and results of operations of the issues as of, and for, the periods presented in the report;
- The signing officers are responsible for establishing and maintaining internal controls and have designed such internal controls to ensure that material information relating to the company and its consolidated subsidiaries is made known to such officers by others within those entities, particularly during the period in which the periodic reports are being prepared. They must also have evaluated the effectiveness of the company's internal controls as of a date within 90 days prior to the report and presented their conclusions about the effectiveness of their internal controls based on their evaluation as of that date.
- The signing officers have disclosed to the company's auditors and the audit committee all significant deficiencies in the design or operation of the internal controls which could adversely affect the company's ability to record, process, summarize, and report financial data and have identified for the auditors any material weaknesses in internal controls and any fraud, whether or not material, that involves management or other employees who have a significant role in the issuer's internal controls; and
- The signing officers have indicated in the report whether there were significant changes in internal control or in other factors that could significantly affect internal controls subsequent to the date of their evaluation, including any corrective actions with regard to significant deficiencies and material weaknesses.

Fraud and abuse know no borders. Three Chinese executives of Zhengzhou Baiwen, a household good wholesaler in China, were charged in 2002 for altering company accounts in 1997 to report a $10.4 million profit rather than an actual loss of $19 million. Fraud 101 states that perpetrators can change their jobs or addresses, but they cannot change who they are.

The Chinese have a tougher policy against white collar crime. In September 2004, Wang Liming, a onetime accounting officer at China Construction, and two other bank employees were executed for defrauding the bank of $2.4 million. In an unrelated corruption case, an officer at the Zhuhai branch of the Bank of China was put to death.[56]

The SEC accused WorldCom senior management of making adjustments to treat $3.9 billion in routine operating expenses as capital investments, which overstated earnings (eventually, $11 billion). The Arthur Andersen audit team had previously asked senior management whether there were any "significant top-side entries."[57]

CEOs are now being squeezed as a result of SOX by BODs, auditors, and lawyers because these watchdogs are finally facing genuine liability for their failures. These watchdogs are trying to protect their hides. Arthur Andersen is out of business, and directors at WorldCom and Enron paid off fraud claims out of their own pockets. Hank Greenberg, former Chairman and CEO of AIG, said that the balance of power in corporate America has shifted.[58]

In March 2005, the SEC said that executives are gatekeepers. Thus, executives can be in trouble if they are in a position to detect wrongdoing below them and do not move forcefully to prevent the fraud. It does not matter if the executive has been lied to. An executive has the responsibility to cut through the lies and try to root out the truth.[59]

A company should have an anti-fraud program, so an auditor or forensic accountant should look for these strategies:

- The company's stance on fraud and other breaches of the ethical code;
- What will be done and by whom in the case that frauds or other breaches are suspected;
- The key initiatives which the company proposes;
- Who will lead these initiatives; and
- Clear deadlines and measures for monitoring effectiveness of implementation.[60]

PCAOB requires an external auditor to evaluate all controls specifically intended to address the risks of fraud that have at least a reasonably possible likelihood of having a material effect on a company's financial statements. A forensic auditor should review this work of the external auditor for the five components on internal controls over financial reporting (see below). These controls include:[61]

- Controls restraining misappropriation of company assets that could result in a material misstatement of the financial statements;
- Company's risk assessment processes;
- Code of ethics/conduct provisions, especially those related to conflicts of interest, related party transactions, illegal acts, and the monitoring of the code by management and the audit committee of the board;
- Adequacy of the internal audit activity and whether the internal audit function reports directly to the audit committee, as well as the extent of the audit committee's involvement and interaction with internal audit; and
- Adequacy of the company's procedure for handling complaints and for accepting confidential submissions of concerns about questionable accounting or auditing matters.

A forensic accountant should not be limited by the materiality principle. The external auditor must perform company-wide anti-fraud programs and controls and work related to other controls that have a pervasive effect on the company, such as general control over the company's electronic data processing. Further, the auditor must "obtain directly the 'principal evidence' about the effectiveness of internal controls."[62]

Once management has assessed the internal controls over financial reporting, their external auditors must evaluate and report on the fairness of management's assessment. If one or more material weaknesses exist at the company's calendar or fiscal year end, an auditor cannot conclude that internal control over financial reporting is effective. If one or more material weaknesses exist at year end, an adverse opinion is necessary. A forensic accountant must be alert to any material weaknesses and focus on these areas.

A material weakness is a deficiency, or a combination of deficiencies, in internal controls over financial reporting, such that there is a reasonable possibility that a material misstatement of the company's annual or interim financial statements will not be prevented or detected on a timely basis. Indicators of material weaknesses in internal controls over financial reporting include:[63]

- Identification of fraud (whether or not material) on the part of senior management (e.g., principal executive and financial officers signing the company's certifications).
- Restatement of previously issued financial statements to reflect the correction of a material restatement.

- Identification by the auditor of a material misstatement of financial statements in the current period in circumstances that indicate that the misstatement would not have been detected by the company's internal control over financial reporting; and
- Ineffective oversight of the company's external financial reporting and internal control over financial reporting by the company's audit committee.

PCAOB's Auditing Standard No. 5 requires the auditor to test the effectiveness of internal control in order to be satisfied that management's is fairly stated. The Board rejects the view that the auditor's work should be limited to evaluating management's assessment process and the testing performed by management and the internal auditors. Instead, the board decided that two opinions were needed to evaluate the effectiveness of internal controls and the requirements of SOX.

Auditing Standard No. 5 suggests that auditors should use a top-down approach to determine the controls to test. Starting at the financial statement level, the auditor should focus on the entity-level controls and work down to the significant accounts and disclosures and their relevant assertions.

The audit of internal controls requires an opinion on management's assessment of the internal controls and another one about the effectiveness of the internal controls over financial reporting. PCAOB has made clear that it attaches equal importance to the evaluation of management assessment and to the direct testing by the auditor of the effectiveness of internal controls over financial reporting (e.g., the accuracy of the financial statements). PCAOB specifically states that the more extensive and reliable management's assessment is, the less expensive and costly the auditor's work has to be.

This Standard No. 5 defines *internal control over financial reporting* to include policies and procedures that:

1. Pertain to the maintenance of records that, in reasonable detail, accurately and fairly reflect the transactions and dispositions of the assets of the company;
2. Provide reasonable assurance that transactions are recorded as necessary to permit preparation of financial statements in accordance with generally accepted principles, and that receipts and expenditures of the company are being made only in accordance with authorizations of management and directors of the company; and
3. Provide reasonable assurance regarding prevention or timely detection of unauthorized acquisition, use or disposition of the company's assets that could have a material effect on the financial statements.

The most common account-specific material weakness occurs in the current accrual accounts (e.g., accounts receivable and inventory accounts). Derivative and income tax accounts often have material weaknesses. Disclosing firms tend to have complex operations, be smaller, and be less profitable.[64]

The most common opinions on the effectiveness of internal control over financial reporting are:

- Unqualified Opinion. An opinion that internal control over financial reporting is effective; no material weaknesses in internal control over financial reporting exist as of the fiscal year-end assessment date.
- Adverse Opinion. An opinion that internal control over financial reporting is not effective; one or more material weaknesses exist as of the fiscal year-end assessment date.
- Disclaimer of Opinion. A report stating that restrictions on the scope of the auditor's work prevent the auditor from expressing an opinion on the company's internal control over financial reporting.

For a regular audit, an unqualified with explanation opinion is probably the most common auditor opinion.

Audit committees, boards of directors, and executives may need to hire forensic accountants if material weaknesses or significant deficiencies are present because these areas have higher potential for fraud. Forensic accountants can play an important role in bridging the gap between a traditional audit and a forensic investigation. Obviously, even an audit cannot (because of cost) and should not be conducted as a full-fledged forensic investigation. In fact, GAAS states that "an auditor typically works within economic limits; the auditor's opinion to be economically useful must be formed within a reasonable length of time and at a reasonable cost."

EYEWITNESS

In February 2005, Ceridian Corp. warned that its accounting firm KPMG would not be able to issue a positive opinion on internal controls, but they expect a clean, unqualified opinion of their financial statements. The material weaknesses include deficiencies in its internally developed software capitalization guidelines; the commencement of amortization of its capital software development costs; its month-end close process; its cost and expense accrual process; its entity-level control process, policies, and practices relating to revenue recognition; and the classification of costs and expenses in the company's consolidated financial statements. The company will change its accounting treatment for its interest-rate and fuel-price derivative securities.

At companies that disclosed a material weakness, more than 60 percent of CFOs either leave or are forced out, according to research firm A.R.C. Morgan. More than 86 percent of these material weaknesses were discovered by external auditors, and not management or compliance consultants. More than one-half of the internal control weaknesses were fraud-related. Audit fees typically grew by 150 percent when a material weakness was found, compared to 30 percent to 50 percent for companies without material weaknesses.[65] By mid-2008, material weaknesses had plunged at large U.S. companies.[66]

These strong indicators, or red flags, of material weakness in the internal control over financial reporting should be noted by forensic accountants:

- Restatement of a previously issued financial statement to reflect the correction of a misstatement;
- Identification by the auditor of a misstatement in financial statement in the current period that was not initially identified by the company's internal control over financial reporting;
- Oversight of the company's external financial reporting, and internal control over financial reporting by the company's audit committee is ineffective;
- The internal audit function or the risk assessment function is ineffective at a company for which such a function needs to be effective for the company to have an effective monitoring or risk assessment, such as for large or highly complex companies;
- For complex entities in highly regulated industries, an effective regulatory compliance function; and
- Identification of fraud of any magnitude on the part of senior management.

PCAOB provides several scenarios illustrating a material weakness. Suppose a company processes a significant number of intercompany transactions on a monthly basis. Intercompany transactions relate to a wide range of activities, including transfers of inventory with intercompany profit between business units, allocation of research and development costs to business units and corporate charges. Individual intercompany transactions are frequently material.

A formal management policy requires monthly reconciliation of intercompany accounts and confirmation of balances between business units. However, there is not a process in place to ensure that these procedures are performed on a consistent basis. As a result, reconciliations of intercompany accounts are not performed on a timely basis, and differences in intercompany accounts are frequent and significant. Management does not perform any alternative controls to investigate significant intercompany account differences.

Based only on these facts, PCAOB says an auditor should determine that this deficiency represents a material weakness for the following reasons: The magnitude of a financial statement misstatement resulting from this deficiency would reasonably be expected to be material, because individual intercompany transactions are frequently material and relate to a wide range of activities. Additionally, actual unreconciled differences in intercompany accounts have been, and are, material. The likelihood of such a misstatement is more than remote because such misstatements have frequently occurred and compensating controls are not effective, either because they are not properly designed or not operating effectively. Taken together, the magnitude and likelihood of misstatement of the financial statements resulting from this internal control deficiency meet the definition of a material weakness.

MATERIAL WEAKNESS INFORMATION NOT USED. Ironically, researchers found that the availability of material weakness information did not appear useful in helping auditors to detect fraud because they did not know how to use the information effectively. This information caused the auditor to assess higher fraud risk and indicated a need to consult with a risk management partner, but they did not generate more risk factors related to fraud or produce higher quality audit programs. The information produced audit programs that were no more effective, and were less efficient. They merely increased the sample size which is ineffective in detecting fraud.[67] Hopefully, forensic accountants can do a better job with this information.

Sarbanes-Oxley requires large companies to have an internal control framework (COSO or similar). PCAOB endorses the COSO model, and it is used more often by U.S. companies. The Committee on Sponsoring Organizations (or COSO) has these five major internal control variables:[68]

1. *Control environment*—management's attitude toward controls, or the "tone at the top."
2. *Risk assessment*—management's assessment of the factors that could prevent the organization from meeting its objectives.
3. *Control activities*—specific policies and procedures that provide a reasonable assurance that the organization will meet its objectives. The control activities should address the risks identified by management in its risk assessment.
4. *Information and communication*—system that allows management to evaluate progress toward meeting the organization's objectives.
5. *Monitoring*—continuous monitoring of the internal control process with appropriate modification made as deemed necessary.

This framework is represented by the COSO Cube:[69]

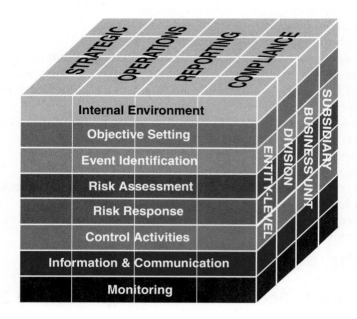

PCAOB outlines these entity-level controls:[70]
- Controls related to the control environment.
- Controls over management override.
- The company's risk assessment process.
- Centralized processing and controls, including shared service environments.
- Controls to monitor results of operations.
- Controls to monitor other controls, including activities of the audit committee and self-assessment programs.
- Controls over the period-end financial reporting process.
- Policies that address significant business control and risk management practices.

PCAOB also provides five principles for establishing a proper environment:[71]
- **Principle 1**: As part of an organization's governance structure, a fraud risk management program should be in place, including a written policy (or policies) to convey the expectations of the board of directors and senior management regarding managing fraud risk.
- **Principle 2**: Fraud risk exposure should be assessed periodically by the organization to identify specific potential schemes and events that the organization needs to mitigate.
- **Principle 3**: Prevention techniques to avoid potential key fraud risk events should be established, where feasible, to mitigate possible impacts on the organization.
- **Principle 4**: Detection techniques should be established to uncover fraud events when preventive measures fail or unmitigated risks are realized.
- **Principle 5**: A reporting process should be in place to solicit input on potential fraud, and a coordinated approach to investigation and corrective action should be used to help ensure potential fraud is addressed appropriately and timely.

The implementation of an anonymous employee hotline is an important device to carry out Principle 5 since tips are the most common method of detecting fraud. SOX requires the Audit Committee to establish and oversee a confidential reporting system. Making the anonymous hotline open to participants beyond employee (e.g., vendors, contractors, and general public) can maximize results.

These are features of a well-designed hotline program:[72]
- Option for anonymity.
- Organization-wide (global) and available 24/7, ideally by telephone, with professionally-trained interviewers in all local languages.
- Single hotline for all ethics-related issues.
- Dual dissemination of the information received so that no single person controls the information, with criteria for immediate escalation where warranted, and for notification of the Audit Committee when financial irregularities or senior management are involved.
- Case management protocols, including processes for the timely investigation of hotline reports and documentation of the results.
- Management analysis of trends and comparison to norms.
- Data security and retention policies and procedures.
- Customization to comply with the laws of foreign jurisdiction and to address the cultural difference.
- Ongoing messaging to motivate everyone in the organization, as well as vendors, to use the hotline.

¶ 4041   FORENSIC ACCOUNTANT'S ROLE

When Forensic Accountants Investigate Where Internal Auditors Fear to Tread

Mentioned previously, financial scandals such as collapses of Enron and WorldCom moved Congress to pass the Sarbanes-Oxley Act. In motion is a sweeping reform program led by the Securities and Exchange Commission, which in turn has mandated a flurry of activity by all the financial and accounting organizations in its regulatory sphere. How much will change?

The Sarbanes-Oxley Act and SAS No. 99 put pressure on management, audit committees, chief executives, CFOs, external accountants, and internal auditors to incorporate forensic accounting techniques into their jobs. Now CEO/CFOs must certify in each 10-K and 10-Q that the signing officer has reviewed the report, and state that based upon the officer's knowledge there are no material misstatements or omissions and the financial statements fairly represent the financial condition and results of operations.

A New Paradigm

One could argue that before Enron and the other scandals surfaced, no one accepted ultimate responsibility for finding fraud. Independent auditors disclaim such responsibility in their engagement letters. Internal auditors put disclaimers in their charters. Management looked to audit committees. Audit committees looked to independent auditors. Independent auditors looked to management. Were it not for the phenomenal amount of investment funds and jobs lost by innocent individuals, the whole business would remind one of the "Who's on first" classic comedy routine.

Will fraud detection now become primarily the responsibility of forensic accountants? Will there be forensic sleuths hired every year for the annual audit or carried on staff? Will forensic accountants have a special role in each internal audit function? Will audit committees insist on the services of a forensic accountant? The answer: No one really knows.

The approach up until now based on Sarbanes-Oxley is to make *everyone* responsible for fighting fraud by increasing all parties' responsibilities for uncovering such fraud in every direction at every step in the process.

A forensic accountant may or may not be a permanent member of an audit engagement. An inhouse forensic accountant may be brought into an external audit for purposes of complying with SAS No. 99. A report by the AICPA Fraud Task Force[73] states that the forensic accountant is required to follow auditing standards. Where the forensic accountant finds that indicia of fraud are clearly present, the audit may change to a forensic or fraud investigation. Thus, investigative techniques may be performed by the forensic accountant that are outside the scope of a traditional audit. Because litigation may be possible, such an investigator is required to follow both the Statement of Standards for Consulting Services[74] and the Code of Professional Conduct.

If, instead, a forensic accountant is brought into an audit engagement to perform a separate investigation (and not as an adjunct to an audit), such an engagement is *consulting*, and consulting standards must be followed. Because litigation may occur in the future, the forensic investigator may eventually be an expert or lay witness.[75]

For example, Bruce Dubinsky was hired by the American Federation of Teachers when they suspected one of their locals had engaged in some "bookkeeping hanky-panky," resulting in as much as $5 million stolen by the local union. Dubinsky "tracks corporate fraud, peeling away layers of fake numbers, phony names and false records to dig up white-collar dirt."[76] Dubinsky says that "fraudsters often use the same pattern most of the time, such as always making up company names with three letters."[77]

Enter the Forensic Accountant

The knowledge, skills, and abilities of the forensic accounting sleuth will become more refined and a well-developed body of knowledge will be created. Improvement in training and education will greatly enhance and standardize competencies. With improved professionalism, demand for the forensic accountant will increase as corporations, audit committees, internal auditors, and management come to appreciate the special talents and objective approach such accountants can take. In some situations the forensic accountant will be brought in to investigate the minute any irregularities surface. In other situations the independent auditors may measure risk factors and create policy that brings the sleuths in when certain scores are attained. In still other situations, the internal audit function may call for bringing in the forensic accountant at random times as a matter of routine. Although forensic accounting services have been used for many years, the specialty itself is in its infancy and will continue to evolve for many years to come. However, past events present clear evidence that external independent auditing, internal auditing, audit committee work, and management review will not eliminate financial report fraud. The cost of such fraud being what it is, such a state of affairs suggests a bright future for the forensic specialists regardless of who actually initiates the assignment.

Forensic Mindset

SAS No. 99 requires external auditors to be skeptical. Forensic accountants must appreciate the fact that financial statements may be wrong. Some companies use creative accounting techniques to disguise damaging information, to provide a distorted picture of the financial health of the business, to smooth out erratic earnings, or to boost anemic or lack of earnings. Forensic accountants should adopt a healthy skepticism in reading and evaluating financial reports. Businesses are often clever in hiding these accounting tricks and gimmicks, so auditors must be ever alert to the signs of outright financial shenanigans. As Charles Manson said, "total paranoid is total awareness." Forensic accountant Bruce Dubinsky says "It's not finding what you can see, but seeing what you can find."[78]

Howard R. Davia divides fraud auditing into two types: reactive and proactive. External auditors, in general, do not audit proactively; instead they are looking for fraud that will result in material misstatements in the financial statements. In proactive auditing, the auditor has few clues that fraud has occurred, so audit procedures for conducting proactive fraud-specific auditing are different from procedures used to practice reactive fraud-specific auditing.[79]

Skepticism means that even trusted employees or executives may be a fraudster. Reverend Michael Jude Fay, former longtime pastor of St. John Roman Catholic Church admitted in federal court to stealing as much as $1 million of parishioners' contributions. He used church money to support a life style, including trips to Europe, the Caribbean, and across the United States. He deposited church monies into several personal bank accounts and bought personal items on the parish's American Express card. Fay was in a romantic relationship with a Philadelphia event planner.[80]

A skeptical mindset encourages a person to ask these questions:

- How might a fraud perpetrator exploit weaknesses in the system of controls?
- How could a perpetrator override or circumvent controls?
- What could a perpetrator do to conceal the fraud?[81]

Forensic accountants note small errors and irregularities because they may point to the modus operandi of corrupt executives, employees, thieves, embezzlers, and defrauders. Because criminals may not be able to bury all of their tracks, forensic auditors look for the tip of the fraudulent iceberg. Basically, external auditors take a big picture, macro view of books, records, and controls, whereas the forensic accountant takes a micro view of a business.[82] Sophisticated software is used to sift through files, flagging relationships or patterns that normally do not occur.[83]

Audit Tests

The SEC expressed concern about the reliability of financial statements and the very concept of audits performed by private-sector auditors who are largely self-regulated. As a consequence, the SEC requested the Public Oversight Board (POB) to sponsor a thorough and objective examination of auditing, from top to bottom, in order to explore the effectiveness of the audit process. An independent private sector body, the POB was created in 1977 by the AICPA to monitor and comment on matters that affect public confidence in the integrity of the audit process.

An auditor should perform either tests of details or precise substantive procedures, not merely test of controls. Because management can override controls, tests of controls may not be effective in detecting fraud. Because of the attitudinal shift in professional skepticism, the external auditor should not use the work of the internal auditors in performing the tests for searching for fraud. External auditors, however, may consider the results of internal auditors' test results designed to detect fraud in deciding which of their own tests to perform.

The Panel on Audit Effectiveness recommended that surprise or unpredictable elements should be incorporated into the audit tests, including:

- Recounts of inventory and unannounced visits to locations.
- Interviews of financial and non-financial client personnel in different locations.
- Requests for written confirmations from client employees regarding matters about which they have made representations to the auditors.
- Tests of accounts not normally performed annually.
- Tests of accounts traditionally or frequently deemed "low risk."

EYEWITNESS

Enron's crude oil trading operation based in Valhalla, New York, was fictitious according to one auditor. "It was pretend. It was a playhouse. There were a lot of expensive people working there, and it was impressive looking, but it wasn't legitimate work." The traders were keeping two sets of books, one for legitimate purposes—to show Enron and auditors from Arthur Andersen—another set in which to record their ill-gotten gains. The auditor must try to think like a crook and think outside the box. SAS No. 99 states that members of an "audit team should not be satisfied with less than persuasive evidence because of a belief that management is honest." Forensic auditors need to have the same skeptical attitude that the United Nations' weapons inspectors needed in Iraq.

SAS No. 99 does not require external auditors to make enquiries of "others," as opposed to management. External auditors and forensic accountants should talk to and make enquiries of others below management level. If asked, employees may be willing to report suspicious activities.

Use independent sources for evaluating management, such as financial analysts. Search the Internet for information about the company and top management. Auditors and forensic accountants need to follow the performance history of executives and directors. If a company has an anonymous reporting system (e.g., a hotline or suggestion boxes), obtain information about the incidents reported and possibly follow up when assessing fraud risk.

Criminal background checks of executives and employees may be appropriate. Here are some Internet sites:

- Federal Bureau of Prisons-since 1982; *www.bop.gov*. Click on "Inmate Info.," then "BOP Inmate Locator."
- Crime Time. *www.crimetime.com*. Click on "Sex Offender Info."
- Background Check Gateway *www.backgroundcheckgateway.com*. Click on "Step 3: Start Your Investigation," then "Criminal History."

All of the above services can be used free of charge.

MONEY TALKED IN ENRON AUDITS. David Duncan, the Arthur Andersen lead auditor for the Enron audit team, was too close to Enron and made too much money from the corporation to be objective ($1 million per year for Duncan). For the year ending August 2000, Andersen received total fees of $58 million from Enron, more than $1 million a week. Duncan was fired by Arthur Andersen and later pleaded guilty to shredding documents in return for cooperating with federal prosecutors. When Duncan invoked his Fifth Amendment rights before Congress, Representative James Greenwood opened questioning by saying: "Enron has robbed the bank, Andersen provided the getaway car, and you were at the wheel."[84]

Duncan had a decade-long relationship with Enron and had been lead auditor for five years. His office was in the Enron building, and he lunched with Enron's CEO and attended U.S. Masters golf tournaments with him. Duncan "hewed to this client's wishes and sparred with his partners" to help Enron to realize its goals with Byzantine transactions. His personality was soft, and he was happiest when playing golf with Rick Causey, Andersen's most important client.[85] Eventually he directed the effort to shred a ton of Enron-related records after Andersen received a request from the SEC for information about Enron.

After Enron collapsed, Duncan's pastor talked about the pressure Enron put on Duncan. "He [Duncan] said it [pressure] was unrelenting. It was a constant fight. Wherever he drew a line, Enron pushed the line—he was under constant pressure from year to year to push the line." Duncan pressed the Enron point of view with Andersen's professional standards group, and sometimes he was less than forthcoming with members of the group.[86]

Brainstorming

SAS No. 99 now requires external auditors to blend consideration of fraud seamlessly into the audit process and continually update it until the audit is completed. Brainstorming is now a required procedure to generate ideas about how fraud might be committed and concealed within the entity. Forensic accountants should attempt to get minutes of these sessions or engage in similar sessions. During such sessions, Michael Ramos, a CPA, says no ideas or questions are dumb. No one owns ideas, and there should be no hierarchy. Ramos suggests that excessive note-taking should not be allowed.[87]

Still another author suggests that it is best to write ideas down rather than saying them out loud. However, for liability and discoverability reasons, notes should be limited. Mr. Wellner, a journalist, makes these recommendations also:[88]

- Take plenty of breaks.
- Best ideas come at the end of a session.
- Important to *not* define the problem too narrowly or too broadly.
- Goal should be quantity, not quality.
- Geniuses develop their most innovative ideas when they are generating the greatest number of ideas.
- No such thing as a bad idea.
- Many companies are great at coming up with good ideas, but lousy at evaluating and implementing them.

There are three types of brainstorming:
- *Open brainstorming*: unstructured; few rules; free-for-all; someone should record ideas.
- *Round-robin brainstorming*: start with no talking, silent period; assigned homework ahead; each individual presents own ideas; each member has a turn.
- *Electronic brainstorming*: shortens meetings, increases ideas, and reduces personalizing ideas because an idea's author remains anonymous.[89]

There are potential pitfalls while brainstorming:
- *Group domination*: one or two participants dominating the process can quickly squelch the creative energies of the group as a whole, reducing the likelihood the team will identify any actual fraud risks.
- *Social loafing*: participants disengage from the process, expecting other team members to pick up the slack.
- *Group think*: team members become so concerned with reaching consensus that they fail to realistically evaluate all ideas or suggestions.
- *Group shift*: avoid allowing the team to take an extreme position on fraud risk.[90]

Financial Statement Fraud Categories and Red Flags

The following paragraphs explore the most important financial fraud categories and red flags. Certain red flags or fraud identifiers may suggest that a company is engaging in financial shenanigans or fraud is present. Fraud identifiers help determine the behavior and origin of the most common fraudsters in the business database.

SAS No. 99 suggests that fraudulent financial reporting may occur as follows:
- Manipulation, falsification, or alteration of accounting records, or supporting documents from which financial statements are prepared.
- Misrepresentation in or intentional omission from the financial statements of events, transactions, or other significant information.
- Intentional misapplication of accounting principles relating to amounts, classification, manner of presentation, or disclosure.[91]

¶ 4051   OVERSTATED REVENUES

Overstated revenues pose such a huge fraud problem that the issue is covered in some detail in the following section. AICPA Statement on Auditing Standards No. 99 provides the following helpful suggestions for uncovering improper revenue recognition:
- Perform substantive analytical procedures relating to revenue using disaggregated data (for example, comparing revenue reported by month and by product line or business segment during the current reporting period with comparable prior periods). Computer-assisted audit techniques may be useful in identifying unusual or unexpected revenue relationships or transactions.
- Confirm with customers certain relevant contract terms and the absence of side agreements, because the appropriate accounting often is influenced by such terms or agreements. Some examples would be acceptance criteria, delivery and payment terms, the absence of future or continuing vendor obligations, the right to return the product, guaranteed resale amounts, and cancellation or refund provisions that often are relevant in such circumstances.
- Inquire of the entity's sales and marketing personnel or in-house legal counsel regarding sales or shipments near the end of the period and their knowledge of any unusual terms or conditions associated with these transactions.
- Be physically present at one or more locations at period end to observe goods being shipped or being readied for shipment (or returns awaiting processing) and performing other appropriate sales and inventory cutoff procedures.

- For those situations for which revenue transactions are electronically initiated, processed, and recorded, test controls to determine whether they provide assurance that recorded revenue transactions occurred and are properly recorded.

AOL created ad revenues out of thin air. With an obsession to get advertising revenue in the door, "Nobody there appears to have paid much attention to whether the business deals at issue were really producing ad 'revenues' by any acceptable definition…." At least $90 million of revenues were expunged by mid-2003, with another $400 million contested.[92]

MiniScribe, one of the world's largest disk-drive makers, in the late 1980s was surreptitiously shipping bricks instead of disk drives to the Far East and receiving credit from the bank for the amount of the shipments. "After all," he says "it's going to be 90 days until they ship the brick back to you." MiniScribe's public accounting firm, Coopers & Lybrand, didn't catch this false-revenue scam during its regular audits—but a forensic accountant did.[93]

¶ 4061   MANAGEMENT ESTIMATES

Management estimates is another area for fraudulent misstatements, such as asset valuation, estimates relating to specific transactions (such as acquisitions, restructurings, or disposals of a segment of a business), bad debt allowance, and pension and other postretirement benefit obligations. Compare current management judgments and assumption with prior periods and with those of other companies in the same industry.

¶ 4071   PRO FORMAS CAN MISLEAD

Forensic accountants ignore the glossy photos and fancy pie charts in annual reports. Pro forma statements are taken with many grains of salt. Pro forma refers to "as if" adjustments to financial information. Pro formas (or cash earnings or operating earnings) are often issued with many expenses excluded, resulting in "hide and seek" earnings. Accountants must focus on the earnings figures that are prepared according to GAAP.

The SEC went after Trump Hotel for making a small gain nearly five times larger in an October 1999 earnings release.[94] The company reported a pro forma profit for Q3 1999 of $14 million, excluding a one-time charge of $81.4 million, and pro forma earnings per share of 63 cents, exceeding First Call estimates of 54 cents. The release quoted then-CEO Nicholas Ribis as ascribing the better-than-expected numbers to improved operating performance.

The SEC claimed that the release failed to mention that the earnings calculation actually included a one-time accounting gain of $17.2 million, stemming from the termination of a lease agreement—the sort of nonrecurring item that pro forma earnings are supposed to ignore. Without that gain, Trump Hotels would have posted a pro forma profit of about $3 million, or 14 cents per share. In other words, Trump Hotels surreptitiously included the one-time gain in the pro forma calculations while publicly excluding the one-time charge.

Trump's share price rose 7.8 percent on the day of the release and fell 6 percent three days later when an analyst discovered the one-time accounting gain. Stephen M. Cutler, director of the SEC's Enforcement Division, said that "the method of presenting the pro forma numbers and the positive spin the company put on them were materially misleading."

¶ 4081   EARNINGS PROBLEMS: MASKING REDUCED CASH FLOW

One of the most significant red flags is a downward trend in earnings. Companies are required to disclose earnings for the last three years in the income statement, so forensic accountants must avoid looking just at the "bottom line." The trend in operating income is just as important as the trend in earnings.

To a certain extent, management can exploit GAAP to produce the appearance of increased earnings. Some popular shenanigans include booking sales on long-term contracts before the customer has paid up, delaying the recording of expenses, failing to recognize the obsolescence of inventory as an expense, and reducing advertising and research and development expenditures.

The accountant can use the cash flow statement to check the reliability of earnings. If net income is moving up while cash flow from operations is drifting downward, something may be wrong. Customers may be paying too slowly or inventory may be ballooning. (Cash from operations should not increase or decrease at a different rate than net income.) Ideally, net cash from operations grows steadily.

In 1998, 1999, and 2000 Xerox improperly used a $100 million reserve to offset related expenses.

Microsoft Corporation survived in 2001 because it had $13.4 billion in cash flow from operations. However, WorldCom, Dynergy, Adelphia Communications, and Tyco International prove that companies can inflate their cash flow by improperly booking expenses as capital expenditures.

¶ 4091   EARNINGS BEFORE INTEREST, TAXES, DEPRECIATION, AND AMORTIZATION (EBITDA)

EBITDA is a popular valuation method for capital-intensive industries. Capital-intensive companies (for which fixed assets are a large part of the balance sheet) offer the best opportunities for shifting expenses onto the balance sheet by aggressive, unethical companies. Auditors should look at the capitalized accounts because of the possible fraud and abuse. Unless amounts paid out will create a long-lasting asset, the expenditures must be expensed.

Roman Weil of the University of Chicago says that most external auditors believe that management is honest and tells the truth. But by taking a small sample audit of capital expenditures, the auditor may miss the fraud altogether, especially when the accounting function is centralized at one location.

WorldCom's improper accounting practice greatly inflated EBITDA ($10.5 billion rather than the real $6.3 billion in 2001). An internal auditor found the WorldCom cooked books, and the resulting financial restatement was more than six times that of Enron Corporation's.

¶ 4101   EXCESSIVE DEBT

Crucial to determining whether a company can weather difficult times is the debt factor. Companies burdened by too much debt lack the financial flexibility to respond to crises and to take advantage of opportunities. Small companies with heavy debt are particularly vulnerable in economic downturns. Investment professionals pay special attention to a company's debt-to-equity ratio, the total debt to stockholders' or owners' equity. Whereas the optimum ratio varies from industry to industry, the amount of stockholders' or owners' equity should significantly exceed the amount of debt. This information is available on the balance sheet and in the subsection of the Cash Flow Statement called *financing activities*. Debt should grow proportionately with sales and earnings.

¶ 4111   INVENTORY PROBLEMS

Forensic accountants uncover inventory problems by looking at the ratio of accounts receivable to sales and the ratio of inventory to cost of goods sold. If accounts receivable exceed 15 percent of annual sales and inventory exceeds 25 percent of cost of goods sold, red flags are raised. If customers aren't paying their bills and/or the company is saddled with aging merchandise, problems will eventually arise.

Overstated Inventories and Receivables

Overstated inventories and receivables are often at the heart of corporate fraud, resulting in future declines in profits. As significant as the ratios are, trends over time are also important. Although there may be good reasons for a company to have bloated or increasing inventory (California Micro being a case in point) or receivables (as with BDO Seidman), it is important to determine whether the condition is a symptom of financial difficulty.

Inventory Plugging

Inventory fraud is an easy way to produce instant earnings and improve the balance sheet.

Crazy Eddie, an electronic equipment retailer, allegedly recorded sales to other chains as if they were retail sales (rather than wholesale sales). For the fiscal year ending March 1, 1985, an accountant, Sammy Antar, falsified inventories by $3 million, and by the next year, the false inventory reached more than $10 million. The fraud may have unraveled because Eddie's wife and sister caught him with another woman on New Year's Eve.

Balancing Act

Inventory, sales, and receivables usually move in tandem because customers do not pay up front if they can avoid it. Neither inventory nor accounts receivable should grow faster than sales. Furthermore, inventory normally moves in tandem with accounts payable because a healthy company does not often pay cash at the delivery dock as purchases are received.

In 2000, Purchase Pro's accounts receivable soared from $13.2 million to $23.4 million, whereas its revenue during the same period was only $17.3 million. Purchase Pro backdated and forged contracts to meet revenue projections.

Attacking Inventory Problems

Inventory quantities fraud may confront an auditor, and SAS No. 99 covers some suggestions such as observing inventory counts on an unannounced basis or conducting inventory counts at *all* locations on the same date. Once one location is counted, someone may have to watch the location overnight to avoid merchandise being removed. An auditor may rigorously examine the contents of boxed items, the manner in which the goods are stacked (e.g., hollow squares) or labeled, and the quality (that is, purity, grade, or concentration) of liquid substances such as perfumes or specialty chemicals. A specialist may be helpful in this regard, and additional testing of count sheets, tags, or other records, or the retention of copies of these records, may be needed to minimize the risk of subsequent alteration or inappropriate compilation.

After the physical count, an auditor may wish to further test the reasonableness of the count quantities. SAS No. 99 suggests comparing quantities for the current period with prior periods by class or category of inventory, location or other criteria, and comparison of quantities counted with perpetual records. Also, computer-assisted audit techniques may be used to further test the compilation of the physical inventory counts (e.g., sorting by tag number to test tag controls or by item serial number to test the possibility of item omission or duplication).

¶ 4121   CPA PROBLEMS

Auditor switching and the financial condition of a company are correlated to a certain extent. Firms in the midst of financial distress switch auditors more frequently than healthy companies. Also, solo auditors are lower quality, and the use of a solo auditor is a red flag according to recent research.[95]

¶ 4131   SALES AND EXPENSES PROBLEMS

Hyped Sales

Sales figures may be inflated in several ways that are difficult to detect:
- Recognizing sales on disputed claims against customers
- Recognizing sales without shipping the goods
- Recognizing full sales amount for partial shipments
- Improperly holding the accounting year open in order to recognize sales
- Recognizing sales on transactions where refunds or concessions are granted
- Understating allowances for sales discounts

Forensic accountants should compare the trend in sales with the trend in net income. Always ask for and read side agreements, especially those involving sales.

EYEWITNESS

From 1999 to 2001, HealthSouth's net income increased nearly 500 percent, but revenues grew only five percent. On March 19, 2003, the SEC said that HealthSouth faked at least $1.4 billion in profits since 1999 under the auditing eyes of Ernst & Young. The SEC said that HealthSouth started cooking its numbers in 1986, which Ernst & Young failed to find over 17 years. HealthSouth also inflated its cash balances.

According to court documents, Centennial CEO Emanuel Pinez used a form of trickery rarely seen: He hyped sales by using his ample personal fortune to fund purchases. "Any auditor would have had a hard time catching that," says William Coyne, an accounting professor at Babson College. Centennial Director John J. Shields, a former CEO of Computervision Corp., says in an affidavit that Pinez admitted to him that he altered inventory tags and recorded sales on products that were never shipped, although Pinez's lawyer maintains his defendant was innocent.

In 2000, Rent-Way disclosed that its CAO had artificially reduced the company's expenses—a reduction of $127 million. There was no one big item, but there were a dozen smaller instances of hiding or understating expenses, from automobile maintenance to insurance payments. The stock plummeted 72 percent, from $23.44 to $6.50.[96]

Possibly the largest accounting fraud, WorldCom, involved the shifting of at least $3.8 billion of line-cost expenses (and possibly labor costs) to capital accounts. Line-costs are the fees WorldCom paid to other carriers for using their networks. These ongoing operating expenses should not have been capitalized, and the growth of the balance sheet should have tipped off the company's auditors, Arthur Andersen, to the oldest trick in the book.[97]

Off-Balance Sheet Items

Special-purpose entities present special opportunities for masking problems in sales and expenses, offering the means to manipulate stock prices, create nonexistent assets, and disguise expenses.

Enron had more than 2,500 offshore accounts and approximately 850 special-purpose entities (SPEs). Enron created and capitalized four special-purpose entities (SPEs) by issuing its own stock in exchange for about $800 million of notes receivable (thereby increasing shareholder equity by $800 million). GAAP requires such notes receivable to be presented as a reduction in shareholders' equity (and not an asset).[98] SPEs are especially troublesome when a company officer is in charge, and the company is engaging in transactions with the entities. Enron's Chewco SPE put $600 million of income onto Enron's books, as well as earning CFO Andrew Fastow $30 million. Had the company given some sort of guarantee to the SPE? Adelphia Communications hid billions of dollars of off-balance debt, much of it owed by the founding family.

In a comparison of published financial statements and tax return book balance sheets, three researchers found that 1998 tax return assets exceeded financial statement assets by $1.9 trillion. Tax return liabilities exceeded financial statement liabilities by $900 billion because of off-balance sheet financing entities. Parent corporations omitted book losses, assets, and liabilities of special-purpose entities from their consolidated financial accounts but included these same amounts on their consolidated returns.[99]

Apparently, Enron did not tell Arthur Andersen that certain Enron limited partnerships did not have enough outside equity and that more than $700 million in debt should have been included on Enron's statements. This oversight caused more than a $400 million reduction in prior period earnings.

¶ 4141   BIG BATH

Forensic accountants should beware of companies making write-offs directly against earnings—especially large amounts. This scheme is called the "big bath." Profits are depressed for that year, but future earnings look much better as the company reduces the unneeded reserves. If accounts receivable are written off, sales may have been inflated.

¶ 4151   BALANCE SHEET ACCOUNT PROBLEMS

Because the balance sheet is a snapshot of a business's financial position at one moment, management may be tempted to manipulate balance sheet accounts to be listed.

For its 1997 fiscal year, America Online, Inc. showed $385 million in assets on its balance sheet called deferred subscriber acquisition costs. This amount represented new subscriber advertising costs that should have been charged against income as an expense.

AOL gave $9.5 million in cash to Purchase Pro.com Inc. for $30 million in stock warrants in the company. Then AOL booked the difference—$20.5 million—as ad and commerce revenue. AOL earned the warrants under a marketing deal that included distributing Purchase Pro software. These warrants gave AOL the right to buy shares in Purchase Pro for a penny, hence booking $20.5 million in advertising and commerce revenue in its December 2000 quarter and another $7 million in the March 2001 period. Thus, AOL recognized a total of $28 million of income.

The Parmalat deceptions illustrate the need to confirm even cash accounts. Parmalat, an Italian dairy company, had a nonexistent Bank of America bank account worth $4.83 billion. A SEC lawsuit asserts that Parmalat "engaged in one of the largest and most brazen corporate financial frauds in history." Apparently, the auditors Grant Thornton relied on a fake Bank of America confirmation prepared by the company.

SAS No. 99 does *not* prohibit clients from preparing confirmations. This fraud continued for more than a decade, and at least $9 billion went unaccounted for. Therefore, the audited company should not be in control of the confirmation process. The owner treated the public company as if it was his own bank account. An unaware phone operator was the fake chief executive of more than 25 affiliated companies. Some $3.6 billion in bonds claimed to be repurchased had not really been bought.

Companies may be tempted to hide debts or liabilities from the balance sheet using these techniques:

1. Using the equity method (rather than trading security and available for sale methods). Nets the assets and liabilities of the investee.
2. Lease accounting (arguing that leases are operating leases). Understates 10 to 15 percent.
3. Pension accounting—netting of the projected benefit obligation and the pension assets. Must un-net them.
4. Hiding debt inside special–purpose entities—trillions of dollars of SPE debt is off the books (e.g., securitization, SPE borrowings, synthetic leases).

Professor Edward Ketz says financial statement readers can make analytical adjustments by searching footnotes for 1, 2, and 3. But there are generally no disclosures for asset securitization, SPE borrowings, and synthetic leases.[100]

Leasing is a favorite way to understate debt on the balance sheet. Airlines have the ability to run their fleet of planes using operating leases whose costs do not have to be fully shown on the balance sheet. David Tweedie, chairman of the International Accounting Standards Board, says his ambition is to fly on an aircraft that is on an airline's balance sheet before he dies.[101]

BAD BALANCE SHEETS. Adelphia acquired a number of companies and as a result increased its debt from $3.5 to $12.6 billion. To improve the balance sheet, the Rigas family created some entities controlled by the family and moved some of the debt onto the special purpose entities without consolidating them. At least $3.1 billion of the debt was owed by the Rigas family, but was not reported on the Adelphia balance sheet.

In a similar fashion, the Baptist Foundation of Arizona (BFA) set up two subsidiaries owned by insiders during the 1989 real estate bubble bust. BFA then sold the depressed real estate to the subsidiaries at book value and recorded notes receivables at the book value amount (and not the FMV). Presto, a cleaner balance sheet.

¶ 4161   PENSION PLAN PROBLEMS

Under pension plan accounting, the expected long-term rate of return (not the actual rate of return or the dollars actually received) is what impacts net income. During rising stock markets, pension fund investments can inflate the bottom line. Small changes in assumptions can make a huge difference in net earnings. Some companies use rates as high as 8 percent, because an upward change of one percentage point can increase the bottom line by more than $100 million.

In 2012, unfunded pension liabilities for private companies were huge, with General Electric having the largest negative liability of $21.6 billion. Companies with more than $10 billion underfunding were AT&T, Boeing, Exxon Mobil, and Ford. At the end of 2011, the value of assets in defined benefit plans in companies in the S&P 500 index was $1.32 trillion, but the value of future obligations was $1.68 trillion, a shortfall of around $355 billion or 22 percent of promised benefits.[102]

The Pension Benefit Guarantee Corporation (PBGC) is a publicly created but privately funded group that insures the U.S. occupational pension plans. In November 2012, the PBGC reported a record gap between available assets and projected liabilities of $34 billion. This shortfall did not consider future premiums or insolvencies.[103]

The inability of the PBGC to set premiums on employers that considers the risk that each company presents keeps the PBGC from stabilizing its finances. The PBGC would like to set premiums on companies like agencies insure deposits at national banks.[104]

Social security is paying out more than the system takes in, and its operating deficit will be more than $800 billion over the next 10 years, and federal and state pension systems also are underwater. The unfunded liabilities for federal employees total more than $630 billion, and state pension plans are underwater by at least $100 billion. All total, unfunded pension liabilities add at least $2.5 trillion to U.S.'s $17 trillion Federal debt and the state and local debt of $2.8 trillion.[105]

¶ 4171   RESERVE ESTIMATES

Companies may play around with reserve estimates that are found on most balance sheets. Reserves are established to cover future adverse developments, such as warranty claims and bad debts. Because companies have huge discretion as to their size, the smaller the reserve, the less costly to the bottom line.

The SEC sued Xerox in 2002 stating that the company increased its earnings by almost $500 million by placing into income so-called cushion reserves. Xerox agreed to pay a $10 million civil penalty to settle the SEC dispute without admitting or denying wrongdoing with respect to approximately 20 reserves. Then in mid-2002, Xerox admitted that its pretax income was inflated by 3.6 percent, or $1.41 billion over the past five years. The SEC said Xerox artificially booked more of lease revenue upfront rather than over the life of the lease.

In August 2002, bankrupt WorldCom disclosed another $3.3 billion of book cooking on top of the $3.85 billion uncovered in June 2002. This new fraudulent accounting involved reversing a "cookie jar" of reserves for bad debts, taxes, and litigation, sometimes called cookie-jar accounting. One week earlier the company's CFO, Scott Sullivan, and controller David Myers were arrested and charged with hiding at least $4 billion of expenses and lying to investors and regulators.[106]

Reserve reversing is common, especially after a merger. A company will overestimate a merger/acquisition reserve, and then inflate earnings after the merger. CUC International (later Cendant) overstated its merger/purchase reserves.

¶ 4181   PERSONAL PIGGY BANK

Family member owners may use a corporation as a personal piggy bank at the expense of public investors and creditors. Forensic accountants must be especially careful with companies that are controlled by a few family members.

The founder and two sons of Adelphia Communication were charged and handcuffed in 2002 by the SEC for allegedly looting the cable TV provider and hiding more than $3.1 billion in off-balance sheet debt from investor. These undisclosed funds were used to buy timberland, invest in a golf course, and help run the Buffalo Sabres hockey team. The company falsified the number of cable television subscribers and created fake management fees to conceal the alleged fraud (all under the watchful eyes of Deloitte & Touche).

Not only was former Tyco executive Dennis Kozlowski charged with sales-tax evasion on art work, but *The Wall Street Journal* accused him of treating his company as a personal piggy bank. He "spent more than $135 million in Tyco funds to finance a lifestyle fit for the Sultan of Brunei. (He had a $6,000 shower curtain!) The company gave him a no-interest loan of $19 million to buy a 15,000–square foot mansion in Boca Raton, and then kicked in another $13 million to help him pay taxes on that loan. None of these benefits was disclosed to Tyco shareholders."[107]

Hong Kong company Akai Holdings Ltd., and Semi-Tech Group, used its acquisition of Singer Sewing Machine Co. as a piggy bank in a case of poor corporate governance. Akai was a holding company owned by James Henry Ting. In 1989, Semi-Tech acquired 138-year-old Singer Sewing Machine Company, and Singer paid $157.5 million to Akai for shares in G.M. Pfaff at twice the value of Pfaff's publicly traded shares. Singer paid a $50 million deposit to purchase a Russian sewing machine factory. Although the acquisition was not consummated, apparently Akai kept $44 million of the deposit. Also, Akai took $1.1 billion from Singer through stock and bond issues, which fatally weakened Singer.[108]

At the beginning of 1999, Akai financial statements showed $2.3 billion in assets, including $262 million in cash. One year later the company was bankrupt. James Ting sold his $5 million Hong Kong compound in June 2000, and disappeared. Semi-Tech became bankrupt in 1999, leaving $528 million in debt. Singer went bankrupt leaving these interesting facts about Ting's empire:

Liquidators found half-a-dozen suspicious transactions in Akai totaling $315 million.

Most of the $2.3 billion assets inside Akai at the beginning of 1999 were gone by the end of the year.

In November 1998, Ting "bought" 50 percent of a U.S. company, MicroMain Corp., for $38.5 million. A year later Akai wrote off the entire amount, and the managing director of MicroMain said no investment was made. What happened to the $38.5 million?[109]

¶ 4191   BARTER DEALS

A number of Internet companies used barter transactions (or noncash transactions) to increase their revenues. For example, 13.4 percent of Seitel 2001 revenue was from noncash transactions. VeriSign received $37 million (3.8 percent) of total revenue in 2001 from barter deals. The problem is how to value this funny money. When an accountant is dealing with advertising, an interpretation of IAS 18 states that a seller can reliably measure revenue at fair market value only by reference to nonbarter transactions that:

- Involve advertising similar to the advertising in the barter transaction;
- Occur frequently;
- Represent a predominant number of transactions and amount of revenue when compared to all transactions to provide advertising that is similar to the advertising in the barter transaction;
- Involve cash and/or another form of consideration (such as marketable securities, non-monetary assets, and other services) that has a reliably measurable fair value; and
- Do not involve the same counterparty as in the barter transaction.

If fair market value cannot be determined, recognize revenue and expenses at cost.

Jeffrey E. Garten, Dean of the Yale School of Management, in FASB's 2002 video entitled *Financially Correct*, says it simply:

> The integrity of the whole society is undermined if financial information is misrepresented, or if it isn't accurate or understandable. Because we live in a market society—and increasingly, the world does—unless the markets can be trusted, then you have widespread corruption…and a market economy that doesn't function.

Financial Fraud Detection Tools

Sherron Watkins discovered the Enron fraud in 2001 when she was working under Andrew Fastow, CFO. She took a simple inventory, using an Excel spreadsheet to calculate which of the division's assets were profitable and which were unprofitable. She discovered the special-purpose entities called Raptors, which were off-the-books partnerships. Enron had hidden losses totaling hundreds of millions of dollars by borrowing money from Raptors and promising to pay the loans back with Enron stock. Enron was hedging risks in its left pocket with money from its right pocket. As the value of Enron stock fell and the losses in the Raptors mounted, Enron had to add more and more stock because Enron had risked 97 percent of the losses, and Arthur Andersen had agreed to the accounting.[110]

Thus, fraud can be found in many ways: by accident, interviewing officers and witnesses, percentage analysis, ratio analysis, using checklists, tips, physical and electronic surveillance, undercover operations, laboratory analysis of physical and electronic evidence, and by accident.

Forensic accountants can learn from an investigating detective, as illustrated by the Spenser novel *Widow's Walk*:

> "How," Susan said, "on earth are you going to unravel all of that?"
> "Same way you do therapy," I said.
> "Which is?"
> "Find a thread, follow it where it leads, and keep on doing it."
> "Sometimes it leads to another thread?"
> "Often," I said.
> "And then you follow that thread."
> "Yep."[111]

Sometimes, however, one must think like a scientist and not a detective. According to Michael Connelly, detectives move on a linear plane. Like detectives, forensic accountants move from clue-to-clue, from red flag to red flag. But these clues may add up to the wrong picture. So Connelly suggest thinking like a scientist:

> Throw out linear thinking and approach the subject from all new angles. Look at the subject matter and then turn it and look at it again. Grind it down to a powder and look at it under the glass.[112]

Professor Cindy Durtschi indicates that there are three phases of fraud:
- The act itself.
- The concealment of the fraud in the financial statements.
- Conversion of the stolen assets to personal use.

Thus, one can study one or more of these phases and possibly find the fraud. For example, if assets are being stolen, conduct surveillance to catch the thief. Or if liabilities are being hidden, look at the financial statement for the concealment. If the thief has an unexpected change in financial status, look for the source of the wealth.[113]

BE AN INVESTIGATOR. "Because I was an investigator," he said.

"O.K.," she said. "Investigators investigate. That, I can follow. But don't they *stop* investigating? I mean, ever? When they *know* already?

"Investigators never know," he said. "They feel, and they guess."

"I thought they dealt in facts."

"Not really," he said. "I mean, eventually they do, I suppose. But ninety-nine percent of the time it's ninety-nine percent about what you feel. About people. A good investigator is a person with a feel for people."[114]

The AICPA, IIA, and ACFE suggest that investigations may involve these tasks:[115]
1. Interviewing, including:
   a. Neutral third-party witnesses.
   b. Corroborative witnesses.
   c. Possible co-conspirators.
   d. The accused.
2. Evidence collection, including:
   a. Internal documents, such as:
      i. Personnel files.
      ii. Internal phone records.
      iii. Computer files and other electronic devices.
      iv. E-mail.
      v. Financial records.
      vi. Security camera videos.
      vii. Physical and IT system access records.
   b. External records, such as:
      i. Public records.
      ii. Customer/vendor information.
      iii. Media reports.
      iv. Information held by third parties.
      v. Private detective reports.
3. Computer forensic examinations.
4. Evidence analysis, including:
   a. Review and categorization of information collected.
   b. Computer-assisted data analysis.
   c. Development and testing of hypotheses.

The forensic accountant needs to track and document the steps in any investigation process, including:[116]
- Items maintained as privileged or confidential.
- Requests for documents, electronic data, and other information.

- Memoranda of interviews conducted.
- Analysis of documents, data, and interviews and conclusions drawn.

A forensic accountant must be careful not to misrepresent his or her identity or the purpose of the contact with a questionable person. Surveillance is not an activity which an accountant normally performs, so in some states surveillance may require a private investigator's license. However, in Florida, a person who holds a professional license (e.g., CPA) is exempt from private investigator licensing requirements if the person is providing services or expert advice in the profession in which that person is so licensed. The forensic accountant should check his state laws.

Public document review may be helpful to a forensic accountant, including:
- Real and personal property records.
- Corporate and partnership records.
- Civil and criminal records.
- Stock trading activities.
- Checking vendors.

An Internet search of a person or company can capture important information. Laboratory analysis may be significant especially for a fraud situation, such as
- Analyzing fingerprints.
- Forged signatures.
- Fictitious or altered documents.
- Mirror imaging or copying hard drives/company servers.
- Using clear cellophane bags for paper documents.

INVESTIGATIVE TECHNIQUE: VIDEOTAPES. The average big city resident is caught on videotape about 75 times a day. This is common in workplaces and stores in the U.S. A former Coca-Cola secretary was convicted of conspiring to steal and sell to Pepsi confidential Coca-Cola documents and samples of products that the company was developing.

A Coca-Cola security expert testified that surveillance cameras were monitoring Joya Williams's movements. The surveillance was a key part of the government's evidence. She stole the materials and was attempting to sell them for at least $1.5 million. She was deeply in debt, unhappy at her job, and seeking a big payday.[117] She is now serving an eight year prison sentence.

Except for four categories, external auditors and internal auditors differ in the degree of fraud detecting effectiveness. The largest category of agreement is the "use of informants," such as talking to people reporting fraud and using employee fraud hotlines. Forensic accountants should investigate all tips or complaints received from disgruntled employees, customers, suppliers/vendors, and whistleblowers. Since "internal auditors perform operational compliance, and financial audits throughout the entire year they seem to be somewhat more creative in developing audit procedures for fraud detection than external auditors."[118]

Check for High Salaries

Many of the companies indicted by the SEC after Enron had one thing in common: CEOs were making about 75 percent *above* their peers. The common thread among the companies with the *worst* corporate governance was richly compensated top executives, as per the Corporate Library, Portland, Maine governance-research firm. Hefty pay checks and perks to current or former chief executives were common. Poor Board of Directors have in common an inability to say no to current or former chief executives.[119]

Some of the biggest offenders have been on Wall Street. Dick Grasso, New York stock exchange chairman, received at least $200 million over eight years. His secretary, SooJee, got $240,000 per year.

Wall Street sets the tone for the highest-paid packages. Citigroup paid Sandy Weill almost $45 million for 2003. "But the real problem is there is a disconnect, where shareholder return is low or negative, but the CEO makes out like a bandit," says Sherron Watkins. "J.P Morgan said that CEOs should not make more that 20 times the average hourly worker. We're above 500 times right now! The average worker gets, let's say, $20 an hour. So the highest CEO salary should be—let's just say it should be $1 million a year," she said.[120]

CEOs' compensation components increased dramatically in the 1990s [mean of $1.68 million in 1992 to $43.2 million in 2000] even after the passage of Code Sec. 162(m) in 1993 [$1 million limit].[121] Compensation increases when the CEO has influence over the outside directors, as measured by the percentage of outside directors appointed by the CEO.[122] CEO compensation is higher when the CEO's tenure is greater than the chair of the compensation committee.[123] The relationship between the change in CEO cash compensation and stock returns weakens with tenure.[124] The greater the percentage of outside board members appointed after the CEO, the more likely the CEO will have a golden parachute.[125]

PwC's 2009 Global Economic Crime survey indicates that in companies where senior executive compensation included a performance-based variable component of more than 50 percent, 36 percent of the companies reported having suffered fraud. Also, each of the three common types of fraud is more prevalent when there is a high variable component in the senior executive's compensation package. PwC hypothesizes that some individuals are tempted to increase their own earnings by fraudulent means because of their perception of the unfairness of their own salaries compared to their senior executives' salaries.

¶4201   INTERVIEWING TECHNIQUES

An important requirement of a forensic accountant, auditor, or IRS agent is to be an effective interviewer. Someone in an organization knows what is going on, so an investigator must know who and how to interview. Listen to rouges and whistle-blowers who complain. Pick someone from customer complaints or employees who have not received pay raises. Ernst & Young's 2002 survey indicates that women and older employees are more likely to report fraudulent activities.[126] Also, employees with a financial incentive to report fraud are more than twice as likely to do so than those with no incentive.[127]

One way to detect fraud is to interview company personnel. The AICPA Fraud Task Force provides an interviewing template of 13 questions for CEOs, CFOs, and controllers:

1. Explain the purpose of the interview—need to assess risk and comply with audit responsibilities.
2. Inquire whether they are aware of any instances of fraud within their organization. Do they have reason to believe that fraud may have occurred or is occurring?
3. Has the CEO or CFO ever approved an accounting treatment for transactions that was not appropriate?
4. Have there been any instances where someone has attempted to inflate assets or revenue or deliberately understate liabilities and expenses?
5. Is there any member of management that has a direct interest or indirect interest in any customer, vendor, competitor, supplier, or lender?
6. Is any member of management related to any other member of management?
7. Does anyone in the company have any personal, financial, or other problems that might affect his or her job performance?
8. If there was an area within the company that might be vulnerable to fraud, what would that be?
9. Has anyone within the accounting department been let go or resigned within the past year?
10. Is there anyone in management that appears to be living a lifestyle beyond their means (expensive cars, trips, jewelry, vices)?
11. Has anyone been involved in civil or criminal proceedings or filed bankruptcy?
12. Does the company have a strong ethics policy?
13. Has anyone ever been fired for committing fraud against the company?[128]

Don Rabon indicates that an interviewer can move an interviewee from the unwilling to the willing chair with the following techniques:[129]

Moving from Unwilling to Willing Chair	
Ask General questions. Win them over.	Make them feel that this is what's best for them.
Take away the foundation.	Gain their confidence.
Explain the facts.	Relate to them.
Deescalate the crisis.	Give them a way out.
Explain the advantages of cooperation.	Give them a chance to explain. Lie to them.
Downplay the disadvantages of cooperation.	Understand them. Hang it on them.
Use deception.	Put it on them.
Play on their sympathy.	Threaten them.
Play on their conscience.	Get them to trust.
Determine their frame of mind.	Mimic their manner.
Talk to them.	Empathize.
Know how far to push.	Show them what they're looking at.
Get on their level.	Show them acceptance.
Speak their language.	Develop a rapport.
Show them.	
Tell them.	

An interviewer must be aware of untruthful answers. As Saint Thomas Acquins said, "Doubt leads to inquiry, and inquiry leads to the truth." Deborah Allen in one of her songs says:

> I swear on my heart
> I was telling the truth
> at the time.
> Baby I lied. Baby I lied.
>
> Deborah Allen

While interviewing executives or suspects, a forensic accountant must try to determine whether the individual is lying or being deceptive. Both words and nonverbal language are important because as much as 60 percent of communication is nonverbal. Previous contact with a person is helpful in determining whether these movements or responses are indicative of lying. For example, during Bill Clinton's testimony he touched his nose several times while he was lying, but did not touch his nose during his truthful testimony.[130]

The accountant should watch for these signs:
- Covering mouth with hand
- Touching nose
- Frequent blinking
- Biting or licking lips
- Moving or tapping foot or finger
- Crossing arms
- Playing with objects (e.g., pencil, paperclip, or pen)
- Avoiding eye contact or averting eyes
- Clearing the throat
- Closing and opening coat
- Picking at lint on clothing
- Playing with collar
- Moving away

- Turning to the side
- Shrug gestures
- Slower response
- Higher or different pitch
- Gap between words becomes longer
- Not answering the question
- Sweating
- Deflecting the question
- Generalities rather than specifics

James R. Brown, Vice-President of Finance at Adelphia Communication, said that he "lied in the company's filings." Brown had no formal training in accounting and finance, and he said Adelphia began manipulating its financial reports soon after the company went public in 1986.

Vice-President Brown said that the company regularly fabricated statistics on the number of subscribers, cash flow, cable-system upgrades, and other closely followed metrics. According to Brown, top executives would meet on Saturdays to determine if they were meeting loan agreements. If not, they would make other types of manipulations of either arbitrarily moving expenses between companies or adding invented affiliate income or interest income from one internal company to another. For more than 10 years they kept two sets of books.[131]

A quote from a Michael Connelly novel is informative for a forensic accountant:

"Bosch didn't say anything. He knew that sometimes when he was quiet, the person he needed information from would eventually fill the silence."[132]

Further in his novel *The Black Ice*, Connelly's detective says:

"Just listen. You are a detective. Detectives are supposed to listen. You once told me that solving murders are getting people to talk and just listening to them."[133] Forensic accountants need to listen also.

At the start of an interview, a forensic accountant should develop a baseline by asking questions to which the interviewer knows the correct answers. The baseline is the reactions and behaviors exhibited by the subject when telling the truth. The interviewer should compare this baseline behavior with the subject's behavior when he or she later has a reason to lie. Differences between the two may suggest deception or lying. If the body language or behavior is not different from the baseline, the person may be truthful.

INTERVIEWING A SUSPECT. In his novel, *Bitterroot*, Burke wrote the following about a character named Temple. "She never asked a question that required only a yes or no response, which forced the subject, if he was dishonest, to search in his mind for ideational associations that would mislead the interviewer. Usually in that moment the subject's eyes went askance. However, if the subject was a pathological liar, his eyelids stayed stitched to his forehead and he leaned forward aggressively, an angry tone of self-righteousness threaded through his answer.

Temple maintained that the first response out of the subject's mouth was always the most revealing, even if the person was lying. She said nouns went to the heart of the matter and adverbs showed manipulation. Honest people erred on the side of self-accusation and took responsibility for the evil deeds others had visited upon them. Sociopaths, when they have nothing at risk, told stories about themselves that made the mind reel and the stomach constrict, then a moment later tried to conceal the fact they had been raised in an alley by a single mother. One way or another, Temple's high-lighter found it all."[134]

A forensic accountant should never block the exit while interviewing someone. The room layouts below indicate the appropriate placement of the interviewee with and without a witness:

Interview Room Layout

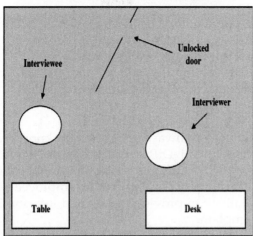

Room Layout with Witness

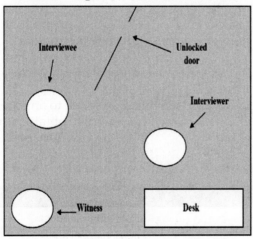

F.E. Inbau gives these hints about room arrangements for an interview:[135]

- Establish a sense of privacy.
- No locks or physical impediments.
- Room plain color (e.g., no pictures, etc.)
- Lighting should provide good, but not excessive or glaring illumination of interviewee's face. Same for interviewer.
- No telephones, cell phones, or beepers.
- Chairs about 4 feet apart. Straight-back. No rollers. Facing each other.
- Both chairs at the same level (both at same eye level).
- Observation room arrangement if possible (or video). Record it, if no video.
- In case of a female, another female should be present.
- Not at suspect's home or office.
- No bad breath odor.

F.E. Inabu when explaining the Reid Technique provides these suggested demeanors of an interviewer:[136]

- Civilian clothes. No uniform. Conservative suit, jacket, or dress.
- Relaxed and comfortable.
- No smoking.
- Questions in conversational tone. Non-accusatory.
- Keep eye contact. Neither person should wear dark glasses.
- Take written notes (but not in an interrogation).
- Use simple language.
- Never scold or reprimand if the suspect is caught in a lie.
- Do not pace around the room.

Lorraine Horton says that there is always someone who knows what is going on. "If you tune in, you will get a feel for it."[137] R.J. DiPasquale suggests "it is important that you select the right person to interview and that you be conversant in interviewing techniques." For instance, pick someone from customer complaints or an employee who didn't get a raise for two years, as they would be likely to provide the needed information."[138] Listen to rogues and whistle-blowers who complain.

There is a difference between an interview and an interrogation. An interview is a non-accusatory process whereby a person asks questions to develop factual information (e.g., who, what, when, where, how). The major advantages of a nonaccusatory interview are:

- Facilitates the development of cooperation.
- Easier to develop rapport.
- More effective way of developing usable information.

An accusatory interview to obtain an admission of guilt is called an interrogation. Disadvantages of interrogation are:

- Interviewee may be alienated and refuse to speak to anyone later.
- If interviewee will not speak to anyone, ability to obtain information or admission is diminished.

Don Rabon differentiates the interview from an interrogation as follows:[139]

Interview	Interrogation
Involves a witness	Involves a suspect
Involves a victim	Involves custody
No Miranda rights	Requires Miranda rights
General information	Specific facts
Less demanding	More demanding
Casual	Highly structured
Interview in the field	Interrogate at the office
Information not known	Confirm known information
Scattershot approach	Pin-down approach

For example, the United States has a confession rate of 60 percent as compared with Germany's 40 percent.[140] John Baldwin found in 600 investigative interviews that 35.7 percent of suspects confessed from the outset, and an additional 16.2 percent confessed initially to part of the allegation.[141]

Information is communicated both verbally and nonverbally. Verbal behavior includes not only words, but timing, pitch, rate, and clarity of the responses. Nonverbal behavior includes body movement, position changes, gestures, eye contact, and facial expressions.[142] Two-thirds of truthful interviewees cross their legs.[143]

Researchers found that nonverbal, vocal, emotional cues successfully classified individuals as misreporters or truth tellers 71 percent of the time while verbal cues showed only marginal ability to detect misreporting.[144]

In research involving deceptive conference calls, "the answers of deceptive executives have more references to general knowledge, fewer non-extreme positive emotions, and fewer references to shareholders value and value creation." Also, "deceptive CEOs use significantly fewer self-references, more third person plural and impersonal pronouns, more extreme positive emotions, fewer extreme negative emotions, and fewer certainty and hesitation words."[145]

The AICPA, IAASB, and Canadian Institute of Chartered Accountants recommend auditors look for behavioral signs of interviewing. However, auditors have a tendency to believe (called truth-bias), and this truth-bias is fairly resistant to red flags that indicate lying. This auditor's truth-bias may occur because of the rarity of lying in interviewing even when red flags are present. Also, auditors may be reluctant to make potentially offensive lie decisions.[146]

Forensic accountants and auditors need to overcome this truth-bias and become deception-detection interviewers to identify deceptive language and behavior. Individuals who are trying to deceive are "marked by caution, nervous behavior, or avoidance of eye contact."[147] They talk in generalties rather than specifics and give responses that are vague and indirect. They use distinct styles of speech and use language that disassociate themselves from the subject matter.

Kathy Reichs in *Cross Bones* gives this advice about interviewing:[148]

> Ryan shook his head. "Friedman's got an interesting approach. Say little. Let the suspect talk, all the while watching for details and inconsistencies he can pounce on later."
>
> "Give a liar enough rope……."
>
> "Kaplan's getting enough to dangle from the top of K2."

Mark Morze, who spent five years in prison for stock fraud, says most frauds fail to unravel because obvious questions are not asked by the auditors. Perpetrators wrap themselves in a veneer of integrity. "Everyone thought Enron was legit. Bernie Madoff people would say—look who his clients are—Steven Spielberg—he must be legit."[149]

By asking questions, the fraud becomes apparent. Morze says "if people get offended when you ask them a question about verification, that's a sign something is up."[150]

He puts a strong hand on my shoulder. "I appreciate you helping us out, Michael." Unlike the FBI polo crew, he's wearing a gray suit with a small stain on his right lapel. His tie is pulled tight, but the top button on his stark white shirt is open. The effect is the most subtle hint of casualness in his otherwise professional demeanor.

"Quite a day, huh, Michael?" It's the third time since we've met that he's said my name, which I have to admit sets off my radar. As my old crime law professor once explained, name repetition is the first trick negotiators use to establish an initial level of intimacy. The second trick is physical contact. I look down at his hand on my shoulder." [151]

UpJohn Warning

During interviews where illegal behavior is suspected and an attorney is present, a proper *UpJohn*[152] warning is appropriate (or corporate Miranda). The attorney should tell the employee that the attorney represents the company and not the employee. Further, the employee should be clearly told that the attorney-client privilege belongs to the company (and not to the employee). The interview notes should state that the *UpJohn* warning was given. Samples of *UpJohn* warnings can be found on the Internet, including one by the American Bar Association.[153]

¶ 4211   ANALYTICS

Analytical procedures involve the study or comparison of the relationship between two or more measures for the purpose of establishing the reasonableness of each one compared. Five types of analytical procedures help find unusual trends or relationships, errors, or fraud:

- Horizontal or percentage analysis.
- Vertical analysis.
- Variance analysis.
- Ratio analysis or benchmarking.
- Comparison with other operating information.[154]

Analytics reveal where to go to audit and for what to search. Analytics can lie, however, and many people do not understand them. For example, Lyndon B. Johnson said that he wanted everyone to have above-average housing. Of course, only one-half can be above average by definition. A good starting point is excerpts from Reference Materials from the Institute of Internal Auditors (see Appendix 1).

Forensic accountants should compare the trend in sales with the trend in net income. For example, from 1999 to 2001, HealthSouth's net income increased nearly 500 percent, but revenue grew only five percent. On March 19, 2003, the SEC said that HealthSouth faked at least $1.4 billion in profit since 1999 under the auditing eyes of Ernst & Young. The SEC said that HealthSouth started cooking its numbers in 1986, which Ernst & Young failed to find over 17 years. HealthSouth also inflated its cash balances.

HealthSouth used PeopleSoft, with at least 2,000 different ledgers. Much of the fraud was pulled off by these simple entries:

Suspense Account	xx	
Revenue		xx
Accounts Receivable	xx	
Inventory	xx	
Property	xx	
Suspense Account		xxx

Most of the entries were inter-company entries, which the external auditors missed or ignored.

After a fraud, the forensic work can be expensive. During 2005, 2004, and 2003, professional fees associated with the reconstruction of HealthSouth's financial records and restatement of 2001 and 2002 consolidated financial statements approximated *$206.2* million and *$70.6* million, respectively.

¶ 4221   PERCENTAGE ANALYSIS

Many financial statement fraud identifiers or red flags are detected by the common-sizing technique and ratio analysis. Common-sizing is done by converting all major financial statement items to a percentage of assets for the balance sheet and revenues for the income statement (both horizontal and vertical analysis). Many accountants forget how these simple techniques could allow them to spot dangerous financial situations.

Horizontal Analysis

Horizontal analysis assists in the search of inequalities by using the financial statements of some prior year as the base and expressing the components of a future year as percentages of each component in the base year. This technique may be used for balance sheet and income statement comparison, but it is used less frequently in the analysis of the statement of cash flow because of the lack of regularity with which items recur in this statement. Typically, horizontal analysis starts with a base year, and each successive year is compared with the base year. The significant changes in account balances (in dollars and percentages) from period to period should be investigated to determine the reason for the change. The changes could signify financial improvement or decline in the specific company or its industry.

For example, suppose advertising in the base year was $100,000 and advertising in the next three years was $120,000, $140,000, and $180,000. A horizontal comparison expressed as a percentage of the base year amount of $100,000 would appear as follows:

	Year 4	Year 3	Year 2	Year 1
Dollar amount	$180,000	$140,000	$120,000	$100,000
Horizontal Comparison	180%	140%	120%	100%

Here are some red flags to find with horizontal analysis:
- When deferred revenues (on the balance sheet) rise sharply, a company may be having trouble delivering its products as promised.
- If either accounts receivable or inventory is rising faster than revenue, the company may not be selling its goods as fast as needed or is having trouble collecting money from customers. For example, in 1997 Sunbeam's revenue grew less than 1 percent but accounts receivable jumped 23 percent and inventory grew by 40 percent. Six months later, in 1998, the company shocked investors by reporting a $43 million loss.
- If cash from operations is increasing or decreasing at a different rate than net income, the company may be being manipulated.
- Falling reserves for bad debts in relation to accounts receivable falsely boosts revenue.

Holly Sharp, a practitioner in New Orleans, used horizontal analysis in an embezzlement situation. An employee was funneling company checks for the IRS into his own personal bank account. The company's history showed that about 25 percent of the revenue was going to federal income taxes. But when the figure jumped to 60 percent, the investigator knew something was wrong.[155]

Vertical Analysis

Vertical analysis (often referred to as common-size statements) presents every item in a statement as a percentage of the largest item in the statement. When vertical analysis is used to compare financial statements from several periods, changes in the relationships between items can be easily determined.

Vertical analysis can be used for all the basic financial statements. In using the income statement, net sales are usually expressed as 100 percent and all other items are compared with net sales. The largest item on the balance sheet is total assets, which is expressed as 100 percent, and the statement of cash flows usually uses the change in cash as the base. A simple case of vertical analysis is shown in Figure 4.1.

Figure 4.1. Vertical Analysis Applied to an Income Statement

	Dollar Amounts	Percent
Sales	$400,000	100%
Cost of Goods Sold	160,000	40%
Gross Profit	240,000	60%
Selling Expenses	40,000	10%
Administrative Expenses	60,000	15%
Operating Profit	140,000	35%
Income Taxes	28,000	7%
Net Income	$112,000	28%

IMPROPER RECORDING OF REVENUE. In November 2002, the SEC brought civil fraud charges against a senior finance officer and a CPA for fraudulently concealing an accounts receivable problem at Peregrine. The SEC claimed that Peregrine's management engaged in myriad deceptive sales and accounting practices to create the illusion of growth, including secretly adding material sales contingencies to what appeared on their face to be binding contracts.

The software company accumulated on its balance sheet millions of dollars of aging receivables that Peregrine management knew the company would never collect. Important indicators of Peregrine's financial health were deteriorating, including days sales outstanding (DSO), an analytical tool used by financial analysts and investors to track the age of a company's aggregate accounts receivable and to assess their quality and, ultimately, the quality of the company's revenue.

Also, the CPA engaged with other persons, including a senior finance officer at the company, in a scheme to conceal Peregrine's difficulties in collecting its accounts receivable. The scheme included, among other things, creating a false $19.58 million invoice and selling it to banks. By selling false receivables to banks, Peregrine materially overstated its cash flow and understated its accounts receivable.[156]

Ratio Analysis

Professor Steve Albrecht says that financial statements tell a story, and the story should make sense. If they do not make sense, they may be fake.[157] Ratio analysis is a subset of trend analysis that can be used to compare relationships among financial statement accounts over time to find the fakes. A number of ratios that may be used to spot red flags and fraud identifiers:

$$\text{Current ratio} = \frac{\text{Current assets (cash and equivalents, receivables and inventories)}}{\text{Current liabilities (payables, accruals, taxes, and debt due in 1 year)}}$$

$$\text{Quick ratio} = \frac{\text{Cash and equivalents plus receivables}}{\text{Current liabilities}}$$

$$\text{Working capital} = \text{Current assets} - \text{Current liabilities}$$

$$\text{Inventory turnover} = \frac{\text{Cost of goods sold}}{\text{Average inventory}}$$

The number of days inventory is on hand can be calculated as

$$\frac{365}{\text{Inventory turnover}}$$

$$\text{Receivables turnover} = \frac{\text{Net credit sales}}{\text{Average receivables}}$$

$$\text{Gross Margin} = 1 - \frac{\text{Cost of goods sold}}{\text{Sales}}$$

$$\text{Expense ratio} = \frac{\text{Selling general and administrative expenses}}{\text{Sales}}$$

$$\text{Operating margin} = \frac{\text{Operating income}}{\text{Sales}}$$

$$\text{Profit margin} = \frac{\text{Net income before extraordinary items}}{\text{Sales}}$$

$$\text{Interest coverage ratio} = \frac{\text{Income before interest and taxes}}{\text{Fixed charges}}$$

$$\text{Margin of safety} = \frac{\text{Income after fixed charges before income taxes}}{\text{Sales}}$$

$$\text{Debt-to-equity ratio} = \frac{\text{Total current and long-term} + \text{Capitalized leases}}{\text{Total stockholder's equity}}$$

Or

$$\frac{\text{Total debt at book value}}{\text{Total debt and preferred stock} + \text{Common stock at market}}$$

$$\text{Return on assets (ROA)} = \frac{\text{Net income}}{\text{Average total assets}}$$

Or

$$\frac{\text{Earnings before interest and taxes}}{\text{Average total assets}}$$

$$\text{Return on equity (ROE)} = \frac{\text{Net income}}{\text{Average common equity}}$$

$$\text{Return on invested capital} = \frac{\text{Earnings before interest and taxes}}{\text{Average invested capital}}$$

$$\text{Years to pay off debt by application of internally generated cash flows} = \frac{\text{Total fixed obligations}}{\text{Operating cash flows}}$$

$$\text{Ratio of senior debt to capital} = \frac{\text{Total senior debt}}{\text{Subordinated debt} + \text{Net worth}}$$

Two professors used many of these ratios on the high profile cases of Enron, WorldCom, Global Crossing, and Qwest.[158] They found the following ratios work well as red flags for reporting problems and financial performance:

- Gross margins and sales growth.
- Price to book and price earnings.
- Profit margin, top-line growth, and bottom-line growth.
- Return on assets and return on equity.
- Current ratio.
- Quality of earnings and effective cash tax rate.

Professor Grove and Cook also found that five qualitative red flags were helpful in determining "cooked books:"[159]

- Falling stock prices.
- Top management (CEO and CFO) resigning.
- Insider stock trading.
- Intentionally opaque and complex financial reporting.
- CEO uncomfortable with criticism from financial analysts.

In 1999, M.D. Beneish[160] suggested five statistically significant ratios for catching earnings management, and Joe Wells[161] and Professors Grove and Cook[162] maintain these five ratios are key fraud detection ratios. These five ratios and index for manipulators are given below. One should use the ratios for two or more successive years and convert them into indexes for benchmarking. For example, a growing Day's Sales in Receivable Index is often a sign that the accounts receivable are impaired due to channel stuffing or other revenue recognition problems.

1.   Day's Sales in Receivable Index:

$$\frac{(\text{Accounts Receivable}_t / \text{Sales}_t)}{(\text{Accounts Receivable}_{t-1} / \text{Sales}_{t-1})}$$

Index for manipulators: 1.5 to 1

---

2.   Gross Margin Index:

$$\frac{[(\text{Sales}_{t-1} - \text{Cost of Sales}_{t-1}) / \text{Sales}_{t-1}]}{[(\text{Sales}_t - \text{Cost of Sales}_t) / \text{Sales}_t]}$$

Index for manipulators = 1.2 to 1

---

3.   Asset Quality Index =

$$\frac{1 - \left(\dfrac{(\text{Current Assets}_t + \text{Net Fixed Assets}_t)}{\text{Total Assets}_t} \right)}{1 - \left(\dfrac{(\text{Current Assets}_{t-1} + \text{Net Fixed Assets}_{t-1})}{\text{Total Assets}_{t-1}} \right)}$$

Index for manipulators = 1.25 to 1

---

4.   Sales Growth Index : $\text{Sales}_t / \text{Sales}_{t-1}$

Manipulators: 60%

Non manipulators 10%

---

5. Total Accruals to Total Assets =

$$\frac{\Delta \text{ Working Capital}_t - \Delta \text{ Cash}_t - \Delta \text{ Current Taxes Payable}_t - \Delta \text{ Current Portion of LTD}_t - \Delta \text{ Accumulated depreciation and amortization}_t}{\text{Total Assets}_t}$$

TATA for manipulators: .031

TATA for non manipulators: .018

Charles Lundelius gives this example of how to compare a company's key ratios with its peers:[163]

Characteristic	MPS	Peer group	% over peers
DSRI	1.56	1.03	51%
GMI	2.00	1.10	82%
AQI	1.23	1.04	18%
SGI	1.50	1.20	25%
TATA	0.10	0.05	100%

Symbol Technologies, Inc. engaged in a number of channel stuffing techniques, such as arranging transactions to make it appear that Symbol was selling products. They would simultaneously eliminate the resellers' obligation to pay for the products. These resellers typically did not need and often could not even afford to pay for the product they ordered, but Symbol negated any risk to the resellers by granting them contingent payment terms and unconditional return rights. Further, the resellers did not have to pay Symbol unless and until they resold the product and received payment from an end user. The resellers also had the right to return any unsold product to Symbol at no cost. These special terms did not appear anywhere in the purchase orders or resulting invoices, which simply recited Symbol's standard "net 45 day" payment terms. Side agreements also superseded the stock rotation terms that Symbol normally granted to channel partners in its standard contracts, which did not permit unlimited returns and provided for a restocking fee in many circumstances.

Since management may override controls, substantive analytical procedures alone are not well suited for detecting fraud. PCAOB indicates that an auditor's substantive procedures must include reconciling the financial statements to the accounting records. Such substantive procedures also must include reconciling the financial statements to the accounting records. The auditor's substantive procedures also should include examining material adjustments made during the course of preparing the financial statements. Also, other auditing standards require auditors to perform specific tests of detail in the financial statement audit.[164] A forensic accountant should consider these suggestions as well.

For example, AU Sec. 316 requires an auditor to perform tests of detail to further address the risk of management override, whether or not a specific risk of fraud has been identified. Also, AU Sec. 330 states that there is a presumption that the auditor will request the confirmation of accounts receivable.[165] Finally, AU Sec. 331 states that observation of inventories is a generally accepted auditing procedure and that the auditor who issues an opinion without this procedure "has the burden of justifying the opinion expressed."[166]

Of the ten prominent companies that had recent scandals, eight of them had CEOs who were also board chairs. Of these ten, only WorldCom and Global Crossing did not have CEO duality, so the CEO should not chair the Board of Directors.[167]

1. Enron
2. WorldCom
3. Tyco
4. Adelphia
5. HealthSouth
6. Global Crossing
7. Waste Management
8. Qwest
9. Homestore
10. Sunbeam

When there are aging Board of Directors, it is easier for management to get away with misdeeds. "They can be hard of hearing;" Enron's Audit Committee Chairman was 72, and nearly 10 percent of Directors in the S&P's 500 stock index are 70 or over.[168]

Some empirical studies found the following about financial statement fraud:[169]
- Fich and Shivdasani found that a tainted director (one sitting on the board of another company that has been sued); weak governance index, larger board, a non-independent, busy, or staggered board, less financial expertise, and zero duality were more likely to result in fraud.[170]
- Zhao and Chen found that SEC allegations of fraudulent financial reporting in Accounting and Auditing Enforcement Releases are negatively related to a staggered BOD (one-third elected each year), negatively related to a BOD and audit committee independence, and positively related to whether the CEO chairs the BOD.[171]
- Beasley *et al.* found that fraud firms have more inside directors on the BOD and audit committee, and shorter average director tenure on the BOD, and less likely to have an audit committee or one composed of at least three members. Average fraud companies had 30 percent inside directors versus 25 percent for no fraud companies. Fraud companies are much more likely to experience turnover of the BOD and other directors than no-fraud companies.[172]

¶ 4231   USING CHECKLISTS TO HELP DETECT FRAUD

It is helpful to look at the fraud risk factors developed over time and create checklists that can be used as part of the fraud fighter's arsenal.

SAS Checklist

The following checklist is based on issues identified by AICPA SAS 99.

Incentives/Pressures
- ❑ Is the client's financial stability or profitability threatened by economic, industry, or entity operating conditions, such as (or as indicated by):
  - High degree of competition or market saturation, accompanied by declining margins;
  - High vulnerability to rapid changes, such as changes in technology, product obsolescence, or interest rates;
  - Significant declines in customer demand and increasing business failures in either the industry or overall economy;
  - Operating losses making the threat of bankruptcy, foreclosure, or hostile takeover imminent;
  - Recurring negative cash flows from operations or an inability to generate cash flows from operations while reporting earnings and earnings growth;
  - Rapid growth or unusual profitability, especially compared to that of other companies in the same industry; or
  - New accounting, statutory, or regulatory requirements.
- ❑ Is the client's management under excessive pressure to meet the requirements or expectations of third parties due to the following:
  - Profitability or trend level expectations of investment analysts, institutional investors, significant creditors, or other external parties (particularly expectations that are unduly aggressive or unrealistic), including expectations created by management in, for example, overly optimistic press releases or annual report messages;
  - Need to obtain additional debt or equity financing to stay competitive including financing of major research and development or capital expenditures;
  - Marginal ability to meet debt repayment or other debt covenant requirements; or
  - Perceived or real effects of reporting poor financial results on significant pending transactions, such as business combinations or contract awards.

❑ Is the client's management or the board of directors' personal net worth threatened by the entity's financial performance arising from the following:

- ● Heavy concentrations of their compensation (for example, bonuses, stock options, and earn-out arrangements) being contingent upon achieving aggressive targets for stock price, operating results, financial position, or cash flow; or
- ● Personal guarantees of debts of the entity that are significant to their personal net worth.

❑ Is the client's management or operating personnel under excessive pressure to meet financial targets set up by the board of directors or management, including sales or profitability incentive goals?

Opportunities

❑ Does the nature of the industry or the entity's operations provide opportunities to engage in fraudulent financial reporting that can arise from the following:

- ● Significant related-party transactions not in the ordinary course of business or with related entities not audited or audited by another firm;
- ● Assets, liabilities, revenues based on significant estimates that involve subjective judgments or uncertainties that are difficult to corroborate;
- ● Significant, unusual, or highly complex transactions, especially those close to year end that pose difficult "substance over form" questions;
- ● Significant operations located or conducted across international borders in jurisdictions where differing business environments and cultures exist; or
- ● Significant bank accounts or subsidiary or branch operations in tax-haven jurisdictions for which there appears to be no clear business justification.

❑ Is there ineffective monitoring of management as a result of the following:

- ● Domination of management by a single person or small group (in a non-owner-managed business) without compensating controls; or
- ● Ineffective board of directors or audit committee oversight over the financial reporting process and internal control.

❑ Is there a complex or unstable organizational structure as evidenced by the following:

- ● Difficulty in determining the organization or individuals that have controlling interest in the entity;
- ● Overly complex organizational structure involving unusual legal entities or managerial lines of authority; or
- ● High turnover of senior management, counsel, or board members.

❑ Are internal control components deficient as a result of the following:

- ● Inadequate monitoring of controls, including automated controls and controls over interim financial reporting (where external reporting is required);
- ● High turnover rates or employment of ineffective accounting, internal audit, or information technology staff; or
- ● Ineffective accounting and information systems including situations involving reportable conditions.

Attitudes/Rationalizations Checklist

Attitudes/rationalizations have been known to be fraud indicators. Certain attitudes/rationalizations held by board members, management, or employees might allow them to engage in and/or justify fraudulent financial reporting. The existence of such attitudes may not be observable by the auditor, but if the auditor does become aware of their existence, he or she should consider it in identifying the risks of material misstatement arising from fraudulent financial reporting. The following questions should be asked:

Are the following factors present in the client's organization:

❑ Ineffective communication and support of the entity's values or ethical standards by management or the communication of inappropriate values or ethical standards by management;

❑ Nonfinancial management's excessive participation in or preoccupation with the selection of accounting principles or the determination of significant estimates;

❑ Known history of violations of securities laws or other laws and regulations, or claims against the entity, its senior management, or board members alleging fraud or violations of laws and regulations;

❑ Excessive interest by management in maintaining or increasing the entity's stock price or earnings trend;

❑ A practice by management of committing to analysts, creditors, and other third parties to achieve aggressive or unrealistic forecasts;

❑ Management failing to correct known reportable conditions on a timely basis; or

❑ An interest by management in employing inappropriate means to justify marginal or inappropriate accounting on the basis of materiality.

The relationship between management and the current or predecessor auditor is strained, as exhibited by the following:

❑ Frequent disputes with the current or predecessor auditor on accounting, auditing, or reporting matters;

❑ Unreasonable demands on the auditor, such as unreasonable time constraints regarding the completion of the audit or the issuance of the auditor's report;

❑ Formal or informal restrictions on the auditor that inappropriately limit access to people or information or the ability to communicate effectively with the board of directors or audit committee; or

❑ Domineering management behavior in dealing with the auditor, especially involving attempts to influence the scope of the auditor's work or the selection or continuance of audit personnel assigned to the engagement.

Specific management questions:

❑ Does management have knowledge of any fraud that has been perpetrated or any alleged or suspected fraud?

❑ Is management aware of allegations of fraud (for example, because of communications from employees, former employees, analysts, short sellers, or other investors)?

❑ What is management's understanding about the risks of fraud in the entity, including any specific fraud risks the entity has identified or account balances or classes of transactions for which a risk of fraud may be likely to exist?

❑ What programs and controls have been established to mitigate specific fraud risks the entity has identified, or that otherwise help to prevent, deter, and detect fraud, and how management monitors those programs and controls?

❑ For an entity with multiple locations, (a) what is the nature and extent of monitoring of operating locations or business segments, and (b) are there any particular operating locations or business segments for which a risk of fraud may be more likely to exist?

❑ Does management communicate to employees its views on business practices and ethical behavior? How do they communicate this?

Further, SAS No. 85 requires an auditor to obtain written representations from management about whether they are aware of any fraud involving (a) management, (b) employees who have significant roles in internal control, or (c) others when the fraud could have a material effect on the financial statements.

Audit Test Activities Checklist

SAS No. 99 provides these audit test activities that may be used to find material misstatements due to fraud:

❑ Perform procedures at locations on a surprise or unannounced basis (for example, observing inventory on unexpected dates or at unexpected locations or counting cash on a surprise basis);

❑ Request that inventories be counted at the end of the reporting period or on a date closer to period-end to minimize the risk of manipulation of balances in the period between the date of completion of the count and the end of the reporting period;

❑ Make oral inquiries of major customers and suppliers in addition to sending written confirmations, or sending confirmation requests to a specific party within an organization;

❑ Perform substantive analytical procedures using disaggregated data (for example, comparing gross profit or operating margins by location, line of business, or month to auditor-developed expectations);

❑ Interview personnel involved in activities in areas where a risk of material misstatement due to fraud has been identified to obtain their insights about the risk and how controls address the risk; or

❑ If other independent auditors are auditing the financial statements of one or more subsidiaries, divisions, or branches, discuss with them the extent of work that needs to be performed to address the risk of material misstatement due to fraud resulting from transactions and activities among these components.

Even after SAS No. 99 was developed, there remains an expectation gap between the professional standards of the AICPA that are broadly written and the jurors' interpretation of professional standards. Mark L. Cheffers and Jeffrey Bourassa believe that more forensic procedures must be used to bridge this expectation gap.[173]

Miscellaneous Fraud Indicator Checklist

This checklist was taken from fraud indicia listed on the AICPA website:

❑ Is there a lack of written corporate policies and standard operating procedures?

❑ Is there a lack of interest in or compliance with internal control policies, especially division of duties?

❑ Are operations disorganized in such areas as bookkeeping, purchasing, receiving, and warehousing?

❑ Are there unrecorded transactions or missing records?

❑ Are bank accounts not reconciled on a timely basis?

❑ Are there continuous out of balance subsidiary ledgers?

❑ Are there continuous unexplained differences between physical inventory counts and perpetual inventory records?

❑ Are there bank checks written to cash in large amounts?

❑ Are there handwritten checks in a computer environment?

❑ Are there continual or unusual fund transfers among company bank accounts?

❑ Are there fund transfers to offshore banks (Enron had more than 880 offshore accounts)?

❑ Are transactions not consistent with the entity's business?

❑ Are there deficient screening procedures for new employees?

❑ Is there reluctance by management to report criminal wrongdoing?

❑ Are there unusual transfers of personal assets?

❑ Are there employees living beyond their means?

❑ Are there vacations not taken?

❑ Are there frequent or unusual related-party transactions (e.g., the Enron special purpose entities)?

❑ Are employees in close association with suppliers?

❑ Is there expense account abuse?
❑ Are business assets dissipating without explanation?
❑ Are there inadequate explanations to investors about losses?[174]

A few other indicia of fraud are:
❑ Heavy selling of stock by insiders (e.g., Enron);
❑ Sudden resigning of an officer (e.g., Jeffrey Skilling at Enron);
❑ Unconsolidated special purpose entities (Enron had more than 3,500 subsidiary companies, some hiding billion-dollars of debts and others used as tax shelters);
❑ Greater than five percent of "other revenue";
❑ Large loans to executives (Baptist Foundation of Arizona loaned companies controlled by one director and two former directors almost $140 million, which they invested in real estate);
❑ Negative cash flow from operations;
❑ Recurring/nonrecurring charges;
❑ Off-balance sheet financing; or
❑ Related Parties—SFAS 57 says a related party is any party that controls or can significantly influence the management or operating policies of the company to the extent that the company may be prevented from fully pursuing its own interests.

¶ 4236   BEHAVIORAL APPROACHES

Some fraud schemes cannot be effectively detected using data-driven approaches. Corruption schemes such as bribery, kickbacks, and bid rigging may go undetected using data-driven techniques. Searching relevant transaction data for patterns and unexplained relationships often *fails to yield results* because the information may not be recorded, *per se*, by the system.

Figure 4.2. The Iceberg Theory of Fraud

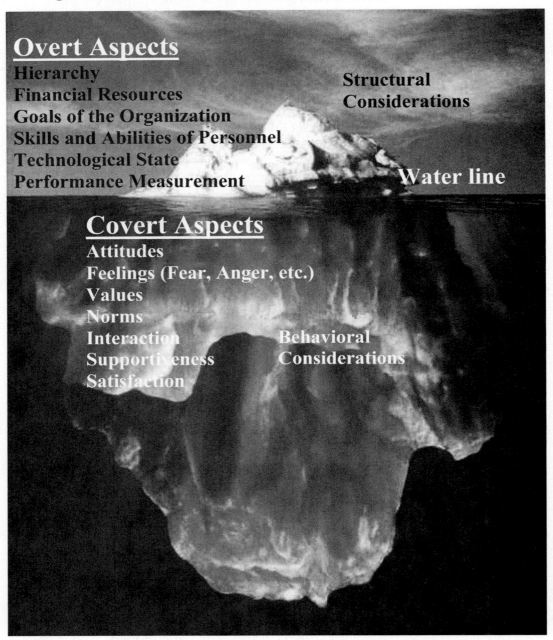

However, behavioral approaches and qualitative factors may allow an auditor to look beyond the raw data.[175] Bologna and Lindquist in their book in 1987 suggested that many of the behavioral considerations lurking beneath the water posed a danger to unsuspecting auditors. Attitudes, feelings, norms, satisfaction, and other behavioral considerations are important for finding fraud.[176] See Figure 4.2. Lifestyles of employees may be important clues to fraud.

EYEWITNESS

For someone who earned a salary of just *$1,000 a month*, Rana Koleilat was able to live a nice life. She traveled by private jet, took along her servant and hairdresser, and stayed at luxurious locality in London and Paris. Back home in Beirut, Lebanon, she lived in a three-story penthouse. To anyone who asked how she lived so well, she would answer that she had a "rich uncle."

Actually, Koleilat helped manage a private bank in Beirut, and thereby hangs a tale. The chairman of the bank said he lost *$1.2 billion*, and depositors lost another *several hundred million dollars*.[177]

The 2012 Wells Report provides important behavorial flags present during fraud schemes sorted by frequency:

Behavioral Red Flags (2012)[178]

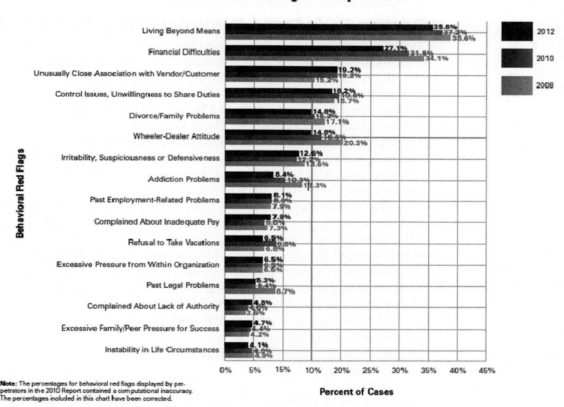

Behavioral Red Flags of Perpetrators

Note: The percentages for behavioral red flags displayed by perpetrators in the 2010 Report contained a computational inaccuracy. The percentages included in this chart have been corrected.

¶ 4241   **CLAWBACK PROVISIONS**

One possible technique for preventing or at least reducing the harm of financial statement fraud is the use of clawback provisions. A clawback clause allows a company to recoup excessive compensation in the event there is an accounting restatement.

Under the Sarbanes-Oxley Act of 2002, in the event of any financial restatement based upon executive misconduct, the public company must recoup compensation incentives to the CEO and CFO that were paid within 12 months preceding the restatement. The Dodd-Frank Wall Street Reform and Consumer Protection Act of 2012 directs the SEC to require listed companies to adopt two key recovery policies.

- A company must disclose any clawback policies for any compensation-based incentives that were paid out based on any erroneous financial information reported under the securities rules.
- Companies must seek recoupment from any current or former executive officer of any incentive-based compensation paid during the three-year period preceding the date that the corporation is required to prepare an accounting restatement that was based on any erroneous data.

Research by three professors found that clawback provisions resulted in significant improvements in both actual and perceived financial reporting quality. They also found an increase in CEO compensation after adoption of new clawback provisions.[179]

Deutsche Bank AG clawed back around $53.5 million in bonuses from a former trader who was involved in attempting to rig interest rates while working for the bank. The trader dealt in derivatives and was paid a percentage of the profits that he made with deferred compensation by a mixture of cash and stock.[180]

Validating Early Fraud Prediction Using Narrative Disclosures

While fraud continues to increase over the years, so have the consequences of fraudulent activity. Companies are more at risk than ever with huge fines being levied (often toping $100 million). There is a need for a timely, accurate predictor of fraudulent activity that will allow fraud to be mitigated.

Chih-Chen Lee, Natalie Tatiana Churyk, and B. Douglas Clinton developed an early fraud prediction method that they claim to be more accurate, more useable by a variety of interest parties, and able to be applied earlier than traditional financial, quantitative fraud predication models. C.C. Lee et al. instead uses a qualitative method to analyze narrative disclosures and, more specific to this study, the Management Discussion and Analysis section of the annual report for signs of fraud. They identified ten narrative variables that were significantly different between fraud and non-fraud companies. Out of these ten, four factors were determined to provide the strongest prediction of deception. Using these four factors, logistic regression and a cross validation procedure, the model accurately classified firms with and without fraud 64.8 percent of the time. Using a holdout sample the model accurately classified the firms with and without fraud 55.9 percent of the time. Tradition fraud prediction models have reported success rates of 30-40 percent.[181]

The four factors used by the model are[182]

1. Fewer terms indicating positive emotion.
2. Fewer present tense verbs.
3. The presence of an increased number of words.
4. Fewer colons.

Deceivers often evidence negative emotions that reflect a negative experience and/or an attempt to disassociate themselves from the experience or message. Deceivers also subconsciously avoid using present tense as another way of disassociating themselves from a deceptive message. Deceivers try to avoid using clarifying language and purposely structure sentences to make interpretation difficult and unclear. Consequently, they tend to avoid colons as they often precede clarifying examples. The expectation of an increased word count stems from the fact the deceiver will take extra time to attempt to be directionally persuasive and more convincing in hopes of avoiding being caught.[183]

The three professors believe that their model will help discover fraud earlier, before it has already caused disastrous financial damage.[184] Their research shows that post-SOX content analysis is still valid even though firms may have tried to over-manipulate the easy to adjust variables such as "for example."[185]

¶ 4246   CONCLUSION

In the absence of internal auditors and external auditors who take responsibility for fighting fraud, the forensic accountant must step into this void. The SEC seems to be moving the traditional players in line, but despite improvements in fighting fraud on all sides, there will be a need for forensic accountants who are specially trained and more suited personality-wise to remain independent and detect and fight fraud. These specialists may become part of one of the auditing teams or may be engaged separately. A comparison can be made between a forensic accountant and a management consultant. Whereas the skilled management consultant arrives from the outside and cuts through the personalities to make the tough calls about waste and assess things like customer focus, marketing prowess, proper infrastructure, and sales organization effectiveness, the forensic accountant can be engaged to take an independent look at controls, systems, personnel, data, etc., to detect fraud.

Efforts of Congress, the SEC, the various stock exchanges, accounting associations and authorities, and others will continue to place more pressure on management, audit committees, accountants, and auditors to fight fraud. Still, the stakes are high and the special skills and knowledge to effectively fight fraud are substantial. Counting on internal auditors and independent public accountants engaged for the financial audit to uncover financial statement fraud in all its complexities is unrealistic. Specialists in fraud detection who possess the required mindset, the proper objectivity, and the required skills will be necessary. Whether these fraud fighters are part of the internal audit team, independent audit team, audit committee, or some yet-unknown entity to approach the problem from another angle remains to be seen.

Although the task is daunting, the fraud-fighting toolset will continue to develop. As more fraudulent activities of the past several years are examined in detail, more inside information will become available and will be used to develop more sophisticated fraud detection skills and techniques. Forensic accountants are needed because the odds that the crime or theft is reported is 2.8 to 1 against.[186]

ENDNOTES

1. Mark Gimein, "What Did Joe Know?," FORTUNE (May 12, 2003), p. 120.

2. Ken Brown, "Auditors' Methods Make It Hard to Catch Fraud By Executives," THE WALL STREET JOURNAL (July 8, 2002), pp. C-1 and C-3.

3. Levitt speech before the Economic Club of New York, New York City, October 18, 1999, *http://www.sec.gov/news/speech/speecharchive/1999/spch304.htm*.

4. Extracted from the "Summary of Conclusions," Report of the Special Audit Review Committee of the Board of Directors of HealthSouth Corporation, May 28, 2004.

5. SEC Rule 10b-5.

6. SAS No. 99, Consideration of Fraud in Financial Statement Audit (New York: AICPA 2002); Rules 3200T and 3500T, PCAOB, 2004, 143-144.

7. International Standards for the Professional Practice of Internal Auditing, IIA, 2004.

8. IIA, AICPA, ACFE, MANAGING THE BUSINESS RISK OF FRAUD: A PRACTICAL GUIDE (2008), p. 5, *http://www.acfe.com/documents/managing-business-risk.pdf*.

9. Discussions on the role of the independent auditor and the following discussion about the internal auditor's role are digested from D.L. Crumbley, J.J. O'Shaughnessy, and D.E. Ziegnenfuss, U.S. MASTER AUDITING GUIDE (Chicago: CCH INCORPORATED, 2002).

10. H.W. Wolosky, "Forensic Accounting to the Forefront," PRACTICAL ACCOUNTANT (February 2004), pp. 23-28.

11. *Ibid.*

12. SAS No. 82, Consideration of Fraud in a Financial Statement Audit (New York: AICPA 1997).

13. George Mannes, "Cracking the Books II: Reliving Equity Funding, Part 2," *TheStreet.com*, accessed October 22, 1999.

14. Larry Neumeister, "Prosecutors Charge Madoff's Accountant with Fraud," YAHOO! FINANCE (March 18, 2009), *http://biz.yahoo.com/ap/090318/na_us_madoff.scandal.html?.v=4*.

15. Mike McNamee and Amy Borrus, "Bill, Show Those CPAs You're the Boss," BUSINESS WEEK (April 28, 2003), p. 84.

16. Adrian Angelette, "Auditors Blamed," BATON ROUGE ADVOCATE (October 23, 2003), pp. A-1 and A-8.

17. H.W. Wolosky, "Forensic Accounting to the Forefront," PRACTICAL ACCOUNTANT (Febraury 2004), pp. 23-28.

18. Public Oversight Board, PANEL ON AUDIT EFFECTIVENESS: REPORT AND RECOMMENDATIONS (August 31, 2000), p. 88.

19. *Ibid*, p. 89.

20 The Public Oversight Board disbanded, per its charter, after the plans for the Public Company Accounting Oversight Board were announced.

21 PCAOB Release 2003-005, April 18, 2003, PCAOB Rulemaking Docket Matter 004.

22 "Securities Enforcement Cracks Down in Post-Madoff World," ACCOUNTANTS WORLD (April 28, 2009), *www.accountantsworld.com/destopdefault.aspx?page=newsstory&category=newsstory&StoryId=tnoHevjQ*.

23 *The Institute of Internal Auditors Professional Practices Framework*, copyright 1999 by the Institute of Internal Auditors, Inc., 249 Maitland Avenue, Altamonte Springs, FL 32100-4201, USA. Reprinted with permission.

24 K.L. James and S.J. Seipel, "The Effect of Decreased User Confidence on Perceived Internal Audit Fraud Protection," JOURNAL OF FORENSIC AND INVESTIGATIVE ACCOUNTING, Vol. 2, No. 1 (January-June 2010), pp. 1-23.

25 Institute of Management and Administration, Press Release, "Employee Fraud #1 Concern of Internal Auditors," (New York: Institute of Management and Administration, September 13, 1999).

26 R.L. Ratliff, W.A. Wallace, G.E. Sumner, and J.K. Loebbecke, INTERNAL AUDITING, 2d ed., (Altamonte Springs, Fla.: Institute of Internal Auditors, 1996), p. 861.

27 *Ibid*, pp. 861–862.

28 CAQ, Deterring and Detecting Financial Reporting Fraud: A Platform for Action, October 2010, pp. 17-18.

29 Rebecca Blumenstein and Susan Pullian, "WorldCom Fraud Was Widespread," THE WALL STREET JOURNAL (June 10, 2003), p. 3.

30 *Ibid*, p. 862.

31 Susan Henry and Kimberly Motala, "Mitigating Trouble-Internal Control Framework," *Litigation Section*, State Bar of Michigan (Spring 2002), p. 2, *www.michbar.org/sections*.

32 IIA, AICPA, ACFE, MANAGING THE BUSINESS RISK OF FRAUD: A PRACTICAL GUIDE (2008), *http://www.acfe.com/documents/managing-business-risk.pdf*, p. 15; see IIA Practice Advisory 2130-1: Role of the Internal Audit Activity and Internal Auditor in the Ethnical Culture of an Organization.

33 *Ibid*.

34 IIA, AICPA, ACFE, MANAGING THE BUSINESS RISK OF FRAUD: A PRACTICAL GUIDE (2008), *http://www.acfe.com/documents/managing-business-risk.pdf*, p. 43-45.

35 Susan Pilliam, Jared Sandberg, and Dan Morse, "Auditor Turns WorldCom Witness," WSJ.com highlights, July 3, 2002.

36 *Ibid*.

37 Julian Borger and Richard Wray, "How Auditor Found $4 Billion Black Hole: Corporate Fraud Uncovered by Second Female Whistleblower," THE GUARDIAN (June 28, 2002).

38 *Ibid*.

39 Susan Pilliam, Jared Sandberg, and Dan Morse, "Auditor Turns WorldCom Witness," WSJ.com highlights, July 3, 2002.

40 Chris Lee, "Ex-WorldCom Exec 'Hindered Auditors," *vnunet.com*, May 07, 2002.

41 R.L. Ratliff, W.A. Wallace, G.E. Sumners, and J.K. Loebbecke, INTERNAL AUDITING, 2d ed. (Altamonte Springs, Fla.: Institute of Internal Auditors, 1996), p. 861.

42 *Ibid*, p. 861–862.

43 Susan Pulliam and Deborah Solomon, "How Three Unlikely Sleuths Discovered Fraud at WorldCom," THE WALL STREET JOURNAL (October 30, 2002), pp. A-1 and A-6.

44 *Ibid*, p. A-1.

45 *Ibid*, p. A-6.

46 *Ibid*, p. A-6.

47 *Ibid*, p. A-6.

48 SEC Release Nos. 33-8220; 34-47654; IC-26001; File No. S7-02-03, Securities and Exchange Commission Standards Relating to Listed Company Audit Committees, 17 CFR PARTS 228, 229, 240, 249, and 274.

49 Center for Audit Quality, Deterring and Detecting Financial Reporting Fraud: A Platform for Action, October 2010, p. 28.

50 W.G. Heninger, Y. Kim, and S. Nabor, "Earnings Mistatements, Restatements, and Corporate Governance," JOURNAL OF FORENSIC & INVESTIGATIVE ACCOUNTING (July-December, 2009), pp. 1-35.

51 S. Ramamoorti, D. Morrison, and J.W. Koletar, "Bringing Freud to Fraud," IFP White Paper, December 22, 2009, p. 14.

52 SEC Accounting and Auditing Enforcement Releases (1982-1992).

53 IIA, AICPA, ACFE, MANAGING THE BUSINESS RISK OF FRAUD: A PRACTICAL GUIDE (2008), *http://www.acfe.com/documents/managing-business-risk.pdf*, p. 12.

54 IIA, AICPA, ACFE, MANAGING THE BUSINESS RISK OF FRAUD: A PRACTICAL GUIDE (2008), *http://www.acfe.com/documents/managing-business-risk.pdf*, p. 13.

55 Sarbanes-Oxley Act of 2002 Sec. 302 Amending Securities Exchange Act of 1934 Sec 13(a) and 15(d).

56 John Goff, "Bank Fraud Brings Executions," CFO MAGAZINE (November 2004), p. 20.

57 D.S. Hilzenrath, "Forensic Auditors Find What Some Companies Try to Hide," THE WASHINGTON POST (November 23, 2002), p. E-1.

58 Diane Brady and Joseph Weber, "The Boss on the Sidelines," BUSINESS WEEK (April 25, 2005), p. 88.

59 Carol J. Loomis, "The SEC Turns the Screws on Gatekeepers," FORTUNE (April 18, 2005), p. 38.

60 David Davies, FRAUD WATCH, 2d ed. (London, ABG Professional Information, 2000), p. 77.

61 PCAOB Release 2004-001, March 9, 2004, par. 24.

62 *Ibid*, par. 111.

63 IIA, AICPA, ACFE, MANAGING THE BUSINESS RISK OF FRAUD: A PRACTICAL GUIDE (2008). Locate on the Internet site of three groups (e.g., *http://www.acfe.com/documents/managing-business-risk.pdf*).

64 Weili Ge and Sarah McVay, "The Disclosure of Material Weaknesses in Internal Control after the Sarbanes-Oxley Act," ACCOUNTING REVIEW (September, 2005), pp. 137-158.

65 Stephen Taub, "How a Material Weakness Will Cost You," *CFO.com*, November 19, 2004.

66 "Material Weaknesses Plunge at Large U.S. Companies, Exclusive Compliance Week Analysis Shows," BUSINESS WIRE (August 5, 2008), http://findarticles.com/p/articles/mi_m0EIN/is_2008_August_5/ai_n27.

67 J.S. Hammersley, K. Johnstone, and K. Kadous, "How Do Audit Seniors Respond to Heightened Fraud Risk?" SSRN manuscript.

68 www.erm.cosous.org.

69 See N. Apostolou and D.L. Crumbley, "Sarbanes-Oxley Fall-out Leads to Auditing Standards No. 2: Importance of Internal Controls," THE VALUE EXAMINER (November/December 2004), pp. 55-60.

70 PCAOB October 17, 2007, pp. 12.

71 Managing the Business Risk of Fraud: A Practical Guide, 2008.

72 Tony Malone and Ralph Childs, Best Practices in Ethics Hotlines, The Network, 2009, pp. 1-25; summarized by Center for Audit Quality, Deterring and Detecting Financial Reporting Fraud: A Platform for Action, October 2010.

73 R.L. Durkin et al., "Incorporating Forensic Procedures in an Audit Environment," LITIGATION AND DISPUTE RESOLUTION SERVICES COMMITTEE (New York: AICPA, 2003).

74 AICPA Technical Consulting Special Report 03-01.

75 R.L. Durkin et al., "Incorporating Forensic Procedures in an Audit Environment," LITIGATION AND DISPUTE RESOLUTION SERVICES COMMITTEE (New York: AICPA, 2003).

76 Luciana Lopez, "Forensic Accountant Uncovers Teachers Union Scandal," Fox News Channel, April 28, 2003, http://www.foxnews.com/story/0,2933,8560,00.htm.

77 Ibid.

78 Ibid.

79 H.R. Davia, FRAUD 101 (New York: John Wiley & Sons, 2000), p. x.

80 "The Con's Lates Ploy," WHITE-COLLAR CRIME FIGHTER, Vol. 9, No. 11, (November 2007), p. 8.

81 IIA, AICPA, ACFE, MANAGING THE BUSINESS RISK OF FRAUD: A PRACTICAL GUIDE (2008), http://www.acfe.com/documents/managing-business-risk.pdf.

82 Paul Shaw and Jack Bologna, PREVENTING CORPORATE EMBEZZLEMENT (Boston: Butterworth, 2000), p. 81.

83 Luciana Lopez, "Forensic Accountant Uncovers Teachers Union Scandal," Fox News Channel, April 28, 2003, http://www.foxnews.com/story/0,2933,8560,00.htm.

84 Sinead Carew, "Duncan Invokes Fifth Amendment Rights," ACCOUNTANCYAGE.COM, January 24, 2002, www.financialdirector.co.uk/news/1127464.

85 Mimi Swartz and Sherron Watkins, POWER FAILURE (New York: Doubleday, 2003), p. 234.

86 Anita Raghavan, "Relentless Pressure to Succeed," BUSINESS SCOTSMAN.COM, May 20, 2002, www.businessscotsman.com/topics.cfm.

87 Michael Ramos, "Auditors' Responsibility for Fraud Detection," JOURNAL OF ACCOUNTANCY (January 2003), pp. 28-36.

88 A.S. Wellner, "Strategies: A Perfect Brainstorm," INC. MAGAZINE (October 2003), pp. 31-35.

89 M.S. Beasley and J.G. Jenkins, "A Primer for Brainstorming Fraud Risks," JOURNAL OF ACCOUNTANCY (December 2003), pp. 33-34.

90 Ibid.

91 SAS No. 99, Consideration of Fraud in a Financial Statement Audit (New York: AICPA 2002).

92 C.J. Loomis, "Why AOL's Accounting Problems Keep Popping Up," FORTUNE (April 28, 2003), p. 86.

93 Jake Poinier, "Fraud Finder," FUTURE MAGAZINE (Fall 2004), http://www.phoneix.edu/students/future/oldissues/winter2004.fraud.htm.

94 T. Reason and E. Teach, "Lies, Damn Lies, and Pro Forma," CFO (March 2002), p. 73.

95 R. D. Fuerman, "Bernard Madoff and the Sole Auditor Red Flag," JOURNAL OF FORENSIC AND INVESTIGATIVE ACCOUNTING, Vol. 1, No. 1 (January–June 2009), pp. 1-38.

96 Q.S. Kim, "Rent-Way Details Improper Bookkeeping," THE WALL STREET JOURNAL (June 8, 2001), p. C-1.

97 Jesse Drucker and Henny Sender, "Strategy Behind Accounting Scheme," THE WALL STREET JOURNAL (June 27, 2002), p. A-9.

98 EITF Issue No. 85-1, Classifying Notes Received for Capital Stock, and SEC Staff Accounting Bulletin No. 40, Topic 4-E, Receivables from Sale of Stock.

99 Amy Hamilton, "Off-Balance Sheet Financing Raises New Suspicions," TAX NOTES (June 17, 2002), p. 1705.

100 J.E. Ketz, HIDDEN FINANCIAL RISKS (John Wiley & Sons, 2003).

101 Jeremy Grant, "Companies Balance Sheets Set to Get a New Lease of Life," FINANCIAL TIMES (February 21, 2007), p. 18.

102 Floyd Norris, "Private Pension Plans, Even at Big Companies May be Underfunded," New York Times, July 20, 2012, http://www.nytimes.com/2012/07/21/business/pension-plans-increasing... V. Monga, "Why the Pension Gap Is Soaring," Wall Street J., February 26, 2013, p. B1.

103 Norma Cohen, "US Pension Insurer Warns of Rising Deficit," Financial Times, January 30, 2013, http://www.ft.com/cms/s/0/20429caa-6a49-11e2-a3db-00144feab49a....

104 Ibid.

105 Michael Sivy, "How Bad is America's Pension Funding Problem?" Time, September 26, 2012, http://business.time.com/2012/09/26/how-bad-is-americas-pension-fun.......

106 Matt Moore, "WorldCom Finds Another $3.3 B in Errors," WASHINGTONPOST.COM, August 8, 2002.

107 Editorial, "Corporate Crime Blotter," THE WALL STREET JOURNAL (August 8, 2002), p. A-12.

108 Mathew Miller, M.L. Clifford, and Susan Zegel, "Dishonored Dealmaker," BUSINESS WEEK (August 5, 2002), pp. 44–45.

109 Ibid, pp. 45–46.

110 Mimi Swartz and Sherron Watkins, POWER FAILURE (New York: Doubleday, 2003), p. 269.

111 R.B. Parker, WIDOW'S WALK, (Berkeley Books, 2002).

112 Michael Connelly, CHASING THE DIME (Hieronymous, Inc., 2002).

113 Cindy Durtschi, "The Tallahassee BeanCounters: A Problem-Based Learning Case in Forensic Audit," ISSUES IN ACCOUNTING EDUCATION 18 (2) (May 2003), pp. 137-173.

[114] Lee Child, ECHO BURNING (New York: Jove Books, 2001), p. 281.

[115] IIA, AICPA, ACFE, MANAGING THE BUSINESS RISK OF FRAUD: A PRACTICAL GUIDE (2008), *http://www.acfe.com/ documents/managing-business-risk.pdf*, pp. 42-43.

[116] IIA, AICPA, ACFE, MANAGING THE BUSINESS RISK OF FRAUD: A PRACTICAL GUIDE (2008), *http://www.acfe.com/ documents/managing-business-risk.pdf*, p. 43.

[117] Myway, "Video Shows Coke Worker Taking Documents," January 26, 2007.

[118] Glen D. Moyes and C. Richard Baker, "Auditors' Beliefs about the Fraud Detection Effectiveness of Standard Audit Procedures," JOURNAL OF FORENSIC ACCOUNTING 4 (2003), p. 211.

[119] Monica Langely, "Big Companies Get Low Marks for Lavish Executive Pay," THE WALL STREET JOURNAL (June 9, 2003), p. C-1.

[120] Deborah Solomon, "Life After Whistle-Blowing," N.Y. TIMES (June 6, 2004).

[121] S. Balsam, AN INTRODUCTION TO EXECUTIVE COMPENSATION (San Diego, CA: The Academic Press, 2002).

[122] J.E. Core, R. Holthausen, and D. Larcker, "Corporate Governance, Chief Executive Officer Compensation, and Firm Performance," JOURNAL OF FINANCIAL ECONOMICS 51 (1999), pp. 371-406.

[123] B. Main, C. O'Reilly, and J. Wade, "The CEO, the Board of Directors and Executive Compensation: Economic and Psychological Perspectives," INDUSTRIAL AND CORPORATE CHANGE 4 (1995), pp. 293-332.

[124] C. Hill and P. Phan, "CEO Tenure as a Determinant of CEO Pay," ACADEMY OF MANAGEMENT JOURNAL 34 (1991), pp. 707-711.

[125] J. Wade, C. O'Reilly, and I. Chandratat, "Golden Parachutes: CEOs and the Exercise of Social Influence," ADMINISTRATIVE SCIENCE QUARTERLY 35 (1990), pp. 587-603.

[126] Ernst & Young, "American Works: Employers Lose 20 Percent of Every Dollar to Work Place Fraud," (2002) Available at *http://www.ey.com/global/Content.nsf/US/ Media_Release_-_08-05-02DC.*

[127] "Who Blows The Whistle On Corporate Fraud?," research paper by Alexander Dyck, University of Toronto, Adair Morse, University of Michigan, and Luigi Zingales, University of Chicago, *http://faculty.chicagogsb.edu/ luigi.zingales/research/PSpapers/whistle.pdf.*

[128] Ronald L. Durkin et al., "Incorporating Forensic Procedures in an Audit Environment," LITIGATION AND DISPUTE RESOLUTION SERVICES SUBCOMMITTEE (New York: AICPA, 2003).

[129] Don Rabon, INTERVIEWING AND INTERROGATION (Durham: Carolina Academic Press, 1992), p. 8.

[130] "Lying 101: There May Be Nonverbal Indicators of Lying," *http://members.tripod.com/nwacc_ communication/id25.htm.*

[131] Chad Bray, "Adelphia Witness Lays Out Lies," THE WALL STREET JOURNAL (May 19, 2004), pp. C-1 and C-2.

[132] Michael Connelly, THE BLACK ICE (St. Martin's Paperback, 1993).

[133] *Ibid*, pp. 92-93.

[134] James Lee Burke, BITTERROOT (New York: Pocket Star Books, 2001), pp. 218-219.

[135] F.E. Inbau, "Essentials of the Reid Technique: Criminal Interrogation and Confessions," Sudbury, MA: Jones & Bartlett Publishers, 2005, pp. 28-33.

[136] *Ibid.*, pp. 41-43.

[137] H.W. Wolosky, "Forensic Accounting to the Forefront," PRACTICAL ACCOUNTANT (February 2004), pp. 23-28.

[138] *Ibid.*

[139] Don Rabon, INTERVIEWING AND INTERROGATION (Durham: Carolina Academic Press, 1992), p. 8.

[140] *http:faculty.nncwc,edu/tocnnor/410/410lecture12.htm.*

[141] "Police Interviewing Techniques," BRITISH JOURNAL OF CRIMINOLOGY 33 (1993).

[142] "Interviewing & Interrogation," THE REID TECHNIQUE, John E. Reid Associates, Inc., L.E.R.C Law Enforcements.

[143] "Lying 101: There May Be Nonverbal Indicators of Lying," *http://members.tripod.com/nwacc_ communication/id25.htm.*

[144] J.L. Hobson, W.J. Mayew, and M. Venkatachalam, "Analyzing Speech to Detect Financial Misreporting," SSRN manuscript, November 8, 2010, *http://papers.ssrn. com/sol3/papers.cfm?abstract_id=1531871.*

[145] D.F. Larcker and A.A. Zakolyukina, "Detecting Deceptive Discussions in Conference Calls," SSRN manuscript, July 29, 2010, *http://papers.ssrn.com/sol3/papers. cfm?abstract_id=1572705.*

[146] C.C. Lee, R.B. Welker, and T. Wang, "Effect of Red Flags on the Inclination to Believe Interviewees: An Experimental Investigation," Unpublished Manuscript.

[147] *Ibid.* D.F. Larcker and B. Tayan, "Financial Manipulation: Words Don't Lie," CGRP-07 (July 23, 2010), Stanford University.

[148] Kathy Reichs, *Cross Bones*, Pocket Book, 2005, p.258.

[149] Kevin Voigt, "Sex, Lies, and Accounting Fraud" Accounting web, *http://www.accountingweb.com/topic/ watchdog/sex-lies-and-accounting-fraud.*

[150] *Ibid.*

[151] Brad Meltzer, *The First Counsel*, Grand Central Pub. NY., 2001, p.86

[152] UpJohn v. U.S., 449 U.S. 383 (1981). For more detail, see U.S. v. Ruehle, 583 F.3d 600 (CA-9, 2009).

[153] For more detail, see L.G. Dunst and D.J. Chirlin, "A Renewed Emphasis on UpJohn Warnings," *White-Collar Crime*, Vol. 23, No. 12, September 2009.

[154] D.L. Crumbley, J.J. O'Shaughnessy, and D.E. Ziegenfuss, 2002 U.S. MASTER AUDITING GUIDE (Chicago: CCH INCORPORATED, 2002), p. 592.

[155] Sonya Stinson, "Accountants Put Skills to Work to Help Nab Criminals," CITY BUSINESS (January 2001), p. 2.

[156] Litigation Release 17859A (November 25, 2002).

[157] J.T. Wells, "Irrational Ratios," JOURNAL OF ACCOUNTANCY (August 2001), p. 80.

[158] Hugh Grove and Tom Cook, "Lessons for Auditors: Quantitative Red Flags," JOURNAL OF FORENSIC ACCOUNTING 5 (2004), pp. 131-146.

[159] Ibid, p. 145.

[160] M.D. Beneish, "The Detection of Earnings Manipulation," FINANCIAL ANALYST JOURNAL (September/October, 1999).

[161] Joe Wells, "Irrational Ratios," JOURNAL OF ACCOUNTANCY (August 2001), pp. 80-83.

[162] Grove and Cook, op. cit., pp. 144-146.

[163] C.R. Lundelius, FINANCIAL REPORTING FRAUD (AICPA, 2003), p. 129.

[164] PCAOB Release 2004-001, A-66.

[165] THE CONFIRMATION PROCESS, par. 34.

[166] Inventories, par. .01.

[167] W.S. Albrecht, C.C. Albrecht, and C.O. Albrecht, "Fraud and Corporate Executives: Agency, Stewardship, and Broken Trust," JOURNAL OF FORENSIC ACCOUNTING 5 (2004), pp. 112-113.

[168] Louis Lavelle, "Directors Know When to Fold Them," BUSINESS WEEK (May 24, 2004), p.14.

[169] J.V. Carcello, D.R. Hermanson, and Z. Ye, Corporate Governance Research in Accounting and Auditing: Insights, Practice Implications, and Future Research, Auditing: A Journal of Practice & Theory

[170] E.M. Fich and A. Shivdasani. "Financial Fraud, Director Reputation, and Shareholder Wealth," J. of Financial Economics, Vol. 86, Issue 2, 2007, pp. 306-336

[171] Y. Zhao and K.H. Chen, "Staggered Boards and Earnings Management," The Accounting Review, Vol. 83, Vol. 5, 2008, pp. 1347-1381.

[172] M.S. Beasley, J.V. Carcello, D.R. Hermanson, and T.L. Neal, Fraudulent Financial Reporting 1998-2007: An Analysis of U.S. Public Companies. Durham, NC: Committee of Sponsoring Organizations of the Treadway Commission (COSO), 2010. Available at: http://www.coso.org/documents/COSOFRAUDSTUDY2010_001.pdf

[173] M.L. Cheffers and J. Bourassa, "Accounting Malpractice Exposure and the Impact of the Panel on Audit Effectiveness Report," OHIO CPA (October–December 2001), p. 28.

[174] AICPA, http://aicpa.org/members/div/mcs/fraudin.htm, accessed April 20, 2003.

[175] Ramamoorti and S. Curtis, "Procurement Fraud & Data Analytics," JOURNAL OF GOVERNMENT FINANCIAL MANAGEMENT 52 (4) (Winter 2003), pp. 16–24.

[176] G.J. Bologna and R.J. Lindquist, FRAUD AUDITING AND FORENSIC ACCOUNTING, 2d ed. (New York: John Wiley, 1995), pp. 36-37.

[177] E.T. Pound, "Following the Old Money Trail," U.S. NEWS & WORLD REPORT (April 4, 2005), p. 30.

[178] 2012 Wells Report, ACFE.

[179] Dehaan, et al. "Does Voluntary Adoption of Clawback Provision Improve Financial Reporting Quality?" Contemporary Accounting Research, 2012.

[180] Laura Stevens, "'Claw' Claims Trader Bonus," The Wall Street Journal, Saturday/Sunday, January 26-27, 2013, p. B2.

[181] C.C. Lee, N.T. Churyk, and B.D. Clinton, "Validating Early Fraud Prediction Using Narrative Disclosures," J. of Forensic & Investigative Accounting, Vol.5, No.1, January – June, 2013, pp. 35-57.

[182] See also N.T. Churyk, C.C. Lee, and B.D. Clinton, "Early Detection of Fraud: Evidence from Restatements," Advances in Accounting Behavioral Research, 2009, Vol. 12, pp. 25-40.

[183] Ibid.

[184] Ibid.

[185] C.H. Lee, E.J. Lush, and H. Halperin, "Content Analysis for Early Detection of Fraud: Evidence from Restatements During the SOX Era. "J. of Forensic & Investigative Accounting, 2013, Vol. 5, No. 2.

[186] Heron House, THE ODDS ON VIRTUALLY EVERYTHING (New York: G.P. Putnam, 1980), p. 188.

EXERCISES

1. What change in auditing may have caused Enron, WorldCom, Xerox, and the other fraudulent situations?
2. What two fieldwork stages gather audit evidence?
3. Define these terms:
   a. Materiality
   b. Control risk
   c. Inherent risk
   d. Detection risk
4. What does Lee Seidler say about external auditors? What overcomes the assumption that separation of duties prevents fraud?
5. Are the GAAS audit standards designed to catch fraud other than financial statement fraud? What is the expectation gap? Did SAS No. 99 close it?
6. What was significant with respect to the recommendations by "The Panel on Audit Effectiveness Report and Recommendations?"
7. What is the key question that an auditor should ask according to the Panel on Audit Effectiveness?"
8. What are some of the main points of SAS No. 99?
9. What is the Public Company Accounting Oversight Board (PCACOB)?

10. What is the Institute of Internal Auditors' definition of internal auditing?

11. What is the internal auditor's task with respect to fraud? Who has primary responsibility?

12. Why are Cynthia Cooper and Scott Sullivan significant in detecting financial reporting fraud?

13. What are some of the requirements for audit committees under the Sarbanes-Oxley Act?

14. Why might management be interested in forensic accounting services?

15. What are pro formas?

16. What is a red flag with respect to earnings?

17. How does a forensic accountant analyze inventories and receivables?

18. What is horizontal analysis?

19. What is vertical analysis?

20. The following information is taken from the accounting records of Donald Company:

Average receivables........................$ 700,000
Cost of goods sold 2,900,000
Sales...8,000,000
Average inventory 1,100,000
Net credit sales................................1,200,000
Operating income 900,000

The inventory turnover is:
a. 1.81
b. 2.2
c. 2.64
d. 2.92
e. None of the above

21. Using the facts in problem 21, the operating margin is:
a. .1125
b. .32
c. 1.1
d. 1.6
e. None of the above

22. A forensic account determines the following facts about a company:

Cash and equivalents.........................$76,000
Receivables 218,000
Current assets.....................................420,000
Current liabilities...............................240,000
Average inventory 310,000
Cost of goods sold 580,000
Advertising expenses.........................255,000

Calculate the following ratio:
a. Current ratio
b. Quick ratio
c. Working capital
d. Inventory turnover

23. Which statement is false with respect to SAS No. 99?
a. SAS No. 99 supersedes SAS No. 82.
b. An audit procedure to address the risk of management override would include examining journal entries and other adjustments.
c. The management characteristics category in SAS No. 82 is significantly more important than those in the other two SAS No. 82 categories.
d. Unlike errors, fraud is intentional and usually involves deliberate concealment of the facts.
e. None of the above.

24. Define these terms:
a. Cooking the books
b. Cookie jar accounting
c. Bottom line
d. EBIT
e. EBITDA
f. Off-balance-sheet financing
g. Channel stuffing
h. Bid rigging
i. Big bath

25. A clerk works in a wholesale business that also operates several retail outlets. Thus, cash sales are common. This clerk is responsible for tallying the day's cash receipts and preparing the daily bank deposit tickets. What is wrong with this situation? What may the clerk do?

26. During the Arthur Andersen obstruction of justice trial, Andersen's attorney Rusty Hardin told jurors that there is "no question David Duncan was a client pleaser." What is wrong with Duncan's approach?

27. Which of these statements is false according to auditing standards?
a. A high degree of competition accompanied by declining margins would be an example of an opportunity for fraudulent financial reporting.
b. Personal guarantees of debt of a company that are significant to one's personal net worth are an example of a pressure/incentive for fraudulent financial reporting.
c. A heavy concentration of one's wealth in a particular company would be an example of a rationalization condition for fraudulent financial reporting.
d. An excessive interest by management in maintaining a company's stock price is

an example of rationalization for fraudulent financial reporting.

e. An anticipated future layoff would be an example of one incentive to misappropriate assets.

f. A large amount of cash on hand would be an example of a rationalization to misappropriate assets.

g. Inadequate internal controls are an example of an opportunity to misappropriate assets.

28. What is meant by the expectation gap?

29. Forensic accounting is governed by the materiality concept. Analyze this statement.

30. What is a material weakness?

31. What is meant by "more than remote?"

32. What are the seven investigative techniques available to a forensic accountant?

33. What public document reviews may be helpful to a forensic accountant?

34. What laboratory analysis may be helpful to a forensic accountant?

35. What could be key points of a company's anti-fraud program?

36. Based upon PCAOB Release 2004-001, what are some strong indicators of material weakness in internal control over financial reporting?

37. Explain the detective approach to solving a forensic problem versus the scientific approach.

38. What are the three major phases of a fraud? How can an accountant find fraud in each phase?

39. What can forensic accountants learn about top executives' compensation?

40. How could auditors have stopped Parmalat's deceptions?

41. How should auditors search for hidden liabilities?

42. A mid-sized company has a standard sales contract, but sales personnel frequently modify the terms of the contract. The nature of the modifications can affect the timing and amount of revenue recognized. Individual sales transactions are frequently material to the entity, and the gross margin can vary significantly for each transaction.

The company does not have a procedure in place for the accounting function to regularly review modifications to sales contract terms. Although management reviews gross margins on a monthly basis, the significant differences in gross margins on individual transactions make it difficult for management to identify potential misstatements. Improper revenue recognition has occurred, and the amounts have been material. Does this scenario meet the definition of a material weakness? Why or why not?

43. A large company has a standard sales contract, but sales personnel frequently modify the terms of the contract. Sales personnel frequently grant authorized and unrecorded sales discounts to customers without the knowledge of the accounting department. These amounts are deducted by the customers in paying their invoices and are recorded as outstanding balances on the accounts receivable aging schedule. Although these amounts are individually insignificant, they are material in the aggregate and have occurred consistently over the past few years. Does this scenario meet the definition of a material weakness? Why or why not?

44. During the assessment of internal control over financial reporting, management identified the following deficiencies. Based on the context in which the deficiencies occur, management and the external auditor agree that these deficiencies individually represent significant deficiencies:

- Inadequate segregation of duties over certain information system access controls.

- Several instances of transactions that were not properly recorded in subsidiary ledgers, transactions were not material, either individually or in the aggregate.

- A lack of timely reconciliations of the account balances affected by the improperly recorded transactions.

Does the combination of these significant deficiencies represent a material weakness? Why or why not?

45. In order to determine how risky a particular company is that you are auditing, you prepare these five ratios along with the same ratios of this company's peers:

	Company	Peers
Day's Sales in Receivable Index	1.51	1.05
Gross Margin Index	1.98	1.11
Asset Quality Index	1.21	1.01
Sales Growth Index	1.53	1.19
Total Accruals to Total Assets	0.11	0.06

What are your thoughts about the risk potential of this company?

46. You are provided the following information about a company for two years (in millions):

	2005	2006
Sales	$23,000	32,000
Cost of Sales	11,960	17,600
Accounts Receivable	4,830	10,560

Calculate:
   a.   Days Sales in receivable index
   b.   Gross margin index
   c.   Sales growth index
   Any thoughts about this company?

47. Find the May 2010, COSO fraud study by M.S. Beasley et al. and answer these questions.
   a.   What is the median fraud amount?
   b.   What percentage of the time was the CEO or CFO involved with the fraud?
   c.   What percentage of the cases involved revenue fraud?
   d.   What percentage of the cases involved overstating assets?
   e.   What percentage of the companies traded on NASDAQ?

48. Suppose you are fired because you would not "cook the books." Do you have any regress? Check out some whistle-blowers websites, especially the Office of Special Counsel.

49. Find the Panel on Audit Effectiveness report by the Public Oversight Board (August 31, 2000) and outline the panel's major recommendations concerning forensic techniques (pp. 1 and 2).

50. Search on the Internet for discussions that distinguish an interview from an interrogation.

51. Using the Internet or print media, find some examples of off-balance sheet ideas.

52. Find websites describing "big bath" situations.

53. On the Internet, find sites describing examples of the bill-and-hold technique.

54. Read about the ZZZZ Best Carpet Cleaning fraud. What schemes did the fraudsters use?

55. Search the Internet for the improper transactions incurred by the A.I.G. What happened to the chairman Maurice R. Greenberg?

56. Search the Internet for Thomas M. Coughlin, former Wal-Mart vice-chairman. What was he accused of in April 2005? What was his annual compensation in 2004?

57. Search the Internet for the outcome of these courtroom scandals:
   a.   Walter Forbes
   b.   Ken Lay
   c.   Jeffery Skilling
   d.   Mark Swartz
   e.   Sam Waksal

58. Using the Internet, learn what type of fraud was found at McKesson & Robbins in the 1930s. How large a fraud?

59. What internal control framework is used most often in the United States?
   a.   Auditing Standard No. 2
   b.   SAS No. 99
   c.   COBIT
   d.   COSO
   e.   Some other framework

60. In baseball analogy, who would be the auditee?
   a.   Pitcher
   b.   Catcher
   c.   Manager
   d.   Umpire
   e.   Some other answer

61. Which would not be one of the six legs on the six-legged table of financial statements?
   a.   The IRS
   b.   Management
   c.   External auditors
   d.   PCAOB
   e.   Board of Directors

62. Who is responsible for internal controls?
   a.   External auditors
   b.   Internal auditors
   c.   Management
   d.   Audit Committee
   e.   Board of Directors

63. Which statement is false?
   a.   Waste Management made top drawer entries.
   b.   Richard Scrushy of Tyco was never convicted.
   c.   Adelphia used special purpose entities to commit their fraud.
   d.   Rationalization reduces an offender's inhibitions.
   e.   None of the above is false.

64. Which statement is false?
    a. SAS No. 99 does not prohibit clients from preparing confirmations.
    b. Enron issued $1.2 billion of stock to an SPE and recorded a $1.2 billion notes receivable.
    c. Most of WorldCom's original entries for online costs were properly placed into expense accounts.
    d. Materiality is not important for an external auditor.
    e. For prosecution for fraud, an accountant needs to find *scienter* (knowingly).
65. "Remote" for purposes of material and control deficiencies refers to:
    a. One out of 20
    b. One out of 25
    c. One out of 30
    d. One out of 40
    e. Some other description
66. What forensic technique was used by Coca-Cola to prosecute the secretary who was convicted for attempting to sell product information to Pepsi?
    a. Invigilation
    b. Interviews
    c. Videotape
    d. Net worth method
    e. Horizontal analysis
67. The _____ theory says that covert aspects of fraud may be as important as overt aspects.
    a. Backdating
    b. Invigilation
    c. Graphology
    d. Iceberg
    e. Game
68. _____ _____ refers to a company pulling revenues into the distribution channel fraudulently.
    a. Constructive intent
    b. Channel stuffing
    c. Gaming strategy
    d. Big bath
    e. Double play

69. Which statement is false?
    a. SAS No. 99 does not mention forensic accounting.
    b. SAS No. 99 does not require auditors to make inquiries of "others" as opposed to management.
    c. Many of the companies indicted by the SEC after Enron had CEOs with compensation 75 percent above their peers.
    d. Bill and hold refers to improper revenue recognition.
    e. According to the 2006 Wells Report, fictitious revenues was the most common financial statement fraud scheme.
70. What would not be an abusive earnings management scheme according to the SEC?
    a. A big bath
    b. Channel stuffing
    c. Postponing repairs and maintenance expenses
    d. Cookie-jar accounting
    e. a. and c. above
71. What is not required by SOX companies?
    a. CEO may not be chairperson of BOD.
    b. Auditors must report to audit committee on a timely basis.
    c. Rotation of lead auditor every five years.
    d. Internal auditing outsourcing outlawed to auditor of company.
    e. Tax services must be pre-approved by the audit committee.
72. What would not be a red flag with horizontal analysis?
    a. Accounts receivable is rising faster than revenue.
    b. Cash flow is increasing faster than net income.
    c. Falling bad debt reserves in relation to accounts receivable.
    d. Inventory is rising faster than revenue.
    e. Inventory, sales, and receivables are moving in tandem.
73. Which statement is false with respect to the PCAOB?
    a. PCAOB issues standards describing auditor's attestation requirements.
    b. D.W. Squires was a former chief auditor of PCAOB.
    c. PCAOB is a five-member oversight board.
    d. PCAOB's reports must be approved by the SEC.
    e. None of the above.

74. Which statement is false with respect to Section 404 of SOX?
    a. The section requires management's assessment of internal control over financial reporting.
    b. The auditor's report on internal control over financial reporting must be included in a company's annual report on Form 10-K.
    c. Implementing Section 404 has been relatively easy and inexpensive.
    d. Registrants must include the internal control report in the annual report to shareholders.
    e. None of the above.

75. According to the SEC, which is not a sign of a possible fraudulent company?
    a. Insiders having greater than 50 percent control of the BOD.
    b. CEO also being chairman of the BOD.
    c. CEO being the company's founder.
    d. Lack of an audit committee.
    e. All of the above are signs.

76. Which statement is false?
    a. Significant deficiencies need only be reported to the BOD.
    b. Material deficiencies must be publicly reported.
    c. The most common area of material weaknesses has been revenue recognition.
    d. PCAOB requires SOX auditors to walk-through company transactions and events.
    e. None is false.

77. Select five of these alleged fraudsters and prepare a two-paragraph discussion of them. Outline their modus operandi.
    1. Frank Abagnale
    2. Jack Abramoff
    3. Kobi Alexander
    4. Eddie Antar
    5. Jim Bakker
    6. Conrad Black (tax fraud)
    7. Dale Brown
    8. Desiree Brown/Lee Farkas (Taylor Bean)
    9. Rita Crundwell
    10. Adrian Dicker (United Kingdom)
    11. Albert J. Dunlap
    12. Bernard Ebbers
    13. Andrew Fastow
    14. Walter Forbes
    15. Martin Frankel
    16. Stanley Goldblum
    17. Leonard Helmsley
    18. Clifford Michael Irving
    19. Mahaveer Kankariya and Atul Shah
    20. Charles Keating
    21. Kwame M. Kilpatrick
    22. Dennis Kozlowski
    23. Ivar Kreuger
    24. Sanjay Kumar
    25. Lyndon LaRouche
    26. Kenneth Lay
    27. Nick Leeson
    28. Bernie Madoff
    29. Michael Milken
    30. Mickey Monus
    31. Philip Musica
    32. Young Hwan Park
    33. Charles Ponzi (tax fraud)
    34. Charles Rangel (tax)
    35. Mark Rich
    36. John Rigas
    37. Dan Rostenowski
    35. Richard Scrushy
    36. Richard Siekaczek
    37. Sir Allen Stanford
    38. Martha Stewart (inside trading)
    39. Scott Sullivan
    40. James Guy Tucker, Jr.
    41. Robert Vesco
    42. Alberto Vilar
    43. Harriette Walters (District of Columbia)
    44. Leonard Weinglass
    45. Mark Whitacre

78. Prepare a one-hour action pack T.V. episode with the main character a forensic accountant or auditor. The main character should be called Dane Striker or Sloane Striker. Your project can include a pitch, a list of characters, and overall plot for the T.V. show. The better projects may include the entire show. Two or three pages are not enough.

79. Develop a reality T.V. show involving accountants (e.g., forensic accountants).

80. You are hired to perform a forensic audit of a movie (e.g., College). Prepare a short term paper on production accounting for a movie or T.V. production.

81. How can vendor allowances be used to cook the books?

82. Below is an interview with Sanjay Kumar, CEO of Computer Associates (April 2001). Point out some red flags or indicators that Kumar may be lying.

Interview with Sanjay Kumar, CEO of Computer Associates (April 2001)

Bill Griffeth (CNBC): [...] Before we get to the specific charges, why do you think these employees would say what they did about your accounting practices?

Sanjay Kumar: Well, I mean, you know, I don't want to play tit for tat with the New York Times, because (unintelligible) somebody who buys paper by the barrel, but let me tell you, there is not a single named employee source in there, there's not a single Wall Street analyst named in the article. To me that is just incredible that the New York Times, a paper of record, would write a story like this without talking to a single accounting source, and he talks to two customers. [...] So I'm not sure where the factual reporting is for the story.

Griffeth: And in the big picture, I mean, the charge that you are trying to mask a decline in sales, I mean, when you are saying that revenues are up, I mean it comes at a time when everybody is, you know, falling on hard times, especially for information technology spending. I mean there is nothing wrong in this climate with having a declining sales rate right now.

Kumar: Well, you are right, there is nothing wrong with it, and we, like everybody else, are seeing tough economic times. You can refer to our April 16th press release where we talked about the fourth fiscal quarter. We clearly said economic times are tough, but we are doing better. [...] Part of the difference here is our new business model. [...] If you look at our press release, in the body of the press release is a very clear sentence that says we also signed $1.3 billion of backlog in the quarter that under the new business model will come into revenue in the future. That is $1.3 billion more than reported revenue that we signed. These are committed customer contracts, signed, done, signed, sealed and delivered, that doesn't come into the [current] period, and to leave that out, I think, is just unfair.

Griffeth: But there is a question posed in the article of how much of what you have booked was maintenance business as opposed to actual new software business.

Kumar: That's right, and we said very clearly today that our maintenance numbers conformed to GAAP accounting, our maintenance numbers conform to accounting statements of position of 972 and 989 of a technical pronouncement...

Griffeth: With all due respect, Sanjay, you can hide behind GAAP accounting methods. Is there a possibility that it is easy to perhaps confuse maintenance business from new software contracts?

Kumar: No, you can't hide [behind] GAAP. GAAP accounting rules are the ones that we all live by and they are very strict. We had both KPMG and [Ernst & Young] yesterday restate that they are ok with our numbers. We have taken the unusual step of getting an attestation to our pro forma numbers. I don't think there's really any confusion at all with respect to the numbers. And we also, by the way, further details on our call this morning and there's information on our Web site as to why our maintenance numbers are in the range, but at the low end of the range, of software companies. And it's a perfectly plausible answer. We don't need to have maintenance numbers like anybody else, but we are not doing anything wrong fundamentally in our business.

[...]

Griffeth: I'm running out of time, unfortunately, but for the record, have you been contacted by anybody connected at all with the SEC about any possible investigation, whether it has, in fact, begun or whether they are in formal inquires about your accounting practices?

Kumar: No, sir. [...] I, my general counsel and CFO have no knowledge whatsoever of any SEC investigation.

Griffeth: Any thoughts of taking action on this on your part?

Kumar: Well, I think we have to do what's right for the company. Today we want to clarify our business model, defend what's right for the company and defend our shareholders. I am most concerned about shareholder value and I think ultimately the truth will prevail. [...]

Griffeth: Mr. Kumar, thank you for taking the time to chat with us.

Kumar: Thank you.

5

EMPLOYEE FRAUD: THE MISAPPROPRIATION OF ASSETS

Unlike other criminal offenses, part of the method of fraud is to conceal its existence. While a bank robber uses overt threats or force, a bank embezzler not only steals money, but also covers up the theft.

—Bruce G. Dubinsky[1]

OBJECTIVES

After completing Chapter 5, you should be able to:

1. Recognize a number of fraud schemes.
2. Understand some of the reasons employees commit fraud.
3. Suggest some ways to prevent fraud.
4. Determine a company's response plan to internal fraud.
5. Assess the financial health of various governments.

OVERVIEW

There are many ways employees can commit fraud and often, they involve false documents that help skirt internal controls. Accountants are perhaps the most valuable employee-fraud fighters because they possess the best understanding of how businesses operate and how transactions flow through the financial or "central nervous system" of the operation.

Employees who commit fraud are motivated by the same factors that influence other fraud perpetrators. Identifying psychological characteristics of employees who commit fraud has not produced much in the way of hard and fast unique descriptors. Some would say that employee fraud may have more to do with what is going on in employees' lives than in what particular character traits they may possess.

Fighting employee fraud and all the various schemes that can be directed at a company's assets involves planning, management, controls, policy, and much more. Fighting fraud, like fighting any loss, calls for prevention as the first step and the preferred tactic. Perhaps no one is as well-suited as the accountant in setting up programs to prevent loss in an organization. Forensic accountants need to understand all the employee fraud schemes so they can apply their knowledge, skills, and abilities to combat them.

Employee fraud is not limited to the private sector. Government entities and nonprofits are targets as well. Fraud creeps into the corporate board rooms of the largest businesses in the world and the most admired government organizations such as NASA. Employees commit fraud at the most benevolent charitable organizations in the world and at the most powerful seats of federal, state, and local government.

The source of fraud is often so surprising and can be so widespread that the forensic accountant, perhaps more than any other professional, must always remain objective and on-guard. In fighting employee fraud, the forensic accountant will work with company management, directors, consultants, lawyers, security managers, and many others who have an interest in the organization. Yet, because fraud can come from any quarter, they must act alone so they can think and operate coolly and objectively.

As Joseph W. Koletar states in his book, *Fraud Exposed*:[2]

> Let's face it, we in the forensic profession labor in an obscure corner of the vineyard. We are the carefully selected, trusted, highly trained guardians of one of the last great secrets remaining on the face of the earth—the $600 billion [now close to $1 trillion] more or less annual problem nobody knows about.

Michael Comer, an English author, breaks fraud into these five broad categories:[3]
1. Corruptions (e.g., kickbacks).
2. Conflicts of interest (e.g., drug/alcohol abuse, part-time work).
3. Theft of assets.
4. False reporting or falsifying performance (e.g., false accounts, manipulating financial results).
5. Technological abuse (e.g., computer related fraud, unauthorized Internet browsing).

Mr. Comer believes that fraud can happen to anyone at anytime, and like a cold, it is hard to keep fraud from spreading. Also, a fraud investigation or litigation support assignment can have more twists and turns than a strand of DNA.

Fraud Schemes and Their Schemers

¶ 5001   COMPANY SUSCEPTIBILITY TO FRAUD

Indiana University Professor Edwin Sutherland coined the term "white-collar crime." He believed that white-collar crime is a learned behavior, a consequence of corporate culture where regulations are regarded as harassment, and profit is the measure of a man or woman. Sutherland felt that white-collar crime violates trust and thus creates distrust. Distrust lowers social morale and produces social disorganization on a large scale.[4]

There are a number of schemes that employees and outsiders may use to commit fraud, so fraud detection is important for most organizations. Just as tax credits are a dollar-for-dollar reduction in tax liability, employee fraud often results in a dollar-for-dollar reduction in net income. Suppose employee fraud reduces the bottom line by $100,000, and a company has a 20 percent profit margin. The company must generate additional revenue of $500,000 to offset the lost income (more than five times the amount of fraud). Factor in that the Association of Certified Fraud Examiners estimates that fraud and abuse causes U.S. organizations to lose five percent of annual revenue. The FBI estimates that fraud is $300 billion in the United States per year. One of the authors of this textbook estimates that fraud may be as high as $1 trillion per year in the United States, and of course, fraud is an international problem.

The loss of cash and other assets due to fraud is not the only damage to an entity. The respondents in the PwC's 2009 Global Economic Crime survey stated these additional damages from fraud:

- Employee morale   32%
- Business relations   23%
- Organization's reputation/brand   19%
- Relations with regulators   16%
- Share price   6%
- Others   4%

Often misappropriations are accomplished by false or misleading records or documents, possibly created by circumventing internal controls.[5] Sometimes random events will bring the fraud to light. Auditors must be more skeptical as well, employing forensic procedures in their audits. Internal and external auditors must demand evidentiary support for all questionable transactions. This chapter surveys the types of misappropriation of assets and explains ways to combat such fraud. For an extensive discussion of employee fraud see *Occupational Fraud and Abuse, Accountant's Guide to Fraud Detection and Control,* and *Fraud 101.*[6]

EYEWITNESS

A secretary was defrauding two medical doctors for whom she was working by submitting the same bill to both doctors individually. This fraud continued until one of the doctors found the duplicate receipts in her desk drawer while she was on vacation.[7]

The 2012 Wells Report indicates that the most common method of detecting occupational fraud is by a tip from an employee, customers, vendor, or anonymous source. The second and third most common methods are by internal auditors and management review, respectively. The most targeted asset is cash.[8]

Impact of Hotlines (2012 Wells Report)

Impact of Hotlines

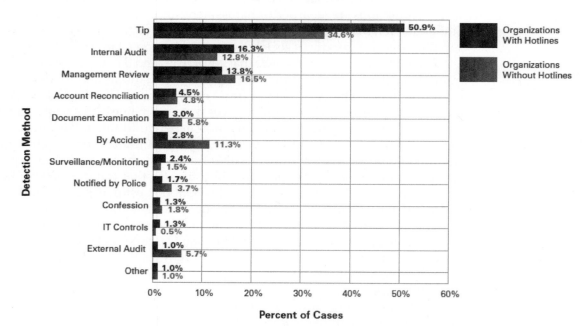

Sources of the tips from the 2012/2010/2008/2006 Wells Reports were as follows:[9]

	2012	2010	2008	2006
Employee	50.9%	49.2%	57.7%	64.1%
Customer	22.1%	17.8%	17.6%	10.7%
Vendor	9.0%	12.1%	12.3%	7.1%
Shareholder/owner	2.3%	3.7%	9.2%	N/A
Anonymous	12.4%	13.4%	8.9%	18.1%
Competitor	1.5%	2.5%	1.0%	N/A
Perps acquaintance	N/A	1.8%	N/A	N/A

Despite advancements in detection technologies and the movement of forensic techniques into the auditing process, fraud is still incredibly challenging to find and eliminate. Fraud is like a leaking row boat. As we bail it out we are happy we can bail it out. The problem is, we have not fixed the holes. Similarly, once fraud is found, the internal controls and other problems must be fixed.

Kessler International was told as part of a due diligence process to find the expensive paintings listed on the balance sheet of a client's acquisition target. The Kessler investigators could not find the paintings anywhere on the premises. One of the accountants went out for a cup of coffee and happened to spot the paintings covered with bubble wrap in the back of a car![10]

A comparison of the main features of three recent fraud surveys appear in Figure 5.1.

Figure 5.1. Comparison of Selected Fraud Surveys

Type	KPMG Fraud Cases	PwC Survey	ACFE Questionnaire
Time Period	2008-2010	2009	2012
Number of participants (population)	348 Cases	3,037	1,388 (34,275)
Response	N/A	Unknown	4%
Estimated fraud in U.S.	Average Loss, $1.4 Million	Unknown	$3.5 trillion (global)
% of companies experiencing fraud	Growing	Growing	Unclear
Highest fraud industry	Public sector (2006)	Government/state owned	Banking/ Financial Services
Second highest fraud industry	Global Manufacturers (2006)	Listed on Stock Exchange	Govt. and Public Administration
Top – Fraud detection – Tips	Not given	34%	43.3%*
Fraud detection – Internal audits	Not given	17%	14.4%
Fraud detection – by accident	13%	13%	7.0%
Some recover of fraud	66%	47% (2005)	51.3% [2012]
Gender of perps - male	87%	60% (2011)	65.0%
Likely age	36-45	31-40 (42%)	41-45
Fraud by senior mgt.	35%	Middle Managers (42%)	Not given
Fraud by Accounting/Finance dept.	32%	Not given	22.0%
Fraud with undergraduate degree	Not given	52% (2005)	36.9%
Common control measure	Not given	External audits	External audit
Second common control measure	Not given	Internal audits (2005)	Code of Conduct
Time in Organization	More than 5 years	3-5 years	Not given
Collusion	61%	Not given	Not given
Duration	3.4 years	Not given	Not given

* Management review, 14.6%

¶ 5011   EMPLOYEE FRAUDSTERS

Chapter 3 describes the fraud pyramid (motive, opportunity, and rationalization) as applied to financial statements, along with some of the characteristics of fraud perpetrators. However, behaviorists have been unable to identify the exact psychological characteristics to distinguish people who commit fraud from those who do not. This is one reason why uncovering fraud is not easy even when dealing with employees whose personalities may be known. The search for fraud is like using a metal detector at the city dump to find some rare coins—the process uncovers a lot of false hits.

Richard Davis says there is no psychometic way to measure integrity, so forget about personality test to pick the fraudsters. They are easily faked. He is more hopeful about new methods involving microexpressions, or those brief expressions that may reveal a person's predisposition to fraud.[11]

A more pleasant analogy of fraud detection is provided in *Fraud Detection and Control*. These authors say that forensic detectives must have a game plan in mind to be successful. Fishermen need special gear and fish at certain times to catch trout. "Like the fisherman whose hook may be dangling inches away from his quarry's mouth, the fish won't even nibble on it" if the fish does not like what is on the hook.[12] The forensic accountant should know something about the "fish" he or she is trying to catch.

Those involved in forensic accounting continue to research information on employee fraud perpetrators that is helping to develop some characteristics even if these are not yielding what might be described as a true profile. Lisa Eversole lists the following characteristics of occupational fraudsters:

- Egotistical
- Risk taker
- Hard Worker
- Greedy
- Disgruntled or a complainer
- Overwhelming desire for personal gain
- Pressured to perform
- Inquisitive
- Rule breaker
- Under stress
- Financially needy
- Big spender
- Close relationship with vendors/suppliers.[13]

Gwynn Nettler in *Lying, Cheating, and Stealing* generalized the characteristics of fraud perpetrators:

- People who have experienced failure are more likely to cheat.
- People who are disliked and who dislike themselves tend to be more deceitful.
- People who are impulsive, distractible, and unable to postpone gratification are more likely to engage in deceitful crimes.
- People who have a conscience (fear, apprehension, and punishment) are more resistant to the temptation to deceive.
- Intelligent people tend to be more honest than ignorant people.
- Middle- and upper-class people tend to be more honest than lower-class people.
- The easier it is to cheat and steal, the more people will do so.
- Individuals have different needs and therefore different levels at which they will be moved to lie, cheat or steal.
- Lying, cheating, and stealing increase when people have great pressure to achieve important objectives.
- The struggle to survive generates deceit.[14]

One difficulty in trying to "sketch out" the type of employee who turns to fraud is that given the right pressures, opportunities, and rationalizations, a large percentage of employees are capable of committing some types of fraud. A Kessler study shows that 13 percent of employees are fundamentally dishonest. Employees outsteal shoplifters. About 21 percent of employees are honest, but 66 percent are encouraged to steal if they see others doing it without repercussion.[15]

Bev Harris says that fraudsters and embezzlers are the nicest people in the world:

> Wide-eyed mothers of preschoolers. Your best friend. CPAs with impeccable resumes. People who profess deep religious commitments. Your partner. Loyal business managers who arrive early, stay late, and never take a vacation. And sometimes, even FAMILY MEMBERS. So if you're looking for a sinister waxed mustache and shifty eyes, you're in for a surprise—scoundrels come in every description.[16]

EYEWITNESS

Robert Hanssen was a nice guy who worked as an FBI agent for 25 years. Married with six children, the Hanssen family lived modestly and had heavily mortgaged their home. He was a CPA and displayed few signs of wealth. Robert Hanssen was a devout Catholic, attending mass everyday. [17]

Yet Hanssen was a Russian mole inside the FBI, who compromised some of our nation's most important counterintelligence and military secrets. He identified at least a dozen human agents, three of which were executed by the Russians. For committing espionage for the KGB, he received life in prison.

Hanssen had poor interpersonal skills and had a dour demeanor. Although he had a high attribute for computer work, he was awkward and an uncommunicative loner. He escaped detection not because he was a master spy (he left many red flags), but because of the FBI's deeply flawed internal security program.

Fraudsters generally start out with baby steps. The fraud will be small. "It begins with little amounts, because the perpetrator is going to test the system. If they get away with it, then they keep on increasing and increasing it."[18] So fraud is accumulative, which is another reason that materiality is not appropriate for a forensic audit.

Statement on Auditing Standards (SAS) No. 99 uses the same three conditions for misappropriation of assets as financial statement fraud: incentives/pressures, opportunity, and attitudes/rationalizations. For example, personal financial obligations may create pressure on an employee to misappropriate assets. Or large amounts of cash on hand or inadequate internal controls may present an opportunity to an employee to embezzle funds. Displeasure or dissatisfaction toward a company may allow an employee to justify fraud.[19] If an employee perceives he or she is being treated unfairly by an employer, the individual may engage in fraudulent activities. Also, employees in large organizations may presume personal ownerships or entitlement by virtue of the position or use of the asset.[20] Incidence of the following discrepancies outlined in SAS No. 99, if found during an audit, may indicate fraud:

- Transactions that are not recorded in a complete or timely manner or are improperly recorded as to amount, accounting period, classification, or entity policy.
- Unsupported or unauthorized balances or transactions.
- Last-minute adjustments that significantly affect financial results.
- Evidence of employees' access to systems and records inconsistent with that necessary to perform their authorized duties. [21]

Fraud Hypothesis Testing Approach

There is a formalized fraud detection method called the fraud hypothesis testing approach. Here a forensic accountant attempts to pro-actively detect fraud that is still undiscovered by formulating and testing null hypotheses. This proactive technique requires a forensic investigator to:

1. Identify the frauds that may exist in a particular situation.
2. Formulate null hypotheses stating that the frauds do not exist.
3. Identify the red flags that each of the frauds would create.
4. Design customized queries to search for the specific red flags or combinations of red flags.[22]

In a refinery, three authors report that after a formalized proactive search for red flags, some unknown frauds were discovered. But applying generic data mining programs to the company's database to detect fraud resulted in a number of Type 2 errors. A Type 2 error occurs when a false null hypothesis fails to be rejected. It is an error to a forensic investigator in the sense that an opportunity to reject the null hypothesis correctly is lost. So in order to be useful the red flags had to be fraud and company specific.[23]

In another situation, the Compliance Division of the Comptroller of Maryland used the fraud hypothesis testing approach to determine the underreporting of sales on sales and use tax returns by liquor establishments. The following steps were performed:

- Obtain data from the files of liquor distributors, sorted by customer tax ID of purchases made by each liquor establishment for the most recent two-year period.
- Use Monarch and ACL software to read the data files from each distributor and convert the data to an Excel spreadsheet.
- Combine the customer data from all of the distributors and sort by the liquor establishment tax ID number using Excel.
- Compare the total amount of purchases made by each liquor establishment, as reported by the distributors, to the total amount of sales reported on the sales and use tax returns.[24]

Auditors then perform an audit on the suspected under-reporters.

Predication

The ACFE group indicates that in the private sector, a fraud investigation should not be commenced without proper predication. Examples of predication events include anonymous tips, complaints, audit inquiries, or conflicts of interests. In other words, predication is the basis for undertaking a fraud investigation. Without predication, the target might be able to sue for real or imaginary damages.

Types of Misappropriations

¶ 5021   EMBEZZLEMENT

Theft or larceny is different than embezzlement. Theft is a generic term for a number of crimes where a fraudster intentionally takes personal property of another without consent or permission and intends to appropriate it to the fraudster's use. *Embezzlement* is the fraudulent appropriation of money or property lawfully in one's possession to be used personally by the embezzler. An embezzler steals from his or her employer.

SAM'S DIVERSION OF UNCLE SAM'S—AND COMPANY'S—MONEY. Bev Harris describes how one employee used many different methods to embezzle from her company, which was growing very quickly at the time. This employee, who is called "Sam" here, diverted payroll taxes meant for the IRS to himself through a dummy account. He also switched the IRS correspondence address to his home and corresponded with the IRS to confuse and delay action. Back payments were disguised as current payments.

Sam set up dummy bank accounts to skim funds before they made their way into legitimate accounts. While sending incoming company payments into his account, he diverted attention by falsely pointing fingers at "slow payers" of accounts receivable.

Diversion was a strategy Sam used repeatedly. At one point he got one employee fired for losing deposits under the employee's control. He also reported missing postage that he himself had actually stolen.

Cash from daily deposits to the bank were skimmed off with corresponding changes made to deposit tickets. He put his wife on the payroll. He padded her hours and "miscalculated" withholding to overpay her, apparently without her knowledge.

Sam was so bold as to set up his landlord, once or twice a year, as an accounts payable.

Sam was a master at fraudulent business expenses. He made reimbursements to himself and his wife for "business expenses" that didn't exist. He also double-reimbursed himself for legitimate expenses by sandwiching in duplicates between proper invoices. He even copied receipts by running them through an old fax machine that used thermal paper to mimic cash register receipts.

Eventually, he made "phone-authorized" wire transfers out of company accounts into his personal checking account.

Eventually, he landed in prison. [25]

Mark A. Siegel provides key principles of investigating the embezzlement of a large sum of money modeled after his work on such a case involving a Middle East country—a case that was settled out of court after his team had finished their investigation. The funds had been dispersed to financial institutions in several European countries. His team of experts comprised two CPAs and an information technology specialist. His principles are as follows:[26]

1. Pool core facts early.
2. Assume someone will testify in court.
3. Tailor the approach by assembling a qualified team, assessing the environment, using visual aids, and making a working plan for identifying and tracking the misappropriated funds.
4. Make sure there was nowhere to hide by using interviews to identify suspect transactions, gather data on the transactions, quantify the claim, and prepare a report.

While they were boxing their files to be sent to London for the first trial, the plaintiff and defendant arrived at a settlement.

EXAMPLE 5.1 Martin Frankel vanished with $200 million of cash and diamonds one day. He accomplished this insurance fraud by buying poorly capitalized insurance companies, cooking the books to show increased premium values, and including nonexistent properties and leases on the balance sheet. He set up a charity in the British Virgin Islands, laundered his money through this account, and eventually moved the ill-gotten gains to Israel through a series of bank transfers.

The tall, skinny guy wearing glasses was found in a posh German hotel with his secretary. J.J. Johnson, Jr. said that Frankel masterminded one of the largest, most bizarre embezzlement schemes in American history. One of his idols was Robert Vesco, who swindled millions of dollars. Vesco had gotten control of Investors Overseas Service, a mutual fund that invested in mutual funds, and disappeared with as much as $500 million.[27]

¶ 5031   CASH AND CHECK SCHEMES

Cash is the favorite target of fraudsters, using skimming, outright larceny, and fraudulent disbursements. Fraud perpetrators use an amazing array of techniques to cipher cash from their employers, such as larceny, skimming, theft of incoming checks, or kiting.

Segregation of duties, mandatory vacations, having two employees open mail, surveillance cameras, encouraging customers to request receipts, and rotation of duties all help to prevent these schemes.

Larceny of Cash

How It Operates

Larceny of cash schemes involve the numerous types of theft of cash after the cash has been recorded on the books, such as directly from a cash register or petty cash. Larceny, in which funds have been documented on a register tape or other bookkeeping method, differs from skimming, in which funds are stolen that have not entered the company's accounting system.

Some fraudulent employees place phony refund forms or voided sales slips in the register to cover the missing funds. Other cashiers doctor register tapes to create a fictitious balance between the tapes and cash on hand. Bookkeepers also can reverse transactions on paper to cover misappropriated cash.

Cash can be stolen by the person taking the deposits to the bank—a type of scheme especially common in small businesses that fail to separate cash-handling roles. Employees who both record deposits and bring cash to the bank can change totals on deposit slips. Or an employee may engage in a form of lapping, stealing the deposit from today, but replacing it with tomorrow's deposit. In such cases the perpetrator justifies the theft as simply a "loan" from the company's funds that he or she plans to replace.

The weakness of larceny is that accounts become out-of-balance and discrepancies are fairly obvious upon audit.

Most fast food restaurants feature two windows at the drive through lane. Having two windows speeds up the traffic somewhat, but two windows also make it more difficult for employees to steal cash and food. To commit larceny with a two-window setup, two employees must work together to take cash and food. Segregation of duties helps prevent cash larceny.

Other restaurants offer a customer a free meal if the customer does not receive a receipt—obviously an attempt to stop employees from taking cash from the register.

How It's Caught

Prevention by segregation of duties is important for stopping cash larceny. One person should not have sole responsibility to receive cash, count the cash, make bank deposits, and post the deposits.

Once recorded on the books, cash larceny schemes are easier to catch by counting the cash a second time unexpectedly. Altering audit schedules may also deter would-be larcenists. Most definitely, cash register tapes or computerized receipts should regularly be reconciled to cash receipts.

To bait a suspected larcenist, a business owner could place marked currency in a location where cash is collected.

A forensic investigator or auditor should review and analyze each journal entry to the cash accounts to reveal cash larceny. The accountant should also check any substantial change in returns to ensure they are not masking larceny.

In the last days of Saddam Hussein's regime, Qusay Hussein presented a note with his father's signature to the Iraqi Central Bank, which resulted in a bank theft of $1 billion—a world record. A team of workers took two hours to load $900 million in U.S. $100 bills and $100 million in Euros into three tractor trailer trucks. This deed was done before the employees came to work. Was this a straight bank robbery or an example of overriding internal controls by a high official?

Skimming

How It Operates

Skimming is an "off-book" technique to remove cash before a company records the receipts. Skimming schemes can involve unrecorded sales, understated sales, ringing no sale, off-hours sales, off-site sales, extra cash registers, theft of incoming checks, and swapping checks for cash.[28]

In some instances, employees first do not record incoming cash, then delay posting the funds in order to divert the funds to personal, interest-bearing accounts. When amounts are substantial, interest earned in short periods in those accounts can be sizable.

How It's Caught

Prevention of skimming can be as simple for some businesses as numbering receipts sequentially and tracking down any missing numbers. Strong internal controls and separation of duties are two vital preventive measures. If receipts themselves are doctored to lower payments received, false discounts are given to understate revenues, or a cashier underrings a sale, more systematic auditing techniques are required to reveal discrepancies. However, sometimes customers will report differences in amounts paid and recorded to their accounts. Lost register tapes are another red flag for misappropriation through skimming. Substantial increases in bad debts recorded also can signal that employees are skimming the company's receivables.

Both skimming and money laundering may be caught with gross profit analysis, as described in Chapter 7. Analytical procedures such as horizontal analysis that evaluate changes in the company's revenue trends can be valuable. Other procedures are to compare receipts with deposits, conduct a surprise cash count, and investigate customers' complaints about inaccurate account balances. The cash flow statement also may give indications of this type of fraud.

Swapping Checks for Cash

How It Operates

A person may take cash, but leave personal checks in the register or petty cash box to cover the money taken in case of a surprise audit. Thus, the cash receipts and register tapes or petty cash records appear to balance. The perpetrator removes the checks before they are cashed, so any personal checks by the cashier found in a register may flag cover-up of a theft.

How It's Caught

An auditor should check for reversing transactions, altered cash counts, or register tapes that are "lost." Most check-swapping cases do not go to trial, but pretrial activities can be a significant opportunity for forensic accounting engagements.

Chasing and finding the assets is only the first step, because getting the assets returned can be a major problem. "Regardless of how quickly investigators locate assets, they are still at the mercy of the legal systems they are finally traced to: typically offshore jurisdictions."[29]

A forensic accountant was hired to find how missing inventory had been disappearing from a grocery store. After several weeks of investigation, everything seemed to be fine—no hints as to the missing inventory. Depressed one rainy evening sitting inside his car outside the store, the accountant noticed that there were only six cash register tapes from seven registers. He soon discovered that the manager would open the seventh cash register when the store was busy, keeping the cash, but not running the seventh cash register tapes through the accounting system.

Check Tampering

How It Operates

During 2010, there were 24.5 billion checks processed in the U.S., down from 30.5 billion in 2006. However, check fraud attempts against deposit accounts only decreased 4 percent from $11.4 billion in 2008 to $11 billion in 2010. The fraud cost to financial institutions in 2010 was $893 million.[30] With such huge numbers of checks it is not practical or cost-effective to visually compare signatures.

There is, however, state-of-the-art automated signature verification technology available to financial institutions to detect and prevent fraud. This technology combines a human-like holistic analysis of a signature and its segmentation with a subsequent analysis of the signature's elements using geometrical analysis (an analytical method based on signature segmentation and finding correlations between the fragments of reference and suspect signatures), dozens of neural networks, and many other innovative techniques. There is also automatic stock verification software to provide scrupulous verification of all preprinted elements on business and personal bank checks.

Fraudsters also may alter check contents by lifting bank officers approval stamps from one check and including it on another check of higher value or altering the MICR line with bogus information. Other alterations are easy. In many situations check writers leave spaces and gaps when populating the various fields; also, dollar amounts, payees and dates can be simply altered using a pen. Parascript, LLC (888.772.7478) offers recognition engines to detect this fraud.

Not all check tampering occurs when the person entrusted to issue checks goes bad. Many phony checks or phony recipients are created by others in a company who gain access to blank checks. Other crimes occur when forgers obtain legitimate company checks and divert them from the intended recipients.

In a common *altered payee* check tampering scheme, an employee may take legitimate invoices from vendors, alter the vendor's name, and revise the invoice number and date. The employee may use his or her own name as payee, or that of an accomplice or fictitious person or company. The employee writes the name of the real vendor in the checking account ledger while writing a different name on the check. Phony supporting paperwork can mask the illegal transaction.

In a *forged endorser* fraud, a forger obtains a legitimate check and simply forges the signature of the payee, then cashes the check.

Larger companies often stamp signatures on checks using automatic check-signing machines, which makes it easy for the check tamperer with access to checks to create unauthorized payments that appear legitimate. Adept fraudsters can even create shell companies to which checks are made payable and easily cashed by the fraudster-owner.

Another twist on check tampering is the interception of already-signed checks. Fraudsters use such checks to alter the payee's name to his or her own or that of an accomplice, or simply endorse the check and attempt to cash it. Alternatively, an insider passes the checks to a crime syndicate, which chemically removes the payee and the amount from the checks (known as *washing checks*). New payees and new amounts are recorded on these "new" checks, and they are deposited in some bank accounts. The cash is withdrawn and accounts closed before the operation is uncovered.[31]

If signed but uncashed checks are returned to a company because the payee's address has changed, a check tamperer has another avenue for obtaining legitimate-appearing checks to alter.

In schemes known as a *forged maker* fraud, the employee steals a check, makes it payable to the thief or an accomplice, then forges an authorized signature.

Additionally, counterfeiting of checks and opening of new accounts in order to cash spurious checks are common check schemes. One popular external scam used by groups is to steal company and government checks from the mail, prepare perfect computer copies, and cash them under other people's names through the new accounts. These fraudsters obtain the identities of bank customers and use the identities to open fraudulent checking accounts.[32]

WASHING CHECKS. A mail fraudster can use a process of washing checks to remove the ink parts on your check with chemicals found in common household cleaning products. A fraudster can prowl the streets with a portable computer, printer, and laminating machine in his car. He steals the mail from mailboxes, washes the ink from the vital areas of the check, making sure not to damage the written signature. He increases the amounts, adds an assumed fake name, and cashes the checks at a local bank.

Avoid putting bills with your checks in a residential mailbox and personally pick up new boxes of checks from your bank. Of course, reconcile bank statements immediately after receiving them. Do not sign your name on an envelope that is mailed. When writing checks, use a gel pen, like the Uniball 207, that allows tiny particles of ink to be absorbed into the check.

How It's Caught

Prevention or early detection of check tampering will minimize its damage. First and foremost, accounts payable groups must practice separation of responsibilities and forced vacations. Employees issuing checks should differ from those reconciling bank statements and receiving canceled checks. Rotations of duties may help present or reveal check tampering. Companies preparing checks with automated check signatures or computerized check-printing software must limit access to the machines and practice strict separation of responsibilities.

For altered payee crimes, the bookkeeping records are covered, so a fraud auditor must contrast the payee in the checking account register with the returned checks. Auditors should also compare amounts listed on the returned checks to those in the checkbook ledger. Nonpayroll checks made payable to employees should have supporting paperwork kept on file. Checks should be imprinted with holographic images, watermarks, inks that cannot be erased, copy void pantograph, chemical voids, security inks, and other security features so that photocopies or counterfeit checks are prevented.

See the subsequent discussion of cut-off bank statements, which can track transactions for dates in between the monthly statements.

An accounting employee for a small business diverted business checks as they arrived at the company, depositing them into her own bank account over a two-and-a-half year period. Her employer did not catch this scheme until the employee quit and started the same scheme at another business. Her ploy was discovered a month later by her new employer, who called the previous employer to relate the details of her scheme. She had stolen more than $800,000 from the now-bankrupt company.

Elma Magkamit, the West Linn, Oregon finance director, stole $1.4 million from 2000 to 2005 to support her gambling habit, expensive clothes, and jewelry. Earning $85,596 a year, Magkamit took blank checks from the city's account stamped with the signature of the city manager, took them home, and typed amounts ranging from $4,250 to $38,992. Checks were made out to a shell company, Magkamit Consulting, or to her husband, Larry Magkamit.

Deputy District Attorney said that "she loved the thrill and adventure of gambling, and when she needed more money, she stole it." After the trial, Elma Magkamit said, "I want to apologize to the finest staff that trusted me."[33]

Kiting

How It Operates

Another cash scheme, *kiting*, involves building up balances in two or more bank accounts based upon floating checks drawn against the other accounts. In kiting schemes, fraudsters write checks or collect cash on an account before the bank has discovered their previous deposits were bogus. Thus, the bank sends money into another account while waiting for funds it will not receive. Kiting is a possibility whenever a bank allows a customer to withdraw cash on deposits for which the bank has not received the cash. Wire transferring makes kiting easier.

The Expedited Funds Availability Act and Regulation CC, in an effort to make funds quickly available to customers, have increased concern about losses through check fraud and kiting schemes. Both banking institutions and their client companies can be stung when employees use kiting to divert deposits to personal or phony accounts.

Three suspicious activities may alert financial institutions to kiting schemes:
- Deposits of large checks drawn on out-of area or foreign banks
- Frequent customer requests for account balances, collected items, or cleared items
- Frequent, large deposits drawn on the same bank

How It's Caught

Forensic investigators detect this type of scheme by looking for frequent deposits and checks in the same amount, large deposits on Fridays, and/or short time lags between deposits and withdrawals. A bank reconciliation audit is an important accounting tool; the bank should send the bank statements directly to the fraud auditor.

A *cut-off bank statement* is similar to a normal bank statement except that it covers a shorter period of time (10 to 20 days). An auditor may compare the cancelled checks and other items with the cut-off bank statement to substantiate outstanding checks, deposits in transit, and similar entries. Online account information helps the investigator to track balances daily, as well. By vouching the reconciling items, one can check for lapping and kiting.

Peter L. Cash, a director of Peoples Bank of Coffee County, Alabama, kited checks between various bank accounts for each of his businesses to create an involuntary overdraft of more than $8 million between October 2005 and July 2008. Cash would continuously draw an insufficient check on one account and deposit that check into another account. This process gave the four victim banks the false impression that there was money in his business accounts. The fraud became apparent when he ended the kiting scheme and all checks and deposits cleared the various banks.[34]

Credit Card Refund and Cancellation Schemes

How It Operates
Fraudulent credit card refunds are common ploys of employees to divert refunds to their own credit card accounts. Fraudsters substitute their own credit card numbers on customers' refund slips. Accomplices also can receive fraudulent refunds, making the acts more complex to identify. Employees often receive kickbacks from confederates for crediting fraudulent returns to other fraudsters.

Another misuse of credit card transactions occurs when a customer service or cashier employee marks actual credit card sales receipts as voided, then withdraws cash for that amount from the cash drawer. If supervisors are not required to verify voided sales or customers neglect to obtain their receipts, fraudsters can doctor the receipts to withdraw comparable amounts with little chance of raising red flags.

How It's Caught
Prevention of these scams requires diligence by supervisors and strong internal controls for cash disbursements. Businesses that accept large numbers of credit card transactions should require immediate approval of voided sales.

Once companies suspect credit card schemes or become concerned about inordinate declines in revenues, a forensic accountant can use trend analysis to pinpoint suspicious increases in refunds. In small businesses, forensic accountants often must systematically match refund records with credit card customers. Inventory reconciliations and surprise physical inventory counts should reveal shortages because the phony product returns were never made.

In extreme cases, surveillance of suspected fraudsters also may reveal clandestine meetings with accomplices to exchange cash from the transactions.

From 62 standard audit procedures, external and internal auditors judged these 19 procedures to be more effective in detecting fraud in the acquisition and payment cycle (in descending order):[35]

- Examine bank reconciliation and observe whether they are prepared monthly by an employee who is independent of recording cash disbursement or custody of cash.
- Examine the supporting documentation such as vendor's invoices, purchase orders, and receiving reports before signing of checks by an authorized person.
- Examine the purchase requisitions, purchase orders, receiving reports, and vendors' invoices which are attached to the vouchers for existence, propriety, reasonableness, and authenticity.
- Examine internal controls to verify that the cash disbursements are recorded for goods actually rendered to the company.
- Discuss with personnel and observe the segregation of duties between accounts payable and custody of signed checks for adequacy.
- Confirm inventories in public warehouses and on consignment.
- Examine internal controls to insure the vendors' invoices, purchase orders, and receiving reports are matched and approved for payment.
- Examine internal controls for the following documents: vendors' invoices, receiving reports, purchase orders, and purchase requisitions.
- Trace a sample of acquisitions transactions by comparing the recorded transactions in the purchase journal with the vendors' invoices, purchase requisitions, purchase orders, and receiving reports.
- Establish whether any unrecorded vendors' invoices or unrecorded checks exist.
- Examine the internal controls to verify the proper approvals of purchase requisitions and purchase orders.
- Reconcile recorded cash disbursements with disbursements on bank statements.
- Discover related party transactions.
- Examine the internal controls to verify the approval of payments on supporting documents at the time that checks are signed.

- Discuss with personnel and observe the procedures of examining the supporting documentation before the signing of checks by an authorized person.
- Examine canceled checks for authorized signatures, proper endorsements, and cancellation by the bank.
- Account for the numerical sequence of prenumbered documents (purchase orders, checks, receiving reports, and vouchers).
- Trace a sample of cash payment transactions.
- Trace resolution of major discrepancy reports.

¶ 5041   ACCOUNTS RECEIVABLE FRAUD

Accounts receivable schemes may include lapping, fictitious receivables, borrowing against receivables, and improper posting of credits to receivables.

Lapping

How It Operates

Lapping involves recording of payment on a customer's account some time after the receipt of the payment. Sometimes called "robbing Peter to pay Paul," in such cases the cash stolen is covered with the receipt from another customer. The process repeats time after time, covering each account with a subsequent payment. Lapping methods are often found as cover-ups of skimming schemes. Lapping is more successful if the same employee has custody of cash paired with recordkeeping responsibilities.

How It's Caught

The forensic investigator compares the checks on a sample of deposit slips to the detail of the customer credits that are listed on the day's posting to the customers' account receivables.

Fictitious Receivables

How It Operates

Fictitious receivables involve covering a phony sale with an equally phony receivable, which may eventually be written off. This process can mask theft of inventory and is recorded under names of actual or phantom customers. Accounts receivable may be backdated to appear current, masking unrecorded payments.

How It's Caught

A forensic auditor should obtain evidence of the existence of accounts receivable and sales, then scrutinize any exception responses from accounts receivable confirmations. He or she should examine any write-offs of accounts receivable. Forensic accountants use the collection ratio, which divides days in the year by receivables turnover to reveal fictitious receivables as well as larceny and skimming. Unexplainable fluctuations in the collection ratio are a red flag for fictitious receivables.

When checking confirmations of accounts receivable, a forensic accountant must be suspicious. Such confirmations may be fictitious. He or she should determine whether the address of the customer is a mail drop or an address in the name of an employee, a related party, or an accomplice. The auditor may check the address in a crisscross (reverse) directory or cold-call the phone number on the invoice. Forensic investigators must be careful to verify sources of faxed confirmations.

Borrowing Against Accounts Receivable

How It Operates

In these fraud cases, the perpetrator puts up accounts receivables as collateral for a loan. An employee may sell accounts receivable at a large discount to a confederate who shares the gains. Perpetrators may also inflate accounts receivable to qualify for large loan amounts and to use part of the loan to cover previous receivables shortfalls.

How It's Caught

Auditing steps to uncover the illegal loan setups include independently verifying account balances of customers who have not paid, reviewing receivables write-offs, and reviewing customer complaints about unrecorded payments or excessive billing.

These 10 audit procedures were judged as being more effective for detecting fraud in the sales and collection cycle (in descending order):[36]

- Observe the proper and appropriate segregation of duties.
- Review monthly bank reconciliation and observe independent reconciliation of bank accounts.
- Investigate the difference between accounts receivable confirmations and customer account receivable balances in the subsidiary ledger and describe all these exceptions, errors, irregularities, and disputes.
- Review sales journal, general ledger, cash receipts journal, accounts receivable subsidiary ledger, and accounts receivable trial balance for large or unusual amounts.
- Verify accounts receivable balance by mailing positive confirmations.
- Examine internal controls to verify that each cash receipts and credit sales transactions are properly recorded in the accounts receivable subsidiary ledger.
- Examine subsequent cash receipts and the credit file on all accounts over 120 days and evaluate whether the receivables are collectible.
- Compare dates of deposits with dates in the cash receipts journal and the prelisting of cash receipts.
- Examine copies of invoices supporting the bills of lading and customers' orders.

¶ 5051   INVENTORY FRAUD

Stealing Inventory

How It Operates

Employees may steal inventory and supplies for personal use or sell the stolen items to outsiders at flea markets and garage sales. Scrap goods may be stolen and sold to outsiders. Faked sales can feature unrecorded "sales" or even a charade in which an accomplice pays the employee a token amount in exchange for a more expensive item.

Kickback schemes often involve a vendor/supplier and an employee who work in cahoots to underreport inventory or payment of an inflated price. Write-offs to discounts or bad debts can conceal thefts, and physical inventory counts can be doctored in computer databases by the technically savvy fraudster. A less technological approach is to cover thefts by padding inventory stocks with empty containers to give the appearance of having the correct supply in storage.

An employee may create a fictitious customer or shell company and sell inventory to this customer. The account can later be written-off as a bad debt.

Some employees use accomplices as "vendors" who return stolen inventory under the guise of delivering new shipments for which the accomplice receives payment. A more complete discussion of bribes and kickbacks is covered in Chapter 6.

EYEWITNESS

A sports bar was experiencing a lower gross margin on drinks. One Sunday evening, a forensic accountant secretly marked the levels of each bottle of wine and liquor. Once the levels of the bottles were checked after a few days and the number of drinks poured was calculated, the skimming bartender was caught.

How It's Caught

Signs the investigator looks for include multiple checks for the same vendor, charged prices that are higher than for other vendors, a purchasing agent who does not take a vacation, or availability of only photocopied invoices. Data-mining software may be used to help find kickbacks from vendors.

Surprise physical inventory counts can reveal discrepancies between actual and recorded stocks. Observing which employees enter the business premises during off hours can help pinpoint fraudsters who steal inventory.

Short Shipments with Full Prices

How It Operates

Fraud by short shipments of inventory/partial shipment occurs when payment is made in full to an outside accomplice. In another type of shipment scheme, once they are entered into inventory at full price, smaller fixed assets may be stolen outright or converted to unlawful personal use.

Collusion may occur between receiving and delivery personnel, whereby a receiving employee signs for less merchandise than was actually delivered. The difference in inventory is later sold, and the receiving and delivery personnel share the proceeds.

An employee may ship merchandise from an employer to an accomplice as a phony sale, using a fake shipping document to conceal misappropriated merchandise. Later the accounts receivable can be written off.

How It's Caught

Companies should prevent the opportunity for shorting shipments by implementing systems of using prenumbered inventory tags matched to count sheets, counting procedures for work-in-process items, and separation of duties between purchasing and logging receipt of shipments.

The forensic investigator reveals short-shipment schemes by closely matching receiving reports with vendor invoices, scrutinizing discrepancies with vendors and employees alike. Random sampling of shipping documents and purchase requisitions enables the forensic accountant to project the error rate in documentation of shipments and costs.

The 1999 Treadway Commission study said that misstated asset valuation accounted for almost one-half of the cases of *fraudulent* financial statements, and inventory overstatement made up a majority of these frauds. Phar-Mor, ZZZZ Best, Equity Funding, the Salad Oil Swindle, and McKesson and Robbins are examples.

These 14 standard audit procedures were judged by external and internal auditors as being more effective for detecting fraud in the inventory and warehousing cycle (in descending order):[37]

- Discover related party transactions.
- Follow up exceptions to make sure they are resolved.
- Review major adjustments for propriety.
- Review inventory count procedures: a. Accounting for items in transit (in and out); b. Comparison of counts with inventory records; and c. Reconciliation of difference between counts and inventory records.
- Review adequacy of physical security for the entire inventory.
- Confirm inventories in public warehouse.
- Review procedures for receiving, inspecting, and storing incoming items and for shipments out of the warehouses.
- Trace shipments to sales records, inventory records, and bill of lading (shipping documents).
- Determine if access to inventory area is limited to approved personnel.
- Observe the physical count of all locations.

- Recount a sample of client's counts to make sure the recorded counts are accurate on the tags (also check descriptions and unit of count, such as dozen or gross).
- Trace inventory listed in the schedule to inventory tags and the auditor's recorded counts for existence, descriptions, and quantity.
- Trace shipments to sales journal.
- Perform compilation tests to insure that inventory listing schedule agrees with the physical inventory counts.

Shoplifting Is Costly

How It Operates

Although employees steal more than shoplifters, inventory does disappear as a result of customers, vendors, delivery personnel, and bookkeeping errors. According to a recent annual survey, total retail losses cost retailers $33.5 billion annually. Employees account for 43 percent, shoplifters 35 percent, administrative error 14.5 percent, and vendor fraud 3.8 percent of the skrinkage.[38]

Safeway officials maintain that a local couple stole more than $5 million in merchandise from their stores in the Portland, Oregon area over a number of years. The couple stole around $400,000 of common items, such as shampoos, razors, Rogaine, teeth whiteners, conditioners, batteries, DVDs, and CDs. Safeway security officers placed a tracking device on their van so they could carefully scan their surveillance videos to gather evidence of their shoplifting.[39]

How It's Caught

A security newsletter indicates many companies use security cameras, but one of the latest trends is to switch from video tapes to digital recording in stores, giving retailers far more flexibility in recording and reviewing events. Remote and live video recording of cameras is another trend allowing businesses to record events centrally at a headquarters location and review them live or at a later time. Point-of-Scale (POS) monitoring is also on the increase, allowing retailers to collect and analyze information on every transaction to identify trends and unusual patterns in each store.[40]

Integrating cameras with loss prevention hardware and POS software is another growing trend, allowing retailers to connect video images to events as they happen. For example, if a cashier has a "no sale" transaction and opens the cash drawer, a camera will record the event. Or, if someone leaves the store with an active security tag on a product, a recording of the event will be saved for review at a later time. These new devices give the retailer an even clearer picture of events in a store, so actions can be taken to correct the situation, if necessary.[41] Forensic accountants should be aware of these ways to obtain evidence.

¶ 5056   ACCOUNTS PAYABLE FRAUD

Accounts payable is an account that shows that a business owes someone, such as a vendor. It is estimated that companies pay as much as two percent of total purchases as duplicate payments. So a business with $80 million of total purchases would have a $1.6 million loss each year ($80 million times 2% = $1.6 million).[42] For example, in 2003 AOL was hit with a class action lawsuit for deliberately double-billing hundreds of thousands of customers by a deceptive scheme involving multiple screen names. Only if a customer carefully examined his or her credit card statement would they realize they were double-billed.

Shell companies may be used to steal through accounts payable. An employee may create a shell company with the secretary of state, open a bank account, and send false invoices to his employer.

In a pass-through scheme, an intermediary shell company inserts itself between a real vendor and a company. The vendor sends a $16,000 invoice to the intermediary company and the invoice is paid. The shell company sends a new, inflated invoice to the victim business for $20,000 in order to make an unauthorized profit of $4,000.

In October 2006, a Federal Court shut down a bogus Canadian billing scheme that was defrauding U.S. companies of millions of dollars for so-called business and travel directory advertising and unordered and undelivered office supplies and consulting services. The Ontario company allegedly would cut advertisements from publications and paste them onto their fake invoices in order to deceive consumers into paying the bogus invoices.[43]

How It's Caught

Duplicate requests for payments of an account may be intentional. Two authors suggest these techniques or red flags to help control payment of duplicate payments and fake invoices.[44]

- Extract only the numerical digits of an invoice number and match on only the numbers portion of the invoice.
- Try identifying the dates that are similar such as dates that are less than 14 days.
- Try matching on the absolute value of the amount.
- Look for rounded-amount invoices.
- Beware of invoices just below approval amounts.
- Search for abnormal invoice volume activity (two invoices one month and 60 the next).
- Be careful of vendors with sequential invoice numbers (LC 0002, LC 0003, LC 0004 are suspect).
- Look for above average payments per vendor.

These five disbursement fraud tests also are helpful:[45]

1. Test for duplicate payments in Excel by sorting by dollar amount and vendor name.
2. Review the accounts payable vendor file by visually comparing vendors with similar names.
3. Check for fictitious vendors, especially for services, looking for P.O. boxes, employee addresses, etc. Google vendor, call, or e-mail them.
4. Compare payroll addresses with vendor addresses.
5. Scan the checks over a short period for appropriate signatures and payee.

Fraudsters may use simple methods to commit their embezzlement. Teri Lyn, an accounts payable clerk at McClelland Equipment, wrote 18 checks to herself for a total of $18,000. She would type her name and address on an address label which she put over the "account" or "to—pay to the order of" person that she had dummied the check out to get it signed.

The fraud was discovered when a check processor peeled back the label on one of the dummied checks and found that the check was supposed to go to a company rather than Teri Lyn's individual account. The processor called Lyn's company, she confessed, and served 13 months of a two-year sentence.[46]

In January 2006, three persons were charged with an elaborate billing scheme to defraud the U.S. government of more than $145 million. One of the individuals was contracts manager with the Department of National Defense, who was charged with fraud, breach of trust, and money laundering. The problem dealt with billing procedures, lack of supporting documentation, unauthorized equipment purchases, extensive use of third-party vendors, and inflated equipment costs. In May of 2004, Hewlett-Packard repaid the government $145 million, but said none of its own employees were involved in the scheme.[47]

¶ 5061   FICTITIOUS DISBURSEMENTS

Doctored Sales Figures

How It Operates
Fraudulent sales schemes include:
- Unrecorded sales
- Understated sales
- Creating fictitious sales
- Padding prices to increase commissions

In retail establishments, an employee may pretend to sell merchandise, failing to ring up the sale, but allowing an accomplice to take the merchandise from the store.

Employees may understate sales through skimming schemes, as described earlier. When sales of services are skimmed, there should be no shrinkage in inventory. However, if sales of merchandise are skimmed, inventory shrinkage occurs.

Fictitious sales may be used to raise the income of a commission-based salesperson. Phony sales orders or credit authorizations are tools for documenting such sales.

In larger sales organizations, an employee can record a higher price than the customer actually pays in order to inflate the revenues on which his or her commission is based.

How It's Caught
Various analytical techniques are used to detect phony sales figures: ratio analysis, statistical sampling, and horizontal and vertical analysis of the sales account. When fictitious sales are created to pump up commissions, documentation of sales should be matched with perpetual inventory paperwork to reveal overages in stock on hand.

Sham Payments

How It Operates
Fraud perpetrators invent myriad fictional accounts payable. Some sham disbursement schemes include:
- Multiple payments to same payee
- Multiple payees for the same product or service
- Ghosts on the payroll (persons on the payroll who do not work for the company)
- Inflated invoices
- Shell companies and/or fictitious persons
- Bogus claims (e.g., health care fraud and insurance claims)
- Overstated refunds or bogus refunds at cash register
- Many fictitious expense schemes (e.g., meals, mileage, sharing taxi, claiming business expenses never taken)
- Duplicated reimbursements
- Overpayment of wages
- False workers' compensation claims

How It's Caught

Here again, prevention is the best defense. Sham payments involve a broad spectrum of transactions and prevention will require some specific tactics depending upon whether payment is a vendor, a benefit claimant, a customer, or employee. Joseph Wells provides the following ideas for detecting and preventing ghost employees:

- Ensure the payroll preparation, disbursement, and distribution functions are segregated.
- Look for paychecks without deductions for taxes or social security. Completely fictitious employees frequently don't have any.
- Examine payroll checks that have dual endorsements. Although most of them are legitimate, two signatures could signal the forgery of a departed employee's endorsement, which the thief also endorses and deposits into his or her own account.
- Use direct deposits. This method, although not foolproof, can cut down on payroll chicanery by eliminating paper paychecks and the possibility of alteration, forgery and most theft, although it doesn't prevent misdirection of deposits into unauthorized accounts.
- Check payroll records for the presence of duplicate names, addresses, and social security numbers.
- On occasion, hand-deliver paychecks to employees and require positive identification. If paychecks are left over, make sure they belong to actual employees, not ghosts.
- Be wary of budget variations in payroll expense. Higher-than-budgeted labor costs can indicate ghost employees.[48]
- Verify the person's social security number, because a ghost employee may have a number that does not exist.

The Chief Administrative Officer of the Ohio branch of the American Cancer Society, Dan Wiant, stole as much as $7.6 million during 2000. He established a number of fictitious companies over three years to steal funds. One such company was for leasing and purchasing cars. He wrote fake consulting expense checks to the companies. Who caught him? His wife turned him into the authorities after he confessed to her. About $6.9 million of the money was frozen in an Austrian bank.[49]

Normal auditing controls, well implemented, can prevent much of this type of scheme. Auditors must investigate suppliers and vendors looking for false billings and fictitious vendors. The employee who is in charge of recording the income should not be the same person who pays the bills. If one person handles both income and expenses, he or she can skim money from the disbursement side and balance the books on the revenue side.

These 11 audit procedures were judged the more effective for detecting fraud in the payroll and personnel cycle (in descending order):[50]

- Sample terminated employees and confirm that they are not included on subsequent payrolls and confirm propriety of termination payments.
- Observe the actual distribution of payroll checks to employees.
- Observe the duties of employees being performed to insure that separation of duties between personnel, timekeeping, journalizing payroll transactions, posting payroll transactions, and payroll disbursement exists.
- Examine internal controls to verify that hiring, pay rates, payroll deductions, and terminations are authorized by the personnel department.
- Sample personnel files and physically observe the presence of personnel in the work place.
- Examine internal controls over payroll records to verify that payroll transactions are properly authorized.

- Discover related party transactions.
- Review the files of new hires for appropriate approvals, pay rates, and dates of accession.
- Review the payroll journal, general ledger, and employee individual pay records for large or unusual amounts.
- Examine internal controls to verify that unclaimed payroll checks are secured in a vault or safe with restricted access.
- Examine internal controls to verify that employee time cards and job order work tickets are reconciled.

Price Manipulations: Land Flipping, Pump and Dump, and Cybersmearing

How It Operates

A *land flip* involves a situation where a company decides to purchase land for a project. A person or group will find the land and buy it using a front name or company. The fraudster then increases the price of the land before selling it to his or her company.

This same concept may be used for stock manipulation between related entities or pump-and-sell schemes. The Internet, with stock chat message boards and online news services, allows people to quickly provide false or misleading information that can cause stock to move rapidly up or down. Numerous messages (or spam) can hype thinly traded stock in what is called *pump and dump,* causing the stock to move up rapidly, at which time the perpetrator sells the stock at a huge gain.

According to the SEC, a high school student bought large blocks of over-the-counter bulletin board (OTCBB) stock, as high as 17 percent to 46 percent of a day's volume. The next day he would sell the stock at a profit. Two professors calculated a fine of $285,000.[51]

Bashing a stock, called *cybersmear,* causes the stock to decline. The perpetrator has sold short, so as the stock declines he or she has a gain. A college student bashed Emulex on August 25, 2000, by spreading a false unfavorable press release supposedly released by Emulex. In early trading the stock dropped 63-1/8 points (or 55.8 percent of its value). The college student had sold 3,000 shares short before the false release.

How It's Caught

A forensic investigator must always question the valuation figure of land by comparing with similar property (*comparables*). Real estate records can be found at county land offices and tax assessor's offices. The investigator should look for quick and multiple sales where the same person starts and ends up with the land, with increased prices. The same lawyer is often used with all of the sales, often with a conflict of interest. Investigators should know the company's Realtor and attorney well.

Proactive measures are key to fighting cybersmears. Larger companies should assign staff to monitor chat rooms and bulletin boards that may post rumors intended to manipulate stock values. Alternatively, clipping services can monitor the Internet as well as print media for articles about the organization. A free service to monitor message board postings about certain companies is *www.companysleuth.com.*

Implementing policies ahead of time to deal with spurious communications will help companies control the damage and issue press releases countering the inaccurate information. Some companies are fighting back against cybersmears using cease-and-desist orders and libel suits. Sometimes it is possible to trace authors of cybersmear using techniques described in Chapter 14 for identifying cybercriminals.

Money Laundering

How It Operates

Money laundering is the use of techniques to take money that comes from one source, hide that source, and make the funds available in another setting so that the funds can be used without incurring legal restrictions or penalties. This discussion focuses on laundering involving employees; Chapter 7 covers money laundering in detail as it is used by governments as well as criminals.

A blatant scheme of the money launderer is to directly involve a person or a business in the crime. The perpetrator could simply ask someone for permission to use his or her bank account for deposits in return for a fee. For example, Ralph Capone, brother of Al Capone, washed $1,751,840.60 through five bank accounts in nominee names in order to hide his illegal alcohol revenues.[52]

Another scenario is to approach a business and ask employees to create transactions in which funds are regularly deposited in the company's account. The business then returns the money as fictitious payments for nonexistent products or services. There are additional ways of laundering money without a business being aware of involvement in a crime. A money launderer can place an order for a customized product and place a large deposit down. Later the perpetrator cancels the order, pays a smaller penalty for the cancellation, and receives "clean" money back. Kickbacks or collusion among purchasing people who participate in the schemes are common.

An example of money laundering and check larceny occurred in the Las Vegas American Cancer Society between 1997 and 1999. Willette Ballard secretly kept open a temporary society's Golf Classic checking account. She would deposit into the secret account checks that belonged in other accounts. She then wrote checks payable to herself. Detective Kai Deger said that Ballard "was taking money coming in throughout the year and used the account, for lack of a better term, to wash it." At least $280,000 was "washed" in the account.[53]

How It's Caught

Accountants use a gross profit analysis to spot money laundering. Most businesses have unique accounting practices and activities, so analytical techniques may vary. A forensic investigator can obtain an insight of various industries in the Internal Revenue Service's Market Segment Specialization Program (MSSP) (see Chapter 6). There are separate Audit Technique Guides (ATGs) for many industry segments. An investigator can learn how to examine and where to search when auditing a particular business (e.g., sport franchises, pizza restaurants, or car wash industry).

Other approaches to revealing money laundering from inside companies is to compare receipts with deposits, conduct surprise cash counts, and investigate customer complaints. The cash flow statement may flag this type of fraud.

Banks and other financial institutions are the main defense against money laundering. Knowing the company's customers and a proper set of internal controls can help banks reduce the risks from money laundering. For more details, see Chapter 7.

In the process of tracking the money trail of Al Qaeda finances, in May 2002 the Spanish government accused Mohammed Galeb of being the Al Qaeda paymaster. With money sent from Saudi-based companies Galeb built apartments and used part of the profits from these properties to give money to Islamic causes. Galeb kept two separate accounting ledgers, allegedly to launder money. He kept a private set of books showing his real profit and a public ledger indicating a loss. The police concluded that some of the profit ended up with entities and people linked to Osama bin Laden.[54]

Bid Rigging

How It Operates

Bid rigging occurs when a vendor is given an unfair advantage in an open competition for a certain contract. For example, a vendor may be given extra information, or the specifications may be established to fit only one vendor. With additional or advance information a vendor can bid low and later obtain more revenue by obtaining variations in the legal contract. Often the rigging schemes feature kickbacks or bribes to the inside informant. Employees can also be paid not to solicit bids from certain of the vendors' competitors or to reveal one competitor's prices to another.

Bid rigging occurred in the stamp industry from the early 1980s until 1997. During that period approximately $20 million in stamps were sold at public auctions at which at least eight dealers agreed to not bid against each other. These conspirators called themselves "The King" and specialized in buying collection lots of stamps. John D. Apfelbaum, one of the biggest names in American stamp collecting, pleaded guilty on January 28, 2002 to two felony accounts of violating the Sherman Antitrust Act.[55]

How It's Caught

Companies should implement policies prohibiting vendor gifts or discounts to employees involved in contract decision making. Policies should explicitly state opposition to bribery and bid rigging. Employees exhibiting a sudden, more extravagant lifestyle should raise red flags.

Bid rigging schemes are often caught by tips or confessions. Forensic accountants can use data mining to identify potentially fraudulent transactions for further investigation and follow-up. Commercial data mining software, such as Audit Command Language (ACL), search databases for suspicious patterns that may indicate fraud schemes. Additional applications analyze past transactions for variables present in fraudulent transactions and for use in flagging similar transactions before they are processed. In small businesses, vendor information can be manually analyzed and compared to employee records to identify payments made to a vendor with the same phone number or address as an employee.

¶ 5071   WALKING THE WALK OF FRAUD DETECTION PROGRAMS

Efforts to create employee fraud prevention programs are not always sufficient to deter the crimes that have been discussed. However, there are actions that should be considered. Three critical self assessment questions an organization might address:[56]

1. Is there a published ethics policy with definitions of fraud?
2. Is fraud included in the company's overall business risk assessment?
3. Is there a plan in place to respond to risk and to limit damage to the business?

The AICPA, IIA, and ACFE suggest these important elements of a fraud risk program:[57]

● Roles and responsibilities (e.g., BOD, audit committee, management, staff, internal auditing department).

- Commitment (e.g., code of conduct).
- Fraud awareness (e.g., periodic assessment, training and communication).
- Affirmation process (e.g., acknowledgement of the code).
- Conflict disclosure (by executives, employees, and contractors).
- Fraud risk assessment.
- Reporting procedures and whistleblower protection.
- Investigation process (documented protocol).
- Corrective action (civil, criminal action, disciplinary).
- Quality assurance.
- Continuous monitoring.

For example, this same group gives the role and responsibility of the internal auditing department:[58]

- Internal auditing should provide objective assurance to the board and management that fraud controls are sufficient for identified fraud risks and ensure that the controls are functioning effectively. Internal auditors may review the comprehensiveness and adequacy of the risks identified by management—especially with regard to management override risks.
- Internal auditors should consider the organization's assessment of fraud risk when developing their annual audit plan and review management's fraud management capabilities periodically. They should interview and communicate regularly with those conducting the organization's risk assessments, as well as others in key positions throughout the organization, to help them ensure that all fraud risks have been considered appropriately. When performing engagements, internal auditors should spend adequate time and attention to evaluating the design and operation of internal controls related to fraud risk management. They should exercise professional skepticism when reviewing activities and be on guard for the signs of fraud. Potential frauds uncovered during an engagement should be treated in accordance with a well-defined response plan consistent with professional and legal standards. Internal auditing also should take an active role in support of the organization's ethical culture.
- Internal auditing should be independent (authority and reporting relationships), have adequate access to the audit committee, and adhere to professional standards.

In the 2012 Wells Report, CFEs list the primary internal control weaknesses in large and small business as follows:

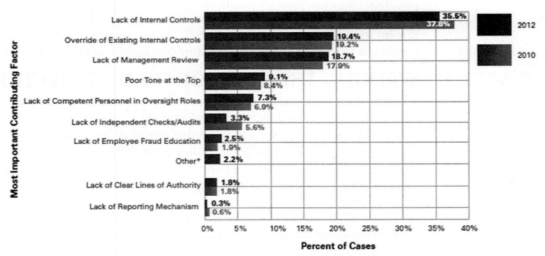

*"Other" category was not included in the 2010 Report.

Source: 2012 Wells Report, ACFE.

KPMG had these responses on their 2009 Fraud Survey to the question "In the event of the discovery of fraud or misconduct, which of the following does your organization have effective protocols to address?

Q. In the event of the discovery of possible fraud or misconduct, which of the following does your organization have effective protocols to address?

	%
Who should perform the investigation	80%
How the investigation should be performed	73%
When the board of directors should be notified	73%
How to administer disciplinary action	70%
How to determine the remedial action	67%
When a voluntary disclosure to the government should be made	62%
No formal protocols exist for how to respond to alleged fraud or misconduct	10%

Business Policies

Many organizations today look at an ethics policy to set the proper tone towards motivating positive behaviors as well preventing negative ones. It stands to reason then that companies would want to have a proper policy in place to battle fraud. An ethics policy can help in prevention, in fighting fraud and mitigating its damages.

Figure 5.2 presented below is an example of a Business Ethics Policy that helps set the tone from the top for an organization that wants to encourage good conduct.[59]

Figure 5.2. Sample Business Ethics Policy

We exist because we maintain our customer base.

The successful operation and reputation of [Company] depends upon the principles of fairness and ethical conduct of our employees. Our reputation for integrity and excellence requires careful compliance with the spirit and letter of all laws and regulations, as well as a personal commitment to the highest standards of conduct and integrity.

The survival and success of this organization depends upon our customers' trust. We must preserve that trust. Employees have a duty to [Company], our customers and our shareholders to act in a way that will always merit the continued trust and confidence of the public and our customers.

[Company], its directors, managers, employees and vendors will comply with all applicable laws and regulations, company policies, and community and industry standards. Directors, officers and employees must conduct business in accordance with the letter, spirit and intent of all applicable laws and refrain from any illegal, dishonest or unethical conduct.

You cannot avoid acting properly.

In general, the use of good judgment will provide proper guidance. However, if a situation arises where it is difficult to determine the proper course of action or you feel you are being pressured to act improperly, the matter must be discussed with your immediate supervisor. If you are uncomfortable discussing the situation with your immediate supervisor, you must contact your supervisor's superior, the head of human resources, corporate general counsel or the president. You must act.

Compliance with this policy is the responsibility of every [Company] employee. Disregarding or failing to comply with this policy will lead to disciplinary action, up to and including possible termination of employment.

Additional policy documents can help to prevent fraud and reinforce a work environment that does not tolerate it. Often the rules of conduct that might be found in an Employee Handbook or other document for employee consumption reflect a company's position on fraud. Figure 5.3 presents a sample rules of conduct document.[60] Fraud related items are in bold.

Figure 5.3. Sample Rules of Conduct

We try to make this a safe and pleasant place to work. The cooperation of all employees is necessary to carry this out. People who have worked together for a long time realize that one person's misconduct may harm all the rest, and they expect certain standards of conduct to be set.

The following list of improper performances is considered to be against the best interest of the majority and will be subject to corrective actions including reprimand, warning, layoff or dismissal:

1. Employees not being at their appointed work places, ready to work, at the regular starting time and failing to remain at such work places and at work until the regular quitting time or until relieved.
2. **Stealing.**
3. **Willful damage to, or destruction or theft of property belonging to fellow employees or the Company.**
4. Fighting, horseplay or disorderly conduct.
5. **Punching another's time card or falsifying any time or production record.**
6. Refusing or failing to carry out a legitimate instruction of a supervisor.
7. Leaving your work station (except for reasonable personal needs) without permission from your supervisor.
8. Inattention to duties, visiting or loafing during working hours.
9. Coming to work under the influence of alcohol or any drug, or bringing alcoholic beverages or drugs onto Company property.
10. Intentionally giving any false or misleading information to obtain employment, a leave of absence, or for any other employment purpose.
11. Smoking contrary to established practice or violating any other fire protection regulation.
12. Willful or habitual violation of safety or health regulations.
13. Frequent tardiness or unexcused absences from work.
14. Carelessness or neglect resulting in abuse to equipment and tools.
15. Unauthorized possession of firearms, cameras, or weapons of any kind on Company property.
16. Use of threatening, harassing or abusive language toward a fellow employee.
17. Unauthorized distribution of literature, or written or printed matter of any description on Company premises.
18. Failure to wear clothing conforming to established standards.

> 19. Employees shall not enter the plant or remain on the premises unless they are on duty, scheduled to work, or are otherwise authorized by the Management.
> **20. Unauthorized use of Company equipment.**

An employer might create any number of such rules of conduct, which may help prevent fraud. The type of business may also be an important consideration. Rules at a professional service company may look a lot different than those at a manufacturer. Some rules may be specifically created to target greater risks such as the following prohibition that focuses on risks from "doctoring" forms and records: "...Falsification or omission of pertinent data when completing applications for employment and/or clearance, accounting forms, personnel records or other company records" are subject to corrective actions.

Punishment and prosecution, or the prospect of either, can be important for reducing fraud. Some companies show a video to all employees (especially new employees) which shows people in jail and the harsh side of imprisonment. The video indicates that the company will prosecute white collar crimes and outlines the step-by-step process towards that end.

Other companies contract with an outside firm to have an "employee" hired, who will later be "arrested" and walked through the company in handcuffs. Perception is important in fighting fraud and abuse. Video cameras throughout a business can be helpful, even if there is no film in the cameras.

EXECUTIONS FOR FRAUD. In September 2004, Wang Liming, a onetime accounting officer at China Construction, and two other bank employees were executed for defrauding the bank of $2.4 million. In an unrelated corruption case, an officer at the Zhuhai branch of the Bank of China was put to death.[61]

Fraud and Company's Risk Assessment

An organization's profile of business risks should be comprehensive and include consideration of fraud. Appropriate systems need to be in place to effectively manage the risks. Risk assessment services should identify and assess primary potential risks faced by the business, independent assessment of risk identified by an entity and evaluation of an entity's systems for identifying and limiting risks. Possible ways to mitigate risks should be identified, such as installation of risk-reduction systems and processes, transferring or sharing of the risks, and avoidance of the risks.

A risk assessment is a comprehensive review and analysis of a company to determine where the risks are and the type of corrective actions needed. Such an assessment helps an auditor or forensic accountant to target the high-risk areas.[62]

A fraud risk assessment should include three key elements:[63]

- *Identify inherent fraud risk*—Gather information to obtain the population of fraud risks that could apply to the organization. Included in this process is the explicit consideration of all types of fraud schemes and scenarios; incentives, pressures, and opportunities to commit fraud; and IT fraud risks specific to the organization.
- *Assess likelihood and significance of inherent fraud risk*—Assess the relative likelihood and potential significance of identified fraud risks based on historical information, known fraud schemes, and interviews with staff, including business process owners.
- *Respond to reasonably likely and significant inherent and residual fraud risks*—Decide what the response should be to address the identified risks and perform a cost-benefit analysis of fraud risks over which the organization wants to implement controls or specific fraud detection procedures.

An internal auditing novel[64] explains the various types of risks in an organization as many small risks, some moderate risks, and one or two huge risks. The "Big R" can destroy an organization (e.g., Arthur Andersen, WorldCom, Enron). Risks can be classified as operational, financial reporting, and compliance. Fleet Walker, an imaginary internal auditor for the New York Yankees, gives this description of his risk assessment:[65]

> Fleet [Walker] realized the importance of risk assessment. Resources are scarce in any organization and especially in internal auditing department. They must be spent wisely where they will do the most good. Risk assessment allows the internal auditor to identify the parts of the organization that are the most risky and to then allocate precious audit resources to ensure the risk associated with those areas is addressed. Fleet annually broke down the Yankee organization into "Auditable Units" and then ranked each auditable unit in terms of riskiness. Fleet measured risk using several "risk factors" such as "impact on operations and customer satisfaction," "legal impact," "degree of computerization," "recent organizational or technological change," and "time since last audit." Audits were placed on the audit schedule based on their total ranking. Fleet was proud of this system because he had purposely designed the risk factors to measure operational and compliance risks.

A simple way to assess the risk in a small entity would be by the "swimming lane" approach. List the various processes along the left side, and across the top list the individuals who can affect the process. One can observe the areas where there is a lack of segregation of duties and, therefore, determine high-risk areas.

Figure 5.4. Swimming Lanes

	Mary	Larry	Jane	Sam
Controls Cash	X			X
Entries in Books	X	X	X	
Deposits Checks		X		X
Does Reconciliation	X		X	
Controls Accounts Receivable		X	X	X

Jonny Frank outlines these steps in a fraud risk assessment process:[66]
1. **Organize** the assessment—integrate into organization's existing business cycle or establish a separate cycle.
2. **Determine** areas to assess—conduct at company wide, business-unit, and significant-account levels.
3. **Identify** potential schemes and scenarios—typically affecting the industry or locations.
   - Fraudulent financial reporting.
   - Misappropriation of assets.
   - Expenditures and liabilities for an improper purpose (cash kickbacks and corruption).
   - Organization commits a fraud against employees or third parties.
   - Tax fraud.
   - Financial misconduct by senior management.
4. **Assess likelihood of fraud**
   - Remote (1 out of 20)
   - Reasonably possible
   - Probable

5. **Assess significance of risk**
   - Inconsequential
   - More than inconsequential
   - Material
6. **Link antifraud controls**—identify the control activities for fraud risks that are both more than likely to occur and more than inconsequential in amount.
7. **Apply assessment results** to the audit plan—consider and document the results of the fraud assessment when developing the audit.

Ernst & Young found that organizations that had not performed fraud vulnerability reviews were almost two-thirds more likely to have suffered a fraud within the past 12 months.[67] COSO provides a comprehensive risk assessment example in *Guidance for Smaller Public Companies,*[68] based upon a risk rating from 1 to 5 across functions (1 being the least risky and 5 the most risky). The analysis is performed in discussion group format, and the results are documented in a table that outlines the specific risks together with the rating and the factors that contribute to the rating. They give an example of risk identified related to revenue recognition.

- Revenue may not be recognized in accordance with GAAP.
- Risk rating = 5.
- Factors contributing to risk rating
  - Complexity of rules for revenue recognition.
  - Knowledge level of people responsible for recording sales transactions.
  - Complexity of promotion and discount transactions.
  - Aggressive sales targets.
  - Incentive and bonus structure.
  - Supporting systems limitations.

A Risk Assessment Matrix of the Balance Sheet is shown in Figure 5.5.[69]

Figure 5.5. Risk Assessment Matrix 1

Risk Identification and Analysis by Significant Account and Disclosure

Financial Statement Account/Disclosure	As a % of Total	Impact on F/S	Account Characteristics	Business Process Characteristics	Fraud Risk	External Factors	Overall Rating	Relevant Assertions10				
								E/O	CO	V/A	R&O	P&D
BALANCE SHEET												
Assets												
Cash & Cash Equivalents	6%	M	H	M	H	H	H	X	X		X	X
Accounts Receivable	30%	H	H	H	H	H	H	X	X	X		X
Prepaid Expenses	4%	L	M	L	L	L	L	X		X		
Inventory	35%	H	M	M	L	L	M	X	X	X	X	X
Property & Equipment	15%	H	L	L	L	L	L	X		X	X	
Intangible Assets Liabilities	10%	M	M	M	M	M	M	X		X	X	X
Accounts Payable	35%	H	H	L	M	M	M	X	X		X	
Accrued Expenses	20%	H	M	M	H	H	H	X	X	X	X	X
Deferred Revenue	30%	H	M	M	M	L	L	X	X	X	X	X
Long-Term Debt	15%	H	L	L	L	H	L	X	X	X	X	X
Shareholders' Equity												
Common Stock	5%	M	M	M	L	L	L	X		X	X	X
Retained Earnings	95%	H	L	L	L	M	H	X	X			X

10   E/O – Existence/Occurrence
        CO – Completeness
        V/A – Valuation/Allocation
        R&O – Rights & Obligations
        P&D – Presentation & Disclosure

A fraud review may include flow charting the major transactions in a business. One way to perform such a review is the "gap analysis" approach.

$$\left\{\left\{\begin{array}{l}\text{Actual Internal Controls}\\\text{Organization's Stated Internal Controls}\\\text{Best Practices Internal Controls}\end{array}\right.\right.$$

A form of risk assessment is the walkthrough of a business' significant processes that auditors are required to do by the PCAOB. An auditor should perform at least one walkthrough for each major class of transactions. In a walkthrough an auditor traces "company transactions and events—both those that are routine and recurring and those that are unusual—from origination, through the company's accounting and information systems and financial report preparation process, to their being reported in the company's financial statements."[70]

An auditor might be able to achieve the objectives of a walkthrough by performing a combination of procedures, including inquiry, inspection, observation, and reperformance of procedures; however, performing a walkthrough represents the most efficient and effective means of doing so. The auditor's work on the control environment and walkthrough is an important part of the principal evidence that the auditor must obtain himself/herself.[71]

Examples of flow-charting or walkthroughs are found in a book explaining the pattern of cash flow inside a casino (see Figures 5.6 and 5.7).

Figure 5.6. Slot Machine Accounting Flow

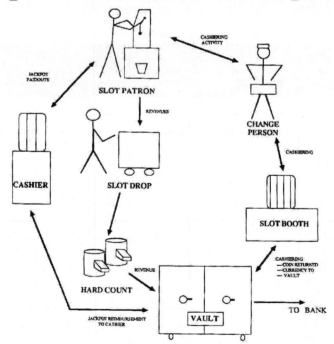

Source: E.M. Greenlees, *Casino Accounting and Financial Management*, University of Nevada Press, 1988, p. 143.

Figure 5.7. Principal Revenue Flows in the Casino

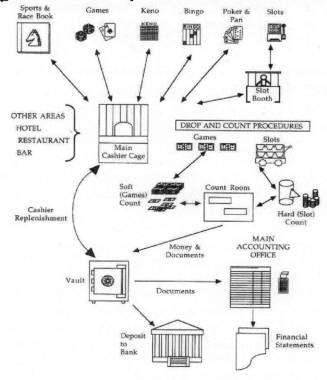

Source: E.M. Greenlees, *Casino Accounting and Financial Management*, University of Nevada Press, 1988, p. 98.

In a similar fashion a forensic accountant or auditor should wander around the entity being audited making informal observations:

- Especially valuable when assessing the internal controls.
- Observe employees while entering and leaving work and while on lunch break.
- Observe posted material, instructions, job postings.
- Observe information security and confidentiality.
- Observe the compliance with procedures.

Proactive Is More Beneficial

There are two major types of fraud investigations: reactive and proactive. Reactive refers to an investigation after there is a reason to suspect fraud or occurs after a significant loss (e.g., predication). Proactive is a preventive approach as a result of normal operations (e.g., reviewing of internal controls or identifying areas of fraud exposure). There is no reason to suspect fraud. Or there is an investigation to detect indicia of fraud.[72]

The threat of a future investigation reduces the occurrence of fraudulent behavior from 75 percent to only 43 percent. The larger the pay-off, the more likely it is a person will commit fraudulent behavior.[73] In other words, give the fox a key to the hen house, and he/she is going to eat hens.

Some proactive and reactive approaches would be outlined as follows.

Proactive approaches include:

- Effective internal controls,
- Financial and operational audits,
- Intelligence gathering,
- Logging of exceptions, and
- Reviewing variances.

Reactive detection techniques include:
- Investigating complaints and allegations,
- Intuition, and
- Suspicion.[74]

THE IRS STRIKES FIRST. When the IRS began requiring banks to issue Form 1099s reporting interest, the reported interest income increased by $8 billion (even though for three years the IRS did not have computer matching capacity).

When the IRS began to require taxpayers to list a social security number for dependents, the next year the number of reported dependents dropped by seven million. More than 11,000 of these taxpayers claimed seven or more dependents in 1986, but they claimed none in 1987.

When the IRS began to require taxpayers to list a name, address, and social security number for babysitters, two years later 2.6 million babysitters disappeared.

Five key proactive principles are provided by the AICPA, IIA, and ACFE:[75]
- *Principle 1*: As part of an organization's governance structure, a fraud risk management program or anti-fraud program should be in place, including a written policy (or policies) to convey the expectations of the board of directors and senior management regarding managing fraud risk.
- *Principle 2*: Fraud risk exposure should be assessed periodically by the organization to identify specific potential schemes and events that the organization needs to mitigate.
- *Principle 3*: Prevention techniques to avoid potential key fraud risk events should be established, where feasible, to mitigate possible impacts on the organization.
- *Principle 4*: Detection techniques should be established to uncover fraud events when preventive measures fail or unmitigated risks are realized.
- *Principle 5*: A reporting process should be in place to solicit input on potential fraud, and a coordinated approach to investigation and corrective action should be used to help ensure potential fraud is addressed appropriately and timely.

Company's Response to Risk

Responsibility for detecting fraud has been illusive since the advent of computer generated accounting and financial statement preparation. However, with the recent financial scandals, new developments such as the Sarbanes-Oxley Act, new SEC rules, and other recent regulatory developments, fraud detection and perhaps to a lesser degree, fraud prevention, seems to be everyone's business from the CEO to the independent auditor, to the internal auditor to the audit committee, and on to the forensic accountant. Getting all capable parties working together to fight fraud is important to controlling risk.

It is also important to have adequate plans and procedures in place to deal with fraud once it has been discovered. Below are some steps that both the company involved and the forensic practitioner should consider.
1. Call legal counsel. If fraud risk has been managed before the event, counsel should have been involved and there may be some legal guidelines that can be immediately referenced. Depending upon the situation, some sure-footed steps can be taken to mitigate damages and avoid compromising any legal or insurance recourse.
2. Get the insurance carrier involved as early as possible. Missteps can compromise insurance coverage and many carriers and insurance brokers have excellent specialists ready to assist.
3. Take immediate steps to safeguard existing assets from further damage. Think of what people do with storm damage—put up the plywood boards to cover the miss-

ing windows. You should have documentation in hand that gives specific guidelines for dealing with computer and other technology that might be affected by fraud.

4. Quietly and confidentially gather evidence. Make sure you don't compromise any legal rights. Calm level-headed rational approaches are best. Consider future ramifications of decisions and actions made in the heat of the moment. Keep an open mind—remember often something that looks like fraud may not be.

5. Manage information on a need to know basis in the early stages of discovery.

6. Consider communications very carefully whether they are to employees or those outside the company.

7. Consider setting aside time immediately to scope out an action plan.

8. Consider those who might assist in the crisis and take steps to eliminate any conflict of interest issues.

9. Consider prosecution which acts as a deterrent for future fraud. As an Islamic proverb states "there is more truth in one sword than ten-thousand words."

The 2003 PriceWaterhouseCoopers fraud survey found that 76 percent of the U.S. respondents were covered by insurance, but fewer than one-half were able to recover from their insurers. Less than one-third of insured companies affected by fraud collected more than 20 percent of the amount lost.[76]

Michael Comer suggests that 85 percent of fraud victims never get their money or property back. Most fraud investigations flounder, leaving the victims to defend for themselves against counter-attack from hostile parties. Further, 30 percent of companies that fail do so because of fraud.[77]

KPMG found in the 2011 "Who is the Typical Fraudster" survey these outcomes or responses to incidents of fraud in the U.S.

- Disciplinary action 54 percent of the time.
- Enforcement action, such as regulatory, legal, and police, 45 percent of the cases.
- Resignation/voluntary retirement (17 percent).
- Settled out of court (6 percent)
- No action of sanction (3 percent).

The KPMG survey also found some details of the fraud communicated internally but little communicated externally. No details were communicated internally 54 percent of the time. Very limited announcements were made 33 percent of the time, and detailed announcements were made only 13 percent internally.

Externally no details were communicated 77% of the time, limited announcements 13 percent of the times, and detailed announcements externally were made only 10 percent of the time.

PricewaterhouseCoopers 2009 Global Economic Crime survey found these actions against *internal* fraudsters:

- Dismissal   85%
- Civil/Criminal action   48%
- Notify appropriate regulatory authority   24%
- Warning/reprimand   22%
- Transfer   4%
- Did nothing   2%

The same survey indicates the actions brought against external fraudsters:

- Civil/Criminal actions were brought   59%
- Cessation of business relationships   51%
- Notify relevant regulatory authorities   46%
- Other actions   16%
- Did nothing   4%

Fraud and Security Policy

Another way the forensic accountant can assist in the fight against fraud is in reviewing or helping to audit the company's security measures. Forensic accountants will not replace security managers and the special services they offer, but it's important for the forensic accountant to become familiar with security plans and controls that can help protect a firm from fraud.

Staffing Role in Fraud Detection and Prevention

Of course, staff selection and promotion based on sound employment practices can fight fraud and help insure that if fraud is detected, it is reported. A workforce that is treated properly with fair promotions and sound compensation practices will help guard against a certain amount of fraud. Excellent training programs exist to help train employees on proper conduct in the workplace to help build some institutional fraud fighting muscle. Fraud detection training can be implemented where needed.

RESIGNATION NAILS EX-EMPLOYEE EMBEZZLER. On October 29, 2002, the Securities and Exchange Commission (SEC) charged an ex-employee of U.S. Lime with financial fraud and other securities law violations related to his embezzlement of nearly $2.2 million from the company during a four-year period.

The perpetrator held a number of positions at U.S. Lime between January 1998 and December 2001, including corporate controller, secretary, treasurer, and vice president of finance. During that period, he forged the signatures of other company officers on dozens of checks and falsified the company's check register to make it appear that the amounts that he personally received or gave to his creditors went to vendors for U.S. Lime's legitimate business expenses. Initially, he embezzled relatively small amounts, but over time his thefts escalated. By January 2002, his thefts were too large to conceal, and he abruptly resigned.

The SEC alleged that this person acted alone, and without the knowledge of other U.S. Lime employees. Throughout the relevant period, he supervised U.S. Lime's internal accounting controls and financial reporting, and he used his position to escape detection by falsifying the company's books and records, lying to its outside auditors, and preparing false financial statements that he then caused the company to file with the SEC (that is, he performed a management override of control).

The company's management, with the help of its outside auditors, discovered the fraud shortly after he resigned. The company immediately reported his misconduct to the SEC, the criminal authorities, and the NASDAQ. U.S. Lime also hired expert securities counsel to conduct an internal investigation, and cooperated fully with the SEC's investigation of the matter.[78]

Company Fraud Prevention, Detection, and Mitigation Measures

¶ 5081   COMPANIES ON THE FRONT LINES IN PREVENTING EMPLOYEE FRAUD

The following are some principles companies should employ to help stop fraud and abuse:
- Maintain a fraud hotline.
- Have a mandatory vacation policy.
- Rotate assignments of employees who handle cash, payables, receivables, and credits.

- Have a written and signed ethics policy.
- Have internal auditors do different procedures each time they audit a unit.
- Observe and listen to employees. Look for lifestyle changes.
- Surprise audits.
- Really understand the business unit, and what functions employees actually perform.
- In a small business, the owner should receive the monthly bank statements unopened.
- Bank statements should *always* be reconciled.
- Supervisors should try to think like criminals.
- Do not assume employees behave honestly.
- Check employee references and resumes.
- Think outside the box.
- Bond employees.
- Use a positive pay system.
- Use a locked box system.
- Count the cash twice in one day.
- Count the cash at irregular intervals.
- Hold unannounced inventory counts.
- Have a fraud risk assessment.
- Beware of related parties.
- Avoid check-signing machines and signature stamps.
- Be careful of allowing employees to make side agreements.
- Beware of perfectionists (e.g., Martha Stewart).
- Pay employees to report fraud.
- Use Uni-ball gel pens.
- For fax or electronic confirmations, verify by telephone with the purported sender.

Fraud auditors need to beware of related entities and parties. In 2007, Nikko Cordial (Japan) was fined for failure to consolidate a special-purpose entity that was 100-percent owned by its subsidiary and for falsifying the timing of an exchange bond issue. This failure created ¥14.5 billion in net profit. An independent panel reviewed more than 507,000 e-mails.

Positive pay is an effective anti-fraud service by many banks whereby a business installs the positive pay software on their computer. As checks are written, important information is transferred to the bank by modem or compact disk. When the checks are subsequently presented to the bank, the transferred information is compared with the incoming checks. If any information on the checks does not match exactly, the bank contacts the business before honoring the checks.

A positive pay system can detect forged checks having duplicate serial numbers, voided checks presented for payment, stale checks, checks with altered or invalid amounts, and checks with altered payee lines. This anti-fraud tool eliminates the need to review each check which helps businesses gain control of the exception process and reduces write-offs. Positive pay can even be integrated into a bank's branch system to detect fraud at the teller window or platform.

Under a lockbox system, invoices are mailed to customers along with a remittance envelope addressed to the bank. The customer mails the remittance directly to the bank, and the bank forwards the details to the business. The money reaches the bank quicker, and the additional interest income earned can offset the bank fee for using the lockbox system.

BOGUS DEGREES! Checking employee references and resumes can be critical. People lie about and exaggerate information on their resumes. In 2004, the General Accounting Office reported that at least 28 high-level federal employees had degrees from bogus colleges or unaccredited schools. The employees serve in eight agencies, and three were supervisors with security clearances in the office overseeing nuclear weapon safety. Two high-ranking Pentagon officials listed degrees from schools identified as diploma mills.

Rigorous Accounting Practices

Reconciling the bank statements and instituting mandatory vacations are important proactive steps to take, especially for small businesses.

A business owner always gave his unopened envelope of canceled checks directly to his trusted assistant for many years. When the assistant went in the hospital, feeling guilty he opened a stack of canceled checks to do the reconciliation himself and made a startling discovery. The assistant had been writing the names of vendors in invisible ink on some of the checks, which the owner would sign. After the ink vanished, she would place her own name on the checks, then cash them for her own use. [There is also erasable ink used for similar ends.] If the owner had merely opened the envelopes before giving them to the assistant, the fraud probably would not have occurred.

Internal controls are important by keeping the person who writes the checks from having access to the bank statements. A company should separate as many duties as possible. There must be clear and uncompromising segregation of duties between record keeping, authorization, asset custody, and reconciliation.

The person in charge of receiving cash or custody of cash should not be in charge of accounting for it. The treasurer should receive cash receipts, and the controller should account for it (e.g., prepare bank reconciliations).

Wells Report Measures

Certified Fraud Examiners (CFEs) rank the controls' importance in detecting and limiting fraud situations as follows:

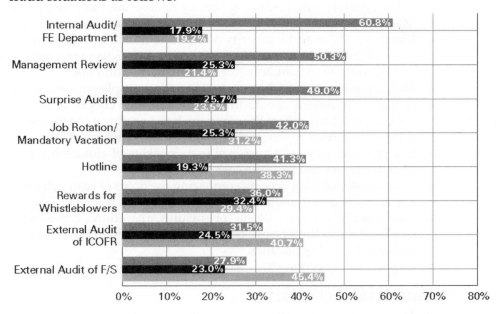

Percent of Respondents

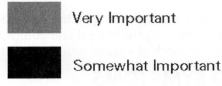 Very Important

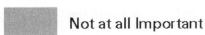 Somewhat Important

Not at all Important

[18]**KEY:**
- External Audit of F/S = Independent external audits of the organization's financial statements
- Internal Audit / FE Department = Internal audit department or fraud examination department
- External Audit of ICOFR = Independent audits of the organization's internal controls over financial reporting
- Management Certification of F/S = Management certification of the organization's financial statements

Source: 2010 Wells Report, ACFE.

Joseph Wells believes that the most powerful audit technique is diligent inquiry (e.g., ask questions). "Experts claim that about 80 percent of all frauds are discovered through tips and complaints compared to 20 percent for other methods, including management oversight and audits." Wells believes that the best clues come from the people who work with the books, rather than the books and records themselves. Auditors need to question the CEO, CFO, and their assistants thoroughly.[79]

Management's Role

Jack C. Robertson, in *Fraud Examination for Managers and Auditors*, provides some excellent extended audit procedures that managers can institute to help find business crime and fraud:
- Count the petty cash twice in a day.
- Investigate suppliers (vendors) to find fictitious vendors being used to make false billings or companies related to purchasing department employees.
- Investigate customers set up by insiders.

- Examine endorsements on canceled checks, looking for second endorsements, especially the name of employees.
- Add up the accounts receivable subsidiary.
- Audit general journal entries, especially nonroutine, nonsystematic journal entries.
- Match payroll to life and medical insurance deductions to catch ghosts on the payroll.
- Match payroll to social security numbers to find an unissued number or one that does not match with the birthdate. Sort the payroll SSNs in numerical order and look for false, duplicate, or unlikely (e.g., consecutive) numbers.
- Match payroll with addresses, looking for multiple persons at the same address.
- Retrieve customers' checks to look for canceled checks showing endorsements and deposits to a bank where the company has no account or that are not available because they are returned to the issuing organization (customer).
- Use marked coins and currency (e.g., pockets of clothes brought to a dry cleaning store or money left near the cash register).
- Measure deposit lag time by comparing the dates of cash debit recording and deposit slip dates to dates credited by the bank.
- Examine documents, looking for erasures, alterations, copies where originals should be filed, telltale lines from a copier when a document has been pieced together, handwriting, and other oddities.
- Inquire; ask questions.[80]

Commercial Activities

Related to management audit procedures above are the following commercial measures that can help prevent fraud:

- Does the company follow strict credit-management practice and enforce credit limits?
- Does the company follow good practice on credit card and counterfeit money?
- Are goods received and their prices checked against delivery notes and invoices?[81]

¶5085   SEARCHING FOR FRAUD SYMPTOMS

There are three major areas to look for fraud symptoms in the typical organization or individual:

- Source documents.
- Journal entries.
- Accounting ledgers.

A red flag is like a ray of sunshine in a cloudy day. A forensic accountant or auditor may have to search numerous source documents to look for red flags. Appropriate source documents are:

- Cancelled checks/bank statements.
- Employee time cards (or time clock records).
- Employee contracts and buy/sale agreements.
- Sales invoices.
- Shipping documents.
- Expense invoices (e.g., travel and entertainment).
- Purchase documents.
- Credit card receipts.
- Cash register tapes.
- Revenue agent report.
- Loan documents.
- Tax returns of related parties.
- Payroll records, W2s, W9s, and 940s.
- Form 1099s.
- Form 990s and Form 941s.
- Insurance documents.
- Brokerage account statements.

Red flags from source documents can include:
- Photocopies of missing documents.
- False/changed documents.
- Missing proper authorization.
- Overstated voids/credits.
- Second endorsements.
- White outs and erasers.
- Duplicate payments to same payee or for some product or service.
- Large number of reconciling items.
- Older items on bank reconciliations.
- Overpayment of wages.
- Ghost employees without necessary reductions.
- Lost cash register tapes.
- Lots of round numbers.
- Too many beginning 9 digits.
- Bogus claims (e.g., healthcare, insurance).
- Many fictitious expense schemes (e.g., meals, mileage, sharing taxi, claiming business expenses never taken).

Forensic accountants should search for these journal entry fraud symptoms:
- Out of balance accounts.
- Lack of supporting documentation (e.g., yellow post.it notes at WorldCom).
- Unexplained adjustments (e.g., suspense account).
- Unusual/numerous entries at end of period (e.g., top side entries).
- Written entries in computer environment.
- Many round numbers.
- Weekend entries.
- Too many beginning 9 digits.
- Entries by unauthorized people.

To check for ledger fraud symptoms, a forensic auditor should look for:
- Underlying assets differences.
- Subsidiary ledger does not agree with general ledger.
- Inconsistencies between control accounts and supporting ledger. Fraud may cause differences.

Four professors have outlined these fraud symptoms or red flags:[82]
- Items that should match, but do not (e.g., invoices for purchases but no receiving report).
- Items that should not match, but do (e.g., vendor the same as an employee's address).
- Outliers and extremes (e.g., employee travels more than others or has significantly more overtime).
- Suspicious trends (e.g., invoice amounts do not match Benford's distribution).
- Accounting anomalies (e.g., employee asked by manager to process a transaction outside the system).
- Internal control weakness (e.g., no separation of duties).
- Analytical symptoms (e.g., unreasonable change in volume, mix, or price of products).
- Extravagant lifestyle (e.g., expensive clothes, jewelry, car, etc.).
- Unusual behavior (e.g., no vacation, unusual work hours, or other eccentric behaviors).

MANIPULATING DOCUMENTS. Michael Hudson in his book *The Monster* provides the following about the activities of Ameriquest Mortgage.[83]

> The sales force at Ameriquest watched the movie Boiler Room as a training film to learn how to pitch overpriced deals to home owners. On page one Mark Grover places two sheets of paper against the window and used the light streaming through to trace a signature from one page to the other.

> Glover's co-workers used scissors, tape, Wite-out, and a photocopier to fabricate W-2s. They would "paste the name of a low-earning borrower onto a W-2 belonging to higher-earning borrower, and like magic, a bad loan prospect looked much better. Their office break room, dubbed the "Art Department," had all the tools they needed to manufacture and manipulate official documents.

The IIA Practice Guide lists these employee red flags:[84]
- Employee acts unusably irritable.
- Employee suddenly starts spending lavishly.
- Overriding of controls by management/officers.
- Consistently exceeding goals/objectives regardless of changing business conditions and or competition.
- Preponderance of non-routine transactions or journal entries.
- Problems or delays in providing requested information.
- Significant or unusual changes in customers or suppliers.
- Transactions that lack documentation or normal approval.
- Employees or management hand-delivering checks.
- Customers' complaints about delivery.
- Poor IT access controls (e.g., password).
- Person living beyond their needs.
- Person conveys dissatisfaction to fellow employees.
- Unusually close association with suppliers.
- Severe personal financial losses.
- Addiction to drugs, alcohol, gambling.
- Change in personal circumstances (e.g., divorce).
- Develop outside business interest.
- Employee consistently rationalizes poor performance.
- Perceives beating the system.
- Rarely takes vacations, and no one performs their work.

Nonprofit Entities as Special Fraud Targets

¶ 5091   REASONS FOR FRAUD IN NOT-FOR-PROFITS

Nonprofit entities, as well as federal, state, and local governments, are increasingly the targets of fraud and abuse committed by employees or volunteers. SAS No. 99 states that the not-for-profit organization faces "incentives and pressures to achieve a given level of financial performance to satisfy its governing boards, contributors, or government agencies or to meet internal targets."[85]

A report in 2008 found that roughly 13 percent of monies given to charities was lost to fraud, and the typical theft from a charity was committed by a female employee with no criminal record who earned less than $50,000 and had worked for the charity at least three years.[86]

What are the reasons for choosing not-for-profits as targets? The website of Clark Schaefer, Hackett & Company pinpointed a couple of major reasons:

> Many smaller not-for-profits just don't have the personnel size required for a real segregation of duties. They often don't require much approval for disbursements. And, when fraud is discovered, they frequently don't prosecute it very aggressively because of the perceived negative publicity.[87]

Fraud within not-for-profits is not that rare. A search of "non-profit fraud" in 2011 on Google found these headlines:

- Vatican bank chief investigated over money laundering claims.
- Pastor Denies Role in Real Estate Fraud
- IRS Looking Closely at What Non-Profits Pay.
- Couple Charged with Food Bank Fraud.
- Treasurer Jailed for Church Fraud (Scotland).
- Wellesly Investment Adviser Sentenced in Church Fraud.
- Catholic Church Swindled in Fraud Racket.
- Georgia Preacher Sued over Church Fraud Scam.
- Tampa Bay: 2 Sentenced in Church-Run Fraud.
- Church Elder Ordered to Repay $4.7 Million to Fleeced Flock.
- Martin Frankel: Sex, Greed, and $200 Million Fraud.
- Affordable-housing non-profit executive forged a $700,000 zoning document.
- Volunteer treasurer uses $65,000 of charity money to buy jewelry and makeup.

A Lake Success, NY, CPA firm had $1 million of forensic billings in 1999. The firm was called when Father Thomas Doyle discovered, while sorting through mail, a check written to an outside consulting company with the pension office manager's signature and bank account number on the back of the check. The manager had been a church employee for 30 years. Within a week the CPA firm found that the employee had deposited over $1.2 million into her own personal bank account over a six-year period. She received probation with restitution of $200 per month over five years. Crime sometimes pays.[88]

Misappropriations at not-for-profits occur from both within and from outside. In December 2002, thieves stole two Van Gogh paintings from the Van Gogh Museum in Amsterdam. These valuable oil paintings were stolen less than one week after a multimillion-dollar gem heist from a Dutch diamond exhibition (Museum in the Hague). John Leighton said, "There is a risk for every museum. You can't have a Fort Knox situation. This is a public institution."[89]

For almost a year in 2002, as many as 2,000 churches and other groups put as much as $18,000 into a church fraud scam. A Georgia minister traveled around the United States offering the right to be awarded a $500,000 grant from a charity operated by Christian businessmen and athletes for a one-time fee of $3,000. The bogus scheme returned little to the churches, but Network International Investment Corporation took in about $9 million from pastors in 41 states. The SEC filed a lawsuit on November 4, 2002, accusing Abraham Kennard, an ex-convict, of fabricating the story about the charitable trust.[90]

LANDMARK CHURCH FOUNDATION FRAUD SHOWS VULNERABILITY TO MISAPPROPRIATION IN NOT-FOR-PROFITS. A high-profile fraud involved the Baptist Foundation of Arizona (BFA), which used investors' funds in real estate ventures. Lawsuits alleged that former BFA Director Lawrence Hoover and his alter ego, D. Hoover & Associates, were key participants in a Ponzi scheme involving fraudulent transactions that allowed BFA to book millions of dollars in fictitious revenues. Suits were also filed against Arthur Andersen, which served as the external auditor for BFA for at least 10 years. A Ponzi scheme is a pyramid-type technique in which early investors are paid with new money collected from later investors, who lose their investments.

The 1999 collapse of BFA led to the largest Chapter 11 bankruptcy filing by a non-profit organization to date. On March 3, 2002, Arthur Andersen agreed to pay $217 million to settle the pending litigation related to its audits of BFA.

Ernst & Young was hired by the Arizona attorney general to perform a forensic audit. E&Y "followed the money through a series of intermediaries and found that the parties buying the property from the foundation got their money from the foundation itself."[91]

¶ 5101   PREVENTION PROGRAMS FOR NOT-FOR-PROFITS

In the vast majority of employee fraud situations, in corporate or not-for-profit settings, prevention is the best medicine. An Enterprise Care Not-for-Profit Services website provides the following practices under which unsuspecting not-for-profits can fall prey to fraud:

- No procedures to detect and report unusual payments
- Increase in amounts owing to creditors
- Inadequate information regarding financial performance
- Regular deferral of capital expenditure
- Explanations of budget variance inadequate
- Liquidity is forecast to be a problem
- Inadequate review and analysis of budgeted versus actual expenses
- Key ratio deterioration
- Expense accounts have increased
- Deferment of statutory payments
- Nonpayment of insurance premiums
- Significant decline in turnover
- Slowdown in receipt of financial reports
- Losses incurred
- No Audit Committee
- No formal external audit and management letter
- Information flow is delayed
- Resignation of key staff or Directors
- Audit reports show disagreement with management and management letters
- Managerial and Board self-indulgence
- Insufficient review of compliance with legislative requirements
- Employee morale low, turnover high
- Key personnel have not had significant holidays for two years
- No separation of check writing and check signing
- No asset register
- No written controls or policies on electronic banking
- No written controls or policies on access/authorization of credit cards
- Qualification in the auditor's report
- Unqualified accounting staff or treasurer[92]

¶ 5111   FRAUD IN FEDERAL, STATE, AND LOCAL GOVERNMENTS

Fraudulent financial statements may not be as great a problem in governmental units as in the private and not-for-profit sectors. But government units also may face incentives and pressures to achieve certain levels of financial performance to satisfy their stakeholders. Further, "corruption and incidents of fraud are much greater in the public sectors than in private industry because people are not dealing with their own money."[93]

Even the guarantor of the soundness of U.S. financial statements, the SEC, has failed at basic accounting according to the Government Accountability Office (GAO). Since the SEC began producing audited financial statements, the GAO has criticized its books almost every year. In November 2010, the GAO said that "the commission's books were in such disarray that it has failed at some of the agency's most fundamental tasks: accurately tracking income from fines, filing fees, and the return of ill-gotten profits."[94] What would the SEC do to a private concern that they said about their business as was reported about the SEC? The GAO said that "a reasonable possibility exists that a material misstatement of SEC's financial statements would not be prevented, or detected and corrected on a timely basis."[95] Who penalizes the SEC?

PricewaterhouseCoopers 2009 Global Economic Crime Survey provides the frauds reported by various types of organizations with percentage of reported frauds:

- Government/state-owned enterprises   37%
- Listed on the stock exchange   31%
- Private sector   28%
- Others   21%

PwC states that although governmental units are more likely to report fraud, listed organizations are more exposed to repeat attacks.

GOVERNMENTAL FRAUDS. Bell, California has 40,000 residents, with 17 percent living below the poverty level. An investigative reporter found that the city manager was paid $787,637 per year to oversee the city. Four of the five members of the Bell City Council were each paid about $100,000 annually.

A total of $111 million from the Obama Administration's stimulus package went to a government agency in Los Angeles to protect 54 jobs. That's more than $2 million per job—apparently very important jobs. The Department of Public Works received $71 million to create 7.76 jobs, for a cost of nearly $10 million per new job. New accounting graduates should look for these jobs. One project spent $4 million to install 65 new left-turn arrows—an average of more than $61,500 per arrow.[96] The Social Security Administration's Inspector General reported that 89,000 stimulus payments of $250 each went to people who were either dead or in prison ($22.25 million).[97] Forensic accountants must look closely at the compensation of employees and executives of all types of entities.

As the FBI closed in, Prince Georges County Executive Jack Johnson had his wife flush a $100,000 check for an alleged kickback scheme down the toilet. With agents knocking on their door, wife Leslie Johnson stuffed almost $80,000 in her bra. She is one of the elected nine-member Prince Georges County Council. They were both charged with tampering with evidence and destruction of records. An FBI team was monitoring wiretaps.[98]

Federal Government Units

According to a 2001 GAO report, increasing globalization, rapid technological advances, shifting demographics, changing security threats, and various quality of life considerations are prompting fundamental changes in the environment in which the U.S. government operates. These changes are placing a premium on increasing strategic planning, using integrated approaches, enhancing results orientation, improving responsiveness, and ensuring accountability within the federal government.[99]

The concept of revitalizing governments is sweeping the world, and forensic accountants can play a key role in this effort. Constituents are holding governments accountable for the resources entrusted to them. Often these resources are misused; when that occurs, the only recourse is the court system. In the same GAO report, the government watchdog said that many federal agencies are mismanaged and unprepared for audit.[100] The same is true for state and local governments. Hence there is great need for forensic accountants who can assist attorneys in recovering misused or stolen assets.

Two of the five improvements suggested by the GAO in 2001 involve fraud and new technologies. The report stresses that government agencies should give high priority to fully implementing existing legislative reforms essential to modernizing performance management, financial accountability, and information technology practices.[101] Also, government agencies must continue to attack government activities at particular risk of fraud, waste, abuse, and mismanagement in order to save billions of dollars, improve services and programs, and strengthen public confidence and trust in government.[102]

Because most of the fraud suggestions for misappropriation of assets are common to both the public and private sectors, the remainder of this chapter will cover ways to detect and cure financial difficulties. However, fraud, abuse, and corruption are prevalent in governmental units.

NASA was defrauded dozens of times in 2001. There were product substitution fraud, false certification of test results, and accepting $27,000 of collect calls from a prison inmate. There was even the theft of a 600-pound safe filled with moon rocks.[103]

WHERE IS $9 TRILLION? The U.S. Federal Reserve cannot account for $9 trillion in off-balance sheet transactions. Also, no one at the Federal Reserve has any idea what are the losses on its $2 trillion portfolio.

On May 12, 2009, Inspector General Elizabeth Coleman could not explain the $1 trillion plus expansion of the Federal Reserve's balance sheet since September 2008. While testifying before Congress, Coleman said the IG does not have jurisdiction to audit the Federal Reserve.[104]

If a U.S. business lost $9 trillion or created $9 trillion on their balance sheet, they would suffer severe penalties.

State and Local Government Susceptibility

Chapter 9 Reorganizations

Although bankruptcy of private sector entities is common, bankruptcy of government units has been rare. Government bankruptcy is an important issue for fraud prevention and detection because like business corporations and organizations, governments facing severe financial difficulties can be fertile ground for fraud. Government bankruptcy may also trigger an investigative need to determine if fraud has contributed to such financial distress. Chapter 9 bankruptcy is used by municipalities, which includes cities, counties, townships, school districts, public improvement districts, bridge authorities, highway authorities, and gas authorities.

Two former Massachusetts state employees pleaded guilty in October 2000 for eight different schemes to steal $9.4 million in state funds. The employees were in charge of Massachusetts' Unpaid Check Fund (UPCF), and they agreed to testify against five other employees (including two lawyers). These brazen and sophisticated embezzlement schemes exposed the lack of internal Treasury controls to detect and prevent the largest theft of public money in the history of Massachusetts. The embezzlers agreed to help the attorney general follow the complex money trail in order to recover the stolen monies. The group devised a complex maze of real estate trusts and financial transactions to conceal the embezzlement before ultimately converting it to personal use.[105]

At the end of 2002, New York City was facing a steep budget deficit, and one writer expressed it, "New York Is Unraveling."[106] New York was not alone. Other states, "sunk in the worst financial doldrums since World War II...faced a possible collective budget shortfall of $40 billion by the end of the fiscal year."[107] Even when the economy recovers, states will require two to three years to become financially robust again. Many of the states had rebounded by mid-2005. However, the recession in 2009/2010 has forced a number of states to consider bankruptcy (e.g., California, Illinois).

Chapter 9 bankruptcy is really a means of reorganization. These communities filed for reorganization after 1980: South Tucson, Arizona; Wellston, Missouri; Waponucka, Oklahoma; and Bridgeport, Connecticut. These governmental units have had stressful situations: Fall River, Massachusetts; Detroit, Michigan; San Jose, California School District; and Philadelphia, Pennsylvania.[108]

ORANGE COUNTY, CALIFORNIA, DECLARES BANKRUPTCY. Orange County, California earned the distinction of being the largest municipality in U.S. history to declare bankruptcy. In November 1994, the auditor told the Orange County Supervisors that their Treasurer, Bob Citron, had lost $1.7 billion of taxpayers' money. Because of fiscal austerity in the State of California as a result of Proposition 19, Citron tried to obtain higher rates of return with some risky investments (e.g., derivatives). Citron increased the investment pool from $7.6 billion to $20.6 billion. He invested in exotic securities (e.g., inverse floaters) that were inversely related to interest rates. He kept buying more and more as the Federal Reserve Board raised interest rates.[109] The result: a $1.7 billion loss and a bankrupt county. Mark Baldassare blamed the bankruptcy on political fragmentation, voter distrust, and fiscal austerity.[110]

Keith Balla gives an example of a housing authority that was buying many appliances (e.g., washing machines, ovens, refrigerators) and stockpiling them at an offsite facility. Then the warehouse sold the appliances to the public at below-market prices. The forensic firm implemented internal controls, with a termination of a number of employees.[111]

Assessing the Financial Health of Governments

How does someone assess the financial health of a governmental entity? Following are early warning signs of possible trouble for municipal entities:

- Current year operating deficit

- Two consecutive years of Operating Fund deficit
- Current year operating deficit that is larger than the previous year's deficit
- A General Fund deficit in the current year – balance sheet – current position
- A current General Fund deficit (two or more years in the last five)
- Short-term debt outstanding (other than BAN) at the end of the fiscal year, greater than five percent of main Operating Fund Revenues
- A two-year trend of increasing short-term debt outstanding at fiscal year end
- Short-term interest and current year-end service greater than 20 percent of total revenues
- Property taxes greater than 90 percent of the tax limit
- Debt outstanding greater than 90 percent of the debt limit
- Total property tax collections less than 92 percent of total levy
- A trend of decreasing tax collections for two consecutive years or a three-year trend
- Declining market valuations for two consecutive years or a three-year trend
- Expanding annual unfunded pension obligations.[112]

Ratio changes may be used to assess the financial health of governmental units, as shown by the office of the New York State Comptroller indicators in Table 5.1. A horizontal analysis over five to six years is recommended, and no single indicator is an indication of a positive or negative trend. Indicators 4, 5, and 6 may be the stronger measurements.[113]

Table 5.1. Indicators of Financial Condition for Municipal Governments

Indicator	Indicator Description	Ratios
1	**Revenue and Expenditures per Capita**	A. $\dfrac{\text{Gross Revenues}}{\text{Population}}$
		B. $\dfrac{\text{Gross Expenditures}}{\text{Population}}$
		C. $\dfrac{\text{Recurring Revenues (Gross Revenues - One-Time Revenues)}}{\text{Population}}$
	Recurring Revenues per Capita (Same as above) Negative Trend: Indicator b increasing faster than indicator a and c.	
2	**Real Property Taxes Receivable**	$\dfrac{\text{Real Property Taxes Receivable}}{\text{Real Property Tax Revenue}}$
	Negative Trend: Percentage increases over time.	
3	**Fixed Costs—Personal Services and Debt Service**	A. $\dfrac{\text{Salaries and Fringe Benefits}}{\text{Gross Expenditures}}$
		B. $\dfrac{\text{Debt Service Expenditures}}{\text{Gross Expenditures}}$
		C. $\dfrac{\text{Salaries and Fringe Benefits + Debt Services}}{\text{Gross Expenditures}}$
	Negative Trend: Percentages increase over time. *	
4	**Operating Surplus/Deficit**	A. $\dfrac{\text{Gross Revenues - Gross Expenditures}}{\text{Gross Expenditures}}$
		B. $\dfrac{\text{Gross Revenues - Gross Expenditures - One-Time Revenues}}{\text{Gross Expenditures}}$
	Negative Trend: Percentages decrease over time.	
5	**Unreserved Fund Balance and Appropriate Fund Balance**	A. $\dfrac{\text{Unreserved Fund Balance}}{\text{Gross Expenditures}}$
		B. $\dfrac{\text{Appropriated Fund Balance}}{\text{Gross Expenditures}}$
	Negative Trend: Percentages decrease over time. †	

6	**Liquidity—Cash and Investment as a Percentage of Current Liabilities**	$\dfrac{\text{Cash and Investments}}{\text{Current Liabilities}}$
	Liquidity—Cash and Investments as a Percentage of Gross Monthly Expenditures	$\dfrac{\text{Cash and Investments}}{\text{Gross Expenditures}/12}$
	Negative Trend: Percentages decrease over time.‡	
7	**Long-Term Debt**	$\dfrac{\text{Long-Term Debt}}{\text{Population}}$
	Negative Trend: Percentage increases over time.§	
8	**Capital Outlay**	$\dfrac{\text{Capital Outlay}}{\text{Gross Expenditures}}$
	Negative Trend: Percentage decreases over time. ‖	
9	**Current Liabilities**	$\dfrac{\text{Current Liabilities}}{\text{Gross Revenues}}$
	Negative Trend: Percentage increases over time.	
10	**Intergovernmental Revenues**	$\dfrac{\text{Intergovernmental Revenues}}{\text{Gross Revenues}}$
	Negative Trend: Percentage increases over time.	
11	**Economic Assistance Costs**	$\dfrac{\text{Economic Assistance Cost}}{\text{Gross Expenditures}}$
	Negative Trend: Percentage increases over time.	
12	**Public Safety**	$\dfrac{\text{Public Safety Cost}}{\text{Gross Expenditures}}$
	Negative Trend: Percentage increases over time.	
13	**Tax Limit Exhausted**	$\dfrac{\text{Tax Levy}}{\text{Tax Limit}}$
	Negative Trend: Percentage increases over time.#	
14	**Debt Limit Exhausted**	$\dfrac{\text{Total Debt Subject to Limit}}{\text{Debt Limit}}$
	Negative Trend: Percentage increases over time.**	

Notes:

* Some analysts use a variation of the 3b ratio based upon debt service expenditures as a percentage of revenues. A ratio of 25 percent for debt service expenditures to "own source" revenues is considered a danger signal.[114]

† Deficits in major funds in excess of 1.5 percent of fund expenditures or $50,000 (whichever is greater) are generally causes for concern. Some analysts use a variation of this ratio: the budgetary cushion. Here the fund balance is compared to revenues. The greater the fund balance as a percentage of revenues, the more likely a local government may weather hard times. A good rule of thumb is that a fund balance should be at least 5 percent of revenues.[115]

‡ A government should generally have year-end cash equal to about 50 percent of current liabilities and 75 percent of average monthly expenditures. A governmental accounting textbook states that this quick ratio (or acid test) omits receivables and amounts due from other funds because of difficulties converting them into cash. They suggest that a large state government should consider a quick ratio of less than 50 percent as an indicator of financial stress.[116]

§ An increase in Indicator 7 would likely trigger a future increase in #3 formula as well as a decrease in Indicator 8.

‖ This eighth indicator is an early warning sign of financial stress.

The tax limit is the maximum amount of taxes that can be levied based upon some statutory authority.

** Debt limit is the maximum amount of debt that can be issued under applicable statutory authority. Compare this ratio with indicators 3 and 7.

State and local government's most pressing problem today is their ballooning unfunded pension liabilities. For example, Illinois' unfunded pension liability is approaching $100 billion, growing at $17 million per day. In November 2012, the pension funding ratio (assets to liabilities) was 39 percent.[117]

Supervisor of the Real Property Tax Adjustment Unit in Washington, D.C., Harriette Walters used at least 92 payments to dummy corporations in a scam to obtain $31.7 million ($344,565 per refund).

Fraud was never noticed by city officials, internal or external auditors. Auditors never examined why the city's property tax refunds were steadily rising. The sham companies' bank accounts were controlled by Walters' brother. Many applications for refund were identical to prior ones.

In a FBI raid of her house, 100 pieces of jewelry, a mink coat, 90 designer purses, 68 pairs of shoes, designer luggage, Rolex watch, silver bar cart, and more were found. Walters had $1.4 million in bills at Neiman Marcus on a $81,000 yearly government salary.

Walters pleaded guilty, and in a plea deal she must pay $48 million in forfeitures and restitutions, $12 million in back federal taxes, and $3 million in D.C. back taxes. She was sentenced to 17 and one half years in prison and ordered to pay as much as $60 million in forfeited assets, restitution, and taxes.

Fraud can be more than just stealing. Cook County, Illinois Treasurer Maria Pappas has been accused of wasting tax dollars. She has a driver making $94,078 a year and a cleaning lady making $57,347, both paid from government funds. The driver, Emanuel Hatzisavas, is hidden in the county budget as a "Project Leader," and the "cleaning lady," Teresa Kawa, is listed in the county budget as an "Administrative Analyst."[118]

Rita Crundwell, the former comptroller of the City of Dixon, Ill., plead guilty to fraudulently obtaining over $53 million from her small town since 1990. Ms. Crundwell used this money to finance her horse breeding corporation and lavish lifestyle.

Crundwell was originally arrested for the misappropriation of more than $30 million since 2006, but further investigation revealed that amount was over $50 million and spanned more than two decades.

According to the indictment, on Dec. 18, 1990, Crundwell opened a bank account in the name of the City of Dixon known as the RSCDA account. Between 1990 and 2012, Crundwell transferred funds from the Dixon's Money Market account into its Capital Development Fund account as well as other accounts. She then transferred city funds into the RSCDA account from those accounts. She used the stolen money for her horse breading ranch with approximately 400 registered quarter horses, a $2.1 million luxury motor home, more than a dozen trucks, trailers and other motorized farm vehicles, a 2005 Ford Thunderbird convertible, a 1967 Chevrolet Corvette roadster, a pontoon boat, almost $225,000 in cash, multiple houses, and many other luxuries. As part of the fraud scheme, Crundwell would create fake invoices to show the city's auditors that the city funds were being used for a legitimate purpose. Crundwell also would tell the mayor and City Council members that the city was low on funds because the state was late in payments to the city, when in fact Crundwell was using the funds for her own use.

Dixon's mayor reported Crundwell to law enforcement authorities in the Fall of 2011 after another city employee assumed her duties during an extended unpaid vacation. Crundwell, whose annual salary was $80,000 annually at the time, received four weeks of paid vacation and took an additional 12 weeks of unpaid vacation in 2011. While Crundwell was absent, her replacement requested all of the city's bank statements. After reviewing them, the employee brought the records of the RSCDA account to the attention of the mayor, who was unaware of the account's existence.

Crundwell is scheduled to be sentenced on Feb. 14, 2013, for her federal wire fraud conviction. She also still faces 60 counts of felony theft in Lee County. Wire fraud carries a maximum sentence of 20 years in prison and a fine of $250,000, or an alternate fine totaling twice the loss or gain, whichever is greater.

When It's Time to Call in Professionals

More forensic techniques should become a part of both external and internal auditing. But Stephen Seliskar says that "in terms of the sheer labor, the magnitude of effort, time, and expense required to do a single, very focused [forensic] investigation—as contrasted to auditing a set of the financial statements—the difference is incredible." It is physically impossible to conduct a generic fraud investigation of an entire business.[119]

Once a forensic accountant (e.g., one holding a Cr.FA, CFE, CFF, or MAFF credential) is engaged, Michael Kessler says that they should not be disruptive. Most employees are not aware that an investigation is taking place. The investigators go in as just another set of auditors, favoring a Columbo-esque investigative style. "We don't wear special windbreakers that say 'forensic accountant.'"[120]

¶ 5121   SOME FORENSIC ACCOUNTANT'S TECHNIQUES

The crisis in accounting is again focusing attention on fraud detection and the use of forensic accounting techniques. As described earlier in this chapter, companies and their auditors should focus not only on detection of fraud, but also on deterrence and prevention.

External auditors, too, are largely responsible for creating safeguards against employee fraud or at the very least, unraveling how it may have occurred once it has occurred. A panel of SEC experts suggests that auditors should make unannounced visits to company locations, conduct surprise counts of inventory items, and request that customers or vendors provide written confirmation of information related to certain transactions.[121]

Covert surveillance observes activities while not being seen. External auditors might watch employees clocking onto a work shift, observing whether they use only one time card. Traveling hotel auditors may check in unannounced, use the restaurant and entertainment facilities, and watch the employees skimming receipts and tickets. Following people on streets and maintaining a "stakeout" should be left to trained investigators, however, according to Professor Jack Robertson.

AU Section 316 talks about the characteristics of fraudulent entries and adjustments. Inappropriate journal entries and other adjustments often have certain unique identifying characteristics, including entries:

1. Made to unrelated, unusual, or seldom-used accounts;
2. Made by people who typically do not make journal entries;
3. Recorded at the end of the period or as post-closing entries that have little or no explanation or description;
4. Made either before or during the preparation of the financial statements that do not have account numbers; or
5. Containing round numbers or consistent ending numbers.

Auditors should be alert to rounded numbers. These are areas where rounded numbers should not be expected:[122]

- Amounts on tax returns (T&E).
- Inventory counts.
- Regulatory filings.
- Accounts receivable balances.
- Journal entries.
- Accounts payable balances.
- Net salary payments.
- Any measure presumed to be exact.

PCAOB indicates that there should be controls over journal entries. Controls that prevent or detect unauthorized journal entries can reduce the opportunity for the quarterly and annual financial statements to be intentionally misstated. Such controls might include, among other things, restricting access to the general ledger system, requiring dual authorizations for manual entries, or performing periodic reviews of journal entries to identify unauthorized entries.

As part of obtaining an understanding of the financial reporting process, the auditor should consider how journal entries are recorded in the general ledger and whether the company has controls that would either prevent unauthorized journal entries from being made to the general ledger or directly to the financial statements or detect unauthorized entries. Tests of controls over journal entries could be performed in connection with the testing of journal entries required by AU sec. 316.

Uncovering Elusive Fraud

Both external and internal auditors should perform some forensic-type procedures on every audit, but suppose the fraud prevention program fails and the external or internal auditors or the audit committee suspects fraud: what then? If the company or auditors have in-house forensic accounting talent, managers should call them into the audit. Lacking that home-grown talent or in cases where the fraud is complex, an outside forensic accountant may be engaged. So the investigatory steps may be as follows: traditional audit, expanded investigative audit, and inside or outside forensic accountant. As an audit moves closer to a forensic investigation, the auditor must comply with the litigation services standards. The outside forensic accountant should be a CFF, Cr.FA, MAFF, or a CFE, or a combination.

Jack Burke's forensic firm uses seven investigative techniques:

- Analyze account records and trace funds.
- Research background and search for assets.
- Develop confidential sources.
- Interview/interrogate persons and find witnesses.
- Conduct surveillance efforts.
- Guide undercover operations.
- Recognize and preserve physical evidence.[123]

EYEWITNESS

In one of Jack Burke's cases a client had two related service businesses. His external auditor had warned of an ever-increasing difference between the general ledger and the subsidiary ledger accounts receivable balance. In a fraud investigation Burke found that two managers were engaged in a diverted checks-for-cash substitution scheme between the two companies operating accounts. One manager would issue credits to cover the diversion and to avoid dunning customers.[124]

FBI ON THE TERRORISTS' CASE. FBI agents used forensic techniques to determine the identity of the September 11 hijackers. Ann E. Wilson says that following the money trail and digging through financial records is like eating a plate of spaghetti. "You start pulling on one piece, and you don't know what you'll pull out and how far you'll have to go. It's a long and tedious process."[125]

In November 2002, FBI agents uncovered financial records that showed a steady stream of payments to two Saudi students in the United States who provided assistance to two of the hijackers. Payments amounting to $3,500 a month came to the students from an account at Washington's Riggs Bank in the name of Princess Haifa Al-Faisal, the wife of the Saudi Ambassador to the United States.[126]

In November 2002, *The Wall Street Journal* reported on how FBI agents traced the money used by terrorists. In March 2002, agents raided the International Relief Organization and a dozen of other related Islamic charities and companies in Northern Virginia. Armed with these records the agents were able to trace the money from a business man, Yassin Qadi, to entities that may have supported terrorists. "An Islamic charity invested $2.1 million with a New Jersey company to which Qadi had ties. The money disappeared. Investigators are looking into whether funds went to terrorism."[127] When investigators follow the money looking for fraud, there are many black holes.

The CIA traced transfers of many millions of dollars from Saudis to Al Qaida during 2002. The CIA tracked the flow of the funds from 12 Saudi businessmen. The Al Qaida network channeled funds through banks, Islamic banks, and money changers. They traded in gold and other commodities to move and store value.[128]

Some research has questioned the effectiveness of searching for red flags and other deceitful clues. Instead, certain deception tactics may be more useful to a fraud auditor, since deceivers use what they know about victims to hinder the discovery of the deceptions they create. The first three tactics below are aimed at concealing the truth, and the other three are aimed at influencing the victim's process of categorizing and interpreting information.

- *Masking* – Failing to record or disclose an expense or a liability.
- *Dazzling* – Disclosing information in the footnotes to the statements rather than showing it in their body.
- *Decoying* – Emphasizing legal issues (blind alleys) that after a close examination turn out to be immaterial or handled appropriately.
- *Re-packaging* – Describing hard to sell inventory as saleable. Reframing issues to maliciously justify the use of favorable accounting procedures.
- *Mimicking* – Creating fictitious transactions or transactions without substance.
- *Double Play* – Improperly applying Generally Accepted Accounting Principles, where an item is not individually material.[129]

¶ 5124 GAME THEORY AND STRATEGIC REASONING

Game theory and strategic reasoning concepts may be used to detect fraud, and certain findings and recommendations have been suggested for fraud risk assessment, audit planning, and audit plan implementations.[130]

Fraud Risk Assessment

- Auditors who use long lists of fraud cues and fraud checklists are inaccurate in their fraud risk assessments.
- Auditors generally overweight cues indicative of management's character even though these cues are most likely cues to be unreliable.
- Audit standards should be designed to persuade auditors to consider how management might manipulate their perceptions of fraud cues.

Audit Planning

- Auditors should develop audit strategies that are unpredictable, especially with regard to the nature of their evidence.
- Audit plans are more predictable and less effective at detecting fraud when auditors use procedures based on prior audits or standard audit programs.
- Audit standards should require auditors to engage in strategic reasoning by considering the types of fraud that management might perpetrate and how these frauds might be concealed from the audit.
- The goal of audit standards should be to encourage auditors to gather new, unusual, or random audit evidence not easily anticipated by management.

Implementation of the Audit

- Learning from experience is critical to effectively performing in a strategic setting.
- Auditors are often insensitive to new evidence regarding fraud risk and can more effectively learn from their interactions with the client.
- Audit standards can improve learning by requiring activities such as documenting and communicating the nature of their interactions with management.[131]

¶ 5126   CONTINUOUS MONITORING

Although not widely used, continuous monitoring (CM) could be used by forensic accountants to detect fraud and abuse. Management hires an outside independent company to install and manage software to continuously analyze every business transaction to detect improper activities and anomalies that indicate errors, control overrides, and fraud.[132]

The detective software can sort incidents into errors, misuse, and fraud. Suspicious transactions can be identified and categorized for future follow-up. CM can flag items such as manual income increasing adjustments, adjustments made late in the year, and large dollar amounts.[133]

Being used by companies with revenues over $1 billion, over the course of a year, monitoring each module (e.g., A/P, Sales, G/L) may be designed to cost approximately the amount the company would pay for one full-time internal auditor per module. One company saved $2 million in external auditing fees using CM in the 404 area.[134]

M.J. Nigrini provides these facts about continuous monitoring:[135]

- Correlation is well suited to environments where there are (1) a large number of audit units (departments, divisions, franchisees, or customers, etc); (2) a series of time-stamped revenues, expenses, or loss amounts; and (3) the goal of developing a formal process to compare each audit unit against a valid benchmark.
- Correlation and time-series analysis are techniques that could be used by forensic accountants in a monitoring role to find evidence of intentional or unintentional errors in situations where there are many audit units.
- These techniques could be used to proactively search for errors without any preconceived belief as to their existence, magnitude, or pervaseiveness, or where the forensic accountant seeks to provide additional evidence showing that such errors occurred after the errors were detected using some other detection method.
- If intentional errors were discovered using other methods of discovery, then the techniques could be used by the forensic accountant to show that the revenue, expenditure, or loss streams of an audit unit differed significantly from a valid benchmark.

ACL Services outlines these benefits of their continuous control monitoring:[136]

- *Independent testing of controls* – through transaction analysis at the source level.
- *Timely notification to management of controls breakdowns* – an "early warning system" of compliance risk, enabling control weaknesses to be fixed before they are reported externally.
- *Fraud reduction and improved risk management* – through identification of control gaps and weaknesses that can lead to error, abuse, and fraud.

- *Improvements to efficiency and effectiveness* – with potential to increase profitability by containing costs, minimizing losses, and improving revenue collection.
- *Extensibility to multiple end-to-end business processes* – with independent assurance of controls effectiveness and transaction integrity across the enterprise.

¶ 5128   SOME FORENSIC TECHNIQUES AND TOOLS

When a potential fraudster is using checking accounts, a forensic accountant may perform a check spread. George A. Manning says the following information is needed to perform a check spread: date, payee, check number, amount, bank from, bank to, first endorsement, second endorsement, and second signatory. Check spreads show patterns of activities and can gather data for the net worth method.[137]

On the other hand, a deposit spread deals with the receipts into a checking account, and shows patterns of activities and gathers data for the net worth and expenditures methods.

Credit card spreads may be used for legal and stolen credit cards to show where a target has been geographically over time.[138]

EYEWITNESS

Forensic accountants are being used by the court–appointed trustees (Irving Picard and Securities Investor Protection Corporation) to reconstruct the books of Bernard L. Madoff Investment Securities (BLMIS). According to Picard, there were paper records, microfilm, and microfiche. But there was nothing that was electronic.

Every customer statement was fiction, so the first task is to reconstruct the books and records of BLMIS. One of the early projects was to digitize the records so they are easier to compare, including customer statements, incoming letters, faxes, and bank records. The forensic accountant will use records from third parties and customers. Every customer account must be reconstructed from the ground up.

Stephen Harbeck, President of Securities Investor Protection Corporation, stated that the forensic accountants "are working as quickly as possible to catalog all the far-reaching aspects of the Madoff scheme and to recover money for investors to the extent possible by law." The cost of the Ponzi scheme may be as high as $65 billion.[139]

Timeline analysis (TA) may be used to show the chronology of a dispute, and certain software tools can prepare trial exhibits. Investigative analysis software can show all details from the beginning of the event until the apprehension of the target. TA helps forensic accountants communicate the timing of case related events and summarizes the investigation. Each link of the timeline chart includes a reference to a source or a direct link to a database.[140]

A **tracing schedule** can be used to show the flow of funds from bank-to-bank, from bank-to-entity, from entity-to-entity, or from person-to-person. A tracing schedule is helpful in money laundering cases.

Link analysis (LA) is a subset of network analysis which shows associations between people and data. For example, a link analysis could compare the mailing addresses of company executives and the cell phone numbers that they have dialed during a given time frame. LA provides crucial relationships between many objects of different types that are not apparent from isolated pieces of data.[141]

EYEWITNESS

Evidence Based Research, Inc. (EBR) states that they can help companies detect and prevent fraud by using advanced analysis and visualization to connect patterns and show links between fraudulent companies and individuals. EBR targets individuals and organizations potentially committing fraud by gathering vast amounts of data on numerous companies and showing their relationships. This process helps detect complex alliances, showing indirect relationships between companies of interest, corporations, organizations, people, and more. EBR utilizes sophisticated tools that search the open source to extract and organize data from thousands of Web pages. They process the language and find meaning in the collected data. When combined with internal data, they develop models to enable link analysis, profile development, and knowledge discovery. They then build illustrative link analysis and multidimensional visualization models to support analysis requirements.

Other companies often use link analysis, especially for the insurance industry. For example, Magnify, Inc. has a Fraud Link Visualizer that helps forensic investigators to connect the dots rapidly between claims, claimants and providers, and other related data in order to identify which claims may be part of larger rings of potential fraud. See Chapter 13 for a discussion of link analysis.

Invigilation

Invigilation is a rather expensive investigating technique that can be used in potential fraud situations to discover the fraud and can later be used in the courtroom. Here detailed records are kept before and after the invigilation period to determine the amount of fraud. During the invigilation period strict controls are imposed (e.g., cameras) so that the fraud is virtually impossible. Or the invigilation period could be while the suspect is on vacation. For example, in Figure 5.9 the suspect is on vacation for two weeks during which there was no fraud. But before and after the vacation the person was embezzling money, $67,000 and $62,000 respectively.

Figure 5.9. Invigilation Technique

No controls	Controls or vacation	No controls
14 days	14 days	14 days
$67,000 lost	$0 lost	$62,000 lost

Genogram

A genogram is a pictorial display of personal relationships among related or unrelated parties. There are software programs that are custom designed for genograms, such as GenoPro 2011 ($49 at *www.genopro.com*). Simple symbols represent the gender (box for male and circle for female), with various lines to illustrate family relationships. People who are not related would not be connected with a line, but could be placed on the genogram. They can lead to determining the motive of a crime or provide evidence that the person had no direct involvement in the fraud.[139]

A genogram could be useful where there is a conspiracy involving vendors or fake vendors. A genogram might be useful for a family business. For example, in Adelphia many of the top management positions—such as CEO, CFO, and members of the Board of Directors—were from the Rigas family, including John Rigas, Tim Rigas, James Rigas, Michael Rigas, and son-in-law Peter Venetis. The Rigas family violated GAAP by transferring debt over to family members' subsidiaries that were not consolidated. The Rigas family stole at least $1.5 billion.

Proof of Cash

The proof of cash procedure is similar to a bank reconciliation, except more detailed and extensive. This procedure can be used to verify that cash accounts on the books are in agreement with the cash transactions recorded by the bank. The Wyoming Department of Audit's proof of cash can be found on the Internet.

Entity Charts

Entity charts show entities and owners with the relationship between them. The charts can show how income and assets are diverted, particularly among seemingly unrelated parties and entities. Microsoft Excel drawing tools may be used to prepare entity charts. For example, an entity chart could show the creation date of off-shore bank accounts and the subsequent decrease in the target's U.S. bank accounts. Identification of other unrelated parties may suggest additional investigation is needed.[143]

Full-and-False Inclusion Tests

These tests are used to ascertain the proper universe of data under investigation, so that no appropriate data is excluded and no extraneous data is included. Full-and-false inclusion tests may be helpful for finding hidden assets.[144] Darrell Dornell says this test is like yellow crime scene tape. Essentially, you can never connect the dots unless you know where all the appropriate dots are.

Financial Models

A financial model may be defined as "an abstract, simplified, mathematical construct related to a part of reality and created for a particular purpose."[145] AICPA Practice Aid 06-2 suggests a financial model could be used in these situations:[146]

- Reviewing or developing planning concepts in the client organization.
- Selecting, gathering, compiling, validating, and assessing data required in the planning process.
- Determining the relationships and interactions among the key factors in client operations and finances.
- Reviewing financial, planning, and operating assumptions with the client.
- Constructing a formal model of key factors, relationships, and interactions.
- Analyzing, testing, and presenting results produced by running the model using various combinations of assumptions, relationships, and activity levels.
- Revising or updating the output as time passes using amended or incremental inputs.
- Submitting the model to the client for future use and maintenance with appropriate documentation and training.

Net Worth Method

Other forensic techniques, the net worth method, and Source and Application of Funds method, are covered in detail in Chapter 6.

Form 1099 Technique

Since employees steal more than shoplifters, some experts suggest that a Form 1099 technique should be used to try to get stolen money and property back from the fraudster. Under this technique the entity supposedly uses the threat of filing a Form 1099 with the IRS for the amount stolen, unless the fraudster signs an installment note agreeing to a payback.

Suppose an employee embezzled $110,000 from a corporation over 2½ years (starting in 2012). Insurance reimbursement was $25,000. An officer explains to the employee that the company must file a Form 1099 unless the fraudster signs an installment note with four percent interest to be paid back in installments of $300 per month. He signs the note.

Receipts from embezzlement, fraud, extortion, bank robbery, and other illegal income are includible in gross income (unless the money is paid back in that year). The Supreme Court in *E.C. James*[147] overturned the prior *L. Wilcox*[148] decision and held that embezzled funds are taxable to a thief under Code Sec. 61(a) in the year the funds are stolen. Any stolen assets are not deductible by the employer until the year the thefts are discovered.

The embezzler must report the assets embezzled or stolen in gross income for each year of the theft which requires the filing of amended returns.[149] Essentially, income is taxable at the time the fraudster takes control of the funds, regardless of future restitution or signing a payback agreement.[150] The stolen funds are taxable even if the employer fails to provide a Form 1099. Stolen funds are taxable in the year taken even if the victim institutes proceedings to recover the full amount prior to the assessment of the tax by the IRS.[151] In other words, even in a debtor-creditor relationship, the fraudster still has taxable income. Further, the illegally acquired funds are taxable even if the victim is reimbursed by an indemnity bond. Also, a self-employed fraudster would report the amount on Schedule C and may be subject to self-employment taxes on the illegally acquired income. Further, the fraudster may be subject to interest and penalties by the IRS for non-payment of taxes on the illegal income.[152]

Any included income can be reduced each year by the amount that is repaid to the employer in that particular year. If, as in our example, the repayment is made in a year after the theft, the fraudster may report the restitution amount as a miscellaneous itemized deduction, subject to the two-percent adjusted gross income limitation.[153]

A deduction is not available unless the fraudster can show that the embezzled assets were previously recorded as taxable income. This tax information could be helpful to a forensic accountant in case of legal proceedings.

There may be a limited exception. A Second Circuit decision[154] in 1977 held that an employee does not have to include the illegally acquired funds in income if four criteria are met:

1. Taxpayer fully intended to repay the funds.
2. Taxpayer expects with reasonable certainty that he/she will be able to repay.
3. The person believes that the withdrawals will be approved by the corporation.
4. Employee makes a prompt assignment of assets sufficient to secure the amount owed.

The installment note option probably would not fall into this exception.

Under Code Sec. 165(a), the victim is allowed as a deduction any loss sustained during a tax year that is not compensated for by insurance. Further, Code Sec. 165(e) indicates that the loss is deductible in the year of discovery. However, where a reasonable prospect of recovery exists, no loss is available. "Reasonable prospect of recovery" is a question of facts to be determined upon examination of all of the facts and circumstances.[155] If in the year of discovery there exists a claim for reimbursement with a reasonable prospect of recovery, no loss is deductible until the tax year in which it can be ascertained with reasonable certainty that the reimbursement will not be received.[156] Thus, a signed installment note by the fraudster would postpone any deduction. A victim is required to report the income to the IRS in each year the employee embezzles assets and may not offer to ignore the reporting in return for a signed installment note. Code Sec. 6721 imposes a penalty if a corporation fails to file correct information. An employer's best choice is to report the income on Form 3949A, rather than Form W-2 or Form 1099-MISC. Form W-2 is used to report compensation for work performed, and Form 1099-MISC is used to report payments to non-employees (e.g., awards, commissions, prizes). Informational Referral (Form 3949A) is used to report possible violations of the tax laws, such as unreported income, kickbacks, and false and altered documents.

An employer can provide the fraudster's name, address, social security number, and describe the alleged violation. By providing the amount of illegal income and the tax years, such information could help prove the amount of the theft loss.

Under the facts in our example, if a company does not allow the fraudster to sign an installment note, the company can take a theft loss deduction in the year of discovery reduced by any insurance recovery. The company does not have to show a conviction for theft, but must prove the amount of the theft. Filing a police report could help substantiate the loss. In the case of stolen assets, the theft loss amount is the adjusted basis of the stolen property.[157]

The signing of the installment note stops the victim from taking a theft loss deduction. Each of the $300 payments in the example to the employer is not taxable, but the interest would be taxable. The fraudster could take a miscellaneous itemized deduction.

In our example, the monthly payment is not sufficient enough to even pay the amount of interest due and thus not enough to reduce the loan principal.[158] Thus, the employee will never be able to pay off the loan. Even if the note is doubled to $600 per month, after 12 months the outstanding loan would still be approximately $107,400.

Based upon the above calculations and the unlikelihood of full repayment by a fraudster, the Form 1099 technique may not be a valuable approach. An employer must use an analysis of a current deduction versus a present value of risky future payments to determine whether to go the Form 1099 route. Any installment note should include a reasonable interest rate or the imputed interest rule would apply.[159] The IRS would impute interest income to the victim.

¶5131   CARBON DATING PAPER AND SIGNATURES

Radioactive carbon dating and microscopy analysis may be used to prove the age of a document or the age of a signature. Dating the writing on a document or a signature can corroborate a suspected forgery. Or a stereoscopic microscope may be used to study signatures for forgery.

For example, if a document is dated 9 years ago and the signature or endorsement on the document is more recent, the document is a forgery.[160] The controversy over President Obama's birth certificate could have easily been settled by carbon dating the paper and the ink (as was suggested in a *Philadelphia Inquirer* editorial, April 28, 2001), and investigating the signature. However, no carbon dating and microscopy analysis was apparently done.

In the mid-eighties a West German newsmagazine paid approximately 9 million German marks for 60 small books that were allegedly diaries of Adolf Hitler. Handwriting analysis appeared to demonstrate that the diaries were Hitler's.

The problem was the police used exemplars written by a notorious forger Konrad Kajan. An ultraviolent-light examination showed that the paper contained an ingredient that was not used in paper until 1954. Hitler died in 1945. Forensic tests on the ink revealed that the ink had been applied to the paper within the past 12 months. Forensic accountants can have suspected documents tested.

¶5136   SOCIAL ENGINEERING

Employees must be taught not to be fooled by fraudsters using social engineering schemes that find ways around internal controls. Hadnagy describes social engineering as "the art or better yet, science, of skillfully maneuvering human beings to take action in some aspect of their lives."[161]

There are a number of social engineering schemes which fraudsters may use to get around internal controls. We are all familiar with the phishing e-mails which we receive weekly trying to pry valuable personal information about ourselves. These phishing e-mails often work.

Similarly, pretexting involves an individual lying to obtain privileged information or data. An individual will gain your trust and then attempt to get you social security number, mother's maiden name, and other facts. An example would be assuming the identity of an authority figure by finding a picture and putting it on an identity badge. The Gramm-Leach-Bliley Act of 1999 made certain types of pretexting illegal. Phreaking involves using a similar technique but using the phone.

Dumpster diving involves sifting through companies' dumpsters to find sensitive information. For example, Proctor & Gamble went through Unilever's dumpsters and found 80 sensitive documents. The legality of dumpster diving varies from state to state. Two preventing measures are locking dumpsters and using across-cut shredders. However auditors should check dumpsters of their clients, such as merchandising companies and restaurants to see if employees are placing valuable merchandise in the dumpster and later that night returning to get the merchandise.

Shoulder surfing involves looking over someone's shoulders to obtain information, such as passwords. Tailgating involves following behind someone wearing an authorizing badge to enter a restricted area.

¶5141   CONFLICT-OF-INTEREST POLICY

Companies should have a conflict-of-interest policy which gives employees explicit guidelines on ethical behavior and situations to avoid. Further, the company should audit the conflict-of-interest policy periodically to ensure effectiveness and compliance. SOX has conflict-of-interest requirements, and not-for-profits can lose their tax-exempt statue if they engage in certain prohibited transactions (e.g., personal loans to executives).

In their Professional Practices Framework Standards Glossary the Institute of Internal Auditors defines a conflict-of-interest as "any relationship that is, or appears to be, not in the best interest of the organization. A conflict-of-interest would prejudice an individual's ability to perform his or her duties and responsibilities objectively." Some examples would be hidden non-arm's length transactions, self-dealing, serving two parties, and related party transactions.

An annual questionnaire should be completed by each employee where they certify that the employee or executive has read and understands the conflict policy and the penalties for noncompliance, will disclose any conflicts, and promises to report any violations that may arise.[162]

Warren Stippich in Grant Thornton's *Corporate Governor* newsletter provides some ways that a conflict-of-interest audit can help an organization:[163]

- Verifying that all employees and other persons of interest are circularized and have responded.
- Examining the organization's conflict-of-interest policy and related documentation.
- Conducting interviews with relevant staff based on their knowledge of the process and their involvement in applying the requirements of the conflict-of-interest policy.
- Analyzing procedures for identification, assessment, and mitigation of conflicts-of-interest.

¶ 5146   CONCLUSION

Fraud in organizations may not be as dramatic as the world record bank theft of $1 billion by Qusay Hussein in Baghdad in the last days of Saddam Hussein's regime, but ordinary employee fraud and abuse costs U.S. organizations as much as $700 billion annually. Auditors must be more skeptical and employ forensic techniques in their audits because only about 21 percent of employees are honest. A combination of motive, opportunity, and rationalization cause the nicest people in the world to commit fraud. If fraud prevention programs and internal controls do not work, companies should prosecute and make a criminal referral.

When you suspect fraud in an organization, think about the parable of the cow in the ditch. You have to do three things. First, get the cow out of the ditch; second, find out how the cow got into the ditch; and third, make sure you do whatever it takes to keep the cow from getting into the ditch again.

Thus, first find the fraud. Second, how was the fraud committed? Third, set up a system to stop the fraud from happening in the future."[164] Under the cockroach theory of fraud, there is never just one fraud incident or red flag of fraud.

Darrell Dorrell says that financial forensics is the art and science of investigating people and money. He indicates "that if you understand financial forensics you understand fraud but not vice versa."[165]

The six white-collar criminals interviewed by the AICPA Fraud Task Force recommend the following policies, practices, and procedures as weapons in the fight against fraud:[166]

1. Organizations need to implement and enforce strong financial controls. Management and boards of directors need to emphasize the importance of testing the controls and closing all loopholes.

2. Board members, executives, and accountants need to closely scrutinize monthly financial statements and other documents, keeping an eye out for signs of suspicious activity.

3. Management should establish a "tone at the top" that encourages ethical conduct and prohibits policies that pressure staff to meet unrealistic financial goals.

4. Organizations should provide a fraud hotline for employees, making it easier for them to act as whistleblowers.

5. Businesses should prohibit CFOs and controllers from simultaneously holding a similar position in another business.

6. Organizations should be wary of entering into an external-audit agreement with an accounting firm that once employed a member of their management team, especially the CEO, CFO, or controller. Knowledge of the accounting firm's audit practice and testing thresholds can be invaluable in designing a fraud scheme to avoid auditors' detection.

7. Organizations should require the use of two-signature checks.

8. Accounting firms should assign auditing fieldwork to seasoned auditors who have received formal education into how to prevent and uncover fraud schemes.

9. CPA firms should teach auditors the value of questioning any discrepancies in client financials. While most occurrences are honest mistakes, a handful point the finger at illicit activities.

10. Accounting firms should prohibit CPAs from serving as trustees for clients' trusts.

11. External auditors should decline any offers of gifts from clients and should notify board members immediately if such an offer is made.

12. Management should take note of any unexpected lifestyle upgrades among staff. If an employee suddenly shows up driving a $100,000 sports car or wearing a $2,500 Italian suit, the employer should determine whether the employee's compensation would allow for such a change in lifestyle.

13. Organizations and auditors should question any unexpectedly high compensation levels for employees and take a closer look at any particularly close relationships between employees, including management and vendors.

14. External auditors should notify the organization's board if any employees, including managers, are delaying or denying the delivery of documents or acting in any other way to impede the auditors.

15. Auditors should verify cash in bank accounts, insist on accurate and timely inventories of fixed assets, research and verify goodwill calculations, and keep an eye out for suspicious patterns.

ENDNOTES

1 Bruce G. Dubinsky, "Fraud Specialists," LEGAL TIMES XXIII (13) (May 27, 2000), *www.legaltimes.com.*

2 Joseph W. Koletar, FRAUD EXPOSED (Hoboken: John Wiley, 2003).

3 M.J. Comer, INVESTIGATING CORPORATE FRAUD (Burlington, Vt.: Gower Publishing Co., 2003), pp. 4-5.

4 Cynthia Crossen, "A Thirties Revelation: Rich People Who Steal Are Criminals, Too," WALL STREET JOURNAL (October 15, 2003), p. B-1.

5 SAS No. 99, Consideration of Fraud in Financial Statement Audit (New York: AICPA 2002), p. 19.

6 Joseph T. Wells, OCCUPATIONAL FRAUD AND ABUSE (Austin: Obsidian Publishing, 1997); H.R. Davia, et al., ACCOUNTANT'S GUIDE TO FRAUD DETECTION AND CONTROL (New York: John Wiley & Sons, 2000); H.R. Davia, FRAUD 101 (New York: John Wiley & Sons, 2000).

7 Eric Winig, "CPAs' Investigate When Numbers Don't Add Up," WASHINGTON BUSINESS JOURNAL (March 16–22, 2001), p. 2.

8 2012 REPORT TO THE NATION: OCCUPATIONAL FRAUD AND ABUSE, (Austin, Tex.: Association of Certified Fraud Examiners), p. ii (called the 2012 Wells Report).

9   2008/2006 Wells Report, ACFE.

10 Eric Krell, "Will Forensic Accounting Go Mainstream?" BUSINESS FINANCE JOURNAL (October 2002), pp. 30–34, *www.investigation.com/artilces/library/2002Articles/15.htm.*

11 S.L. Mintz, "The Gauge of Innocence," CFO (April 2009), p. 57.

12 H.R. Davia, P.C. Coggins, J.C. Wideman, and J.T. Kastantin, FRAUD DETECTION AND CONTROL, 2d ed. (New York: John Wiley & Sons, 2000), p. 60.

13 Lisa Eversole, "Profile of a Fraudster" (1998), *http://www.lsu.edu/accounting/faculty/lcrumbley/fraudster.html.*

14 Gwynn Nettler, LYING, CHEATING, AND STEALING (Cincinnati, Ohio: Anderson, 1982).

15 "Studies Show 13% of Employees Are Fundamentally Dishonest," KESSLER NEWS (November 1, 2001), *www.investigation.com/articles/library/2001articles.*

16 Bev Harris, "How to Unbezzle a Fortune," *www.talion.com/embezzle.htm,* p. 1.

17 Office of the Inspector General, "A Review of the FBI's Performance in Deterring, Detecting, and Investigating the Espionage Activities of Robert Phillip Hanssen" (August 14, 2003).

18 H.W. Wolosky, "Forensic Accounting to the Forefront," PRACTICAL ACCOUNTANT (February 2004), pp. 23-28.

19 SAS No. 99, Consideration of Fraud in Financial Statement Audit (New York: AICPA 2002), pp. 49–50.

20 Duffied and Grabosky, *op. cit.,* p. 4.

21 SAS No. 99, Consideration of Fraud in Financial Statement Audit (New York: AICPA 2002), pp. 38–39.

22 C.C. Albercht, W.S. Alberccht, and J.G. Dunn, "Conducting a Pro-Active Fraud Audit: A Case Study," JOURNAL OF FORENSIC ACCOUNTING 11 (2000), pp. 203-218.

23 *Ibid.*

24 J.T. Loftus and T.E. Vermeer, "Pro-Active Fraud Auditing: Technology, Fraud Auditing and Liquor," JOURNAL OF FORENSIC ACCOUNTING 4 (2003), pp. 307-309.

25 Bev Harris, "How to Unbezzle a Fortune," *www.talion.com/embezzle.htm.*

26 M.A. Siegal, "Recovery of Embezzled Assets Half a World Away," JOURNAL OF ACCOUNTANCY (August 2001), pp. 45–51.

27 Rachael Bell, "Fugitive," Court TVs Crime Library, *www.crimelibrary.com/notorious_murders/classics/frankel/l.html*; Ellen J. Pollack, "The Pretender," THE WALL STREET JOURNAL *(*2002).

28 Barbara Apostolou, "Conduct an Internal Fraud Investigation," SMARTPROS (February 7, 2000), *http://finance.pro2net.com/X8741.xml.*

29 "Pursuing Justice Across Boards," FORENSIC ACCOUNTING BULLETIN (June 2002), p. 1.

30 ANDREW TILBURY, "BEST PRACTICES IN REDUCING CHECK LOSSES," BLUEPOINT SOLUTIONS, BLUEPOINTSOLUTIONS.COM.

31 Fraud Alert, KPMG Forensic Accounting (March 2000).

32 "Thieves Get More Bang for Bucks," CRAIN'S NEW YORK BUSINESS (November 2000), *www.investigation.com/articles.*

33 Grace Lednicer, "Embezzler Gets Eight Years," THE OREGONIAN (November 18, 2006); *http://www.nogorgecasinos.com/index.php?option=com_content&task=view&id=20&Itemid=2.*

34 "Elba Businessman Pleads Guilty to Bank Fraud Charges," U.S. Attorney's Office, 25 October 2010, available at *http://www.justice.gov/usao/alm/press/current_press/2010_10_25_cash.pdf.*

35 Glen D. Moyes and C. Richard Baker, "Auditors' Beliefs About the Fraud Detection Effectiveness of Standard Audit Procedures," JOURNAL OF FORENSIC ACCOUNTING 4 (2003), pp. 204-205.

36 *Ibid*, p. 209.

37 Glen D. Moyes and C. Richard Baker, "Auditors' Beliefs About the Fraud Detection Effectiveness of Standard Audit Procedures," JOURNAL OF FORENSIC ACCOUNTING 4 (2003), pp. 206-207.

38 National Retail Federation, "Retail Fraud, Shoplifting Rates Decrease," *http://www.nrf.com/modules.php?name=News&op=viewlive&sp_id=945.*

39 KGW Staff, "Couple shoplifted $5 million from Portland Safeway stores, police say," February 17, 2011, *http://www.nwcn.com/home/Couple-shoplifted-5-million-from-Portland-Safeway-stores-police-say.html.*

40 Survey Estimates Shoplifting Costs Retailers Billions, *http://www.docstoc.com/docs/24668102/Survey-Estimates-Shoplifting-Costs-Retailers-Billions.*

41 *Ibid.*

42 C. Warner and B.G. Dubinsky, "Uncovering Accounts Payable Fraud," FRAUD MAGAZINE (July/August 2006), pp. 29–51.

43 News, "Court Shuts Down Bogus Billing Scheme" (October 17, 2006); *http://www.consumeraffairs.com/news04/2006/10/ftc_bogus_billing.html.*

44 C. Warner and B.G. Dubinsky, "Uncovering Accounts Payable Fraud," FRAUD MAGAZINE (July/August 2006), pp. 29–51.

45 C.B. Hall, "Five Disbursement-Fraud Tests," http://www.printfriendly.com/print?url=http://cpa-sribo.com/five-disb.....

46 The Montel Williams Show, "My Life As a Thief," June 11, 2004, 2004 Paramount Pictures Corp.

47 CBS News, "Charges Laid in $100-million DND Billing Scheme" (January 31, 2006); *http://www.cbc.ca/canada/story/2006/01/31/dnd-hp-scheme-charges.html.*

48 J.J. Wells, "Keeping Ghosts off the Payroll," JOURNAL OF ACCOUNTING (December 2002), p. 82.

49 "Former Cancer Society Exec. Stole $8 M" *CBSNews.com,* Columbus, Ohio (August 25, 2000); The Forensic Group, "The Fraud Detective" newsletter (August 30, 2000), *www.frauddetectives.com/fdcnn108.shtml.*

50 Glen D. Moyes and C. Richard Baker, "Auditors' Beliefs About the Fraud Detection Effectiveness of Standard Audit Procedures," JOURNAL OF FORENSIC ACCOUNTING 4 (2003), p. 208.

51 A.J. Cataldo and L.N. Killough, "The 'Pump and Dump' and 'Cybersmear:' An Investigation of Two Cases of Internet Based Stock Price Manipulation," JOURNAL OF FORENSIC ACCOUNTING 111 (2002), pp. 225–244.

52 Elmer Irey, THE TAX DODGER (New York: Greenberg, 1948).

53 Michael Squires, "29 Counts: Theft Alleged at Nonprofit," LAS VEGAS REVIEW JOURNAL (October 12, 2001), *www.lvrj. com/lvrj_home/2001/Oct-12-Fri-2001/news/17210138.html*.

54 Keith Johnson, "Mapping the Trail of Terror Money Proves Daunting," THE WALL STREET JOURNAL (May 15, 2003), p. A-7.

55 "Apfelbaum Pleads Guilty to Bid-Rigging Conspiracy," (2001–2002), *stampsmauritius.com*.

56 M. Moody, "Fraud—Enemies Within," DIRECTOR (April 2000), p. 16.

57 IIA, AICPA, ACFE, MANAGING THE BUSINESS RISK OF FRAUD: A PRACTICAL GUIDE (2008), *http://www.acfe.com/ documents/managing-business-risk.pdf*, p. 6.

58 *Ibid*, p. 15.

59 CCH HUMAN RESOURCES MANUAL: PERSONNEL PRACTICES (Chicago: CCH INCORPORATED, 2003), ¶852.

60 *Ibid*, ¶2365.

61 John Goff, "Bank Fraud Brings Executions," CFO (November 2004), p. 20.

62 B.I. Derby, "Data Mining for Improper Payments," JOURNAL OF GOVERNMENT MANAGEMENT 52 (4) (Winter 2003), pp. 10-13.

63 IIA, AICPA, ACFE, MANAGING THE BUSINESS RISK OF FRAUD: A PRACTICAL GUIDE (2008), *http://www.acfe.com/ documents/managing-business-risk.pdf*, p. 20.

64 D.L. Crumbley, D.E. Ziegenfuss, and J.J. O'Shaughnessy, THE BIG R: AN INTERNAL AUDITING ACTION NOVEL (Durham, N.C.: Carolina Academic Press, 2000), p. 75.

65 *Ibid*, p. 76.

66 Jonny Frank, "Fraud Risk Assessments," INTERNAL AUDITOR (April, 2004), pp. 43-47.

67 J.W. Koletar, FRAUD EXPOSED (John Wiley & Sons, 2003), p. 167.

68 *www.ic.coso.org*.

69 *Ibid*.

70 PCAOB Release 2004-001.

71 *Ibid*.

72 H.R. Davia, "Fraud Specific Auditing," JOURNAL OF FORENSIC ACCOUNTING 111 (2002), pp. 111-120.

73 S. L. Tate, et. al, "The Small Fraud Paradigm: An Examination of Situational Factors That Influence the Non-Reporting of Payment Errors," JOURNAL OF FORENSIC ACCOUNTING 7 (2006), p. 406.

74 Jack Bologna and Robert Lindquist, FRAUD AUDITING AND FORENSIC ACCOUNTING, 2d ed. (New York: John Wiley, 1995), p. 137.

75 IIA, AICPA, ACFE, MANAGING THE BUSINESS RISK OF FRAUD: A PRACTICAL GUIDE (2008), *http://www.acfe.com/ documents/managing-business-risk.pdf*, p. 6.

76 J.D. Glater, "Survey Finds Fraud's Reach in Big Business," *www.nytimes.com/2002/07/08/ business/08CHIE.html*.

77 Michael J. Comer, INVESTIGATING CORPORATE FRAUD (Burlington, VT: Gower Publishing, 2003), p. 9.

78 SEC Litigation Release No. 17816 (October 30, 2002).

79 J.T. Wells, "Why Ask? You Ask," JOURNAL OF ACCOUNTANCY (September 2001), p. 88.

80 Jack C. Robertson, FRAUD EXAMINATION FOR MANAGERS AND AUDITORS (Austin, Tex.: Viesca Books, 2000), pp. 221–224.

81 M. Moody, "Fraud—Enemies Within," DIRECTOR (April 2000), p. 16.

82 C.C Albrecht, M.L. Sanders, D.V. Holland, "The Debilitating Effects of Fraud in Organizations," in Michael Jones, CREATIVE ACCOUNTING, FRAUD AND INTERNATIONAL ACCOUNTING SCANDALS (West Sussex, England: John Wiley & Sons, 2011), pp 179-180.

83 Michael W. Hudson, THE MONSTER (New York: Henry Holt & Company, 2010), 266 pp.

84 IIA Practice Guide, Internal Auditing and Fraud, December 2009, pp. 8-9.

85 SAS No. 99, Consideration of Fraud in Financial Statement Audit (New York: AICPA 2002), p. 35.

86 Stephanie Strom, "Report Sketches Crime Costing Billions: Theft from Charities," NEW YORK TIMES (March 29, 2008).

87 "Not-for-Profits Need to Focus on Internal Controls," NOT-FOR-PROFIT INSIGHT (Fourth Quarter 1999) *www. cshco.com/letters*.

88 Melissa Klein, "NY CPAs Uncover $1.2 m Church Fraud" ACCOUNTING TODAY 13 (5) (March 15–April 4, 1999), p. 1.

89 Arthur Max, "2 Van Goghs Stolen from Amsterdam Museum," LAS VEGAS SUN (December 8, 2002), *www. lasvegassun.com*.

90 D.B. Caruso, "Georgia Preacher Sued Over Church Fraud Scam," HOUSTON CHRONICLE (November 29, 2002), p. 12A.

91 D.S. Hilzernath, "Forensic Auditors Find What Some Companies Try to Hide," WASHINGTON POST (November 23, 2002), p. E-1.

92 Enterprise Care Not-for-Profit Services website, *www. enterprisecare.com.au*.

93 Stuart Kahan, "Minding the Store," PRACTICAL ACCOUNTANT (December 5, 2002), *www. electronicaccountant.com/practicalaccountant/index*.

94 Edward Wyatt, "S.E.C. Hurt by Disarray in Its Books," NEW YORK TIMES (February 3, 2011), p. 81.

95 *Ibid*.

96 C.N. Davis, "A Costly Temptation," THE IRE JOURNAL (Summer 2010), p. 16.

97 Stephen Ohlemacher, "72,000 stimulus payments went to dead people," *Yahoo! news, http://finance.yahoo.com/ news/72000-stimulus-payments-went-apf-3512346589. html?x=0*.

98 Terry Frieden, "Maryland Official, Wife hid money as FBI approached, affidavit says," cnn.com, *http://www.cnn. com/2010/CRIME/11/12/maryland.official.custody/index. html?iref=allsearch*.

99 GAO, "Major Management Challenges and Program Risks" (January 2001), p. 6; *www.gao.gov/pas/2001/d01241.pdf*.

100 *Ibid.*, p. 13–14.

[101] GAO, *op.cit.*, p. 7. Information technology (IT) reform legislation, including the Paperwork Reduction and Clinger-Cohen Acts, which attempts to ensure that agencies' information technology projects are implemented within reasonable cost and time frames and that costly investments contribute to tangible improvements in performance.

[102] *Ibid.*, p. 7.

[103] "NASA Records Show Faulty Parts, Fraud, and Theft of Moon Rocks," THE NEW YORK TIMES (October 31, 2002), p. A-19.

[104] Julie Crawshaw, "Federal Reserve Cannot Account for $9 Trillion," Newsmax.com (May 12, 2009), *http:// moneynews.newsmax.com/financenews/feds_lost-nine-trillion/2009/05/12/213463.html.*

[105] News Release, Office of the Massachusetts Attorney General (October 18, 2000).

[106] Steven Malanga, "New York Is Unraveling," THE WALL STREET JOURNAL (November 25, 2002), p. A-14.

[107] Christina Ling, "States Face $40 Billion Budget Deficit Report," YAHOO! NEWS (November 26, 2002).

[108] H.C. Grossman and T.E. Wilson, "Assessing Financial Health," HANDBOOK OF GOVERNMENTAL ACCOUNTING & FINANCE (Somerset, N.J.: John Wiley & Sons, 1992), pp. 38-1–38-13.

[109] "The Orange County Bankruptcy: Who's Next?" RESEARCH BRIEF #11 (April 1988), Public Policy Institute of California.

[110] *Ibid.*

[111] *Ibid.*

[112] Grossman and Wilson, *op. cit.*, pp. 38.13 and 38.14.

[113] Office of the New York State Comptroller, *www.osc.state. ny.us/localgov/muni.*

[114] J.R. Razek et al., *op. cit.*, p. 412.

[115] *Ibid,* p. 411.

[116] *Ibid,* pp. 410–411.

[117] "Squeezed," The Economist, January 26 to February 1, 2013, pp. 27-28.

[118] Pam Zekman, "Is Treasurer Maria Pappas Wasting Your Tax Dollars?" CBS Chicago, January 12, 2011, *http:// chicago.cbslocal.com/2011/01/12/is-treasurer-maria-pappas-wasting-your-tax-dollars/.*

[119] Eric Krell, "Will Forensic Accounting Go Mainstream?" BUSINESS FINANCE JOURNAL (October 2002), pp. 30–34, *www. investigation.com/artilces/library/2002Articles/15.htm.*

[120] *Ibid.*

[121] S.J. Paltrow, "Accounting—Overhaul Plans Draw Skepticism," THE WALL STREET JOURNAL (July 8, 2002), p. C-16.

[122] Shows Estimation, Approximation, or Fraud. XL Audit Commander, free, Excel add-on; *http://ezrstats.com.*

[123] From *www.jackburkeassc1.com.*

[124] *Ibid.*

[125] K. Kaplan, "Tracing the Money Trail of Terrorism," LOS ANGELES TIMES (September 24, 2001), p. 1.

[126] "The Feds Probe a Possible New Saudi Link to Al Qaeda," *Live Talk*, MSNBC (November 22, 2002), *www. msnbc.com/news/838867.asp?ocv=KB10.*

[127] G.R. Simpson, "Tracing the Money, Terror Investigators Run into Mr. Qadi," THE WALL STREET JOURNAL (November 26, 2002), p. A-1.

[128] "CIA: Saudis Still Sending Tens of Million to Al Qaida," *WorldTribune.com* (November 27, 2002).

[129] S. Grazioli, K. Jamal, and P.E. Johnson, "A Cognitive Approach to Fraud Detection," JOURNAL OF FORENSIC ACCOUNTING 7 (2006), p. 70.

[130] T.J. Wilks and M.F. Zimbelman, "Using Game Theory and Strategic Reasoning Techniques to Prevent and Detect Fraud," ACCOUNTING HORIZON (September 2004), p. 182.

[131] *Ibid.*

[132] Oversight Systems, "Continuous Transaction Integrity Monitoring for Real-Time Defense Against Fraud and Errors," (Atlanta: Oversight Systems, Inc., 2004).

[133] D.R. Hermanson, B. Moran, C.S. Rossie, and D.T. Wolfe, "Continuous Monitoring of Transactions to Reduce Fraud, Misuse, and Errors," JOURNAL OF FORENSIC ACCOUNTING 7 (2006), p. 17.

[134] *Ibid,* p. 28.

[135] M.J. Nigrini, "Monitoring Techniques Available to the Forensic Accountant," JOURNAL OF FORENSIC ACCOUNTING 7 (2006), pp. 321-344.

[136] *http://www.acl.com/products/ccm.aspx.*

[137] G.A. Manning, FINANCIAL INVESTIGATION AND FORENSIC ACCOUNTING (Boca Raton, FL: CRC Press, 1999), pp. 196-198.

[138] *Ibid.*

[139] WebCPA staff, "Forensic Accountants Reconstruct Madoff Books," (May 15, 2009), *http://www.webcpa. com/news/Forensic-Accountants-Reconstruct-Madoff-Books-50484-1.html.*

[140] Wikipedia, the free encyclopedia, *en.wikipedia.org.* Stuart Weiss, "Forensic Accounting Tools and Techniques," THE VALUE EXAMINER (January/February 2007), pp. 12-13.

[141] D.D. Dorrell and G.A. Gadawski, "Forensic Accounting: Counterterrorism Weaponry," FINANCIAL FORENSICS II 3 (3) (May 2005), p. 50.

[142] *Ibid.*

[143] *Ibid,* p. 49.

[144] *Ibid.*

[145] Edward A. Bender, AN INTRODUCTION TO MATHEMATICAL MODELING (New York: John Wiley & Sons, 1978), p. 3.

[146] Preparing Financial Models, PRACTICE AID 06-2 (New York: AICPA, 2006), pp. 2-3.

[147] *E.C. James,* SCt, 61-1 USTC ¶9449, 366 US 213, 81 SCt 1052. See Rev. Rul. 65-254, 1965-2 CB 50 and Rev. Rul. 61-185, 1961-2 CB 9.

[148] *L. Wilcox,* SCt, 46-1 USTC ¶9188, 327 US 404, 66 SCt 546. *Wilcox* held that embezzled funds were not taxable because the thief had no "claim of rights" over the funds.

[149] Rev. Rul. 61-185, 1961-2 CB 9.

[150] *B.S. Fox,* 61 TC 704, Dec. 32,484 (1974).

[151] *R.M. Horn,* 25 TCM 1133, Dec. 28,135(M), TC Memo. 1966-220.

[152] Code Sec. 165(c)(2); Rev. Rul. 82-74, 1982-1 CB 110; *J.T. Stephens,* CA-2, 90-2 USTC ¶50,336, 905 F2d 667.

[153] Rev. Rul. 65-254, 1965-2 CB 50; Code Sec. 165(c); *J.T. Stephens,* CA-2, 90-2 USTC ¶50,336, 905 F2d 667 at 671.

[154] *E.M. Gilbert,* CA-2, 77-1 USTC ¶9324, 552 F2d 478.

[155] Code Sec. 165(c)(2).

[156] Reg. §1.165-1(d)(3).

[157] Reg. §1.165-7(b).

[158] In fact, the principal of the loan will be increased by $66.67 the first month.

[159] Code Sec. 7872(a)(1). For more details, see C.C. Cheng, and D.L. Crumbley, "Fraudsters and Form 1099," J. of Forensic & Investigative Accounting, Vol. 5, No. 1, January-June 2013, pp. 58-84.

[160] FORENSIC FILES: CARBON DATING THE PAPER AND THE SIGNATURE TO PROVE FORGERY, Neil Garfield, January 25, 2011; Joe Nickell, Detecting Forgery: Forensic Investigation of Documents, Lexington, Ky.: Press of Kentucky, 2005.

[161] C. Hadnagy, Social Engineering: The Art of Human Hacking. Indianapolis, IN: John Wiley, 2011, p.10.

[162] Warren Stippich, "Conflict-of-Interest Internal Audit, Corporate Governor, Winter 2010, pp. 4-5; M.R. Simmons, "What You Should Know About Conflict of Interest," Internal Auditing and Fraud Investigation, Facilitated controls.com/fraud-investigation/coiknow. shtml.

[163] Stippich, ibid.

[164] Suggested by Anne Mulcahy in "The Best Advice I Ever Got," FORTUNE (March 21, 2005), p. 104.

[165] Darrell Dorrell, FINANCIAL FORENSICS BODY OF KNOWLEDGE (John Wiley, 2011).

[166] Jeff Drew, "Criminal Minds," *J. of Accountancy*, August 2012, p.28.

EXERCISES

1. Define *misappropriation of asset.* What are other terms for this concept?

2. How may misappropriations be accomplished?

3. Multiplier, Inc. has a 25 percent gross profit margin during a year when there is a skimming scheme which reduces the bottom-line by $1,200,000. What increase in revenue is needed to replace this bottom-line loss?

4. SAS No. 99 gives what ways assets may be misappropriated?

5. Define these terms:
   a. Skimming
   b. Kiting
   c. Lapping
   d. Kickbacks

6. What are the three conditions for misappropriation of assets in SAS No. 99?

7. Review the generalizations that Gwynn Nettler provides about fraud perpetrators.

8. What four discrepancies are outlined in SAS No. 99 that indicates the presence of fraud?

9. What statement(s) is false?
   a. Personal financial obligations may create pressure on an employee and encourage fraud.
   b. Disappearance or dissatisfaction toward a company may allow an employee to justify fraud.
   c. Large amounts of cash on hand may create pressure on an employee to misappropriate assets.
   d. Cash is the favorite target of fraudsters.
   e. None of the above.

10. What are four fraudulent disbursement schemes?

11. What are some ways to steal cash? What can help to prevent cash and check thefts?

12. Why do fast food restaurants have two windows at the drive through lanes? At many cafeterias, why do you pay after you eat and not when you get food?

13. If there is a substantial increase in bad debts, what might this mean?

14. Missing inventory may indicate what is happening in a grocery store?

15. You find short time lags between deposits and withdrawals and large deposits made on Fridays. What should you suspect?

16. What is called "robbing Peter to pay Paul?" How do you catch it?

17. What is meant by "white-collar crime?" Who first coined the term?

18. What are some audit steps to catch skimming and money-laundering schemes?

19. What is kiting? How can one spot a kiting scheme?

20. What is not especially helpful for spotting kiting?
    a. Confirming accounts receivables.
    b. Look for frequent deposits and checks in the same amount.
    c. Check for large deposits on Fridays.

    d. Look for short time lag between deposits and withdrawals.

    e. None of the above.

21. What is meant by "washing checks?"

22. Describe a lapping scheme and an audit step to discover lapping.

23. What is a cut-off bank reconciliation?

24. Outline the typical kickback scheme.

25. What is a land flip?

26. What is money laundering? How do you catch it?

27. What is the most common response to the discovery of fraud by an organization? How often does an organization report a fraud to a law enforcement agency?

28. What should an organization avoid when a fraud is discovered?

    a. Hiring an external fraud investigator.

    b. Check the target's personal computer.

    c. Discuss with as few people as possible.

    d. Remove access to computers and servers.

    e. None of the above.

29. List the things that should not be done in a fraud investigation.

30. What three conditions are normally present when misappropriation occurs?

31. What are some incentives or pressures to misappropriate assets?

32. Which risk factor should be considered an incentive or pressure per SAS No. 99?

    a. Significant related party transactions.

    b. Unstable organizational structure.

    c. High turnover of senior executives.

    d. Ineffective communication.

    e. Recurring negative cash flow.

33. Is an auditor likely to know the attitudes or rationalizations of employees or executives that may cause misappropriation of assets?

34. Which factor would not be an opportunity for misappropriation of assets?

    a. Personal financial obligation (e.g., wife is sick).

    b. Inventory items are small in size and valuable.

    c. Inadequate physical safeguards of assets.

    d. Lack of mandatory vacation policy for employees.

    e. None of the above.

35. List some principles to follow to stop fraud and abuse.

36. The 2010 Wells Report found which two measures to be more effective in detecting fraud?

37. Should forensic accountants engage in covert surveillance?

38. Do not-for-profit organizations face incentives and pressures to cook their books? Discuss.

39. Review the warning signs for not-for-profit organizations provided by Enterprise Care Not-for-Profit Services internet site.

40. Are fraudulent financial statements a great problem in government units?

41. Can a government unit go bankrupt? Explain.

42. Using the Internet, find some government units having financial problems.

43. Determine whether the following situations are negative indicators of the financial health of a government unit:

    a. Cash and investments divided by current liabilities ratio is decreasing over several years.

    b. Current liabilities divided by total revenues ratio is decreasing.

    c. Fixed costs divided by total expenditures ratio is increasing.

    d. Real Property Taxes Receivables divided by Real Property Tax Revenue ratio is increasing over time.

    e. Debt Service expenditures as a percentage of revenues is greater than 25 percent.

    f. Debt Service Expenditures divided by Gross Expenditures ratio is decreasing over time.

    g. $\frac{\text{Gross Revenues} - \text{Gross Expenditures}}{\text{Gross Expenditures}}$: Decreasing over time.

    h. The debt service expenditures as a percentage of revenues is 25 percent or larger.

    i. A fund balance is greater than 10 percent of revenues.

    j. Unreserved fund balance divided by gross expenditures ratio is decreasing over time.

    k. The quick ratio of a large state government is 2.2 to 1.

    l. Long-Term Debt divided by population ratio is decreasing over time.

    m. Current Liabilities divided by Gross Revenues ratio is increasing over time.

    n. Tax Levy divided by Tax Limit ratio is decreasing over time.

44. How much year-end cash should a local government have?
45. You have the following data for a city in the southwest. Calculate the quick ratio. Is this ratio favorable or unfavorable?
    Current Liabilities.........................$28 million
    Cash ....$27 million
    Investments ....$36 million
    Accounts Receivables.................$12 million
    Due from other funds................$2.5 million
46. You have the following information about a midwest city. Calculate the ratios of fund balance to revenues and determine if they are favorable or unfavorable.
    General Fund...............................$62 million
    Unreserved Fund ....$54 million
    General Fund Revenues...........$401 million
47. You determine the following data about a local government in the southeast. Determine the ratios of unreserved fund balance and reserved fund balance to total revenues. Are these ratios favorable?
    Revenues from Property Taxes.....$36 million
    Unreserved Fund Balance ....$5 million
    Reserved Fund Balance.............$3.5 million
48. Assume the following facts about a local government. Determine the Tax Limit Exhausted and the Debt Limit Exhausted ratios.
    Tax Limit ....$11 million
    Debt Limit.....................................$13 million
    Tax Levy ....$8.5 million
    Total Debt subject to Limit ....$9 million
49. Assume that Debt Service Expenditures is $16.2 million and Total Revenues is $70.1 million. Calculate the Debt Service/total revenue ratio. Is the ratio favorable?
50. Outline the steps in the fraud hypothesis testing approach. What are Type II errors? How does one avoid Type II errors?
51. Explain the so called "gap analysis approach" to fraud deterrence.
52. Go to the Internet and listen to the song by Johnny Cash called "One Piece at a Time." Outline some lessons from the song.
53. Flow chart the normal flow of cash in a casino.
54. You receive a tip on the company's hot line that there has been some fraud in the collections area. What five audit steps would you suggest using in order to find the fraud?
55. During a brainstorming session, a suggestion is made that the most likelihood of fraud in a particular division is in the area of acquisition and payment cycle. Outline five audit steps to help find any potential fraud.
56. While auditing a company you notice an employee in payroll who is living beyond his means (e.g., clothes, automobiles, housing). His wife does not work. Suggest six audit steps to help satisfy you there is no fraud in the payroll and personnel cycle.
57. An anonymous e-mail is sent to an internal auditor that there is fraud in the inventory/warehousing cycle. Suggest some appropriate audit steps.
58. What is meant by the hockey stick pattern?
59. What is meant by the cockroach theory of fraud?
60. Explain how a shell company could be used to engage in a pass-through billing scheme.
61. How much do companies lose through payment of duplicate invoices?
62. The FBI estimates that fraud in the United States is annually what amount?
    a. $652 billion
    b. $1 trillion
    c. $300 billion
    d. $400 billion
    e. Some other amount
63. What was the major fraud scheme used by the Baptist Foundation of Arizona?
    a. Ponzi scheme
    b. Created many fake purchase orders
    c. Improperly capitalized a number of expenses
    d. Bill and hold strategy
    e. None of the above
64. According to the 2012 ACFE Report, organizations lose how much to fraud and abuse?
    a. Five percent of annual revenue
    b. About $4,500 per employee each year
    c. About $12 per day per employee
    d. About $652 billion annually
    e. All of the above
65. What percent of occupational fraud involves asset misappropriation?
    a. 55 percent
    b. 65 percent
    c. 70 percent
    d. 80 percent
    e. 90 percent

66. In the 2012 Wells Report, what was the third most common way of detecting fraud?
    a. Tips
    b. Internal audits
    c. External audits
    d. By accident
    e. Reports from the police

67. What would not be a type of prediction for purposes of a CFE?
    a. Anonymous tip
    b. Complaint
    c. Audit inquiry
    d. Conflict of interest
    e. None of the above

68. Who coined the phrase "white collar crime?"
    a. Joe Wells
    b. Edwin Sutherland
    c. Michael Comer
    d. D.R. Cressey
    e. James McCleland

69. Which would not fall under corruption?
    a. Conflict of interest
    b. Bribery
    c. Falsifying performance
    d. Extortion
    e. All of the above fall under corruption

70. Which statement is false?
    a. Women are more likely than men to report fraudulent activity.
    b. Older employees are more likely to report fraudulent activities than younger employees.
    c. For each $1 of compliance spending an organization saves about $7.21.
    d. Theft of asset fraud is increasing.
    e. Expense account abuse is increasing.

71. Which statement is false?
    a. In terms of actual numbers of events, women commit more fraud than men.
    b. Fraudsters act alone about 70 percent of the time.
    c. Employees are the largest number of tipsters.
    d. It is physically impossible to conduct a generic fraud investigation of a large business.
    e. Maybe 20 to 40 percent of employees are honest.

72. What would be the worst strategy to catch ghost employees?
    a. Insure segregation of payroll preparation, disbursement, and distribution functions.
    b. Check for inflated invoices.
    c. Examine payroll checks that have dual endorsements.
    d. Use direct deposit.
    e. Hand deliver paychecks to employees occasionally.

73. What is not a proactive approach to forensic accounting?
    a. Investigating complaints
    b. Effective internal controls
    c. Logging of exceptions
    d. Reviewing variances
    e. Financial audits

74. According to the 2010 Wells Report, the most costly form of fraud was:
    a. Asset misappropriations
    b. Fraudulent disbursements
    c. Check tampering
    d. Fraudulent financial statements
    e. Bribery and corruption

75. The measure most helpful in preventing fraud is:
    a. Anonymous hot line
    b. Fraud training
    c. Established fraud policy
    d. Willingness for company to prosecute
    e. Strong internal controls

76. _____ refers to the basis for undertaking a fraud investigation.
    a. Alter ego
    b. Predication
    c. Wildcatting
    d. Invigilation
    e. Shenanigan

77. _____ is a pictorial display of personal relationship among related or unrelated parties.
    a. Timeline
    b. Entity charts
    c. Genogram
    d. Graphology
    e. Full-inclusion

78. _____ _____ refers to software continuously analyzing every business transaction to detect improper activities.
    a. Double play
    b. Game theory
    c. Continuous monitoring
    d. Timeline analysis
    e. None of the above

79. _____ _____ shows associations between people and data.
   a. Link analysis
   b. Game theory
   c. Timeline analysis
   d. Tracing theory
   e. Invigilation analysis

80. Search the FBI site or other sources and determine how money laundering was used in
the fraud at Riggs Bank.

81. Go to the Internet and listen to the 1976 coun-
try-western song by Johnny Cash, "One Piece
at a Time." What is the moral of this song?

82. Fraud Bingo

		T	I	G	E	R
R		Ohio Congressman who has 2002 act named after him that responded to Enron crisis.	Big accounting firm that bit the dust because of alleged wrongdoings.	The federal agency uses forensic accounting to catch mafia types	A person on payroll but does not work there.	"Sunny" company went bankrupt because of shady dealings; trying to "iron" out its problems.
U		CEO in big fraud scheme has the same last name of great snack food company.	Garbage co. with garbage financial statements. Hint: they should stick to "Managing Waste".	CEO at HealthSouth who almost got off.	Carpet Cleaning fraud company of the '80s.	An analyst who almost went to jail for lying.
L		Name of the movie about Frank Abagnale.	Auditors for HealthSouth during fraud	FREE SPACE	Madoff's $50 billion fraud scheme.	CFO of WorldCom who was the architect of the epic fraud.
E		First person to coin the phrase forensic accounting.	Whistleblower at Enron.	Government agency in charge of regulating companies traded on the stock market.	Famous Internal Auditor at WorldCom.	Recording of payment on a customer account sometime after receipt of payment.
S		Term for building up balances in bank account by floating checks.	AICPA SAS# dealing with fraud	Organization formed by the Sarbanes-Oxley Act to oversee auditors of public companies	Italian Diary Company with huge fake bank account.	First forensic accountant in Scotland.

Be a Sleuth:
Use your answer to "catch" one of the first and most infamous fraudsters:

S-G	R-T	E-E	U-E	E-I

Now that you've caught the fraudster, tell us a little about him and his scheme.

_____
_____
_____
_____
_____

83. A victim/employer of embezzlement's best choice to report the taxable income would be:
    a. Form W-2
    b. Form 1099-Misc
    c. Form 3949 A
    d. Form 1040
    e. Some other form
84. When may a business take a deduction for money stolen by an employee?
85. If an embezzler signs a payback agreement to repay the victim, may the fraudster postpone reporting the amount as income? Why?
86. Explain the concept of bid rigging?
87. Which would *not* be considered a source document?
    a. Bank statement
    b. Form 1099
    c. Weekend entry
    d. Purchase document
    e. Credit card receipt
88. Which would *not* be a journal entry fraud symptom?
    a. Out of balance
    b. Unexplained adjustment
    c. Number of rounded numbers
    d. Underlying assets disagree
    e. All of the above are possible fraud journal entry
89. From the Internet, determine the common chemicals that can be used to "wash checks."
90. Prepare a paper to be given to your forensic accounting professor about the fraud of former Detroit Mayor Kwame M. Kilpatrick (1 to 2 pages).

91. The following are questions about Jack Abramoff. You are to answer the questions in this scavenger hunt.
    a. When was I born and in what city?
    b. From what undergraduate university did I graduate and when?
    c. From what law school did I graduate and when?
    d. When was I chairman of a college political national committee and when?
    e. Who is my wife and how many children do I have?
    f. Name my children (if any)?
    g. Where do I live, and what is my telephone number?
    h. What is my religion?
    i. What movie did I produce?
    j. I was a lobbyist for which companies?
    k. What is my political affiliation?
    l. What movie was based upon my fraudulent activities? Who was the star?
    m. What president and prime minister did I pay money to meet?
    n. What was the name of my lobbying firm?
    o. When was I found guilty to commit wire fraud, mail fraud, tax evasion, fraud, and conspiracy?
    p. Name the four Indian tribes that I defrauded?
    q. Name some of my partners in crime?
    r. Where did I serve my prison term, and how much did I earn per hour?
    s. What was my inmate number?
    t. How much time did I serve in prison?
    u. Where was my halfway house?
    v. Where did I work after my prison term?
    w. Who was my whistleblower?
    x. Name the two documentary films about my fraud?

6

INDIRECT METHODS OF RECONSTRUCTING INCOME

I am amazed at the creativity of those who like being Americans but dislike their American tax obligation. Since tax cheats are endlessly creative, the IRS has to be just as creative to catch the crooks.

—Senator Charles Grassley[1]

OBJECTIVES

After completing Chapter 6, you should be able to:

1. Distinguish which indirect methods may be used by the IRS.
2. Know how to look for lifestyle changes indicative of fraud and unreported income.
3. Understand which sources of information should be used in financial status audits.
4. Choose the proper indirect method to apply to reconstruct income and expenditures based on information sources available.

OVERVIEW

Internal Revenue Service (IRS) agents were some of the earliest and most successful forensic accountants in the United States. Whereas other law enforcement agencies tried to pin a crime on 1930s gangster Al Capone and failed, a Criminal Investigation (CI) special agent, an IRS forensic accountant, penetrated the organized racketeering gangs resulting in the tax evasion conviction of Capone and other reigning gangsters. Al Capone failed to report large profits from gambling, bootlegging, and racketeering. Capone's defense that all the money came from illegal activities did not pass muster. All income is taxable and must be reported.[2] According to former IRS Assistant Commissioner for Criminal Investigation Donald K. Vogel, "the Capone investigation was certainly not one of our biggest tax evasion investigations; however, it is a perfect example of what we do. When more conventional investigative techniques fail, we follow the money trail—the proceeds of crime eventually lead to the criminal."[3] Capone was convicted and sentenced to an 11-year prison term based on evidence from financial ledgers and bank statements.[4]

Forensic accountants working in the private sector can learn much from their public sector counterparts in the IRS. Some techniques used by IRS agents may be useful in the private sector. This chapter looks at some of the methods and means employed by the IRS to fight crime. For more than 80 years the IRS Criminal Investigation Division has been solving financial crimes and the stakes are huge. Relatively recent IRS estimates of the gross tax gap—the amount of tax imposed by law that is not paid voluntarily and timely—is roughly $345 billion for all income and employment taxes.[5]

Although private sector forensic accountants lack some of the access to tax return information and the authority to summon third-party records available to IRS agents, many of the techniques used by the IRS may be used by forensic accountants to indirectly calculate net income, expenditures, and net worth.

To prove unreported income and fraud, IRS agents use both direct and indirect methods. The direct methods (or transaction methods) involve probing missing income by pointing to specific items of income that do not appear on the tax return. A taxpayer may have omitted sales, a large real estate transaction, or stock sale from his or her tax return. In direct methods, the agents use conventional auditing techniques such as looking for canceled checks of customers, deed records of real estate transactions, public records, and other direct evidence of unreported income.[6]

When conventional direct methods prove unproductive and the IRS has a reasonable indication that there is a likelihood of unreported income, indirect methods may be employed. Indirect methods use economic reality and financial status techniques in which the taxpayer's finances are reconstructed through circumstantial evidence.

This chapter identifies the major indirect methods of proof used by the IRS, discusses the significance and application of these methods from the viewpoint of an IRS agent, and describes which method is appropriate for each type of business. Understanding the IRS practices helps a forensic accountant gain an understanding of the special tools and concepts involved in the indirect methods.

Forensic Audit Approaches Used by the IRS

The IRS suggests to Revenue Agents that the specific items method (or direct method) of determining income is preferable to an indirect method as it is based upon direct evidence of income. For example, copies of suppliers' invoices and cancelled checks can establish the amount of income that a restaurant owner receives from rebates from suppliers. Thus, the specific items method relies on evidence gathered from source documents, rather than indirect estimates an investigator may have to obtain from third parties.[7]

Professor Charles Price and Len Weld give some examples of the specific or direct method. A trip down to the courthouse can provide evidence of real estate transactions, and state motor vehicles records may reveal sales and transfers. Checking billing invoices of major customers can help spot unreported sales. Jewelry and artwork sold and removed from policy riders may be found in insurance records.[8]

EYEWITNESS

The specific items method of establishing income, supplemented by the bank deposit method, is illustrated in *W.R. Ketler*.[9] During 1990 and 1991, Warren Ketler operated two sole proprietorships, including a catering operation doing business as "California Barbecue." Since Mr. Ketler failed to file federal income tax returns for 1990 and 1991, the IRS determined Mr. Ketler's unreported income for these years by reference to Forms 1099 provided by payers. Before trial, the IRS obtained 1990 and 1991 bank records for all of Mr. Ketler's accounts and identified various nontaxable transfers and deductible business expenses. Based on this analysis, the IRS asked that the U.S. Tax Court find increased income tax deficiencies. After trial, the Tax Court found that Mr. Ketler received the income reflected on these Forms 1099. This trial court also found that the IRS had properly performed the bank deposits analysis, and, therefore, Mr. Ketler also was liable for increased income tax deficiencies.[10]

The IRS's use of indirect methods exemplifies the pros and cons of techniques that can prove fraud as well as invade taxpayers' privacy. In the plus column, indirect methods have been used in the successful prosecution of a significant number of criminal tax fraud cases. In the negative column are listed overzealous intrusions of privacy by agents, prompting congressional limits to be imposed.

In 1995, concerned about estimates of the amount of income escaping taxation, the IRS introduced Economic Reality (Lifestyle) Audits. These audits did not introduce any new techniques. The techniques were the same indirect techniques that had been successfully used for many years. What changed was the emphasis on the use of the techniques. The techniques were used regardless of whether they were necessary or lawful. In 1998, reacting to the overemphasis of these techniques, Congress enacted Code Sec. 7602(e) which limits the use of indirect methods by IRS agents.

¶ 6001   MINIMUM INCOME PROBES

The IRS's authority to use an indirect method is contained in Code Sec. 446(b). The Code Section provides that "if no method of accounting has been regularly used by the taxpayer, or if the method of accounting does not clearly reflect income, the computation of taxable income shall be made under such method as, in the opinion of the Secretary, does clearly reflect income."[11]

The use of indirect methods to reconstruct income by the IRS is limited by Code Sec. 7602(e), which prohibits financial status or economic reality techniques to determine the existence of unreported income unless the agent has a reasonable indication that there is a likelihood of such unreported income.

The Internal Revenue Manual (IRM)[12] sets forth minimum income probes. For non-business returns (having no Schedule C or F), an agent is to question the taxpayer or the representative about possible sources of income other than those reported on the return. If there is no other information in the file indicating potential unreported income, such as a currency transaction report or an unreported Form 1099 report, the minimum income probe is met. However, for taxpayers who are self-employed and file a Schedule C or F, an analysis is made from tax return information to determine if reported income is sufficient to support the taxpayer's financial activities.

¶ 6011   LIFESTYLE PROBES

Just like an IRS agent, a forensic accountant should be aware of the lifestyles of employees of companies as well. The lifestyle of a taxpayer or employee may give clues as to the possibilities of unreported income. Jack Bologna and Robert Lindquist[13] refer to this approach of looking at events, transactions, and environments in their covert aspects. They believe that fraud auditing is like an iceberg with many of the behavioral, covert aspects of the fraud below the water line, including:

- Attitudes
- Feelings (fear, anger, etc.)
- Values
- Norms
- Interactions
- Supportiveness
- Satisfaction

Of course, many of the structural, overt aspects are important, but the behavioral aspects below the surface can be extremely important. For example, a great deal of information about fraud can be found by listening, especially around the copy machine or break room (or wherever the employees congregate on breaks). Stakeouts and sifting through garbage may be off-beat ways to gather evidence. Interviewing peers, workers, and neighbors may be helpful. Further, in addition to examining financial documentation, a forensic accountant must focus on the individuals involved by interviewing witnesses and suspects.

EYEWITNESS

Niamh Brennan and John Hennessy state that forensic accounting demands an awareness of motive. "Often a pattern of evidence only becomes apparent and understandable when the forensic accountant considers possible motive."[14] Robert J. Lindquist states: "You've got to have knowledge of fraud, what it looks like, how it works, how and why people steal. You're the bloodhound much more than the watchdog."[15] Sandi Smith says that often a suspect's lifestyle will give him or her away. "Forensic accountants can study computerized banking records, tax records, and the employee's human relations department records to create an individual profile."[16]

Certainly, obvious lifestyle changes may indicate fraud and unreported income:
- Lavish residence
- Expensive cars and boats
- Vacation home
- Private schools for children
- Exotic vacations
- Expensive clothes and jewelry

However, the investigator must keep in mind that a high-living style may be obtained by going into debt or through "family money" such as gifts and inheritances.

EXOTIC LIFESTYLE OF THE CIA MOLE. The most damaging mole in CIA history, Aldrich Hazen Ames, survived for many years because the CIA would not use financial lifestyle probes and audits. In a bizarre twist, the KGB used financial lifestyle techniques to capture a number of the unidentified human assets that Aldrich Ames delivered to the KGB.

Ames, the most cold-blooded traitor in U.S. history, received more than $1.8 million, and more than $900,000 was placed in a Moscow bank account for him. Traitor Ames sold the KGB the names of at least 10 U.S. spies in Russia, who were executed. He sold the first three names for a mere $50,000, to pay off his accumulated debt at that time.

Ames drove a new Jaguar to work, which cost more than his annual salary. He took a lover on weekend jaunts to Acapulco, and dined in some of the finest restaurants in Mexico City. He wore a Rolex, had capped teeth, wore $1,500 custom tailored silk suits, monogrammed shirts, and hand-sewn leather shoes.[17] Yet none of the spooks in the CIA were suspicious, which makes the old saying believable: A CIA agent cannot track a wounded, bleeding elephant over a field of fresh snow.

David R. Saunders indicates that a good forensic accountant has "the ability to suspect fraud by some means that is better than pure guessing. It is an intuitive process, not subject to predictable forms of logical reasoning."[18]

Proactive forensic audits may not discover a fraud, but the risk of detection may act as an effective deterrence. Howard R. Davia gives this advice for inexperienced forensic auditors:[19]

1. Find out who did it. Do not worry about all the endless details.
2. Be creative, think like the fraudster, and do not be predictable. Lower the auditing threshold without notice.
3. Take into consideration that fraud often involves conspiracy.
4. Internal control lapses often occur during vacations, sick outages, days off, and rest breaks, especially when temporary personnel replace normal employees.

¶ 6021   IRS'S FINANCIAL STATUS AUDITS

In 1995, the IRS began a program known as Economic Reality Audits, which was also known as Lifestyle Audits. The emphasis of this program was to attempt to uncover unreported income by comparing the taxpayer's reported income with the taxpayer's lifestyle. These audits resulted in third-party contacts and searches of public records even when there was no indication of any wrongdoing. In 1998, Congress added Code Sec. 7602(e) to limit these techniques to situations where there was a *reasonable* indication of unreported income.

In a memorandum dated August 6, 1998, the Assistant Commissioner (Examination) cautioned that due to privacy issues and the intrusiveness of inspecting a person's residence, such inspections should be limited to resolving specific issues such as the validity of deductions for an office or business located in the residence.

The IRS, in Chief Counsel Advice 200101030, concluded that a revenue agent may drive by a taxpayer's home and conduct a LEXIS search to determine whether a person purchased real estate during the year without violating the statutory prohibition against financial status audits.[20] Both of these activities are available to determine whether there is a reasonable likelihood of unreported income, which then allows the agent to use an indirect method.

The theory in the use of lifestyle audits is valid for both IRS agents and private sector forensic accountants. If someone is spending beyond his or her apparent means, there should be a concern. Making these concerns known to neighbors, business associates, financial institutions, and customers through third-party contacts based upon superficial information is prohibited for IRS agents and quite likely will result in legal action against forensic accountants.

RESIDENTIAL RAIDS. Sometimes tax returns may be found in raids. Although obtaining tax returns in criminal cases is more difficult, the federal government searched former Governor Edwin Edwards' residence and obtained massive amounts of documents. Laura East, an employee of the FBI, then reviewed and deciphered the evidence.

According to Ms. East, "I spent weeks just cataloging and inventorying the documents." The government then subpoenaed documents from over a two-year period, obtaining any type of financial documents in order to try to create a financial picture of Edwards. The government interviewed anyone who had anything to do with financial aspects of Edwards' businesses.[21]

If a forensic accountant suspects fraud or unreported income, a form of financial status audit may be appropriate that will enable the investigator to check the lifestyles of the possible perpetrators.

KATO EMBEZZLEMENT. Consider one of the larger embezzlements in U.S. history. Between 1991 and 1997, Yasuyoshi Kato, the CFO at Day-Lee Foods, Inc., obtained off-book loans from U.S. affiliates of Japanese banks and issued checks to himself and his wife for about $62 million. The fraud was caught by the IRS, possibly as a result of an anonymous tip. Kato's opulent lifestyle gave him away: He owned two $10,000 macaws and a zoo-sized aquarium containing sharks and other exotic fish.

Kato forged daily accounting entries. He started stealing when he agreed to pay his wife and two daughters $50,000 a month for support in a divorce settlement although he earned only $150,000 a year in salary. He was sentenced to 63 months imprisonment and ordered to repay the embezzled funds at a rate of $500 per year.[22] The lesson for the agent or auditor here is that the lifestyle of an employee can be important in discovering fraud or finding unreported income.

Indirect Methods

An indirect method should be used when the taxpayer has inadequate books and records, the books do not clearly reflect taxable income, or there is a reason to believe that the taxpayer has omitted taxable income. An indirect method also is appropriate when there is a significant increase in year-to-year net worth, when gross profit percentages change significantly for that particular business, or when the taxpayer's expenses (both business and personal) exceed reported income, and there is no obvious cause for the difference.

The four major indirect methods to spot unreported income are: cash T, source and application of funds, net worth, and bank deposits. Other methods used in specific industries are contained in the IRS's Market Segment Specialization Program (MSSP) Audit Techniques Guides, which are available on the IRS website, *www.irs.gov*. A sample from the guides appears in Figure 6.1. Among these additional methods are Percentage of Markup, and Unit and Volume, which are used for businesses dealing primarily in cash and having a limited number of products and suppliers, such as, bars, restaurants, and gas stations.

¶6031　MARKET SEGMENT SPECIALIZATION PROGRAM

The Market Segment Specialization Program focuses on developing highly trained examiners for a particular market segment. A market segment may be an industry such as construction or entertainment, a profession like attorneys or real estate agents, or an issue like passive activity losses. An integral part of the approach used is the development and publication of Audit Technique Guides (ATGs). These Guides contain examination techniques, common and unique industry issues, business practices, industry terminology, and other information to assist examiners in performing examinations.

Audit Technique Guides are available here in *Adobe PDF* format, and must be viewed with the *Acrobat Reader*. Several guides are now also available to View On-Line in HTML.

Figure 6.1. Sample from MSSP Descriptions on IRS Website

A B C D E F G H I J K L M N O P Q R S T U V W X Y Z

Alaskan Commercial Fishing: Part 1 – Catcher Vessels (7/95 229K)
Specifically structured around the Alaskan industry but may be used as an outline for commercial fishing industry in other regions.

Alaskan Commercial Fishing: Part II – Processors & Brokers (7/95 280K)
Concentrates on issues to be considered during audit of fish processing plants; larger, vertically integrated organizations; and fish brokers. Specifically capital assets and transactions and foreign related party transactions.

Alternative Minimum Tax For Individuals (12/99 304K)
(View On-Line)
Discusses brief history of Alternative Minimum Tax (AMT). Provides line-by-line instructions for computing AMT on Form 6251. Includes prior law (prior to 1993) and current law (1993 to 1998).

Investigators are cautioned that the extent to which an indirect method is used is to be determined on a case-by-case basis. There is no one indirect method applicable to each case.[23]

Forensic accountants may use ATGs to quickly and efficiently learn of the distinct and detailed practices in a particular industry. Internal controls within an industry and the procedures that a business may use to help prevent employee fraud and theft are sometimes covered. For example, the ATG for business consultants contains an internal control questionnaire. The ATG for Bars and Restaurants provides a checklist of the items to notice when doing a walkthrough of a restaurant. Many of the ATGs have a glossary listing of many of the important terms in a particular industry. "Armed with terms and jargons used in the business gives the forensic investigator a head-start as the actual case work begins, and may provide information as to what types of useful industry-specific documents might be available during the examination and discovery process."[24]

USING ATGs. Suppose a forensic accountant is investigating a trucking company. The ATG for the trucking industry suggests that an investigator request two documents: the driver's manifests and trip settlement sheets used to prepare the Form 1099s for each driver. These documents may be used to tie in expenses to the related revenue sources in order to determine if truckers' specific trips were included in gross income to determine if there is unreported income.[25]

Forensic accountants can learn from the investigative techniques used by IRS agents. For example, agents are told that these public resources may be accessed by the Internet.[26]
1. Sale and transfer of property
2. Mortgages and releases
3. Judgments, garnishments, chattel mortgages and other liens

4. Bankruptcy records
5. Conditional sales contract
6. Births, deaths, marriages, and divorces
7. Change of name
8. Auto licenses, transfers, and sales of vehicles
9. Drivers' licenses
10. Hunting and fishing licenses
11. Occupancy and business privilege licenses
12. Building and other permits
13. Police and sheriff records of arrests
14. Court records of civil and criminal cases
15. Registration of corporate entities and annual reports
16. Parole officers' and probation departments' files
17. Registration of non-corporate business entities
18. School and voter registrations
19. Professional registrations
20. State income tax returns
21. Personal property tax returns
22. Real estate tax payments
23. Inheritance and gift tax returns
24. Wills
25. Letters of administration
26. Inventories of estates
27. Welfare agency records
28. Worker's compensation files
29. Bids, purchase orders, contracts, and warrants for payments
30. Minutes of board and agency proceedings
31. Health Department records
32. State Unemployment Compensation records

¶ 6041   CASH T

For a taxpayer who files a Schedule C or F, an agent may prepare a cash transaction account (cash T) to determine the understatement of income. A *cash T* is an analysis of all of the cash received by the taxpayer and all of the cash spent by the taxpayer over a period of time. The theory of the cash T is that if a taxpayer's expenditures during a given year exceed reported income, and the source of the funds for such expenditures is unexplained (e.g., taxpayer had no loans or nontaxable sources of income), such excess amount represents unreported income.

If the taxpayer spent more than he or she received, there is taxable income, unless the taxpayer can prove otherwise. The cash T in a simpler form is usually used in the preliminary stages of the audit. When an IRS agent is assigned a business tax return, the agent generally prepares a preliminary cash T using the information shown on the return. On the left (debit) side of the cash T, the agent would list all sources of income, and on the right (credit) side of the cash T, the agent would list all applications of funds. In addition to the amount gathered from the tax return, an agent also would estimate personal living expenses using guidelines based on income and family size. If there is a preliminary understatement of income, this understatement would indicate to the agent to begin probing for evidence of the source of the preliminary understatement. An example of a preliminary cash T is shown in Table 6.1 below, and a proof of cash worksheet can be found in Figure 5.13 in Chapter 5.

Table 6.1. Preliminary Cash T[27]

Cash In		Cash Out	
Wages	XX	State/Fed. Withholding	XX
Interest Income		FICA Withholding	XX
Taxable	XX	Other Withholdings	
Nontaxable	XX	on Form W-2	XX
Dividends	XX	Estimated Tax Payments	XX
Tax Refunds/		Tax payments for	
per Return	XX	Prior Years-IDRS	XX
Tax Refunds/		Investment Interest	XX
on IDRS	XX	Schedule C Purchases	XX
Alimony Received	XX	Schedule C Expenses	XX
Schedule C Receipts	XX	(Net of Depreciation)	
Schedule D Gross Sales	XX	Rental Expenses	XX
Sale of Business		(Net of Depreciation)	
Property—Form 4797	XX	Schedule F Expenses	XX
IRA/Pension/Annuity		(Net of Depreciation)	
Distributions	XX	Assets/Invest. Purchases	
Rental Income	XX	Form Schedule D	XX
Schedule F Receipts	XX	Form 2119 Sale of	
Unemployment		Residence	XX
Compensation	XX	Form 4562	
Social Security		Depreciation	XX
Benefits	XX	Motor Vehicle Records	
Other Income	XX	(If Available)	XX
Unreported IRP Amts.	XX	IRA/Pension/Annuity	
Cash Distributions		Contributions*	XX
(If Available)		Penalty—Early	
From S-Corps	XX	Savings Withdrawal	XX
From Partnerships	XX	Personal Living	
From Fiduciaries	XX	Expenses (PLE)†	XX
Sale of Personal		Other "Cash Out"	
Residence (2119)	XX	Items	XX
Advanced EITC	XX		
Other "Cash In"			
Items	<u>XX</u>		——
Total	<u>XXX</u>	Total	<u>XXX</u>
Potential Understatement			XXX
<Excess Funds Available>	<u>XXX</u>		

* Contributions to retirement plans can be made after year end and still be deductible. This factor should be considered when inspecting prior and subsequent years.

†The entry for Personal Living Expenses (PLE) on the preliminary cash T is an estimate. Determine the personal living expenses (PLE) in the preliminary cash T by using information from the return and information in the case file. The resulting estimated PLE can be compared to Bureau of Labor Statistics to test for reasonableness.

Form 4822

During the initial interview, an IRS agent is instructed to discuss potential understatements with the taxpayer or representative to attempt to reconcile the understatement. Two items not apparent in the preliminary cash T analysis that the agent needs to address at the initial meeting (if income understatement is indicated) are personal living expenses and the existence of a cash hoard. To arrive at living expenses, which is an application of funds, the agent, with the help of the taxpayer, completes IRS Form 4822, Statement of Annual Estimated Personal and Family Expenses, shown in Figure 6.2.

Figure 6.2. Form 4822 Used to Determine Living Expenses

Form **4822** (Rev. 6-83)	Department of the Treasury - Internal Revenue Service **STATEMENT OF ANNUAL ESTIMATED PERSONAL AND FAMILY EXPENSES**				
TAXPAYER'S NAME AND ADDRESS				TAX YEAR ENDED	

	ITEM	BY CASH	BY CHECK	TOTAL	REMARKS
1. PERSONAL EXPENSES	Groceries and outside meals				
	Clothing				
	Laundry and dry cleaning				
	Barber, beauty shop, and cosmetics				
	Education *(tuition, room, board, books, etc.)*				
	Recreation, entertainment, vacations				
	Dues *(clubs, lodge, etc.)*				
	Gifts and allowances				
	Life and accident insurance				
	Federal taxes *(income, FICA, etc.)*				
2. HOUSEHOLD EXPENSES	Rent				
	Mortgage payments *(including interest)*				
	Utilities *(electricity, gas, telephone, water, etc.)*				
	Domestic help				
	Home insurance				
	Repairs and improvements				
	Child care				
3. AUTO EXPENSES	Gasoline, oil, grease, wash				
	Tires, batteries, repairs, tags				
	Insurance				
	Auto payments *(including interest)*				
	Lease of auto				
4. DEDUCTIBLE ITEMS	Contributions				
	Medical Expenses — Insurance				
	Medical Expenses — Drugs				
	Medical Expenses — Doctors, hospitals, etc.				
	Taxes — Real estate *(not included in 2. above)*				
	Taxes — Personal property				
	Taxes — Income *(State and local)*				
	Interest *(not included in 2. and 3. above)*				
	Miscellaneous — Alimony				
	Miscellaneous — Union dues				
5. PERSONAL ASSETS, ETC.	Stocks and bonds				
	Furniture, appliances, jewelry				
	Loans to others				
	Boat				
	TOTALS				

STF FED5305F

Form 4822 (Rev. 6-83)

Searching for a Cash Hoard

An agent is instructed to question a taxpayer regarding beginning and ending cash-on-hand and to specifically inquire regarding the existence of a cash hoard. A *cash hoard* consists of money that is not in a bank account, or other readily verifiable location that the taxpayer alleges should be in the beginning cash balance. The instructions to the agents regarding questioning for possible cash hoards can be found in the IRM.[28] The discussion here is summarized to illustrate how forensic accountants can uncover cash hoards using similar strategies to those of the agents.

Because cash on hand is an important aspect of all indirect methods, it is imperative that an investigator establish the amount and verify the taxpayer's statements of cash accumulations. Cash on hand information is a must in every indirect method. An adjustment for unreported income can be lost if this item is not determined at the beginning of the audit. If taxpayers are faced with an understatement, they will probably try to explain it away. The "cash in the mattress" defense cannot be used if the actual cash on hand has already been established.

In order to avoid any misunderstanding by the taxpayer, the meaning of cash on hand must be explained to him or her prior to answering any inquiry. Taxpayers must understand the term "cash on hand" in this context: any undeposited currency and coins they have for whatever purpose. Once this term is understood, the investigator should inquire about the existence of any cash on hand.

If a taxpayer attempts to avoid answering questions concerning cash, agents should try to pinpoint amounts by requesting an estimate such as "under a thousand dollars" and narrowing the range until the taxpayer agrees with a general amount.

A commitment should be sought concerning whether an individual had any large accumulations of cash during the period. Agents should pursue questions in this area until the taxpayer makes an affirmative statement regarding the existence or nonexistence of a cash hoard.

If taxpayers allege that they have what appears to be an inordinate amount of cash on hand (a cash hoard), the examiner should further inquire to establish:

- The amount of cash on hand at the end of each year under examination to the present (at the time of the interview)
- How it was accumulated
- Where it was kept and in what denominations
- Who had knowledge of it
- Who counted it
- When and where any of it was spent

Information regarding cash hoards is necessary to establish the consistency and reliability of the taxpayer's statement. Usually no direct corroborating evidence is available, but statements made about the source and use of the funds can be verified. A forensic accountant may look for the following discrepancies, for example:

- The taxpayer may not have had sufficient taxable or nontaxable income in prior years to accumulate cash.
- Claims of a prior substantial cash hoard also might be rebutted by showing that the taxpayer lived frugally, borrowed money, made installment purchases, incurred large debts, was delinquent on accounts, had a poor credit rating or filed for bankruptcy.
- Financial statements filed by the taxpayer at banks and other places can be reviewed to see whether the taxpayer disclosed the cash hoard on these statements.

A taxpayer's explanation for a cash hoard may change during an examination. The investigator should document the information *as it is received*. The documentation should include when and where the information was received, who was present, what was said, and when the documentation was prepared.

CASH HOARD ARGUMENTS FOR GAMBLING CASE. The cash hoard defense figured in the Edwin Edwards' gambling corruption trial in 2000. An IRS agent testified that Governor Edwards spent hundreds of thousands of dollars more in cash than he reported in earnings.[29]

A financial analyst testified for the prosecution about how the former Louisiana governor hid money he extorted from riverboat casino owners and spent his cash.

Don Semesky, a special agent for the Internal Revenue Service, used a chart to show that Edwards spent $872,000 more in cash than he reported receiving from 1986 to 1997.

Semesky said Edwards started 1986 with $82,000 in cash. He based that figure on Edwards' own testimony in an unrelated trial in 1985.

In the current trial, Edwards testified he always had between $250,000 and $500,000 in cash during the mid-1980s. Using $250,000 as a starting point, Semesky said, Edwards still spent $704,000 more in that period than he reported receiving.

"I believe the evidence in this case is that Mr. Edwards received cash from other, unreported sources," Semesky told prosecutor Mike Magner.

In either calculation, Edwards started spending more cash in 1996, Semesky said. He agreed with Magner's allegation that the increase in spending coincided with Edwards getting extortion payments from Robert Guidry.

Guidry, the former owner of the Treasure Chest casino in Kenner, testified he paid Edwards and his son along with Edwards' former aide, Andrew Martin, $100,000 a month from early 1996 until August 1997.

Semesky's total for cash spent by Edwards included $383,500 the FBI seized from his safe-deposit box on April 29, 1997.

Edwards testified that cash was left over from $400,000 Eddie DeBartolo, Jr. had given him in a legitimate business deal on March 12, 1997. He said the amount was primarily to prepare for a gambling election in Bossier City, where DeBartolo was applying to put in a casino boat.

DeBartolo, who had pleaded guilty in the case, testified for the prosecution that Edwards extorted the $400,000 from him.

But while Semesky showed the $383,500 as cash spent, he did not show the $400,000 from DeBartolo as cash received, defense attorney Small said.

"Isn't it a fact that you screwed up and you missed the $400,000?" Small asked Semesky.

"Mr. Small, you're not understanding the concept of this chart," Semesky said. "The government's contention in this case is that it (the $400,000) came from extorted payments."

The purpose of the chart was to show legal sources of cash, Semesky said. That included $1,586,800 in net gambling winnings Edwards had from 1986 until 1997, he said.

But defense attorney Small said the cash shortfall that Semesky found—about $872,000—could be made up by starting with $500,000 in cash in 1986, as Edwards testified he might have had.

Add the $400,000 from DeBartolo and the shortfall disappears, Small said.

Later in 1997, DeBartolo reported to the IRS he had given Edwards the money, Small said.

But Semesky maintained that the $400,000 could not be counted as a legitimate source of cash.

"It doesn't belong on that schedule," he said.

Preparing the Final Cash T

The sample in Table 6.2 is the format of an in-depth cash T, prepared with tax return information and information available in the case file prior to taxpayer/representative contact and then updated based upon information obtained during the examination process. The final cash T includes both internal and external sources of information.

Table 6.2. Final Cash T[30]

Cash In		Cash Out	
Wages		State/Fed Withholding	XX
Interest Income		FICA Withholding	XX
Taxable	XX	Other Withholdings	
Nontaxable	XX	on Form W-2	XX
Dividends	XX	Estimated Tax Payments	XX
Tax Refunds/Return	XX	Tax Payments for Prior	
Tax Refunds/IDRS	XX	Years-IDRS	XX
Alimony Received	XX	Investment Interest	XX
Sch C Receipts	XX	Sch C Purchases	XX
Sch D Gross Sales	XX	Sch C Expenses	XX
Sale of Business		(Net of Depreciation)	
Property—Form 4797	XX	Rental Expenses	XX
IRA/Pension/Annuity		(Net of Depreciation)	
Distributions	XX	Sch F Expenses	XX
Rental Income	XX	(Net of Depreciation)	
Sch F Receipts	XX	Asset/Invest. Purchases	
Unemployment Comp.	XX	Form Schedule D	XX
Social Security		Purchase of	
Benefits	XX	Residence	XX
Other Income	XX	Form 4562	
Unreported IRP Amts.	XX	Depreciation	XX
Cash Distributions:		Motor Vehicle Records	
From S Corps.	XX	(If available)	XX
From Partnerships	XX	Contract Amounts	XX
From Fiduciaries	XX	Insurance Policies	XX
Sale of Personal		Cash on Hand-End of	
Residence (2119)	XX	Year*	XX
Advanced Earned		Ending Bank Balances†	XX
Income Credit	XX	IRA/Annuity/Pension	XX
Other "Cash In"		Contribution‡	XX
Items	XX	Penalty-Early Savings	
Sale of Personal		Withdrawal	XX
Property	XX	Loan Repayments	XX
Cash on Hand-		Beginning Credit	
Beginning of Year*	XX	Card Balances	XX

Beginning Bank		Personal Capital		
Balance(s)†	XX	Acquisitions	XX	
Ending Credit Card		Personal Living		
Balances	XX	Expenses (PLE)§	XX	
Loan Proceeds	XX	Other "Cash Out"		
Child Support		Items	XX	
Received	XX			
Nontaxable Amounts	XX			
(Inheritances,				
gifts, etc.)				

Accrual Bases T/Ps:		**Accrual Bases T/Ps:**	
Decrease-Accts/Rec	XX	Increase-Accts/Rec	XX
Increase-Accts/Pay	XX	Decrease-Accts/Pay	XX
Total	XX	Total	XX
<Excess Funds Available>	XXXX	Understatement	XXXX

* Cash on hand represents the coins and currency that a taxpayer has on their person, in a safe deposit box or any other place outside the banking system.
† Cash in banks should be the reconciled balances at the beginning and end of the year; not the balances indicated on the bank statements.
‡ Contributions to retirement plans can be made after year-end and still be deductible. This entry will be adjusted for the cash outlay(s) occurring in the year of examination.
§ The entry for Personal Living Expenses (PLE) on the final Cash-T is the actual expenses determined by the examination process.

¶ 6051 SOURCE AND APPLICATION OF FUNDS METHOD (EXPENDITURE APPROACH)

The *source and application of funds method* (also referred to as the *expenditure method*) was approved for IRS use by the Supreme Court in 1942.[31] This technique is a variation of the net worth method (discussed later in this chapter) that shows increases and decreases in a taxpayer's accounts at the end of the year. Often the IRS agent uses the expenditure approach when a taxpayer is spending income lavishly rather than purchasing assets or investments. The expenditure approach is similar to the cash T, except that the data used are the increases and decreases in the taxpayer's accounts. As with the cash T, if the person's spending exceeds explainable total income, any difference may be unreported income (such as stolen funds or drug money). When dealing with taxpayers, the IRS often uses a cash expenditure approach because taxpayers can understand this approach. In the courtroom the IRS may use a net worth calculation to reconstruct income.[32]

The format of this method is to list the applications of funds first and then subtract the sources (see Figure 6.3). If the taxpayer's known cash sources exceed his or her known cash receipts (including cash on hand at the beginning of the year), any difference is unreported income. However, the IRS has the responsibility to perform reasonable net worth analysis, investigate all reasonable leads, and establish a likely source for the omitted income.

Figure 6.3. Source and Application of Funds Format[33]

Sample of Application of Funds Method Layout

1. Funds Applied:

Increase in cash on hand	$ 4,000
Increase in cash in banks	5,000
Increase in accounts receivable	21,400
Increase in loans receivable	13,000
Increase in inventory	19,000
Increase in stocks and bonds	12,500
Increase in furniture and fixtures	11,100
Increase in real estate	135,000
Increase in personal automobile	24,000
Decrease in accounts payable	11,500
Decrease in mortgage payable	23,000
Personal living expenses	29,700
Federal income tax paid	6,500
Nondeductible personal loss	3,500
Gifts made	10,000
Total Funds Applied	$329,200

2. Sources of Funds:

Decrease in cash on hand	$ 3,100
Decrease in bank balance	2,000
Decrease in securities	13,500
Increase in accounts payable	11,800
Increase in notes payable	22,100
Increase in mortgage payable	121,500
Increase in accumulated depreciation	23,300
Tax exempt interest	1,700
Inheritance	42,000
Total Sources of Funds	$241,000

3. Understatement of Taxable Income:

Total Application of Funds		$329,200
Total Sources of Funds		241,000
Adjusted gross income as corrected:		88,200
Less: Itemized deductions	31,600	
Personal exemptions (2)	5,000	(36,600)
Taxable income as corrected		51,600
Taxable income per return		23,700
Understatement of taxable income		$27,900

When the application of funds is greater than the source, a taxpayer is deemed to have an understatement of income. Both the cash T and the source and application of funds methods are appropriate for taxpayers when a substantial amount of the income is not deposited in bank accounts and the expenditures on the tax return are not proportionate to the income reported.

¶ 6061   NET WORTH METHOD

The net worth method is a common indirect balance sheet approach to estimating income. To use the net worth technique, an IRS agent must calculate the person's net worth (the known assets less known liabilities) at the beginning and ending of a period. The agent adds nondeductible living expenses to the increase in net worth. If there is a difference between the reported income and the increase in net worth during the year, the agent tries to account for the difference as (1) nontaxable income and (2) unidentified differences. Any unidentified difference may be an approximation of the amount of a theft, unreported income, or embezzlement amount (e.g., an inference of unreported income).

The net worth method of estimating income is illustrated in *N.G. Michas*.[34] During 1984, some taxpayers owned several sole-proprietorships, including a liquor store. The IRS determined that the books and records of these sole-proprietorships were inadequate and analyzed the taxpayers' net worth to determine whether all taxable income had been reported. The IRS performed this analysis by determining the cost of the taxpayers' business and personal assets at the beginning and end of 1984. The IRS then reduced these amounts by the taxpayers' liabilities at the beginning and end of the year. Then, the difference was adjusted by adding nondeductible expenditures (for example, living expenses) and by subtracting nontaxable sources of income (for example, gifts and loans).

The Tax Court largely agreed with the IRS, but found that certain adjustments to net worth were not proper. Accordingly, the trial court reduced the amount of unreported income determined by the IRS.

Revealing Unreported Income

This technique may be used when there is a year-to-year increase in net worth and the taxpayer does not have adequate records to determine taxable income or when fraud is strongly suspected. This indirect method was sanctioned by the Supreme Court in 1954 by *M.L. Holland*.[35] The courts have established several safeguards to prevent the misuse of this method. An IRS agent must determine beginning net worth with reasonable accuracy, track down all leads given by the taxpayer to explain the source of the unreported income, and establish a reasonable source for the omitted income. If the person's net worth increase (as adjusted) exceeds the reported taxable income, there may be unreported income (or a previous cash hoard or large gift).

This technique may be appropriate for any taxpayer when two or more years of returns are being audited and the agent determines that there have been substantial changes in assets and liabilities from year to year.

EXAMPLE 6.1 During 2013, John Connors sold his personal car for $2,500. He had purchased the car in 2009 for $6,000. In March 2013, he sold 500 shares of stock for $10,000. He had acquired the stock in December 2008 for $22,000. On January 11, 2013, he gave his nephew a truck that had been used solely in his business. The truck cost $9,000 in 2010. Depreciation totaling $6,500 had been previously deducted on the truck at the time of the gift. John paid the following personal expenses in 2013:

Food	$ 3,000
Real Estate Taxes on Home	2,500
Repairs to Home	300
Utilities	900
Personal Auto Expenses	1,800
Vacations	1,100
Department Store Purchases	1,700
Interest on Home Mortgage	2,000
Charitable Contributions	500
Life Insurance Premiums	1,500
Medical Bills	600
Entertainment	900
Other	300
Total	$17,100

For 2013, John reported adjusted gross income of $19,000. The balances in his bank accounts were $1,500 at the end of 2012 and $18,900 at the end of 2013. Assuming that John correctly reported his income for 2013, the net worth computation would appear as follows:

	12/31/12	12/31/13
Assets		
Cash in Banks	$ 1,500	$18,900
Personal Auto	6,000	-0-
Truck	9,000	-0-
Stock	22,000	-0-
Total Assets	$38,500	$18,900
Liabilities		
Reserve for Depreciation (Truck)	6,500	-0-
Net Worth	$32,000	$18,900
Net Worth 12/31/13		$ 18,900
Net Worth 12/31/12		(32,000)
Net Worth Increase (Decrease)		($13,100)
Plus: Nondeductible Expenses and Losses		
Gift of Truck		2,500
Loss on Sale of Car		3,500
Loss on Stock in Excess of $3,000		9,000
Personal Living Expenses		17,100
Reconstructed Adjusted Gross Income		$19,000
Reported Adjusted Gross Income		$19,000
Understatement of Income		-0-[36]

Determining Living Expenses

The determination of nondeductible living expenses may not be easy. Kalman A. Barson made the following suggestions for determining expenses:

> For that you need to go into the checking and savings accounts of the individuals and, depending on the extent of the accuracy of the records involved, you may have to make certain assumptions. Interview the parties involved

and reconstruct their standard of living, making some educated guesses as to what they spend on such mundane expenses as food, clothing, and various other elements of living that often leave little or no residual financial trail. Be as thorough as possible inasmuch as you are on less stable ground (even though the ultimate result may be a very supportable one) than if you had come up with proof in the form of actual cash deposits that were not reconcilable to reported income.[37]

The net worth analysis may be used when the forensic investigator is searching for hidden income in drug trafficking and insurance fraud situations. A person's lifestyle and spending habits may not match his or her reported income. Alternatively, in a divorce case a spouse may be showing a substantial *decrease* in income.

EYEWITNESS

A defendant argued that an auditor should have followed the "net worth method" applicable in tax prosecutions under *M.L. Holland*.[38] But Holland need not be followed in non-tax cases according to the Eight Circuit. Unlike tax prosecutions, narcotics conspiracy charges do not involve financial gain as a necessary element of offenses, so less stringent standards are permissible.[39]

¶ 6071   BANK DEPOSIT METHOD

Whereas the focus of the net worth method is on the year-end bank balances, as well as other assets and liabilities, the bank deposit method looks at the funds deposited during the year. This method attempts to reconstruct gross taxable receipts rather than adjusted. This bank deposit method was approved by the court almost 70 years ago in *L.M. Gleckman*.[40] An agent does not have to corroborate the unreported income by another method.[41]

The Fifth Circuit provided an excellent description of the bank deposit method in 1978 in the *Boulet* case:[42]

> In this case, the government used the bank deposit and cash expenditure methods. In order to use this method the government must establish a likely source of the income, that the taxpayer made deposits in a bank account and make a distinction between taxable and non-taxable income. The assumption is that the taxpayer's gross income is the total of the deposits minus loan proceeds, transfers and other non-taxable items. Nontaxable items include loans, gifts, transfers between accounts and cash the taxpayer had on hand at the beginning of the year. The doctor received fees in cash, which he gave his wife for groceries. This amount is added to the net bank deposits to arrive at gross receipts. The amount is compared with gross receipts on the tax return. If there is an excess amount, this will be unreported gross receipts.

The bank deposit method is appropriate when most of the income is deposited in banks and most of the expenses are paid by check. This technique may be used to audit income of physicians or dentists who normally receive payments from patients and insurance companies in the form of checks as mentioned in the Supreme Court decision above. A formula for computing gross income taken from the IRM is shown in Figure 6.4,[43] and Figure 6.5 shows business gross receipts.

Figure 6.4. Gross Receipts Formula

The formula for computing gross receipts is:

1.	Total bank deposits	$XXX
Less:		
2.	Nontaxable receipts deposited	(XXXX)
3.	Net deposits resulting from taxable receipts	$XXX
Add:		
4.	Business expenses paid by cash	$XXX
5.	Capital items paid by cash	XXX
6.	Personal expenses paid by cash	XXX
7.	Cash accumulated during the year from receipts	XXX
8.	Sub-Total	$XXX
9.	Less: Nontaxable cash used for (4) through (7)	(XXX)
10.	Gross receipts as corrected	$XXX

The following is a step-by-step explanation of the specific items used in the above computations of gross receipts.

Item 1 — Total bank deposits means total deposits in all of the taxpayer's bank accounts. This amount includes the taxpayer's business and personal accounts, the spouse's accounts, and dependent children's accounts. (Note: This figure could vary if the spouse files a separate return.) The deposits should be reconciled, if possible, so that only the receipts during the current year are included. This is accomplished by totaling deposits as shown on the bank statements, and adding to this amount any current year's receipts, which were deposited in the subsequent year, and deducting any prior year's receipts, which were deposited in the current year.

EXAMPLE:

Deposits during 2012, per bank statements	$150,000
Add: 2012 Receipts deposited in 2013	13,000
Less: 2011 Receipts deposited in 2012	(11,500)
Reconciled Bank Deposits—	$151,500

Item 2 — Nontaxable receipts deposited represent the duplicated and nontaxable items. Duplicated items include checks to cash where the proceeds are redeposited. An example is when the taxpayer writes a check payable to cash and obtains currency and/or coins from the bank in exchange for the check. This currency is then used to cash customers' checks which are deposited into the taxpayer's bank account; in effect, redepositing the funds withdrawn. This deposit must be eliminated in determining deposits from taxable receipts. Transfers between accounts are another example of nontaxable receipts. Transfers can occur between different checking accounts, different savings accounts, and between savings accounts and checking accounts (Note: All such transfers do not represent additional receipts since they are merely a shifting of funds from one account to another). Deposits from transfers must be eliminated in determining deposits from taxable receipts. Other common types of nontaxable receipts that are often deposited and must be eliminated in determining deposits from taxable receipts include loan proceeds, gifts, inheritances, Social Security benefits, nontaxable Veterans Administration benefits, etc.

EXAMPLE:

Reconciled Bank Deposits—2012		$151,000
Less: Nontaxable receipts deposited:		
Loan proceeds	$12,000	
Checks to cash redeposited	3,500	
Transfers between checking accounts	6,000	
Nontaxable Veterans		
Administration pension	<u>14,000</u>	<u>($35,500)</u>
Net deposits from taxable receipts		<u>$116,000</u>

Item 4 — Business expenses paid by cash are computed in a negative manner by determining the business expenses paid by check and subtracting this amount from the total outlays reported on the return. Note: Total outlays on the return include only business expenses which require a cash outlay. Items such as depreciation, depletion and bad debts are not included in total outlays. This step is based on the assumption that outlays as disclosed on the return were actually made and could only have been paid for by either check or cash. The amount of business expenses paid by check can be negatively determined by subtracting the nonbusiness checks from the total checks written. This approach is used because an analysis of nonbusiness checks is necessary since the personal expenses and capital items paid for by check have to be known in order to determine the amounts of these items paid for by cash.

EXAMPLE:

Total outlays per return		
Computation of business checks for year:		
Balance @ 1-1-12	$10,000	
Add: Deposits	<u>150,000</u>	
Subtotal	$160,000	
Less: Balance @ 12-31-12	<u>(8,000)</u>	
Subtotal	$152,000	
Add: Checks written in 2012 but cleared in 2013	<u>3,000</u>	
Subtotal	$155,000	
Less: Checks written in 2011 but cleared in 2012	<u>(6,000)</u>	
Total checks written in 2011	$149,000	
Less: Nonbusiness checks:		
Checks to cash	$3,500	
Check transfers	6,000	
Personal expenses	34,500	
Capital items	<u>15,700</u>	<u>($59,700)</u>
Total business checks		<u>$89,300</u>
Total business expenses paid by cash		<u>$50,700</u>

Generally, the number of nonbusiness checks written is less than the number of business checks. Nonbusiness checks include checks for personal living expenses, capital purchases (personal and business), checks to cash redeposited, check transfers between accounts, and payments on liabilities. Checks for these items would be included even if the taxpayer deducted them on the return. Total checks written can be quickly computed by adding the total deposits to the beginning bank balance and subtracting the ending bank balance from that amount. The resulting figure must then be adjusted for checks written during the year, which have not cleared the bank, and checks written in the prior year, which cleared during the current year. This is merely a reconciliation of the checks which insures that only the current year's checks are taken into account.

NOTE:

The examiner should be satisfied that all checks have been presented. Should the taxpayer remove any portion of the nondeductible checks, the total, as computed, of deductible disbursements would be overstated. The result would invariably be distorted and reflect, although incorrectly, in favor of the taxpayer.

Item 5 — Capital items paid by cash includes cash purchases of capital assets, cash deposited in savings accounts, and cash used to make payments on liabilities.

Item 6 — Personal expenses paid by cash includes living expenses, income taxes, etc.

Item 7 — Cash accumulated is the cash received by the taxpayer during the year which is on hand at the end of the year (it was neither expended nor deposited). It is the difference between the cash on hand at the beginning and end of the year.

Item 8 — Nontaxable cash used for (4) through (7) is nontaxable cash used to pay expenses, purchase capital assets, deposit into savings accounts, make payments on liabilities, and to accumulate. Nontaxable cash includes: loans, withdrawals from savings accounts, gifts, inheritances, collection of loans receivable, nontaxable income, etc., not deposited.

Suppose an investigator is attempting to determine if a service station owner is underreporting his income in a divorce dispute. The ATG for Gas Retailers suggests that a bank deposit analysis may be used for service stations because more people are using debit and credit cards to pay for gasoline and diesel fuel purchases. Since service bay repairs are often paid with checks, it is now easier to use a bank deposit analysis as an indirect method to determine possible hidden income. The key to such a bank deposit technique is to remember to add to bank deposits the amount of credit card sales and cash payouts. The oil company then gives the IRS station owner credit for the daily credit card sales against the fuel purchases.

Figure 6.5. Gross Business Receipts Formula

The formula for computing gross business receipts is:

1.	Total bank deposits		$XXX
2.	Less: Nontaxable and nonbusiness receipts deposited		(XXX)
3.	Net deposits resulting from business receipts		$XXX
	Add:		
4.	Business expenses paid by cash	$XXX	
5.	Capital items paid by cash	XXX	
6.	Personal expenses paid by cash	XXX	
7.	Cash accumulated during the year from receipts	XXX	
8.	Sub-Total		$XXX
9.	Less: Nontaxable and nonbusiness cash used used for (4) through (7)		(XXX)
10.	Gross business receipts as corrected		$ XXX
11.	Adjustments for accrual basis taxpayers		$XXX

The following is a step-by-step explanation of the gross business receipts computation.

Item 1 — Total bank deposits is the same as discussed in the gross receipts formula. See IRM subsection 4.6.3.6.1.

Item 2 — Nontaxable and nonbusiness receipts deposited includes the same items as the gross receipts formula *plus nonbusiness receipts deposited*. In computing gross business receipts it is necessary to eliminate all nonbusiness deposits, whether taxable or not. Nonbusiness deposits include salaries, wages, dividends, rent, etc. In other words, deposits from any source but business receipts are eliminated.

Item 4 — Is identical for both formulas. See IRM subsection 4.6.3.6.1(2)d.

Item 5 — Is identical for both formulas. See IRM subsection 4.6.3.6.1(2)e.

Item 6 — Is identical for both formulas. See IRM subsection 4.6.3.6.1(2)f.

Item 7 — Is identical for both formulas. See IRM subsection 4.6.3.6.1(2)g.

Item 8 — Nontaxable and nonbusiness cash used for (4) through (7) includes the same items as the gross receipts formula (See IRM subsection 4.6.3.6.1(2)h) plus nonbusiness cash used to pay expenses, purchase capital assets, deposit into savings accounts, make payments on liabilities, or accumulate. Nonbusiness cash is received from any source except business receipts.

Item 10 — Is identical for both formulas. See IRM subsection 4.6.3.7 for explanation.

Ratio Analysis

The IRS suggests to agents that operating ratios may be used in examining businesses. For example, large percentage changes or non-standard percentages for an industry can highlight potential fraudulent areas. Statistical and ratio analyses are useful to a forensic accountant in analyzing large and unusual items and in focusing on which items on the financial statements to examine and the scope of that examination. Statistical and ratio analyses are not tests of the reliability of reported income or expenses and cannot be substituted for an income probe audit step. Rather, the use of statistics and ratio analysis may indicate that additional audit steps are warranted. An investigator still needs to perform audit tests to determine if the books and records can be relied upon and must use direct or indirect methods to determine gross income. If necessary, however, ratios can be used to support audit conclusions arrived at using these indirect methods. See ¶4221 for more on ratio analysis.

EYEWITNESS

It works like this: the casino advertises (and reports to the tax authorities) a given return on the slot machines. If that return is even a little lower than the rate reported, the income increases sharply. That is, if you report that your machines will return 95 percent to the players, but you really only return 94 percent, and a million bucks a night goes through the slots, you're skimming $10,000 a night. In a few months, that adds up to real money.

Of course, you have to be careful about state auditors. For a politically well-connected company, in Mississippi, that wasn't a major problem: "Them boys is crookeder than a bucket of cotton-mouths," Bob said.[44]

¶6081 CONTRACT AND PROCUREMENT FRAUD

Indirect methods may be useful for determining contract and procurement frauds. In the case of a contract, there are generally six requirements for a valid contract:

- Offer and acceptance
- Lawful objective
- Capacity of parties to perform
- Something of value exchanged

- Appropriate form (e.g., in writing)
- Entered into freely

A breach of a contract may occur when a party fails to perform or says he or she will not perform. In either situation, the injured party may sue for damages. Damage calculations are covered in Chapters 10 and 12.

The intentional failure to perform a contract does not necessarily result in fraud. The injured party must show that the other party did not intend to perform the contract and deliberately mislead the other party. For both civil and criminal actions, there must be proof that the party knowingly and willfully knew that the contract was false with the intent to deceive or defraud. With such a heavy burden, it may not be worthwhile to try to prove fraud.

Procurement Fraud Techniques Are Numerous

There are numerous ways to commit procurement fraud, and H.R. Davia outlines these major techniques for engaging in a procurement fraud scheme:[45]

1. Bribes and kickbacks
2. Bid rigging
3. Defective pricing
4. Phantom vendors
5. Product substitution
6. Conflict of interests
7. False claims
8. Cost mischarging
9. Contract specification failures
10. Duplicate, false, or inflated invoices
11. Split purchases
12. Unnecessary purchases
13. Defective delivery

Bribes are universal and are the most damaging of these corrupting schemes. Often bribes and kickbacks are entwined with one or more of the other schemes. Whether called a grease payment, expediting fee, a tip, or envelope, they are often disguised as some type of exchange. Nigerian police personnel may ask for a "little something for the weekend," or a bribe to a border guard may be placed inside the passport. Since proving intent to exchange one favor for another is necessary to convict, a universal rule is to never hand over the cash or check at the same moment of the lobbying attempt. Wait until later.[46]

According to *The Economist*, by giving people power and discretion, whether border guard or grand viziers, some will use their position to enrich themselves. They cite a study that shows that bribes account for eight percent of the total costs of operating a business in Uganda, and corruption boosts the price of hospital supplies in Buenos Aires by 15 percent.[47]

Ernst & Young's 12th Global Fraud Survey entitles "Growing Beyond: A Place for Integrity" found that bribery and corruption is pervasive. For example, in Brazil, 84 percent responded that corruption was widespread. Overall, 39 percent of the respondents said that bribery and corruption practices occur frequently in their countries.

Since CFOs have a significant impact on the payment of bribes, E&Y provided the responses of nearly 400 CFOs to these actions to help their business survive.

- Entertainment to win/retain business   34%
- Cash payments to win/retain business   15%
- Personal gift to win/retain business   20%
- Misstating company's financial performance   4%

As examples, in Indonesia 60 percent of respondents considered making cash payments to win new business acceptable. In Vietnam, 36 percent of the respondents considered it acceptable to misstate their company's financial performance.

EYEWITNESS

In Germany, a sales director once bragged at an office party about how he had bribed several large retail customers. Some only responded to large gifts, he said, recalling one situation when he discreetly pushed a car key to the other side of the negotiating table. The trick was to find out what they liked.[48]

One of his employees commented that what was disturbing about his remarks was the way he bragged about it. In that company, as in countless others, bribery was not only tolerated, it was cool. If a person wanted to become a successful marketing executive, this behavior was what was expected.[49]

What follows is a potpourri of bribe schemes around the world, even at the highest levels of government:

- City Council member Monica Conyers, wife of Michigan congressman John Conyers, plead guilty of accepting cash bribes in exchange for supporting a sludge contract with a Houston company. She received cash envelopes in parking lots of a Detroit community center and a McDonalds.
- In March 2007, a Brazilian federal congressman and former governor of Sao Paulo was charged in New York for stealing more than $11.5 million from a Brazilian public works project in a construction kickback scheme. He allegedly transferred the money to a New York bank and then to an offshore account. The scheme involved inflated and false invoices to contractors involved in the building of a giant highway.
- Two prominent Baton Rouge restaurateurs and four other businessmen were accused of bribing a parish tax auditor and an undercover FBI agent with cash, diamonds, trips, whiskey, and women to avoid paying taxes on $10 million. An indictment alleges Laymon offered an undercover FBI agent posing as an East Baton Rouge Parish auditor $800, a weekend trip to Costa Rica, and two prostitutes a day if he concluded that Arzi's didn't owe any sales tax.
- A Greek prosecutor is investigating claims that Siemens Greece paid up to $550 million in bribes to officials at the defense and interior ministries in order to win a security contract for the 2004 Olympic games in Athens. A senior Siemens accountant said bribery was a common practice at Siemens.
- A Paris judge launched an investigation into allegations that Total, a French oil and gas group, paid bribes to win a $2 billion gas contract in Iran. The investigation stems from the discovery of $82 million in two Swiss bank accounts, allegedly by Total to an Iranian intermediary to help the French company consortium to win an Iranian contract.
- A report claims that AWB, the company responsible for selling Australia wheat, paid over $221 million to Alia, a Jordanian hauling company, ostensibly to distribute its wheat in Iraq. In fact, the money was going to the Iraq government.
- Armstrong Williams, an American columnist and television host, was paid $240,000 by the Department of Education to comment regularly on "No Child Left Behind," an education-reform bill.
- Nineteen individuals were indicted for receiving bribes and rigging bids for school window washing contracts in New York State.
- Congressman Randy Cunningham, R-Calif., resigned from Congress in 2005, hours after pleading guilty to taking at least $2.4 million in bribes to help friends and campaign contributors win defense contracts. Prosecutors said he received cash, cars, rugs, antiques, furniture, yacht club dues, moving expenses, and vacations from four co-conspirators in exchange for aid in winning defense contracts.
- In January 2007, Peter Hartz, former Volkswagen executive, was given a two-year suspended prison sentence and fines for bribing the head of the labor union ($3.25 million) for secret bonuses and fake consultancy fees. The bribe involved sex holidays and paying for prostitutes for German labor officials.

- In the 1950s in the United States, record companies would pay money for the broadcast of records on radio, called payola. This practice is now outlawed.
- In England, police interviewed Prime Minister Tony Blair in February 2007 about allegations that honors, including seats in the House of Lords and Knighthoods, were given to individuals who loaned money to the Labour party ($9.8 million).
- Under President Bill Clinton, Democratic National Committee donors were allowed to spend the night in the Lincoln bedroom for a contribution of $150,000 (e.g., Chairman of Occidental Petroleum). Then in 1997, Clinton made an exception so that Occidental Petroleum could pursue a venture in Sudan.
- A lawsuit in February 2007 alleged that Intel provided secret kickbacks to Dell in order to ensure it remained the computer maker's sole microprocessor supplier.
- Former Bank of America executive Luca Sala told investigators that over seven years he took $27 million in a kickback scheme involving Parmalat. He obtained the monies by a kickback arrangement with an outside broker who helped organize bond issues from Parmalat.
- Former New Orleans Mayer Ray Nagin was charged in February 2013 by a federal grand jury for taking cash bribes and gifts from three city contractors involving a granite installation contract with Home Depot.

The normal bribe/kickback scheme generally involves something being transferred to someone (e.g., cash, vacation, etc.) and a later influence of a business or official action. See Figure 6.6. Transferring cash is not the best approach since cash is easier to detect and harder to deduct. The more sophisticated scheme is to give noncash favors to an entity set up for such purposes, possibly owned by a relative.

Figure 6.6. Bribe/Kickback Scenario

Something Transferred	Later Influence on a Decision
Cash	Awarding contract
Gifts	Later higher prices
Trips/Vacations	Excessive quantity purchases
Entertainment	Accepting lower quality
Drugs/Gambling	Delayed or short delivery
Sexual favors	
Favored loans	
Debit/Credit cards	
Fees/Commissions	
Spouse's salary	
Discounts (e.g., house)	
Sporting events	

For example, Vernon Jackson admitted to bribery of Rep. William Jefferson, D-LA. More than $400,000 to $1 million was paid to a company controlled by the congressman's wife in exchange for promoting iGate. Jackson gave 24 percent stake in iGate and paid $80,000 of traveling expenses to Africa. The FBI found cold cash of $90,000 in Jefferson's freezer, but he was subsequently reelected (57 percent–43 percent) to the U.S. Congress. In June 2006, the House did remove him from the powerful House Ways and Means Committee. In 2008, he was defeated.

One of the world's largest property investors, Brookfield Asset Management, had bribery civil charges filed against them in Sao Paulo, Brazil. The prosecutor said a high system of bribery was used to gain project approvals by the Toronto firm.

By collecting copies of invoices the prosecutor was able to link permit-issuance with payments allegedly made to public officials. The defendants include both a former and current public officials and a vendor. The vendor allegedly overstated invoices at Brookfield's request and gave the extra money to the public officials. The scheme was reported by a fired CFO who refused to participate in the bribery scheme. [50]

Wolfgang Schaupensteiner has a downtown Frankfurt office with his walls decorated with cartoons about corruption. As head of the financial crime unit in Frankfurt, he has a backlog of bribery, fraud, and white-collar crime cases running into the hundreds. He says corporate profits have surged across many businesses, and German executives have used illicit dealings to fuel their success. Many executives believe that crime does pay.

"Globalization has become a motor for corruption in Germany," Mr. Schaupensteiner says. Siemens, BMW, Volkswagen, and DaimlerChrysler have been raided and put under investigation, or some employees have been taken into custody. An employee of BMW was jailed for accepting bribes from an auto parts supplier.[51]

Two authors provide these red flags of possible bribery and kickbacks:[52]
- Lack of standard invoices.
- Requests for funds to be routed to a foreign bank.
- Requests for checks made payable to "cash" or to "the bearer."
- Commission substantially higher than going rate.
- Requests for a large line of credit from a customer.
- Insistence by a government official that a certain third-party agent or supplier be used.
- Lack of staff or facilities to actually perform the service.
- Request by a local agent for a rate increase in the middle of negotiations.
- Suggest need to utilize more than one local agent.

Joe Wells provides these red flags of phantom vendors that might be established to facilitate a bribery scheme:[53]
- Invoices for unspecified consulting or other poorly defined services.
- Unfamiliar vendors.
- Vendors that have only a post-office-box address.
- Vendors with company names consisting only of initials. Many such companies are legitimate, but crooks commonly use initials when naming companies.
- Rapidly increasing purchases from one vendor.
- Vendor billings more than once a month.
- Vendor addresses that match employee addresses.
- Large billings broken into multiple smaller invoices, each of which is for an amount that will not attract attention.

Certain steps are important to help prevent procurement fraud through phantom vendors:[54]
- There should be an approved vendor list, and all new vendors should be evaluated for legitimacy. Are they listed in the phone book, and do they have an Internet site?
- There should be separate job responsibilities, so that the purchasing agent cannot approve the vendors.

- There should be an anonymous hotline for whistleblowers.
- Be careful of cliques inside and outside the business.
- Get insurance protection.
- Do the parking lot test. Does the purchasing agent drive an expensive car? Own an expensive home?

Finding, proving, and prosecuting procurement fraud is not easy. A forensic accountant may try to prove the corrupting influence circumstantially through the five factors on the right side of Figure 6.6 (e.g., higher prices). Or evidence can be gathered to show that the outsider received more business as the insider received more and more bribes. If the forensic accountant can obtain the appropriate personal records about the insider through subpoena power, indirect methods may be used to determine the amount of bribes the insider is receiving. An alternative is to try to turn the outsider to testify against the insider.

Two important concepts are important in fighting procurement fraud: duty to cooperate and audit rights. In the United States an employee has the duty to cooperate. So it is important to interview the inside target before firing him. Even if you cannot prove the fraud, at least the company can fire the insider if he refuses to cooperate.

Many contracts have an audit right clause, such as "the contractor must participate promptly and cooperatively in any audit conducted by [the company] or its nominee." Thus, through the audit a forensic accountant may be able to prove some of the influences on the right side of Figure 6.6, or evidence may be found pointing to the bribes given to the insider.

KICKBACK SCHEME. Former Bank of America executive Luca Sala told investigators that over seven years he took $27 million in a kickback scheme involving Parmalat. He obtained the monies by a kickback arrangement with an outside broker who helped organize bond issues from Parmalat. Mr. Sala (corporate finance head) helped organize several bond placements for Parmalat for which the bank regularly received fees.[55]

A Virginia businessman paid a $47,000 penalty for rigging bids during North Carolina's foreclosure auctions. Bruce McBarnette and his company Summit Connection would enter into agreements with other bidders to stop bidding on certain properties in exchange for payments from the other bidders. The auctions took place in Durham and Mecklenberg counties in North Carolina. McBurnette said he did not know the activity was illegal because he had seen the practice before.[56]

¶6086   PIERCING THE CORPORATE VEIL

Normally the corporate entity provides shareholders the protection of limited liability. However, with a single corporation, parent-subsidiary situations, or in brother-sister situations attempts can be made to pierce the corporate veil to get to the shareholders around this corporate protection (or even to the board of directors).

Also known as alter ego or single enterprise theory, forensic accountants may be called upon on either side of a legal dispute to treat the rights or duties of a corporate entity as the rights or liabilities of its shareholders. Plaintiffs often try to pierce, lift, or collapse the corporate veil and make the shareholders responsible for wrongful acts. Or the technique can be used to make shareholders liable for debts where the business is unable to pay its creditors. If the court pierces the corporate veil, then creditors can have a claim on the shareholders' assets to satisfy any company debt.

Courts may consider a number of issues before piercing the corporate veil, such as:[57]
- Corporate debt was intentionally incurred when the company was insolvent.
- Annual board of directors meetings were not held.
- Corporate formalities were not fulfilled.
- Corporate records were not timely maintained and updated.
- Shareholders used corporate funds for personal reasons.
- There was a general commingling of corporate activity and/or funds with those of the person(s) who control the company.
- There was a failure to maintain separate identity. The company had little or no other business and was only a façade for activities of the dominant shareholder who was in fact, the corporate "alter ego."
- Pattern of consistent non-payment of dividends.
- Undercapitalization because shareholders removed unreasonable amounts of funds from the company's account.

There are five steps to help avoid the lifting of the corporate veil:[58]
1. Undertaking necessary formalities such as creating and regularly updating bylaws, issuing shares to shareholders, holding annual meetings with the board of directors, and paying necessary filing fees and corporate taxes.
2. Documenting major business actions and decisions (such as contracts).
3. Do not comingle business and personal assets by keeping separate checking accounts and using business credit cards only for business expenses.
4. Ensure adequate business capitalization for smooth operations of the business.
5. Make corporate status known by creating business cards, creating invoices in the company's name, and signing contracts in the company's name.

There are many ways that a forensic accountant can help an attorney defend or develop a piercing conflict:[59]
- Determining whether assets are commingled requires an inspection of accounting and other business records that memorialize the transactions in question.
- Common business practices and shared services between related companies might (or might not) be undue domination by a parent or controlling shareholder. Accountants experienced with larger enterprises can provide insights as to whether the practices used are common, appropriate, and benefit the potentially-dominated corporation.
- Adequacy of capital is a judgmental determination that necessarily considers the risks of the business, and how these business activities were financed. In making these judgments a forensic accountant must consider the business model of the company being studied, and make comparisons to what other well-managed enterprises are doing.
- The existence of common vendors, employees, and processes can be determined through an inspection of the accounting records of the parents, subsidiary, and other related firms.
- Transactions between related parties may be appropriate (or not), depending upon the price and terms used for the transactions. This issue can be determined by an appraisal of the fair market value of exchange.
- Whether the potentially-dominated corporation is too dependent on its shareholders, or vice versa, can be determined by analyzing the operations of each. These transactions and operations are recorded in business records which an accountant will be able to understand and interpret.
- Are the shareholder's personal transactions being paid by the potentially-dominated corporation? Sometimes this payment is readily apparent, but any payment also might require an inspection of the underlying business records.
- The nature and timing of shareholder withdrawals and/or loans must be determined. Creditors appropriately want to know where the money went and when. Forensic accountants can make this determination through an inspection of the accounting records, checks, and deposits of the sending and receiving entities.

- For all of the above inquires the accounting records may be incomplete or not trustworthy. A forensic accountant can assess the completeness and accuracy of the records obtained in discovery.

¶ 6091   CONCLUSION

Tax compliance and fraud are growing problems for the IRS and the accounting profession. Unfortunately, not all taxpayers disclose all sources of income and are in full compliance with the tax laws, so there is a huge underground economy. Some people believe the Beatles' song, "Taxman," by George Harrison: "If you drive a truck, I'll tax the street; if you try to fix it, I'll tax your seat. If you get a cold, I'll tax the heat; if you take a walk, I'll tax your feet." But the possibility of being audited by the IRS has dropped as low as 1 in 100.

Over the years, through tax laws and court cases the IRS has been provided with many tools to help foster tax compliance. The tax laws have been somewhat effective for individuals who are not self-employed. For example, the present tax laws require employers to report to the IRS the amount of wages paid to employees. However, for self-employed individuals there are fewer methods of using a third party to determine taxable income. Therefore, in order to determine unreported income for a self-employed taxpayer, the IRS is allowed to use indirect methods. These methods are both time consuming and costly to the IRS (or to us as taxpayers) and place an undue burden on taxpayers who do comply with the tax laws.

Although Code Sec. 7602 limits the use of indirect methods, the Code does not prohibit or preclude its use. Until better methods of determining unreported income are provided, the IRS will probably continue to use the methods discussed in this chapter and sanctioned by tax law. The lack of better or less costly methods of determining taxable income for persons who are self-employed provides motivation for future research in this area. Likewise, forensic accountants may use these methods under appropriate circumstances. The lifestyles of taxpayers and employees may give clues to the possibility of unreported income or fraud.

ENDNOTES

[1] Charles Grassley Press Release, "IRS Pursuit of Credit Card Records," March 25, 2002.

[2] IRS Digital Daily, "Criminal Investigation (CI) Special Agents are a Part of a "Bigger" Law Enforcement Team," http://www.irs.gov/irs/article/0,,id=107041,00.html.

[3] Statement of IRS Assistant Commissioner for Criminal Investigation Donald K. Vogel Before the House Subcommittee on Treasury, Postal Service and General Government, March 12, 1996.

[4] Thomas A. Buckhoff, "Forensic Accountants: Fraud Busters," NEW ACCOUNTANT, High School ed. (2002), pp. 9–10.

[5] There is a wide range of estimates on the tax gap found in tax literature. This gap is no doubt a difficult number to estimate. The $345 billion figure comes from IR-2006-028, Feb. 14, 2006.

[6] For a detailed discussion of IRS practices, see Robert E. Meldman and Richard J. Sideman, FEDERAL TAXATION: PRACTICE AND PROCEDURE, 6th ed. (Chicago: CCH INCORPORATED, 2001).

[7] IRM 4.10.4.5.2. "IRS Audit Technique Guide: Bars and Restaurants: Market Segment Specialization Program," April 9, 2003, Training 3149-118 (Rev 11-2002).

[8] Charles Price and Leonard Weld, "Income Reconstruction," THE CPA JOURNAL (August 1998).

[9] TC Memo. 1999-68, 77 TCM 1495, Dec. 53,276(M).

[10] Ibid.

[11] Code Sec. 446(b).

[12] See IRM 4.10.4.

[13] G.J. Bologna and R.J. Lindquist, FRAUD AUDITING AND FORENSIC ACCOUNTING, 2d ed. (New York: John Wiley, 1995), pp. 36–37.

[14] N. Brennan and J. Hennessy, FORENSIC ACCOUNTING, (Dublin: Round Hall Sweet & Maxwell, 2002), pp. 122-123.

[15] Terry Carter, "Accounting Gumshoes," ABA JOURNAL (September 1997), p. 36.

[16] Sandi Smith, "Meet the Forensic Accountant: Sherlock Holmes of the Information Age," INTUITADVISOR (2002), www.intuitadvirsor.com.

[17] "An Assessment of the Aldrich H. Ames Espionage Case," Senate Select Committee on Intelligence (November 1, 1994), Parts I and II.

[18] R.K. Elliot and J.J. Willingham, MANAGEMENT FRAUD: DETECTION AND DETERRENCE (New York: Petrocell; Books, 1980).

19 H.R. Davia, Fraud 101 (New York: John Wiley & Sons, 2000), pp. 42-45.

20 Chief Counsel Advice 200101030 (October 25, 2000), Financial Status Audits.

21 Sonya Stinson, "Accountants Put Skills to Work to Help Nab Criminals," City Business (January 2001), p. 2.

22 "Steal a Million, Pay a Pittance," Earth Island Journal 13 (1) (Winter 1997–1998).

23 IRM 4.10.4.6.2.

24 E.D. Fenton, Jr., "Audit Technique Guides from the IRS: Useful Tools for Industry Specific Investigations," J. of Forensic Accounting 5 (2004), p. 38.

25 Ibid.

26 IRM 4.10.4.5.2. "IRS Audit Technique Guide: Bars and Restaurants: Market Segment Specialization Program," April 9, 2003, Training 3149-118 (Rev 11-2002).

27 IRM 4.10.4.3.3.1.

28 IRM 4.10.4.6.8.3.

29 C. Baughman, "Prosecution Concludes Case in Edwards Trial," The Advocate Online (April 4, 2000).

30 IRM 4.10.4.5.3.7.

31 W.R. Johnson, SCt, 43-1 USTC ¶9470, 319 US 503, 63 SCt 1233.

32 R.E. Meldman and R.J. Sideman, Federal Taxation: Practice and Procedure, 6th ed. (Chicago: CCH Incorporated, 2001), p. 764.

33 IRM 4.10.4.6.4.7.

34 TC Memo. 1992-161, 63 TCM 2452, Dec. 48,084(M).

35 M.L. Holland, SCt, 54-2 USTC ¶9714, 348 US 121, 75 SCt 127. See also C.T. Conaway, CA-5, 94-1 USTC ¶50,009, 11 F3d 40.

36 Robert E. Meldman and Richard J. Sideman, Federal Taxation: Practice and Procedure, 6th ed. (Chicago: CCH INCORPORATED, 2001), p. 781.

37 K.A. Barson, Investigative Accounting (New York: Van Nostrand Reinhold Company, 1986), p. 98.

38 M.L. Holland, SCt, 54-2 USTC ¶9714, 348 US 121, 75 SCt 127.

39 P.J. Cuervo, CA-8, 354 F3d 969 (2004), cert. denied, 543 US 865, 125 SCt 199 (2004).

40 CA-8, 35-2 USTC ¶9645, 80 F2d 394, cert. denied, 297 US 709, 56 SCt 501.

41 N. Stein, CA-7, 71-1 USTC ¶9209, 437 F2d 775, cert. denied, 403 US 905, 91 SCt 2205.

42 R.M. Boulet, CA-5, 78-2 USTC ¶9628, 577 F2d 1165, 1167, cert. denied, 439 US 1114, 99 SCt 1017.

43 IRM 4.10.4.6.3.6 (5-14-1999).

44 John Sandford, The Hanged Man's Song, (Berkley: 2003), pp. 14-15.

45 H.R. Davia et. al, Accountant's Guide to Fraud Detection and Control (John Wiley, 2000), p. 62.

46 "How to Grease a Palm," The Economist (December 23, 2006), p. 115.

47 Ibid.

48 Wolfgang Munchau, "A Dangerous Precedent for Corporate Corruption," Financial Times (December 28, 2006), p. 15.

49 Ibid.

50 Craig Karmin and Paulo Trevisani, "Brookfield Faces Bribery Charges in Brazil," The Wall Street Journal, February 6, 2013, p. C6.

51 Carter Dougherty, "Germany Battling Rising Tide of Corporate Corruption," New York Times (February 15, 2007), http://www.nytimes.com/2007/02/15/business/worldbusiness/15scandal.html.

52 M.T. Biegelman and J.T. Bartow, Executive Roadmap to Fraud Prevention and Internal Controls (John Wiley, 2006), pp. 325-326.

53 J.T. Wells, "Billing Schemes Part I: Shell Companies That Don't Deliver," Journal of Accountancy (July 2002).

54 "Six Steps to Prevent Procurement Fraud," Baseline (June 6, 2006), http://www.baselinemag.com/article2/0,1540,1972097,00.asp.

55 A. Galloni and C. Mollenkamp, "Ex-Parmalat Banker Admits Stealing $27 Million," Wall Street Journal (February 27, 2004), p. A-3.

56 Raleigh (AP), "Va Businessman Pays Fine for Bid-rigging in N.C.," Independent Tribune (December 28, 2010), p. A-6.

57 http://www.flangasmcmillan.com/blog/BOSVIEW/PIERCING-THE-CORPORATE-VEIL/

58 http://www.bizfilings.com/learn/avoid-piercing-corporate-veil.aspx

59 http://www.fulcrum.com/Corporate_Veil.htm

EXERCISES

1. What is the difference between direct and indirect methods of income verification?
2. Under what circumstances may an IRS agent use indirect methods?
3. Which of the following is not a major indirect method?
   a. Net worth
   b. Cash T
   c. Balance sheet evaluation
   d. Source and application of funds
4. What are some lifestyle changes that may indicate fraud and unreported income?
5. Describe the cash T method.
6. What is a cash hoard?
7. What is the theory behind the cash T?
8. Describe the source and application of funds method. When is this technique appropriate to use?
9. Describe the net worth method.

10. Suppose under the net worth method a person's net worth increase (as adjusted) exceeds the reported income. What may be inferred?

11. What statement is false with respect to the net worth method?
    a. The focus of the net worth method is on the year-end bank balances as well as other assets and liabilities.
    b. The bank deposit technique looks at the funds deposited during the year.
    c. The net worth analysis may be used when searching for hidden income in drug trafficking and insurance fraud situations.
    d. The bank deposit method has not been approved by the U.S. Supreme Court.
    e. None of the above.

12. What is the focus of the bank deposit method? When is this technique appropriate?

13. Given the following facts about Sammie Bright, calculate his preliminary understatement using the cash T method.

Schedule C expenses	$102,000
Personal living expenses	59,000
Schedule C receipts	112,000

14. In question 13, do you have enough information to determine that Sammie has understated income? If not, what else is needed?

15. When a taxpayer is being questioned by an IRS agent, is it advantageous when asked to estimate living expenses to estimate on the high side or low side when exact figures are unavailable? Why?

16. If any IRS auditor is assigned a tax return for audit that has a Schedule C for a tavern, where could the agent locate information to provide assistance in the audit?

17. Search for discussions of Leona Helmsley on the Internet. Describe her tax problems. What is her famous comment about taxes?

18. Look on the Internet for some professional sports players who have failed to report some of their income from the sale of memorabilia (e.g., Pete Rose). How were these failures discovered?

19. Find websites that list estimates of total unreported taxable income in the United States as well as other countries. In which countries is the problem most severe?

20. Check the IRS website to view Audit Technique Guides. Report on one of the professions.

21. How did an accountant figure in bringing Al Capone to justice? In what other ways may forensic accountants fight organized crime?

22. How are minimum income probes used by forensic accountants?

23. What are economic reality audits? Can forensic accountants investigate the lifestyles of fraudsters?

24. What indirect methods of reconstructing income are especially helpful when the disclosed income level of a divorcing spouse is suspected of being artificially low?

25. Compare the lifestyle of CIA mole Aldrich H. Ames and FBI mole Robert Hanssen (Chapter 5). Compare with Al Capone (Chapter 1) also.

26. You are investigating possible hidden income in a divorce dispute involving an automobile repair shop with five bays. There are five mechanics, charging approximately $60 per hour for 7 hours per day. Assume 315 days worked with each person's wage of $30 per hour for 8 hours. Compute gross profit per year. If the owner reports $42,500 of gross income, what is your opinion?

27. Go to the IRS's ATG for Gas Retailers and determine some initial interview questions to help a forensic accountant to accurately estimate the income from a service station.

28. Go to the IRS's ATG and obtain the definitions of these terms:
    • Assemblage [Construction industry]
    • Flooring Statement [Auto dealership]
    • Full IRS restaurant [Bars and restaurants]
    • The "Z" key [Bars and restaurants]

29. Go to the IRS's Bars and Restaurants ATG and review the 101 ways to steal from a restaurant. The IRS advises agents to focus on what three items? What is a point-of-sales system?

30. Using the ATG "Bars and Restaurants" guide, develop a checklist of items to observe while doing a walkthrough of a restaurant.

31. You are reviewing the books and records of a local restaurant trying to determine the reliability of the reported income. What are some appropriate audit procedures using the books and records? Suppose you find some red flags; what are some other income probes?

32. Locate *Big H. Ng*, 73 TCM 2900, Dec. 52,067(M), TC Memo. 1997-248. What indirect method was used here by the IRS? Summarize the decision.

33. You determine the following information about a local bar:

Cost per liquor quart	$4.48
Quart has 32 ounces	
1-1/4 ounces per drink	
Sales tax per bottle	$1.97
Total purchase of quarts	$5,000

Determine the pouring cost percent. Determine gross receipts and gross profit. What are other variables to consider?

34. Locate *M. Cebollero*, 60 TCM 1379, Dec. 47,018(M), TC Memo. 1990-618, aff'd CA-4, 92-2 USTC ¶50,327, 967 F2d 986. What indirect method was used here by the IRS? Summarize the decision.

35. Locate *A.J. McQuatters*, 32 TCM 1122, Dec. 32,197(M), TC Memo. 1973-240. What is the McQuatters formula?

36. While investigating a gas retailer, you compute the following ratios:

COGS	83.7%
Gross profit	16.3%
All other expenses	3.4%
Profit before taxes	0.61%

What are some tentative conclusions? You may wish to refer to the IRS's ATG on Gas Retailers.

37. While investigating a gas retailer, you notice some invoices for naphtha and alcohol. What should you do?

38. Using Internet resources, develop the revenue flow (walkthrough) for the slot operations of a casino.

39. Explain proactive auditing. Compare with reactive auditing. Give specific techniques.

40. You prepare a Cash T of an automobile dealer, as follows:

CASH IN		CASH OUT	
Gross receipt	$ 5,000,000	Cost of Goods Sold	$ 4,900,000
		Sch. C Expenses	$ 95,000
		Sch. C Depr	$ 10,000
		Meals	$ 1,250
		Bureau of Labor Statistics data	$ 40,000
Cash In	$ 5,000,000	Cash Out	$ 5,026,250

Do you have any thoughts and what questions would you ask?

41. You prepare a comparative analysis of an automobile dealership. What questions should you ask?

	2011	2012	2013
Gross Receipt	$3,000,000	$4,000,000	$5,000,000
Cost of Sales	$2,800,000	$3,850,000	$4,900,000
Expenses	$180,000	$140,000	$95,000
Gross Profit	$20,000	$10,000	$5,000
Gross Profit %	0.67%	0.25%	0.10%

42. All income statement accounts are run through the balance sheet, but not all balance sheet accounts are run through the income statement. Analyze this statement. Give an example of a balance sheet account not affecting the income statement.

43. Refer to the IRS's ATG "Auto Dealership," and answer these questions.
    a. What is the difference between LIFO and non-LIFO inventory values called? What does it represent?
    b. What is a simple way to obtain a "ball park" estimate of a company's LIFO reserve?
    c. What is a car dealer's average holdback on new cars?

44. While investigating an auto dealership you calculate the following [refer to the IRS's ATG on Auto Dealerships]:

From "window sticker":

MSRP	$10,000
Destination Charges	400
MSRP Retail Total	$10,400

From Dealer Invoice:

Vehicle Factory Wholesale Price	$9,000	
Destination Charges	400	
Advertising Association	100	1% of MSRP
Holdback	300	3% of MSRP
Total Invoice Price	$9,800	
Holdback: coded amount is	(300)	3% of MSRP
Inventory Cost to the Dealer	$9,500	

a. What entry should the dealer make initially and when the holdback is received?
b. Should the dealer include the holdback in inventory? Why?

45. Refer to the IRS's ATG on Auto Dealership.
Suppose a dealer sells a car to a customer for the following:

Sales Price	
(including Sales Tax and license fees)	$10,000
Less: Down payment	1,000
Balance to be Financed	$9,000
Finance Charge @ 10%	900
Face amount of Installment Note	$9,900

The dealer sells the note to a finance company who agrees to pay the dealer a 20 percent commission on the finance charge, or $180.
   a. What is the correct entry to make?
   b. Referring to *J.R. Hansen*, SCt, 59-2 USTC ¶9533, 360 US 446, 79 SCt 1270, when is the amount held back taxable to the dealership?

46. What are some ways that a forensic accountant gathers evidence?

47. What are the requirements for a valid contract?

48. Why is it difficult to prove procurement fraud?

49. List some procurement fraud schemes. Which scheme is more common?

50. Describe the normal bribe/kickback scheme. What would be a sophisticated procurement fraud scheme? Why is cash a poor "something of value?"

51. What was the purpose for the passage of the Foreign Corrupt Practices Act of 1977?

52. According to Wolfgang Schaupensteiner, what has been the motor for corruption in Germany?

53. List some red flags of bribery and kickbacks.

54. List some red flags of phantom vendors.

55. What are some ideas to help prevent procurement fraud through phantom vendors?

56. How can a forensic accountant find and prove procurement fraud?

57. What is meant by:
   a. Duty to cooperate
   b. Audit rights

58. Which would be the best source for a forensic accountant to gather information and learn about a new industry?
   a. RIA Federal Tax Articles
   b. Audit Technique Guidelines
   c. Daubert Tracker
   d. CCH Citator
   e. Shepardizing

59. Which would *not* be a procurement fraud scheme?
   a. Bid rigging
   b. Phantom vendors
   c. Cost mischarging
   d. Bill-and-hold
   e. Split purchases

60. What famous U.S. Congressman resigned from Congress in 2005 after pleading guilty to taking $2.4 million in bribes?
   a. Armstrong Williams
   b. William Jefferson
   c. Vernon Jackson
   d. Peter Hartz
   e. Randy Cunningham

61. What would probably not be helpful in trying to find and prosecute someone for accepting bribes and kickbacks?
   a. Audit right clause
   b. Chain-of-custody
   c. Duty to cooperate
   d. Foreign Corrupt Practices Act
   e. Trying to turn someone

62. It is the usual accountant's story…a friend of yours (John Dough) has purchased a small business and knows that you are proficient at analyzing financial information. He has asked you to help him with his financial analysis. He informs you of the following background information:

After 20 years of service at his prior job, John was burned out and considering a change. While Christmas shopping, he was talking with a retail owner at a local mall and was informed that most retail stores mark up their prices 200%. John decided to quit his job and purchase and operate a retail toys and hobby shop. So after finding the right opportunity, in January of year 1, he purchased a small store and inventory of toys / games for $300,000. He financed the purchase through the local bank, which loaned him 80% of the money at 7% for 10 years and required John to personally finance the other 20%. Since he is the owner of a small business, he has been operating it as a sole proprietor and not issued any stock. He is not paid a salary, but draws money out as needed. He has a full-time bookkeeper who handles all his books and accounting functions. There are two full-time sales clerks that work in the store and stock inventory in storage or on the shelves as it is delivered. All three of these employees have worked for him since he opened his business. John started each of them out at about $25,000 per year and has given each of them raises every year (approximately 3% per year). Additionally, if the company has a good year (net income), he rewards the employees by paying each of them a bonus of 3% of the net income amount. The bonuses are paid in the following year (February).

For years 1 and 2, he had some external accountants prepare a compilation report. For years 3, 4 and 5 he had a different set of external accountants prepare the compilation reports. The compilation reports state that the books are kept on an accrual basis of accounting according to GAAP and that Property & Equipment is capitalized at cost and depreciated using the straight-line method over the useful life of the property (Equipment 3 years, Furniture 5 years and Buildings 15 years).

Required: Analyze the information provided from the accountants and advise John on his business and which accounts, if any, that you would like more detailed information (investigate), what type of information you would like and why you want it. Be prepared to explain why you are requesting each piece of information for the specific time period (year) you are requesting it. Keep in mind that unnecessary additional accounts analyzed is a waste of your resources (time), but you should utilize your professional skills to analyze and advise John on his business. You should use all the financial analysis tools available to you (vertical, horizontal and ratio analysis, as well as calculations and estimations). One suggestion is to analyze related accounts when performing your analysis. For example, analyze the balance sheet account and the related income statement account together (accounts receivable and bad debts expense). Use the spreadsheet provided, place the number 1 in the specific accounts and years that you would investigate and want more information for on the worksheet titled "Answers". All the accounts have been pre-filled with the number 0 to represent the account is OK until you change it (if needed – it is a waste of resources (time) to investigate an account that is OK). When finished, save the file to turn in, print out the "Answers" worksheet, and provide explanations as to why you would investigate each item.

Source: Adapted from teaching materials developed by David Hayes, while at Louisiana State University.

		Year ended 12/31				
		1	2	3	4	5
Current Assets:						
	Cash	$12,351	$19,553	$42,862	$31,055	$21,908
	A/R	$17,459	$22,725	$46,826	$57,357	$68,606
	Investments - CD	$-	$20,000	$40,000	$20,000	$5,000
	Inventory	$83,457	$78,958	$107,763	$67,915	$88,749
	Prepaid Insurance	$5,922	$6,355	$6,988	$7,419	$7,988
	Total current Assets	$119,189	$147,591	$244,439	$183,746	$192,251
Property:						
	Equipment	$36,599	$37,596	$37,596	$39,458	$44,187
	Furniture & Fixtures	$27,495	$27,495	$30,509	$30,509	$30,509
	Buildings	$157,976	$157,976	$157,976	$157,976	$157,976
	Total Property, Plant & Equipment	$222,070	$223,067	$226,081	$227,943	$232,672
	Less Accumulated Depreciation	$(18,580)	$(38,050)	$(64,216)	$(84,803)	$(103,634)
	Net Property, Plant & Equipment	$203,490	$185,017	$161,865	$143,140	$129,038
Total Assets		$322,679	$332,608	$406,304	$326,886	$321,289

		Year ended 12/31				
		1	2	3	4	5
Current Liabilities						
	Accounts Payable	$12,897	$20,589	$22,477	$25,688	$27,195
	Accrued Wages Payable	$1,233	$2,241	$1,685	$1,957	$2,391
	Short term portion of LT debt	$18,426	$19,758	$21,186	$22,718	$24,360
	Total Current Liabilities	$32,556	$42,588	$45,348	$50,363	$53,946
Long-Term Liabilities						
	Long-Term Note Payable	$204,391	$188,135	$171,392	$153,799	$135,762
	Total Long-term Liabilities	$204,391	$188,135	$171,392	$153,799	$135,762
Total Liabilities		$236,947	$230,723	$216,740	$204,162	$189,708
Equity						
	John Dough, Equity	$85,732	$101,885	$159,564	$122,724	$131,581
	Total Equity	$85,732	$101,885	$159,564	$122,724	$131,581
Total Liabilities & Equity		$322,679	$332,608	$376,304	$326,886	$321,289
Revenues:						
	Sales	$373,492	$452,781	$449,685	$362,755	$399,975
	Less Returns & Allowances	$(2,895)	$(1,670)	$(8,477)	$(9,317)	$(11,179)
	Net Sales	$370,597	$451,111	$441,208	$353,438	$388,796
	Less Cost of Goods Sold	$128,968	$158,987	$176,388	$169,589	$162,832
	Gross Profit	$241,629	$292,124	$264,820	$183,849	$225,964
Expenses:						
	Advertising & Promotion	$10,725	$4,343	$8,289	$6,131	$5,700
	Bad Debt Expense (write offs)	$399	$1,483	$125	$2,349	$1,300
	Bank Charges	$1,940	$2,177	$1,803	$1,799	$1,998
	Depreciation	$18,580	$19,470	$26,166	$20,587	$18,831
	Insurance	$3,948	$4,477	$4,695	$5,143	$5,637
	Interest Expense	$16,256	$16,743	$17,593	$18,037	$18,397
	Legal & Professional	$8,697	$6,602	$6,419	$8,627	$8,885
	Miscellaneous	$261	$426	$778	$1,875	$2,972
	Office Supplies	$4,265	$3,871	$4,825	$4,385	$4,000
	Payroll Taxes	$9,215	$10,982	$14,397	$15,183	$16,831
	Repairs & Maintenance	$5,042	$10,928	$11,472	$18,035	$15,849
	Salaries & Wages	$77,587	$79,915	$85,619	$90,590	$94,715
	Telephone	$1,840	$2,770	$2,812	$3,871	$3,700
	Travel	$1,982	$2,279	$1,806	$3,092	$3,240
	Utilities	$4,788	$5,819	$6,392	$11,471	$6,100
	Total Expenses	$165,525	$172,285	$193,191	$211,175	$208,155
Net Income (Loss)		$76,104	$119,839	$71,629	$(27,326)	$17,809

63. The following is a list of alleged facts concerning Jeffrey K. Skilling.
   1. I was born January 27, 1969.
   2. My social security number is 241-85-5532.
   3. I became the CEO of a major energy company in February 1, 2001, but I resigned from the company on August 14, 2001. I joined the company in June 1990.
   4. My last name means a former silver coin of Denmark.
   5. I currently reside near Littleton, Colorado.
   6. I have two daughters and two sons.
   7. I graduated in the top 10 percent of my Harvard Business School class.

8. I received total cash compensation in 1999 of $5,678,171.20.
9. In 1999, my social security taxes were $76,200 and my medicare taxes were $81,996,134.79.
10. I paid $697,246.40 of Texas state income taxes.
11. My credit score is 550.
12. I have not been sued or had a prior arrest.
13. I previously worked for McKinsy.
14. I attended a conference in Aspen, Colorado in February 1994.
15. I currently qualify for the earned income credit.

Your assignment is to verify whether the statements by Mr. Skilling are true. All of these questions have an absolute definitive answer, but you may not be able to find a single definitive source that provides you with the answer. In that case, you will need to make some investigative conclusions based on the evidence at hand that you have collected including verification with multiple sources in some instances. Be skeptical; not every statement a person makes can be trusted.

Your answer to each question should include the following:
a. The source(s) of the information.
b. The information from the source that you are using.
c. The reasoning behind your conclusions. A simple reiteration of a source is not sufficient. We want to be able to understand your reasoning. This reasoning is especially important if you are using multiple sources and need to reason out a conclusion.
d. Your final conclusions.

64. Using the same instructions for problem 63, determine the accuracy of these facts about Frank Abagnale.
   a. I was born on June 27, 1948.
   b. I impersonated an airline pilot and attorney.
   c. I cashed fraudulent checks in 42 states and 19 countries.
   d. I spent no time in prison.
   e. What is my current job(s)?
   f. How many entities use my fraud prevention programs?
   g. I was named a member of Fox's Pinnacle 400.
   h. Most of my frauds were committed between ages 16 and 27.
   i. I have written 14 books.
   j. My middle name is James.
   k. I escaped prison four times.
   l. My I.Q. is 130.
   m. One of my names was Skywayman.
   n. I have four sons and one daughter.
   o. I speak on college campuses.

65. A major part of forensic accounting, auditing, or life is gathering evidence. Go out into the real world and start a conversation with a stranger (e.g., on a plane, at a store, party, library, etc.). You can not use anyone you know, work with, or related to you. You may not pose as an interviewer, break the law, or engage in unethical behavior. Attempt to obtain as much personal information as possible, such as name, age, address, date of birth, social security number, employer, spouse's name, children's names, likes, and dislikes. The more personal facts you obtain, the better your grade.

66. Obtain a copy of the first or second series of Fox's "Lie to Me." Watch several episodes and summarize some of the tips for catching lies.

7

MONEY LAUNDERING AND TRANSNATIONAL FINANCIAL FLOWS

O money, money, money, I'm not necessarily one of those who think thee holy,

But I often stop to wonder how thou canst go out so fast when thou comest in so slowly.

—Ogden Nash[1]

OBJECTIVES

After completing Chapter 7, you should be able to:
1. Provide a definition of money laundering.
2. Describe the parties involved in money laundering.
3. Describe the role of the banking system in money laundering.
4. Describe the role of others in money laundering.
5. Illustrate the techniques used to break the audit trail to launder money.
6. Outline guidelines for organizations to use in combating money laundering activities.

OVERVIEW

The financial world is increasingly borderless. There are electronic financial transactions occurring 24 hours a day at any place on the globe. The transnational flows of financial information occur on a continuous basis. Some of these transactions are of a criminal nature and are used to launder cash receipts received from illegal activities. The purpose of this chapter is to learn how money laundering occurs and to determine whether anything can be done to trace it and prevent it.

Money Laundering: An Introduction

The traditional money laundering process can be divided into three steps. First, the money is deposited in a bank or financial institution and is called placement. Second, a set of complex transfers is made to disguise the original source of the money and to hide the audit trail. This is called layering the transactions. The final step called integration takes place when the money is integrated back into the legitimate money supply.

¶ 7001   LEGAL AND ILLEGAL LAUNDERING

Money laundering has become big business, and although the amount of illegal money that is laundered each year is unknown, it is estimated to range between $300 billion to $1 trillion. In the past, illegal money laundering has been recognized as a collateral crime. It was considered a collateral crime to other activities such as drug running, illegal gaming, or arms sales, for example. For this reason, only recently has money laundering been recognized as a separate crime in many jurisdictions.

Most people associate money laundering with drug running, but the procedures used to launder drug money can also be used to "launder" money within a legal context. The latter methods can be questioned on ethical grounds but not on technical grounds as they use the same procedures adopted by money launderers. All money laundering techniques have the same objective: to disguise the funds' origin.

Money Laundering Defined

A definition of *money laundering* that covers both legal and illegal contexts is to take money that comes from one source, hide that source, and make the funds available in another setting so that the funds can be used without incurring legal restrictions or penalties.

Purpose of Money Laundering

The primary purpose for money laundering is to make the funds spendable in a context that would have been unavailable otherwise. Consequently, the definition extends money laundering activities beyond the realm of drug dealers and criminals. It is possible to find accounting practices used within legitimate businesses and governments that closely follow the techniques used by international drug dealers to conceal the source of funds. For example, a government department attempting to remove spending restrictions from designated funds may use laundering procedures by charging the department with restricted monies for "services" from another de-partment. The second department then does not have a restriction on funds paid for its services and such monies can be used for discretionary spending. Or, a successful business executive might use similar methods to hide assets in a divorce settlement by setting up a series of back-to-back bank loans ending in cash payment and a loan default.

THE ONE STOP. Western Express advertised one-stop shopping to enable persons in Eastern Europe to conduct business in the United States. Their clients used fictitious identities, and often multiple identities, to conduct their business in the United States. Western Express performed various services for their clients, in addition to transmitting money and cashing checks: they exchanged digital currency (such as recently closed E-Gold and currently operating WebMoney), provided clients with stored value gift cards, ATM cards, and U.S. Taxpayer Identification Numbers, and rented U.S. addresses for their clients to use as mail drops. Investigations revealed that their clients were involved in widespread illegality beyond the mere receipt of funds under fictitious aliases and addresses, including a variety of cyber-crimes such as "re-shipping" schemes and "phishing," "spoofing," and spamming. See *http://www.manhattanda.org/whatsnew/press/2006-02-22.shtml.*

¶ 7011   CYBERCASH AND GOLD-BASED E-CURRENCY CREATES NEW LAUNDERING OPPORTUNITIES

Most of the money laundering activities that occurred in the past would have required the collusion or ignorance of several organizations, with the most important being the bank that knowingly or unknowingly transferred money from one location to another. But now, using the Internet, it will be possible for anyone to transfer large sums of money from one location to another without using a bank and with the transfers being totally anonymous. Today, cybercash transactions are beginning to take place without the need for third parties and the consequential scrutiny that might otherwise exist. Furthermore, cybercash transfers can be structured so that they originate in jurisdictions where such activities under regulatory scrutiny are not considered illegal.

There are a number of alternative business models for electronic currency or cybercash. PayPal (*paypal.com*) is a prepaid e-cash service that is available for making cash payments once a balance is deposited into the user's account. PayPal requires eventual cash deposits and transfers to and from user's accounts. The success of PayPal is related to its ability to exchange for payments in online auctions.

Bitcoins do not follow the same business model. Bitcoins are considered to be encrypted currency and an alternative to national currencies. Its value is based on trades taking place in an online market. These coins have value in themselves and do not require the deposit of cash into an account. Their immediate value is determined by market trades much as stock values. The number of coins circulating on the Internet is closely controlled to prevent their value from dropping. At the same time, each coin is encoded with an encrypted electronic code. Bitcoins can be issued by anyone with enough computer power, the proper algorithm, and being a member of the bit mining network. The weakness of the system is a computer containing Bitcoins can be hacked and the coins stolen. The coins are accepted for purchases by e-merchants around the world especially in countries where credit card controls are weak and open to hackers. The coins may also be exchanged for national currencies. When Bitcoins are used with Tor (anonymous websurfing) and purchases made with them, such as drug deals on Silk Road, they are untraceable. Double spending of the same coin and counterfeit coins are avoided by using third-parties to verify the authenticity of the coins being spent. With Bitcoin, when a coin is spent, the exchange is broadcast to the Bitcoin network and verified. At the same time, new ownership of the Bitcoin is recognized. As of 2013, the valuation of Bitcoins in circulation is $275M. See: https://en.bitcoin.it/wiki/FAQ

Another example of online currency use with Linden dollars is found in Second Life. Second Life (*secondlife.com*) is a free 3-D world that exists online where money is traded for services or electronic products. These services and products include computer training provided by Second Life members or digital clothing designed for the avatars that exist in the islands of Second Life. There are reportedly millions of Second Life members from all around the world. SL members have netted over $100,000 selling designer clothes for Second Life avatars. The Financial Accounting Standards Board, many accounting firms, and universities have office complexes in Second Life. All the money that changes hands is called Linden dollars. Linden dollars are readily convertible into U.S. currency at prevailing exchange rates through PayPal. Linden dollars can be earned within the community or U.S. currency deposited into Second Life will be converted into Linden dollars. Thus, the business model is based on exchanges taking place within a fantasy world and not be directly used to purchase goods outside the online community.

The identification for using these systems is generally an e-mail address. These methods of distributing cybercash have the potential to create a world of web electronic money with flows that are virtually untraceable and with the actual purchaser of goods unknown to the seller.

Digital Cash (e-Currency) Transactions

Why use banks and real dollars when you can use "digital currency" or e-currency to send payments from one person to another anywhere in the world? There are two ways a digital exchange works. First, the exchange can begin with an e-currency exchanger whose payment system is based on the digital currency of another company responsible for the exchange of e-currency. For example, an e-currency exchanger can use the Pecunix payment system which is based on Pecunix gold currency. A second approach is to not use an e-currency exchanger as a middleman, i.e., Pecunix and e-exchanger can create its own e-currency. Once an account is set up on the Pecunix website using only an e-mail address, it is possible to begin exchanging currencies. Pecunix uses gold to underwrite Internet transfers and the site makes it easy to encrypt all transaction information with PGP. The attractiveness of Pecunix is that its system is backed by gold.

Digital currency or e-currency should not be thought of as a digital token with an electronic ID and useable for small purchases at a number of online websites. Digital currency is controlled by online, privately-owned payment systems that allow members to transfer large amounts of digital currency from a member's account to anyone at any location. These digital currencies may be backed by precious metals or national currencies that fluctuate in value. If so, the gain or loss in the members' account varies depending on the underlying value of the metal or currency backing the digital currency. In such cases, the provider of digital currency is acting in the role of a national government by issuing their own currency. For examples of digital money companies and their policies, see EuroGoldCash *http://www. eurogoldcash.com*; Network Pay *http://www.networkpay.com*; or Perfect Money *http://www. perfectmoney.com*.

When a digital exchange system is implemented, electronic fund transfers are made from one bank account to another or from one individual to another. The transaction is confirmed with a simple click on a "confirm" button. Often times, an e-Voucher is used for this purpose. An e-Voucher is a special code used to fund an account. A member transfers or sells this code to any other person who uses the code to fund his/her account. Thus cash transfers are not officially recorded within the national banking system. Digital accounts are anonymously funded when a member makes a deposit with online bank transfers, checks, credit cards, Paypal, cash deposits, e-currency, money grams, or electronic money orders, for example.

Exchangers keep bank accounts in a number of international locations and arrange for the movement of monies as requested by a member. E-currency companies using gold keep certified gold bullion in secure locations anywhere in the world. A member may use digital currency to pay for services, purchase a product, send cash to a specific individual, or put it on a debit card for someone else's use. Money is sent worldwide using only a recipient's e-mail address. It can be sent to mobile devices whereby the recipient receives an e-voucher that allows the recipient to transfer the funds into their bank account. It is even possible to request money from anyone even if the request is coming from individuals who are not members of the network.

These transactions are instantaneously made from any electronic device connected to the Internet without the difficulties of traditional wire transfers. Such instantaneous transactions can be made as quickly as account numbers can be punched into a cell phone or other mobile device. The servers running these exchanges do not have to be physically located in the United States, but they are accessible from any location in the United States. Additionally, IP addresses in the United States can be hidden making it virtually impossible to trace the source of the funds deposited into these accounts. Today, it is possible to transfer funds around the world without the interference of financial institutions or governments.

EXAMPLE 7.1 It is interesting to note that in June 1, 2003, Dole's first online loyalty promotion put $10 in electronic currency on each of 30 million packages of Dole Fruit Bowls. In addition to four-ounces of mandarin oranges, peaches, pineapples, or mixed fruit, each package has a code number redeemable at Dole.com for online cash from SoftCoin Inc. Customers could use it at seven participating e-retailers, including Art.com, Cooking.com, KBkids.com, and SunglassHut.com. The second wave of the 18-month promotion, starting on January 1, 2004, puts SoftCoin cash on another 30 million packages, redeemable at seven additional E-retailers.[2]

Another example of the potential for circulating money in an online environment is Second Life (*http://secondlife.com*) with close to 1 million monthly players. Second Life is an online 3D game that uses Linden dollars to buy and sell virtual property and objects in the game. Just as in real life, Second Life buyers and sellers can incur profits or losses, and the Linden dollars they own can be converted into U.S. dollars based on a fluctuating conversion rate. Currently, Second Life (Linden Labs) is generating revenues of about $75M a year. In order to buy or sell property within the Second Life, players must pay a monthly fee of $9.95. Region fees can be $1,000 for set up and $295 per month. Presently, there are millions of dollars circulating within the parameters of the game.

¶ 7021   WHO USES MONEY LAUNDERING PRACTICES?

No list can contain all the examples of those who would use the techniques of money laundering. It should be remembered that the reason for money laundering is to convert resources into a format that makes them usable to their recipient.

Grant Recipients

In recent years, a number of universities were caught using methods similar to traditional money laundering as they converted federal grant monies into discretionary spending. Yet, it would be unlikely for university administrators or controllers to consider themselves to be money launderers even as they adopted money laundering techniques to move restricted grant monies into a fund with no spending limitations. These methods can be questioned on ethical grounds, but in most cases, such activities would not be considered illegal.

An example within a government context occurs in the following manner. Universities receive federal, state, and grant monies that restrict expenditures to specific spending purposes. These monies must be accounted for in separate funds to show that restricted monies are spent appropriately. Such monies cannot be used for discretionary purposes without converting them from their restricted fund classification. One method to complete the conversion would be to record a charge against the restricted fund for "services" rendered by the university. Such a charge may be for the rent of facilities or IT support charges as long as they are allowable charges under the grant. Once the monies are cleared out of the grant and paid to the university as revenues for the services rendered, they become available for discretionary spending.

Criminals

Besides drug trafficking, there are wide arrays of nefarious activities that can create questionable profits and require conversion of cash into a usable and totally spendable resource: extortion; bribes; protection rackets; terrorism; smuggling of goods, weapons, nuclear material, precious metals, and gems to avoid customs; smuggling of people to avoid immigration laws; white slavery and trafficking in women for prostitution; pedophiles' activities; intellectual property theft or the theft and resale of commodities, art, antiques, and historical artifacts; revenue from counterfeiting currency or documents; crimes of violence (contract killing, arson, and bombing); illegal logging; trade in endangered species of animals and plants, and even in human body parts; environmental crimes; usury; investment and VAT fraud; false invoicing and financial fraud; automobile thefts; tax evasion; illegal gambling; maritime crimes (piracy, cargo deviations, phantom ships, marine theft); illegal weapon sales; and identity theft and fraud over the Internet.

All these initial crimes, if successful, have the potential to generate large pools of money whose origin cannot be explained, thus prompting the use of money laundering procedures.

These four examples illustrate how the results of an initial crime made it necessary to launder large sums of money.

EXAMPLE

EXAMPLE 7.2 *Fraud proceeds:* Abu deposited $1,600,000 at a bank with five different checks ostensibly from the sale of land in a foreign country. No documents were provided to support the transactions. The bank was suspicious about the source of the funds and disclosed it to U.S. Treasury officials. Through cross-checking Abu's background, agents from the Justice Department determined that Abu's father was sentenced to jail after a foreign bank collapsed as a result of financial fraud organized by Abu's father. Abu was eventually arrested on attempting to launder money obtained through his father's fraud scheme. In this case, the money launderer was identified as a result of suspicious bank management.

EXAMPLE 7.3 *Bribes:* Fred worked for a state government, and he was responsible for proposing and approving capital expenditures (not a good practice) in a large public works project. For a positive approval on submitted RFPs, contractors were willing to remit a bribe to him. As the expenditures on the capital projects were large, the bribes were also large, equaling close to $10 million. In order to launder the money, Fred got his sister's husband Ted to set up a fruit company that supposedly purchased fruit from overseas and imported it into the U.S. The subcontractors paid their bribes to the fruit company's bank and were provided with invoices to justify their cash payments. The fruit company transferred the money out of its business bank account to various overseas accounts. These transfers were supposedly to pay for fruit imports and supporting invoices for the fruit purchases were given to the fruit company. Eventually, the money laundering operation was identified through a tip from a subcontractor and the tracing of wire transfers between the company's bank and the foreign bank accounts. Additionally, no fruit inventory had ever been kept nor had the fruit company incurred transport charges.

EXAMPLE 7.4 *Tax evasion:* Maury started a business to order, distribute, and resell RAM chips for PCs to computer manufacturers. The company had four branches in several countries selling the RAM chips. In order to reduce his tax payments, he set up a plan whereby the Asian company selling them the chips would send two invoices for the product. One was for the actual price of the RAM and the second was only for 90 percent of the first invoice. The invoice with the lowest price was given to Customs authorities as the basis for the import tax. Maury was able to avoid paying more than $1 million in import duties. The saving in unpaid tax was accumulated within the company and then transferred into Maury's personal account. Maury's bank became suspicious when account transaction tracking software used by the bank identified Maury's account as containing transactions that were outside the normal criteria boundaries for this account. Maury's bank notified Treasury officers and the tax evasion scheme was uncovered when the fake invoices at the Customs office were compared with the dollar amounts remitted to the Asian supplier for the purchased chips.

EXAMPLE 7.5 *Internet fraud:* Valentine, a citizen of France, registered DotGambling as a gaming company in Hungary. It was established to provide gambling services on the Internet, but Valentine did not get a license to operate a gambling business in Hungary. In Mexico, there was already another legitimate company called DotGaming that provided gambling services on the Internet. Valentine arrived in Canada and opened an Internet business account for DotGambling in a local bank accessible from anywhere. He used this account to establish his creditability in Aruba, the next location where he was going to open a bank account.

Valentine next traveled to Jamaica where he set up a website to "establish" his Internet gaming operations. Once there, he focused his advertising on gamblers in Great Britain. There was a large group of gamblers in Great Britain who were using the legitimate company DotGaming. He was able to get e-mailing lists from various Internet marketing companies that provide information about the purchasing habits of e-consumers and he targeted those consumers. As with any Internet gambling operation, DotGambling required that gambling deposits be paid prior to placing a wager. Another Internet bank account in Aruba was set up to handle these cash deposits. The Internet e-mails had convinced the gamblers they were using the same company, DotGaming, where they had placed bets in the past. When the account in Aruba contained $3 million, Valentine used a satellite phone during a flight to France to withdraw $1 million of the money into his personal account in France. The bank in Aruba got suspicious and refused to transfer such a large sum of money. Clearly, it is not certain in which jurisdiction the crime was actually committed.

These examples indicate the creativity that can be involved in a money laundering operation. The main reason that these particular money laundering schemes were not successfully executed was because a third party (i.e., bank or coconspirator) revealed the operation to authorities. Consequently, a chain of custody was documented between the criminal parties and the cash. The establishment of a chain of custody can be done in a traditional paper trail or as required with   today's web-based operations in electronic data and documents.

As previously stated, the methods of money laundering can be adopted by legitimate businesses to avoid the payment of taxes. For example, in the manufacturing process, it is necessary to transfer manufactured commodities from one jurisdiction to another. It is unlikely that the tax rates in these various states or countries are the same. Therefore, it would be advantageous for the manufacturing company to be taxed at the lowest rate. It is illegal to falsify invoices to achieve this end, but it is not illegal to develop a transfer pricing policy that creates profit in the country with the lowest tax rates and the results are the same as falsifying invoices… avoiding taxes.

Political Asylum Seekers

Money laundering is usually viewed as an illegal activity, but in some cases it may be performed for good reasons. People persecuted for religious or ethnic reasons within a specific country may need help in escaping from that country as well as help in taking their personal wealth with them.

SHOULD MONEY LAUNDERING PRACTICES BE CONDEMNED AND SANCTIONED IN EVERY SITUATION? White Zimbabwean farmers have exported their wealth because it was likely to be confiscated by the Zimbabwean government.

U.S. GOVERNMENT LAUNDERING MONEY? The Iran-Contra political scandal during 1985 and 1986 involved money laundering activities. High-ranking members of the Reagan administration secretly sold weapons to Iran. Then, they gave the profits from the $30 million sale to the Nicaraguan Contra rebels. Lieutenant Colonel Oliver North, who was the military aide to the National Security Council, was the chief negotiator of these operations and reported first to National Security Advisor Robert C. McFarlane and then to his successor, Vice Admiral John M. Poindexter. The sales to Iran were initially made at Israel's suggestion in order to improve its relationship with Iran and to free some American hostages who were being held by pro-Iranian terrorists in Lebanon. North set up the entire network for distributing this support to the Contras in the form of ships, aircraft, and bank accounts.

Financial Institutions' Role in Money Laundering

International banking plays a role in identifying money laundering activities, but it also plays a role in creating an environment where money laundering can exist.

¶ 7031 CORRESPONDENT BANKING

International banking is interconnected through a series of correspondent and respondent banks that allow for the 24-hour transfer of cash to and from any point in the world. Correspondent banks have relationships with thousands of other banks around the world, and large money center banks can process up to $1 trillion in wire transfers per day.

Correspondent banking takes place when one bank provides services to another bank, usually smaller bank, to move funds, exchange currencies, and access investment services such as money market accounts, overnight investment accounts, CDs, trading accounts, and computer software for making wire transfers and instant updates on account balances. Another service provided by foreign respondent banks to their clients through these correspondent-banking relationships is a *payable-through account*. Such an account enables the respondent bank's clients within the country where the bank is registered to write checks that are drawn directly on the respondent bank's correspondent account in the United States. Thus, U.S. correspondent banks provide all their foreign clients with direct access to the U.S. banking system. Since the passage of the Patriot Act in 2001 and the issuance of subsequent Treasury regulations, the activities of correspondent banks with shell banks has been curtailed. Additionally, the Patriot Act requires that U.S. banks establish stronger due diligence programs, such as know-your-customer rules, for all correspondent accounts and private banking accounts belonging to non-U.S. citizens and foreign banks.[3] Such due diligence risk assessment is enhanced for correspondent banks with banking licenses issued from jurisdictions with known money laundering problems.

The Report from the Senate Committee on Governmental Affairs states:

> The result of these due diligence failures has made the U.S. correspondent banking system a conduit for criminal proceeds and money laundering for both high-risk foreign banks and their criminal clients.[4]

The previous four money laundering cases were foiled, but if correspondent-respondent banking relationships along with a cash-intensive business cover such as a taxi cab company had been used, it would have been much harder to identify these money launderers. Money laundering was used in the 2006-2010 UBS tax avoidance scheme identified by the Justice Department. The bank which paid a large fine was alleged to have used its private bank in the U.S. to launder millions of dollars into European accounts for its rich clients and allow these clients to avoid U.S. taxes.

¶ 7041 TOOLS BANKS USE TO IDENTIFY MONEY LAUNDERERS

Monitoring Software

Banks do attempt to identify those individuals who might be laundering money at the point where illegal money enters the banking system. Banks have purchased software that allows them to monitor account transactions and identify suspicious activity. For example, the analysis provides for account/routing number comparisons to analyze the trail of deposits between banks; whether deposited amounts were the same or different between accounts; risk evaluations are made based on length of time the account has been open; the dollar amount on checks is analyzed to determine if they are divisible by 100, 1,000, etc.; duplications in the dollar amounts of deposits and withdrawals are compared; and periods of activity are evaluated to develop an evaluative risk factor based on the number of the days between deposits and withdrawals.

Fiserv provides antimoney laundering (AML) software that allows for suspicious account transactions to be statistically identified and monitored based on irregular transaction activity as compared with expected account profiles developed from historical data. Such a red flag may include a high-level of under-monetary legal limit transactions, for example. The system includes peer group analysis and watch list alerts. The collected information can be categorized by country and branch locations.

Ontrack Data International's data-collection software allows for the quick recovery of electronic data. Electronic memos and e-mail, when available, can be searched to establish relationships among the parties to these transactions.

These programs help banks satisfy the Bank Secrecy Act, Section 5318(h) of Title 31 of the U.S.C., and Section 352 of the Patriot Act whereby all U.S. banks are required to have antimoney laundering practices in place including an AML compliance officer.

CTRs and SARs and Form 8300

At a minimum, banks are supposed to have a set of policies and controls, a compliance officer, employee training, and independent audits to test their AML programs. Further, the U.S. Department of the Treasury requires banks to file Currency Transaction Reports (CTRs) about transactions above a specified dollar amount—currently $10,000—and Suspicious Activity Reports (SARs) for transactions as noticed by bank personnel. Figure 7.1 shows pages 1 and 2 of the Currency Transaction Report (Form 104), and Figure 7.2, the Suspicious Activity Report (Form 109) for money transmitter businesses (MSB). The transactions has to be considered "suscipious" and in excess of $2,000. MSBs provide traveler's checks, money orders (Walmart) that are sent to other countries, and/or exchange currencies. Even the U.S. Postal service is responsible for filing these forms. Similar reporting forms have to be filed by depository institutions and investment firms in the securities and futures industry.

The number of SARs annually filed with the Treasury is in the millions. In 2004, the Intelligence Reform and Terrorism Prevention Act provided millions of dollars in funding for improving and more efficiently operating SAR reporting practices as well as using the FinCen databases containing these documents. Today, no paper filings are accepted. These forms can only be electronically filed with the Treasury.

Bankers use a policy of know-your-customer (KYC) guidelines for identifying suspicious activities. Unfortunately, KYC guides may mean that innocent parties' personal financial information is forwarded to government agencies for scrutiny. As the privacy of banking transactions is important, the reasons for identifying a transaction as "suspicion-based" needs to be clearly defined in bank policy guidelines. Before he resigned, the governor of New York, Eliot Spitzer, was discovered to be making unlawful wire transfers of cash to shell company accounts. His activities were uncovered when the banks holding these accounts filed SARs with the Treasury Department. In addition, an individual must file a Report of International Transportation of Currency or Monetary Instruments (CMIR) (Figure 7.3) when the individual or members of a family group physically transport more than $10,000 in currency or monetary instruments into or out of the United States at one time. Examples of monetary instruments are traveler's checks, bearer stocks and bonds, and promissory notes.

GOT YOU. U.S. Customs and Border Protection (CBP) officers seized $53,000 in unre-ported currency Friday on the M/V Caribbean Fantasy ferry departing to Santo Domingo, Dominican Republic.

CBP Officers selected Dominican Republic citizen Mr. Felipe Alvarez, 69, for examination. During the interview, Mr. Alvarez declared to be traveling alone and transporting less than $10,000. Intensive examination revealed that he was traveling with two other passengers, US citizen Manuel De La Rosa, 47, and Dominican Republic citizen Cristian De La Rosa, 35, both nephews of Mr. Alvarez.

Subsequent interview and exam of the three passengers revealed non reported currency within their clothing and in their carry-on items totaling $53,726. Mr. Alvarez later admitted that the money transported by him and his nephews were proceeds of his business in the Dominican Republic. U.S. Department of Homeland Security, U.S. Customs and Border Patrol, Newsroom, January 28, 2013 (http://www.cbp. gov/xp/cgov/newsroom/news_releases/local/01282013.xml).

The U.S. Treasury's Financial Crimes Enforcement Network (FinCEN) reviews all the reports data. FinCEN uses artificial intelligence software to put together relevant information from the universe of reported data. The system then connects disparate pieces of information, such as banking transactions and accounts, and with this linking process, it reveals a pattern of financial transactions that are likely being used to launder money. This system also allows for the identification of potential suspects during the analysis.

Beyond these reporting requirements, businesses must file Form 8300, *Report of Cash Payments Over $10,000 Received in a Trade or Business,* with the Internal Revenue Service (IRS) for business sales that result in the receipt of more than $10,000 in cash. The cash may have been received in a single transaction or a series of related transactions in the seller's business operations. Such transactions are related if it involves a rental agreement or loan repayments along with the initial sale transaction. The business is obligated to notify their customer that they have filed a Form 8300 with the IRS. The rules apply to business such as car dealers, contractors, universities, taxi drivers who make lease payments to a cab company that are over $10,000, and advance payments of more than $10,000 to a bail bondsman. Failure to file the form can result in a minimum penalty of $25,000. There are two interesting exceptions to the reporting requirements. First, personal checks and wire transfers are not considered to be cash under the reporting guidelines, and second, although universities are filing Form 8300 for normal operations, most nonprofit organizations are largely exempted from the reporting requirements. (See *http://www.irs.gov/Businesses/Small-Businesses-&-Self-Employed/ FAQs-Regarding-Reporting-Cash-Payments-of-Over-$10,000-%28Form-8300%29*)

Figure 7.1. CTR Form Completed by Bank Personnel for Transactions Exceeding $10,000

FINCEN Form **104** (March 2011) Department of the Treasury FinCEN	**Currency Transaction Report** ▶ Previous editions will not be accepted after September, 2011. ▶ Please type or print. *(Complete all parts that apply--See Instructions)*	OMB No. 1506-0004

1 Check all box(es) that apply: a ☐ Amends prior report b ☐ Multiple persons c ☐ Multiple transactions

Part I Person(s) Involved in Transaction(s)

Section A--Person(s) on Whose Behalf Transaction(s) Is Conducted

2 Individual's last name or entity's name	3 First name	4 Middle initial
5 Doing business as (DBA)		6 SSN or EIN
7 Address (number, street, and apt. or suite no.)		8 Date of birth __/__/__ MM DD YYYY
9 City	10 State 11 ZIP code 12 Country code (if not U.S.)	13 Occupation, profession, or business

14 If an individual, describe method used to verify identity: a ☐ Driver's license/State I.D. b ☐ Passport c ☐ Alien registration

d ☐ Other _____ e Issued by: _____ f Number: _____

Section B--Individual(s) Conducting Transaction(s) (if other than above).
If Section B is left blank or incomplete, check the box(es) below to indicate the reason(s)

a ☐ Armored Car Service b ☐ Mail Deposit or Shipment c ☐ Night Deposit or Automated Teller Machine d ☐ Multiple Transactions e ☐ Conducted On Own Behalf

15 Individual's last name	16 First name	17 Middle initial
18 Address (number, street, and apt. or suite no.)		19 SSN
20 City	21 State 22 ZIP code 23 Country code (If not U.S.)	24 Date of birth __/__/__ MM DD YYYY

25 If an individual, describe method used to verify identity: a ☐ Driver's license/State I.D. b ☐ Passport c ☐ Alien registration

d ☐ Other _____ e Issued by: _____ f Number: _____

Part II Amount and Type of Transaction(s). Check all boxes that apply.

	28 Date of transaction
26 Total cash in $_____ 0.00 27 Total cash out $_____ 0.00	__/__/__ MM DD YYYY

26a Foreign cash in _____ 0.00 27a Foreign cash out _____ 0.00
(see instructions, page 4)   (see instructions, page 4)

29 ☐ Foreign Country _____ 30 ☐ Wire Transfer(s) 31 ☐ Negotiable Instrument(s) Purchased

32 ☐ Negotiable Instrument(s) Cashed 33 ☐ Currency Exchange(s) 34 ☐ Deposit(s)/Withdrawal(s)

35 ☐ Account Number(s) Affected (if any): _____ 36 ☐ Other (specify) _____

Part III Financial Institution Where Transaction(s) Takes Place

37 Name of financial institution	Enter Regulator or BSA Examiner code number ▶ (see instructions)
38 Address (number, street, and apt. or suite no.)	39 EIN or SSN
40 City	41 State 42 ZIP code 43 Routing (MICR) number

Sign Here ▶	44 Title of approving official	45 Signature of approving official	46 Date of signature __/__/__ MM DD YYYY
	47 Type or print preparer's name	48 Type or print name of person to contact	49 Telephone number (__ __)__ __ __-__ __ __ __

▶ For Paperwork Reduction Act Notice, see page 4.   Cat. No. 37683N   FinCEN Form **104** (Rev. 03-2011)

FinCEN Form 104 (Ef. 03-2011)   Page 2

Multiple Persons
Complete applicable parts below if box 1b on page 1 is checked

Part I   **Person(s) Involved in Transaction(s)**

Section A--Person(s) on Whose Behalf Transaction(s) Is Conducted

2 Individual's last name or entity's name	3 First name	4 Middle initial

5 Doing business as (DBA)	6 SSN or EIN

7 Address (number, street, and apt. or suite no.)	8 Date of birth ___/___/___ MM DD YYYY

9 City	10 State	11 ZIP code	12 Country code (if not U.S.)	13 Occupation, profession, or business

14 If an individual, describe method used to verify identity: a ☐ Driver's license/State I.D.   b ☐ Passport   c ☐ Alien registration

d ☐ Other _____   e Issued by: _____   f Number: _____

Section B--Individual(s) Conducting Transaction(s) (if other than above).

15 Individual's last name	16 First name	17 Middle initial

18 Address (number, street, and apt. or suite no.)	19 SSN

20 City	21 State	22 ZIP code	23 Country code (if not U.S.)	24 Date of birth ___/___/___ MM DD YYYY

25 If an individual, describe method used to verify identity: a ☐ Driver's license/State I.D.   b ☐ Passport   c ☐ Alien registration

d ☐ Other _____   e Issued by: _____   f Number: _____

Part I   **Person(s) Involved in Transaction(s)**

Section A--Person(s) on Whose Behalf Transaction(s) Is Conducted

2 Individual's last name or entity's name	3 First name	4 Middle initial

5 Doing business as (DBA)	6 SSN or EIN

7 Address (number, street, and apt. or suite no.)	8 Date of birth ___/___/___ MM DD YYYY

9 City	10 State	11 ZIP code	12 Country code (if not U.S.)	13 Occupation, profession, or business

14 If an individual, describe method used to verify identity: a ☐ Driver's license/State I.D.   b ☐ Passport   c ☐ Alien registration

d ☐ Other _____   e Issued by: _____   f Number: _____

Section B--Individual(s) Conducting Transaction(s) (if other than above).

15 Individual's last name	16 First name	17 Middle initial

18 Address (number, street, and apt. or suite no.)	19 SSN

20 City	21 State	22 ZIP code	23 Country code (if not U.S.)	24 Date of birth ___/___/___ MM DD YYYY

25 If an individual, describe method used to verify identity: a ☐ Driver's license/State I.D.   b ☐ Passport   c ☐ Alien registration

d ☐ Other _____   e Issued by: _____   f Number: _____

Figure 7.2. Suspicious Activity Report

FinCEN form **109** March, 2011 Previous editions will not be accepted after September 2011	**Suspicious Activity Report by Money Services Business** ▶ Please type or print. Always complete entire report. Items marked with an asterisk * are considered critical. (See instructions .)	(FINANCIAL CRIMES ENFORCEMENT NETWORK) OMB No. 1506-0015

1 ☐ Check this box only if amending or correcting a prior report (see item 1 instructions)   1a ☐ Check this box if this is a recurring report

Part I   Subject Information   2 ☐ Multiple subjects (see item instructions)

3 Subject type (check only one box) a ☐ Purchaser/sender   b ☐ Payee/receiver   c ☐ Both a & b   d ☐ Other

*4 Individual's last name or entity's full name	*5 First name	6 Middle initial

*7 Address

*8 City	*9 State	*10 Zip Code	*11 Country Code (If not US)	

*12 Government issued identification (if available)

a ☐ Driver's license/state I.D.   b ☐ Passport   c ☐ Alien registration   z ☐ Other _____

e Number | | | | | | | | | | | | | | | | | | | f Issuing state/country _____

*13 SSN/ITIN (individual) or EIN (entity)	*14 Date of birth ___ / ___ / ___ MM DD YYYY	15 Telephone number (___) ___ – ___

Part II   Suspicious Activity Information

*16 Date or date range of suspicious activity From ___/___/___ To ___/___/___ MM DD YYYY MM DD YYYY	*17 Total amount involved in suspicious activity a ☐ Amount unknown $ _____ .00

*18 Category of suspicious activity (check all that apply)

a ☐ Money laundering   b ☐ Structuring   c ☐ Terrorist financing   z ☐ Other (specify) _____

*19 Financial services involved in the suspicious activity and character of the suspicious activity, including unusual use (check all that apply).

a ☐ Money order   b ☐ Traveler's check   c ☐ Money transfer

z ☐ Other _____   e ☐ Currency exchange

Check all of the following that apply

(1) ☐ Alters transaction to avoid completing funds transfer record or money order or traveler's check record ($3,000 or more)

(2) ☐ Alters transaction to avoid filing CTR form (more than $10,000)

(3) ☐ Comes in frequently and purchases less than $3,000

(4) ☐ Changes spelling or arrangement of name

(5) ☐ Individual(s) using multiple or false identification documents

(6) ☐ Two or more individuals using the similar/same identification

(7) ☐ Two or more individuals working together

(8) ☐ Same individual(s) using multiple locations over a short time period

(9) ☐ Offers a bribe in the form of a tip/gratuity

(10) ☐ Exchanges small bills for large bills or vice versa

If mailing, send each completed SAR report to: **Electronic Computing Center - Detroit** **Attn: SAR-MSB** **P.O. Box 33117** **Detroit, MI 48232-5980**	**A free secure e-filing system is available to file this report.** Go to http://bsaefiling.fincen.treas.gov/index.jsp for more information and to register

Catalog No. 34944N   Rev. 3/01/11

Part II   Suspicious Activity Information, Continued   `2`

*20 Purchases and redemptions (check box "P" for purchase or box "R" for redemption)

Instrument	P	R	Issuers	Total Instruments	Total Amount (US Dollars)
Money Orders:	☐	☐	_____	_____	$_____.00
	☐	☐	_____	_____	$_____.00
	☐	☐	_____	_____	$_____.00
Traveler's Checks:	☐	☐	_____	_____	$_____.00
	☐	☐	_____	_____	$_____.00
	☐	☐	_____	_____	$_____.00
Money Transfers	☐	☐	_____	_____	$_____.00
	☐	☐	_____	_____	$_____.00
	☐	☐	_____	_____	$_____.00

*21 Currency Exchanges:

	Tendered Currency/Instrument	Country	Received currency	Country	Amount (US Dollars)
☐ If bulk small currency	_____	_____	_____	_____	$_____.00
☐ If bulk small currency	_____	_____	_____	_____	$_____.00

Part III   Transaction Location   22 ☐ Multiple transaction locations

23 Type of business location (check only one)   a ☐ Selling location   b ☐ Paying location   c ☐ Both

*24 Legal name of business | 25 Doing business as

*26 Permanent address (number, street, and suite no.) | *27 City | *28 State | *29 Zip Code

*30 EIN (entity) or SSN/ITIN (individual) | *31 Business telephone number ( ) ___ — ____ | 32 Country Code (If not US) | 33 Internal control/file number (If available)

Part IV   Reporting Business   34 ☐ The Reporting Business is the same as the Transaction Location (go to Part V)

*35 Legal name of business | 36 Doing business as

*37 Permanent address (number, street, and suite no.) | *38 City | *39 State | *40 Zip Code

*41 EIN (entity) or SSN/ITIN (individual) | *42 Business phone number (include area code) ( ) ___ — ____ | 43 Country Code (If not US) | 44 Internal control/file number (If available)

Part V   Contact for Assistance

*45 Designated contact office | *46 Designated phone number (Include area code) ( ) ___ — ____ | 47 Date filed (See instructions) ___/___/_____ MM DD YYYY

48 Agency (If not filed by a Money Services Business)

Figure 7.3. Report of International Transportation of Currency or Monetary Instruments

FinCEN Form **105** March 2011 Department of the Treasury FinCEN ▶ **Please type or print.**	DEPARTMENT OF THE TREASURY FINANCIAL CRIMES ENFORCEMENT NETWORK **REPORT OF INTERNATIONAL TRANSPORTATION OF CURRENCY OR MONETARY INSTRUMENTS** 31 U.S.C. 5316; 31 CFR 1010.340 and 1010.306	OMB NO. 1506-0014 ▶ To be filed with the Bureau of Customs and Border Protection ▶ For Paperwork Reduction Act Notice and Privacy Act Notice, see back of form.

PART I FOR A PERSON DEPARTING OR ENTERING THE UNITED STATES, OR A PERSON SHIPPING, MAILING, OR RECEIVING CURRENCY OR MONETARY INSTRUMENTS. (IF ACTING FOR ANYONE ELSE, ALSO COMPLETE PART II BELOW.)

1. NAME (Last or family, first, and middle)	2. IDENTIFICATION NO. (See instructions)	3. DATE OF BIRTH (Mo./Day/Yr.)

4. PERMANENT ADDRESS IN UNITED STATES OR ABROAD	5. YOUR COUNTRY OR COUNTRIES OF CITIZENSHIP

6. ADDRESS WHILE IN THE UNITED STATES	7. PASSPORT NO. & COUNTRY

8. U.S. VISA DATE (Mo./Day/Yr.)	9. PLACE UNITED STATES VISA WAS ISSUED	10. IMMIGRATION ALIEN NO.

11. IF CURRENCY OR MONETARY INSTRUMENT IS ACCOMPANIED BY A PERSON, **COMPLETE 11a OR 11b, not both**

A. EXPORTED FROM THE UNITED STATES	**COMPLETE "A" OR "B" NOT BOTH**		B. IMPORTED INTO THE UNITED STATES
Departed From: (U.S. Port/City in U.S.)	Arrived At: (Foreign City/Country)	Departed From: (Foreign City/Country)	Arrived At: (City in U.S.)

12. IF CURRENCY OR MONETARY INSTRUMENT WAS MAILED OR OTHERWISE SHIPPED, COMPLETE 12a THROUGH 12f

12a. DATE SHIPPED (Mo./Day/Yr.)	12b. DATE RECEIVED (Mo./Day/Yr.)	12c. METHOD OF SHIPMENT (e.g. u.s. Mail, Public Carrier, etc.)	12d. NAME OF CARRIER

12e. SHIPPED TO (Name and Address)

12f. RECEIVED FROM (Name and Address)

PART II INFORMATION ABOUT PERSON(S) OR BUSINESS ON WHOSE BEHALF IMPORTATION OR EXPORTATION WAS CONDUCTED

13. NAME (Last or family, first, and middle or Business Name)

14. PERMANENT ADDRESS IN UNITED STATES OR ABROAD

15. TYPE OF BUSINESS ACTIVITY, OCCUPATION, OR PROFESSION	15a. IS THE BUSINESS A BANK? ☐ Yes ☐ No

PART III CURRENCY AND MONETARY INSTRUMENT INFORMATION (SEE INSTRUCTIONS ON REVERSE)(To be completed by everyone)

16. TYPE AND AMOUNT OF CURRENCY/MONETARY INSTRUMENTS		17. IF OTHER THAN U.S. CURRENCY IS INVOLVED, PLEASE COMPLETE BLOCKS A AND B.
Currency and Coins	▶ $	A. Currency Name
Other Monetary Instruments (Specify type, issuing entity and date, and serial or other identifying number.)	▶ $	
(TOTAL)	▶ $	B. Country

PART IV SIGNATURE OF PERSON COMPLETING THIS REPORT

Under penalties of perjury, I declare that I have examined this report, and to the best of my knowledge and belief it is true, correct and complete.

18. NAME AND TITLE (Print)	19. SIGNATURE	20. DATE OF REPORT (Mo./Day/Yr.)

CUSTOMS AND BORDER PROTECTION USE ONLY

THIS SHIPMENT IS ☐ INBOUND ☐ OUTBOUND	PORT CODE	CBP QUERY? Yes ☐ No ☐	COUNT VERIFIED Yes ☐ No ☐	VOLUNTARY REPORT Yes ☐ No ☐
DATE	AIRLINE/FLIGHT/VESSEL	LICENSE PLATE STATE/COUNTRY NUMBER		INSPECTOR (Name and Badge Number)

FinCEN FORM 105

¶ 7051   DUE DILIGENCE LAWS FOR BANKS

An antimoney laundering law, enacted in 1986, is the Money Laundering Control Act was the first law that made money laundering a separate crime. The law makes it a crime for an individual to engage in a financial transaction that involves the proceeds from illegal activities. In 1992, the Annunzio-Wylie Anti-Money Laundering Act outlawed the operation of "illegal money transmitting business," and the Act provides that if a bank is convicted of money laundering, proceedings to terminate its bank charter or its insurance will be initiated. Usually, these banks receive large fines but they are not terminated.

These laws and regulations require that a bank perform due diligence in its relationships with other banks and important clients as well as continually monitor account transactions. Within banks, due diligence must co-exist with the client's need for privacy and the secrecy laws existing in many foreign jurisdictions that prevent access to bank documents. The *Report from the Senate Committee on Governmental Affairs* has described U.S. banks anti-money laundering activities toward their foreign correspondent accounts as "weak." Thus, many banks are facing conflicting roles and statutes as they try to monitor themselves. Additionally, the fees earned from correspondent banks are lucrative.

There are no valid business reasons for a foreign bank to provide services to its U.S. customers without the need for that bank to incur the costs of obtaining a physical presence, employees, and a U.S. bank license. Without access to these correspondent bank services, foreign shell banks and offshore banks could not exist.

¶ 7061   SHELL BANKS

Shell banks are a link for people in foreign countries to have access to the United States banking system. Unfortunately, the link has been identified with money laundering activities. *Shell banks* are generally high-risk banks that exist without any physical presence in *any* legal jurisdiction. These banks have a banking license in a specific country, but they are not likely to have a staff and may be operated as part of another business or operated out of an individual's personal residence. These banks should not be thought of as branch banks without a physical presence in a country and affiliated with a home-country financial institution. Since the passage of the Patriot Act, shell banks without any physical presence in any jurisdiction are prohibited from operating in the United States, but they can still have a relationship with a correspondent bank that operates through a U.S. bank. Thus, their appeal as a money laundering institution has been reduced.

Locations Conducive to Shell Banking

Such banks may be licensed in the Nauru, Vanuatu, Montenegro, Cayman Islands, or Antigua, but the actual banking operations can be anywhere in the world.

EXAMPLE 7.6 Nauru is said to have issued 400 licenses for offshore shell banks. Nauru offers the possibility of setting up a bank with no requirement for local directors or any local presence apart from a registered office and company secretary in Nauru.

The Internet ad reproduced here provides the basic information and contact details for establishing a bank in Nauru. Another South Pacific Island is Vanuatu that currently has more than 50 offshore shell banks. Caribbean governments also provide shell bank licensing.

Petro Funds advertisement

http://bpcapital.org/petrodollar_12/opecapital/bank_own_Nauru.html or http://bpcapital.org/lloyds/bank_own_Nauru.html

Your Own Bank In
Republic Of Nauru

For Only US $9,500

Advantages to owning a Nauru Bank include:

Minimum formation time

Low formation costs

Minimum pre and post incorporation legal formalities

Low capitalization

Freedom to issue bearer shares

Complete secrecy of operations

Anonymity of promoters

Noninterference in operations

Absence of individual and corporate tax structure

Complete freedom in conducting all legal activities

The capital requirements for a bank are very low—US$ 100,000—and the time for incorporation is in the order of one to three months.

Offshore Banks Versus Shell Banks

Offshore banks are slightly different than shell banks, although neither is mutually exclusive from the other. There is a caveat in an offshore banking license that prevents the organization from transacting banking activities with any citizens of the licensing jurisdiction or transacting business with the currency of the licensing jurisdiction. These bank operations solely exist within international financial transactions, and they are set up, in many cases, to avoid taxes in the U.S. These accounts allow account holders access to many different world currencies. Such services are provided by most national banks to their well-off customers. Monies in the accounts can be withdrawn using any AMT.

Nested Services

Both shell and offshore banks provide nested correspondent services where a foreign bank's private clients use U.S. correspondent accounts. In such a case, the first foreign bank has access to the U.S. financial system through a correspondent banking relationship with a U.S. bank. Nested services occur when a second or third foreign bank has a correspondent relationship with the first foreign bank without the knowledge of the U.S. bank. Consequently, there may be shell banks with anonymous access to the U.S. financial system. These foreign shell banks have private bank clients who are very exclusive customers with large deposits and consequently receive VIP bank services not available to regular customers. Bank secrecy laws in most of these countries, until recently, would not permit the disclosure of information about such client transactions.

Internet-based Shell and Offshore Banks

Today, shell and offshore banking operations can be entirely Internet-based. An Internet bank does not need to have the normal bank physical facilities anywhere, because all transactions occur over the web. Consequently, a PC in a room is adequate to conduct banking activities. These banks are difficult to regulate because they can be located anywhere in the world. It becomes difficult for bank officials to monitor unusual activity in these accounts. As Internet banking expands, it provides for account queries, transfer of funds among accounts, bill payments, security trading, applications for loans, downloadable information about accounts, stock trading, transfers to third-party accounts, and check and deposit slip imaging.

Before Bank One was taken over by Chase, Bank One allowed its customers to send, receive, and request money over the Internet. Today similar Internet worldwide cash transfer services are available from from MoneyBookers (*http://www.moneybookers.com*) a U.K. based company. The sender identifies the account from which the money will be withdrawn, and the receiver identifies the account into which the money will be deposited. Citibank allows for the international transfer of funds between a Citibank linked account and any other linked account. Western Union also provides for the international transfer of money between countries (*http://www.westernunion.com/Home*). Also see Xoom, an international money transfer service, for an online way to send money to friends around the world.[5]

As these services expand, they will make it difficult to identify which country's banking laws and bank supervisors have jurisdictional authority over these cross-border transactions. They also make it more difficult for law enforcement to catch sophisticated money launders.

The Internet, combined with offshore and shell banks, provides money launderers with the opportunity to layer cash transactions among numerous virtual entities in such a way that the transactions are almost impossible to trace; the audit trail is nonexistent or completely falsified. The secrecy laws of many countries further exacerbate the problem by making the underlying transactional data totally unavailable. By carefully choosing the jurisdiction in which to locate cash, money launderers essentially import the weakest overseas bank regulations into the United States.

EXAMPLE 7.7 A recent instance of using these correspondent and shell bank relationships to launder money is the M.A. Bank of the Cayman Islands. The M.A. Bank was licensed in the Cayman Islands as an offshore bank with most of its clients in Argentina although it had no Argentinean banking license. This bank also had correspondent banking relationships with Citibank in New York and other banks in Europe and South America. The organizational chart for the M.A. Bank follows:

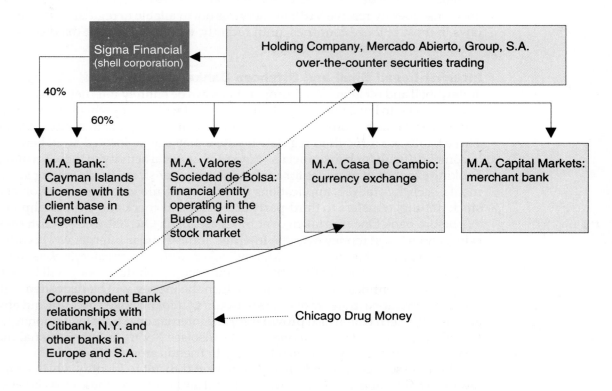

Mercando Abierto, S.A. acted as a holding company that controlled the M.A. Bank in order to allow its investors to have access to investments in U.S. and European financial markets. Mercando held a 60 percent ownership in M.A. Bank, and its Cayman Islands shell corporation Sigma Financial held the other 40 percent. Argentinean laws restrict its citizen's access to non-Argentinean financial markets, but the M.A. Bank provided access through its Cayman Island bank. The only physical presence for the organization was in Argentina.

The money laundering operation began when a client account was opened in the M.A. Bank for an account holder in Argentina. The account holder was an Argentinean real estate agent, and the real estate agent was allegedly helping a U.S. buyer purchase properties in Argentina. The account was eventually part of the money trail that was used to wire transfer $43 million in drug money into the Citibank correspondent accounts in the United States held by both the M.A. Bank and M.A. Casa de Cambio. Money was wired from Chicago directly into two correspondent bank accounts at Citibank and consequently into the real estate agent's account. Thus, the bank that was initially accepting the cash deposits into the financial system was the M.A. Bank and not Citibank. The Juarez Cartel obtained the money from drug sales in Chicago, and the cash was being laundered from Chicago to Argentina and elsewhere. The real estate agent acted as the collection and distribution person in Argentina.

The M.A Bank could not operate as a bank in Argentina, but its customers could pick up cash from Mercando Abierto, S.A., holding company for the bank. If there was not enough cash on hand at Mercando Abierto, S.A., customers could receive cash by having M.A. Casa de Cambio wire cash to a U.S. bank that also had a local branch in Argentina. Initially, the money would be wired from the U.S. Citibank correspondent accounts to a second U.S. bank. An employee from Mercando Abierto, S.A. would then go into the second U.S. bank's local branch in Argentina and pick up the cash. Thus, the M.A. Bank always used other financial institutions, and consequently it did not have to file reports about its banking activities in Argentina, Cayman Islands, or in the United States. The M.A. Bank's administrative offices (i.e., back-office operations) are located in Montevideo, Uruguay further supporting the fact that the bank was not operating in Argentina. Thus, the paper trail was even more difficult to follow as it criss-crossed national borders.

The drug money obtained in Chicago was being laundered from Chicago directly into the banking system through correspondent accounts and then on to Argentina for distribution. Even though the U.S. Treasury eventually seized the monies remaining in the correspondent accounts through a sting operation, a portion of the cash was returned to the M.A. Bank because under the law the bank argued it was an "innocent bank" that had been duped.[6]

Other Businesses' Role in Money Laundering

Businesses besides banks are affected by money laundering activities as money launderers look for ways to legitimatize their cash collections. Small businesses also can be used to launder money. Businesses that typically receive large amounts of cash are especially vulnerable to infiltration by money launderers.

¶ 7071 CASH-ORIENTED BUSINESSES

Businesses with large amounts of cash sales include vending machine companies, taxicab companies, car washes, currency exchanges, nightclubs, bars, restaurants, real estate agencies, casinos, online auctions, and brokers. All these businesses are attractive operations for money launderers. By acquiring or investing in one or more of these businesses, a money launderer can identify a legitimate source of cash receipts, and with businesses such as a tavern there are almost no sales invoices to falsify.

Currency Exchanges

With a *currency exchange*, the large amounts of cash flowing through in wire transfers provides an easy means to convert criminal proceeds into legitimate money. All documentation can be falsified, making it difficult to prove that these operations are not legitimate business transactions.

Online Auctions

An *online auction* provides another good way to launder money into legitimate cash when items are overpaid for in an auction sale. Overpaying for the item, listed on the auction site by confederates shuts out other buyers except for the launderer. The seller of the item receives the money, through PayPal, for example, and the transaction is legitimized at that point through the sham sale.

Overseas Shell Companies

The launder sets up a shell company for a few hundred dollars in a few hours and transfers money to it from their untraceable overseas bank account. The shell company does not have any real business operations. Next the launder's U.S. company borrows money from the shell company with the hope that the loan documents will show monies came from a corporate loan.

Looking for a paper trail through a series legal documents is unlikely to yield any clues about who was involved in setting up the shell company only a search of electronic communications can yield useful results. Many times the relationship between shell companies stretch around the world as in one recent drug laundering case the money trail ranged from New Zealand to Latvia to Mexico to Wachovia in the U.S. through correspondent banks. All these organizations were involved in laundering money for the Sanaloa drug cartel, and eventually Wachovia paid a fine of $160M for being involved in laundering $420 billion.

Shell companies can be easily set up by fictitious persons. A recent study showed that the international rules and regulations over requiring proof of identity to set up a shell company are largely ineffective.[7] For a fee, incorporation service companies in various countries provide all the legal work that is needed to incorporate a shell corporation. U.S. incorporation services located in Delaware and Nevada were found to be the least interested in securing proper identification from parties incorporating shell companies. The study was based on 7,400 emails sent to more than 3,700 corporate incorporation services that make and sell shell companies in 182 countries.

EXAMPLE 7.8 A money launderer wants to set up an online business to launder monies that are already in accounts held in two offshore banks. These offshore banks are in the Cayman Islands and Nauru, two countries having strong bank secrecy laws.

The launderer sets up a web business located on a web server in the United States. A legitimate Internet service provider (ISP) is used to establish the online business. The business accepts credit card orders. The offshore money has been distributed among a number of bank accounts in the two island banks. These accounts have legitimate credit or debit cards issued with them. These bank accounts, controlled by the money launderer, are used to purchase consulting services from the web company, and the web company invoices the credit card companies for the fictitious services provided. The credit card company invoices the offshore banks, and the money from the fictitious sales is transferred into a Canadian bank account opened by the money launderer in the locale where the alleged company headquarters is located. All components of the scheme are separated from one another and involve cross-border transfers of financial information. Thus, an audit of one business entity in one country would not normally uncover the scam. The documentation generated by the credit card company and the banks is legitimate, and the cash in the banks is assumed to come from legitimate business transactions.

In Example 7.8, the weakest point in the laundering transaction would be the continual purchase of services from the web business through the same accounts at the same two banks. Concentrating an investigation on these specific transactions would be the most useful way to uncover the scheme. Any ISP would be expected to maintain computer logs of all transactions coming through its web servers. These logs would identify the IP address and access phone number with the ISP subscriber. If the ISP does not maintain these logs, this should immediately raise a red flag about its operations. Even if the web business established its own web server, suspicions would be raised if the business did not keep computer logs. If the logs are available, an auditor should review them to determine if any suspicious activity is occurring at the site. For example, if all the IP numbers and phone numbers for the various clients purchasing services are the same or all coming from the same ISP, an investigator should be suspicious.

Casinos

Money launderers use *casino gambling* as a way to launder money. There are a number of techniques to launder money through a casino. The simplest method is for the money launderer to take cash into the casino. A few small normal bets are placed and afterward the launderer leaves the casino, redeeming his cash at the cashier's cage. In this way, a legitimate source for the cash can be documented. Such activities are used with casinos based in the United States.

Casinos where Americans bet their money do not have to be based in the United States. Online and offshore casinos can be based in any country or in several countries. Another way to legitimize money received in criminal activities is through online gambling. Such gambling has been prosecuted under the Federal Wire Act which was passed in 1961 to control organized crime activities and betting activities where wire communication was used. More recently, Internet gambling in Internet casinos have come under question with the Congressional passage of the Unlawful Internet Gambling Enforcement Act of 2006 ("Act"). The Act illegalized payment processing for Internet gambling operations. Under the law, it is illegal for a bank or financial institution to engage in transferring money to an online gambling website. Prior to the passage of the Act, large amounts of money could be transferred to accounts at businesses that operated Internet gambling websites. Transfers from these accounts to other nongambling accounts would legitimize the money flows. The effectiveness of the law is in question because it has been found to violate World Trade Organization commercial service accords. The E.U.'s European Commission has declared the law protectionist and a violation of E.U.-U.S. free trade guidelines, and many online U.S. gamblers have simply jumped to online services such as UseMyBank (based in Canada) and just continued to gamble with no problems. Due to the nature of the Internet, the Act is largely unenforceable. It is likely that Congress will change the legislation to regulate online gambling in the U.S. rather than outlaw the practices. Many states in the U.S. are seeking other sources of revenue and are considering legalizing online gambling.

SUSPICIOUS ACTIVITY REPORTING REQUIREMENTS. Nevada casinos and tribal governments have been filing FinCEN Form 102, Suspicious Activity Report by Casinos and Card Clubs (SARC), with FinCEN to report potentially suspicious transactions and activities that may occur by, at, or through a casino. Of course, it may be difficult for the casino to identify an individual and file an SARC if they do not have account numbers from credit cards, playing card numbers, or checking accounts. Using cash to buy chips and not using a player's card should circumvent the casino reporting system.

Purchasing Departments

Even normal business purchasing activities can be easily converted into a money laundering operation. By setting up a retail computer company in a country outside the United States, the means are provided for laundering money overseas and back into the United States. Assume that large-scale purchases of computer equipment are made in the United States with money that has been placed in the banking system through *smurfing*. Smurfing is a money laundering technique in which confederates of the money launderer deposit random amounts of less than $10,000 into variously named accounts at a number of different banks. Due diligence procedures such as CTR and SAR filings usually are not triggered by such transactions. Thus, smurfing is most often used to launder smaller amounts of money.

In money laundering schemes involving purchases, the purchased equipment is then sent and sold overseas below cost. A U.S. shell company may be involved. At the point of sale, the money has been legitimized. Once the sales are made, the money can be transferred back through the banking system to the U.S. drug dealer or other criminal as money received from computer sales through export operations. This technique may or may not involve the falsification of invoices below cost to the foreign sales office in order to show a profit on the sale of the equipment.

Credit Cards

A bank's business credit card operations can unknowingly be used to launder money. When a legitimate largely cash-based business in the United States is taken over by criminal elements or if those criminals establish a legitimate new business, credit cards issued to the business by a bank can be used to launder money. Assuming U.S. criminals make prepayments on their company credit cards issued through a variety of different banks that have business relationships with the company, all these credit cards can be taken into a foreign country and the prepaid balances refunded as cash or just used to make purchases. The underlying technique is to use the credit card as a means to transfer cash into another country regardless of whether it is an advance on the credit card or a refund of a prepaid balance. Online banking services that allow for the transfer of monies from checking accounts to credit cards make this process easy to perform from any geographical location. Similar procedures have been used by legitimate businessmen to launder money and avoid paying taxes on their U.S. income. These tax cheats illegally put real cash into banks in the Cayman Islands, for example, and then use the bank's credit or debit cards to make purchases in the United States. Through off-shore banks may issue anonymous credit cards that are not traceable to the tax cheats. The offshore bank has no obligation to file a CTR or SAR with the U.S. Treasury Department.

THE CROOKED CONTROLLER. Jane Wood Brooks was sentenced to 46 months in prison and ordered to pay $1,358,662 in restitution. Brooks pleaded guilty in August 2006 to mail fraud and money laundering charges. Brooks was the Controller for BACHO North American, a division of Snap-on Tools. Brooks had the authority to request and issue checks for payments to vendors and for other services related to the business. Brooks devised a financial fraud and money laundering scheme to defraud BACHO. She issued forty BACHO checks made payable to "MBNA" in amounts from $9,000 to $33,987. MBNA is a legitimate credit card company in Wilmington, DE. These checks were going into her account to prepay her credit card account. Any excess above credit card charges was transferred to Brooks' personal checking account at another financial institution. Once the monies were in her checking account, she was able to use the funds to make large purchases or transfer them into other accounts. The total loss to BACHO was $1,462,797. (Internal Revenue Service, Examples of Money Laundering Investigations.)

¶ 7081   AUDIT TRAIL FOR BUSINESS MONEY LAUNDERING SCHEMES

The more transactions through which illegal money can be churned, the more difficulty one has in following and identifying the audit trail. The more countries through which the money can be transferred (especially targeting those countries with strong bank secrecy laws or weak anti-money laundering laws), the more difficult the money trail becomes to follow.

Churning

The Internet has made the churning of monies and cross-border flows instantaneous to implement, and without the subpoena power of law enforcement, the needed documents to trace the trail of such cash are unavailable. Even with subpoena powers, the information may be unobtainable due to overseas secrecy laws.

Of course, the best laundering operation would not even begin with illegal cash in the hands of the criminal. With an investment fraud, the proceeds would be electronically wired to the criminal's bank account by the victims. Thus, the cash would already be in the banking system. Many Ponzi schemes are based on naïve investors happily sending their funds to the person running the fraud. Afterwards, the scammer must then launder the cash.

Laundering Cycles

Figure 7.4 illustrates the basic cycle of cash in a laundering operation. All the steps are supported by falsified documents and are passed through several international borders.

Figure 7.4. The Basic Cycle of Money Laundering Cash

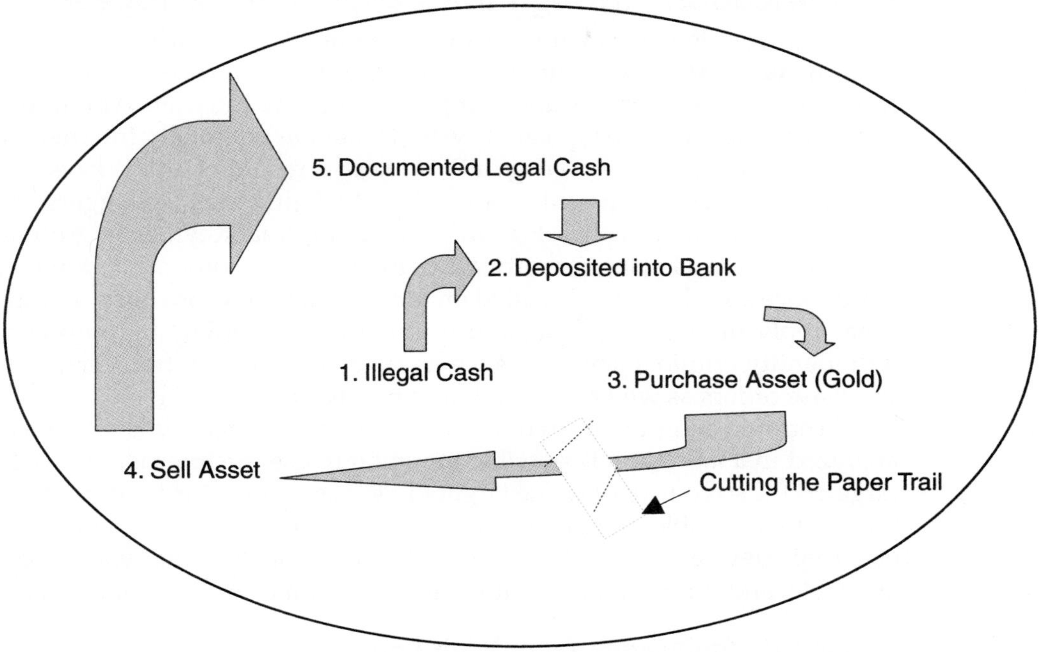

The illegal cash in Figure 7.4 is shown as being deposited into a bank in Step 1. As shown illegal cash is only deposited into one bank, but in actuality deposits may be made into a sequence of banks to obscure the paper trail. Steps 1 and 2 in Figure 7.4 are called placement, and it occurs when illegal sources of money are deposited into the financial system. The source of such initial cash may be falsely attributed to a restaurant or other high-cash receipt business. Steps 3 and 4 are known as layering the transaction. The purposes of these steps are to hide the original source of the cash through various types of deposits and asset purchases. Step 5 is called integration as the monies are now documented to be from a legitimate sale, in this case the sale of gold. Now the money can be spent by the criminal. In this cycle, only at the initial entry point of the cash into the banking system is the illegal cash likely to be detectible as laundered money.

Finding Money Laundering Schemes

¶ 7091   ## LIKELY SOURCES

Under most money laundering schemes, the traditional paper trail only exists in a fraudulent form. In other words, the audit trail exists to convince investigators and auditors that the sources of cash are legitimate. Support for the fraudulent trail can be completed through the warehousing of inventory items, false purchase orders, false sales invoices, ghost staffers, etc. Furthermore, traditional accounting controls are only in place to make the system look good. Once this fact is realized, one must also understand that traditional methods of testing for proper controls and following a paper trail are only going to be successful when the falsified audit trail is weak or not properly maintained by the criminals.

Digital information is more difficult to falsify and may provide a more reliable source of information for forensic accountants who are trying to trace a money laundering scheme. Web logs, IP addresses, Internet activity, wire transfers, and metadata are more difficult to falsify.

Identification Through Web Logs and Keyloggers

Although web logs and wire transfers are not 100 percent reliable, they are more reliable than the falsified books maintained by a criminal enterprise. Web logs are related to data flows between webservers and computers over the Internet. Wire transfers and electronic fund transfers are more typical of systems that are not totally Internet-based.

Keyloggers can be placed on a PC to keep a record of all the keystrokes made on a specific keyboard and then sent to a third party. Numerous keyloggers are available for free from download.com such as Free Keylogger or Actual Keylogger. Although your anti-virus software may tag keylogger software as malware, the software at download.com is not malware. Once a keylogger is installed on your PC, it will record every keystroke along with the time, application path, e-mail, and user name. The typing log produced with a keylogger will identify criminal activities such as suspicious money transfers, falsified invoices, and purchase orders as well as user IDs and passwords.

Electronic equipment used in a crime may be seized by law enforcement officials and analyzed in a lab, but it is possible to remotely use the Internet to install a program on the targeted PC so control over the targeted PC passes to a third party. Although all these techniques are available, the perspective taken here is that access to the criminal's PC or other electronic device is limited. The PC, cell phone, or PDA that was used in the crime is not available, and information about what occurred has to be obtained from other sources.

Tracing IP Addresses from Web Logs

Every web server maintains a record of the events occurring on that server. Each message sent over the Internet goes through a long series of web servers to its final destination. A traceroute program shows the path taken by the packet over the Internet to reach its destination. At each of those servers, a record is kept of the incoming and outgoing messages. A hacker may take over an "innocent" web server as a base to send out cash transfer orders, but the hacking skills needed and the additional complications this creates for the criminal reduces the possibility of this form of falsification. Therefore, the trail of a transaction across the Internet can potentially leave more reliable fingerprints than would falsified paper documents.

HTTP (Hypertext Transfer Protocol) log files used over the Internet should include the following information as requests to a web server are logged:

- The IP address of (exact host name of the person making the web request, such as http://24.1.155.15)
- Date and time of the request recorded in Greenwich Mean Time (GMT)
- File name of the requested file
- Size of the requested file
- Pages visited on the site
- Type of browser that the requester is using
- ID and password, if used, along with internal cookie tracing
- Address of the website from which the requestor linked

In addition, the Referer Field (if the address of requested field was typed directly into the browser, it was not referred) shows:

- Whether the requested page has been bookmarked and location of the bookmark on the computer's hard drive
- Whether a search engine was used to locate the site
- The words typed into the search engine to find the site

The requestor may have a dynamic or static IP address. A *static IP address* does not change and is usually given to a user who is continually connected to the Internet with a cable modem, satellite, or broadband connection. A *dynamic IP address* is a changing IP address that is assigned to an Internet user each time they dial into the ISP connection with a dial phone connection. As dial-up services disappear so will dynamic IP addresses. Although it is easier to trace a static IP address, logs on dynamic IP addresses also can be traced back to the time of connections and then through a process of elimination identified with a user.

HTTP Common Logfile Format

The HTTP Common Logfile Format appears as follows. Each component is explained in Table 7.1.

```
212.212.41.33 jdoe ships [06/Nov/2001:02:14:37
-0500] GET/library.html/books HTTP/1.1 200 4839
```

Table 7.1. Components of HTTP Common Logfile Format

Component	Explanation
212.212.41.33	This is the IP address.
Jdoe	This is the user name used to gain access to the site.
Ships	This is the unencrypted password used to enter the site.
[06/Nov/2001:02:14:37 -0500]	This string represents the date and time of access (day/month/year:hour:minute:second zone). All times are in Greenwich Mean Time (GMT). To convert GMT to Eastern Standard Time, subtract 5 hours from GMT, as shown.
"GET/library.html/books	This is the web file that is being requested on the site, along with the method of request: "GET." The request can relate to a graphic, a CGI script, a web page, or other items.
HTTP/1.1	This is the HTTP protocol (language) that is being used.
200	This is the HTTP response code. Code 200 means the request was successful. Code 404 means "Document not Found."
4839	This shows the number of bytes that have been transferred.

The *Extended* Common Logfile Format (CLF) provides the previously described data as well as information about the page the visitor was at prior to entering a visited site, whether the site is bookmarked, and the browser version used by the visitor. The following log entry is an example of the additional information provided with an Extended CLF. Table 7.2 explains its components:

```
Mozilla/2.0 (compatible; MSIE5.0;Win98; I)
http://www.une.edu.au/computer/internet/access/
->phonerec/name.html
```

Table 7.2. Components of Extended Common Logfile Format

Component	Explanation
Mozilla/5.0 (compatible; MSIE4.01; AOL4.0; Win XP; I)	This format shows the browser that is used. Netscape is code named Mozilla and Explorer is MSIE. "Mozilla/2.0 compatible" indicates that the browser is Netscape compatible, and the visitor is also using AOL Version 4.0. An international version of Windows XP is being used.
http://www.une.edu.au/ computer/internet/access/ ->phonerec/name.html	This format shows the URL address from where the visitor came from to get to the site (*www.une.edu.au/computer/internet/access*). If a search engine was used to find the site, it could also show the name of the search engine used and the term that was searched. The second part of the log shows the file that was requested from the site (*->phonerec/name.html*).

On a popular website, thousands of log-ins would be recorded every hour. In addition, log-ins would occur on other web server ports open to the Internet, such as SMTP and FTP ports. Logs for these ports also would need to be reviewed. Error logs are maintained on a web server to provide detailed information about the time, date, and errors that took place on a web server. All these logs would be analyzed using various log review software. Although more for webmasters than forensics, Google Analytics (free version) does provide disclosures of web log information.

Uses by Forensic Accountant

The log data is of interest to a forensic accountant who is reconstructing financial transactions in an investigation or trying to locate the physical location of a fraudster who has stolen money from the accountant's client. Such logs show information about access made to a website to collect information or to execute a web-based business transaction such as the transfer of funds or graphic files, for instance. Particularly interesting to the forensic accountant are the IP address, user name, and password (if used), GMT time adjustment, files requested, and the previous URL. This information is kept on the individual's PC or on a company's webserver, and it can be used to identify and trace the person and their Internet activity.

With the IP address, it is possible to trace the person back to an internet service provider's (ISP) phone number, and a geographical location For example, assume the IP address 212.111.41.33 was found in the web logs of a suspect's workplace computer. Searching for the IP at ARIN will show that this IP address is assigned to a European user. Contact information can be found in the RIPE database (http://www.ripe.net/data-tools/db) which lists contact information on European IP addresses.[8] Such information helps identifies the suspect's activities.

A search at the RIPE database will identify the following company as the user of that IP address along with a phone and fax number (the numbers are not shown):

Telecity Group (UK) Ltd
Manchester Science Park
Lloyd St. North
M15 6SE Manchester
UNITED KINGDOM

Within a few seconds, one may trace back an IP address to an ISP and possibly the individual using the IP address.   ARIN is one way to search for the geo-graphical location of an IP address. After finding the contact person for an IP ad-dress (who is likely to be the system administrator or sysad), the investigator then contacts the sysad to find out if logged data is available. Much of this information about a ISP's customer would not be forthcoming from an ISP without a subpoena. Even if the logs are unavailable to trace directly to the suspect, such tracing provides background information about the suspect's Internet activities as well as geographical information.

EXAMPLE 7.9 A laundering operation with funds in an offshore bank wants to move the funds into the United States. The operation decides to use the anonymity of the Internet to launder the cash. As indicated, one way to launder funds is to establish a website and business in Canada and make credit purchases of nonexistent online products using the bankcard issued by the offshore bank. The purpose of making fake purchases from one's own business is to get a check from the bank sent to the business that can be cashed at a local bank. Although all the invoices and sales records are in order in this situation, the logs records are not. Even if the web business does not keep logs, the ISP does and there are logs on all the other servers over which the Internet transactions passed.

In some cases, such as with instant messaging, it is more difficult to identify an IP address. A direct connection identifying the IP address is revealed if the investigator sends a file to the individuals in the instant message group. Yahoo Messenger logs every file transmission in the sender's computer in the server log. A check of that log will reveal the IP address of everyone that opened the file. Again cooperation form the Yahoo would be necessary. Technically it is possible for law enforcement investigators to to check the logs on a PC that is constantly connected to the Internet without the knowledge of the owner and without leaving a trace on the PC. Finding the IP on a Skype call, which allows instant messaging, is more involved and requires the use of a network analysis tool such as Wireshark.[9] Even so, the IP address on Skype calls can be quickly identified. Once the IP address is identified, it provides the possibility of finding the geographical location of a suspect.

Time stamped information is also useful in identifying an individual's location. The Greenwich Mean Time (GMT) automatic time adjustment is also helpful in identifying the world-wide geographical location of the visitor. In the map in Figure 7.5, it can be seen that the GMT for the East Coast of the United States is -5 hours from GMT. A logged entry would reveal that information.

The time stamp is from the computer where the request originated; therefore, this information provides an indication of whether someone is on the east or west coast of the United States, for example. The time stamps also provide information as to when a website was viewed or when an e-mail was sent. Of course, those internal computer times may be inaccurate. To determine if the internal time clock in your computer is accurate, check it against GMT time at *http://wwp.greenwichmeantime.com/gmt-timestamp.htm.*

Figure 7.5. Map of the World GMT Locations

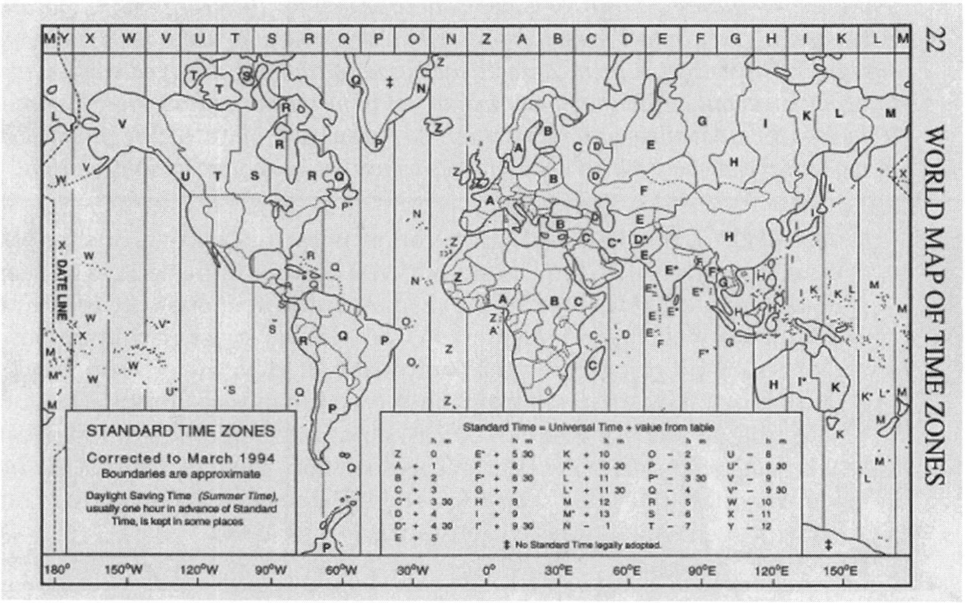

Source: *crh.nooaa.gov*

The different types of web files viewed and the files downloaded from a site provide additional information about a person's actions when he or she was at a website that provided gambling services, money transfer services, graphic downloading, or paid for personal information about other individuals. For example, if an information broker sells social security numbers over the Internet, each sale should be identifiable with a trail to the IP address that requested such information. This is also true for unauthorized movie and music downloads from the Internet sites.

All of these procedures provide information about the electronic trail individuals followed as they used the Internet. Although tracing the perpetrator's sequence of net surfing is not the same as obtaining a traditional paper trail of invoices, bank reconcilations, and purchase orders, there *is* a paper trail in the sense of reading the log records. This trail may also be harder for a criminal to distort than with a traditional paper trail. If this Internet activity is done on a company's workplace PC or a company laptop assigned to an employee, then any logged information is available for scrutiny by the forensic accountant in most cases without the employee's permission. If the logs are on a computer outside the company's control, then the logged information is going to be impossible, or at least much more difficult, to obtain without a subpoena for the computer's internal logs.

Identification Through Wire Transfers

Modern financial systems allow for electronic transfer of funds using PCs. Traditional wire transfers go through the Clearing House for Interbank Payments System (CHIPS), Society for Worldwide Interbank Financial Telecommunication (SWIFT), or Fedwire. These transfers are made over the Internet using IP protocols. Thus, they are subject to the same scrutiny of logged web activities as previously described. All these organizations accept cash or negotiable instruments and make wire transfers of these funds to various recipients. The threshold for filing reports (CTRs) on these transactions under the Bank Secrecy Act is $10,000. Thus, criminal activity taking place through wire transfers can go unreported as long as the transfer amount is less than $10,000, but banks become suspicious when a large number of wire transfers are made to unrelated third parties. Wire transfers occur between U.S. banks and their correspondent banks.

Underground Banking Systems Are Off the Grid

Underground banking systems work with two agents located in two geographical locations (for example, the United States and Colombia). If money needs to be used in Colombia, the agent in the United States collects the money and sends a fax or encrypted e-mail to the agent in Colombia. The money is made available from funds held by the coconspirator in Colombia based on that communication. The system is sometimes called "hawala" and can involve more than two co-conspirators as untraceable monies are transferred around the world.

When the money is needed in the reverse order, the agent in the United States makes it available from funds already held by the U.S. agent. The two agents make bookkeeping entries debiting and crediting their reciprocal accounts or simply use chits as records, and periodically the accounts are reconciled through occasional transfers. These transfers of money do not generate the normal paper trail found in normal banking wire or electronic fund transfers, which makes them more difficult to trace. Eventually, accounts may need to be reconciled between the underground bankers and at that time, a trail may possibly exist. Yet another aspect of the system making it hard to trace is that the balances between the agents could be settled with goods or services. This form of "banking" is expected to grow in the future as legitimate banks continue to expand their due diligence operations.

Identification Through Bank Reports

The mandatory information on a Fedwire transfer includes:

- The receiving bank's nine-digit American Bankers Association (ABA) number
- Type/subtype classification: regular transfer
- The sending bank's nine-digit ABA number
- The dollar amount of the transfer
- Name of the originator of the transfer

The Fedwire system is operated by Federal Reserve Banks for the international transfer of large deposits among its members. Wire transfer rules provide more information about the origin and destination of money in a wire transfer. These rules are intended to provide a trail of the parties involved in a wire transfer. A bank sending a wire transfer should include more information than just the account number to the recipient bank. Only a well-placed public official or criminal would try to use Fedwire to launder money. The U.S. Treasury and the Federal Reserve Board have directives in place that require transmittal information be retained by banks about wire transfers. Yet, these rules have not always been useful in preventing wire transfers from being used to launder funds and these rules are under revision. Currently, technology is being adopted to identify correlations among SARs, CTRs, and Currency and Monetary Instrument Reports (CMIRs) filed with the Treasury and the Fedwire forms are being reformatted to incorporate those changes. These software tools are one method to help pinpoint which organizations repeatedly trigger these reports.

Electronic Fund Transfers

Just as logging occurs within PCs on the Internet, so too logs can be kept when electronic fund transfers (EFTs) are made. The origination of EFTs differs slightly from wire transfers. EFTs are made directly by a business using the PCs within that business to another organization, such as a bank, and prior authorization may be needed for the transfer. EFTs occur when salaries and wages are directly deposited into an employee's bank account, for example. Also, EFTs occur when withdrawals are made through an ATM, home banking deductions occur, or cash balances are changed on smart cards. When employees are paid with smart cards through electronic fund transfers, they can withdraw their salary from any ATM.

When an EFT is made, an electronic funds transfer file is created, and thus an audit trail of the transaction is available.

RETENTION OR TRANSMISSION OF EFT FILES. With FedComp software, credit unions' transaction files are stored in the PC's working directory. In addition, files contained in a directory called (in most cases) *shdraft* record the unfiltered or "raw" data files that come directly from the processor. Even if the posting files in the working directory are deleted, there is still a copy of the same data in its "raw" form. This dual system allows for compliance with regulations concerning the retention or transmission of EFT files.

Depending on the logging system, the following information can be retained:
- Generation data about the EFT file used to transfer the funds,
- Date and time information,
- Changes to the database containing EFT data,
- A type of log entry,
- Record of EFT user IDs,
- Details about the EFT transmission to the other financial institution, and
- Transaction summary.

Again depending on the system, the log could appear as follows:
- Description
- Length of the log entry
- Type of log activity
- Controller ID
- Transaction Number
- Date and Time
- Operator ID
- Servicer ID
- Day of settlement
- Response action code
- Response reference/approval number

With both wire transfers and EFTs, there is a great deal of information logged about these transactions. EFTs and wire transfers are monitored using rules-based analysis software, such as Nice Actimizer (http://www.niceactimize.com/index.aspx?page=news624) to build a profile of unusual business transactions involving transfer-related checks or even in complex interest rate swaps. With Nice Actimizer each transaction, such as a payment, transfer, or SARs Report, is individually analyzed and compared against the expected "normal" or peer group behavior. The purpose of the analysis is to detect patterns among account relationships and the flows among these accounts that may be an indication of money laundering or fraud. Algorithms and statistics are used to generate risk scores and alerts for further review. Timelines of the suspect activities are automatically generated. The system can check over 15 million transactions per day.

A single wire transfer may pass through several banks, and the money involved may be held in suspense accounts and commingled with other banks funds before it is transferred to its final destination. A *suspense account* is a temporary ledger account that can be used to "store" dollar amounts until the organization decides how to record the transaction. The balance in the account is closed prior to preparing the financial statements and its use is never disclosed.

As the money transfer continues from one financial institution to another, certain information about the sender and receiver of the wire transfer may not appear on the final document. Nondisclosure of this information may be a deliberate action by a bank to keep certain information confidential under the banking secrecy laws of that jurisdiction.

In the past, money transfer activities could be so blatantly obvious as to have a series of individuals enter the same money transmittal service and send the same dollar amount of money with an international wire transfer to the same account in the same foreign country during less than a one-hour period. Any legitimate business should have suspicions about such activities. In more recent cases, laundering activities may be more complicated and harder to detect.

EXAMPLE

EXAMPLE 7.10 Want to make wire transfers for $100 million? Or more? Private banking can provide a means for laundering funds into the banking system. Private banking exists for wealthy clients. For these clients, a host of VIP banking services is provided. Prior to accepting a private banking client, bank officials need to apply due diligence standards regarding the client and the client's business. Due diligence procedures ensure that the bank officials know their client, and they are familiar with the client's normal business operations. Due diligence standards were not adequately followed in this instance.

Raul Salinas, brother of the former president of Mexico, initially established a private banking relationship with Citibank through the referral of an existing private bank customer who was an agriculture minister in Mexico. Once this banking relationship was created, Salinas was able to transfer more than $100 million out of Mexico (where he was accused of murder and providing protection to drug lords). Citibank locations in New York City and Mexico were involved in sending and receiving the wire transfers. Money was withdrawn from five banks in Mexico. The money was already in the banking system in Mexico, and the objective of the money laundering operation was to remove the money from Mexican banks while making its trail untraceable. Using an alias, Salinas's wife, Paulina, hand carried checks to Citibank's Mexico City offices. These funds were wire transferred from Citibank's Mexico office to Salinas's private banker in Citibank's New York offices. In New York, all transferred funds were put into a concentration account. (A *concentration account* is a suspense account that banks use to temporarily commingle their funds until they are transferred out or otherwise assigned.) This practice leads to tracing problems in associating client's names with account numbers and account activity.

Once the monies had been commingled with other funds, they were later transferred to the Trocca shell company's bank accounts in the Cayman Islands. The board of Trocca was composed of three other shell companies established in the Cayman Islands. All these shell companies were set up by Citbank, which maintains dormant investment companies for assignment to clients.

Finally, the money was sent from the Cayman Islands to accounts in Switzerland and London where it was invested in stocks and bonds. Initial investigations would not reveal the paper trail of the money transfers. In fact, the paper trail was only explainable by someone who was involved in making the transactions. After Raul Salinas was arrested in Mexico in 1995, an investigation was launched into these transactions, which eventually led to Raul Salinas serving a 27-year jail term. Investigators estimated that approximately $120 to $250 million went through these offshore accounts.[10]

Guarding Against Money Laundering

Today every business has to be careful not to become unintentionally involved in money laundering operations. A number of steps should be taken when a bank establishes a relationship with a new client, especially when private banking is involved. But, even though these policies are particularly important for a bank, they also are important for a business that is considering accepting an investment from another company or group of individuals. Without good advice from its professional accountant or accounting firm, a business can find that it is being used as a money laundering operation.

¶ 7101   INDIVIDUAL DUE DILIGENCE USING IDENTITY CHECKS

Becoming familiar with the background of a new client or investment partner is important. The first step in this process is the verification of his or her identity. If third parties are acting for underlying beneficiaries, the identity verification process also applies to the third party and the underlying parties.

Identity verification includes photo IDs, such as passports or drivers' licenses, sending correspondence to the address on the ID, and the address being used for documents established in the new business relationship, referrals from other businesses, and confirmation of identity by legitimate banks. Documents used for verification should be original documents and not photocopies.

Business Associations

Money launderers may be interested in purchasing or obtaining a partnership in a legitimate business to show that their funds come from legal sources. When an individual is opening a bank account or is being considered as a new business partner, identity confirmations should involve credit checks, phone directory checks, possibly requesting a utility bill from listed addresses, verifying driver's licenses, checks of Internet records such as property records listed for the given address, and introductions from trusted individuals. Many documents can be easily forged, so crosschecks are made on documents against public records that are easily available on the Internet, such as performing reverse phone number searches (*http://www.reversephonedirectory.com* or *http://www.whitepages.com/reverse_phone*). Independently obtaining a phone number is one means of checking the authenticity of the number. For state property records, see *http://publicrecords.netronline.com*. Additional public records are available at *http://www.brbpub.com/free-public-records/* and social security numbers at *http://www.docusearch.com*.

Employment

Salary details as recorded on a pay stub can be used to help verify identities. Information should verify the person's name; date and place of birth; nationality; occupation and employer's name; permanent address; telephone, fax, and mobile phone numbers; passport details; and signature and confirming details from a collaborating financial institution where personal bank accounts are maintained.

Social Media and Due Diligence

There is an explosion in the amount of information that is available about individuals on social media websites such as Twitter, Facebook, and LinkedIn. Such sources can provide due diligence information about potential businesses and individuals that was not previously available. These sources need to be considered as part of any due diligence investigation. Such investigations are not related to the hiring of employee, rather they are related to the merger of a business with another group or individual.

Facebook will be considered here, but similar approaches can be used with Twitter or LinkedIn. The purpose of performing a search of a business or personal Facebook page is to be able to study the links and comments that other people have made on that page. The next step is to learn more about the people and associates making comments. Where is their geographical location for example? What kinds of comments are being made? All the information may be harmless, but if the comments are coming from people located in a country noted for money laundering, it may raise the suspicions of the forensic accountant as to the advisability of forming a partnership with these groups or individuals.

The downloading of information of a number of linked Facebook pages can be a time consuming process. Fortunately, Belkasoft has developed a free automated utility which will quickly download public information from Facebook profiles (http://forensic.belkasoft.com/en/facebook_profile_saver). It does not capture private, hidden, or protected information. It is called Facebook Profile Saver (FPS). FPS downloads publicly available photo albums and their accompanying comments. It shows the names of the individuals who made those comments with links to their public pages. The utility will download the text and images in wall contents. If it is necessary to login to Facebook prior to downloading the data, the software provides for that step. The software helps the investigator to develop a series of linked relationships among Facebook users. Investigation of social media is a valuable step in due diligence practices.

¶ 7111 COMPANY DUE DILIGENCE IN VERIFICATION PROCEDURES

Corporate Ownership and Governance

Networks of shell companies can be fronts for money laundering, so investigators must verify the legal existence of a company and ascertain that the company has a true economic purpose. It is necessary to verify that the person acting on behalf of a company is really authorized to be an agent of the company and, if not, identify the true identity of the parties who have ultimate control over the business. If these parties cannot be found , a red flag should be raised. The nature of the business and intercompany relationships should be clearly understood. For this reason, information such as the names of customers, trading partners, or suppliers may be needed. If a banking relationship is being established, a normal profile of the business's operations should be developed and later monitored for unusual activity.

Normal due diligence procedures for a company includes determining whether the company is listed on a registered stock exchange or is the subsidiary of a listed company. Any company insurance documents, board meeting minutes, organiza-tional charts, employee agreements, supplier and vendor lists, customer lists, and special company licenses or permits should be reviewed. Copies of its directors' names and any owners with more than a 10-percent interest in the company should be obtained, along with confirming evidence about the identity of at least two of its directors. There should be checks with investment regulators in the company's country of incorporation for violations; confirmations of its branch office locations; checks with the company's correspondent bank about its activities; and a review of any business license or authorization to conduct business and the company's audited financial statements and tax returns. If a new bank account is opened, the identity of any authorized signatories on the account that are different from those individuals already identified as company officials should be verified.

Bearer Shares

Some legal jurisdictions allow for the formation of a company with "bearer" shares. Essentially, the bearer (i.e., custodian) of the shares is the recognized owner. The underlying ownership of the shares is not identified with the true owner's name. If a business is developing a partnership with a company that has been formed with bearer shares, additional precautions should be taken. The shares may be used to hide the identity of the owners of the company. The potential business partner using these shares for collateral on the investment may have operations spread around the world with minimum or nonexistent legal requirements for business formation. Once a business relationship is established, the shares are transferred to the real owners of the company. At that time, the real owners may be discovered to be money launderers who have just found a way to legitimize their ill-gotten cash in new businesses.

¶ 7121   TRUST DUE DILIGENCE USING TRUST DEEDS

Trusts also are used as a money laundering tool. A *trust* is generally a legal relationship that is established by one person when assets have been placed under the control of another person for the benefit of the beneficiary. Typical arrangements form family trusts, pension trusts, and charitable trusts.

Trusts provide an easy means for criminals to remain unidentified while retaining control of the trust's assets. Therefore, the forensic accountant must be suspicious if the person establishing the trust and the trust beneficiary are not related in any apparent manner. Usually, a trust is used in a money laundering scheme after the money has already been put into the banking system. If a trust is established in one of the countries that are typically used to set up shell companies and are known to be used by money launderers, additional procedures need to be taken to ensure the authenticity of the trust. The purpose of such trusts may be another way to disperse funds from the trust to the launderers.

Trust Deed

Due diligence procedures include obtaining copies of the original trust deed and any subsidiary trust deed regarding the appointment of the trustees. Confirming identities is important because the trustee may be yet another trust, and the beneficiaries also may be trusts. If the beneficiaries are only identified as a general category, information is still needed about the identity of the beneficial owner of the funds, who is providing the funds, and the name of any person who has the power to remove trustees. Information should be obtained about the nature and purpose of the trust. If a "flee clause" is included in a deed of trust, such a clause provides for the automatic transfer of the trust to another legal jurisdiction if the trust comes under investigation.

Beneficiaries

Letters of confirmation should be obtained from the trustee to prove that the trustee is aware of the true identity of the underlying beneficiaries in the trust and that there are no anonymous principals in the trust. As much as possible, such information should be independently confirmed. When monies are received on behalf of a trust, the source of the funds should be identifiable.

Most of these verifications described up to this point are related to business dealings that are initiated in a face-to-face relationship. Today, many business transactions can occur over the Internet. In these cases, the processing may need to be slowed down to enable adequate verifications. The verifications for Internet transactions need to be performed in the same manner as for traditional business operations.

¶ 7131   ORGANIZATION-WIDE SUSPICIOUS ACTIVITIES

A number of suspicious transactions are performed by individuals, corporations, or trusts that raise red flags identified with money laundering. Although one factor in itself does not indicate that money laundering is occurring, a combination of these factors should be considered suspicious. Examples of these red flags are:

- An individual for whom verification of identity is unusually difficult
- A corporate client that has long delays in providing copies of accounts or documents of incorporation
- Clients with distant overseas addresses who have no underlying reason for using the services or purchasing a business interest in the local area
- Unnecessary use of a third-party intermediary in the transaction
- Transaction settlement with cash or proceeds received from a number of different accounts
- Transfers of investments from/to unrelated third parties
- Payments with money transfer where there are variations in the account holder and the customer
- Payments to unconnected third parties

- Identification of sales invoices that are above the known value of goods
- Continually selling goods at a loss without concern
- Payments in several currencies
- Unnecessary use of agents
- Subsidiaries with no apparent business purpose
- Interest premiums on investments paid to persons other than the recorded creditor
- Unexplained wire transfers
- Receipt of large amounts of low-denomination currency
- Large number of bank deposits or payments to a business, all under $10,000
- Payments in traveler's checks or wire transfers from overseas
- Proceeds raised from loans against assets held by third parties where the origin of the assets are unknown
- Transactions with offshore banks and shell companies
- Loan proceeds quickly sent overseas
- Company directors who never meet
- Commingling of cash in suspense accounts
- Questionable breaks in paper trails
- Company dividends paid to persons other than the shareholders

¶ 7141   THE ACCOUNTANT'S ROLE AS GATEWAY KEEPER

Enough laws to prevent money laundering have been enacted so that if these statutes were going to have a serious impact on deterring laundering, reductions in this criminal activity would have occurred by now. Unfortunately, the techniques of money laundering change so rapidly that these laws are ineffective and their enforcement—especially at the financial system entry points—has not been enthusiastically carried out. Generally, antimoney laundering laws have focused their attention at the gateway where the illegal money enters the financial system (i.e., largely banks).

SPOTLIGHT

PROTECTING THE INTERESTS OF THIRD PARTIES. Some writers suggest that responsibility should be extended to accountants as protectors of the interests of third parties.[11] PricewaterhouseCoopers found money laundering occurring in The Bank of Credit and Commerce International, which was the seventh largest bank in the world, and following events eventually led to the seizure of the bank by regulators.[12]

The methods used in money laundering transactions to avoid exceeding legal monetary limits may not be as visible to individual banks receiving those deposits as they would to the company accountant or auditor who observes the network of transactions. In the United States, no confidential accountant–client privilege exists in the courts similar to the attorney–client relationship, and auditors have an overriding duty to the public above those of their client's interests. Therefore, the disclosure of illegal activities such as money laundering is considered by the courts to be a superseding obligation.

In Europe, the Financial Action Task Force, Groupe d'action financiere, called for auditors to develop a risk assessment model for money laundering. It was suggested that the model be used for certain clients for whom they were providing auditing services. The report provided general guidelines as to the nature of those risk assessments.

An effective risk-based approach will allow accountants to exercise reason-able business and professional judgement with respect to clients. Application of a reasoned and well-articulated risk-based approach will justify the judgements made with regard to managing potential money laundering and terrorist financing risks. A risk-based approach should not be designed to prohibit accountants from continuing with legitimate business or from finding innovative ways to diversify their business.[13]

AICPA Auditing Standards Governing Money Laundering

Currently, U.S. auditors have two auditing standards that provide some guidance with money laundering activities. These standards relate to the overall effects on the entity's financial statements. Guidelines are provided in AICPA's Statement on Auditing Standards (SAS) No. 54, *Illegal Acts by Clients,* and Statement on Auditing Standards (SAS) No. 99, *Consideration of Fraud in a Financial Statement Audit.* SAS 54 requires auditors to be aware of illegal acts, such as money laundering that may have occurred and affected the financial statement reports. In addition, if these acts have a "material" effect on the entity's financial statements, an auditor must apply additional auditing procedures. In many cases, however, money laundering activities will not materially affect the organization's financial reports. It is not necessary for the auditor to actively search for money laundering activities.

SAS No. 99 went into full effect during 2003. Under this new SAS, the rules for investigation are expanded. An auditor must identify the risks of material misstatement in a company's financial reports and must write up the results of the analysis. Additionally, audit teams must continue to "brainstorm" during the audit to identify ways in which fraud could be committed in the audit client's organization. Inquiry levels under SAS No. 99 also have been expanded as well as perspectives on accounting reporting. As such, the number of people questioned will be expanded and the accounting methods used by management are to be viewed from a more long-term and comparative perspective. In January 2007, the Public Company Accounting Oversight Board issued Release No. 2007-01. The Release re-emphasized the need for proper practices to be followed by auditors as they assess the risk of fraudulent practices during an audit engagement, and described those practices that are not currently up to that standard. Today none of the SASs directly deal with those typical suspicious business activities that would be expected to alert accountants to possible money laundering, such as:

- Continual changes in internal accounting staff,
- "Accidental" destruction of documents such as invoices,
- The use of unnumbered invoices,
- Making out a large number of checks to "cash,"
- Cancelled checks with second or third party endorsements, especially payroll checks,
- The selling of assets but keeping them in the facility,
- Selling assets for excessive or discounted prices,
- Completion of business transactions that have no true economic purpose,
- Ratio of business costs to sales significantly different than competitors,
- High level of transactions with off-shore companies,
- Bank accounts being used as pay-through accounts,
- Inventory turnover ratio goes unexplained,
- Differences between the goods listed on an invoice and the goods received in a warehouse,
- Commission payments made without justification or documentation,
- Differences between invoice amounts and amounts paid to suppliers,
- Money received through a third party trust for no business reason,
- No written documentation on loan agreements,
- Loan interest is nonexistent or materiality different from market rates,
- When loan is not repaid, no efforts are made to collect the principal and interest payments,
- Journal entries are made for loan repayments without any cash receipts, or
- Amounts paid to consultants is out of line with the going fee for these services, i.e. accounting, legal, or IT services.

Lack of Reporting Requirement

Accounting firms also may act as intermediaries to provide due diligence verifications. A third party may need to rely on the due diligence procedures provided by an accounting firm in making a business decision. In these situations, if money laundering is identified, it should be reported to the third party and government authorities. Yet there is no requirement that these money laundering activities are to be reported by the organization's auditors if they are immaterial. Without an expansion in auditors' responsibilities beyond current generally accepted auditing standards, there is no requirement for the accounting profession to uncover or report money laundering activities by any U.S. auditor.[14]

The view in the U.S. and Europe are different toward detecting and deterring money laundering. The view in Europe is for the development of a money laundering risk assessment model. In the U.S. the view is more for "tick box" evaluation of a company's antimoney laundering (AML) policies. Although it may appear there is no difference, a risk assessment model goes much further into analyzing a company's risk for money laundering beyond whether specific AML procedures are in place. Increases in client risk assessment would be affected by the geographical regions where a company operates, evaluation of suspicious transaction frequency, prevalence of cash transactions, identification of underlying reasons an accounting firm was chosen to provide services (small sole practitioner), extraordinary auditing fee payments, trading of merchandise for other goods, and confidence percentage associated with client/subsidiary identifications, for example.

¶ 7151   USA PATRIOT ACT OF 2001

In October 2001, the USA Patriot Act (the Act) was signed into law. Although many of the working provisions of the Act are under scrutiny by Congress and have been interpreted through the issuance of Treasury regulations, a number of the original Act's statutes apply to money laundering. These original statutes are found in the section of the Act entitled International Money Laundering Abatement and Financial Anti-Terrorism Act of 2001 (MLAA). MLAA increases the penalties for money laundering as well as extends the power of the Federal government in controlling money laundering activities. The Act requires that bank and nonbank financial institutions have AML policies and programs in place. Nonbank financial institutions include broker/dealers, insurance companies, mutual funds, casinos and card clubs, loan and finance companies, money service business, travel agencies, dealers in precious metals, investment advisors, pawn shops, and operators of credit card systems. Within the provisions of the MLAA are guidelines that allow the U.S. Treasury Department to require U.S. financial organizations to file specific information about transactions occurring in countries identified as primary money laundering havens.

MLAA significantly increases the disclosure requirements for U.S. banks and their correspondent banks. The information required to be disclosed under MLAA includes a complete description of a specified transaction, the identity and address of participants, the relationship of the participants involved in the transaction, and the beneficial owner of the monies involved in the transactions. Specific guidelines are to be followed in verifying identities. Note that the term *account* can be broadened to include more than just a checking or savings account under MLAA statutes. In general, the bar that government agencies must meet for requests of private information under MLAA has been lowered. In fact, confidential requests for complete files on individuals from consumer reporting agencies only requires a certificate signed by a supervisory official at a federal agency.

Payable-Through Accounts

Use of payable-through accounts, correspondent accounts, and concentration accounts are specifically mentioned in the Act. Payable-through checking or pass-through accounts have been in use for a number of years. These accounts allow U.S. banks to provide check writing privileges in the United States to foreign banks and their customers. This practice allows non-U.S citizens, who have not been scrutinized as well as U.S. citizens, to use the U.S. banking system.

With payable-through accounts, complete disclosure of the names of each customer with these privileges now can be required based on Treasury Department needs. With correspondent banking accounts, the Treasury has the power to require domestic banks to shut down any accounts with countries that are deemed to be a money laundering risk. In addition, the identities of the customers using these accounts need to be disclosed along with additional information typical of that required of customers who have noncorrespondent bank accounts.

MLAA gives the Treasury the power to ensure that procedures are in place that document all transactions in a concentration account, where funds are commingled, so that the identity and the specific deposits belonging to each customer are identified.

Enhancements and Restrictions Under MLAA

MLAA statutes require that due diligence be used to enhance the scrutiny of funds that are deposited for senior foreign political officials or their immediate family members or close associates as these funds may have been obtained from the proceeds of corrupt activities. In addition, due diligence procedures have been expaned by the U.S. Treasury in regard to private accounts (maintained by non-U.S. citizen with more than a $1M balance) and offshore banking activities. Shell banks with no physical presence in any country are prohibited from using correspondent banking services in the United States under MLAA. This change is not going to cause shell banks to disappear.

MLAA eliminates legal liabilities so that financial institutions can share information about account activities and business transactions among themselves. The new law specifically does away with notifications to the parties about whom the banks are collecting information. The jurisdiction of the Act applies to foreign persons and foreign institutions in the United States.

Reporting Requirements Under MLAA

In a break from the past, the statutes in MLAA provide for steps to "encourage" foreign governments to require the name of the originator of a wire transfer be documented from its origin to its point of fund disbursement.

Securities brokers and dealers as well as futures commission merchants, commodity trading advisors, and commodity pool operators will have to meet suspicious activity reporting requirements under the Act. In addition, all underground banking systems are required to keep all records maintained by other financial institutions currently under the Federal Deposit Insurance Act authority. Of course, that is unlikely to happen with the underground banks.

MLAA is so broad that it touches most of the practices of money laundering in its statutes. The passage of the USA Patriot Act will make it more difficult for money launderers to operate. But, if the past is any indication, as soon as better controls are exercised over one technique or procedure, the money launderer quickly shifts to other methods. In addition, the slow pace of enforcement allows laundered funds to move out of the reach of law enforcement officials. For example, in 2004 after six years of investigation, the Riggs Bank in Washington, D.C. was fined for its weak anti-money laundering policies that allowed money to be laundered through the bank from Chile and Equatorial Guinea. Those weak procedures included accepting for deposit bags of cash.

¶ 7161   CONCLUSION

The objective of all money laundering methods is to make a questionable source of money untraceable to its source and then legally spendable. Many of these methods are directed at placing monies into the banking system. Once illegal money is in the banking system, the cash is difficult to trace.

Money laundering is a transnational crime that can potentially corrupt financial systems around the world with bribes and payoffs. When money laundering is used to convert illegal proceeds into spendable resources, these activities should be considered a serious crime by all jurisdictions. If laundering techniques are adopted within a legal context to remove government restrictions from funds, for example, they should be considered a violation of organizational ethical codes.

The USA Patriot Act of 2001 was intended to deter and close loopholes in financial procedures related to correspondent banking, wire transfers, and identity verification that allows money launderers to operate. As these Treasury regulations are used to strengthen the provisions of the law, they will determine whether the Act is effective in curtailing money laundering. Yet in some cases where oppressed groups of people are fleeing for their lives from their countries' leaders, the use of money laundering techniques may be the only available method these people have of bringing their resources with them.

ENDNOTES

1   O. Nash, "Hymn to the Thing That Makes the Wolf Go," January 1934 in FAMILIAR QUOTATIONS, John Bartlett, 14th ed., edited by E.M. Beck, Boston: Little Brown and Company, 1968.

2   Cheryl Rosen, "Doling Out E-cash," INFORMATIONWEEK 840 (June 4, 2001), p. 79.

3   Due diligence is considered to be a program of reasonable checks to uncover all potential risks related to a particular business decision or action. Such due diligence procedures for banks include reviewing Treasury and public information to determine if a foreign financial institution has any legal or other actions against it related to money laundering. Further due diligence policies require the bank to determine if the financial institution is operating with a banking license from a "non-cooperative" country in regard to prevention of money laundering activity within that country.

4   U.S. Congress, Senate. Committee on Governmental Affairs. Permanent Subcommittee on Investigations. *Report on Correspondent Banking and Money Laundering: A Gateway to Money Laundering.* Report prepared by the Minority Staff, 107th Congress, 1st Session, Washington, D.C.: Government Printing Office, February 2001; p. 4, *http://handy.gslsolutions.com/gov/senate/hsgac/public/_archive/020501_psi_minority_report.htm*).

5   "Virtual world" payment systems were identified as the number two threat, after identity theft, to retail banking as identified by 44 percent of compliance officers surveyed at global, national, and regional financial institutions with assets ranging from $5 billion to $1 trillion ("Financial Crimes Survey," THE FORTENT REPORT, (Winter 2008)).

6   Minority Staff Report (February 5, 2001).

7   Finley, M., Nielson, D., and Sharman, J. 2012. Global Shell Games: Testing Money Launderers' and Terrorist Financi-

ers' Access to Shell Companies. *http://www.griffith.edu.au/business-government/centre-governance-public-policy/research-publications/?a=454625*

8   For Asia, the same information can be found in the Asia Pacific Network Information Centre (APNIC) at (*apnic.net*).

9   See *http://newhax.com/forum/index.php?threads/find-user-ip-on-skype.3070/* to learn how IP address on Skype can be collected with Wireshark. Wireshark is a free network analysis tool.

10 "How Can You Hide $100 Million? Read This," TIME 152 (24) (December 14, 1992), and U.S. General Accounting Office, *Private Banking: Raul Salinas, Citibank, and Alleged Money Laundering* (GAO/OSI-99-1) (October 1998), printed in *Miami Herald* (October 10, 1999).

11 J. Humphries, "Preventing Electronic Funds Transfer Fraud Pays," *Information Security Reading Room,* Sans Institute (April 14, 2001).

12 S. V. Melnik. "The Inadequate Utilization of the Accounting Profession in the United States Government's Fight Against Money Laundering, JOURNAL OF LEGISLATION AND PUBLIC POLICY 143 (4) (2000–2001).

13 Financial Action Task Force, Groupe d'action financiere, *RBA Guidance for Accountants, Guidance on the Risk-Based Approach to Combating Money Laundering and Terrorist Financing*, June 2008. par. 28,, p 5.: (Paris, France).

14 Under SEC reporting requirements, auditors are required to file reports about illegal activities uncovered during an audit. The auditor's obligation begins with a report to the company; observation of corrections made by the company; and if no significant corrections are made and the company has not filed the report with the SEC, then the auditor must file a duplicate of the report with the SEC. *See* SEC Financial Reporting Release No. 49, Implementation of Section 10-A of the SEC Act of 1934.

EXERCISES

1. Give a succinct definition of money laundering.

2. What is the primary purpose of someone engaging in money laundering?

3. Explain the two ways a digital exchange work.

4. Can a gain or loss be recognized when dealing with digital currencies?

5. What is an e-Voucher? Explain.

6. On the Internet go to Second Life (secondlife.com) and explain how this online game works.

7. Explain how a college or university might engage in money laundering.

8. Explain how money laundering might be used in a bribe situation.

9. Explain how money laundering might be used in a tax evasion scheme.

10. What is correspondent banking?

11. When must a bank file a Currency Transaction Repots (CTRs).

12. When must a business file Form 8300?

13. What is the penalty for the failure to file a Form 8300?

14. Are wire transfers considered to be cash under the Form 8300 reporting guidelines? Are nonprofit organizations exempted from Form 8300 Reporting requirements?

15. What is a shell bank? What locations are conductive to shell banking?

16. Explain how money launderers can use casino gambling.

17. Assume that you work for Able, Bold, and Cowing as an auditor, and you are auditing Texas Pizza, a chain located in and around Brownsville, Texas. Explain how important you think it is to account for the exact origin of the large percentage of cash revenues your client receives.

18. Explain the statement: Banks are part of the solution and part of the problem when it comes to money laundering.

19. Log into the FBI wesite (fbi.gov) and find a case dealing with money laundering. Copy the case description. Describe the placement, layering, and integration activities that are occurring in the case.

20. What does it mean if a bank is described as a "virtual" bank?

21. A large cash donation has been made to Howard Tech University from a non-U.S. citizen whose son graduated from Howard Tech. Before accepting the donation, what should the university have investigated about the source of these funds?

22. Name some techniques that can be used by money launderers to break the audit trail.

23. Discuss the conflict between the need for personal privacy and confidentiality in banking transactions and the need for the government to curtail money laundering activities.

24. Why is money laundering considered a serious criminal activity if it only involves the transfer of money from one location to another?

25. Go to the PayPal website and determine the requirements for setting up a PayPal account. Do you think PayPal could be useful to a money launderer?

26. Find an IP address that you use. Go to a traceroute service and trace the IP address. Print out all the information that is provided by the service. Bring the printed description to class with you.

27. **Almost Over the Line?** The accounting firm of Glofry and Tammar (G&T) has been asked to arrange for a $2 million loan for Tang Enterprises by its client Ted Hoover at Hoover Company. Hoover Company is involved in a number of different business operations and has a net worth of $20 million. A senior partner at G&T instructed Henry Morgan, a G&T accountant, to make sure that the loan was secured by collateral. Tang forwarded ownership shares from a foreign company as collateral for the loan. Upon investigation, it was determined that these shares were worthless. Tang Enterprises then sent prime bank guarantees that—had a fair value of $5 million. Upon the receipt of the guarantees, Glofry and Tammar arranged for the transfer of the money to Tang. A month after the money had been transferred to Tang, Ted Hoover asked G&T for a letter to certify the authenticity of the bank guarantees so that they could be sold. What should the accounting firm of Glofry and Tammar do under these circumstances?

28. **Over the Line?** The Wang Consulting Group is headquartered in the United States with subsidiaries in Canada and the Cayman Islands. Proceeds from its Canadian subsidiary are sent directly into its U.S. bank accounts using electronic fund transfers. Fore and Moore, auditors of its U.S. company, noted that several times the transfers were made prior to the date that the services had been rendered by the Canadian subsidiary. The monies in its U.S. headquarters are invested in commodity trades and, once completed, the trades' proceeds are transferred to the Cayman Islands subsidiary. The U.S. company recognizes Deferred Trading Assets on its books related to the transfers and these deferred assets are supported by contracts with its Cayman Islands subsidiary. Harry Morgan has recently been put in charge of the Wang audit, and he thinks these cash transfers are of a questionable legal nature. When he approached Frank Bobbister, a senior partner at the accounting firm handling the audit, Frank told him that the auditors' main concern is with the year-end figures unless one of the financial transactions threatens the viability of the company. He closes his discussion with Harry by telling him to "forget about it." Are the activities of Wang Consulting so suspicious that they should be reported to authorities and which authorities?

Should Harry collect any additional information before making a final decision?

29. **Leases.** Betty Gosh runs ByGosh Realtors in Seattle, Washington. The company is a multi-million dollar agency, and the realty company has been in business for twenty years. Besides selling real estate, the company provides a rental management service for landlords' apartments and commercial properties. All properties that are for sale and for rent are listed on ByGosh's website. The terms of the rental contract follow the requirements of the city statutes that require a two-day cooling off period whereby the lessee may cancel the rental contract. The refund can be made with a check or as a credit to the card used to make the original payment. At the time of cancellation, there is a five-percent penalty.

It is normal for Betty to request a credit check on any renter and this is the procedure followed with all accounts. The rental contract is not consummated until payment is received. Many of the payments are made over the Internet with a credit card after the lessee has requested a rental property. Betty's accountant, Mary Stans, prepared a report showing that the number of cancellations on rental properties with one-year advanced payments has increased by more than 100 percent in the last year, and the vast majority of cancelled accounts have requested a check rather than a credit to their card. This has resulted in the collection of substantial revenue in penalty fees for ByGosh.

Betty is worried about this unusual trend in cancellations, and she casually discussed it with a friend who happened to be a member of the local police force. Betty's friend joked, "It sounds like money laundering to me." Mary checked and all the credit card numbers are different.

How could it be determined whether the Internet payments are the basis for a money laundering scheme?

30. **Correspondent Banking.** Harold Macronic is a businessman in Zurich. He has three companies under his control. Select Gems (SJ) is a registered company in France run by his cousin Thomas. SJ was purchased by Harold 10 years ago. Prior to the purchase, SJ had been in the wholesale jewelry business for 35 years. Moran Gold is a company run by Richard Macronic, Harold's brother, and it is registered in the Czech Republic. The company is inactive at the present time. The third company TDH, Inc., is a shell company in the Cayman Islands with Harold and Richard as the sole members of the board.

SJ has had a correspondent account with Citibank in Los Angeles for 15 years. In the past, its sales to private customers in the L.A. area accounted for a substantial portion of its business. Cash and checks are directly deposited into the Citibank correspondent account in L.A. During the last 10 years, money deposited into the correspondent account has increased by 100 percent over in each five-year period.

The money deposited in the account is transferred into bank accounts controlled by Moran Gold in the Czech Republic and by TDH, Inc. in the Cayman Islands. Electronic fund transfers, not wire transfers, are used to move money out of the companies the bank accounts in the Czech Republic and the Cayman Islands to other locations.

How could it be determined whether the cash transfers are the basis for a money laundering scheme?

31. **Please Donate to My Favorite Charity.** UARB is a charity based in the United States. Its mission statement states that UARB's goal is "to help the poor, sick and oppressed people of the world reach their individualized goals of achievement." UARB has been very successful in obtaining donations from its American nationals who have recently moved to the United States. Millions of dollars have flowed into UARB's U.S. bank accounts from these donations. None of the money collected from these donations is from illegal sources. Once the donations are collected, they are sent to a Nauru bank account and from this bank account checks, money orders, and wire transfers are sent to numerous bank accounts in Europe and Asia.

What is the weakest point in this network on which forensic investigators should concentrate their efforts for determining whether money laundering is occurring?

32. **My Keylogger.** Go to the website download.com and pick a keylogger to download. Two examples are: (1) Free Keylogger or (2)

Actual Keylogger. In order to put keylogging software on your PC you may have to override your antivirus software warnings and you must have administrative rights on your PC.

Once the software is installed, write a short report describing the characteristics of the software, how it would be useful in an accounting situation, and its effectiveness in logging information.

33. **What's the Balance in My Credit Card Account?** Cavos Metdolas is a money laundering organization for a drug cartel in Wisconsin and Illinois. A money laundering method that Cavos Metdolas has been using is to prepay, from an Internet bank account, balances on credit cards controlled by the organization. Visa and MasterCard will send refund checks back to the credit card holder when the positive balances remain unused. The card owners have addresses that are listed in Argentina, Colombia, and the United States. Once these checks are received from the credit card companies, they are deposited into legitimized accounts.

Cavos Metdolas has been using up to 1,000 credit cards in this scheme. There are only 30 different "real" card owners. Cavos Metdolas has a private banking relationship with First Bank of Boston through its Brazilian shell company, Perzola. Staff are able to write checks from the Perzola account within U.S. borders using their shell company's correspondent account at First Bank of Boston.

What would be the weakest point in this money laundering scheme?

34. **International Inc.** In the western provinces of Canada, the Mock-Lee drug ring owns a series of Dollar Stores in 10 medium-sized towns. It uses these stores to launder the money it collects from drug sales. The stores are operated by coconspirators of the drug ring. Each of the stores has separate accounts in different banks, whenever possible. Although a deposit into an account will occasionally be over the threshold reporting limit, the vast majority of cash deposits are under the threshold.

Merchandise sold in the stores is imported from another coconspirator, China Merchandising, operating in a free-trade zone in Singapore. Dollar Stores purchases all its retail merchandise from China Merchandising or other related dummy corporations in the free-trade zone. Wire transfers are made to China Merchandising and its dummy corporations from the 10 different Dollar Stores based on doctored invoices for dollar amounts that are above the true value of the goods. China Merchandising operates completely within the free-trade zone after its merchandise shipments are received from its Chinese vendors. Its bank accounts are in the free trade zone, and the rules of the zone allow the bank to operate under expanded client confidentiality guidelines. Drug shipments to the Mock-Lee organization are separately routed to Canada by drug producers in Thailand. Once the drug shipments have arrived safely in Canada from Thailand, payments are made from the various bank accounts in the free-trade zone to designated accounts of dummy corporations in Thailand or to couriers coming into the free-trade zone to collect cash.

What is the weakest point in this network that Canadian forensic investigators should concentrate their efforts on for investigating the money laundering scheme?

35. **Print Me Up Some Money.** Michael Bloom is an executive manager in a federal contract review office in the District of Columbia. He has final review and authorization authority over reconstruction contract bids in the southeast region of Afghanistan. Bloom has agreed to take a bribe of $500,000 to make certain that Alburton Construction receives the contract for building new schools in the region. This government contract involves multimillions of dollars in expenditures.

In anticipation of the bribe, Bloom has set up a new company called Island Printing LLC, a shell company, along with a company bank account. He is the sole owner of Island Printing, which is registered on the island of Nauru. Bloom owns shares in Z-Print LLC, a small printing company registered in the District of Columbia. He has operated the printing company along with his father-in-law for a number of years. Bloom has checked the operating agreement for Z-Print, and there are no restrictions that would prevent him from selling his shares in Z-Print to an outsider in a non-public offering of these company shares.

Alburton gets the Afghanistan contract, and Bloom tells Alburton to invoice Island Printing for $500,000 in printing services and deposit the money in Island Printing's bank account in Nauru. From there, Bloom uses the money to buy out his shares in Z-Print. The purchase price is $500,000. Bloom's father-in-law says he will go along with the deal for $50,000. The $50,000 is recorded as an increase in his salary. The sale documents are signed, and the money is moved from Island Printing to Bloom's personal bank account in two transfer payments of $250,000 each over a four-month period. Although he knows the deposits will require the bank to report the transactions, he believes the sale documents will deflect any questions that may be asked.

Describe the placement, layering, and integration activities that are occurring in this case.

36. **Internet Exercise**: Using Internet Explorer, visit at least two websites and then go to the following website *http://network-tools.com* to determine the information that can be collected about your web surfing activities. List the information that was collected about you. List the one piece of information that would be most useful for a forensic accountant to collect about you in trying to determine if you are laundering money through an Internet bank account.

37. **Pay Me With Virtual Money or Gold?** Your accounting client, Ted Longview, is the CEO of Longview Industries, Inc. Longview Industries sells their engineering products worldwide with a number of salesmen located at various cities throughout the world. Currently, the company has been paying these salesmen's salary and commissions with money transfers into their overseas bank accounts. The cost of fund transfers has been increasing over the years. Mr. Longview has come to you to ask about the risk of using a cash payment system called Pecunix. He tells you that the currencies in the payment system are backed by gold so there is little risk of loss, and the price of gold may increase making it possible to have a gain on the funds. He wants to use Pecunix and debit cards to pay his salesmen. You tell him you will prepare a risk assessment on Pecunix.

Write a formal memo addressed to Mr. Longview and Longview Industries, Inc., outlining any the financial risks of using the Pecunix Payment System. Identify the physical location of the company as well as any other information you develop from Network-Tool.com and other Internet sites.

38. **The Dirty Accountant?** Logan Johnson is a recent graduate of MidUniversity's accounting program. She has begun her work as the accountant for Platinum Automotive run by Joe and Tom Younger. Platinum has a series of car lots where they sell top-end "previous driven" cars in Baltimore, Maryland. On February 6, 2011, Joe Younger sold a 2010 BMW X3, 3.01 SUV for $38,000. Logan entered the following entry into the accounting database for the sale:

Feb. 6, 2011	Cash	9,800	
	Note Receivable	28,200	
	BMW X3		38,000

Logan thought nothing of the sale. On February 10, Joe Younger dropped off documentation that showed $9,900 of the loan had been paid off. Logan booked the proper entries. On February 15 and again on February 20, documentation showed that the loan was being repaid and paid off with payments of $9,500 and $8,800, respectively. Shortly afterward, Logan received an envelope with $250 in cash on her desk. On the front of the envelope, the word "bonus" was written. Logan is happy that her work is being favorably recognized by the owners.

Do you have any advice for Logan?

39. **Sell It to Me.** Oakland Mortgage, Inc. has received funding from the BCCI Bank in Washington, D.C. for a housing development in Maryland's Eastern Shore. When completely finished, the condominium development will consist of 125 units. Appraisals of the property development have supported the price at which the units are being sold. Oakland Mortgage invested and wire transferred $5M as a deposit into the BCCI Bank. The completed project is appraised to be worth $50M. Oakland Mortgage, Inc. will originate the loans to the condo buyers and sell the mortgages to BCCI Bank. The Bank is funding 75 percent of mortgages loans.

All financial payments required by Oakland Mortgage have been met on a timely basis. You, senior accountant at BCCI, recently met Mr. Winky Cohen who is head of Oakland Mortgage. Although the meeting went well, you became suspicious when he mentioned having a house in the Cayman Islands. In order to make a full investigation of the Oakland Mortgage, Inc. what additional actions might you take?

40. **How Big a Bag Do I Need?** On November 8, 2008, within a 30-minute period, dozens of criminal "cashers" in the United States, Hong Kong, and Russia withdrew $9M from approximately 130 ATMs at convenience stores and other locations in 49 cities as they executed a world-wide scam of RBS, World Pay, Inc. (RBS). The cashers are assumed to have made repeated rapid-fire withdrawals using 100 ATM cards, and then walked away with the cash. RSB is the U.S based payment processing branch of the Royal Bank of Scotland. RSB issues payroll cards. Payrolls cards are like debit cards, and they can be used by companies to pay salaries to people who do not have bank accounts, for example. These individuals redeem their salary by withdrawing cash from an ATM. The crime is one of the first times computer hackers altered information inside a company's "accounting" records to commit a financial crime. Hackers usually attack a website to steal proprietary information such as credit card numbers, for example. To commit this crime, cybercriminals made a final penetration of RBS's computer system in Scotland prior to November 8. The purpose of the attack was to obtain unencrypted PIN numbers, eliminate or substantially raise the withdrawal limits on specific payroll cards, and later use this information to counterfeit the magnetic-strip on 100 payroll cards. At the time, when they knew the ATMs would be filled with cash, the cashers attacked the machines. (a) Assume each casher walked away with $70,000 in cash and that the ATM disperses $20 bills only. Also assume that 100 bills are equal to ½ inch. How big a pile of bills would each casher carry? (b) Assume the weight of 10,000 bills is 22 lbs. How much weight would each casher carry? (c) Assume 100 ATMs were robbed in the United States. What is the total weight of the cash accumulated in the United States? (d) How can this stolen cash be laundered into the banking system?

41. **The "Hammer" Gets Hammered.** In 2010, Tom DeLay, former Texas Congressman and U.S. House Majority Leader, was convicted of money laundering and sentenced to a three-year prison term. At the time of this writing, that case is under appeal. During his years in Congress, DeLay was known as the hammer for his political style. Study this money laundering case and flowchart the flow of money. Describe how the money laundering scheme was executed. Why is this called "money laundering"?

42. **Please Give Me the Cash....or Take It?** Mr. Thomas Oversight is the external auditor for I&J Manufacturing. I&J is a small manufacturer of metal trailers, horse trailers, and other tow-behind rigs. In the economic downturn, I&J has been facing cash flow problems. Casey Turnbull is the President of I&J, and he believes the decline in company's sales is only temporary. Recently, Mr. Turnbull was in Orlando attending an annual business conference for U.S. trailer manufacturers. While at the conference, he was introduced to Michael J. Carter. Mr. Carter is a loan originator, and he indicated his business is providing short-term loans to small manufacturers like the company operated by Mr. Turnbull. Casey knows that Mr. Carter has been talking to other businesses about providing financing. Casey thinks Mr. Carter can provide the financing for Casey. Casey's normal lines of credit have not been available during the economic slump, and he is getting desperate to increase his cash flow. Although the loan from Mr. Carter would be at a higher interest rate, the rate is acceptable considering the alternatives. Mr. Carter has asked for a loan origination and upfront fee of $100,000 for a $950,000 loan. Casey has the money, but it would just about use up his entire cash balance. Casey asks Mr. Oversight, his auditor, if he thinks the arrangement is on the "up-and-up"? Mr. Oversight checks to determine where the $100,000 check is to be sent, and he finds the check is going to an ac-

count at the Bank of New York. The Bank of New York is a well-recognized bank in New York City that has been in business for decades. Based on that information and the documents sent to Casey by Mr. Carter, Mr. Oversight recommends that Casey go ahead and sign the loan documents and forward the check to the Bank of New York. Do you believe there are other due diligence measures that should have been taken? If so, list and describe those measures.

43. **Where's My Lawyer?** Mr. Larce Fenning is an estate attorney in Toledo, Ohio. He has represented clients there for over 15 years. One of his clients is Maddy Cole, who is a retired school teacher, has a $3.5 million stock portfolio, and is in poor health. Maddy never married and most of her relatives are dead. Larce encouraged her to write a will. In the will, Maddy left a small inheritance to a distant cousin, who she had not seen in years, with the remainder of her estate going to the World Wildlife Fund and St. Jude's Children Research Hospitals. Larce is the executor of Maddy's estate and has the power of attorney to her accounts.

Larce has been married three times, and he is desperate to pay off gambling debts. He wants Maddy's money after she dies. He knows that he has little risk of being caught if he can get her money out of the United States. If he can, he will leave his fourth wife and move to a remote island in the South Pacific. Advise him how to launder the money into the banking system and send it out of the United States. Draw a flow chart of the cash flows as they are laundered through a series of accounts.

PART 3

COURTROOM PROCEDURES AND LITIGATION SUPPORT

8

LITIGATION SERVICES PROVIDED BY ACCOUNTANTS

You should know the difference between giving an opinion as an expert witness as opposed to giving an opinion in an audit situation. You should be able to prepare exhibits (including charts and schedules, as and if necessary) that are, in addition to factual, easily understandable to nonaccountants. You must be able to objectively analyze other experts' reports, and succinctly, point out to the attorney with whom you are working, the strengths and weaknesses of those reports.

—Kalman A. Barrson[1]

OBJECTIVES

After completing Chapter 8, you should be able to:
1. Learn the standards of conduct for performing litigation services.
2. Understand what it means to be an expert witness.
3. Know how to qualify as an expert witness.
4. Follow the dos and don'ts of testifying at a deposition or trial.
5. Know the circumstances in which expert witnesses can be held liable for their testimony.

OVERVIEW

Accountants may provide consulting services with respect to potential and pending judicial and regulatory proceedings. Accountants may be retained as a consultant, summary witness, expert witness, or master. This chapter explains what standards apply to accountants when they perform litigation services, discusses how to qualify as an expert witness, gives tips for testifying at a deposition or trial, and points out the potential liability that accountants risk when they testify at trial.

There are many ways for an expert witness to be excluded from the courtroom. Both simple and complex *Daubert* and *Frye* challenges are becoming frequent as tort costs climb. Accountants must take the qualification process seriously in order to avoid adversely affecting clients and their personal reputation. Lack of independence, conflicts of interest, side-taking, and result-oriented work are some of the situations to avoid.

Litigation in the United States

¶ 8001   U.S. TORT COSTS CLIMBING

The U.S. tort system cost $248.1 billion in 2009, which was $808 per U.S. citizen ($12 in 1950). U.S. tort costs accounted for 1.74 percent of GDP.[2] An economist, Lawrence J. Mcquillan, puts a much higher $865 billion per year, or $2,457 person.[3] Some of these costs are expert witnessing fees. A cartoon on a legal advertisement by Rose. Walker., LLP shows a lecturer pointing to a power point slide saying "OK, repeat after me," to a room full of lawyers. The slide says bill, bill, bill, settle.

A Justice Department study found that in state courts of general jurisdiction, 33 percent of civil trials were for alleged breach of contract. Judges were significantly more likely than juries to find for the plaintiff over the defendent. Plaintiff won 68 percent of bench trials versus 54 percent of jury trials.[4]

"Cases that might have been expert-free 30 years ago now involve as many as eight experts, four on each side," says Russell Frackman, an intellectual-property lawyer at Mitchell Silberberg & Knupp in Los Angeles. "Even if you don't think the other side's expert will have much influence, you don't want the jury to wonder why you couldn't find another expert to offset him or her."[5]

EYEWITNESS

Executives and directors often have employment contracts and company by-laws to protect or indemnify them against liabilities such as lawsuits. From January 1, 2004, to July 2011, after the government took over Fannie Mae and Freddie Mac, taxpayers have spent more than $466.4 million defending the companies and their former top executives.[6]

Freddie Mac was caught understating its income from 2000 to 2002. Fannie Mae overstated its financial results for six years.

In addition to $466.4 million in taxpayer money, Fannie and Freddie spent millions of dollars defending former executives and directors before the government take-over. Apparently, there is little chance of recouping these legal fees, even though they put their own personal interests ahead of their shareholder's interest.[7]

Along with the major CPA firms, these are some of the dozens of other companies that supply financial analysis for legal disputes (sometimes called corporate investigators):

- CRA International
- FTI Consulting
- Huron Consulting Group
- Kroll, Inc.
- K2 Intelligence
- Navigant Consulting

FTI Consultants is a publicly traded firm with a forensic and litigation services division with revenues of $177 million and a profit margin of 17 percent in 2012. FTI with 3,800 employees did much of the work on the Bernie Madoff fraud.[8]

These corporate investigators are getting a great deal of business as a result of the Foreign Corrupt Practices Act. Multi-nationals must make sure that their employees are not violating anti-bribery laws. The increase in whistleblowing also has created more work, and due diligence work running background checks is a growth area. The recession causes scams to collapse and creates fraud litigation, asset-tracing, and insolvency billable hours.[9]

K2 Intelligence website indicates that they conduct investigative, analytic, due diligence and advisory assignments all over the world. The firm employs a wide range of traditional investigative techniques—often amplified by the application of proprietary technology especially to interrogate large data sets or monitor public sentiment.[10]

Counsel for Omnicom retained Cornerstone Research in a dispute stemming from Omnicom's stock price decline following a 2002 *Wall Street Journal* article. The plaintiffs claimed that the article was a class-period-ending corrective disclosure that revealed allegedly improper accounting for Omnicom's investments in certain interactive advertising companies. The plaintiffs alleged damages in the billions of dollars.[11]

Cornerstone Research supplied three experts, including Professor William Holder of the University of Southern California, for the defendant, Omnicom. Professor Holder reviewed Omnicom's accounting for its investments in interactive advertising companies and concluded that the accounting judgments of Omnicom's management were reasonable. Cornerstone Research also supplied a loss causation expert who examined the role that the article played in Omnicom's stock price decline and an industry expert who discussed typical business practices in venture capital transactions.[12]

The U.S. District Court of Southern New York granted summary judgment in favor of Omnicom, rejecting the claims in their entirety because the plaintiffs had not proven loss causation. The court found that the plaintiffs had failed to "distinguish the alleged fraud from 'the tangle of [other] factors' that affect a stock's price," as required by the Supreme Court's *Dura* ruling.[13]

THE PAID EXPERT. David Teece was born in New Zealand but moved to the United States in the early 1970s. While working on a Ph.D. at the University of Pennsylvania, he worked on a summer project for $3,000 to help fight price-fixing against Exxon. Today he owns 7.3 percent of LECG, currently valued at $17 million. In 1997, when LECG went public, his faculty members were shocked to see that Dr. Teece was earning $700,000 a year as an expert witness. He does not dispute that his career earnings from expert consulting amount to at least $50 million.[14]

In one case testifying for Philip Morris, much of his testimony was as plain spoken as a tenth-grader in a social-studies class. Philip Morris' executives or lawyers could have said the same, but since Professor Teece was a prominent scholar and independent thinker, his remarks carried extra weight. The jurors ruled in favor of Philip Morris.[15]

However, in a 2001 dispute, District Court judge Robert Payne said that Dr. Teece royalty estimates were "a wild guess." The judge remarked that "I have the impression, from what I have read, that Mr. Teece will say just about anything."[16]

¶ 8006   A DISPUTE BEGINS

John Grisham gives two major ways to sue in the civil courts: (1) by ambush, or (2) serve and volley. With an ambush, the attorney prepares a skeletal framework of the allegations, runs to the courthouse, files the suit, leaks it to the press, and hopes he or she can prove what is alleged. A serve and volley begins with a letter to the defendants, making the same allegations, but rather than suing, the attorney invites a discussion. Letters go back and forth trying to reach a compromise so litigation can be avoided.[17]

There are two different courtroom environments: civil and criminal. Some experts believe it is more difficult to convict in a criminal trial. E.J. McMillan says "you have to remember one thing, and this is the fact that our laws aren't designed to punish guilty people; they're intended to protect innocent people."[18] And Clinton McKinzie says "I have never come to terms with a system based on the principle that it is better to let hundreds of guilty people go free rather than wrongly convict one innocent person. It's okay for people to be victimized again and again as long as no one is mistakenly locked up."[19] In a civil trial, however, the jurors try to give away as much money as possible, because it is not their money, and there are no guilty feelings. Plaintiffs generally wish a jury trial. Accountants may be used in both civil and criminal situations.

There is now a so-called "CSI effect" because of the three shows on television. Peoria State's attorney Kevin Lyons says that the shows "project the image that all cases are solvable by highly technical science, and if you offer less than that, it is viewed as reasonable doubt. The burden it places on us is overwhelming."[20] Barbara La Wall, the county prosecutor in Tuscon, Arizona, says that jurors expect criminal cases "to be a lot more interesting and a lot more dynamic. It puzzles the heck out of them when it's not."[21]

Winning in a civil trial may only be a pyrrhic victory because the plaintiff may never receive payment of any judgment. For example, O.J. Simpson never paid the $474 million judgment against him. Also, Robert Blake had a $30 million civil judgment against him, but he declared bankruptcy.

EYEWITNESS

A disappointed jury can be a dangerous thing. Just ask Jodi Hoos. Prosecuting a gang member in Peoria, Illinois for raping a teenager in a local park, Hoos told the jury, "You've all seen CSI. Well, this is your CSI moment. We have DNA." Specifically, investigators had matched saliva on the victim's breast to the defendant, who had denied touching her. The jury also had gripping testimony from the victim, an emergency-room nurse, and the responding officers. When the jury came back, however, the verdict was not guilty. Why? Unmoved by the DNA evidence, jurors felt police should have tested "debris" found in the victim to see if it matched soil from the park. "They said they knew from CSI that police could test for that sort of thing," Hoos said. "We had his DNA. We had his denial. It's ridiculous."[22]

The six major phases of litigation are:
● Pleadings
● Discovery
● Pre-trial conferences
● Trial
● Outcome
● Possible appeal

Much of the work for forensic accountants occurs in the discovery stage.
The pleadings consist of:
● *Complaint*—Plaintiff files.
● *Service of process*—Served on defendant.
● *Answer*—Defendant must admit or deny allegations.
● *Demurrer*—No cause of action exists.
● *Possible cross-complaint*—Defendant files.

An attorney's job is to ultimately avoid trial and the resulting lost time and expenses. Thus, the goal of a forensic accountant is to help the attorney to avoid the cost and uncertainty of a trial.[21]

Discovery refers to the right to know and access the evidence that the government or the other side has against a defendant and intends to use at trial. The methods of discovery include interrogatories, depositions, admissions of facts, request for production, subpoenaing, and asking to examine documents for authenticity. Discovery is not automatically granted to a defendant in federal court as it may be in state courts. Exculpatory evidence tends to exonerate the defendant (otherwise known as Brady material) and always has to be handed over by the government. In federal court, the prosecutors play their hand close to the chest, and according to Jilliane Hoffman (in her novel, *Last Witness*), trial by surprise may be the rule of the game. There are not as many depositions taken in federal court, no right to interview the witnesses and victim before trial. That's why the federal conviction rate is so high. It is hard to block the punch you don't see coming. Of course, the government has enough money, manpower and resources to pack a mean punch.[24]

Before trial there are pre-trial conferences to encourage settlement, but if there is no settlement there is a settlement conference. During the settlement conference both parties agree on certain facts, called stipulations.

Both sides may serve on the other party up to 25 written interrogatories, including all discrete subparts. These interrogatories are written questions that the other side must answer in writing under oath within a specific time period (often 30 days). Hopefully, the forensic accountant is asked to help to develop the financial or accounting questions.

One has the right to a jury trial in district courts, but jurors can only determine the facts and not the law. There is no jury trial in probate, family law, estate issues, equitable issue, U.S. Tax Court, and U.S. Court of Federal Claims. There is an automatic right to appeal from trial courts to the first level of the appellate process. But higher courts (e.g., Supreme Court) must decide whether to hear a dispute. To get to federal courts, one must raise the question of a federal law or diversity of citizenship (e.g., different state). For the federal court, the controversy must exceed $50,000. State courts have trial courts, appeal courts, and Supreme Court.

MAKING A DECISION. The following quote from Hoffman's novel, *Last Witness*, provides a good illustration. "Judge Leopold Chaskel sat at his desk in chambers, reading and rereading the legal briefs before him, thick with attached case law from every court in the country. Only cases that are directly on point from Florida's Third District Court of Appeal, the Florida Supreme Court, and the United States Supreme Court are binding on any decision he would make. But the decisions of other courts, even those outside the jurisdiction, that had faced the same or similar issue were called 'legally persuasive.' In other words, if four out of five dentists say it's good, then he should, too."[25]

During the trial the attorneys each act in the role of opposing movie directors—calling witnesses and orchestrating carefully timed presentations. All of it is designed to sway the jury's disposition in favor of their respective client's position. Civil cases are decided based only on which side has the greatest preponderance of evidence in its favor. Evidence of guilt or innocence beyond a reasonable doubt is the criterion for deciding criminal cases only, and therefore do not apply to civil cases.[26]

¶ 8008 TYPES OF WITNESSES

There are different types of witnesses in the courtroom: fact or lay, expert, summary, and special masters.

Under Federal Rule of Evidence 701 a fact witness is limited to opinions and inferences that are rationally based on the perceptions of the witness, helpful to a clear understanding of the witness' testimony or the determination of a fact in issue, and not based on scientific, technical, or other specialized knowledge. A non-expert witness can only refer to documents already in evidence and cannot testify about hearsay evidence. A fact witness is paid a small statutory daily fee.

A witness with specialized knowledge, training, and experience may help a court to understand technical issues. Once a judge has determined a witness to be an expert, the expert can testify about documents that have not been introduced into evidence. An expert can testify about hearsay evidence, and he or she is entitles to a reasonable hourly rate. An expert can testify from first-hand knowledge, information admitted into evidence during the trial, and any information made known to the expert before the trial.

Summary witnesses are used as a means of effectively and efficiently presenting voluminous and complex data in the courtroom. Summary witnesses are fact witnesses who testify about matters of which they have direct knowledge, so they do not have to survive Daubert or Frye challenges. There are three types of summary witnesses:

- 1006 Summaries – Primary-evidence summaries
- 611 Mode and order of interrogation and presentation – Pedagogical-device summaries
- Hybrid 1006 and 611 – Secondary-evidence summaries.[27]

Since 1968, the use of summary witnesses has steadily increased in tax cases, especially in the U.S. District Courts. In the majority of disputes, the government presents summary witnesses in tax fraud, false statements, and attempts to evade taxes. More than 75 percent are IRS employees, and more than 50 percent present Rule 611 pedagogical-device summaries.[28]

Types of Litigation Services Provided by Accountants

¶ 8011 CONSULTANT

An accountant may be hired by an attorney to gather and interpret facts, prepare analyses, help the attorney interpret evidence, advise about issues and strategies involved in a legal matter, locate other accountants to act as consultants or expert witnesses, and help expert witnesses form their opinions. Accountants acting as consultants will not be asked to testify in a judicial or regulatory proceeding, and their work usually will be protected from disclosure by the attorney work product privilege.

EYEWITNESS

She considered the usual battalion of expert witnesses, who would testify if needed about things they hadn't seen based on texbook science and likelihoods and their own professional experience. I have never trusted professional witnesses. I understand the need for them in this day and age, but in the end they are hired guns lined up to discredit the same witnesses for the other side. An expert is impressive as hell until suddenly the opposite truth comes out. They are trained to know things, yet we have seen even the best of them make mistakes. I remembered the handwriting experts with impeccable credentials who got hoodwinked by that ingenious murderous forger, Mark Hoffman. The experts knew everything about paper and inks, they knew all the tricks, while Hoffman was nothing but a self-taught madman. And he fooled them.[29]

¶ 8016   EXPERT WITNESS

An accountant may be retained by an attorney or court as an expert witness to testify in a judicial or administrative proceeding. Accountants often are asked to lend their expertise to shareholder disputes, valuation controversies, and commercial damage claims.

Accountants retained as expert witnesses will be expected to give their opinion in a judicial or administrative proceeding and can expect their work for a lawyer or court to be available to others involved in the litigation.

An excerpt from an educational novel provides an informative description of an expert testifying in the courtroom:[30]

> "Briefly, forensic accounting is a science that deals with the relationship and application of facts to business and social problems." Lenny smiled and turned towards the jury. "As I tell my students, a forensic accountant is like the Columbo or Quincy character of yesteryears, except he or she uses accounting records and facts to uncover fraud, missing assets, insider tradings, and other white collar crimes." Lenny turned back to the pinstriped lawyer.

Keep in mind that the forensic accountant is "trying to piece together a puzzle where you do not have the picture on the box to know what it looks like. The facts are unsettled, and actually it's the facts that are in dispute."[31]

¶ 8021   MASTERS AND SPECIAL MASTERS

Accountants sometimes are appointed by a court as a master to assist the court in some matter (e.g., to determine certain facts or compute damages).[32] They also may be appointed to act as the court's representative (referred to as a *special master*) in a particular transaction.

The powers and duties of masters and special masters depend on the terms of the order making their appointment and applicable court rules.[33] The compensation paid a master or special master is set by the court and paid by the parties or out of any fund or subject matter of the litigation.[34]

When Sir Paul McCartney split from Heather Mills, there was a battle between the forensic accountants as to the value of his assets. Mills wanted 125 million pounds for her short four year marriage to the Beatle.

Ernst & Young placed a value of 400 million pounds on his fortune, and the judge accepted this figure over the value suggested by Mills' accountant, Lee and Allen. The judge said that Mills' accountant dealt mainly with claims for damages and admitted that he had never valued a recording catalogue.

Heather Mills received only $48 million, but still that was $12 million per marriage year.[35]

Standards of Conduct for Performing Litigation Services

¶ 8031   KNOWLEDGE, SKILLS, EXPERIENCE, TRAINING, AND EDUCATION

The skills, knowledge, experience, education, and training (SKEET) that accountants are expected to have and use in performing litigation services are the same that they must have and use when performing other professional services.[36] They also must satisfy the standards established by the court or other dispute-resolution forum controlling the litigation.

¶ 8041   PROFESSIONAL CODES OF CONDUCT

An accountant who performs litigation services may be subject to professional codes of conduct. For example, a CPA who is a member of the American Institute of Certified Public Accountants, Inc. (AICPA) will be expected to comply with the AICPA *Code of Professional Conduct*, the AICPA *Statement on Standards for Consulting Services No. 1*, the AICPA *Statement on Responsibilities for Litigation Services No. 1*, and *Statement on Standards for Valuation Services No. 1*.

Certain AICPA rules are particularly relevant to CPAs who perform litigation services:

- Professional competence. CPAs must undertake only those professional services that they reasonably can expect to complete with professional competence.[37]
- Independence. Independence from a client is not required when a CPA performs litigation services without a related attestation service.[38] However, CPAs who testify as expert witnesses should try to maintain at least the appearance of independence so that jurors and judges will be more likely to accept their opinions.
- Objectivity and integrity. CPAs must maintain their objectivity and integrity, and avoid conflicts of interest.[39] They must not "blindly offer only evidence and opinions helpful to the client;" although they may resolve doubt in favor of their client, they may not subordinate their judgment to their client's.[40]
- Confidential client information. CPAs are obligated to preserve the confidentiality of information that they obtain about a client.[41] CPAs acting as expert witnesses cannot use confidential client information as the basis for an opinion without first obtaining the client's consent.
- Conflicts of interest. CPAs must consider whether they have a conflict of interest with any of the parties involved in litigation and their attorneys.[42]

¶ 8051   CONFLICTS OF INTEREST

Before agreeing to perform litigation services, accountants should consider whether they have, or have had, any relationships that would, or might lead others to think would, impair their integrity and objectivity in performing the litigation services. They also should consider whether their work might conflict with their duty to preserve client confidences. Once they have agreed to perform litigation services, accountants should be sensitive to conflicts of interest that arise during the course of their work.

Practice Aid 10-1 indicates conflicts of interest are actual or apparent incompatible interest between a practitioner and others connected to an engagement. Examples include the potential client and legal counsel, and opposing parties' and legal counsel, and unnamed but associated third parties to a dispute.[43] Statement on Standards for Consulting Services No.1 states "that a conflict may occur if the CPA or the firm has a significant relationship with another person, entity, product, or service that could be viewed as impairing their objectivity."[44]

Any actual or apparent conflicts of interest should be disclosed. The need to avoid even potential conflicts of interest is particularly important when accountants perform litigation services because any appearance of a conflict can make judges and jurors question a practitioner's credibility.

Unlike the case with attestation engagements, independence is not a factor used to determine whether a CPA performing litigation services has a conflict of interest.[45]

¶ 8061   WRITTEN AGREEMENT
TO PERFORM LITIGATION SERVICES

Accountants asked to perform litigation services should enter into a written agreement with the employing attorney.

The written agreement should cover the following matters:

1. The name of the attorney's client.
2. The litigants' names and place for the legal proceeding.
3. The nature of the litigation services to be performed.

4. Whether the practitioner will be asked to testify as an expert witness.
5. What restrictions will be imposed on use and disclosure of the practitioner's work.
6. Whether the practitioner has any conflicts of interest with the litigants and/or their attorneys.
7. Whether the practitioner's work will be protected by the attorney work product privilege.
8. Circumstances under which the practitioner may terminate his or her engagement.
9. Fee (including payment arrangements).

A four page Model Consulting Agreement may be found in *The Comprehensive Forensic Services Manual*, Appendix V.[46]

Confidential communication between a client and lawyer is considered a protective privilege. If a forensic accountant is hired to testify as an expert, he or she may not use the attorney–client privilege. However, a nontestifying expert may fall under an attorney work product privilege.[47] Thus, a forensic accountant hired as a consultant is immune from discovery under Rule 26(b)(4)(B). A forensic accountant should be hired directly by the attorney, and any agreement should be between the expert and attorney.

Becoming an Expert Witness

¶ 8071   EXPERT WITNESSES DISTINGUISHED FROM LAY WITNESSES

An accountant may testify as a lay (fact) witness or as an expert witness. A *fact witness* testifies as to facts. An *expert witness* is an individual who, because of specialized training or experience, is allowed to testify in court to help the judge or jurors understand complicated and technical subjects.[48]

As a general rule, an individual may not testify as a witness unless he or she has personal knowledge of the matter being litigated.[49] However, if specialized knowledge will help the jurors or judge understand the evidence or determine a fact in issue, a witness qualified as an expert may testify.[50] Expert testimony is not needed "to explain an issue or fact that the average person can understand by the use of common knowledge or common sense."[51] Expert testimony about matters that are readily intelligible is unhelpful to a jury and is inadmissible.[52]

Expert witnesses may rely on inadmissible facts or data if they are of a type reasonably relied upon by experts in the particular field in forming opinions or inferences upon the subject.[53] They may give an opinion on an ultimate issue to be decided by the trier of fact.[54] Expert witnesses may be asked to answer hypothetical questions in deposition and on the stand.

Generally, nonexpert witnesses cannot give opinions. However, an exception is made for opinions that amount to "shorthand statements of fact" or are otherwise helpful to an understanding of the witness' testimony. A typical example would be testimony that a person "looked drunk." The lay opinion rule may be thought of as one of preference. If a witness can make a statement more specific, then the more specific language is preferable. But if a witness probably cannot do so or if requiring a more detailed description would unduly consume time without benefit to the fact finder, it may be better to hear it as it is. Courts often take the view that so long as a witness had a sufficient opportunity to observe, the details can be inquired into on cross-examination.

Another situation in which lay opinions may be admissible can occur when character is in issue. Under such circumstances, in some jurisdictions a witness may be permitted to provide an opinion regarding the good character of the person in question.

¶ 8081   WHAT LAWYERS LOOK FOR IN AN EXPERT WITNESS

Accountants interested in becoming an expert witness should take steps to make themselves attractive to attorneys. The following is a list of what lawyers look for in an expert:[55]

- Individuals with extensive, focused, undiluted experience with the facts and events in dispute.
- Individuals with maturity who are established and experienced in their career.
- Individuals who are active and current in their field.
- Individuals who have earned the respect and recognition of their peers in their area of expertise.
- Individuals whose relevant area of expertise is undiluted by unrelated degrees and credentials.
- Individuals who cannot be dismissed as a "professional" witness.
- Individuals who have no history of having gone on record with any position inconsistent with the position that will be taken during the case in point.
- Individuals who will be likable and credible to the jurors.
- Individuals who are flexible, quick on their feet, and noncombative.
- Individuals who will talk to the jurors, in their own language.
- Individuals who are good teachers.
- An individual who is "guaranteed to entertain and interest the jury—the hallmarks of an expert who will be able to persuade."[56]

Subscribers to Daubert Tracker[57] have access to a searchable database of all reported cases to track an expert's history.

There are a number of ways for the other side to attempt to challenge an expert:

1. *Daubert* challenges.
2. *Frye* challenges.
3. Does not qualify as an expert by skills, knowledge, experience, education, and training (SKEET).
4. Requires a valid connection to the pertinent inquiry as a precondition to admission.
5. Courts remain vigilant against the admission of legal conclusions.
6. *In re Paoli Railroad Yard PCB Litigation*,[58] lists others.
    a. Relationships of technique to methods already established to be reliable.
    b. Existence and maintenance of standards controlling technique's operation.
    c. Expert witness' qualifications and nonjudicial uses to which method has been put.
7. Side-taking or result-oriented work.
8. Conflict of interest.
9. Ghost-written report.
10. Spoliation.
11. Name not disclosed within time limit.
12. Improper expert witness designation.

Many of these challenges are discussed in this chapter.

¶ 8091   QUALIFYING AS AN EXPERT WITNESS

How an individual can qualify as an expert witness varies depending on whether the litigation is in federal or state courts. The federal courts and many states have adopted the Daubert standard. Some states follow the older Frye standard, and other states have their own standard (e.g., North Carolina balances relevancy or materiality against prejudicial effect). The following internet sites keep track of the states: *http://faculty.ncwc.edu/toconnor/daubert.htm*, and *http://www.effingham.net/michael/dbtp.html*.

Frye Standard

Before *Daubert* was decided, the dominant standard for determining the admissibility of expert testimony was the Frye standard. Under the Frye standard, which no longer is used in federal courts but still is used by many state courts (at least 14), the test for admitting expert testimony is (1) whether the expert's testimony will assist the trier of fact in understanding the evidence or in determining a fact in issue, (2) whether the theories and/or techniques relied upon by the expert are generally accepted by the relevant professional community, and (3) whether the particular expert is qualified to present expert testimony on the subject at issue.[59]

Judges applying the Frye standard review what an expert's peers have written and said about the expert's theories and/or techniques to determine whether those theories and/or techniques have gained general acceptance in the relevant professional community. Judges applying the Frye standard defer to an expert's peers to determine whether the expert's testimony should be admitted into evidence. By contrast, under the Daubert standard, judges themselves are required to assess the reliability of an expert's theories and/or techniques.

Daubert Standard

In *Daubert v. Merrill Dow Pharmaceuticals, Inc.*,[60] the United States Supreme Court established the rule for federal courts that trial judges have a special responsibility to ensure that scientific testimony is not only relevant, but also reliable. In *Kumho Tire Company, Ltd. v. Carmichael*,[61] the Supreme Court decided that a judge's "gatekeeping" obligation applies not only to scientific testimony but to all expert testimony. The *Daubert* case and its progeny have had a substantive impact on forensic accounting methods and reasoning in general. These cases have resulted in heightened scrutiny in many instances of not only the methods used but the underlying factual support for the conclusions presented.

There may be simple *Daubert* challenges or complex *Daubert* challenges. A simple *Daubert* challenge involves a motion of limine and a motion of summary judgment. Once documents are filed, there is a hearing with the judge and lawyers. The motion for summary judgment may or may not be granted. A complex *Daubert* challenge may involve multiple-day hearings. There can be live witnesses with challenged experts and rebuttal experts.

Simple Daubert Challenge
- Motion of limine.
- Motion of summary judgment.
- Documents filed.
- Hearing with judge and lawyers.
- Motion for summary judgment may or may not be granted.

Complex Daubert Challenge
- Multiple day hearing.
- Live Witnesses.
    - Challenged Expert
    - Rebuttal Expert

THE WITNESS'S ROLE. My job is to provide credible expert opinions on complex accounting issues. The opposing attorney's job is to make me look like a lying idiot. Any anger, loss of confidence, or other emotional lapse he can drive or insult me into, will inure to his purpose. My experience as a professor would work to my favor, since my career centers around explaining complex accounting issues in clear understandable terms.

What I need to guard against is treating the jury like my students. The opposing lawyer will accuse me of grandstanding and thinking I'm back in my ivory tower. He'll try to make me look like a fool. The judge *owns* the courtroom. The witness is just a guest, and one that not every party appreciates.[62]

QUALIFICATIONS FOR TESTIFYING. Under the Federal Rules of Evidence, a judge will permit an accountant to testify as an expert witness only if the judge decides that:

The accountant's testimony will help the jurors or judge understand the evidence or determine a fact in issue.[63]

The accountant is qualified as an expert by knowledge, skill, experience, training, or education.[64]

The accountant can show that his or her testimony (a) will be based on sufficient facts or data and (b) will be the product of reliable principles and methods that have been applied reliably to the facts of the case.[65]

Before permitting an individual to testify as an expert, a judge will determine whether the expert's reasoning and methodology can appropriately be applied to the facts of the dispute.[66] Also, the judge must take into consideration the expert's background and practical experience when deciding whether an expert is qualified to render an opinion.[67] A judge may decide that an expert is insufficiently qualified because his or her expertise is too general or too deficient.[68] A judge also may decide that studies cited are too dissimilar to the facts involved in the litigation.[69]

Foundation of Testimony

Various factors are considered to determine whether an expert's testimony rests on a reliable foundation and can be applied properly to the facts at issue. In *Daubert*,[70] the United States Supreme Court suggested that judges consider the following factors:

- Whether the theory or technique in question can be (and has been) tested
- Whether the theory or technique in question has been subjected to peer review and publication
- The theory's or technique's known or potential error rate
- Whether the theory or technique has attracted widespread acceptance within the relevant community

The Ninth Circuit Court of Appeals[71] added another consideration: whether the theory or technique existed before litigation began.

Daubert decisions are made at the trial court level. The U.S. Supreme Court has held that the abuse-of-discretion standard ordinarily applied to review evidentiary rulings is the proper standard by which to review a trial court's decision to admit or exclude expert testimony.[72]

DAUBERT CHALLENGES. Litigants are increasingly making successful Daubert and Frye challenges. One searchable database of Daubert and Frye challenges is the Daubert Tracker, which had 1,108 challenges to financial expert witnesses from 2000-2010. Twenty-eight percent were completely excluded, 17 percent were partially excluded, and 52 percent were admitted.[73]

Trends and outcome from a PWC study include:[74]

- Number of challenges to financial expert witnesses fell in 2010, but the success rates increased to their highest level since 2005.
- Five federal circuits adjudicate the majority of all *Daubert* challenges to financial expert witnesses.
- Plaintiff financial expert witnesses are challenged more frequently, consistently two to three times as often as defense experts, but their exclusion rates have been lower than defense experts in five of the last six years.
- Economists, accountants, and appraisers are the more frequently challenged financial expert witnesses but also the ones more likely to survive the challenge.
- Case type affects the frequency and outcome of *Daubert* challenges to financial expert witnesses.

- For the 11th consecutive year, lack of reliability is the top reason financial experts are included.
- Exclusions more commonly result from the misuse of accepted methodologies than from the introduction of unusual or untested analytical methods.

Just saying that one is a CPA (or has some other professional designation) will not automatically qualify an accountant as an expert. CPAs who wish to testify as an expert witness have to convince a judge that they should be considered an expert about the matter being litigated and that their testimony will be relevant and reliable. A CPA must carefully set out what the AICPA professional standards are, explain what CPA certification requires, and why he or she is entitled to be an expert in a particular situation. The accountant must put this CPA evidence in every case so that on appeal the information is in the record.[75] If a trial judge says that the testimony of an expert is admissible, there is almost no way that the decision to admit evidence will be reversed on appeal.[76] But this is not a hard-and-fast rule.

A CPA's testimony about an insider trading defendant was inadmissible because the methodology used for the CPA's opinion was no more than speculation.[77] An accounting expert who valued property using a discounted cash flow analysis and assigned no value to raw land and a large office building was not allowed to testify.[78] An economist's testimony concerning loss figures for guidance or counsel for financial support was inadmissible because it was not based on scientifically valid methodology.[79] The testimony by a former tax prosecutor that the government should not have filed a criminal tax case was inadmissible.[80]

Daubert Challenges

Paschal Baute has advised experts to include the following information in their expert's affidavit to overcome Daubert challenges:[81]

- State that the conclusion or opinion rendered is "within reasonable degree of medical or scientific certainty."
- Specifically state the conclusion of the independent research relied upon.
- Name the scientific scrutiny and peer review to which the studies or methodologies have been subjected.
- Name the independent objective sources supporting the conclusion reached.

Accountants should take the qualification process seriously. Their disqualification can adversely affect not only their client but also their personal reputation. If their expert testimony is inadmissible, the lawsuit may be over.

A plaintiff lost a breach of contract and breach of fiduciary duty dispute by summary judgment because the plaintiff's accounting expert report was "pure speculation, based upon utterly implausible assumptions and unreliable methodology."[82]

If accountants claim expertise about a matter, do work for a litigant, and are rejected as expert witnesses, a litigant may bring a malpractice claim against them. Accountants who are excluded several times on Daubert challenges may find themselves discredited.

Judges can hurt an expert witness' reputation by making negative comments about the expert in open courtroom. A judge in Florida's Fourth District Court of Appeal said the following about an expert when a defense attorney asked why he excluded the expert: "Dr. ____ is an insidious perjurer who wouldn't know the truth if it leapt up and bit him on the ***." The expert is a doctor since 1963 and has testified for 25 years. On appeal the appellate court upheld the judge's ruling that the expert's claim lacked merit.

On January 6, 2005, Andrea Yates' capital murder conviction for drowning her children was overturned by an appeals court because of a celebrated psychiatrist Dr. Park Dietz's erroneous testimony about a nonexistent TV episode on "Law & Order." His photo was shown on "Fox News," and the talking heads called him a "hired gun" and a "whore." One talking head said that "he's dead." Dr. Dietz is part medical examiner, part detective, and part scholar. He has a complete set of serial killers trading cards in a wall-length display case in his home.[83]

In an antitrust dispute a District Court excluded an economist and awarded summary judgment to plaintiff. The Fourth Circuit affirmed the exclusion, saying that the expert had an MBA and significant executive experience in the relevant industry, but he subscribed to no economics journals, could identify no economics journals, had published no economics-related articles, was unfamiliar with basic terms employed by economists in antitrust analysis, had never conducted any relevant market analysis, and had read only materials provided to him by counsel.[84]

In another dispute, the Fifth Circuit said just because the expert had a MD degree was not enough to qualify him to give an opinion on every conceivable question.[85]

In *F.J. Laureys, Jr.*,[86] the IRS offered the testimony of Dr. Bradford Cornell, a professor of finance and economics at UCLA, to demonstrate that a taxpayer was never "at risk" as to his option trading activities. About his proffered testimony, Tax Court Judge Mary Ann Cohen commented:

> We agree with taxpayer that the factual premises of Dr. Cornell's report are unreliable and that neither his testimony nor his qualifications assist in determining taxpayer's purpose in engaging in the transactions in issue.

> We do not believe that the type of economic analysis set forth in Dr. Cornell's report is relevant to the type of risk covered by Section 465(b). Further, Dr. Cornell's testimony is tainted by his perception that, from an economic standpoint, wash sales are not legitimate. Second, his isolation of data as to certain transactions, on certain dates, chosen from a few transactions selected by the IRS among hundreds engaged in by taxpayer, is not reasonably representative. It is also inconsistent with his own statement that his analysis must consider "the investor's overall strategy." Third, his assumption of predictability of stock prices is inconsistent with reality and with the existence of an active national options exchange in which differing views of the future create buyers and sellers at different prices.[87]

Accountants can run afoul of Daubert if they do not stick with generally accepted principles, they do not apply generally accepted accounting principles (GAAP) consistently, they cannot explain how their conclusion follows from GAAP, or they rely on bad information. Accountants should be skeptical of *any* information given to them by their client.

Figlewicz and Sprohge have provided 10 guidelines to help experts avoid legal challenges:[88]

1. Know the relevant professional standards.
2. Apply the relevant professional standards.
3. Know the relevant professional literature.
4. Know the relevant professional organizations.
5. Use generally accepted analytical methods.
6. Use multiple analytical methods.
7. Synthesize the conclusions of the multiple analytical methods.
8. Disclose all significant analytical assumptions and variables.
9. Subject the analysis to peer review.
10. Test the analysis—and the conclusions—for reasonableness.

Justifying Methodology

If accountants plan to use a new methodology to analyze a matter at issue, they will have to convince the judge that the new methodology makes sense. Ideally, they will be able to point to other experts who find the new methodology acceptable.

Once accountants have been qualified more than once as an expert witness, Daubert challenges are likely to become rarer. More frequently, opposing counsel will be willing to stipulate that they are experts, but the friendly side's attorney should enumerate the accountant's qualifications on the stand in order to impress the judge or jury.

Weight vs. Admissibility

There is a difference between using a Daubert challenge for admissibility versus weight. Daubert analysis should not replace trial on merits, but any defects in an expert's methods should be addressed through cross-examination.[89] The duty of a district court is to ensure that the basis of an expert's opinion is not so fatally flawed as to render his or her opinion inadmissible as matter of law.[90] For example, an appellate court said that the defendant did not argue that the expert fails to comport with Daubert factors, but rather argued that his calculations did not support his conclusion. This attack is not a true Daubert challenge, but rather goes to weight.[91]

Creditors argued that a company's quarrels with the expert's approach went to weight, not admissibility, but district court identified no fewer than eighteen deficiencies, and testimony was riddled with implausible and unexplained assumptions. The Second Circuit said that there was no abuse of discretion.[92] However, in another situation the Ninth Circuit said that a plaintiff's expert was qualified and used mathematical extrapolation, straight line linear progression, and averaging to arrive at his figures. Defendants attacked none of these methodologies, and their objections went to weight, not reliability.[93]

Also, the First Circuit said that defendants did not object at the trial court level and so review is for plain error. Defendants said the expert is unqualified, but he had spent 33 years as an IRS agent, mostly investigating financial fraud. Defendants also fault the expert for basing analysis solely on bank records supplied by plaintiffs, rather than a broader array of transactions, but this objection goes to weight, not admissibility.[94]

¶ 8101   COURT-APPOINTED EXPERT WITNESSES

Courts may, on their own motion or on the motion of any party to the litigation appoint an expert witness.[95] Courts may appoint an expert witness agreed upon by the parties or may select their own expert witness.[96] That a court appoints an expert witness does not prevent parties from calling expert witnesses of their own selection.[97] An individual may not be appointed as an expert witness unless the individual agrees to act as an expert witness.[98]

An individual appointed by a court as an expert witness will be informed of his or her duties by the court.[99] Court-appointed expert witnesses must advise all parties to the litigation of their findings.[100] They may be deposed by any party and may be called to testify by the court or any party.[101] When testifying, court-appointed experts may be cross-examined by each party, including the party who called the witness.[102]

Court-appointed expert witnesses are entitled to reasonable compensation, whatever sum the court may allow.[103] Their compensation may be paid by the parties in such proportion as the judge directs or from funds provided by law for such purposes.[104]

Preparing to Testify as an Expert Witness

¶ 8111   MAINTAINING INDEPENDENCE FROM THE CLIENT

Although accountants serving as a consultant to an attorney may be an advocate for a client, accountants who act as expert witnesses must be concerned about maintaining at least the appearance of independence from their client. Their relationship with a client must not be such that it would lead jurors and judges to question whether they can be impartial and fair in reaching their opinions. For example, accountants should not agree to a fee contingent on the success of their testimony. They should be paid for their time and expenses, *not* for their opinion.

Lack of independence not only may undermine an expert witness' testimony (and perhaps disqualify the individual from testifying) but also may make an expert witness' working papers with respect to the client and other engagements subject to discovery by the opposing party.

¶ 8121   EVIDENCE UPON WHICH EXPERTS MAY RELY

Experts may base their opinions on facts or data that they themselves perceived or which were made known to them at or before a judicial hearing.[105] The facts or data need not be admissible in evidence in order for the expert's opinion to be admitted if the facts or data are of a type reasonably relied upon by experts in the same field in forming opinions.[106] Otherwise inadmissible facts or data may not be disclosed to the jury unless the court determines that their probative value in assisting the jury in evaluating the expert's opinion substantially outweighs their prejudicial effect.[107]

Unless the court requires otherwise, experts need not testify to the facts or data underlying their opinions before giving their opinion and the reasons for their opinion.[108] However, they may be required to disclose underlying facts or data on cross-examination.[109] Although expert witnesses are allowed to present naked opinions, if their testimony has an inadequate foundation, the court can exclude their testimony.

¶ 8131   USE OF CONFIDENTIAL CLIENT INFORMATION

Accountants acting as expert witnesses should not rely on any confidential client information as the basis for their opinions without first obtaining the client's consent to disclose such information. If an accountant acting as an expert witness is required by a judge to disclose the source of information and the accountant refuses to disclose the source because the information is confidential client information, the judge may bar the accountant's testimony.

¶ 8141   EXPERT REPORTS

Witnesses retained or specially employed to provide expert testimony, or whose duties as an employee of a party to litigation regularly involve giving expert testimony, must prepare and sign a written report (referred to as an *expert report*).[110] A well-written report can be a vital tool in litigation. Such a report helps experts collect their thoughts and express them in a clear and cogent manner. The judge or jury may be particularly impressed with a thorough, persuasive report.

Information in the Report

An expert report usually must be signed and contain the following information:

- A complete statement of all opinions to be expressed and the basis and reasons for those opinions;
- The data or other information that the accountant considered in forming the opinions;
- Any exhibits to be used as a summary of or support for the opinions;
- The accountant's qualifications, including a list of all publications that he or she has authored within the past 10 years;
- The compensation the accountant is to be paid for the study and testimony; and
- A list of any other cases in which the accountant has testified as an expert at trial or by deposition within the preceding four years.[111]

The AICPA suggests four hold-harmless provisions to be included in engagement letters. Practice Aid 04-1 suggests attaching your curriculum vitae (CV) as an exhibit to the engagement letter, with the following clause:

> As an exhibit to this engagement letter, I have attached my CV. If a court later determines that I am not qualified to offer testimony, such determination will not be deemed a breach of this agreement, and you will still be liable for the payment of fees and expenses as set forth herein.[112]

A statement similar to this one should be at the end of a report:

> I have not attempted to set forth verbatim every detail of my expected testimony and every fact that supports my opinion. Thus, I may provide additional topics in response to arguments or assertions offered during the course of deposition and testimony.

Types of Expert Reports

An expert report may be fact or opinion-oriented, or a combination of both. For a *fact-oriented report,* a forensic accountant gathers and evaluates facts and uses them to prepare a report. The challenge is to gather enough documentation and support for one's opinions. "I have to check and recheck the numbers. The last thing I want to be nailed on is where I got the numbers." But generally the numbers do not lie.[113] *Opinion reports* (e.g., valuation reports) are more subjective and rely more on the professional judgment of the expert. The accountant must be able to demonstrate in the judicial process the adequacy and competency of the research in forming such an opinion.

Organization of the Report

The format for an expert report varies from court to court. A typical expert report is organized as follows:

- The name and docket number of the case
- A statement of qualifications
- Information considered in formulating opinions
- A list of other cases in which the individual has testified as an expert within the preceding four years
- Compensation to be received for expert testimony
- Opinions to be expressed and the reasons for those opinions

Unless otherwise directed by the court or stipulated by the parties, the report must be furnished to the other parties involved in the litigation at least 90 days before the trial date or the date that the case is to be ready for trial or, if the expert witness' testimony is intended solely to contradict or rebut evidence on the same subject matter identified by any other expert witness, within 30 days after the disclosure made by the other party.[114] The reason for requiring a timely report is to eliminate unfair surprises to the opposing parties and to conserve resources.[115]

If expert witnesses learn that information disclosed in their report is incomplete or incorrect in some material respect, they should notify their employer so that the report can be supplemented.[116]

This expert report has been described as an accountant's "best friend" because expert witnesses can refer to it, and even read from it, whenever necessary, even while they are being questioned.[117]

Ghost-Written Reports

An expert report must be prepared by the expert and not by his or her attorney. An expert report prepared mostly from interrogatory answers prepared by the party's lawyers is not sufficient.[118] "Rule 26(a)(2)(B) does not preclude counsel from providing assistance to experts in preparing the reports, and indeed, with experts such as automobile mechanics, this assistance may be needed. Nevertheless, the report, which is intended to set forth the substance of direct examination, should be written in a manner that reflects the testimony to be given by the witness, and it must be signed by the witness."[119]

In one dispute an attorney assisted an expert in preparing a report by providing assistance in retyping and incorporating changes authorized by the expert. A trial attorney "may well have legitimate cause to give assistance to an expert witness in the preparation of the report." But the court also emphasized that in no way does it suggest that the attorneys have license to change the opinions and report of the expert witnesses.[120]

In an Indiana dispute an attorney actually wrote the expert report, but the attached opinions and work papers were those of the expert, and the expert testified at deposition that the report reflected his opinions.[121] Still in another case, a Virginia court found "significant evidence of teamwork and collaboration between ATE (a government litigation consultant) and the U.S.'s testifying expert." There was "extensive substantive assistance in drafting the expert's report."[122] In still another dispute an expert report was "substantially derived" from a prior case, which was "substantially similar" to a different expert's report in another dispute. Since there was substantial similarity among the three expert witness reports derived from the authorship of this common language by plaintiff's counsel, the Michigan court struck an expert's report because it had "not been prepared by the expert," in violation of FRCP 26(a)(2).[123]

The U.S. Tax Court indicates that certain kinds of help are clearly available to assist an expert. For example, a lawyer's assistance with the preparation of documents required by Rule 26, such as a list of cases in which the expert has testified, or fine-tuning a disclosure with expert's input to insure that a report complies with the various rules, is permissible. Preparing an expert's opinion "from whole cloth and then asking the expert to sign it if he or she wishes to adopt it, conflicts with Rule 26(a)(2)(B)'s requirement that the expert 'prepare the report.' Preparation implies involvement other than pursuing a report drafted by someone else and placing one's name at the bottom to indicate agreement. In other words, the assistance of counsel contemplated by Rule 26(a)(2)(B) is not synonymous with ghost-writing."[124]

In *Bank One Corporation*, the Tax Court rejected a jointly prepared 20-page expert rebuttal report on the behalf of two experts since it was prepared primarily by only one expert and by taxpayer's counsel. The report went through 12 revisions. The Tax Court complained that the expert never explained to their satisfaction that the words, analysis, and opinions in that report were his own work and a reflection of his own expertise. This court was not persuaded that the expert played any meaningful role in preparing the contents of the rebuttal report. "He was vague, uncertain, and unfamiliar with the contents of the report, and he was uncomfortable and evasive, and he was uncomfortable about his role in its preparation."[125]

Hurwitz and Carpenter say that permissible assistance certainly should include familiarizing an expert with the requirements of Tax Court Rule 143(f)(1) and helping the expert understand what information must be included in the expert report. By contrast, an expert's report written entirely by an attorney is automatically suspect. Behavior falling between these two extremes poses more trouble.[126] They assert that it is likely that the U.S. Tax Court will allow an expert to serve as a scribe only when the expert is not capable of articulating his or her thoughts in the form of a written report.[127]

Side-Taking

Side-taking or result-oriented work may result in a trial judge dismissing an expert. Hints at a lawyer's line of arguments provided before reviewing evidence can influence an accounting expert's decision about an auditor's compliance with GAAS.[128] For example, in a fifty-seven page decision involving the valuation of a company, the U.S. Tax Court attacked a valuation expert, Dr. Shannon Pratt.[129] The IRS used as its expert on the valuation questions Dr. Shannon Pratt, managing director of Willamette Management Associates and the acknowledged guru of business appraisers. Tax Court Judge Renato Beghe nevertheless concluded that "Willamette's report was result-oriented and this was reflected in Dr. Pratt's testimony." The Judge noted that appraisers "have third-party responsibilities—just as certified public accountants do—to those who rely on their opinions, and their determinations must be independent and objective...."[130]

The judge said that Dr. Pratt strayed from the standard of objectivity and cast aside his scholar's mantle and became 'a shill' for respondent." Thus, Judge Beghe rejected most of both the Willamette report and Dr. Pratt's testimony, but did take into account Dr. Pratt's criticism of the taxpayer's expert reports and testimony.

Tips on Preparing an Expert Report

Following are dos and don'ts accountants should remember in preparing an expert report:[131]

- *Discuss the report with the attorney.* Ask the attorney to list the issues that should be addressed in the expert report.
- *Focus on empirical and market-derived data.* Courts expect empirical and market-derived data to drive an expert's conclusions, not vice versa. Avoid phrases such as "in my opinion" and "based on my experience" and instead explain what the data shows.
- *Rely on authoritative treatises, professional standards, and accepted industry practices.* The foundation for an expert's opinions should be authoritative treatises, professional standards, and accepted industry practices. Avoid relying on the opinions of single individuals, no matter what their level of knowledge, skill, experience, training, and education.
- *Relate theories and formulas to the specific facts and circumstances of the case.* Explain why and how any theories and formulas used apply to the specific facts and circumstances of the matter being litigated.
- *Clearly state opinions.* State opinions clearly and confidently. Do not hedge opinions with such words as I believe, it seems, probably, possibly, apparently, evidently, or supposedly.
- *Use objective language.* Use objective language, not language that is biased or argumentative.
- *Do not state an opinion on the law in the report.* Do not give an opinion on what the law is, and be careful about citing law, code sections, and court decisions. Stating an opinion about the law may result in the exclusion of the report and testimony from the trial. For example, in *FPL Group, Inc.,*[132] Michael M. Wilson, an attorney, filed a report on behalf of FPL. Tax Court Judge Robert P. Rume, observing that the report stated legal conclusions, granted the government's request to exclude Wilson's report.
- *Stay within the field of expertise.* Do not offer opinions on issues outside the specific field of expertise.
- *Use first-person singular and active voice.* Write the expert report in the first-person singular (i.e., "I found") and use the active, not passive, voice.
- *Define technical terms.* Provide definitions of all technical terms that are used in the expert report.

- *Avoid mistakes.* Mistakes in an expert's report can be deadly. Opposing counsel will generally seize on such mistakes, no matter how small, on the theory that if the expert is mistaken about one thing, he or she may be mistaken about other things (including, perhaps, the entire opinion).

¶ 8151   WORKING PAPERS

Expert witnesses should bear in mind that any notes, memoranda, working papers, and similar materials prepared in anticipation of litigation may have to be disclosed to opposing counsel and can be used during cross-examination. Unlike attorneys, there is no work product rule protecting an expert's working papers from discovery.

According to U.S. District Court Judge Robert E. Payne "the basic precepts of the Federal Rules of Civil Procedure relating to the work of testifying experts requires…the retention and production of draft reports and the correspondence reviewed by the testifying expert."[133] Judge Payne has written that the rule in force since the Daubert decision requires that any "information reviewed by an expert will be subject to disclosure, including drafts of reports sent from and to the testifying experts….The party requesting disclosure no longer bears the burden of demonstrating that the expert actually relied on the document."[134] Thus, the work product of nontestifying consultants will be discoverable if the testifying expert uses it.

Need for Completeness

There are no specific rules governing the form and content of an expert witness' working papers. What expert witnesses include in their working papers is left to their professional judgment. However, the documentation should be sufficient to justify the expert's opinion. In their working papers, expert witnesses should include the bases for their opinions, copies or references to materials that they have used to form the bases for their opinions, details of any calculations, and all assumptions made.

Poor paperwork is what attorneys dislike the most about expert witnesses.[135] If an expert's files are disorganized and/or incomplete, then the other side's counsel will spend time harping on the expert's poor method. If the file contains a mass of notes and preliminary thoughts about the case (particularly if based on discussions with the lawyer who prepares the expert), these, too, will be a fertile ground for cross-examination. Worst of all, if the file contains obvious omissions, which indicate that the expert has destroyed documents, there may be intense inquiry (and sometimes an adverse inference) concerning the missing materials.

Disclosure of Problems

Lawyers generally dislike working with expert witnesses who view paperwork as a nuisance, or who think that they can make up for lack of preparation on paper with a facile courtroom presentation. Perhaps the worst sin, in this regard, is for an expert witness, once confronted with problems in a file or report, to insist that there is no problem. The expert witness generally should admit, candidly (and preferably even before cross-examination exposes the problem) what the problem is (with an explanation for why the problem is not material).

¶ 8161   EVALUATION OF OTHER EXPERTS

One of an expert witness's duties is to evaluate the opinions of other expert witnesses and help prepare attorneys to question those other experts. As an expert witness, the forensic accountant will be expected to review the expert reports prepared by other experts, identify problems with the conclusions reached by opposing experts, and help the attorney he or she is working for frame questions to expose those problems.

The forensic witness will be expected to help attorneys develop a working knowledge of the technical area at issue and recommend treatises for attorneys to consult. He or she may be asked to suggest questions for attorneys to ask opposing experts and may be asked to be present at the examination of an opposing expert witness to clarify the meaning of answers and suggest follow-up questions.

It is not sufficient to say that another expert's conclusions are incorrect. The expert witness has to help an attorney communicate *why* those conclusions are incorrect. The expert witness should help the attorney develop questions that make it clear to nonexpert jurors that those conclusions are incorrect.

¶ 8171   EXHIBITS AND OTHER DEMONSTRATIVE EVIDENCE

Demonstrative evidence (such as charts, graphics, and animations) is useful because it can make testimony more understandable and interesting. Such evidence should be prepared well before trial because a court ruling on its admissibility may be needed.

Before experts prepare any exhibits, they should consult with the attorney who hired them. Whether a graphic, summary chart, or animation is "evidence" or "demonstrative evidence" depends upon the particular court and possibly the judge. In general, demonstrative evidence does not go to the jury room because it "has no independent probative value." Exhibits may be used in the jury room, as long as the exhibits have been admitted into evidence. The circuits are split as to whether a summary chart is allowed in the jury room.[136]

Studies show that the average person retains as much as 87 percent of information presented visually and as little as 10 percent of information given orally. Furthermore, computer animations are even more persuasive. Both types of delivery impact the weight given to the evidence by jurors.[137] Thus, forensic accountants should use visual aids and computer animations whenever possible in order to communicate more memorably than an expert of the opposition.

EYEWITNESS

Conrad Black and his former cohorts at Hollinger International were compared by a prosecutor in March 2007 to "bank-robbers" who wore suits rather than black masks. They systemically stole $60 million through disguising payments that they received following the sale of dozens of Hollinger publications.

The 12 jurors were shown slides explaining Hollinger's complicated corporate structure and the elaborate scheme that Lord Black and his fellow defendants allegedly used to steal from the company. Prosecutor Jeffrey Cramer presented e-mails in which Lord Black referred to himself as a "proprietor."

"These are the most sophisticated businessmen you will ever see," Mr. Cramer said. "We all know what a street crime looks like...[This case is] exactly the same thing... [except] they did it with memos and documents."[138]

Testifying as an Expert Witness

¶ 8181   TESTIFYING AT A DEPOSITION

Expert witnesses are expected to answer questions from opposing counsel at a deposition. At a *deposition or examination before trial in some states,* which takes place outside a courtroom, witnesses known as the deponent are required to answer oral questions under oath. The rules for depositions vary from state to state, but the Federal Rules of Civil Procedure Rule 30 cover disputes in the federal courts in all fifty states. If a report is required from an expert, a deposition may not be conducted until after the report is provided under FRCP 26(b)(4). An expert may receive a notice of deposition subpoena, because if an expert does not receive a subpoena and fails to show up for the deposition, the attorney can be responsible for court costs.[139]

Depositions may be recorded by a written transcript, audio, or by a video outside the courtroom. A videotaped deposition may be used if an attorney plans to submit the video testimony in lieu of the party's live testimony. A videotaped deposition may be more economical because one does not have to pay for the expert to testify at trial. Videotaped depositions are used when the witness may not be available for trial due to illness, travel plans, or some other reason.

FRCP limits the number of depositions to 10 per side, and around 35 states use versions of the FRCP. Generally, the deposition is limited to one day (7 hours). Often after all depositions, a compromise may be reached, or the deposition transcript will be used to impeach the witness. A deponent should read and sign the deposition transcript making corrections on an errata sheet.

SPOTLIGHT

VIDEO IN THE COURTROOM. FTI, one of a number of consultants that advise lawyers on trial technology, specializes in such techniques as putting someone's image alongside a smoking-gun document and freezing the film on a phrase or facial expression. For example, the firm digitized more than 600 hours of videotaped testimony for Mr. Bartlit for a trial. As a result, any fragment could be called up within seconds by typing a page number of the written transcript into a laptop computer.

Videos can help lawyers underscore points. In Minnesota's landmark trial against the tobacco industry to recover the health-care costs of treating sick smokers, which settled in 1998, the state played a large portion of a deposition of Philip Morris Company's former research director, Thomas Osdene, invoking his Fifth Amendment protection against self-incrimination 135 times.[140]

Expert witnesses can expect to be asked about the following:
- The scope of their assignment
- Their current employment (job title, duties)
- Their educational background
- Licenses
- Work experience
- Memberships in professional organizations
- Publications and lectures
- Fields in which they are qualified as an expert
- Other work they have performed as an expert witness or other litigation consultant
- What compensation they are receiving (and what percentage of their compensation is derived from testifying as an expert witness)
- What opinions they have formed
- The bases for their opinions

Any written materials that they have relied on to form their opinions usually will have to be furnished to opposing counsel at the deposition. So may all written communications between an expert and counsel. Draft copies are no longer required to be furnished in federal courts.

Sample Deposition Questions

LESTER E. HEITGER, Ph.D., CPA

having been first duly sworn to tell the truth, the whole truth, and nothing but the truth took the stand and testified as follows:

DIRECT EXAMINATION BY MR. NOFFSINGER:

Q: State your name.

A: My name is Lester E. Heitger. That's L-e-s-t-e-r: middle initial E as in Edward: last name Heitger, H-e-i-t-g-e-r.

Q: And your professional address?

A: That would be Indiana University, Kelley School of Business, Department of Accounting and Information Systems. I guess the street address is 10th and Fee Lane, Bloomington, Indiana, 47405.

Q: And what is your profession?

A: I'm a professor of accounting/information systems.

Q: Let me show you what's been marked as Plaintiff's Exhibit 16 and ask if you can identify that.

A: This is a subpoena, for this deposition which asks me to provide you with certain items here at the deposition.

Q: And did you bring with you the items listed on that subpoena?

A: Not one of them.

Q: Which one?

A: That would be Item No. 4.

Q   And that is your calendar and date book, journals, itineraries, etc.?

A: Correct.

Q: And why did you not bring that one?

A: I didn't see that that was relevant to the case, and I had discussed that with Ms. Brown.

MR. NOFFSINGER: I've been out of town for three weeks. Has anyone sought relief from the Court?

MS. BROWN: I did. I filed for a Protective Order last Thursday.

MR. NOFFSINGER: Did you either fax or e-mail me a copy?

MS. BROWN: I faxed it to you and regular mailed it to you and the Court, and there's your copy (indicating).

MR. NOFFSINGER: It has not yet been ruled upon?

MS. BROWN: No, it hasn't. My feeling would be before Dr. Heitger answers that question, if you want him to produce his calendar, we call the judge because I don't think he's required to answer that because I don't think his personal calendar is relevant.

MR. NOFFSINGER: It's funny I didn't get that.

MS. BROWN: It has the little mark on the bottom showing it went through the fax machine.

MR. NOFFSINGER: Okay.

Q: Dr. Heitger, do you have a title?

A: I'm a professor with Indiana University School of Business.

Q: And how long have you been here at IU?

A: Thirty-one years last December.

Q: And you were retained to testify as an expert witness in this case?

A: Initially, I was retained just for some evaluation. I was eventually retained as an expert witness in the case, yes.

Q: Do you know when you were first retained?

A: Late January or early February.

Q: Would you have any records that would show that?

A: I don't think so. It was a telephone conversation with Ms. Brown.

Q: Do you charge by the hour?

A: Yes.

Q: And did you charge for that initial conversation?

A: I don't recall.

Q: If you did, those records would show when you were first retained; correct?

A: Probably.

Q: What do you do on a daily basis with regard to the evaluation of business losses?

A: I don't understand that question.

Q: In this particular case did you make calculations to determine the loss to William J. Plaintiff, as a result of a breach of the contract in this case?

A: Yes, I did.

Q: Do you do that on a regular basis?

A: I do that from time to time.

Q: And could you tell me what from time to time is?

A: It means that as part of my activities, I serve as expert witness and as litigation consultant in a variety of cases. Some of those involve situations where there is lost wages either from wrongful discharge cases or from injuries or other circumstances of that sort.

Q: And when you are retained, is that for consultation in lawsuits? Let me re-ask the question. Give me the circumstances under which you would be retained to do that.

A: Generally, I would be retained to do that where there was some either litigation in process or some disagreement between parties about what the magnitude of the loss or damages might be in the circumstances.

Q: And when you say you do this from time to time, can you tell me how many times per year you are retained to do such a thing?

A: Well, some years I may do one or two cases. Other years I may do four or five cases. It varies. It's not something that I do routinely every other day or every other week or whatever. I mean, I perform these services when they're requested.

Q: And how is it that they are requested of you? Do you advertise or how do people know to get a hold of you to do this?

A: There are several reasons. One is that I have been doing this for over twenty years. I've done a wide variety of cases—testified in Federal Court, State Court, arbitrations, mediations in a wide variety, and I testified for the U.S. Federal Tax Court, in St. Paul, Minnesota. So some of the cases that I get involved in, I will do one case for an attorney through a referral or whatever and we will work well together, understand each other's principles, etc., and I'll get asked to do more cases. In other circumstances, I would be referred by one attorney to another, by one client to another. That would be one way. Another way is that I have been teaching—and this year will be my fifth year—the forensic accounting or investigative accounting course at the graduate level, in the accounting graduate programs here at Indiana University. In the process of teaching this course, there has been a fair amount of interest and publicity about this activity. I occasionally get calls from people who hear about that, read about that. I bring in practitioners from large firms to talk to my students about what they're doing—Price WaterhouseCooper, Pete Marwick Mitchell, a variety of other firms. Occasionally, I am asked by them to fill certain roles in cases that they are involved in. It's hard to say precisely. I don't advertise. I don't have a website which people go to to find me. It's more referral, word of mouth, knowledge about what I do.

Q: How long have you been teaching forensic accounting? Five years?

A: This year will be the fifth year I've offered the forensic accounting class.

Q: Four previous years and then this year?

A: Correct.

Q: Are you familiar with the National Association of Forensic Economics?

A: No, I'm not.

Q: When did you last testify in Federal Court?

A: It wasn't actually testify. Deposition counts or just trial?

Q: Either a trial or deposition.

A: The last Federal case I was deposed in—and this just recently settled—was last August. Case was set to go to trial and just recently settled.

In the case of a written deposition a deponent generally has the right to read and sign the deposition transcript. However, under the Federal Rules of Civil Procedure, the right to read and sign is not self-executing, and the deponent must request reading and signing the transcript prior to the completion of the deposition. "An expert should never allow an attorney to waive your right to read and make changes in form or substance."[141]

During a deposition the stenographer records only what is said "on the record." There may be "off the record discussions" during the deposition, but an expert should be careful what he or she says during these discussions. The other side can use what is said in these "off the record discussions" even though the material is not recorded. Further, the other side can ask what you talked about during the break.

OFF THE RECORD? Q. Dr. Baloney, during our break you mentioned that you had a great deal of difficulty reaching your second opinion. Could you please explain?

A. But we were "off the record."

Q. True, but now that we are on the record, please explain how you can have any confidence in your opinion with respect to my client.

A. But I was "off the record!"

The purpose of deposition is to lock an expert into their testimony at trial. If an expert changes an answer at trial, the opposing attorney can bring into evidence the expert's inconsistent statements in the deposition. This process is called impeachment, which can have an unfavorable effect on the credibility of the witness at trial (as well as future work).[142]

INCONSISTENT STATEMENTS. "Where credibility is at issue, counsel should be permitted to first question the witness and then confront the witness with a prior inconsistent answer in the witness' deposition; counsel need not give the witness an initial opportunity to admit or deny allegedly inconsistent statements before reading them from the deposition."[143]

Under rules of discovery a party can bring a motion to compel a party to provide requested discovery. A court may issue protective orders to protect an expert from annoyance, embarrassment, oppression, or undue burden or expense. An expert may receive a subpoena duces tectum to produce and permit copying and inspection of designated books, documents, or tangible things in the custody or control of the expert.[144]

Keep in mind that you are not required to produce anything not in your possession, and the requesting attorney cannot keep the inspected original documents, books, and records. You are not allowed to intentionally disorganize any requested documents.

Generally, the attorney taking the deposition has the option to take a deposition at the expert's office or the attorney's office. Thus, an expert may ask his or her counsel to be deposed at their office. The major disadvantages are:

1. Interruptions and distractions.
2. Disclosure of unwanted information may occur.
3. Time of your staff may be wasted.
4. On-site records may be requested.
5. You may prepare less.[145]

There are, of course, these advantages:
1. Less travel involved.
2. More time available for other activities.
3. Feeling more comfortable on "your own turf."
4. Control of logistics: seating, temperature, etc.
5. Staff available to assist.
6. Records available when needed.[146]

Tips on Giving Depositions

The following tips can help the forensic expert witness testify during a deposition:

- Do not bring notes, diagrams, books, or other written material to the deposition unless a subpoena or the attorney requires it. Review your curriculum vitae to make sure it is up-to-date and accurate.

- Always tell the truth, but answer only the question asked.
- Think before answering.
- Never answer a question you do not understand.
- Answer the question asked, and then stop. Do not volunteer any information.
- Answer questions directly, then stop.
- Do not guess or speculate.
- Do not use words that leave you vulnerable to attack (such as *always, never, I think, I believe, I guess,* or *it's possible*).
- Stop talking when an attorney or judge makes an objection and wait for a ruling.
- Do not argue or become angry or hostile to the examining attorney.
- Even if a question calls for a yes or no answer, ask to explain your response if you feel a qualification or explanation is required to complete your answer.
- Be wary of questions that involve absolutes.
- Do not memorize your answers before the deposition.
- Ask for a break any time you need one to collect your thoughts or refresh yourself.
- If the deposition is being videotaped, look directly at the camera when answering a question; avoid long pauses; make sure any exhibits you use can be seen; and do not eat, drink, or chew anything while testifying. Women should consider wearing makeup, and men should consider shaving before testifying.
- Review the court reporter's transcript of your testimony and correct all errors, including typographical errors. Do not waive the reading and signing of the transcript of your deposition.[147]

The second tip may be the most important one. David Malone and Paul J. Zweir have pointed out that experts "may lose sight of the deposing attorney's goal, which is to find means to diminish the expert's credibility or to challenge the bases for the expert's opinions."[148] "Because they think they are safe within their own field, experts at deposition may be more willing to provide explanations and lengthy answers, to volunteer information, and to educate their ignorant but interested students."[149] Malone and Zwier advise lawyers to smile, nod, lean forward, maintain eye contact, and ask open questions to "play" the expert. They advise lawyers to encourage experts to teach at the deposition.

Answers That Suffice
Malone and Zwier suggest these seven answers to most deposition questions:

1. Yes.
2. No.
3. Green.
4. I don't know.
5. I don't remember.
6. I don't understand the question.
7. I need a break.[150]

The third answer above—Green—is the response to the question, what is the color of your car? Do not answer "it is an old green Ford." Answer only the question; nothing else.

Expert Report Used as a Reference Tool by Witness
Expert witnesses should bring their expert report with them to a deposition. They may refer to their report as often as they want and even can read from the report when necessary. They are not required to memorize every item in their report.

If expert witnesses discover that information that they provided at a deposition is incomplete or incorrect in some material respect, they should notify their employer so that their testimony can be amended.[151]

¶ 8191   PREPARING TO TESTIFY AT TRIAL

Experts need to prepare themselves to testify in court. Tips on preparing oneself to testify at court are:

- Refresh your memory about the facts of the case.
- Review your expert report and any notes and papers, and prepare yourself to explain your analyses and conclusions.
- Convince yourself that your conclusions are correct. Successful expert witnesses are convinced that their opinions are true and convey that conviction to the judge and jurors. They demonstrate to the judge and jurors "an apostolic—almost religious—conviction in the truth" of their testimony.[152]
- If possible, become familiar with the courtroom in which you will be testifying.
- If you need to use any audio or visual equipment during your testimony, you should test the equipment before trial and see where it can be set up.

¶ 8201   TESTIFYING AT TRIAL

At a trial, expert witnesses (like other witnesses) usually undergo four phases of interrogation: direct examination, cross-examination, redirect examination, and recross-examination.

During *direct examination,* an expert witness is questioned by the attorney for the party for whom the witness is testifying. Leading questions (i.e., questions that suggest a desired answer, usually a "yes" or a "no") may not be asked on direct examination unless directed to the opposing party or hostile witness.

During *cross-examination,* the attorney for the opposing party questions the expert witness. The opposing counsel generally can question an expert witness only about the credibility of the witness and matters covered by the direct examination. However, under certain circumstances a court may permit questions regarding matters not covered during direct examination. While cross-examining a witness, an attorney may ask leading questions.

During *redirect examination,* the direct examiner gives the expert witness the opportunity to clear up any confusion that may have been caused by the cross-examination and complete any answers that the witness could not complete during cross-examination. Questions asked during redirect examination must be within the scope of the direct examination.

Unless there is an introduction of new matter on redirect examination, a *recross-examination* is not required. Unless there is something new, an attorney has the last word with his or her own witness.[153] If a new subject is raised in redirect examination, courts will allow new matters to be subject to recross-examination.[154]

"EVERYBODY LIES. Cops lie. Lawyers lie. The victims lie. A trial is a contest of lies. And everybody in the courtroom knows this. The judge knows this. Even the jury knows this. They come into the building knowing they will be lied to. They take their seats in the box and agree to be lied to.[155]

The trick if you are sitting at the defense table is to be patient. To wait. Not for just any lie. But for the one you can grab on to and forge like hot iron into a sharpened blade. You then use that blade to rip the case open and spill its guts out on the floor."[156] The previous quote from Michael Connelly captures the courtroom spirit in his novel, *The Brass Verdict.*

Courts have discretion whether to permit witnesses to hear each other's testimony. At the request of a party or on its own motion, a court can exclude witnesses from the courtroom except while testifying. Courts often permit experts to listen to each other's testimony so that they may comment in rebuttal. Courts usually instruct witnesses to refrain from discussing the case or their testimony with each other.

ROUNDS OF QUESTIONING. "Trial rules permitted *direct examination* by the side giving its case-in-chief, then *cross examination* by the opposition, then another round of questioning should they be required by the side that had called the witness in the first place. This last round was the *redirect*, and Powell was up and rolling before Freeman got back to the defense table."[157]

LIES V. TRUTH

● Prosecutors in the Lay/Skilling/Enron criminal trial used a poster board divided into black and white parts.
● The black side said "lies" and the white side said "truth."
● The four month case boiled down to a simple decision over who had told the truth and who had lied.
● The prosecutors said the defendants were evasive and had used the answer "could not recall" more than 200 times.[158]

Goals of Testimony

According to Bursztajn and Bordsky, the following should be the primary goals of an expert witness:

● To communicate the truth to the jury in an ethical, objective, and effective way.
● To maintain your autonomy, authenticity, and integrity.
● To uphold the values of your profession.
● To interact with attorneys and with the judge and jury in an atmosphere of mutual respect.
● To engage in an ongoing dialogue with your attorney so that, together, you can educate as well as learn from the judge and jury as to what questions each may have.
● To speak directly to the issues.
● To make complex matters understandable without oversimplifying.[159]

An expert has to be careful not to state a legal opinion while testifying. Mentioning a legal opinion may result in testimony being disqualified by the judge. A court expects helpful and reliable testimony from an expert witness—not opinions about the law. A judge does not wish to be concerned with questions of reliability and helpfulness of expert testimony. Instead, a judge wishes to take helpfulness and reliability for granted.[160]

Tips on Testifying on the Stand

The following tips can help make a forensic accountant a more successful expert witness:[161]

● *Be punctual.* Arrive on time at the courtroom.
● *What to bring to court.* Bring your expert report. Bring only those other files, documents, and materials that your attorney says you should bring and/or are required by any subpoena that has ordered your attendance at trial.
● *Dress.* Dress neatly and conservatively. Dark suit is preferred. Do not wear shoes that squeak as you walk to the witness stand.
● *Body language.* Keep your hands visible to jurors (i.e., on top of the furniture).
● *Show modesty as well as expertise.* Arrange to have the friendly lawyer question you in detail about your qualifications; do not stipulate your own credentials.
● *Taking the oath.* When taking the oath as a witness, say loudly, "I do."
● *Answer only when asked.* Do not speak unless addressed by an attorney or the court.
● *Listen to the entire question before responding.* Listen carefully to the entire question and don't respond until you completely understand what you are being asked.
● *Pause before answering a question.* Take some time before responding to a question. That will allow you time to consider what you will say and give your counsel time to object to the question, if necessary.

- *Answer only what you've been asked.* Listen carefully to the question and answer only the question that you have been asked. Do not make gratuitous comments.
- *Use plain language.* Speak clearly, use unambiguous language, and avoid jargon. If you need to use a technical term, explain its meaning to the trier of fact.
- *Give reasons for your opinions.* Opinions are more persuasive if reasons for them are given.
- *Stick to the facts.* Experts may find their testimony excluded from trial if they give opinions about the law. For example, in a tax dispute, a CPA was disqualified for testifying that he believed the defendant violated the law.[162]
- *Stop talking if an objection is made.* If one of the attorneys objects to the question asked or the answer given, stop talking until the judge instructs otherwise.
- *Maintain your composure.* While you answer questions, do not become agitated or defensive or argue with the person asking a question.
- *Answer only when asked.* Do not speak unless addressed by an attorney or the court.
- *Addressing others.* Address the judge as "your honor" and the attorneys by their names.
- *Be interesting.* Try to keep the jurors' interest at all times.
- *Don't be defensive about your credentials.* You should be confident (and express that confidence) that you have the expertise to help the trier of fact come to the correct conclusion regarding the litigation. Don't be afraid to admit that you lack certain credentials and don't hesitate to mention credentials that make you an expert.
- *Be prepared for indirect attacks on your expertise.* Accountants should be prepared for indirect attacks on their expertise. For example, accountants testifying in a matter involving a particular business often are asked whether they are an expert in the company's industry. The questioner hopes to undermine the witness' credibility by having the witness answer "no." Rather than answer "no" (even if true), the witness can respond by answering that the witness is an expert in analyzing companies (or particular aspects of companies) in the industry. Accountants who say something not included in their expert report should be prepared for opposing counsel to ask such questions as: "You didn't say _____ in your report, did you?" or "Where did you say _____ in your report?" Such questions are intended to imply that your expert report is inadequate, that your testimony is inconsistent with your expert report, and/or that you have changed your opinion since you wrote your report. An appropriate response is to explain that you tried to make your report as comprehensive as possible and that in answering opposing counsel's question you were elaborating on what you wrote in your report.
- *Maintain your independence.* You should testify as an expert, not an advocate for a particular litigant. You should be objective, not a hired gun. Avoid making statements (such as "it is our position") that suggest a lack of independence.
- *Don't make personal attacks against another expert witness.* It undermines your professionalism if you make personal attacks against another expert witness.
- *Talk directly to the jurors.* When testifying, you should talk directly to the jurors (or the judge, if the judge is acting as the trier of fact).
- *Be sincere and respectful.* When speaking to the jurors or judge, be sincere and respectful.
- *Refer to your expert report, notes, and supporting documents whenever you're unsure of an answer.* You should bring your expert report, notes, and supporting documents with you when you testify at a deposition, trial, or other legal proceeding. Whenever you're not absolutely sure of an answer, you should refer to those papers and documents to refresh your memory. You're not expected to have memorized your expert report, notes, and supporting documents.
- *Take as much time as you need before answering a question.* Don't feel that you have to quickly answer a question to show your expertise. Take as much time as you need to review your expert report, notes, and supporting documents to find the answer to a question.

- *Answer questions completely.* If a questioner cuts you off before you can complete an answer, make it clear that you have more to say.
- *Don't answer "yes" or "no" if a more complete response is required.* Don't let an attorney intimidate you into answering "yes" or "no" to a question that requires a more detailed answer. Instead, say that a "yes" or "no" answer would not be complete and could mislead the jurors (or judge, if the judge is the trier of fact).
- *Avoid using words that make you vulnerable to attack.* Try to avoid using the words "never," "always," "I guess," "I believe," "I think," "it's possible," or "it seems" when expressing an opinion, but always be truthful. Avoid "very," "just," "pretty," and "really."
- *Don't be afraid to say "I Don't Know" or "I Can't Remember."* Don't be afraid that the judge and jurors or others will think less of you if you have to admit that you don't know an answer or can't remember a detail—if that response is truthful.
- *Admit when you've made a mistake or an omission.* If you find that you have made a mistake or omission, admit it and explain how the new information affects your opinion.
- *If you've changed your opinion, admit it.* If at one time you expressed a different opinion, don't be reluctant to admit that you've changed your opinion. Explain what information has made you change your opinion.
- *Don't feel compelled to read, or agree with, statements taken out of context.* As an expert witness, you should be prepared to be asked whether you agree with particular statements taken from your expert report, expert reports prepared by other witnesses, treatises, and other sources. Before agreeing or disagreeing with a particular statement, you should read the statement and the context in which the statement is made. You should read the material to yourself and then out loud. Don't hesitate to read several paragraphs or several pages if those paragraphs or pages are pertinent to how you answer a question regarding a particular statement culled from those paragraphs or pages.
- *Don't try to answer a question you don't understand.* Instead of trying to answer a question that you don't understand, explain why you have a problem with the question and ask that it be rephrased.
- *Don't answer a question that is ambiguous or includes incorrect jargon.* Rather than try to answer a question that is ambiguous or that includes incorrect jargon, explain any problem you have with the question and ask that it be rephrased.
- *Don't answer questions that combine two or more questions.* Instead of trying to answer a question that combines multiple questions, you should ask the questioner to rephrase the question as a simple query. If you try to answer a question combining multiple questions, your answer is likely to confuse the judge and jurors.
- *Educate, don't advocate.* As an expert witness, your role is to educate listeners, not to advocate one party's position.
- *Determine whether you have any continuing obligations to testify.* After you have completed your testimony and been excused by the judge, determine whether you are obligated to remain in court for additional testimony or may have to return at a later time.

Barbara Tannenbaum says if you use PowerPoint slides, use gestures that are fewer and neater and made with a finger rather than the hand. She believes the impact of an expert is 60 percent visual, 30 percent vocal, and only 10 percent message.[163]

In the fraud-related trial of WorldCom Chief Executive Bernard Ebbers, the judge ruled that the defense could question the prosecution's star witness [CFO Scott Sullivan] about his "marital infidelities" because it reflects on his truthfulness. U.S. District Court Judge Barbara S. Jones said that "the defense is entitled to wide latitude."[164]

The demeanor and communication skills of an expert are important in the courtroom. Advice from two Seak, Inc. experts is informative:

> Is the expert attractive and well groomed? Does he or she communicate well, or does the expert speak with an accent or talk over people? Is the expert arrogant or evasive? How does this person respond to surprise questions? Is the expert prepared and well organized? Does he or she speak loud enough that the jury will be able to hear? Even innocent sounding "jokes" or flip remarks by an expert during deposition may give counsel insight into how an expert's testimony will appear to the jury or fact finder. How an expert will play in front of a jury is crucial for evaluating the settlement value of the case. It is also crucial in determining how valuable a certain expert is.[165]

Babitsky and Mangraviti argue that since 90 percent of most contested disputes never get to trial, the demeanor of the expert witness may have an important impact on the settlement terms.[166] There are no penalties for pausing and taking your time at a transcribed deposition, so take plenty of time. Ask the attorney to repeat the question when in doubt. Pauses and uncertainty, however, will show up on a videotaped deposition. Babitsky and Mangraviti suggest that attorneys will look at your five "Cs:" confidence, calmness, control, care, and coolness under fire.[167]

LEADING WITNESS. "Did you hear her? Was she, for example, singing in the shower or something like that? Moving furniture around?" Freeman was taking advantage of the rules that allowed defense in cross-examination to lead witness, and Freeman was also using this bantering tone to get back into a more relaxed mode with Fred, showing him what a regular Joe he could be.[168]

Defending the Testimony

Expert witnesses should be aware of possible attacks against their testimony and plan to defend against them. Fourteen possible attacks against the testimony of an accountant have been described by Albert S. Osborn[169] (and summarized by Max Lourie):[170]

- Insufficient preparation and experience to qualify as an expert witness.
- Inadequate examination of the issues presented.
- Improper presentation of the issues to the witness.
- Suspicion cast upon the testimony, based upon the witness' personal record and character.
- Use of misleading illustrations, selection of unfair examples, drawing of inferences not justified by the facts, and improper emphasis or exaggeration.
- Impossibility of reaching a conclusion meriting serious consideration on an issue not permitting adequate inquiry.
- Expression of an opinion unjustified by the reasons given.
- Basing an opinion upon vague and trivial facts insufficient to sustain any opinion, and arriving at a conclusion by guesswork.
- A biased and unfair attitude of the witness in the examination of the facts.
- The possibility that the problem is so difficult or unusual that even a competent and careful witness may be mistaken.
- Influence of things other than technical findings on the opinion of the witness, and basing conclusions on reasons other than those given.
- Technical errors in the testimony of the expert witness.
- Serious errors made by the witness in other cases or at other times.
- Corruption or perjury of the witness.

Carl N. Edwards has warned expert witnesses not to let their ego be turned against them:[171] A good lawyer will find a witness' point of vulnerability and use it. For most people, that is ego. "Force the expert to stake his reputation on every opinion" is the motto some attorneys adopt. The forensic accountant shouldn't fall for it! He or she should let the logic of the evidence speak for itself—not to the opposition but to the jury. The wise witness lets the opposition appear the bully while remaining calm and likable.

Some Research Findings

D. N. Ricchiute provides the following information about testifying:[172]

- 65 percent of surveyed jurors were influenced by expert testimony.
- Merely referring to a witness as an "expert" affords the witness credibility.
- Jurors assign more credibility to government rather than AICPA standards.
- Jurors hold auditors to higher standards of care when the audit failure is severe.
- Juror decision-making is not independent of the use and reliability of decision aids.

David Yale shows that a picture is worth a thousand words:[173]

- Studies show that the average person retains as much as *87 percent* of information presented *visually* and as little as *10 percent* for information given *orally*.
- Computer animations are *even more persuasive*.
- Both types of delivery impact the weight given to evidence by jurors (or judges).
- Use visual aids, computer animations, and other visual help whenever possible while on the stand.

D.S. Scott and R. Laguazza give the following suggestions for courtroom behavior:[174]

- Storyboard your testimony (series of sketches).
- Do *not* overdo it.
- Design illustration so jurors can take away the message in 5 seconds. Title should give your conclusion.
- Color is important.
- Put the most important information in the *top* right-hand corner of the chart.
- Do not simply enlarge a document. Highlight important stuff.
- Practice with your exhibits.
- Give your exhibits to the jurors in a plastic protective folder.

Steven Babitsky and J.J. Mangraviti point to a bulletproof expert: one who gives opposing counsel little or nothing productive during cross-examination. This situation is dangerous to the other side because the jury expects counsel to make some good points during cross-examination. When few or no good points are made during cross-examination, the expert's stature is likely to grow significantly and opposing counsel's stature is likely to diminish.[175]

These same Seak, Inc. experts also believe that "jurors are far more influenced by an expert's relevant practical experience, perceived honesty, and demeanor than the expert's academic record or lack of publications."[176] They suggest that if an expert is honest and has a "good amount of relevant hands-on experience," such an expert is more credible to jurors than a professor with many publications, "but who no longer does hands-on work and who has a pompous demeanor."[177]

A novel by J.T. Lescroart provides this advice:[178]

> Further, even though Gage and Terell hadn't gotten them any points, neither had they put too many on the boards for Powell. That, though, could change in an instant. One false move now could turn the momentum of the entire

trial. It was a time to be conservative in the literal sense—conserve what you've already got. Don't let the other side score.

Judge Mary Lisi of the U.S. District Court in Rhode Island keeps her eyes glued to two flat-screen panels on the bench. One displays evidence, and the other displays testimony translated from the court reporter's shorthand into English in real time. With an optical mouse, she flags key testimony and makes notes on the screen.

Both counsel tables are equipped with a flat-screen monitor, and the jury box is equipped—one for every two jurors—with monitors as well. The courtroom has at its disposal a digital camera that projects the image of documents or objects onto each monitor in the courtroom. Judge Lisi affectionately refers to it as ELMO, the manufacturer's name.[179]

KEEPING IT SIMPLE. In the 2007 insider-trading trial against CEO Joseph Nacchio, of Qwest Communication, defense attorney Herbert Stern showed jurors documents demonstrating public statements about Mr. Nacchio's stock sales and revenue projections. "Mr. Stern seemed to lose jurors in tiny print projected on a video screen detailing millions of dollars in Mr. Nacchio's stock sales and Qwest's revenue estimates."[180]

The government prosecutor's presentation, however, "to the jury was slow and simple, but became confusing when Mr. [James] Hearty tried to explain that Qwest was relying on one-time revenue, which he labeled risky, instead of recurring revenues."[181]

Liability of Expert Witnesses

¶ 8211   WITNESS IMMUNITY

For many years, expert witnesses have been protected by the same absolute immunity afforded other witnesses. The administration of justice requires that the testimony of witnesses be unrestrained by the risk of being subject to vexatious litigation. The words that witnesses utter should be protected and not be subject to an action for slander.[182] "Communications made in judicial or quasi-judicial proceedings carry an absolute privilege so that witnesses, bound by their oath to tell the truth, may speak freely without fear of civil suits for damages."[183]

The importance of truthfulness is illustrated by ink expert Larry F. Stewart in the Martha Stewart trial. Prosecutors said that Larry F. Stewart committed perjury on the stand during the obstruction-of-justice trial of Martha Stewart. Mr. Stewart, laboratory director for the U.S. Secret Service, was charged with two counts of perjury, facing five years in prison if convicted. Prosecutors said that Mr. Stewart lied when he said he participated in the testing of ink on a worksheet supposedly showing a pre-existing agreement with Martha Stewart to sell her shares of Imclone stock.[184]

Larry Stewart was acquitted on October 5, 2004. He had said, "I performed a test to determine…," when in effect, he did not participate in analyzing the critical documents. One juror said, "He put his foot in his mouth, and he couldn't take it out because of his ego. He did not walk into the courtroom intending to lie."

An investigator was asked in cross-examination: "'You said that you wrote your notes contemporaneously. Is that correct?'

'Yes,' replied the witness.

'And was the interview conducted at normal conversation speed?' counsel asked, and the witness agreed that this was true.

'They are very neat and tidy, Mr. Jones, aren't they?'

'Yes,' replied the witness and then added a fatal piece of humor: 'Unlike lawyers and doctors, I have been trained to write nicely.'

'Very good, Mr. Jones. I am now going to dictate a passage to you at normal conversational speed, and I would like you to write down notes of everything I say.'"

Within two minutes the witness was a blubbering wreck, because he could not keep pace with dictation. The case was thrown out.[185]

THE CHALLENGE OF TESTIMONY. I liked the grueling task of preparing beforehand and participating in a courtroom battle over accounting principles. There was the challenge to react and respond to the many innuendoes and leading questions asked by the opposing attorney. Probably the stress was not worth the daily fees I received, but I kind of enjoyed it. I sometimes imagined the opposing attorney to be a black-clad medieval knight racing towards me on horse-back with a long, sharp lance. I always toppled the vicious knight in my daydreams, though not always in court.[186]

Threat of Lawsuit

In recent years, state courts have narrowed the protection afforded expert witnesses by ruling that friendly expert witnesses can be sued for negligently preparing their opinions or evidence (e.g., for making a mathematical error), but not for an opinion itself.[187] Typical policy concerns that promote absolute immunity for fact witnesses do not apply to expert witnesses because expert witnesses generally are hired. Because their testimony is expected to benefit their employer, courts have argued that freedom for expert witnesses to testify negligently would not result in more truthful expert testimony.[188] They have been reluctant to shield a professional, otherwise held to the standards and duties of his or her profession, from liability for malpractice simply because he or she was engaged to provide services in relation to a judicial proceeding.[189]

Claims of Negligence

Witness immunity has been held not to protect even court-appointed experts from a claim of negligence.[190] However, even among courts that permit suits against expert witnesses for negligence in preparing their opinions or evidence, there has been a reluctance to permit one litigant to sue another litigant's expert witness for negligence.[191] Those reluctant to permit such suits have argued that litigants do not rely on their opponents' expert witnesses and that permitting such suits would encourage retaliatory lawsuits. Those in favor of permitting such suits have argued that litigants should be able to expect adverse expert witnesses to exercise the same standard of care they are expected to exercise outside litigation.

¶ 8221   BASES FOR LIABILITY

Lawsuits brought by clients against their expert witnesses generally involve breach of contract (for not performing promised services) or negligence.

Breach of Contract

A claim for breach of a contract generally is brought in a state court using state laws, but under certain circumstances a breach of contract dispute may be brought in a federal court (e.g., when there is diversity of citizenship and a claim in excess of $75,000[192]). Sometimes a client's claim is that the defendant failed to exercise the degree of care reasonably expected from an accountant. This negligence-type claim is brought as a breach of contract dispute because the statute of limitations for a negligence or malpractice claim is shorter than for a breach of contract claim.

Breach of contract covers several areas, such as whether the expert failed to perform according to the explicit terms of the service contract, breached an implied duty to perform in good faith, or violated an implied or express warranty. A majority of the courts require these implied duty and care disputes to be brought as negligence claims rather than breaches of contract.

A client may win a breach of contract dispute by showing that the expert failed to (a) perform a specific contracted service, (b) perform a contracted service in a timely fashion, (c) perform in a satisfactory manner, or (d) comply with professional standards.[193]

Negligence

A lawsuit against an expert for negligence is one type of tort action. A negligence claim has a shorter statute of limitations than a breach of contract action.

In order to prove negligence, a plaintiff must show (a) a duty was imposed on the expert in favor of the plaintiff, (b) the expert violated that duty, (c) the plaintiff suffered damages, and (d) the expert's breach was the proximate cause of the damages to the plaintiff. Expert's have a duty to perform their services with care, skill, reasonable experience, and faithfulness. Because an expert possesses special auditing, accounting, or valuation skills, he or she must exercise the average degree of skill, care, and diligence exercised by members of the accounting profession in the same or similar locality.

Criminal Process

In a criminal fraud situation a suspect is arrested or the prosecutor obtains a grand jury indictment. A judge selects and swears in a group of jurors called the *grand jury.* Often composed of retired people or people with flexible work schedules, these 16–23 sworn people meet biweekly or monthly and hand down indictments when at least 12 votes favor them, without the prosecutor present. Because a grand jury has the power to accuse but not the power to convict, the accused has no right to be informed. If the accused person attends, he or she has no right to an attorney.[194]

A grand jury may subpoena witnesses and documents, and witnesses may be compelled to testify under a grant of immunity. If an immunized witness refuses to testify, he or she can be found in contempt and jailed. Once indicted, a party is arraigned by the reading of the indictment in an open court. In a criminal trial the burden of proof on the prosecutor is much higher: beyond a reasonable doubt. Also, under the U.S. Constitution, a person is innocent until proven guilty.[195]

EYEWITNESS

In 2004 and early 2005, Robert David Madrid was getting as much as $175 an hour as a forensic witness in Anniston, Alabama. His resume said he had a master's degree from Georgetown University, a medical degree from Harvard, and a Ph.D. from MIT. He was reading and interpreting medical records for defense lawyers.[196]

In February 2005, sheriff's cars came to his house and officers confiscated two computers and took some personal records. At the Talladega County jail a deputy snapped his arrest mug. The investigator and forensic expert had lied about his degrees.[197]

Dr. Michael Welner received a fee of $30,000 to testify for the prosecution in a criminal case in Pittsburgh. He had this to say about the state of affairs of forensics in criminal trials:

"Expert witnesses testify the way they are paid to testify, and it is almost always the prosecution that has all the money. Some paid experts testify exclusively for the prosecution side, knowing that if they ever testify for the defense, they will be blackballed."[198]

Harsher White-Collar Prison Sentences

The line from Bob Dylan's song "Hurricane" may no longer be true: "All the criminals with their coats and ties, are free to drink martinis and watch the sun rise." WorldCom's Bernard Ebbers received a 25-year jail sentence, and Enron's Jeffrey Skilling received 24 years. Dennis Kozlowski of Tyco got 8 to 25 years. Lord Black of Hollinger International received a prison sentence of 78 months, and was required to pay Hollinger $6.1 million, plus a $125,000 fine. There were 78 counts in the indictment against Enron's Andrew Fastow.[199]

Prosecutor Jeffrey Cramer said this about Lord Black: "Bank robbers are masked and they use guns. Burglars wear dark clothing and use crowbars. These men dressed in ties and wore a suit."[200] But should white-collar crimes be punished more than violent crimes since few burglars get 25-year sentences? At least one writer says no. "Guns and crowbars are used to violate people physically, which is a qualitatively different matter to defrauding them." Christopher Caldwell continued: "Throwing the books at white-collar criminals has provided a dramatic and efficient way of doing that—but not a just or intellectually coherent one."[201]

Federal Sentencing Guidelines

Federal Sentencing Guidelines were adopted in 1984 to emphasize fairness, consistency, punishment, incapacitation, and deterrence in sentencing. This mandatory sentencing regime was in place until the Supreme Court in 2004[202] and 2005[203] converted the guidelines to advisory status, stating that these guidelines violated the Sixth Amendment. District court judges are now required only to consider guideline ranges.

Under the sentencing guidelines the base offense level is determined for a specific offense.[204] For example, the basic offense level for larceny, embezzlement, and other forms of theft is 6 where the loss is $5,000 or less. However, if the loss is more than $2.5 million, add 18 to the 6. Other adjustments are made for victim, role, obstruction of justice, multiple counts, and defendant's criminal history. Negative adjustments can be made for accepting responsibility.[205]

If a company has an effective ethics and compliance program (i.e., internal audit department), three offense points are deducted from the total score. So if the total score is 29 before the reduction of three points, the fine would be $ 8.1 million; whereas a score of 26 results in a fine of only $3.7 million.

If an individual has an offense level of 16 and falls into the first criminal history category, the guideline sentence is 21 to 27 months. If, however, the criminal history category is 5, the guideline prison sentence is 41-51 months.

A Department of Justice Fact Sheet date March 15, 2006 said that as a result of the *U.S. v. Booker* decision, the fairness, consistency, predictability, and accountability that were the hallmarks of the mandatory guidelines are in serious jeopardy as a result of a decline in compliance with the guidelines. Within one year the number of sentences imposed within the guidelines has dropped 62.2 percent.[206] A July 11, 2010, Department of Justice annual letter to the U.S. Sentencing Commission stated that there are now two dichotomous regimes that over time will breed disrespect for the federal courts: some judges follow the guidelines and others ignore them.[207]

¶ 8231   CONCLUSION

As Herbert Rosenthal has said, "a lawsuit is like a parachute jump; you have to get it right the first time." Litigation breeds litigation, so an expert witness may be swimming with sharks when he or she testifies in a courtroom. A knowledge of courtroom procedures is essential to the success of a litigation consultant. Bear in mind that there are biases toward experts:

"The courts hold them in disdain; the parties are offended by their expenses; and the jurors are resentful because the experts arrogantly claim superior knowledge."[208]

Sarah E. Murray summarizes the expert's paradox as an advocate hired by one party in an adversarial dispute. However, an expert "will only be persuasive if the jurors or judge believe that you are a neutral and objective expert (like a scientist), with an opinion that has not been influenced by the adversarial nature of the forum."[209]

David Booth says that business people often believe that their goal in a presentation is to deliver information. The reality is that information presented in a speech is rarely remembered. Images, metaphors, and anecdotes are what stick in listeners' minds.[210] "An expert makes his testimony relate to something the jury can understand from their own experience gained from buying lumber at a lumber yard."[211]

For 16 days Johan Van der Walt was on the stand during the trial of Durban businessman Schabir Shaik. He said, "I don't stress, and I am afraid of nothing. The adrenaline sometimes catches up with me, but I sleep well at night. My job is to find and communicate the facts. I like being cross-examined. Giving evidence is the ultimate test of my work. If I am proven wrong, I will admit it. I do not get emotionally involved in my cases."[212]

The Shaik case was "an enormous task," Van der Walt said. "After we had gone through 152,000 pages of documents, I had to write my report. At one stage I was working 360 hours a month. When we were on deadline we decided it took too long to travel between Johannesburg and Pretoria. We just stayed in Pretoria."[213]

In early June 2005, Shaik was found guilty of two counts of corruption and one of fraud.[214]

ENDNOTES

1. Kalman A. Brown, INVESTIGATIVE ACCOUNTING (New York: Van Nostrand Reinhold Company, 1986), p. 105.
2. Tillinghast-Tower Perrin, U.S. TORT COSTS: 2008 Update (2008).
3. "Cost of the Tort System," ECONOMIST'S VIEW (May 27, 2007), *http://economistsview.typepad.com/economistsview/2007/03/the_cost_of_the.html*.
4. "Civil Bench and Jury Trials in State Courts," 2005 (NCJ 223851), *www.ojp.usdoj.gov/bjs/abstract/cbjtsc05.htm*.
5. George Anders "An Economist's Courtroom Bonanza," WALL STREET JOURNAL (March 19, 2007), p. A-1.
6. Elizabeth MacDonald, "Fannie and Freddie: Shangri -La for Lawyers," Fox Business, March 1, 2013, foxbusiness.com/industries/2012/03/01/fannie-and-freddie-shangri-la-for-lawyers/.
7. G. Morgenson, "Mortgage Giants Leave Legal Bills to Taxpayers," NEW YORK TIMES (January 24, 2011), pp. 1-3.
8. "The Bloodhounds of Capitalism," *The Economist*, January 5, 2013, pp. 47-48.
9. *Ibid.*
10. K2intelligence.com/our-business/
11. *www.Cornerstone.com*.
12. *Ibid.*
13. *Ibid.*
14. George Anders "An Economist's Courtroom Bonanza," WALL STREET JOURNAL (March 19, 2007), p. A-1.
15. *Ibid.*
16. *Ibid.*
17. John Grisham, THE STREET LAWYER (New York: Bantam Dell, 1998), p. 274.
18. E.J. McMillan, THE AUDIT (MD: Harwood Publishing, 2000), p. 259.
19. Clinton Mckinzie, THE EDGE OF JUSTICE (New York: Bantam Dell, 2002).
20. Kit R. Roane, "The CSI Effect," U.S. NEWS & WORLD REPORT (April 25, 2005), p. 50.
21. *Ibid.*
22. *Ibid.*
23. H. Silverstone and M. Sheetz, FORENSIC ACCOUNTING AND FRAUD INVESTIGATION (Hoboken, N.J.: John Wiley & Sons, 2004), p. 233. For more details of the steps in a lawsuit, see Steps in a Trial, American Bar Association (ABA), *http://www.americanbar.org/groups/public_education/resources/law_related_education_network/how_courts_work/steps_in_a_trial.htm*; American Institute of Certified Public Accountants (AICPA) 2009. Introduction to Civil Litigation Services. Special Report 90-1, FVS Section, 7-13.
24. Jilliane Hoffman, LAST WITNESS (New York: G.P. Putnam's Sons, 2005), p. 208.
25. *Ibid.*, p. 234.
26. I.W. Collett and D. Forgione, COSTLY REFLECTIONS IN A MIDAS MIRROR, (Thomas Horton and Daughters, 1995), p. 131.
27. B.W. Muehlmann, P. Burnaby, and M. Howe, "Summary Witness Testimony in Federal Tax Litigation Cases as Identified in Court Opinion," J. of Forensic & Investigative Accounting, January-June, 2013, pp. 1-34.
28. *Ibid.*, p.20
29. John Dunning, THE SIGN OF THE BOOK (New York: Pocket Books, 2005), p. 366.

30   D.L. Crumbley, M. Smith, and L.D. DeLaune, TRAP DOORS AND TROJAN HORSES: AN AUDITING ACTION ADVENTURE (Durham: Carolina Academic Press, 2009), p. 78.

31   Andrew Bernstein, "Forensic Accounting: Exponential Growth," *accountingtoday.com* (February 1, 2007).

32   See, e.g., Rule 53(a) of the Federal Rules of Civil Procedure.

33   See, e.g., Rule 53(c) of the Federal Rules of Civil Procedure.

34   See, e.g., Rule 53(a) of the Federal Rules of Civil Procedure.

35   Penny Sukhraj, ACCOUNTING AGE (18 March 2008).

36   See, for example, the AICPA's *Proposed Statement on Responsibilities for Litigation Services No. 1* (December 1, 2001); AICPA, Communicating in Litigation Services: Reports, Practice Aid 96-3

37   Rule 201 of the AICPA *Code of Professional Conduct.*

38   Rule 101 of the AICPA *Code of Professional Conduct;* AICPA's *Proposed Statement on Responsibilities for Litigation Services No. 1* (December 1, 2001).

39   Rule 102 of the AICPA *Code of Professional Conduct.*

40   AICPA *Proposed Statement on Responsibilities for Litigation Services No. 1* (December 1, 2001), pp. 19–20, 24.

41   Rule 301 of the AICPA *Code of Professional Conduct.*

42   AICPA *Proposed Statement on Responsibilities for Litigation Services No. 1* (December 1, 2001), pp. 19–21.

43   AICPA, *Practice Aid 10-1, Conflict of Interest*, paragraph 55.

44   AICPA, *Statement on Standards for Consulting Services No.1*, 3. Rule 102-2

45   *Ibid*, p. 19.

46   S. Babitsky, J.J. Mangraviti, and C.J. Todd, THE COMPREHENSIVE FORENSIC SERVICES MANUAL (Falmouth, Mass.: Seak, Inc., 2000), pp. 569–572.

47   *Hickman v. Taylor*, 329 US 495, 67 SCt 385 (1947).

48   BLACK'S LAW DICTIONARY, 7th ed.

49   See, e.g., Rule 602 of the Federal Rules of Evidence.

50   See, e.g., Rule 702 of the Federal Rules of Evidence.

51   4 WEINSTEIN'S FEDERAL EVIDENCE § 702.03[3], Mathew Bender, 2d ed.

52   *H.J.F. Montas*, CA-1, 41 F3d 775 (1994).

53   See, e.g., Rule 703 of the Federal Rules of Evidence.

54   See, e.g., Rule 704 of the Federal Rules of Evidence.

55   Carl N. Edwards, "Scientific Evidence: A Short Course in the Applied Forensic Sciences," ACFEi-Core Course-111 (November 1, 1999), pp. 24–25.

56   D.M. Malone and P.J. Zwier, EFFECTIVE EXPERT TESTIMONY (Notre Dame: NITA, 2000), p. 93.

57   The Daubert Tracker website is *www.mdexonline.com.*

58   *In re Paoli Railroad Yard PCB Litigation*, 35 F3d 717 (3rd Cir. 1994).

59   *Frye v. U.S.*, 293 F. 1013 (DC Cir. 1923).

60   509 US 579, 113 SCt 2786 (1993).

61   526 US 137, 119 SCt 1167 (1999).

62   I.W. Collett & M. Smith, TRAP DOORS AND TROJAN HORSES (Thomas Horton & Daughters, 1991) p.127.

63   Rule 702 of the Federal Rules of Evidence.

64   *Ibid.*

65   *Ibid.*

66   *Stagl v. Delta Airlines, Inc.*, CA-2, 117 F3d 76 (1997).

67   *McColluck v. H.B. Fuller Co.*, CA-2, 61 F3d 1038 (1995).

68   *Trumps v. Toastmaster*, 969 F. Supp. 247 (S.D. N.Y. 1997).

69   *General Electric Co. v. Joiner*, 522 US 136, 118 SCt 512 (1997).

70   509 US 579, 113 SCt 2786 (1993).

71   *Daubert v. Merrell Dow Pharmaceuticals, Inc.*, CA-9, 43 F3d 1311 (1995).

72   *General Electric Co. v. Joiner*, 522 US 136, 118 SCt 512 (1997).

73   PricewaterhouseCoopers, "Daubert Challenges to Financial Experts: An 11-Year Study of Trends and Outcomes" (2011), p. 6.

74   *Ibid.*, p. ii.

75   Alex Kozinski, "Expert Testimony After Daubert," JOURNAL OF ACCOUNTANCY (July 2001), pp. 59–60.

76   Alex Kozinski, "Expert Testimony After Daubert," JOURNAL OF ACCOUNTANCY (July 2001), p. 60; V.J. Love and D.L. Goldwasser, "Update on the Preclusion of Financial Experts Under Daubert," THE CPA JOURNAL, July 1999; *Irvine v. Murad Skin Research Lab.*, CA-1, 194 F3d 313 (1999).

77   *SEC v. Lipson*, 46 F. Supp. 2d 758 (N.D. Ill. 1999).

78   *Frymire-Brinati v. KPMG Peat Marwick*, CA-9, 2 F3d 183 (1993).

79   *Cochrane v. Schneider Natl. Carriers, Inc.*, 980 F. Supp. 374 (D. Kan. 1996).

80   *J.V. Rice*, CA-10, 52 F3d 843 (1995), cert. denied, 116 SCt 2536 (1996).

81   For more information, see *Mealey's Daubert Report,* Mealey's Publications, King of Prussia, PA. P.O. Box 62090, 19406-0230.

82   *Target Market Publishing Co. v. ADVO, Inc.*, CA-7, 136 F3d 1139 (1998).

83   Dale Keiger, "The Dark World of Park Dietz," jhu.edu/jhumag/1194 web/dietz.html

84   *Berlyn, Inc. v. Gazette Newspapers. Inc.*, No. 02-2152 (CA-4, Aug. 18, 2003) (unpublished).

85   *Christopherson v. Allied Signal Corp.*, CA-5, 939 F2d 1106 (1991).

86   *F.J. Laureys, Jr.,* 92 TC 101, Dec. 45,446 (1989).

87   B.J. Raby and W.L. Raby, "Reasonable Compensation, Expert Witnesses, and the Tax Practitioner," TAX NOTES (September 15, 2003), pp. 1417-1418.

88   R.E. Figlewicz and Hans-Dieter Sprohge, "The CPA's Expert Witness Role in Litigation Services: A Maze of Legal and Accounting Standards," THE OHIO CPA JOURNAL (July–September 2002), p. 35.

89   *Mathis v. Exxon Corp.*, CA-5, 302 F3d 448 (2002).

90   *In re Visa Check*, CA-2, 280 F3d 124 (2001), cert. denied, 122 SCt 2382 (2002).

91   *TFWS v. Schaefer*, CA-4, 325 F3d 234 (2003).

92   *Lippe v. Bairnco Corp.*, 288 B.R. 678 (S.D. N.Y. 2003), aff'd No. 03-7360 (CA-2, Apr. 9, 2004) (unpublished).

93   *CDM Mfg. v. Complete Sales Representation, Inc.* No. 01-56138 (CA-9, Oct. 29, 2002) (unpublished).

94 *Microfinancial, Inc. v. Premier Holidays Int'l, Inc.*, No. 04-1493 (CA-1, Oct. 5, 2004).

95 See, e.g., Rule 706(a) of the Federal Rules of Evidence.

96 *Ibid.*

97 See, e.g., Rule 706(d) of the Federal Rules of Evidence.

98 See, e.g., Rule 706(a) of the Federal Rules of Evidence.

99 *Ibid.*

100 *Ibid.*

101 *Ibid.*

102 *Ibid.*

103 See, e.g., Rule 706(b) of the Federal Rules of Evidence.

104 *Ibid.*

105 See, e.g., Rule 703 of the Federal Rules of Evidence.

106 *Ibid.*

107 *Ibid.*

108 See, e.g., Rule 705 of the Federal Rules of Evidence.

109 *Ibid.*

110 Rule 26(a)(2)(B) of the Federal Rules of Civil Procedure. See *Walter International Products, Inc. v. Salinas*, 2011 WL 3667597.5.7 (CA-11, 2011), where six experts were not allowed to testify because they did not submit an expert report.

111 *Ibid.*

112 C.L. Wilkins and J.H. Kinrich, Business Valuation/Forensic and Litigation Services Practice Aid 04-1, "Engagement Letters in Litigation Services," a practice aid issued by the AICPA Forensic and Litigation Service Committee.

113 Becca Mader, "The Gumshoe of CPAs: Forensic Accountants Look Beyond the Financials," September 14, 2001, *www.sequence-inc.com/journalsandpubs*.

114 Rule 26(a)(2)(C) of the Federal Rules of Civil Procedure.

115 *Sylla –Sawdon v. Uniroyal Goodrich Tire Co.*, CA-8, 47 F3d 284 (1995), cert. denied, 516 US 822 (1995).

116 Rule 26(b)(2)(C), (e)(1) of the Federal Rules of Civil Procedure.

117 Robert F. Reilly, "Expert Witness Procedures for Accountants: Do's and Don'ts for Success in the Courtroom," 69 CPA JOURNAL (3) (March 1999), pp. 24–28.

118 FRCP 26(a) (2) (B). *Smith v. State Farm Fire & Cas. Co.*, 164 FRD 49 (SD VA 1995).

119 Advisory Committee notes to FRCP 26.

120 *Marek v. Moore*, FRD 298 (DKS 1997).

121 *Indiana Ins. Co. v. Hussey Seating Co.*, 176 FRD 293 (D. IN 1997).

122 *Trigon Insurance Co.*, 88 AFTR 2d 2001-6883 (E.D. Va. 2001).

123 *In re Jackson Natl. Life Ins. Co. Premium Litigation*, 1999 WL 33510008 (DC Mich, 1999).

124 *Bank One Corp.*, 120 TC 174, Dec. 55,138 (2003).

125 *Bank One Corp.*, 120 TC 174, Dec. 55,138 (2003): Judge Laro's Order dated 1/15/03, p. 29.

126 S.M. Hurwitz and R. Carpenter, "Can An Attorney Participate in the Writing of an 'Expert Witness' Report in the Tax Court?" JOURNAL OF TAXATION (June 2004), pp. 358-362.

127 *Ibid.*

128 D.N. Ricchiute, "Effects of an Attorney's Line of Argument on Accountants' Expert Witness Testimony," ACCOUNTING REVIEW (January 2004), pp. 221-245.

129 *Estate of B.I. Mueller*, 63 TCM 3027, Dec. 48,225(M), TC Memo. 1992-284, Doc 92-4343.

130 See B.J. Raby and W.L. Raby, "Reasonable Compensation, Expert Witnesses, and the Tax Practitioner," TAX NOTES (September 15, 2003), p. 1417.

131 See, for example, Robert F. Reilly, "Expert Witness Procedures for Accountants: Do's and Don'ts for Success in the Courtroom," 69 CPA JOURNAL (3) (March 1999), pp. 24–28.

132 83 TCM 1463, Dec. 54,708(M), TC Memo. 2002-92.

133 *Trigon Insurance Co.*, 88 AFTR 2d Par. 2001-5558 (E.D. Va. 2001).

134 *Ibid.*

135 Steven C. Bennett, "On Becoming an Expert Witness," JOURNAL OF FORENSIC ACCOUNTING (December 2002).

136 Courtroom 21 Research Report, "The Use of Technology in the Jury Room to Enhance Deliberation," *www. courtroom21.net*.

137 David Yale, "Computers on the Witness Stand: Expert Testimony That Relies on Data Generated by Computers in the Age of *Daubert*," FORENSICS AND THE LAW (University of Connecticut Law School, 1997) *www. dcyale.com/law_paper/daubert.html#n_16*.

138 Stephanie Kirchgaessner, "Hollinger Chiefs 'Bank Robbers' in Suits, Court Told," FINANCIAL TIMES (March 21, 2007), p. 1.

139 FRCP 30 (g) (2).

140 "In Videotape Depositions, Every Twitch Tells a Tale," The WALL STREET JOURNAL LEGAL BEAT (December 8, 1998), B1.

141 FRCP 30 (e).

142 Steven Babitsky and J.J. Mangraviti, Jr., HOW TO EXCEL DURING DEPOSITION (Falmouth, MA: Seak, Inc., 1999), pp. 20-21.

143 FEDERAL PROCEDURE, Lawyer's Edition (Rochester, NY: Lawyers' Cooperative Publishing, 1994), p. 686.

144 FRCP 45 (a)(1)(c).

145 S. Babitsky and J.J. Mangraviti, Jr., HOW TO EXCEL DURING DEPOSITIONS (Falmouth, MA: Seak, Inc., 1999), pp. 145-148.

146 *Ibid*, p. 144

147 B.P. Brinig, "The Art of Testifying," HANDBOOK OF FINANCIAL PLANNING FOR DIVORCE AND SEPARATION (New York: John Wiley, 1990), pp. 85–87; J.H. Kinrich, M.F. Reiss, and E.R. Kabe, "Forensic Accounting and Litigation Consulting Services," ACCOUNTANT'S HANDBOOK (New York: John Wiley & Sons, 1999), pp. 40-23 and 40-24.

148 D.M. Malone and P.J. Zwier, EFFECTIVE EXPERT TESTIMONY (Notre Dame, Ind.: NITA, 2000), p. 57.

149 *Ibid.*

150 *Ibid,* p. 81.

151 Federal Rules of Civil Procedure Rule 26(e)(1).

152 Robert F. Reilly, "Expert Witness Procedures for Accountants: Do's and Don'ts for Success in the Courtroom," CPA JOURNAL 69 (3) (March 1999), pp. 24–28.

153 WHARTON'S CRIMINAL EVIDENCE, 14th ed., vol. 2 (1986), p. 698.

154 *J.M. Riggi*, CA-3, 951 F2d 1375 (1991).

155 Michael Connelly, THE BRASS VERDICT (New York: Little, Brown and Company, 2008), p. 3.

156 *Ibid.*

157 J.T. Lescroat, THE 13TH JUROR (New York: Dell Publishing, 1994), pp. 337-338.

158 Sheila McNulty, "Enron Case Hanges in the Balance as Jury Retires," FINANCIAL TIMES (May 18, 2006), p. 16.

159 H.J. Bursztajn and A. Brodsky, "Ethical and Effective Testimony During Direct Examination and Cross-Examination Post-Daubert," Lifson, L.E. Simon, R.I, eds. THE MENTAL HEALTH PRACTITIONER AND THE LAW (Cambridge, Mass: Harvard University Press, 1999), pp. 262–280.

160 *Bank One Corp. v. Comm.*, Tax Ct. Dkt. Nos. 5759-95 and 5956-97; See Lee A. Sheppard, "Bank One: The Court's Experts Testify," TAX NOTES (July 9, 2001), pp. 163–169.

161 See, for example, Robert F. Reilly, "Expert Witness Procedures for Accountants: Do's and Don'ts for Success in the Courtroom," CPA JOURNAL 69 (3) (March 1999) pp. 24–28; Jay W. Danker, Communicating with the Jury, Handout materials for the Fifth Annual National Expert Witness and Litigation Seminar, Hyannis, Massachusetts (June 20, 21, 1996), p. 2; 73 Kalman A. Barson, INVESTIGATIVE ACCOUNTING (New York: Van Nostrand Reinhold Co., 1986), pp. 8, 105–108; a United Kingdom expert witness survey prepared by Smith & Williamson and reported at *www. smith.williamson.co.uk/corporate/litigation.html.*

162 *Garnac Grain v. Blackley*, CA-8, 932 F.2d 1567 (1991).

163 Barbara Tannenbaum, "Expert Advice for the Expert Witness," FOCUS, AICPA, November/December 2008, Vol. 4, No. 6, p. 3.

164 A. Latour, S. Pulliam, and S. Young, "Ebbers Defense Rings Up a Win Over Testimony," THE WALL STREET JOURNAL (January 19, 2005), pp. C-1 and C-4.

165 Steven Babitsky and J.J. Mangraviti, Jr., HOW TO EXCEL DURING DEPOSITIONS (Falmouth, MA: Seak, Inc., 1999), p. 22.

166 *Ibid.*, pp. 157-158.

167 *Ibid.*, p. 158.

168 J.T. Lescroat, THE 13TH JUROR (New York: Dell Publishing, 1994), p. 310.

169 Albert S. Osborn, THE PROBLEM OF PROOF, 2d ed. (Newark, N.J.: Essex Press, 1926), pp. 394–395.

170 Max Lourie, "Forensic Accounting," NEW YORK CPA (November 1953), pp. 696–705.

171 Carl N. Edwards, "Scientific Evidence: A Short Course in the Applied Forensic Sciences," ACFEi-Core Course-III (November 1, 1999), p. 38.

172 D.N. Ricchiute, "Effects of an Attorney's Line of Argument on Accountant's Expert Witness Testimony," ACCOUNTING REVIEW (January 2004), pp. 221-245.

173 David Yale, "Computers on the Witness Stand" (Univ. of Conn. Law School, Fall 1996), *www.dcyale.com/law_papers/daubert.html.*

174 D.S. Scott and R. Laguzza, "Communication with the Jury," LITIGATION SERVICES HANDBOOK (John Wiley, 2001), pp. 15-2 and 15-3.

175 Steven Babitsky and J.J. Mangraviti, CROSS-EXAMINATION (Seak, Inc. 2003), p. 392. See AICPA, Serving as an Expert Witness or Consultant, Forensic and Valuation Services Section, Practice Aid 10-1, 2010.

176 Steven Babitsky and J.J. Mangraviti, Jr., HOW TO EXCEL DURING DEPOSITIONS (Falmouth, MA: Seak, Inc., 1999), p. 75.

177 *Ibid.*

178 J.T. Lescroart, THE 13TH JUROR (New York: Dell Publishing, 1994), pp. 343-344.

179 Jim Mckay, "Show & Tell," GOVERNMENT TECHNOLOGY (January, 2005), p.16.

180 Dionne Searcey, "Nacchio Trial Tests Emotions," THE WALL STREET JOURNAL (March 21, 2007), p. B-11.

181 *Ibid.*

182 *Murphy v. A.A. Mathews*, 841 S.W. 2d 674 (Mo. Sup. Ct. 1992).

183 *Briscoe v. LaHue*, 460 US 332, 103 SCt 1108 (1983).

184 Chad Bary, "Stewart Ink-Test Trial Starts," THE WALL STREET JOURNAL (September 24, 2004), p. C-4.

185 M.J. Comer and T.E. Stephens, DECEPTION AT WORK (Burlington, Vt: Gower Publishing Company, 2004), p. 397.

186 I.W. Collett and D. Forgione, COSTLY REFLECTIONS IN A MIDAS MIRROR (Thomas Horton and Daughters, 1995), p.131.

187 See, e.g., *Murphy v. A.A. Mathews*, 841 S.W.2d 671 (Mo. 1992); *Lythgoe v. Guinn*, 884 P. 2d 1085 (Alaska 1994); *Mattco Forge v. Arthur Young & Co.*, 60 Cal. Rptr. 2d 789 (Cal. Ct. 1997); *LLMD of Michigan Inc. v. Jackson-Cross Co.*, 559 Pa 297, 740 A.2d 186 (1999); *Marrogi v. Howard*, 805 So.2d 1118 (La. 2002). However, see also *Bruce v. Byrne-Stevens & Associates Engineers, Inc.*, 113 Wash.2d 123, 776 P.2d 666 (1989) (using witness immunity to protect expert witnesses to ensure their objectivity). The Washington court felt that, in the absence of immunity for expert witnesses, two forms of censorship would occur. First, imposition of liability would discourage anyone who is not a full-time professional expert witness from testifying, because one-time or infrequent experts might not carry the necessary insurance to cover the liability risk in testifying. Second, an expert witness might shade or distort his or her testimony out of fear of subsequent liability, possibly losing objectivity or adopting an extreme position favorable to a client.

188 *Marrogi v. Howard*, 805 So.2d 1118 (La. 2002).

189 *LLMD of Michigan Inc. v. Jackson-Cross Co.*, 559 Pa 297, 740 A.2d 186 (1999).

[190] *Levine v. Wiss & Co.*, 97 N.J. 242, 478 A.2d 397 (1984) (court-appointed expert).

[191] See the discussion in *Davis v. Wallace*, 565 S.E.2d 386 (W. Va. 2002). Texas has permitted suits against an adverse expert witness. *James v. Brown*, 637 S.W.2d 914 (Texas 1982).

[192] 28 U.S.C. §1332(a).

[193] "Breach of Contract," New York Practicing Law Institute (January 2000) Ch. 3.2[B].

[194] The Grand Jury, "Changing the Defendant in the Courtroom," THE WHITE PAPER 15 (5) (September–October 2001), *www.udayton.edu/~grandjur*.

[195] *Ibid.*

[196] Fredrick Burger, "For the Expert Witness, a Few Tough Questions," *Washington Post.com* (April 10, 2005), p. D-01.

[197] *Ibid.*

[198] Paul Carpenter, "Expert Illuminates Perjury Problem Involving Experts; There Is Virtually No Accountability," ALLENTOWN MORNING CALL (Sunday, March 31, 2002).

[199] Christopher Caldwell, "Financial Crime and Punishment," FINANCIAL TIMES, (March 24, 2007), p. 7.

[200] *Ibid.*

[201] *Ibid.*

[202] *U.S. v. Blakely*, 542 U.S. 296 (2004).

[203] *U.S. v. Booker*, 543 U.S. 220 (2005).

[204] U.S. Sentencing Commision, *Guideline Manual*, §3E1.1 (November 2008), *p. 16.*

[205] *Ibid*, p. 395.

[206] Department of Justice, Fact Sheet: *The Impact of the United States v. Booker* on Federal Sentencing, March 15, 2006.

[207] Fascinating Assessment of Federal Sentencing in DOJ Annual Letter to U.S. Sentencing Commission, July 11, 2010, *http://sentencing.typepad.com/sentencing_law_and_policy/2010/07/fascinating-assessment-of-federal-sentencing-in-doj-annual-letter-ot-sentencing-commission.html.*

[208] D.M. Malone and P.J. Zwier, EFFECTIVE EXPERT TESTIMONY (Notre Dame, Ind.: National Institute for Trial Advocacy, 2000), p. *X.*

[209] Sarah E. Murray, "Standing at the Crossroads of Truth and Advocacy," NACVA Conference, Miami, June 3, 2004.

[210] David Booth, "An Actor's Guide to Giving a Great Speech," BOTTOM LINE PERSONAL, (March 1, 2004), p. 8.

[211] Judge Joseph B. Morris, TODAY'S CPA, (May/June 1991), pp. 48-49.

[212] "Following the Cash Trail with the Dogs of War," (November 21, 2004), IOL, *www.iol.co.za/general/news/newsprint.php?art_id=vn20041121104424188C3275774&sf.*

[213] *Ibid.*

[214] John Reed, "Political Fallout from S. Africa Fraud Case," FINANCIAL TIMES (June 3, 2005), p. 7.

EXERCISES

1. Explain the differences between a civil trial and a criminal trial.
2. Outline the five major phases of litigation. Where would a forensic accountant do most of his or her work?
3. List the various types of pleadings.
4. What should be the goal of a forensic accountant in litigation support?
5. Where can one obtain a jury trial?
6. List some trial courts.
7. How can someone get a federal court to hear a dispute?
8. How does the knowledge, skill, experience, training, and education that accountants are expected to have and use in performing litigation services compare with what they are expected to have and use when performing other types of professional services?
9. What professional standards apply to accountants who perform litigation services?
10. What is a conflict of interest?
11. What should be included in a written agreement by an accountant to perform litigation services for an attorney?
12. What is the difference between an expert witness and a lay witness?
13. What does it mean to have to qualify as an expert witness?
14. Outline some ways to challenge an expert witness.
15. What are the normal steps in a simple *Daubert* challenge?
16. What was the major holding of *Kumho Tire Company, Ltd. v. Carmichael*?
17. A *Frye* challenge is appropriate in a District Court dispute. Determine the reliability of this statement.
18. Discuss the difference between weight versus admissibility with respect to *Daubert* challenges.
19. What is a hold-harmless provision?
20. What is the *Frye* standard?

21. What is the *Daubert* standard?
22. Can accountants acting as expert witnesses be advocates for their client? Is advocacy possible for accountants who serve as consultants?
23. On what types of evidence may expert witnesses rely? Give examples.
24. Can accountants acting as expert witnesses base an opinion on confidential client information?
25. What is an expert report? What should the report contain?
26. Can the accountant state his or her opinion about the law in an expert report?
27. Can the attorney who hires the forensic accountant as an expert witness help in drafting an expert report?
28. Can the opposing side see the forensic accountant's working papers if he or she is acting as a consultant? Is access by opposing counsel possible if the accountant is acting as an expert witness?
29. Can the forensic accountant refer to the expert report when he or she testifies at a deposition or trial?
30. What is the difference between direct examination and cross-examination?
31. When testifying at a trial, should the forensic accountant use as much technical language as possible to impress listeners with his or her expertise?
32. If the expert witness does not understand a question, should he or she try to answer it anyway?
33. Can the client sue a forensic accountant if his or her testimony hurts the client's case?
34. What do lawyers dislike the most about expert witnesses?
35. Draft a sample agreement to perform litigation services for an attorney.
36. Draft the qualifications section of an expert report by you as an expert. You may make up credentials, or you may find Larry Crumbley's resume online and prepare the qualification section of an expert report.
37. What is wrong with this question in the courtroom during direct examination: "Didn't the defendant appear to you to be stealing money from the cash register?" Substitute better questions to cover this situation. When might the question be used?
38. On the Internet find (a) cross-examination testimony and (b) recross-examination testimony.

39. On the Internet find information about Joe Nacchio (Qwest). What type of corporate corruption charges might be brought against him and other insiders?
40. Use the Internet to search for the "Federal Grand Jury" site by Susan Brenner. Read some of the FAQs. What is a "runaway" Grand Jury? See what a subpoena looks like. Read the federal grand jury indictment returned against Timothy McVeigh and Terry Nichols.
41. Research states that allow lawsuits against friendly experts.
42. Who bears the burden of proof in a criminal trial and what is it?
43. Explain the metaphor that a lawsuit is like a parachute jump.
44. Look on the Internet for definitions and illustrations of:
    a. *mens rea*
    b. *actus reus*
45. Using the Internet determine the states that allow a friendly client to sue an expert witness. Which states protect an expert witness from lawsuits?
46. Using the Internet, determine the various types of lawsuits against accountants.
47. What does it take to prove negligence in a court of law?
48. What is meant by proximate cause? Use the Internet.
49. What is meant by restrictive privity in Pennsylvania? Near-privity approach? Reasonably forseeability approach?
50. Searching the Internet, find some red flags of risky clients.
51. You are preparing to testify as an expert witness for a fraud issue in an oil/gas industry dispute. Find Larry Crumbley's resume online and then prepare questions and answers for the friendly attorney to ask Professor Crumbley. An instructor may wish to divide the class into groups of three and have each group video the Qs and As. An instructor could use his own resume or other faculty members' resumes.
52. What are Bates numbers? Find some examples on the Internet.
53. What are Audit Technique Guides? Find some on the IRS Internet site. How may an expert use them?

54. Explain the following:
    a. Ambush; serve and volley.
    b. Complex *Daubert* challenge.
    c. Weight versus admissibility.
    d. Hold-harmless provisions.
    e. Side-taking.
    f. Motion to Compel.
    g. Impeachment.
    h. *Subpoena duces tecum.*
    i. Bulletproof expert.

55. Here is a question to and answer from an expert during a fraud trial. Do you consider the answer to be appropriate? Defend your answer.
    Q. Professor, it is agreed that at least $254,000 was embezzled from Sands, Inc. The question that I have today is whether this money was stolen by James Jones. Do you have an opinion?
    A. Yes, he stole it.

56. Here is a question to and answer from an expert during a deposition for an accounting dispute. Do you consider the answer to be appropriate? Defend your answer.
    Q. Doctor, since this dispute involves both auditing strategy and fraud detection, do you consider the textbook *Forensic and Investigative Accounting* to be authoritative?
    A. Yes, I do. It is an excellent book.

57. Locate *Anthony v. Abbot Laboratories*, 106 F.R.D. 461 (1985). What ten factors did this court use to determine a reasonable expert witness fee?

58. Locate *Haarhuis v. Kunnan Enterprise, Ltd*, 223 B.R. 252 (D.D.C. 1998). What was the expert entitled to charge as a fee per hour, portal to portal for travel time?

59. Divide large classes into groups or for small classes students may work alone. Have students or groups take pictures of the various internal controls they can observe. They may use digital, Polaroid, or disposable cameras. Examples of internal controls are locks, safe, passwords, etc.

60. Go online and search for types of retainers for forensic accountants. Bring one to the classroom. One example would be Presentation Dynamics.

61. Locate Judd Robbins' Internet site (*www.computerforensic.net*) and find his curriculum vitae. Prepare questions with answers to ask Mr. Robbins at trial for a forensic accounting dispute.

62. Go online and find some basic fees charged by forensic accountants (i.e., *www.forensiceconomics.net/retainer*).

63. Locate the National Litigation Support Services Association (NLSSA) on the Internet and determine what this group does.

64. Locate Statistical Evidence in Litigation on the Internet. List some court cases on "Economic Damages in Anti-Trust and Price-Fixing."

65. What is a 30(b)(6) deposition of the custodian of records?

66. Locate on the internet and read the Louisiana State Bar Association consumer brochure on "Preparing to be a Witness, Including Deposition and Trial Testimony."

67. Go to the National Clearing House for Science, Technology and the Law (*ncstl.org*) and look through its General Information Resources.

68. Find the Internet site of the National Association of Forensic Economics. Read the NAFE Ethics statement and answer these questions.
    a. When should a practitioner decline involvement in a dispute?
    b. Can a practitioner accept a contingency fee arrangement?
    c. Explain the consistency statement (No. 5).
    d. What is the knowledge statement?
    e. What is the name of the journal?
    f. What type of certificate does it offer?

69. Using the Internet, determine why these expert witnesses got into trouble themselves.
    a. Sandra Anderson (dog handler)
    b. James Bolding, Criminalist IV
    c. Ira S. Dubey, Deputy Director, Suffolk County Crime Lab
    d. Graham Halksworth, Fingerprint Examiner, Scotland Yard

70. Locate *Emanuel M. Sistrunk v. Nicholas Armenakis*, No. 99-36000 (CA-9, 2001).
    a. What did the court say about Dr. Jan Bays?
    b. What is the *Schlup* gateway?

71. Locate *Long Term Capital Holdings*, 330 F. Supp. 2d 122 (D. Conn. 2004), and answer these questions.
    a. The name Scholes is cited often in this case. Who is he?
    b. How large of a special partnership allocation did Scholes receive for his work on the OTC tax shelter scheme (around p. 123 of the decision)?
    c. Scholes, a Nobel Prize winning author, claimed that he lacked detailed tax knowledge. Do you believe that statement?
    d. Was there a conflict between Scholes and the investment banker?

e. On page 72 of the court opinion, who said "if we are careful, most likely we will never have to pay long-term capital gains on the 'loan' from the government?"

72. Is punishment for financial crimes too harsh now when compared to violent crimes?

73. Locate the resume of your instructor on the Internet or obtain a copy from him or her. Prepare a list of sample deposition questions to ask your professor to show the professor as an expert.

74. Using the Internet and other sources, develop a dispute that could be used as a mock trial.

75. Using the Internet and other sources, answer these questions about Bernard L. Madoff.
   a. I am a collector of _____.
   b. When was I born?
   c. I wrote and performed a(n) _____ when I was in the fifth or sixth grade.
   d. I graduated from _____ High school in _____.
   e. I attended University of _____ for one year before transferring to _____ College.
   f. I served three one-year stints as head of _____.
   g. My social security number is _____.
   h. I married _____. Her social security number is _____.
   i. I studied law for one year at _____ law school.
   j. Who reported me to the authorities about my ponzi scheme?
   k. Which of my sons committed suicide?

76. After an auditing firm signed off on Acme's financial statements, Acme's CFO and the head of its sales department were indicted for falsely reporting sales and earnings over a three year period by creating phony invoices on non-existent sales. Acme's CEO and chairman professed ignorance of the scheme and fired the CFO and head of sales once the scheme came to light.
   a. Do you believe these three groups knew of the fraud?
   Acme's CEO _____
   Acme's Board of Directors _____
   External auditors _____
   b. Using a seven-point scale (1=no responsibility; 7=complete responsibility), rate how much responsibility did these parties have to uncover the fraud.
   Acme's CEO _____
   Acme's Board of Directors _____
   External auditors _____
   c. On which side would you support in a lawsuit for professional negligence brought by investors against Acme's accountants?

COMPREHENSIVE PROBLEM

Scott E. Miller, CPA, CVA has given an example of an expert witness in his article entitled "You Got the Litigation Engagement, So Now What," in *The Value Examiner*. Read his example and then prepare a list of mistakes that the expert made in his expert witnessing engagement.

Let's assume there is a CPA, Calvin P. Anderson. Calvin has been a practicing CPA for 15 years. He has a successful CPA firm providing a full range of traditional accounting and tax services but does no litigation support or business appraisal services. Neither Calvin nor his staff have any experience in litigation support or business valuation.

Calvin hears from another CPA that litigation support and business valuation can provide profitable growth areas for CPA firms. He remembers hearing and reading a lot about these practice areas being growth areas for CPA firms and decides that he is interested and wants to look into providing this type of work. His friend tells him there is a three-day seminar on litigation support being held soon and he should take it. Calvin takes the class and gets fired up about the prospects of entering into this new and exciting practice area.

When he gets back to his office, he immediately calls all his attorney prospects and lets them know he can provide these services. He develops some marketing literature and mails it out to his attorney contacts and many other attorneys in his local area.

It's now mid-July and he gets a call from an attorney with a large firm in his home town. Calvin is excited. Working for such a large firm like this one could really help get his litigation practice going. The attorney, Justin C. Esquire, with Peterson, Jones, Haskins and Dingle, LLP asks him about his current practice, education, amount of experience, and whether or not he has any experience with economic analysis. Calvin says, "Of course, I have been doing financial analysis for over 15 years as a part of assisting my clients and besides, you have to analyze financial statements when you do financial statement work." When Esquire asks if he has any experience testifying before, Calvin says yes, knowing that the only time he did was when a client was getting divorced and they asked him to comment on the income reported on his client's tax returns. He thinks, "It was so easy, this can't be much different." Esquire asks his fees and Calvin tells him $150 per hour. Calvin had heard that you could get premium rates for litigation work, so he quoted 20 percent above his normal rate of $125 per hour. Esquire tells Calvin he is willing to pay $135 per hour. Calvin, thinking he is getting a $10 per hour premium, jumps at the chance. Esquire realizes $135 per hour is cheap and that Calvin is not asking for a retainer. Esquire thinks he is getting a great deal for his client.

Mr. Esquire says, "Okay. Let me talk to my client, and I will call you in a couple of weeks." Calvin is excited but nervous. He can't wait to start, but realizes this is new territory for him. Two weeks go by, and he doesn't hear from Esquire. Three weeks later, he gets the call from Esquire. His client has approved the cost of hiring Calvin. Esquire says he will prepare the engagement letter and mail it to Calvin for signature.

Calvin waits for the engagement letter. It is now late August and the engagement letter hasn't come. He sends Esquire an email about the status of the engagement letter, and Esquire responds that he is busy now but will get to it. In late September, the engagement letter comes; Calvin signs it and immediately returns it to Mr. Esquire without carefully reviewing it first.

Esquire calls him in the first week of October and discusses the engagement. It is a wrongful termination action and Esquire represents the employer. He explains to Calvin that he needs to make sure the damages figure is low, because he thinks his client could lose. Calvin tells Esquire that he will do the best that he can but can't guarantee the result will be what his client wants. Esquire ignores the comment and says he will be sending over a package of information for Calvin.

In the third week of October, the package arrives. The package contains a copy of the plaintiff's (Emily Broke) last three paychecks showing she earned a salary of $4,000 per month, a copy of her last two years' tax returns, a typed list of her benefits, and a brief letter stating that Emily Broke was a senior training manager at a manufacturing company. She started in May 1991 and was terminated on December 23, 2001, after complaining about her manager's sexual advances.

Calvin reviews the information and begins to calculate her potential damages. The benefits listed are medical and dental insurance, three weeks of vacation, and two weeks of sick pay per year. He includes in his analysis her lost wages, lost medical and dental benefits, lost vacation, and lost sick pay. There is no information about the actual employer cost of her medical and dental insurance. Calvin thinks about it and decides that since it is only an estimate, he could use a "reasonable" proxy for the cost, so he looks at his own medical and dental insurance bill and uses his cost of $450 per month to project her lost benefits.

Calvin calls a friend of his who is an account executive at a temporary placement firm to find out how long it normally takes someone to find a job similar to Ms. Broke's. His friend tells him that most people find a job in three to six months. Thinking he is being generous, Calvin calculates six months of wages and medical and dental benefits and the accrued vacation and sick pay she would have received had she remained with the company.

Calvin adds it all up and emails the amount to Mr. Esquire in the first week of November. His analysis is as follows:

Lost wages (6 x $4,000)	$24,000
Lost benefits (6 x $450)	2,700
Lost vacation (3/4 x $4,000)	3,000
Lost sick pay (2/4 x $4,000)	2,000
Total lost wages & benefits	$31,700

Esquire looks at the figure and is quite excited. It is less than he thought and way below the $1,000,000 the plaintiff is seeking. He emails Calvin and tells him of his pleasure and asks Calvin if he is done with his work. Calvin responds that he is done.

Two weeks later, Mr. Esquire calls Calvin asking where his expert report is. Calvin is confused. He provided the amount. "What the heck is an expert report?," he thinks. He was never told one was required or when it was due. Then Esquire tells him he has three days until it has to be submitted to the court. Calvin tells Esquire he already started it (although he hadn't) and it will be done in time.

He hangs up the phone with his hand shaking and asks himself, "What do these things look like? What information do I need to include?" He doesn't want to let Esquire know he doesn't know what he is doing, but he needs to find out how to prepare his expert report. So, he calls his friend, Oscar Ripley CPA, and asks what an expert report looks like. Mr. Ripley tells him that expert reports aren't required in Oregon so he can't help. Calvin can't understand why one is due if they aren't required. He then decides to call one of his friends who is an attorney for help. His friend, Justin C. Scales, tells him not to worry and faxes him a copy of the Federal Rules of Civil Procedure rule 26 [FRCP (26)]. Calvin reads rule 26 but is unclear exactly what he needs to do. He takes a stab at it anyway.

Calvin is feeling better now but is still quite nervous. A light bulb goes off over his head, and he calls Mr. Esquire and asks if he has any particular format he likes for expert reports based upon FRCP (26)(a)(2)(B). Esquire is impressed; he thinks, "This guy knows the rules." He tells Calvin he will have his secretary fax him one tomorrow and hangs up before Calvin can object and ask for it today. Calvin says to himself, "Oh great, all I have is 24 hours to get this report done."

He gets the fax around 11 a.m. the next day with a note that his report is due to Esquire by 3 p.m. He has only four hours. Yikes!! He has a lunch appointment with a prospective new client that is supposed to last from noon to 2 p.m. Calvin realizes that no matter what he does, he loses. He has his secretary call the new client to reschedule the lunch and to pick up a sandwich for him, since he will have to work through lunch.

He puts everything aside and dives into his work. He prepares his report which contains sections for the parties, background of the lawsuit, the amount of damages, and the signature block. The parties section simply states "Emily Broke—Plaintiff," "Ding Bells Manufacturing—Defendant"; the background section is a few lines stating that Ms. Broke was fired for not being a team player; in the damages section he indicates he used the data provided by Mr. Esquire regarding Ms. Broke's earnings and benefits, and then he states the total amount of damages. He signs the report and faxes it to Esquire at 2:30 p.m.

At 4:30 p.m., Calvin is just leaving to take his wife out to dinner for her birthday when Esquire calls screaming, "This won't work! I thought you knew how to do one of these things!" Calvin stutters and fortunately for him, Esquire blurts out that he needs his CV and that Calvin needs to detail all of the information sources he used to form his opinion, the work he did to come to his conclusions, a list of any testimony he gave by deposition or at trial over the past four years, and a list of the articles he has authored in the past seven years. Esquire tells him he needs it NOW. Esquire immediately hangs up and calls the plaintiff's attorney, Dudley Doright, to see if he is willing to give him a one-day extension so he can go over Calvin's report prior to submitting it to the court. Dudley knows he doesn't have to give the extension and his refusal could harm Esquire's defense, but he decides that he will allow it anyway. Esquire thanks him for the professional courtesy and hangs up.

Calvin panics. "What should I do?," he thinks, "What happens if I don't get this to Esquire in time?" He calls his wife and tells her something came up and he has to work for a while. His wife reminds him that they have reservations at 6:30 p.m. and he tells her not to worry and that he will meet her at the restaurant.

Calvin realizes he doesn't have a CV prepared and knows he testified several years ago in a client's divorce but can't remember when. He isn't exactly sure what a "CV" is, but based upon how Esquire was talking, he thinks it is a resume. He prepares his CV like a resume for a job interview by listing all of his previous jobs, salary and positions, length of employment, transferable skills, and educational background.

He sits back and tries to remember when he testified for his clients, the Dorfenburgers. To find out, he goes into his storage room and scours his "dead" files. He finally finds the box with the Dorfenburgers' files. As he pulls the box out of the storage rack, he catches his shirt on the frame and tears it. To make things worse, he scraped the back of his wrist on the frame and it is bleeding. Now he is not only scared about his work for Esquire, he is angry.

He looks through the file and finds the date. He puts a sentence in his CV stating he testified in the divorce of his ex-clients, the Dorfenburgers, in 1998. He hasn't written any articles, so he doesn't indicate anything.

At 6:15 p.m. the phone rings and it's his wife. She asks where he is and if he will be at the restaurant in time. He tells her not to worry that he may be a few minutes late but to have a drink and he will be there soon.

He then starts working on his report again. He struggles with it and finally faxes it to Esquire at 7:10 p.m. He dashes out of his office and races to the restaurant. He gets there at 7:30 p.m. By this time, his wife is just finishing her third martini and ordering a fourth. Not only is his wife extremely angry with him, she is tipsy. He looks awful because he is covered with dust, his shirt is ripped, and there is blood on his shirt and pants. Needless to say, dinner did not go very well.

The next morning, he gets a call from Esquire telling him he got his report and it still doesn't have everything that is required. "Calvin, I thought you had experience and knew what you were doing. Well, do you?," Esquire says. Calvin's tongue gets stuck in his throat and he coughs and manages to stammer, "Well, not doing reports, but I am an excellent analyst." Esquire realizes Calvin doesn't know what the heck he is doing and starts to think about how he can save face with his client and get a reasonable report submitted by the end of the day.

Esquire tells Calvin to email him his files and that he will pull it together into the right format. At 4 p.m., he gets a call from Esquire's legal assistant who tells him that she will be emailing him the signature page and he needs to print it, sign where indicated, and fax it back immediately. He grabs the signature page, signs it, and faxes it back to her immediately. Calvin is swamped with work from a large audit that he dropped to do Esquire's work, so he just files the signature page away and gets back to his other work. Calvin never reviews the report.

On December 29th, Calvin is preparing his month end invoices and statements and notices that Esquire hasn't paid any of his invoices. He sends Esquire an email, and Esquire replies that per the engagement letter, he doesn't get paid till the end of the case. Calvin reviews the engagement letter and realizes that not only is Esquire correct, he only gets paid if the client prevails!

Calvin doesn't hear from Esquire until February 2nd. Esquire calls to tell him that they have had no luck settling, so trial is scheduled for February 10th and he needs to meet with him at 2 p.m. on the 8th for trial prep and to bring his files with him. Although it is in tax season, Calvin takes some (minor) consolation that it is early February and not in March or April.

At noon on February 8th, Calvin tells his staff to hold all his calls and leave him alone because he has to prepare for his meeting with Esquire. At 1:30 p.m. as he is getting ready to leave his office, he gets a call from Esquire telling him the trial has been postponed and he will let him know when the trial will be rescheduled. Calvin is finally having something go his way! He heard that most cases settle and hopes that this one will so he will never have to testify.

On March 1st, he gets a call from Esquire. The trial has been rescheduled for April 4th and should last three days. Esquire tells Calvin they should meet on Saturday the 2nd for trial prep and that he isn't sure what day or what time so he will call Calvin. He also tells Calvin that he should be prepared to be at the courthouse two hours after he calls him. Calvin is speechless. "What do I do?," he thinks, "How will I be able to handle my regular tax client appointments and be ready at a moment's notice to be in court?" If Calvin hadn't already had questions about what he got himself into, he sure does now.

When they meet on April 2nd, Calvin asks Esquire when he anticipates being called and is told that the Plaintiff will put their case on first, so he doesn't anticipate calling him on the 4th but to be ready on the 5th, 6th, or 7th depending on how things go. Calvin stops for a moment and asks, "I thought you said it was only a three-day trial. How can it go longer?"

Esquire chuckles and says, "You are a newbie aren't you? Do you really think trials go exactly the length they are planned for?" He adds, "It doesn't happen as often as you might think, so be prepared to be called at any time."

Calvin gets depressed again. "How will I deal with the many client meetings I have scheduled on those days and be available to Esquire when he needs me?," Calvin thinks. He tries rescheduling some of his appointments and having his staff cover for him, but there are still some clients that can only make the originally scheduled days. He forces the issue and tells those clients that he must reschedule because he has to be available for Esquire.

The clients are not as understanding as he would have liked, and they tell him they will call back when they know when they can come in. Calvin thinks he better make Esquire happy with his testimony, or he will have gone through this for nothing, because he will probably lose some or all of the clients he has put off.

April 4th, 5th, and 6th come and go and at noon on the 7th, Calvin gets "the call" to be at the courthouse at 2 p.m. Calvin immediately rushes to his calendar and looks at his schedule. He has to cancel three more appointments and more if he doesn't get back by 5 p.m.

At 1:30 p.m., he grabs his file and heads to the courthouse. At 1:45 p.m. he walks into the courtroom and is told by the judge, "Get out! Witnesses aren't allowed during the testimony of other witnesses." "Well, that started off well," Calvin says to himself. So he leaves and sits down outside the courtroom.

Two o'clock comes and goes and still no Esquire. By 3:30 p.m., he still hasn't been called to testify. He has read every document in his (admittedly thin) file over a dozen times by now. It is now 4 p.m. and Esquire comes out to call him in to testify, "Are you ready, Calvin?" He replies, "As ready as I can be."

Calvin enters and is sworn in. He sits down and for the first time realizes it is a jury trial. Esquire begins by asking him a few questions about his education and experience and then makes a motion to have Calvin admitted as an expert. Opposing counsel does not oppose the motion because the CV attached to Calvin's expert report shows a great deal of experience. Esquire asks Calvin just a few questions and lets plaintiff's counsel, Dudley Doright, cross examine Calvin.

Well, Dudley is a pretty good attorney and after reading Calvin's report, he knows Calvin hasn't done his work properly. Mr. Doright begins his cross examination by asking Calvin if he brought all his work papers with him today. Calvin says yes. Doright then asks the judge for a brief recess so he can review Calvin's work papers. The judge grants a 15-minute recess. Mr. Doright takes Calvin's work papers and sits down to review them.

The judge and jury reenter and Doright begins his cross examination. He starts by asking Calvin how many times he has calculated damages in a wrongful termination matter, and does he have any training specifically doing these types of damages calculations. Calvin squirms and says, "Ah, no." Doright then asks him if his practice is primarily tax related. Calvin says, "We do other things than just tax work." Doright then asks, "Well what do you do, and what is the percentage breakdown?" Calvin thinks for a moment and says, "70 percent tax, 20 percent financial statement services, and 10 percent personal financial planning and business consulting." Calvin is then asked, "What percentage of your work is calculating economic damages?"

Doright asks, "In reviewing your file, Mr. Anderson, I noted your engagement letter with Mr. Esquire's firm says that you only get paid if they win this case. Is that true?" "What?," Calvin says. Doright approaches, shows him the engagement letter, and asks the question again. This time Calvin has no choice but to say yes. Doright knows that he can get Calvin immediately excluded as an expert but decides that he can have more fun with Calvin by not doing so. Calvin, for the first time, realizes that he has fed himself to the wolves and will be lucky to leave the courtroom with his head intact.

Mr. Doright then pulls out Calvin's report and questions him about his damages analysis. Doright asks Calvin to describe the elements of damages and why they are relevant in this case. Doright then asks Calvin if there are any others that he may have inadvertently missed. Calvin is totally stunned. He looks at Esquire while franticly flipping through his work papers, and then he gives Doright a blank stare not knowing how to respond. Doright then reiterates, "Well Mr. Anderson, are there any elements of damages you may have missed?" Hoping it is a trick question (he has seen that many times on *Matlock* and *Law & Order*), he answers, "No, it's all there."

Unfortunately for Calvin, television is not reality, and Mr. Doright asks Calvin about social security taxes, worker's compensation, unemployment insurance, and pension benefits. By this time, Calvin wants to just crawl into a hole and die as that will be easier than going through this. Calvin answers, "Social security and unemployment insurance are taxes, so no, and she voluntarily withdrew all of her vested pension funds and lived on them after her termination so she gave up any potential gain they might have had."

Mr. Doright is now smiling from ear to ear. Everyone in the courtroom knows that Calvin has just committed hari-kari. Mr. Doright sits back in his chair and looks at Calvin. He is contemplating whether or not to continue or just let Calvin leave with his tail between his legs.

Doright decides that he wants to bring it all out so he asks Calvin about where he got the variables used in his analysis. "Why did you choose six months? Where did you get the $450 per month for the cost of insurance? Did you know that Ms. Broke was disabled and therefore may have a more difficult time finding employment?," he asks. All Calvin can do is to sink lower and lower into his chair, say no, and pray for the torture to end.

Doright knows that Calvin has been destroyed but decides he needs to be sure that his expert's damages figure of $1,000,000 is the only one the jury thinks of, so he asks Calvin for his file and then pulls out some emails between Calvin and Esquire. He begins to ask Calvin a question about one, when Esquire objects but the judge overrules him. Doright intends to read the email to the jury. He stands up, walks in front of the jury box, then turns and asks Calvin if he had a conversation with Mr. Esquire about the quality of his case. Esquire objects again on the grounds of attorney client privilege. The judge overrules his objection.

Calvin doesn't know what Doright is talking about so he tells the truth and says he's not sure. Doright reads the notes of the conversation between Calvin and Esquire in which Esquire tells Calvin that he was "probably going to lose" and needs the damages to be as low as possible. After reading it out loud in front of the jury, Doright asks Calvin if it is true. Calvin stammers, "Ah, ah, ah, yes?" Doright then hands the notes in Calvin's own handwriting to the jury to see for themselves. Mr. Doright decides to drive the point further (into Calvin's heart) and continues to ask Calvin about the comment and why Esquire told him that. Calvin says he doesn't know.

Doright, knowing better, asks if it was to keep the potential losses down. Calvin looks at Esquire and thinks he is about to have a heart attack. With what seems to be his last breath, Calvin says, "Yes." Doright then asks the final question, "Do you believe your damages calculation is correct?" Calvin hangs his head and with a whimper he says, "No sir." Mr. Doright says that is all and sits down giving Esquire a chance for redirect. Esquire knows the case is now over, and he has no way of countering the plaintiff's expert who says her damages are $1,000,000. All Esquire can think about is why did that idiot make that note? Esquire determines the best thing to do is to cut his losses and not question Calvin again.

It is now approaching 5 p.m., so the judge ends the trial for the day and says it will start up again at 9 a.m. with any further witnesses Mr. Esquire may have. Calvin dashes out of the courtroom nearly in tears. When he gets back to the office, he finds five messages from other CPAs asking for information on Calvin's "ex-clients" so they can prepare their current year tax returns. Calvin sits at his desk sobbing. He has just lost a couple of thousand dollars a year of income, pissed off his clients, and will never get any business from Esquire again, not to mention the potential malpractice issues. Calvin decides after that fiasco never to do it again.

Back at the courthouse, Esquire knows he has just lost his case; he approaches Doright and asks if he can still accept their last offer of $700,000. Doright says he is not predisposed to do that, but he will talk to his client. Esquire watches as Doright speaks to Ms. Broke. He can see they are both laughing at him and Calvin. Doright calls Esquire over and says, "We never thought we would get a million bucks and actually were hoping to settle this thing for about $400,000 to 500,000. Given the risk of getting less, my client has decided to take your gracious offer. Can you have a check to my office within three business days?"

Back at his office, Esquire thinks back to his original interview with Calvin. He remembers how he thought he was pulling the wool over Calvin's eyes with a $135 per hour rate and getting an inexperienced guy to give him the low damages figure he wanted.

When Calvin submits his final bill, Esquire sends him an email saying that the engagement letter said he would only get paid if they prevailed. Calvin thinks Esquire may be right and even if he pushes the issue he will be sued for malpractice, so he writes off the $4,000 bill.

9

PROPER EVIDENCE MANAGEMENT

The admissibility of different forms of evidence varies widely from jurisdiction to jurisdiction. Testimony which is customary in one city may be prohibited in the community next door. Evidence is governed by statute, case law, and federal regulations.

—Carl N. Edwards[1]

OBJECTIVES

After completing Chapter 9, you should be able to:

1. Understand the rules of evidence and their importance to your work as a litigation consultant.
2. Know how communications between accountants and their clients can be protected and what steps to take to protect such communications.
3. Protect the integrity of evidence and ensure its admissibility into evidence at trial.
4. Be aware of technology that can help the forensic accountant to gather evidence.

OVERVIEW

Accountants who perform litigation services need to base their conclusions and opinions on sufficient relevant evidence. In general, forensic accountants can gather evidence from accounting records and legal documents (depositions), interviewing, employee searches (e.g., desks, computers), internal control charts, observation, invigilation, and possibly undercover work. This chapter explains the basic rules of evidence, examines basic evidence issues that affect accountants when performing litigation services, explains what needs to be done to preserve the integrity of evidence and make sure it is admissible at trial, and discusses various types of technology that can help accountants gather evidence. Since forensic accounting is often used in legal forums, forensic accountants must be familiar with legal concepts and procedures. Nothing spoils a great case quicker than the lack of evidence. Expert opinions are evidence.[2]

In a humorous movie, *The Other Guys*, Allen Gamble (played by Will Ferrell) is a straight-laced, gullible detective/ forensic accountant. Allen says in the movie script:

> Until there is a piece of paper with the word guilty on it, justice cannot be served. Paperwork is the oxygen Justice breathes. So feel free to make fun of me behind my back.

Robert Frost once said that "a jury consists of twelve persons chosen to decide who has the best lawyer." The same can be said about expert witnesses. A passage from *Retribution* is instructive:[3]

> C.J. knew that you could find an expert somewhere who would say almost anything, refute even the most airtight evidence with conviction, if paid enough. Psychologists who would blame pro wrestling for a teenager's act of cold-blooded murder; doctors who would blame death on a heart attack rather than on a drunk driver. For the right price, there were witnesses for any defense, any legal theory. And sometimes it worked.

As Colin Evans has suggested:[4]

> It is one of the curiosities of human nature that experts tend to gain gravitas with the number of air miles they rack up. This is particularly true in a court of law. For some reason, when a witness has flown across a continent - - or in this case, halfway around the world - - to deliver his or her testimony, it invariably carries considerably more weight than if the same testimony had emanated from a local lab.

As Arthur Conan Doyle said in The Hounds of the Baskervilles, "It is not what we know, but what we can prove."

Basic Rules of Evidence

¶ 9001   WHAT ARE THE RULES OF EVIDENCE?

The rules of evidence are the rules governing the admissibility of evidence in a legal proceeding and the weight to be given to evidence that is admitted.[5] The U.S. federal courts follow the Federal Rules of Evidence. State courts usually follow their own rules.

Rules of evidence are designed "to secure fairness in administration, elimination of unjustifiable expense and delay, and promotion of growth and development of the law of evidence to the end that the truth may be ascertained and proceedings justly determined."[6]

¶ 9011   WHAT IS EVIDENCE?

Evidence is testimony, writings, and material objects offered to prove an alleged fact or proposition.[7] Evidence other than oral testimony is sometimes referred to as *real evidence*. This term represents mere terminology and does not express a preference for or superiority of tangible over oral evidence.

There are two basic types of evidence: direct and circumstantial. Although the media often deride circumstantial evidence, the law does not value it any less than direct evidence.[8]

Direct evidence is evidence that directly proves a fact at issue, without the need for any inference or presumption.[9] The most common form of direct evidence is testimony based on a witness's personal knowledge or observation of facts in controversy.

Circumstantial evidence is evidence from which a fact at issue may be proved indirectly.[10]

Think of the difference between the two types of evidence this way: Suppose during the night it snows around your house. If you wake up during the night and see it snowing, that is direct evidence. However, if you sleep during the night and only observe the snow the next morning, that is circumstantial evidence.

The novel *The 13th Juror*[11] provides a somewhat humorous definition of documents:

> "Documents" is used herein in the broadest sense and includes all written, printed, typed, graphic or otherwise recorded matter, however produced or reproduced, including non-identical copies, preliminary, intermediate, and final drafts, writings, records, and recordings of every kind and description, whether inscribed by hand or by mechanical, electronic, microfilm, photographic or other means, as well as phonic (such as tape recordings) or visual reproductions of all statements, conversations or events, and including without limitation, abstracts; address books; advertising material; agreements; analysis of any kind; appointment books; brochures; calendars; charts; circulars; computer cards; contracts; correspondence; data books; desk calendars; diagrams; diaries; directories; discs; drawings of any type;
>
> Estimates; evaluation; financial statements or calculations; graphs; guidelines; house organs or publications; instructions; inter-office or intra-office communications; invoices; job descriptions; ledgers; letters; licenses; lists; manual; maps; memoranda of any type; microfilm; minutes; movies; notes; notebooks; opinions; organization charts; pamphlets; permits; photographs; pictures; plans; projections; promotional materials; publications; purchase orders; schedules; specifications; standards; statistical analyses; stenographers' notebook; studies of any kind; summaries; tabulations; tapes; telegrams; teletype messages; videotapes; vouchers; and working drawings, papers and files.

An expert may base his or her opinion on business records reviewed even though these records are not placed into evidence.[12]

The courts are even using Wikipedia, The Free Encyclopedia on the Internet as a resource. Wikipedia, with more than three million articles, had 606 cites in the federal and state cases database on LexisNexis as of April 11, 2010, and 2,086 document cites in Westlaw's Journal and Law Reviews as of April 18, 2010. Courts also have cited other websites, such as Wiktionary and the Urban Dictionary.[13] Judge Richard A. Posner of the Seventh Circuit says that "Wikipedia is a terrific resource, partially because it is so convenient; it often has been updated recently and is very accurate."[14]

Cass R. Sunstein, visiting Professor at Harvard Law School, says "I love Wikipedia, but I don't think it is yet time to cite it in judicial decisions." Many citations by judges are in footnotes, outside the main judicial point, essentially soft facts, or tangential. So if judges can use information from Wikipedia to make their opinions more readable, expert witnesses should be able to do the same, selectively.[15]

Law reviews are being cited less and less; Chief Judge Dennis G. Jacobs of the Federal Appeals Court in New York says, "no one speaks of them. No one relies on them." So the legal academy has become much less influential at the same time the courts' case-load has exploded. Some professors suggest that judges may not have the intellectual curiosity to appreciate legal scholarship, as the articles in law reviews have become more obscure. Possibly judges are now using Lexis or Westlaw, rather than searching law review articles.[16] For an expert witness, however, a law review article can be an excellent resource, especially for learning a new area.

¶ 9021　PROCESS FOR DETERMINING THE ADMISSIBILITY OF EVIDENCE

The evidence that a fact finder may use to support a finding is determined through a process of admission and exclusion based on offers by the proponent and, sometimes, objections by the opponent. With limited exceptions, a failure to object is treated as a party's waiver of any right to appeal a judge's ruling on the admission of particular evidence.

In addition to offering evidence, a proponent may make an offer of proof in order to make a record on appeal to show that substantial prejudice resulted from exclusion of particular evidence. In the case of testimony, the offer of proof may be in the form of an oral offer by counsel, who sets forth the substance of the testimony. The court also may take the testimony out of the presence of the jury in order to make a record. When a party knows in advance that evidence will be offered that will prejudice the jury if it is heard even if it is excluded, the opponent can bring a motion *in limine* to exclude the evidence or request that the offer be made outside the presence of the jury. Courts usually are attentive to the opponent's reasonable concerns in this regard.

For evidence to be admissible, sometimes a specific factual foundation is required. For example, in order for hearsay to come in under an exception, facts on which the exception is based must be proven. A court may be required to make a preliminary finding of fact prior to admitting the evidence. The concepts of conditional and limited admissibility can play an important role, however. Evidence may be admitted on condition of its being "linked up" to other evidence. If that does not occur, the evidence may be stricken, and the jury will be instructed to disregard it. Also, evidence can be admitted for a limited purpose. Evidence that is objectionable when offered on general grounds may be admissible when offered for a limited purpose.

Under the concept of judicial notice, a court can take as proven certain matters that are considered indisputable, matters of common knowledge, and certain ascertainable facts from unquestionably accurate sources, such as a calendar, road map, or government mortality table. The process of taking judicial notice can be confusing. A court may be more likely to decline to take judicial notice when an opposing party objects. Therefore, the process of taking judicial notice can resemble a stipulation, although it is conceptually different.

¶ 9031　RELEVANCE REQUIREMENT

To be admissible in court, evidence must be *relevant*.[17] As a general rule, all relevant evidence is admissible, except as otherwise provided by law or the rules of evidence.[18] Evidence that is not relevant is not admissible.[19]

Even though evidence is relevant, the evidence may be inadmissible in court if its probative value is substantially outweighed by the danger that it will unfairly prejudice a litigant by suggesting a decision on an improper basis, confuse the issues, or mislead the jury.[20] Relevant evidence also may be inadmissible if its probative value is substantially outweighed by considerations of undue delay, waste of time, or needless presentation of cumulative evidence.[21]

An expert is not needed for common knowledge. "An expert who supplies nothing but the bottom line supplies nothing of value to the judicial process."[22] In another dispute, a trial court held that a manager of an accounting firm's "fairly simple pass" opinion was not acceptable merely because he was an expert in accounting. This expert conceded that he did not employ the methodology that experts in valuation find essential. The accounting expert used a discounted cash flow analysis, assigning a value of zero to a number of projects that had low or negative net cash flow.[23]

Circumstantial Evidence

Evidence is *relevant* if it has "any tendency to make the existence of any fact that is of consequence to the determination of the action more probable or less probable than it would be without the evidence."[24]

Evidence can prove a fact directly, such as direct testimony that states the fact to be proved. For example, a witness's testimony based on personal knowledge that a person was present on a given occasion (e.g., during the time of a theft), offered to prove that fact, would be direct evidence. An expert witness' testimony is considered to be direct evidence. However, evidence does not have to prove an issue directly but instead may be part of a chain of inferences. This type of evidence is called circumstantial evidence. Despite arguments disparaging circumstantial evidence, direct evidence is not necessarily more compelling.

EXAMPLE 9.1 For circumstantial evidence to be relevant, it must be supported by a logical inference. To prove that Ms. A and Ms. B were doing business together, it would probably be appropriate to show that they had lunch together in a prominent financial district restaurant. People who "do lunch" together are more likely also to do business than those who do not do lunch. The fact that they had lunch does not in and of itself prove that they engaged in business. They may merely be friends. A finding based solely on this evidence would probably be inappropriate. But the evidence has a tendency in reason to support the inference that they had a business relationship. This is "logical relevance," as opposed to those concepts of relevance that really express judicial policy.

Inflammatory Evidence

Although evidence may be logically relevant, its probative value may be outweighed by the likelihood that the jury will use it for a purpose that is improper, such as a conscious or unconscious bias against a party. This action often happens with evidence that tends to show that the party engaged in some sort of immoral or illegal conduct that is in and of itself irrelevant to an issue in the case. If the same result can be obtained by use of different evidence or if the value of the evidence is minimal, the court may exclude the inflammatory evidence, because one or more jurors may become prejudiced against that party who is unfavorably portrayed. There are also other creative ways in which a court can exercise its discretion regarding inflammatory or prejudicial evidence, such as redacting the offending parts or accepting a stipulation by the other side to the fact in issue.

Evidence About Plaintiff's Character

There is a general rule that evidence of good or bad character is inadmissible to prove conduct on a specific occasion. The same can be said for bad acts. The usual exception is where "character is in issue," such as in a defamation action. In that situation the plaintiff claims the defendant's conduct damaged his or her good name. The defendant has the right to prove the plaintiff had no or minimal good name to damage. Evidence of relevant specific conduct would also be admissible. Furthermore, character evidence is admissible if it is offered for some other, limited purpose, such as impeachment.

In a Michigan District Court dispute a CPA spent 2,000 hours assisting in the prosecution of a claim for damages because of alleged wrongdoings of defendants. The judge said that an expert may not opine on the ultimate liability of defendants even though an expert may give the jury all of the information from which the jury can draw inferences as to the ultimate issues.

Further, expert testimony is not needed to determine if someone is telling the truth. After listening to the expert's testimony, the judge said that the expert was trying to "weave a story." He "selected those portions of the available material which support his client's position, and has deliberately ignored other portions that do not support his client's claim."[25]

Evidence of Habit

Evidence of habit may be admissible, especially when it tends to be repeated or nearly invariable. The point at which it becomes clear as to whether there is a habit is one for the jury, provided there is at least enough information to support a finding of a habit. "Custom and practice" or "routine practice" is a form of habit evidence and is often used to establish business practice, including authentication of business records.

Exclusionary Rules

There are special exclusionary rules based on policies determined by the courts over time to promote justice. One of these involves subsequent remedial measures. Evidence of such conduct is often excluded because parties would be discouraged from doing something about dangerous or improper conditions if their doing so would be used as evidence against them. A special exclusionary rule also applies to offers of settlement and similar matters. In order to promote resolution of disputes, evidence of offers of compromise or settlement, settlements, plea bargaining, and pleas of *nolo contendere* are inadmissible. The rule of exclusion also applies to discussions or negotiations relating to settlement or compromise.

Evidence of Liability

If offered to prove liability, evidence of liability insurance is admissible in the federal courts.[23]6This special rule seems unnecessary and represents a historical outgrowth because the evidence is not logically relevant. Evidence of liability insurance can be used for other, limited purposes, such as showing proof of ownership of a car. However, since it could be viewed as prejudicial, the court would probably exclude it under its discretionary authority, if other equally satisfactory means of proof existed, such as the motor vehicle registration.

¶ 9041   PRIVILEGED COMMUNICATIONS

Individuals within certain protected relationships (such as attorney–client, doctor–patient, and priest–penitent) cannot be forced to disclose on the witness stand statements made during the course of their relationship. Such statements are referred to as *privileged communications*. The nature, extent, and application of the rules of privilege can vary widely from jurisdiction to jurisdiction. Each privilege represents a policy determination for that jurisdiction.

In analyzing issues relating to privilege, the accountant needs to identify and understand the policy that supports the privilege. Every privilege represents a determination that the decision-making process should be deprived of relevant evidence for overriding policy considerations. A further helpful concept in understanding privileges is to identify who the "holder" is. The holder is usually the person who should have the right to complain if the allegedly privileged information is disclosed. For example, in the case of the spousal witness privilege, one view might be that the testifying spouse is the one who should be the holder. This privilege is for the purpose of preserving the marriage relationship. If a testifying spouse is willing to testify over the other's objection, arguably there is not much to preserve. However, these rules are not always perfectly rational. In some jurisdictions one spouse can prevent the other from testifying even when willing to do so.

Exceptions to Privilege

Once it has been determined that a privilege applies, this information cannot be used for any purpose, including discovery. There are usually exceptions for disputes between the parties to the privilege. Also, in general, there is usually an exception where the asserted privileged communication or advice is for commission of a crime. Privileges can be waived by failure to object or by voluntary disclosure. However, if the evidence is protected, the court and counsel are prohibited from commenting on it, and the jury or other fact finders may not properly draw an inference from the fact of its assertion. In order to establish the existence of a privilege, a factual foundation may be necessary.

Attorney–Client Privilege

One of the most commonly encountered privileges is the attorney–client privilege. In general, for the privilege to exist there must be an attorney, a client, and a confidential communication between them relating to legal advice. Definitions vary and are subject to complex nuances. For instance, the privilege does not apply to physical objects, including documents prepared by or addressed to third parties, merely because the client deposited the documents with the attorney. Exceptions to the privilege include malpractice cases and disputes between joint clients.

Employee Communications

Whether statements secured from employees of a company for purposes of litigation fall within the attorney–client privilege is controversial. A communication may be protected by the privilege when the subject matter of the communication is within the course and scope of the declarant's employment, the employee knows that the statement is confidential and will be used to obtain legal advice for the company, and the information is not obtainable from a higher source. A forensic accountant who is charged with obtaining such statements must find out from the attorney under what circumstances employee communications fall within the scope of the privilege.

Work Product Rule

The United States Supreme Court has recognized a qualified privilege for certain materials prepared by an attorney acting for his or her client in anticipation of litigation.[27] Under this rule, known as the *work product rule*, personal memoranda, written statements of witnesses, and other materials prepared by an attorney in anticipation of litigation need not be disclosed to other parties involved in litigation. The work product rule was developed to prevent an attorney's work product from being used against a client and undermining the attorney–client privilege.

Accountants, unlike attorneys, have no accountant–client privilege under federal or state common law.[28] The United States Supreme Court has noted that barring disclosure of communications to accountants would "ignore the significance of the accountant's role as a disinterested analyst charged with public obligations."[29] Some states (e.g., Louisiana) have recognized an accountant–client privilege (usually rather limited) by statute.

Although no accountant–client privilege has been recognized under the common law, a limited privilege has been provided with respect to tax advice.[30] With respect to tax advice, the same common law protections of confidentiality that apply to a communication between a taxpayer and an attorney apply to a communication between a taxpayer and any federally authorized tax practitioner (e.g., an individual authorized under federal law to practice before the IRS) to the extent that the communication would be considered a privileged communication if it were between a taxpayer and an attorney.[31] This privilege applies only to noncriminal tax matters before the IRS and noncriminal tax proceedings in federal court brought by or against the United States.[32] This privilege does not apply to any written communication between a federally authorized tax practitioner and a director, shareholder, officer, or employee, agent, or representative of a corporation in connection with the promotion of the corporation's direct or indirect participation in a tax shelter.[33] Such protection does not apply to accountants and other federal authorized tax practitioners when they engage in work other than lawyers' work (e.g., protection does not extend to communications between a tax practitioner and a client simply for the preparation of a tax return).[34]

This area of blocking the IRS's access to some communication under Section 7525 is very fluid. In general, the work product doctrine does not protect audit opinion letters, tax opinion letters, accountant worksheets, tax accrual workpapers, tax pool analyses, or items prepared by a company's in-house counsel to assist outside auditors in preparing financial disclosure statements.[35] Although the First Circuit may be an exception,[36] tax accrual workpapers probably do not qualify as protected work product.[37]

Attorney-Requested Accounting Work

The attorney–client privilege covers work by accountants performed at an attorney's request for the purpose of helping the attorney give proper legal advice.[38] After confirming with counsel that the privilege applies, a forensic accountant should carefully document that the work is pursuant to the privilege. One way to document this is to label each page of privileged work papers as such.

Work done for an attorney by a forensic accountant that does not fall within the attorney–client privilege may nevertheless be protected by the attorney work product privilege. However, the scope of the attorney work product privilege may vary with the subject matter. Generally, an attorney's own work product (e.g., the thought processes of the attorney) receives special protection and is nearly absolutely protected. The work of a forensic accountant who assists the lawyer is conditionally protected. The other side may be able to obtain the information for good cause shown if compelling enough circumstances are demonstrated. Obtaining such information is generally difficult, however. The party who is seeking discovery must show substantial need and inability to obtain equivalent information by other means. However, if the expert is to serve as a witness, then all work performed by that expert from inception is subject to discovery. This rule applies even if the work was originally a privileged work product while the expert was serving only in an advisory capacity and had not been designated as a testifying witness. The decision to make the expert a witness waives the work product privilege from inception.

No work product rule has been applied to accountants. Code Sec. 7525, which provides a limited confidentiality privilege for communications between a taxpayer and a tax practitioner, has not created a work product rule for accountants and other federally authorized tax practitioners.[39]

Must Draft Copies Be Saved?

A practitioner may be engaged as a consultant or an expert witness. The engagement letter generally determines whether a practitioner is a consultant or expert witness. Sometimes a consultant may eventually become an expert witness. Generally, an expert witness's documents are discoverable, but a consultant's documents are not discoverable (with exceptions).[40]

In federal courts and many state courts an expert witness must prepare a written report. Due to the practice of electronically-prepared draft reports, these drafts are often not recorded on paper. Not retaining draft copies is quite common among litigation experts and consultants. Often if a consultant's report is provided to the expert, these draft reports are requested from opposing counsel.

Is an expert required to save all drafts? Saving a new version of every keystroke is extremely burdensome. However, each time an expert makes a revision to an original draft, there is a "write over" of the initial draft document. Since draft reports provide a glimpse into an expert's understanding of a dispute, opposing counsel wish these draft reports in order to cross-exam the expert with respect to the input provided by counsel and the evolution of the final opinion.

Attorneys try to use this work product privilege to avoid sharing the work of consultants (non-testifying) and expert witnesses (testifying). In general, to gather protection under this privilege, a non-testifying consultant should follow these tips:[41]

- Attorney should directly retain the consultant/ expert witness.
- Agreement (engagement letter) should be between attorney and expert.
- Expert should obtain facts through, or at direction of the attorney.
- Investigation should be done at the direction of the attorney.
- Attorney included when meeting with client (at least initially).

Before December 1, 2010, there was a split in the Federal courts as to the discoverability of an attorney's work product provided to an expert and draft expert reports. A majority of the courts held that any material provided by an attorney to an expert (including draft reports) are discoverability.[42] This bright-line approach was outlined by the Sixth Circuit:[43]

> The bright-line approach is the majority rule, represents the most natural reading of Rule 26, and finds strong support in the Advisory Committee Notes. Therefore, we now join the "overwhelming majority" of courts . . . in holding that Rule 26 creates a bright-line rule mandating disclosure of all documents, including attorney opinion work product, given to testifying experts.

A minority of courts had held that opinion work product (as opposed to fact work product) is not discoverable, even if the communication is given to a testifying expert. A minority of courts believed that an attorney's opinion or core work product (e.g., mental impressions, opinions, legal opinions, and conclusions) as stated in FRCP 26(b)(3) are not discoverable unless there is substantial need. *Hickman v. Taylor*[44] stated in 1947 that the work product doctrine generally protected parties from disclosing documents prepared by or for an attorney in anticipation of a court battle. Further, a Michigan District Court held that an attorney's work product was not discoverable merely because the material is shared with a testifying expert.[45]

Key positive changes to the Federal Rules of Civil Procedure became effective on December 1, 2010. These new practical rules extend the work-product privilege to include certain communications between testifying expert witness and the retaining attorney.

Rule 26(b)(4)(A) and (B) now protect drafts of any reports or disclosures required, regardless of the form in which the draft is recorded (e.g., handwritten, electronic, typing, etc.). Further, Rule 26(b)(4)(C) protects communication between the party's attorney and any witness required to prepare a report, regardless of the form of the communications (e.g., e-mail, depostion). There are three exceptions:

1. Relate to compensation for the expert's study or testimony;
2. Identify facts or data that the party's attorney provided and that the expert considered in forming the opinions to be expressed; or
3. Identify assumptions that the party's attorney provided and that the expert relied on in forming the opinions to be expressed.

These changes will not apply to states that have not adopted the Federal Rules of Civil Procedure.

In these states, attorneys should instruct their experts in writing to preserve draft documents and communications. Once an expert or consulting expert has finished a preliminary draft and sent it to counsel for review, the expert should preserve that version and create a new document for any revisions. The same practice should be followed for each subsequent draft. Counsel also should save each draft in both electronic and hard-copy formats.[46] A failure to preserve drafts and e-mails may result in sanctions, such as exclusion of expert's report and testimony as well as adverse inferences.

Other suggestions for state courts include:

1. Both sides can agree in writing that draft documents will not be requested, and they need not be retained by the experts.
2. Limit written communications with attorneys, including e-mails.
3. When drafting written communications, consider how it will appear to opposing counsel.
4. Counsel should avoid giving opinion work product to the testifying expert.
5. Avoid ghost written reports (e.g., reports written by or improved by counsel).
6. Maintain a clear delineation between the consulting function and the expert function.[47]

Medical Privilege

Medical privileges are sometimes encountered in civil litigation, particularly cases involving personal injury. Generally, these privileges consist of the physician-patient and psychotherapist-patient privileges. For the doctor or physician/patient privilege to apply, a confidential communication relating to treatment or diagnosis must be made between a doctor and patient. This privilege is usually deemed waived by a patient who tenders his or her physical condition as an issue in litigation (e.g., a personal injury claim). The privilege often does not apply in criminal cases. Generally, the psychotherapist/patient privilege applies only to confidential communications relating to diagnosis or treatment. This result is considered controversial. A frequently expressed view is that there should be an exception for dangerous patients.

Spousal Privilege

The spousal testimonial privilege allows a party to litigation to refuse to testify against his/her spouse or to prevent the spouse from testifying against that party. A separate privilege, the spousal communication privilege, applies to confidential communications between spouses. There are many exceptions, such as for intrafamily crimes, interspousal litigation, and collusive marriages.

Other Types

Communications between a cleric or priest and a penitent usually are privileged. Some states limit the privilege to sacramental communications. The penitent is usually the holder of the privilege, which has no exceptions.

There are now a variety of governmental privileges, such as for state secrets, official information, and information from informants. A forensic practitioner in business disputes may be more likely to encounter these privileges than some of the more commonly known ones, especially when attempting to assist counsel to obtain governmental records. Generally, information that has been preserved as a trade secret will be protected. But the privilege is not absolute and may be easily waived by a showing that confidentiality has not been properly preserved.

¶ 9051   HEARSAY RULE

As a general rule, hearsay is not admissible as evidence in a legal proceeding.[48] The reason for excluding *hearsay*—which is an oral or written assertion (or nonverbal conduct intended as an assertion), other than one made by the declarant while testifying at the trial or hearing, offered in evidence to prove the truth of the matter asserted[49]—is that such statements are considered untrustworthy.

Whether a statement has been offered to "prove the truth of the matter asserted" has been one of the most frequently litigated issues in the law of evidence. Most of the time, a statement is easily recognizable as hearsay, and the real question is whether an exception applies. Nevertheless, in some frequently encountered situations a statement that appears to be hearsay is offered for a nonhearsay purpose (i.e., to prove a fact other than the matter asserted):

- *Legally operative fact.* Sometimes the fact that a declarant made a statement, not whether the declarant was lying or mistaken about the substance of the statement, is legally significant. For example, that a customer gave notice of a breach of warranty may be offered to prove that notice was given but not to prove that there was a breach of warranty.
- *Effect on the listener.* If the importance of a statement lies in its effect on the listener, it is not hearsay. For example, someone's statement to Joe's employer that "Joe is a thief" may be offered to show why the employer fired Joe but may not be offered to prove that Joe is a thief.
- *State of mind of the declarant.* A statement made by a declarant may be evidence of the declarant's state of mind, regardless of the truth or falsity of the statement. For example, Susan's statement to a business colleague that "Mike is a crook" may be offered to prove that Susan was not likely to have made an oral business agreement with Mike but may not be offered to prove that Mike is a crook.
- *Impeachment.* Prior statements of a declarant may be offered to impeach the declarant. Generally, the fact that a person made an inconsistent statement may support the inference that the person cannot be believed, regardless of which statement is the truth. Therefore, the statement is being offered for a purpose other than the truth of the matter asserted.

Evidence that otherwise would be hearsay can be used to support an expert opinion if it is of the sort reasonably relied on by experts in the same field. However, a court may limit the ability of counsel to present the hearsay evidence to the jury and may limit the expert to simply describing it. Nevertheless, as discussed below, some hearsay evidence that is relied on by expert witnesses may come into the courtroom indirectly through the expert's testimony.

When hearsay is admitted into evidence, it is often through one or more of the exceptions. There are three concepts underlying the exceptions to the general rule barring hearsay:

- *Trustworthiness.* Some types of hearsay are considered sufficiently trustworthy to merit admission into evidence. For example, an excited utterance is thought to be more reliable because of its spontaneity, although this assumption has been disputed.
- *Unavailability of the declarant.* Some exceptions apply only if the declarant cannot testify at trial. However, a declarant's unavailability will not make an exception available if the reason the declarant cannot testify at trial is because the person wishing to present the declarant's statement as evidence made the declarant unavailable.
- *Practical considerations.* Because prior inconsistent statements, which can be admitted to impeach a witness, and prior consistent statements, which can be admitted to rehabilitate a witness, are in evidence before the jury, it is considered just as well to let the jury consider such statements on their merits. The rationale is that it is almost impossible for jurors to listen to such statements for impeachment or rehabilitative purposes alone and otherwise disregard matters asserted.

The Federal Rules of Evidence treat some types of statements traditionally excepted from the hearsay rule as not being hearsay.[50] For example:

- *Prior statements by a witness.* A statement made at a prior trial or hearing that is subject to cross-examination may be presented into evidence if (1) inconsistent with the declarant's testimony and was given under oath, (2) consistent with the declarant's testimony and is offered to rebut an express or implied charge against the declarant of recent fabrication or improper influence or motive, or (3) a statement of identification of a person made after perceiving the person.[51]
- *Admissions by a party-opponent.* The following types of statements may be offered against a party: (1) a party's own statement in either an individual or representative capacity, (2) a statement that a party has manifested an adoption or belief in its truth,

(3) a statement by a person authorized to make such a statement, (4) a statement made by the party's agent or employee during the existence of their relationship concerning a matter within the scope of the agency or employment, and (5) a statement made by a party's coconspirator during the course and in furtherance of their conspiracy.[52]

Some of the hearsay exceptions are available regardless of whether the declarant is available as a witness:

- *Business records.* A record, report, memorandum, or data compilation of an act, condition, opinion, or diagnosis is excepted from the hearsay rule if made at or near the time by, or from information transmitted by, a person with knowledge, was kept in the course of a regularly conducted business activity, and was the regular practice of the business activity to make the record, report, memorandum, or data compilation.[53] The absence of a matter in admissible records of a regularly conducted activity can be presented in a legal proceeding to prove the nonexistence or nonoccurrence of the matter if a record regularly was made and preserved about such matters.[54] Normally, the custodian or another qualified witness must testify about recordkeeping, and the method of preparation must not suggest untrustworthiness. In many states, custodians need not personally testify but instead may submit affidavits. The opposing side can subpoena and cross-examine the custodian, nevertheless. For the convenience of the trier of fact, summaries are often admitted if the records are voluminous.
- *Commercial publications.* Market quotations and other published compilations are exempted from the hearsay rule if they are generally used and relied upon by the public or persons in particular occupations.[55]
- *Learned treatises.* Statements in published treatises may be relied on by an expert witness during direct examination or called to the attention of an expert witness on cross-examination if the treatise is established as a reliable authority by the testimony or admission of the witness, other expert testimony, or by judicial notice.[56]
- *Public records.* The record of a document purporting to establish or affect an interest in property may be presented in a legal proceeding as proof of the content of the original recorded document and its execution and delivery if the record is a record of a public office and applicable law authorizes the recording of such documents in that public office.[57] Statements in such documents are exempted from the hearsay rule if relevant to the purpose of the document, unless dealings with the property have been inconsistent with the truth of the statement since the document was made.[58] Record, report, statement, or data compilation of a public agency is excepted from the hearsay rule if the record, report, statement, or data compilation sets forth the agency's activities or matters as to which the agency had a legal duty to report.[59] Records and data compilations of births, deaths, and marriages are exempted from the hearsay rule if they were made to a public office as required by law.[60]
- *Past recollection recorded.* A memorandum or record concerning a matter about which a witness once had knowledge but now cannot recall in sufficient detail to testify about fully and accurately may be read into evidence under an exception to the hearsay rule if the memorandum or record was made or adopted by the witness when the matter was fresh in the witness's memory.[61]
- *Statements in ancient documents.* Statements made in documents that have been in existence for a specified number of years (e.g., 20 or more) are exempted from the hearsay rule if the authenticity of the documents can be established.[62]
- *Present sense impressions.* A statement describing or explaining an event or condition that an individual makes while perceiving the event or condition or immediately thereafter is exempted from the hearsay rule.[63] An example would be the statement "I see Mac striking a match" just before the explosion occurred, as evidence of the cause of an explosion.
- *Excited utterances.* A statement relating to a startling event or condition that an individual makes while under the stress of excitement caused by the event or condition is excepted from the hearsay rule.[64]

- *Declarant's existing mental, emotional, or physical condition.* An individual's statement regarding his or her state of mind, emotion, sensation, or physical condition is exempted from the hearsay rule.[65] This exception does not include statements of an individual's memory or belief to prove the fact remembered or believed.[66]
- *Statements made for medical diagnosis or treatment.* A statement made by an individual regarding the individual's symptoms and medical history is exempted from the hearsay rule if made for the purpose of medical diagnosis or treatment.[67]

Some hearsay exceptions apply only if the declarant is unavailable:

- *Former testimony.* Testimony given as a witness at another hearing of the same or different proceeding or in a deposition in the course of the same or another proceeding is excepted from the hearsay rule if the party against whom the testimony is now offered (or a predecessor in interest) had an opportunity to develop the testimony by direct, cross, or redirect examination.[68]
- *Dying declarations.* A statement made by a declarant while believing that his or her death was imminent is excepted from the hearsay rule if the statement concerned the cause or circumstances of what the declarant believed to be his or her impending death.[69] Statements about other subjects, including someone else's death, do not fall within the exception. The traditional rule required that the declarant must have actually died and was limited to murder cases. In at least one jurisdiction, California, the exception today applies in any type of situation.
- *Statement against interest.* A statement that, when made, was contrary to the declarant's pecuniary or proprietary interest or tended to subject the declarant to civil or criminal liability or render invalid a claim that the declarant had against another is excepted from the hearsay rule if a reasonable person in the declarant's position would not have made the statement unless he or she believed that the statement was true.[70]

A declarant is "unavailable" as a witness if the declarant is exempted by privilege from testifying, the declarant refuses to testify despite a court order to do so, the declarant testifies that he or she has no memory of the statement, the declarant cannot testify because of physical or mental illness or infirmity, or the proponent of the statement has been unable to procure the declarant's attendance by process or other reasonable means.[71] A declarant will not be considered "unavailable" as a witness if the exemption, refusal, claim of lack of memory, inability to attend, or absence is due to the procurement or wrongdoing of the proponent for the purpose of preventing the witness from testifying.[72]

Equivalency Exception

A statement not specifically covered by a rule of evidence nevertheless may be excepted from the hearsay rule if a court determines that the statement has equivalent circumstantial guarantees of trustworthiness, the statement is more probative on the point for which it is offered than any other evidence that the proponent can procure through reasonable efforts, and the interests of justice will best be served by admitting the statement into evidence.[73]

Hearsay Within Hearsay

Sometimes a hearsay statement contains a hearsay statement. This situation is referred to as "multiple hearsay" and is fairly common in business records. In such situations, each statement must qualify for an exception, but each statement may qualify for a separate exception.

An expert must be careful during deposition and testimony not to suggest that certain written material is authoritative. Federal Rule of Evidence 803(18) permits the introduction of relevant material from written sources to get around the hearsay rule if an expert states that a particular source is authoritative. If an opposing attorney can get the expert to "concede the existence of reliable authorities in the field," the material later may be used at trial to help their side.[74] Or the attorney may spend hours questioning you about material in the document.

¶ 9061   AUTHENTICATION REQUIREMENT

To be admissible as evidence in a legal proceeding, a document or other material usually must be authenticated or identified as what its proponent claims it to be.[75]

Great latitude is allowed parties in authenticating evidence. For example, an item may be authenticated by a witness with knowledge of what the item is claimed to be. An item also may be authenticated by its distinctive characteristics (e.g., appearance, content, substance, or other distinctive characteristics). Evidence that a document's condition creates no suspicion concerning its authenticity, the document was where it likely would be if it were authentic, and the document has been in existence for a number of years (e.g., 20) may be sufficient to authenticate the document.

Voices sometimes can be authenticated by recognition. In the case of telephone calls, however, the caller may not know the voice on the other end of the call, such as a call to a business. Nevertheless, a telephone call can be authenticated in the same manner as writings, including authentication by content and the number dialed or by showing it was made in reply to an earlier communication.

A showing that the process by which computer records were prepared was accurate may serve as adequate authentication. Computer records increasingly are being subpoenaed as evidence, especially with regard to business litigation. Because of the complexities that can arise with authentication of computer records, notice to the court and opposing counsel may soften some of the difficulties or issues relating to admissibility.

Certain materials are exempted from the authentication requirement because they are considered self-authenticated.[76] Examples of self-authenticated materials are: public documents; certified copies of public records; official publications; newspapers and periodicals; acknowledged documents; and inscriptions affixed in the course of business that indicate ownership, control, or origin.[77] The original or duplicate of a record of a regularly conducted activity is admissible as self-authenticated if its custodian certifies that the record was kept in the course of the regularly conducted activity; was made by the regularly conducted activity as a regular practice; and was made at or near the time that the matters set forth occurred by, or from information transmitted by, a person with knowledge of those matters.[78]

Ultimately, the jury decides authenticity. The court need only determine that there is sufficient evidence for the jury to make a factual determination.

¶ 9071   BEST EVIDENCE RULE

Under the *best evidence rule* (also referred to as the *original writing rule*), to prove the contents of a writing, recording, or photograph, the original writing, recording, or photograph usually must be presented.[79] The best evidence rule historically required that original documents be produced, rather than "secondary" evidence, including oral testimony. Historical rules permitted "duplicate originals" when a copy was executed and intended to have the same effect. Then came typewriters, and carbons became duplicate originals. Photocopies never were duplicate originals, however. They were just copies. Today the rule is influenced by practicality and is often governed by statute. For example, usually a computer printout is admissible as an "original," provided that it is authenticated and a foundation of accuracy is laid.

Exceptions for secondary evidence traditionally have been made where the original was lost, destroyed, or unavailable and cannot be obtained by process. There are also exceptions for documents in the possession of the opponent. Other practical exceptions include official writings that are otherwise properly authenticated, voluminous evidence where a summary is more appropriate, and copies where the original is produced for inspection. There is also an exception for "collateral" writings, whose contents are not important to the issues in the case. A duplicate is admissible into evidence if there is no genuine question as to the authenticity of the original, and it would not be unfair under the circumstances to admit the duplicate in lieu of the original.[80] If all of these exceptions do not enable forensic accountants to get by the best evidence rule, they are really having a bad day.

¶ 9081   DEMONSTRATIVE EVIDENCE

Demonstrative evidence is an item that illustrates testimony but has no probative value in itself (such as a chart, diagram, photograph, video, or model). Trial counsel may have the forensic expert prepare exhibits that set forth calculations and analyses. These exhibits are sometimes referred to as "chalks," by analogy to a witness drawing a diagram on a chalkboard.

Whether demonstrative evidence can be presented at trial depends on whether it is considered relevant. Does it have a tendency to assist the fact finder? If the judge thinks so, it will be admitted, unless it contains inappropriate content or is prejudicial. If the evidence is designed to appeal to the jury's passions or prejudices or if it is distorting or may be confusing, then the court will keep it out. Because demonstrative evidence has no probative value, there is no need to authenticate it in a technical sense.

Easy to read charts, tables, and graphs are helpful aids for an expert witness. But Dean E. Hienberg indicates that demonstrative exhibits must be accurate. He gives the example where an expert's large spreadsheet exhibit had a significant mathematical mistake early in the exhibit.

The opposing attorney gave his expert a calculator and a large red marker. The opposing attorney then asked his expert to add two numbers near the top of the exhibit. When the numbers did not add, the expert would cross out the original amount and place next to it on the exhibit the correct figure.

"Unfortunately, when the testimony was completed, the expert's exhibit had mostly red lines through it. Looked as if the chart had been bleeding. Unfortunately, so did the expert's credibility. The jury sided with the other side."[81]

¶ 9091   SPECIAL RULES FOR CRIMINAL CASES

The rules of evidence in criminal cases are more complicated than those in civil cases because the government is a party and an individual's personal liberty is at stake. Many of the rules of evidence in criminal proceedings have been modified to take into account an individual's special constitutional rights with respect to criminal matters. For example, the Fourth Amendment protects individuals against unreasonable searches and seizures, the Fifth Amendment protects defendants against self-incrimination, and the Sixth Amendment gives defendants the right to confront witnesses against them.

Constitutional issues often are raised by defense motions to suppress evidence and prosecution motions for discovery of such items as blood samples and writing exemplars. Because of a defendant's right against self-incrimination, the prosecution's opportunity for discovery of evidence is much more limited than a plaintiff's discovery rights in a civil action. The Confrontation Clause of the Sixth Amendment may be raised with regard to out-of-court identifications.

Some states have enacted specific legislation regarding what evidence can and cannot be introduced regarding a victim's past. The defendant may proffer evidence of his or her good character only in regard to the character trait that is an aspect of the crime charged. For instance, in a prosecution for assault the defendant may offer evidence of his or her character for nonviolence. But the defendant who chooses to testify may not offer evidence of veracity, unless first impeached. The prosecution can attempt to rebut any evidence of character once the defendant tenders the issue. Rules differ from jurisdiction to jurisdiction as to the method by which character may be proved and rebutted.

The following quote from Connelly's novel, *The Brass Verdict*, discusses the art of discovery.

"Wouldn't that come out in the discovery material?"

"Not always. There is an art to discovery. Most of the time it's what is not in the discovery file that is important and you have to watch out for. Jeffrey Golantz is a seasoned pro. He knows just what he has to put in and what he can keep for himself."[82]

PROSECUTOR'S ADVANTAGE. In his novel, Connelly states, "There is an unfair advantage to the prosecution built into every trial. The state has the power and might on its side. An assumption in every juror's and onlooker's mind that we wouldn't be here if smoke didn't lead to a fire. It is that assumption that every defense has to overcome."[83]

¶ 9101   SPECIAL RULES IN ADMINISTRATIVE PROCEEDINGS

Like criminal courts, administrative agencies often have their own particular procedures. Many follow the Federal Administrative Procedure Act or state equivalents and may have their own special procedures as well. Forensic accounting experts are advised to seek guidance from counsel regarding which procedural aspects relate to their engagement obligations.

Tone of the Proceedings

Generally, administrative agencies are subject to a broad standard requiring procedural due process. However, the applications to particular agencies can vary widely and provide little guidance for the forensic accountant. Parties with experience in the courts but who are not familiar with administrative procedures may be surprised to find that much of the customary procedural formality of the courts is lacking in administrative proceedings. For example, traditional notions of separation of powers between the prosecution and the judicial functions do not necessarily apply in administrative proceedings. In some agencies, the same party that presents the evidence also renders the decision. Often, however, the agency provides a significant degree of separation between presentation of the case and the decision-making function for purposes of fairness and impartiality.

Usually, the technical rules of evidence do not apply in administrative proceedings, and the agency has wide discretion in admitting relevant evidence that does not comply with the formal rules of evidence. However, a forensic accounting expert should not be surprised when counsel vigorously objects and challenges the admissibility of evidence on a hotly contested issue of fact in an administrative hearing, regardless of how informal the proceedings may appear. The challenge is apt to be on substantive, rather than mere technical, grounds. Therefore, forensic accounting experts should be just as prepared to document and support any opinion as they would in a court proceeding where the technical rules of evidence apply.

Residuum Rule

The *residuum rule* is one major exception to the relaxation of the formal rules of evidence in administrative proceedings. In substance, the residuum rule is that no finding may be supported solely by hearsay evidence. There must be some amount of nonhearsay evidence to support each finding. Of course, the nonhearsay evidence may be circumstantial, and there is no requirement that the evidence must be particularly compelling. Therefore, the residuum rule alone is rarely a problem. However, because of this rule, counsel will need to object to the admissibility of hearsay evidence. The presiding officer will admit the evidence "as hearsay." Often, counsel is allowed an ongoing objection to particular lines of hearsay evidence, once the objection has been made, to avoid the need for repeated objections.

Management of Evidence

¶ 9111 MAXIMIZING CLIENT CONFIDENTIALITY

Attorneys, accountants, and clients should structure their relationships to minimize the amount of information conveyed to each other that has to be disclosed to opposing parties. Attorneys, accountants, and clients should decide ahead of time what services each will provide, how those services will be provided, who is responsible for preparing written materials, and to whom written materials should be sent.

Advice given by accountants with regard to tax shelters is not privileged, whereas the same advice given by attorneys is protected. As mentioned earlier, if an accountant acts as an attorney's agent for the benefit of a client, the accountant's work can be protected under the attorney work product rule.

Michael Mostek provides the following advice for protecting the work product privilege:[84]
- The attorney should directly retain the consultant.
- The agreement should be between attorney and expert.
- The expert should obtain facts through, or at direction of, the attorney.
- The investigation should be done at the direction of attorney.
- The attorney should be present when the consultant meets with client.

¶ 9121 USING TECHNOLOGY TO GATHER EVIDENCE

As Fred Smolen stated, a business-like approach to investigation management is important. Target dates should be set for completing segments of the investigation, charts should track interrelations between the segments, and a decision tree should be drawn to complete the big picture. Streamlining is essential because of mushrooming costs.[85] A business-like approach is necessary to answer the question identified by Graham Soutar: "where is the smoking gun in 55,000 pieces of paper" or 55 disk drives that have been tampered with?[86]

Digital evidence is akin to the fingerprint in today's courtroom. The sight of hard drives, Internet files, and e-mail as courtroom evidence is increasingly common. In the wired world almost every crime intersects with the digital realm at one time or another.

Laptops, digital cameras, phones, and hard drives provide mountains of raw data for experts to sift through, part of the expanding field of computer forensics. A single file, credit card purchase, or stray e-mail message can provide the proof that clinches a decision for a party.[87]

Forensic accountants must use information technology to gather, manage, and use evidence. They must use software to store, sift through, and organize large amounts of information with great speed and accuracy. Each year the AICPA Top Technologies Task Force identifies the top 10 most important technology issues for the current year. The task force found the following 10 technologies for 2010 in descending order of importance:[88]

1. *Security of data, code & communications / data security & document retention / security threats.* Proper Information Security Management protects the integrity, confidentiality and availability of information in the custody of an organization and reduces the risk of information being compromised.
2. *Connectivity / wireless access / high speed Internet connections / voice and data.* The ability to make and maintain an instantaneous connection between two or more points using connection devices is more eminent than ever In order to stay competitive in the marketplace.
3. *Backup solutions/ disaster recovery/ business continuity.* Business Continuity Management and Disaster Recovery Planning are the holistic processes organizations use to mitigate the risks to systems and people when unexpected events occur.

4. *Secure electronic collaboration with clients–client portals.* Portals enable employees, customers, vendors, and other contacts to securely access and share information and documents. Collaboration tools allow multiple users to work together on files of all kinds.

5. *Paperless workflow/ paperless technology/ electronic workpapers.* A paperless office environment is essential to supporting mobile users who want to access and collaborate on digital documents from remote locations.

6. *Laptop security / encryption.* Stored data can be altered to commit fraud, intercepted by an unscrupulous person en route and altered, and laptops storing vast amounts of confidential information can be lost or stolen.

7. *Small business software / Office 2010 / Windows 7.* There is a new generation of productivity applications available from Microsoft and others, including Office 2010, Windows 7, and Google Apps to improve the user experience.

8. *User mobility/ mobile computing/ mobile devices.* Enabling people to work from anywhere and at any time is the goal of Mobile and Remote Computing. Technologies used include Citrix, Virtual Desktop Interface, Cellular broadband, and other applications.

9. *Tax software/ electronic transmittals of tax forms/ modern e-file.* A paperless office environment is essential to supporting mobile users who want to access and collaborate on digital documents from remote locations.

10. *Server virtualization and consolidation.* Virtualization is running computing resources in an emulated and consolidated environment. Server virtualization is a method that allows computing resources to be installed, used, and supported more efficiently.

"In today's internal forensic accounting investigations, massive amounts of electronic data, transactional detail, electronic communications and historic reports comprise the full universe of information that is typically available to the forensic team to perform the fact finding and corresponding analysis of the investigation.

Dealing with this enormous amount of data is time consuming, challenging and costly. However, when you add the complexity associated with a growing number of electronic data types, password cracking and restoration of information on historical media (e.g., backup tapes), the challenges of accessing the relevant information are even more difficult."[89]

Drill-Down Functionality

The *drill-down functionality* technique enables financial managers and forensic accountants to make reports interactive and multidimensional. Microsoft Excel enables viewers to go "below the surface of a statement and uncover the source of any number and how it was calculated." Basically, one can click on a number in a financial report and bring up all of the details.[90]

Electronic Imaging

Forensic electronic imaging is a process of scanning evidential and case-related documents onto a magnetic medium (e.g., a computer hard drive or an optical disk, such as a CD-ROM). A person then can sort, analyze, and retrieve these documents without having to go through massive amounts of paper materials. Electronic imaging may be indispensable to satisfy legal obligations to complete a civil or criminal case within a reasonable timeframe and force full disclosure of the materials collected.[91]

DOCUMENT IMAGING. In June 2000, the Dutch branch of KPMG Forensic Accounting installed a document imaging and full-text retrieval software called ZyIMAGE. This software allows KPMG to add scanning and full-text indexing of large paper collections to their services. They can fully disclose the full contents of large amounts of paper in a short period of time. After scanning and indexing the paper collections, not only a 100 percent copy of the original is available, but KPMG can also search for every word or every combination of words, even if the word is misspelled or unrecognized by the scanning system. Additionally, documents can be structured, organized, and shared easily within KPMG Forensic Accounting or with customers.[92]

In complex investigations, a manual system of locating documents is time-consuming and probably does not provide as high a degree of confidence as an imaging system does. Cases involving large numbers of transactions, fund tracing, and relationships among companies and individuals require some type of relationship database (which can create links between two or more pieces of information). One such relational database is a chronological database. A chronological database helps investigators to compile a timeline of events, people, companies, and places associated with the alleged wrongdoing. By sorting the recorded information so that the date and time of movements of funds are identifiable, a sophisticated database can even help investigators establish links among transactions in different locations and currencies.[93]

Benford's Law

Dr. Frank Benford in the 1930s discovered that the distribution of initial digits in natural numbers is not random, but instead follows a predictable pattern based upon his formula.[94]For example, there is an approximately 30.1 percent chance that the first digit in a number will be 1, and only a 4.6 percent chance that the first digit will be a 9. The likelihood of 2 is about 19 percent, 4 is 9.7 percent, and 6 is 7 percent. With computers, Benford's Law may be used to detect anomalies in financial, tax and economic data that might escape traditional methods of detection. The accountant can detect invented numbers and errors in bookkeeping or accounting by comparing the frequency of the appearance of initial digits in a list of numbers.[95] Benford's Law makes fraudulent activities more difficult to conceal and reduces the benefits of fraud. For example, if you examine the check amounts on 10,000 random checks, the number 1 should appear as the first integer about 30 percent of the time (and not one-ninth of the time).

Figure 9.1. Benford's Law of Predictable Patterns

1st digit	2nd digit	3rd digit
0= -----	12%	10.2%
1= 30.1%	11.4%	10.1%
2= 17.6%	10.9%	10.1%
3= 12.5%	10.4%	10.1%
4= 9.7%	10%	10%
5= 7.9%	9.7%	10%
6= 6.7%	9.3%	9.9%
7= 5.8%	9%	9.9%
8= 5.1%	8.8%	9.9%
9= 4.6%	8.5%	9.8%

Richard Lanza believes that Benford's Law can be used to identify fraud in large data sets by detecting potentially invented numbers in the following situations:
- Investment sales/purchases
- Check register amounts

- Sales history/price history
- 401 contributions
- Inventory unit costs
- Expense accounts
- Wire transfer information
- Life insurance policy values
- Bad debt expenses
- Asset/liability accounts[96]

David G. Banks developed a Benford's Law analysis with Microsoft Excel using a five-step process. First, he selects a population for analysis. Second, he assembles the raw data in a format acceptable to Excel. Third, he cleans nonnumeric leading characters (such as letters or dollar signs) and decimal points. Fourth, he extracts leading digits and stores them for analysis. Finally, he executes the final analysis. Although these steps can be executed manually in Excel, he says the task is shortened through the use of Excel macros.[97]

Three professors have presented these situations in which Benford Analysis is or is not likely useful. See Figure 9.2.

Figure 9.2. When Benford Analysis Is or Is Not Likely Useful[98]

When Benford Analysis Is Likely Useful	Examples
Sets of numbers that result from mathematical combination of numbers — result comes from two distributions	Accounts receivable (number sold times price). Accounts payable (number bought times price).
Transaction-level data — no need to sample.	Disbursements, sales, expenses.
On large data sets — the more observations, the better.	Full year's transactions.
Accounts that appear to conform — when the mean of a set of numbers is greater than the median and the skewness is positive.	Most sets of accounting numbers.

When Benford Analysis Is Not Likely Useful	Examples
Data set is comprised of assigned numbers.	Check numbers, invoice numbers, zip codes.
Numbers that are influenced by human thought.	Prices set at psychological thresholds ($1.99), ATM withdrawals.
Accounts with a large number of firm-specific numbers.	An account specifically set up to record $100 refunds.
Accounts with a built in minimum or maximum.	Set of assets that must meet a threshold to be recorded.
Where no transaction is recorded.	Thefts, kickbacks, contract rigging.

DATAS

Digital Analysis Tests and Statistics (DATAS) is another deductive analytical tool that can help forensic auditors be more effective and efficient by presenting various high level evidence along with the ability to drill down deeper as needed.[99] This tool identifies process inefficiencies, errors, and fraud by searching for abnormal (1) digit and number patterns, (2) round number occurrences, and (3) duplications of numbers.[100] This powerful tool is easy to use, requiring no programming experience. DATAS uses menus to guide the user through the audit, and requires minimal set-up time.[101]

Data Warehousing/Mining

Data mining is a technique that uses mathematical algorithms to seek hidden patterns or associations in data. Data mining may be statistical in nature or may augment statistical analysis. Thus, data mining is a methodology that enables the forensic accountant to sift the appropriate information and compare data to obtain unknown relationships and trends. Data mining may be used by management, external and internal auditors, and forensic accountants to review controls and discover fraud, abuse, and corruption.[102] There are many data mining software vendors on the market, and there are frequent product upgrades.[103]

Using data mining tools that search for signs of fraudulent activity, such as bogus loans, stolen shipments, and shady fund transfers, forensic accountants can identify potentially fraudulent transactions for further investigation and follow-up. For example, vendor information can be analyzed and compared to employee records to identify payments made to a vendor with the same phone number or address as an employee. Additional applications can analyze past transactions for variables present in fraudulent transactions and for use in flagging similar transactions before they are processed.

Data warehousing is a process, not a product, for assembling and managing data from various sources for the purpose of gaining a single, detailed view of part or all of a business.[104] Data warehousing is an ongoing process and is never really complete. It is designed to give management a unified picture of the business but can be used for other purposes as well. For example, the Pentagon has a data mining project designed to use data "fabricated to resemble real-life events" such as police arrests in order to pinpoint indicators of terrorist activities.[105]

Deloitte & Touche used data-mining tools to discover procurement fraud by an Asian company. After reviewing 1.5 gigabytes of data (an amount equal to several encyclopedias), the investigators found that someone was consistently overpaying one of the company's suppliers. Deloitte's findings led to litigation against the perpetrator.

MINING ONE'S OWN BUSINESS. Ironically, one of the largest decision-support vendors, MicroStrategy, had to restate its revenues and earnings for 1998 and 1999. MicroStrategy produces data-mining software that analyzes large amounts of corporate data on marketing and customer relationships. The earnings restatement announcement caused the firm's stock price to drop more than 60 percent in a single day. The SEC accused MicroStrategy of inflating revenue and earnings on contracts that had not been properly executed in the same fiscal period. Three of its top executives agreed to pay $11 million to settle the accounting fraud charges of the SEC.

Data warehousing may involve the reconstruction of records. Deloitte & Touche was involved with an Australia-based company with subsidiaries throughout the region. Shareholders sued the company for alleged financial mismanagement, but the company claimed that key records had disappeared, making it impossible to prove the allegations. Deloitte was able to recreate the missing records with electronic data downloaded from various banks and stockbrokers.[106]

Julie S. David and Paul J. Steinbart have listed steps of the process in building a successful data warehouse:[107]

1. Identify the business need for the data warehouse.
2. Determine the scope of the project.
3. Organize the metadata and develop a data model.
4. Acquire hardware and software.
5. Load the data into the warehouse.

Despite the proven success of data mining, at least one accountant, Michael Kessler, maintains that solving most fraud cases involves instinct and that there is no substitute for gut feelings.[108] But by using a combination of statistical analysis algorithms, exploratory analyses, modeling techniques, and database technology, *data mining finds patterns and subtle relationships in data*. One cannot push a button and expect the software to pick the one bad apple out of the panel, however.[109]

Data Extraction versus Data Investigation

There is a difference between the procedures used for traditional data extraction (i.e., data mining) and data investigation for evidentiary purpose. With traditional data extraction, tools such as Interactive Data Extraction and Analysis (IDEA) or ACL software are used to interactively extract, sample, and analyze data.

Yet by simply checking a client's files or cross comparing data, files for forensic investigations are damaged. Such actions are similar to sending a housekeeper in to tidy up a murder crime scene before the forensic investigative team is allowed to start analyzing the evidence. For forensic purposes, software tools collect digital data without changing it. After the data is collected, it is analyzed. Examples of forensic software tools are Encase, SafeBack, or Ontrack's Easy Recovery software. Increasing the time lag between initial fraud suspicions and the recovery of the related digital data makes the evidence less valuable.

Internal auditor Gene Morse used data mining software to find the fraud at WorldCom. The beauty of the software system to Mr. Morse was that it enabled him to scrutinize the debit and credit side of transactions. By clicking on a number for an expense on a spreadsheet, he could follow it back to the original journal entry—such as an invoice for a purchase or expense report submitted by an employee—to see how it had been justified. In a short time, Mr. Morse had turned up a total of $2 billion in questionable accounting entries.[110]

Mr. Morse grew increasingly concerned that others in the company would discover what he had learned and try to destroy the evidence. With his own money he went out and bought a CD burner and copied all the incriminating data onto a CD-ROM. He told no one outside of internal audit what he had found.[111]

Inductive versus Deductive Method

The two most acceptable scientific methods for deriving truth are the deductive and inductive approaches. Under the deductive approach, one goes from general to specifics. The inquirer starts from a general principle to specific findings. Deductive methods in accounting are fairly simple and economical. Discovery sampling and digital analysis are deductive approaches and are appropriate for smaller companies.

Under the inductive approach, one starts with specific experiences and then draws inferences. An accountant starts from individual cases and moves to a general conclusion. Custom data mining and analysis of all data are inductive approaches, suitable for larger companies. Steve and Conan Albrecht provide an excellent table describing the two approaches,[112] shown in Table 9.1.

Table 9.1. Pick the Fraud-Detection Method Best for a Company

Deductive Approach	Inductive Approach
Generic data mining	Custom data mining
Digital analysis	Analysis of all data
Discovery sampling	Custom software
Generic software	For larger organizations
For smaller organizations	Sophisticated features
Basic features	Requires advanced skills
Easy to learn	More expensive
Relatively inexpensive	

Discovery sampling involves the use of a random-number-generating software to select the checks or other items that an auditor is auditing. Once the auditor has examined some of the checks, etc., the auditor may refer to a Discovery Sampling Table (appearing in most auditing text books) to determine the frequency of certain occurrences in a sample with approximations of the likelihood of their existence in the sample population.

M.J. Comer cautions against using generic data mining packages, arguing that they have given disappointing results and are expensive. He does, however, support specially written computer programs for use in special situations.[113]

¶ 9131 COMPUTER EVIDENCE

Forensic accountants often deal with electronic documents as part of their investigations and in the courtroom. The term *computer forensics* is used to describe the procedures applied to computers and peripherals for gathering evidence that may be used in civil and criminal courts of law. For more detail, see Chapter 13.

Electronic evidence (including e-mails) is gathered for both criminal and civil proceedings. For criminal investigations, electronic evidence is sought with a warrant or subpoena. When a court issues a subpoena for documents, included is a demand for all appropriate electronic data. This electronic evidence is everywhere—on desktop PCs, network servers, notebook computers, tape back-up systems, web-enabled cell phones, PDAs that store e-mail, and digital cameras that store images. Workplace searches are legal under the Fourth Amendment to the U.S. Constitution, but they must be for a reasonable purpose. The area to be searched must not be covered by an employee's expectation of privacy. Electronic evidence for civil action is sought through discovery requests such as interrogatories or deposition. Courts have been imposing penalties on businesses that cannot produce electronic evidence subpoenaed.

A federal judge admonished Medo Health Solutions, Inc. for violating his order to turn over documents in the company's legal battle with the Justice Department. Medco, one of the country's largest pharmacy-benefit managers, had been "dilatory" in its disclosure of certain documents that were supposed to be turned over, so the judge stated that "any further violations of this court's orders may result in sanctions."[114]

If a judge or jury agrees with the Justice Department, Medco could technically be liable for an $11,000 fine on each of the millions of prescriptions Medco processed for government employees.[115]

In his order, the judge said Medco had turned over documents on disks that had technical defects, and that the plaintiffs have complained about the defects to Medco. Medco argued that it has not been made aware of any defects in electronic document production. But the judge wrote: "Clearly, this is disingenuous."[116]

Protecting Data in Hardware Seizures

Computers and related equipment may be seized as evidence in a criminal matter. When such equipment is seized, care must be taken to prevent evidence from being mishandled or accidentally destroyed. Here are some tips:

- Close phone line connections to the modem so data cannot be removed from a remote location.
- Videotape and label all connections and cables so that equipment can be successfully reconnected at the lab, and possibly returned without damage.
- Do not turn on seized electronic equipment without advice from a forensic expert. Booby traps may erase data if correct passwords are not used.
- Do not use the software on the system being examined to boot the system for fear of destroying evidence.
- Thoroughly document the examination.
- Determine whether the system is operational.
- Write-protect all diskettes and hard drives and identify the computer to be used for examination.
- Review all files in a bit-system or "read only" mode to legally ensure that no alterations could have been made to the evidence.
- After converting the directory/subdirectory listings, check for hidden and deleted files using appropriate commercial or custom software. Next, display and then print files.
- Send the printouts and report to the contributor or subject matter expert for additional analysis. Repack the computer and all disks and return the evidence.
- A chain of custody should be recorded and signed by all parties. Verified copies should be reviewed, and the original copy should be sealed.[117]

FIGHT CYBER-CRIME. Shoring up vulnerable software is crucial for public and private organizations as cyber-threats grow in sophistication. Organized crime, terrorist groups, and hostile countries now account for most major attacks. They are making huge amounts of money from identity thefts and extortion. Alan Paller says the FBI estimates that organized crime now reaps more profits from cyber-crime than from the drug trade. These profits are plowed back into research to produce more sophisticated attack methods.[118] For more detail, see Chapters 14 and 15.

There are reports that a vast electronic spying operation has infiltrated at least 1,295 computers in 103 countries, including those belonging to embassies, foreign ministries, and governmental offices. This malware has been whaling for important topics. This GhostNet can even turn on the camera and audio-recording functions of the infected computer.[119]

Insidious E-Mails

E-mails are called the cockroaches of mass communication because they are so difficult to eliminate. Delete an e-mail, and it is still in the trash bin. Delete the trash bin, and the evidence is still on the server. Purge the electronic closets of a company, and messages remain stored on the employees' hard drives, remain as printed copies filed away by employees, and e-mail sent or forwarded to people outside the company remains on their machines.[120]

E-MAIL IS VALUABLE EVIDENCE. E-mails may be particularly valuable as evidence. Saved e-mails are a "goldmine of information, documenting date, time, source, potentially incriminating content, and more."[121] Bill Gates' e-mail showed up in Microsoft's antitrust trial. In one e-mail, he asked AOL executives: "How much do we need to pay you to screw Netscape?"[122] E-mails were useful in the investigation of former President Bill Clinton with respect to Monica Lewinsky. Research indicates that people offer more accurate and complete information about themselves when filling out questionnaires on a computer than in face-to-face interviews or on a paper form.[123] In the SEC's case against Symbol Technologies, Inc., the SEC produced a March 2001 e-mail to a distributor showing the fraudulent nature of their transactions:

> Frank [Borghese] talked to me today and he wants you...to think about giving him an order of US$ 7 million with a revenue of...US$ 5 million. He needs for you to take it and put it in a warehouse that is not Symbol. He is prepared to pay you for the storage fees by you invoicing us some form of consulting fees to hide the fact that [it] is storage fees. The factory created for me a list of product mix which they would like the order to be constructed as. I realize this is a bit crazy...but he needs as usual all he can get.

Other electronic files also are difficult to eliminate. As Michael S. Kridel has noted, few people understand what happens when the delete button is pushed to erase a file. Although the file is no longer visible to the user, the material remains intact until fully erased by a special type of software. Unless fully erased by that special software, the material can be restored easily.[124]

SAS No. 80 states that substantive tests may not be sufficient for a system predominantly consisting of electronic evidence. Thus, an auditor must perform tests of the system controls to determine whether they are strong enough to mitigate the risks with electronic evidence. By combining system control tests with substantive evidence, an auditor may issue an opinion. SAS No. 94 provides guidance to external auditors about the effect of information technology on internal controls, and on the auditor's understanding of internal controls and assessment of control risk.

Aiding and abetting is a favorite phrase on cop shows and courtroom dramas. For Motorola Inc. and Scientific-Atlanta Inc., the phrase is hitting close to home these days.

The names of both companies surfaced frequently in the federal fraud trial of four former executives of Adelphia Communications Corp., most recently in an e-mail message read aloud in court that indicated top Scientific-Atlanta executives approved a transaction that allegedly helped Adelphia cook its books.

The electronic message, read by a defense attorney, came on top of earlier testimony about the same set of transactions by the government's star witness, former Adelphia finance executive James R. Brown.[125]

Documenting Computer Evidence

Forensic auditors should follow these guidelines when examining computer evidence:[126]

- Upon receipt of evidence, log the evidence into an appropriate evidence control system and assign it to an examiner. Use a unique numbering system to record the date and time that the evidence was received.
- Identify the examiner and prepare documentation for the chain of custody from evidence control to examiner.
- When transferring evidence to an examiner, determine if other expert analyses, such as accounting, drug record analysis, etc. are necessary.

- Prepare chain of custody documentation for other experts as necessary for complete examination, and determine that all pieces of equipment listed as having been submitted are actually present. Mark and initial each piece of evidence as required by the laboratory and prepare notes.

Computer Online Forensic Evidence Extractor

Forensic accountants may be able to make use of evidence obtained by law enforcement officers by a free Microsoft device called Computer Online Forensic Evidence Extractor (COFEE). The COFEE device is installed on a USB flash drive or other external disk drive to gather digital evidence. The digital forensic tool contains 150 commands that can dramatically reduce the time it takes to gather digital evidence by decrypting passwords and analyzing a computer's Internet activity as well as data stored in the computer. The investigator does not have to seize the computer, which would involve disconnecting from the network, turning off the power, and possibly losing data. Essentially the investigator scans for evidence on site with a pre-configured COFEE device by inserting the USB device into the suspected computer.[127]

Other Digital Multifunctional Devices

Forensic accountants can obtain evidence from other digital multifunctional devices (MFDs). For example, digital copiers store thousands of records in internal memory when documents are copied, printed, scanned, and faxed. Even when the individual walks away from the machine, the information remains in memory. Billions of pages of information also are stored on printers, copiers, and facsimiles. Forensic auditors should conduct an inventory of data storage devices that may contain appropriate evidence.[128]

EVIDENCE STORED ON MFDS.[129] Mr. Thief, a mid-level manager, supervises several engineers in his company's R&D department. Ms. Vendor, an entrepreneurial business woman, convinces Mr. Thief to sell her schematics and blueprints for a new hydraulic press his company is developing. Excited by the potential for financial gain, Mr. Thief agrees. However, he does not want to get caught with paper or electronic copies of the documents either on his person or his desktop workstation.

Mr. Thief, staying late one evening, simply goes to the company's photocopier and selects the scan and email options and in a matter of mere minutes (possibly seconds), copies, scans, and emails the schematics and blueprints, saved as a PDF formatted file to Ms. Vendor. Mr. Thief meets Ms. Vendor, receives his payment, and agrees to send Ms. Vendor additional proprietary documents as they become available.

Alerted by a competitor to whom Ms. Vendor attempted to sell the documents, Mr. Thief's company launches an investigation into the "leak." As part of the investigation, Mr. Thief's computer is seized and an audit/cyber forensic examination is performed on it. No incriminating evidence is uncovered as a result of the investigation. A forensic accountant should look for the MFD evidence, also.

¶ 9141   ENSURING THE ADMISSIBILITY OF EVIDENCE IN COURT

Accountants who provide litigation services should assume that any documents or other evidence that they handle will be used in a legal proceeding. They should not mark, staple, or otherwise alter any documents or other evidence that might find its way into court. They should record how they obtained the evidence and who has handled it. They should keep the evidence in a secure location and limit who can handle the evidence. To avoid putting their or others' fingerprints on documents, accountants should use see-through holders.

¶ 9151   SECURITY FOR EVIDENCE AND WORKING PAPERS

A key task of evidence management is to preserve the integrity of evidence. Original documents should be stored in safes or locked cabinets accessible to a limited number of persons. Safes or cabinets used to store evidence should be fireproof. If there is a risk that someone might want to steal or destroy (e.g., by arson) any evidence, steps should be taken to minimize that risk.

Working papers also need to be safeguarded, not only to protect them from theft and damage but also to preserve the confidentiality of the information in those papers. Material stored on a computer should be password protected, and a backup copy of such files should be made on a regular basis and stored in a separate, secure location.

I got started on Carp's laptop by working my way around the password security. I plugged my laptop in his via a USB cable, ran a program that took control of his hard drive from my laptop, deleted his password file, and I was in. It ain't rocket science.[130]

¶ 9161   EVIDENCE DATABASE

Evidence should be copied, inventoried, and indexed so that it can be readily found when needed. A document database is helpful not only in keeping track of what evidence has been obtained but also in identifying what other evidence needs to be obtained.

If there are many items of evidence, a computerized database should be established to manage them.

¶ 9171   EVALUATING THE QUALITY AND PERSUASIVENESS OF EVIDENCE

Although the attorney for whom a practitioner performs litigation services is primarily responsible for determining what evidence the practitioner may rely on, practitioners should inform attorneys of any suspicions that documents are missing, questionable, or irrelevant. They also should tell attorneys whether they lack sufficient relevant evidence upon which to reach an opinion and, if so, what information is needed to prove facts at issue.

The following are guidelines for measuring the persuasiveness of evidence:

- The evidence must be relevant to the related conclusion.
- Objective evidence usually is more persuasive than subjective evidence (e.g., a physical count of inventory is more persuasive than an estimate).
- Documented evidence is typically more persuasive than undocumented evidence (e.g., 10 letters from customers praising a product is more persuasive than testimony that customers have said they like a product).
- Third-party evidence is generally more persuasive than evidence from within an organization involved in litigation.
- Large samples generally are more persuasive than smaller samples.
- Statistical samples usually are more persuasive than nonstatistical samples.
- Corroborated evidence is usually more persuasive than uncorroborated evidence.
- Timely evidence is typically more persuasive than evidence produced after a delay.
- Authoritative evidence usually is more persuasive than nonauthoritative evidence.
- Direct evidence usually is more persuasive than indirect evidence (e.g., a physical count of inventory is more persuasive than perpetual inventory records).
- Evidence from a well-controlled and reliable system usually is more persuasive than evidence from a poorly controlled or questionable system.[131]

ACTORS IN COURT. "Did you hear her? Was she, for example, singing in the shower or something like that? Moving furniture around?" Defense attorney Freeman was taking advantage of the rules that allowed *defense* in *cross-examination* to lead witness, and Freeman was also using this bantering tone to get back into a more relaxed mode with Fred, showing him what a regular Joe he could be.[132]

Suppose the previous testimony of a witness is needed in a case, but the witness is not available or refuses to testify? That was the situation when Scott Sullivan took the Fifth Amendment in a class-action lawsuit in which WorldCom investors were suing Arthur Andersen.[133]

Neil Intraub, a 48-year-old-actor, was called upon to impersonate Mr. Sullivan and deliver some of his most dramatic lines, such as "I falsified the financial statements of the company." The actor spent about two and a half hours giving the previous testimony of Sullivan when he was the prosecutor's star witness against Bernard J. Ebbers.[134]

Actors are sometimes used rather than a dull paralegal or a court reporter. At the retrial of investment banker Frank Quattrone, a public prosecutor took on the role of giving testimony from Mr. Quattrone's first trial.[135]

Questioned Documents

A forensic accountant may question whether a document is counterfeit, forged, or fraudulent. With the use of a magnifying glass or enlarged photograph, a forensic accountant may inspect a document. Invoices and other documents may be fake or altered when:

- Font sizes or types are not consistent.
- No address is shown for the vendor or customer; this situation is especially suspicious if a vendor has not identified an address to which a check can be sent.
- The document has no identifying numbers such as invoice number, purchase order number, or customer number.
- All invoice numbers on invoices from vendors are numbered sequentially, with no numbers skipped.
- No tax is shown for taxable items.
- No shipping or freight cost is shown for items that would have been shipped at the purchaser's expense.
- Little or no detail is provided on the invoice or document.[136]

By obtaining legitimate similar documents, called exemplars, an investigator may compare them with the questioned document. If there are differences in quality of paper, print style, ink color, or watermark, one may need to have the document examined by a questioned document expert.

The FBI Laboratory, Questioned Document Unit examines and compares data appearing on paper and other evidentiary material. On their Internet site, the FBI indicates

> that surface data includes handwriting, hand printing, typewriting, printing, erasures, alterations, and obliterations. Impressions in the surface of paper, such as those from indented writing or use of a check writer.

In addition to data contained on the surface of documentary evidence, data *within* paper or other surfaces—watermarks, safety fibers, and other integral features—may be components of document examinations. Unit examiners also match the torn or perforated edges of items such as paper, stamps, or matches.

Other Unit examinations include analyses of typewriter ribbons, photocopiers, facsimiles, graphic arts, and plastic bags.[137] Three exhibits taken from the FBI Internet site are shown below in Figure 9.3.

Figure 9.3. FBI Exhibits[138]

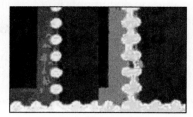

A stamp perforation match

Paper shreds demonstrating different optical properties
under ambient and specialized lighting

Inks of different intensities used on the same document

A business owner made massive improvements to his personal residence, not paid for with personal funds. His company showed many corporate payments to home remodeling and landscapers, even though the industrial park was not owned by the company.

Only photocopies of invoices were provided to the forensic accountant in a divorce dispute. The forensic accountant demanded original documents, and finally original documents were given. The original documents had white-outs of job locations and work descriptions. When the forensic accountant turned the originals over, she could read the real data from the back side.[139]

Although there is no state licensing for forensic document examiners, the American Board of Forensic Document Examiners was established in 1977 to identify qualified forensic scientists capable of providing professional services. This Board provides a program of forensic document examination requiring at a minimum:[140]

- Possession of a baccalaureate degree.
- Completion of a two-year, full-time training program at a recognized document laboratory.
- An additional two years of full-time independent document work.
- A full-time practice of forensic document examination.
- Passing a comprehensive written and/or oral examination.

An example of altering documents involves an obscure pardon document of Abraham Lincoln in the National Archives. Thomas Lowry, an amateur historian, apparently altered the "4" in 1864 and changed it to a "5" in order to promote his book.

An Inspector General of the National Archives said that Dr. Lowry confessed to sneaking a Pelikan pen into the archives, erasing the "4," and changing it to a "5."[141]

Graphology is not forensic document examination, since it is the study and analysis of handwriting in relation to human psychology.

In selecting a qualified document examiner, be sure the individual has an extensive up-to-date library along with this technical equipment:

- A stereoscopic binocular microscope and hand magnifiers to view documents under proper magnification.
- An Electrostatic Detection Apparatus (ESDA) to detect and visualize indentations on paper.
- A Video Spectral Comparator (or similar device) to detect differences in inks with ultraviolet and infrared irradiation.
- Test grids to detect alterations to typewritten documents.
- A variety of cameras with special filters and film.[142]

Here are rules that a document examiner should follow:[143]

- Handle the documents with gloves or tongs. Do not assume, just because the opposing examiner or attorney handles the documents with ungloved hands, that fingerprints on the documents will not be an issue later. Avoid being accused of mishandling the evidence.
- Place documents in the kind of transparent, plastic sleeves that will not lift writing off the paper.
- Do not fold the documents or reverse already existing folds.
- Do not make cuts or tears or apply staples, paper clips, or chemicals that could alter or damage the documents. If a document must be changed or altered, secure written permission to do so from the opposing attorney.
- Avoid subjecting the documents to dampness and extreme temperature variances.
- Do photograph or scan the documents.
- Copy the documents using the manual feed only, one document at a time. Auto-feed could introduce new marks or indentations on the documents. Also, make sure that the glass copy bed is clean.
- Do not mark questioned and known documents, front or back, with identification numbers or initials. These marks may be placed on photographs, scans, or copies of the documents.

A number of these rules should be followed by a forensic accountant handling a questionable document or item.

Han Searman Kelly works as a questioned document examiner for the Las Vegas Metropolitan Police. Her job is the equivalent of finding a needle in a haystack.

Kelly's job consists of examining checks and other materials to determine their authenticity and to see if they have been manipulated. What she examines is not apparent to the naked eye. She uses a microscope to see characteristics of handwriting. She looks at a check to see if it's a machine-generated document, such as a photocopy, and examines the style of the signer's handwriting.

"Questioned document examination is based on the fact that everyone has their own style of writing. It involves shapes and strokes, the size of letters, speed of the writing. They tend to be more minute characteristics."

"Sometimes I'll ask someone to provide me with a writing sample to compare. They may try to change capital letters or change the slant of the handwriting. That doesn't work."[144]

¶ 9181   RECORD RETENTION

Practitioners should establish a policy on retaining records used in litigation support. They should ask the attorney employing them what records they must and should retain.

If practitioners receive a subpoena or notice of deposition, they should be careful not to dispose of any of their records.

Which records must be retained and which can be destroyed is now clearer. The U.S. Supreme Court heard the Arthur Andersen appeal of its criminal conviction of destroying records. Chicago headquarters had directed the Houston Andersen office to shred the Enron records, which the government argued was equivalent to wiping down the crime scene before the police arrive. Andersen argued that FBI agents throw away their interview notes that defendants would love to get. The agents retain only their typewritten notes. Andersen had told 89 employees in a videotaped training session that they could destroy documents before the filing of litigation. The jury in the Andersen trial watched the video twice.[145]

On May 31, 2005, the Supreme Court voided the Andersen verdict based upon improper instructions to the jury. Writing for the Supreme Court, Chief Justice William H. Rehnquist said that a company may have a document retention policy and may destroy documents unless it destroys documents consciously knowing it is committing a fraud.[146]

In both criminal and civil situations, electronic evidence often will be collected for prosecution purposes. Reasonable workable searches are legal under the Fourth Amendment to the U.S. Constitution, but there must be a reasonable purpose. The areas to be searched must not be covered by an employee's expectation of privacy. *Computer forensics* may be defined as the procedures applied to computers and peripherals for gathering evidence that may be used in civil and criminal courts of law. For criminal investigations, electronic evidence for civil actions is sought through discovery requests, such as interrogatories or depositions.

The courtroom itself is becoming more sophisticated, so an expert should check out the place he or she will be testifying beforehand. ELMOS, digital cameras, PowerPoint slides, flat-screen monitors, laptops, and video conferencing are replacing yellow legal pads. Having monitors at the lawyer's tables, judge's bench, and in the jury box allows everyone to see the evidence at the same time, rather than having to hand around a piece of evidence. If the litigant has 90 documents, technology clearly can save time.

EYEWITNESS

"Presenting evidence electronically—PowerPoint slides and scanned material—and showing it to jurors on their monitors makes for a more powerful presentation, and jurors appreciate the efficiency," said Judge E. Dana Winslow of the New York State Supreme Court.

"If you have records of 1,000 or 2,000 pages and you want to get to page 134, electronically it will take you about three to five seconds. If you try to do the same thing with massive documents through the witness and through the attorneys, it will take you a substantial amount of time. I've seen it take 10 minutes."

"Having monitors at the counsel tables also saves time by cutting down on objections because lawyers have the precise language in front of them."[147]

¶ 9186   CHAIN OF CUSTODY

Just as in the movies or on a television show such as CSI, a forensic accountant must safeguard evidence through a financial chain of evidence. Since documents and other items in a dispute are generally admissible in the court, a judge must be confident that a writing or document is in the same condition as it was when the crime was committed. There is a need for an accounting for this evidence from the time it was first obtained until the item is offered into evidence: who touched it, when, and what did they do to the evidence.

There must be a way to show that the evidence has not been tampered with or damaged by the forensic accountant or some other party. If documents are seized, the forensic accountant should put his or her initials and date of the seizure on the back of each document. Or better yet, put the document in a transparent envelope and write a description on the envelope. Store the original and work only with a copy.

An example of a U.S. Department of Labor custody form is shown in Figure 9.4. Basically, create a written report that identifies the item of the evidence, tells where it is found, shows its quantity (e.g., number of pages), and assigns a control number to it (e.g., Bates number). A photo of the document or item is helpful, especially if it's damaged.[148] Care must be taken to document in work papers the capture of forensic images of electronic information to assure the court that the evidence has not been altered.

Figure 9.4. Custody Form

History and Custody of Documents   **U.S. Department of Labor**
Pension and Welfare Benefits Administration

Date _____

Case Number _____
Case Name _____

1.   How were the documents obtained?

_____ By consent (note any significant comments of the principal or third party witness and any unusual circumstances which occurred)?

_____ By legal process (describe).

2.   What is the relationship between the documents and the person submitting them?

3.   Were manual transcripts or facsimile copies made of any of the documents either in whole or in part?

_____ Yes   _____ No
If Yes, list documents copied.   Manner of reproduction

4.   Have all copies been compared with the original documents and identified?

_____ Yes   _____ No
If No, why not?

5.   Were the original documents described herein under your control or supervision at all times prior to their return to the principal, third party witness, or representative?

_____ Yes   _____ No
If No, set forth circumstances of any transfer in control.

6.   Did the principal, third party witness, or a representative request access to the documents during your custody?

_____ Yes   _____ No
If Yes, who requested access and what action was taken?

Signature _____

Title_____

PWBA 219
(May 1987)

FROM TREES TO TABLES. A chain of custody is important in the forestry industry. From logs, to lumber, to furniture, to wood pulp, a chain of custody is the path wood products take from the forest to the consumer, including all manufacturing, transportation, and distribution links.

To demand Chain-of-Custody, customers fill in a straightforward questionnaire covering operation background, company details, and any supply chain knowledge. With these details, SGS assessors inspect the relevant manufacturing, transformation, or distribution sites. If everything is in order, customers will then receive a full report and product certification.[149]

¶ 9191   CONCLUSION

Great care must be taken in gathering and handling evidence to make sure that it will be available when needed and that the evidence will be admissible at the legal or regulatory proceeding. The same technology that has so changed how we live has been recording more and more aspects of our lives and giving great fodder to forensic accountants and others who need to see how we have lived.

Benford's Law, electronic imaging, and data mining techniques are useful in both fraud detection and litigation consulting. Forensic accountants must exercise care when dealing with computer evidence, especially in hardware seizures. Proper, uncontaminated evidence is vital to being on the winning side in the courtroom. A forensic accountant must have and apply a basic understanding of the rules of evidence.

Prosecutor Billy Downer, in the fraud case against Durban businessman Schabir Shaik, said that "if you have a forensic auditor who knows what he is doing, there is nothing to worry about." Then John Van der Walt took the stand for 16 days, explaining, defending his findings, making jokes, and presenting the paper trail of the fraud.[150]

KPMG auditor Walt dropped his files only twice, but managed without fail to find whichever one of the 20-plus behind him held the documents he was looking for. "The secret," he confided, "was when we realized that the witness stand was too small for our files." He and Anton Steynberg, one of the advocates assisting Downer, fashioned an extended shelf to hold the files. "After that it was easy," he said.[151]

Gil Grisson (William Petersen) tells Catherine Willows (Marg Heigenberger) on a CSI–Las Vegas episode entitled "The Execution of Catherine Willows:"

> It's just about the evidence. It's not up to you if he lives or dies. The case has no face.

BEST EXPERT WITNESS. In his novel, Michael Connelly provides this example of an expert witness:

"Her personality was going to win over the jury, and her facts were going to seal the deal. So much of trial work comes down to who is testifying, not what the testimony actually reveals. It's about selling your case to the jury, and Shami could sell burnt matches. The state's forensic witness was a lab geek with the personality of a test tube. My witness had hosted a television show called Chemically Dependent."[152]

ENDNOTES

1 C.N. Edwards, "Scientific Evidence: A Short Course in the Applied Forensic Sciences," ACFEi Core Course III, November 1, 1999, p. 31.

2 D.W. Squires, "Problems Solved with Forensic Accounting: A Legal Perspective," JOURNAL OF FORENSIC ACCOUNTING 4 (2003), p. 132. FRE 702.

3 Julliane Hoffman, Retribution, New York City: Berkley Publishing, 2004, p.390.

4 Colin Evans, A Question of Evidence, Hoboken, N.J.: John Wiley, 2003, p.177.

5 BLACK'S LAW DICTIONARY, 7ᵗʰ ed.

6 See, e.g., Rule 102 of the Federal Rules of Evidence.

7 BLACK'S LAW DICTIONARY, 7ᵗʰ ed.

8 Ibid.

9 Ibid.

10 Ibid.

11 J.T. Lescoart, THE 13TH JUROR (New York: Dell Publishing, 1994), p. 102.

12 Carter v. Steverson, & Co., 106 S.W. 3rd 161 (Tex. App. 2003).

13 J.C. Miller and H.B. Murray, "Wikipedia In Court: When and How Citing Wikipedia and Other Consensus Websites Is Appropriate," St. John's Law Review, Vol. 84, 2010, pp. 633-656.

14 Noam Cohen, "Courts Turn to Wikipedia, but Selectively," NEW YORK TIMES (January 29, 2007), p. C-3.

15 Ibid.

16 "When Rendering Decisions, Judges are Finding Law Reviews Irrelevant," NEW YORK TIMES (March 19, 2007), p. A-8.

17 See, e.g., Rule 402 of the Federal Rules of Evidence.

18 Ibid.

19 Ibid.

20 See, e.g., Federal Rules of Evidence Rule 403.

21 Ibid.

22 Zenith Elecs. Corp. v. WH-TV Broad. Corp., No. 04-1635 (CA-7, Jan. 20, 2005).

23 Frymire-Brinati v. KPMG Peat Marwick, CA-7 2 F3d 183 (1993).

24 Rule 401 of the Federal Rules of Evidence.

25 DeJager Construction v. Schleininger, 938 FSupp 446 (D.Ct. Mi, 1996).

26 Rule 411 of the Federal Rules of Evidence.

27 Nobles, 422 US 225, 95 SCt 2160 (1975).

28 L.V. Couch, SCt, 73-1 USTC ¶9159, 409 US 322, 93 SCt 611; A. Young, SCt, 84-1 USTC ¶9305, 465 US 805, 104 SCt 1495.

29 L.V. Couch, SCt, 73-1 USTC ¶9159, 409 US 322, 93 SCt 611.

30 Code Sec. 7525.

31 Code Sec. 7525(a)(1).

32 Code Sec. 7525(a)(2), (3)(A).

33 Code Sec. 7525(b).

34 KPMG LLP, DC D.C., 2003-1 USTC ¶50,174, 237 FSupp2d 35.

35 Dennis J. Ventry, Jr., "A Primer on Tax Work Product for Federal Courts," TAX NOTES (May 18, 2009), p. 878.

36 U.S. v. Textron, Inc., No. 07-2631 (CA-1, March 25, 2009).

37 Ventry, Jr., op. cit., pp. 875-884.

38 L. Kovel, CA-2, 62-1 USTC ¶9111, 296 F2d 918.

39 R.A. Frederick, CA-7, 99-1 USTC ¶50,465, 182 F3d 496.

40 FRCP 34(a) and (b). ESI include e-mail, e-mail attachments, instant messages, word processing files, spreadsheets, database files, internet files, and so forth.

41 Zeph Telpner and Michael Mostek, EXPERT WITNESSING IN FORENSIC ACCOUNTING (Boca Raton, Fla.: CRC Press), pp. 209–237.

42 Fed. Rul. Civ. Proc. 26 Advisory Committee Notes; In re-Pioneer Hi-Bred International, Inc., 238 F3d 1370 (Fed. Cir. 2001). See footnote 12 in M.W. Tindall and S.D. Fried, "Protecting Attorney Work Product in Communications with Testifying and Consulting Experts," Enviromental Litigation Committee Newsletter (Summer/Fall 2006) for a list of decisions.

43 Regional Airport Authority of Louisville and Jefferson County v. LFG, LLC, 460 F3d 697 (CA-6, 2006).

44 329 U.S. 510 (1947).

45 Haworth, Inc. v. Herman Miller, Inc., 162 F.R.D. 292 (W.D. Mich. 1995). See also Toledo Edison Co. v. GA Techs., Inc., 847 F.2d 335 (CA-6, 1988).

46 J.T. Pinnell, "Does Your Litigation Expert 'Write-Over?'" E-Discovery Bytes, http://ediscovery.quarles.com/2008/01/articles/practice-tips/does-you.

47 M.W. Tindall and S.D. Fried, "Protecting Attorney Work Product in Communications With Testifying and Consulting Experts," Environmental Litigation Committee Newsletter (Summer/Fall 2006).

48 See, e.g., Rule 802 of the Federal Rules of Evidence.

49 Rule 801(c), (a) of the Federal Rules of Evidence.

50 Rule 801(d) of the Federal Rules of Evidence.

51 Rule 801(d)(1) of the Federal Rules of Evidence.

52 Rule 801(d)(2) of the Federal Rules of Evidence.

53 See, e.g., Rule 803(6) of the Federal Rules of Evidence.

54 See, e.g., Rule 803(7) of the Federal Rules of Evidence.

55 See, e.g., Rule 803(17) of the Federal Rules of Evidence.

56 See, e.g., Rule 803(18) of the Federal Rules of Evidence.

57 See, e.g., Rule 803(14) of the Federal Rules of Evidence.

58 See, e.g., Rule 803(15) of the Federal Rules of Evidence.

59 See, e.g., Rule 803(8) of the Federal Rules of Evidence.

60 See, e.g., Rule 803(9) of the Federal Rules of Evidence.

61 See, e.g., Rule 803(5) of the Federal Rules of Evidence.

62 See, e.g., Rule 803(16) of the Federal Rules of Evidence.

63 See, e.g., Rule 803(1) of the Federal Rules of Evidence.

64 See, e.g., Rule 803(2) of the Federal Rules of Evidence.

65 See, e.g., Rule 803(3) of the Federal Rules of Evidence.

66 See, e.g., Rule 803(3) of the Federal Rules of Evidence.

67 See, e.g., Rule 803(4) of the Federal Rules of Evidence.

68 See, e.g., Rule 804(b)(1) of the Federal Rules of Evidence.

69 See, e.g., Rule 804(b)(2) of the Federal Rules of Evidence.

70 See, e.g., Rule 804(b)(3) of the Federal Rules of Evidence.

71 See, e.g., Rule 804(a) of the Federal Rules of Evidence.

72 *Ibid.*

73 See, e.g., Rule 807 of the Federal Rules of Evidence.

74 D.M. Malone and P.J. Zwier, EFFECTIVE EXPERT TESTIMONY (Notre Dame, Ind.: NITA, 2000), p. 73.

75 See, e.g., Rule 901(a) of the Federal Rules of Evidence.

76 See, e.g., Rule 902 of the Federal Rules of Evidence.

77 *Ibid.*

78 *Ibid.*

79 See, e.g., Rule 1002 of the Federal Rules of Evidence.

80 Rule 1003 of the Federal Rules of Evidence.

81 D.E. Heinberg, "The Use of the Financial Expert (or Consultant)—from Both the Attorney's and Expert's Perspective," VALUE EXAMINER (May/June 2005).

82 Michael Connelly, THE BRASS VERDICT (New York: Little, Brown and Company, 2008), p. 141.

83 *Ibid.*, p. 272.

84 Zeph Telpner and Michael Mostek, EXPERT WITNESSING IN FORENSIC ACCOUNTING (Boca Raton, Fla.: CRC Press), pp. 209–237.

85 Terry Carter, "Accounting Gumshoes," ABA JOURNAL (September 1997), p. 37.

86 "Super Sleuths," FAR EASTERN REVIEW (October 7, 1999) *www.investigation.com/articles.*

87 Michael Coren, "Digital Evidence: Today's Fingerprints," *http://cnn.law.printthis.clickability.com/pt/cpt?action=cpt&title=CNN.com+ Digital+evi.toptechs.aicpa.org.*

88 See *http://infotech.aicpa.org.*

89 Matthew Greenblatt and Stephen O'Mally, "Inside an Internal Accounting Investigation," NEW YORK LAW JOURNAL (May 29, 2007).

90 Jeff Lenning, "Drilling for Information," JOURNAL OF FORENSIC ACCOUNTING (August 2000), p. 39.

91 Basil Orsini, "Electronic Imaging," THE WHITE PAPER (July/August 1999), p. 24.

92 See *www.zylab.nl/zylab2000.*

93 Helen Ehlers, "Fraud Investigations Need to Start with a Plan for Gathering and Handling the Evidence," INTERNAL AUDITOR (October 1996), pp. 38–43.

94 Probability (x is the first digit) = Log 10 (x + 1) – Log 10(x).

95 David G. Banks, "Benford's Law Made Easy," THE WHITE PAPER (September/October 1999), p. 20.

96 Richard B. Lanza, "Using Digital Analysis to Detect Fraud," JOURNAL OF FORENSIC ACCOUNTING: AUDITING, FRAUD & TAXATION 1 (2000), p. 293.

97 David G. Banks, "Benford's Law Made Easy," THE WHITE PAPER (September/October 1999), p. 21.

98 Durtschi, Hillison, and Pacini, "The Effective Use of Benford's Law to Assist in Detecting Fraud in Accounting Data," JOURNAL OF FORENSIC ACCOUNTING 5 (2004), p. 24.

99 See *www.digitalanalysisonline.com.*

100 Richard B. Lanza, "Using Digital Analysis to Detect Fraud," JOURNAL OF FORENSIC ACCOUNTING: AUDITING, FRAUD & TAXATION 1 (2000), p. 291.

101 *Ibid,* p. 295.

102 See K.H. Pickett and J.M. Pickett, FINANCIAL CRIME INVESTIGATION AND CONTROL (New York: John Wiley & Sons, 2002), pp. 257–266.

103 For an evaluation of five fraud data mining products, see D.W. Abbott, I.P. Matkovsky, and J.F. Elder IV, "An Evaluation of High-end Data Mining Tools for Fraud Detection," *www.datamininglab.com/pubs/smc98_abbott_mat_eld.pdf.*

104 S.R. Gardner, "Building the Data Warehouse," COMMUNICATIONS OF THE ACM (September 1998), p. 54. For more information, see Jeff Lenning, "Drilling for Information," JOURNAL OF ACCOUNTANCY (August 2000), pp. 39–51.

105 Robert Burns, "Pentagon Defends Data-Mining Project," THE ADVOCATE (November 21, 2002), p. 10A.

106 "Super Sleuths," FAR EASTERN REVIEW (October 7, 1999), *www.investigation.com/articles.*

107 Julie S. David and Paul S. Steinbart, DATA WAREHOUSING AND DATA MINING: OPPORTUNITIES FOR INTERNAL AUDITORS (Altamonte Springs, Fla.: The Institute of Internal Auditors Research Foundation, 2000), p. 5.

108 "Super Sleuths," FAR EASTERN REVIEW (October 7, 1999), *www.investigation.com/articles.*

109 B.L. Derby, "Data Mining for Improper Payments," JOURNAL OF GOVERNMENT FINANCIAL MANAGEMENT 52 (4) (Winter 2003), p. 11.

110 Susan Pulliam and Deborah Solomon, "Uncooking the Books – How Three Unlikely Sleuths Discovered Fraud at WorldCom," WALL STREET JOURNAL (October 30, 2002).

111 *Ibid.*

112 W.S. Albrecht and C.C. Albrecht, "Root Out Financial Deception," JOURNAL OF ACCOUNTANCY (April 2002), p. 33.

113 M.J. Comer, CORPORATE FRAUD, 3d ed. (Aldershot: Gower Publishing Ltd., 1998) p. 11.

114 Barbara Martinez, "Judge Admonishes Medco on Case Documents," THE WALL STREET JOURNAL (February 4, 2005), p. A-5.

115 *Ibid.*

116 *Ibid.*

117 G. Stevenson Smith, "Collection and Control of Electronic Evidence," JOURNAL OF FORENSIC ACCOUNTING 5 (1) (2000), pp. 285–286. *See also* Mark Bigler, "Computer Forensic," INTERNAL AUDITOR (February 2000), pp. 53–55.; David Icove, Karl Seger, and William VonStorch, COMPUTER CRIME, A CRIMEFIGHTER'S HANDBOOK (Sebastopol, Calif.: O'Reilly & Associates, 1995), pp. 190–194.

118 Steve Towns, "Fighting Cyber-Crime," GOVERNMENT TECHNOLOGY (April 2009), p. 42.

119 John Markoff, "Vast Spy System Loots Computers in 103 Countries," THE NEW YORK TIMES (March 28, 2009), *http://www.nytimes.com/2009/03/29/technology/29spy.html.*

120 Nicholas Varchaver, "The Perils of E-mail," FORTUNE (February 17, 2003), p. 99.

121 Sandi Smith, "Meet the Forensic Accountant," INTUIT ADVISOR (2002), *www.intuitadvisor.com.*

122 Nicholas Varchaver, "The Perils of E-mail," FORTUNE (February 17, 2003), pp. 96–100.

[123] *Ibid*, p. 99.

[124] S.H. Cytron and R. Tie, "A CPA's Guide to the Top Issues in Technology," JOURNAL OF ACCOUNTANCY (May 2001), p. 77.

[125] Jesse Drucker and Mark Maremont, "An E-Mail Casts Two Key Suppliers As Adelphia Abettors," THE WALL STREET JOURNAL (June 1, 2004), p. C-1.

[126] David Icove, Karl Seger, and William VonStorch, COMPUTER CRIME: A CRIMEFIGHTER'S HANDBOOK, Sebastopol (Calif.: O'Reilly & Associates, 1995), pp. 190–194.

[127] B.J. Romano, "Microsoft Device Helps Police Pluck Evidence from Cybercrime of Crime," THE SEATTLE TIMES (April 29, 2008). *http://seattletimes.nwsource. com/html/microsoft/2004379751_msftlaw29.html*.

[128] Al Marcella and R.J. Dippel, "Technical, Legal, and Internal Control Implications of Today's Digital Multifunctional Devices," JOURNAL OF FORENSIC AND INVESTIGATIVE ACCOUNTING, Vol. 2, Issue 2 (2010), pp. 255-275.

[129] *Ibid*.

[130] John Sandford, THE HANGED MAN'S SONG (Berkley: 2003), p. 139.

[131] R.L. Ratliff and I.R. Johnson, "Evidence," INTERNAL AUDITOR (August 1998), pp. 55–61.

[132] J.T. Lescroart, THE 13TH JUROR (New York: Dell Publishing, 1994), p. 310.

[133] Shawn Young, "Courtroom Drama: Why Good Actors Are Playing Bad Ones," THE WALL STREET JOURNAL (April 19, 2005), p. A-1.

[134] *Ibid*.

[135] *Ibid*., p. A-14.

[136] T.W. Golden, S.L. Skalak, and M.M. Clayton, A GUIDE TO FORENSIC ACCOUNTING INVESTIGATION (Hoboken, N.J.: John Wiley & Sons, 2006), pp. 156-157.

[137] See *http://www.fbi.gov/hq/lab/org/qdu.htm*.

[138] *Ibid*.

[139] Mark Kohn, "Unreported Income and Hidden Assets," FORENSIC ACCOUNTING IN MATRIMONIAL DIVORCE (Philadelphia: R.T. Edwards, 2005), pp. 49-57.

[140] See *http://expertpages.com/news/select_document_examiner.htm*.

[141] Sam Roberts, "A Stroke of Pen Altered Date, and a Tale of Lincoln, Too," NEW YORK TIMES (January 25, 2011), p. A-11.

[142] See *http://expertpages.com/news/select_document_examiner.htm*.

[143] L.C. Liebscher, "Conducting an Observed Document Examination," THE FORENSIC EXAMINER (Spring 2007), p. 62.

[144] Monique Frigard, "Newsmakers: Document Examiner Keeps a Sharp Eye Focused to Fight Crime," Reviewjournal.com, April 5, 2004, *http://reviewjournal.com/ lvrj_home/2004/Apr-05-Mon-2004/living/23571098.html*.

[145] Pete Yost, "High Court Probes Arthur Andersen Trial," YAHOO! FINANCE, April 27, 2005, *http:/biz.yahoo.com/ap/050427/scotus_ Arthur_Andersen.html?. v=7 & printer=1*.

[146] *Arthur Andersen LLP*, 544 US 696, 125 SCt 2129 (May 31, 2005).

[147] Jim Mckay, "Show & Tell," GOVERNMENT TECHNOLOGY (January, 2005), pp. 18-20.

[148] T.W. Golden, S.L. Skalak, and M.M. Clayton, A GUIDE TO FORENSIC ACCOUNTING INVESTIGATION (Hoboken, N.J.: John Wiley & Sons, 2006), pp. 427-428.

[149] See *http://www.sgs.com/forestry_chain-of- custody?serviceId=10010031&1obId=5554*.

[150] "Following the Cash Trail with the Dogs of War," IOL, November 21, 2004, *www.iol.co.za/general/news/newsprint. php?art_id=vn20041121104424188C327574&sf=*.

[151] *Ibid*.

[152] Michael Connelly, THE BRASS VERDICT (New York: Little, Brown and Company, 2008), p. 367.

EXERCISES

1. What are the rules of evidence? Where are they found? Are expert opinions evidence?
2. Is taking judicial notice the same as a stipulation? Explain.
3. What is the difference between direct and circumstantial evidence? Which is better?
4. When is evidence relevant?
5. When may relevant evidence be inadmissible in a court of law?
6. What is a privileged communication?
7. Are these items admissible?
   a. Offer of compromise
   b. Settlement offer
   c. Plea-bargaining
   d. Plea of *nolo contendere*
   e. Liability insurance
8. What is the attorney–client privilege?
9. What is the accountant–client privilege? When is it honored?
10. Who is the holder of the privileged communication?
11. What are some exceptions to the privileged communication rule?
12. Under what circumstances are communications between taxpayers and tax practitioners protected by federal tax law?
13. What is the work product rule? Does it apply to accountants?
14. Can communications between an accountant and a client be protected under the attorney–client privilege? Does the attorney work product rule apply to accountants?
15. What is hearsay evidence?
16. What is the hearsay exception for business records?

17. What is the hearsay exception for commercial publications?

18. Can market reports be admitted under the hearsay evidence exception?

19. What is the hearsay exception for learned treatises?

20. What is the hearsay exception for public records?

21. Explain Fed. Rul. of Evidence 803 (18). Why must expert witnesses be careful here?

22. What is the authentication requirement?

23. How may computer records be authenticated?

24. What is the best evidence rule?

25. What is demonstrative evidence? When can demonstrative evidence be introduced at trial?

26. What are some special evidence rules for criminal matters?

27. Define the residuum rule.

28. What is a chronological database?

29. What are fingerprints in the modern courtroom?

30. What are the AICPA's 2005 top 10 technology issues?

31. Explain electronic imaging.

32. What is drill-down functionality?

33. What is Benford's Law and when is the technique useful?

34. What are the odds that these numbers will be the first digit in a particular number?
    a. One
    b. Two
    c. Four
    d. Nine

35. What is Digital Analysis Tests and Statistics (DATAS) and when is this technique useful?

36. What is data warehousing/mining and how is it used?

37. Explain the difference between data extraction and data investigation. What are some tools for doing both?

38. How did Gene Morse find the WorldCom cooked books?

39. How must computer evidence be handled?

40. Can anything be done to retrieve lost e-mails and files?

41. What steps must be taken to preserve the integrity of evidence?

42. Using the Internet for definitions and illustrations, describe:
    a. Peripheral witness
    b. Hostile witness
    c. Percipient witness

43. Explore Internet examples of the laboratory analysis of physical and electronic evidence.

44. Find information about the Sahlen and Associates fraud on the Internet. What happened to the auditors in this case?

45. Go to the AICPA Internet site and list the current top 10 technology issues.

46. Prepare a paper on sophisticated courtrooms throughout the United States.

47. From the Internet, define these terms:
    a. Vacatus
    b. Demurrer
    c. Ipse dixit

48. Determine whether these are direct, circumstantial, hearsay, or not evidence.
    a. The gun left behind at a crime scene.
    b. Argument presented by a prosecutor.
    c. Sworn testimony of a witness.
    d. Testimony excluded from trial.
    e. When you wake up in the morning and your driveway is wet. You decide it rained during the night.
    f. Samples of your work performance.
    g. Sam testifies that Larry said he left home early.

49. Locate the 2005 Supreme Court decision involving Arthur Andersen's appeal of its criminal conviction of destroying records. What is the Supreme Court's opinion with respect to record retention?

50. On the Internet, locate the Brief of Amici Curiae of the Washington Legal Foundation and the U.S. Chamber of Commerce dated December 8, 2004, on behalf of Arthur Andersen.
    a. What does *amici* mean? See footnote 1.
    b. Give the purpose of the Washington Legal Foundation.
    c. Explain the split in the courts with respect to the phrase "corrupt persuasion."
    d. What is the "rule of lenity?"

51. On the Internet locate Appellate.net by Evan M. Tager.
    a. Outline his tips for preserving arguments for appeals.
    b. Locate and read his article "Bad Faith Experts after Kumho." At note 24, is a course of self-study adequate to create an expert?
    c. In the article in b above, at note 23, can someone become an expert by accumulating experience in testifying?
    d. Pick one of his Amicus Briefs and summarize the position set forth.

52. "Graphology is forensic document examination." Determine the validity of this statement.

53. What is some of the equipment that a forensic document examiner might use in his or her work?

54. What may alert a forensic accountant that an invoice is fake or altered?

55. "Each state has a licensing board for forensic document examiners." Determine the validity of this statement.

56. Frank Abagnale says it is 3,000 times easier to commit fraud today than when he was operating. Why?

57. Find the U.S. Eastern District Court of New York *SEC v. Symbol Technologies, Inc.*, June 3, 2004. Explain the so-called three way round trip transactions or the candy deals.

58. Benford analysis is *not* useful in which of the following situations?
    a. Accounts receivable
    b. Accounts payable
    c. Amounts on checks
    d. Invoice numbers
    e. c and d

59. Benford's law states:
    a. The digit 9 occurs as the first, second, or third digit in a set of numerical data with a probability of about 10 percent.
    b. Any digit occurs as the first or second digit in a set of numerical data randomly.
    c. Any digit occurs as the first, second, or third in a set of numerical data with a probability that is predictable.
    d. The digit 1 occurs as the first, second, or third digit in a set of numerical data with a probability of about 15 percent.
    e. None of the above.

60. Using the Internet and other sources, answer these questions about an individual.
    a. My birth name is Martha Hellen Kostyra. What name do I go by today?
    b. I am of _____ decent.
    c. My birthday is _____, and I was born in _____, N.J.
    d. I earned a degree in European and Architectural history in 1962 at _____ College in Manhattan.
    e. I was married to _____ in 1961, but divorced him in _____.
    f. The name of my one daughter is _____.
    g. I became a(n) _____ in 1967.
    h. In 1991, I changed the name of my company to _____.
    i. I have contributed approximately $_____ over the years to the _____ party.
    j. When and where were my prison sentence(s)?
    k. My prison inmate number was _____.
    l. Do I have anything copyrighted?
    m. Where do I currently reside?
    n. What is my current net-worth (2011)?
    o. My mother died at age _____ in _____ (year).

chapter

10

COMMERCIAL DAMAGES

A forensic accountant is more likely to be used when damages are difficult to determine or prove. The type of case and the parties involved will determine the forensic accountant's role.

—W.G. Bremser[1]

OBJECTIVES

After completing Chapter 10 you should be able to:

1. Discuss the types of damages claims.
2. Understand basic damage calculation approaches.
3. Be able to use the various methods available to determine commercial damages.
4. Be able to determine lost profits.

OVERVIEW

When harm comes to one person or party who suffers an economic loss as its result, there are financial considerations. If the loss is sustained from the harmful act of another, there may be damages. Damages may be defined as money claimed or paid by law to make up for some harm done to a person (or other entity) or his or her property.[2] Often the party harmed ought to receive compensation for the damages suffered. The fact-finding surrounding such damages and the quantifying of those damages is often complex. In a legal setting, the person harmed (plaintiff) and the person who harmed the plaintiff (defendant) may not agree as to the facts surrounding the harm and the damages. Often experts are called in to resolve the issues and present them in court. The forensic accountant role in such disputes can vary from case to case, but it is often concerned with the calculation of damages.

Understanding the nature of the harmful acts involved in damages is fundamental to the study of damages. If the occurrence of the harmful act itself is wrongful, it is a *tort,* a wrongful act other than a breach of contract that injures another and for which the law imposes civil liability. A second harmful act that involves damages is a breach of contract. A *breach of contract* is a failure without excuse or justification to fulfill one's obligations under a contract.

In a legal setting, the plaintiff must show that he or she was harmed or injured (usually financially) by the defendant. Eventually, comes the most important question: "What is the amount of the damages?" In virtually every commercial dispute, there is a difference of opinion—often significant—about the size of the damages. Often, the amount of the damages rests on accounting concepts, measurements, and assumptions. Thus, accountants often are involved in the determination of damages and in presenting and defending their damages estimates in the dispute. Because damages estimates involve these accounting concepts, measurements, and assumptions, the court typically relies on expert witnesses who possess accounting, financial, or economic backgrounds to assist the court in reaching the damages verdict.

Commercial damages may relate to either loss of profits or the reduction in value of a business entity. In rare cases, there may be both lost profits and reduction in business value. However, in these cases, care must be taken to avoid an "overlapping" count (or double dipping).

THE EXPERT

¶ 10,001   EXPERT WITNESSES' QUALIFICATIONS

Sources differ on what qualifications are desirable for an expert witness in damages. Certainly, the expert should be trained and experienced in quantitative analysis. According to the Federal Judicial Center's Reference Manual on Scientific Evidence,[3] the method used and the substance of the damages claim dictate specific areas of specialization that experts need. The accountant who serves as expert witness will often be a CPA or hold a Ph.D. Often the accountant may also have an MBA degree and a growing number of practitioners are seeking a forensic-type credential. Economists who offer expert witness services will generally hold a Ph.D. Patrick Gaughan emphasizes economics and finance education and experience as desirable qualifications of an economic expert who could provide expert testimony on commercial damages.[4]

Selecting the right expert witnesses for a specific case is a matter of matching the accountant's qualifications with the relevant issues at hand. For example, a lost earnings case may require someone with a labor background; a case involving securities may require a finance background.

¶ 10,011   EXPERT WITNESSES' TESTIMONY REQUIREMENTS

Daubert Factors

Perhaps more important than the expert witnesses' qualifications is the testimony provided. In the milestone *Daubert* case,[5] the bar was raised for introducing expert witness testimony. In this case, the U.S. Supreme Court characterized the Court's function as that of a "gatekeeper" in determining whether an expert's testimony constitutes "scientific knowledge" that will assist the trier of fact to understand or determine a fact in issue. A judge performs this function by ensuring that an expert's testimony is relevant and reliable. The Supreme Court in *Kuhmo Tire Co.*[6] extended the principles of *Daubert* applicable to scientific experts to all experts possessing "technical" or "other specialized" knowledge. In determining the admissibility of nonscientific expert testimony, the Court may consider the following *Daubert* factors:

- Whether a theory or technique can be or has been tested,
- Whether it has been subjected to peer review and publication,
- Whether a technique has a high rate of error,
- Whether there are standards controlling the technique's operation, and
- Whether the theory or technique enjoys a general acceptance within the scientific community.

The Supreme Court in *Kuhmo Tire Co.*[7] citing *Daubert*, stated that in assessing an expert witness's reliability, the court must determine whether the expert "employs in the courtroom the same level of intellectual rigor that characterizes the practice of an expert in the relevant field."

Federal Rule of Evidence 702 (Testimony by Experts) follows along the same lines as *Daubert* as the federal courts are more and more trying to eliminate "experts" who do not follow generally accepted methods in formulating their testimony.

Voir Dire Challenges

Voir dire (examination of a witness's competency) is another legal obstacle to expert testimony in a damages case. Usually the opposing attorney is questioning the expert's skills, education, training, knowledge and/or experience to be an expert witness.

Daubert and *voir dire* challenges are courtroom obstacles that the damages expert must be prepared to encounter. The expert must prove that he or she possesses sufficient skills, education, knowledge, training, and experience to be accepted as an expert and he or she has used the proper methods based on the facts and circumstances to arrive at a reasonable estimate of the damages. See Chapter 8 for more information on challenges to expert witnesses.

BASICS OF DAMAGES LITIGATION

¶ 10,021   THE LEGAL FRAMEWORK OF DAMAGES

In order to win an award for damages, the injured party must generally prove two points:

- That the other party was liable for his damage.
- That the injured party suffered damages as the results of the actions or lack of actions of the offending party.

This usually requires the proof of three issues by the legal team:

- *Proximate (direct) cause.* The damages caused was a direct result of the offending party's actions or lack of actions.
- *Reasonable certainty.* That it is "reasonably certain" that the injured party would have earned the claimed amount of damages "but-for" the actions of the other party.
- *Foreseeability.* That a prudent person could look into the future and see that the actions of the offending party would damage the other party to the litigation.

The above three required issues that must be proved in litigation serve as the basis for many law suits. For example at the heart of the *Scott v. Johnson* case were the first two issues stating that:

> It appears to be the general rule that while a plaintiff must show with reasonable certainty that he has suffered damages by reason of the wrongful act of the defendant, once the cause of existence of the damages have been so established, recovery will not be denied because the damages are difficult of ascertainment.[8]

In another case related to this issue, *Parker Tractor & Implement Company, Inc. v. Johnson* the court stated that "when the cause of the damages is reasonably certain, recovery is not to be denied because the data in proof does not furnish a perfect measure thereof….It is reason enough that sufficient facts are given from which a jury may safely make at least a minimum estimate."[9]

Pennsylvania law illustrates these principles. In Pennsylvania, lost income or profit is recoverable for the destruction or interruption of an established business, "whenever they are not merely speculative or conjectural."[10] Damages are allowable where (1) there is evidence to establish the lost profits with reasonable certainty, (2) there is evidence to show that the lost profits were proximately caused by defendant's wrongful acts, and (3) in a contract action, there is evidence that lost profits were reasonably foreseeable.[11] The lost profits damages "must be a proximate consequence of the breach, not merely remote or possible," and "the element of causation requires not only 'but for' causation in fact but also that the conduct be a substantial factor in bringing about the harm."[12]

Generally, the harm that has been caused by the plaintiff can be either a breach of contract or a tort. This distinction is important in understanding the legal framework of damages and determining how they are calculated.

¶ 10,031   TWO TYPES OF HARM: TORT AND BREACH OF CONTRACT

Two types of harm are the focus of damages awards. As mentioned in the Overview, one type of harm is a *tort,* or an act that is harmful in itself. The second type of harm is a *breach of contract,* which is a failure to fulfill one's contractual obligations.

Generally, torts leading to economic loss can involve personal injury, wrongful death, and commercial damages. In personal injury cases and wrongful death, damages assessment is somewhat straightforward. It is in commercial damages cases, where expert testimony is most often complex and driven by unique circumstances. Most of the application of this chapter focuses on commercial damages situations.

Some tort lost-profits situations include:
- Theft/conversion of funds
- Trademark/patent infringement
- Professional malpractice
- Fraud (e.g., kickbacks)
- Defamation
- Simple/gross negligence
- Slander/libel

Some contract breaches include:
- Employment contract
- Insurance contract
- Failure to pay/provide services
- Broken covenant to compete
- Stock sales
- Sales of a business
- A construction contract
- Sale of inventory
- Real estate contract

¶ 10,041   TWO TYPES OF DAMAGES: RESTITUTION AND RELIANCE

Two types of damages must be understood in loss studies. Damages from a tort are determined under the principle that compensation should place the plaintiff in a position economically equivalent to that person's position absent the harm. When the harmful act unjustly enriches the defendant at the expense of the plaintiff, the term *restitution* is used to describe the damages. When the harmful act is fraud and the intent of damages is to restore the plaintiff to the position as if no promises had been made, the damages are described as *reliance*.[13]

Damages Estimation as Unique Accounting Activity

When an expert witness provides a damages estimate in a dispute, he or she typically makes many calculations, using accounting assumptions and accounting measurements in arriving at the damages estimate. But damages estimates are different from most accounting reports. Weekly product cost reports, monthly sales revenue reports, and quarterly warranty cost reports are all based on historical events. For example, actual costs of production are divided by units of output to determine per unit product costs for the week. Similarly, sales units and sales dollars are accumulated for all stores to determine the amount of sales in units and dollars for the month. Also, warranty service centers measure and report the amount of product repair costs, replacement costs, and allowances granted to determine quarterly warranty cost data.

Most of these accounting reports are based on historical data. Although the timing of the reports may vary, the level of report detail may change from company to company, or some other aspects of the reports might change at management's request, the basic nature and final amounts in the reports are fundamentally going to be the same regardless of who prepares the report.

Forensic analyses typically are quite different from traditional accounting and reporting activities. Although two different experts may look at fundamentally the same accounting data, they may see the damages in a different way. Why? There are a variety of reasons for this different view. In general, the expert's orientation is toward higher or lower damages depending on which side he or she represents in the dispute. All other things being equal, a plaintiff would like damages to be large, and a defendant would like damages to be small. Consequently, whenever there are facts, issues, measurements, or assumptions that can be interpreted differently, the experts for the plaintiff and defendant will tend to interpret those items in a way that is most favorable for their respective client.

In theory, however, experts should be objective, and both sides should arrive at similar damages estimates. Obviously, experts should not distort facts related to the dispute or make illogical assumptions related to the situation, or in other ways manipulate case-related issues so that their client benefits. However, even in traditional accounting activities there often are issues that cause one accountant to record a transaction differently than another accountant. Similarly, one accountant may interpret some financial information differently than another accountant. These differences related to accounting activities occur even when accountants are reviewing historical business activities and historical accounting data in the evaluation and analysis.

Experts use more than just historical accounting data to make damages calculations. Thus, there can be significant differences of opinion about what other data is important for a given set of circumstances. One major additional issue in damages calculations is that the expert must incorporate estimations about what would have happened absent the tort that occurred. Thus, an expert must make a number of predictions. The expert must look at the actual (historical) accounting data to see what actual results were (e.g., sales, profits, costs, market share, etc.), and then the expert must predict what would have happened to those same variables had the tort event or harm not occurred. Making such predictions is not easy, and when experts have different orientations, the predictions differ widely.

Although the general inclination of the plaintiff and defendant is for damage estimates that are larger/smaller respectively, damage estimates that are clearly inappropriate and/or poorly documented and supported may work to the disadvantage of the party. Courts tend to frown on damage estimates that seem to have little relevance to the facts. Therefore, parties need to consider carefully as to the damage estimates they submit to the court and the supporting arguments that they use to defend their damage estimates. In addition, courts tend not to allow experts to "manufacture" profit where none existed beforehand. If a company has struggled making small profits or no profits for a number of years, an expert will have difficulty convincing the court that the firm would have earned large profits absent the event caused by the defendant. Most often the plaintiff can only recover for lost profits where there is concrete data of past profit history.[14] A plaintiff needs a history of profitability for a reasonable time prior to breach of contract.[15] As is discussed later in the chapter, damages for lost profits are based upon net profits rather than gross receipts.

APPROACHES TO LOSS ESTIMATION

¶ 10,051   DAMAGES CALCULATION APPROACHES

Two major theories are used to determine damages; the one selected depends upon state laws. The theories are the out-of-pocket method and the benefit-of-the-bargain method.

Out-of-Pocket Approach

The *out-of-pocket loss* (California and New York) refers to the difference between the actual value received and the actual value conveyed. What is the difference between what a plaintiff paid for something and the actual value received? In other words, the damages award includes no opportunity costs in certain jurisdictions. The plaintiff can recover nothing beyond his or her investment.

In New York, a plaintiff may be awarded only out-of-pocket damages rather than expectation damages.[16] Generally adhering to the legal framework of damages principles described at ¶10,021, a New York District Court explains what a plaintiff must do to obtain damages:[17]

> First, it must be demonstrated with certainty that such damages have been caused by the breach and, second, the alleged loss must be capable of proof with reasonable certainty. In other words, the damages may not be merely speculative, possible or imaginary, but must be reasonably certain and directly traceable to the breach, not remote or the result of other intervening causes…
> In addition, there must be a showing that the particular damages were fairly within the contemplation of the parties to the contract at the time it was made.

Benefit-of-the-Bargain Approach

Under the *benefit-of-the-bargain theory* (or *expectations remedy*), the damages include not only the money invested but also other expenses such as increased costs (i.e., interest expense), lost profits, and decreased value of the investment.

In benefit-of-bargain jurisdictions (which a majority of states use), experts can include money invested plus any lost profits and extra costs. Computation requires at least five major factors:

- Method
- Damages period
- Definition of profit
- Growth rate
- Discount rate

EXAMPLE 10.1 Debra (defendant) sells Paula (plaintiff) an asset with an alleged value of $2 million for $1.8 million. However, the asset really had a market value of only $1.6 million. The fraud damages can be calculated in two ways.

Out-of-Pocket loss rule: $1.8 million – $1.6 million = $200,000.
Benefit-of-the Bargain rule: $2 million – $1.6 million = $400,000.

¶ 10,061   THE LOST PROFITS METHODS

There are three major methods to calculate lost profits: before-and-after method, yardstick approach, and the "but-for" method. In addition, the direct method and the combination method are also available to the analyst. Each method is used to determine the plaintiff's lost profits. Care must be taken to select the appropriate method considering the facts and circumstances of the assignment.

- *Before-and-after method.* Take sales or sales growth before the act and compare to the comparable figures afterward.
- *Yardstick (or benchmark) approach.* Compare sales or sales growth of the company to other companies or to other industry averages.
- *"But-for" method.* The difference in the estimated profits (but-for the actions of the defendant) and the actual profits.
- *Direct method.* Any agreement may indicate how to calculate.
- *Combination method.* May use a combination of methods

The before-and-after method is better for more mature businesses but fails to consider the possibility of sales increases in the future. Thus, the before-and-after method is not the best approach for a rapidly growing business.

The yardstick approach measures what a plaintiff would have done or accomplished without interference from the defendant. A yardstick may be the growth in sales by the industry as compared to the plaintiff's actual sales growth.

The "but-for" method is based upon a market model or sales projection created to compute lost profits. Often, a computerized financial model is based upon a number of assumptions about revenues and expenses. An expert witness testifying about this method would require a strong background in computer modeling and statistics.[18]

Damages may also be calculated by lost asset value, lost personnel earnings, and lost royalties and licensing fees.

AWARDS AND SETTLEMENTS MADE IN MAJOR DAMAGES CASES

Case	Resulting Damages
Honeywell v. Litton	$1.2 billion
Polaroid v. Eastman Kodak	$873.2 million
Smith v. Hughes	$204.8 million
DCS Communication v. General Instruments	$140 million
Fonar v. G.E.	$128 million
Honeywell v. Minolta	$128 million
3M v. Johnson & Johnson	$107.3 million

¶ 10,071   STUDY OF LOSSES PROCESS

When an economic loss takes place and damages need to be applied in an established legal framework, a "study of losses" is made. The primary elements in such a study are the quantification of the reduction in earnings, the calculation of interest on past losses, and the application of financial discounting to future losses.[19] In most situations, current and future earnings of the plaintiff are measured against estimates of current and future earnings that would have been received by the plaintiff had the harmful event not occurred. Interest on the losses occurring before the trial are also calculated and future losses are often calculated and discounted.

Figure 10.1 presents the standard formula offered in the Federal Judicial Center's *Reference Manual on Scientific Evidence.*[20]

Figure 10.1. Standard Formula for Damages

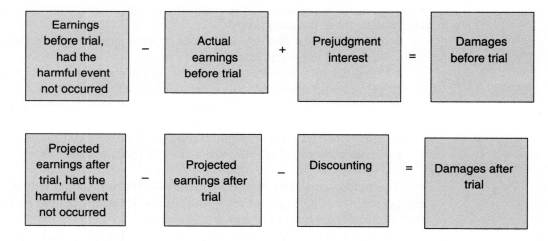

¶ 10,081   ECONOMIC FRAMEWORK FOR THE LOST PROFITS ESTIMATION PROCESS

Not unlike a business valuation, a damages projection must include an economic analysis of the macroeconomic, industry, and company environments.[21] The discussion below is a very simplified look at this process.

Macroeconomic Analysis

First, an analysis of the economy is made looking at measures of overall economic performance. Gross domestic product (GDP) is one measure of economic activity that is often used for such purposes. GDP is the total amount of goods and services produced in the United

States in a year. If the measure of GDP is increasing over the period being reviewed, and the company being analyzed is one that improves with the economy, one may posit that the company performance would have improved over the period as well.

Often, the macroeconomic analysis will drill down further to look at regional performance as well. This process can be especially important for a company that does all of its business within a specific region or produces goods and services that target the needs of a specific region. It is less important for a company that conducts business throughout the United States or a company that produces goods and services of use throughout the country.

Industry Analysis

Industry analysis is the next level of economic analysis performed. A specific industry may grow with the macroeconomic trends, or it may not. A specific industry may experience its own peaks and valleys. An industry analysis looks at the industry's recent performance, its current status and outlook. Some of the issues an industry analysis may review are as follows:

- Size—by both revenue and number of firms
- Growth trends and sales trends
- Employment
- Historical perspective
- Factors influencing new entries or barriers to entry
- Factors influencing growth or decline
- Trends expected that may influence industry
- Statistics on new entries into market
- Government regulations that impact the industry
- Common structure and management in industry

Many companies provide industry analysis data and other help. Increasing services online can provide immediate up-to-date information. Some sources are available in both print and online. Some of the companies offering such information are as follows:

- Standard and Poor's Industry Survey
- Hoover's Industry Group Snapshots
- Value Line Investment Survey
- Dunn and Bradstreet Industry Report
- Ibbotson Associates

Company-Specific Analysis

After the accountant looks at the macroeconomic conditions and the industry conditions, a company-specific analysis is needed. At this level, the forensic accountant may truly excel over other experts. This analysis will include scrutinizing the financial statements, including the income statements, balance sheet, and statement of cash flows (if available). This step may well involve a fraud audit type review if circumstances call for it. Case-specific data also will be gathered and financial ratio analysis may be needed to further ascertain the health of the company under study.

Financial Analysis Conclusion

After reviewing the economic conditions and performance from a macroeconomic, industry, and firm-specific vantage point, the expert is ready to draw some conclusions. Was the firm's performance trending in a clear direction before the harmful event? Did the firm's performance follow macro and industry trends in the past? Can one make a strong correlation between macro trends and the firm trends; between industry trends and the firm trends?

MEASURING THE LOSS

¶ 10,091   LENGTH OF THE LOSS PERIOD

The period of time in which losses are measured is important. Losses must be measured over the time period in which sales recover from the wrongful harm. Defining the loss period is the starting point for the loss measurement process. Defining the loss period requires a determination of what type of loss period is involved with the damages claim. As Figure 10.2 shows, it might be a "closed" period, in which revenue declines and has already recovered. It might be an "open" period during which revenue losses continue. Or it may be an "infinite" period in which the firm has gone out of business.[22]

Figure 10.2. The Three Outcomes of Business Damages

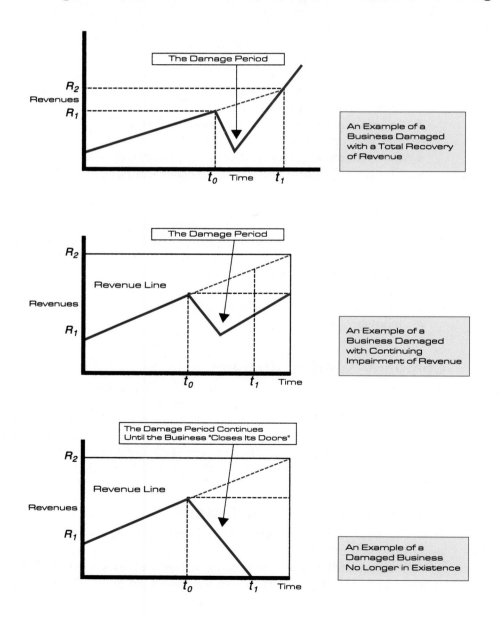

Source: Adapted from EXPERT ECONOMIC TESTIMONY: REFERENCE GUIDES FOR JUDGES AND ATTORNEYS, Figures 9, 10 and 11, pages 128 and 129. ©1998, Lawyers & Judges Publishing Company, Inc., Tucson, Arizona, product #5546. Adapted with permission of the publisher.

Projecting Lost Revenues

Next, the expert projects lost incremental revenues and applies a profit margin to the projected lost revenues. The profit margin should reflect all of the incremental costs that would have been incurred to achieve the forecasted incremental revenues. Lost revenue projection can be obtained using simple methods or sophisticated ones.

Using the projected revenue growth rate is perhaps the simplest method of forecasting lost revenues. It begins by establishing a revenue base and then follows with determining the appropriate growth rate form with which to project "but for" revenues. Basic growth rate used in the calculation may be a simple extrapolation of the historical rate of growth.

Sophisticated methods may involve defining an equation for a line or curve that "best fits" the historical data.[23] Regression analysis quantifies the relationship between variables. In linear regression, the data points determine an amount or function that follows a straight line. In its most simple application for lost revenue forecasting, sales might be one dependent variable to be forecast and one independent variable might be used for such forecasting. For forecasting purposes, the quantified relationship between the variables must be known. The values of the independent variable "cause" or determine the values of the dependent variable. For an analysis, a data file containing the values of the dependent and independent variables for a set of observations must be available. The more observations provided, the more accurate will be the estimate of the parameters to create the line. The difference between the forecast amounts and the actual value of the dependent variable is the deviation. If a linear function cannot describe accurately the function or value, a nonlinear regression analysis may be used. Before offering too complex an analysis to forecast revenues however, the expert witness needs to consider the following important factors:

- Judges and juries are normally not schooled in sophisticated statistical techniques, and the more complex the analysis, the more difficult it might become to provide effective evidence.
- Other tools exist that might help verify the reasonableness of the forecast. Some of these, such as statistical banding, are in and of themselves complex, adding to the complexity of the presentation in a courtroom.
- Common sense must be used to verify the findings. Does the company have the capacity to produce the number of products the forecast shows will be sold? Are projected sales reasonable for the industry, region, and physical location?

New businesses represent a greater forecasting challenge than older ones because there is no history to project from going forward. However, experts can use data from firms that are similar to project growth rates and other statistics that can be used.[24]

Measuring Profitability

Forecasting revenues is not the same thing as forecasting profitability. True economic losses are lost incremental revenues minus lost incremental costs. The margin associated with these lost incremental revenues is usually equal to, or less than, the gross margin but greater than, or equal to, the net margin.[25] The reason that lost revenues would typically have a higher margin than overall gross margins relates to fixed and variable costs. Generally, the incremental lost revenues have lower costs than the base revenue because fixed costs such as overhead would not necessarily increase as revenue increases. This result may not be the situation however, in cases where capacity or other elements of the enterprise structure must be modified to adapt to the additional sales.

Mitigation and Offsetting Profits

Lost profit analysis also must consider mitigation and offsetting profits. A plaintiff needs to have taken reasonable steps to mitigate or reduce its damages. If reasonable steps are not taken, the defendant may argue successfully that the damages should be reduced accordingly.

Another consideration in lost profit calculations involves offsetting profits. A company may be able to adjust its activities so that profits lost in the harmed business segment were made up for by increases in another segment that were the result of juggling redirected assets or capacity from the harmed segment. This would generally involve two companies owned by the same entity or persons. The defendant might successfully argue that damages should be reduced.

Time Value of Money Considerations

Accounting students understand the time value of money. In determining damage awards, consideration is given to economic loss that has taken place prior to the trial and loss that will take place after trial. Prior losses must be measured and then a present value of the past losses must be calculated. Likewise, future losses must be projected, and then projected future losses must be converted to present dollars. After trial, damages may also need to be discounted. See ¶10, 221 for additional information on discounting after-trial damages.

The *Guide to Litigation Support Services*[26] provides the recovery rules for certain types of claims. These rules appear in Table 10.1.

Table 10.1. Recovery Rules for Damages Claims

Types of Claims	Recovery
Buyer of goods	Difference between purchase price and market value + incidental damages − expenses saved
Sellers of goods	Difference between resale price and contract price + incidental expenses − expenses saved
Breach of warranty	Difference between value of goods accepted and value if had been warranted
Agency contracts	Lost profits
Covenants not to compete/unfair compensation	Difficult. Maybe defendant's gain
Fraud	Out-of-profit or benefit-of-the bargain theory

Source: Brining, et al., GUIDE TO LITIGATION SUPPORT SERVICES.[27]

DIFFERENCES IN THE OPPOSING EXPERT'S OPINION. In the *Mobil Oil Corp. v. Amoco Chemical Company*[28] dispute, the claimed damages by the two sides were quite different. At dispute was a patent infringement of paraxylene (MVPI) a precursor of polyester. Plaintiff Mobil claimed damages of $584 million, which was equal to one-half of the cost savings that Amoco had received as a result of this new technology. Mobil approximated the amount that the two sides would have reached if they had derived a licensing arrangement for MPVI in hypothetical negotiations.

The defendant, Amoco, looked at a number of licenses that Mobil had with other manufacturers. These royalty rates were used as a benchmark for reasonable royalties of about $70 million (e.g., the damages). The Ninth Circuit has defined reasonable royalties as "an amount which a person, desiring to use a patented article, as a business proposition, would be willing to pay as a royalty and yet be able to use the patented article at a reasonable profit."[29]

The Mobil court also considered a "lost profits" approach, making an estimate of lost profits on the incremental sales and royalties Mobil could have obtained if Amoco had never made use of the paraxylene. However, the Federal Circuit has held that the lost profits approach is not appropriate in patent disputes, and the reasonable royalties approach is more appropriate.[30] Ken Emanuelson states that reasonable royalties is considered the "minimum floor for calculation of damages" for patent infringement, which probably will not bankrupt a defendant. Lost profits may well bankrupt a defendant, particularly where a large patent holder sues a small infringer. Some courts may award both reasonable royalties and lost profits.[31]

¶ 10,101   COMPONENTS OF DAMAGES

A 1986 AICPA publication lists the following possible types of damages:[32]

- Lost profits
- Lost value
- Lost cash flows
- Lost revenue
- Extra costs

This list is not exhaustive; often more than one of these elements will be part of the final damages estimate. Clearly, accounting data would typically be of value in making the damages estimates, but some components of the damages estimate are not available from the accounting records.

For example, usually there would be no accounts in the general ledger titled "Lost Revenue," or "Lost Profits," or even "Extra Costs," although one might think of unfavorable standard cost variances as "extra costs." Most litigation damages are not found directly in the accounting records. Instead, accounting experts must intelligently use the available accounting information to logically and persuasively provide the court with an appropriate measure of damages.

EXAMPLE 10.2 There was a contract that called for the Lumber Supply Corporation to furnish 100,000 board feet per month of number one grade red oak lumber to a furniture company, the Real Wood Furniture Company, at a price of $2.00 per board foot. The supplier satisfied the contract for the first two months of the year, but then defaulted on the agreement for some reason. What is the amount of damages incurred by the Real Wood Furniture Company?

The court found that Lumber Supply Corporation was liable under the contract for not providing lumber for the last ten months of the contract. Typically, two experts will prepare estimates. The defendant wants the damages to be as small as possible (zero would be optimal). The plaintiff would like the damages to be as large as possible (a really big number would be optimal). (This example is expanded upon throughout the chapter to illustrate several points that follow.)

¶ 10,111   THE DEFENDANT'S DAMAGES ESTIMATE

In order to arrive at a "zero" damages estimate, a defendant must demonstrate to the court that the plaintiff suffered no financial damages. In order to substantiate this position, the defendant must show among other things that the Real Wood Furniture Company could have purchased the 100,000 board feet a month of number one oak lumber from other suppliers for $2 a board foot or less. This information would not come from the accounting records of the Real Wood Furniture Company or the accounting records of the Lumber Supply Corporation. Instead, the information comes from external sources such as lumber price list, industry guide data, or other potential sources of lumber pricing data. For example, there may be an industry price guide for the relevant time periods and locations that shows that the lumber could have been purchased from other suppliers for $1.90 per board foot during the time period covered by the dispute.

If there is no data supporting the previous scenario, the expert for Lumber Supply Corporation would attempt to minimize the damages by limiting it to the "extra cost" the furniture company had to pay for the defaulted lumber shipments. Assume the defendant's expert identified relevant lumber prices for the type and grade of lumber required under the contract as shown in Table 10.2.

Table 10.2. Lumber Prices Identified by Defendant's Expert

Month	Price per Board Foot
March	$2.10
April	2.10
May	2.25
June	2.30
July	2.35
August	2.40
September	2.30
October	2.30
November	2.25
December	2.35

The calculation of the loss is in Table 10.3.

Table 10.3. Defendant's Calculation of Damages

Month's	Price per Board Foot Contract	Actual	Monthly Amount	Monthly Damages
March	$ 2.00	$ 2.10	100,000	$10,000
April	2.00	2.10	100,000	10,000
May	2.00	2.25	100,000	25,000
June	2.00	2.30	100,000	30,000
July	2.00	2.35	100,000	35,000
August	2.00	2.40	100,000	40,000
September	2.00	2.30	100,000	30,000
October	2.00	2.30	100,000	30,000
November	2.00	2.25	100,000	25,000
December	2.00	2.35	100,000	35,000
Total damages				$270,000

Clearly, this simple calculation demonstrates that the Real Wood Furniture Company's damages were $270,000. In the eyes of the defendant's expert, this is "extra cost" that the plaintiff incurred because the defendant did not supply the red oak lumber for the last 10 months of the contract. Further the defendant's expert is of the opinion that the *only extra cost* suffered by the plaintiff in this situation is the extra cost of purchasing the lumber as described above.

The defendant's expert report would include his or her damages estimate along with support for the numbers presented. The report may contain a variety of issues upon which the expert will give opinions. But often the main opinion the accounting expert provides for the court is about damages in the dispute. The form and the content of the expert report will vary somewhat depending on the nature of the dispute and on the venue of the case. State and federal cases may have somewhat different formats and rules. In all disputes, however, the basic nature of the expert report is to provide the experts' relevant opinions in the case.

¶ 10,121   THE PLAINTIFF'S DAMAGES ESTIMATE

The plaintiff clearly thinks the damages are greater than zero. If that were not true, there would have been no logic in filing a lawsuit. But what are the components of the plaintiff's expert damages estimate? The answer depends on the plaintiff's expert and his or her understanding of the issues in the conflict. Much of the support for the damages estimate for the plaintiff come from various accounting records of the Real Wood Furniture Company, but the use of those supporting data also shows that damages estimates are both an art and a science. The scientific part is primarily the understanding and appropriate use of accounting information. The art part of the process is in knowing how the accounting information is used in creating components of the damages estimate. In addition, expert witnesses frequently use many other kinds of information other than traditional accounting records in arriving at and defending damages calculations. For example, an expert witness may use a company's sales records during a 36-month period immediately prior to a contract violation, to estimate the lost sales caused by violation of a "no-compete" clause of a business sales contract. But an expert also may need to look at industry national and regional sales data to clearly identify the appropriate measure of lost sales. The more unbiased the supporting information, the better the expert can support his or her expert report.

The defendant's expert witness only includes the extra cost of purchasing the red oak lumber in the damages estimate. This position may be an accurate reflection of the defendant's expert opinion on what the actual damages were in connection with this dispute. Certainly, the defendant's expert will be more inclined towards fewer items of damages and lower dollar amounts for each component of the damages estimate.

The plaintiff's expert, on the other hand, will be inclined toward higher damages estimates if the issues in the conflict support doing so. Higher damages suggests a higher dollar amount for individual components of the damages estimate and/or more areas in which the expert believes there are damages resulting from the issues in the dispute. The plaintiff's expert may believe there are many other components in his or her damages estimate. Some other common damages components in a contract situation of this sort might be (1) lost sales and profits, (2) production or other cost increases, (3) customer ill will that will result in future lost sales and profits, and (4) other adverse effects. How would the plaintiff's expert go about calculating and supporting damages relating to these other damages components?

¶ 10,131   LOST SALES AND PROFITS

Because calculations and supporting evidence is as much an art as a science, a clear knowledge of accounting information and business operations is essential to the process. The actual process, however, requires ingenuity and sometimes imagination to achieve the desired results. Here the plaintiff's expert made the following analysis on lost sales and profits resulting from the lumber supply contract default as shown in Table 10.4.

Table 10.4. Plaintiff's Calculation of Damages

Month	Monthly Sales 2011 Sales	Monthly Sales 2012 Sales	Average G/M Last Two Years	Monthly Damages
January	$ 400,000	$ 420,000	35%	N/A
February	410,000	450,000	35%	N/A
March	440,000	460,000	35%	N/A
April	500,000	350,000	35%	$52,500
May	550,000	360,000	35%	66,500
June	600,000	480,000	35%	42,000
July	540,000	460,000	35%	28,000
August	500,000	450,000	35%	17,500
September	500,000	480,000	35%	7,000
October	540,000	580,000	35%	N/A
November	600,000	720,000	35%	N/A
December	650,000	750,000	35%	N/A
Total damages caused by lost sales				$213,500

For this damages estimate component, the plaintiff's expert argues that the disruption in lumber deliveries caused by the contract violation caused the furniture company major problems in filling special orders, producing regular stock for off-the-shelf-deliveries, and, in general, meeting customer demand. A look at the monthly sales shows that January/

February sales were actually higher than the previous year by about 7.4 percent. Even March sales were up slightly from the prior year. This increase, of course, was for the first month of the lumber supply contract violation. The small March increase in sales can be explained, according to the plaintiff's expert, by the fact that the company was "selling down inventory" made during prior months. By April, however, the interruption in the steady production flow of number-one grade red oak lumber from the defendant caused major production interruptions and other production, sales, and distribution problems. These problems resulted in a string of six straight months of lower than expected sales. These lower sales had a significant negative impact on the company's profits as shown by the $231,800 lost profits. Starting in October, the lumber supply problems were solved and the company was back on track.

¶ 10,141   PRODUCTION OR OTHER COST INCREASES

The defendant's expert identified only one area of cost increase to the Real Wood Furniture Company as a result of the contract violation. The plaintiff's expert identified four areas of cost increase resulting from the contract tort. The first cost increase component is the one identified by the defendant, the cost of purchasing the lumber.

Lumber Supply

The only component of the defendant's expert damages estimation was the extra cost Real Wood Furniture Company had to pay to replace the red oak wood supply that resulted from the contract default of the Lumber Supply Corporation. This "cost increase" is a type of damage. Both the plaintiff's and the defendant's expert agree that this component is a legitimate "extra" cost that the furniture company had to pay because of the contract violation. Both agree that the purchase price presented by the defendant's expert for number one red oak lumber is correct. Further analysis shows, however, that the prices used were for a supplier using FOB shipping point prices. The furniture company's contract with Lumber Supply Corporation was an FOB destination contract. The shipping cost for the oak lumber would have been $0.20 per board foot for the supplier in question. This additional fact changes the damages estimate for this component as shown in Table 10.5.

Table 10.5. Damages Estimate Including Lumber

Month	Price per Board Foot Contract	Actual	Shipping	Monthly Amount	Monthly Damages
March	$2.00	$2.10	$0.20	100,000	$30,000
April	2.00	2.10	.20	100,000	30,000
May	2.00	2.25	.20	100,000	45,000
June	2.00	2.30	.20	100,000	50,000
July	2.00	2.35	.20	100,000	55,000
August	2.00	2.40	.20	100,000	60,000
September	2.00	2.30	.20	100,000	50,000
October	2.00	2.30	.20	100,000	50,000
November	2.00	2.25	.20	100,000	45,000
December	2.00	2.35	.20	100,000	55,000
Total damages					$470,000

Changing this seemingly minor item—a $0.20 per board foot shipping cost—nearly doubles the damages estimate for this one component. Was the defendant's expert wrong in omitting this item from his analysis? One cannot say without more information. Perhaps the expert was not aware of the shipping terms in the pricing data. Perhaps there is some question of whether the shipping cost would apply to a large regular customer such as Real

Wood Furniture Company. There are many possible explanations about why these two accounting experts arrived at different amounts for one particular component in a damages dispute, and often the court must sort out the details. Of course, the experts in their trial testimony will try hard to convince the court as to the proper estimate.

Other Cost Increases

Frequently, when there are unexpected interruptions in the flow of production resources (such as materials or labor), temporary or permanent production cost increases occur. Sometimes production interruptions can cause increases in the costs of other value-chain activities. For example, there may be pricing penalties if products are not delivered on time or the company may have to use other, more expensive, shipping methods. These are but a few of a wide range of possible cost increases caused by contract torts.

Labor Cost Increases

In our example, the plaintiff's expert believes the lumber supply interruption caused a number of production and other cost increases. One possible area of cost increase is an increase in the amount of unfavorable direct labor variances. The plaintiff expert's analysis is shown in Table 10.6.

Table 10.6. Labor Costs

Month	Standard DLC	Actual DLC	Variance	Monthly Damages
January	$ 78,000	$ 80,000	$ 2,000	N/A
February	80,000	82,000	2,000	N/A
March	56,000	77,000	21,000	$21,000
April	55,000	75,000	20,000	20,000
May	60,000	72,000	12,000	12,000
June	62,000	68,000	6,000	6,000
July	68,000	70,000	2,000	2,000
August	74,000	72,000	(2,000)	N/A
September	80,000	74,000	(6,000)	N/A
October	86,000	75,000	(11,000)	N/A
November	88,000	75,000	(13,000)	N/A
December	80,000	70,000	(10,000)	N/A
Total damages caused by production cost increases				$61,000

The plaintiff's expert can argue that Real Wood Furniture Company experienced significant labor inefficiencies as a result of the lumber supply contract failure. For the period March through July, production cycle adjustments, varying quality of lumber, and other production factors relating to the efficiency of labor caused higher labor costs. This expert further argues that by August these labor inefficiency issues caused by the contract tort were no longer a problem. In total, these extra labor costs are reflected in the $61,000 unfavorable labor variance for March through July of the year.

Shipping Cost Increases

The plaintiff's expert also asserts that there was an increase in the cost of shipping the product. As the result of short product supply during much of the year, the company often had to use a faster means of shipping the product, which was more expensive. During the year, the company shipped 650,000 pounds of product at a total cost of $117,000. During the previous year, the average cost of shipping product was $0.12 per pound. Therefore, the increase in shipping cost required because of the lumber supply contract failure was:

Actual current year cost	$117,000
Expected shipping cost at old rate (6,500,000 × $0.12)	- 78,000
Damages caused by increased shipping costs	$ 39,000

Advertising Cost Increases

Another cost increase suggested by the plaintiff's expert is an increase in advertising costs. The plaintiff argues that the lack of an adequate quality lumber supply during much of the year caused many product shortages. To keep customers happy and to attract new customers, the Real Wood Furniture Company increased its advertising spending from $55,000 last year to $90,000 this year. The expert claims that the entire increase in advertising expense of $35,000 ($90,000 – $55,000) is an element of the total damages estimate.

¶ 10,151   CUSTOMER ILL WILL AND FUTURE LOST PROFITS

This component can contain a wide variety of possible items. Exactly what is included and how the expert defends the numbers depend on the circumstances surrounding the dispute. A word of caution is in order. Although it is desirable for the plaintiff's expert to assert a large amount of damages, an expert must be cautious. If the court believes that the expert is attempting to add illogical or unsupported items, the more solid damages items in the estimate may be discounted by the court as well.

Based on discussions with the marketing staff and an analysis of sales growth trends during the last five years, it is estimated that there will be lost sales for the next three years caused by unhappy customers who could not get the products they wanted. This lack of desired product is alleged to be caused by the missing lumber supply. The expected lost sales for the next three years are measured in terms of a percentage of sales during 2011.

Based on the discussions with the company's marketing staff, lost sales in 2010 are estimated to be 15 percent of 2011 sales, in 2013 lost sales are estimated to be 10 percent of 2011 sales, and in 2014 lost sale are estimated to be 5 percent of 2011 sales. To find the total sales dollars for 2011, use the sales data shown earlier in the lost profits table for the current year.

Table 10.7. Lost Sales

	Monthly Sales	
Month	2011 Sales	2012 Sales
January	$ 400,000	$ 420,000
February	410,000	450,000
March	440,000	460,000
April	500,000	350,000
May	550,000	360,000
June	600,000	480,000
July	540,000	460,000
August	500,000	450,000
September	500,000	480,000
October	540,000	580,000
November	600,000	720,000
December	650,000	750,000
Total sales	$6,230,000	$5,960,000

The calculation of lost sales would be as follows:

Year	2009 Sales	Estimated Percent of Lost Sales	Lost Sales For Year
2012	$6,230,000	15%	$934,500
2013	$6,230,000	10%	623,000
2014	$6,230,000	5%	311,500

The lost profits from these expected lost sales are calculated the same as the lost profits on current year (2011) sales shown earlier as shown here in Table 10.8.

Table 10.8. Lost Profits

Year	Lost Sales For Year	Average G/M Last Two Years	Estimated Lost Profits From Future Lost Sales
2012	$934,500	35%	$327,075
2013	623,000	35%	218,050
2014	311,500	35%	109,025
Total lost profits from lost sales 2012–2014			$654,150

¶ 10,161   OTHER ADVERSE EFFECTS

Contract torts and other causes of action in litigation can give rise to a wide variety of alleged damages in a particular situation. Plaintiffs sometimes have a long laundry list of issues that they believe have resulted in damages from a particular dispute. Some of these issues may be legitimate causes of damages that the plaintiff is aware of from personal knowledge of the business and the events surrounding the dispute. Whenever possible, the expert witness for the plaintiff will be asked to provide support for the plaintiff's positions on damages issues.

Other times there may be some facts alleged by the plaintiff that are not accurate, logical, or defendable. For example, plaintiffs have argued that they were harmed because they had to use personal funds to cover business losses. Had the business losses not occurred, the plaintiff argues that they could have invested in other alternative investments yielding better returns during the time period covered by the dispute. This "lost profit" on an alternative investment would typically be called an opportunity cost. Usually courts are not friendly toward awarding damages for opportunity-type losses. However, certain base rates of return on investments in general, often are part of damages awards. This concept is reflected in the time value of money, which is essential to certain types of damages calculation.

Experts must use experience, wisdom, and common sense in sorting through damages allegations. The various components of the expert's damages estimate are combined into a total damages estimate that composes a major part of the expert report. The total damages estimate for this plaintiff is shown in Figure 10.3.

Figure 10.3. Damages Report

Damages Report
Plaintiff's Expert Witness
July 4, 2012

The following report identifies the damages suffered by the Real Wood Furniture Company when the Lumber Supply Corporation defaulted on its supply contract for number one red oak lumber. There are several components to the damages suffered by the company.

Current year lost sales and profits:..		$ 213,500
Increased costs:		
Increased cost of buying red oak lumber..	$470,000	
Increased cost of labor..	61,000	
Increased cost of shipping..	39.000	
Increased cost of advertising..	31,000	605,000
Future years' lost sales and profits..		654,150
Total damages caused by the contract default..		$1,472,650

The total damages estimate of the plaintiff's expert is $1,472,650. This amount is $1,202,650 more than the damages estimate of the defendant's expert. Expressed as a percentage, the plaintiff's damages estimate is 445 percent more than the defendant's damages estimate. Often damages estimates by experts on opposite sides in a dispute are significantly different. At trial, each expert has an opportunity to explain to the court his or her damages calculations and the reasoning behind those numbers. Each expert's estimate of damages makes up a major component of the expert report. These expert reports are the foundation for much of the trial testimony of the expert witnesses.

THE EXPERT'S JOURNEY THROUGH THE LEGAL SYSTEM

¶ 10,171   TESTIMONY EARLY IN CASE

Pretrial Summary Judgments

Expert testimony at trial comes late in the litigation process. Long before the trial occurs, experts are busy working with attorneys providing insights, interpretations, guidelines, and advice on accounting and financial issues. Many of the pleadings and other case-related documents prepared by attorneys contain, at least in part, components that are directly influenced (and sometimes written) by accounting expert witnesses.

Often the information and opinions provided by accounting experts will result in a settlement before the dispute goes to trial or even a verdict. Attorneys may file a petition for *summary judgment*, which implores the court to side with them immediately and throw out the arguments of the other side. The theory is that the arguments of one side are so persuasive, and/or the arguments of the other side are so poor, that surely the court will see things the one side's way and rule in that side's favor without even going to trial. Summary judgments are not often granted by a court, but when they are granted, they usually are granted to the defendant.

Decision to Try the Case

When a summary judgment is not granted, and there is no pretrial settlement by the litigating parties, the dispute then goes to trial. The arguments of the attorneys, the fact witnesses, and the expert witnesses are heard by the court.

The court listens to and evaluates the testimony of the expert witnesses. As in the earlier example, often there are significant differences between the damages estimates expressed by both sides. The court must decide who is correct or what the appropriate middle ground is between the two positions taken by the experts. This decision is not an easy task for the court. Experts are called to shed light on complex issues that the average person may have trouble understanding without special training or education. Typically, juries and judges have little or no knowledge of accounting and financial issues. The logic and the persuasiveness of the experts are the primary determinants of how the court arrives at its decision. Successful experts find that complex accounting issues must be reduced to simple and understandable terms if the court is to be persuaded that their position is correct.

¶ 10,181 DEFENDING THE EXPERT REPORT

Deposition Testimony

Typically, the expert has to testify *twice* about the expert report submitted. The first time is deposition testimony when the expert is questioned, under oath, about many issues. Usually, the first questions are about the expert's qualifications in general and then about qualifications as specifically related to issues in the dispute. Other questions are about what the expert was hired to do, how he or she went about the tasks, and other issues related to the conflict. The main reason for the deposition of an expert, however, relates to the expert report itself.

The questioner, who is one or more attorneys for the other side, attempts to learn as much as possible about the report and how it was developed. But the main purpose of the deposition is to find "flaws" and weaknesses in the expert report. The exact nature of the flaws can be many, and the seriousness of the flaws may not surface until the dispute goes to trial. For example, the opposing attorney may believe that the deposition exposed serious flaws in the assumptions the expert used in the report. Perhaps the attorney believes there are flaws in the way the calculations were made in the report. Whatever the problems, the other side with the help of their expert(s) are looking for ways to discredit the opponent's expert report.

Of course, after making the damages calculations and preparing the expert reports, each expert is questioned intensely about his or her report. The questioning is under oath. Each question and answer is recorded. If the expert lies about something or stretches the truth, there is a good chance the truth will be discovered. If so, at the very least the offender will be embarrassed. This issue is stressed here to illustrate the circumstances under which experts operate. Knowing that the expert will be questioned under oath about the report and other case-related issues is important to remember. The forensic accountant is a professional, and every practitioner hanging out the forensic shingle must work and act like a professional at all times.

Trial Testimony

Deposition testimony occurs during the discovery phase of the damages litigation. If the conflict is not settled out of court, the trial phase is next. At trial, the expert may testify again about his or her expert report, assuming there is no successful *Daubert* challenge. Usually the expert reports are the heart of the expert's testimony.

Questioning by Client's Attorney

Unlike deposition testimony, the first questioner at trial probably will be the expert's attorney. The objective of the accountant's testimony and of the attorney's questions is to present the accountant's side of the conflict as it relates to his or her expertise. The friendly attorney wants the expert to appear as a knowledgeable and believable expert witness. The attorney also wants testimony about the expert report to be persuasive to the judge and/or jury in evaluating the issues in the dispute. The friendly attorney will ask questions designed to bring out the key persuasive points in the expert report. Often the expert will be involved in preparing the questions that will be asked, and he or she will have the opportunity to practice the questions and answers a number of times. For trials involving potentially large sums of money, the expert may even practice his or her testimony in front of a mock jury.

Questioning by Opposing Attorney

Once the friendly attorney has finished questions about the expert report, one or more opposing attorneys will cross-examine the expert. The objective of the opposing attorneys is the opposite: to discredit the witness as an expert and to discredit the expert report. It is not personal; it is business. But often it feels personal when the expert is being cross-examined. Typically, the questions will attempt to discredit the accountant as a witness in general or as it relates to the issues in the conflict.

EXAMPLE 10.3 "Ms. Expert you have testified in a number of trials related to contracts in retail businesses, but you have never testified in a trial relating to an electric utility, have you?" Questions of this sort are designed to persuade the judge or jury that Ms. Expert really does not have expertise appropriate in this situation. Sometimes this line of questioning can backfire, and the attorney may actually engender support for the expert witness.

A second major line of cross-examination is designed to discredit some or all of the expert report. Much of the questioning here may come from information learned during the accountant's deposition testimony. But the deposition can be a two-way street. Many times an expert can anticipate cross-examination questions from the type and nature of the questions asked at the deposition. In preparing for trial testimony, the forensic expert should anticipate likely questions during cross-examination, then prepare good answers for the anticipated questions. Often experts prepare answers for 20 or more anticipated cross-examination questions and get asked only one or two of those questions. But being prepared to answer a couple of tough cross-examination questions is valuable and worth the effort of preparing for many others. Some experts argue that major points the expert makes on cross examination are far more important than any other testimony he or she may give.

Preparation for Trial Testimony as Essential

Trial testimony is the accountant's chance as an expert witness to influence the outcome of the trial for his or her client. The expert's ability to articulate his or her positions in the dispute to the court is crucial. The best analysis possible is lost if the accountant cannot clearly, succinctly, and persuasively convey his or her position to the judge and/or jury. Even then, the "best" arguments are not always successful.

Experienced expert witnesses relate that they have testified in cases where they were certain their side clearly had a much stronger position, yet they lost. At other times they went into the trial knowing they had a really weak position, and they won. Regardless of the strength of the arguments, an expert must do the best possible job of expressing his or her position in the courtroom. The bottom line: An inability to communicate well is a fatal career flaw in testifying in the courtroom.

A forensic accountant's primary role as an expert witness is to provide the court with understandings of issues that otherwise would not be clear to the court. Of course, the expert's services are being paid for by a client who expects the accountant to shed the best possible light on the conflict from the client's point of view. The expert's persuasiveness is driven by what is said and how it is said. The most exceptional analysis, if not properly delivered at trial, may be worthless in the final outcome.

Trial testimony is usually much shorter than deposition testimony. There is no rule of thumb as to the amount of time the expert will typically spend in deposition testimony versus trial testimony. In general, however, deposition testimony usually is four to five times as long as trial testimony.

Developing a Theoretical Framework for Damages

Accounting expert witnesses provide the court with valuable information and insights about concepts and topics that absent the experts' views the court might misunderstand, misinterpret, or not view in the proper perspective. Using their knowledge of accounting and financial issues, accounting experts identify the key issues, analyze the relevant financial data, and calculate the appropriate damages in the case. The outcome of this process usually results in an expert report that is the basis for the expert's testimony both at deposition and at trial.

Of course, different accounting experts on opposite sides in a case often arrive at different (sometimes very different) views of what the damages are and how the damages should be calculated. This should not be a surprise because in many cases there are legitimate differences of opinion about the issues involved in the case and what accounting/financial information is relevant to determining appropriate damages.

Because the court, the judge and jury, typically have little or no knowledge about accounting and financial issues, it is difficult for them to evaluate the differing messages that are being provided by the opposing experts' testimony. The experts' opinions should be based on a sound accounting foundation that supports the damages that the expert provides the court. If an expert provides the court with a damage estimate without explaining why those numbers were used and other numbers were omitted, and what was the basis or accounting framework for the calculation model, the court may have a lot of trouble making a valid decision.

In order to provide structure to damage deliberations, courts like to have some accounting foundation or framework to intelligently evaluate competing damage estimates. Depending on the issues in a case, virtually any accounting concept may be important and relevant in evaluating damages. For example, in a case involving an electric utility and the U.S. Environmental Protection Agency key issues revolved around the appropriate nature and timing of the capitalization or expensing of plant repair and maintenance expenditures. Many damage analyses and calculations are based on essential cost/managerial accounting concepts. Some of the more commonly used Cost/Managerial accounting concepts include:

- Cost behavior
- Differential costs/incremental costs
- Relevant costs
- Matching concept
- Identifying the cost objective
- Direct costs
- Allocated cost and allocation bases
- The entity concept

Many of the above concepts are important in an expert's decisions about what costs to include in the analysis, how should the costs be measured, and what is the appropriate timing of the costs/revenues given the case issues. Perhaps the most important accounting concept in damage estimates is cost behavior. Fixed, variable, and mixed costs enter into the calculation of damages in virtually every case. Cost behavior is also critical in determining whether or not predatory pricing occurred in antitrust cases. Another very commonly used accounting concept used in damage measurements is differential/incremental costs. Many damage calculations revolve around the issue of absent the event that is the basis for the law suit, what would the costs and profits have been. So the issue is what costs are incremental to or different from the costs that would have occurred absent the law suit event.

In one U.S. Tax Court case, the judge wanted the expert witness to provide a theoretical framework for evaluating a "cost reconstruction system" in connection with a plaintiff's claim for tax credits under the "research and experimentation tax credit" (RETC) act. The law, designed to help U.S. companies remain on the cutting edge in research, was passed by Congress but it took the U.S. Treasury several years to establish the regulations to implement the law for all users. By the time the regulations were in effect, the plaintiff in the case had to go back and "reconstruct" the costs that applied to the RETC. The judge wanted the expert to create the theoretical framework for such a cost reconstruction system and, to determine if the plaintiff's costs used in applying for the tax credits before the court complied with the cost reconstruction model.

As this example demonstrates, there are many different accounting concepts that have relevance in a wide variety of cases that confront courts each day. Effective and ethical experts will identify what accounting framework is most appropriate for the issues before the court and wisely choose the ones that support the analysis at hand. In order to be successful, the expert must be diligent and thorough in explaining to the court what accounting framework was used and why it was the appropriate framework given the issues in the case. The expert must also remember that most jury members and many judges will have little knowledge of accounting and the expert must do a good job of "teaching" the court what it needs to know in order to intelligently evaluate the accounting issues in the case and evaluate the appropriate damages.

Rebuttal Testimony

In addition to preparing and submitting an expert report, the defendant's expert probably will be asked to provide insight and support for evaluating the other expert report and testimony of the plaintiff's expert. Usually, the opposing expert is asked to act as a rebuttal witness against the plaintiff's expert report and testimony. Sometimes rebuttal testimony is more valuable than direct testimony.

At trial, the plaintiff's expert attempts to convince the judge/jury that the defendant has significantly underestimated the amount of damages. The plaintiff's expert testifies that each of the components of his or her damages estimate is logical, appropriate, and supported by evidence provided in the expert report and put into the trial record.

The defendant's expert witness at trial attempts to undermine much of the plaintiff's damages estimate. There are a variety of arguments that the defendant's expert witness might use to persuade the court that the plaintiff's alleged damages are too high. For Real Wood Furniture, starting with the lost sale/profit calculation, the expert might state that the $213,500 estimate for this damages component includes only the months in which sales were lower in 2010 than in 2009. After the contract violation, there were four months in 2010 when sales were actually higher than in 2009 (e.g., March and the last three months of 2010). If these months were included in the analysis of lost sales/profits the alleged damages for this component would fall from $213,500 to $115,500. But even this amount is too high because the 35 percent used in the damages calculation is lost gross profit, not lost net profit.

Analysis of Real Wood Furniture Company's income statements for the last five years shows that its average net income as a percentage of sales was eight percent. Using eight percent times the alleged lost sales results in lost profits damages of only $26,400. Even this amount assumes that the lost sales were solely the result of an interruption in lumber supply caused by the contract, and this assumption may not be true. Of course, the plaintiff's expert will counter with other arguments, such as:

> My damages estimate for lost sales is conservative because it does not take into consideration the increased sales trend that the company has been experiencing. Over the last several years, sales at the company have been growing at the rate of nine percent compounded annually. If this sales growth had been taken into account, lost profit damages would have been higher by ap-

proximately $78,000. Further, many of the operating expenses of the firm are fundamentally fixed in the range of sales covered in this dispute. Therefore, lost gross profit is a good surrogate for lost profits to the firm.

As the judge and jury hear these accounting arguments, they may become quite confused. The concepts of gross profits, net profit, operating expenses, fixed and variables costs, and sales trends may be unfamiliar terms to most members of the jury (and to the judge as well). Who will they believe? It is hard to predict. Clearly, the experts' skills during trial testimony will be as important as the damages calculations themselves.

Most of the damages estimate components in this illustration are contested in court as well. For example, the damages component for labor inefficiency may be appropriate, but the defendant would certainly want to do some analysis of that component. The plaintiff's expert included in the analysis only those post-contract months in which there were unfavorable variances. The months with favorable labor efficiency variances were ignored. Additionally, the defendant's expert asked for previous year labor efficiency reports so that current year variances can be compared with prior period experiences. Each of the damages components requires scrutiny by the opposing expert.

Probably the most aggressive damages component of the plaintiff is the future years' lost sales and profits, and it is the largest single component of the plaintiff's expert damages estimate. First, will an interruption in the company's lumber supply early one year have far-reaching sales effects for years to come? Perhaps an expert in marketing and customer behavior could help with this issue. Certainly, the accounting expert would want to look at sales trend and industry trend data to see if there is a flaw in the analysis performed by the other expert. Again in this calculation, the plaintiff's expert used lost gross profit to determine the dollar amount of damages from alleged lost sales. Over the longer run, can one really claim that expenses of any sort are fixed? Therefore, the more appropriate measure of lost profits could be a percentage based on lost net income rather than a gross profit percentage.

The Role of the Expert Witness and Ethical Challenges

We know that the role of the expert witness is to provide enlightenment to the court in areas where the court might otherwise misunderstand items such as technical issues, issues that require interpretation, and complex or comprehensive accounting issues that the judge or jury need help understanding. Typically experts have knowledge, skills, or other attributes not possessed by the average person. An ethical challenge that is faced by the expert and that impact on the courts evaluation of the expert's testimony is the fact that both the plaintiff and the defendant pay their experts for testifying. Even though experts are paid by one side in the case, experts are not allowed by the court to be "advocates" for their client. Unlike attorneys who clearly are advocates for their client, experts must walk an ethical line as they prepare for and testify in a case. The challenge of maintaining an ethical posture in a case given the adversarial nature of litigation is referred to as *adversarial bias*. The concept of adversarial bias refers to witness bias that arises because a party to an adversarial proceeding retains experts to advance its cause in a case. Commonly cited forms of adversarial bias include: (1) conscious bias: opinions for hire "hired guns," (2) unconscious bias: wanting to help the side that is paying your bills, (3) selection bias: the attorney has the ability to select from a wide range of expert positions "picking an unrepresentative expert for testimony."[33]

Of the three forms of adversarial bias listed above, the one that is most relevant for experts to address is number two, unconscious bias. Of course we know that courts have standards of performance for experts such as the Daubert standard that we have discussed before, but it is necessary for experts to be conscious of their role in avoiding adversarial bias.

If experts recall the ethical standards that are often faced, it is possible to keep the ethical role of the expert in sight. For example, independence and objectivity should always be recalled. You are the expert for the court, not a pawn of your client. Sometimes this can be a challenge when dealing with aggressive lawyers. Another issue is confidentiality when experts possess and use significant amounts of confidential information. Conflicts of interest may arise when an expert least expects them and that may change the nature of the role of the expert, and of course experts cannot charge their clients based on contingency fees.

In the final analysis, it may bode well for an expert to remember what the court expects of expert witnesses. Included are:

- People who have earned the respect of peers and others in this area of expertise.
- People who have a consistent record on matters at issue in the case.
- People who cannot be dismissed as a "professional" witness.
- People who are likeable and credible to the judge and jury.
- People who are good under pressure when answering tough questions and who do not become combative.
- People who can take difficult financial concepts and explain them to a jury/judge in understandable form.
- In the final analysis, often it is not what you say but rather how you say it that makes the most difference with a judge/jury.

COST BEHAVIOR AND DAMAGES CALCULATIONS

An understanding of cost behavior and related issues is essential for a forensic accountant. Virtually all damages calculations performed by accounting experts requires the use of cost behavior concepts and the estimation of cost behavior patterns for relevant accounting data in the dispute. In calculating lost profits before trial and after trial, variable costs are subtracted from the lost revenues to arrive at lost profits. Cost of goods sold is considered to be a variable cost, so if a company's gross profit percentage averages 45 percent, then cost of goods sold will be approximately 55 percent of lost revenues. Additionally, some conflicts, such as antitrust cases, may require the use of cost behavior data in proving or defending against liability issues. Antitrust disputes are discussed in Chapter 11.

¶ 10,191   COST BEHAVIOR DEFINED

Cost behavior is a simple concept, but if not used correctly, can lead to illogical decisions. In its simplest form, *cost behavior* is the way that cost(s) change with respect to changes in the volume of activity. For example, when sales commissions are based solely on a percentage of sales dollars achieved, sales commission costs increase or decrease in proportion to the dollar amount of sales. Costs that behave in this manner are called *directly variable costs* or just *variable costs*. Notice that there are two components to the definition of cost behavior. The first is a change in the cost and the second is with respect to some change in the volume of activity. This relationship is crucial when accountants do cost behavior analyses. For example, the cost behavior patterns for the cost category direct labor may be different when the volume variable is sales dollars versus using units of products produced as the volume measure.

There are many reasons why managers may want to know about cost behavior in their company:

1. To use in many different types of cost-volume-profit (CVP) analyses.
2. For use in flexible (dynamic) budgeting activities.
3. For use in determining Manufacturing Overhead (MOH) application rates.
4. For use in standard costing, in particular, MOH variance analysis.
5. For use in litigating or defending a wide variety of cost-related legal issues:
   a. Federal antitrust cases (e.g., predatory pricing)
   b. Alleged contractual violations
   c. Measurements of damages for lost sales/profits/etc.

The primary purpose for forensic accountants to use cost behavior is the one enumerated as reason 5 above. This section reviews the common types of cost behavior and how to estimate cost behavior from traditional accounting data.

¶ 10,201   COMMON TYPES OF COST BEHAVIOR

Fixed Costs

Fixed costs fundamentally are not driven by changes in the volume of activity. Notice that the definition does not say that fixed costs never change. Frequently, fixed costs do change because of contractual agreement, government actions, and management decisions. A lease agreement may call for monthly rent payments of $1,200 the first year, $1,400 the second year, and $1,500 the third year. Some costs that usually are fixed in nature are depreciation, property taxes, supervisory salaries, and plant fire insurance. A simple equation that describes fixed costs is:

$Y = a$, where a is the amount of fixed cost

Variable Costs

Variable costs change directly and proportionately with the volume of activity. Notice that variable costs are not merely costs that change, but they change directly and proportionately with activity. Some examples of costs that usually are variable include direct materials, direct labor, and sales commissions. A simple equation for variable costs is:

Variable Costs $= bx$
Where b is the increase in volume and x is the measure of the volume of activity.

Mixed Costs

A third cost classification useful in cost behavior analyses relating to litigation support is mixed cost (or semivariable). These are costs, or cost pools, that contain *both* a fixed and a variable component. There are many costs in business that usually contain both a fixed and a variable component. For example, many shopping center store lease agreements require the store operator to pay a fixed monthly charge such as $1,200 per month plus a variable component such as 1.5 percent of each sales dollar at the store month. Store labor costs, utility costs, maintenance costs, overhead costs, and marketing costs are just a few other examples of costs that usually are mixed costs. A simple equation for mixed costs is:

$Y = a + bX$
where a equals the fixed component and bX is the variable component.

There are two other categories of cost behavior that should mentioned. Both of them are common cost behavior patterns, but neither are used often in litigation analyses. The three cost behavior patterns already mentioned—fixed costs, variable costs, and mixed costs—are used most frequently in cost behavior analyses in litigation support. Two other cost behavior patterns are semivariable costs and semifixed costs.

Semivariable Costs

Semivariable costs change with the volume of activity, but not proportionately with activity changes. Costs of this nature are often called *learning curve costs* because they increase at a decreasing rate with the volume of activity.

EYEWITNESS

When a new product is manufactured or a new service is provided, the labor related costs of that new product or service decline as employees become more familiar with the process. This decline in the cost overtime can be measured and used by accountants to estimate production or other costs once the learning process has stopped. The steady state is reached when the learning curve effect is over.

The importance of the learning curve effect has become more important in business as product life cycles have shortened and automation rates have accelerated.

Semifixed Costs

Another type of cost behavior pattern is *semifixed costs.* These costs increase in steps or jumps. Some argue that all fixed costs are really semifixed costs at various levels of activities. A good example of a semifixed cost might be the depreciation cost of a finished goods warehouse. When the warehouse becomes too small because of the addition of new product lines, the company needs to build another warehouse. The depreciation cost increases by a significant amount when the warehouse is completed rather than increasing in small increments as production ratchets up with the new product lines. Both semivariable costs and semifixed costs provide valuable information for certain types of management analyses and decisions, but they generally are not used as cost behavior models in litigation support.

¶ 10,211   COST BEHAVIOR ASSUMPTIONS

Basis of Cost Behavior Estimates

Two basic assumptions underlie the concept of cost behavior. They are the relevant range assumptions and the time assumption. Although it is convenient to think of costs as being fixed, variable, mixed, or something else, few costs exhibit the same cost behavior pattern for all levels of activity. Instead, costs exhibit a particular cost pattern for a specified range of activity called the *relevant range.* Cost behavior estimates are usually based on historical cost observations and analyses.

EXAMPLE

EXAMPLE 10.4 An expert may want to determine the cost behavior pattern of a store's operating costs. To evaluate this cost pool, the expert analyzes 52 weeks of store operating costs to determine how they increase or decrease with the level of sales each week. During the 52 weeks covered by the data, the activity measures sales ranged from $520,000 to $740,000. Because all of the cost data come from that range of sales activity, it is difficult to estimate what store operating costs would be at sales of either $300,000 or $900,000. These activity levels may be outside of the relevant range. The relevant range is usually deemed to be close to the range of activity from which the analyzed data were drawn.

The further one moves from the range of activity used in the data analysis, the more likely the cost behavior pattern may be different than that shown by the analysis. The relevant range can be illustrated by the chart in Figure 10.4.

Figure 10.4. Relevant Range Illustration

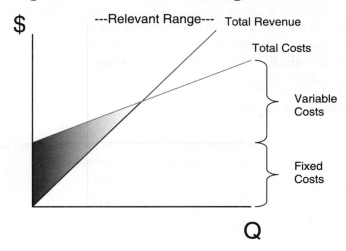

Total Costs = FC + VC
Total Costs = FC + Q (Variable Cost per unit)
Total Revenue = Price X Q
B.E. = Break Even Point
█████ = Loss zone

A second important cost behavior assumption is the *time assumption*, which means that as time passes, the business environment changes, and cost behavior may change as well. Many factors can cause a cost to change patterns over time. Management may have a hydraulic press maintenance agreement that costs $1,500 per month. The amount is fixed regardless of whether production is high or low. Management then decides to switch to a pay-as-you-go plan in which the firm pays an hourly repair rate plus a charge for replacement parts. Under this plan there is a strong relationship between the amount of production output and the amount spent repairing hydraulic press machinery. This serves as an example in which management's decision about the type of maintenance plan used changed the cost behavior pattern of this maintenance cost from a fixed cost to a variable cost. Management decisions, government regulations, and contract commitments are but a few reasons why cost behavior for a particular cost can change over time.

Ways of Estimating Cost Behavior

There are several ways of estimating cost behavior:
- Account analysis method.
- High-low method.
- Regression analysis.
- Engineering or work-measurement method.

Account Analysis Method

The account analysis method classifies the cost accounts in the subsidiary ledger as fixed, variable, etc., based upon experience and judgment. This method is cheap, but subjective.

High-Low Method

The high-low method is the simplest quantitative analysis based upon the basic formula $y = a + bx$, where b is the unit variable cost per measure of activity. Solving for b,

$$b = \frac{\text{Cost at high activity level} - \text{Cost at low activity level}}{\text{High activity level} - \text{Low activity level}}$$

$$b = \frac{\text{Change in total cost}}{\text{Change in activity level}}$$

b = Unit variable cost per measure of activity.

	Independent Machine Hours	Dependent Associated Total Cost
High activity	9,000	$350
Low activity	4,600	218
Change	4,400	132

$b = \$132 \div 4{,}400 = 0.03$ per machine hour.
High level: Total variable costs = 0.03 (9,000) = \$270
Low level: Total variable costs = 0.03 (4,600) = \$138
High level: $a = \$530 - \$270 = \$80$ fixed cost
High level: $a = \$218 - \$138 = \$80$ fixed cost

Regression Analysis

Regression analysis takes all available data and estimates the cost function. That is, this statistical analysis determines the average amount of the change in the dependent variable by using all available data. Thus, regression analysis is more accurate than the high-low method. Regression analysis is more accurate using computer programs to find relationships between cost driver or volume (independent variable) and a cost (dependent variable).

Engineering (Work-Measurement) Method

The engineering or work-measurement method uses industrial engineering, which can be expensive.

SPOTLIGHT

"BUT-IF" ANALYSIS. Professors Avi Rushinek and Sara F. Rushinek give an example of the use of "but-if" analysis in a day-trading dispute.

Late one afternoon, in the middle of a trade, the trader complained to his broker. The broker got offended and told the trader to leave and go to another trading room with another broker. The trader replied that he had just started a trade and asked the broker to let him finish this, his last trade. The broker became restless and threatened to pull the plug on the PC if the trader did not move out immediately. When the trader refused to move, saying that he had to complete his transaction, the broker pulled the power plug, suspending the trade before the trader could cover a short position. The trader planned to cover his short by earning $2 per share on 10,000 shares, a total of $20,000. Instead, the trader lost the opportunity to earn $20,000 due to his inability to cover his short position during that trading day. Because the stock market closed in the meantime and the market value trend reversed on the next day, the trader sued for $20,000 damages due to the broker disrupting his trade and causing $20,000 in lost profits.

The broker claimed that the trader should have left earlier when the broker told him to leave in the first place. The broker claimed that the trader was not authorized to stay there and continue to trade because the broker had told him to leave.

The forensic accountant has to determine whether the lost profits would have amounted to $20,000. Using a but-if analysis combined with a regression and ANOVA, the forensic accountant demonstrated that indeed the trader would have earned about $20,000, if he would have covered his short position before the market closed, which the trader planned to do. The trader kept a written plan of transactions and exit points, which were available to all parties. However, because of the uncertainty of the adjusted R-square of .65 prior to the trade, the forensic accountant could not conclude the entire $20,000 in damages.

The forensic accountant could show that "but if" the action of the broker would have not occurred, the trader would have most probably made $20,000 on covering his short position, with a better than 65 percent probability (based on the R-Square value of about 65 percent). However, combining this 65 percent and the $20,000, results in lower total damages than the trader alleged. [34]

¶ 10,221   DAMAGES PERIOD AND DISCOUNT RATE

Because the largest component of a plaintiff's dispute is the future years' lost sales and profits, the future damages period is important (e.g., after trial). The longer the damages period, the more difficult to establish that any lost profits relate to the harmful event. Besides, a plaintiff must take whatever steps or actions necessary to overcome or mitigate any damages. The longer the recovery period, the more likely the lost profits result from the plaintiff's failure to mitigate the damages or some other irrelevant factor.

Discounting After-Trial Damages

The after-trial damages should be discounted back to present value. There are two major approaches to discount amounts to present values. One approach is to project a plaintiff's hoped-for income stream, by modifying losses to a realistic expectation by factoring in future losses to a present value at a risk-reduced relatively low discount rate.

Another approach is to project the hoped-for-but-lost amounts and then apply a higher discount rate that already includes risk or uncertainty in order to determine the present value. In other words, an expert may either adjust for risk and uncertainty (1) when future profits are projected, or (2) when selecting the discount. Thus, two experts can arrive at similar damages estimates with widely different discount rates. Robert L. Dunn and Everett P. Harry believe that the first approach is best: Modify the losses to a realistic expectation. [35]

Case Law for Discounts

Generally, the courts will not approve a discount rate above 20 percent. [36] Some court decisions that involve discounts are as follows:

- *Knox v. Taylor*, 992 S.W.2d 40 (Tex. App. 1999): 7 percent risk-free discount rate is acceptable.
- *Burger King Corp. v. Barnes*, 1 F. Supp. 2d 1367 (S.D. Florida 1998): 9 percent discount rate was approved.
- *Olson v Nieman's, Inc.*, 579 N.W.2d 299 (Iowa, 1998): 19.4 percent was awarded for patent royalties.
- *American List Corp. v. U.S. News & World Report, Inc.*, 72 N.Y. 2d 38, 550 N.Y.S.2d 590 (1989): 18 was deemed too high according to the Appeals court.

¶ 10,231   CONCLUSION

Calculating commercial damages represents another legal and accounting touch-point where the knowledge, skills, and abilities of the accountant are put to good use in a forensic context. The complexity of the process is apparent to those who must understand the legal and accounting concepts, the various calculation methods and the economic framework. Measuring commercial loss can involve practically all the complexities of business valuation and thus it should only be undertaken by those practitioners trained in the requisite competencies of the valuation expert. Forensic accountants need to understand the fundamentals regardless of whether they intend to take on such engagements because like business valuation, damage calculations will enter into the forensic fray in many different circumstances involving the forensic specialist.

ENDNOTES

1. W.G. Bremser, FORENSIC ACCOUNTING AND FINANCIAL FRAUD (Watertown, Mass.: American Management Association, 1995), p. 5.

2. Clarence L. Barnhart and Robert K. Barnhart, THE WORLD BOOK DICTIONARY, vol. 1 (Chicago: World Book-Childcraft International, Inc., 1982), p. 523. See BLACK'S LAW DICTIONARY (St. Paul: West Group, 2000) for definitions of the many types of legal damages.

3. Federal Judicial Center, REFERENCE MANUAL ON SCIENTIFIC EVIDENCE, 2d ed. (Washington, D.C.: Federal Judicial Center, 2000), p. 282, *www.fjc.gov*.

4. Thomas R. Ireland, Stephen M. Horner, et al., EXPERT ECONOMIC TESTIMONY: REFERENCE GUIDE FOR JUDGES AND ATTORNEYS (Tuscon: Lawyers and Judges Publishing Co., Inc.), p. 112.

5. *Daubert v. Merrell Dow Pharmaceuticals, Inc.*, 509 US 579, 592, 125 L. Ed. 2d 469, 113 SCt 2786 (1993).

6. *Kuhmo Tire Co., Ltd. v. Carmichael*, 526 US 137, 143 L. Ed. 2d 238, 119 SCt 1167 (1999).

7. *Ibid.*

8. Koeber, James A, and Crumbley, D. Larry, "Lost Profits Disputes: A Primer," OIL, GAS, & ENERGY QUARTERLY, (Rel. 58-03-3/2010 Pub. 520), p. 475.

9. *Ibid.*, p. 476.

10. *Delahanty v. First Penn. Bank*, 318 Pa. Super. 90 (Pa. Super. 1983).

11. *Bolus v. United Penn Bank*, 363 Pa. Super. 247 (Pa. Super. 1987).

12. *Advent Systems v. Unisys*, CA-3, 925 F2d 670 (1991).

13. Federal Judicial Center, REFERENCE MANUAL ON SCIENTIFIC EVIDENCE, 2d ed. (Washington, D.C.: Federal Judicial Center, 2000), p. 283.

14. *TDS, Inc. v. Shelby Mut. Ins. Co.*, CA-11, 760 F2d 1532 (1985); *Ronald Re. v. Gannett Co. Inc.*, 480 A.2d 668 (Del. Super. Ct. 1984).

15. *Niagara Therapy Mfg. Corp. v. Niagara Cyclo Massage, Inc.*, 196 So.2d 476 (Fla. App. Ct. 1967); *Radio of Georgia, Inc. v. Little*, 199 S.E. 2d 837 (Ga. App. Ct. 1973); *Message Center Management v. Shell Oil Products Co.*, 2002 Conn. Super. LEXIS 1029.

16. *Telewide System, Inc.*, CA-2, 794 F2d 766 (1986).

17. *Schonfeld v. Hilliard*, 62 F. Supp. 2d 1062 (S.D.N.Y. 1999).

18. W.G. Bremser, FORENSIC ACCOUNTING AND FINANCIAL FRAUD (Watertown, Mass.: American Management Assoc., 1995), pp. 65–66.

19. Federal Judicial Center, REFERENCE MANUAL ON SCIENTIFIC EVIDENCE, 2d ed. (Washington, D.C.: Federal Judicial Center, 2000), *www.fjc.gov*.

20. *Ibid*, p. 281.

21. The coverage presented here is very basic and simplified. For a more detailed discussion of this process see Thomas R. Ireland, Stephen M. Horner, et al., EXPERT ECONOMIC TESTIMONY: REFERENCE GUIDE FOR JUDGES AND ATTORNEYS (Tuscon: Lawyers and Judges Publishing Co., Inc.) An excellent source for additional information on financial analysis for students is the Association for Investment Management and Research (AIMR), an international, nonprofit organization of more than 50,000 investment practitioners and educators in over 100 countries. For more information on this organization and educational opportunities see *http://www.aimr.com*.

22. Robert R. Trout and Carroll B. Foster, "Economic Analysis of Business Interruption Losses" in LITIGATION ECONOMICS, Patrick A. Gaughan and Robert Thornton eds. (Greenwich, CT: JAI Press, 1993).

23. Thomas R. Ireland, Stephen M. Horner, et al., EXPERT ECONOMIC TESTIMONY: REFERENCE GUIDE FOR JUDGES AND ATTORNEYS (Tuscon: Lawyers and Judges Publishing Co., Inc.), p. 114.

24. *Ibid*, p. 133.

25. *Ibid*, p. 134.

26. Brining, et al, GUIDE TO LITIGATION SUPPORT SERVICES, 7th ed. (Fort Worth, Tex.: Practitioners Publishing Co., 2002), pp. 3.5 and 3.6.

27. *Ibid*.

28. 915 F. Supp. 1333 (D. Del. 1933).

29. *Faulkner v. Gibbs*, CA-9, 199 F2d 639 (1952).

30. *Gargoyles, Inc.*, 113 F3d 1580 (1998). See also *Vermont Microsystem, Inc. v. Autodesk, Inc.*, CA-2, 138 F3d 449 (1998).

31. Ken Emanuelson, "Intellectual Property Coverage: Are You Naked?" *www.irmi.com/expert/articles/warren003.asp*.

32. AICPA Practice Aid No. 7, Litigation Services (New York: AICPA, 1986).

33. "Expert witnesses, Adversarial Bias, and the (Partial) Failure of the Daubert Revolution," IOWA LAW REVIEW (2008).

34. A. Rushinek and S.F. Rushinek, "The Role of the Forensic Accountant in Calculating Damages Using the "But If" Analysis in a Case of Internet Day Trader & Online Broker Misconduct Litigation," JOURNAL OF FORENSIC ACCOUNTING 1 (2000), p. 246.

35. R.L. Dunn and E.P. Harry, "Modeling and Discounting Future Damages," JOURNAL OF ACCOUNTANCY (January 2002), pp. 49–55.

36. *Ibid*, p. 55.

EXERCISES

1. Define damages.
2. Point out some contract breaches.
3. What is a tort?
4. Point out some tort lost profits situations.
5. What would the recovery rule for these claims be?
   a. Agency contract
   b. Buyer of goods
   c. Breach of warranty
   d. Fraud
6. Describe the two major theories used by the courts to determine damages.
7. Sam agrees to buy an asset from Pam for $205,000, but six months later Pam says no sale. The asset is now worth $325,000. What would the damages be under the benefit-of-bargain rule?
8. What five major factors are required for the benefit-of-the-bargain computation?
9. Describe the four major ways to calculate lost profits.
10. What three elements must be proven to win a fraud dispute?
11. Describe what is meant by the term *damages* in connection with litigation.
12. "I'm not sure how strong our case is on the issue of liability, but our damages case is really strong and easy to defend." If you were the plaintiff in this case and your attorney made the previous statement, how would you feel about the statement?
13. Two equally competent and equally educated expert witnesses who have been provided the same information and documents should arrive at about the same amount of estimated damages in a particular dispute most of the time. Comment on the previous statement.
14. Describe the difference in orientation between the plaintiff's and the defendant's experts. Is the job of either expert generally easier?
15. Auburn Furniture Company makes a variety of wood furniture for the home and office. The company uses a standard costing system for its manufacturing costs. During a recent unexpected surge in demand, the company decided to use temporary employees from a local employment agency. The company used the temporary employees for two months, after which managers stopped using them. There were many complaints from production foremen that the temporary employees were not very efficient. Additionally, customer service staff noted that during the two month time period when the temporary employees were working there was an increase in the number of units that had to be reworked and the number of units being returned by customers.

    Management is considering filing a lawsuit against the temporary employment company for providing workers who did not perform at the level of regular employees as had been promised by the employment company. Before filing the lawsuit, management would like to have some information about the possible damages in the case. What accounting and other information would you look at to assist management in evaluating possible damages?
16. Why is it important for a forensic accountant to have knowledge of cost behavior patterns in providing services in a litigation support situation?
17. What are the most commonly used cost behavior patterns in forensic analysis? Define and describe these cost behavior patterns.
18. Name and describe the two basic assumptions that underlie cost behavior patterns.
19. Can an experienced forensic accountant look at the financial information of a company and tell which costs are fixed and which costs are variable?
20. Acme Aviation (AA) entered into an agreement with the Express Deliveries (ED) to fly packages for ED on an "as needed" basis. The agreement was for three years. After the first year, Acme Aviation was not making any money on this agreement and notified Express Deliveries that it would no longer honor the agreement. Express Deliveries was forced to find another company to fly the packages that previously would have been flown by Acme. Express Deliveries claimed that the cost of the new carrier added $250,000 a year to its expenses. Four years after Acme Aviation defaulted on the contract, Express Deliveries filed for bankruptcy.

    In a subsequent lawsuit, Express Deliveries sued Acme Aviation for $6 million, claiming that the AD's default on the delivery contract caused Express to incur significant additional costs and this eventually forced them into bankruptcy. During discovery the following issues were uncovered:

- ED used AA for about 20 percent of its deliveries during the one year the contract was operating.
- An internal AA memo states that the marketing manager said, "I don't care what our legal obligations are under the contract with ED, we are losing money so end it." (the contract).
- During the three years prior to the start of the AA/ED contract, ED had earnings (losses) of $125,000, $(150,000), and $(175,000) respectively.
- In an AA internal memo the company stated that it had lost about $300,000 in the first year of the ED contract due, in part, to the varying volume of deliveries requested by ED throughout the year.
- AA fired the marketing person who secured the ED contract and used the ED contract as an example of poor analysis of potential sales contracts as part of the documentation for the firing.
- An ED accounting department analysis of ED's delivery costs showed that direct costs of delivery were $140,000 per year higher for the delivery service used to replace AA. The other $110,000 of additional costs was corporate overhead allocated to the delivery service contract.
- Ed's financial statements showed that it had losses of $175,000 and $260,000 during the two years after the end of the AA contract but before ED filed for bankruptcy.
- Express Delivery's asset book value at the date bankruptcy was filed was $3,500,000, but the estimated liquidation value of its assets was estimated at only $1,000,000.
- An ED accounting department analysis estimated that during a six-month period after AA defaulted on the delivery contract, ED had trouble finding acceptable delivery alternatives. As a result, the analysis found that the firm lost approximately $800,000 in delivery sales.

The issue of liability here is primarily a legal one. There is little chance that account-

ing issues will be addressed in determining liability. For purposes of this conflict, assume that the three-year contract was binding and that AA is liable for damages resulting from the two years it did not honor the contract.

a. You are an expert that has been hired by Express Delivery to develop a damages estimate for them that you will defend in deposition and at trial, if necessary. Using the information provided prepare a preliminary damages estimate and explain the basis for your opinion on each item. Identify any questions or information you would like to see or analyze to support your damages estimate.

b. You are an expert that has been hired by Acme Aviation to develop a damages estimate for them that you will defend in deposition and at trial if necessary. Using the information provided prepare a preliminary damages estimate and explain the basis for your opinion on each item. Identify any questions or information you would like to see or analyze to support your damages estimate.

21. The Fernald Corporation manufactures commercial shipping containers and trailer bodies for trucks. Several years ago, Fernald bought $160,000 of coating materials to rustproof and paint 500 units of containers. Fernald alleged that the coating products were faulty, claiming that shortly after the products were completed, many of the units started rusting and the paint began peeling off. Most of the units were sandblasted to remove the old coating materials, then the units were recoated. The coating materials were supplied by the Industrial Paint Products Company (IPPC). IPPC claimed that Fernald personnel attempted to apply the coating to surfaces that were not properly prepared for the coating. Fernald denied that allegation. In an effort to keep a good customer happy, IPPC did not bill Fernald for the alleged bad coating and provided new coating materials for the 500 units free of charge.

Fernald's management continued to pursue the idea that it had suffered far more damages than just the cost of the coating materials. On several occasions during the last several years Fernald has asked Industrial Paint Products to make an offer to settle the dispute between the two companies. Last year, Fernald asked its attorney to file suit against IPPC for alleged damages associated with supplying the bad coatings. An expert, Karen Scott, has been hired, and she has prepared a damages estimate for the dispute. Before the conflict goes any further, Fred Culter, vice president, finance for Fernald, sent a letter to John McCoy, CEO at IPPC, in an effort to settle the dispute before the litigation process. The letter is presented below.

Mr. John McCoy, CEO
Industrial Paint Products Company
2929 South Cedar Drive
Yorktown, Ohio, 32850

Dear Mr. McCoy:

Fernald has been a customer of IPPC for over a decade. We have never had any real problems with your company before this situation. We believe we have been patient about this matter. We have hired a professional accounting expert witness to compute the damages associated with the events in this case. She has talked with many of our operations people and has carefully calculated damages based on the facts. We hope you will review this information and be willing to settle the case so we can get on with normal business relationship with your firm.

Mr. McCoy, I hope you will agree with me that the time has come to put this issue behind us. We have been waiting patiently for four years now for your firm to settle this matter. It is hard to envision us continuing to have a positive business relationship with this hanging over our head. Below are the most recent calculations Karen has prepared:

Cost to sandblast and recoat
shipping containers $540,000
Cost of coating materials 160,000
Cost of lost production 800,000
Cost of labor inefficiencies 490,000
Lost sales (4,000 units @ $700) 2,800,000
Cost of negative goodwill 1,000,000
Total Damages...$5,790,000

If you have any questions about any of this, please give me a call. I look forward to bringing this matter to a close and getting on with our solid business relationship.

Fred Culter
Vice President, Finance

You have been hired by IPPC as an accounting expert witness. Initially, you will be providing litigation advice to the IPPC's attorney, but you may have to prepare an expert report and testify in the case. Currently, the attorney needs some advice about the nature and probable validity of Fernald's expert's damages estimate. Provide some guidance and advice on the following:

a. For each component of the damages estimate, indicate what documents, accounting records, or other information you would need to review to evaluate the validity and the amount of the item.

b. Based on the limited case information you currently posses, do any of the damages estimate components appear to be questionable?

c. What kinds of analyses do you plan to do to evaluate each of the components of the damages estimates?

22. Mr. Snow has worked for the Jones Auto Parts Store for 12 years. He started as a sales clerk and worked his way up to assistant store manager. He was the assistant store manager for six years before he was fired by the owner after a heated argument. Mr. Snow started working at the store for $16,000 per year. Right before he was promoted to assistant manager, he was earning $21,400. His first year salary as assistant store manager was $25,000, and he was earning $33,500 when he was fired. Mr. Snow was 45 years old at the time he was fired.

In his damages claim, Mr. Snow is seeking $2,250,737 in lost compensation. In the expert report filed on Mr. Snow's behalf, the expert explained his calculation of damages as follows. Mr. Snow's salary grew at an average annual rate of 9.11 percent. This rate was calculated by dividing his final year salary of $33,500 by his first year salary of $16,000. The result showed an increase of 109.375 percent ($33,500 ÷ $16,000) = 2.09375. He then divided by 12 years to get an average annual increase of 9.11 percent (109.375 ÷ 12) = 9.11 percent. Next, the expert projected a 9.11 percent salary increase compounded annually for Mr. Snow for the remaining 20 years that he expected to be employed by the Jones Auto Parts Store. He then summed the expected annual salaries to arrive at the alleged damages amount.

You have been hired as an expert witness by Jones Auto Parts Store to provide rebuttal testimony to the expert hired by Mr. Snow. Without regard to the issue of liability in this case, critique the damages estimate of Mr. Snow's expert providing as much reasoning and support for your position as possible.

23. Following is a letter received from a prospective client.

Mr./Ms. Unknown, CPA
Unknown, Johnson, and Becker, CPAs
2900 Fee Lane
Bloomington, Indiana, 47405

Dear Mr./Ms. Unknown:
You have been recommended to me as a person with considerable accounting knowledge and skills. I am an attorney here in Bloomington, and I have been retained by two men in connection with a possible contract-violation case. A brief description of the circumstances surrounding the case is presented below.

Don Williams and Willie Nelson are local carpenters that work on construction projects in and around the Bloomington area. As a hobby, both men are avid automobile race fans. During one of their visits to the Indianapolis Speedway track, they allege they came up with the idea for a line of souvenir products called "Brickhead Products." Williams and Nelson claim they developed ideas, sketches, and models for seven different souvenirs, and they went to Indianapolis Speedway management with the "Brickhead" idea and the examples of typical products. They allegedly offered Indianapolis Speedway management a contract for the "Brickhead" idea in which Williams and Nelson would continue to develop ideas for souvenir products, which would be sold at the track and around the Indianapolis area. In return, Williams and Nelson would receive five percent of the gross proceeds from the sale.

According to Williams and Nelson, they had two meetings with Indianapolis-Speedway management, and some telephone calls as well. Williams and Nelson stated that Indy 500 management liked the idea and would get back to them in the near future. No further contact occurred, and the proposed contract was never signed. A year after the meetings took place, however, the Indianapolis Motor Speedway came out with some "Brickhead" products that were being sold at the track and around town at other stores. Williams and Nelson were furious and claim their idea was stolen by Indianapolis-Speedway management. Williams and Nelson claim that sales this year will be significant and over the years the sales will be in the mil-

lions. They estimate that sales will be over $20,000,000 over the next ten years, and they want to seek damages in this dispute of $20,000,000 plus punitive damages.

The above description currently is a bit sketchy, but I am still gathering information and documents. In the meantime, I would like to ask your advice in evaluating the merits of this conflict. Clearly, at the heart of this dispute are a number of important accounting issues. Accounting is where I need your help and advice. Would you please give me an idea of what you think the merits of this situation are, and what you think about my clients' damages estimate?

Please indicate what information, in particular accounting information, should we seek during discovery. Also, who do you think we need to depose to get the information you would need for your analysis and testimony on damages or other issues?

Please give me some information about your professional background. You were recommended by another attorney, but she had no vita or other written information about you.

Thank you in advance for your help.

Sincerely,

Jenny Jones
Attorney at Law

Write a response to this letter with the intent of securing Ms. Jones as a client. Provide whatever information you believe is appropriate under the circumstances.

24. Dexter Manufacturing entered into an agreement with the Delta Salt Mining Company to build and be the exclusive supplier of heavy duty product conveyor belt systems for the company's mining operations. The conveyor belt systems are used to move mined salt from the working surfaces to the crusher rooms, where it is crushed and sifted into various sizes and grades of marketable salt. Additional conveyor belt systems are used to send the crushed and graded salt to shipping areas above ground.

Until this contract, Delta purchased conveyor belt systems from several different suppliers. Delta entered into the agreement with Dexter Manufacturing in order to have a stable supply of product conveyor belts at a reasonable and constant price for a three-year period. During the first 15 months of the contract Dexter supplied $2,700,000 of conveyor belt systems to Delta at nine different mine sites. At this time

Dexter approached Delta with a proposition to raise the price of conveyor belt systems by 15 percent for the remaining life of the contract. Dexter claimed that during the first 15 months of the contract the company had actually lost 10 percent on the sale of belt systems. They further stated that they would be happy to continue with the contract if they could earn just 5 percent on the remaining contract sales.

Delta management is not pleased with the Dexter Manufacturing proposal. Management of the Delta Salt Mining Company is considering litigation to force Dexter to honor the remaining terms of the agreement or to pay the damages caused by the breach of contract. In order to get some idea about the various issues and costs associated with legal action, Delta's management committee has asked you, as head of the accounting department, to perform some analyses to help with the decision. In particular, the committee would like to know the following:

a. How much in losses do you think Dexter may have experienced on the current contract so far? How much more in losses might Dexter experience if the contract runs for its intended life? What information would you like to have from Dexter to do further analysis on this issue?

b. What extra costs might Delta experience if it goes along with the Dexter proposal?

c. What costs, other than the ones already mentioned, might Delta want to consider before it went forward with litigation against Dexter Manufacturing?

d. If Delta did sue Dexter, what would be the basis for its damages in the case?

e. Are there any nonaccounting issues Delta should consider in this case? If so what are they?

25. Using the Internet, determine what is meant by "goodness of fit."

26. Using the Internet, find and summarize the following damage court case: *Lithuanian Commerce Corp. v. Sarah Lee Hosiery*, 177 F.R.D. 245 (D.N.J. 1997). What did Sarah Lee and the court think about Mr. Cummiskey's expert report?

27. Assume you have been retained as an expert witness for a client who is the defendant in the case, and your client is alleged to have breached a contract and caused damages of $3,000,000 which includes added costs and lost profits. The contract required that your client supply hardwood lumber to a furniture manufacturer for a three-year period. After six months your client found it could not supply the lumber in the quantity required by the plaintiff in the case and quit shipping lumber. Your client states that there is no way the damages could be anywhere near the amount alleged in the suit because your client was selling hardwood lumber to the plaintiff at "about the market rate." The plaintiff alleges that because it could not get the lumber from our client, it had to buy in the open market and it paid more for the lumber and lost production output and gross margin on its furniture products. Your preliminary analysis of the case data finds the following:

1. The plaintiff purchased a total $1,200,000 of hardwood lumber from your client during the first six months of the contract.

2. Your client was supplying hardwood lumber under the contract at about eight percent below market rate for similar hardwood sales.

3. The plaintiff's average gross margin on sales is 35 percent and its average profit on sales is 10 percent.

4. The plaintiff's average sales volume over the last five years has been $10,000,000 per year.

5. During the six months immediately after the contract was breached, the plaintiff's average sales were $800,000 per month.

6. Your analysis of the Plaintiff's average variable costs for operating expenses is 70 percent fixed and 30 percent variable.

Required: As the defendant's expert witness:

a. What is your best estimate of the damages that the plaintiff has suffered as a result of your client's breach of contract?

b. Based on the information provided, does the plaintiff's "lost profits and added costs" allegation have any basis in fact? Show necessary calculations to support your position.

c. If asked to provide the court with a "theoretical model" of the basis of your damages, what would you provide?

d. What additional information, if any, might you like to have to refine your damage estimates a bit more?

LITIGATION SUPPORT IN SPECIAL SITUATIONS

Antitrust analysis is highly fact-specific. And as much as we can all agree on that, we must constantly remind ourselves of it, lest we get hijacked by naked theory.

—Deborah Platt Majoras[1]

OBJECTIVES

After completing Chapter 11, you should be able to:

1. Understand the accountant's role in antitrust litigation.
2. Know what *predatory pricing* is and how to prove whether a company has practiced it.
3. Be able to use cost behavior estimation methods to calculate a company's average variable costs.
4. Understand the accountant's role in Federal False Claims Act litigation.

OVERVIEW

This chapter discusses the litigation support accountants can provide in two important types of business disputes: antitrust litigation and Federal False Claims Act litigation. Both types of disputes typically require significant input from accountants and involve many different accounting issues.

Accountants are uniquely qualified to provide advice and assistance in these types of cases. In antitrust cases, accountants are called upon to identify and analyze relevant historical accounting case data. Typically, the analyses must then be explained and interpreted in light of the case issues. In Federal Fraudulent Claims Act cases most of the case issues relate to accounting measurements, reports, and billings. Often forensic accountants are the ones best able to sort out the relevant accounting issues in the dispute and to explain the accounting case issues to the judge and jury evaluating the case.

Antitrust Litigation

¶ 11,001   OVERVIEW OF ANTITRUST LAWS

Antitrust laws are an outgrowth of the early years of the Industrial Age in the United States when a small number of powerful businessmen used any tactic at their disposal to force competitors out of business. Once the competition was eliminated, the surviving business became a monopoly, at least in some parts of the country, and would charge relatively high prices for the goods and services sold. This practice was particularly common in the railroad and oil businesses. Some of the most successful players in creating monopolies were called "robber barons."

Because such business practices were not in the best interest of the country, federal legislation was passed that prohibits the formation and continuation of monopolies except when in the best interest of the public. For example, many electric, gas, and water utilities are monopolies that service a specified geographic area.

INFAMOUS MICROSOFT ANTITRUST BATTLE ENDS WITH A WHIMPER. It is easy to say that whenever a monopoly forms, it should be eliminated. However, to know when or whether a monopoly has formed is not easy. Few monopolies have nationwide significance. One possible exception was Microsoft Corporation. Antitrust litigation against Microsoft Corporation by the United States Justice Department, however, claimed Microsoft had a national monopoly. Microsoft vigorously fought the allegations, and a settlement was reached that some people believed favored Microsoft's positions. Interestingly, the judge appointed a Harvard professor as a Special Master to handle much of the work. Microsoft fought the appointment, and an appellate court refused to accept the Special Master.

Monopolies have not ceased despite widespread deregulation in formerly monopolistic industries. There are still claims that a company has monopolized or is attempting to monopolize some business activity in a specific geographic area.

Someone might allege that a particular company, say, the Busy Bee Egg Company, had monopolized the sales and distribution of chicken eggs in a *specific geographic region*, such as southern Indiana. The allegation would have to specify clearly that the Busy Bee Egg Company enjoyed the alleged monopoly in the southern Indiana area.

EXAMPLE 11.1 A consultant was engaged in an antitrust case in which one large city was the alleged area of monopolistic activity. When that alleged area of monopolization did not prove to be accurate, the plaintiff changed the scope of the suit to one area of the city, rather than the city as a whole. The area of alleged monopolization is central to such cases, because it impacts the experts' analyses as well as the documentation demanded by the court during the discovery phase of the litigation.

What happens if someone argues that a company is in violation of antitrust laws? First, one may file a complaint with the U.S. government. If the government agrees with the complaint, an attempt will be made to remedy the situation by negotiations and other activities designed to solve the problem. If this attempt fails, the U.S. Justice Department may start proceedings against the offending business with the intention of having the court force the company to come into compliance with the antitrust laws.

Sometimes complaints of a monopoly filed with the government are not accepted. The government may believe there could be a problem, but the complaint does not provide enough information or evidence to pursue the issue. The Justice Department may not have enough time or staff to pursue some complaints even when there does seem to be a problem. Thus, an individual or another company may file a lawsuit under the antitrust laws. Many antitrust actions are filed in this manner.

¶ 11,011   ROLE OF ACCOUNTANTS IN ANTITRUST LITIGATION

In antitrust cases, accountants may be called upon to determine whether there is liability under the antitrust laws. The primary issue that forensic accountants address is whether the defendant has engaged in predatory pricing. Accountants are uniquely skilled to provide insight into whether predatory pricing has occurred. Accountants also may be asked to calculate the damages a party has sustained as a result of a violation of the antitrust laws.

In an antitrust suit in Indianapolis, a grocery chain was accused by another grocery company of engaging in predatory pricing activities during an 18-month period. The accused grocery chain had gone from a profitable position in earlier periods to significant losses during the alleged predatory pricing period. The plaintiff in the case alleged that the defendant's change from profitable operations to major losses were evidence of predatory pricing. The defendant countered by saying its losses were due to efforts to compete on a price basis with another major new grocery retailer that had entered the Indianapolis marketing area.

The defendant hired a forensic accountant to demonstrate that the company was not engaged in predatory pricing. The accountant pointed out that merely experiencing business losses were not a clear sign of predatory pricing. The forensic accountant spent considerable time running regression analyses on store data of both the defendant and the plaintiff. He found that the defendant's stores had in all periods priced its products above average variable costs and therefore, in his opinion, had not engaged in predatory pricing. He also found that the plaintiff in the case also had experienced major losses during the time period in question and, in his opinion, the plaintiff was closer to the predatory pricing benchmark than the defendant.

The plaintiff changed the geographic area covered by its complaint to smaller geographic areas in an effort to find some areas of operation in which the defendant had priced products below average variable cost. The defendant's forensic accountant analyzed store cost data for each of these new geographic areas of alleged antitrust law violations. He found that in each instance, the allegations were false. The analysis and information provided by the forensic accountant were instrumental in the court's decision for the defendant.

¶ 11,021   ACTIONS THAT CONSTITUTE PREDATORY PRICING

Predatory pricing is the act of pricing a product so low that the only logical explanation is that the pricing is designed to drive competitors out of business. This definition, although descriptive, is not very operational. The definition does not give a judge or jury much guidance in determining whether predatory pricing has occurred. Because of that, the courts have used a simpler definition to apply the concept of predatory pricing in actual situations. The operational definition is whether a company prices its products or services below "average variable cost;" if so, predatory pricing is present. In other words, if a company is charging customers less than the company's average variable costs for its products or services, there is evidence that the company is guilty of engaging in predatory pricing.

¶ 11,031   DETERMINING A COMPANY'S AVERAGE VARIABLE COSTS

The definition and concept of *predatory pricing* seem simple enough. However, knowing what types of cost behavior patterns are common in business is not enough to allow an expert or analyst to merely look at a company's ledger accounts and identify which costs are fixed, variable, or mixed. Most organizations have few costs that are captured, recorded, and reported by their cost behavior pattern. Instead, costs typically are identified and recorded by their functional characteristics, such as product cost and period cost. For example, period costs include most operating costs, such as marketing, customer service, personnel, product warranty, accounting, and administration. Product costs include direct materials, direct labor, and manufacturing overhead. Management, investors, and lenders find functional classifications useful, but such classifications are of little use in determining whether predatory pricing has occurred.

Without more information about individual costs, it is necessary to determine the cost behavior pattern of each cost. How to estimate cost behavior patterns is discussed in ¶11,041.

¶ 11,041   ESTIMATING COST BEHAVIOR PATTERNS

An analyst can use a variety of methods to estimate cost behavior patterns.

Getting Started

The first step in gaining an understanding of the cost behavior patterns of a firm is to look for experienced accounting employees or those who have some intuition about cost patterns of the firm. Often a working knowledge of a firm's accounting system provides some knowledge of the nature of cost behavior in the firm's accounting system. Sometimes account titles are misleading, and accounts are used to record items not originally intended for the account. A quick way for an expert to become familiar with an accounting system of a new client and the system's characteristics is to spend time talking to one or more seasoned veterans with the firm who know about its history and how the accounting system works.

Graphic Analysis and High-Low Method

Scatter Diagrams

Although experience and intuition are valuable in giving an expert insight into an accounting system, it is seldom enough. A better approach to gain insight into cost behavior patterns is graphic analysis. Plotting data and creating *scatter diagrams* can be useful in showing an expert the general trend or nature of a cost or a pool of costs. Analysts can easily plot data from spreadsheet files and use that information to form an initial understanding of cost relationships and cost behavior patterns.

High-Low Method

Another cost analysis method used frequently by consultants is the *high-low method*. With this approach, the highest and lowest costs are identified, along with their related activity levels. The difference is calculated between the two costs and the two activity levels. The difference in costs is then divided by the difference in activity levels to determine an estimate of the variable cost per unit. The variable cost is then inserted into the total cost equation to find the fixed cost component.

EXAMPLE 11.2 A company is analyzing 20 months of overhead cost data. The highest overhead cost for any month was $300,000, at an activity level of 100,000 units. The lowest overhead cost for any month was $280,000, at an activity level of 90,000 units.

$$\text{Variable cost} = \frac{\$300,000 - \$280,000}{100,000 \text{ units} - 90,000 \text{ units}}$$

$$= \frac{\$ 20,000}{10,000 \text{ units}}$$

$$= \$2 \text{ per unit}$$

Fixed cost = $300,000 − (100,000 units × $2 per unit)

= $100,000

Total cost = $100,000 + $2 × (the number of units)

The high-low method of cost analysis is a quick and easy approach to obtain some understanding of cost behavior information in a dispute. But this approach does have potential flaws. For example, this approach only uses the highest and the lowest values of the cost data in the analysis. If these values are *outliers* (representing data that is not usual), the resulting cost behavior information will probably be distorted. Business phenomena (such as wildcat strikes or malfunctioning machinery) can cause such anomalies, and cost analyses or projections should not be based on that unusual level of activity. Also, there are only two data observations used in the analysis. If the high-low method is used with 20 months of data, only the highest and lowest cost observation is used in the analysis. The other 18 months of cost and activity data are ignored.

Graphic analysis and the high-low method both are intended to help an analyst obtain an understanding of the nature of the client's accounting system and the characteristics and nature of the client's costs. The high-low method is particularly useful early during a dispute when the expert has little company data or highly aggregated company data. Usually financial information gathered and analyzed in this way is preliminary and designed to help the expert provide the attorney(s) with some initial observations and guidelines. Sometimes such analyses are useful in determining what documents should be requested during the discovery process, or to determine in a general sense what if any damages might be present in a dispute.

Although graphic analysis and the high-low method are potentially useful to experts and their clients early in litigation, they are seldom of much value as a dispute proceeds.

Regression/Correlation Analysis

The most powerful and common method of analyzing cost behavior is regression/correlation analysis. *Regression* or *correlation analysis* is a statistical technique for measuring the nature and strength of the relationship between two variables. When applied to cost accounting data, regression/correlation can be used to determine the relationship between specific cost data and some measure of activity, such as sales dollars or production volume. *Regression analysis* is used to determine the *nature* of the association between two or more variables in the analysis. In other words, as one variable moves up, does the other variable move in the same direction, or does it move in the opposite direction? *Correlation analysis* is used to measure the *strength* of the association between the variables. If one variable is moving with or in the opposite direction of the other variable, how strong is the relationship between the movements of the two variables?

Simple Linear Regression

Variables

The most common type of regression/correlation analysis used in cost behavior analysis is simple linear regression. This method uses two sets of variables in the analysis. The two variables comprise a *dependent variable*, which usually is *cost*, and an *independent variable* or *predictor variable,* which usually is the measure of the volume of activity. In simple linear regression, an accountant enters cost and activity data into the regression model. The regression model will use the data to compute a regression line, which is represented by the formula:

$$Y = a + bX$$

Where:

Y   is the computed value of the dependent variable obtained from a specific value of the independent variable.

a   is the constant or intercept where the regression line crosses the vertical axis. (It is the value of Y when X = 0).

b   is the slope of the regression line. Describes the change in the value of Y for each unit change in the value of X.

X   is the value of the independent variable.

A positive (+) value for *b* indicates that the dependent and the independent variables are positively correlated (moving in the same direction). A negative (–) *b* value indicates that the dependent and the independent variables are moving in opposite directions. An example of negative correlation might be that increases in interest rates often are inversely related to the amount of new construction. The graph in Figure 11.1 shows cost and activity data and the resulting regression line:

Figure 11.1. Sample Regression Line

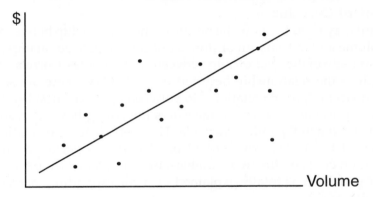

Least Squares Regression Line

The regression line is often referred to as the *least squares regression line* or the *line of best fit.* Least squares refers to the fact that the regression line is the line which does the best job of minimizing the squared distance between the regression line and the individual data observations used in computing the regression line. The regression line is the best fitting straight line that can be drawn through the observed data. No other straight line would do a better job of minimizing the distance between the observed data and the regression line.

Standard Error of the Estimate

Of course, business cost data seldom show perfect correlation. Instead, a variety of factors cause the data to not be perfectly correlated to the activity variable. Most cost categories are not created to include only costs that are fixed, variable, or of some other cost behavior characteristic. In addition, there are a number of other factors that cause cost pools to not behave in any specific pattern. Therefore, when actual cost data are regressed against some measure of the volume of activity, that data likely will have some amount of variability. A measure of the variability of the cost data in the regression analysis is called the *standard error of the estimate,* which indicates the variability of the data used in the regression calculations. The greater the variability of the data, the less precise the results from estimates made from using the regression data.

Typically, many estimates are point estimates. *Point estimates* are single estimates made using the regression parameters. For example, the expert may use the "a" and "b" values obtained in a regression to estimate the total costs that a business should have incurred at a given volume of activity. Because there is some variability in the regression data, an expert may want to enhance the strength of the estimate by incorporating some measure of the regression variability and some desired confidence level in determining a range of possible values of cost at the given volume level.

To accomplish this enhancement, a consultant can use the standard error of the estimate and values from either a *T table* or a *Z table* for the desired confidence level. For example, assume the point estimate for a cost is $256,000 and the standard error of the estimate is $25,500. The expert wants to find the range of costs within which the cost should fall 95 percent of the time. The sample size used in the regression analysis was 60 months of data. Either the T table or the Z table gives a value of 1.96 for a 95 percent confidence interval. So the range of projected cost is $256,000 ± ($25,500 × 1.96) or $206,020 to $305,980. T tables are used to find values for sample sizes less than 60. The smaller the sample, the larger the T value, which adjusts for sampling error with smaller sample sizes. Z tables are used for large sample sizes. Because many business regressions are run using samples smaller than 60, T tables are commonly used. T tables can be used for all sample sizes by referring to the last row of the T table values.

Correlation Analysis

Coefficient of Correlation

A consultant may need to know the nature of the relationship between two variables, such as sales volume and the amount of store labor costs. But of equal importance is knowledge about the strength of the relationship between two variables. Correlation analysis measures the strength of the relationship between the variables. There are several measures that describe the strength of the relationship between the two variables. The first is called the *coefficient of correlation,* or *r,* which measures the strength of the association between the dependent and the independent variable. The coefficient of correlation ranges in possible values from –1 to +1. An *r* value of +1 or –1 indicates perfect positive or perfect negative correlation between the two variables, meaning that each increase or decrease in the dependent variable *Y* is totally explained by a corresponding increase or decrease in the independent variable *X.*

Coefficient of Determination

If the coefficient of correlation is squared, one gets *r squared,* which is called the *coefficient of determination.* This coefficient ranges in value from 0 to +1. The coefficient of determination measures the *amount of explained variance* [referring to the total variance of the dependent variable about its mean (average) value, the amount of that variance that can be explained by changes in the independent variable is measured by the coefficient of determination]. For example, a coefficient of determination of .84 or 84 percent means that 84 percent of the dependent variable's total variance can be explained by changes in the independent variable. High values of r squared means that there is a strong linear relationship between the dependent and the independent variables.

Coefficient of Nondetermination

The *coefficient of nondetermination* (1 – r squared) is the portion of the relationship between the two variables that is not explained by the coefficient of determination. This unexplained variance may be random fluctuations or it may be a variation that is explained by some other independent variable.

Association Versus Causation

Movements in the Independent Variable

Regression/correlation analysis shows the degree of association between variables, but it does *not* prove causation. There is a tendency to think that, if a regression/correlation analysis shows a high degree of correlation, movements in the independent variable clearly cause changes in the dependent variable. Although such a conclusion is tempting, one must look to other supporting information before making such a claim.

EXAMPLE 11.3 If regression-correlation results show relationships that seem illogical, factors affecting the results may need to be evaluated. For example, the relationship may be merely a spurious correlation (i.e., two variables just happened to be moving in the same direction at the same time). Suppose Alexander goes to the grocery store and buys a shopping cart full of groceries and the checker totals the bill at exactly $100. Alexander's immediate thought is: "Something is wrong. My bill cannot be exactly $100." But after he checks and adds the amounts, he finds that the receipt is correct. That one time out of hundreds of trips to the store, the bill was a nice round $100.

EXAMPLE 11.4 Sometimes in regression/correlation analysis, the numbers just happen to be ripe for a relationship that just does not make any logical sense. A California state representative reputedly ran a regression of teacher salaries in the state of California against gambling revenues in Las Vegas and found a high coefficient of correlation. He then stated that there was no logic to supporting higher teacher salaries because he had proof that teachers were all squandering their raises at the Las Vegas casinos. Although teachers may have been doing just that, the fact that teachers' salaries and revenues in Las Vegas were moving in the same direction did not prove that one caused the other.

Reasons for the Unexpected

There are many reasons why accounting data regressions may not result exactly the way a forensic accountant expected. Some of the accounting reasons that regressions may yield unexpected or perplexing results include:

- *Allocations.* Many costs included in cost analyses contain costs allocated from shared services. How these costs are allocated and the timing of these allocations can make a big difference in the cost behavior results from the analysis.
- *Transfer prices.* When products or services are transferred (sold) between various parts of a company, there is a question of what amount should be charged for the exchange of products or services. The amount charged is called a *transfer price* or a *chargeback*. For example, a manufacturing division may charge an internal customer the market price for electric motors that it makes and sells to another division for use in the manufacture of radial arm saws. The market price transfer price, when regressed against units produced, will appear to be a directly variable cost. The manufacturing costs of the electric motors for the division that makes them, however, are 55 percent fixed and 45 percent variable. Therefore the transfer pricing method has an impact on the cost behavior analysis.
- *Entity concept.* The preceding example raises another interesting cost behavior analysis issue. Viewed from the division buying the electric motors, the cost of the motors is clearly fixed, but viewed from the division that makes the electric motors, the cost behavior is clearly mixed (part fixed and part variable). The issue then is: Which entity does the forensic accountant study to determine the cost behavior pattern for

the electric motors? To answer that question, he or she needs to know the objectives of the cost analysis.

- *Accounting policies.* Many accounting policies have an important impact on the analysis of cost behavior. If the accounting policy is to charge depreciation to units only once each year rather than each month, cost analysis will have different results. Similarly, accounting policy may state that various costs are allocated based on the number of units receiving the allocation rather than dollars of sales. The difference in allocation method can have a major impact on the perceived nature of the cost behavior.

Need to Become Familiar with Accounting Systems

The obvious conclusion one should reach from the preceding discussion is that forensic accountants must be adequately informed about the nature and operation of the accounting system for each and every business that he or she is evaluating. If two companies differ in their accounting treatment of a particular type of cost, an analysis may suggest different cost behavior for the same cost.

EXAMPLE 11.5 Assume two companies allocate corporate marketing costs to all of their stores on a weekly basis. Assume also that the two companies have virtually the same types and amounts of marketing costs. One company allocates weekly marketing costs on a per store basis (e.g., each of the company's 50 stores gets 1/50 or two percent of the weekly marketing cost). The weekly sales dollars achieved by each store have no impact on the amount of cost allocated to it. Likewise, sales trends up or down have no impact on the allocations to each store.

The other company also allocates weekly marketing costs to its 50 stores, but its allocation is based on each store's actual sales for the week as a percentage of the company's total sales for that week. Therefore, a store with $5,000,000 in sales out of a company total sales volume of $100,000,000 in sales will be allocated ($5,000,000/$100,000,000) or five percent of the company's marketing costs for the week. If a store's sales volume increases or decreases in relation to company sales as a whole, the store's allocation of corporate marketing costs will increase or decrease accordingly.

This example illustrates how a company's accounting policies (i.e., the policy on corporate cost allocations to stores) can have a significant impact on the cost behavior estimates that result for the regression/correlation analysis. Many accounting policies have an impact on accounting data analysis. Company policies on when to write off prepaid items, at what level the firm records depreciation and in what timeframes, and policies on how to record employee fringe benefit costs can all impact the results of regression/correlation analysis.

The U.S. Justice Department brought action against the National Council on Problem Gambling, Inc., a trade association, to stop its unlawful territorial allocation system. This system was designed to prevent state affiliates from offering or selling problem gambling products and services outside their states, thereby eliminating competition among the state affiliates.

On June 13, 2003, the U.S. District of Columbia Court enjoined the trade association from a number of actions, including any move that would prevent a problem gambling service provider from engaging in many practices that would create competition.

¶ 11,051   CASE STUDY: COHO GROCERY

Assume that the Coho Grocery store chain has been sued by Ohio Grocery under federal antitrust laws. Ohio Grocery alleges that Coho is trying to monopolize the grocery business in the Columbus, Ohio area. Ohio Grocery claims Coho has engaged in a variety of anti-competitive activities, including predatory pricing. The alleged time period during which the predatory pricing and other anticompetitive activity occurred is the calendar years 2010 and 2011. In order for Ohio Grocery to prevail on the predatory pricing issue, the company must prove that Coho for some period of time and in a geographic area (here the Columbus, Ohio area) has been selling products below average variable cost.

To prove predatory pricing, Ohio Grocery's attorneys retain a forensic accountant to serve as an expert witness. The company asks the expert to evaluate the accounting data of the Coho Grocery store chain in order to prove that Coho has engaged in predatory pricing. Of course, Ohio Grocery and its attorneys do not have direct access to Coho's accounting records. So, during the process of discovery, Ohio Grocery's attorneys go to the court and ask for the accounting records needed to prove their claim.

In order to analyze the cost behavior data of Coho Grocery, the Ohio Grocery's attorney requests monthly store operating data for the years 2010 and 2011 for Coho's 22 grocery stores in the Columbus, Ohio, area. The court requires Coho to provide Ohio Grocery's attorneys with the requested monthly operating data plus store operating data for the three years of operations prior to the alleged antitrust violations. During the production of documents stage of the discovery process, Coho also is required to produce its chart of accounts and a description of the nature of each account listed.

Accounting Data Analysis for Coho Grocery

Once the attorneys for Ohio Grocery have obtained the necessary store accounting data, their consultant can analyze the data in order to form an opinion whether predatory pricing has occurred. But the expert cannot merely look at the reports and make a determination. Instead, the consultant must analyze the accounting data provided and determine the cost behavior patterns of the costs in the accounting reports and other information secured through the discovery process. The term *average variable cost* will not appear in Coho's accounting records or statements. In fact, there is a good chance that cost behavior terms will not appear in any of Coho's accounting reports or other documents. The reason, of course, is that most companies develop their accounting system to satisfy functional reporting requirements.

Beginning with Income Statements

How does the expert determine whether Coho Grocery sold products below their average variable cost during the time period covered by the dispute in the litigated geographic area? First, the consultant analyzes the store data for Coho's Grocery stores in the Columbus, Ohio area. The expert should begin with the monthly income statements of the stores. If Coho had store profits during most of the months identified in the complaint, then Coho could not be engaged in predatory pricing. (Selling products or services below average variable costs is the benchmark for predatory pricing.) If Coho had store profits, the company covered *all costs* and not just variable costs. If Coho had losses each month during 2010 and 2011, the expert would need to do more analysis. In order to achieve some understanding of whether Coho engaged in predatory pricing (knowingly or unknowingly), the costs for Coho Grocery stores must be analyzed to determine the cost behavior characteristics at the stores.

Choosing the Independent Variable

Ohio Grocery's expert may use whatever analytical methods that he or she chooses to evaluate Coho's cost behavior, but the expert probably will incorporate regression/correlation as part of the cost behavior analysis. First, the expert must make some choices. What variable should be used for the independent variable? In situations involving retail sales operations, the most common choice for the activity variable is sales dollars or sales units. If the mix of products sold is quite diverse, such as in a grocery store, sales dollars is usually the variable of choice.

Cost Analysis

The dependent variable in the analysis is the costs. But how should the costs be analyzed? The expert could use large pools of costs, such as cost of goods sold and store operating costs. Another choice would be to separate the larger costs pools into more specific cost categories. For example, store operating costs could be divided into store labor costs, store marketing costs, store maintenance costs, store delivery costs, store customer service costs, and allocated corporate overhead costs. Because cost behavior characteristics can cancel out or net out when accounts are aggregated, the expert can get different results depending on the level of the analysis used.

During 2010 and 2011 period, Coho grocery stores in the Columbus area reported profits in only 7 of the 24 months of operations. Monthly profits (losses) ranged from $377,000 to ($625,000). The combined store operating data for Coho's 22 grocery stores shows that, during 2010 and 2011, the company had an average of $6,650,000 in sales, $5,187,000 in cost of goods sold, and $1,870,000 in store operating expenses. The average monthly loss was $407,000.

Merely finding that Coho experienced losses, however, does not show that predatory pricing occurred. Instead, the Ohio Grocery expert must show through his or her analysis that, during at least some of the reported 24 months of store operations, Coho priced its products below its average variable costs. The more reporting periods Ohio Grocery can show in which Coho priced products below average variable costs, the better its chances of proving to the court that Coho violated the antitrust laws.

Ohio Grocery's expert uses regression/correlation to analyze the cost behavior patterns of the two major cost categories for Coho. The results for the combined data of the 22 stores in the Columbus area are as follows:

- Cost of goods sold regressed against Sales had an r squared of .98, a b value of .78 and an a value or constant of $156,000.
- Store operating costs regressed against Sales yielded an r squared of .77, a b value of .16, and a constant of $396,000.

Using the regression data to assist in the determination of the cost behavior of the Coho Grocery stores, Ohio Grocery's expert can only identify two months in which the stores appeared to be close to selling products below their average variable costs. The data analysis does not seem to support the predatory pricing allegation. If the expert for Ohio Grocery does not find significant evidence of Coho pricing products below its average variable costs, one would conclude that the predatory pricing charge is without merit.

Alternative Courses for Plaintiff

The plaintiff may choose to continue the case without the predatory pricing allegation. An alternative strategy might be to modify the complaint. For example, the original complaint alleged that Coho was engaged in predatory pricing in the Columbus, Ohio area in which the firm had 22 stores. The Ohio Grocery expert analyzed the store operating data in aggregate for Coho's 22 grocery stores in the area. An alternative approach would be to look at and analyze the store operating data for each of the 22 grocery stores to see whether any of the stores seemed to be selling products below their average variable costs. Another approach would be to group the 22 grocery stores into areas that are smaller geographic areas than the entire Columbus, Ohio, area. For example, Coho has seven stores in the east Columbus area, five stores in the west Columbus area, four stores in the south Columbus area, and six stores in the north Columbus area. The expert could combine and analyze the store operating data for the stores in each of the four parts of the Columbus operating area.

In the north Columbus area, where Coho has six stores, competition between them and other grocery store chains has been particularly fierce. The competition in this area has created some special pricing strategies on the part of all competing parties. An analysis of cost data for the combined store operating reports for Coho's six stores in north Columbus shows the following.

Average monthly sales were $1,950,000, cost of goods sold was $1,740,000, and operating expenses were $555,000. These amounts result in an average monthly loss of ($345,000). In the north area, Coho only had two profitable months in the years 2010 and 2011. Monthly net income (loss) ranged from $135,000 to ($460,000). Ohio Grocery's expert uses regression-correlation to analyze the combined store costs of just the north region. Using this cost data, the expert determines that the stores in the north area did not appear to cover their variable costs in 13 out of the 24 months. Based on this analysis, Ohio Grocery intends to pursue the predatory pricing allegations at trial, and the expert will present his or her evidence and reasoning behind the findings.

Whether the allegation is sustained by the court depends on a variety of issues. One, of course, is the persuasiveness of the expert's testimony and the effectiveness of the testimony of Coho's expert. Another issue is the court's view of monopoly. A geographic area like Columbus, Ohio, may be viewed as large enough for the court to envision a monopoly to have occurred. As a complaint narrows the geographic area of alleged illegal activity to smaller areas, there is more difficulty to sell the concept of effective monopoly to the court. For example, suppose Coho has one store that clearly is selling products below average variable costs. Is it engaging in predatory pricing practices? Can one store effectively create a monopoly in a general geographic area in which there are many grocery stores? In all likelihood, the court would not find a single store monopoly in a geographic area in which there are many stores.

Damage Estimation

Assume for the moment that the court finds Coho Grocery liable under the antitrust laws for the six stores in the north area of Columbus, Ohio. What is the next step in the legal process? Next, the court would seek to determine what—if any—damages were incurred by the plaintiff. If damages occurred, what was the amount of damages, if any, that occurred as a result of the illegal actions of the defendant? Now the expert's analysis shifts from Coho store data to Ohio Grocery store data. Until now Ohio Grocery's expert concentrated on the combined store operating data of Coho for its north area stores to determine their cost behavior patterns and to determine whether the stores were selling their products below their average variable costs. Once that has been accomplished, one needs to determine how much Ohio Grocery was harmed by these actions.

Because Ohio Grocery chose to concentrate its complaint on the Coho's stores in the north area of Columbus, the damage estimates is limited to the Ohio Grocery stores that compete with the Coho store in the north area. Ohio Grocery, of course, would like to identify as many stores as possible as north area competitors to maximize its damages. Coho, of course, will attempt to limit Ohio Grocery to the fewest possible stores in the damage analysis.

During the two years of alleged antitrust violations, the five Ohio Grocery stores located in the north area had average monthly losses of ($387,000) from average monthly sales of $1,590,000.

Ohio Grocery's expert analyzes the combined store operating costs of the five Ohio Grocery stores that were deemed to be competitors in the north area. To accomplish this analysis, the expert uses data from two years immediately prior to the alleged antitrust violations to evaluate what Ohio Grocery's "normal" sales, costs, and profits should be. The expert finds that, during the 24 months prior to the alleged antitrust violations, the five stores in the north area had average monthly sales of $1.550 million during 2008 and 2009. Average monthly cost of goods sold for the two years was $1.190 million and average store operating costs were $250,000. These figures resulted in an average monthly net income of $110,000 during 2008 and 2009. Sales grew in 2009 by 10 percent compared with 2008 levels.

During the two years of alleged antitrust violations, the five Ohio Grocery stores in the north area had average monthly losses of $387,000 from average monthly sales of $1,590,000.

A simple, but easy to explain estimate of the damages is that instead of averaging monthly losses of $387,000, Ohio Grocery would have earned profits of $110,000 per month *if it were not for the illegal actions of Coho*. This simple damage calculation would make damages $11,928,000 (($110,000 × 24) + ($387,000 × 24)).

Ohio Grocery's expert might argue that the company's sales were growing at the rate of 10 percent a year, and had it not been for the actions of Coho it would have experienced the same sales growth rate in 2010 and 2011. That reasoning would mean that average monthly sales would have been $1,705,000 per month in 2010 ($1,550,000 × 1.10) and $1,875,500 per month ($1,705,000 × 1.10) in 2011. The average monthly sales then would have been $1,790,250 per month. This amount is much higher than the average sales of $1,590,000 that actually occurred in 2010 and 2011.

Of course, damages are not lost sales, but the lost profits on those sales. To find the lost profit at this sales level, the expert must analyze the cost behavior of Ohio Grocery and then apply those finding to the expected sales volume without the antitrust actions of Coho. Assume that the expert, using data from 2008 and 2009 (normal years), found that for cost of goods sold the b value was .76 and the constant was $35,000 with an r squared of .95. For store operating costs, the b value was .075 with a constant of $108,000, and an r squared of .74.

Using the preceding information, the average projected monthly profit for Ohio Grocery for these five stores is $152,391 ($1,790,250 – ($1,790,250 × .76 + $35,000) – ($1,790,250 × .075 + $108,000)). Using this analysis the damages for the five store for the years 2010 and 2011 is $12,945,384 (($152,391 × 24) + ($387,000 × 24)).

The damage estimate that is shown here and other uses of regression data in this chapter have used point estimates in the calculation. That is, we substituted the regression coefficients for a and b into the total cost formula and determined a single value for the expected costs or damages. Because the values of a and b were obtained from samples of cost data, they are only estimates of the true values for these variables. The sample used in our regression analysis should be representative of the population from which it was drawn. The amount of the variability of regression data can have a significant impact of the use of the regression data. Regressions with high correlation coefficients tend to have the sample data tightly packed around the regression line. In such cases, the dispersion of the regression data about the regression line is small. A measure of the amount of dispersion of the regression data about the regression line is called the standard error of the estimate. The regression line parameters and the standard error of the estimate can be used to find the probability of data points falling within a certain distance from the regression line.

In this example, assume the standard error of the estimate for the regression of sales against cost of goods sold was $23,000, the standard error of the estimate when sales were regressed against store operating expenses was $11,000. Previously, Ohio Grocery's expert computed a point estimate of the average monthly profit of $152,391 for the years 2010 and 2011. The expert could compute a range of values for the average monthly profit and could assign a probability that the actual profit would be within the range of computed values 95 percent of the time (or some other confidence level). In the example, the calculation of the range of values for a 95 percent confidence level is as follows:

Sales	$1,790,250	$1,790,250
COGS: (($1,790,250 × .76) + $35,000 ± ($23,000 × 2.074)	1,443,292	1,347,888
Oper. Exp. (($1,790,250 × .075) + $108,000 ± ($11,000 × 2.074)	265,083	219,455
Range of damages with a 95 percent confidence interval	$ 81,875	$ 222,907

The high and low cost estimates are derived by computing the point estimate as before and then adding and subtracting from the point estimate the standard error of the estimate times the appropriate "t value" from the point estimate value. The t value factor is based upon the desired confidence interval and the size of the sample. Here we wanted to be 95 percent confident that the actual average monthly costs and related profit would fall within the range that was calculated. In this situation, the factor is 2.074, which is the value for a 95 percent confidence interval with 22 degrees of freedom. The 22 degrees of freedom comes from our sample size of 24 months minus 2 degrees of freedom for the two parameters calculated in the regression analysis. The T table, also called the "student t table," is the appropriate table to use when the sample size is smaller than 60.

Instead of making a monthly income point estimate of $152,391, now there is a range of values from $81,875 to $222,907. Of course, by extending this to the alleged damages for the two-year period, there is a range for the damages. Here the range is $11,253,000 (($81,875 × 24) + ($387,000 × 24)) to $14,637,768 (($222,907 × 24) + ($387,000 × 24)). This range with a 95 percent confidence interval gives the evaluators some concept of the range of possible damage values if the jurors and/or judge believe the analyses and assumptions used are appropriate.

The Defendant's Expert Analysis

Determining Plaintiff's Below-Average Costs

Of course, the defendant in an antitrust dispute does not merely sit back and see what the other side does with its analysis. Often antitrust cases result from fierce competition in markets in which one of the competitors believes a competitor (usually a large firm) is engaging in anticompetitive practices (usually predatory pricing). The plaintiff alleges that the goal of the defendant is to drive the smaller firm out of business, and then significantly raise prices and reap monopolistic profits. The defendant often claims that the plaintiff is engaged in the same business practices that it claims are anticompetitive. Therefore, while the plaintiff's expert is analyzing the defendant's store operating data, the defendant's expert is typically doing the same with the plaintiff's data. The initial goal of the defendant's expert is to show that the plaintiff itself had some periods in which its stores sold products for below its average variable costs. If the plaintiff appears to be engaged in predatory pricing, then the plaintiff has a more difficult time claiming wrongdoing on the part of the defendant (even if there were some evidence of defendant predatory pricing).

Defendant's Damage Calculations

If the court finds that the defendant is liable for antitrust activities, the defendant's expert needs to perform similar damage calculations. Usually the defendant's expert will rebut the plaintiff's expert damages opinion and prepare his or her own report estimating the damages. As with other types of disputes, the damage estimate of the defendant's expert will tend toward the lower side. Here, for example, the defendant's expert might point out that Ohio Grocery's 10 percent sales growth in north Columbus during 2008 and 2009 was due largely to the closing of a major competitor chain in the area. Other grocery stores, such as Coho's, actually increased sales during the same time period by 25 to 30 percent.

Armed with this information, the defendant's expert may project a sales decline during 2010 and 2011. The defendant's expert may determine different cost behavior for Ohio Grocery's stores than Ohio Grocery's expert, and the resulting cost structure may yield less profit per dollar of lost sales. In general, the defendant's expert uses the best professional skills he or she has to minimize the damage exposure of the client within the framework of ethical and professional behavior.

Federal False Claims Act Litigation

¶ 11,061   ## OVERVIEW OF THE FEDERAL FALSE CLAIMS ACT

Federal False Claims Act litigation frequently relies heavily on the expertise of forensic accountants. The Federal False Claims Act[2] was passed to protect the government from the unscrupulous acts of a few government contractors that intentionally or carelessly overcharge the government for goods and services. The Internet site of Ashcraft & Gerel indicates that 10 percent of the U.S. annual budget is paid to companies or persons who are defrauding the government.[3]

Depending on how they are counted, products and services that are purchased by governments and government agencies in this country amount to nearly half of the country's gross national product. The U.S. government is the biggest customer. From military aircraft to decals, the government buys all kinds of products. The array of purchased services is just as great. Some items, such as paper, pens, computers, and other common products, are purchased on the open market where there are many buyers. There are many other items, however, such as high-tech weaponry and specialized products and services, that are purchased on fixed contracts or on a cost-plus contract basis.

Whenever there are contracts or other agreements governing the amounts to be paid and the products or services to be delivered, there are often disagreements. Everyone has heard about the $500 toilet seats and the $200 hammers that were sold and billed to the government. Although these incidents make good sound bites for television news, they are insignificant in comparison with many of the contracts and other disputes the government has with contractors. Many items sold to the government develop disputes, and sometimes such disputes can be settled only with litigation. Sometimes the issues are clearly contractual disputes, and these conflicts are settled in civil trials or at settlement hearings prior to trial.

Fraud Allegations

Some government/contractor disputes are more serious because they involve allegations of fraud. The fraud allegations can and do come from various sources. One source is the audit process. Most government contracts have audit clauses that allow or even require periodic audits of the contract by the contract parties, government agencies, or both. If in the course of these periodic audits, there appears to be fraud by the contractor as defined by the Federal False Claims Act, the government may choose to start a proceeding against the contractor. False Claims Act cases, like all government litigation, are prosecuted by the U.S. Department Justice (U.S. DOJ). The U.S. DOJ has a distinct group that specializes in litigating False Claims Act cases.

Whistle-blower Allegations

Another source of False Claims Act cases is whistle-blowers. These people usually are current or former employees of the contractor who allege that the contractor has intentionally overcharged the government for goods or services. Whistle-blowers can proceed in two ways against a contractor when False Claims Act charges are alleged. They can contact the U.S. Department of Justice directly and provide it with whatever descriptions and evidence of the fraud is currently available. Often this evidence is not enough to cause the case to proceed. Sometimes the whistle-blower will personally file a False Claims Act case in federal court against the contractor on behalf of the federal government. Such a case is referred to as a *qui tam suit*.

Qui Tam Suits

Qui tam suits have a special and interesting history. The law allowing such suits was enacted during the Civil War at the urging of President Abraham Lincoln. The impetus for this law was the widespread bilking of the Union Army by vendors selling it wagons, guns, food products, and many other items that did not meet standards or were, in some cases, just plain worthless. At that time there was no General Accounting Office (GAO), Army Audit Agency (AAA), or any other government agency in place to look for and pursue fraud cases. The qui tam suit allows any concerned citizen to seek relief in the name of the government.

The qui tam suit still exists, and many whistle-blowers initially file qui tam suits to get the dispute started and on the books. Once a qui tam suit is initiated, the U.S. Department of Justice will evaluate the case to see whether it believes there are sound reasons to pursue the conflict. Typically, most False Claims Act cases have many allegations. The U.S. DOJ can take as its own any or all parts of any qui tam suit that it believes has a good chance of successful prosecution. Whatever parts of the qui tam suit the U.S. DOJ does not take, the whistle-blower and his or her attorney can continue to litigate.

LAW & ORDER

WHISTLEBLOWER GETS $1.35M IN FIRING CASE. A former employee of Rockland Community College has been awarded $1.35 million by a federal jury that found she was wrongly fired after warning the school that federal funds were being misused.

Rockland County will appeal Friday's verdict in favor of Sara Schmidt, said Lewis Jefferies, the county's insurance coordinator.

Schmidt, 69, of Isreal, filed the lawsuit 14 years ago, two years after she was fired as director of the Judaic studies program. She said she told former school President F. Thomas Clark about lax academic standards in the program and told his two top aides about the possible misuse of federal funds.

The college denied any knowledge of Schmidt's concerns and said she was fired because she interfered with communications and acted outside the boundaries of her job description.

A state audit later found that more than $10 million in tuition subsidies had been improperly obtained for students in the program. Five men were convicted and the college had to repay $5.2 million to the U.S. Department of Education.[4]

Reasons for Bringing Action

Why would a whistle-blower file a False Claims Act case in the first place, and why would he or she continue to pursue those parts of the dispute that the U.S. DOJ did not pick up and litigate on its own? The answer is *money*. The court may choose to provide the whistle-blower with 15 to 25 percent of the damages awarded if the government proceeds with the action and 25 to 30 percent of the damages awarded if the government does not proceed with the action.[5]

Occasional media stories about large amounts received by a whistle-blower lead the public to believe that they typically get large amounts of money for "just doing what is right." Actually, most whistle-blowers receive little or nothing from the actions they pursue. In addition, negative publicity from former employers and the press in general often makes life difficult for whistle-blowers. Whistle-blowers may have a difficult time finding new jobs with the same responsibilities and compensation, because they are not perceived as "team players." This trouble is not to suggest that one should not blow the whistle on a contractor who is fraudulently charging the government; however, such an act may affect the person's life for many years to come.

¶ 11,071 THE ACCOUNTANT'S ROLE IN FALSE CLAIM ACT LITIGATION

Accountants typically provide a significant service in Federal False Claims Act disputes. They may act as an expert witness for the defense, the government, or a whistle-blower litigating the qui tam parts of the case.

Typical questions that accountants help courts to answer are:
- What costs should be included in the contract?
- How should costs be measured under the contract?
- What is the correct timing of the costs and/or revenues under the contract?
- What accounting concepts, rules, etc., apply under this contract?
- What is the magnitude of the damages that occurred because of the fraud that took place?

By analyzing a company's business records and practices, accountants can help courts determine whether the company acted *knowingly*. Under the Federal False Claim Act, no proof of specific intent to defraud is required.[6] Under the Federal False Claims Act, a person acts *knowingly* with respect to information if the person has:[7]

- Actual knowledge of information;
- Acts in deliberate ignorance of the truth or falsity of the information; or
- Acts in reckless disregard of the truth or falsity of the information.

Intellectual Property

¶ 11,075   THE NATURE AND CHARACTERISTICS OF INTELLECTUAL PROPERTY

Another interesting and often challenging area of practice in dispute resolution is the area of intellectual property. It is a term referring to a number of distinct types of creations of the mind for which property rights are recognized—and the corresponding fields of law.[8] Intellectual property includes such assets as copyrights, patents, trademarks, trade secrets, business processes, and other intangible rights that are conveyed to owners via legal rules and regulations. You can find a significant amount of information about patents and trademarks and the laws that govern them at *http://www.uspto.gov/*. Most intellectual property rights are conveyed for a period of time such as 20 years for patents. All "original works of authorship" created after January 1, 1978 in a fixed tangible form are protected for the duration of the creator's life plus 70 years. Companies hold copyrights for 95 to 120 years depending on whether or not the work has been published.[9] Other types of intellectual property such as trademarks may have an indefinite life. One of the most famous trademarks in the world is Coca-Cola which was registered in 1892. Its value has been estimated at more than a billion dollars. Companies spend huge amounts of money advertising and promoting their products and their images for quality, reliability, and many other positive attributes. One can scarcely go anywhere without seeing all kinds of company and product trademarks. When others violate the rights legally conveyed to owners by copyrights, trademarks, or other intellectual property, the owners typically seek remedy for violations of their property rights.

When unauthorized entities use trademarks, copyrighted materials, trade secrets, or other intellectual property, they are liable for the damages that they cause to the owners of such items. The question of what the amount of damages is, however, may be more complex to estimate than in other types of disputes. Unlike most tangible assets, intellectual property may be taken and used without the owner even knowing about it. Additionally, the nature and quantity of the damages may not be obvious. Although the calculation of damages in intellectual property cases may include lost sales and profits just like breach or tort cases, there may be other components to the damages as well. For example, if the value of a plaintiff's firm is diminished because someone sells pirated products or performs other acts that decrease the market value of the offended business, the plaintiff may recover the lost value. In most intellectual property cases, the plaintiff may sue for damages caused by lost sales, lost customers, and the loss of reputation caused by an unauthorized user selling lower or differing quality of products or services that are represented as the protected products or services.

According the U.S. Copyright Office, "a Copyright is a form of protection provided by the laws of the United States (title 17, *U.S. Code*) to the authors of "original works of authorship," including literary, dramatic, musical, artistic, and certain other intellectual works. This protection is available to both published and unpublished works."[10] When seeking damages in a copyright infringement case, it is important to determine if the copyright is registered. Original works created in the United States are instantly copyrighted, without the author doing anything except putting it into a tangible form. If you also register your copyrighted material with the U.S. Copyright Office, you have a stronger ability to seek damages if there is a copyright infringement of your property.[11] When seeking damages in a copyright infringement case, the plaintiff may be able to seek statutory damages or actual damages. If the copyrighted material that was infringed upon has been registered with the U.S. Copyright Office, the plaintiff can seek statutory damages. Such damages tend to be much greater than actual damages. Statutory damages are set by law, and they range from hundreds of dollars to thousands of dollars per infringement regardless of the actual damages incurred by the plaintiff. "In the United States, statutory damages are set out in Title 17, Section 504 of the U.S. Code. The basic level of damages is between $750 and $30,000 per work, at the discretion of the court. Plaintiffs who can show willful infringement may be entitled to damages up to $150,000 per work."[12]

Additionally with statutory damages, the plaintiff is relieved of the necessity of calculating and defending actual damage amounts. For example, assume that a defendant sold just one copy of registered copyrighted material. The plaintiff lost $10 in profit on the sale but suffered no other damages. The statutory damage for this event is $9,000 per incident. Clearly the statutory damages are much greater than the actual damages in this case, and the plaintiff's strategy would be to seek the statutory damages.

If the copyright is not registered or for some other reason statutory damages are not relevant, actual damages must be computed for the copyright infringement. Actual damage calculations have many of the same components as damages in other types of disputes. Actual damages would be the amount of lost profits, increased costs, or other elements that caused the plaintiff to be worse off because of the infringement. Typically the plaintiff will attempt to show what profits would have been higher than the profits actually achieved if it were not for the infringement that occurred. As with any effort to measure actual damages, it is essential that the plaintiff provide the court with as much documented evidence as possible to support the damage calculations. Of course, estimating and supporting actual damages in an infringement case is more difficult than claiming statutory damages which are spelled out by the law.

Patents infringements are common points of dispute in business. Many companies produce products that are covered by patents, and many production processes are protected by patents. Patent rights provide logical protection for companies that invest large sums of money developing new products and creating new manufacturing processes. In an effort to successfully compete in a market, some companies will produce and sell products that are similar or even identical to the successful patented products and production processes of other companies. When this happens it is very common for the harmed company to file a patent infringement law suit. The purpose of such suits is to get the offending company to cease and desist from its actions and to recover any damages that may have accrued because of the patent infringement. Patent infringements have a number of possible damage components. Common damage components include lost profits from sales, lost customer base, lost company value, and other damage elements that the plaintiff can identify and support as a component of harm caused by the actions of the offending party.

¶11,078   COMMON ISSUES IN PROVING/DEFENDING PATENT INFRINGEMENT CASES

Patent infringement cases constitute a major area of litigation for many businesses. Patent infringement cases involving major corporations frequently make headline news. One of the most visible cases is Apple's lawsuit against Samsung for alleged violations of Apple's touchscreen technology. Initial damages in the case topped $1,000,000,000, but the case is under appeal. Apple is also reopening cases against Google's Motorola subsidiary. Companies through litigation and other dispute resolution approaches seek to protect their investment in the development of new products and the development of new processes that provide competitive advantages for firms in their constant efforts to generate attractive levels of profit. Knowingly or unknowingly, other companies sometimes violate the patent protection enjoyed by other entities by producing products or using processes that are protected by patents.

When that allegedly occurs, the parties involved in the dispute should be aware of the typical strategies used in pursuing or defending a patent infringement case. Below we discuss some of the more common issues and approaches in litigating patent infringement cases.

The Georgia-Pacific Factors

In a well-known case between Georgia Pacific Corporation and United States Plywood Corporation, the court used 15 factors to determine the monetary damages in the case. The factors were:

1. The royalties received by Georgia-Pacific for licensing the patent to prove an established royalty.
2. The rates paid by the licensee for the use of similar patents.
3. The nature and scope of the license.
4. Georgia-Pacific's policy of maintaining its patent monopoly by licensing the use of the invention only under special conditions designed to preserve the monopoly.
5. The commercial relationship between Georgia-Pacific and the licensees.
6. The effect of selling the patented specialty in promoting sales of other Georgia-Pacific products; the existing value of the invention to Georgia-Pacific as a generator of sales of non-patented items; and the extent of such derivatives or convoyed sales.
7. The duration of the patent and the terms of the license.
8. The established profitability of the patent property, its commercial success, and its current popularity.
9. The utility and advantages of the patented property over any old modes or devices that had been used.
10. The nature of the patented invention, its character, its characteristics, and the benefits to those who used it.
11. The extent to which the infringer used the invention and any evidence probative of the value of that use.
12. The portion of the profit or selling price that is customary in the particular business or in comparable businesses.
13. The portion of the realizable profit that should be credited to the invention as distinguished from any non-patented elements added by the infringer.
14. The opinion testimony of a qualified expert.
15. The amount that Georgia-Pacific and a licensee would have agreed upon at the time the infringement began if they had reasonably and voluntarily tried to reach an agreement.[13]

As you can see, the court selected many different issues to use in determining the damages in this case. Many of them had case-specific importance, but these 15 factors have been used as a guideline is evaluating many other cases through the years. The Georgia-Pacific factors have been widely used and cited by courts in evaluating patent infringement case damages. The 25 Percent Rule

In the late 1950s Robert Goldscheider completed an empirical study relating to 18 commercial licenses from a Swiss subsidiary of an American company.[14] The licensing referred to patents, trademarks, and copyrights. The licensees paid royalties of 5% of sales and typically generated operating profits of 20% of sales resulting in the 5%/20% or "25% rule".[15]

This 25% rule was used frequently in estimating damages in intellectual property disputes. One of the many intellectual property cases in which the 25% rule played a major role in estimating damages in an intellectual property dispute was the *Uniloc v. Micorsoft* case. The effective use of the 25% rule in this case resulted in a jury award for Uniloc of $388,000,000 in damages. On appeal, the Court of Appeals for the Federal Circuit ("CAFC") issued a procedural ruling that as a matter of Federal Circuit law the 25% rule of thumb is a fundamentally flawed tool for determining a baseline royalty rate in a hypothetical negotiation. Evidence relying on the 25% rule of thumb is thus inadmissible under Daubert and the Federal Rule if Evidence, because it fails to tie a reasonable royalty base to the facts of the case.[16] The result of this appeal will result in a new trial on the questions of damages in this case.

Cost of Next Best Alternative

One possible analysis in evaluating damages in a patent infringement case is to identify the next best alternative technologies and use that information to forecast the costs savings or the price premium that is conveyed patent technology at issue in the case.[17] For example, if a technology offers the owner a 10 percent pricing premium over the next best technology, a royalty rate of 10 percent or less might be a reasonable estimate of the damages from the patent infringement. Of course, determining the "next best technology" for a given patent protected technology may be a challenge, and even more challenging may be the calculation of the cost savings and/or pricing premium offered by the protected technology. Although the implementation of "cost of next best alternative" may be challenging, it is a methodology that is conceptually easy for the court to understand and it provides a framework for evaluating the alleged damages from the patent infringement.

Running Royalty vs. Upfront Payments

Royalty agreements can contain both upfront royalty obligations and royalties that are based on the ongoing use of the intellectual property. Upfront royalty obligations typically result when the licensing agreement calls for a lump sum payment at the start of the agreement that allows the buyer of the product to use the licensed product. Typically the buyer will also pay an ongoing (running) royalty for the actual quantity of use of the product. If the upfront royalty is significant, it is common to allocate the amount over the expected useful life of the agreement in order to accurately measure the cost of the royalties each period. The issues can be further complicated when the product licensing agreement addresses the use of the product across different geographical areas and across different state of country lines. Because many royalty agreements include substantial negotiations between the two parties, the agreement should clearly spell out the relationship between the upfront payments and the running royalty.

Because patents and other intellectual property typically have specific territorial context, many companies and multinational operations must be careful that patent rights conveyed by an agreement are clearly understood and that the products and territories in which the firm operates are in compliance with the licensing agreements. When patent infringement cases are litigated in this type of environment, the calculation of damages and the defense against alleged damages can be very complex. The accounting experts may have to make hundreds of calculations for each product and each territory covered by the patents in an effort to evaluate alleged patent infringement damages.

Cost of Designing Around

Designing around a patent is a legal strategy to create a new product/technology/process that provides the user with an alternative to a patented item without violating the rights of the patent holder or the holder of other intellectual property rights.[18] Although this is an acceptable strategy for competing with patented property rights, it is essential that the new item of intellectual property does not violate the property rights of the original patent holder. In order to avoid this problem, entities that choose to "design around" an existing patent often seek legal advice on issues related to the patent. Sometimes patent holders attempt to defend against design-around attempts by competitors. One approach is to develop a large portfolio of interlocking patents, called a patent thicket, that causes a competitor to design around a large number of patents.[19] Designing around a patent can be a way to avoid very high royalty fees that may be charged by a patent holder, sometimes referred to as patent trolls, but the cost of designing and developing the newly designed product, process, or invention must be justifiable in light of the royalty charged by the original patent holder.

Anti-Trust Issues

Patents and antitrust laws seem to be internally inconsistent. On the one hand patents provide a form of limited monopoly and anti-trusts laws prohibit monopoly. Patents are intended to provide the patent holder with a limited monopoly for the product, process, or invention covered by the patent.[20] This right is conveyed by the United States constitution and it authorizes the Congress to grant such rights to the patent holder. The exclusive rights grated to a patent holder, however, do not void anti-trust laws, and when patent holders reach beyond the privileges granted by a patent they run the risk of being successfully sued under antitrust laws.[21]

Of course, patent holders are eager to enforce their patent rights and sometimes they attempt to enforce their patent rights beyond those that were conveyed by the patent that they hold. Often third parties sue patent holders alleging that the patent holder has exceeded the bounds of the patent and therefore are in violation of anti-trust laws. When this occurs it is up to the court to determine the boundaries between patent and anti-trust law. Plaintiffs in such cases can be the patent holder alleging that a third party is in violation of the patent(s) held by the plaintiff. In other situations a third party can be the plaintiff claiming the patent holder has exceeded the bounds of the patent and are in violation of anti-trust laws.

One area in which there are many patent infringement/anti-trust cases is the pharmaceutical industry. Because of the myriad of medications, both over the counter and prescription, that are constantly being developed and produced and the complex nature of the products, it is very challenging for a court to understand and evaluate many pharmaceutical cases. Many cases against pharmaceutical firms allege that patent holders on certain medicines exceed the privilege granted by the patent and impair the ability of other pharmaceutical providers to manufacture and sell generic drugs. The alleged result is that consumers must pay a lot more for these drugs and both state and federal anti-trust laws are violated.

¶ 11,081   CONCLUSION

Accountants often play a vital role in proving liability in antitrust disputes. Sometimes accountants are called upon to determine what costs should have been incurred in a contract, and their opinion may have an impact on proving liability. In other scenarios, accountants' testimony goes to the issue of liability, but primarily accounting experts testify about damage measurements.

Accountants also play a significant role in Federal False Claims Act disputes. Most False Claims Act cases relate to accounting-based contracts (usually cost-based). Accounting experts are used on both sides to provide insights for courts on the relevance, significance, and magnitude of the accounting issues.

Another major area of forensic practice is disputes involving intellectual property. Patents, copyrights, trademarks, and other intellectual property are the source of many litigation disputes. Each type of intellectual property has its own unique issues and challenges, but typically forensic accountants are called upon to measure the type and extent of damages that have occurred because of the wrongful act of the defendant. Some areas such as copyrights may be covered by statutory law, but most areas of intellectual property disputes require forensic accountants to perform actual damages calculations using their knowledge and skills.

ENDNOTES

[1] Introductory remarks, DOJ/FTC Hearing on Health Care and Competition Law and Policy, *http://www.usdoj.gov/atr/public/speeches/200828.htm*.

[2] 31 U.S.C. §§3729-3733.

[3] Ashcraft & Gerel, "Whistle Blower Litigation Under the Federal False Claims Act—Qui Tam Claims," *www.ashcraftandgerel.com/whistleb.html#History*.

[4] Associated Press, *Las Vegas Sun*, accessed June 18, 2003, at *http://www.lasvegassun.com/sunbin/stories/natgen/2003/jun/18/061800942.html*.

[5] 31 U.S.C. §3730(d).

[6] 31 U.S.C. §3729(b).

[7] *Ibid.*

[8] Richard Raysman, Edward A. Pisacreta and Kenneth A. Adler, "Intellectual Property Licensing: Forms and Analysis," LAW JOURNAL PRESS (1999-2008).

[9] "What are copyrights and patents?" (18 October 2000). HowStuffWorks.com. *http://www.howstuffworks.com/question492.htm* (23 April 2011).

[10] *www.copyright.gov.*

[11] *Ibid.*

[12] *http://en.wikipedia.org/wiki/Statutory_damages_for_copyright_infringement.*

[13] *Georgia-Pacific Corp. v. United States Plywood Corp.*, 318 FSupp 1116, 6 USPQ 235 (SD NY 1970):

[14] Robert Goldscheider, "Litigation Backgrounder for Licensing", *Les Nouvelles*, 29 (March 1994), p. 20-25.

[15] G. Smith and R. Parr, "Use of the 25% Rule in Valuing Intellectual Property", *Intellectual Property*, (Wiley & Sons, 2005).

[16] (*hhtp://www.cafc.uscourts.gov/stories/opinions-orders/10-1035.pdf*)

[17] (*hhtp://journalofaccountancy.com/Issues/2004/20StepsForPricingAPatent.htm*

[18] *http://en.wikipedia.org/wiki/Design_around*

[19] Rubinfeld, Daniel L.; Maness, Robert (2005). "The Strategic Use of Patents: Implications for Antitrust". In Leveque, Francois; Shelanski, Howard. *Antitrust, Patents and Copyright: EU and US Perspectives*. Northampton: Edward Elgar. pp. 85–102. ISBN 1-84542-603-7.

[20] *www.stanford.edu/dept/law/ipsc/pdf/feldman-robin.pdf*

[21] *http://www.thefreelibrary.com/The+statutory+presumption+of+patent+validity+in+antitrust+cases*

EXERCISES

1. Are all monopolies illegal in the United States?
2. What does geographic area have to do with alleged violations of the antitrust laws? Can there be a monopoly in part of a city?
3. What is predatory pricing?
4. Why is it difficult to determine a company's average variable costs?
5. How is graphic analysis used to estimate cost behavior patterns?
6. What is the high-low method?
7. For what is regression analysis used?
8. For what is correlation analysis used?
9. What is the coefficient of correlation?
10. What is r squared?
11. What is the coefficient of nondetermination?
12. Can regression/correlation analysis prove causation? If not, why not?
13. What role can accountants fill in a Federal False Claim Act suit?
14. A travel agency had its highest operating costs in June ($26,250), and its lowest operating costs in November ($21,750). The agency sold 1,500 tickets in June and 900 tickets in November.
    a. Using the high-low method of cost estimation, compute the fixed and variable components of the travel agency's monthly operating costs.
    b. If the travel agency expects to sell 1,900 tickets in December, estimate its operating expenses for December.
    c. What concerns might arise about making the December operating expense estimate?

15. The Shannon Valley manufacturing plant used regression-correlation to evaluate cost behavior. Using sample data for 20 weeks, the controller regressed prime production costs against the number of units manufactured. The following regression data were obtained:
    $a = \$3,430$
    $b = \$35.60$
    $r = .94$
    a. Write the equation for the regression line.
    b. Discuss the meaning of, a, b, and r.
    c. How much variation in the value of the dependent variable can be explained by changes in the value of the independent variable?
    d. If anticipated production for next week is 900 units, what are the estimated prime costs for the week?

16. An expert is analyzing the cost behavior patterns of the defendant in an antitrust dispute. The expert plans to use the information to prepare a damage estimate. The expert analyzed 30 months of cost and sale data for the Downtown Department Store. The results of regression-correlation analyses on the store's six cost categories regressed against sales dollars are as follows:

Account	a value	b value	r squared
Cost of goods sold	$45,000	.46	.88
Store salaries	$65,000	.055	.72
Store utilities	$26,000	.015	.34
Store maintenance	$14,000	.08	.035
Advertising	$26,000	.01	.001
Corporate overhead	$75,000	.025	.045

a. Use the cost behavior data presented above to make a point estimate of expected costs and net income for the month of July (assuming sales of $980,000).

b. How would you describe (categorize) each of the costs?

c. How strong do you feel about estimations you made in part a?

17. The Movietown Movie Theater Company operates movie theaters in 15 different towns throughout the Midwest, including Harborview, a small city of 250,000 people with a major state university. In Harborview, Movietown owns and operates five different movie theaters with a total of 38 screens. Movietown operates the only theaters in Harborview and the only ones within a 30-mile radius around the town. Movietown charges $6.00 for matinee movie times and $8.50 for evening movies. These prices are about 10 percent higher than the prices charged around most of the rest of the state. There are no discount ticket prices of any sort for senior citizens, students, or any other group. Most movie theaters around the rest of the state offer some, if not all, such special group discounts.

Several other movie theater companies have sought to build movie theaters in Haborview over the last 10 years. Each of these efforts has failed. In addition, Movietown has actively lobbied town authorities to keep out any other movie theater companies.

a. What are the issues with Movietown's operation?

b. Is there a possible case of monopoly here under federal law?

c. During discovery, what if any accounting records should be requested?

d. What other information would be needed?

e. What are the services that a forensic accounting expert witness might be asked to provide in connection with this dispute?

18. A whistle-blower in her allegations made in a qui tam suit, alleged that her former employer fired her because she told the company that it was "padding the bills" to the federal government for the cost-plus contract it had to build ejection seats for fighter aircraft. She alleges that the company overcharged for materials, ran up labor costs,

threw "all kinds of stuff in overhead," and illegally plugged corporate administrative costs into the contract billings.

As the forensic accountant hired by the U.S. Justice Department to litigate this case, answer the following:

a. What documents will you seek during discovery to address the whistle-blower's allegations?

b. What will you be looking for in each of the requested documents?

c. What will be the basis/foundation for the opinions you will provide in this case?

d. How will you utilize the whistle blower in pursuing your opinions in this case?

19. Jamestown Electric has a contract with an agency of the federal government to provide electrical power to the agency for a five-year period. The contract stipulates, in part, that the power will be provided "at the lowest reasonable cost without compromising safety." In connection with this contract, Jamestown Electric buys and uses coal from its wholly-owned subsidiary Great Plains Coal Company. The sale of this coal to Jamestown Electric specifically for this contract represents 40 percent of the coal sales for Great Plains. The profit for Great Plains Coal Company during the life of the contract averaged $1.2 million per year.

Jed Jones, a former employee of Jamestown Electric was fired by the firm and immediately filed a qui tam suit alleging Jamestown had intentionally overcharged the government throughout the life of the power supply agreement

a. You are the forensic accountant for the whistle-blower's attorney. What are the accounting issues in this case? What are the damages in this case? What documents and other information do you intend to seek? What is the basis for your opinion?

b. You are the forensic accountant for Jamestown Electric. What are the accounting issues in this case? What are the damages in this case? What documents and other information do you intend to seek? What is the basis for your opinion?

20. Up North Marina is and has been the only marina on Lake Woodward for the last 20 years. There have been numerous efforts to open other marinas during this time period. Each

attempt, however, was unsuccessful. A recent lawsuit was successful in proving liability on the part of Up North Marina management is keeping many of those other marina operations off the lake. The court is now addressing the liability issue in this case.

a. You are the forensic accountant for the plaintiffs in the case. What documents and other information will you seek to compute damages? What will be the basis for you damage estimate? What is your theory of damages, and what are the components of your damage model?

b. You are the forensic accountant for the defendant in the case. What documents and other information will you seek to compute damages? What will be the basis for your damage estimate? What is your theory of damages, and what are the components of your damage model? What are your plans to counter the plaintiffs' damage calculations?

21. Visit the Internet page of the Justice Department's Antitrust Division and read the highlights. Summarize a recently released antitrust case against a defendant.

22. Access the Internal page of the Taxpayers Against Fraud (TAF), the Federal False Claims Legal Center. Describe the TAF's resources, especially the Qui Tam Attorney Network.

23. Using the Internet, read about the history of the Qui Tam provision on the Ashcraft & Geral site.

12

COMPUTING ECONOMIC DAMAGES

OBJECTIVES

After Completing Chapter 12, you should be able to:

1. Recall the differences between measuring commercial damages and measuring personal injury damages.
2. Understand the role played by the forensic accounting expert witnesses for both sides in a personal injury case.
3. Identify the common components of the damage calculation found in a personal injury case.
4. Understand the role of assumptions that may be needed to calculate personal injury damages.

OVERVIEW

Damage calculations were discussed in Chapter 10, Commercial Damages. Most of the issues discussed in that chapter have general applicability to many areas of damage calculations in providing litigation support services. There are some areas of damage calculations, however, that require additional knowledge and skills. Cases involving wrongful death, wrongful discharge, complete or partial disabilities, and other similar situations that take into account the economic value of persons, require the use of economic concepts that have not been covered yet. This chapter will address some of those additional issues that are useful in calculating economic damages in other types of dispute situations.

Many of the situations discussed in previous damage calculation chapters covered situations in which the act or event created a contract breach for some specified time period such as the breach of a two-year purchase agreement. In this chapter, issues raised by events that cause damages over some long or unspecified time period in which there is a range of possible outcomes for the damage period are discussed. For example, if a person sustains permanent work-related disabilities, there are a variety of issues that impact on the amount of damages that will accrue to the injured person over his or her remaining lifetime. For example, how long will the injured person live? What level of injuries were sustained? What is the impact of those injuries on the employee's remaining work effort and abilities to perform services outside of the work place? The calculation of economic damages would be based on a variety of issues including, but not limited to, the following four relevant factors:

- What are the characteristics of that person's work life?
- What is the employee's educational background?
- What is the employee's gender?
- What is the employee's expected time left in the work force?

There would be a number of other relevant factors in the evaluation of economic damages as well. Fortunately, there is a wealth of statistical data on many relevant issues and facts that may be of use to the expert in evaluating the situation and in computing economic damages for each specific case. Most of these statistics are compiled and published by the Federal government and they cover a wide variety of labor, health, and other personnel and economic statistics. Government data can be very helpful in preparing and explaining economic damages in many personal damage situations.

The Nature of Economic Damages

The purpose of this chapter is to introduce some of the key issues in measuring economic damages. Many common issues that arise in measuring economic damages are examined. This chapter is an overview. The complexity of the issues involved in measuring economic damages and the depth of some of the more complex issues in evaluating economic damages situations are challenging and support the continuing publication of many volumes and countless articles on the topic. One well recognized and instructive book is *Determining Economic Damages*, by Gerald D. Martin and Ted Vavoulis.[1] A web-based search of economic damages, personal injury damages and other relevant terms will provide many books and sources of additional information.

It is difficult and confusing to discuss the calculation of economic damages in general terms. Specific references to a particular case or situation are more instructive. Therefore, this chapter presents two illustrations. The first example is a case in which a person was wrongfully discharged (fired) from a job with an agency of a county government and sues the county for lost wages and benefits. The second example involves a woman who was permanently disabled in a work-related accident and sues for lost wages and the loss of nonwork services at home that she is no longer able to perform because of the accident. This type of nonwork services is usually referred to as household services.

¶ 12,001   WRONGFUL DISCHARGE CASE

Case Description

Jeff Evans has operated the Evans Marine Services business for the last twenty years. His business is located across the street from the Lakeside County Marina. This marina, located on a large lake in south Florida, is a popular stopping point for many South Florida boaters. One of the main services of the county marina is the gas docks that are located at the marina.

In 2003, Evans secured a five-year renewable contract to operate the Lakeside County Marina. The contract with Lakeside County covered the period from 2003 through 2007 and required Jeff Evans to provide various services to transient boaters. At the end of 2007, the county did not renew Jeff's contract. During the five years of the contract, Jeff earned a salary from Lakeside County and also earned additional income from the sale of gasoline at the Lakeside County Marina gas docks. Jeff Evans purchased the gasoline and sold it at the Lakeside County Marina boat dock. Jeff paid Lakeside County 10 cents for every gallon of gasoline that he sold at the county marina. The 10 cents per gallon Jeff paid the county for the gasoline sales is reflected in the gasoline "Cost of Goods Sold" numbers shown in Figure 12.1. Figure 12.1 presents data relating to the Evans Marine Services business operations of Jeff Evans during and after his five-year contract with the county. Figure 12.2 summarizes Federal tax return data for Jeff Evans for the years 2003 through 2009. This period includes the five years of the contract with Lakeside County and the two years immediately following his firing by the county.

Figure 12.1. Business Operations

Evans Marine Services	2003	2004	2005	2006	2007	2008	2009
Sales:							
Parts	$18,450	$17,468	$19,810	$9,810	$11,690	$13,880	$17,940
Labor	34,660	28,911	31,442	23,410	22,112	26,525	28,717
Gasoline	41,750	44,821	65,654	62,770	71,212	-	-
Other income	5,456	7,631	4,125	1,867	3,848	2,911	3,777
Total Sales	$100,316	$98,831	$121,031	$97,857	$108,862	$43,316	$50,434
Cost of Goods Sold:							
Parts	16,740	15,111	14,789	8,221	7,470	9,789	12,674
Gasoline	34,766	38,917	58,287	44,211	57,462	-	-
Other Income items	121	2,317	1,123	-	877	368	1,121
Total Cost of Goods Sold	$51,627	$56,345	$74,199	$52,432	$65,809	$10,157	$13,795
Gross Margin	$48,689	$42,486	$46,832	$45,425	$43,053	$33,159	$36,639
Operating Expenses	45,319	44,220	39,879	46,534	43,229	28,770	29,333
Net income (loss)	$3,370	$(1,734)	$6,953	$(1,109)	$(176)	$4,389	$7,306

Figure 12.2. Summerized Tax Data

Jeff Evans Summarized Tax Data	2003	2004	2005	2006	2007	2008	2009
Salary and Wages:							
Salary from Evans Marine Services	$18,000	$18,000	$18,000	$18,000	$18,000	$18,000	$18,000
Salary from Lakeside County contract	15,200	16,400	15,800	16,300	16,100	-	-
Total Salary and wages	$33,200	$34,400	$33,800	$34,300	$34,100	$18,000	$18,000
Schedule C income: Evans Marine Ser.	$3,370	$(1,734)	$6,953	$(1,109)	$(176)	$4,389	$7,306
Adjusted gross income	36,570	32,666	40,753	33,191	33,924	22,389	25,306

Jeff Evans received a salary from the county which is shown in Figure 12.3. In addition, he received a profit on the sale of fuel sold at the county dock. This fuel-sale income is reported as part of the Schedule C income for Evans Marine Services. The Schedule C income is shown in Figure 12.1 and it is summarized in Figure 12.2.

At the end of the five-year contract, the county did not renew its contract with Jeff Evans. The county cited various complaints that it alleged it received over the life of the contract. Jeff Evans claimed that the complaints were minimal and that the county should not have used such issues to void the contract. He sued the county in state court and he won on the issue of liability. The issue currently before the court is the determination of the appropriate amount of damages that Lakeside County owes Mr. Evans.

At the time the contract was terminated, Jeff Evans was 55 years old. In court documents, Mr. Evans stated that he planned to work until the age of 65, and he planned to operate the county marina during that entire 10-year period.

During the five-year life of the contract, Mr. Evans received some additional benefits from Lakeside County. These benefits were summarized by Mr. Evans and are reported in Figure 12.3.

Figure 12.3. Additional Benefits

	2003	2004	2005	2006	2007
Salary	$15,200	$16,400	$15,800	$16,300	$16,100
Employer's FICA taxes	1,193	1,287	1,240	1,280	1,264
Emloyer's Health Insurance Plan	1,700	1,780	1,890	2,100	2,300
Sick pay and vacation	1,520	1,640	1,590	1,680	1,710

Measuring Economic Damages

The economic damages model that the expert prepares will include those components that the expert believes are relevant to the accurate and appropriate measurement of damages under the circumstances of the case. Of course, as is always true in such cases, experts may differ about what issues are important or relevant. There may also be differences of opinion about how the damage calculations should be performed and how the damage measurements should be interpreted. Sometimes the differences between contending expert reports rest on the measurement of the amounts that should be reported as damages and sometimes experts disagree on what are the relevant assumptions that must be made to determine appropriate measures of damages. Questions about what should be included in the economic damages model and what amounts should be reported for each damage component rest in part on the expert's understanding of the nature and character of the circumstances and events that transpired in connection with the case. The expert must then convert this knowledge into an accurate and understandable measurement of the economic damages arising from the case issues.

The measurement of damages is based on the assumption that absent the wrongful discharge (in this case the termination of the contract with the county), Mr. Evans would have continued to enjoy the various benefits provided to him under the agreement. In the case used in this illustration, any issues related to liability are over. The court has ruled that the county is liable for not renewing the contract. Even if the issue of liability had not been determined yet, typically the financial expert's role in this type of case would be limited to issues of damages. The liability issues would be litigated based on legal and other matters that typically are not the domain of most financial expert witnesses.

Usually in a case of this sort, both sides will retain an expert to provide the court with an appropriate view of the issues involved in the damage calculations and to help the court understand the damage estimates that the experts provide. To illustrate the issues that may be involved in a case of this type, and to show how an expert might measure economic damages in a case like this, the respective figures provide the economic damage measurements of the experts for both Mr. Evans and for the county. Although the two experts have somewhat different views of the nature of the components that should be included and of the amounts that should be reported as damages, both experts do provide a similar view of the process of preparing their reports.

The Damage Calculations of Mr. Evans's Expert

Figure 12.4. Damages

Jeff Evans Damages	2008	2009	2010	2011	2012	2013	2014	2015	2016	2017
Salary	$16,583	$17,080	$17,593	$18,121	$18,664	$19,224	$19,801	$20,395	$21,007	$21,637
FICA Taxes	1,269	1,307	1,346	1,386	1,428	1,471	1,515	1,560	1,607	1,655
Health Insurance	2,415	2,536	2,663	2,796	2,935	3,082	3,236	3,398	3,568	3,746
Fuel Sale Profits	16,155	16,963	17,811	18,701	19,637	20,618	21,649	22,732	23,868	25,062
Total Damages	36,422	37,886	39,412	41,004	42,664	44,395	46,201	48,085	50,050	52,100
Present Value Factor	1	1	1	0.943	0.89	0.84	0.792	0.747	0.705	0.665
Present Value of Damages	$36,422	$37,886	$39,412	$38,667	$37,971	$37,292	$36,591	$35,920	$35,285	$34,647
Total Damages Before Adjustments	$370,093									

Figure 12.4 presents the damage calculations of Jeff Evans's expert. Included in the expert's damage calculations are a number of components. Some of the larger items are lost wages, lost profits on fuel sales, and also several other smaller items. Each of these items is discussed below. The alleged time period covered by the expert of Mr. Evans is ten years. This time period was selected because Mr. Evans, in his complaint, claimed that he planned to work and keep his job as manager of Lakeside County's Marina until he was 65 years old. His age at the time the county fired him was 55.

Lost Salary

Probably the most obvious item of lost benefits for Mr. Evans is his salary from the county. In general the approach to calculating the salary damages for a wrongful discharge case is to (1) determine the earnings history for the plaintiff during time of employment, (2) determine any appropriate growth rate for the plaintiff's earnings during the time period covered by the complainant in the case, and (3) take the computed total lost salary and discount it to its present value.

In *Determining Economic Damages*, Dr. Gerald Martin and Ted Vavoulis state, "The economist will rely, first on the earnings history of the plaintiff as a starting point for the evaluation of the loss."[2] In our case illustration, Jeff Evans' salary from the county ranged from $15,200 to $16,300 during the five years of the contract as shown in Figure 12.2. His average annual salary was $15,960. Although the general trend in his salary was a small increase, there was no steady salary increase for the period.

There are a number of options for calculating the trend in salary amounts over the time period covered by the damage period alleged in the case. One possibility is to compute the average increase in salary during the period of time that the plaintiff was employed by the defendant and use that actual trend for the time period covered by the damages. The average salary increase would then be used to compute the expected salary amounts for each of the years used in the damages calculation. If the employer had any stated or written policies that pertained to salary data or any of the other possible damage calculation issues, those items could be included in the analysis.

A second possibility for computing the expected growth in salary during the time period covered by the damage estimate is to use some national average for wage and salary growth for the United States. The United States government maintains a wealth of statistics relating to all aspects of labor and labor related activities. Many of these databases are available to practitioners online. For example, one can go to the United States Census Bureau, Statistical Abstract of the United States (*http://www.census.gov/prod/www/statistical-abstract-us.html*) and find a large amount of potentially useful statistics to assist in measuring damages in a wide variety of economic damages cases. Another very useful source is the Economic Report of the President.

In looking at the actual or historical growth rate of the wages of Mr. Evans from 2003 to 2007, the growth rate is approximately 1.5 percent a year compounded annually. Mr. Evans's expert may choose to use the U.S. Department of Labor, Bureau of Labor Statistics average wage increase for nonagricultural workers from 2003 through 2008.[3] That average is approximately three percent. The expert should choose the measure of damages that he or she believes best describes the appropriate measure of damages given the circumstances of the case and the issues involved in the case. Of course, all other things being equal the expert will tend to choose those variables that are more favorable to his or her client.

The plaintiff's expert in this case used the salary data of Mr. Evans during his five-year contract with Lakeside County as the base for starting the salary projections for the damage period. Then his expert took the 2007 salary of $16,100 as a base year and multiplied it by 1.03 to arrive at a projected 2008 salary loss of $16,583. The three percent salary increase was derived by using the U.S. Department of Labor, Bureau of Labor Statistics average wage increase for nonagricultural workers from 2003 through 2008 mentioned above. The expert reasoned that the national average wage growth was a more realistic measure of the kind of salary growth that Mr. Evans could have experienced over the remaining ten years of his management of the marina. The expert suggested that Mr. Evans might even experience higher salary growth during the damage period because Lakeside County had been stingy with its salary increases during the first five years of employment. The lost salary amount for the entire ten year period of the damage estimate assumes a consistent three percent growth rate each year.

Lost Fuel Sale Profits

The second major component of damages in the plaintiff's expert report is "lost fuel sale profits." The expert used *lost gross profit* on fuel sales as the measure of damages. Figure 12.1 provides Schedule C information from Mr. Evans's tax return. Included in the data are revenue by business category, including fuel sale revenues, and cost of goods sold by business category, including cost of goods sold for fuel sales. These data are provided in Figure 12.1 for all five years of Mr. Evans's contract with Lakeside County. Below is a schedule of fuel sale revenue, cost of goods sold, and gross profits for the five-year period:

	2003	**2004**	**2005**	**2006**	**2007**
Fuel sales..................	$41,750	$44,821	$65,654	$62,770	$71,212
Fuel COGS..................	34,766	38,917	58,287	44,211	57,462
Gross Profit..............	$ 6,984	$ 5,904	$ 7,367	$18,559	$13,750
Gross Profit %..........	16.73%	13.17%	11.22%	29.57%	19.31%

The expert used the last two years of the fuel sales activity as the basis for the lost fuel sale profits component of the damage estimate. The gross profit for the last two years was averaged ($18,559 + $13,750)/2 = $16,155. This was used as the first year (2008) estimate of lost profits from fuel sales. The explanation of using this amount was that the last two years were a better indicator of future fuel sale profits than a longer term average that included much lower sales of fuel. Subsequent years of lost profits on fuel sales were computed by assuming a five percent per year increase in fuel sale gross profits. This treatment was supported by the argument that fuel sale gross profits were much larger in years 2006 and 2007 than they were in earlier years Therefore, the expert felt that the five percent increase was fairly conservative.

Other Components of the Damage Calculation

Two other components of the damage calculation are the FICA tax payments that the employer would have made on the lost salary and the health insurance premiums that the employer would have paid had Mr. Evans not been fired. The FICA tax payments would be the amounts the employer would be required to pay as its share of FICA taxes. In this case it would be 7.65 percent of the lost salary that Mr. Evans was not paid because he was fired. For example, in 2008 the lost salary in the damage model is $16,583. This amount is multiplied times 7.65 percent yielding $1,269. This same calculation is made for each of the other years covered by the expert's damage model.

Lakeside County paid health insurance premiums for Mr. Evans and his family throughout his five year contract with the county. The $2,415 health insurance damage estimate for 2008 is determined by using the $2,300 health insurance paid by Lakeside County for Jeff Evans in 2007 and multiplying that amount by a growth rate of five percent. The expert feels that a five percent growth rate in health insurance costs is quite conservative. In fact, the actual growth rate in health insurance payments for Mr. Evans by Lakeside County during the life of his employment contract was nearly eight percent. The five percent growth rate for health insurance costs was used throughout the ten years of the damage period. For example, the estimated health insurance amount for 2009 is the 2008 estimate of $2,415 plus a five percent increase. Therefore the 2009 health insurance amount is $2,536.

You may have noticed in Figure 12.3, which lists the benefits received by Mr. Evans while he was employed by Lakeside County, an amount identified as "sick pay and vacation pay." This amount is *not* included in the damage calculation. A common mistake that some individuals make in estimating economic damages is to include vacation, holiday, and sick pay as components of the employee's fringe benefit package. Actually, these amounts are already included in the employee's gross wages payroll data. To include sick pay and vacation pay as components of an employee's fringe benefits would "double count" these employee benefits. Potentially there are many legitimate components of an employee's fringe benefit package that are not included in the employee's gross payroll data. Items such as the employer's payments for health insurance, educational programs, cafeteria subsidies, and recreational programs would all be examples of possible fringe benefits paid on behalf of an employee.

Discounting Amounts to Their Present Value

In their book, *Economic/Hedonic Damages: The Practice Book for Plaintiff and Defense Attorneys*, Brookshire and Smith explain the need for discounting damage estimates to their present value and the authors describe many considerations for selecting the appropriate discount rate.[4] In simple terms, it is necessary to discount damage estimates to their present value in order to incorporate the time value of money into the analysis. It is common knowledge that a dollar received today is worth more than a dollar received at some time in the future, because having the money today allows the privilege of either using the money now or investing it so it will grow to a larger amount in the future. The present value of an amount that will be received in the future is a function of two issues: (1) how long must I wait to receive the money and (2) what is the interest rate that I would have available to me to invest the money? The longer I must wait for the money, the lower its current (present) value is to me. Likewise, the higher the interest rate is, the less the present value of an amount is.

Of these two variables, the time period and the interest rate, the interest rate (often called the discount rate) is the more challenging variable for the expert to determine. Typically the time period of the cash receipt is known or easy to estimate. For example, in the case we currently are analyzing, the expert estimated cash damages for each of the ten years covered by the remaining stated work life of the plaintiff in this case. Therefore, it is a simple matter to apply the discount rate to each of the ten years of the damage calculation.

The discount rate on the other hand is not as obvious. Discount rates (interest rates) are determined by a number of issues such as the type of investment that is being used to determine the interest rate and the level of risk of the investment. There are many possible variables that the expert may want or need to consider in determining the appropriate discount rate for a case. There are a number of standards that can be used in cases, but a detailed discussion of this topic is beyond the scope of this chapter. For purposes of this discussion it will suffice to say that cash flows should be discounted to their present value using some appropriate discount rate.

The plaintiff's expert used a six percent discount rate. In Figure 12.4, you can see the present value factor that is applied to each of the estimated annual cash flows. Notice in years 2008, 2009, and 2010, the present value factor is "1." This occurs because the alleged damages in the case started immediately after Mr. Evans was fired by Lakeside County. Therefore the years 2008 and 2009 are already past. The case is going to trial in 2010 and by the time the court renders an opinion, 2010 will be over. The present value of cash flows that are already here is merely the actual amount of the cash flow. For future years, the estimated annual cash flows are multiplied by the present value factor for that period. For example, the estimated annual cash damages in 2011 is multiplied by the present value factor of 0.943 and the estimated annual cash damages in 2015 is multiplied by the present value factor of that period of 0.747. The estimated annual damages of each of the ten years covered by the case are converted to their present value and those present value amounts are summed yielding a total present value of the damages according to the plaintiff's expert of $370,093.

The Damage Calculations of Lakeside County's Expert

Figure 12.5. Damages

Jeff Evans Damages	2008	2009	2010	2011	2012	2013	2014	2015	2016	2017
Salary	$16,341	$16,587	$16,835	$17,088	$17,344	$17,604	$17,869	$18,137	$18,409	$18,685
Minimum Wage Earnings	$10,712	$10,819	$10,927	$11,037	$11,147	$11,258	$11,371	$11,485	$11,600	$11,716
Net Wage Loss	$5,629	$5,768	$5,908	$6,051	$6,197	$6,346	$6,497	$6,652	$6,809	$6,969
FICA	431	441	452	463	474	485	497	509	521	533
Health Insurance	2,415	2,536	2,663	2,796	2,935	3,082	3,236	3,398	3,568	3,746
Total Damages	8,475	8,744	9,023	9,310	9,607	9,914	10,231	10,559	10,898	11,249
Present Value Factor	1	1	1	0.943	0.89	0.84	0.792	0.747	0.705	0.665
Present Value of Damages	$8,475	$8,744	$9,023	$8,779	$8,550	$8,328	$8,103	$7,887	$7,683	$7,480
Total Damages Before Adjustments	$83,053									

The damage estimate of defendant Lakeside County's expert is presented in Figure 12.5. As might be expected, this estimate is lower than the damage estimate of the plaintiff's expert. The damage estimate of the defendant's expert is less than 25 percent of that of the plaintiff's expert. Some of the differences between the two damage estimates in this case are fairly minor issues such as the growth rate of the salary of Mr. Evans. Other differences are fairly major issues such as what to use as the appropriate measure of lost profits from fuel sales. Each of these issues is discussed below.

Lost Salary

Both experts started their evaluation of lost salary by using Mr. Evans's 2007 salary of $16,100 which was his salary the last year of his contract with Lakeside County. The plaintiff's expert used a salary growth rate of three percent that was taken from the U.S. Department of Labor, Bureau of Labor Statistics average wage increase data for nonagricultural workers. The defendant's expert chose to use the actual salary growth rate of Mr. Evans's salary during the five years of his employment with the county. This was 1.5 percent a year. This difference between 1.5 percent and 3 percent may seem very small, but by the end of the ten-year period of the damage calculation it results in a $2,952 difference in estimated salary loss for year 2017 ($21,637 - $18,685).

The major difference in the lost wage calculation between the two experts' damage estimates is that the defendant's expert includes an adjustment for minimum wages earnings for Mr. Evans. Many states require that a person who has been wrongfully discharged must seek other employment to "mitigate" the amount of damages caused by the wrongful discharge. If there is an available market for the type and quality of the fired employee, he or she must seek such employment. In such case, the damages would be limited to the difference between the wages and the benefits of the job at issue in the case versus the wages and the benefits provided by the new job.

If a person cannot find similar employment, the issue of mitigated wage damages may be more complex. For example, if a person has a unique job or a job with significant responsibility and income in a particular geographic area, and there are no other similar jobs in that geographic area, the court may determine that finding a similar job in the area is not possible and the wage mitigation requirement will not stand. In this case, the defendant's expert did include a salary mitigation component. Acting on the belief that the job skills required for attending the county gas docks at the marina are not unique to that activity, it was assumed that such skill could be applied to many other job options in the geographic area. The amount included as wage mitigation is based on a minimum wage job. The defendant's expert believes that this is a conservative measure of the possible job options that would be available to Mr. Evans. The minimum wage amount is allowed to grow by one percent a year. Although there is no current legislation designed to increase the minimum wage amount, the expert felt that over the ten-year life of the alleged damage period, this small growth amount would allow for some increase in the wage rate or allow Mr. Evans to move to a somewhat higher salary job opportunity.

In each of the ten years of the damage estimate, the estimated salary for the year is mitigated (reduced) by the minimum wage job that Mr. Evans is assumed to have taken. The difference between these two numbers is the "net wage loss" as calculated by the defendant's expert. In other words, this is the "net amount" of salary that Mr. Evans lost as the result of being fired by the county.

This amount of "net wage loss" is what is used to calculate the amount of employer FICA payment that was lost because of the wrongful discharge. The model assumes that Mr. Evans's new employer would pay the FICA taxes on the minimum wage job.

Lost Fuel Sale Profits

Another major difference between the damage estimates of the plaintiff's and the defendant's experts is the "lost fuel sale profits." The plaintiff's lost fuel sale profits is the largest single component of the damage model. The plaintiff's expert based the lost fuel sales profit component of the model on lost gross margin on fuel sales. In addition, the plaintiff's model assumes a fairly significant growth in gross profit on fuel sales over the life of the damage estimate.

The defendant's expert used the same fuel sale data as the plaintiff's expert (found in Figure 12.1) and came to a very different conclusion about the "lost fuel sale profits." The first major difference is that the plaintiff's expert states that gross profit on fuel sales is not the same as lost profit on fuel sales. Gross profit is merely the difference between the amount a vendor pays for a product and the amount of the sales price the vendor receives for that product. To find the *actual lost profit* from the sale of a product one must next deduct the related operating expenses.

Using the data provided in Figure 12.1 Lakeside County's expert determined that during the five years of the Lakeside County contract, Evans Marine Services earned little or no profit on its operations as a whole. In particular, the two years the plaintiff's expert used as its base for its estimate of lost profits from fuel sales the company actually experienced a net loss for each of the two years in the period. Additionally, the two years after the county contract was lost, Evans Marine Services experienced two of its most profitable years.

Based on this information, the county's expert is prepared to testify that the evidence shows there was very little or no profit from fuel sales. In order to claim lost profits, a plaintiff must show that profits did occur before the alleged violation occurred and that there is good evidence such profits would continue into the future. A careful review of the data shows that no net profits resulted from the fuel sales. Damages claimed by a plaintiff must be actual lost profits and not merely lost gross profits. To determine the amount of actual lost profits, an entity must deduct any operating business expenses from gross profits to determine net profit. The plaintiff's expert merely used lost gross profits without deducting any operating expenses. The defendant's expert is prepared to testify that the plaintiff used an incorrect measure of lost profits and that the plaintiff has not shown any lost net profits from fuel sales. Additionally, Lakeside County's expert will claim that because there is no evidence that Mr. Evans earned *any net profit* on the sale of fuel, it is illogical and improper to include any component for this in the damage model.

Other Components of the Damage Calculation

As with the plaintiff's expert damage estimate, there are two other components of the damage calculation. One is the FICA tax payments that the employer would have made on the lost salary, and the other is the health insurance premiums the employer would have paid had Mr. Evans not been fired. In the defendant's damage estimate the amounts of the employer FICA tax payments are less than in the plaintiff's damage model, because the FICA tax payments of the defendant are based on only the "net wage loss" as discussed earlier. The estimated damage amount is 7.65 percent of the "net" lost salary that Mr. Evans was not paid because he was fired. For example, in 2008 the net lost salary in the defendant's damage model is $5,630. This amount is multiplied times 7.65 percent yielding $431. This same calculation is made for each of the other years covered by the expert's damage model.

Discounting Amounts to Their Present Value

As with the first estimated damage report, the estimated annual damages are discounted to their present value. In this illustration, the same six percent discount factor that was used by the plaintiff's expert is used. Frequently, experts will disagree in cases on the appropriate discount rate and that will be a point of contention during the litigation. An extensive discussion of evaluating appropriate discount rates is beyond the scope of this chapter.

Other Possible Issues in Determining Damages

There are a number of possible additional issues that may arise in estimating the damages in a case of this nature. For example, Mr. Evans was 55 years old at the time he was fired by Lakeside County. By the end of the alleged damage time period, he will be 65. Although he has a good chance of still being alive and healthy at the age of 65, it is not a certainty. Additionally, Mr. Evans states that he plans to work until he is 65 years old. Many factors, such as health, injury, layoffs, changes in plans, and other issues may arise during the ten-year period that will cause him to leave the work force at an earlier date.

The United States Government maintains a wealth of statistics on the probability of many of these events happening. For example, the U.S. Department of Labor Bureau of Labor Statistics provides tables of "Worklife Estimates: Effects of Race and Education." An expert can use the work life expectancy tables to adjust the previously computed damage estimate to include the probability of the plaintiff leaving the workforce before his stated intended retirement date. Work life expectancy tables take into account a variety of variables such as life expectancy, probability of being disabled, probability of being laid off, and a variety of other issues that may cause a person to leave the work force before he or she originally intended. Of course, the work life expectancy statistics and other government statistics do not relate specifically to Mr. Evans, but there is a widely based set of statistics for the United States population as a whole. Also, many of the statistical categories separate the population by potentially useful characteristics such as education, sex, and race.

Another possible variable that can be used to reflect a more accurate measure of economic damages is life expectancy. At the time of his firing, Mr. Evans was 55 years old. At the time of the illustrated damage calculation, it is three years after the firing of Jeff Evans and he is still alive. Therefore, the issue is what—if any—impact is there of the probability that he will not be alive for some portion of the remaining seven years of the alleged damage period.

To answer this question the National Vital Statistics Report in Table 2, which shows the number of people alive out of an initial population of 100,000 persons, can be used.[5] Statistics are provided for males, females, whites, blacks, and all other categories. "Number alive" data are provided for each age within the various categories mentioned above. The "base year" for Mr. Evans is 58 because that is his age at the current time when this calculation is being made. His probability of being alive right now is 100 percent. From here forward his probability of being alive is less than 100 percent. The probability of being alive during the next seven years of the alleged damage period is computed as follows:

Age	Number Alive	Probability of being Alive
58	92585	1.000
59	91984	0.994
60	91317	0.986
61	90579	0.978
62	89767	0.970
63	88884	0.960
64	87934	0.950
65	86918	0.939

The above probability of life values are used to adjust the Present Value of Damages amounts each year by the probability Mr. Evans will be alive. Notice that the first three years the probability of life is 1.0 because those years are already past and Mr. Evans is alive. As the calculation looks into the future, the probability of life decreases, and the damage amounts reflect this change. The probability of life amounts are plugged into the damage model as shown in Figure 12.6.

Figure 12.6. Damages

Jeff Evans Damages	2008	2009	2010	2011	2012	2013	2014	2015	2016	2017
Salary	$16,341	$16,587	$16,835	$17,088	$17,344	$17,604	$17,869	$18,137	$18,409	$18,685
Minimum Wage Earnings	$10,712	$10,819	$10,927	$11,037	$11,147	$11,258	$11,371	$11,485	$11,600	$11,716
Net Wage Loss	$5,629	$5,768	$5,908	$6,051	$6,197	$6,346	$6,497	$6,652	$6,809	$6,969
FICA	431	441	452	463	474	485	497	509	521	533
Health Insurance	2,415	2,536	2,663	2,796	2,935	3,082	3,236	3,398	3,568	3,746
Fuel Sale Profits	-	-	-	-	-	-	-	-	-	-
Total Damages	8,475	8,744	9,023	9,310	9,607	9,914	10,231	10,559	10,898	11,249
Present Value Factor	1	1	1	0.943	0.89	0.84	0.792	0.747	0.705	0.665
Present Value of Damages	$8,475	$8,744	$9,023	$8,779	$8,550	$8,328	$8,103	$7,887	$7,683	$7,480
Probability of Life	1.000	1.000	1.000	0.994	0.986	0.978	0.970	0.960	0.950	0.939
P.V. of Damages With Prob.of Life	8,475	8,744	9,023	8,727	8,430	8,144	7,860	7,572	7,299	7,024
Total Damages	$81,298									

In this case, the amount of decrease in the estimated economic damages was not that large. Of course, in some cases in which case participants are older, the probability of life calculation can have a big impact on the expected value of the present value of the damages.

¶ 12,101   PERMANENT DISABILITY CASE

This case illustrates many of the issues that may arise in a situation in which the plaintiff has suffered a permanent disability due to a work-related accident. Of course there are countless variations to the possible cases that may arise from an accident causing economic losses. The severity and length of the injury as well as the cause and nature of the accident all may have a significant impact on the determination of liability and the measurement of damages. Similarly, the personal, educational, and other characteristics of the person injured play a major role in measuring economic damages in a personal injury case.

Case Description

Haley Mills has been employed by the C&C Manufacturing Company for 20 years. She is a machine operator who has operated a variety of production machines during her tenure with the company. On January 4, 2005, she was operating company equipment that malfunctioned while she was using it. She was thrown to the floor and severely injured her back. Ms. Mills has had some back trouble before and now she claims that her back has been permanently impaired and that she has trouble standing. An occupational therapist will testify on the plaintiff's behalf that she is no longer able to work and that she is permanently disabled and unable to work for the rest of her life. Ms. Mills further alleges that her back causes her almost constant pain and that she is unable to perform many of her household duties that she was able to perform before the injury.

The forensic accountant has been hired by the plaintiff to prepare a report on estimated damages relating to Haley Mills's job related injury. There is considerable debate over the extent of the injuries in this case and the company's insurance company is contesting the nature and extent of the injuries to Ms. Mills. Although the financial expert plays no role in the determination of the extent of the injuries in a case, the expert must use assumptions about the extent of the injuries and the impact of the injuries on the level of the plaintiff's disability in measuring the amount of economic damages. The role of the financial expert is to assess the damages based on the information provided.

At the time of the injury, Haley Mills was 50 years old. Her stated work goal was to work to the age of 62. Her alleged total disability precludes her from working again. She also claims that her disability has reduced her ability to perform household duties by about one-third.

Based on this information the plaintiff's expert has prepared two schedules in support of the economic damages in this case. Figure 12.7 identifies the present value of the lost wages from the plaintiff's job, and Figure 12.8 depicts the damages she and her husband suffered for lost domestic (household) services. The sum of these two amounts is the economic damages she alleges she suffered from the work-related accident.

Figure 12.7. Lost Earnings

Haley Mills Lost Earnings	2005	2006	2007	2008	2009	2010	2011	2012	2013	2014
Wages	$31,589	$33,042	$34,562	$36,152	$37,815	$39,554	$41,374	$43,277	$45,268	$37,880
Fringe benefits	$6,950	$7,269	$7,604	$7,953	$8,319	$8,702	$9,102	$9,521	$9,959	$8,334
Job-related expenses	$(5,370)	$(5,617)	$(5,876)	$(6,146)	$(6,429)	$(6,724)	$(7,034)	$(7,357)	$(7,696)	$(6,440)
Total Damages	$33,168	$34,694	$36,290	$37,959	$39,706	$41,532	$43,443	$45,441	$47,531	$39,774
Present Value Factor	1.000	1.000	0.943	0.890	0.840	0.792	0.747	0.705	0.665	0.627
Present Value of Damages	$33,168	$34,694	$34,222	$33,784	$33,353	$32,893	$32,452	$32,036	$31,608	$24,938
Adjusted for unemployment rate	$31,858	$33,324	$32,870	$32,449	$32,035	$31,594	$31,170	$30,770	$30,360	$23,953
Present Value of Damages	$31,858	$33,324	$32,870	$32,449	$32,035	$31,594	$31,170	$30,770	$30,360	$23,953
Total Damages	$310,384									

Damage Calculations for Haley Mills

Lost Wages

The damage calculation for Haley Mills includes two components: lost wages and lost fringe benefits. The most obvious component is the lost wages Mills suffered by virtue of the accident and the resulting inability she has of not being able to earn any income. The starting point for measuring Haley Mills's lost wage damages is to evaluate her earnings while she was employed at C&C Manufacturing Company. Her gross wages for the last five years she worked for the C&C Manufacturing Company were as follows:

Year	Wages
2000	$25,600
2001	$26,880
2002	$28,100
2003	$29,100
2004	$30,200

As mentioned in our first example, the starting point for determining lost wages typically is the plaintiff's immediate past work experience. Ms. Mills earned $30,200 in her last year of employment. Additionally, it is determined that over the last five years of her employment she enjoyed wage growth that averaged a bit over 4.2 percent a year. This wage growth is very similar to the average annual compound increase in hourly compensation in the non-farm business sector from 1980 to 2001: 4.6 percent, as provided by the Bureau of Labor Statistics. Therefore, the plaintiff's expert has selected this average annual growth in wages as a good surrogate for the wage growth that Ms. Mills would have experienced during the time period covered by this economic damage calculation.

The first year, 2005, of the lost wages damage estimate is $31,589 which is the plaintiff's 2004 wages of $30,200 times the average wage growth rate of 4.6 percent. Thus, the estimated 2005 salary is $31,589 ($30,200 × 1.046). Each subsequent year's estimated wage loss is the wages of the current year multiplied by 1.046.

Fringe Benefits

Next it is necessary to estimate the amount of employee fringe benefits that were lost as the result of the plaintiff's inability to work because of the accident. In their book, *Economic/Hedonic Damages: The Practice Book for Plaintiff and Defense Attorneys*, Brookshire and Smith define fringe benefits as:

> that residual part of the total compensation provided by an employer to an employee, other than such direct elements of compensation as wages, salary, commission, bonus, overtime, and shift differential payments. Thus,

employer contributions to social security; workers' compensation; unemployment compensation; health, life, and dental insurance; private pension plans; and cafeteria-style benefits plans are among the possible elements of a fringe benefit package. The proper treatment of employer contributions to employee fringe benefit benefits, as a major element of lost earning capacity and economic damages, becomes more important each year.

Brookshire and Smith cite several theoretical bases for including fringe benefits into the calculations of economic damages. Included in their list are (1) the "market theory" which states that an employee has the ability to earn some total package of compensation that includes fringe benefits as a part of the earnings package; (2) the "replacement theory" which states that an employee who is no longer able to work must "replace" all of the components of his or her wage and benefits package; and (3) the "interchangeable nature" of the wages and benefit components meaning that compensation components are fundamentally interchangeable with various components moving from wages to benefits and back as the work compensation package changes.[6]

A careful review of the fringe benefits provided to Ms. Mills and her fellow employees by C&C Manufacturing Company under the union contract suggests that the benefits average about 22 percent of wages. The exact amount of fringe benefits as a percentage of wages is a bit difficult to compute. Some benefits are fixed dollar amounts per person and because some employees earn more than others, the percentage of wages for those benefit items varies with each employee's earnings. Additionally, as wages rise and as various employee benefits and benefit amounts change, employee benefits as a percentage of wage changes as well. Nonetheless, the expert believes that the actual fringe benefit package for employees in Ms. Mills's work class average in the range of 22–26 percent of wages. Therefore, the plaintiff's expert believes the 22 percent fringe benefit amount is fairly conservative.

If the expert believes that the employee benefits data for the plaintiff's company accurately reflect the correct amount of fringe benefits received by the plaintiff while she was working, then those amounts should be used in the calculation of the economic damages in the case. If, however, there is some question about the benefit amounts, it may be logical to use national average statistics for the type of business at which the plaintiff was employed. For example, the U.S. Census Bureau, Statistical Abstract of the United States: 2001 in Schedule No. 615 the "Annual Total Compensation and Wages and Salary Accruals for Full-Time Equivalent Employees by Industry." For "private industry manufacturing" it shows total annual compensation of $50,641.[7] It also shows annual wages and salary of $42,862. Dividing total compensation by wages and salary yields a value of 1.18 ($50,641/$42,862). This means that on average for this business group total compensation includes benefits above the wages and salary that average approximately 18 percent of the wage/salary base.

This average fringe benefit percentage for manufacturing firms of 18 percent could be used as a logical surrogate for the amount of wage fringe benefits that Ms. Mills would lose as a result of the accident. In our example, the expert is reasonably confident about the quality of company-specific fringe benefit data that was developed. Therefore, the estimated company benefit amount of 22 percent is used in Figure 12.7 on wages losses.

Job Related Expenses

When employees lose their job, they lose wages and other benefits, but they also avoid job-related expenses. Union dues, special work clothing or shoes, and job commuting expenses are but a few expenses that employees may avoid when they are no longer employed. To accurately assess economic damages in a job loss case, it may be necessary to estimate the job-related expenses that the employee will be able to avoid.

Haley Mills commuted 25 miles each way to work. The round trip mileage of 50 miles is multiplied by approximately 47 weeks of work yielding 235 days a year of commuting. The total number of commuting miles is multiplied by the IRS mileage rate of $0.385 per mile yielding a commuting cost of $4,524. In addition, Ms. Mills expects to save annual union dues of $240 and annual clothing and shoe costs of $350. The worked-related expenses total to $5,114. This amount represents approximately 17 percent of Haley Mills's 2004 wages. It is assumed that these expenses would grow at approximately the same rate as Ms. Mills's lost wages. Therefore, the damages for wage losses are adjusted to reflect the expected work related expenses that will be avoided with the lost employment.

Adjustment for Unemployment

In order to prepare a realistic measure of lost wages, it is necessary to adjust for common variables that can impair an employee's ability to work. One of those variables is unemployment. The Economic Report of the President provides a significant history of unemployment data. To estimate the probability that Ms. Mills might be unemployed, her expert took a twenty year average of unemployment statistics for "white women over the age of 20." The average for the twenty year period was 3.95 percent. In Figure 12.7, the expert reduced the present value of each year's lost wages and benefits by 3.95 percent.

Discounting Values to their Present Value

As with virtually all damage reports, it is appropriate to discount the estimated annual damages to their present value. In this illustration, a six percent discount factor is used. Frequently, experts will disagree on the appropriate discount rate and that will be a point of contention during the litigation. There are many issues that impact on the selection of an appropriate discount rate. An extensive discussion of evaluating appropriate discount rates is beyond the scope of this chapter. It is worth noting, however, that—all other things being equal—the higher the discount rate, the lower the present value of the damage estimate will be and vice versa.

Adjustment for Expected Worklife

Haley Mills stated that, absent the work-related accident, she intended to work until she was 62 years of age. That would be an additional 12 years of employment after the accident before her intended retirement date. This may well be a reasonable estimate of the time period she would have worked had it not been for the accident that she suffered.

There are factors, however, that may cause an employee to work some period of time less than his or her intended retirement date. Things such as health problems, accidents, probability of death, and probability of being disabled are examples of factors that are incorporated into the U.S. Department of Labor Bureau of Labor Statistics tables on "Worklife Estimates: Effects of Race and Education."[8]

In computing the lost earnings of Haley Mills, the expert used Table A-5 and found an average "worklife expectancy" of a 50-year-old white woman who is currently active in the workforce of 9.8 years. Therefore, instead of using Ms. Mills's stated remaining time in the workforce (until age 62 or 12 years of lost wages) a period of 9.8 years was used. This provides for a fairly conservative and defendable estimate of lost earnings because it adjusts for a variety of factors that may adversely impact on the ability of the plaintiff to work throughout her intended remaining work life. A second factor that makes this a conservative and therefore defendable economic damages estimate is that the government's tables for expected work life are not very current. The participation of women in the work force has increased significantly since the tables were last issued. Therefore, it is likely that more current statistics would provide a longer expected work life than the tables show.

The 9.8 years of expected work life is reflected in the lost earnings damages schedule by including only 9.8 years of damage data rather than the twelve years that would have been indicated by Ms. Mills's statement about her intended retirement age 62. Therefore, the first nine years in the damages schedule (2005–2013) are full years of employment. Year ten in the schedule, which is 2014, is 80 percent of the tenth year's work data.

When all of the factors discussed above are incorporated into the economic damages model for Ms. Mills's lost earnings, the present value of the earnings is $310,384. Of course, this is the major component of the alleged damages for Haley Mills. There is, however, another significant component for damages in disability cases. That is the value of the lost household services that may have occurred because the injured party is no longer able to perform some or all of the duties that the victim was previously able to perform. Below the calculation of damages from the loss of household services is discussed.

Lost Household Services

An accident that causes disabilities that prevent an employee from performing any job-related activities often also causes a decline or elimination of a person's ability to perform household duties. Brookshire and Smith define the loss of household services as "the value of services provided, not to an employer, but rather to a family unit which needs and benefits from those services...The value of these services...is now lost, just as were wages and fringe benefits." They go on to say, "we logically go to the relevant market to value a service performed within the household (but now lost)...Not only does it seem logical and proper to evaluate this element of damages,...it may be a major element of economic loss."[9]

There are a number of factors that influence the measurement of the economic damages related to the loss of household services. Several key issues are how many hours of household services were typically provided by the accident victim, how much of the victim's household services have been lost because of the accident, and what is the dollar value of those lost services.

Each of these issues, as well as other related issues, may be crucial to estimating accurately the economic damages from lost services. When it comes to determining the amount of hours of lost household service time, studies indicate that the sex of the accident victim is important. Although there is some variability of the data on this issue, all studies show that females (whether they are not employed outside the home or whether they are employed full time outside the home) provide far more hours of household services than men. One illustration of this phenomenon can be found in Gerald D. Martin's book *Determining Economic Damages* in his section on "The Value of Household Services."[10]

When preparing an estimate of economic damages for lost household services, the expert should use one of a number of widely cited and peer-reviewed documents that relate to the issue of the value of household services. The plaintiff's expert prepared and reported the damages from loss of household services for Ms. Mills in Figure 12.8. The expert selected one of the commonly cited and utilized studies on measuring the value of household services. The study used by Ms. Mills's expert was performed by D. Peskin and is often referred to as the Peskin study.[11] In the Peskin study, the average hourly time spent by a female on household services is measured for females who work full time outside the home and for those females who do not work outside the home. As would be expected, females working full time outside the home have less time to spend on household services than those who are not employed outside the home. (Nonetheless, full time employed females still spend a significant amount of time engaged in household duties in total and compared to their male counterparts.)

Figure 12.8. Projected Present Value of Lost Household Services

Haley Mills's Projected Present Value of Lost Household Services	Year	Ms. Mills's Age	PESKIN'S 1987 Values	PESKIN'S Adjusted to Current Values	PV Factor	PROJECTED PRESENT VALUE OF LOST HOUSEHOLD SERVICES
1	2005	50	7,725	13,553	1.000	4,518
2	2006	51	7,725	13,553	1.000	4,518
3	2007	52	7,725	13,553	0.971	4,388
4	2008	53	7,725	13,553	0.944	4,263
5	2009	54	7,725	13,553	0.917	4,141
6	2010	55	7,717	13,539	0.890	4,018
7	2011	56	7,717	13,539	0.865	3,903
8	2012	57	7,717	13,539	0.840	3,792
9	2013	58	7,717	13,539	0.816	3,683
10	2014	59	8,759	15,367	0.793	4,061
11	2015	60	12,928	22,681	0.770	5,822
12	2016	61	12,928	22,681	0.748	5,656
13	2017	62	12,928	22,681	0.727	5,494
14	2018	63	12,928	22,681	0.706	5,337
15	2019	64	12,928	22,681	0.686	5,184
16	2020	65	12,605	22,114	0.666	4,910
17	2021	66	12,605	22,114	0.647	4,770
18	2022	67	12,605	22,114	0.629	4,633
19	2023	68	12,605	22,114	0.611	4,501
20	2024	69	12,605	22,114	0.593	4,372
21	2025	70	8,975	15,746	0.576	3,024
22	2026	71	8,975	15,746	0.560	2,937
23	2027	72	8,975	15,746	0.544	2,853
24	2028	73	8,975	15,746	0.528	2,772
25	2029	74	8,975	15,746	0.513	2,693
26	2030	75	6,103	10,707	0.498	1,779
27	2031	76	6,103	10,707	0.484	1,728
28	2032	77	6,103	10,707	0.470	1,678
29	2033	78	6,103	10,707	0.457	1,630
30	2034	79	6,103	10,707	0.444	1,584
31	2035	80	3,546	6,221	0.431	894
						$115,535

The amounts shown in Figure 12.8 in "Peskin's 1987 values" are the amounts that the study showed for the value of household services while employed full time outside the home (the first 9.8 years of the damage calculation). In 2015, the model assumes Ms. Mills no longer would be employed outside the home and the amount of time she would have available to perform household services would therefore increase (absent her injuries of course). In 2025, because of advancing age the study shows that her household service potential would decline.

All of the values in the "Peskin's 1987 values" need to be adjusted to current year wage values. Therefore, the expert used the U.S. Department of Labor, Bureau of Labor Statistics Major Sector Productivity and Cost Index to adjust the 1987 dollars in the Peskin Study to current labor dollar values.[12] The data in this report, which included the index for wage values for "Nonfarm Business," was used to adjust the 1987 wage values to the current period. Thus, the amounts in the column "Peskin's adjusted to current values" are determined by merely adjusting the previous column values to current wage rate values.

The next column to the right is the PV (present value) column in which the current value amounts are adjusted to their present value. This column actually accomplishes two important functions. One function is to adjust (grow) the future values of the household services just as we adjusted the 1987 wages values to the current period. This is done by increasing the value of the household service wages using the average annual compound increase in hourly compensation in the non-farm business sector from 1980–2001: 4.6 percent, as provided by the Bureau of Labor Statistics. In the same column, with one algebraic function the amounts are discounted using the average yields of three-year Treasuries from 1981–2001. Throughout this 20-year period, the yields on 3-year Treasuries have remained quite steady at 7.68 percent. The net discount rate (the difference between growing the earnings 4.6 percent and discounting the amounts 7.68 percent) yields a "net discount rate" of 2.94 percent.

The above discussion addresses the issues of "What is the number of hours of household services that are typically provided by a female?" and "What is the value of those services?" The final issue that must be addressed is, "What is the amount of lost household services time Ms. Mills lost because of the accident?" This is a tough issue that typically is not the expertise of the financial expert witness. Instead, the financial expert usually must rely on the expertise of others. In this case, the expert met with an occupational therapist who is an expert in assessing the skills and abilities of a person who has lost some or all of the household or other skills. After meeting with Haley Mills and performing a number of tests and evaluations, the occupational therapist concluded that she permanently had lost about one third of her abilities to perform her household services. Based on this information, Ms. Mills's expert multiplied the present value of each year's lost value of household services by one third. The amounts for each year are shown in the far right hand column of Figure 12.8. The total of the present value of all lost household services is $115,535 and is shown at the bottom of the column.

The Economic Damages Report of Haley Mills

When the two damage schedules are completed, the expert is ready to prepare the report. The schedule of damages will include a summary of the two schedules that have been discussed in Figures 12.7 and 12.8. The report summary would present something like the following:

> Based upon the information provided and other supporting information listed below, it is my opinion that Ms. Haley Mills suffered damages of $425,919 as the result of this accident. The calculations of these damages are presented in Figures 12.7 and 12.8.

> Figure 12.7 shows the present value of the expected lost income to Ms. Mills. In addition to the amount of damages suffered by Ms. Mills for lost wages, she and her husband also suffered damages for lost household services of $115,535. Below are the assumptions and facts upon which I based my calculation of economic damages for Haley Mills.

Assumptions and facts used in my opinion:
- Haley Mills's birth date is January 4, 1955.
- The accident occurred January 6, 2005.
- Ms. Mills has a high school diploma.
- Ms. Mills was a full-time employee at C&C Manufacturing Company.
- Ms. Mills intended to work until the age of 62.
- As a result of the accident, Ms. Mills lost about one third of her ability to perform her normal domestic household services.
- The interest rates used to discount cash flows to the present are presented in the U.S. Treasury Yield Curve.
- Post-injury earning capacity: None.

Facts Ascertained from Research:
- Age as of January 6, 2005: 50.0 years.
- Work life expectancy of a 50.0 year old white female: 9.8 years remaining.
- Average annual compound increase in hourly compensation in the non-farm business sector from 1980 to 2001: 4.6%.
- Business expenses as a percentage of 2004 earnings: 17%.
- Average yield on three-year United States Treasury securities from 1981 to 2001: 7.68%.

Of course the actual expert's report will contain a complete description of the expert's assumptions, calculations, data sources and other salient factors that related to the research, development, and preparation of the expert report. The expert also will provide whatever supporting materials and persuasive arguments that he or she feels appropriate to provide a professional expert report.

¶ 12,201 CONCLUSION

Determining economic damages for wrongful discharge, personal injury, wrongful death, and other types of issues requires special knowledge and understanding of those factors that typically impact on the measurement of economic damages. This chapter presented an overview of many of the factors that influence an expert's evaluation of and calculation of damages in such cases.

The issues considered in this chapter often are complex and comprehensive. The facts in each case dictate what the expert must evaluate and how the expert should approach the measurement of economic damages. When faced with an actual case of the sort discussed in this chapter, it would be necessary to delve into the various topics presented in this chapter to achieve a better working knowledge of the relevant issues related to the case at hand. In some cases, the issues can become very complex.

ENDNOTES

[1] Gerald D. Martin and Ted Vavoulis, *Determining Economic Damages* (James Publishing, Incorporated, 2002).

[2] *Ibid*, pp. 3-8.4-10.

[3] U.S. Department of Labor, Bureau of Labor Statistics average wage increase for nonagricultural workers from 1999 through 2004.

[4] Brookshire and Smith, *Economic/Hedonic Damages: The Practice Book for Plaintiff and Defense Attorneys* (Cincinatti: Anderson Publishing Company, 1990).

[5] NATIONAL VITAL STATISTICS REPORT, Vol. 47, No. 13, Table 2, December 24, 1998, p. 9.

[6] Brookshire and Smith, *Economic/Hedonic Damages: The Practice Book for Plaintiff and Defense Attorneys* (Cincinatti: Anderson Publishing Company, 1990), pp. 69-71.

[7] The U.S. Census Bureau, Statistical Abstract of the United States: 2001 presents in Schedule No. 615 the "Annual Total Compensation and Wages and Salary

Accruals for Full-Time Equivalent Employee by Industry."

[8] Labor Bureau of Labor Statistics tables on "Worklife Estimates: Effects of Race and Education," 1986, table A-5, p. 19.

[9] Brookshire and Smith, *Economic/Hedonic Damages: The Practice Book for Plaintiff and Defense Attorneys* (Cincinatti: Anderson Publishing Company, 1990), pp. 87-89.

[10] Gerald D. Martin and Ted Vavoulis, *Determining Economic Damages* (James Publishing, Incorporated, 2002), p. 6-12.

[11] Douglass, Kenney, and Miller, "Which Estimates of Household Production are Best?" JOURNAL OF FORENSIC ECONOMICS 4 (1) (1990), pp. 25-45.

[12] U.S. Department of Labor, Bureau of Labor Statistics Major Sector Productivity and Cost Index, Series ID:prs85006103, March 26, 2003.

EXERCISES

1. What makes measuring damages in personal cases different from the cases described in Chapter 10?

2. What are some of the characteristics of a victim in a personal injury case that might impact on the calculation of economic damages?

3. Given that typically both the plaintiff's and the defendant's experts start their estimation of damages with the plaintiff's actual wages data, how can they come to different conclusions about the amounts of wage loss damages?

4. What are commonly used components when measuring economic damages in a wrongful discharge case? Describe each component and explain why it should be used in the damage calculation.

5. What are fringe benefits? What are common components of fringe benefits?

6. Should fringe benefits be used in the computation of economic damages in a wrongful discharge case? Why or why not?

7. Describe some of the commonly used theories for the inclusion of fringe benefits in the computation of economic damages.

8. What are some of the commonly used resources that experts use in evaluating a personal injury case and in computing economic damages?

9. What kind of information can be found in the "Economic Report of the President?" Find a web site that contains the "Economic Report of the President" and review the information that is available there. What did you find that (1) was unexpected, (2) was most interesting to you, and (3) you think might have the greatest value to an expert in measuring economic damages?

10. If a plaintiff in a case is currently alive and healthy, why is it appropriate to adjust damage estimates for "probability of life?"

11. If a plaintiff states clearly that he or she plans to stay in the workforce until the age of 65, then there is no need to adjust any damage calculations for "expected work life." Do you agree with this statement? Why or why not?

12. Go to the web and find the U.S. Department of Labor: Bureau of Labor Statistics. Review the materials that you found. What did you find that (1) was unexpected, (2) was most interesting to you, and (3) you think might have the greatest value to an expert in measuring economic damages?

13. What, if anything, would be different in evaluating the economic damages between a case in which an employee was permanently disabled in a job-related accident and a case in which an employee was killed in a job-related accident?

14. Describe the nature of damages that result in the loss of household services.

15. What are the components of measuring the economic damages from the loss of household services?

16. Describe how an expert would evaluate the economic damages resulting from the loss of household services.

17. Go to the web and find The U.S. Census Bureau, Statistical Abstract of the United States. Review the information provided. What did

you find that (1) was unexpected, (2) was most interesting to you, and (3) you think might have the greatest value to an expert in measuring economic damages?

18. What is the role of a financial expert in the determination of the extent of injuries and the amount of disability resulting from an accident?

19. What, if any, use does a financial expert witness make of information relating to the extent of injury or disabilities a plaintiff experienced as the result of an accident?

20. What is meant by "job-related costs?" What are some common components of job-related costs?

21. Do job related costs enter into the calculation of economic damages? If so, how are they used? What is the logic for using job-related costs in a damage calculation?

22. What is meant by "mitigation" of damages with respect to lost wages?

23. You were a "whistle-blower" in a case in Montana. You successfully proved to the court that you were wrongfully discharged. During the damages phase of the case, the company that fired you argued that you did not mitigate your wage loss damages by getting another job. You argue that you have applied at over 30 businesses in the region over the last six years and no one has been willing to hire you. What is the most likely outcome of these arguments? Why?

24. Go to the web and look for The U.S. Census Bureau, Statistical Abstract of the United States: 2001. What kind of information did you find? What information that you found seems like it would be useful in measuring economic damages?

25. Jimmy Jones was on his way to work when he was hit broadside by a truck that ran a red light. Jimmy suffered twenty seven broken bones, numerous lacerations, and a variety of other medical problems. Mr. Jones was in the hospital for two months and he has been recovering at home for the past four months. He is certain that he will never be able to work again. At the time of the accident, Mr. Jones was 35 years old. The insurance company for the trucking company that hit Jimmy Jones is not sure that he is completely disabled and they intend to contest that issue. You have been hired as a financial expert witness by the

attorney of Jimmy Jones to assist in this case. You have visited Jimmy several times and you are certain he is never going to return to his pre-accident health.

   a.   What is your role in supporting Jimmy's disability claim?
   b.   What are the possible/probable components of Jimmy's economic damage claim?
   c.   What information will you seek from Jimmy/his lawyer and what information/research will you pursue on your own?
   d.   What information, if any, will you seek from Jimmy's attorney about the nature and severity of Jimmy's injuries and the extent of his disability?

26. Fred is a successful dentist in Boston. He has a comprehensive injury and a disability insurance policy that he has carried since shortly after he started his practice. During the first 15 years of his practice he has experienced the following net income:

Year	Net Income
1	$56,000
2	64,000
3	70,000
4	77,000
5	85,000
6	93,000
7	101,000
8	110,000
9	124,000
10	135,000
11	145,000
12	156,000
13	120,000
14	117,000
15	121,000

At the beginning of his 13th year of practice he experienced an accident at the office in which he fell and hit his head. Ever since the accident he has experienced serious headaches and dizziness that he had not experienced before. As a result of these symptoms, Fred is unable to work the long hours that he once did and he has been unable to grow his practice. He fully expected to grow his income from his practice by about 10 percent a year. He has filed a claim (which is being contested) with his insurance company.

Fred has hired you to prepare a measure of economic damages resulting from the accident. Fred was 42 years old at the time of the accident and he just turned 45 last week.

   a.   What information will you seek from Fred to help with your measurement of economic damages?
   b.   What do you think will comprise the components of your damage measurement?
   c.   Based on the information available to you, prepare your best estimate of the damages that you will seek on behalf of Fred.

PART 4
CYBERCRIME

chapter

13

INVESTIGATION OF ELECTRONIC DATA: A BRIEF INTRODUCTION

RAM disk is not an installation procedure.

– Anonymous

They have computers, and they may have other weapons of mass destruction.

– Janet Reno

Those parts of the system that you can hit with a hammer are called hardware; those program instructions that you can only curse at are called software.

– Anonymous

OBJECTIVES

After completing Chapter 13, you should be able to:
1. Define computer forensics.
2. Use several basic computer forensic techniques.
3. Understand the difference between digital and paper-based evidence.
4. Understand the technical skills needed to perform computer forensics investigations.
5. Understand the fragility of electronic evidence and the importance of preserving such data.
6. Become familiar with data mining concepts and strategies.
7. Understand the difference between computer forensics and data mining methods.

OVERVIEW

Computer forensics is the analysis of electronic data and residual data for the purposes of its recovery, legal preservation, authentication, reconstruction, and presentation to solve or aid in solving technology-based crimes. Useful digital courtroom evidence is evidence that can be legally viewed as "witnessing" an event and providing reliable identification of the user of a computer. Generally, useless digital courtroom evidence is classified as hearsay evidence *albeit* documentary hearsay. Computer forensics is restricted to the investigation of computer data. When the forensics investigations go beyond computer, it is called digital forensics.

Although it may appear that computer forensics is outside the purview of the forensic accountant, it needs to be recognized that there is little financial fraud committed today not involving a computer. For that reason, the forensic accountant and accountants, in general, need to be aware of the ways that computer evidence is collected and the ways that it is different from paper evidence. Paper evidence is still important, but a complete understanding of financial fraud cannot be completed without analyzing computer evidence.

THE DISAPPEARING PAPER TRAIL. What's wrong with these fraud detection techniques?

1. Exam erasure marks.
2. Exam typed documents for traces of counterfeiting and unique characteristics of the typewriter's key marks.
3. Examine paper documents for double folds.
4. Use of correction fluid on documents.
5. Missing paper checks.
6. Identify false paper vouchers.

And the answer is:

It is hard to find rubber erasure marks on digital data, and with today's accounting systems, unauthorized modifications to documents are done electronically. Although these fraud detection methods were cutting edge in the 1960s, they only provide minimum value with today's electronic forensic investigations. The paper audit trail is disappearing. Today, it is necessary to electronically examine and map the flow of funds, immediately investigate suspicious transactions and supporting documentation from a database, and create reports with charts and graphs that demonstrate the financial fraud. The number of transactions needing to be examined can only be done electronically. Further, the client will not accept the billing charges needed to manually examine these documents or the charges to develop unique spreadsheets for the analysis. Third party software, such as Crystal Reports, allows for the reporting and analysis of large amounts of financial data without the possibility of corrupting the electronic information.

Paper evidence and electronic evidence are so different that if investigators are largely familiar with the use of paper evidence in crime investigations, they are likely to have difficulty incorporating electronic evidence into their crime analysis or brain storming activities. Even thinking about the nature of the digital-based crime has to change from the linear view used with paper evidence to a more dynamic view present with electronic evidence. For example, handwritten signatures using a pen are only going to be found on paper documents. Paper evidence only displays the dates printed on the document. Finding dates on electronic documents differs significantly as there are many dates. There are the dates on the document as well as the date when the document was created, accessed, or last modified. In addition, there may be dated cached versions of the document that also need to be reviewed for the investigation. The investigator needs to know how to determine if any of these dates have been altered by the technically savvy criminal.[1] Thus, electronic data provides the investigator with a more complex set of steps in a financial investigation than piling up stacks of paper documents and going through them to find erasure marks.

WHO DID WHAT? Evidence collected for a criminal trial showed Harry Towns, a clerk at Hobarts Department Store, had diverted payroll funds from nonexistent employees into an offshore numbered account. Harry's username and password had been used 20 times to divert payroll monies. One of the store's internal auditors testified the clerk was fraudulently diverting funds from the organization's payroll accounts. The store wanted Harry to repay $25,000 of diverted monies and face a prison term. Harry's lawyer hired a forensic accountant who was familiar with computer forensics methods. The accountant quickly determined that although Harry's username and password were used, the network logs showed the IP address was from a computer belonging to the Vice President of Operations. Further checking on this computer determined the VP had been diverting monies using Harry's IDs. Eventually, the VP returned the missing cash and resigned. Harry decided to resign, too, after receiving a large cash settlement from Hobarts.[2]

Introduction to Electronic Evidence[3]

¶ 13,001   PERSPECTIVES ON INVESTIGATION

Electronic evidence of a crime is contained on employer-owned personal computers (PCs) and mainframes, employees' personal laptops, the company's network, personal data assistants, blackberries, digital cameras, pagers, iPads, external drives, dongles (security devices that must be connected to a computer in order for certain software to run), memory sticks, scanners, floppy disks, smart cards, cell phones, and web servers in external networks.[4] Such electronic evidence easily and unintentionally can be destroyed or made inadmissible as courtroom evidence by the actions of those who first find the evidence and are uninformed as to how such data should be handled.[5] Further, electronic evidence is likely to vanish more quickly than any paper evidence. For example, original paper documents can be copied and used in court, but when original digital files are copied, they are essentially destroyed for evidentiary purposes.[6]

A computer may contain electronic evidence of criminal activity for two reasons. First, when the PC is the target of a criminal, it contains evidence of the attack. Stealing financial data, such as credit card or pin numbers, on a server is an example of such an attack. Second, a PC may be a tool or instrument used to commit a crime. Such an example is an employee's workplace computer being used to carry out a financial fraud. Although it is unlikely the traditional auditor would be responsible for the final analysis of the data contained on the hard drive of such PCs, it is likely that an auditor may be the first person on the scene when such crimes are uncovered. The auditor's actions from initial fraud suspicions to the beginning of evidence analysis by the forensic specialists will determine whether the electronic data on these computers can be used to identify who was responsible for the crime. Taking correct actions at the initial discovery point is vital for preserving such evidence.

HOW MANY E-MAILS DO I HAVE TO READ? If an employee receives 30 e-mails per day or 7,500 e-mails per year and there are 500 employees in a company, the total number of e-mails received through the company's e-mail system is 3,750,000 each year. If 20 percent of those e-mails contain attachments, then there are 750,000 attachments and 3,750,000 e-mails that have the potential for containing electronic evidence. Yet if e-mail collection is not properly handled, for example the improper shutting down of a mail server, this evidence is unusable as it is considered altered.

¶13,011   AUDITOR'S JOB AS RELATED TO COMPUTER FORENSICS

A question that should be asked is: "Does computer forensics have anything to do with the auditor's job functions?" Bigler states that auditors often have responsibilities for investigations of computer-based "frauds, harassment, theft, pornography, or deception committed by employees, contractors, vendors, customers or other third parties."[7]

Currently, auditors have several auditing standards to provide them with guidance in dealing with fraud and illegal acts by their clients. American Institute of Certified Public Accountants' (AICPA) Statement on Auditing Standards (SAS) No. 31, *Evidential Matter*, provides guidelines for audit engagements encountering electronic documents.[8] It states that for an accounting system predominately evaluated through the use of electronic audit evidence, it may not be practical or possible to reduce detection risk to an acceptable level using only substantive tests for financial statement assertions. In these cases, the auditor should perform tests of system controls to show they are strong enough to mitigate the risks inherent in electronic audit evidence. Together with system control tests, substantive evidence should be strong enough for the auditor to issue an opinion. Such an audit may require the use of generalized audit software or a continuous audit module to test controls.

SAS No. 80, *Amendment to SAS No. 31, Evidential Matter*, updates SAS No. 31 and provides guidance for audits of entries processing, maintaining or accessing significant amounts of information electronically.[9] Under situations where detection risk levels cannot be reduced with increased substantive tests, auditors are required to test controls in order to make satisfactory assertions regarding reporting risks in the organization and provide the basis for an unqualified opinion. SAS No. 80 defines evidential matter as consisting of both written and electronic information, e.g. written checks and electronic fund transfers, respectively. The SAS recognizes that time lapse is an important consideration for substantive and control tests as electronic evidence is not retrievable after a certain time period. *The Information Technology Age: Evidential Matter in the Electronic Environment* (ITA) was issued to provide additional nonauthoritative guidance for SAS No. 80.[10] Its recommendations include the need for the auditor to have a good understanding of how electronic evidence is extracted from networks, and it discusses issues related to the deliberate manipulation of electronic data.

Further guidelines are provided in SAS No. 54, *Illegal Acts by Clients*, and SAS No. 99, *Consideration of Fraud in a Financial Statement Audit*.[11] SAS No. 99 provides guidelines for testing digital data. It states that:

> In an IT environment, it may be necessary for the auditor to employ computer-assisted audit techniques (for example, report writers, software or data extraction tools, or other system-based techniques) to identify the journal entries and other adjustments to be tested.[12]

SAS No. 99 went into effect on December 15, 2002. Under the SAS, the rules for fraud investigation have been expanded and the auditor is expected to display an increased attitude of skepticism throughout the audit.[13] The auditor must identify the risks of material misstatement in the financial reports and write up the results of the analysis. Auditors must brainstorm to identify ways that fraud could be committed in the audited organization.

In January 2007, the Public Company Accounting Oversight Board (PCAOB) issued Release No. 2007-001 titled "Observations on Audits' Implementation of PCAOB Standards Relating to Auditors' Responsibilities with Respect to Fraud." The somewhat critical Release contains observations on the manner auditing firms are implementing their fraud responsibilities under SAS No. 99.[14] In regard to the role of computer analysis, the PCAOB reiterated that brainstorming team sessions should involve information technology specialists, and such experts should be used to evaluate computer records to detect the manipulation of electronic journal entries. These PCAOB recommendations imply that financial auditors need a clear understanding of the fraud implications found in warnings provided by computer forensic experts.

SPOTLIGHT

WHO'S THAT PUTTING ENTRIES IN MY ACCOUNTS NOW? Herb Lowe worked in accounts payable at Safe and Good, a large supermarket. The company's management discovered the company had been paying fraudulent invoices. With a warrant, police seized a computer in Herb's home. Upon digitally examining files in the computer, it was determined that Herb had been scanning legitimate numbered invoices into his computer and using them to produce false invoices for a bogus company. Further examination of the digital entries and slack space in the corporate computers uncovered a repeating list of unauthorized changes in payees' names.[15] It was determined that Herb would enter the invoices into the accounting system as being from one of Safe and Good's regular vendors. The company printed its payable checks once a week. Just before the checks were run, Herb would electronically change the payee's name on the check to his bogus company. After the checks were printed, he would change the payee back to the company's regular vendor. Herb is now in jail. Although this crime was committed by an employee, it could have been just as easily committed by an outside hacker who gained unauthorized access to Safe and Good's computer network.[16]

Sarbanes-Oxley's Extensions

The primary purpose of the Sarbanes-Oxley Act[17] is to help avoid the financial frauds of the last decade. The approach taken in the legislation is (1) to make management directly responsible for the integrity of the company's financial statements and (2) to require a strengthening of internal control procedures. Added assurances need to be made regarding the level of information integrity, protection of financial records, accuracy of financial representations, and assertions that reporting systems are working as designed. Section 404 requires that these validations need to be performed by the external auditors. Auditors need to map and monitor the electronic path of applications as they go through networks, servers, databases, various operating systems, and software programs in order to perform these validations.

Digital security over data and electronic transactions is critical if a company is going to demonstrate that it has adequate corporate financial controls under Sarbanes-Oxley. Therefore, if a company and its external auditors cannot recover and preserve digital data, for example, it is questionable whether they are meeting the need for corporate financial controls under Sarbanes-Oxley. Further, if there are design failures or weaknesses in the financial reporting of digital data, it may mean there is a significant deficiency or a material weakness under Sarbanes-Oxley.[18] This is a different perspective than was found in the practices promulgated by the AICPA's Auditing Standards Board.

The Securities and Exchange Commission (SEC), in developing its rules under Section 404, identified the internal control framework developed by the Committee of Sponsoring Organizations of the Treadway Commission (COSO)[19] as the recommended guide to use in evaluating the effectiveness of management's internal control procedures.[20] The SEC stated in 2003 that the COSO framework satisfies its criteria for internal control.[21] The COSO framework recognizes strong internal controls for preventing financial frauds. In making this recommendation, the SEC stepped away from existing AICPA accounting practice guidelines used in preventing or detecting digital fraud.[22]

The general information technology (IT) guidelines under the COSO framework have been established for the following eight areas:
1. Internal control environment,
2. Objective setting,
3. Event identification,
4. Risk assessment,
5. Risk response,
6. Control activities,
7. Information and communication, and
8. Monitoring.

Evaluating the internal control environment means the underlying corporate culture is evaluated for its views on risk including risk-taking, ethical values, and adequate controls. Objective-setting evaluates whether there is a process in place for setting objectives that correspond with the organization's mission. Event identification tries to determine how internal and external occurrences are separated by the organization into risk and opportunity classifications and then how they correlate with objectives. Risk assessment determines whether there is an effective response for managing IT risks faced by the organization. Risk response deals with avoiding, accepting or reducing such identified risk. Control activities evaluate controls to determine whether effective controls are in place to work effectively in controlling IT risk. Communication must be established so that it allows information to be broadly shared up and down the organization. It is also important to have assurances that the proper information is identified and captured. Correct monitoring is in place if it can be verified that the controls in place are effective enough so that when weaknesses are detected there are corrective actions taken.

If it is found that users' access to the organization's network is not occurring correctly, this is a potentially serious risk event. An organization with a good internal control environment has immediate concerns about this situation and identifies it as a risk event. Risk assessment policies are then used to access the level of risk, and risk response in this case is applied to correct the network access problem. Management is immediately made aware of the problem and encourages others to identify other instances of improper access to the system. A clear understanding is given to employees as to why these organizational changes are instituted and why these changes will reduce fraud risks. Afterwards, monitoring of the system is necessary to make certain the enacted remedies are (1) actually being used and (2) evaluate their effectiveness.

During an audit, serious weakness in IT controls should be recognized as a weakness in the financial system. Consideration should be given to using a standard network vulnerability analysis as part of the risk assessment procedures. Network vulnerability software is commercially available to test a system's weakness to attacks and any unauthorized access.

WHAT DO'YA WAN'NA BE? What knowledge, skills, and abilities do you need to become a forensic accountant? The following job advertisement from a large oil company for a forensic accountant provides an indication:

Fraud/Forensic Accountant:
- Thorough knowledge and experience with PC's including Microsoft Office, SAP, and Guidance Encase software.
- Strong verbal and written communications and interpersonal skills are required.
- Experience in executing audits/investigations relating to allegations of fraudulent activities using forensic accounting principles, computer forensic procedures, data-mining techniques, and witness/subject interview methodology is desired.
- Minimum ten years audit experience, with at least five years experience in forensic and/or fraud auditing.
- Bachelors or Master's degree with a professional certification such as Certified Internal Auditor (CIA), Certified Fraud Examiner (CFE), Certified Information Forensics Investigator (CIFI), Certified Forensic Computer Examiner (CFCE) or Certified Electronic Evidence Collection Specialist (CEECS).

The PCAOB

The Public Company Accounting Oversight Board (PCAOB) was created by Sarbanes-Oxley (SOX) legislation, and it was given authority over auditors' attestation standards with the purpose of protecting investors from the recent financial fraud abuses.[23] The PCAOB has taken over setting auditing standards for auditors from the Auditing Standards Board of the

AICPA.[24] The PCAOB, under an SEC approval process and SOX Section 404, is responsible for adopting auditing and practice rules over public accounting firms auditing public companies listed on U.S. stock exchanges that are registered with the SEC. One of the most significant actions taken by the PCAOB in fraud prevention has been the approval of Auditing Standard No. 2, *An Audit of Internal Control Over Financial Reporting Performed in Conjunction with an Audit of Financial Statements.*[25] Standard No. 2 is directed at evaluating internal control design and operating effectiveness as it relates to financial reporting. The PCAOB recognizes the importance of the underlying role played by technology in the process:

> The nature and characteristics of a company's use of information technology in its information system (IS) affect the company's internal control over financial reporting.[26]

PCAOB guidelines require auditors to understand the flow of electronic transactions from their introduction to their aggregation on an organization's financial reports. The PCAOB stresses the importance of IT to good internal control with much more emphasis than did the Auditing Standards Board. The purpose of these guidelines is in providing assurances that the financial statements generated by an automated system can be relied upon.

PCAOB Standard No. 2 does not outline, other than in a general fashion, the steps necessary to achieve proper internal IS controls needed to prevent financial fraud. For example, antifraud programs and controls are mentioned,[27] but little detail is provided about what composes good antifraud programs. For those who need more detailed guidelines, the Control of Business Information Technology (COBIT) model is more helpful. In 2010, PCAOB Standard No. 12, Appendix A, B4, indicated the auditor should evaluate risks related to unauthorized access to a network that might cause the destruction, manipulation or incorrect recording of financial data. Assurances need to provided that electronic data cannot be manipulated through unauthorized access.[28] Without control over electronic data, there can be no assurances regarding annual financial statements themselves so it is important to know what controls are being used, but also to know what controls should be used to prevent unauthorized access. For example, an electronic transaction system should provide assurances that: (1) There are there controls to assure that records coming out of one database are actually entering a second; (2) The total dollar amount sent equals the total dollar amount received; (3) Transfers are reconciled; (4) Duplicated transfers can be detected; (5) The system provides for checks to prevent specific transactions from disappearing; and (6) Time data provides information as to whether the transfers occur instantly or whether there is a time delay between when the data is sent and when it is received.

COBIT's Extensions

An IT audit should be tightly coordinated with a company's financial audit. The Information System Audit and Control Association (ISACA) issued guidelines to use in evaluating the internal control for high-tech networks with a special orientation toward financial audits in its most recent COBIT publications.[29] Two such publications are *IT Control Objectives for Sarbanes-Oxley: The Importance of IT in the Design, Implementation and Sustainability of Internal Control over Disclosure and Financial Reporting*[30] and *IS Standards, Guidelines and Procedures for Auditing and Control Professionals.*[31] COBIT guidelines provide a set of detailed IT control practices that can be used to evaluate company standards against established benchmarks. The COBIT guidelines expand the general guides found in the COSO requirements, recommended by the SEC, and provide a specific framework for evaluating and reducing high technology fraud risks present in a networked environment. *IS Standards, Guidelines, and Procedures for Auditing and Control Professionals* provides certification standards for IT guidelines that should be followed during an IT audit. These guidelines include evaluations of control objectives and practices as well as audit practices. The guidelines describe management practices related to performance measurement, IT profiling, and benchmarking.

IT Control Objectives for Sarbanes-Oxley defines IT controls specifically within the context of financial reporting issues and under Sarbanes-Oxley legislation. The ISACA is coordinating its internal control issues, normally the bailiwick of the accounting profession, to meet Sarbanes-Oxley directives. The ISACA believes that monitoring the effectiveness of internal control over financial reporting can only be successful if IT is correctly implemented.

Good network security includes: (1) limited access to financial applications, (2) limited access within the financial application, (3) access controls over digital documents prepared within the application, (4) monitoring of security violations through reviews of audit logs, (5) required changes in passwords, and (6) the monitoring of application access logs. Computer job applications must be monitored showing job scheduling, actual job runs, and anomalies related to these applications. Without such controls, the financial reporting system is at risk.

For example, one aspect of COBIT's internal control begins with identifying the risks to financial reporting, mitigating them, and monitoring to ensure that risk reduction methodologies and policies remain effective. Risk assessment identifies those events that can impact financial reporting goals, such as a network security failure and its corresponding effects on financial reporting. Regarding unauthorized access points, *IT Control Objectives for Sarbanes-Oxley* states:

> Effective access security controls can provide a reasonable assurance against inappropriate access and unauthorized use of systems. If well designed, they can intercept unethical hackers, malicious software and other intrusion attempts.[32]

ISO/IEC 17799:2005 Information Technology—Security Techniques— Code of Practice for Information Security Management

This ISO is published by the International Organization for Standardization and the International Electrotechnical Commission. ISO guides were first used in Europe, but they have gained global acceptance and use as quality standardization measures for the protection of valuable information assets. ISO 17799 provides 139 control guides for information security. In July 2007, the ISO was renumbered to ISO/IEC 27002:2005, but except for this numbering revision, it is the same as ISO 17799. The ISO standardizes international best practices for corporate information security. The sections of the ISO are: (1) security policy; (2) organization of information security; (3) asset management; (4) human resources security; (5) physical and environmental security; (6) communications and operations management; (7) access control; (8) information systems acquisition, development, and maintenance; (9) information security incident management; (10) business continuity management; and (11) compliance. The guidelines in these chapters help organizations meet the IT security control requirements under the Sarbanes-Oxley Act. When information assets are not properly protected, it creates questions regarding business continuity, potential increases in abnormal losses, lower return on investment, and reduced business opportunities.

An important purpose of implementing the ISO's guidelines is to create confidence in inter-organizational interactions and lower vulnerability risks. For example, if a cybercriminal cannot directly penetrate the organizational security at one business entity, their next step is to identify a trusted partner or subsidiary with weaker security and gain unauthorized access through the weaker partner. With effective implementation of ISO security guidelines and continued monitoring, world-wide business organizations have less concern that access to their computer systems is set by the security at their weakness link.

Under ISO guidelines, one of the first steps in securing information assets is to inventory information assets. These intangible assets have to be located before security measures can be implemented. The Big Four along with Grant Thornton and BDO International note:

> The value of many companies resides in various "intangible" assets (such as employee creativity and loyalty, and relationships with suppliers and customers). However, information to assess the value of these intangibles is not consistently reported.[33]

There are many cases in which the accountant can help in the identification of intangible information assets critical to the company's business operations especially current and archived digital financial data. For financial statements, the typically-recognized intangible assets are patents, licenses, and copyrights. Although the information in these assets needs to be secured, there are other valuable intangible assets recorded in databases such as business contracts, mathematical algorithms for encryption, archived e-mail, intellectual property for cloning, customer lists, digital images, business computer model for targeting new customers, specific project e-documents, submitted bid proposals, financial model for picking stocks, in-house developed add-on software, financial databases, information processing methodology, and other cyber property that have value. Also there are digital assets that have independences that would make losing one create a usage loss with a second digital asset. These interrelationships and their ultimate effect on business operations must be understood in valuing the identified assets. The accountant needs to ensure that information security measures are extended to this digital property. Once these information assets are identified, the accountant needs to determine who is responsible for maintaining and updating the digital data.

What should you, as a financial auditor, consider in making a security risk assessment at a small-to-medium size company and their recently outsourced payroll functions? Obviously there are numerous areas related to the security risks ranging from securing information to possibly the flow of information across international borders. Yet, one common aspect of securing financial information is related to encryption and potential data breaches. To assess the security risks in outsourcing payroll functions, the following questions should be asked about encryption.

- What is the encryption algorithm being used? (Hopefully not DES!)
- What is the encryption's algorithm's vulnerability to cracking?
- At what points in the sending and receiving process are the documents encrypted and decrypted?
- How is the outsourced system continually monitored for keyloggers?
- Do computer audit logs record the what, when, and who encrypted data?
- Do computer audit logs record errors in the decryption process and analyze the reasons for those errors to determine if data has been compromised?

SPOTLIGHT

LET IT DO IT! The IT security at a Midwest financial services company was described as "first rate." The department followed a strong IT audit schedule and had funding to adopt new technologies. The financial services company had always received a "clean" audit opinion from their accounting firm which relied on risk assessment reports provided by the IT Department. The Department was shocked when it was uncovered that one of their IT employees had been "doctoring" his payroll records and increasing the amount of overtime pay that he was receiving in each pay period. The financial fraud was uncovered because the employee's pay stub was accidently seen by a third party who knew those levels of overtime were not legitimate. Although the dollar value of the loss to the Company was not significant, the fraud is an indication that auditors did not fully understand the flow of electronic transactions from their introduction to their aggregation on the organization's financial reports. Further, it is provides an example where the financial audit team needs to be more conversant with underlying issues of access security as well as the other common information risks associated with such a problem.

Computer Forensics: Electronic Evidence Collection

¶13,021 CAN DIGITAL EVIDENCE REALLY BE DESTROYED?

Auditors who discover financial files that appear fraudulent in their testing procedures must know how to use or at least understand the purpose of electronic data investigative tools, or quickly bring in a specialist who knows how to use these techniques. It should be noted there is a difference between the procedures used for traditional data extraction, i.e., data mining, and data investigation for evidentiary purposes. With traditional data extraction in an auditing environment, tools such as Interactive Data Extraction and Analysis (IDEA) or ACL software are used to interactively extract, sample, and analyze data during an audit. Yet by simply checking a client's files or cross comparing data, digital files for forensic investigations are contaminated. For forensic purposes and courtroom use, imaging software tools collect digital data without affecting data integrity.[34] Examples of these forensic investigative tools are EnCase, SafeBack, Helix, and Ontrack's Easy Recovery software. EnCase provides bitstream copies of the hard drive.[35] The bitstream copies are images of the original electronic files including the unused space in the file, thus providing a key to information from previously deleted files. It should be understood that deleting a file by clicking on the delete key does not really delete that file. It simply records a notation in the computer's master database that the space previously used by the deleted file is now available for new data. Such "deleted" data that is partially overwritten can be recovered with imaging tools so it is difficult to really delete electronic files, but it is easy to contaminate them.

Another effect that lessens the investigative usefulness of digital evidence is the passage of time. Increasing the time lag between initial fraud suspicions and the recovery of the related digital data makes the evidence less valuable. Time lags will increase as managerial clearance decisions are made about whether to use a forensic team. The problem is critical because data contained on the organization's workplace machines are continuously in use, so data are overwritten and losses continue. In addition, an extended time lag allows a suspect to become aware that an investigation is about to occur, and the suspect can then begin to change and denigrate the electronic evidence to better hide the fraud.

Auditors need to use data extraction tools on imaged copies and not create more problems for the forensic investigator by unknowingly changing original evidence files. Computer forensics training can help accountants gain the needed technical skills to understand how to work with digital forensic evidence.

¶13,031 THE AUDITOR'S COMPUTER FORENSICS SKILL SET

The underlying evidence from electronic financial frauds is found in text files, swap file space (i.e., space on a hard disk used as a memory extension), cache (i.e., memory used for the temporary storage of data to speed up data transfers), deleted files, e-mail, slack space in clusters (i.e., the amount of excess and unused hard disk space found in a newly saved file), logs from the local area network (LAN), WiFi connections, or external networks. Such digital information needs to be properly collected and secured. Shackell writes, "Conversely, the wrong actions at this early stage [of the fraud investigation] can lead to a botched investigation, destruction of evidence, financial loss and possibly, action against you [the accounting firm] and/or the company."[36] Any audit data mining software used to search for underlying patterns in records or extracting data from files must not alter the underlying data needed for the digital investigation.[37]

The technical skills needed for working with digital evidence collection are based on the following six requirements.

1. *Understanding of Various Operating Systems.* The auditor may have to conduct a preliminary review of electronic financial data. The analysis needs to be conducted quickly with an evidentiary search of the target data on various operating systems (OSs). Thus, the auditor needs a basic familiarity with different OSs and their network file architecture in order to locate pertinent files.

2. *Quickly Identifying Pertinent Digital Data.* The auditor needs to know how to perform a read-only search that will not alter the data in order to quickly investigate any fraud suspicions. If there is a time constraint for collecting data, the most volatile data, such as cached data, needs to be collected first. At one time, there was only 516MB of random access memory or RAM, but today it is measured in GBs.[38] It is important to preserve such extensive sources of electronic evidence as it may contain the remnants of altered documents, for example.

3. *Properly Preserving Data.* The auditor needs to know how to preserve the date and timestamps within any files that are being analyzed for a possible financial fraud. Such skills require a basic familiarity with OS timestamp and data protocols. Date and timestamp information show when changes to files were being made and help in identifying who made the changes.[39]

4. *Properly Securing Data.* The auditor should be able to use hashes to find out if critical financial files have been altered. (A hash, or hash value, is a number representing a string of text. The hash is much smaller than the text itself, and it is very unlikely that some other text would ever produce the same hash value.) The hashes quickly identify if a file's integrity has been compromised.[40]

5. *Properly Collecting Data.* When an initial review of the financial system data is done, the auditor may have to use mirror imaging software to immediately identify and collect electronic evidence by making a bitstream, read-only image. Once the data is secured, it can be given to computer forensic analysts for further investigation.

6. *Maintaining a Proper Chain of Custody.* The chain of custody provides a record of who collected and handled the data, whether it is write-protected, and how collected electronic data is controlled during an investigation. The auditor needs to carefully record the steps taken in identifying the fraudulent financial data and recording who handled the data before turning the evidence over for computer forensic analysis. The chain of custody for any collected data is important for the investigation as it helps prevent claims of evidence contamination.

These six requirements are only the beginning procedures in electronic fraud investigations. They stress examination without changing the data and saving the data for a standard computer forensic investigation. The technical skills needed to perform these activities are already partially embedded into the auditing profession as information systems security auditors use software tools such as Nmap (a port scanner), John the Ripper or Ophcrack (password crackers), TCPDump and Dice (a sniffer combination), Tripwire (a file integrity checking tool), and still possibly THC-Scan (a wardialer for left over modems) in their audits.[41] If necessary, the computer forensic expert will take the investigation onward, but if an auditor is suspicious that fraud is present, the evidence must be securely collected before the electronic data vanishes or is purposefully destroyed.[42] Further, if an investigation is being performed to determine whether an employee should be dismissed, the actions of company's "computer investigators," including accounting staff, may jeopardize the company's leverage and reasons for justifying the dismissal. For example, if a computer is simply powered off using the normal Windows shutdown procedures, it can result in writing entries into the PC's log or registry files and changing the digital evidence so that is it not usable.[43] In addition, cached memory contents, volatile in-transit data, and state of network connection information will disappear.

WHAT TIME DO YOU WANT IT TO BE? The date and time information in a Microsoft Word file or other files are disclosed as part of the information in the Properties of a file. To see this information in Windows 7, right click on any file. A long list of choices will appear. The properties information box will show the dates and times when the file was created, modified, and accessed. If you open the file and change anything, the last access and modified dates will be the current date. Information such as this provides the investigator with information about the times and dates that files were being used.

It is relatively easy to change the timestamp information associated with a file to any date you choose on your computer. To see how this is done download the free utility eXpress TimeStamp Toucher from download.com eXpress TimeStamp Toucher allows the user to change the creation, last accessed, and modified date on most files. The opening screen for eXpress follows. By selecting a file and simply entering a new date stamp and time, the modified date in the file can be changed to any date the user selects. If the forensic investigator does not understand that these dates can be manipulated, the investigator will not know when files were actually being used and possibly who was using them. This simple example is of how a cybercriminal can alter electronic evidence. By changing the timestamp, it allows a criminal to show he was not present when the file was last used, i.e., it gives him an alibi supported by falsified files that he was elsewhere when the crime occurred. One job of a forensic investigator is to be familiar with the methods used by cybercriminals to escape detection. Such a simple analysis moves from the data mining of thousands of transactions as applied by the auditor into the analysis of internal electronic data held in a file. Such data is called metadata. Metadata is information about the nature of a file. Its collection is important in any investigation of a financial fraud.

The trained forensic investigator knows that it is possible to modify electronic files, and therefore for forensic purposes, it is necessary to use imaging software that detects attempts to change electronic evidence.[44] Once someone has modified data stamp information in an electronic file for nefarious purposes, they have taken a first step into cyber crime.

¶ 13,041   ENCASE AND THE FORENSIC ENVIRONMENT

Most financial information is available in an electronic format. Underlying the generation of this transactional data are relational databases and underlying the databases are the deeper internal workings of the computer such as the command shell and kernel. The auditor's Computer Assisted Audit Tools (CAATs) and other application programs, such as Excel, sit on the surface of these underlying command lines or machine language programs. What occurs below the application-level processing is not apparent to the auditors as they use their CAATs. Application programs or "apps" can be described as a program allowing the user to interact with the underlying computer architecture in a user-friendly manner. Unless care is taken, such applications can change the information in slack space found in the clusters on the hard drive and the swap file used by the operating system to swap between memory and virtual memory.

A Windows cluster is the smallest piece of hard drive storage space where data is kept. Cluster size can vary. If the clusters are larger, the hard drive can move and use data more quickly. When new data is allocated to a previously used cluster, i.e., a deleted file, it leaves some empty space in the cluster called slack space. This unused space contains data from the previously deleted file. Such data can still be recovered. Thus, an investigation may hinge on the slack space in a cluster. Improperly opening and using a file can cause the information in the slack space to disappear for forensic purposes.

A swap file is used as a temporary memory location on the hard disk. It is a virtual extension of computer RAM and thus acts as if the computer has more active computer storage than is really available. The data stored in the swap space is very temporary, but it can be recovered. RAM data is another matter. If the PC is disconnected, the temporary data in the RAM is lost.[45]

Forensic accountants use a different approach toward fraud detection than traditional financial auditors. The forensic accountant is concerned with identifying anomalies that are an indicator of a fraud. Anomalies are more easily identified using forensic tools to examine the metadata in electronic files. Metadata is embedded in computer files to show the electronic history and use of a file. Auditors are more concerned with knowing if there may be something significantly amiss in the financial statements and whether the problem might affect their audit opinion or create legal after-audit liabilities for their accounting firm. Those latter concerns are easier addressed with CAAT analysis. Although the forensic accountant will not reject information collected in a CAATs analysis, the forensic accountant will want to make sure e-evidence is preserved in a manner that allows it to be presented in a courtroom.

Encase is an example of the computer forensic software used by forensic accountants.[46] It can recover deleted files, timestamp data, and identify unauthorized applications. The approach does not extract data or make copies but captures a read-only image of the entire hard drive so none of the data above or below the application level is changed. Using an image has a different goal than using an extraction method, as imaging is a noninvasive method. Imaging is the process of converting the contents of a hard drive sector by sector into a digital image, and then storing the image in another location or on another media, essentially making a duplicate of the original hard drive. Such a method will collect data from deleted files so the investigator can understand the sequence of actions, e.g., what the dollar total or address was on the original invoice before it was changed. Encase provides a graphic timeline of file events such as date created, modified, last written, last access, and deleted times.

SPOTLIGHT

EXERCISE FOR POTENTIAL FORENSIC INVESTIGATORS. In Oscar Wilde's story, *The Picture of Dorian Gray*, Dorian Gray had an image of himself, painted by a friend, which retained and reflected all the evidence of his evil lifestyle. Using software, forensic accountants have a much more efficient means of creating an image for collecting evidence of evil doing. EnCase software packages can cost close to $10,000, and its imaged files are accepted for courtroom use. Although we cannot use EnCase imaging software here, we can make images using other software. Making an image includes all slack space, deleted files, and free space on the disk; copying files does not include that information, and depending how the copy is made it may change the timestamp information in a file. The following optional exercise is one method to make images.

To demonstrate how to make an image of a drive, the free software product DriveImageXML(DiX) is used. See an explanation of how to use this software at YouTube. There are a number of videos available on the use of this product, for example: *http://www.youtube.com/watch?v=PTEnKA7tOXM*. The free software is available at download.com. In addition, a USB drive will be used to demonstrate how to make an image of files.

Step 1: Download and install DriveImageXML onto your computer.

Step 2: Insert your USB drive into your computer.

Step 3: Double click the new icon on your desktop.

Step 4: The opening screen will appear. Click on "Backup Drives to Image Files."

Step 5: DiX will identify your USB drive for backup. At this point, you do not want to back up your C: drive. If you are unsure which drive is your USB Drive, go to "Computer" and remove your USB drive, and the USB drive letter will disappear from the list of drives identified by your PC.

Step 6: Select your USB drive and click "Next."

Step 7: The Wizard appears to help you back up your drive. Click "Next" again.

Step 8: The software asks where you want the backup image stored. It wants to place it into your Documents. Just to the right of the box is an small folder icon that will allow you to store the image file on your desktop. Select the desktop as the storage location.

Step 9: Before clicking on "Next," select "Raw Mode" and deselect "split large files." The raw mode will image everything on the USB drive including slack space. When looking for a forensic image, all sectors of the drive have to be imaged for later read-only analysis. If you were imaging your entire C: drive for restoration purposes, you would not save it in raw mode.

Step 10: DiX will show you the progress it is making as it images the drive. See the next illustration. For a USB drive, imaging will take less than five minutes. For a large hard drive, it could take an hour or more to make an image. Once the process is completed, two files will be on your desktop. One is a Drive "letter".dat file and the other is a Drive-G file. You have now imaged your USB drive.

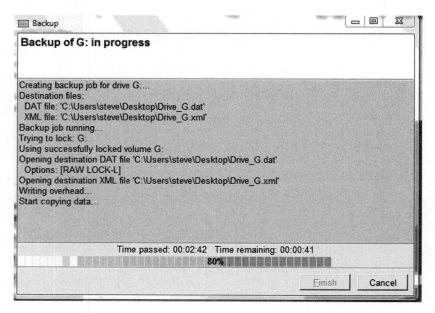

Step 11: To view your imaged files, click on the "Browse" button on DiX's opening screen, find your drive.XML, and open it. It should appear as follows:

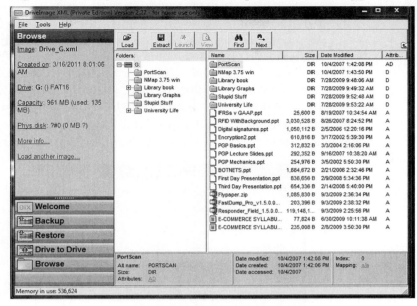

Note: If your results do not show the file structure in the USB drive, restart your PC and try it again. If necessary, you can download the DiX a second time.

Once the USB has been imaged, the forensic investigator would use a read-only copy and investigate the file structure for evidence of a financial fraud. In the above example, it can be seen that the USB device was found on the PC's G drive. All the folders and files are shown as they appear on the imaged drive. The exercise provides an easy way to image electronic data. One forensic technique would be to compare the file structure of the USB drive at different dates to see the changes that have occurred in the folders and files. Such a comparison would allow the forensic investigator to focus their attention on suspicious changes in the drive. More expensive software automates this process and identifies hidden files within the file structure.

EnCase and Helix provide for a Preview mode that allows the image of the drive and file structure to be viewed before collecting the image. EnCase and Helix can do this without contaminating the electronic evidence. For example, the investigator's computer launches EnCase for Windows, and the Acquire button is used to image the drive. EnCase associates a unique hash with each acquired file and keeps it in its hash library. The hash code shows the stored file matches exactly the original file and nothing has been added to or deleted by the investigator, i.e., the message is intact in its original format. Knowing that the two files have the same information on them at the beginning of the forensic analysis is important as the original file will be sealed and the investigator will only investigate the read-only imaged file for electronic evidence. Hashes, such as the MD5 hash, are based on mathematical algorithms. MD5 hashes on files can be compared with each other to identify the same files even if they are saved under different file names and with different file extensions, i.e., doc. zip, exe, docx, jpeg. Furthermore, if the cybercriminal tries to hide his activities by changing an extension from .jpeg to .txt for example, EnCase will not be misled, and it will identify the file as containing an image.

HASH AIN'T ALWAYS FROM POTATOES. MD5 hashes verify that two files are exactly the same. It is extremely unlikely that two different electronic files would have the same MD5 hash numbers. To see this in operation, download Hash Calculator which is a free software program (*http://www.slavasoft.com/hashcalc*) or HashCalc (http://download.cnet.com/windows/). These programs provides hash algorithms for MD2, MD4, MD5, SHA1 and SHA2.[47] By simply clicking on the Calculate button, the program can hash any of the following files: .doc, .tiff, .zip, .gif, .pdf, .MP3, .wav, and others. (Please note that there are a number of other websites that provide free hash calculators.[48])

The opening screen should appear as follows. One can see that a file on the A drive has been already selected for an MD5 and SHA1 hash sequence.

Once the files are hashed using the proper algorithm, HashCalc shows the hash values in the next screen. Calculating the hash value for a file in this manner may not seem to hold value, but the separate hash value on two separate files will show if they are the same or have been altered in any manner. Hash values allow the forensic accountant to determine if two large financial files are exactly the same or not. The screen shot shows the MD5 and SHA1 hash results for a file titled Computer Forensics.doc. This analysis can be performed on large financial files to determine if they are identical.

Most web browsers also allow users to download and use basic hashing plug-ins provided by various developers. For example, Fire Encrypter is a plug-in for the FireFox browser. See download.com. Or Encrypeted Communication as a FireFox Add-On. Fire Encrypter allows the user to hash terms, not files, and use nine encryption methods to create cipertext for passwords.

Try HashCal on two files. Use an original file and the second which you copied to see if the hash codes are the same on the two files. If you used DiX earlier, use your original USB drive hash and compare it with the XML file on your desktop.

With large hard drives, the imaged files are changed to read-only, password protected, compressed, and burned onto a CD, DVD, or another hard drive. The drive's files are then examined for a number of aspects that are not considered in a financial audit. For example, discrepancy checks between a file's extension (e.g., .txt, .bmp or .doc) and its header help to discover the file's real origin, and searches for specific text strings are made. On a hard drive registry, reviews are conducted to identify installed programs, to determine how they are programmed to run, and to view slack space in the registry.[49] If manipulations were made by anyone to financial data to "spruce it up" before it was entered into the accounting databases, recoveries from slack space and swap files would uncover such changes. Also, grep searches of text with a known format, such as logon commands, command line instructions, or a "get record" command used by a specific user, can be conducted to identify possible suspicious activity.[50] Download.com provides a free utility to perform grep searches of binary files and text. See GrepWin (64-Bit).

As one can see, the complete forensic analysis of digital data requires familiarity with the computer's architecture, data file structures, and some limited programming skills. Software solutions from EnCase and Helix allow for the automatic imaging and hashing of large hard drives filled with electronic evidence. The previous two demonstrations have illustrated the process with free software and utilities. Forensic accountants performing these evaluations generally need higher technical skills than those held by the traditional financial auditor who uses application programs.

¶ 13,051 COLLECTION OR SEIZURE OF ELECTRONIC EVIDENCE

Back in 1997, 30 percent of written documentation never reached a printed format and in 2001 it was estimated at 93 percent,[51] and one might expect that that percentage has increased somewhat since then. At one time, printed documentation was the primary source of information for investigation, but now it is the electronic data that is being used in analysis and legal proceedings. In many legal jurisdictions, collection of evidence is automatically assumed to mean electronic documents without requiring that "electronic documents" *per se* be specifically described in the request for information.

In using electronic evidence, it must be remembered that an electronic document can be easily changed (as has been illustrated here). More frightening, a knowledgeable technician can change electronic documents and corresponding logs without leaving a trace that a change occurred. Consequently, the nature and verifiability of evidence in criminal and civil procedures have changed drastically within the past 10 years.[52]

¶ 13,061 HOW CAN ELECTRONIC EVIDENCE BE LEGALLY COLLECTED?

Many electronic devices may contain evidence needed by prosecutors and companies who are investigating a financial cybercrime or the illegal electronic activities of employees.[53] In internal investigations of employee's unauthorized or illegal activities, it is important to assume that all electronic evidence may eventually appear in the courtroom. For that reason, the practices followed in developing courtroom evidence need to be followed to correctly uncover and collect any useable digital data.

In order to determine if the evidence can be legally collected, the role of the electronic device in the crime needs to be ascertained. Without such a determination, the seizure of evidence and the legal seizure of evidence may become separated. For example, the Federal Rules of Criminal Procedure 41(b)(2) allow for the seizure of contraband, fruits of crime, or things criminally possessed. When a hacker uses stolen credit card numbers to purchase computer equipment, the equipment is contraband and it can be seized.[54] When legitimate software, such as Microsoft Office 2010, is downloaded from a warez site, it is contraband.[55] On the other hand, the computer, along with other equipment, may be seized as evidence when it is not contraband, but when it played a significant role in the crime, i.e., it was an instrumentality of the crime. For example, a financial criminal could have used the computer to send financial and proprietary data through Internet service providers (ISPs) and over the Internet. Such a computer is an instrumentality of the crime (as are the documents themselves). From the financial fraudster's point of view, a legal argument could be put forth that the electronic equipment (e.g., computers, modem, PDAs, fax machines, etc.) was illegally seized because it was not contraband (it was legally purchased), and it contained other legitimate data. For example, if criminal evidence is mixed with newsletters or book materials published or to be published by the accused criminals, it may come under First Amendment privileges and protections that prohibit the use of search warrants against members of the press. Therefore, the defendants make the legal argument that any electronic evidence found on these devices should not be admitted into the court proceedings as evidence. Furthermore, if a computer is seized under a warrant and as it is examined other, unrelated criminal activity is uncovered and collected, that evidence is not likely to be admissible in court. The court views the additional evidence as not under the umbrella of the first warrant. Upon initially finding evidence of a second crime, the investigator needs to secure a second warrant for the investigation of that crime to ensure the evidence is admissible in a courtroom.

In the financial fraud case, the computers used by the ISP are also electronic evidence because of the information logged and recorded about transmissions through the site. Consequently, these computers have important evidence for the case and such evidence also needs to be collected. Unfortunately, if another legitimate business has its Web site hosted by the same ISP, this business may also be shut down along with the financial thieves' operations when the ISP's web servers are collected by the authorities as evidence. Law enforcement personnel do not have the right to seize all properties, and courts exercise the "reasonable person" doctrine in determining whether seizures go beyond those boundaries. Restrictions on wide seizures of property by law enforcement are based on Fourth Amendment rights that require specific descriptions of the places, people, and things to be searched and seized.

In many computer-related crimes, evidence will be only available from equipment that *does not* belong to the criminal. For example, distributed denial of service (DDOS) attacks conducted by hackers are launched through botnets so that they cannot be traced back to the attacker.[56] In a DDOS attack, the attacker uses computers belonging to others to assist in attacking the target computer system.[57] These "zombie" computers, legitimate in themselves, have been compromised by the attacker. In order to solve such a crime, law enforcement may need to collect the electronic evidence that is left on the zombie computers. As a result, evidence collection by law enforcement agencies may mean the disruption of legitimate services conducted by those businesses whose computers were unknowingly involved in the crime. Today, it is beginning to be more likely that companies whose computers have been turned into zombie computers may face civil proceedings for damages because they negligently allowed their computers to be used in a DDOS attack.

Of course, the decision as to the admissibility of evidence occurs after the electronic evidence, along with the equipment in which it resides, has been seized, and evidence is collected and summarized. The process of developing electronic evidence is likely to occur both at the crime scene and at the laboratory where the equipment is taken for a full analysis. Once the evidence has been collected, preserved, and reconstructed, it is necessary to present the evidence in a courtroom to a jury. Proceedings can either be in a civil or criminal trial.

The burden of proof in a criminal case is higher than in a civil proceeding. The evidence presented will either be physical evidence or direct evidence. Physical evidence could be the logs collected after a cyber attack that show the intruder's activities on a network or the employee's fraudulent financial actions. The forensic accountant is likely to provide testimony to support physical evidence that has been introduced in the trial. Such testimony is called direct evidence. Direct evidence could also be the testimony of a person such as the tech security employee who printed out the log that was admitted as physical evidence in the case. When testimony is made about cybercrimes in a courtroom, a balance must be made between technology and the jury's knowledge about networks and computer events. Direct evidence must be presented in a way that is understandable to the jury and others in the courtroom. Within most trials, it can be assured that one line of questioning to be raised by a defense attorney is related to the chain of custody that was maintained over the electronic evidence. This line of questioning is to ensure that the evidence was not contaminated.

Electronic documents can be contaminated or destroyed more easily than it was ever possible to destroy paper records. Thus, it is very important for cautions to be exercised as electronic evidence is collected. Such cautions include:

- Document the scene with notes and photographs. Photos and notes should clearly show the computer, cables connections, and all peripherals.
- Close phone line connections to a modem or shut down all wireless networks. Live connections allow for the remote removal of data to another location or the placing of a Trojan from a network connection. Caution: Shutting down the wireless network may result in the loss of volatile data being used at the time.
- Turn off power to network hosting machines before they are disconnected from the network to ensure digital evidence is preserved. Caution: Shutting down the network connection may result in the loss of volatile data streaming between the suspect's computer and the network, such as file transfers.
- Do not turn on computer equipment. Boot up procedures without a timed password may be set to permanently delete files or destroy the hard drive. Caution: Standard boot up procedures change time stamp and other data.
- Laptops should have their batteries disconnected first to ensure they have no energy source once their electrical power cord is disconnected. Caution: When power is disconnected from a running computer all RAM data is lost.
- Only view files in a bitstream or read-only mode to ensure that evidence is legally secure.
- Use accepted algorithms to hash all evidence files.
- Search files, slack space, swap space and undeleted files working with the evidence files (not original files).
- Document file creation dates, modified dates, and last accessed dates…the real ones.
- Make a chain of custody record to ensure the legality of the evidence.
- Keep all electronic evidence in a secured forensic environment.

In addition to these cautions, organizations, such as accounting firms, must be wary of legal requests that include a preservation of evidence letter and discovery notification. It is common practice for organizations to rotate their backup computer tapes or online repositories. Following this practice, tapes or recordable DVDs used for backups of data may only be stored for a limited time. After this time period, new data is recorded over the old data. Once legal requests for electronic evidence are received, such normal business practices need to be stopped and hard drives need to be imaged. Evidence requests are likely to include all e-mail; e-mail headers; e-mail logs; all data files created with word processing, spreadsheet, accounting software, sound recordings, or presentation software; network activity logs; task lists; databases; and e-calendars. All such requests encompass the data on servers, workstations, laptops, floppy disks, online repositories, tapes, voice messaging systems, CDs, DVDs, memory sticks, cell phones, iPads, and all stored backups of data. After this request and until the pertinent drives are imaged, new files should not be saved to working computers. No new software should be loaded or upgraded. No systems checks, defragging, erasing, or disk optimization procedures should be started. Without such changes in operating procedures, court orders will be violated and electronic evidence requested by parties to the lawsuit is destroyed.[58] Such intended or unintended actions can result in large fines, court sanctions for "spoliation" of evidence, and the loss of a case. Spoliation occurs when a party to a legal case destroys, hides, or changes pertinent evidence to the case. The most notable example in accounting was when Arthur Andersen tried to destroy all their paper documents related to the Enron case before the order to preserve evidence was issued. Eventually, they were convicted of obstruction of justice and the accounting firm went out of existence. Even though the conviction was later reversed, Andersen surrender its CPA licenses. The following spotlight illustrates excerpts from a preservation letter for electronic evidence.

ELECTRONIC EVIDENCE PRESERVATION LETTER EXCERPTS

1. Plaintiffs demand that you preserve documents, tangible things, and electronically stored information potentially relevant to the issues in this cause.
2. You are directed to immediately identify and modify or suspend features of your information systems and devices that cause the loss of potentially relevant electronically stored information (ESI).
3. You should anticipate that your officers, employees, or others may seek to hide, destroy, or alter ESI. You must act to prevent and guard against such actions.
4. In the event you deem it impractical to sequester systems, we believe that forensically sound imaging of the systems, media, and devices is expedient and cost effective. As we anticipate the need for forensic examination of relevant evidence in forensically accessible areas of the drives, we demand that you employ forensically sound ESI preservation methods. Failure to use such methods poses a significant threat of spoliation and data loss. The products of forensically sound duplication are called "bitstream images" or "clones" of the evidence media. A forensically sound preservation method guards against changes to metadata evidence and preserves all parts of the electronic evidence, including deleted evidence within "unallocated clusters" and "slack space."

Source: Adapted from Craig D. Ball, "The Perfect Preservation Letter," *http://www. craigball.com/Preservation_Letter.pdf*

Electronic messages go over the Internet through an expanse of routers and servers. The message's path can be traced backwards to the sender, and the residual data stored in routers, such as the computer used to access the network, its sequence numbers, and IP addresses, can be collected. Transmission information and copies of messages and documents may be retained after the recipient deleted the message from his or her PC. Other sources of unexpected electronic information are sometimes found in chat rooms or social posting sites such as YouTube. Chat rooms are places for groups to meet and exchange information. Information such as documents, executable programs, and photographs may be distributed among chat room members. Consequently, investigators have used scanning software to search chat room logs and YouTube postings for leads in investigations. Without encryption, these messages and postings are open for anyone to read and can help identify a fraudster who is bragging about his or her exploits to others in a chat room or displaying them on YouTube.

Additionally, information can be stored on devices connected to a PC. For example, a laser printer may retain copies of the last page printed in its internal memory or the laser printer may have software that uses the hard drive within the PC for storage and the message is retained there. E-mails printed on such peripheral devices may be obtainable even though the printed copy has been destroyed and the hard drive completely swiped clean.

For an accounting firm that is requested to preserve ESI as part of a legal proceeding, the accounting staff must understand metadata so as to not destroy it. If a letter to preserve

ESI is received by an accounting firm, a paragraph such as the following would be included to cover the metadata in electronic files:

> You should further anticipate the need to disclose and produce system and application metadata and act to preserve it. System metadata is information describing the history and characteristics of other ESI. This information is typically associated with tracking or managing an electronic file and often includes data reflecting a file's name, size, custodian, location, and dates of creation and last modification or access. Application metadata is information automatically included or embedded in electronic files, but which may not be apparent to a user, including deleted content, draft language, commentary, collaboration, and distribution data and dates of creation and printing. For electronic mail, metadata includes all header routing data and Base 64 encoded attachment data, in addition to the To, From, Subject, Received Date, CC, and BCC fields.[59]

Johnson identifies electronic data as available in either active, inactive, archival, or residual formats.[60] Active data is data that is used and changed on a daily basis such as data used in calendaring applications. Inactive data is electronic data that PC users may not be aware is stored on the hard drives such as timed backups that have not been removed. Some word-processing programs will automatically make and retain timed backups of files in temporary storage. Archival data is data that has been purposefully backed up. Archival data can contain rich sources of information for discovery purposes and in criminal cases. When discovery motions are begun in civil proceedings, all the normal deletion procedures for all the various backups of requested information must be curtailed to prevent electronic evidence from being destroyed. In criminal proceedings, attempts will be made to seize this information and, possibly, the equipment on which it is stored. Even when electronic tapes are reused or hard drives are overwritten, the information may still be available for collection. Magnetic force microscopy is an expensive technique that can be used to recover information on a magnetic tape or hard drive that has been overwritten.[61] The use of this recovery technique makes it difficult to ever delete electronic information. For example, deviations of the drive head from the original track made in recording the information on the disk may make portions of the previous track of information recoverable. Inconsistent circuit frequencies used in rewriting the disk may also result in recoverable information. To prevent recovery of information on a magnetic medium, the rewrite has to be performed using lower than normal circuit frequencies, deep drive head penetration on the disk, and random passes before and after the erasure process to confound the reconstruction. Circumventing recovery from magnetic media can also be attempted with costly magnetic equipment that will neutralize the magnetic field on the disks or tapes.

Assurances that it is impossible to recover information from magnetic media is important to legitimate businesses that discard their old PCs, servers, and routers to the trash heap and later find that business secrets and confidential information, such as social security numbers, have not been deleted from their discarded equipment. But, to really ensure that a magnetic disk is destroyed, it is necessary to melt the disk. If the disk is taken out of its protective metal covering, and physically damaged, it is still possible to recover information.

THE DIGITAL PERSPECTIVE. When looking at a paper document used for financial evidence, we see a very flat, linear view of the document. When this same document is stored on a computer in digital form, the information contained within it becomes both dynamic and historic.

¶13,065   THE FORENSIC ACCOUNTANT RECOVERS DATA ON A DISK

Disk Investigator is a freeware program available from Kevin Solway (*http://download.cnet. com/windows/*). Disk Investigator allows the user to identify hidden and deleted files and directories on a disk. These deleted files are not in the Recycle Bin. Disk Investigator's opening screen follows with an examination of the same USB drive that was imaged with DiX. It is highlighted as Drive G in the following screen.[62] The opening screen on Disk Investigator shows the same directory structure as found with DiX except with Disk Investigator all the deleted files and directories are shown at the top of the screen. When Disk Investigator is used, the opening screen is color coded to show the status of the files and directories. It cannot be seen in the black and white illustration, but the deleted files are: Fale-Mailer.exe, IFRS v GAAP.ppt, and First Day Presentation.ppt. The deleted directories are: New Folder, Port Scan, and friendflag.winxp. The file BOTNETS.PPT is a normal file on the drive. A quick review of the files gives you the dates they have been modified and created, and the file extensions identify the file type. These files could have been deleted e-mails or fraudulently-modified financial reports crucial to the investigation of a financial fraud.

By highlighting any of the deleted files or directories on the drive, it is possible to restore them to any other drive on your computer. If they have been partially overwritten, only the original, unchanged part of the file will be recovered. For the forensic investigator, it is important to know there are deleted files available for recovery on any disk. Once the deleted drives are restored, they can be examined for evidence of falsified documents such as doctored invoices or purchase orders. It may mean that an original file was altered for fraudulent purposes. Such nonlinear tracking of a paper document is not available for investigation.

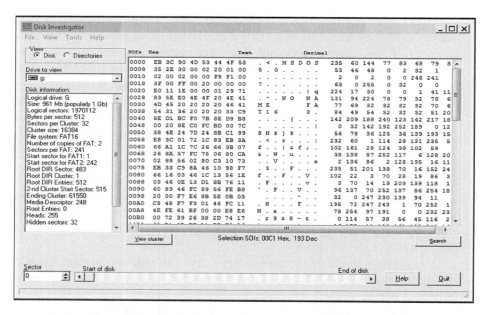

This screen is a hexadecimal or disk view of the USB drive.[63] To counter a forensic investigation, a cybercriminal may try to hide his activities by using software that allows clusters on the hard drive to be designated as "damaged." Such "damaged" clusters may be overlooked and thus used to hide evidence of fraudulent activity. Only a complete forensic examination of the disk could reveal the files hidden in such areas on the disk. This brief introduction into computer forensics does not allow for the explanation of all the material shown in the screen, but without such an explanation, it should be clear that the digital information is much more complex than the information found in paper documents. By only viewing paper documentation, important information in a fraud investigation is lost.

In the screen shot (above), the version of MS-DOS is disclosed as 5.0. Such information could possibly be important if the file under review was not saved with the same DOS version the suspected fraudster had on his or her machine. This information is not available from a paper document. The structure of the drive is FAT16 which determines how the drive is partitioned or divided into sections, and cluster size information is also provided. Hidden sectors are not hidden files; rather they are used each time the disk is opened. For the forensic investigator, such an analysis allows him to better understand the activities of the cybercriminal.

¶ 13,067   DATA MINING: ELECTRONIC EVIDENCE COLLECTION

Collecting electronic evidence with data mining methods is different than applying forensic methods to electronic data. Data mining does not delve into the inner shell of a computer and its architecture, a practice followed in electronic data analysis. Data mining is used to investigate vast amounts of data and thousands of line items in financial databases for evidence of fraudulent activities. With data mining, fraudulent activities are uncovered through statistically analyzing the patterns in the data in order to find suspicious cases. In data mining, methods such as link analysis, case based reasoning, cluster analysis, classification formatting, sequence analysis, and user event patterns are used. Both methods need to perform their investigations on bitstream backups to prevent the corruption of the electronic data. Also, in both cases hash codes have to be used to show the files being analyzed are identical to the original files. When data mining evidence is presented in the courtroom, the emphasis is on validating the tests methods to ensure their validity as well as their courtroom acceptability. It is assumed that the data records are unaltered, i.e., they have not been manipulated or edited by a hacker or employee to hide or remove electronic evidence. For example, the logs of the electronic audit trails are assumed to be legitimate and show what actually occurred. Data mining evidence will not deal with the metadata in a file.

Data Mining Strategies for Analyzing Electronic Data

The first steps in data mining analysis are to (1) ensure that a working file has been imaged, (2) the hash code of the working file is initially the same as the original file, and (3) make certain the working data has been "cleaned" to eliminate obvious errors such as typos, for example.[64] Unless the first two steps are taken, there is no guarantee that the data will be accepted in the courtroom. With data mining, it is more important to be certain the data in the working file has been cleaned. Computer forensics delves into the interior of the PC and data mining reviews the actual entries in accounting records. For that reason, it is more important to ensure that cleaned data is being reviewed as the data is mined.

Once these steps are completed, the analysis of the data can begin. Such an analysis cannot be done manually because of the size of the databases being examined. Three commercial data mining programs that are useful in this analysis are ACL, ActiveData, and IDEA. For more details about ActiveData please see Appendix 8. For more details about IDEA please see Data Mining Software for Analyzing Electronic Data below and Appendix 9. Even with these software programs, the approach to analysis needs to be strategically patterned in order to successfully uncover fraudulent activity. The following procedures can be helpful in identifying anomalies in the data.

Link Analysis

The underlying assumption in link analysis is that there are some fundamental correlations or associations between the items in a database. With link analysis, an algorithm of that relationship is developed and used to as a means to identify cases that do not fit what would be expected. For example, assume a database of purchase orders are under review. There is an underlying relationship in the orders between a series of products. If we purchase Product A from Vendor 1, we are also likely to purchase Product B. Such a purchase might be gasoline and oil.

Transaction Number	Component Purchased	Purchased Item	Support (A is purchased 75% of the time)
5678	A, B, Q	A	75%
5679	A, B	B	50%
5680	A, F	A, B	50%
5681	Q, F	Q	50%

Rules of Assocation:

IF A is purchased then B is purchased, with a certainty of: xx % (a)

IF A is purchased then B is purchased, in xx % of cases (c)

In the list of purchases, A and B are purchased together 50% of the time (c) and the certainty of the association is 67% (a).[65]

Although this is a very simple example, it illustrates the steps in a strategic approach to data mining. The associations in the data allow the investigation to make some "first cuts" so all purchase orders do not have to be reviewed in the analysis. Those cases that have no association to the items under investigation can be dropped from the analysis. Software such as with Financial Investigation System (FIS) from Actionable Intelligible Technologies is useful in establishing a visual pattern of the links in data. FIS provides graphic linkages between various data points in identifying associations. The purpose of link analysis is to uncover relationships that can be studied in more detail. For example, if it is noticed that a number of purchases included Item A but not Item B, it might be worthwhile to determine the reasons those specific purchases, A alone, are not following an established relationship.

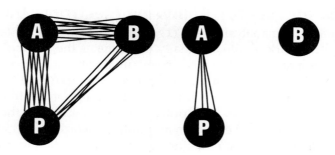

The first illustration shows the linkages between purchases (P) and Products A and B. It can be seen that most purchases include both Product A and B. Through linkage analysis, the purchases that only include Product A can be quickly highlighted in the linkage graphic. Now the purchase orders related to only Product A can be investigated in more depth. It may be that fraudulent purchase orders were issued by fraudsters for only Product A as they did not understand the linkage relationship underlying the two products.

Case Based Reasoning

Case based reasoning uses the closest approximations from the past in order to adapt a correct past solution to a current situation. Case based reasoning can be considered to be memory-based problem solving. It is based on predicting future events as a result of studying previous events. The Help Desk at a large call-in center makes available to each employee a list of steps to follow to answer incoming questions based on the matching characteristics of the new question to similar, previous calls. This is an example of case based reasoning. In fraud detection, it might be useful to uncover similar characteristics in current accounts that are indicative of past fraudulent accounts. To analyze large databases, there must be a "matching engine" that quickly sorts thousands of accounts to retrieve similar cases for examination. The database sort is based on a selected number of matching characteristics using cases with the least amount of differences between specific data points. The following flowchart illustrates the feedback loop that can be used in case based reasoning to select possible fraudulent accounts when there is a suspicion that fraud has occurred in the organization.

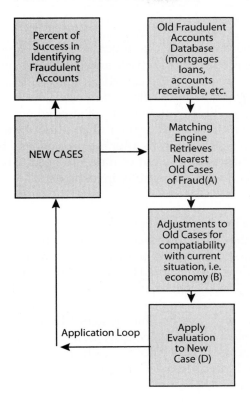

In the flowchart, the matching engine compares the new cases with the nearest examples of the old cases. The comparison may be based on a combination of items such as missing information, phone numbers, addresses, ratio analysis, external certifications, and employee authorizations, for example. The A-D loop in the flowchart can be used repeatedly to develop a higher success rate in identifying fraudulent accounts or to adapt to the changes in the fraudster's *modus operandi*. The success of the approach is dependent on how closely the old and new cases are matched, and adjustments to the old cases which may require a weighted matching of a selected number of similarities between the cases.

Sequence Analysis
Although case based reasoning can help to model past transactions to current ones, it does not necessarily evaluate the time relationship between these events. Sequence analysis is concerned with evaluating patterns in time series data to uncover fraudulent activity. It is assumed that an ordered set of events ($s=a_1, a_2,...a_n$) will be encountered together. The transaction order is separated by a time delay. For example, sequence analysis might uncover the timing of an event that occurs immediately after the end of each quarter such as the rewriting of addresses on invoices. Or, it might uncover large purchases on a credit card shortly after a small purchase was made. In the former case, someone is changing addresses on invoices back to the correct address after they used a fake address on the invoice. In the latter case, a criminal is making a small purchase to ensure the stolen credit card will work, and then he is using it to buy everything he can before it is cancelled. A time series pattern can be used to help identify frauds. The best sequence is one that is unique and not part of other sequences. The goal is to model the data sequence and finding either similar patterns or derivatives from the pattern.

Assume the following sequence exists in the purchase of merchandise by a national retail store. It is assumed there are interdependencies in the sequence.

Purchase order for merchandise sent.	Merchandise inventory ordered is received.	Received merchandise units are checked. Damaged items are returned.	Good units are added to the merchandise inventory.
Sequence: 1	2	3	4

It is found that 80 percent of the transactions to record returns on inventory are made within an average of one day of the receipt of the orders, and four hours after that the good units are added to the merchandise inventory. We can check this sequence flow of events from the information in our inventory database. After data mining thousands of purchase orders, you discover that there are a significant number of purchases where the returned items were recorded after the inventory was increased for the full amount of the purchase order. Some of these returns were recorded several months after the product had been received. Is this a red flag of fraud or are the products simply out-of-date and need to be returned to the vendors? Obviously, this finding needs to be more fully investigated.

Cluster Analysis

Cluster analysis is used to divide data into nonoverlapping groups containing similar characteristics. A simple example illustrating the concept is the separation of different marbles into their distinctive characteristics. Each group should have a strong level of "sameness" that separates it from the other data groups. The data in a cluster should be closer to the mean in that cluster than the mean in any of the other clusters formed from the data under analysis. The underlying data forming a cluster can be based on a single characteristic or on multiple characteristics measured in different ways, just as long as they are similar within clusters.[66] Dividing groups alphabetically or using pre-set labels is not implementing cluster analysis. If upon separating the groups, there are outliers discovered in the groupings, they need to be identified. Such outliers may be an indication of fraud in the data set. It needs to be determined if the outliers have a particular characteristic that may make them a red flag of fraud. For interval data, it is possible to calculate the z score (at the .05 level of significance) to identify outliers in the cluster under investigation. The z score shows how many standard deviations above or below an individual data item is from the population mean.[67] Z scores in combination with other factors can be used to identify outliers that may exist in the clustered data. One underlying assumption is the data is represented by a normal distribution. If it is not, there are other ways to apply cluster analysis.

As an illustration of cluster analysis, assume the following two clusters have been identified from county property records regarding appraisals performed to value homes for tax purposes in Sanilac County. The appraisals are performed by both independent contractors and county employees. A regression model is used to calculate residuals for each appraisal, i.e., in each cluster, in the database. The residual is the difference between the actual property appraisal less the predicted appraisal as calculated by the regression model. In other words, it is the amount of error from the predicted appraisal.

Cluster	Appraisal Cases	Avg. Appraisal 1	Avg. Appraisal 2	Avg. Increase (Decrease)
Independent Contractor	1010	$104,750	$185,950	$81,200
County Employee	678	$101,325	$178,433	$77,108

The z scores are calculated for each residual, and any outliers can be flagged for further investigation. The z score identifies those residuals that are the most extreme, i.e., statistically significant. Assume every case in the two clusters where the z score is greater than 2.5 and the average appraisal increase is less than or equal to $12,000 is flagged for additional review. We are trying to determine if a group of appraisers is receiving incentives, such as kickbacks, to lower the appraisal value of property in the county.

ZIPF'S LAW AND WORD FILTERING FOR FRAUD. One method of data mining for fraud detection that has received recent attention is Zipf's law.[68] With Zipf's Law, it is understood that word documents have sequential patterns identifiable with a Zipf analysis. Like Benford's Law, Zipf's law deals with the identification of a natural phenomenon. Benford's Law deals with the distribution of digits showing that in a series of random digits 1 is found in about 30 percent of the cases, 2 in about 18 percent of the cases, and 3 in about 12 percent of the cases. The relationship was uncovered in 1881 by Simon Newcome who noticed the first pages of books of logarithms were more soiled than the latter pages. Benford later formalized the law which carries his name.

Zipf's Law was identified by George Zipf and was later modified by Benoit Mandelbrot. Zipf's Law is applied to the frequency of English words rather than the frequency of digits. Basically Zipf's law states that the quantity under analysis is inversely proportional to its rank (1, ½, 1/3, etc.). The most frequently observed word occurs X times. The second-most frequently occurring word X/2 times, the third ranking element X/3 times, etc. Therefore, if the most frequently occurring word occurs 10 percent of the time within a document, the second most frequently occurring word should appear five percent of the time and on down. In language, the second most common word "and" will appear ½ as many times in a text as the most common word in the English language "the." If "the" =1, then "and" occurs ½ as often.[69] It has been suggested[70] that Zipf's Law can be used in fraud detection by filtering out cases that do not follow the frequency distributions found in the law. A similar approach is applied with Benford's Law. By comparing actual distributions to expected distributions, it is possible to identify anomalies for further investigation. The steps in the analysis include identifying significant attributes (vendor invoice: date sent, name, address, date, billing date, payment date, ID, authorization) in line with a fraud objective and then using software to count the frequency pattern of each attribute. In this pattern, a rank of 1 is given to the most frequent occurrence. Next the expected frequency of the distribution is calculated as determined by Zipf's Law. The purpose of this step is to separate pattern anomalies within the data. This can be done with regression analysis. Once this is done, z scores can be calculated for the residuals as done in cluster analysis to identify significant differences in the patterns. At this point, a forensic investigator will determine the underlying reasons for these differences.

Data Mining Software for Analyzing Electronic Data

When mining electronic data, a software tool is essential. Such tools are often referred to as CAATs (computer assisted audit tools software). Examples of such tools are IDEA- Data analysis software (Appendix 9) and Prosystem fx ActiveData (Appendix 8). IDEA allows investigators to find anomalies that help identify fraudulent behavior. As previously stated, data mining software should be used in combination with computer forensic analysis and after the hard drive information has been properly imaged.

Mining data is easy in IDEA with its Windows-based interface and point-and-click navigation. Users import the data so that IDEA can keep the integrity of the original file. Once the file has been imported, the user can begin analyzing and mining the data. All steps are retained in History for documentation purposes. Some of the many pre-programmed features included in IDEA are: Summarization, Stratification, Duplicate Detection, Gap Detection, Benford's Law, various Sampling techniques, and Aging.

IDEA and other CAATs use these pre-programmed features to identify missing check numbers, duplicate invoice payments, thresholds where fraudulent activity could occur just below a dollar limit, name searches and many others. In order to successfully detect fraud through data mining, one must think like a fraudster. Tests in IDEA can easily be automated without knowledge of programming languages.

CAATs like IDEA help identify potential fraud which should further be investigated, such as:

- High number of transactions just below an authorized level
- Unusual write-offs or returns of merchandise
- High number of partial payments by customers
- Duplicate or missing social security numbers or invoices
- Addresses that do not match addresses in the Human Resources database
- Discrepancies between company policies on hiring contractors and actual contractor hiring patterns
- Recording a large number of repeat invoices from vendors
- Terminated employees with log on access after termination date
- High or unusual payments made to vendors

The following graphic is an example of what IDEA looks like when it is first opened. IDEA projects are easily managed through the Home menu. A demo version of IDEA can be downloaded for free at: *www.caseware.com/IDEACDBook1* To learn how to use IDEA and get started on the IDEA Project in the Spotlight, the Tutorial is available to be downloaded at the install screen.

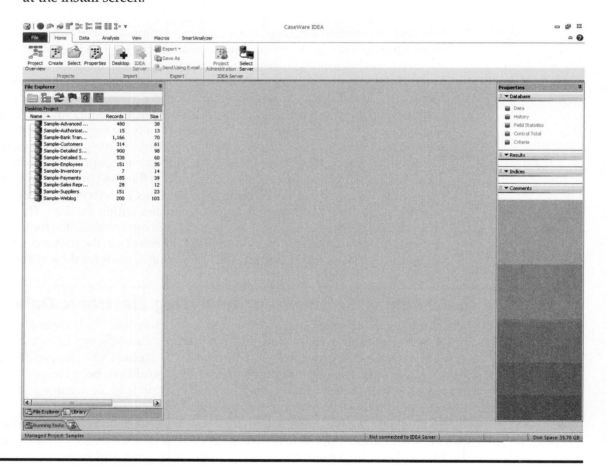

You have been hired as a data mining expert in HR by Newman & Associates to evaluate their payroll and HR files. The CEO has a suspicion there may be some discrepancies in the HR data and payroll reports, especially since hiring their new HR Manager 2 years ago. Using IDEA, you will run various tests on Payroll and HR databases looking for discrepancies. Payroll fraud can be implemented by employers or employees. The red flags of such frauds include employees without payroll deductions, employees without social security numbers or with duplicate social security numbers, the same address for nonfamily member/employees, only a post office box address, the same electronic deposit number for several employees, mismatched names in payroll compared with human resource lists, overtime given to salaried employees, and payroll checks being issued to employees who have been terminated. With unauthorized access to a payroll database, even cybercriminals can commit a payroll fraud by adding fake employees to the payroll, assigning them a high monthly salary, and withdrawing these salaries from the organization's bank accounts.

After each test, discuss the purpose of running such a test and the objective that is being met. At the end you should have a good understanding of how IDEA can be used to data mine and search for potential fraud. Keep in mind the findings will need further investigating, but IDEA leads you in the right direction.

Once you have downloaded IDEA from the student demo site at *www.caseware.com/IDEACDBook1*, you can obtain the data files at: *http://ideasupport.caseware.com/public/downloads/datafia.zip*. If you encounter difficulty downloading the demo software you may contact: *ideasupport@caseware.com*.

The zip file contains two Excel folders: (1)HR_Master.xlsx and (2) Payroll_Extract.xlsx. The step-by-step instructions in Appendix 9 explain how to use these files and where to save them on your computer. Please check the instruction under "Load Data" as to where to save these files. If you have an older computer, WinZip or 7-Zip (free) can be used to open a compressed zip file. As each of the databases on the website is an Excel file, you will also need MS Excel to open them. The payroll problem procedures are outlined step-by-step in **Appendix 9**. This solution is provided as an introduction into the use of IDEA software for investigations.

It should be remembered that avoiding payroll fraud also involves good internal control procedures. These methods may include a periodic check to verify employees' social security numbers with the Social Security Administration, mandatory vacations for employees maintaining payroll records, and thumb prints ID for clocking time worked.

EYEWITNESS

"Vancouver, British Columbia, December 10, 2008... Canada Revenue Agency (CRA) investigators have charged five individuals alleged to have evaded taxes through the use of specialised computer software at restaurants they operate. The software was designed to work with point-of-sale systems and electronic cash registers to erase, or electronically suppress, sales records. As part of this investigation, a series of search warrants were executed at various restaurant locations, as well as at the offices of Richmond based InfoSpec Systems Inc. (InfoSpec), a software company that is alleged to have designed and sold electronic sales suppression software.

"The search of InfoSpec was the culmination of an eight-month undercover operation by the Royal Canadian Mounted Police (RCMP). *During the search, the CRA seized both paper and electronic records consisting of invoices, e-mails, point-of-sale software and other electronic data* [emphasis added]. It is alleged that InfoSpec knowingly provided four restaurants with computer programs designed to erase sales and thereby allow for the evasion of taxes."[71]

How are both computer forensics and data mining used in this example? Do you think the restaurants would have received a "clean" audit opinion before the crime was discovered?

Using Audit Trail Logs to Trace Fraud

Another tool useful in uncovering financial frauds is the logged audit trail. In accounting, an electronic audit trail is a chronological record of every transaction that is electronically entered into the accounting system. Application software such as PeopleSoft and SAP are used to record audit trails. Audit trails can also refer to paper documents used to trace a single transaction from entering to exiting the accounting system. Audit trails may also mean the electronic traces of computer activity recorded as employees use the Internet and bounce from one site to another.

Besides the actual electronic accounting entry, accounting audit trails should record the identity of the employee making the entry, and the time the entry was made at a minimum.[72] Consequently the audit trail provides a traceable path of all the employee actions as entries are entered into the accounting system. Rather than tracking a specific business transaction through the system, log entries would be more beneficial in identifying employees who are making suspicious or unauthorized transactions. It may be discovered that an employee is making continual changes to company invoices at their final payment date. Such actions may be considered suspicious and require further investigation and a review of log entries. Audit logging software should maintain modification logs that show the ID of the person making changes, additions or deletions to master files, and before and after information relating to accounting changes. Two examples of audit logs follow.

```
ID                Real Time       PC time        PC Usage       Command
                                                                Executed

smith87           0.51re          .13cp          4372K          upd4
```

The computer logs record the user ID, the clock time (military time), PC usage time, computer space used in the PC, and the command executed—in this case an update command. The example shows that the user entered a command to update data in the computer. Each event that is used to change the computer operating procedures should be logged. It would be expected that thousands of such log events are recorded on a daily basis.

The next log is related to changes made in an accounting application program used to maintain a company's ledgers.

```
APSyst008 456784 JE-AP 3 JE56709 459896 1 0 S
```

The logged information is updating accounts payable by the employee APSyst008, and the transaction posted was JE56709. The other information recorded in the log follows.

ID	APSyst008
Control No.	4567894
Description	JE-AP
Number of Transactions	3
Last Transaction Posted	JE56709
Total Amount Posted	459896
Number of Errors	1
Number of Warnings	0
Result	Success

In the table, it can be seen how the information can be used to track the entry of accounting transactions throughout the general ledger. There several ways for a criminal to defeat this system. Users of the system who have administrative access, i.e., root access, will be able to make any changes to the system such as removing those logs that identify their fraudulent activities or using other employee's IDs. Such super users may be external hackers or employees who have stolen administrative passwords. Another issue may be the software itself. For example, assume an error from a previous fiscal period is found. If the correction is made as an adjusting entry, all changes are correctly noted in the log. If the software's procedures allow a correction to be made by replacing the incorrect balances with the correct balance, without adjusting entries, and this process continues over a long period, the entries in the audit trail will become totally misleading. It may appear a fraud has occurred when none exists.

It should also be apparent that logging all these entries will also result in the generation of gigabytes of logged data. A retention policy for storing logs needs to be in place. Also there must be a method to quickly and effectively review the raw logs and to report only suspicious entries or a combination of entries that together are suspicious. In other words, the logs need to be parsed to identify the components of the log record.

Trying a Log Parser

Although we cannot use a program like SAP or Peoplesoft to generate log entries and parse them, Microsoft does provide a log generator for free. Event Viewer is part of Vista and Windows 7 operating systems.

Event Viewer is an example of how logs are generated and reviewed. The Event Viewer is opened by typing Event Viewer in the Search box under Start. The logs themselves are already recorded in the PC. Similar conceptual processes are followed to generate log reports from systems such as mySAP and other ERP systems. Again, it needs to be noted that any log files used to solve a cybercrime need to be imaged and hashed before they are investigated. The illustrative examples here are not implementing those steps. A parser program is used to query the internal records in the PC and produce the log report shown. The log report is extensive and may go back several years unless the computer user has cleared her log files. The logs generated by the Event Viewer make it easier to identify events on a PC that might be an area of concern for a forensic investigator.

The Event Viewer logs information about administrative tasks, applications, security, setup, system, applications and services logs, and forwarded events. Forwarded events are logs generated when information is forwarded to your computer from remote computers. Clickable steps allow for the operation of the Event Viewer and diagnosing problems. Under the "Details" tab, additional information is provided about the nature of the log entries. The information in the Detail window is particularly important for understanding anomalies in the logs. For example, the security logs show valid and invalid attempts to logon to the computer, and if logon auditing is active, it records each logon. The Event Viewer logs events that are unsuccessful, such as when a printer does not print due to a driver problem. The following illustration provides an example of a printer problem log entry in which the "Error" code is recorded. Errors are recorded when some process fails to properly load. The reason for the error is provided in the lower Detail window. The date and time and event ID of the error are shown. In the example, the printer called upon to print was not connected to the computer. For additional information about various error messages search *http://msdn.microsoft.com.*

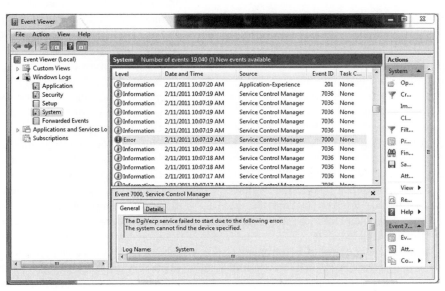

¶13,071   CONCLUSION

Historically, auditors have viewed their job functions as almost solely related to ensuring that the proper accounting practices are being followed by corporate managers in preparing the company's financial reports. In the past, this was done by relying on paper documentation and reviewing these documents in a linear fashion related to document dates and audit check lists. At this time, it was an approved practice to "audit around the computer." In auditing around the computer, auditors would look at what when into the computer on one side and what came out on the other side with assurances that proper systems controls were excised by management. This practice allowed auditors to avoid developing the technological skills they would have otherwise needed. Such practices seem so naïve in today's world of electronic fraud.

Today if the auditor or the accountant does not have the technical ability to understand the company's digital network, they have little hope of identifying the fraudulent manipulations so easily carried out in cybercrimes. Without accounting assurances regarding the integrity of the company's digital network, there can be no assurances regarding corporate financial reports either. Such integrity has been legislated into law by the Sarbanes-Oxley Act.

On a daily basis and usually remotely, computers are used to commit financial fraud by malicious employees, unlawful hackers, writers of malware, deceitful executives, and organized criminal gangs. Without being able to help identify the technologically-skilled culprits committing these digital financial crimes, accountants are only contributing to the chaos. The chapter has provided a glimpse into some of the electronic forensic techniques, such as alternating timestamps, imaging, hashing, identifying deleted files, and developing and evaluating electronic logs. These techniques can be used to help forensic and other accountants identify financial fraud. The basic methods explained in the chapter form the foundation for understanding digital forensics and the future technology role for the accounting profession.

ENDNOTES

[1] Beyond the tech savvy criminal altering time and date stamps, there is the PCs time drift and differing time zones that influence time and date stamp data. Time drift occurs when the clock in the computer leads or lags the correct time.

[2] Adapted from 2004 Australian COMPUTER CRIME AND SECURITY SURVEY, Published by the Australian High Tech Crime Centre, Australian Government.

[3] Many of the topics covered in this chapter have also been discussed by the author, G. Stevenson Smith, in a series of articles and columns written in the JOURNAL OF FORENSIC ACCOUNTING, AUDITING, FRAUD & TAXATION including the following:
"Post-Enron Guidelines for Financial Frauds: Where Are They? And How Effective Are They?" JOURNAL OF FORENSIC ACCOUNTING, AUDITING, FRAUD & TAXATION: BLACK TECH FORENSICS. Vol. IV (June 2005) 273-280.
"Computer Forensics: Helping to Achieve the Auditor's Fraud Mission?" JOURNAL OF FORENSIC ACCOUNTING, AUDITING, FRAUD & TAXATION. Vol. IV (June 2005) 119-134.
"Divergent Views and Approaches Toward the Digital Evidence of Financial Fraud," JOURNAL OF FORENSIC ACCOUNTING, AUDITING, FRAUD & TAXATION: BLACK TECH FORENSICS. Vol. V (June 2004) 265-270.
"The Collection, Seizure, and Control of Electronic Evidence," JOURNAL OF FORENSIC ACCOUNTING, AUDITING, FRAUD & TAXATION: BLACK TECH FORENSICS. Vol. 1 (December 2000) 283-290.

[4] In 2002, Ernst & Young's fraud survey of directors and managers of large organizations across the world found that slightly more than half the respondents to the survey were concerned with *computer* crime and corruption. Yet in only five percent of reported frauds was electronic evidence used in the investigation. It is surmised that one possible reason for the low level use of digital evidence is because "investigation competencies have not yet moved to match this new source of evidence." M. Savage, FRAUD: THE UNMANAGED RISK. (South Africa: Ernst & Young 2002), p. 12.

[5] Two good sources for guidelines on handling electronic evidence can be found in: (1) ELECTRONIC CRIME SCENE INVESTIGATION: A GUIDE FOR FIRST RESPONDERS, U.S. Department of Justice, National Institute of Justice, Washington, D.C. July 2001; and (2) FORENSIC EXAMINATION OF DIGITAL EVIDENCE: A GUIDE FOR LAW ENFORCEMENT, U.S. Department of Justice, National Institute of Justice, Washington, D.C. April 2004.

[6] The normal copying or opening of digital files alters the file's date stamps, for example, and allows the defense attorney to argue that someone other than their client tampered with the files.

[7] M. Bigler, "Computer Forensics." INTERNAL AUDITOR. 57 (February 2000): 53-55.

[8] SAS No. 31, EVIDENTIAL MATTER (New York: AICPA 1980).

9   SAS No. 80, Amendment to Statement on Auditing Standards No. 31, Evidential Matter (New York: AICPA 1996).

10 The Information Technology Age: Evidential Matter in the Electronic Environment (New York: AICPA 1997).

11 SAS No. 54, Illegal Acts By Clients (New York: AICPA) (Effective on or after January 1, 1989). With the frauds at Enron and WorldCom, SAS No. 82 was revised as SAS No. 99, under the same title, Consideration of Fraud in a Financial Statement Audit. SAS No. 99, Consideration of Fraud in a Financial Statement Audit (New York: AICPA) (Effective on or after December 15, 2002).

12 SAS No. 99, Consideration of Fraud in a Financial Statement Audit (New York: AICPA 2002), par. 61.

13 M. Beasley, "SAS No. 99: A New Look at Auditor Detection of Fraud." Journal of Forensic Accounting: Auditing, Fraud & Risk. 4 (Jan/June 2003): 1-20. M. Ramos, "Auditors' Responsibilities for Fraud Detection." Journal of Accountancy. 195 (January 2003) 28.

14 SAS No. 99, Consideration of Fraud in a Financial Statement Audit (AICPA, Professional Standards, vol. 1, AU sec. 316).

15 Slack space is the undeleted data that is left in a cluster (smallest data storage area used by an operating system) on a hard drive after the cluster is reused by the operating system for storing a new file. Slack space is created when the data in the new file does not completely fill up the cluster. Consequently the old data is not overwritten by the new file and remains in the "slack space" of the cluster. For this reason, it is possible to recover the old data which most users assume has been deleted. An analogy is when a person with a size 8 foot does not fill up a size 12 shoe. Standard cluster storage sizes can vary, and with a larger storage size on a hard drive, there is likely to be more undeleted data available for forensic recovery.

16 Adapted from 2004 Australian Computer Crime and Security Survey, Published by the Australian High Tech Crime Centre, Australian Government.

17 P.L. 107-204.

18 Under Sarbanes-Oxley, a significant deficiency is defined as an internal control deficiency in a significant control or an aggregation of such deficiencies that could result in a misstatement of the financial statements that is more than inconsequential. More serious is a material weakness. Under Sarbanes-Oxley, a material weakness is a significant deficiency or an aggregation of significant deficiencies that preclude the entity's internal control from providing reasonable assurance that material misstatements in the financial statements will be prevented or detected on a timely basis by employees in the normal course of performing their assigned functions. In this case, the auditors cannot issue an unqualified opinion.

19 The sponsoring organizations of COSO include the American Institute of Certified Public Accountants (AICPA), American Accounting Association (AAA), Financial Executives International (FEI), Institute of Internal Auditors (IIA) and Institute of Management Accountants (IMA).

20 COSO is a voluntary organization whose mission is to improve the quality of financial reporting. See COSO, Internal Control-Integrated Framework (1992). In 1994, COSO published an addendum to the COSO Report. The addendum addresses the scope of internal controls pertaining to the safeguarding of assets. In 1996, COSO issued a supplement to its original framework to address the application of internal control to financial derivatives.

21 Final Rule: Management's Reports on Internal Control Over Financial Reporting and Certification of Disclosure in Exchange Act Periodic Reports, Securities and Exchange Commission, 17 CFR PARTS 210, 228, 229, 240, 249, 270 and 274, [Release Nos. 33-8238; 34-47986; IC-26068; File Nos. S7-40-02; S7-06-03], RIN 3235-AI66 and 3235-AI79. Effective Date: August 14, 2003. "The COSO Framework satisfies our criteria and may be used as an evaluation framework for purposes of management's annual internal control evaluation and disclosure requirements. However, the final rules do not mandate use of a particular framework, such as the COSO Framework...." [Section B (3)(a)].

22 It should be remembered that SAS No. 94, The Effect of Information Technology on the Auditor's Consideration of Internal Controls in a Financial Statement Audit (New York: AICPA) (effective June 1, 2001), was available to be used as a defining document.

23 Section 105 of Sarbanes-Oxley grants the PCAOB broad authority over registered public accounting firms. The PCAOB has both investigative and disciplinary authority over public accounting firms.

24 As the PCAOB is responsible for setting auditing standards for public companies, the Accounting Standards Board will focus its attention on setting audit standards for nonpublic entities such as governments, academia, and other nonprofit organizations, and companies not listed on U.S. stock exchanges or registered with the SEC.

25 Auditing Standard No. 2, An Audit of Internal Control Over Financial Reporting Performed in Conjunction with an Audit of Financial Statements (PCAOB 2004).

26 Auditing Standard No. 2, An Audit of Internal Control Over Financial Reporting Performed in Conjunction with an Audit of Financial Statements (PCAOB 2004), par. 75.

27 Auditing Standard No. 2, An Audit of Internal Control Over Financial Reporting Performed in Conjunction with an Audit of Financial Statements (PCAOB 2004), par. 40.

28 PCAOB, Auditing Standard No. 12, Identifying and Assessing Risks of Material Misstatement (Release No. 2010-04), Appendix B, Consideration of Manual and Automated Systems and Controls. Difficulties arise when auditors uses system-generated data to perform substantive analytical procedures but then do not test the completeness and accuracy of the system-generated

data or the controls used to generate such data. Are some transactions or records missing? It is important for auditors to perform their own analysis of these systems and not rely on IT staff opinions and documentation to reach a conclusion as to adequacy of controls.

29   The Information System Audit and Control Association (ISACA) is an international information system audit and information security organization that administers the Certified Information Systems Auditor and Certified Information Security Manager designations.

30   Christopher Fox, CA, and Paul Zonneveld, CISA, CA. IT CONTROL OBJECTIVES FOR SARBANES-OXLEY: THE IMPORTANCE OF IT IN THE DESIGN AND IMPLEMENTATION OF INTERNAL CONTROL OVER FINANCIAL REPORTING, 2nd Ed. (IT Governance Institute 2006).

31   IS STANDARDS, GUIDELINES AND PROCEDURES FOR AUDITING AND CONTROL PROFESSIONALS (ISACA 2005).

32   Christopher Fox, CA, and Paul Zonneveld, CISA, CA. IT CONTROL OBJECTIVES FOR SARBANES-OXLEY: THE IMPORTANCE OF IT IN THE DESIGN AND IMPLEMENTATION OF INTERNAL CONTROL OVER FINANCIAL REPORTING, 2nd Ed. (IT Governance Institute 2006), p. 17.

33   Global Public Policy Symposium, GLOBAL CAPITAL MARKETS AND THE GLOBAL ECONOMY: A VISION FROM THE CEOS OF THE INTERNATIONAL AUDIT NETWORKS. (November 2006), p. 2.

34   The objective of imaging is to duplicate all the forensic information from one magnetic medium such as a hard drive, leaving the original source untouched, and making the copy available for forensic analysis.

35   Bitstream copies duplicate everything on a disk including slack space. Bitstream copying continuously and sequentially records the entire hard drive without change. Simply copying a disk duplicates the files but ignores the forensically important slack space on the disk.

36   M. Shackell, CORPORATE FRAUD: PREVENTION, DETECTION AND INVESTIGATION. (NSW, Australia: PriceWaterhouseCoopers 2000), p. 11.

37   For example, there is software that uses the principles of Benford's Law to interactively analyze data for fraud. If the analysis is performed on a working PC rather than an imaged disk (i.e., identical copy) of the data, the files analyzed have been destroyed for courtroom use. For an example, see Audit Commander.

38   Random Access Memory is a form of computer storage for the short-term. Its storage pattern allows for quick access and overwrites because the protocol for storage is random rather than highly structured as on a PC's hard drive. The purpose of RAM is to allow the computer to work more quickly by storing more commonly used data where it can be accessed more quickly. Unless there is a battery backup when the computer is shut down all information in RAM is lost.

39   Reviewing date and timestamps on files allows the investigator to determine when the fraud event occurred. These dates provide information as to when the file was created, accessed, and last modified. Most

forensic investigative tools used to analyze digital files automatically report date and timestamp information as soon as the file is opened. For an example of a software tool, see WinHex. For a simple Windows example, open a file and click on File, then on Properties, and Statistics. Date and time information will be shown.

40   Investigators can use the hash to show that a file matches exactly the original file and nothing has been added or deleted, i.e., the document is intact in its original format. MD5 and SHA-1 hashes are based on mathematical algorithms, and they are more reliable than simple checksums, which can be faked.

41   National State Auditors Association and U.S. General Accounting Office. Management planning guide for information systems security auditing: Joint information systems security audit initiative, management planning guide committee. (Washington, D.C.: Government Printing Office 2001).

42   The analysis can be performed on an individual computer in about three or four hours without the computer user ever knowing it was done or the need to remove the computer from its workstation. T. Satov, "Forensics on the Fly." CA MAGAZINE. 135 (June/July 2002) 12.

43   To avoid this problem, the power should not be disconnected from the machine until all the volatile data has been collected.

44   A good computer forensic analyst will know that not all the timestamps have been changed at every point in the computer. Deep within the computer, the Filename Attribute list will remain unchanged and it identifies the discrepancies.

45   RAM data can be recovered if it is collected before the power is disconnected from the computer. Data found in the RAM may be important to the investigation. For example, rootkits may be running in the RAM, and identification of the code in the rootkit may identify the hacker. Furthermore, RAM data may be waiting to be encrypted, and if captured, it is readable by anyone. A dump of the RAM from a running system will recover such data prior to disconnecting the PC; otherwise such RAM information is lost. X-Ways Capture software (*http://www.x-ways.net*) allows the forensic investigator to collect such data from Windows 2000, XP, and Linux operating systems.

46   Encase is used here as a typical example of investigative software employed by forensic accountants. It is used by the large international accounting firms and the Securities and Exchange Commission.

47   There are other hashing programs that will work with Vista such as DPASHA.

48   Another free hash calculator is HASHX.

49   The registry is a database that contains information about all the software installed on a computer as well as network information. Registry data includes information about the shared users of a PC and their preferences. If AutoComplete in Internet Explorer is activated, text

string information will report private information about a person's web activities and indicate whether they used a password to visit a specific website, for example.

50 A grep (global-regular-expression-print) search focuses on a pattern inside a file. It acts as a search engine. Searches can be made on words or specific symbols (^) on all the files on a disk. To see how EnCase is used in searching a hard drive, see the YouTube Video, Encase Computer Forensics Demo (*http://www.youtube.com/watch?v=O4ce74q2zqM*).

51 J. Jessen, "The Perils of Disk-covery." ELECTRONIC PERSPECTIVES. (1997) 22, 48. G. Johnson, "Symposium: Emerging Technologies and the Law: Practitioner's Overview of Digital Discovery." GONZAGA LAW REVIEW. (1997/1998) 33, 347-263. J. Krause, "Frequent Filers." ABA JOURNAL, August 2003.

52 O. Kerr, "Digital Evidence and the New Criminal Procedure." Accepted paper COLUMBIA LAW REVIEW (2005).

53 The Department of Justice defines a computer crime as: "any violations of criminal law that involve knowledge of computer technology for their perpetration, investigation, or prosecution." NATIONAL INSTITUTE OF JUSTICE, U.S. DEPARTMENT OF JUSTICE, COMPUTER CRIME: CRIMINAL JUSTICE RESOURCE MANUAL 2 (1989).

54 Seizure occurs through the issuance of a warrant. A warrant is issued under probable cause guidelines by a judge authorizing a law enforcement officer to seize property or make a search. A warrant for a search only may culminate in the seizure of property. The warrant itself needs to be written as narrowly as possible yet include descriptions of property to be seized or searched.

55 A warez site is one that provides cracked versions of commercial software or movies.

56 In a standard denial of service attack, targeted machines are overwhelmed with a flood of transmissions that prevent legitimate users access to the system. A botnet is a network of computers that have been taken over by a computer hacker. A botnet can include 10,000 or more compromised computers that the hacker uses to launch attacks over the Internet.

57 In order to help prevent an attack from zombie computers, websites use CAPTCHA programs. These programs are used to try to ensure that a request from a webserver is being made by a human and not a chain of zombie comput-ers. Usually the test is a distorted digital image of a word or a series of letters and numbers that a computer user is asked to type into open box before being admitted to the website. It is assumed that only a real person can pass the test.

58 When data is purposely or inadvertently destroyed at this point in the discovery process, it is referred to as spoilation.

59 Adapted from: *http://www.craigball.com/Preservation_Letter.pdf*.

60 G. Johnson, "Symposium: Emerging Technologies and the Law: Practitioner's Overview of Digital Discovery." GONZAGA LAW REVIEW. (1997/1998) 33, 347-263.

61 P. Gutmann, "Secure deletion of data from magnetic and solid-state memory." SIXTH USENIX SECURITY SYMPOSIUM PROCEEDINGS. (San Jose, CA, 1996).

62 It is possible to run eXpress on any disk.

63 Hexadecimal notation is used with the base 16-number system. The digits used are 0, 1, 2, 3, 4, 5, 6, 7, 8, 9, A, B, C, D, E, and F. Hexadecimal notation allows for the examination of the binary data (0 and 1's) on a disk by using four binary digits per hexadecimal digit. For example, 15 is 1111 in binary and F in hexadecimal. Thus, it is possible to search for data on a large disk that uses a known hexadecimal notation. Although the file may be deleted or its extension changed, the search for its known hexadecimal notation provides a good chance for recovering the file. For example, searching for FFD8 will uncover the beginning of a jpeg image. It is known that jpeg pictures will have the FFD8 notation at the beginning of a file and FFD9 at the end of file. Once the location of the file is found on a disk, the file can be saved to another location and examined with other software used to bring up the image in the jpeg picture. Encase and other imaging software have automated this process for most hidden files.

64 The clever criminal would use typos to hide his tracks. For example, by purposefully placing typos in the letters in an address line would make two addresses appear as separate addresses to a software program looking for the same address. Unless the software program used fuzzy logic, the two addresses would not be identified as the same address.

65 Item (a) is calculated as follows: .50/.75 =.67. This percentage indicates the two purchases are not independent of each other. Purchases of B without A never occur.

66 This is called partition clustering.

67 The z score is calculated as follows: individual score – population mean/population standard deviation.

68 Huagn, S. Yen, D., Yang, L., and Hua, J. "An investigation of Zipf's Law for fraud detection." DECISION SUPPORT SYSTEMS. (2008) 40, 70-83.

69 See Hermetic Word Frequency Counter, Advanced Version (*http://www.hermetic.ch*).

70 Huagn, S. Yen, D., Yang, L., and Hua, J. "An investigation of Zipf's Law for fraud detection." DECISION SUPPORT SYSTEMS. (2008) 40, 70-83.

71 *http://www.cra-arc.gc.ca*.

72 For an example of an article describing how logs can be used to identify fraudulent activities, see Best, P., Rikhardsson, P., and Toleman, M. "Continuous Fraud Detection in Enterprise Systems through Audit Trail Analysis." JOURNAL OF DIGITAL FORENSICS, SECURITY AND LAW. (2009) Vol. 4, 39-60.

EXERCISES

1. Define computer forensics.
2. What is wrong with these fraud detection techniques: erasure marks and missing paper checks?
3. List where some electronic evidence may be found of a crime.
4. Summarize the guidelines SAS No. 31 provides for auditors.
5. Which data extraction software should be used by a forensic accountant? Why?
6. Discuss any three of the technical skills needed for working with digital evidence collection.
7. From the internet, determine the use of these software tools:
   a. Nmap.
   b. John the Ripper.
   c. TCPDump.
   d. Tripwire.
   e. THC - Scan
8. What are a windows cluster and a swap file?
9. What is the purpose of Encase and Helix?
10. What does FRCP 41(b) (2) say about the seizure of contraband?
11. Describe COBIT's goals.
12. What is slack space and how is it created?
13. Can deleted files always be recovered? Explain your answer.
14. How can timestamps be altered?
15. For what purposes do computer forensic specialists analyze electronic data?
16. What are the dates found on an electronic file that is currently being used?
17. In what ways can electronic evidence be destroyed so that it is no longer admissible in court? Explain your answer.
18. The Securities and Exchange Commission recommended the internal control framework used by which organization?
19. Under the COSO framework, what general IT guidelines have been established?
20. What organization is now responsible for setting the auditor's attestation standards?
21. List some examples of imaging software.
22. List some examples of data mining software.
23. What technical skills are needed for electronic evidence collection?
24. What does comparing the hash values of two files show?
25. What is John the Ripper?
26. Hashing can be done on what types of files?
27. What legal instrument (document) is needed for the seizure of a computer considered to be part of a cybercrime?
28. Which Amendment to the U.S. Constitution might restrict the seizure of electronic property that is part of a cybercrime investigation? Why?
29. What is magnetic force microscopy?
30. Which software tool can be used to view and investigate hexadecimal data on a disk?
31. **Using HashCalc.** Use HashCalc to check the hash codes on the two identical files. Once it is determined the two files have the same hash codes, delete a word in one of the files. Now run another hash on the two files. It should be clearly seen that the two hash codes are now different. What does this show?
32. **Right On.** Describe what is meant by the "linear view" used with paper documents.
33. **Changing Times and Dates**. Use files that you have been working with in the chapter to complete the following.
   a. Use *Properties* to view the electronic dates on the two files. Record all information about the times and dates.
   b. Now use eXpress to change the time and dates on the two files.
   c. Use *Properties* to again view the dates on the two files. Write all information about the times and dates.
   Write up a brief report about the changes in the files that occurred as you carried out each step. Indicate how such time and date information could be important in a forensic investigation.
34. **Focus**. Describe why weak IT controls and security may be the Achilles' heel of financial reporting.
35. **Delete It and Go Free!** Henry C. Yuen, the former chief executive officer of Gemstar-TV Guide International, was under investigation by the Securities and Exchange Commission (SEC) for committing an accounting fraud that resulted in billions of dollars of lost market value for investors. The SEC's case was being developed with the use of e-mails and other electronic documents. During the continuing investigation, Mr. Yuen installed

a software tool called Eraser on his company PC and proceeded to wipe the entire contents of his hard drive, including unallocated space, so that no electronic courtroom evidence could be recovered. The hard drive contained e-mails, corporate documents, and other electronic documents that had been subpoenaed by the SEC. Eraser is sold by Heidi Computers, Ltd, an Irish company, and costs about $21, and it is available at *http://www.heidi.ie/node/6*.

Yuen's action destroyed needed electronic evidence for the fraud case. Consequently, Mr. Yuen, unlike the top officers at Enron, could not be effectively prosecuted for a complex securities fraud that included recognizing millions of dollars in phantom and kickback revenues on Gemstar's audited annual report. Instead of charging Yuen with securities fraud, he was charged in a civil case and with obstruction of justice.

What should have been done to prevent the destruction of electronic evidence contained on a company's computers?

36. **Cross Word.** Solve the following crossword puzzle dealing with the chapter's terminology.

ACROSS		DOWN	
1.	an algorithm used to compare files	2.	residual data on a hard drive
3.	volatile data	4.	a method to efficiently review audit logs
5.	a law dealing with a natural phenomenon		
6.	international standardization guidelines		
7.	a method to strategically filter data for fraud analysis		

37. **Career Focus.** Identify: (a) the characteristics of each of the following certifications; and (b) the professional group that provides these certifications.
    a. Certified Internal Auditor
    b. Certified Fraud Examiner
    c. Certified Information Forensic Investigator
    d. Certified Forensics Computer Examiner
    e. Certified Electronic Evidence Collection Specialist

38. **Ten-Second Car Mistakes.** Review the following payroll files for the last two years for Felix Tao, a ten-second car builder from Dallas, Texas. Felix rebuilds Hondas to run the quarter mile in ten seconds, and he is not interested in accounting. Can you detect any problems in Felix's payroll?

Wage Paid during 2013:					
Name	#SS	Employment Period	Gross Wages	Deductions	Net Wages
Henry Jones	577845356	Jan 2013-December 2013	33,210.00	4,981.50	28,228.50
Douglas Reeder	660252600	Jan 2013-December 2013	33,210.00	4,981.50	28,228.50
Peter Litton	598275631	June 2013- October 2013	13,840.00	2,076.00	11,764.00
Douglas Witty	446998322	July 2013-December 2013	13,840.00	2,076.00	11,764.00
Joseph Mills	546703589	July 2013-December 2013	13,840.00	2,076.00	11,764.00
John Fields	629810229	July 2013-December 2013	12,890.00	1,933.50	10,956.50
Michael Bias	615372066	July 2013-December 2013	13,840.00	2,076.00	11,764.00
Richard Durst	505035018	July 2013-December 2013	12,567.00	1,885.05	10,681.95
Evan Bacon	695507758	Aug 2013-December 2013	12,990.00	1,948.50	11,041.50
Wages Paid during 2014:					
Name	#SS	Employment Period	Gross Wages	Deductions	Net Wages
Henry Jones	577845356	Jan 2014-December 2014	34,040.25	5,106.04	28,934.21
Timothy Stout	855995459	Jan 2014-December 2014	34,040.25	5,106.04	28,934.21
Teddy James	661700793	Feb 2014-April 2014	8,234.00	1,235.10	6,998.90
Jessica Della	729791932	March 2014-November 2014	28,125.00	4,218.75	23,906.25
Cory Dean	641745169	April 2014-July 2014	11,110.00	1,666.50	9,443.50
Charles Big-ley	423327643	May 2014-December 2014	22,110.00	3,316.50	18,793.50
Douglas Witty	446998322	July 2014-December 2014	17,020.12	2,553.02	14,467.10
Joseph Mills	546703589	July 2014-December 2014	17,020.12	2,553.02	14,467.10
John Fields	629810229	July 2014-December 2014	17,020.12	2,553.02	14,467.10
Michael Bias	615372066	July 2014-December 2014	17,020.12	2,553.02	14,467.10
Jane Lilox	878860793	July 2014-December 2014	16,970.00	2,545.50	14,424.50

39. Which of the following software packages is used to investigate slack space?
    a. PeopleSoft
    b. Encase
    c. SAP
    d. IDEA

40. **You Spoiled It.** Motorola, Inc., fired its CFO, Paul Liska, in January for a number of reasons related to his performance as stated by Motorola. Liska has filed a suit against Motorola for the conditions of his dismissal. Motorola, accused its former CFO of destroying evidence needed in the case, and asked the Cook County Circuit court to sanction Mr. Liska for "spoiliation" of evidence in the case. When he was fired on January 29, Mr. Liska left the company with his company laptop, and when he returned his laptop on February 17, the laptop had been "wiped." Motorola's forensic investigators had found that a data destruction program was run on the laptop numerous times to destroy any usable data needed by Motorola to show what Mr. Liska had been working on prior to his dismissal. Mr. Liska states that he only deleted personal files.
    a. Do you believe that all files related to the case have have been destroyed?
    b. Are there any other places that work files related to the CFO's accounting activities would be kept?
    c. What would have to been done to files collected from a source other than Mr. Liska's laptop?
    d. Would these files be acceptable in a courtroom case?

41. **E-mail Linkages.** NodeXL is a social media graphing tool that is available for free. It works in an Excel format and allows for the entry of datasets that can easily be graphed. The software graphs the linked relationships in social media sites such as Twitter. It allows the analyst to study the communications that occur between individuals in social media. For example, it will map the contacts between "friends" in Facebook. It can also be used to study the communication relationship in e-mails between company employees. Normal contacts between employees do not have to be

investigated, but if a fraud has occurred and one employee has been identified in the fraud, then the e-mail contacts of that one employee could be important to identify the extent of the fraud in the organization. Hundreds of e-mail relationships would need to be reviewed.

A screen shot from NodeXL follows. It shows e-mail communication among a number of company employees. The direction of the e-mails is shown with arrows. Can you surmise anything about the relationships among these employees and determine who might be the leader of this group?

42. Compare and contrast Zipf's and Benford's Law.

43. **Zipf's Law and an Internet Problem.** Download Wolfram's CDF Player from *http://demon-strations.wolfram.com/download-cdf-player.html*. Afterward search the Wolfram's application projects for *Zipf's Law Applied to Word and Letter Frequencies*. The demonstration is an application of Zipf's Law to word frequency counts. Select JFK's Inaugural Speech.

a. How many times does "the" appear in the speech? Make a digital copy of the screen display to turn in with your solutions?

b. What is the Zipf sequence between the most common word and the next three?

c. Describe a way Zipf's law could be applied to uncover fraudulent documents.

44. **Identifying Anomalies.** Use the Event Viewer to analyze the logs on your computer. In your logs, find an event that is an anomaly such an error or warning. The anomaly can come from application, security, setup, system, or forwarded event logs. Once the anomaly is found, (a) copy the screen display; (b) search the Internet and find an explanation of the anomaly as described in the Event Viewers "Detail" box. Turn in both the copy of the screen display and your explanation. For help with this exercise, see *http://www.youtube.com/watch?v=J6vUOyxmU1o*.

45. **Save It All.** When an accounting firm receives a legal request for the preservation of e-evidence, what steps should it take?

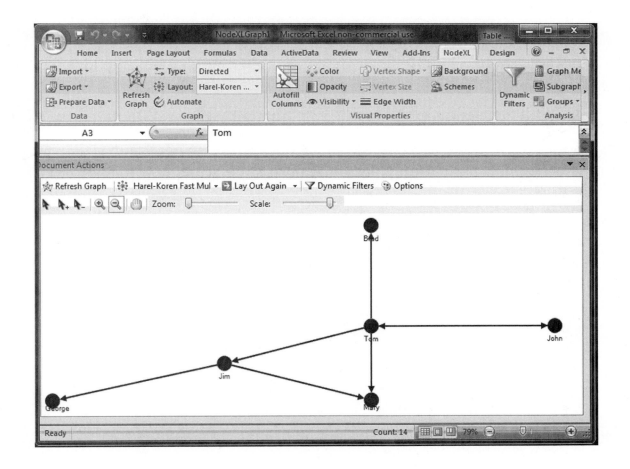

14

DIGITAL FORENSICS ANALYSIS

An Easter egg, Mr. Yamata. That's what we call it.

It keys on two stocks. If General Motors and Merck go through the system at values which I built in, twice and in the same minute, the egg hatches, but only on a Friday, like you said, and only if the five-minute period falls in the proper time range.

—Tom Clancy, Debt of Honor[1]

I don't know how that got on my computer.

—Famous last words spoken by many about their computer

OBJECTIVES

After completing Chapter 14, you should be able to:
1. Describe Internet protocols.
2. Find IP addresses in TCP/IP packets.
3. Identify the sender of an e-mail.
4. Trace IP addresses to their source.
5. Recognize the potential of a forensic audit.
6. Use the Internet to perform due diligence.

OVERVIEW

Today's tech-savvy cybercriminal can steal more money with a keyboard than any of the 1930s bank robbers and criminals would have ever imagined. The potential financial damages that can be created by a well-executed cyber attack are astronomical. For example, in March 2007, billion-dollar retailer TJX had the encrypted credit card information from approximately 46 million customers stolen. The cyber thefts took place undetected over a 17-month period. While the thefts were occurring, the intruders scrubbed their tracks out of computer logs and altered time stamps. Stolen credit card numbers are usually rapidly sold over the Internet to others who use them for making purchases from retailers or other purposes. Today, there are so many stolen credit card numbers being sold over the Internet that their prices have been drastically dropping due to the economics supply and demand. Such criminal actions call the integrity of a company's entire financial system into question and raise audit control issues under the Sarbanes-Oxley statutes.

Beyond direct monetary losses, the risks of an attack extend to system shutdowns, introduction of false information into a system, and stealing corporate proprietary information and other confidential information. The attack on a company's payroll program can result in the theft of thousands of employees' identities in just 10 seconds.

In the past, a distinction was made between the malicious attack from a *cracker* and a curious but nonmalicious intrusion from a *hacker.* Today the term *hacker* has changed to refer to a cybercriminal whose intent is to gain access to a computer network for malicious purposes. Many Internet hacker websites provide free software to use in attacking other websites. At one time, hacker sites brag about their latest successful attack against business and government agencies, but now cybergangs want money, not bragging rights. In fact, cybercriminals are selling their services to launch attacks for others. The typical cost to rent a botnet with 10,000 zombie computers, which is enough to bring down most Internet sites, is around $200 per day and the botherder, who runs the botnet, may also provide the potential purchaser with a three-minute free trial. (http://blog.damballa.com/archives/330)

Contributing to these problems is the reluctance of victims of cyber attacks to disclose that their network has been successfully breached. A well-known company does not want to reveal to the general public and its customers that they have been successfully hacked. This silence makes it is difficult for others to know how to protect themselves against similar attacks, and for corporations and customers to prevent their financial information from being sold and resold over the Internet.

In recent years, many high profile financial frauds have been committed by unethical top executives at companies like Enron, WorldCom, Waste Management, Inc., Adelphia, Health-South, Tyco International, and Dell, for example. All these financial crimes and cybercrimes could have been analyzed with digital forensics. Digital forensics is the investigation of any digital or electronic media (flash drives, webcams, cell phones, Internet, printers, etc.) for evidence of unethical behavior and financial malfeasance. Digital forensics overlaps computer forensics which is specifically related to computer platforms. In this chapter, digital forensics will begin with an explanation of Internet protocols.

EXECUTIVES: CAN'T LIVE WITH THEM AND CAN'T LIVE WITHOUT THEM. *Executives at American International Groups and Brightpoint, Inc are Charged in Securities Fraud.* Brightpoint, Inc. is a firm with a global sales and distribution network and total revenues of over $1 billion. It has products such as handsets, personal digital assistants (PDAs), and software. Brightpoint executives committed a financial fraud to hide a substantial decrease in annual profits. The fraud involved a complex financial accounting conspiracy among high-level executives at Brightpoint and American International Group (AIG). AIG is a large holding company whose subsidiaries sell a wide range of insurance products. In 1998, Brightpoint forecasted a $13 to $18 million one-time charge against its 1998 revenues. The charge was related to losses from the closure of Brightpoint's U.K. middleman trading operations for their wireless products.

Prior to the issuance of the annual report, it became obvious the trading loss was close to $29 million. In order to report the loss within the forecasted range in Brightpoint's 1999 annual report, Brightpoint's Chief Accounting Officer and Director of Risk Management purchased for $15M a "retroactive insurance" policy from AIG. Essentially, Brightpoint paid AIG a bribe for a fake insurance policy and the later return of their payment to them as insurance proceeds. All documents were pre-dated to August 1, 1998. The "insurance policy" was specifically structured to smooth annual income and fool Brightpoint's auditors. In 1999, the receivable on the policy was used to cover $12 million in 1998 losses and to show the reported loss within the forecasted range as well as hiding the round trip $15M payment to AIG and back to Brightpoint. The result of the deception was an overstatement of Brightpoint's income before taxes by 61 percent. Brightpoint's CFO was also charged by the SEC. The fraud was uncovered by tips received by the SEC and later confirmed with the collection of electronic evidence found in e-mails sent by executives.

Biovail pays $10M to settle case with SEC. The SEC has accused Biovail's chief executive, CFO, former CFO and Controller of accounting fraud involving the use of three separate accounting schemes to hide the company's true earning picture from 2001 to 2003. The company moved $47M in R&D expenses from its corporate accounts to a shell company, used a bill-and-hold scheme to generate $8M in fake revenues, and understated foreign exchange losses by $3.9M. All steps were executed under the direction of C-group executives. Today an investigation of digital data would have quickly identified these activities.

AIG, Brightpoint, and Biovail are all illustrations of significant financial frauds where traditional financial auditing techniques, such as the separation of duties, testing internal controls, and confirmations, have little chance of uncovering these events. In the case of Brightpoint, the insurance contract was specifically written to meet all the accounting criteria needed to hide the true nature of the transaction. The co-conspirators in many high profile frauds are executives who can override all the accounting controls and bribe almost anyone who might report on their activities. Such conspirators are usually uncovered through tips from a third party and not by the auditors or the SEC. The investigative methods described in the current chapter are directed at changing that unfortunate record. The described methodology and tools are used to stop and uncover these frauds. Consequently, these methods must go beyond checks of internal financial controls. As will be explained, these investigative techniques form the foundation for performing a forensic audit and identifying unethical executives, cybercriminals, and thieving employees.[2]

Sifting for Cyber Clues

¶ 14,001   COLLECTING EVIDENCE

All computers connected to the Internet are protected under federal law (18 USC §1030). Federal investigators can use subpoenas, court orders, search warrants, and electronic surveillance, as well as traditional investigative methods to search for the cybercriminal. Investigators without supporting legal authority are faced with using Internet forensic research to try to identify criminals before the electronic trail disappears. Most cybercrimes leave clues for the forensic investigator provided the investigator knows where to look.

The savvy financial cybercriminal will not make it easy to find these clues. The real PC used to make the attack can be hidden. If electronic use logs are kept by the victim of an attack, they may be altered by the hacker to disguise the location of the attacking PC or to hide the fact that the victim's PC had been compromised. If an attacker is located outside the United States, a crime may not have occurred in the foreign country where the criminal lives and little cooperation can be expected from authorities. For example, countries where widespread malicious activities such as spamming, malware generation, phishing, and botnets can be found are in the Rus-sian Federation, Luxemburg, Latvia and the Ukraine.[3]

When cybercrimes are launched from such locations, the only hope for the victim is if the forensic investigator and the accountant can document the dollar value of the destruction that has occurred as well as provide law enforcement with viable clues about the identity of the attacker. In those instances, the victim is more likely to receive law enforcement support. Furthermore, the auditor, who should stumble across the clues of a financial fraud, must be careful not to destroy or alter electronic evidence before it is properly collected.

¶ 14,011   CLUES VERSUS EVIDENCE

In tracking down these clues, both legal and technological factors should be considered. Most clues collected by the forensic investigator are not going to meet the rigorous requirements of courtroom evidence unless the information is uncovered by legal authorities and its evaluation is strictly controlled. Still, the clues collected by the independent forensic investigator may provide legal authorities with enough preliminary information for them to issue a search warrant, and thus speed up the collection of electronic evidence before it disappears.

TURN ME OFF? If a forensic investigator simply turned on an employee's computer during an internal investigation, regardless of the findings, all evidence would not be admissible in court. In this case, it would be easy for the defense attorney to charge that the electronic evidence had been changed and become tainted. Furthermore, the turning off of a computer would cause volatile data, such as swap files, to be unrecoverable.

The forensic investigator needs to be familiar with the protocols used on the Internet to be able to collect clues about unethical executives, or internal or external attackers. In addition, when law enforcement officials send requests or subpoenas for information about a company's electronic logs, the forensic analyst must understand the type of information being sought. Lacking this understanding, the analyst can create a situation where legal authorities may view the company as part of the crime rather than as another possible victim. Finally, it is difficult to understand how the financial auditor can "brainstorm" about the possibility of fraud, as required under SAS No. 99, without a basic understanding of the technology behind electronic financial files and crimes. These technologies and investigative methods are explained in the remainder of this chapter.

Technical Searches

¶ 14,021   **INTERNET PROTOCOLS: TECHNICAL SEARCHES BEGIN HERE**

The Internet is being used for transferring large amounts of confidential financial data, and forensic accountants have a role as investigators to protect financial information, prevent their clients from being defrauded, work with computer forensic technicians, and assist law enforcement in identifying the perpetrators of these crimes. The developers of the Internet never expected that the system would be used for so many business purposes. For these reasons, the forensic accountant should acquire a basic behind-the-scenes understanding of how network traffic flows over the Internet. An understanding begins with Internet *protocols*, which are those rules allowing different operating systems and machines to communicate with one another over the Internet. Whenever *http* is typed into a web browser, it is signaling which protocol is being used. In this case, it is the protocol that allows for browsing a hypertext document on the Internet.

Transmission Control Protocol (TCP) and Internet Protocol (IP)

TCP/IP protocols are the communication guidelines used and widely supported over the Internet. When a user is surfing the Internet with a browser such as Firefox, Chrome, or Internet Explorer, all this communication activity is unobtrusively occurring within the browser package. The user is unaware of the way packets of information appear on the computer screen, how this data is logged, or how unauthorized and potentially damaging code can be sent within those packets to create financial havoc. The browsing of websites is done with TCP/IP protocols. There are other communication systems such as File Transfer Protocol (FTP) and User Datagram Protocol (UDP), but TCP/IP is the protocol examined here.

Almost every packet of information sent over the Internet uses the *datagrams* contained within a TCP/IP envelope. The datagram consists of layers of information needed to verify the packet and get the information from the sender's to the receiver's location following traffic control guidelines. These protocols enable different applications and equipment to communicate with one another over the Internet. The packets are continuously changed as they move along the Internet from one router to another. Thus, there is path information contained in the packet.

Message encapsulation is used in sending the packets. In message encapsulation, each layer of information in the sent packet is interpreted by the same layer at the receiving end of the transmission. Additionally, each layer can only communicate with the one directly above or below it. Figure 14.1 shows the layering that exists in a TCP/IP system known as the Operating System Interconnection (OSI) model. The figure illustrates five layers. In addition to these five layers, there are presentation and session layers, respectively, below the application layer.[4] Using just the first five layers, however, adequately explains the functions of the OSI model.

Figure 14.1. The Layered Operating System Interconnection (OSI) Model Used with TCP/IP

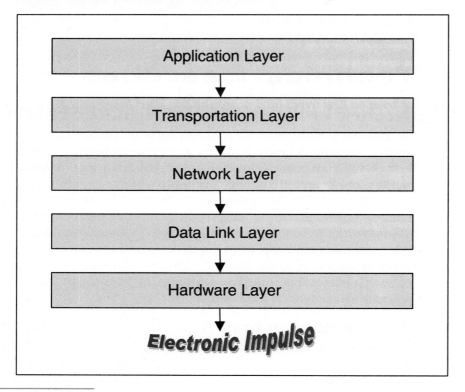

Application Layer

The application layer issues the commands that define the operations such as those required for an e-mail or the interpretation of the software protocol for a financial transaction request. It interacts with the user's operating system and exists just below the user's operating system level. The user sees the effect of transfers between the operating system level and the application layer as files are transferred. Applications for Hypertext Transfer Protocol (HTTP), Telnet, Simple Mail Transfer Protocol (SMTP), and FTP reside in this layer. Each of these applications provides for a connection and data transfers between a local and a remote computer. When a user views the number of bytes being downloaded in the Windows screen, they are seeing the application layer in action. As shown in Figure 14.1, the application layer is the topmost in the stack.

THE HOKE HOAX. *The Cybercrime.* On the morning of April 7, 1999, users of Internet bulletin boards hosted by Yahoo! Finance, devoted to discussing a company named PairGain, saw a message from an individual identifying herself as Stacy Lawson of Knoxville, Tennessee. The message reported that PairGain, a telecommunications equipment company located in California, would be purchased for $1.35 billion by an Israeli company. The message contained a link to a Bloomberg News story. No one at either company involved in the transaction could be reached for comment because of time zone differences and holidays. The story and the Bloomberg web page were false. Consequently PairGain's market price rose over 31 percent on the NASDAQ with 10 times its normal volume. When the hoax was revealed, thousands of people lost money in the stock's decline.

The Trace. All the information the cybercriminal had placed into the free web hosting services (Anglefire) and distributed through e-mails (Hotmail) was false. Both the free web hosting service and the e-mail provider logged subscriber information such as the suspect's IP number. The logs showed the suspect had logged onto the web hosting service and an e-mail provider using several different IP numbers. A search of free web-based IP tracing services revealed that the IP numbers were located at PairGain and Mindspring. Mindspring is a large Internet service provider (ISP). A list of IP numbers and times was presented to Mindspring along with a subpoena to identify the account user who had used the web hosting service and e-mail address. The IP address allowed Mindspring to identify the e-mail address as ghoke@mindspring. In addition, Mindspring's logs identified the phone number used to dial into the e-mail account. Gary Hoke, a PairGain employee, was quickly identified and arrested. Further investigation led to Gary Hoke pleading guilty to securities fraud. Hoke never used the crisis to trade in PairGain stock to make money so the only way to trace the fraud back to him was through IP logs, and not through traditional stock trade information.[5]

Transportation Layer

The layer directly below the application layer in Figure 14.1 is the transportation layer, which functions to provide reliable message delivery. This layer provides data to make the connection to the receiving host computer. The transportation layer is responsible for ensuring the integrity, control, and proper connections between the sending and receiving hosts. This responsibility includes finding the proper entry port on the recipient's web server. With more than 65,000 possible ports, numerous messages can be simultaneously arriving at a web server. TCP resides in this layer and for web transmission, it creates a TCP header incorporating data coming from the application layer.[6] The envelope created consists of user data, an application header, and a TCP header, at this point. The TCP header is shown in Figure 14.2.

Figure 14.2. TCP Header Information

Source Port								Destination Port	
Sequence Number									
Acknowledgment Number									
HLEN	RES	URG	ACK	PSH	RST	SYN	FIN	Window	
Checksum								Urgent Pointer	
Options									
Data									

Source: Excerpted from "When Is a Cybercrime Really a Cybercrime?"[7]

The TCP header in Figure 14.2 contains information about the correct delivery of the message. The destination and source ports allow for connections to the correct web server port. Out of the 65,536 ports, there are 1024 ports standardized for well-known operations, i.e., HTTP uses port 80. The next set of data—the sequence and the acknowledgment numbers—ensure reliable message delivery. When a TCP connection is launched, the sending server forwards a sequence number to the recipient server. The initial sequence number is based on the computer's system clock and is therefore predictable. The recipient server adds a one to the initial sequence and sends it back as an acknowledgment number. This exchange continues as data is sent back and forth. The pattern of exchanges shows which bytes have been sent and acknowledged as received. The process is used to ensure that sent messages have been reliably received.[8]

The next set of data is called flags. Flag data is used to signal the connection state of the data exchange. The HLEN flag provides information about the bit size of the TCP header. The classification Reserved (RES) comprises actual bits in the datagram reserved for future use, i.e. they are unused. The URG (urgent) flag indicates the significance of the data in the upcoming Urgent Pointer field and provides an end marker for the urgent data in the packet. The ACK (acknowledgment) flag provides the information that the data was successfully received, and it is always sent with data after initial connection. The PSH (push) flag processes data so it is not waiting to be sent nor is it waiting to be processed when it is received. Thus, the data is not queued to wait for more data to arrive. The RST (reset) flag will be set if the received packet does not appear to be the one that was expected to be received. It tells TCP to reset the connection. A SYN (synchronization) flag indicates the significance of the sequence number and the initiation of a connection (an initial sequence number is sent). When the first packet is sent, only the SYN flag is set. With all the other packets both the SYN and the ACK flags are set. The FIN (finish) flag, which must be acknowledged, shows there is no more information to be sent in the message.[9] The sophisticated cybercriminal has the ability to change the expected sequence of information in the flags to confuse the recipient's computer and gain unauthorized access to the network, bypassing any firewall.

The next section of the datagram in Figure 14.2 is the window field. The window field shows the size of the open window through which data packets can be sent. The window tells the sender the amount of packets the recipient is capable of accepting. If a window is close to zero and there are no acknowledgments forthcoming, it indicates the recipient server's port is congested. The larger the window, the more packets that a server can accept. A port may become inaccessible due to a denial of service attack.

The checksum field is used to ensure data integrity by checking for errors in the data, TCP header, and IP header. The sender's server calculates a checksum for each TCP packet sent based on the data in the packet. The checksum is placed in this field. The recipient's server recomputes the checksum and compares it with the one that was sent. If they are the same, it is assumed there are no errors in the received packet and the message is ACK'ed. If they are not the same, then a request for retransmission will be made and no acknowledgment is sent.

The urgent pointer is commonly used in the datagram to indicate the transfer of a large file. If the recipient server needs to interrupt the large transfer, the URG pointer will be set to point to the end of this large file. The options field follows the URG pointer. One use of the options field is to limit the size of the data segments sent. After the options field, the message data is entered. It is amazing to know that all these actions are completed in nanoseconds.

Network Layer

The next layer is the network layer, which controls the route the data takes to get to its destination. IP operates at this layer and sends the packets from the source to its destination network across various subnets and through numerous routers. At this point, the envelope has a "phone number" or in this case the IP address of its destination. The IP address is a 32-bit address field. Each packet sent out has the correct IP address. Therefore, a set of information may be sent in several packets and must be reassembled by TCP protocols. There is no guarantee that sent data will arrive in a properly ordered sequence at their destination. In fact, duplicate packets can be created and sent to the destination. When one router sends a packet to a second router but does not receive a receipt acknowledgment, the first router resends the packet. Thus, two packets with the same information, except for different arrival times, will have to be dealt with by TCP protocols in reassembling the correct message for the recipient.

HIDING YOUR IP ADDRESS. The IP address in the network layer can be changed using software, which allows a web surfer to be anonymous as he goes to websites across the Internet. Such software provides the user with a fake IP address and a fake country of origin. A fake IP is generated by using a proxy server. Using a proxy server is the same as borrowing a friend's cell phone to make a call. In such a case, the call is traceable to the friend's cell phone but not the caller's phone. On the Internet, a person can use another server with a different IP address (untraceable back to him) as he surfs the Net. Thus, the proxy's IP address (i.e., same as a friend's cell phone number) replaces the true IP address. Examples of software used to hide IP addresses are Hotspot Shield, Anonymity 4 Proxy, NetConceal, and the Anonymizer. The streaming of TV programs may cause a determined viewer to hide her IP address. Hulu, a U.S. TV steaming service, is not available to computers displaying a European IP address due to copyright restrictions. By first connecting to a U.S. proxy service and then connecting to Hulu, the European user's IP address appears as a U.S. IP, and the programs are available for viewing. It is not recommended that this procedure be used as it is a violation of U.S. copyright laws.

Figure 14.3 illustrates the header information contained in an IP datagram. In the datagram, Version 4 is the IP edition used. The header length describes the length of the header.[10] The Type of Service (TOS) signals the quality of the service requested as the message is transmitted over the Internet from router to router. The choices are low delay, high reliability, and high throughput. These service levels are not independent of each other as one choice such as high throughput may affect reliability. The total length field refers to the entire size of the datagram in bytes (the largest acceptable length is 65,535 octets or eight bits).

Today, IP version 6 (IPv6) is beginning to supplement version 4 (IPv4; for example, 192.168.1.50). The switch to IPv6 is being made because all the IP addresses under IPv4 have been allocated (4.3 billion). The last top level IPv4 addresses were allocated in February 2011. IPv6 (2001:0:5ef5:79fd:2c80:2592:3f57:feed)allows for the expansion of IP addresses from a 32 bit to 64 bit format. Also, the packet format in IPv6 is different than in IPv4. Version 6 provides a larger address space, simplified packet header, no checksum is used, no fragmentation of messages, there are integrated security features, and a hop limit for packets is used instead of time to live fields (see next section). IPv6 has the capacity to efficiently send jumbo packets with a length of 4294967295 octets. As IPv6 becomes more widely used, Figure 14.3 in the text will be revised to reflect the new format. At the end of 2012, IPv6 was approximately 1% of Internet traffic.

PING OF DEATH. Internet Control Message Protocol (ICMP) provides for monitoring controls between Internet hosts, redirects of messages, packet time exceeded messages, and pings. A ping is an echo request sent as an ICMP packet by one host to another to determine whether the pinged host is active and listening. It derives its name from the ping echoes used in Navy submarines. Over the Internet, the machine sending the ping knows the second machine is reachable over the network if a return ICMP ping is received. An attack called the Ping of Death was developed by exploiting the IP maximum size of 65,535 bytes to crash systems in denial of service attacks. The fragmented packet sent in the ping attack was more than 65,535 bytes in size, thus causing a system reboot or possibly a system crash as the packet was incorrectly processed. In these attacks, the header length field was set to a minimum value, such as 1. Today most servers do not allow a response to pings, so the Ping of Death attack is dead, but the basic approach of this attack is still being applied in other contexts.

The identification field shown in Figure 14.3 is assigned by the sender, and it is used to help reassemble the fragments of the datagram upon receipt. Flags are used to control how the datagram should be fragmented when it is transmitted. With IPv6, the data is not fragmented; rather it is sent in one data packet. With IPv4, the reason a router may transmit a fragmented datagram is because the router controlling the communication between two different networks does not use the same size packet criteria. With IPv6, it is expected a route will be selected that can carry the entire packet. As IPv6 can send the entire packet along the same route, the flags signaling whether the packet is fragmented (0) or not (1) are not used, thus simplifying the packet's structure. The flags in IPv4 also indicate whether a fragment is the last fragment (0) or if more fragments are being transmitted (1). The fragment offset field identifies a packet's position among all the fragments received.

Figure 14.3. The IP Header Information

Version	Header Length	TOS		Total Length
Identification		Flags		Fragment Offset
TTL		Protocol		Header Checksum
Source IP Address				
Destination IP Address				
Options (if any)				
Data				

Source: Excerpted from "When Is a Cybercrime Really a Cybercrime?"[11]

TTL stands for *time to live*. TTL is the time the datagram is allowed to be active on the Internet. Once that time period is over, the datagram is destroyed. Without a limited life, lost datagrams would endlessly loop around the Internet using up bandwidth.[12] Every unit that processes the datagram over its route reduces the packet's time left to live. The protocol field is the next higher level protocol to be used in processing the datagram such as TCP, ICMP, or UDP. The Header Checksum field is used to detect transmission errors. It is calculated based on the content of the entire IP header, and it is updated whenever the packet header enters a router on its way to its destination. If an error is detected in the checksum, the packet is discarded. The Source IP address is the 32-bit IP address of the sender. An *IP address* is a 32-bit number (four bytes) that identifies the sender and recipient who is sending or receiving a packet of information over the Internet. It acts as the phone number for the Internet.[13] The Destination IP address is the final destination of the packet. The Options field may be used in the datagram. One option that can be provided for in this field is a time stamp to record when the datagram was sent. Another option is to record the route the first fragment of the datagram followed in arriving at its destination. After Options, the data is entered into the datagram. These features are all simplified or eliminated in IPv6 but both versions will continue to be used on the Internet for some time to come.

Data Link Layer

The data link layer transfers the datagram from one network node to another. Initially, the data link layer packages data into frames for the physical layer. A frame has a header and trailer, error checking bits, and a manufacturer's physical machine address that is different from an IP address. The data link layer also transmits the frames sequentially to the network layer. It handles incoming acknowledgments showing the data has been successfully received by the recipient. It is responsible for error checking on incoming frames from the physical layer.

The data link layer is split into two separate layers called the media access control (MAC) and logical link control (LLC). MAC maintains a link to the network with permissions to broadcast data locally or to a remote location. MAC carries the physical address of each device as related to an Ethernet card on the network.[14] This physical address is useful as a means to identify an employee's computer on the company's internal network. LLC encodes data into a proper format in transmission such as with or without acknowledgment at this layer. In this way, the data link layer provides for network interface.

Hardware Layer

The hardware layer, or physical layer, provides the means of sending and receiving data on a network by converting bits into voltages for transmission to a coax cable. This layer includes the cables, cards, connectors, and other equipment connected to the network, such as the T-1 physical connector. The job of the physical layer is to send and receive electronic transmissions.

WHO IS MONITORING MY COMPUTER ACTIVITY: KEYLOGGERS. A keylogger is a software program or hardware device that can be used to log all the keystrokes made on the keyboard. If the user has encryption software, all the keystrokes are made in plaintext, i.e., before encryption. Thus, keyloggers can be very useful for collecting passwords, IP addresses, and all e-mails. When keylogger software is used, it must be secretly installed on the PC without the user's knowledge, which may be hard to accomplish.

WebWatcher is a keylogger software program that costs around $99 and allows for remote access to a monitored computer, once it is installed. It monitors e-mails, logs websites visited, and captures screen shots, as well as records keystrokes. Obviously, installation of such software must be done without the computer user's knowledge. Such installations should only be performed in legally approved circumstances. Keylogger software is available from numerous sources including ActualSpy and Actual Keylogger, which is a free software product. Numerous free keyloggers are available from http://download.cnet.com/windows/

Companies can use a keylogger as one method to catch an employee suspected of misusing company assets or selling valuable proprietary information.

¶ 14,031 DECODING PACKET INFORMATION

To learn who is visiting a website, it is necessary to decode the previously described packet information. Most web users would be surprised about the information contained in the packets that are sent over the web as they surf the Internet. Once it is understood there is important information hidden in Internet packets, the need to study such information becomes more obvious. Without such understandings, the accountant can only review paper documents. Today, the only way to quickly trace a fraud perpetrated through a company's computer network is by tracing the information left behind by the attacker's packets.

For a forensic investigator, it is important to be able to successfully identify the perpetrator of a cybercrime, whether that perpetrator is an employee or an external attacker. Such crimes may occur as e-mail threats, destruction of data files, or as unauthorized access to a company's network, for example. The forensic investigator needs to trace such cybercrimes back to a perpetrator, before all the electronic tracks have disappeared. The experienced cybercriminal will try to hide his or her electronic trail just as the forensic investigator is trying to find it. A traditional financial auditor must aid the forensic investigator, at a minimum, by not destroying evidence useful in identifying the perpetrators of a financial fraud.

Forensic investigators employ several techniques to follow the trail left by the cybercriminal. The previously described information contained in TCP/IP packets provides basic clues in the search.

Web Log Entries

Information in TCP/IP packets can be uncovered in several ways. One important method for finding the web trail of the attacker is in examining web logs. Recorded network logs provide information needed to trace all website usage. This information includes the visitor's recorded IP address, geographical location, the actions the visitor performs on the site, browser type, time on page, and site the visitor used before arriving. When company employees use their work computers to visit websites, this activity is recorded in logs. Skilled cybercriminals may attempt to alter these logs to hide their activities. Therefore, one caution is to store the logs on a computer separated from the web server hosting the site. Another preservation problem is that these logs are only kept for a short time. Once they are deleted and the media is continually overwritten, it is almost impossible to find information about unauthorized network use or trace employee web activities.

Figure 14.4 shows an example of a raw log entry created when a visitor used his web browser to visit a website.

Figure 14.4. The Raw Log and Its Interpretation

```
200.55.243.2 [25/Nov/2005:01:20:15 +0900] GET/finasset/gates/gif
HTTP/1.1
200 7560 Mozilla/6.0 (compatible: MSIE 5.0; AOL 5.0; Windows98; DigExt)
```

200.55.243.2 is the accessing IP address or host name of the visitor. The IP address can be traced to a specific geographical location.

25/Nov/2011:01:20:15 +0900 stands for day/month/year:hour:minute:second and GMT time zone. The time zone will provide a means to identify the geographical location of the PC sending the request. This location may be different than the visitor's PC.

GET is the code request from the browser. In this case, GET is a request to get a file.

finasset/gates/gif is the file that is being requested from the website.

HTTP/1.1 is the HTTP version being used.

200 is the HTTP response code. In this case, 200 shows that the page was successfully retrieved. A 404 code would show an error occurred in retrieving the page.

7560 is the size of the file in bytes that is being requested.

Mozilla/6.0 (compatible: MSIE 5.0; AOL 5.0; Windows98; DigExt) shows that Netscape (Mozilla) was the browser used by the visitor to the site.

Log entries vary depending on the communication protocol used. For example, there would be differences in FTP and HTTP logs, but the information contained in the secured logs will give the forensic investigator an opportunity to trace criminal or unethical activity back to its perpetrator. Most important in Internet tracing is identifying the IP address and geographical location of the attacker. For example the identification of this IP 78.2.22.164 would show it is from Croatia/Hrvatska(HR) region in Eastern Europe, and it is an IP assigned to Croatian Telecom Inc., Zagreb, Croatia. In this case, entry point to the Internet is from the city of Pula.

The time zone from where the message was sent provides added identifying information. The IP address is shown in Figure 14.4. The raw log also provides information about a visitor's activity while on the website. The IP address enables the investigator to trace the visitor back to a specific Internet hosting service and possibly a specific PC. The log can also show the version of the visitor's web server such as Apache 2.0.54, whether Etags for more efficient operation are used, and last modification dates.

GUESS WHO I AM. There are many websites that can and readily identify you. For example go to *http://myip.sonyonline.net.* This site identifies your IP address, port number, and web browser. Other sites will identify the geographical location of your ISP. See http://network-tools.com/. For my work computer the following information is shown: You are coming in from IP Address 78.2.22.164, port 59083, Using Mozilla/5.0 (Windows; U; Windows NT 6.1; en-US; rv:1.9.2.13) Geck-o/20101203 Firefox/3.6.13

TCPDUMP

Besides reviewing the raw log entries, the investigator can use more tools to analyze Internet traffic information in packets sent to a compromised website by the attacker. One such tool is a Unix-based program called TCPDUMP. TCPDUMP is a form of network sniffer that can disclose most of the information contained in a TCP/IP packet. A *sniffer* is a program used to secretly capture datagrams moving across a network and disclose the information contained in the datagram's network protocols. Sniffers have earned a bad reputation because hackers use them to identify network passwords, but they are the friends of the forensic investigator.

A Windows version of TCPDUMP, called WINDUMP, is a free download from a number of websites (such as, *http://winpcap.org/windump)*[15] for those who are unfamiliar with Unix coding. There are other free sniffer programs available on the Internet. Most of these programs reveal the same information about data flowing over a network. A sample of the information disclosed by TCPDUMP is shown in Figure 14.5.

Figure 14.5. An Example of a TCPDUMP

```
18:20:01.743609 0b:a0:4d:f2:0d:e1 0a:50:b1:44:8f:1d 160.173.10.1
10.1301>125.25.10.11.1501: S2896914311:2896914311(0) win 512 [tos
0x10]
```

18:20:01.743609 stands for hour:minute:second:microsecond.

0b:a0:4d:f2:0d:e1 is the MAC address of the sender.

0a:50:b1:44:8f:1d is the MAC address of the recipient.

160.173.10.110 is the source's (sender) IP address.

1301 is the source port from where the packet came.

125.25.10.11 represents the destination IP address for the packet.

1501 is the destination port for the packet.

S is the SYN flag setting.

2896914311:2896914311(0) shows the sequence number for the packet with no data (0).

win 512 represents the size of the window. 512 bytes is the minimum size that can be used.

[tos 0x10] shows the level of service that the packet should receive as it is sent.

In Figure 14.5, the data reveals several useful pieces of logged packet information. The time stamp on the message is shown. The source and destination IP addresses are shown as well as the MAC addresses on the source and destination network. The IP address allows for tracing the packet back to a source, and the MAC address allows for a more extensive search on the source network for a specific computer. The port activity enables the investigator to see the access port through which the packet entered the web server. In some cases, the port entrance may occur through a little used port and raise the investigator's suspicions or the packet may be suspicious in other ways. Of course, there would be hundreds of packets, not just this one, coming into a website and TCPDUMP would provide the same information about each one. Figure 14.5 provides an example of a TCPDUMP, but the extent of the information revealed in the log will depend on the options chosen by the investigator as they use the software. Such choices would change the information shown in the figure.

Web logs and TCPDUMP reveal information that enables the investigator to try to trace the perpetrator of a financial fraud or hacking attack. For example, this information will show whether the crime was launched from outside or inside the company. It will show whether or not the criminal activity came from an ISP used by one of the employees. When logs are available from several sources, it is important to correlate criminal activities to time and time zones in the different logs to substantiate the case against the perpetuator.

Web logs show when the suspect was on the Internet. Log comparisons among different ISPs show attacker activity across these ISPs. Report summaries of such comparisons make a strong case as an investigator tries to get law enforcement support and subsequent legal action against the attacker.

Before the process of an IP traceback is described, it is also important to review how identity information can be collected from headers in e-mail messages. All this supporting evidence can be combined to make a case against a suspect in an internal financial fraud or hacking attack. The importance of these identification methods is increasing as cybercriminals enhance their efforts to steal intellectual and proprietary information, such as research and development designs or strategic marketing plans, from companies.

GET READY FOR NEW ONLINE FRAUD SCHEMES: Crowdfunding

The new Jumpstart Our Business Startups Act signed in 2012 allows for companies to raise up to $1M in equity over the Internet on Securities and Exchange registered websites. The Act eliminates many of the previous legal safeguards on selling stock over the Internet. The $1M in funding can be raised by small businesses from small investors without the need to file standard registration documents with the Securities and Exchange Commission. Many of these investment websites are likely to be based in home basements and oriented toward specific groups.

An analysis of Internet domain names by state and Canadian securities regulators found nearly 8,800 domains with 'crowdfunding' in their name as of Nov. 30, up from fewer than 900 at the beginning of the year," NASAA said in a statement. "Of these websites, about 2,000 contained content, more than 3,700 had no content and more than 3,000 appeared to be 'parked' and serving as placeholders to reserve a domain name for later use or sale. Of the domains with 'crowdfunding' in their name, about 6,800 have appeared since April 2012, when the JOBS Act was signed into law. http://www.nasaa.org/18951/nasaa-sees-sharp-spike-in-crowdfunding-presence-on-the-internet/

For examples of crowdfunding sites see: http://www.ulule.com/ or http://www.crowdcube.com/

¶ 14,041   DECODING SIMPLE MAIL TRANSFER PROTOCOL (SMTP)

The information obtained from e-mail messages is a key factor in influencing and affecting business decisions. It is also an invaluable source for investigators to track the relationships between corporate financial fraudsters and their accomplices. Consequently, it is important to have assurances about the integrity of such messages. Unfortunately, e-mail provides an easy means of misrepresenting both the source of the message and the sender. As a result, spoofed e-mail messages containing malware have been a major contributing factor to the destruction of asset values around the world.

Attachments to e-mail have at numerous times crippled corporate computer networks, as did the infamous "Melissa" and "Love Bug" viruses and the more recent versions of the W32/Kelvir worm or the Phish-Bank Fraud Trojan. Today, virus makers have developed nonmalicious code can be loaded on a computer. Once is is on a computer it will pull together parts of other common programs already resident in a computer to construct a virus. The code combining software copies coding from other commonly used programs to create malware. Beyond these attacks, misinformation about a company's financial prospects received as e-mail messages have contributed to stock price drops that resulted in the disappearance of millions in market capitalization within a few hours.

SMTP is the protocol used to send e-mail over the Internet. SMTP servers accept incoming messages into Port 25, check addresses, store local messages, and forward messages to remote addresses. SMTP protocols are standardized in e-mail servers. It is possible to directly communicate with an SMTP mail server by telnetting into Port 25 if that port is left open. Once the connection is made, Telnet allows for bi-directional communication between the two computers, and it allows for execution of commands on the remote computer such as sending e-mail. The command language is relatively simple and easy to use. Using "Run" to obtain a command line and typing "telnet" will open a telnet session on the user's computer. Once opened, the next step is to use a remote computer's IP address and port number to enter and begin the telnet session on the remote computer. Logins may or may not require passwords. It is possible to check to see if the relay port is open at http://www.mailradar.com/openrelay/.

GUESS WHO I AM NOW. SMTP mail servers operating on Port 25 sometimes have open relays that will forward mail as a service to third parties without checking the identity of that third party. If the mail port relay is open, it allows spammers and others to bounce mail through this relay service to any e-mail address and fake the return address to be anyone … such as the President of the United States, for example. Spammers use automated software to search for open relays on servers throughout the world. Once they find an open relay, they telnet into Port 25 and funnel thousands of e-mails through that open relay. All the sent e-mails show the IP address of the server with the open relay. Malicious e-mails can be easily sent through these open relays to misdirect people or to assume others' identities. Such fake e-mails were being sent long before cybercriminals began using compromised servers for phishing attacks. This problem can be avoided by closing Port 25, using verification procedures for accessing SMTP ports, or using digitally signed e-mail that include the sender's encrypted ID information.

Path Checking

SMTP server logs are a useful source of information about the origin of e-mail messages. If these logs are correctly maintained, they can be used to check the path of the e-mail from the sending host to the receiving host. Such path checking also requires the cooperation of two administrators from two different ISPs; otherwise, it is impossible to get copies of these logs and correlate them. The SMTP command settings control the exact information that will be recorded in a log entry. A sample SMTP log is shown in Figure 14.6 for the acceptance of an e-mail message.

Figure 14.6. An Example of an SMTP Log

```
[2002/11/26 15:50:10 -0500] cross.smtp[7654]: General
Notice:SMTP-Accept:078EXC987.W466782GD:<786490346.B78662D4@msn.
com:[125.12.11.1]:125.12.11.1:<p2@msn.com>:516:1:<trash4@you.
com>
```

[2002/11/26 15:50:10 -0500] shows the year/month/day/hour/minute/second/time zone. In this case, the time zone is the East Coast of the United States.

cross.smtp [7654] is the name of the SMTP module that recorded the event.

General Notice:SMTP-Accept describes the event that occurred: acceptance of an e-mail message in this case.

078EXC987.W466782GD is the unique message ID assigned to the message by the mail server.

786490346.B78662D4@msn.com is the sender's e-mail address.

125.12.11.1 is the IP address of the sending server.

p2@msn.com is the message ID in the message header assigned by the sending server.

516 is the size of the message in bits.

1 is the number of recipients.

trash4@you.com is the e-mail address of the recipient.

The log in Figure 14.6 shows the time the message was received, the message ID assigned to the message by the mail server, the sender's e-mail address, the IP address of the sending server along with the ID given to the message by that server, the number of recipients, and the e-mail address of the recipient. Much of this information is also available in the e-mail's header, but secured information in the log is more difficult for a hacker to falsify.

A web server has thousands of port connections that may be open to the Internet. Some of these ports allow anyone from anywhere to use the web server's ports to download files.

Port 25 is the SMTP port on a web server, and the software for the server's e-mail is hosted in that port. As has been stated, if relay control is open on Port 25, it is possible to bounce unauthorized e-mail messages through an unsuspecting web server using a fake e-mail address and send it to another real e-mail address with a fake message. The fake e-mail can contain viruses, spam, or fraudulent information that directly cause losses for a business. Websites that leave Port 25 open for such activity are blacklisted and the e-mail from their IP address are blocked by Internet Service Providers (see: http://www.blacklistalert.org).

SMTP logs and e-mail headers provide the forensic investigator with the potential means to identify the criminal suspect behind such attacks. Such information also provides for the identification of employees who are conspiring to commit a financial fraud and are using the company's e-mail system to send their messages.

In today's workplaces, disgruntled employees can anonymously use the Internet to harass and retaliate against their colleagues, bosses, or companies by sending falsified information in e-mail. Offers of sex or allegations of child abuse committed by a targeted colleague are common ploys. Such malicious slander should be traced not only to stop the perpetrator from more abusive behavior but also to end the economic toll on the employer.

DON'T SAY IT IN AN E-MAIL. Defamatory and anonymous e-mails were received by company employees regarding their managing deputy director, Brian Cone, at Takenaka. The e-mails stated he had an affair, fathered an illegitimate child, and made death threats. Takenaka is a large Japanese construction company with world-wide projects. These anonymous e-mails were written to destroy the director's reputation, and they originated from a fake Hotmail account and CompuServe's ISP service. To find the sender of these e-mails, investigators examined the e-mail headers to trace the email's path. Using IP traces through ISPs, time stamp information, and computer forensic analysis of deleted data on a company laptop, it was discovered that David Frankl, a former employee of Takenaka, was the sender of the e-mails. Frankl had previously worked for Cone. Although the e-mails had originated from a laptop assigned to Thames Water Utilities in Turkey, only two employees had access to the account. The forensics analysis.....

> ... of matching the dates and times between the ISP's billing information, the Hotmail access logs and the computer traces (from the file structure, the file content, unallocated space, cluster analysis and cache indices' (Takenaka (UK) Ltd and Brian Corfe v David Frankl (unrep, High Court, 11 October 2000)

....revealed that only Frankl was responsible for the sending of the e-mails.

Frankl insisted the e-mails had been sent from the laptop by malware not by him, but he was specifically identified with the use of the laptop when the e-mails were sent. Furthermore, there was no trace of malware on the laptop. He was fined £26,000 and required to pay court costs of £100,000.

Headers

In trying to trace a suspect, the information in e-mail headers should not be ignored. To understand how perpetrators who send viruses and financial misinformation are traced through their e-mail headers, it is necessary to understand some of the technical information found in e-mail headers. If we see any header information in our e-mail messages, it is the short form of the header, and it shows the e-mail address of the sender and the recipient, the subject, date, and time. The time zone information is in relationship to Greenwich Mean Time (GMT).

In the following date line, the time zone from which the message was sent was five hours after GMT, which is Eastern Standard Time.

```
Sun, 20 Mar 2011 21:06:31 -0500 (EST)
```

This date shows the date on the sender's computer when the message was written, thus allowing for the identification of information about the geographical location of the sender's computer. The date line on the following message shows it was sent from the East Coast of the United States. If 0500 were replaced with +1300, the message would have been sent from New Zealand. Of course, all this header information can be faked, and there is no chance of knowing whether a fake message has been sent by viewing the short form of the header.

Most of the important information about the origin of an e-mail message is in the long form of the header that most e-mail users never see. All e-mail packages should allow users to set their preferences for viewing the long form of the header. To trace an e-mail message back to its source, it is necessary to begin with the long form of the header. In Hotmail, for example, the long form of the header can be viewed by right-clicking on the e-mail message in question, and then clicking on "view message source." The next screen will identify the e-mail's originating IP address and routing information.

Here a message is being sent from a Hotmail account to a university e-mail account. The expanded header follows:

```
X-Message-Delivery: VjOxLjE7dXM9MDtsPTA7YTOwOOQ9MjtTQOw9NA==

X-Message-Status: n

X-SID-PRA: Stevenson G. Smith <sgsmith@se.edu>

X-Message-Info: M98loaKOLo3AhpqODr2oVSmJfWPq+xAWX60gu5nqdeRwFnClh-
M2YLUvaoWbGfzrMYk0aco5sau3AnyZO2vNlmXub3ldBYVjyRvhUJFrxpdtUTM6VQho
2zQ==

Received: from lily.se.edu ([164.58.120.25]) by SNTO-MCl-F32.SntO.
hotmail.com with Microsoft SMTPSVC(6.0.3790.4675);
 Tue, 29 Mar 2011 05:25:34 -0700

Received: from EXCHANGE.se.edu (10.0.0.102) by lily.se.edu
(172.17.120.22) with Microsoft SMTP Server (TLS) id 8.1.436.0; Tue,
29 Mar 2011 07:25:29 -0500

Received: from schefflera.se.edu ([::1]) by EXCHANGE.se.edu ([::1])
with mapi;
 Tue, 29 Mar 2011 07:25:33 -0500

From: "Stevenson G. Smith" <sgsmith@se.edu>
To: "figure_man@hotmail.com" <figure_man@hotmail.com>
Date: Tue, 29 Mar 2011 07:25:18 -0500
Subject: Test Message
Message-ID: <6A52550ABC05CA489F378FAAD70CFF7F427D1496F9@schefflera.
se.edu>
Content-Language: en-US
Content-Type: text/plain; charset="us-ascii"
MIME-Version: 1.0
Return-Path: sgsmith@se.edu
X-OriginalArrivalTime: 29 Mar 2011 12:25:34.0290 (UTC) FI-
LETIME=[66DBF320:01CBEE0C]
```

The message is a test message sent from a university account (sgsmith@se.edu) to a Hotmail account (figure_man@hotmail.com). The expanded header contains information that allows for tracing the e-mail message in a manner that cannot be done with the short header. Although there is a vast amount of pertinent information in the expanded header, the most important data for tracing purposes are the IP addresses and the message ID. The message ID is assigned internally by the sending server, and it can be used to trace the message to the e-mail logs where more details about the message are available.[16]

In the headers, the first received message (lower most) provides information about where the message originated: Received: from schefflera.se.edu ([::1]) by EXCHANGE.se.edu ([::1]) with mapi; Tue, 29 Mar 2011 07:25:33 -0500. The first received message in every header identifies where the message originated and other "received" messages shows the hops the e-mail made from one mail server to the next on its way to the recipient. The message was sent from a university e-mail system: se.edu. The server sending the message was on the East Coast of the U.S. (-0500). The term "mapi" (messaging application program interface) indicates that an e-mail feature is active for allowing the different e-mail systems, i.e., within an organization or between a sender and recipient to work together and decode the message.

In the logged example, there is one originating IP address, 172.17.120.22. The trace on 172.17.120.22 identifies it as a U.S. IP address, but it is only documented as a "private IP address on a LAN" (http://www.ip2location.com/).17 Addresses within such private address space are unique to a specific organization (se.edu). A private internet is used internally by an organization. Private hosts can only communicate with other hosts inside the organization. Private IP addresses do have access to external communications through application level gateways. This is the reason the IP address is shown in the e-mail log. But, this IP address cannot be directly identified through an IP address search. Information as the assignment of this IP address could only be obtained with a warrant for the university's mail server's logs. On the other hand, a trace on 164.58.120.25 IP address is identified with se.edu. The sender of the e-mail logged into their se.edu e-mail from a Croatian ISP, but there is no record of that information in the e-mail headers. To find information about the Croatian ISP requires a review of the mail logs on the university's mail server.

It should also be noted that the receipt of the e-mail by initial Hotmail server recorded its arrival time on the Hotmail server not at the time it was sent by the university e-mail system. The message ID was given by the originating mail server at se.edu. The ID will allow for an immediate trace back to its source. The term "MIME" in the message refers to Multipurpose Internet Mail Extension, and it allows for images, sound, and text to be inserted into the e-mail message. In order to quickly parse, the information in a e- mail header use the website MX Toolbox at: http://mxtoolbox.com/EmailHeaders.aspx.

¶ 14,051   DECODED IP ADDRESSES: TRACING TOOLS

Once the information such as IP and MAC addresses are obtained from the server logs, it is necessary to try to trace the criminal's activities back to their source.

SPOTLIGHT

EMULEX E-MAIL HOAX. According to *The Wall Street Journal*, identifying the perpetrator of the Emulex hoax was largely based in tracing an IP address in an e-mail message. The Emulex hoax was the result of a bogus press release sent to Internet Wire, a news service. The news release stated that Emulex's CEO was resigning under the cloud of an investigation of the company's accounting practices by the Securities and Exchange Commission, and there would be downward restatement of company earnings. The stock fell about 61 percent, and market capitalization of more than $2 billion was lost once the announcement was picked up by other market wire services. The press release was allegedly from the head of a fictitious public relations firm called Porter & Smith. Because of the way the release was written, employees at Internet Wire assumed it was a legitimate news release.

The news release had been sent by a former employee of Internet Wire named Mark S. Jakob. His purpose in sending the e-mail was financial gain. He was maintaining a short position on the company's stock and needed the price to drop. He sent the message from a computer lab at El Camino Community College in California using a free Yahoo! e-mail account opened just for sending the release to Internet Wire. Jakob had been enrolled at the community college.

The authorities used the IP address in the e-mail message to quickly trace it back to El Camino Community College and learn the time it was sent from the lab. After that, they used traditional police investigative practices to correlate factors such as names of students in the lab with former and present Internet Wire employees, and stock trades to identify Jakob as the sender of the bogus e-mail message. The first key to successfully identifying Jakob was the IP address in the long form of the e-mail header.[18]

Traceroute

Several methods can be used to back trace an IP address. One such commonly used program is traceroute.[19] Traceroute provides the means to determine where an e-mail message or TCP/IP packet originated. Traceroute follows the route taken on the Internet between the source IP address and the destination IP address. It provides information about the hops a packet takes from one router to another by listing the IP address and optionally the domain name of the various routers along with the time it takes for the packet to traverse its Internet route to its destination. Some traces may time out because the servers along the route do not answer traceroute queries. Some traceroute programs allow the investigator to see the route taken over a map of the United States or the world to the exact geographical location of the originating IP address (for an example, see *http://www.visualware.com/demo/index.html*). For a large number of links to Internet traceroute gateways, see *http://www.traceroute.org/#USA .html*. If a visual trace is not required, Windows operating systems include a traceroute utility program. To use this utility, it is necessary to access a command line (C:\ prompt). By clicking on Run and typing *cmd*, a screen will open in Windows. The utility allows for a trace from the initializing PC to the IP address.[20] In the command line, type in *tracert Dell.com*, for example, or use the actual IP address.

In some cases, the trace will time out because some servers have turned off this option or because of the long number of hops between the originating PC and the IP address. Traceroute programs are now providing the user with choices as to whether to use IPv4 or IPv6 (http://centralops.net/co/)

Whois

Whois searches can provide collaborating information after a traceroute search is used. Whois is another freely available service providing identification information on almost any domain name and the administrators who run it. Using the IP address from a web server log or e-mail header, Whois tells the investigator the name of the organization running the domain name and its address, administrative and technical contact names and e-mail addresses, country location, billing address, domain servers, and usually contact phone numbers. Whois and traceroute enable the investigator to identify an IP address with the originating organization and in some cases, with the computer on the network that sent the message. All this tracing can be completed in a few seconds.[21] Figure 14.7 shows the results of a fictitious Whois search. The Whois search shows a contact administrator (Greg Homer), his contact phone number (1–555–555–5555), and his extension number (2000).

Figure 14.7. Results of a Whois Search at American Registry for Internet Numbers (ARIN) (https://www.arin.net/)

```
Name: Homer, Greg
Handle: GH50-ARIN
Company:
Address: Brainer Corporation
16000 Tree Boulevard, 224 Lammeroot Beach FL
Country: US
Comment: RegDate: 1990-02-16
Updated: 2000-04-24
Phone: +1-555-555-5555-2000 (Office)
Phone: +1-555-555-5556 (Fax)
```

There are Whois gateways on the Internet to check IP addresses for Europe (RIPE Network Coordination Centre—RIPE): *http://apps.db.ripe.net/search/query.html*), in the U.S. ARIN (American Registry for Internet Numbers) currently charges for access but try free access at: (*http://whois.marcaria.com/domain-whois/North-America/USA-domain-US/*) and Asia (Asia Pacific Network Information Centre—APNIC): *http://www.apnic.net/apnic-info/search*). Also see: *http://www.internic.net*). Other, similar identification tools can be employed, such as Dig (*http://www.kloth.net/services/dig.php*), and Network Solutions (*http://www.networksolutions.com/whois/index.jsp*) or GoDaddy for everything except .edu sites (*http://who.godaddy. com/?prog_id=GoDaddy*). Whois searches for items such as domain names, IP networks, and e-mail addresses. This information can be supplemented with the search engine Shodan (*http://www.shodanhq.com*). The Shodan search engine interrogates the ports on webservers to determine the locations and character of specific routers, servers, industrial control systems, switches, and even refrigerators connected to the Internet. For example, Shodan provides information about the software that is running on the web server at an IP address or all the Apache servers in a country. If a user wanted all the Apache servers in a particular domain name they would type "apache hostname.se.edu" After the first period, different domain name would be added such as .af.mil.

SPAM. Spam is an irritating problem in everyone's e-mail, but it can cause a substantial economic loss for businesses that unknowingly pay for such junk mail to be sent through their e-mail systems. In many cases, web servers are compromised as soon as they are put online, and the unsuspecting business is left paying for the increased bandwidth as thousands of spam messages are sent via the company's servers. If such losses arise, forensic investigators should trace the source of the spam and ensure corporate mail relay ports are closed. Accounting practitioners may need to make formal determinations as to the loss incurred by the company from such spam floods. To use a spam calculator to estimate how much spam costs a company in lost salary and lost productivity, use the calculator at *http://www. cmsconnect.com/marketing/spamcalc.htm.*

Ping

Ping is another tool that is used over the Internet to electronically query an identified IP address. Today, not all websites are guaranteed to return a ping query. Conceptually, an Internet ping is similar to a sonar ping used by the Navy to identify an object in the water. The pings sent are echoed back by the queried machine showing it is alive and listening and able to receive datagrams. If a machine is listening, additional information can be collected from its open ports. Pings do not use TCP protocols but instead they use another protocol called Internet Control Message Protocol (ICMP). ICMP is related to IPv4, and it is used among webservers as a diagnostic and reporting tool. For example, if the datapacket has exceeded its TTL, ICMP protocols are used to notify the source of the message. ICMPv6 is the protocol that will be used with IPv6. ICMPv6 acts in a similar manner as its predecessor with more extensive diagnostic features.

Machines on a network have either a static or dynamic (changing) IP address.[22] A ping to a dynamic IP address only provides temporary identification with a user as dynamic IP addresses are continually reassigned by an ISP to new users coming online. An example of static IPs are the old dial-up Internet services. A ping to an attacker's IP address will help establish the status of the perpetuator's PC at that time. A ping to a static IP address identifies the specific machine with the queried IP. Identification is also related to the physical MAC address of the machine, i.e., its burned in Ethernet adaptor ID.[23] If the MAC address is obtained, it specifically identifies the computer was involved in the criminal act. Identification to a specific machine does not mean the owner of that machine was the culprit as the machine could have been taken over by the real attacker, i.e., the compromised machine acted as an unknowing zombie host or the WiFi system was breached.

Figure 14.8 shows the results of a ping on a web server. The server was pinged three times. Each sequenced line is the echo reply received from the pinged machine. Time information on the round trip shows minimum, average, and maximum times to send and receive a response. The information indicates the host is alive and listening to Internet requests.

Figure 14.8. Ping Results from Using the Ping Gateway at fifi.org (http://www.fifi.org/services/ping?hostname=dell.com&packet-count=1&packetwait=1&formatted=yes&submit =Ping) and Pinging the Server at 202.84.251.189

Sequence number	Answer From	Time To Live (TTL)	Delay
1	202.84.251.189	247	20.1
2	202.84.251.189	247	19.6
3	202.84.251.189	247	19.8

Sent	Received	Loss	Delay: Minimum	Average	Maximum	Mean Deviation
3	3	0%	19.630	19.859	20.102	0.192

To perform a ping, the forensic investigator can use one of the gateway pages (see *http://www.tracert.com/tracegw.html*) on the Internet (or download a free ping program, such as that available at *http://download.cnet.com/Ping-Test-Easy/3000-2651_4-10523393. html*. A ping program is also available from a command line prompt in Windows. A simple identification service also is provided by Nslookup. Nslookup provides a service to either identify an IP address (such as 122.89.10.1) from a domain name such as amazon.com or the reverse, identify a domain name from its IP address. Nslookup is also available from a command line prompt in Windows.

Finger Searches

Finally, finger searches are a helpful alternative for the investigator trying to identify usage patterns of a suspect on a network. Finger programs take the identified e-mail address and provide information about the user such as their home directory, real and login names, the last time they logged onto the system, received or read their e-mail, the time they currently logged into the system, and how long they stayed on the system. The information provided will vary with the fingering program used and some programs only provide information about the users who are currently on the network. To use a finger tool on a network, it is necessary to Telnet into port 79 on the server. Protocols with the finger port would require you to type "finger" finger a host @se.edu for example, or finger <e-mail address>. Telnet is available from the Windows command screen.[24] Also, there are various finger gateways on the Internet, but they do not provide the specific information available from finger tools on an internal network. Access to webservers using finger have been severely limited in recent years. (Finger and other tracing tools are available at *http://www.subnetonline.com/pages/network-tools/online-finger.php*)

The usefulness of these searches depends on the services that a queried web server has running. For example, ping responses have been turned off by many system administrators to prevent hackers from using ping as an exploit or as a means to begin an attack against a web server. Finger may have been turned off also.[25] Regardless, all the identification methodologies should be used as an attempt is made to trace the activities of an internal or external suspect.

THINK...THINK...THINK. FRAUD VERSUS FORENSICS. In the typical fraud model of crime, the criminal is in close proximity to his victim at the time the crime occurs. Thus, the traditional fraud model analyzes the crime scene in a house or in a company, i.e., a crime limited to a specific area. With a financial cybercrime, the criminal can be anywhere in the world, and so can the victim. The crime occurs anywhere the victim's PC is located. Additionally, the crime can be executed on thousands of victims at the same time, providing staggering returns to the criminal. Forensic analysis looks at this bigger picture of financial crime, and thus it must use an investigative model and methods that extend investigations to anywhere in the world—from the corporate office to the hacker on the other side of the world.

¶ 14,061   DECODED IP ADDRESSES: NARROWING THE SEARCH

Once the trace back has led investigators to an IP address outside the company's network, additional information cannot be collected without the support of the ISP controlling the IP. The ISP is under no obligation to provide any information to a private investigator about its clients. Yet, it is important to perform a trace back on the suspect because without an immediate search the electronic evidence will quickly be deleted and unrecoverable.

At this point, if the investigation is related to a cyber attack, the forensic investigator has two choices. First, the description of the attack and the information that has been collected can be reported to law enforcement. At a minimum this information should include the suspect's screen name, how the attack was discovered, suspect's e-mail address, date, GMT time, duration of the incident, all appropriate time zone information, IP addresses, and ISP host names as well as contact information. The report should provide the following information about the attacked system: hardware and operating system information, firewalls and other security measures in use, copies of pertinent logs along with any correcting information on the times recorded in the logs, i.e., checking whether the computer clock is accurate. In order for such information to be complete, a description of the exploit, its success, damage done, and a dollar valuation of the damages should be made. The description of the incident should provide as much when, where, how, what, who, and why information as can be reasonably collected.

If the collected information is part of a forensic investigation of a corporate executive who is suspected of being involved in a financial fraud, the information will need to be initially handled inside the company. After the information is reviewed by the company's legal counsel, it will be determined whether law enforcement should be contacted.

Preliminary Incident Response Form for a Cyber Attack

Figure 14.9 provides an example of a Preliminary Incident Response Form to record incident information before it is filed as part of a police report about the cybercrime. The investigator must be familiar enough with cyber attacks to be able to complete all the information on the form. All incident information should be compiled prior to approaching law enforcement officials for assistance. The investigator should retain an electronic image, not copy, of the victim's drives after the attack. Items 12 and 13 on the response form require calculations made by an accountant who is familiar with cybercrimes and can determine the full extent of damages. Such calculations may require present value and real option determinations (see Chapter 16). All intangible losses should be included in this estimate. The supporting documentation of the damage calculations should be retained for a possible insurance claim. Furthermore, if the investigator knows that the attack is part of a coordinated effort by a hostile group against a number of sites, the evidence for such a conclusion should be clearly disclosed in the Response Form.

Figure 14.9. Sample Preliminary Incident Response Report

PRELIMINARY INCIDENT RESPONSE REPORT

Part I: Description of Victim

1. Name of company_____
2. Company host and sites involved_____
3. Company Contact:
a. Name of Individual_____ Position_____
b. E-mail_____ c. Phone_____
d. Mailing Address_____

_____

Part II: Description of the Incident

1. Date of the incident:_____
2. GMT time of the incident:_____
3. Physical location of the attacked system (company headquarters, other site or sta te):_____
4. Operating system on the attacked system:_____
5. Hardware:_____
6. Security systems in use on the attacked system (name and version):

_____
7. Mission of the attacked system (What is its function?):_____

_____
8. Describe how the attack was detected._____

_____
_____
9. Describe the attacker's activities (DOS, virus, sniffer, spoofing, social engineering, etc.)._____

_____
10. Estimate time duration of the incident from detection to completion._____

_____
11. If possible, estimate how long the attacker was on the system before being detected. _____
12. Description of the damage done in the attack._____

_____
13. Provide an estimated dollar valuation of the damage (show calculations)._____

_____
14. Describe activities taken by the victim up to the time of filing the report._____

_____
15. Attach copies of appropriate logs (up to 20) and collaborate the times on the logs. If the times on the logs are not correct, reconcile them to the correct times.

Part III. Suspect(s) Information

1. Source IP address for the attack_____
2. Provide a complete description of how this IP address was collected._____

_____
_____

3. Organization responsible for IP address_____

_____

4. Contact information for the organization in Item #3.
   a. Name of Individual_____ Position_____
   b. E-mail_____ c. Phone_____
   d. Mailing Address_____

_____

5. E-mail address of the attacker, if known_____
6. ICQ ID number of the attacker, if known_____
7. Name of the attacker, if known_____
8. Address of the attacker, if known_____
9. Description of further contact that the attacker has requested_____

_____

10. The date and time when the attacker is demanding further contact_____

_____

11. If possible describe the suspected reason for the attack (extortion, fraud, terror, mischievous behavior, etc.)._____
12. Attach copies of messages or threats left by the attacker (e-mail messages, coding and messages on web defacement, etc.).
13. Attach appropriate copies of Whois, Rwhois, Traceroute, Ping, Nslookup, and Finger searches on the suspect(s).

At the present time, not all local law enforcement officials are familiar with Internet fraud. Few local law enforcement officials will be familiar with the technical information that is provided to them which makes redress for victims an unlikely outcome. If the attack is part of a coordinated attack by hackers on several sites and the dollar value of the damages is significant, federal or state law enforcement will likely have an interest in the crime. If law enforcement accepts the case, agents or officers can serve subpoenas for the disclosure of additional evidence such as the needed ISP logs.

REPORTING THE CRIME. The Internet Complaint Center is a national site supported by the FBI for reporting Internet crimes (*http://www.ic3.gov/default.aspx*). A number of states have set up special cybercrime units within their police agencies to deal with financial crimes. Examples of these include: New Jersey (*http://www.state.nj.us/njsp/divorg/invest/cyber-crimes-unit.html*), and Florida (*http://www.fdle.state.fl.us/content/getdoc/f3b576fc-83c8-45ac-bfe3-72f5c39900d7/Home.aspx*). A worldwide site is (*http://www.4law.co.il/6.html*). Due to the large number of computer-based crimes and the resulting work backlog at these agencies, investigations of electronic evidence can take months, at a minimum. Outside of law enforcement, Deloitte, one of Big Four accounting firms, is a leader in cybercrime investigations. Deloitte has lab facilities located worldwide for collecting electronic evidence. For over 10 years, the accounting firm has recognized digital forensics as an important service area for their accounting clients.

John Doe Subpoena

A second possibility for the corporate victim is to file a *John Doe subpoena* under a civil suit. If the case is in any way related to defamation, copyright or trademark infringement, or breach of contract issues that have occurred over the Internet, it is possible to file a John Doe subpoena to obtain ISP logs. Financial hoaxes can financially damage a company, and they may be considered a form of defamation as the hoaxer may not try to obtain financial gains in the hoax. Additionally, if an employee discloses information covered under a nondisclosure agreement he or she signed on being employed, a John Doe subpoena may be filed. Under a typical John Doe subpoena, the evidence being requested from an ISP is the identity of an unknown person who used the ISP in performing an act against the company. Usually the demand for identity information is filed with the ISP hosting the traced IP address used by the suspect. These subpoenas are sent directly to the ISP, and they are not reviewed by a court before they are sent. If the ISP or the target of the subpoena files a motion with the court to quash the subpoena, then a court will review the legality of the subpoena. If the ISP or unknown target of the civil suit (who is likely not informed of the subpoena) does not object, the information will be released.

Usually, there are only seven days available for the ISP or target of the investigation to file a brief with a court to quash the subpoena. Thus, the requested information is usually released by the ISP as the ISP cannot just ignore the subpoena, and it may not want to fight the request in court. If a court becomes involved, the court usually views such subpoenas as potential violations of the unknown individual's First Amendment rights, and the court is not likely to allow for the enforcement of the subpoena.[26]

DON'T MAKE IT DIFFICULT....OR IT WILL COST YOU. When an employee was required to surrender his laptop under a subpoena for computer records, the laptop was found to contain only systems files needed to run the computer. Deloitte was called in to investigate whether the employee had destroyed incriminating electronic evidence.

- Deloitte found that time stamps on the operating system showed it was installed in 2003. Additionally, no other documents or applications were on the computer.
- Deloitte decoded the manufactured date of the computer's hard drive as mid-2007. This demonstrated the time stamps were faked.
- Deloitte examined the slack and unallocated spaces on the hard drive and found them to be clean indicating the computer had not been turned on since the operating system was installed.

The forensic investigation was sufficient to show spoliation and have the case against Deloitte's client dismissed. Court costs, including the cost of the digital forensic analysis, were paid by the plaintiff. (See deloitte.com)

¶ 14,065   TRACING FINANCIAL FRAUDS IN THE EXECUTIVE BOARDROOM

The financial frauds committed by the top executives at large public companies have resulted in the losses of millions of dollars to stockholders, the collapse of public companies and accounting firms, the unjustified payment of executive performance awards and stock bonuses, contracts issued based on favored status of the contractor only, illegal conspiracies to prepare misleading financial statements, kickbacks from customers and vendors, generation of numerous false financial documents, and inaccurate performance projections to the investing public. All the while, these executive's dealings ignored company's codes of ethics while each company received a clean audit opinion from their auditor.

It is obvious that at these executive levels the conspirators evaded internal controls and ignored the company's code of ethics. A company's system of internal control is usually effective in controlling financial frauds as long as the fraudster does not have the authority to override the control system. Under current internal control systems, the only evidence of an override might be the recognition of an unusual transaction, out of millions made during the year. Internal control measures have not been effective in controlling boardroom frauds. Usually boardroom frauds are only uncovered when a third party comes forward to disclose evidence of the events.

The tracing and investigative methods described in this chapter have outlined a number of measures that can be used to trace fraudulent activity back to a perpetrator. If a serious attempt is going to be made to trace financial frauds back to the executive board room and prevent millions of dollars in asset losses, it is time to apply digital methods to identify fraudsters in the boardroom. Today, there is no justification for allowing high-level executives to circumvent a company's internal controls. As traditional controls do not work in these cases, another method of controlling for fraud needs to be used. One way to expand control over the executive boardroom is with a *forensic audit*.

Forensic audits have not been defined by the accounting profession, but they have been discussed in several white papers.[27] The concept is considered to be the application of a forensic investigative approach where traditional internal controls under a financial audit are not effective in controlling financial frauds. For our purposes, a forensic audit is a process of applying investigative methodologies and technologies by an independent entity to obtain an understanding of the underlying economic risks facing an organization. Although a forensic audit could be implemented across an organization's entire management team, the cost would be prohibitive. Therefore, it is being suggested here that such an audit be limited in scope to investigating the activities of the organization's top-level executives and deterring boardroom frauds.

SPOTLIGHT

BRING ON ALL THE FORENSICS. Gov. Robert Bentley has engaged a Birmingham auditor to conduct a forensic audit of Alabama State University, rattled in recent weeks by shifts in leadership and allegations of improper contracts.

The ASU board of trustees, of which Bentley is a member, had already requested the Montgomery firm .....to conduct an audit. ..Bentley said while he supported the continuation of that audit, he believed having Forensic Strategic Solutions also do a forensic audit was in "the best interest of Alabama State and all of us who love this university." Bryan Lyman, Bentley orders forensic audit: Birmingham firm's examination 'will help provide transparency' Montgomery Advertiser, December 15, 2012 http://www.montgomeryadvertiser.com/article/20121215/NEWS/312140031/ASU-Bentley-orders-forensic-audit-Birmingham-firm-s-examination-will-help-provide-transparency-

There are organizations that have been described as "too big to fail" on a national and regional basis. Therefore, the executives in charge of these organizations have more responsibility to act in the interest of the public, i.e., a public trust. If they act only in their own self-interests, their acts can create economic damage extending far beyond their companies' boundaries. Responsibility for the public's trust requires transparency and disclosure. The tools of a forensic audit allow for such disclosures and should be applied in reverse order to the organization's authority structure. Those managers with more hierarchical authority and the ability to more easily override internal controls would find themselves come under more forensic scrutiny than those managers with less ability to override internal controls. Traditional financial controls are still needed to prevent financial fraud but as has become apparent, managers with unrestricted authority in an organization have abused traditional internal controls to achieve their own financial goals while causing damage to their companies and the general public. The consequences of these executive's actions go beyond negative effects on their "too big to fail" companies as their activities damage the economic welfare of the general public.

In developing the policy and procedures for implementing a forensic audit that goes beyond a traditional audit, it must be remembered that employee communication sent or received over a company's computer network is not confidential. It is not necessary to contact an outside legal authority to collect the e-mails or computer logs generated by company employees. Therefore anyone working for a corporation can be subjected to a high level of monitoring. Management models such as agency theory hold that director's activities need to be monitored in order to prevent managers from committing aberrant acts. As has been shown earlier in the chapter, the monitoring of corporate communication can be done in a cost effective manner.[28] There are three factors that support the implementing of a forensic audit for deterring boardroom financial frauds. They are: (1) limited privacy protections in the workplace, (2) agency theory which recognizes manager's tendency toward their self-interest unless they are monitored, and (3) cost-effective monitoring software of all electronic communications.

In the Brightpoint, fraud case discussed at the beginning of the chapter, monitoring of executives' e-mails would have set off red flags and identified a pattern of financial fraud among the co-conspirators at Brightpoint and AIG. As there was no monitoring of executive communications at Brightpoint, these e-mails were only recovered after the financial fraud was uncovered due to a third party tip to the SEC.[29]

Who Falls Under a Forensic Audit?

The managers subjected to monitoring under a forensic audit depend on the operating structure of an organization. In general, executives who have the potential ability to override internal controls and whose incentive plans are based on profit performance should be monitored. For example, a CEO whose bonus is tied to meeting EPS performance goals is highly motivated to reach those targets whether they are achieved in fact or fiction. Any executive whose compensation is strongly tied to meeting targeted financial goals, i.e., sales, return on investment, return on sales, etc., has the motivation to manipulate financial results in her favor, including orchestrating a fraud.

In identifying the specific extent to which monitoring should be carried out under a forensic audit, it is necessary to assess the organization's "ethical way of life" or how it does business. The assessment begins with an evaluation of the organizational culture, company business practices, and specifically ethical attitudes. A cultural assessment is done with quantitative methods with surveys or qualitative method with interviews, focus groups, or observation briefs. Taped interviews and focus group comments are collected and observation briefs are compiled from attending executive board meetings. Here the assessment is directed at top-level managers. An organization's culture is exemplified by the top executive's ethical attitudes, values, assumptions, and behavioral norms which trickle down to other company managers. The consequence is a set of unwritten behavioral rules for managers to follow if they expect to survive and succeed within the organization. These results help to identify how executives deal with day-to-day events.[30] When the tone at the top includes a causal disregard toward stakeholders and is exemplified by luxury purchases or extravagant corporate parties coupled with a stress on single profit performance measures and dominant overriding executives, the potential risk of financial fraud increases exponentially. For example, the fraud risk in a company with a *laissez faire* attitude toward its customers, employees, product quality, and vendors exhibits characteristics of fraud risks that require more monitoring than managers in corporations without such traits. Once a cultural assessment is completed, the potential for fraud risk determines the base level of monitoring needed to reduce the potential for executive financial frauds. Such base-level monitoring is not static. Forensic audit procedures would increase across the organization as targeted events occur within an organization. One such targeted event is the disposal or acquisition of a business segment. Therefore, the answer to the question *Who falls under a forensic audit?* is: It depends on the ethical culture prevalent within each organization. The higher the potential for fraud risk, the higher is the level of monitoring.

Who Performs a Forensic Audit?

In order for a forensic audit to be effective, it must be continuous, it is not a periodic audit, and it does not have to be performed by financial auditors. It requires an independent third party who reports directly to independent members of the Board of Directors or other independent body. Communications about the audit are limited to prevent details about an investigation from being circulated among possible fraud conspirators. The company's operational executives should not have detailed knowledge about the forensic firm's monitoring and investigation activities. With today's technology, it is not necessary for the forensic firm to be located in the company's headquarters, and monitoring is best performed in a separate facility. Yet great care needs to be taken so that no employee is unjustly accused of fraudulent activity. To aid in preventing unjust accusations, a fraud response team is brought together if a monitored transaction or event is deemed to have the appearance of a financial fraud. After a potential fraud event is identified, selected members of a fraud response team meet in emergency session to assess the event, mitigate the fallout and possible damages to the company from the fraud, and decide on the next course of action. The team should know the policies that should be followed when a fraud is suspected or detected, and the team is responsible for ensuring evidence of the fraud is properly collected and preserved.

At a minimum, a fraud response team should be composed of a chief investigator to oversee broad aspects of the investigation. In many cases this would be an attorney who can ensure that legal guidelines are being followed and help make sure, as much as possible, the team's reports are covered under attorney client privilege. A liaison to upper-level management, such a member of the board, can advise senior management without disclosing the confidential details of a case. Upper management needs to support the investigation, but if upper-level managers are under investigation they should not be tipped off about the investigative process. Obviously, a forensic accountant needs to be part of the fraud response team. Most fraud investigations would require the use of an external, independent forensic accountant as most companies do not have these specialists on their staff. The forensic accountant would be involved in analyzing the details of the fraud under the supervision of the chief investigator. It would be important to have computer forensic specialists as part of the team. The trail of fraudulent documents is an electronic trail and the collect and preservation of those electronic documents needs to be competently completed by digital investigators. Members of the company's IT department should not be used as digital investigators as they do not have the training for such investigative work. It would also be expected that the company's internal auditors would be part of the team. Their familiarity a company's internal controls would help focus the investigation on those control areas where there are the weakness and the most likely location for fraudulent activity. An assessment of the interviewing skills of the fraud team up to this point would determine if others professionals with interviewing skills need to be added as team members. A human resources officer needs to help the team to ensure that no company employee's rights are violated by the investigation. If these investigations are handled in a heavy-handed manner and violate an individual's right with false accusations, other law suits against the company are a likely result. Finally, the developments from the investigation need to be explained to the public and legal authorities so as to create the least amount of damage to the company's reputation, and its stock price. Public relations managers should be part of the team to mitigate the negative fallout from a fraud investigation. In this scenario, digital investigators along with the forensic accountants are responsible for convening the entire fraud response team when fraudulent activities are suspected or detected.

What Is Monitored?

Electronic data from the company's LAN and WiFi networks is monitored. The extent of monitoring, whether it is continuous or periodic and the specific executives monitored, is determined after the completion of the cultural assessment. The data collected includes executive-level e-mails and website activity. All collected data is automatically searched for potential "fraudulent activity." Internal policies would identify the meaning attached to fraudulent activity. Depending on the size of the organization, thousands of e-mails would be pass through the company's network. In order to simplify the review process, the preliminary review is automated. For example, the terms "destroyed"or "post-date" or e-mails with subjects related to quarterly or year-end financial results would cause the e-mail to be logged for further review by a forensic investigator. Such a review requires an analysis of cross linked messages among executives connected to the initially logged e-mails. As necessary, analysis would be expanded to the web activities of an identified executive or group of executives. For example, if an executive is identified as making Google searches for countries without extradition treaties with the United States, banks in the Cayman Islands, or looking for software that will erase a hard drive, it might be a cause for concern, at a minimum.

The reviews of electronic company documents go beyond the collection of e-mails and web activity. Interrelated business activities create an electronic footprint among its participants, identifying the interconnections for insights that are otherwise unapparent. Software is available to provide a link analysis of communications between executives and others either inside or outside the organization. The identification of damaging links and hidden associations provide the opportunity to stop relationships that violate policy guidelines for protecting proprietary assets.

With electronic monitoring, logs are collected and analyzed to provide information about the approval process for new contracts, for example. Investigative efforts are used to determine if the contracting process falls within the organization's policy guidelines. Why was an employee on a bid project sending e-mails to a competitor's attorney? Electronic authorizations for purchases can be immediately compared with the IP address (not passwords) on computers making the authorization with the IP address of computers authorized to make these approvals. Stock option documentation can be analyzed to prevent the backdating of stock options or the creation of stock option slush funds.[31] Fictitious stock trading related to Ponzi schemes are recognizable as falsified paper or electronic documents and are not supported by electronically logged entries.

During specific time periods when the stress for performance becomes more intense, such as mergers, acquisitions, discontinuation of segments, and recognition of non-operating gains and losses, the forensic investigators expand their survey of electronic communication and events. At these times, the web of cross communications among the company's executives needs to be intensified to help identify any schemes used to falsify business events.

Consequence of the Forensic Audit

The results of a forensic audit are a report, not an opinion. The report summarizes the results of any emergency meeting held by the fraud team members. Therefore, the report is only compiled after there has been a meeting of the fraud team. The report should contain recommendations for action, and it should be addressed to the Board of Directors. The documentation, such as logs, used to identify any executive officers who have committed unethical or fraudulent acts is part of the report.

Depending on the severity of the conclusions reached in the report, the next step is to take administrative, civil, and/or legal action against identified corporate executives for unethical or fraudulent practices. If the outcome is a prosecution for fraud, all electronic evidence must be collected in a manner that makes it useable in the courtroom. These forensic audit procedures and the collection of extensive logged evidence can prevent corporate officials from saying they were ignorant of the fraudulent events, i.e., "It is impossible to know about everything that is occurring in a large company"; "I was unaware of these events."[32] With the collections logs and the monitoring of other information, it will be harder for unethical corporate officials to squander or steal a company's assets or mislead their stockholders.

WE ARE WORTH IT! *Executives at Comverse Technology Backdate Millions in Stock Options while Operating a Stock Options Slush Fund.* The Securities and Exhange Commission (SEC) charged the former CEO, CFO, and General Counsel with securities, mail, and wire fraud. The executives are charged with issuing false and misleading financial statements for 14 years. Stock options are supposed to be based on fair market value of stock on the date the stock option is granted. Top executives at Comverse Technology backdated option grants to the dates of low points in stock's trading price, thus allowing the grantee to realize the difference between the option and higher current market price as immediate profit. These executive gains were reductions in profit to the company. In addition, the CEO and CFO created a slush fund of backdated options which they gave to favored employees. The scheme was only accidently uncovered and reported by a third party.

Due Diligence Searches

¶ 14,071 **INTERNET DATABASES: INFORMATIONAL SEARCHES BEGIN HERE**

If the name of the suspect can be learned with a John Doe subpoena or by other means, the investigator may also want to collect as much information about that person as possible. If an e-mail is sent from a high-level company executive to a suspicious party, the investigator wants background information about that individual. Background searches of individuals, executives, or corporate investment groups may be necessary for other reasons as well.

Due diligence procedures in partnership revisions or private investments require a background check of individuals or groups forming the new partnership or investment group to avoid after-the-fact problems. If a client is taking in any sort of new partner, an accountant needs to provide assurances regarding the legitimacy of the new partner. Beyond reviewing paper documents submitted by the parties and other personal contacts, it is advisable to check online sources of background information. If the valuation of assets is important in a business transaction, it is helpful to make online searches of the parties involved to ensure no collusion has occurred such as the selling and reselling of property between the parties to raise its valuation. Incorporation papers on shell companies or affiliated subsidiaries may be a source of valuable information. If suspicions of financial fraud arise with asset identification and valuation in a divorce case, online property checks may uncover hidden assets. Several search engines and databases on the Internet allow for collecting all manner of information about individuals and groups. Such information includes property records; maps to suspects' homes or businesses; political contributions; birth, marriage, and death certificates; web cam feeds; personal postings to various social websites; voting records; resumes; telephone numbers; and e-mail addresses, for example. Even social security numbers are found online for a price. Several of these information resources are reviewed below.

General Searches

In beginning a search on a person, the first step would be to use a search engine and type in several variations of the person's name. One of the most widely used general search engines is Google *(http://google.com)*. When the Advanced Features of Google are selected, one can conduct searches of military and government sites, Linux sites, and Microsoft related pages.

Besides Google, there are several other good search engines:

- Altavista: *http://www.altavista.com*
- Yahoo: *http://www.yahoo.com*
- Excite: *http://www.excite.com*
- Lycos: *http://www.lycos.com*
- Ask: *http://www.ask.com*
- Bing: *http://www.bing.com*
- Kurrently: *http//kurrently.com (Twitter and Facebook)*
- Canadian Company Public Filings: *http://www.sedar.com/homepage_en.htm*
- U.S. Company Public Filings: *http://www.sec.gov/edgar.shtml*
- TinEye: *http://www.tineye.com/ (searches for the location of images)*

THROUGH THE LOOKING GLASS. Many times the information on the Internet is amazing even with a Google Search. For example, hackers can use simple Google searches to identify companies using outdated software with known attack vulnerabilities or to find unencrypted password files. For an example of an unusual search, type the following data into Google's search box and click on the results showing an IP address: inurl:/view.shtml

What did the webcam show you? Many webcams send their video stream over the Internet without encryption, allowing anyone to view the feed. The example here is for one type of webcam but there are many such unencrypted sites without passwords using numerous webcam codes.

For country-specific searches, there is a list of search engines at Beaucoup *(http://www. beaucoup.com)* under their "geographical" groupings and Search Engine Colossus *(http:// www.searchenginecolossus.com)*.

Some search engines are called *metacrawlers*. These engines simultaneously check other search engines and automatically throw out any duplicated information. Such metacrawlers are Dogpile *(http://www.dogpile.com)*, Webcrawler *(http://www.webcrawler.com)*, and IXQuick *(http://www.ixquick.com)*. Finally, Adobe .pdf documents can be searched on Google when the basic search is changed to an advanced search mode. If you need to search a webpage other than the current version of that page, there are two search engines for that purpose. One is the Wayback Machine *(http://www.archive.org/web/web.php)* and the other is Archive-It *(http:// www.archive-it.org/public/all_collections)*.

Name, Telephone Number, and E-Mail Address Search Engines

A good database to perform a meta search for e-mail addresses is at My Email Address Is *(http://my.email.address.is)* but it charges for its services. In each search, the site checks five other e-mail search engines. Its searches are based on the individual's name. A Usenet e-mail address search for dated materials can be made at Usenet Address *(http://usenet-addresses. mit.edu)* for the period from 1991 to 1996. Searching a known e-mail address in Google will identify a large amount of information about the person who owns the e-mail address.

Investigators should remember that e-mail addresses can be faked, and they can be made anonymous by remailers. A remailer strips off an e-mail address, sender's name, and other traceable information from the e-mail header so the recipient does not know who sent the e-mail. The remailer replaces the subscriber's real identification with a dummy address, sometimes a new name, and eliminates any traceable information in the header. One example of a remailer is the George Mason Society at *http://gilc.org/speech/anonymous/remailer.html*. The Society will send anonymous e-mails which is different than faked e-mails with phony return addresses visible to a recipient.

Switchboard.com *(http://switchboard.com)* provides for telephone searches based on the individual's name and location. Telphone Number Identification is good search engine for phone number identification (http://tnid.us). If the address is unknown, the search can still be made. Once the person's address and phone number are found, Switchboard. com has a map directory so map directions are provided to the person's street address. At YahooPeople Search *(http://people.yahoo.com)*, it is possible to search for an e-mail address as well as phone numbers based on an individual's name. A number of free and chargeable services are available at Freeality.com *(http://www.freeality.com)* including cell phone numbers and reverse address searches. The latter searches for addresses based on phone numbers. Another people search engine is called "Yoname" at http://www.yoname.com/.

To find out information about a person at a corporation or university without directly searching that corporation's or university's website, the investigator can use Google. For a corporation, type in the search box: site:xxxxxx.com<*space*>name of the person in quotes.

Google will search the corporation or university site using the domain name and the name of the individual to find information. Such an indirect search method is less likely to tip off a suspect. A service that charges a fee for personal information is IRB Search *(http://www. irbsearch.com)*. The database covers addresses and phone numbers. Birthdays can also be checked at the Steve Morse site *(http://stevemorse.org/birthday/birthday2.html)* for free. Another service with limited free trials is Zoominfo *(http://www.zoominfo.com)* in which background information is collected about individuals. SpiesOnline *(http://www.spiesonline.net/public.shtml)* provides links to a number of public databases in which personal information is available. Docusearch.com *(http://www.docusearch.com)* provides searches, again for a fee, on financial and bank searches, property records, driver's licenses, social security numbers, and VIN number searches. Merlin Information Services *(http://www.merlindata.com)* charges minimum fees for small searches in a real-time telephone directory and skiptrace directory. For name searches in the U.K., 192.com can help to identify individuals *(http://www.192.com)*. All of these information service sites have become more sensitive about selling an individual's personal information due to the enormous increase in identity theft cases. Yet, if it is necessary to check or more intensively investigate a person's background, the Internet provides the location as to where such information can be found. Additionally, state governments provide an abundance of information on birth, marriage, and death certificates as well as property records, tax, and map locations. Most of the online information from states is provided without fees unless paper copies are requested. Such searches can be useful in collaborating background information provided by new clients, job applicants, investment advisors, the business activities of corporate executives, or potential business partners.

Internet Relay Chat (IRC), Listserv Searches, and Blogs

IRC is a chat room on the Internet following the rules of client/server software. For example, free software, such as ChatZilla, is available for setting up an IRC connection. Although communications through Twitter and Facebook receive more attention, it is still worthwhile to investigate IRC rooms. Some search engines will search IRC files. Two such search engines are ISOHunt *(http://isohunt.com)* and Search IRC *(http://searchirc.com)*. The information collected may show that a company executive, employee or potential partner has been active in chat rooms in which financial hoaxes or misrepresentation are discussed. Employees may use chat rooms to discuss their company's proprietary operations or express their opinions about company acquisitions. Depending on the chat site, personal communications, a chatter's physical location on specific dates, personal relationships with others, and IP logs (for law enforcement) can be collected.

Another way of online communication is the listserv. A listserv uses an e-mail program to automatically distribute e-mail to the names on a mailing list. Individuals with a common interest, such as forensic accounting, are able to post and receive e-mail based on discussion topics. Many websites provide for searches of the topics that are discussed in a listserv such as L-Soft *(http://www.lsoft.com/lists/list_q.html)*. Once a potential listserv is identified, the site must be individually searched with the listserv's search engine, or if none is provided, it is possible to use e-mail commands to search the site.

With today's blog, i.e., web logs, explosion on the Internet, it is good idea to search blogs for the disclosures they may provide about the subject of the search. Blogs have provided financial news and views about companies that may not be available from any other sources. Google provides a blog search engine *(http://blogsearch.google.com)*. Two other blog search engines are Icerocket *(http://www.icerocket.com)* and Technorati *(http://technorati.com)*. The former also allows for searches on Twitter and Facebook. Although restrictions in the length of tweets on Twitter may not allow for the collection of significant information about an individual, it is still worth investigating. Twitter searches can be done with *http://search.twitter.com/*.

Carlos Salgado, Jr. (aka SMAK) was indicted on five counts: three counts of computer crime under 18 USC §1030 and two counts of trafficking in stolen credit cards. The events leading up to Salgado's arrest and indictment began in an IRC chat room where another person was initially offered a database with 60,000 credit card numbers. Salgado had used several well-known hacker exploits to gain access to these databases in three different companies and steal credit card files. He received payments for the credit card numbers through anonymous Western Union wire transfers.[33]

Usenet Postings Search

Usenet is an Internet discussion system consisting of a set of user's submitted messages or notes to a group, and each collection of similar notes or messages is called a newsgroup. It is a precursor and similar to the blogs that are found on the Internet today. Members must be admitted to the group. There are eight main group discussion hierarchies in Usenet. They are computer-related topics, humanities, miscellaneous, news about Usenet, recreational issues, science, social issues, and general talk. Messages are posted to the newsgroup by its members, or the moderator, and then broadcast to other members of the newsgroup. A search of Usenet group postings can be made from Google *(http://groups.google.com/group/news.lists.misc/topics)*. The search engine allows for searches on specific individual names, company names, and the threads of the discussion that follow. Although Facebook and LinkedIn are used to do background searches, postings on Usenet are just another way of collecting information about an individual's activities. For information about using a Usenet, see *http://www.how-to-usenet.com/*.

COLLECTING EVIDENCE. If a disgruntled employee is a suspect in a propriety theft case, making a search of Usenet postings, chat rooms, or blogs may be worthwhile in collecting further evidence. The postings on Facebook may reveal who else is involved in unlawful or unethical activities.

Legal Records

A number of legal jurisdictions provide information about their citizens on websites. Such information may be provided for free or for a small fee. For example, numerous states allow searches of their sex offender databases. The Texas Department of Public Safety allows visitors to check their conviction record database after creating an account and paying a fee *(https://records.txdps.state.tx.us/DpsWebsite/Index.aspx)*. The State of Florida also allows searches of its criminal databases for a fee *(http://www.fdle.state.fl.us/content/getdoc/2952da22-ba08-4dfc-9e45-2d7932a803ea/Obtaining-Criminal-History-Information.aspx)*. Some companies charge a fee for criminal records such as Justice.com for the State of Colorado *(http://www.cojusticebeyond.com/)*, but guarantees real-time information. Pacer *(http://www.pacer.gov/)* provides case and docket information from Federal, Appellate, District, and Bankruptcy courts for its registered users. Netronline *(http://www.netronline.com)* is a portal providing freely searchable links to state-by-state public records all the way to those states' county offices that have an online records database. If a county does not have an online database, a contact phone number is provided. Public records include deeds, maps, tax data, and property ownership information. The Federal Bureau of Prisons provides an inmate locator as well as identifies anyone who has been incarcerated since 1982 *(http://www.bop.gov)*. Marriage and birth certificates may also be available in these public databases. Search Systems *(http://publicrecords.searchsystems.net/)* offers more than 25,730 free searchable public record databases from all over the world. Black Book Online (*http://www.blackbookonline.info*) also lists numerous free search sites such as one for ABA bank routing number identification and interactive crime maps. eInvestigator is another source that acts as an aggregator of many sources of information on individuals (*http://www.einvestigator. com/links/index.html*). Finally, Owens Online (*https://www.owens.com*) offers search sites from U.S. and international databases on credit and education verifications and government records for a fee. All these online information sources are available for anyone performing a due diligence investigation or trying to collect information about an employee's suspicious activities.

Socializing Websites

Individuals are joining websites that allow them to post information about themselves and run blogs with like-minded groups of other people they meet on the Internet. One site that allows for the posting of intimate thoughts and videos is Myspace (*http://myspace.com*). The site provides a search engine to identify specific individuals, company names, or other topics catalogued on the website. Another site, filled with video postings, is YouTube (*http://www. youtube.com*), which can be easily searched for individuals' names, topics, or company information. Facebook (*http://www.facebook.com/srch.php*) can also be searched for individuals who have not restricted their profiles. Facebook searches are available at Cue, (*https://www.cueup. com/auth#login*), which requires registering for a tool bar or with the Bing browser. Facebook information comes from postings, e-mail, and photos on the individual's "wall". LinkedIn (*http://www.linkedin.com/ns*) is a similar website. To see a LinkedIn member's full profile, it is necessary to register, but the website does provide a summary profile without registration. These sites should be considered to be part of a due diligence review in determining the legitimacy of new business contacts or as part of an individual's background review. Currently Kurrently.com allows for searches on Facebook, LinkedIn, and Google (*http://www. kurrently.com*). Using a search engine called Graph, Facebook itself is allowing nonmembers to make searches of the site. It is expected that this search engine will expand beyond Facebook to LinkedIn and other social networking sites. Basic searches on twitter can be done at *https://twitter.com/search* and topic searches are available at Tinker at *http://www.tinker.com*, but to understand the linked relationship between individual a datamining search of social media is necessary. One example of a data mining site for twitter comes from Arizona State University at TweetTracker (*http://tweettracker.fulton.asu.edu*). It is only through a through datamining search that data about individuals can be completely analyzed.

Instant Messaging (IM)

IM and ICQ (I Seek You) are programs set up to enable individuals to know when a group of their friends are on the Internet. Afterward they can join an IRC-like chat room and exchange real-time messages. Instant messaging is finding wider usage in corporations as a means to instantly communicate with colleagues who are inside and outside the company network. In this way, needed decision-making information can be quickly exchanged. Texting is also being used for instant communications, but with texting you need to know the recipient's phone number as the messages generally go between cell phones. With IM, you need to only know the recipient's screen name. Additionally, text messages are kept like e-mails whereas, IM is not stored communications. IM is based on real-time communication.

When using IM, which is PC-to-PC, it is possible to determine detailed information about the person with whom information is being exchanged. Netstat is part of the DOS package in most computers. Netstat allows for the identification of the other person at the other end of a chat through their IP address and using whois identification. By knowing you are communicating with a trusted IP, the sender is more assured they are not being spoofed or a cell phone has been stolen. In Windows, by typing in Netstat at the C prompt, it is possible to see all connection programs and IP addresses. Once an IP address is identified, it is possible to identify the person chatting with more certainty. Identification can occur as the chat continues. Figure 14.10 shows a Netstat active connection report. The report shows a TCP connection, the local address of the PC, and IP addresses.

Figure 14.10. Netstat Reports the Connections and IP Addresses in an ICQ Chat

```
C: WINDOWS>netstat

Active Connections

Proto Local Address Foreign Address State
TCP oemcomputer:1026 baym-cs77.msgr.hotmail.com:1863 ESTABLISHED
TCP oemcomputer:1029 205.188.7.246:5190 ESTABLISHED
TCP oemcomputer:1037 64.12.28.37:5190 ESTABLISHED
TCP oemcomputer:1038 205.188.4.120:5190 ESTABLISHED
TCP oemcomputer:1058 1800expedia.com:80 ESTABLISHED
TCP oemcomputer:1064 207.68.175.99:80 ESTABLISHED
TCP oemcomputer:1100 207.46.249.61:80 TIME WAIT
TCP oemcomputer:1101 207.46.249.61:80 TIME WAIT
TCP oemcomputer:1103 msimg.com:80 ESTABLISHED
```

It is also possible to use ICQ numbers to trace the owner of an e-mail address. When users register and download the ICQ software, they receive an ID called an ICQ number. At the ICQ web page *(http://www.icq.com/people/)* searches by ICQ number reveal the person's name, phone number, nickname, address, or cell phone number.

¶ 14,081   WEB PAGE SEARCHES

If a personal or company web page is included in the investigation, the web page should be viewed so the coding in the page can be seen. With Firefox, this is possible by clicking on Page Source (Tools>Web Developer>Page Source). The information disclosed shows date information and the location of servers where pictures on the website are stored. Such image storage does not have to be on the same server where the web page is hosted, and it may provide a clue about the real geographical location of an individual.

The investigator should bear in mind that there are web-forwarding services that provide their customers with proxy web servers. For example, the RU-Center *(http://www.nic.ru/dns/service/en/webforwarding.html#redirect)* charges a fee and allows a web page to have a URL that is not its real URL. Thus, a Russian webpage can be given a U.S. URL. Web page forwarding can be confusing in developing a background on a suspect.

Additionally, U.S. companies can be duped into providing restricted products to unauthorized companies, thus incurring heavy government fines. U.S. companies may be restricted from providing services or products to certain countries due to copyright laws or government bans. To circumvent such restrictions, a foreign company or individual places an order through a proxy web server in Florida. Services are immediately downloaded over the Internet flaunting copyright protections. For purchased products along with a proxy server, a Florida drop mail address is used for receipt of the order. Once the restricted product is received, it is forwarded by co-conspirators in Florida to the foreign address, again circumventing the government's bans on shipments. If a company or individual's web page is being checked in a due diligence investigation, its HTML code should be reviewed. All browsers will show a web page's coding. For example, with Explorer one would right click on the Page and View Source, then the HTML code will appear. The true URL should be shown in the coding and at least raise the forensic accountant's suspicions.

¶ 14,091   GOVERNMENT DATA SEARCHES

For information about the U.S. government, the best sites to use are FirstGov *and* DataGov *(http://www.usa.gov/; http://www.data.gov/).* DataGov is a relatively new site providing federal datasets of information available for download and analysis. The states all have their own sites, and there is no consistency in the information contained on these sites. European Union laws are searchable at *http://europa.eu/index_en.htm.* For a long list of country-specific web pages see the WWW

Virtual Library *(http://www2.etown.edu/vl)*. CourthouseDirect *(http://www.courthousedirect.com)* charges a fee for digital images of documents, but it also provides a link to several free databases related to real property documents throughout the United States and other government reports. Such government datasets can provide information about property ownership, for example, by executives that they would like to keep hidden.

¶ 14,101   MISCELLANEOUS SEARCHES

Hoax e-mails endlessly circulate over the Internet. Although hoaxes are not directly related to finding information for a specific investigation, hoaxes sent by individuals are continuously appearing in e-mail messages and wasting valuable work hours. They demonstrate the underlying basis used in phishing attacks. These e-mail hoaxes are misinformation about the latest virus and how to prevent it, for example. The message includes instructions as to how to disable the virus that unsuspecting victims follow until they disable their computer. Other hoaxes are less crippling and describe some fictitious event.

EYEWITNESS

One of the early examples of such a fictitious event was the $250 recipe for Neiman-Marcus cookies that circulated over the Internet for several years.

Another example of an Internet hoax is the following e-mail:

All mobile users pay attention. If you receive a phone call and your Mobile Phone displays (ACE) on the screen, don't answer the call. END THE CALL IMMEDIATELY. If you answer the call, your phone will be infected by a virus.

This virus will erase all IMEI and IMSI information from both your phone and your SIM card, which will make your phone unable to connect with the telephone network. You will have to buy a new phone. This information has been confirmed by both Motorola and Nokia. There are over 3 million mobile phones being infected by this virus around the world. You can also find this information on the CNN website.

PLEASE FORWARD THIS PIECE OF INFORMATION TO ALL YOUR FRIENDS WHO HAVE MOBILE PHONES.

Before one forwards any chain letters, petitions, or virus warnings, HoaxKill *(http://www.hoax-slayer.com/)* or Hoaxbusters *(http://www.hoaxbusters.org)* should be checked to see whether the information is false.

In developing an Incident Response Report or Forensic Report, pertinent information should be collected. There are many Internet databases containing information about everyone, and they should be quickly checked before contacting legal authorities. Additionally, the search methods described here can be used to help confirm information for forming a new relationship with a business partner or check on the suspicious activities of company executives.

¶ 14,111   CONCLUSION

This chapter presented an overview of some of the more important steps and tools to use in tracing and collecting digital evidence, profiling individuals, and performing Internet due diligence.

The forensic accountant must understand basic network concepts and the technologies that can help prevent and solve financial frauds. Without an understanding of logs, message IDs, IP addresses, tracing tools, search methods, and Internet databases, a forensic accountant's hopes of solving an electronic-based crime are slim.

Logged data is volatile and may only be available for a short time before it is deleted. Unlike a traditional financial fraud, where the evidence may remain available in paper records for years, computer logs are only preserved for brief periods because of their extensive and expensive storage requirements. A forensic accountant needs to understand the detailed electronic tracks left behind in a financial fraud case and the actions needed to quickly preserve that data.

ENDNOTES

1   Tom Clancy, DEBT OF HONOR, New York: G.P Putnam's Sons, 1994, p. 202.

2   See G. Smith and L. Crumbley, "Defining a Forensic Audit" JOURNAL OF DIGITAL FORENSICS, SECURITY AND LAW, Special Edition (2009), Vol. 4, 61-79.

3   Global Security Report: *http://hostexploit.com/ downloads/viewdownload/7-public-reports/39-global-security-report-may-2012.html*

4   The presentation layer defines how data received appears and is formatted for display in the other layers. The session layer keeps the session open and ensures packet recovery. It maintains and ends communication with the receiving machine. The session layer provides for full duplex or half-duplex transmissions. It establishes termination and restart procedures. These seven layers compose the open systems interconnection (OSI) model. The OSI is a model of agreed-upon networking architecture that allows for communication between different products.

5   C. Painter, "Tracing in Internet Fraud Cases: PairGain and NEI Webworld" U.S. ATTORNEYS BULLETIN (May 3, 2001). *United States v. Hoke* (PairGain), CR 99-441.

6   Another, less reliable communication protocol used on the Internet is User Datagram Protocol or UDP. It is a send-and-forget type of communication, i.e., it provides no reliability checks or checks that the datapacket was received.

7   G. Smith, "When Is a Cybercrime Really a Cybercrime?" JOURNAL OF FORENSIC ACCOUNTING, AUDITING, FRAUD, AND TAXATION 3 (December 2002), pp. 301–314.

8   The sequence and acknowledgment numbers can range from 0 to 4,294,967,295.

9   The SYN, ACK, and FIN flags are important in establishing and concluding communications between the sender and the recipient servers. The sender forwards a TCP SYN packet to the receiver. In this TCP packet, the SYN flag is active, and there is an initial sequence number in the packet. Upon receipt of the packet, the recipient server transmits an acknowledgment. The acknowledgment contains the recipient's new sequence number, which is the sender's sequence number plus one, and an active ACK flag. Upon receipt of the TCP acknowledgment packet, the sender's server sends an acknowledgment with a new sequence number by adding one to the sequence again. The exchange is known as a *three-way handshake.* After the handshake is completed, the two servers are open and sending TCP data packets containing messages back and forth to each other.

10   Measurement is in octets, sequences of eight bits (*octo* meaning eight in Latin). A *bit* is the smallest unit of data in a computer, i.e., either 0 or 1. Consequently, an octet is a sequence of bits. In this case, an eight-bit byte. A byte is used by computer systems to represent a letter, number, or symbol. Thus, a byte holds a string of bits. A byte is not necessarily eight bits in all computer systems; therefore, using octets provides for commonality among disparate computer systems. All hosts must accept messages of 576 octets in length, and there are 32 bits in 4 octets.

11   G. Smith, "When Is a Cybercrime Really a Cybercrime?" JOURNAL OF FORENSIC ACCOUNTING, AUDITING, FRAUD, AND TAXATION 3 (December 2002), pp. 301–314.

12   It is interesting to note that not all lost datagrams disappear. Some old lost and broken packets examples are saved at The Museum of Broken Packets, found at *http:// lcamtuf.coredump.cx/mobp/.*

13   When a web page is requested or an e-mail sent, IP protocols include the IP address in the message and every machine on a TCP/IP network that has an IP address. An IP address is composed of two parts: the network section and the host section (PC within the network). The network address is externally assigned (134.6.0.0) and the host section within a network is assigned by the network administrator, i.e., a subnet address within the organization (135.6.75.0). The IP address as read by humans is based on a Domain Name System (such as amazon.com) that is translated into dotted decimal number for computers with each 4 byte address written as a decimal number from 0 to 255 (125.10.4.74) and with that decimal number address correlating with a hexadecimal value (BEE50A). In some cases, a cyber attacker may try to confuse the investigator by using a ten-digit number in place of a normal IP dotted decimal number address.

The Domain Name System for a large website such as amazon.com usually covers a wide range of IP addresses. Hexadecimal notation is a numbering system with 16 sequential numbers as base units before adding a new position for the next number (16 decimal number '10 hexadecimal). The change from decimal to hexadecimal can easily be performed on the Windows calculator (Start\Programs\Accessories\Calculator) using the scientific mode. If an IP address appears in a ten-digit integer format (2551685664), it is possible to change the integer format first to a hexadecimal (9817A220) and then to a decimal notation by separately converting each pair of two hexadecimal notations to a normally viewed IP address (152.23.162.32). Ping, traceroute, or a browser such as Firefox or Explorer will automatically convert the ten-digit integer format into the IP address.

14   If a device's MAC address is unknown, the network uses Address Resolution Protocol (ARP) to locate the unknown device. A MAC address is a hardware address composed of a 12-digit hexadecimal number (00AA0600A267). The first six digits are a manufacturer's ID; the last six, the serial number of a specific device. If a broadcast is sent over the network to all devices, it looks like ff-ff-ff-ff-ff-ff. All machines on the network listen to the message to determine whether the request is for them. If it is, the device responds

with its address, and it receives its message. But all devices on the network have listened to the open message request. To see how MAC addresses can be located, see NetworkTracer, a free download, at: *http://www.pc-help.org/trace.htm*. Network Tracer can identify MAC addresses. Also on Windows machines, type ipconfig –all after the C prompt. The disclosed data about the computer shows the MAC address. It is called the "physical address." It appears as a six group hexadecimal. MAC addresses are normally unobtainable outside a network's gateway to the Internet, and it must be remembered that in some cases, it is possible for internal attackers to change or spoof MAC addresses with software (see *http://www. klcconsulting.net/smac/#PriceList*). Also see *http://www. tech-faq.com/how-to-change-a-mac-address.html*. Even though computers have their real MAC address burned into their Ethernet card, the address can be spoofed with software.

15 Every attempt has been made to ensure all websites mentioned in this chapter are current. If a website is no longer active using the address listed here, type the name of the site into a search engine to find its new address.

16 The illustrated e-mail message passed through three servers and left traces of its presence in logs at those servers before arriving at its destination. Each of the Received headings shows the message's path.

17 IP addresses in the following range are used for private internets: 172.16.0.0- 172.31.255.255

18 There are anonymous remailers who will freely send anonymous e-mail messages. The remailer strips away the mail headers from the original e-mail and substitutes its own mail headers to make the message untraceable. There are remailers in many countries, making it difficult for U.S. law enforcement officials to subpoena logs and records from these remailers. The use of a remailer requires the user to download an encryption key and use a program like mixmaster. Remailer sites are operated in various countries around the world and one the e-mail is properly formatted it will be sent through a series of webservers that make the encrypted e-mail untraceable. If a financial hoax or supposedly friendly e-mail with a virus attachment is to be sent, it not likely to be considered creditable if the header shows the sender as "anonymous." See: *https://ultimate-anonymity.com/web-based-remailer. htm or https://dizum.com*

19 T. Ewing, M. Rose, R. Rundle, and G. Fields, "E-Mail Trail Leads to Emulex Hoax Suspect," The Wall Street Journal (September 1, 2000), p. C.1.

20 The amount of information that a website can collect about a visitor is extensive. The following information is collected and disclosed at Privacy.net *(http://privacy.net/ analyze)*: the browser type, browser's requests at website, CPU and screen information, time stamp information, number of web pages visited, and traceroute. In addition, there is commercial software for tracing hackers such

as Hacker tracker *(http://hacker-tracker.com)* and Sam Spade *(http://www.pcworld.com/product/947049/sam-spade.html)*.

21 The initial DOS screen for tracert will appear as follows. It can be seen that tracert switches allow for various options to be made during the search:

```
C:WINDOWS>tracert
Usage: tracert [-d] [-h maximum hops]
[-j host-list] [-w timeout] target name
Options:
-d Do not resolve addresses to
hostnames.
-h maximum hops Maximum number of hops to
search for target.
-j host-list Loose source route along
host-list.
-w timeout Wait timeout milliseconds for
each reply.
```

22 There are Internet gateway locations that allow for the identification of the path taken between the gateway's server and any other IP address. A link to many of these gateways is available at *http://tracert.com/* or *http:// www.traceroute.org/#USA* or *http://www.abika.com/help/ IPaddressmap.htm*. IP addresses can also be traced using software developed for this purpose, such as Sam Spade. Nslookup, whois, and traceroute are all available for tracing e-mail messages in the Sam Spade package. By typing in the IP address obtained from a suspect's e-mail header, it is possible to determine the exact location of the sender in just a few seconds.

23 A *static IP address* does not change. Usually, company employees have static IP addresses. Cable ISP services also provide a static IP address. A *dynamic IP address* is one that changes each time a connection is made to the Internet. The dynamic IP address is assigned from an available pool of IP addresses that the ISP has been given. Dynamic IP addresses are more commonly associated with home users and dial-up services.

24 An Address Resolution Protocol table correlates the IP address in the ping request and the MAC address of the specific machine on the network. If the MAC address of a network computer is spoofed, it cannot be found in the ARP table and messages directed at the PC will not be received.

25 Telnet is available on Port 23. It is a bidirectional interface enabling the user to log into a remote machine and execute commands on that machine. The Telnet program is available on Windows by clicking on Start\ Run and then typing telnet into the command line. The IP address and port number of a remote host is then typed into the new screen. User and password identification may be required for a login. Some web servers have restricted the use of Telnet because of the abuses.

26 There are partial solutions if finger has been turned off. Telnetting into the mail server port (25) and typing vrfy

smith will provide for the verification of an e-mail address and other information about the owner—in this case, Smith—of the e-mail account. Of course, port 25 must be open.

27 Three cases that deal with this area are: *Brief Amicus Curiae of America Online, Inc.*, *Melvin Doe* Letter Opinion, and *Dendrite v. Does.*

28 The PCAOB has stated that "forensic audits can be performed to achieve various objectives and can include a variety of different procedures" (Public Company Accounting Oversight Board 2007b). Thus, forensic audits have been discussed but not defined in any set of established auditing standards. See Standards/Standing Advisory Group Meetings 2007 (02 22) Forensic Audit Procedures. See also *http://www. cfonet.com/article.cfm/8759510?f=search*. Recently, the Big Four along with Grant Thornton and BDO International released a white paper entitled "Serving Global Capital Markets and the Global Economy" (Global Public Policy Symposium 2006). The Global Report's authors suggest that all public companies have forensic audits conducted.

29 There are a number of software programs that can be used to analyze the risks facing an organization. For examples of cost effective monitoring see: (1) Visual Analytics' software package called Visual Links *(http://www. visualanalytics.com)* uses a graphical screen to uncover patterns, associations, and relationships among masses of unrelated data. (2) Maltego *(http://www.paterva.com/ web5)* is a software monitoring program used to establish links between corporate employees and others with whom they communicate to determine if they are violating corporate guidelines. (3) Perceptive Software, formerly ISYS Search Software *(http://www.perceptivesoftware. com/products/perceptive-search)* is used to make forensic searches of e-mails and information on hard drives over the entire intranet. (4) RFID technologies that raise alerts when company notebooks are removed from company premises. (5) NetMap Analytics *(http://www.netmap. com/)* is used for mapping unrecognized relationships by mapping common links. (6) SpectorSoft CNE Investigator *(http://www.spectorcne.com)* surveillance software that records everything that employees do on the Internet. Background arguments for using these approaches

can be found in the paper "Empowering Board Audit Committees: Electronic Discovery to Facilitate Corporate Fraud Detection" (Michaud, Dutton, and Magaram 2006). The authors recommend the continuous monitoring of e-mail messages within a corporation. For examples of computer forensic software, see the "Buyer's Guide to Audit, Anti-Fraud, and Assurance Software" (Brooks, Goldman, and Lanza 2007).

30 Securities Act of 1933, Release No. 8284, September 11, 2003; Securities Exchange Act of 1934, Release No. 48474, September 11, 2003; Accounting and Auditing Enforcement, Release No. 1854, September 11, 2003; and Administrative Proceeding File No. 3-11251. *In the Matter of Brightpoint, Inc., Respondent.* Order Instituting Cease-and-Desist Proceedings, Making Findings, and Imposing a Cease-and-Desist Order Pursuant to Section 8A of the Securities Act of 1933 and Section 21C of the Securities Exchange Act of 1934 as to Brightpoint, Inc.

In the actual case, only with warrants was the SEC able to collect the following two e-mails between executives at Brightpoint:
"I need to support for [the Auditors] the recording of an insurance receivable related to the losses in the UK (in the amount of $12MM—Whoa)"
"The binder you signed (I looked at it again) has January 6, 1999 (in one case 1998) all over it. This is not good and that copy must be destroyed and [sic] with an August date executed."

31 Yauch, C. and Steudel H., (2003) Complementary use of qualitative and quantitative cultureal assessment. Organizational Research Methods. Vol 6 (4) 465-481.

32 Stock option slush funds are set up by high-level executives for fictitious employees. The stock options in the slush fund are later dispersed to individuals who have provided favors to the executive who set up the fund.

33 It is interesting to note that company executives use this defense even in the face of Section 302, *Corporate Responsibility for Financial Reports* in the Sarbanes-Oxley Act of 2002 where these company executives are required to sign their company's financial reports attesting that they have fully reviewed the report, and they are aware of the company's financial condition.

34 R. Power and R. Farrow, "Are You Ready for Electronic Commerce Crime?" (1997).

EXERCISES

1. Define
   a. Hacker.
   b. Cracker.
   c. Botnet.
   d. Zombie computer.

2. List some significant frauds where traditional auditing techniques and internal controls did not uncover the events.

3. Why does a forensic accountant need to be familiar with protocol used on the Internet?

4. Explain these terms.
    a. Message encapsulation.
    b. Transportation layer.
    c. Checksum field.
    d. Flag data.
    e. Network layer.
    f. Keylogger.
    g. Sniffer.
5. List some of the famous computer viruses.
6. Explain how an employer can trace a defamatory and anonymous e-mail.
7. Describe the function of the Windows field in the TCP/IP headers.
8. Explain two methods, as briefly described in the chapter, a hacker might use to tamper with a network.
9. Describe how an initial TCP/IP connection is made.
10. Identify the following IP addresses with the organization that owns them.
    a. 207.246.6.128
    b. 209.3.112.1
    c. 164.58.120.10
    d. 211.213.248.213
11. What is the difference between a bit and a byte?
12. What are the main advantages of adopting the OSI model throughout the world?
13. Using the general search engines Google and Altavista and the meta search engine Dogpile, look up the term *leptospirosis.* Print out the top three websites returned by the search engines and comment on the results of the search. In your answer, state whether there were any duplications by the search engines. Compare the three searches and explain why you think one might be a better search engine than the other.
14. Use the Address Resolution Protocol (ARP) utility in Windows to identify the MAC address on a PC. Print out the results and identify the MAC address on the print out.
15. **Incident Response Report.** On June 30, 2004, Hank Law, webmaster at the MacVee Software Company located in Hyattsville, Maryland, detected suspicious activity on its web server. After checking, he detected a sniffer had been placed on Windows.NET Server. He assumed it was being used to record passwords and user names. The server is run on a 960 series Gateway box (2.4 GHz, 1024 MB and 1600 SDRam with a Xeon Processor) and a WinNT4

operating system. A Black Ice firewall system is used. Hank had updated all software with the most recent patches and last performed maintenance on the system May 1, 2004. TCP-DUMP, a sniffer, was running on the network connected to the server.
    a. In checking the sniffer's logs, he found that some log entries had been altered. He switched to early logs, and found the following log entry: 05:25:10.695000 0A:E5:4D:F3:00:E10 0E:6B:00:F8:00:00 250.14.130.1.5112>135.135.75.6.80: 1386754311:1386754311(0) win855. The unusual aspect of the log entry was the source port 5112. This port is not a commonly used one, and the attacker may have been trying to hide his presence on the compromised computer that he was using to attack MacVee's website. Currently, Hank has not shut the web server down, but he has hardened the access to other parts of the network from the web server, and he added a new sniffer program to the web box called the Effe Tech sniffer v.3.4. Hank is hoping the hacker will come back and Hank will get more identity information about the hacker.

      Based on the information provided, complete Part II of the Preliminary Incident Response Report in Figure 14.9 in the chapter.
    b. Identify the probable IP address the attacker used to enter MacVee's system.
    c. What are the advantages and disadvantages of not shutting down the server?
    d. Would law enforcement authorities be interested in further pursing this crime through the courts?
16. **Attack! Attack!** White Florist is a large distributor of flowers on the U.S. East Coast. The company has a web server farm where customers can bulk order flowers online. Two days before Christmas, one of the company's busiest periods, its web server was subjected to a denial of service (DOS) attack. As a result on December 23 and 24, their customers could not place orders on the web server. Frank Folk, the CEO, estimates the loss at $1 million. The system administrator, Carol George, did not notify anyone in the company about the DOS attack until after the first day of the at-

tack: December 24. At the present time, the attacker or attackers have not been identified. Carol George does not believe they will ever be able to identify the attackers. Frank Folk believes that the loss could have been reduced and the hacker identified if the proper people in the company were immediately notified about the attack.

You, as a noted forensics expert, have been contacted to help White Florist determine who in the company should be immediately involved in an investigatory role if such an attack is made on the company again. Identify departments in the company to notify and the role they should play.

17. **Finding Ports of Call.** Netstat shows you the ports that are open on your computer. It also allows you to detect any unauthorized programs that might be running on your computer's ports and collecting confidential information about you. Run Netstat on your computer, save the information that it discloses, and determine what ports are open on your computer. Are all these open ports authorized?

   Note: Before performing this exercise, you should be connected to the Internet and running another operation such as downloading a file.

18. **The First Step.** Assume members of a fraud response team have identified electronic e-mails they believe are an incident of unethical behavior by the company's CFO. If a fraud response team meeting is called, under a limited scope forensic audit, what are the first steps you believe should be taken by the group?

19. **Where's the Teeth in Ethics?** HP executives admitted that outside investigators had used a technique called "pretexting," or posing as someone else to obtain phone records of reporters and board members suspected of involvement in press leaks. Then-board Chairman Patricia Dunn, who ordered the investigation, said she had been unaware of the technique's use and called it "embarrassing." "It was not consistent with the values of our company, our privacy policy and our practices, and it was certainly not consistent with decades of ethical behavior," said Scott Taylor, who was named as HP's Chief Pri-

vacy Officer in June. While addressing the company's top-ranking 150 executives at an internal conference, HP CEO Mark Hurd said one of his top dozen priorities was "building a world-class ethics and compliance program," Hoak said. Do you feel that an unethical event such as pretexting could occur again at HP? Why or Why Not? Can you suggest steps to use to put more teeth into the ethical procedures at HP and ensure the 150 executives at the meeting will not commit unethical or fraudulent acts?

20. **Transfer it Here.** Viria Ventures is a venture capital firm run by Henry J. Kyler and Larry Wills (LW). Viria is thinly funded without a track record, and as a consequence the investment opportunities available to the firm are limited. Jeffrey Wills (JW), the son of Larry Wills, is a senior treasury analyst in SureSouth's finance group. SureSouth is a mortgage company. As a treasury analyst at SureSouth, JW has the authorization to make wire transfers of cash to and from a list of approved investment accounts. LW convinces his son, JW, to make wire transfers from the SureSouth treasury accounts that JW controls to Viria. Kyler and LW only want to use the money as "face" capital to impress investors. Additionally, the money is to be wired transferred back to SureSouth at the end of each quarter and prior to the annual audit to prevent the auditors from identifying the unauthorized transfers. After each of these periods, the money is again returned to Viria.

   In order for Viria to get the money, JW transfers the money to a series of approved investment accounts. The money remains there for a short period and then JW moves the money out of these accounts to Viria. In this way, the SureSouth's internal controls are circumvented. It appears the transfers were made to approved investment accounts. JW is able to transfer $25M to Viria in this manner. When the funds are returned to SureSouth, they are first moved through the approved investment accounts and then back to SureSouth. JW uses the wire transfer paperwork to show the funds only moved through approved accounts. Viria uses the transfers to qualify for high-yielding accounts.

The following e-mails were logged between JW and LW:

JW (4/2/09) Made the $10 transfer to your account today. More transfers later. Jeff

LW (4/2/09) Let me know the name of transfer account so I can tell the bank. Thanks. Dad

JW (4/7/09) Remaining 15 transfer on way today from STP Account. Jeff

JW (4/16/09) Need funds back as of 6/30. Auditors are expected after that date. Jeff

LW (6/27/09) We can't get the remaining $2M back. They stole it. Dad

JW (6/27/09) I am dog x$@xy.

Assume you are a forensic accountant working with the digital investigators who have logged these e-mail messages and called them to your attention. You have seen each one in the sequence as it was sent. At which date in the sequence of messages, if any, would you feel the need to call a meeting of the fraud team? Justify your decision and indicate what actions should be taken.

21. **Footnote Number 27.** Morgan Stanley's Prime Brokerage Division provides financial and administrative services to numerous hedge funds. As a consultant to Morgan Stanley and its Information Technology Department, Ted Michaels is responsible for securing computer connections between Morgan Stanley and its Prime Brokerage clients. Ted has access to numerous confidential and proprietary documents. These documents include a list of all of Stanley's Prime Brokerage hedge fund clients along with the formulas used to calculate the rates paid by clients to Stanley for prime brokerage services. Ted is approached by Sarah Pearl who is a former Morgan Stanley client service representative. Sarah wants to start a consulting firm with Ted using the confidential client list. She believes together they can provide the same services to these clients at a lower cost. After a number of phone calls and e-mails, she talks Ted into sending the client list to her as an e-mail attachment. Using Footnote 27, decide which software listed in the footnote could have been used to detect this conspiracy, and describe in detail your reasons for your software selection. You may want to search the Internet to collect more

information about the software packages you have selected before you submit your reasons as to why you have decided your software list is the best solution.

22. **Forensic Audits.** Present arguments that you believe a forensic audit will never become an accepted fraud detection practice.

23. **LinkedIn.** Select a student team and develop a LinkedIn page *(http://www.linkedin.com/)*. The LinkedIn page can be based on a fictitious or real person. The purpose of the LinkedIn page is to promote the job potential of the selected person. Once the LinkedIn page is set up, a second group of students will evaluate the page. Your instructor will give you the criteria that your group will use to evaluate the LinkedIn page that your team has created.

24. **Profiling.** Go to the FBI website *(http://www.fbi.gov)* and find a description of a financial fraud. The FBI site provides numerous descriptions of financial fraud cases that they have prosecuted. After selecting one of the financial fraud cases, select one of the convicted defendants named in the case and use the profiling methods described in the chapter to collect all the Internet information that you can about this individual. The information that you collect can include news reports, addresses either physical or virtual, education background, etc. Document where you found the information by including the name of the website and its URL.

25. **Ethics at the Top.** In response to the number of financial frauds that had been occurring in the United States, AIG made the following statement in their 2003 Annual Report and 10-K. In the statement, AIG sympathizes with stakeholders who were financially damaged by numerous financial frauds that had come to light in 2002.

"The whole country is paying a price for the gross misdeeds of relatively few executives who shirked their responsibility to create value for all of their corporate constituencies – shareholders, customers and employers – and abused the system to create wealth for themselves and their close associates. It is unfortunate that the misbehavior of a few companies and their executives could have a negative impact on so many . . . *The focus on integrity and building long-term value must start at the top if it is to permeate throughout an organization."*

Search the Internet to determine how well AIG has done in following its code of ethics and developing long-term value for its stakeholders from 2003 to 2010.

26. **Ping Me.** On your computer, use "ipconfig" to identify your IP address. You will have to go to a C prompt. Trade that IP address with a friend's IP. Now ping your friend's IP address. Again, you will need a C prompt and type "ping" followed by the IP address. Copy the resulting screen and turn it in with an explanation of the event.

27. **Finding a Criminal.** Five customers at the Tartu Bank had complained about unauthorized monies being withdrawn from their accounts. The Bank has a business fraud team which was called together to investigate the thefts from the accounts. The team could determine the account receiving the funds, times the events occurred, the amount of the cash withdrawn from the accounts, whether or not a bank password had been reset, but they did not have the skills to develop additional information about the IP address used in the thefts. They could not determine the source country or region, the IPS involved, and whether the session used to withdraw the cash was from an IP used by their customer. Tell them how they can use Internet tools to further identify the cyber criminals and describe the job each tool should perform.

15

CYBERCRIME MANAGEMENT: LEGAL ISSUES

Run, run, run as fast as you can

You can't catch me

I'm the Gingerbread Man.

These efforts [new statutes], are, like much of the law's attempts to play catch up with technology, too little, and too late. The legal system, inherently conservative, is perpetually a decade behind the technology....

—Curtis Karnow[1]

Cybercrime is a truly global problem and to tackle it we need strong partnership between countries and across private and public sectors.[2]

OBJECTIVES

After completing Chapter 15, you should be able to:
1. Provide a definition of cybercrime.
2. Describe the models used for cyber fraud and unauthorized system access.
3. Review Federal and state computer statutes.
4. Outline the role for the forensic investigator in combating cybercrimes.

OVERVIEW

This chapter deals with identifying cybercrimes, developing a basic understanding of how such crimes can occur over the Internet, and trying to find a way to deal with these criminal activities. Initially, it needs to be understood that the legal definition of a cybercrime varies within different government jurisdictions. An activity may be considered illegal in the United States, but not under the existing laws of another country. As Internet crimes can be committed from any location, the criminal can select the location with the most lenient laws, and the forensic investigator cannot offhandedly assume alleged "criminal" activity is really a crime. The activity may be considered only a nuisance. As a result, a victimized client or corporation cannot prosecute an offender. Today, business models such as online auctions, banking, and retail stores are under threat due to these Internet crimes. Without a basic understanding of the cyber laws along with Internet security skills, it is impossible for the investigator to advise a client about their legal rights, the nature of a systems attack, or an online fraud.

The definition of *cybercrime* is illusive, and so are cybercrime statistics. When an identity thief only uses the Internet to collect initial information about the victim, is the crime a cybercrime, or is it a traditional crime? How should such a crime be reported? If proprietary information is hidden in another file and encrypted, has a cybercrime been committed? What if the information is not encrypted? Cybercrime statistics need to be reported in order to develop legislative policies addressing such crimes and they are not fully reported.

The Business Alliance, which reports on software piracy, *(http://portal.bsa.org/globalpiracy2009/index.html)* estimated that $51 billion of software was stolen in 2009. Over 300,000 complaints the Internet Crime Complaint Center (IC3) referred to local, state, and federal law enforcement for further consideration in 2011, and the reported losses associated with these complaints totaled more than $485 million. It was also noted that in 2011, Alaska was the state with the most complaints per capita. The median average loss due to reported cybercrime in 2011 was $636 but ballooned to $4,187 when using the mean average of all losses (*http://www.ic3.gov/media/annualreport/2011_IC3Report.pdf*). For small business, the most serious crime is the loss incurred from the non-delivery of purchased merchandise.

These statistics are not reflective to the entire losses incurred as no more than 10 percent of computer crimes are reported largely because there is a belief that law enforcement is unable to catch the criminals. All sorts of financial frauds are rampant over the Internet and the true loss is immeasurable. The Internet has not changed the basic manner of conducting a fraud, but it has made it easier to rapidly reach a larger target audience. For example, a crime can be successfully committed against a person on a laptop located in his or her bedroom without having to even meet the victim.

The cybercrimes described in this chapter are purposefully committed; they do not occur because of the perpetrator's incompetence or negligence. The perpetrators *intend* to commit these crimes.

Cybercrimes: An Introduction

For 2011, cybercrime statistics are available from CSI Computer Crime and Security Survey. The most costly attacks for the surveyed organizations came from financial frauds with two separate cases resulting in a $20M and $25M loss. The latter loss occurred from the theft of mobile devices. These loss estimates underreport intangible losses from lost profits due to website inaccessibility. A sampling of the information in the report shows the most common complaints from the respondents:

Most common problems:
- Malware infections.....................................67%
- Misrepresented as sender of Phishing ...39%
- Laptop/mobile device theft.....................34%
- Bots on network...29%
- Insider abuse of Internet or email...........25%
- Denial of service 17%
- Password sniffing......................................11%
- Financial Fraud...9%

Survey data indicates a decrease in the reported financial frauds over the last few years and an increase in the percentage of malware infections.

A number of criminal activities fit under the mantle of cybercrime: fraudulent spam, financial frauds, unauthorized access, industrial espionage, illegal use of encryption, cyberstalking, denial of service, damaging networks or computers, child pornography, fraudulent e-mail, illegal use of resources obtained from hacking activities, and sending viruses or mail bombs. It is unsettling that these attacks are beginning to be launched by organized criminal gangs. Although today's misdeeds may be committed in combination with traditional crimes in use prior to the existence of the Internet, cybercriminals cannot be pursued in traditional ways.

Net frauds and unauthorized system access used in the chapter are examples of introductory cybercrimes. They are introduced to provide the forensic accountant with cybercrime case examples that improve the forensic accountant's ability to protect their clients against such attacks. Later, these case examples are compared with existing computer laws. Such a comparison is informative in evaluating how effective today's cybercrime statutes are in preventing criminal activities.

SPOTLIGHT

CRIME BREAKTHROUGH: HACKING AND FINANCIAL EXPERTISE COMBINED.
Blue Bottle Limited and Matthew C. Stokes are defendants in an SEC lawsuit. The defendants' U.S. assets have been frozen, and they have been legally required to repatriate funds transferred to overseas accounts. The defendants are from Hong Kong and the Island of Guernsey. The SEC's complaint alleges that the defendants hacked into the computer systems of 12 U.S. companies (including Symantec Corporation) and gained unauthorized access to financial news prior to its release to the public. Using this advance information, they traded in these companies' stock. The defendants made profits of close to $3 million. This is one of the first instances where cybercriminals used hacking methods and sophisticated financial expertise together in a scheme to manipulate stock trading. The defendants are not in the United States; therefore, they cannot be prosecuted under U.S. statutes related to computer fraud. Instead, their U.S. assets have been frozen under SEC statutes.[3]

The 12 companies whose networks were successfully attacked had high risk profiles and low assurances that their financial systems were protected as required under SOX. As a forensic accountant working with these companies, it would be necessary to identify these security risks prior to the attack and possibly disclose the risk to financial records in the financial statements.

¶ 15,001   NET FRAUDS: NO SKILLS NEEDED

Net frauds ensnare unsuspecting Internet users and companies into giving up their resources to an online criminal. These frauds could be performed with or without the Internet, and when they are conducted with the Internet, they do not adopt technologically sophisticated techniques. In contrast, more technological sophistication is needed to gain unauthorized access to a computer network. In those cases, the attacker wants to steal propriety information, such as software codes, bid projections, confidential information, or account numbers. Several traditional techniques for gaining access to networks are introduced in the chapter.

The number and variety of frauds that have occurred on the Internet defy classification. In traditional cases of fraud, the victim's greed and unwariness lead to exploitation by the criminal. Victim's greed and unwariness underlie net frauds also. Net frauds are based on the same psychology of past approaches with the receipt of fraudulent letters, knocks on the door followed by the swindle, and deceptive phone calls, but now criminals, with no more technological skill than knowing how to send e-mail, are successfully executing these "new" cybercrimes.

A net fraud can range from bank fraud, in which a victim's bank account number is stolen, money withdrawn, and sent to the perpetrator's account, through an intermediary, for example, to other schemes requesting a victim go to a spoofed website to verify personal and account information.[4] A website may be penetrated and credit card numbers or other financial data stolen.

NIGERIAN BANK OR 419 SCAM. The Nigerian bank scam begins with a letter received in an e-mail from the scam's perpetrators. The Nigerian criminals involved in the scam call themselves the "yahoo boys," i.e. based on their e-mail addresses, and their take from the scams is one of the largest revenue sources for the country.

REQUEST FOR AN URGENT ASSISTANCE:

I am Mr. Kaloma Alli a former special adviser on petroleum and economic matters to the late Head of State of Federal Republic of Nigeria General Sani Abacha.

Because of my strategic position in the former Government, and also being a close confidant of the Head of State, I was able to acquire personally, the sum of $45,000,000.00 USD (Forty five Million United States Dollars) presently lodged in a security company. I made this money legally through "CONSULTANCY FEE" and "Good Faith Fees" paid by Water Oil Blocks and other Lifting/prospecting right.

Nigeria is the 6th largest Producer/Exporter of Crude Petroleum in the World. As you are probably aware Nigeria is prone to political/Economic Instability, hyper Inflation, and among other problems, I therefore resolved to invest my money abroad, preferable in Real Estate Properties and Importation of Goods for safety and optimum returns on Investments.

However, straight transfer of this money into a bank abroad will present two major problems:

1. The tax incidence will be too high, as much as 60 percent of this money will go up in Taxes, Levies, Penalties, etc.

2. As an Ex serviceman in a former military government on which the present democratic government of Chief Olusegun Obasanjo is fighting very hard to freeze the accounts of the men that serve in the government of General Abacha.

So, as a result of Government deliberate restrictions on flight of capital Abroad. The solution is to Courier this money in cash abroad, through a security company here in Nigeria, the money would be packed in a Diplomatic trunk boxes and tagged Diplomatic luggage, while the documents to courier the consignment would be on your name/address, the security company has assured me of conveying the consignment to their offshore/regional office in Europe. This system is secret and the money is therefore untraceable. It is the system used by most top Government officials in Nigeria to remove their fortunes/loot to safety abroad.

I have therefore concluded every arrangement with the security Company in Nigeria to Courier this money abroad using the courtesy and safety of Diplomatic trunk boxes. All I now need is an honest partner who can receive the money on my behalf and help me to invest as forementioned. There is no risk involved in this transaction as the money will be delivered to you in United States Dollar Bills.

If you are interested in assisting me, please send me by email immediately your preferred contact address which would be used to register you as the beneficiary to the fund. Upon delivery, we are to finally arrange on how to transfer the fund to your country.

For your help and assistance in this deal, you will receive 30% of this money in cash, 10% will be set aside to offset all expenses while the remaining 60% is for me.

Expecting to hear from you.

Best regards,

Mr. Kaloma Alli.

NOTE: UPON RECEIPT OF YOUR RESPONSE I WOULD SEND YOU MY TELE-PHONE NUMBER. IF YOU ARE TO CONTACT ME ON THE PHONE PLEASE CONFIRM THIS CALL CODE "KIWI" BEFORE ANY DISCUSSION. YOU ARE TO ASK FOR THE CALL CODE, I'M TO GIVE YOU THE ANSWER KIWI.

The scam letter only requests an address. Once the victim returned an address, he or she was asked to transfer monies to a Nigerian bank as an advance fee. The request usually read something such as:

However, to be a legitimate transferee of these moneys according to Nigerian law, you must presently be a depositor of at least US$100,000 in a Nigerian bank which is regulated by the Central Bank of Nigeria.

In the United States, this scam resulted in the loss of millions of dollars as well as deaths of those who went to Nigeria hoping to recover their money. Usually, individuals are defrauded of their savings, but the largest known from an advance-fee scam was $242 million in a Nigerian-Brazil business fraud.[5] In such a large business fraud, it might be worthwhile to ask how the company's accountants could allow such a financial fraud to occur.

EYEWITNESS

GOING PHISHING. The following examples are of phishing scams used on the Internet. Phishing occurs when a phisher pretends to be from a legitimate company and requests confidential information, such as passwords, from either a business or a consumer. With an official looking e-mail, the phisher asks the victim to go to a website and fill out their personal information. Once the phisher obtains this confidential financial information, they assume the victim's identity. In February 2005, an Anti-Phishing Act with jail terms and fines was introduced into the Senate by Senator Patrick Leahy, but not currently passed into legislation. The phishing scam usually involves an e-mail and a fake website, but the phisher scams, called pharming, place a web bug on the victim's computer to execute the fraud. When the victim gets ready to go to their online bank, the bug redirects the victim to a fraudulent bank website, set up by the phisher, for spoofing the victim's bank login page. With pharming, opening an e-mail from the phisher results in the placement of a Trojan on the victim's computer. Such a fraud can also occur when the Trojan logs passwords and later e-mails them to the phisher.

Customers of Discover Card and Morgan Stanley Dean Witter and Company have been tricked into disclosing confidential account numbers and online passwords on a fake website.[6] Using a membership list of Discover Card or other companies' online customers, the e-mail used in this ploy may state: "We regret to inform you that your username and password have been lost." Afterward, a site with a web address similar to the legitimate company's web address is listed as the place to correct the problem. Using the stolen account numbers and passwords, the criminals can then go on their own Internet purchasing spree or just sell the thousands of collected credit card numbers and let others do the rest.

Variations on this scheme include the sending of e-mail for the victims to opt out of a plan whereby credit bureaus will be releasing personal credit information. Victims must report their personal information including their social security number on the listed website.

The following two e-mails are examples of phishing frauds.

Save Your Social Security Number Fraud with a Phone Call

```
END DISTRIBUTION OF YOUR SOCIAL SECURITY NUMBER

CALL: 1-888-567-8688

Just wanted to let everyone know who hasn't already heard,
the four major credit bureaus in the US will be allowed,
starting July 1, to release your credit info, mailing ad-
dresses, phone numbers, etc., to anyone who requests it. If
you would like to "opt out" of this release of your info, you
can call 1-888-567-8688. It only takes a couple of minutes
to do, and you can take care of anyone else in the household
while making only one call, you'll just need to know their
social security number. Once the message starts you'll want
option #2 (#1 sounds like the right one but it's not) and then
option #3 (#1 is only for 2 years). Make sure you wait until
they prompt for the third option, which opts you out forever.
```

Save Your Bank Account with a Fraudulent IP Address (Clicking on the link can put a trojan on your computer)

We recently reviewed your account, and suspect a fraudulent ATM transaction, proceed without authorization.

Therefore, as a preventative measure, we have temporarily limited access to your online banking access. To restore your account access, please follow the steps listed below.

1. Log in to your Internet Banking account. In case you are not enrolled for Internet Banking, you will have to use your Social Security Number as your User ID and the first 6 digits of Social Security Number as Password, then, fill in all the required information.
2. Review your recent account history for any unauthorized withdrawals or deposits, and check your account profile to make sure no changes have been made. If any unauthorized activity has taken place on your account, report this to KeyBank staff immediately.

To get started, please click the link below:

https://accounts2.keybank.com/ib2/Controller?requester=signon

Thank you for your prompt attention to this matter and thank you for using KeyBank!

Key Bank, N.A. Member FDIC. Equal Housing Lender
Copyright 2004 KeyBank, N.A. All rights reserved

Frequent fraud occurs at online auction sites as well. The scam may be that items purchased are not sent or differ from the items purchased. Although it is possible to check on the satisfaction of previous sales made by the online seller, the seller may fake such testimonials by using various online e-mail addresses purported to be from previously satisfied customers, thus fraudulently boosting the seller's reputation score. Auction frauds are typically person-to-person frauds, but they are expanding into the business-to-business area. In B-to-B auction frauds, accomplices may enter the bidding to raise the price of the item being auctioned—or never ship the ordered item.

An online auction scam that defrauds a number of third parties occurs when fake credit cards obtained in an identity theft are used to purchase legitimate goods from an e-business, then the goods are sold at a legitimate online auction site. The online auction company is duped into acting as a "fence" for the criminal. An innocent victim, individual or company, has its credit history destroyed and the credit card company and the e-business have been swindled.

Another variation on this approach uses illegal funds that are being transferred to launder money. When the victim, i.e., online auction seller, is unknowingly acting as a money launderer, they receive a money order for much more than the purchase price of the item being sold, and they are asked to send the item along with a check for the excess payment back to the buyer. The money order is a way to legitimize illegal funds, and the seller is victimized into laundering illegal money into a U.S. bank account. A similar scam occurs when the victim accepts an e-mail job offer to act as a "financial manager" who cashes mailed checks in their bank account and wires the cash to a foreign account, less a commission. In these cases, the checks are counterfeited and the wired monies are collected by the criminal before the paper checks clear through the banking system.

SPOTLIGHT

ENTRY LEVEL POSITION FOR MULES. The following spam e-mail was sent to entice recipients into unknowingly participate in a money laundering operation.

Velocity Global is a one stop project management agent. It is virtually managed B2B designed to cater advanced programming services ranging from web application, C++ modules, web designing to data conversion from text to SGML, XML.

We have many ways to save our clients' money.

One of these ways to save money is hiring a Financial Manager. In case of getting an order from another country we have to pay 15% fee for international bank transfer according to US law. To reduce the transfer cost we are looking for Financial Managers all over the world. When we get an order from another country, the Financial Manager in this country gets the payment and sends it to us through Western Union. Commission rate of Financial Managers is 3%.

In order to qualify for the position, you must be aged 21 and above. The prospective candidate should be good with numbers, committed and a good communicator. No special education is required; however, any experience in accounting/finance/client relations/database management is an advantage. You will receive your commission as soon as the transfer is carried out. There are no probation periods, no rolling reserves and no hidden fees or deductions.

For more information: Click here

Source: Computer Crime and Security Survey (*http://www.auscert.org.au/render.html?it=2001*).

Customer education is the best method to protect individuals and companies from being defrauded in these Net scams. A forensic accountant who provides her clients with periodic round table discussions about new Net frauds is reducing the fraud risk level in a company. Additionally, ensuring that computer logs are maintained and suspicious logs are analyzed is another way of diminishing the success of such Net frauds.

Unauthorized Access Via Social Engineering

In Table 15.1, the fourth method shown in gaining unauthorized access is called *social engineering*, which is any technique that is used to deceive an employee into revealing a password or access code. Although this method does not use technology, it is effective. A phone caller pretends to be an authorized user who has forgotten or lost his or her password. Or, the attacker may pretend to be an employee who is running a test on the system but who needs a password to complete the test. The criminal may pretend to be a temporary employee who cannot get into the system and is calling the help desk for assistance. The criminal cajoles someone in the organization into revealing a password so that the criminal can access the system. If an employee is being impersonated, the attacker already has collected enough personal information about the employee to effectively carry off the impersonation. Information about the employee's boss, his wife and kids' names, office location, and fellow employees' names are used to make the impersonation effective. Social engineering has been recently called pretexting, but it is the same approach of pretending to be someone else to get information that otherwise would be unobtainable.

¶ 15,011   UNAUTHORIZED ACCESS TO NETWORK ASSETS

It is somewhat arbitrary to separate cybercrimes into different categories because these crimes are executed in combination with each other. Yet, unauthorized network access using hacking tools to steal proprietary and financial information can be considered a distinct crime from the previous old-school fraud approaches. A separating point is that such crimes require more technological skills. The key characteristic of this crime it is a technology attack that allowed attacker *unauthorized access by breaching the organization's information system.*

Ransoming Information

One now-classic extortion cybercrime is executed by a criminal group of hackers who breaks into a business's computer networks. Once in the system, the hackers collect information such as customers' credit card numbers or unreleased financial reports. Afterwards they contact the business and pose as "security consultants" with recommendations as to how to correct the network's holes. They also make it clear that they will not release any customers' account numbers or other stolen information if the business purchases security services. In return for this security service, the business must deposit money into an untraceable foreign bank account.[7] Another crime of this nature is to access a production system in a manufacturing facility and insert a virus, in an attempt to damage or disrupt the company's production schedule. As billions of financial transactions move to the Internet such as FedLineWeb and the global banking network with critical bank payment services; as health organizations move payment information and health records; or as cash treasury management becomes web-based, it is anticipated these changes are providing target rich environments for cybercriminals. Again, "security consultants" will send e-mail to explain how to correct an information system problem for a consulting fee. Years ago these cybercrimes began with benign attempts by young hackers to gain h unauthorized system access for various reasons, and now such activities have turned into traditional criminal gang extortion schemes.

Keeping Up with the Criminals

Although Internet financial frauds, such as the Nigerian letter scam, do not require a high level of technical skill to implement, fraud schemes that begin with unauthorized information system access require a criminal with advanced technological skills. If the forensic investigator or law enforcement personnel cannot match the criminal's tech skills, the crime will remain unsolved as investigators are left in the dark as to how the crime was committed. Furthermore, cybercriminals are not waiting for their adversaries to become better skilled. As a result, cybercriminals' technical skill levels continually advance as investigators struggle to match them.

MY AVATAR WAS ROBBED! If your avatar on Second Life was robbed, what law enforcement agency would you go to for help? Could local city police help you get restitution? Could the state police help? Second Life is an online community with millions of members, including businesses, from around the world.

This was an actual crime and the only help available came from the computer programmers at Second Life who could identify the avatar that was stealing the money and they made restitution and kicked the offending avatar off their website.

¶ 15,021   THE UNAUTHORIZED ACCESS SKILL SET

Unauthorized access can come from inside the company as a disgruntled employee collects proprietary data with the intention of selling it to competitors. Just as easily, the attack can come from outside the company. Outside attacks may come from individuals in other countries where such cyber activities are not considered illegal. The five methods that can be used to gain access to a system without authorization are listed in Table 15.1.

Table 15.1. Five Traditional Methods and Technologies Used for Gaining Unauthorized Access to Computer Systems

Access Method	Technology Used
1. Modem Attack	Wardialing/Brute force password crack
2. Port Access	Nmap stealth scan/Apply downloaded exploit
3. Trusted Server	Zone transfer/IP spoofing
4. Social Engineering	None
5. Wardriving	Wi-Fi/inSSider/aircrak-ng (run from a Linux CD)

Access Using Wardialers in Modem Attacks

The first method listed in Table 15.1 is a phone modem attack. The use of modems has decreased in recent years as faster DSL systems have taken their place, but the lower cost modems have not entirely been replaced. Additionally, some cell phones may be used as "modems", tethering, to allow laptops to connect to the Internet when no WIFI is available and the user has a wireless data access plan. In 2012, software is available to perform wardialing on Skype, and WarVox (http://warvox.org/install.html) allows for wardialing using VoIP audio tones. Therefore, modems may still provide the hacker with a means to gain unauthorized access to a network or attach malware to a laptop or PC which will later be connected to a network. The concept of wardialers has been adapted in today's online voting for talent contestants, where automatic phone dialers are used to log votes for a favored candidate on TV shows at thousands of votes per minute. These automated callers use the same concept as wardialers.

Unauthorized modems still may be installed on computer networks by employees to allow them to access files while they are traveling. Small businesses in rural communities may use a modem to connect to the Internet. Only a password is required to gain access to these modems and the network they support.

A *wardialer* is a downloadable software cracking program that allows a modem attacker to rapidly dial and check all phone numbers within a given range such as from 293-5000 to 293-7000. The wardialer produces a log to identify those numbers that are tied to a modem or fax machine based on the handshaking tones. Once a modem is identified, the next step is to uncover the password used to access the modem. In some cases, there may be a default password to access and check the modem's operation. If the attacker knows the equipment's published default password, then the first step would be to try the default password. If the default password is unknown, a dictionary and brute force password attack is implemented to find the password. A dictionary used to check passwords may already come with the wardialer. If not, there are freely available dictionary packages on the Internet. Once access is gained, the specifics of further access to the network will vary greatly from site to site. Cellphones being used as a modem for a laptop are not likely to use a password for access.

WARDIALING. There are a host of free wardialers available on the Internet. Modem-Scan (http://www.security-science.com) provides a downloadable wardialer for use with Windows XP and older Windows systems. Before using a wardialer, state statutes need to be reviewed to determine if wardialing is legal in the jurisdiction where the wardialer is being used. The opening screen for ModemScan is shown here. ModemScan will dial a range of phone numbers in a random sequence to detect faxes and modems.

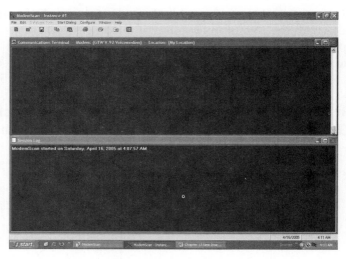

To prevent an attack based on wardialing, no unauthorized access to the Internet from a company's network should be allowed.   A company needs to periodically check its system for unauthorized Internet access set up by its employees. The forensic accountant needs to advise his clients about the need to reduce fraud risk and meet SOX guidelines by conducting periodic reviews to remove these unauthorized access points.

Access Via Buggy or Unpatched Software

Port Scans

The next method used to gain unauthorized access to a system is to exploit unpatched software. Web servers have 65,535 possible access ports. Not all these ports may be connected to the Internet, but many of them are active. The task of the attacker is to find the active ports and determine the software that is used on these ports. Port scanning allows an attacker to make these determinations. A quick scan of the most common 1,024 ports on a server can be done in a few minutes, at the most. Depending on the scanner used, the attacker can log the software that is being used on the active ports. A stealth scan allows a scan to be made in such a way that it is undetectable. With a stealth scan, the server does not report in its logs that it has been scanned.

Port scans are used to identify potential targets for gaining network access. As previously noted, this procedure begins with a ping sent to a web server. Once it is determined that a port is running software with a known bug or an unpatched version of the software, the attacker downloads the published exploit, i.e., code to implement the attack, compiles the code for the specific system, and uses the compiled program to enter the network. Once inside the network, there are various actions that might be taken to collect proprietary information and place backdoor Trojans on the entry port which allow the hacker to re-enter the system at will. Access to these systems can be completed in less than 15 minutes by a skilled hacker.

PORT SCANNING WITH NMAP. Nmap (*http://nmap.org/download.html*) is a free port scanning tool downloadable from Nmap.org. It works on all Windows systems, and it is executable without command lines, only clicks. In most jurisdictions, port scanning is not considered to be any more illegal than making a phone call. Nmap has a number of options for making a scan available in its drop down menu. Nmap will identify vulnerability risk levels of the software running on each port scanned. Many firewalls filter their ports and do not allow Nmap to collect information about the software running on their ports. The following screen is a simple Nmap port scan run. It identifies the most popular systems and their open port numbers. After the user identifies a target website and types in the website or IP address, clicking on "Scan" completes the process.

Nmap is as useful for preventing attacks against a web server as it is in launching them. Network administrators can use Nmap to determine which of their web server ports are open and have potential vulnerabilities on them. If there is unauthorized backdoor software running on their server, it may be detectable by Nmap's. At the same time, attackers can use Nmap to find vulnerabilities that should have been patched by network administrators. The tool is not the culprit. It is how the tool is used.

To assist their clients in meeting SOX guidelines about protecting the financial records from unauthorized access and ensure financial information integrity, forensic accountants should recommend periodic penetration testing be conducted. In a penetration test, a computer forensic group attacks a company's computer network with the most powerful tools used by the hacking community to break into a company's network. Once the weaknesses are identified by accessing the network, they are corrected.

Access Via Trusted Server

Zone Transfers and IP Spoofing

Another traditional method for gaining unauthorized access to a network is with zone transfers and IP spoofing. A zone transfer is a request for all the information that is available about a domain name. Zone transfers allow for updated connectivity information about new web hosts being added to a network or the Internet.[8] A zone transfer provides a blueprint on the trusted IP addresses used by a website. From an attacker's perspective, the objective of a zone transfer is to develop basic reconnaissance on a targeted website. For example, finding all the IP numbers associated with a domain name. Such an analysis may begin by checking Edgar for identify the subsidiaries companies associated with a primary target. A Windows based utility for identifying IP numbers associated with a primary target is EZDig and it is available from download.com.

Such an attack takes a two-pronged approach to gain unauthorized access. As stated, the normal purpose of a zone transfer is to provide automatic, periodic up-dates of information about changing network data, such as IP changes, for all trusted servers on that network. Once those IP addresses are identified, the attacker may decide that the best way to gain access is to spoof the trusted servers.

The attack begins with a zone transfer. One method for making zone transfers is with Nslookup.[9] Not all servers allow zone transfers to be made. By performing a zone transfer, the attacker gets a list of the trusted servers. The next step is to spoof (falsely pretend to be another IP address) the IP address and connection sequence number of the connect request coming from the trusted server. As a consequence, the firewall will not stop the unauthorized entry. Before that can be done, the trusted server must be disabled so that no services will be duplicated while the attacker is actively spoofing. The disabling of the trusted server can be done in a number of ways, but most commonly it is done with a denial of service attack.[10]

FAKE IP ADDRESSES. Another reason for spoofing an IP address is to be able to privately surf the Internet. As one surfs the Net, websites pick up a great deal of information about the surfer and their computer operating system. Invisible Browsing allows the Internet user to hide their real IP address and substitute another IP address (or proxy) from a drop down list of U.S. and overseas servers. Any preliminary "Whois" checks on this Internet surfer would lead to incorrect data. The opening screen for Invisible Browsing shows that the user's real IP address is hidden and the user's IP address appears to be 168.12.2.103. Invisible Browsing sells for around $30.

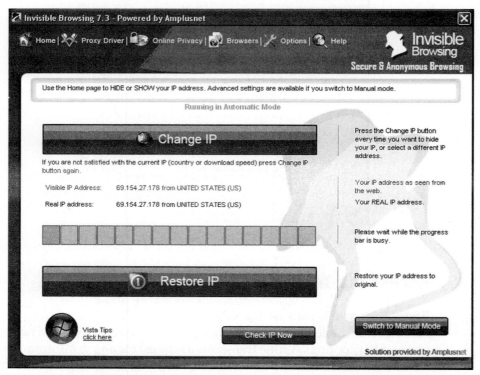

Invisible Browsing will allow you to pick your IP address. When proxy servers are used, such as TOR, they hide your real IP address, but they do not allow you to pick or spoof a specific IP address.

THE 10-MINUTE E-MAIL ADDRESS. Everyone talks about the disposable phones used by criminals. How about a disposable e-mail address that will last for 10 to 20 minutes and then disappear? It is another way to remain anonymous on the Internet and not have e-mail traced directly back to you. What could you do with a disposable e-mail address? Maybe send untraceable messages. *http://10minutemail. com/10MinuteMail/index.html*

Backdoor Entry

With spoofing, there is a limited time period for the attacker to get into the targeted system. Consequently, the attacker will place software, such as a backdoor Trojan, on the targeted system to allow reentry at a later date. At this point, the hacker has taken over the PC. The Trojan can be placed on an open port, or in the registry, and waits for communications from the attacker. This process creates an open backdoor into the entire hnetwork. Once the system being spoofed is back online, the IP spoofing attack cannot be continued, but the attacker can get back into the targeted system through the backdoor placed on the target during the attack. At a later date, the attacker will come back and download proprietary information or take other illegal actions against the business. Such infections can result in the altering of financial files and records. In many cases, the backdoor Trojan can be inserted simply by having the victim visit a webpage listed in a "trusted" e-mail. Trojans are difficult to guard against, and anti-virus software may not be able to detect the infections as the program signature within the Trojans morphs from antivirus identified information. To remove a Trojan, it may be necessary to view the PC's registry with a free utility such as "HijackThis." The utility will scan the registry, prepare a log file for identifying possible Trojan software, but it is up to the user to determine if an identified program is a Trojan and should be removed.

THE PSP2-BBB TROJAN: SAY WHAT? During the first three months of 2011, an average of 73,000 new strains of malware had been created every day—10,000 more than during the same period last year, according to stats from Panda Security. Around 70 percent of these malware strains were Trojans, with viruses making up 17 percent of the sample, the second most common category (*www.pandasecurity.com*).

The PSP2-BBB Trojan was used to launch a "man-in-the browser" attack to gain unauthorized access to 138 bank accounts in the U.K. that netted cyber criminals approximately £600,000. The PSP2-BBB Trojan is not stopped by two-factor authentication logins as it is an exploit developed specifically to overcome two-factor authorization. In this attack, unauthorized access begins the moment the bank customer logs into her account. The customer's web browser could become infected with the Trojan from e-mail or just by visiting a compromised webpage and clicking on the wrong link. For bank customers whose browsers had been infected with the Trojan, a special web page would be inserted into their online banking activity asking for confidential information. Once the information was collected from the customer, it allows the Trojan to automatically transfer money out of the customer's account during the banking session. Preventing such an attack is very difficult because the transfer is made from within the customer's browser at the time the customer is logged into her online account. Consequently, the IP address or cookies in the customer's browser appear correct. The automated transfer is made to a "collection" account belonging to a mule. The mule uses Western Union to transfer the money to the home base of the criminals in Eastern Europe. Several of the cyber criminals from Uzbekistan, Angola, Portugal, and Venezuela have been implicated or sentenced for the U.K. thefts.

One way of guarding against such attacks is with Trusteer Rapport software (*http://www.trusteer.com/product/trusteer-rapport*). The software is specifically developed to stop man-in-the browser or man-in-the-middle attacks.

It is difficult to establish defenses against zone transfers, IP spoofing, ten-minute e-mail addresses, and constantly changing Trojan software. The forensic accountant needs to have assurances from their accounting client that the best methods of cyber protection are being used to prevent and preserve the client's financial records from such attacks. In order to know if the best methods are being adopted, the forensic accountant needs to have a basic familiarity with attack methodologies. If client assurances regarding cyber risks are obviously lagging or not implemented and a significant financial loss potential exists, it may be necessary to add footnote disclosures to the financial statements identifying the higher level of vulnerability risk faced by a company.

Wardriving

Wardriving is the process of using an exploit to gain unauthorized access to a wireless system. There are free and open wireless systems used at motels, libraries, airports, and fast-food restaurants such as McDonalds. Other private wireless systems have been set up by corporations or homeowners for their own uses. In latter cases, these are private WIFI networks not open to everyone and access is restricted. For a corporation, unauthorized access to its wireless network may also mean that the attacker has access to the entire company network. Wireless networks have an access point (AP), and the AP sends a beacon signal out allowing users with wireless cards in their laptops to connect through the AP to the internal network.

A wireless network can be considered to be open or closed. An open network is available for anyone to use whereas a closed network requires the user to at least know the Service Set Identifier (SSID, i.e., network name) and usually another password to join the network. A network also may control access based on the MAC address of the connecting PC. Of course, any network can bleed signals into a city street where anyone with a laptop and a wireless card may gain unauthorized access to a closed network. This is also true of a neighbor's wireless networks.

Wardriving gets its name because a slowly moving vehicle using a laptop was used to locate wireless signals bleeding into city streets. Of course, it could be done by walking down a sidewalk. In both cases, the airwaves are being searched for wireless signals bleeding from buildings with active WIFI networks. Bleeding of wireless signals occurs because the radio wave transmissions do not simply transmit in a single path to a receiver. Instead, these transmissions have signal offshoots that reach unintended areas such as parking lots outside highly secured corporate buildings.

A freely downloadable wireless network analyzer called inSSIDer2.0 (*http://download.cnet.com/windows/*) can be used to find and identify data in wireless transmissions. inSSIDER2.0 analyzes 802.11 headers to determine SSID, MAC address, WEP packet usage, RSSI (signal strength), channel, router vendor, type of encryption (WEP or stronger), GPS data, and other information; it also develops a time graph of activity on each identified wireless network. SSID is the name of the identified wireless network and MAC is an identifier for a specific PC on a wireless LAN (WLAN). inSSIDER2.0 works on the most recent Windows operating systems. By itself, it does not allow the attacker unauthorized access into a wireless network. The opening screen for inSSIDER2.0 is shown here. It reveals the network name or SSID by sniffing the communication authentications protocols. Also, the MAC addresses are shown in the clear. Even if encryption is used, the MAC address is still shown in the clear. Once the MAC address is obtained, it is easy to change the MAC address on the attacker's PC to one of the authorized MAC addresses with free software such as SpoofMac. If the wireless network should be WEP encrypted, it is necessary to use a packet sniffer to collect wireless packets and then crack the encryption in those packets. A free sniffer that can do this is called aircrack-ng.or which is updated only through Windows XP. With more recent operating systems, you will have to use a Slitaz live CD boot on your system. Today old 104 bit WEP-protected systems can be cracked for open access to a wireless network in about one minute.

One of the easiest exploits for attackers today is to gain access to unprotected or WEP encrypted wireless networks. As can be seen in the insider screen shot, all the wireless systems are encrypted with WEP or RSNA-CCMP. Today, WEP beginning to be replaced with WPA/WPA2 encryption. The change is based on access speed issues more than stronger encryption. These access methods are performed with Linux OS and will not be discussed here.

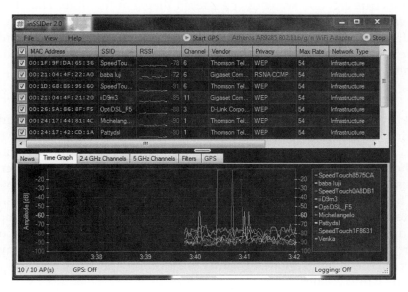

These methods of unauthorized access, and there are others, have been presented here as an illustration of network vulnerabilities. Is knowing about vulnerable networks important for a forensic accountant? Would it be considered unethical for an accountant to post all of his client's confidential financial information on the side of a public building? Is it wrong for an accountant to write his tax client's social security number on the side of his house? If not, then there is no problem with putting unprotected financial information into a vulnerable computer network and creating unreported financial losses for a company.[11] In order for an accountant to determine if s/he is or is not protecting a client's financial records, assets, and even family members from harm, the accountant needs to understand basic computer attack strategies.

Criminality of Cybercrimes

Computer crime legislation is in effect to help protect innocent victims of financial and other computer crimes. Such legislation must be written in a manner to stop unauthorized access and fraud techniques from being used. Currently, U.S. court cases have adopted a "socialization" view rather than a strictly legislative view toward the authorization to use a network. Basically, the courtroom view is that if use was not authorized, it is unauthorized. With wireless communication, this becomes confusing as normally it is not unlawful to intercept communications that are accessible to the general public, such as radio station signals. If these radio signals are open access, then WIFI should be open access? Courts, especially state courts, are likely to take a more restrictive view on the matter. All these issues make effective legislation difficult to write and even more difficult to implement, as described next.

¶ 15,031   WHEN IS A CYBERCRIME REALLY A CYBERCRIME?

The previous section described activities that might be cybercrimes, but what is *really* a cybercrime is an activity that has been made clearly illegal by the jurisdiction in which the crime was committed. Internet criminal activities can come from anywhere in the world. The laws of different countries do not uniformly consider every activity described in the previous section as an illegal act.

SPOTLIGHT

"I LOVE YOU VIRUS." The "I Love You" virus was written in the Philippines where the virus creation was not considered illegal at the time. The "I Love You" virus was sent around the world, and it was described as creating billions of dollars in damages to computer systems. If the creator of the "I Love You" virus had initially released the virus in the United States instead, he would have joined the U.S. creator and sender of the "Melissa" virus in jail.

It is vital to determine in which jurisdiction a cybercrime was committed. If the criminal is sitting at a computer in South Africa, the web page is on a server in Aruba, money is transferred to a bank in Canada with a final destination to the criminal's bank in London, where did the crime occur? It may be difficult to decide on the jurisdiction. A criminal who is aware of these jurisdiction differences may be able to execute a cybercrime without prosecution.

There are over 240 countries with domain registered country codes.[12] The countries with registered domains include Afghanistan (AF), Cook Islands (CK), and Tuvalu (TV). Each country has active web servers and each country has different laws, or no laws, to define cybercrimes. Complicating jurisdictions issues, smaller countries may have their domain servers maintained in another country. In addition, they may not have an extradition treaty with the United States.

Intangible Assets

Before the forensic accountant can review jurisdiction issues, the legislative stance toward cybercrimes needs to be understood. Criminal codes are written to prevent fraud or protect tangible assets or intangible rights such as intellectual property. Tangible assets have a physical presence and intellectual properties have legal property rights attached to them. Information on the Internet and in computer databases represents intangible assets composed of bits and bytes. Early statutes, enacted in the 1970s, viewed computer crimes as attacks against computers or computer supplies, i.e., tangible assets.[13] In some cases, fraud statutes may be written to specifically require that a *person* was deceived. If the fraud is perpetuated on a computer, technically it may not be considered a crime because no *person* was defrauded.

Yet the most valued assets in a network are the bits and bytes that flow within it. Data in a computer or on the Internet consists of electronic representations or pulses. Data needs to be analyzed before it becomes information and receives protections under property statutes. The destruction of electronic representations may not be considered the destruction of information or stealing because *information* is legally another formation that was not affected. For this reason, the erasure of data, caused by a data-eating virus, without physically damaging a tangible computer asset may not be considered to be a crime or at most a minor misdemeanor. Such activity is not considered equivalent to the theft of a physical asset by a criminal.

Under some jurisdictions, if the data is accessed but not used for any purpose, then no crime may have been committed. For this reason, the scanning of ports on web servers and learning the type of software running on a port is not considered to be an illegal activity. A scan is largely viewed as a phone call to see if anyone is at home. Additionally, the appropriation of the data for different purposes than it was originally collected is not considered a significant event compared to the misappropriation or misuse of physical assets. Unauthorized access to data may not include the interception of wireless transmissions that go through the walls of a building where I live or that can be received off-site with special detection equipment.

These views form the underlying basis in which physical assets are recorded, and compared with digital assets, in the financial statements. Today most companies do not place a value on the bulk of their digital assets and in some cases, do not recognize that their existence.

The unauthorized use of tangible assets means that the criminal had to be physically present on the owner's property, i.e., a building or home. When computer data is misused or misappropriated, the criminal may only have an electronic presence within the owner's property. Statutes may not provide for the recognition of criminal trespass, a property crime, based on a virtual presence. How can I trespass, if I was not there?

If statutes were expanded to include electrical pulses as "property," it would create more crimes than possibly could be investigated. For example, the loss of a person's e-mail would be considered a crime and changing downloaded open-source coding could also be considered a violation. Under such an approach the electric pulse generated by my computer, as I surfed the Internet, would belong to only me. Interference with my electrical pulses such as investigating where I was surfing would be a criminal violation.

Using bots, such as search engines, to investigate websites or perform activity on their own may be considered illegal. Is it possible to prosecute an electronic impulse, generated by a bot that took action predicated on its own learning? Thus, creating laws that recognize electrical pulses as legal property may not be the best approach.

OECD Recommendations

It is difficult to attempt to write current laws in the face of continually changing Internet technology. Yet in 1986, the Organization for Economic Cooperation and Development (OECD) wrote a series of recommendations for its member states. The OECD defined the computer crimes as illegal acts and recommended that member states adopt similar definitions in their national legislation.[14]

INITIAL RECOMMENDATIONS FOR COMPUTER LAWS BY THE OECD IN 1986

1. The input, alteration, erasure and/or suppression of computer data and/or computer programmes made willfully with the intent to commit an illegal transfer of funds or of another thing of value;

2. The input, alteration, erasure and/or suppression of computer data and/or computer programmes made willfully with the intent to commit a forgery;

3. The input, alteration, erasure and/or suppression of computer data and/or computer programmes, or other interference with computer systems, made willfully with the intent to hinder the functioning of a computer and/or telecommunication system;

4. The infringement of the exclusive right of the owner of a protected computer programme with the intent to exploit commercially the programme and put it on the market;

5. The access to or the interception of a computer and/or telecommunication system made knowingly and without the authorization of the person responsible for the system, either (i) by infringement of security measures or (ii) for other dishonest or harmful intentions.

Although these recommendations were made in 1986, it is interesting to consider how they would affect the hacking technologies that are used today to gain access to computer networks. Since 1986, there have been numerous new technologies used to attack computer networks. In beginning a network attack, a hacker performs a scan of the server's ports. Under none of the five recommendations would a scan be considered illegal. Sniffer programs, not available in 1986, can be used to collect passwords today. The installation of a sniffer program on a network to collect information may be illegal under recommendation five. Yet, the collection of the password is not "dishonest or harmful" unless the password is used and if no harm were done inserting a sniffer, what was the crime that was committed? There may not have been an "infringement of security measures" required to place the sniffer program on the network if the security measures were not active on the access point that the hacker used. In fact, accessing the network may not have required the hacker to alter the server's software. Access may only require running a program that created no changes in the server's programs. So, there may not be a violation under recommendation five either.

Spoofing

Spoofing occurs when one misappropriates the identity of another. The entity whose identity is stolen does not know misappropriation has occurred. On the Internet, one purpose of the spoof is to gain unauthorized access to a network by assuming the IP identity of a trusted website. Spoofing would fall under recommendation three because spoofing a website is a form of forgery. Yet, the spoof is located on the attacker's computer not the targeted system so there has been no access to the targeted network. Without access to the targeted system, has a computer crime been committed? What is spoofed or anonymous e-mail? *Spoofed e-mail* is, or can be, an alteration of data. But if the data is not stored on the computer where the e-mail message is read, is it a violation of the OECD recommendations? An anonymous e-mail is different from a spoofed message as the former is an attempt to hide the sender's e-mail address not to pretend to be someone else by using their e-mail address through a spoof.

WHO ARE YOU? No one can automatically assume that a received e-mail is really sent from the person listed in the message's "From" line unless the e-mail has a digital signature that has been checked by the recipient. Negligently responding to e-mails can result in the release of confidential corporate and personnel information. For example, spoofed e-mails can be used to induce an employee to leave his workstation while a keylogger is installed on their PC. When anonymous or fake e-mails are sent, the sender wants to hide their real identity or spoof someone else's identity. Usually, the identity of the real sender remains undisclosed in the short version of the e-mail header. Anonymailer.net allows e-mail to be sent through an open SMTP port, i.e, the e-mail port. The annual cost is less than $20. An example of such an e-mail, with the short header, from Omar Kadefi is shown below. As previously mentioned, the short version of the header does not allow for the identification of the true sender of the e-mail. The site stresses that spoofed e-mails are not to be used for illegal purposes meaning that a spoofed e-mail is only as illegal based on the reason purpose for which it is sent. Yet in some jurisdictions, the sending of a fake e-mail is considered illegal. It is up to the recipient of the e-mail to understand the limitations of short headers and if an e-mail is suspicious, it is up to them to check the IP addresses or domain name in the long header.

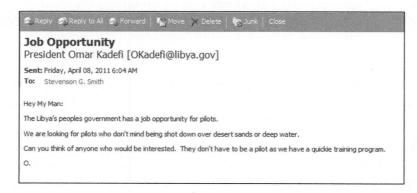

Bots

Bots is an abbreviation for robots. Bots are software programs on infected computers constructed to perform specific actions usually with little human input, acting on behalf of the person who installed them. Bots can act as friendly agents for a person to help make decisions based on information the bots collect.[15] When bots become part of a network of computers that have been taken over by a hacker, the network is called a botnet. These bots potentially can interact with other bots to launch Internet denial of service (DOS) attacks with minimum input from their human user. The communication to coordinate the attack of the infected computers is done with Internet Chat Relay (IRC), a basic chat system, which is secretly installed on one of the infected computer's lesser-used ports and listens for its commands.[16] The botherder who runs the botnet authenticates himself to the bot using the IRC channel and then sends out action commands used to communicate with the bot network. These malicious bots are used to launch DOS attacks that can shut down Internet services for Fortune 500 companies as well as some small countries. The bots can search for proprietary information stored on the infected computer. The number of bots in a botnet can number into the hundreds of thousands.

If software bots are used to randomly search websites for data, is that a violation of the OECD's recommendations? Bots may only be searching for the lowest price on merchandise. Yet such bots may be a violation of recommendation five because they do not have the "authorization of the person responsible for the system" to make these searches. If true, it would be illegal to use commercial software to follow a web surfer in order to collect information about the surfer's web habits. Thus, the enforcement of recommendation five may put commercial infomediaries, such as DoubleClick, in jail. Along with infomediaries, Google executives would have to be jailed as they use webcrawling bots to search websites for information. These OECD recommendations are so broad that they result in creating problems for legitimate Internet businesses.

SPOTLIGHT

DO ACCOUNTANTS HAVE A DUTY TO SAFEGUARD A CLIENT'S PHYSICAL ASSETS? HOW ABOUT DIGITAL ASSETS? Digital assets are those assets that do not have a physical presence such as the bandwidth a company pays for access to the Internet or the unused capacity of its computers. If a cybercriminal virtually steals those valuable virtual company resources, does it have anything to do with safeguarding a company's real assets? If my company's avatars are maliciously destroyed in the company's online community, should this be reported in the financial statements? If my avatar's Linden dollars are stolen by another avatar in the SecondLife on-line community, has a cybercrime been committed? Or are digital resources only recognizable as expenses? How can anyone steal an expense?

Jeanson Ancheta pleads guilty to four felony charges related to planting bots on computers including U.S. government computers at the China Lake Air Facility and the Defense Information System Agency. Ancheta used a botnet and zombie computers to generate profits of $61,000 over a 14-month period. Ancheta rented his bot army out through PayPal to people who wanted to launch denial of service attacks. Later, he expanded his revenue operations into installing display ads on the compromised computers in his botnet and got paid for this activity. It is estimated that he controlled over 400,000 zombie computers.[17]

Many times bots will install keyloggers on the compromised computer to log all key strikes such as user names and passwords. The logs are kept on the compromised computer, and at periodical intervals, the collected and formatted information is sent as an e-mail to the owner of the bot. The collected information is then sold or used by the hacker.

For an example of a more benign chatterbot see Alice (at *http://www.alicebot. blogspot.com/* and chat with A.L.I.C.E. or a somewhat unresponsive Captain Kirk). The Alice bot has the virtual face of a woman with blinking eyes that follow the movements of the cursor on the screen. Alice will answer text questions about various topics. Bots of this nature are known as avatars. If you want to quickly construct your own avatar in your own likeness or with even better features, see Second Life (*http://secondlife.com*).

Technologies Not Foreseen by OECD

The OECD's recommendations were effective for the technology that was available in 1986. Twenty-eight years later, these recommendations are not effective. All computer crime statutes face a similar situation: They become quickly outdated by new technologies or they are so general as to be unenforceable. In all the federal and state statutes that will be reviewed in this chapter, none mention wireless communication technologies.[18] Today low-power radio signals are being used to connect to the Internet. When does unauthorized access take place on a radio wave that is passing through my house on its way to its destination? As cloud computing becomes a reality, it changes the way corporations use software packages and store financial data.[19] Cloud computing puts all software and files on a webserver that is remotely accessed from the employee's work computer, but none of the application software or any files are stored on their work computer.

Regulation of Investigatory Powers Act

When the laws are focused on specific activities, they become easier to circumvent. An example of an attempt to circumvent an enacted law occurred when the Regulation of Investigatory Powers Act (Act) was passed in the United Kingdom in 2000.[20] The section dealing with the Investigation of Electronic Data Protected By Encryption provides the government with authority to demand disclosure of any protected information traveling in the United Kingdom as well as the key needed to decrypt any encrypted data in order to protect national security, detect crime, or for economic well-being. Protected information is information that cannot be readily accessed or shown in an intelligible format without a digital key. Encrypted information readily falls under the provisions of the Act. A number of governments have enacted similar restrictions on encryption.

The Theory of Chaffing and Winnowing

Chaffing is a term that is used to describe an Internet-based methodology for sending hidden messages.[21] It is a technique whereby the packets that route data over the Internet use hidden files in their headers.[22] Headers contain information to identify the packets that are sent over the Internet so that these packets can be reassembled when the message is received at the recipient's site. Chaffing mixes packets of real information with random packets of white noise, i.e., mixtures of wheat with the chaff. *Message authentication codes (MACs)* are used to identify all real information in the packets, but only the recipient can separate the real packets from random packets using the authentication codes to "winnow" them out.[23] Hidden messages can be sent by participants who are not even aware of the other hidden messages in the transmission. The messages can be sent without using encryption and yet the recipient cannot decode them except with the correct key.

The packet is still "in the clear"; no encryption has been performed. Software that merely authenticates messages by adding MACs is automatically approved for export, as it is deemed not to encrypt.[24]

Chaffing hides information in plain sight, and the information does not have to be encrypted. As such, it is already in an "intelligible format" and does not violate the encryption provisions of the Act. Does it violate any provisions of the Act? It depends on how the terminology "readily put into an intelligible format" is defined. What does the term "readily" mean? Encryption cannot be cracked but unencrypted chaffing messages may be more easily put into an intelligible format without the required key. It is not as clear whether chaffing is a violation of the Regulation of Investigatory Powers Act. Technological modifications to a program can be introduced that do not violate a newly-enacted law and consequently circumvent the letter of the law.

Steganography

Is steganography a violation of the Act if the hidden file is not encrypted? With *steganography* an unencrypted financial file can be hidden in a digital photo or wave file. The file is compressed. Is the compression of data that, if found, can be readily placed into an intelligible format a violation of the Act? Unencrypted steganography is just another form of chaffing and winnowing.

A simple example of how to hide a secret message in plain sight for someone who has never used steganography can be found at spammimic.com. Typing a short message such as "Pick up financials at Coral Gables 1300 the 16th" is encoded into a large, innocuous paragraph of spam to be used by the sender of a secret message. The recipient of the spam e-mail message can cut and paste the entire spam paragraph into a decoding form at spammimic to decrypt the message. The recipient of the message will arrive at the correct place at the correct time to pick up the files without anyone else having knowledge of the exchange. The example meets the definition of "covered writing," and implementation of steganography.

Steganography works with graphics, movies, digital images (.bmp, .gif, or .jpeg) and sound (.wav) files when a hidden file or the message file is encrypted and embedded, not attached, within the image or .wav file without changing the picture or sound quality. The cover file is the document into which the message file is placed. Encryption, by itself, ensures that a message sent between two parties cannot be read by a third party. Thus, stolen company proprietary information or unreleased financial data can be sent in an e-mail attachment or taken from company premises in an image file without detection.

Within a digital image, the hidden file is stored within the cover file's least significant pixels. The software determines the best locations to separate and store the message bits by checking the luminosity of the picture's pixels to locate those areas where the variance between pixels is not very strong or weak for the placement of the information.

Stego software can be purchased from a number of commercial vendors as well as downloaded for free from the Internet. There are several stego packages available from download.com. The example illustrated here uses a program called Our Secret and it works with all photos. The opening screen is shown. The steps for using the software are clearly shown. Basically, the user needs to pick a file in which the second file will be hidden. At this point it is possible to post the picture on any website with its secret message; no one will know it's there. After posting the picture, send the password to others who can download the pictures from the Internet and then open the confidential files or hidden message.

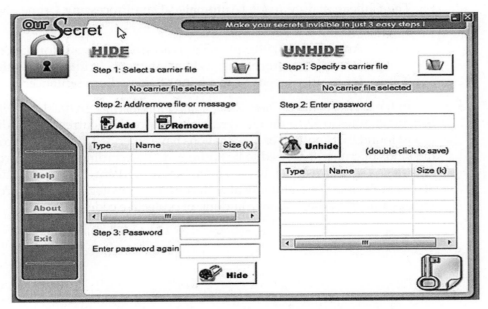

Most stego packages use strong encryption, and their clickable format makes their use simple. Usage is largely composed of selecting the cover file, identifying the message file, picking a password, and clicking "Hide" file. Decoding is as simple as clicking on "Unhide" after entering the password." The simplicity of using these software packages is remarkable considering that they produce a cover file in which the message is visually undetectable. The best method of preventing the theft of confidential files and valuable propriety documents with the use of steganography is not to allow any unauthorized laptops or a media device capable of using stego software in a sound or photo format on the company's premises.

¶ 15,041   LAGGING TECHNOLOGY LEGISLATION

It is difficult to enact legislation to incorporate specific restrictions for technologies that are continually changing.[25] It is expected that as legislation becomes specific in defining illegal activities, programmers will write code to attempt to circumvent such statutes. On the other hand, broad-scoped legislative rules may entrap legitimate businesses. Although legislation may lag behind the changing attack technologies, the forensic accountants' skill set should not.

The forensic accountant needs to know the controls and assurances that need to be in place to protect financial records from unauthorized access. It is not adequate to rely on the security assurances from IT personnel alone. If the financial records are stolen, , the potential loss, if it can be reasonably estimated, needs to be disclosed in the footnotes to the financial statements. Such a valuation calls for an understanding of the nature of the attack and a clear valuation of lost digital assets. After such breaches, advice should be provided as to whether restitution is available under international, federal, or state cybercrime statutes. A brief review of these statutes follows.

Cybercrime Statutes

¶ 15,051   INTERNATIONAL LAW

Although around 240 countries currently have IP domain registrations, the countries with cybercrime statutes are fewer. Schjolberg surveyed the penal legislation in 44 countries for references to "computer crimes."[26] Schjolberg found that countries like Argentina had no legislation, whereas countries like Chile with three articles in its law has limited provisions, and other countries incorporated broader provisions for computer crime such as unlawful access, computer fraud, taking computer data, releasing code that causes damage or hindering access.[27]

The Chilean statute reads (Automated Data Processing Crimes No. 19.223, published June 7, 1993):

> Anyone (who) illegally obtains access to or uses information contained in an information processing system, intercepts or interferes with it, shall be liable for imprisonment from a minor to a medium sentence.[28]

In the report entitled *Cyber Crime…and Punishment? Archaic Laws Threaten Global Information*, the statutes in 52 countries were evaluated for their currency regarding cybercrime.[29] The report found that "only 10 of these nations have amended their laws to cover more than half of the kinds of crimes that need to be addressed."[30] According to the report those 10 nations are: Australia, Canada, Estonia, India, Japan, Mauritius, Peru, Philippines, Turkey, and the United States. In Estonia, the statutes deal with computer sabotage, damaging computer connections, viruses, unlawful use, and mishandling of protective codes.

When the attack on a company's website is launched from one of the countries with weak cybercrime statutes but with IP domain registrations, the forensic investigator may find little hope in providing a victimized company with restitution. Cybercrimes involve the theft or destruction of proprietary data. Networks can be shut down or sabotaged. The cybercriminal can distribute viruses and Trojan horses. Forgery and fraud continually occur over the Internet. Balances in bank accounts can be stolen from locations around the world. Currently, there are a number of national jurisdictions where cybercrimes expose the criminal to little risk. Generally, the cooperation in joint international prosecutions is so low as to allow the careful criminal to operate without fear of prosecution.

In 1989, the Council of Europe recognized the transnational nature of computer crimes and made calls for harmonization in national computer crime legislation of their member nations and improvement in legal cooperation among law enforcement agencies.[31] The Council of Europe is a separate body from the European Union. Its objectives are to develop a more unified Europe. Another example of attempts to define computer crimes occurred in 1995. At that time, the U.N. Commission on Crime and Criminal Justice published the *Manual on Prevention and Control of Computer-related Crime* (Manual).[32] It helped member nations identify computer crimes, but the Internet was just beginning to become important so cybercrimes were not identified in that publication.

On November 23, 2001, the Council of Europe Convention on Cybercrime (*http://conventions.coe.int*) issued a model law for its member states including transactional cooperation recommendations. The Council's model law has 48 sections for incorporation into national laws on cybercrime. The Council's recommendations provide a definition of cybercrime and call for international cooperation in prosecuting cybercriminals. The issues in the model law range from mutual assistance to illegal access to networks. An excerpt of the first 28 recommendations is in Appendix 3. The adoption of the model law have been slow because provisions in the law are considered by some countries to violate international law and a country's sovereignty such as trans-border access to computer data. After ten years, thirty-two countries have ratified the treaty and another fifteen have signed it but not ratified it.

The forensic investigator needs to be familiar with the nature of cybercrime statutes if the investigator is going to provide advice to the client regarding the best actions to take against these borderless attacks. In the United States, there are two jurisdictional sets of laws that apply to cybercrimes. They have been written at the Federal and at the state level. Each of these areas will be considered next.

¶ 15,061   FEDERAL LEGISLATION

A number of federal statutes deal with cybercrime (for example, see the Department of Justice, Computer Crime and Intellectual Property, Federal Computer Intrusion Laws at *http://www.usdoj.gov*). These laws outlaw "counterfeit" access devices that are used for fraudulent purposes (18 U.S.C. §1029). The statutes deal with fraud in connection with computers (18 U.S.C. §1030 also known as the Computer Fraud and Abuse Act), communication lines (18 U.S.C. §1362), interception of electronic communications (18 U.S.C. §2511), unlawful access to stored communications (18 U.S.C. §2701), the disclosure of confidential information obtained as a provider of communication services (18 U.S.C. §2702), and disclosure of information to government agencies (18 U.S.C. §2703). Section 1030, Fraud and Related Activity in Connection with Computers, is an important federal statute related to cybercrime. Portions of it are highlighted in Table 15.2 along with segments of Sections 1029 and 2701. These laws have been expanded and strengthened under the Patriot Act.

Table 15.2. Three Relevant Federal Statutes Related to Cybercrimes

Federal Statute	Title of Code	Focus of Statute	Loss Criteria
18 U.S.C. 1029	Fraud and Related Activity in Connection With Access Devices	Prevent use of counterfeit access devices to get account numbers, mobile ID, card, or PIN to steal funds or make fund transfers. The term "access device" has a broad definition and includes any card to any "instrument identifier."	The theft must be for $1,000 or more during any one-year period. The loss includes the cost of responding to an offense, doing a damage assessment, restoring the system, revenue losses, cost incurred, or other damages because of an interruption of service.
18 U.S.C. 1030	Fraud and Related Activity in Connection With Computers	Under the statute a "protected computer" is (A) exclusively for the use of a financial institution or the United States Government, or, in the case of a computer not exclusively for such use, used by or for a financial institution or the United States Government and the conduct constituting the offense affects that use by or for the financial institution or the Government; or (B) which is used in or affecting interstate or foreign commerce or communication, including a computer located outside the United States that is used in a manner that affects interstate or foreign commerce or communication of the United States. A criminal act against a "protected computer" is the sending of code that causes damage, trafficking in passwords, threatening with the intent to commit extortion and/or accessing files without authorization or without proper authorization, for example.	Slight variation with the criminal activity, but is generally considered to be at $5,000 per year. The law also allows victims to bring civil actions against a perpetrator.*
18 U.S.C. 2701	Unlawful Access to Stored Communications	Unauthorized access to an electronic communication service and the alteration of stored files.	None listed.

* Under amendments in the USA Patriot Act of 2001, the losses of $5,000 can be aggregated on a network and not considered separately for each individual computer as had been the case in the past.

Source: JOURNAL OF FORENSIC ACCOUNTING. ©R.T. Edwards, Inc.

Section 1030 is written to prevent unauthorized access to a "protected computer" to obtain confidential information, transmit damaging malicious code, or perpetrate a fraud as defined in the code. The criteria for identifying a protected computer under the statute are so broad that any computer connected to the Internet of interest to the federal government is essentially "protected." Section 1030 as well as the other U.S.C. sections fails to meet the extensive provisions in the Council of Europe's model law (see Appendix 3). Even with the strengthening of these cyberlaws with the passage of the Patriot Act, U.S. law enforcement has not been highly successfully in bringing justice to those criminals who launch their attacks from outside the borders of the United States.

USA Patriot Act

The USA Patriot Act (Act), enacted by Congress in 2001, has strengthened U.S. cyber laws and expanded cybercrime definitions.[33] Congress has renewed authority for the Patriot Act with the most recent extension in February 2011. It is expected that the Act will continued to be renewed in the future. Under the Act, an activity covered by the law is considered a crime if it causes a loss exceeding $5,000, impairment of medical records, harm to a person, or threat to public safety.

Previously, laws did not specify that causing $5,000 in damages without having the "intent" was a crime. Under Act Sec. 814 revisions, Deterence and Prevention of Cyberterrorism, causing such damages is now considered a crime. Also, the definition of losses from computer attacks has been codified in Act Sec. 814 to include the losses of responding to the attack, conducting a damage assessment, restoring the system to its previous condition, and any loss of revenue or costs incurred due to the interruption. The loss definition is in line with the one provided by the 9th Circuit Court in *N. Middleton*[34] as well as the loss definition in 18 U.S.C. §1030. Additionally, the dollar losses from an attack are described as aggregated losses, where they were not in the past.

Today, if 10 computers are damaged but the damage on each is only $600, the aggregated loss is $6,000, and the crime is covered under the law's threshold loss criteria.

Amendments to Section 212 of the Act, Emergency Disclosures by Communications Providers and the 2002 enactment the Cyber Security Enhancement Act, make it easier for an Internet service provider (ISP) to make disclosures to the government about unlawful customer actions without the threat of civil liability. Under the revisions, the ISP can disclose information to "protect their rights and property" or if it believes a "serious crime" is involved. The right to make additional disclosures may allow ISPs to disclose information requested by a forensic investigator. If such voluntary disclosures were not made to the forensic investigator, then under threat of a lawsuit from the damaged party, the ISPs may feel compelled to provide the requested information in order to "protect their property" from legal damage.

Also of interest to forensic investigators are the revisions in Act Sec. 217, Intercepting the Communications of Computer Trespassers, whereby victims of hackers can request law enforcement help in monitoring trespassers on their computer systems. Under the revisions, law enforcement may intercept, with wiretaps, any unauthorized communication going through a protected computer. Such interceptions by law enforcement personnel were not allowed prior to the passage of the Act. Restrictions on communications previously available under wire and electronic communication protections are no longer provided under the Act. Consequently, it may be possible for forensic investigators to use these provisions of the Act to assist victims of cyber attacks. The Act has expanded the federal government's authority to investigate and punish cybercrimes as well as providing clear definitions of the nature of such crimes.

In addition to revisions in federal statutes, a number of state laws provide protection against cybercrimes. These laws are reviewed next.

¶15,065   PROPOSED FEDERAL LEGISLATION

On March 31, 2009, draft legislation was introduced into the 111th Congress to provide additional cybersecurity protections for the U.S. computer networks using the Internet. The bill was never passed but it is interesting to review the bill's provisions. The legislation begins with this statement: "America's failure to protect cyberspace is one of the most urgent national security problems facing the country." The draft legislation is titled *Cybersecurity Act of 2009.* Quoted testimony in the introduction to the legislation states that "a successful cyber attack against a major financial service provider could severely impact the national economy..." The legislation calls for the President to appoint members to a Cybersecurity Advisory Panel to advise the President on cybersecurity issues facing the nation. The legislation also calls for the establishment of regional Cybersecurity Centers to work with small and medium sized businesses to help them secure their networks from attack. The National Institute of Standards and Technology (NIST) is required to set benchmarks for cybersecurity standards once the legislation is enacted. The national licensing of cybersecurity professionals is also called for under the legislation. Concerns are expressed in the legislation in regard to protecting the privacy of information stored on distributed systems or transmitted over networks, how to determine the origin of messages sent over the Internet, and requiring cybersecurity to be a factor in bond ratings. Funding is provided for universities to build test beds for testing system vulnerabilities, scholarships, competitions, and grants in cybersecurity. Under the legislation, the President may declare a cybersecurity emergency and shut down parts of the Internet related to critical infrastructure in the United States. Although the legislation has not been enacted, a push in this direction occurred with an executive order from the President in 2013. The executive order called for business-government information sharing. Of course, information must be collected before it can be shared.

This legislation makes it clear that there is a great deal of concern within the federal government of a possibly of a cyberattack. These nationwide cyberattacks that have closed the Internet have already occurred in Estonia, South Korea, Sweden, and the Ukraine. These attacks were launched from outside these countries' borders.[35]

Under the Act, the level of emergency that is being planned for is one so serious the President could shutdown all Internet services until the emergency situation subsided. For U.S. business, the closing of Internet connections could be disastrous and damages losses would be in the billions of dollars. For the accounting profession, it could be mean the loss of data that would never be recovered and the loss of clients' digital assets. Data connectivity relating to stock trading, payroll and other distributed accounting services, shared files, cloud computing, online banking, sales, and credit card payments would disappear. If the U.S. government is concerned about the seriousness of such an attack, it important for accounting practitioners to consider how to manage such an emergency.

¶ 15,071   STATE LEGISLATION

When new state computer crime statutes are enacted, they are usually added to that state's existing property offense or criminal statutes. Such cybercrimes are viewed as part of traditional crime. Although these statutes are being updated, legal protections for "punched cards" of computer code and data can still be found.[36] Today, it is difficult to even find a punched card, and most of today's college students have never seen one.

Table 15.3 highlights computer crime statutes for the 50 states.[37] Many of the states have separately-enacted money laundering, identity theft, unlawful use of encryption, illegal spam, computer tampering, interruption of computer services, online gambling, cyberstalking, and other Internet statutes in their codes.[38] Additionally, the interpretation of these statutes is left up to the judges in the various states. The statutes listed in the table are state laws that are related to *computer crimes*. These statutes do not refer to "cybercrimes" as the statutes were originally enacted when there was no Internet. Thus, legislative oversight in the acts tends to focus on "computer crimes," "unlawful access," or "property crimes."

Table 15.3. Summarized State Statutes Specifically Related to Computer Crimes

See Legal Information Institute (*http://www.law.cornell.edu/statutes.html*) for these state statutes.

State	Code Sections	Title of Code	Focus of Statute and Pertinent Code Definitions
Alabama	Ala. Code Article 5: 13A-8-102, and 13A-8-103	Alabama Computer Crime Act	Unauthorized access; crimes against intellectual property, destruction of data, programs, systems, networks, or internal or external supporting documentation; modification of equipment or supplies.
Alaska	Alaska Stat. Sections 11.46.484 (a) (5), 11.46.740, 11.46.985, and 11.46.990	Offenses Against Property: Criminal Use of Computer	Use of a computer without right to use it with the objective of introducing false information into the system.
Arizona	Ariz. Rev. Stat. Ann. Sections13-2316, 13-2316.01, and 13-2316.02	Computer Fraud	Alteration of computer systems to commit fraud and the outright destruction of computers, systems; Accessing, altering, damaging or destroying any computer, system or network, or any part of a computer, computer system or network, with the intent to devise or execute any scheme or artifice to defraud; introducing a computer contaminant into any computer, system or network; causing the denial of computer or network services; unauthorized acquisition of confidential public information or proprietary information.
Arkansas	Ark. Stat. Section 5-41-203 and 5-41-206	Computer Related Crimes	The statute defines encryption as the use of any protective or disruptive measure, including, without limitation, cryptography, enciphering, encoding, or a computer contaminant. "Computer contaminant" is a virus, worm, or Trojan horse or any other similar program, signal, or sound that is designed to prevent, impede, delay, or disrupt the normal operations. Any unauthorized modification, damage, alteration, destruction, disclosure, use, concealment, retention or taking possession of, copies, acquisition or attempts to obtain access to, permits access to or causes to be accessed, a computer, system or network; causes a denial of service to rightful users; uses encryption to commit a criminal offense; falsification of e-mail; discloses a code, password, or other means of access to a computer or computer network.

California	Ca. Penal Code, Section 502(c)	California Penal Code	The statute defines internet domain name as a globally unique, hierarchical reference to an Internet host or service, assigned through centralized Internet naming authorities, comprising a series of character strings separated by periods, with the rightmost character string specifying the top of the hierarchy.
			Unauthorized access to alter, damage, delete, destroy, or otherwise use any data, computer, computer system, or computer network; destroy computer data, cause denial of computer services, create computer contamination, or avoid telephone charges or other frauds; provides assistance in accessing a computer system; introduces a computer contaminant; falsifying e-mail.
Colorado	Colo. Rev. Stat. Section 18-5.5-102	Computer Crime	Using a computer to commit a fraud or unauthorized access to a computer to destroy, alter, damage it, or commit a theft.
Connecticut	Conn. Gen. Stat. Section 53-451	Computer Crimes	Unauthorized access to disable, cause a malfunction, erase, or alter, computer data, computer programs or computer software from a computer or computer network; falsify or forge e-mail or routing information; provide software that is primarily used to falsify e-mail; theft of computer services; interruption of computer services; misuse of computer information; and destruction of computer equipment.
Delaware	Del. Code tit II, Part 1, Ch. 5, Sub Ch. III, 931-939	Offenses Involving Property	The statute defines originating address as the string used to specify the source of any electronic mail message (e.g. *company@sender.com*). Further receiving address is defined in the statute as the string used to specify the destination of any electronic mail message (e.g. *person@receiver. com*), and the Internet is described as a hierarchy of computer networks and systems that includes, but is not limited to, commercial (.com or .co), university (.ac or .edu) and other research networks (.org, .net) and military (.mil) networks and spans many different physical networks and systems around the world.
			Unauthorized access; theft; interruption or degradation of computer services; misuse of computer with unauthorized display or alter; delete, tamper with, damage, destroy or take data intended for use by a computer system; destruction of computer equipment; distribution of unsolicited bulk commercial electronic mail; forge e-mail; failure to cease e-mail distribution upon request.

State	Statute	Title	Description
Florida	Fla. Stat. Ann. Sections 815.04, 815.05	Florida Computer Crimes Act	The statute defines computer contaminant as any set of computer instructions designed to modify, damage, destroy, record, or transmit information within a computer, computer system, or computer network. Unauthorized access leading to crimes against intellectual property, trade secret disclosures, offenses against computer users such as the denial of services or the destruction taking, injury, or damage of equipment or supplies.
Georgia	Ga. Code Sections 16-9-91 and 16-9-93 to 16-9-94	Computer Theft	Computer theft; trespass through deletion, obstructing, altering, interrupting of a program or data through unauthorized access; invasion of privacy through the examination of records without authorization; password disclosure; forgery.
Hawaii	Hawaii Rev. Stat. Sections 708-890 to 709-895.7	Various computer crime statutes	Unauthorized access causing computer damage; using a computer in another crime; perpetuating a fraud using a computer, or using unauthorized information obtained from a computer in a fraud scheme. Students, or curious computer hackers, may gain unauthorized access to computer systems and do no damage to those systems. Although these people have committed a serious breach of privacy, they do not deserve to be charged with a felony.
Idaho	Idaho Code Section 18-2202	Computer Crime	Unauthorized access for fraud or theft; destruction or damage to a computer, data, program, or software.
Illinois	Ill. Rev. Stat. Sections 16D-3, 16D-4, 16D-5	Computer Crime Prevention Law	Computer tampering (unauthorized access) to falsify e-mail, or insert damaging programs; distribute software whose purpose is to falsify e-mail; aggravated computer tampering (disruption of government services or public utility); computer fraud, and unauthorized password access.
Indiana	Ind. Code Sections 35-43-1-4	The statutes are found under: Arson—Mischief and Burglary—Trespass	Unauthorized access is considered computer tampering and classified as mischief and trespass.
Iowa	Iowa Code Sections 702.1A, 702.14, 714.1, 716A-716A.16	Unauthorized computer access	A person who knowingly and without authorization accesses a computer, computer system, or computer network commits a simple misdemeanor.
Kansas	Kan. Stat. Ann. Section 21-3755	Computer crime; computer password disclosure; computer trespass	Computer trespass through unauthorized access (or exceeding authorization) and damaging or altering, taking possession of a computer, system, network, or other property; using a computer for fraudulent purposes; or disclosing computer passwords.

Kentucky	Ky. Rev. Stat. Sections 434.845, 434.850, 434.855	Unlawful Access to a Computer	Unlawful access to computer software, programs, data, systems to commit fraud, and misuse of computer information as recognized through involvement with unlawful access.
Louisiana	La. Rev. Stat. Sections 14:73.2 to 14:73.5	Computer Related Crime	Stealing intellectual property, damaging computer equipment or supplies, offenses against computer users, and computer fraud (i.e., insertion of programs).
Maine	Me. Rev. Stat. Ann. Sections 432 and 433	Computer Crimes	Criminal invasion of privacy is unauthorized access to a computer resource; copying a program, software, or information.
Maryland	Md. Criminal Code Ann. Section 7-302	Unauthorized Access to Computers and Related Material	Unauthorized access, causing a malfunction of network, altering, damaging, or destroying data; attempting to identify access codes or publicizing such codes.
Massachusetts	Mass. Gen. Laws Ann. Chapters 266, 120F	Unauthorized access to computer system	Access to a computer without authorization.
Michigan	Mich. Comp. Laws Sections 752.791 to 752.797	Fraudulent Access to Computers, computer systems, and computer networks	Using a computer to generate a fraud; insert a program for accessing, damaging, altering, destroying computers, programs or data; use of a computer to commit other crimes under the Michigan statutes.
Minnesota	Minn. Stat. Sections 609.89 and 609.891	Computer Theft and Unauthorized Computer Access	Computer theft includes stealing a computer or computer system or computer services through unauthorized access; intentional and unauthorized attempts to or actual penetration of a computer security system. The law defines destructive computer programs that can be introduced to alter or damage a PC.
Mississippi	Miss. Code Ann. Title 97, Sections 3, 5, 7, 9	Computer Crimes	Accessing a computer to commit fraud; computer crime against users by causing denial of service or disclosure of passwords; offenses against computer equipment through their destruction; stealing or destruction of intellectual property.
Missouri	Mo. Rev. Stat. Sections 569.094 to 569.099	Robbery, Arson, Burglary and Related Offenses	Computer tampering is the modifying destroying, damaging, or taking of a computer, system or network without authorization; disclosing passwords or other identifying code; taking data, documentation or other information without authorization; causing a denial of service to authorized users.
Montana	Mont. Code Ann. Section 45-6-311	Theft and Related Offenses: Unlawful use of a computer	Acquiring use of a computer without owner's consent; altering or destroying a computer program, network, or part thereof.

Nebraska	Neb. Rev. Stat. Sections 28-1344, 28-1345, 28-1346, 28-1347, 28-1348	Computer Crimes Act	Unauthorized access or the exceeding authorization to a computer and harming or disrupting computer operations such as through the distribution of a destructive program or altering or destroying data; depriving another of services; obtaining confidential public information.
Nevada	Nev. Rev. Stat. Sections 205.476 to 205.513	Unlawful Acts Regarding Computers and Information Services	One of the few state laws that mentions encryption (205.4742) and the Internet (205.4744). Unauthorized access and denial of service to authorized users; forgery of data, image, program, signal, or sound; unlawful use of encryption to commit a crime; forging routing, domain name, sender's name, subject or header lines in e-mail; an ISP will keep information about a subscriber confidential; it is illegal to obtain subscriber services through fraud or help others do the same.
New Hampshire	N.H. Rev. Stat. Ann. Sections 638:17, 638:18 and 638:19	Computer Crime	Unauthorized access or service that causes a denial of service or disrupts or degrades the service; and altering, destroying or damaging data. Introduction of contaminants.
New Jersey	N.J. Rev. Stat. Sections 2A:38A-1 to 2A:38A-6 and 2C:20-23 to 2C:20-32	Computer Related Crimes	Without authorization altering, damaging, or destroying data, a computer or system; the same for fraudulent purposes; a financial instrument is specifically mentioned as a target; disclosure of data is also considered an offense; and access without alternation, destruction, or damage is only considered a disorderly offense.
New Mexico	N.M. Stat. Ann. Sections 30-45-3 to 30-45-7	Computer Crimes Act	Unauthorized access with intent to defraud or embezzle or copy, take, conceal data; computer abuse is recognized as the altering, damaging, or destroying of computer, network, service, or system as well as the introduction of false data to the system.
New York	N.Y. State Penal Law Sections 156.05 to 156.27	Offenses Involving Computers	Unauthorized use; computer trespass to commit a crime; computer tampering is destroying computer material; unlawful duplication of material.
North Carolina	N.C. Gen. Stat. Section 14-454 to 14-457	Computer Related Crime	Accessing computers to commit fraud or falsify educational testing scores; altering, damaging, or destroying computer; computer data, software, network, program or part thereof including introducing a self-replicating or a self-propagating computer program) into a computer; computer program, computer system, or computer network; creating a denial of service to an authorized user; committing extortion; computer trespass and forging e-mails addresses and sending unsolicited bulk e-mails.
North Dakota	N.D. Cent. Code, Section 12.1-06.1-08	Racketeer Influenced and Corrupt Organizations	The computer crime statute is included under a racketeering statute and it simply provides a list of definitions.

State	Statute	Title	Description
Ohio	Ohio Revised Code Ann. Section 2913.04	Unauthorized use of property; computer or telecommun- ication property	Unauthorized use of property is to attempt to gain access to computers, systems, network, and telecommunications device without consent; if unauthorized use is related to fraud it is considered a felony.
Oklahoma	Okla. Stat. tit. 21-1953 to 21-1958	Oklahoma Computer Crimes Act	Unauthorized access and damage to a computer, computer system, network or commit a fraud after gaining access; provide assistance in gaining access.
Oregon	Oregon Rev. Statutes, Section 164.377	Computer Crime	Unauthorized access to alter, damage, or destroy computers, networks, software, programs; or attempted access to do the same.
Pennsylvania	18 Pa. C.S.A. PA ST Pt. II, Art. C, Ch. 39, Art. G, Ch. 76, SubCh. A-E	Computer Offenses	Unlawful use is defined as the distribution of a computer virus. This distribution may result in the unauthorized access or exceeding authorization to alter, damage, or destroy any computer system, World Wide Web site, software, or to interrupt the functioning of an organization, commit fraud, publish passwords, unauthorized duplication, and commit a denial of service attack. The statutes have provisions against the transmission of forged or falsified e-mail.
Rhode Island	R.I. Gen. Laws. Sections 11-52-2 to 11-52-8	Computer Crime	Access to computer for fraudulent purposes; unauthorized access and alteration, damage, or destruction; computer theft; trespass including forging of mail headers, cyberstalking; tampering with computer sources documents and falsifying information.
South Carolina	S.C. Code Ann. Sections 16-16-10 to 16-16-40	Computer Crime Act	DEF: Refers to computer hacking as a misdemeanor. Defines computer hacking as accessing a computer, system, or network for the purpose of establishing contact only without the intent to defraud or commit any other crime after such contact is established and without the use of computer-related services except such services as may be incidental to establishing contact. Use of a computer for fraudulent purposes; unauthorized access to alter, damage, or destroy computer, data, programs, networks, and software or introduces a computer contaminant..
South Dakota	S.D. Codified Laws Ann. Sections 43-43B-1 to 43-43B-8	Unlawful Use of Computer System	Unauthorized access for fraudulent purposes or alternation, destruction or damage of computer system or any part thereof; the disclosure of codes or passwords or other means of access; alters software or data; destroys or disables a computer system.

Tennessee	Tenn. Code Ann. Sections 39-14-602 to 39-14-603	Computer Offenses	The Code defines a virus as a migrating program which, at least, attaches itself to the operating system of any computer it enters and can infect any other computer that has access to an "infected" computer. A worm is defined as a computer program or virus that spreads and multiplies, eventually causing a computer to "crash" or cease functioning, but does not attach itself to the operating system of the computer it "infects." A hacker is any person who knowingly accesses and without permission alters, damages, deletes, destroys, or otherwise uses any data, computer, computer system, or computer network.
			Access to commit fraud; altering, damaging, or destroying the proper computer, system, software, network, program or data internal or external to the foregoing; tampering with computer security devices; alteration of a financial instrument or an electronic fund transfer; introduction of a computer contaminant; and commit acts of terrorism.
Texas	Tex. Penal Code Ann. Sections 33.02 to 33.04	Computer Crimes	The statute defines a computer virus as an unwanted computer program or other set of instructions inserted into a computer's memory, operating system, or program that is specifically constructed with the ability to replicate itself or to affect the other programs or files in the computer by attaching a copy of the unwanted program to other computer programs.
			Unauthorized access, or commit fraud, damaging or deleting data, software, programs, network system.
Utah	Utah Code Ann. Sections 76-6-703	Utah Computer Crimes Act	The Act defines security systems as a computer, computer system, network, or computer property that has some form of access control technology implemented, such as encryption, password protection, other forced authentication, or access control designed to keep out unauthorized persons.
			Unauthorized accessing and altering, damaging, destroying, disclosing, or modifying any computer, network, computer property, system, program, data or software.
Vermont	Vt. Stat. Ann. tit. 13-87-4102 to 13-87-4107	Computer Crimes	Unauthorized access to any computer, system, network, software, program, or data; access for fraudulent purposes; unauthorized access to damage, interfere; theft of a computer or its components.
Virginia	Va. Code Sections 18.2-152.2 to 18.2-152.15	Virginia Computer Crimes Act	Computer fraud; trespass causing a malfunction; erasing data, programs or software; falsifying e-mail transmissions' routing information; distributing software that enable falsification of e-mail; computer privacy invasion when one person examines personal information of another person without authority; theft of computer services; harassment with a computer when viewed as profane, lewd, lascivious, or indecent language, or making any suggestion or proposal of an obscene nature; embezzlement; using encryption in criminal activity.

Washington	Wash. Rev. Code Sections 9A.52.010, 9A.52.110, 9A,52.120, and 9A.52.130	Section of the Burglary and Trespass Code	Computer trespass is unauthorized access to the database of another.
West Virginia	W. Va. Code Section 61-3C-4 to 61-3C-21	Crimes Against the Government	Computer fraud; unauthorized access; unauthorized possession of computer data or programs; altering, deleting, damaging, or destroying a computer, network, resources, software, data, or program; degrading computer services; disclosure of passwords or other security information; obtaining confidential public information; invasion of a system to examine confidential information; deletion of computer data as part of a forgery.
Wisconsin	Wis. Stat. Section 943.70	Computer Crimes	Unauthorized access that modifies, destroys, takes (data), copies computer programs or supporting documentation; interruption of service through the submission of multiple messages; hiding the location of a computer while committing the offense may cause the penalty to be increased. The Code includes punch cards, paper tape, magnetic tape, and microform in its definition of computer supplies.
Wyoming	Wyo. Stat. Section 6-3-502 to 6-3-505	Computer Crimes	Unauthorized access; intellectual property; crimes against computer equipment or supplies; modifying equipment or supplies used in a computer system; interruption or impairment of governmental operations or public services; denial of access to authorized users.

Source: JOURNAL OF FORENSIC ACCOUNTING. ©R.T. Edwards, Inc.

It can be seen in Table 15.3 that in the more recently updated statutes, states have begun to legislatively define Internet-related terminology such as encryption, computer contaminant, Internet domain name, World Wide Web, originating-receiving address, and virus. The following cybercrimes are mentioned in the states' statutes:

- Extortion/embezzlement
- Unauthorized access to commit an unlawful act
- Intellectual property crimes
- Computer or computer material property crimes
- Denial of service to legitimate users
- Harmful virus introduction
- Using encryption to commit a crime
- Falsification or forging of e-mail
- Disclosing passwords or other access codes
- Providing assistance for unauthorized access to a computer
- Using a computer to commit a crime
- Computer theft
- Distributing unsolicited bulk e-mail
- Failure to cease e-mail distribution upon request
- Trespass
- Computer Tampering or mischief
- Invasion of privacy

- Specifically forging routing information, domain names, sender name or the subject of an e-mail
- Falsifying computer-based educational test scores

In addition to these crimes, Virginia outlaws profane computer harassment.[39] Several states have restrictions against the sending of multiple messages or bulk mail, i.e., spam. Although there are strong similarities in the descriptions of computer crimes related to "unauthorized access," there are also significant differences in how the states view such unlawful acts. Some statutes view any unauthorized access as a felony, whereas the Hawaii Code provides an exception in this area for harmless computer hackers.[40] A number of statutes make it unlawful to commit an offense against a computer or computer supplies.

The penalties and the dollar amount of loss recognized under the statutes vary considerably from state to state. Some states define how the loss is to be recognized—usually market value or replacement value—but in general, states leave the loss undefined within their statutes.

States appear to be revising their statutes to incorporate the prevailing criminal activity being used on the Internet, but contemporary cybercrimes still would not be considered illegal in a number of jurisdictions. In 2001, California was the first state to enact a statute under its Civil Code that requires disclosure to any resident of California of the fact that his or her personal unencrypted information has been acquired by unauthorized persons. Such laws are called security breach laws, and by 2012 46 states had enacted similar consumer protection laws. Credit card information, health records, names, social security numbers, driver's license numbers, and other account numbers are covered under the statute. If this information is obtained in a cyber attack on a company's database, the company must notify its customers that such information has been stolen. The 2001 law applied to all California residents regardless of whether they are doing business with a California company or one based in Delaware. Thus, it had implications for all companies in the United States.[41] Congress has been considering enacting the Data Accountability and Trust Act. If enacted, such a Federal law would likely override provisions of the state security breach laws.

WHO DID WHAT? SAYS THE ELECTRONIC FRONTIER FOUNDATION

The *Laws are too strong and too open to interpretation, according to the EFF. In response, the EFF is calling for legislators to lessen the penalties specified by the US Computer Fraud and Abuse Act (CFAA), starting with the way that it defines unauthorised access.*

"Here is the CFAA's greatest flaw: the law makes it illegal to access a computer without authorisation or in a way that exceeds authorisation, but doesn't clearly explain what that means. This murkiness gives the government tons of leeway to be creative in bringing charges."

Shaun Nichols and Dave Neal, The Inquirer, February 5, 2013, EFF wants a rewrite of e-crime laws (http://www.theinquirer.net/inquirer/news/2241514/eff-wants-a-rewrite-of-us-ecrime-laws).

In summary, the nature of computer crime state legislation creates a network of problems for the forensic accountant in determining the legality of an activity and whether it is a recognized crime under state laws.

Guidelines for Cybercrime Management

Due to the borderless nature of Internet crimes, the forensic accountant, who is trying to advise a client, faces a quandary in trying to identify where and if a cybercrime has been committed within a legal jurisdiction. Such is the case in both international and state jurisdictions. Consequently, the investigator may find it difficult to identify the proper jurisdiction under which the client should file civil or criminal legal action.[42] Further complicating the issue is that law enforcement agencies may not have enough trained personnel to adequately investigate the majority of Internet crimes. For that reason, only high-profile cybercrimes receive the necessary law enforcement attention.

¶ 15,081   KSAS FOR FIGHTING CYBERCRIME

The forensic accountant needs a set of basic technological knowledge, skills, and abilities (KSAs) in order to help an employer or client who has been victimized by a cybercrime. IT personnel cannot be relied upon for assistance because they are not trained to investigate such crimes. The investigator needs to rely on a skill set that allows for the successful tracing of the cyber criminal, collection and documentation of meaningful information and courtroom electronic evidence about the act, interviewing skills, ability to value the loss, and development of recommendations in security policy changes. Many times the auditor is the first person uncovering a financial fraud, and the auditor's technical skill set includes those computer forensic skills needed for preserving data at the time initial fraud suspicions are raised and before the computer forensic investigators have arrived. The following list describes the basic skill set needed:

- Ability to build an Internet audit trail.
- Skills needed to collect "usable" courtroom electronic evidence, i.e., a proper chain of custody to prevent the contamination of evidence.
- Ability to recognize and trace an unauthorized system user.
- Knowledge base to use in recommending or reviewing Internet security policies.
- Knowledge of the most recent computer fraud techniques.
- Basic understanding of the information that can be collected from various computer logs.
- Ability to place a valuation on any incurred losses from attacks.
- Technical familiarity with the Internet, web servers, firewalls, general attack methodologies, security procedures, operating systems, and penetration testing methods.
- Understanding of organizational and legal protocols in incident handling to prevent employee rights violations.
- Ability to identify the legal code providing for client restitution from an attack.
- An established relationship with law enforcement agencies.[43]

Although the last item in the list is not a skill *per se*, it is important to have an established relationship with law enforcement agencies that have cybercrime investigation units. Without this basic skill set, the forensic accountant is at a loss in: (1) providing assistance to an employer or client regarding the steps to take in securing a site; (2) collecting creditable evidence and loss valuations for presentation to a law enforcement agency; (3) mounting a successful disciplinary action against an internal attacker; and (4) recommending and guiding reasonable legal actions. The forensic accountant may find he has no choice but to collect evidence of a system breach due to the limited resources available from law enforcement; if the evidence is not collected quickly, it is lost. Without correctly executing an investigation, accountants can create more serious legal problems for their employers or clients than initially arose from the attack.

¶ 15,091   FILING REPORTS OF CYBERCRIMES

In addition to collecting evidence of the cybercrime, the investigator should know where, besides law enforcement, such crimes can be reported. There are a number of websites that collect information about events that may be cybercrimes. Among businesses, there may be a concern that reporting such incidents will create adverse publicity but every report helps to develop a better picture of the way cybercrime is evolving.[44] Table 15.4 provides a list of organizations where Internet criminal activity and complaints can be reported.

Table 15.4. Sites for Filing Cybercrime Complaints and Hacking Alerts

Organization	Website	Function
Internet Fraud Complaint Center	http://www.ic3.gov	A partnership between the Federal Bureau of Investigation and the National White Collar Crime Center.
Department of Justice	http://www.justice.gov/criminal/cybercrime/reporting.html	Lists numbers and web addresses for reporting computer crimes. The site needs updating.
National Fraud Information Center	https://secure.nclforms.org/nficweb/nfic.htm	A private organization related to reporting Internet frauds.
Australian Computer Emergency Response Team	http://www.auscert.org.au/	Deals with computer crime incidents and their prevention.
FTC Consumer Complaint Form	https://www.ftccomplaintassistant.gov/	A site on which an online form can be submitted to the FTC Consumer Complaint Department.
Securities and Exchange Commission	http://www.sec.gov/complaint.shtml	File complaints about investment fraud or practices.

The Internet Fraud Complaint Center is a focal point for filing complaints about Internet crimes, but other sites, such as the Securities and Exchange Commission's (SEC) site for financial fraud, are important. The SEC has become particularly concerned with the rash of "pump and dump" e-mails or message board postings purporting to be from reputable analysts or investors who are providing breaking information about a company that is shortly going to drive the company's stock price rapidly upward. Unfortunately, the e-mails are a fraud. The e-mail sender makes enormous profits selling their already-purchased stock as buyers rush into the market and drive up the stock price based on the rumor. Eventually, buyers stop entering the market, the market price collapses, and most investors lose their money. Several of the sites listed in the table provide online forms for filing complaints.

¶ 15,101   CONCLUSION

After reviewing international, federal, and state statutes dealing with computer crimes and several attack methodologies, it may be surmised that: "You can get away with more than you get caught for." But, that situation is changing as international organizations begin to call for reforms that bring the borderless Internet under a more systemic set of laws and regulations. Additionally, revisions are taking place in existing laws to make them compatible with new attack technologies. Yet in order for the revisions and new laws to become effective they have to be written in a way to prevent innocent actions from becoming "illegal activities." At the same time, it cannot be easy for criminals to circumvent the law. Currently we are not at the point where our networks are secure.

The forensic accountant is faced with constant threats against a company's financial system. These threats will not diminish in the future as criminal gangs become more organized in executing these attacks on a company's financial assets. To meet the guidelines of SOX, the forensic accountant needs a forensic skill set to handle cybercrimes and deal with cybersecurity issues. Although it may appear that these problems are nothing more than what has been dealt with in the past, today's cybercrime is executed with an electronic pulse....a series of electronic 1's and 0's. If these pulses are not correctly captured as evidence, no illegal activities can be proven to have occurred. If a company's assets are not secure from these pulses, the company's very existence can be threatened. To successfully assist their employer or client, the forensic accountant must understand the new world of cybercrime and cybersecurity.

HACKING CLOSES EU CARBON MARKET....IS WALL STREET NEXT? January 2011. European carbon market, used to limit carbon emissions, was effectively shut down in the middle of last week after permits worth 6.8M had been stolen in a hacking attack. Hackers gained unauthorized access to log-in details which allowed the criminals to quickly access and sell the permits. Shortly afterward, the European Commission halted its 72B Emissions Trading Scheme (ETS).

ENDNOTES

1   Curtis Karnow, "Recombinant Culture: Crime in the Digital Network," (July 1994), DEFCON II, Las Vegas, NV, *http://cpsr.org/prevsite/cpsr/privacy/crime/karnow.html/*.

2   Statement by UK Crime Prevention Minister James Brokenshire on the formation of the International Cyber Security Protection Alliance International body ICSPA to fight cybercrime globally (July 5, 2011). BBC New Technology (http://www.bbc.co.uk/news/technology-14032989).

3   *SEC v. Blue Bottle Limited and Matthew C. Stokes*, 07 Civ. 01-CV-1380 (CSH)(KNF)(S.D.N.Y.)(February 26, 2007).

4   *Spoofing* is any method that is used to pretend to be another person (e-mail spoofing) or another web server (IP spoofing). One purpose of the technique might be to identify passwords.

5   Internet Fraud Complaint Center, IFCC 2002 Internet Fraud Report, The National White Collar Crime Center and the Federal Bureau of Investigation, 2003.

6   Dispatches, "Net Fraud Cost Americans $18 million," INTERNATIONAL HERALD TRIBUNE: THE IHT ONLINE (April 12, 2002).

7   Sam Skolnik, "Two Russians Accused of Operating Hacking Scam to Defraud Americans," SEATTLE POST-INTELLIGENCER REPORTER (September 20, 2001).

8   RIPE does a zone transfer to identify new web hosts. In this way, RIPE can accurately calculate growth statistics on new web hosts joining the Net. Restrictions in zone transfers results in miscounts.

9   For information about using Nsloopup which is DOS command see: http://www.windowsnetworking.com/kbase/WindowsTips/WindowsXP/AdminTips/Network/nslookupandDNSZoneTransfers.html

10 A *denial of service attack* floods a web server with messages until it either crashes or is shut down by the system administrator.

11 Economic espionage inflicts costs on companies that range from loss of unique intellectual property to outlays for remediation, but no reliable estimates of the monetary value of these costs exist. **Many companies are unaware when their sensitive data is pilfered**, and those that find out are often reluctant to report the loss, fearing potential damage to their reputation with investors, customers, and employees. *Foreign Spies Stealing U.S. economic Secrets in Cyberspace* (October 2011). Office of the National Counterintelligence Executive, Report to Conress on Foreign Econommic Collection and Industrial Espionage, 2009-2011.

12 *See* Internet Assigned Number Authority *(http://www.iana.org/)*.

13 U.N. Commission on Crime and Criminal Justice, UNITED NATIONS MANUAL ON PREVENTION AND CONTROL OF COMPUTER-RELATED CRIME (New York: United Nations, 1995), par. 127, *http://www.uncjin.org/Documents/EighthCongress.html*.

14 *Ibid*, par. 118.

15 An example of an IRC chat system used to control bots is Unreal IRCd or Conference Room.

16 At the present time, automated bots are being used to sign up for multiple free e-mail accounts to mail spam messages or for multiple PayPal accounts. To stop these bots and only allow humans to register on these sites, the sign-up procedures require that warped graphics be read and the letters or numbers they represent to be typed into a box before the sign up procedures can continue. This registration procedure is a form of Turing Test. The test is used to separate humans from bots because the bots cannot read the graphics.

17 CNN.com, Botnet Hacker Pleads Guilty, *Technology* (January 23, 2006). A zombie computer is a PC that has been taken over by a hacker without the owner's knowledge. This act is performed by placing a bot on the computer. When hundreds of computers are controlled by bots, it is called a botnet.

18 For example, until 2006, denial of service attacks were a legal grey-area for law enforcement in the U.K. In 2006,

The Police and Justice Bill makes it makes it an offense to impair the operation of any computer system, prevent or hinder access to a program or data held on a computer, or impair the operation of any program or data held on a computer. The maximum sentence for such cybercrimes has also been ramped up from five years to 10 years.

19   Cloud computing is based around virtual networks. Using their computers, users log on and off virtual machines and use application programs that are physically located elsewhere within the "Internet cloud." These applications are provided by the company setting up the virtual network and generating revenues on subscription fees.

20   Regulation of Investigatory Powers Act 2000, Chapter 23, Part III, Investigation of Electronic Data Protected By Encryption Etc., *http://www.legislation.gov.uk/ukpga*.

21   Ronald Rivest, "Chaffing and Winnowing: Confidentiality Without Encryption," MIT Lab for Computer Science (March, 1998), *http://people.csail.mit.edu/rivest/Chaffing.txt*.

22   Electronic packets act as the mail of the Internet. The packets or datagrams contain information about their source and destination. When a message is sent over the Internet, it is broken into packets of data that must be reassembled when arriving at its destination. The packet contains a header and in the header is information about the length of the packet, synchronization bits, sequence number of the packet in the series sent, type of packet or protocol information, origination address, and destination address, as well as the data and error checking numbers.

23   Message authentication codes are an algorithm contained in a series of bits used to ensure authenticity and integrity of the transmitted message. Data authentication is confirmed through a message authentication code and a key. This process ensures that the data sent is the same as the data received. It is not encryption.

24   Ronald Rivest, "Chaffing and Winnowing: Confidentiality Without Encryption," MIT Lab for Computer Science (March 1998), *http://people.csail.mit.edu/rivest/Chaffing.txt*.

25   Partially in response to the Regulation of Investigatory Powers Act, a program called "WhiteNoise—Multi-Message Package Chaffing" was developed. This software program was written specifically to provide a loophole around the Act through the use of chaffing. The sites hosting the software have been closed. These secret messages can be hidden and sent undetected without the need for standard fixed encryption. The key that is sent with the message is used to discard the packets containing white noise thus leaving packets that contain the message. Theoretically, all packets with information in them could be sent without being encrypted, thus avoiding provisions of the Act. WhiteNoise software does provide for the encryption of messages.

26   Stein Schjolberg, "The Legal Framework - Unauthorized Access to Computer Systems Penal Legislation in 43 Counties" Moss District Court, Norway (April 17, 2003), *http://www.mosstingrett.no/info/legal.html*.

27   For a list of international cyber crime statutes, see *http://www.cybercrimelaw.net/Cybercrimelaws.html*.

28   Law on Automated Data Processing Crimes, No. 19.223, Article 2 (June 7, 1993), *http://www.mosstingrett.no/info/legal.html*.

29   McConnell International, Cyber Crime…and Punishment? (December 2000), *http://www.witsa.org/papers/McConnell-cybercrime.pdf*.

30   *Ibid*, p. 1.

31   Council of Europe, Committee of Ministers, *Recommendation No. R (89) 9 of the Committee of Ministers to Member States on Computer-Related Crime, http://www.coe.int*.

32   U.N. Commission on Crime and Criminal Justice, United Nations Manual on Prevention and Control of Computer-related Crime (New York: United Nations, 1995), par. 127, *http://www.uncjin.org/Documents/EighthCongress.html*.

33   U.S. Congress (HR 3162), Uniting and Strengthening America Act by Providing Appropriate Tools Required to Intercept and Obstruct Terrorism (USA PATRIOT) Act of 2001, P.L. No. 107-56, October 25, 2001, *http://www.cdt.org/security/usapatriot/title1.pdf*.

34   *N. Middleton,* 231 F3d 1207, 1210-11 (2000).

35   If you would like to see a real time map of attacks on the Internet, view the Akamai map at *http://www.akamai.com/html/technology/dataviz1.html*.

36   Ind. Code § 35-43-1-4.

37   Ala. Code, Art. 5, §13A-8-100 - §13A-8-103; Alaska Stat. §11.46.484(a)(5), §11.46.740, §11.46.985, §11.46.990; Ariz. Rev. Stat. Ann. §13-2316, §13-2316.01, §13-2316.02; Ark. Code Ann. §5-41-201 - §5-41-206; Cal. Penal Code §502; Colo. Rev. Stat. §18-5.5-101 - §18.5.5-102; Conn. Gen. Stat. §53-451; Del. Code Ann. tit. II, part 1, ch. 5, sub. ch. III 931-939; Fla. Stat. ch. 815.01 - 815.07; Ga. Code Ann. §16-9-9 - 16-9-94; Haw. Rev. Stat. Ann. §708-890 - §709-895.7; Idaho Code §18-2201 - §18-2202, §26-1220; Ill. Comp. Stat. 5, 16d-1 - 16d-7; Ind. Code §35-43-1-4; Iowa Code Ann. tit. XVI, subtitle 1, §622.51A, §702.1A, §702.14, §714.1, §716.6B; Kan. Stat. Ann. §21-3755; Ky. Rev. Stat. Ann. §434.840 - §434.860; La. Rev. Stat. Ann. §14:73.1 - §14:73.5; Me. Rev. Stat. Ann. tit. 17, §431-433; Md. Code Ann., Art. 27, 146; Mass. Gen. Laws ch. 266, §30, §33A, §120F; Mich. Comp. Laws §752.791 - §752.797; Minn. Stat. §609.87 - §609.894; Miss. Code Ann. tit. 97, §§3, 5, 7, 9; Mo. Rev. Stat. §569.094 -§569.099; Mont. Code Ann. §45-6-310 - §45-6-311; Neb. Rev. Stat. §28-1343 - §28-1348; Nev. Rev. Stat. Ann. §205.473 - §205-513; N.H. Rev. Stat. Ann. §638:16 - 638:19; N.J. Stat. Ann. §2A:38A-1 - §2A:38A-6 and §2C:20-23 - §2C:20-

32; N.M. STAT. ANN. §30-45-1 - §30-45-7; N.Y. PENAL
LAW §156.00 - §156.50; N.C. GEN. STAT. §14-453 - §14-
457; N.D. CENT. CODE §12.1-06 - §1-08; OHIO REV. CODE
ANN. §2913.04; OKLA. STAT. ANN. tit. 21, §1951 - §1958;
OR. REV. STAT. §164.125, §164.377; 18 PA. C.S.A. PA
ST PT. 11, ART. C., CH. 39, ART G., CH. 76, SUBCH. A-E;
R.I. GEN. LAWS §11-52-1 - §11-52-8; S.C. CODE ANN.
§16-16-10 - §16-16-40; S.D. CODIFIED LAWS §43-43B-1 -
§43-43B-8; TENN. CODE ANN. §39-14-601 - §39-14-603;
TEX. PENAL CODE ANN. §33.01 - §33.04; UTAH CODE ANN.
§76-6-701 - §76-6-705; VT. STAT. ANN. tit. 13, §87-4101
- §87-4107; VA. CODE ANN. §18.2-152.1 - §18.2-152.15;
WASH. REV. CODE §9A.52.010, §9A52.110 - §9A52.130;
W.VA. CODE ANN. §61-3C-1 - §61-3C-21; WIS. STAT.
§943.70; WYO. STAT. ANN. §943.70; WYO. STAT. ANN. §6-
3-501 - §6-3-505.

38 Susan W. Brenner, "State Cybercrime Legislation in the
United States of America: A Survey," RICHMOND JOURNAL
OF LAW AND TECHNOLOGY 7 (3) (Winter 2001) *http://law.
richmond.edu/jolt/v7i3/article2.html.*

39 VA. CODE ANN. §18.2-152.1-18.2-152.15.

40 HAW. REV. STAT. ANN. §708-890, §708-895.7.
41 CAL. CIVIL CODE §2, §1798.29. Effective July 1, 2003.
42 Several U.S. sites that may be able to provide assistance
with cybercrimes are: U.S. Customs Service, *http://www.
cbp.gov/*; Federal Bureau of Investigation, *http://www.
fbi.gov*; U.S. Treasury Department, *http://www.ustreas.
gov/*; and National Security Agency, *http://www.nsa.gov/.*
43 Local and state law enforcement organizations are
establishing special cybercrime units to combat Internet
fraud activities. The Justice Department is providing
training for such operations. One example of a state with
established units is Ohio. There are cybercrime units
in Akron and Columbus, the Miami Valley Regional
Crime Lab—Regional Computer Crime Unit, Ohio
Attorney General's Computer Crime Task Force as well
as other units. (See *http://www.ohiohtcia.org/resources/
cybercrime.*)
44 Matt Loney, "Lack of Reporting Hits Cybercrime Fight,"
ZDNet (2002), UK, *http://www.zdnet.co.uk/news/it-
strategy/2002/04/25/lack-of-reporting-hits-cybercrime-
fight-2109168/.*

EXERCISES

1. What is the most common complaint about cybercrime from respondents?
2. List some of the criminal activities that fall under the mantle of cybercrime.
3. List some net frauds.
4. What is the so-called 419 scam?
5. What is phishing?
6. Explain the wardialer software.
7. What is the purpose of port scans? Explain.
8. What is the purpose of zone transfers? Explain.
9. What is a cybercrime?
10. Which of the state statues in Table 15.3 makes it a crime to send fake e-mails even if they are not malicious?
11. Discuss the reasons a forensic accountant may need to know about viruses, denial of service attacks, forging e-mail, and unauthorized computer access.
12. What is the best way to prevent attackers from exploiting well-known bugs to gain access into a web server?
13. Why are all these hacker tools and techniques so readily available on the web?
14. If social engineering is the reason that confidential financial information was revealed, what needs to be done to prevent this from occurring in the future?
15. Discuss the problems that may be created for the forensic investigator if "unauthorized access" is legislatively viewed as a property crime.
16. Explain why the OECD's recommendation No. 3 may not be effective in deterring IP spoofing.
17. What provisions in the Patriot Act have been enacted to make it easier to apprehend cybercriminals?
18. Discuss whether it would be better to contact federal or state law enforcement officials if an Alaskan business has become the victim of a cybercrime.
19. Discuss how it might be possible to detect whether a message is hidden in a digital photo.
20. Compare the computer crime-related statutes that have been enacted in the states of: a) Nevada; b) Alaska.
21. **Unauthorized Access.** Ted Munice has recently been fired. He had been the payroll accountant at Texas Shipping in Galveston, Texas. The systems administrator had determined that someone had logged into the payroll system twice on December 25. A forensic investigator hired by Texas Shipping questioned Ted. Ted admitted that he had logged onto the network, but denied that he had done anything while on

the network. The Company wants to take legal action against Ted and has asked a forensic accountant for advice. What should the forensic accountant tell Texas Shipping?

22. **Computer Fraud?** Marcie Lewis and Fred Cisco worked as accounting mangers at Save-Lot Food Stores. The Company distributes stock options to its 10,000 employees as part of their compensation package. Marcie and Fred both work with the ACE computer system that is used to distribute the stock options to employees. The ACE computer system creates a control number and broker transaction summary. After broker transaction summary is created, the request for the stock option is faxed to Second Boston, which handles the distribution of the option to the employee's brokerage account. Once the option is in the brokerage account, the employee can request the issuance of the shares and sell them. The broker will confirm the existence of options with Second Boston and take care of the sale. In auditing transactions, Marcie found that Second Boston reused account control numbers essentially negating its controls. Also, the ACE computer system issued control numbers that were never sent to Second Boston. Second Boston expected control numbers received from the ACE system to be out of sequence. Marcie and Fred knew it would be easy to create a broker transaction summary and fax requests with a forged signature to Second Boston for stock options to be sent to their brokers. They could easily use an extra control number from the ACE system that had not been sent to Second Boston. Considering all the federal and state statutes described in the chapter, if Marcie and Fred were to execute this scheme, what would they be guilty of doing?

23. **Cybercrimes and Cybercrimes.** The recommendations from the Council of Europe's *Convention on Cybercrime* contain some of the most recent descriptions of cybercrimes.
    a. Review the Convention in Appendix 3 and list the cybercrimes that the Council identified in its recommendations.
    b. List and provide examples of the cybercrimes that are found in your answer to *a* that are not mentioned in the state statutes in Table 15.3.

24. **In-flight Crime.** Nicole Freedman, a U.S. citizen, was on an Air India flight from New York to London on May 15, 2003. Midway over the Atlantic, she used an airplane phone to execute the transfer of $1 million in cash from a bank account in the Cayman Islands to another account in Ireland. The monies were obtained in a web-based gambling scheme committed in Canada. Nicole used the phone call on the flight as a means to escape the jurisdiction of all law enforcement. If all countries had adopted the recommendations contained in the Council of Europe's *Convention on Cybercrime*, which country would prosecute Nicole?

24. **Cyber Skill Set.** List two organizations that could help an accountant develop the basic skill set listed in the chapter section, *Guidelines for Cybercrime Management*. These may be training organizations or other bodies that can help the investigator develop the skills they need to investigate cybercrimes.

25. **Backdoors.** Your consulting firm, Higher Associates, installed an online ordering system for Lotus Flower shops two months ago. On Monday, you have received a frantic call from Mark Wellmen, the owner of Lotus Flower. Mark tells you that someone has been sending flowers through their online ordering system without paying for them. So far, this has resulted in a $4,000 merchandise loss to the company. The web server has a firewall and the standard security procedures, i.e., passwords for users, encryption on credit card numbers, etc. Mark wants your advice as to what he should do to prevent further losses.

26. **Sniffing Around.** Many times sniffers are used to collect and analyze data going across a network. Sniffing software can be used to collect passwords and other confidential information. Sniffers are able to collect this information because computer's communications are sent over a shared network almost like the old party lines that telephone companies used in the 1950s. Consequently, any computer can listen in on the communications directed at another computer. One sniffer that is relatively easy to use on a Windows system is called WinDump. WinDump is available for free from a number of websites (*http://www.winpcap.org/windump/install/*).

    Instructions: Download and install WinDump. A program that is used to analyze the raw data collected from WinDump is Dice. Download and install Dice (*http://www.ngthomas.co.uk/dice.html*). *Dice is optional but it classifies the* *information in a more readable format and it is recommended.* Use the two programs to analyze data on your own computer. In order to collect a lot of data, make sure your computer is connected to the network and/or to the Internet.

27. **Hot Tip.** Dan Wilmer, a small businessman, was facing a cash crunch in business operations at his company Always-Behind-You Trailer Sales. He is desperate to locate a source of short-term financing or cash to be able to pay

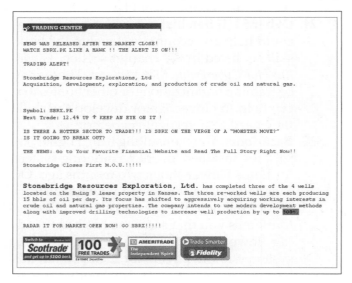

his accounts payable for the next 30 days. His bank will not lend him anymore money in the short-term. Yesterday, he received the following e-mail.

Dan has a small amount of cash, and he has called you, his accountant and financial adviser, to ask what you think about the possibility of investing in Stonebridge Resources as mentioned in the e-mail to make a short-term killing on this oil stock. Provide Dan with a short memo regarding this e-mail tip.

28. **Do You Know More Than a 15-Year-Old?** The U.S. government is highly concerned that critical infrastructures in the United States are vulnerable to a cyber attack from criminal gangs, terrorists, or hostile governments. Assume you are working for a medium-sized accounting firm in Shamrock, Texas. One of the partners in the firm has asked you, as a recent graduate, to write a report that (1)

makes a list of the five critical infrastructures that could be damaged by such an Internet attack, and then (2) using your list of five infrastructures, pick one and determine how damages to it would affect the firm's operations, and (3) make suggestions as to how to mitigate these problems. In answering part (2) develop a timeline for the shutdowned infrastructure showing how the firm's operations would be affected the longer the shutdown extended into the future.

29. Make a list of valuable digital assets and describe why they have value.

30. In Appendix 3, under Article 3, *Illegal Interception,* of the Council of Europe's Convention in Cybercrime model law, evaluate if you would be in violation of Article 3 if you used your neighbor's WIFI network without their knowledge?

31. **Using Nmap.** The most recent version of Nmap can be downloaded from nmap.org. Download and install the software program on a PC. Once installed, you can double click on the icon to open the program. Pick a friendly IP address or domain name and run the program. The results will appear in the Nmap output box. Print out or image the output screen and turn it in with your answers to the following questions: (a) What kind of scan was made? (b) What was the IP address and domain name that you used for the scan? (c) How many ports were scanned? (d) How many open ports were discovered? (e) What were the numbers on the ports that were open? (f) Were any operating systems detected on the open ports? If so, identify them.

32. **Communication and Financial Risks.** WIFI services have recently been introduced into the geographical area where Thrifty Fast, a convenience chain, has 10 of their stores. Up until now, they used phone lines and modems as one form of communication with the head office. Thrifty wants to know about the increase in financial risks to their company if they switch to WIFI services from modem dial up connections. Compare the differences and potential for cybercrime risk between the two systems.

16

CYBERCRIME LOSS VALUATIONS

Cyber terrorism could also become more attractive as the real and virtual worlds become more closely coupled, with automobiles, appli-ances, and other devices attached to the Internet.

—Dorothy Denning[1]

In amending Section 192.001(19), it [the Florida Legislature] made a sharp distinction between the information program or routine (the "imperceptible binary impulses"), and the medium on which the information, program or routine is carried. That is to say, as the court interprets this amendment, the Legislature determined that the disk or tape itself was tangible personal property, [for tax purposes] but the information, program or routine was not.

—Court of Appeal of Florida, Fifth District[2]

OBJECTIVES

After completing Chapter 16, you should be able to:

1. Review federal and state statutes that provide computer loss descriptions.
2. Identify the types of tangible and intangible losses that can occur during a cyber attack.
3. Place a dollar valuation on losses from cyber attacks.
4. Develop an understanding of the coverage available from insurance companies for protection against such losses.

OVERVIEW

Intangible losses incurred in a cyber attack generally compose a larger percentage of the total loss incurred compared with traditional financial crimes. For example, in a traditional loss that occurs from a building fire suspected to be arson, the forensic accountant must determine the dollar loss in inventory, equipment, and buildings. Little in the way of intangible property has been destroyed. Loss valuations for a traditional crime such as check kiting emphasize cash losses. Again, the intangible aspects of the crime are not proportionally the largest percentage of the total loss. In *most* traditional financial crimes, the largest proportion of the loss occurs from the theft or destruction of tangible properties. Businesses—and forensic accountants—have years of experience in measuring the loss from such crimes.

In contrast to traditional crimes, cybercrimes are relatively new, and they create large losses of intangible properties.[3] Thus, an entirely different perspective must be used when placing a value on the losses from cybercrimes. Such loss evaluations must closely investigate the loss of all intangible assets. It is no longer acceptable for a forensic accountant to tally the direct labor costs attributed to software development or other proprietary information lost in a cyber attack and stop there. Cybercrime valuations must at a minimum include the company's diminished prospects for future opportunities.

Intangible losses may be paramount in traditional patent infringement suits. Yet again, this typifies loss determination in a traditional format whereby a second or third party is alleged to have misused the ownership rights of another. Such investigations rely on years of courtroom litigation support, case law, and comprehension in a legal arena. When an individual's personal data is released over the Internet without authorization or when a network is shutdown for four hours due to a denial of service attack, the question is raised: "Where is the intangible loss?" Thus, traditional forensic investigations have not generally defined and recognized intangible losses with any success. Consequently, with cybercrimes, significant intangible losses can go unrecognized.

Today no online business or organization can assume it is safe from an external cyber attack or a criminal act against its network from a rogue employee. When these cyber attacks occur, businesses need to assess their losses. Losses can occur from the removal or destruction of proprietary information, unauthorized access, access above clearance levels by either employees or others, and lessening a company's reputation or loss of shareholder confidence with trauma to the company's stock price. Losses are usually considered tangible if they can be correlated with direct costs such as material and labor charges. However, the most significant damage from a cyber attack is the intangible losses.

There are several important reasons to quantify the loss from a cybercrime. One reason is to report the entire valuation of the losses to law enforcement. If the loss from the crime does not exceed a specified dollar amount, the attack is not considered a statutory crime.[4] Another reason for loss determination is for insurance purposes. If a quantified loss has occurred, the organization may be able to recover damages under its insurance policies. The loss recognized for an insurance claim usually differs from loss recognition calculations in a courtroom proceeding. Also, the victim may want a loss determination for internal purposes and at the same time, the victim may not want to report the crime to law enforcement or to file an insurance claim. If these attacks are not disclosed, managers believe the companies' total intangible losses will be minimized, i.e., reputation damage, etc. Each case raises different issues the forensic investigator needs to consider in developing loss estimates.

BREACH NOTIFICATION LAWS. In 2003, a privacy law went into effect that requires those companies storing sensitive information about California residents to notify those residents when such data has been accessed without authorization (California Civil Code, Sections 1798.29 and 1978.82-.84). Prior to the passage of this law, consumers were not notified if their confidential information had been stolen. This law affects any U.S. company holding confidential information about California residents in its databases. Today, several state legislative bodies have passed similar legislation.

EXAMPLE 16.1 DAILY LOSSES OF ID INFORMATION Lexis-Nexis disclosed on March 9, 2005, that in January of that year the confidential data for 32,000 people had been stolen. Choice Point learned in late September and disclosed in February that personal data on 145,000 individuals has been fraudulently released to a bogus company. On February 15, Bank of America announced that it had lost confidential personal data on company tapes at the end of December. Such tardy disclosures are usually too late for consumers to protect themselves from identity thieves. Examples of such losses are continuing and are constantly reported. For example, in February 2011, Jeremey Parker admitted hacking into servers owned by an e-commerce company and making off with about $275,000. He also admitted to breaking into servers maintained by NASA's Goddard Space Flight Center in Maryland and causing $43,000 of damage.

Attacks on Tangibles and Intangibles

¶ 16,001 EXTENT OF THE PROBLEM

Estimates for losses from the "Melissa" virus are $80 million, "Love Bug," $10 billion, and the "Code Red" virus, $1.2 billion.[5] Some of the more destructive viruses include "Anna Kournikova," "Nimba," "Klez-H," "Slammer," "Blaster," "Sir Cam," "MyDoom," "W32.Beagle," and "SoBigF." The losses from these viruses are attributed to slowed access and lost productivity, added monitoring of systems security, and restoring infected systems or destroyed files. It is difficult to find out how these estimates are compiled. For example, estimates of damages from the "Code Red" virus ranged from $1.2 to $8.7 billion—a wide estimate. A loss estimate is usually made by multiplying the number of computers thought to have been infected times an estimated cost to repair each PC. Yet, these estimates of worldwide damages are questionable because they do not take many standard financial valuation methods into account.

Although cyber attack statistics are difficult to find, the 2010 CSI Computer Crime and Security Survey based on 351 returned surveys determined that:

- ___ percent of respondents experienced malware infection, compared to 2009's 64.3 percent;
- ___ percent experienced denial-of-service attacks, compared to 2009's 29.2 percent;
- ___ percent experienced password sniffing, compared to 17.3 percent in 2009;

Additionally, insider abuse of net access or e-mail was 24.8 percent and attacks re-lated to financial frauds were 8.7 percent down from 20 percent in the previous year. Phishing frauds and zombie computer attacks continued to increase and were experienced by 39 percent and 29 percent of the respondents, respectively. In 2010 , the CSI Computer Crime and Security Survey reported that the most expensive computer security incidents cost responses $25M and $20M each. In a survey of 50 U.S. companies, the Ponemon Institute determined that the mean cost of cyber crime was $5.9M.[6]

The Computer Crime and Security Survey prepared by the Australian Computer Emergency Response Team (AusCERT) reports extensively on losses and abuse sustained by respondents to its annual survey (*http://news.softpedia.com/news/CERT-Australia-Releases-First-Cyber-Crime-and-Security-Survey-Report-330325.shtml*).[7] The 255 respondents represent a wide range of industry sectors including education, manufacturing, mining, and financial organizations. The 2012 survey found:

- 28 percent of the respondents had experienced a malware attack
- Reasons for the attacks were made malicious damage (17 percent) and financial gain (15 percent)
- 17 percent suffered loss of proprietary information
- 20 percent did not report the incident to law enforcement because of the fear of negative publicity

It must be remembered that these are self-reporting surveys and consequently, the information that is reported is subjected to self-reporting biases. Businesses do not want to report how vulnerable they are to cyber attacks or how many times they have been attacked in an annual period.

All such criminal activities create losses and damages for business organizations. Unfortunately the amount of losses experienced by business organizations is expected to increase as the source of these attacks changes from those launched by lone, geeky hackers out to "showoff" to those strategically executed attacks to gangs of cyber criminals located in jurisdictions where their prosecution is difficult. Russia, the Ukraine, China, Turkey, Brazil, and Estonia are the top locations for these gang activities. Furthermore, the use of automated attack systems only increases the damages from cyber criminals. The business model for these criminal operations is broken into specialized units, i.e., developing malware code, bot herding, or penetration hacking for example, that only have limited contact with each other. Such a loose organizational structure allows for high levels of anonymity and untraceability. It also provides the opportunity for its various elements to morph together and then separate and combine with other cyber criminals. The common objective among these groups is to attack financial institutions for financial gain.

Experts and legislators have attempted to identify losses from specific activities in various state and federal laws. These legal guidelines provide a starting point for the forensic accountant in determining a dollar value for losses due to cyber attacks. However, losses recognized for statutory purpose are likely to differ from losses filed under insurance claims. Therefore, each approach toward loss calculations is separately considered in this chapter.

THE CYBER STORM. Damages arising from a cyber attack do not necessarily have to come from attacks directed at a specific company.

What would you do if your smart phone stopped working or the power grid on the East Coast crashed because of a cyber attack? Many government agencies, industry sectors, and large companies are concerned about the effect of a large, sophisticated cyber attack on U.S. commerce and our communication system. During 2011–2012, Cyber Storm IV was launched by the Department of Homeland Security, National Cybersecurity Division. The purpose of the biannual exercise is to determine how well public and private organizations would respond to a large-scale or multi-faceted cyber attack and to have an effective national incident response plan. The exercise includes representatives from the banking, chemical, communications, dams, defense industry, information technology, nuclear, transportation, and regional water suppliers as well as 12 international partners. During the exercise, a simulated attack is run against participating organizations, but not against real-time production systems, to determine how prepared they are to successfully respond to such an attack. The exercise is oriented at identifying responses to a large-scale threat to the Internet that can destroy both digital and physical assets. Additionally, the Electric Power Research Institute has established policies under its Energy Information Security Program and PowerSec

Initiative to prepare for the possibility of a cyber attack against the U.S. power grid. The possibility of an attack on a country's Internet infrastructure is real. In April 2010, China used erroneous IP addressing to route 15 percent of all Internet traffic through servers in China, including those coming from U.S. government and military websites.

¶ 16,011   STATUTORY LOSS VALUATIONS

State computer crime codes provide broad descriptions of how losses should be recognized when a computer crime takes place. Table 16.1 contains a list of the 13 state statutes that provide guidance in making loss determinations.

Table 16.1. State Statutes Describing Losses/Damages from Cybercrime

See Legal Information Institute (*http://www.law.cornell.edu/*).

State	Code Sections	Title of Code	Code Definitions of "Loss"
California	Penal Code, Section 502	California Penal Code	Loss is defined as any expenditure reasonably and necessarily incurred by the owner or lessee to verify that a computer system, computer network, computer program, or data was or was not altered, deleted, damaged, or destroyed by the access.
Delaware	Title II, Part 1, Ch. 5, Sub Ch. III, 931-9	Offenses Involving Property	Loss is recognized as the market value of the property destroyed or replacement cost of the property.
Georgia	16-9-91 and 16-9-93 to 16-9-94	Computer Theft	"Victim expenditure" means any expenditure reasonably and necessarily incurred by the owner to verify that a computer, computer network, computer program, or data was or was not altered, deleted, damaged, or destroyed by unauthorized use as well as any lost profits.
Hawaii	708-890 to 709-895.7	Various Computer Crime Statutes	Loss defined as costs associated with diagnosis, repair, replacement, or remediation and damages are related to the impairment of the availability of data, a program, a system, a network, or computer services.
Iowa	Title XVI, Sub-title 1, 622.51A, 702.1A, 702.14, 715.3, 716.6B	Unauthorized Computer Access	Loss is considered to be the greater of retail value or repair/replacement cost. Damage is impairment to the integrity or availability of data, software, a system, or information. Property lost includes both tangible and intangible property, labor, and services.
Massachusetts	Chapter 266, 120F	Unauthorized Access to Computer System	None listed, but computer crime fits under crimes against property that carries various loss criteria.
Minnesota	609.89 and 609.891	Computer Theft and Unauthorized Computer Access	Loss is considered to be the greatest of the market value of property, its replacement value, or the reasonable value of loss created by the unavailability of the property until it is repaired.

Nevada	205.4765 to 205.513	Unlawful Acts Regarding Computers and Information Services	Such costs include: investigation costs to determine the facts surrounding the crime; determine any past or future loss, injury or other damage; cost to mitigate any past or future loss, injury or other damage; or the testing and restoring the integrity of or the normal operation or use of any Internet or network site, electronic mail address, computer, system, network, component, device, equipment, data, information, image, program, signal, or sound.
New Hampshire	638:17, 638:18 and 638:19	Computer Crime	Aggregated losses are defined as the market value of the property or its replacement value. The statute mentions the cost of reproducing or replacing the property or computer services at the time of the violation.
New Jersey	Section 2 of P.L.1984, c.184 (C.2C:20-23)	Computer Related Crimes	Losses are the cost of repair or remediation of any damage caused by an unlawful act and the gross revenue from a lost business opportunity caused by the unlawful act. The value of any lost business opportunity may be determined by comparison to gross revenue generated before the unlawful act that resulted in the lost business opportunity.
Oklahoma	21-1953 to 21-1958	Oklahoma Computer Crimes Act	Loss is defined as costs incurred to verify that a computer system, network, program, or data was or was not altered, deleted, disrupted, damaged, or destroyed.
Pennsylvania	Title 18, Chapter 76, 603	Crimes and Offenses, Restitution	Loss is the cost of repairing or replacing the system and lost data as well as the lost profit for the period that the computer, computer system, computer network, computer software, computer program, computer database, World Wide Web site, or telecommunication device is not usable.
West Virginia	61-3C-4 to 61-3C-21	West Virginia Computer Crime and Abuse Statute	Loss is described as the market value or the cost of replacing the property as well as lost profits.

The statutes in Table 16.1 have been revised in recent years to recognize lost profits as an additional form of damages. As Table 16.1 is reviewed, the following factors are shown as remediable activities and loss classifications:

- Verification costs to check systems (diagnosis-remediation)
- Restoration costs to put systems back online (testing)
- Market value or replacement value of the property destroyed or services
- Lost profits
- Reasonable value of loss caused by "unavailability"
- Investigation costs
- Past or future losses
- Injury suffered
- Loss of computer time (lost productivity)
- Cost of replacing lost data

The list includes tangible and intangible losses. The damages from injury suffered and system unavailability are intangible losses. Tangible losses can be determined from employee work hours associated with verification, restoration, investigative actions, lost productivity, and replacing lost data.

The federal government identifies the following damage losses in cyber attacks as described in Section 18 U.S.C. 1029 and in Section 814 of the USA Patriot Act:

- Responding to an attack
- Costs of making a damage assessment
- Time and costs of restoring the system
- Loss of revenues from the interruption
- "Other damages" related to an interruption of service

SHOULD WE BOOK HACKER RISKS?....NOT YET. The following disclosure note appeared in Intel Corporation's 2009 financial statements. This note represents the first disclosure in a financial statement in which a major U.S. company recognizes the risk of hacking attacks against its digital assets. In October 2011, the Securities and Exchange Commission has issued a recommendation that potential attacks from cyber criminals need to be disclosed in financial statement footnotes. These disclosures should include information about the business significance of a potential attack, risks of an attack that may remain undetected, insurance coverage from an attack, costs related probability of an attack, and adequacy of pre-ventive measures related to outsourced operations. Materially is a significant issue in these disclosures. (CF Disclosure Guidance: Topic No. 2 http://www.sec.gov/divisions/corpfin/guidance/cfguidance-topic2.htm)

We may be subject to intellectual property theft or misuse, which could result in third-party claims and harm our business and results of operations.

We regularly face attempts by others to gain unauthorized access through the Internet to our information technology systems by, for example, masquerading as authorized users or surreptitious introduction of software. These attempts, which might be the result of industrial or other espionage, or actions by hackers seeking to harm the company, its products, or end users, are sometimes successful. One recent and sophisticated incident occurred in January 2010 around the same time as the recently publicized security incident reported by Google. We seek to detect and investigate these security incidents and to prevent their recurrence, but in some cases we might be unaware of an incident or its magnitude and effects. The theft and/or unauthorized use or publication of our trade secrets and other confidential business information as a result of such an incident could adversely affect our competitive position and reduce marketplace acceptance of our products; the value of our investment in R&D, product development, and marketing could be reduced; and third parties might assert against us or our customers claims related to resulting losses of confidential or proprietary information or end-user data and/or system reliability. Our business could be subject to significant disruption, and we could suffer monetary and other losses, including the cost of product recalls and returns and reputational harm, in the event of such incidents and claims.[8]

¶ 16,021   HIGH-TECH "TANGIBLE" LOSSES ATTRIBUTED TO CYBER ATTACKS

Examples of tangible losses from a cyber attack are destroyed web servers, routers, physical equipment, PCs, infrastructure damage such as the shutdowns of production lines. Additionally tangible losses include the cost of system restoration and lost worker productivity. In traditional manufacturing companies, tangible assets are purchased physical assets or constructed assets developed from using resources such as labor, materials, and overhead. With high-tech companies, the same ingredients—labor, materials, and overhead—are used to develop the bits and bytes in software. Because software and physical assets use the same ingredients, lost or destroyed program code is considered a tangible loss when the loss is related to work hours used to create the code. At the present time, courts have placed different interpretations on "intangible" losses. The value of tangible assets is easily identified with their market or replacement cost, and the value attributed to lost productivity and system restoration costs are based on the work-hours used to restore the system.

THE LOCUSTS ARRIVE. When one hacker finds a hole on a network, the presence of the hole is broadcast to other hackers through e-mail and chat sites. Although the first hack may not have had a criminal intent, the hundreds of other hackers who capitalize on the information may not be so innocent.

Hack Attack Shuts Down System

The value of a cyber asset includes the employees' wages used in developing the asset. If the asset is lost in an attack, the workers' time needed to re-develop the asset is used in determining the extent of the loss. Additionally, workers' time used in diagnosing, restoring, checking, and testing the network as well as possibly replacing lost data is part of the tangible loss from a cyber attack. *Productivity losses* arise from the reduction of efficient, "normal" production of work due to an event such as a cyber attack.

The process used to determine cost estimates for workers' time and overhead incurred to restore a system are shown in the following example for the Maxer Company.

EXAMPLE 16.2 The Maxer Company has been victimized by the hacker known as *Lobospider*. The company's website, critical to its client base, had to be shut down for four hours on Saturday, November 15. The systems administrator (sysad) was called in to work and was in the company's office with two IT employees over the weekend. They worked a 20-hour shift to restore the system. The sysad is salaried and the two IT employees, Ted and Fred, are hourly workers. The systems administrator's annual salary is $70,000, and the IT employees' hourly rate is $50 with time and a half for overtime hours plus benefits of approximately 20 percent. Company overhead is charged to client jobs at 110 percent of direct labor dollars (without benefits). The forensic accountant brought into Maxer to calculate the losses must determine how much salary expense and overhead should be considered to be part of the loss charged to the attack.

The cost of the salary expenses attributed to the attack and the loss experienced by Maxer is calculated as follows:

1. The sysad has a fixed salary that does not change because the sysad had to work over the weekend. Therefore, the sysad's salary of $70,000 is not part of the cost of the incident.

2. The added salary paid to the two IT workers is a cost of the incident along with benefits and overhead tied to the cost of their wages.

Workers	Direct Labor (20 hrs. × $50) × 1.20 for benefits	Overhead (1) Overtime (20 Hrs × $25*) × 1.20	Overhead (2) Applied Overhead (Direct Labor × 110%)	Total Cost of Incident
Ted	$1,200	$600	$1,100†	$2,900
Fred	$1,200	$600	$1,100†	$2,900
Total Cost				$5,800

* Overtime premium is: $50 × 1.5 = $75; $75 − $50 = $25.

† $1,000 × 1.10 = $1,100. Overhead was calculated on direct labor only.

In calculating the loss for the example, it is important to separate the overhead from the direct labor costs of the two IT workers. Overtime is considered to be part of the overhead and not part of the cost of direct labor. By only calculating the direct labor costs involved in correcting the attack, there would only be a loss of $2,400 ($1,200 + $1,200). When the cost of the loss includes overhead, the loss exceeds the $5,000 minimum threshold for the crime to be investigated by federal law enforcement officials.

TJX TAKES A HACKER HIT. BOOK THE ENTRY NOW! On January 17, 2007, TJX announced that it had suffered an unauthorized intrusion(s) into portions of its computer systems that process and store information related to customer transactions. In the first quarter of fiscal 2008, the Company recorded an after-tax charge of approximately $12 million, or $.03 per share, for costs incurred during the first quarter, which includes costs sustained to investigate and contain the intrusion, enhance computer security and systems, and communicate with customers, as well as technical, legal, and other fees.

In the second quarter, the Company expects to continue to incur these costs related to the intrusion(s), which the Company estimates will total $.02 – $.03 per share. Beyond these costs, TJX does not yet have enough information to reasonably estimate the losses it may incur arising from this intrusion, including exposure to payment card companies and banks, exposure in various legal proceedings that are pending or may arise, and related fees and expenses, and other potential liabilities and other costs and expenses. The Company will record known losses when they become both probable and reasonably estimable.

Other Tangible Costs

Other tangible costs of an attack as listed in states' statutes are the market value or replacement cost of property destroyed in an attack, external investigation costs, valuation of lost productivity, and the cost of replacing lost data. Depending on the attack scenario, tangible property may be destroyed. Market values for standard electronic equipment such as web servers, routers, plant equipment, and PCs are readily determinable as the invoice price of a new asset. Replacement cost is considered to be the current cost of replacing the old asset with a new asset with the same capability as the old asset. The replacement cost may be different from the market price if the destroyed asset has been in use for several years. For example, if a PC has been in use for five years, its speed and capability would be obsolete. Therefore, the market value instead of replacement cost would be a better measure of the loss because it would be difficult to find an exact replacement for a five-year-old PC. With specialized equipment, the replacement cost would have to be determined on a "best estimate" basis.

Another cost that is also easily determined is the cost of hiring a private high-tech security firm and its team of forensic specialists to collect evidence about the intrusion and bring the system back online. Security firms are likely to send a group of security specialists specifically trained to quickly bring a network back online. These high-tech security specialists are referred to as a "tiger team." Private security costs related to such engagements are easily quantifiable from the billings sent by the security service firm.

TIGER TEAMS. Tiger teams are groups of forensic and IT professionals who are hired to determine why network security has been broken. In addition, the team can be hired proactively to test network security in facilities prone to attack. The product of their work is a vulnerability report and recommendations for corrections and security enhancements. Such procedures, called "penetration testing," are often used to break into a site, with the site owner's permission. Thus, they receive a "get-out-of-jail" card from their client, i.e., they incur no legal liability for penetrating the network.

Lost Productivity Analysis

Lost worker productivity, another tangible cost, is determinable from the labor time during which company operations are diminished or shut down. The following example shows how the Excelsior Tech Company assigned a dollar value to the productivity that was lost because of a virus attack on its e-mail system.

EXAMPLE 16.3 At 10:00 A.M., a virus infected Excelsior Tech's e-mail system, entering the system from a file attachment. IT staff quickly determined that the entire network was under virus attack. The virus was spreading and destroying files on the infected PCs in the San Francisco office. Mach Security, a high-tech security and investigative firm, was called. Mach advised Excelsior to shut down its entire network and all its PCs to prevent the spread of the virus. Mach would send a tiger team to investigate the intrusion as soon as possible.

Excelsior's San Francisco office houses 25 employees. Three employees are salaried and earn $150,000 annually (2,000 work hours annually figured at 40 hours per week times 50 weeks). The other 22 employees earn an average hourly rate with benefits of $35 per hour. The system was shut down for six hours before Mach could rid the system of the virus. Thus, employee productivity was lost from 10:00 A.M. until the end of the workday. Chad Mange, the office director, knows that the productivity losses increased the longer the system was down. At first, employees continued working with other business such as meetings, but eventually the work that was being accomplished declined to such a level the employees were dismissed by 4:00 P.M. Chad believes the employees would make up for the lost time over the next couple of days. If necessary, they could shift work to other offices or pay staff overtime to get caught up. Excelsior wants to calculate the cost of losing six hours of employee time, i.e., a productivity loss.

Chad and the other two managers estimate that during the first hour little productivity was lost as employees worked around the problem. During the second and third hour, productivity decreased to 70 percent, then during the next two hours to 30 percent. Finally, at the end of the day when only the managers were in the office, productivity was only 10 percent of normal. Using this information, the forensic accountant constructed the following lost productivity table.

Downtime Hours	Productivity Level	Productivity Loss	Dollar Loss (rounded)
First Hour*	100%	0%	$ 0
Next Two Hours†	70%	30%	597.00
Next Two Hours‡	30%	70%	1,393.00
Last Hour§	10%	90%	972.50
Total Loss			2,962.50

* {[(22 × $35) + ($150,000 ÷ 2,000 hrs) × 3)]} = $995 × 1 hour × 0% = 0.

† {[(22 × $35) + ($150,000 ÷ 2,000 hrs) × 3]} × 2 hours = $1,990 × .30 = $597.00.

‡ {(22 × $35) + [($150,000 ÷ 2,000 hrs) × 3]} × 2 hours = $1,990 × .70 = $1,393.00.

§ {[($150,000 ÷ 2,000 hrs) × 3] × .90} = $202.50 × 1 hour = $202.50; all hourly workers have been sent home. [(22 × 35) × 1] = 770

The total productivity loss from the virus attack was $2,962.50, comprising the productive time lost from both salaried and hourly employees. Excelsior is also including six hours of lost Internet service from its hosting service as part of the cost of the attack. The charge for lost service is $2,000. The loss of $4,962.50 ($2,962.50 + $2,000) is not above the $5,000 threshold loss level under federal law. If Mach Security charges more than $37.50 for restoring and securing the network, however, the damages from the virus attack will exceed the minimum threshold loss in the federal statutes.

MAIL BOMB. It is not necessary to shut down an entire e-mail system to create productivity losses. By targeting a high-level employee in the organization with a mail bomb, it is possible to curtail that employee's work activities by preventing him or her from accessing e-mails. A mail bomb is designed to automatically flood an individual e-mail address with messages until the mailbox is unusable. Of course, mail bombs may be used to send enough spam e-mail messages through a network to shut down the entire system and prevent access. Thus, larger productivity loss is created.

¶ 16,031   HIGH-TECH INTANGIBLE LOSSES

The cyber attack just described as a mail bomb would not be viewed with much law enforcement interest because of the small loss attributable to the attack. Traditional business insurance policies covering property losses are not likely to provide coverage for lost productivity from the mail bomb either, because it is generally considered an "intangible" loss.

The tangible loss attributed to workers' time, valuations of destroyed property, external investigation costs and lost productivity can be quickly determined, but such losses usually do not make up the most significant loss from a network attack. The most significant losses are the intangible losses such as unavailability of the website, lost profits, general injury, and values attributed to destroyed or lost information contained on compromised PCs. Such lost information may only have a virtual presence, such as in the coding for software.[9] Therefore, estimating the value attributable to an intangible loss is more complicated than summing the hourly wages of affected workers.

Loss Attributed to Unavailability

Website unavailability is also part of the cost of an attack. When an attack shuts down a website, the loss arising from the unavailability of a website to customers and clients must be calculated. The unavailability loss arises from the inconvenience caused to customers who want to use the website but are unable to do so. Denial of service or spoofing attacks typically close websites especially when directed from a botnet.

Although lost sales are not the same as unavailability, sales figures can help to evaluate the loss from the unavailability of the website. Growth of sales is an indication of consumer satisfaction with a business, its products, and its services. Unavailability of access to a company's website decreases consumer satisfaction; therefore rates of sales growth provide an indication of the loss suffered from a disabled website.

EXAMPLE 16.4 Both the Maxer Company and Excelsior Tech should attribute a reasonable loss to the unavailability of their website during the period when their systems were down. Maxer had its website shut down for four hours and a charge for the downtime should be determined, as website unavailability is a loss recognized under various state statutes. Although no online sales are occurring over the Maxer Company's website, unavailability of the site creates client/customer inconvenience and the consequential loss of customer goodwill. The system was down for four hours and an intangible charge should be calculated for the period the system was unavailable.

Maxer Company has had two percent annual average increase in profits over the last five years before setting up a website for the company. The first year after the website was used, company profits increased 2.5 percent. Maxer credits 0.25 percent of the profit increase to customer visits to the website. Yearly, a 0.25 percent profit increase is equivalent to $250,000. Maxer assumes this trend will continue at the same rate in the future. Therefore, a four-hour shutdown is equal to about $114

{[$250,000 ÷ (365 × 24)] × 4}. The unavailability loss is not significant for Maxer, but it would be a significant loss for an e-business that only sells online and had its website shut down for the same length of time.

Lost Profits Analysis

The unavailability loss is based on profits, but the lost profits, themselves, are a separate issue. The unavailability loss is an intangible charge due to the loss of an intangible item—customer convenience. Lost profits occur when customers cannot gain access to a website and consequently go to another e-retailer or bricks and mortar store to make their purchases.

Analyzing the intangible loss from profits forgone because of the crash of a website involves several considerations. First, it will be necessary to combine financial sales data and nonfinancial data collected about the website activity. The data needed to calculate lost profits is based on marketing information about the customer base, website statistics, and financial data. If an e-business is not collecting website statistics as well as financial information, it is not possible to analyze the profits lost in a cyber attack. Website data about the number of customer visits and marketing information about the sales from these visits is needed as well as revenue and cost information to determine profit data.

Most companies should keep a wealth of information about their customers' purchasing habits, visits to the site, activity on the site, and the retention rates of its customers. Such website statistics may be crucial for insurance recoveries. Yet sometimes, the e-retailer may not even keep a log of website visits. Without records of website activity and customers' purchasing habits, there is little that an investigation into damage losses can uncover. Lost sales are considered an identifiable loss under state statutes, but as they are an intangible loss, they may not be recoverable under traditional business insurance.

EXAMPLE 16.5 MacLeary Mart, an online music retailer, uses its website for selling music CDs, music downloads, and other items such as posters, hats, and band logo items to a large customer base. New customers are asked to register before they make any purchases. MacLeary places cookies on each customer's PC to determine the number of customer visits as well as other information about their buying habits. Thus, they know the percent of visitors to their site who register and those who do not. They are aware of the average number of purchases, average sales, and profits generated on the site by their registered customers.

On October 14, MacLeary's website was shut down for four hours by hackers supporting Animal Friends who objected to certain lyrics in music CDs of the *DeadDog Band* that are sold on the site. MacLeary is concerned about the lost sales that occurred during the four-hour period. The managers know some of these lost sales will be recovered, but some customers will never return. The following analysis has been prepared by Lou Lewis, a forensic accountant with DBDirect, a consulting firm. Lou has discussed the situation with Alice Fayer, marketing head of online sales. Based on that discussion, estimates have been made using judgmental probabilities of the number of lost customers and sales.

Lou realizes the analysis will need to be broken into short-term and long-term losses. The immediate profits lost are identified as those lost within the next year. Long-term profit effects from the shut down are those occurring beyond the one-year period, and they are separately calculated using present value analysis. He makes the following estimates. Any computations beyond one year should include time value of money computations.

The website statistics in the following table were already collected by MacLeary's webmaster. (The webmaster is the person or group responsible for designing and running the company's website, collecting visitor usage statistics, and ensuring that the website is usable.)

Immediate Lost Sales Analysis. The online sales on the website show the following pattern:

Website Visitor:	Avg. Profit per Visit	Normal Probability of Selling Merchandise on Visit	With Downtime, Probability of Return and Making Purchase
New–first visit customer	$100	20%	5%
Registered customer	$200	50%	25%

Using the website statistics, Lou determined the immediate loss from having the website shut down for four hours was $242,000 as follows:

Website Visitor (a)	Avg. Profit per Visit After Registration (b)	% of Customers Lost from Downtime (c)	Dollar Loss from Downtime (b) × (c) = (d)	Average No. of Visits per Hour from Each Group (e)	No. of Hours Website Was Down (f)	Immediate Lost Sales (d) × (e) × (f) = (g)
New–first visit customer	$100	15%*	$15	700	4	$42,000
Registered customer	$200	25%	$50	1,000	4	$200,000
Total Lost Sales from 4-hour downtime on website						$242,000

*From first table 20% − 5% = 15%

A few of the customers who were not immediately able to gain access to the website to make a purchase will return. Registered customers are more likely to return to the website and make a purchase. New customers visiting the website for the first time are less likely to return to make a purchase. New customers are more likely to go to an alternative site and make their purchases. In Column (c), the percent of lost customers is calculated. The sales and profits that could have been received from these customers will never be regained.

Long-term losses from nonreturning new customers. There is a 15 percent probability (20 percent − 5 percent) that a new visitor to the site who was not able to access the web page will never return to the site. The potential profit obtainable from these customers is lost forever. There were 420 visitors to the site who are lost to MacLeary as customers during the four hours the site was shut down [.15 × (700 × 4 hours)]. From discussions with Alice, Lou learns that in the first year after a customer registers with the site they visit it 12 times or about once a month to make purchases. Lou calculates the annual profit lost from these permanently lost customers is $1,008,000, determined as follows:

No. of Annual Visits by Customers	Average Profit of Customer (no longer new)	Potential Customers Lost	Annual Loss of Profits from Permanently Lost Customers
12	$200	420	$1,008,000

Although many long-term registered customers have been using the site for a number of years to buy CDs or make music downloads, website statistics show the average retention period for registered customers is about five years. It is believed the chances of these lost customers returning to the site over the next five years are minimal. In such a case, the present value of the annual lost sales must be calculated to account fully for the damages to MacLeary for its inaccessible site. MacLeary has not calculated a cost of capital to use as a discount rate. Recently, MacLeary refinanced a large loan at a seven-percent interest rate. Lou uses the seven-percent rate to discount the annual loss of $1,008,000 to determine the present value of the total loss over the five years the lost customers would have otherwise made purchases from the site. The present value of the lost profits is equal to $4,132,800.[10] The long-term loss needs to be added to the immediate profit loss of $242,000.

If it can be shown that some of the lost customers would return to the MacLeary website during the five-year period to make purchases, the present value of the lost profits would be reduced. In such a case, reasonable estimates would have to be provided about the percentage of returning customers in each of the five years with a decrease in the annual loss.

Because of the inaccessibility of the website to its customers, MacLeary decided to offer an incentive to its registered customers to come back and visit the site. MacLeary estimates the discount coupons it is providing its registered customers will eventually cost $70,000. The $70,000 cost would not have been incurred if the website had not been brought down by the hackers from Animal Friends. Lou tallies the costs to determine the total cost of the four-hour crash of the site as $4,444,800 ($242,000 + $4,132,800 + $70,000). This is a damage estimate that should interest law enforcement personnel.

Lost Data Analysis

Credit card numbers at a bank website, lists of tax clients' probability scores for possible IRS tax challenges on a CPA's computer, or a bid strategy document to be used on a government contract are examples of data that can be stolen when a hacker gains unauthorized access to a network. Often the first phase of such a cybercrime is to steal the data, and often the second phase is to sell the data back to the victim company or a competitor. The second phase of the crime comprises a traditional extortion scheme. In some cases, the intruder may simply destroy the data. Destroying the data is reflective of a political attack rather than a crime committed for financial gain. In either case, the data has been lost because there is no assurance any returned data subsequent to an extortion has not been altered.

If an intruder steals and then destroys information or software code, the loss to a company comprises the original developmental costs, the cost to restore the information or program, and the possible business opportunities lost or reduced because of the attack.[11] If the loss affects a revenue stream beyond a one-year period, the loss analysis includes present value computations. Financial effects can occur from canceled contracts, delayed implementation of a new product, and a consequential reduced market share.

EXAMPLE 16.6 Swipe Tech, a leader in steganographic detection software, developed a prototype monitoring system called Carnor for the Department of Defense (DOD). The Carnor system is to be used for checking digital images for possible hidden terrorist messages or other illegal activity against U.S. military installations. Swipe spent two years and 12,750 work hours (developmental time 70 percent; testing time 30 percent) to create the system. Swipe was ready to demonstrate Carnor to DOD.

On Christmas Day, Carnor was stolen and files related to its development destroyed. The attackers entered Swipe's system through its web server. It is estimated that restoring Carnor will require 10,000 work-hours. If DOD had signed a contract with Swipe for the system, Swipe estimates the nine-year contract would have been worth $2 million per year. Before the attack, Swipe estimates it had a 60 percent chance of signing a contract with DOD. After the attack the probability of a successfully signed contract has been cut in half.

Swipe's chief financial officer, Lois Freed, is developing an estimate of the loss from the attack. The original cost of developing the program included salaries of $55 and $70 per hour for development and testing, respectively. Overhead is charged to development at $8 per direct labor hour for all jobs at Swipe. It is also estimated that managerial personnel were directly involved in developing the program for 100 days during each of the last two years. Total annual managerial salaries at Swipe are $250,000. Swipe estimates the original developmental costs of the software as follows:

Original Cost (12,750 hours)	Dollar Cost Lost
Technician Wages [$55 (12,750 × .70)]	$490,875
Support Services ($8 × 12,750)	$102,000
Managerial Support to Carnor*	$138,889
Testing [$70 (12,750 × .30)]	$267,750
Total Developmental Cost of Carnor	$999,514

*Total annual salaries devoted to Carnor: ($250,000 × 100 ÷ 360) × 2 years = $138,889.

The attacker was methodical in destroying coding, and Swipe managers will have to devote 150 days to restoring the Carnor system during the next year. Because of the ramifications from the attack and the consequential delays, the Carnor system's chances of acceptance by DOD have been halved. Swipe believes there is a $125,000 unbooked cost to restoring Carnor because Swipe will be required to divert its computer resources to rebuild Carnor and ignore other potentially profitable work. Swipe has decided the best way to analyze the loss from restoring the codes for Carnor is to compare the net present value (NPV) of getting the DOD contract before and after the attack. Swipe believes this is a better estimate of the loss than just adding the reconstruction costs to the original development costs. Swipe estimates its direct costs of restoring Carnor as follows:

Reconstruction Cost (10,000 hours)	Dollar Cost Lost
Technician Wages [$55 (10,000 × .70)]	$385,000
Support Services ($8 × 10,000)	$80,000
Opportunity Cost of Computer Time	$125,000
Managerial Support to Carnor*	$104,167
Testing [$70 (10,000 × .30)]	$210,000
Total Reconstruction Cost of Carnor	$904,167

* $250,000 × 150 ÷ 360 × 1 year = $104,167.

If Swipe can restore Carnor in time for a demonstration to DOD and win the contract, Swipe would earn $2 million per year over the next nine years. With Swipe's cost of capital of 10 percent, the present value of this revenue stream is $11,518,000 ($2,000,000 × 5.759 present value of an ordinary annuity table factor). This potential loss should not be considered "lost profits" as in the previous example as these returns were only assured if the DOD contract was awarded to Swipe.

Before the attack, Swipe estimated it had a 60 percent chance of winning the DOD contract. The NPV of the contract is estimated as follows:

Chance of Earning $11,518,000 × .60 = $6,910,800

Less: Cost of Developing Carnor = 999,514

Net Present Value $5,911,286

Now, Swipe's chances have been reduced to 30 percent, and its net present value from the contract must include the original development costs as well as its reconstruction expenses as follows:

Chance of Earning $11,518,000 × .30 = $3,455,400

Less: Cost of Developing Carnor   =   999,514

Less: Reconstruction Costs   =   904,167

Net Present Value $1,551,719

Assuming reconstruction, Swipe does not view its loss as $1,903,681 or the lost developmental costs added to its new restoration expenditures ($999,514 + $904,167). Instead, Swipe views its loss from the attack as the difference in NPV before and after the attack of obtaining the DOD contract or $4,359,567 ($5,911,286 – $1,551,719). Swipe will suffer this potential loss in earnings from the attack if it does not receive the contract. If Swipe should get the DOD contract, then the loss would be considered to be just the $1,903,681, i.e., the original development costs and the costs to restore the system. Currently, it is unclear whether Swipe will win a contract with DOD. The attack has reduced Swipe's chances of success in receiving the contract. The consequential negative effects on Swipe's profits must be recognized in this loss analysis. Most traditional business insurance policies consider data losses to be intangible losses not recoverable under their policy protections.

Loss of Optioned Opportunities

In the previous example, Swipe's data loss was valued at more than the cost of developing and restoring the data. Beyond the developmental and restoration losses, Swipe's losses included lost business opportunities. Another example of a lost business opportunity is a lost business option. Managers often strategically position a company to be able to quickly exploit a new business opportunity. Such business decisions are made to ensure a company is correctly positioned to enter a new market, build a new plant, capture a defined market share, or develop a new product, for example.

Importance of Optioned Opportunities

Decision making of this nature requires managerial flexibility to respond to changing conditions in markets and the economy. Managerial flexibility allows for a decision made in one point in time to be revised and modified as conditions change. Thus, managers are able to begin and plan a project, but they are also ready to cut short its level of development or abandon it as market conditions change. For example, managers who commit to a small pilot project and thus delay carrying out the entire project—possibly forever—are exercising managerial flexibility.

An initial software expenditure incurred by a high-tech company or even a new pilot store built by a grocery chain may be made to allow the company to later fully expand into a new market. The expenditures enable the company to be positioned to enter the market without fully committing the company to the project until market conditions stabilize. Consequently, a company involved in software development provides support for a beta version of its software, but the full funding for a commercial version is held back until the potential sales picture becomes more certain. Yet, if the company had not made the initial expenditures to develop the beta software, it would not be in a position to expand into a new market. Such company planning has created a strategic option for product expansion, and such an option has a value that can be lost.

Real Options

If an intruder destroys the beta version of the new software, the intruder also destroys the company's strategic positioning to enter the new market. Consequently, two losses have occurred. One loss is the developmental costs of the new software, but the more substantial loss is the lost strategic option as the company has lost its ability to expand into a new profitable market. In such a case, a value must be placed on both the developmental costs and the option. Such options are called *real options.*[12]

Real options have a value if uncertainty about a business action can be resolved during a future time period. If there is no uncertainty to a future action, the option has no value. If it is clear that developing beta software will lead to a retail version of the software, no uncertainty exists about future events. Also, underlying the option's valuation is flexibility in management's response to change. For example, if the market for the beta version of software is not developing, managers need to have the flexibility to abandon the project. On the other hand, if the market for the software is growing, managers must have the flexibility to inject more resources into the project to develop a commercial version of the software. Managerial flexibility is related to decisions on whether to abandon the project, go ahead, shrink the size (and cost) of the project, temporarily shut it down, expand the project, defer the start date until later, or default on the investment. If these choices are available to managers, such options have a value to the firm.

Standard present value analysis does not work well as a valuation technique in projects where there is significant uncertainty about future events. The ability to delay a project arising from managerial flexibility is not directly recognized in net present value (NPV) analysis. To overcome this problem, NPV computations may have to be highly positive for managers to be willing to financially commit to the investment. Essentially, a highly positive NPV assigns a value to intangible causes that cannot be properly evaluated with present value analysis.

Real option valuation requires that: (1) there is uncertainty with an unknown probability to the outcome of a project; (2) a project can be delayed, up to a point, without risking it; (3) managers are willing to undertake a project with a negative NPV; (4) managers are willing to give up—i.e., lose—the funds they have initially invested in a pilot project such as in beta software, and (5) managers are not obligated to make the investment, i.e., it is not a legal contract.

EXAMPLE 16.7 VitiTech has developed a new beta browser called FivePack. VitiTech's business strategy has all the preconditions for the software investment to be considered a real option. The labor and overhead developmental costs of FivePack are $800,000. On July 1, a hacker attacked VitiTech's network and destroyed the coding and backup copies of FivePack. The beta version of FivePack was positioned as a pilot project for a new generation browser. With its coding lost, VitiTech is being forced to reconstruct the project. Reconstruction will be completed during the second year—a one-year delay in FivePack's release—and cost $500,000 in reconstruction costs. VitiTech has to pay a licensing fee of $1 million before any software can be sold. VitiTech plans to delay the $1 million payment until the launch date. In addition, VitiTech will only pay the licensing fee if future projected profits justify the additional cost. VitiTech is trying to determine the loss from the attack.

Besides FivePack's developmental costs of $800,000, a loss value must be attributed to the strategic option that VitiTech lost. If FivePack had been released on July 1, VitiTech estimated future profits would be $2 million with a successful product launch, and at a minimum FivePack would produce a profit of $600,000 after its first year of product sales. With the loss of the coding and a year of re-development ahead, the high and low profit estimates in the second year are $2.5 million and $800,000, respectively. VitiTech assigned a 50 percent probability to all these upward and downward profit levels. In addition, VitiTech's cost of capital is assumed to be five percent.

In assigning a value to the lost option, VitiTech uses a binomial tree to analyze the upward and downward change in future profits. A binomial tree is a branched decision tree with nodes broken into upward and downward probabilities of the decision occurrences facing a manager. When using a binomial tree, valuation is determined by beginning with the final nodes in the tree, and then working back toward the first node in the tree. The values at each node are calculated using present values. If a node results in a loss, the outcome at that node does not affect the option's valuation as no business would decide to incur a loss if they knew about it ahead of time. The upward and downward probabilities extending from a node are based on volatility and time factors.

A two-year binomial tree for VitiTech is shown in the following figure with the estimated profit levels. The timeline at the bottom of this figure shows the profit possibilities at Year 1 and Year 2.

The Future Estimated Profit from FivePack

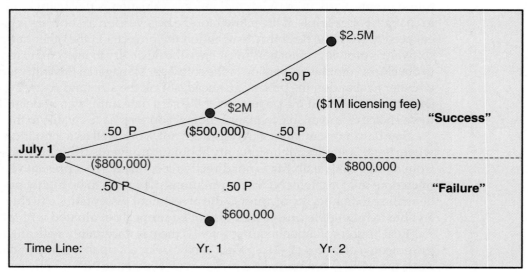

The dotted line in the middle of the figure shows the division of successful profit outcomes (above the line) compared with unsuccessful outcomes (below the line). The developmental cost of the beta version of FivePacks is $800,000 as shown in the figure. If the profit outcomes are less than $800,000, VitiTech is not interested in making further expenditures on FivePack. The only outcome in this product "failure" range in the figure is if a profit of $600,000 is earned.[13] If the profit outcomes equal $2 million, VitiTech considers it a successful outcome. Before the attack, the value of the option was equal to the projected positive profit reduced by licensing fee, discounted for the time value of money, and affected by its 50 percent chance of occurrence or $476,191 [.5($2,000,000 − $1,000,000) ÷ 1.05)].

After the cyber attack, the value of the option has changed. In the second year, FivePack is restored, and there is a 50-50 probability that profits will either be $2.5 million or $800,000.

In valuing the option that VitiTech lost in the attack, the present values of the successful profit outcomes must be summed along with the probability of obtaining those outcomes. The following figure provides an illustration of the profit values for FivePack and a valuation of the business option that was lost.

The Real Option Value After the Attack: $340,136

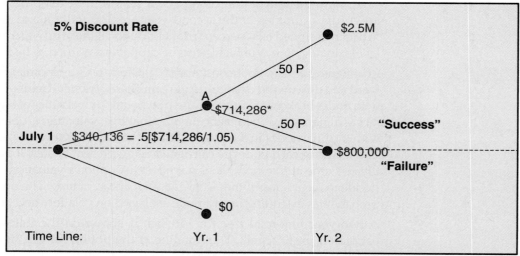

*The option value at Point A is $714,286 {.5[($2.5M − $1,000,000)/1.05]} + {.5[($800,000 − $1,000,000 ÷ 1.05]}

In this figure, only the profitable outcomes are discounted to the present period, and the value of the option after the attack is shown as $340,136. When the coding for FivePack system was destroyed, it prevented VitiTech from being in a position to launch FivePack into the browser market as planned. Thus, the value of the business option that VitiTech had developed for earning future profits was reduced in value. The difference in the value of the option before and after the attack needs to be recognized as part of VitiTech's business loss.

VitiTech has lost a valuable intangible asset as VitiTech had strategically developed an option to launch a new business product. Its real option positioned VitiTech in the browser market so it could take over a market share. The loss of this intangible option is as important to VitiTech as an option contract on land or a mineral reserve. For VitiTech, the total option loss from the attack is $136,055. The option value loss is the difference in the value of the option before and after the cyber attack ($476,191 − $340,136).[14] The total loss from the attack is $1,436,055 which is equal to the lost developmental costs ($800,000), the restoration costs ($500,000), and the diminished value of the option ($136,055). The $800,000 in developmental costs have already been incurred and do not affect the decision to reconstruct FivePack. These expenditures are part of the loss but not part of the option's value. The valuation of the option is related to whether the $1 million will be paid. The $1 million will be paid if there are sales of $2.5 million, i.e., a "successful outcome." The $500,000 in reconstruction costs should not be deducted from the option's valuation as a comparison needs to be made on the distinct difference in the option's value before and after the attack. The $500,000 in reconstruction costs are separately considered as part of the loss.

Losing a business option is an intangible loss and is not covered under general business insurance policies. But it is a real business loss. From a legal perspective, damages attributed to intangible losses, such as lost options, should be tallied whether the attack is on one website or a simultaneous attack on thousands of websites around the world.

The forensic accountant may be called upon to determine cyber losses for management and legal purposes. In addition, a loss report may be required as part of an insurance claim. Usually, the general business policy carried does not provide significant coverage for losses typically incurred in a cyber attack. Thus, it is important for the forensic accountant to be familiar with types of coverage recognized under an organization's cyber insurance policies. The next section provides an overview of cyber insurance coverage.

Loss Valuations and Insurance Claims

¶ 16,041   INSURERS

Today, insurers write contracts providing coverage from cyber attacks. The forensic accountant needs to know the amount recoverable under an insurance policy to place a valuation on the dollar amount of the entire loss. Although it may be possible to convince a court of the need for restitution from intangible losses described in federal or state statues, insurance payments for damages from a cyber attack are only for losses specifically described in the contract. Traditional business insurance policies have not been forthcoming in providing insurance coverage for lost computer data because such losses are considered intangible.[15] Traditional property damage policies are intended to cover only tangible property. The insured party needs to understand the method used by the insurance company to calculate the loss in each instance for which coverage is provided. Lloyd's of London, Chubb, and AIG provide hacker insurance or cybersecurity insurance for companies.[16] Several insurance companies are teaming with security consulting firms to assess the company's networks before providing such insurance.[17] If these evaluations indicate the network is a high risk system, the policy premium is increased or worse the insurance cannot be obtained.

¶ 16,051   COSTS AND TYPES OF COVERAGE

Insurance coverage provides for first- and third-party liability coverage up to $50 million each. Premiums for these policies can cost $20,000 to $40,000 annually. First-party liability coverage is for direct damage to the insured from a cyber attack. With the development of cloud computing, first-party policies provide for contingent business interruption losses that arise when another party such as a cloud service provider is shut down. Third-party liability provides for coverage from the negligent acts of the insured as, for example, when the insured's computers are unknowingly used to launch an attack against a primary target

First-party cyber insurance usually includes coverage of losses from:
- Malicious destruction or alteration of information
- Theft of data such as credit card numbers
- Lost business income up to 12 months after the attack
- Extortion from threats such as introducing viruses into a network
- Introducing fraudulent information into a network
- Defamation
- Cost to repair and replace data
- Unintentional virus transmission
- Denial of service attacks
- IP infringement from website squatters
- Illegitimate use of network
- Defacement of a website and related losses
- Coverage of extra expense incurred during a disruption
- External consultant fees
- Intellectual property infringement from the disclosure of trade secrets
- Rehabilitation expenses to reestablish the insured's reputation and market share
- Crisis communication expenses with clients to provide assurances the system is reliable and safe

The list is similar to those losses recognized in the federal and state statutes, but loss interpretation is likely to be more restrictive.

¶ 16,061   QUALIFYING FOR COVERAGE

Risk Survey

Before providing cyber attack coverage to a client, the insurance company would conduct a survey of the client's site to assess the nature of the insurance risks. Such a risk evaluation would determine how much the company should be charged for cyber insurance. Extensive and proper use of encryption and an updated and properly patched operating system would have the effect of reducing the cost of the policy. A risk survey would collect information about the:
- Public, customers, vendors, and subcontractors who have access to the network and data
- Company's role in providing Internet hosting services to clients
- Number of computer users with access to the network
- Level of Internet web publishing
- Type of e-commerce conducted
- Number of servers in the network
- Operating system used on the network

- Number of external network connections
- Security software and firewalls used
- Implementation of a written network security policy
- Use of encryption
- Use of security audits
- Written policies used to prevent invasion of privacy
- Copyright, patent, and trademark infringement
- Written policies in use to prevent the unauthorized copying of trade secret data
- Use of backup tapes or disks

Security Audit

The actuarial risk tables for companies seeking coverage against hacking attacks do not exist. Therefore, an insurance company may require a complete security audit of any client's network as well as a risk survey before providing insurance coverage. An experienced security assessment firm will provide a thorough due diligence security audit of the network before issuing any policy.

The analysis of the company's network will affect the insurance risk and the premiums. If there are no written policies on security, privacy, intellectual property, or unauthorized computer use, the insurance risk and the premium need to be higher. As can be seen in the risk survey, more access points to the network also increase the risk.

What Should Be Known About Coverage

From the insured's viewpoint, it needs to be ascertained that loss coverage is for all destroyed data, text, images, sounds, collections, and compilations as well as intellectual property such as computer programs and coding. The method used to calculate business income losses should be clearly described in the insurance policy as well as the inclusive time period covered *after* the incident, i.e., does coverage begin immediately or after a designated time lag?[18] The insured should understand the difference between coverage of the *income* losses compared to coverage of the *revenue* losses from the attack. The insured needs to know whether a discount will be received on the policy premium if the insured has a service contract with an insurer-certified security firm.

Third-Party Lawsuits

Third-party coverage arising from computer systems liabilities come from lawsuits against the insured related to negligence of the insured or their employees from errors, libel, slander, invasion of privacy, plagiarism, infringement of a copyright, weak security on a company web server that results in losses to a third-party, mega tags with other company's names on company web page, or the negligent provision of professional services.

Intangible Losses

Today, cyber security insurance can protect companies against loss of intangibles such as computer data. These policies provide for security services as well as insurance coverage. High-tech companies should not rely on their traditional business policies against property losses as a means to protect themselves from cyber attacks. In general, traditional policies only provide coverage for the loss of tangible physical assets.

¶ 16,071   CONCLUSION

Loss valuations need to be made for both tangible and intangible assets that are destroyed in a cyber attack. Some of the most valuable assets for a high-tech company are its intangible assets. Although there may be a tendency for some companies not to want to disclose the loss incurred in an attack, it is important for law enforcement, the insurance industry, security assessment firms, and forensic investigators to have accurate statistics on the number, type, and losses from these attacks. Without a good background of attack statistics, the reports of losses are distorted and the organizations that deal with these cybercrimes have a more difficult job of analyzing them. Press reports on the dollar value attributed to these cybercrimes are inaccurate and cannot be relied upon as many of a company's most valuable resources are not reported as a loss.

Agreed upon methods have to be established for assessing the damages incurred from these attacks. Such assessments should include standard financial measures that are applied consistently to each situation to determine both the tangible and intangible loss insured. The forensic investigative community needs to agree upon how losses described in federal and state statutes are to be interpreted. Courtroom precedents need to be established to recognize the substantial intangible losses that can occur from these attacks. A great deal of standardization needs to be done before the actual losses incurred from these criminal activities can be accurately quantified.

SEC and Sony and Hacking

Three weeks after Sony Corp. was forced to shut down its PlayStation network by hackers who stole users' information. Senate Commerce Committee Chairman Jay Rockefeller of West Virginia sent a letter to the SEC asking it to issue guidance stating that companies must report when they have suffered a major network attack and disclose details on intellectual property or trade secrets that hackers may have stolen.

The PlayStation network was shut down, and the estimated loss from the attack was estimated to be $171M. (http://online.wsj.com/article/SB10001424052748704681904576317571066403808.html#ixzz1M9H4hH50)

ENDNOTES

[1] http://essays.ssrc.org/10yearsafter911/is-cyber-terror-next

[2] *Gilreath v. General Electric Co.*, 751 S2d 705 (Fla App 2000).

[3] G. Stevenson Smith, "Security Management: Recognizing and Preparing Loss Estimates from Cyber Attacks," INFORMATION SYSTEMS SECURITY 12 (Jan/Feb 2004), p. 46-57; G. Stevenson Smith and Anthony J. Amoruso, "Using Real Options to Value Losses from Cyber Attacks," JOURNAL OF DIGITAL ASSET MANAGEMENT 2 (May/Jul 2006), p. 150-172.

[4] For a federal crime, the damages must exceed $5,000. For state computer crimes, the dollar damages vary.

[5] K. Poulsen, "Justice Delayed for Melissa Author," SECURITY FOCUS, *http://online.securityfocus.com* (July 30, 2001); P. Svensson, "'Love Bug' Costs Billions in Time and Data Losses," THE CINCINNATI ENQUIRER (May 6, 2000); T.C. Greene, "Code Red Hysteria - $8.7BN in Damage Estimated," THE REGISTER (August 1, 2001); M. Godoy, "Code Red II Nastier Bug," TECHTV (August 6, 2001).

[6] Second Annual Cost of Cyber Crime Study August 2011. ArcSight and Ponemon Institute., p. 2

[7] Australian Computer Emergency Response Team (AusCERT) 2012.

[8] Intel Corporation, 10-K, Risk Factors, December 26, 2009.

[9] True cyber assets do not have a physical presence. Cyber assets characteristically have a virtual presence in the bits and bytes that exist in a network. In fact some cyber assets may not *have* a value except on the network. If there is no network, the cyber asset has no value. For example, in Second Life the payments made for your avatar's clothes only have value within Second Life. This is true for the islands purchased there also.

[10] The calculation should also include the lost sales for the remaining portion of October, November, and December of the current year as the shutdown occurred on October 14. This was ignored in the illustration. The present value factor for seven percent over five annual periods is 4.1. The $4,132,800 is calculated by multiplying the present value factor times the annual loss of $1,008,000. The result is the present value of the annual loss of profits from the lost customers over a five-year period.

[11] If a company experiences a natural disaster, such as an inventory fire or earthquake damage, the loss should be confined to the cost to replace the inventory less any insurance or salvage proceeds. With a cyber attack, the criminal loss should include both the original developmental costs and the restoration development costs.

[12] See M. Amram and N. Kulatilaka, REAL OPTIONS: MANAGING STRATEGIC INVESTMENT IN AN UNCERTAIN WORLD (Boston, Mass.: Harvard Business School Press, 1999); L. Trigeorgis, REAL OPTIONS IN CAPITAL INVESTMENT: MODELS, STRATEGIES AND APPLICATIONS (Westport, Conn.: Praeger, 1995); and L. Trigeorgis, REAL OPTIONS: MANAGERIAL FLEXIBILITY AND STRATEGY IN RESOURCE ALLOCATION (Cambridge, Mass.: The MIT Press, 1999). For a single-period model, the present value, *PV*, of a binomial decision tree is calculated as:

$$PV = \frac{pCF_u + (1-p)CF_d}{(1+k)}$$

where p = objective probability of up state
$(1-p)$ = objective probability of down state
CF_u = cash flow in the up state

CFd = cash flow in the down state
k = weighted average cost of capital.

[13] Sales of $600,000 are not considered to be a viable choice because they would have resulted in a loss of $400,000 after payment of the $1 million licensing fee ($600,000 – $1 million) even without considering the development costs.

[14] The before and after option values are compared with one another by adjusting all time values to the beginning of Year 1.

[15] C. Rivard and M. Rossi "Is Computer Data 'Tangible Property' or Subject to 'Physical Loss or Damage'? Part 1," *International Risk Management Institute, Expert Commentary (*August 2001) *http://www.irmi.com*; "Is Computer Data 'Tangible Property' or Subject to 'Physical Loss or Damage'? Part 2," *International Risk Management Institute, Expert Commentary (*November 2001) *http://www.irmi.com.*

[16] L. Enos, "Lloyd's of London to Offer Hacker Insurance," E-COMMERCE TIMES (July 10, 2000).

[17] AIG's netAdvantage product suite covers four broad categories of cyber-risk. The security liability coverage defends the insured against legal liability arising from security failures, paying legal fees, and amounts the insured is obligated to pay, such as reissuing new credit cards. First party coverage pays for any direct damage suffered by the insured, such as extortion by hackers. Information asset coverage pays costs to recreate or restore electronic data damaged or lost in an attack, such as customer databases. Business interruption pays for loss of income resulting from disruption to computer systems, such as loss of sales to retailers. "Only 25 Percent of Companies Have Cybersecurity Insurance," *CIO* (October 4, 2005), *http://www.cio.com/article/12656/Only_25_Percent_of_Companies_Have_Cybersecurity_Insurance.*

[18] For example, the business loss may be calculated as the revenue reasonably projected as lost over the next 12 months less the variable costs related to such revenues. This net income is often called the *contribution margin.* For the insured, this calculation is more generous than if overhead charges also had to be deducted before determining the business income loss. But, these methods are less generous than if total revenues were covered under the policy. Additionally, expenditures should be covered that the insured makes, after the attack, to lessen the business income lost. For example, if the insured temporarily uses web servers located at an off-site ISP to provide a network for the company while the company's real network is being restored, such costs should be covered.

EXERCISES

1. Clearly distinguish between tangible and intangible assets. What are the tangible and intangible values attached to a computer software program?

2. The Nevada Code (refer again to Table 16.1) provides that damages from a cyber attack will include "past" losses. Describe the past losses that could be incurred from a computer crime.

3. When would the replacement cost of an asset be a more valid measure of the loss sustained in a cyber attack?

4. If a company website is penetrated by a hacker, why should that company report the attack and a damage estimate to law enforcement officials?

5. The legal statutes and insurance policy coverage identify a number of loss categories from a cyber attack. In the list of losses is one for "general injuries." Identify one general injury that might be suffered during a cyber attack. How should a loss estimate be determined for the item you have identified as a general injury loss?

6. What is the difference between a loss arising from the unavailability of a website and the lost profits that are incurred when that website is disabled?

7. What role should judgmental probabilities play in determining losses from cyber attacks?

8. What role should opportunity costs play in determining the loss from a cyber attack?

9. Corporation XW recently discovered that their network had been penetrated by a hacker six months ago. The hacker has not been active on their network for the last two months. No damages to the system are detectable. Should XW recognize a loss?

10. Define a real option. Why is there any value attributed to a real option?

11. Use an Internet search engine such as Google to search the terms *cyber insurance* and *hacker insurance* until you find an example of an insurance policy that provides coverage for cyber attacks. Read the policy's provisions and identify the specific cybercrimes, as per the statutes in Table 1, that are covered under the policy.

12. Determine if your university has had an Internet security breach. If such a breach occurred, was it revealed by your university? Was the university required to disclose

information to the public that their system had been hacked?

Note: If no breaches occurred at your university, pick another university and answer the same questions. An Internet search will quickly provide information about universities that have had cyber attacks.

13. **My Avatar was Robbed! Help!** The Big Four Accounting Firms, FASB, and large U.S. corporations have a presence in Second Life. The Second Life Community consists of avatars and islands that are owned by organizations and individuals. A virtual market-based economy exists on Second Life. Assume that your avatar has been given $2,000 Linden dollars by one of the Big Four Accounting Firms as an incentive to attend a recruiting seminar. Your avatar flies to the seminar site. As you walk past another avatar in front of the meeting site, you notice your avatar blinks on the screen several times. Your avatar attends the meeting with a number of other student avatars, and you are pleased with the presentation. After the presentation, you want to buy a new suit and tie for your avatar. You notice the $2,000 in Linden dollars is missing. You think your avatar was robbed by the avatar that walked past you on the way to the meeting. Write up a report of the crime for local law enforcement in your community.

14. **When Will It Be Available?** The 2012 and 2013 income statements for Webster Stores follow. Webster Stores is an e-retailer that sells high-end clothing over the Internet. Although its website has generated high sales, Webster Stores has lost money over the last two years, but sales have increased. Bill Forrester, the general manager, predicts the company will be profitable in 2014 and sales for 2014 will be up between 15 percent and 20 percent over sales in 2003. During 2004, the site was attacked by hackers from Animal Friends who objected to the fur on several of the jackets sold on the website. The website was shut down for one day. The disabling of the site is a significant loss for Webster Stores. Because of the branding of its products Webster believes that some customers will return to the website to make future purchases. The disabling of Webster's website has created both lost sales for Webster as well as an unavailability loss.

	2012	2013
Sales	$11,000,000	$14,000,000
Less: Cost of Sales	8,250,000	10,920,000
Gross Margin	$ 2,750,000	$ 3,080,000
Less: Operating Expenses	3,000,000	3,100,000
Operating Profit	($250,000)	($20,000)
Less: Taxes	–	–
Net Income	($250,000)	($20,000)

a. Using the comparative 2002 and 2003 summary income statements, discuss the best income statement statistic to use in evaluating the unavailability loss for 2004.

b. Determine the unavailability loss from Webster's disabled website from the measure decided on in Part (a).

15. **Turn Me Off, Turn Me Off.** Myman Pharmaceuticals uses centrifuges in its labs to remove product solids from its finishing processes. The labs five engineers are responsible for running the machines and each of the ten machines is closely monitored with digital control displays. The centrifuges cost $500,000 each and the engineers are paid an average salary of $125,000 including benefits. On October 14, without warning the machines begin to self-destruct. Six of the centrifuges are shut down before they are damaged, but the other four are destroyed. An investigation determined that the Stuxnet worm had infected the software running the machines and caused them to spin out of control while hiding these effects from appearing on the display monitors. The lab will lose 50 percent of its productivity over the next six months as it will take that long to replace the destroyed centrifuges. In estimating the loss from the cyber attack, the CFO assigned an annual revenue to each centrifuge of $2.5M. In recent years, Myman had earned a 15-percent return on its sales. Vendors have indicated that the replacement cost of new machines will be approximately $600,000. Estimate the loss from the attack and whether any other factors need to be considered.

16. **My Sales Are Lost, and I Can't Find Them.** Archer Meddleton, Inc. has developed a successful e-tail business related to the sale of

antiques. Archer keeps numerous marketing statistics about its web sales.

For example:

Total average sales
per registered customer
per visit $75
Number of annual visits
by registered customers 6
Most commonly visited
page at the site ....antique books
Number of monthly
hits on the page..............................8,675
Total registered customers 980

The Archer website was subjected to an attack in December and shut down for one day. At the time, a great deal of customer Christmas purchasing was occurring. Archer believes it has lost a significant amount of Christmas sales, from approximately 300 registered customers. Due to the nature of the site, Archer believes roughly 10 percent of its lost customers will return and continue to make purchases over the next several months.

Month After Attack	Customers Returning Who Originally Left (%)	Cumulative Number of Customers Returning
1	5	15
2	4	27
3	1	30
4–20	0	—

Assume a registered customer remains active on Archer's site for approximately twenty months, and Archer has a five percent cost of capital. Determine the sales loss from the attack over a 20-month period.

17. **No Toys for the Kids.** Boise Toys, an e-retailer, had its vendor website shut down for two days due to a denial of service attack. The company's vendor website is an auction-based system where vendors compete to supply specific toy products at the lowest price. As Boise Toys uses a JIT system, it could not fill orders on its e-tail website which remained open for customer's orders during the two days. Charles Backus, the controller, estimates the dollar value of the unfillable customer's orders over the two-

day period is $825,000. He believes that forty percent of those orders can be filled. The restoration and analysis labor costs of repairing the system are $220,000. The normal rate of return on sales for Boise Toys is 20 percent due largely to the Internet auction systems used with vendors. The shutdown of the vendor site required the emergency purchase of toy product from higher-priced vendors and increased shipping costs that together totaled $175,000. Mr. Backus believes the shut-down will affect Boise's rate of return. He provides the following estimates: (1) 40 percent chance of a 10-percent decrease; or a 60 percent chance of a 25-percent decrease.

Estimate the preliminary loss for Boise Toys. Is there anything else that Mr. Backus should consider in making the loss estimate?

18. **The Bank that Wasn't.** The President of the MayFair Bank, Mike Morgan, has received an e-mail from Yurie Bronco, an "IT consultant." The e-mail stated that as a consultant Yurie would like to notify the bank that their network has a vulnerability that could shutdown the bank's entire financial network. For $125,000, Yurie is happy to assist the bank in repairing the problem. Yurie has indicated that the "consultant fee" should be wired to a bank account in Switzerland within three days. If the bank agreed, the account number would be provided.

Visibly upset, Mike Morgan visits with Gordon Jenkin. Gordon is the head of IT and network systems for the bank. Gordon emphatically declares, "there are no problems with our systems, that Russian is trying to extort us."

Gordon is partially correct. On the fourth day, the bank's network is completely shut down. Customers cannot use online banking, tellers have to keep deposits at their stations, make paper notations regarding withdrawals, and all business services are stopped. After five days, the network hole is found, and the system is back up and online.

Mr. Morgan has assigned you the task of determining the long-run financial effect on the bank. The bank uses a discount rate of nine percent as criteria for its investments. The annual loss from business clients is expected to range from $2M to $5M in profit over the next five years. Two thousand individual bank accounts are expected to be closed. The average balance in these accounts is $10,000, and the bank earns nine percent on these accounts. Due to the press reporting of the incident, new business profits are expected to decrease. Mr. Morgan estimates that the drop in business profit over each of the next five years will exhibit the following pattern.

Year	Decrease in New Business Due to the Cyber Attack
1	$2,000,000
2	$2,000,000
3	$1,500,000
4	$1,000,000
5	$ 500,000

Determine the long-term loss to MayFair Bank from the cyber attack.

19. **Really, It's an Option**. Burleigh Tech has developed an optioned strategy to compete in a new software market. Its new software package is a security product that identifies a cyber attacker entering a network and responds to the attack with a counterattack on the hacker's system. The counterattack is designed to disable the attacker's PC. Burleigh has named its system Seeker. Currently, Seeker is in a beta version, and Burleigh is awaiting legal clearances before Seeker can be released. There are three to four other high-tech firms developing similar counterattack software. Burleigh has invested $250,000 in developmental costs for the software, and the company is positioned to be the first high-tech firm to release such a package. Burleigh's lawyers have estimated there is a 75 percent probability that legal issues will be settled after one year. At that time, Burleigh can invest another $500,000 into the development and release a commercial version of Seeker. Assuming all legal hurdles are overcome and the software is released, Burleigh estimates it has a 50-50 chance of earning either $1,000,000 or $4,000,000 in profits during the first year Seeker is sold.

On Thanksgiving Day, Melvin Poluce, one of Burleigh's programmers, came into the office and stole the coding for the software. At the same time, he destroyed the files that would have allowed Burleigh to restore the coding for the software. As of the end of the year, Melvin has not been caught. Burleigh's leading edge in the counterattack software market has been destroyed and Burleigh has decided to abandon the project.

Determine the option loss that Burleigh has suffered assuming the company's cost of capital is six percent.

20. **Rockie II.** PaperDyne is a high-tech company that installs its own firewall system called "The Rock" for its clients. A new version of the Rock—"Rockie II"—was in development. Last year, company sales were $10 million with a profit margin of 15 percent. Prior to Rockie II's launch, there was a cyber attack on the company resulting in the destruction of files and documents related to the new version of the firewall.

Sean Gannon, the President of Paper-Dyne, does not want the attack or its effect revealed to anyone outside the tech group working on the project, if possible. PaperDyne's network has been hardened, at a cost of $75,000, to prevent another attack. Sean has told clients of a "technical delay" in the project, but he has promised them the new version of the firewall will be available in three months.

In order to meet the deadline for the reconstructing of Rockie II, programming staff overtime charges will be incurred. Currently, IT project staff are paid at $38 per hour with benefits and time and a half for overtime. It is estimated the IT project staff will have to work a 55 hour work week for the next three months in order to reconstruct the loss data.

Tim McCagbe, who is project director of Rockie II, is upset about the loss of the project's data. He has decided that he will put in ghosted hours to help meet the three-month deadline, i.e., Tim will work without asking for any overtime pay.

Not counting Tim, there will be 10 workers reconstructing the Rockie II project. PaperDyne charges overhead at the rate of 80 percent per direct labor dollar, and it is expected the reconstruction will require 6,600 hours of IT staff time. In addition, another project will have to be abandoned in order to meet Rockie II's three-month release date. The new project was estimated to have a profit of $700,000.

After two months have passed, the project is going well, but there are concerns about meeting the project deadline. In the final month, Sean contracted with an outside IT firm, Breakers, to bring in additional programming assistance on the reconstruction. The one-month contract was for $15,000. Breakers was largely responsible for checking codes.

PaperDyne wants to calculate the cost of the cyber attack. PaperDyne estimated that the original cost of developing the Rockie II firewall was $300,000.

a. Determine the loss to PaperDyne from the cyber attack.

b. Evaluate Sean's decision to keep the cyber attack a secret. How would a valuation be placed on the additional loss the company would sustain if the PaperDyne's clients became aware of this successful cyber attack?

c. Evaluate Tim's decision to ghost his work hours in the reconstruction phrase of the project.

21. **Who Did It, at Who U?** Chance Percell works at Who U, a large university, on the East Coast, as an IT employee. His hourly salary is $18 per hour. During the week of March 7, the School of Business and Economics website is defaced by a hacker. Chance spends three hours restoring the webpage and another two hours ensuring the unauthorized access will not re-occur. Chance's benefit package is approximately $2 per hour, and he works 2,000 hours annually. Who U charges an overhead rate of 45 percent on its government research grants. What is the cost to Who U of this cyber attack?

PART 5
BUSINESS VALUATIONS

17

BUSINESS VALUATIONS

A valuation analyst should be able to explain and defend his or her valuation, including both the valuation analysis and conclusion. Further, this explanation and defense may often be performed within a contrarian's environment.

—G. S. Gaffen[1]

OBJECTIVES

After completing Chapter 17, you should be able to:

1. Understand the importance of business valuation in business and law.
2. Determine the many reasons for business valuations.
3. Appreciate why business valuations can be contentious.
4. Understand the basic principles and techniques employed by business valuation specialists.
5. Comprehend the complexity and rigor involved in proper business valuations.

OVERVIEW

Forensic practitioners are asked to perform a variety of economic and accounting measurements for many important purposes that relate to legal rights. One of the most complex and pervasive measurements made is the business valuation. Business valuations require professionals who are knowledgeable and skilled in finance, law, and accounting. Valuations are so complex, in fact, that the majority of professionals who perform them are specialists. Nevertheless, a forensic accountant who is not a business valuation specialist may be asked to review specific issues involved in a valuation. Thus, all forensic accountants need to understand the basic principles involved.

Business valuation is an increasingly specialized field with a variety of guidelines, case law, and techniques affecting valuations for different purposes and continually advancing the state of the art. However, business valuation is also an "easy entry" profession with wide variances in the background, training, and experience of practitioners. The quality of a business valuation and its findings is directly related to the skill, training, and experience of the professional.

Entire college courses are devoted to the issues of business valuations and even those courses do not fully cover the complexities of the topic. This chapter provides an overview of the most significant business valuation concepts and reviews common methods of valuing businesses. Much of this chapter is derived from the *CCH Business Valuation Guide* by George Hawkins and Michael Paschall. Specifically, the Fundamentals, The Three Valuation Approaches, Gathering Initial Information, Financial Analysis, Business Valuation Standards, and Business Valuation Reports sections appear in part in the *CCH Business Valuation Guide*. The authors of this book are indebted to Hawkins and Paschall for its use.

This chapter concentrates on business valuations of specific closely held businesses that are performed for specifically stated needs at a single point in time. Most publicly traded companies have market-determined values at any given date in time.

Fundamentals

¶ 17,001   VALUATION AND APPRAISER ACCREDITATIONS[2]

Organizations Certifying Valuation Professionals

Rapidly growing demand for qualified business valuators has led to the development of four national certifications. Each certification was developed by one of four national accrediting organizations, which provide their own education and testing programs. Business appraisers have traditionally come from either a finance background or an accounting background. Some organizations cater more to individuals with one or the other background. The designations by organization are as follows:

- Accredited senior appraiser (ASA) and accredited member (AM) awarded by the American Society of Appraisers (ASA)
- Certified business appraiser (CBA) awarded by The Institute of Business Appraisers (IBA)
- Certified valuation analyst (CVA) awarded by the National Association of Certified Valuation Analysts (NACVA)
- Accredited in business valuation (ABV) awarded by the American Institute of Certified Public Accountants (AICPA)

All four organizations provide excellent training for prospective business appraisers, and their certifications strive to enhance valuation professionalism. Some of these organizations offer additional accreditations with less stringent requirements for those professionals wanting to limit their business valuation engagements to pursue litigation support engagements that relate to business valuation. Each group offers an array of introductory and advanced valuation courses, along with continuing education programs, seminars, and conferences. All of the groups also work closely together in various ways to develop valuation standards and terminology.

Financial Analyst Accreditation

A fifth accreditation and organization is the chartered financial analyst (CFA) awarded by the Association for Investment Management and Research (AIMR), parent organization of the Institute of Chartered Financial Analysts. Although not specifically a business valuation certification, the CFA covers valuation in depth, both of public and private companies, along with a broad-based, inclusive study of other investment subjects. Some believe the CFA is among the most prestigious of all certifications in the field of corporate finance and on Wall Street.

¶ 17,011   ENGAGEMENT AGREEMENTS THAT CREATE SUCCESSFUL CLIENT RELATIONSHIPS[3]

An engagement agreement is needed in any valuation or client-related undertaking. An engagement agreement:

- Clearly sets forth the expectations of the business valuator and client
- Reduces the chance for misunderstanding and, therefore, the risk of malpractice litigation and claims against the business valuator
- Increases the likelihood of the valuator being paid, since it establishes a clear obligation on behalf of the client

A standardized engagement agreement should be drafted and reviewed by an attorney to meet the needs of the valuation practice. Although attorneys draft many types of contracts, they may not be familiar with issues that are unique to business valuation.

The following specifics need to be considered in drafting an engagement agreement:
- Identify the client
- Specify the interest, date, purpose, and intended use of the valuation
- Define the standard of value
- Assign responsibility for fees and costs
- Price the engagement
- Specify responsibility for real estate and other appraisal costs
- Obtain a retainer
- Protect against the use and misuse of forecasts by clients
- Include indemnification language
- Include other terms and conditions

¶ 17,021   PURPOSES FOR OBTAINING BUSINESS VALUATIONS

Valuations are needed for various purposes:
- Tax purposes (estate tax, gift tax, charitable contributions, casualty loss, sale of securities, state tax, etc.)
- Divorce distributions (often referred to as *equitable distributions*)
- Liquidations (partnerships, sole proprietorships, and corporations)
- Employee stock ownership plans (ESOPs)
- Lost profit analyses
- Mergers and acquisitions
- Minority shareholder distributions
- Buy-sell agreements
- Bankruptcies
- Recapitalizations
- Management buyouts
- Allocations of purchase price

In business valuations, the practitioner is asked to provide a valuation for a business or some other economic unit. The vast majority of all businesses in the United States are privately held companies in which ownership (stock, partnership, or proprietorship interests) is held by a small number of people. Ownership rights are not typically traded on any market such as the New York Stock Exchange or the American Stock Exchange.

Conflicts Giving Rise to Business Valuations

Many situations involving business valuations of partnerships are resolved quite amicably with departing and remaining partners agreeing on the amount that is paid for the departing partner's interest. Sometimes, the partnership's value or methodology for determining the value, is spelled out in advance in the partnership agreement. Many times, however, there are differences of opinion about the amount that should be paid for the business interest that is being sold. Such disputes are often litigated in a legal forum in "forensic" fashion.

Additionally, many business sales or dissolutions are fraught with conflict from the start. Family business dissolutions that result from divorce are often contentious. Typically, divorces involve significant conflict already, and when the issue of valuing large commonly owned assets such as a business is involved, there are major disagreements.

Even in the best of situations, however, generally the seller of the business interest wants the most he or she can get, and the buyer wants to pay as little as possible for the business ownership interest. To resolve such differences, business valuators are asked to provide an impartial valuation that is developed in a professional and systematic manner.

Often business valuations are attacked or defended in court. The business appraiser who performs the appraisal is one expert, but the opposing side may introduce other experts to give testimony on the flaws in the report. Some experts may be brought in to look at parts of the appraisal; some may be asked to look at the entire appraisal. Thus, in some situations, expert appraisal witnesses may need extensive and broad understanding of the process and issues; in others, the expert may need specialized knowledge on a narrow portion of the appraisal or specific issues regarding it.

General Types of Valuations

In general, there are three types of valuations:

- *Asset-based*. This type of valuation is used to value asset-intensive businesses such as retail and manufacturing. The focus is on what the equipment and real estate are worth.
- *Income approach*. This type of valuation is useful for service companies. The focus is on how much money a buyer can make from the business.
- *Market approach*. This type of valuation looks at what the market is paying for similar businesses and is used to value many different types of businesses. The focus is on the marketplace: what others have paid for similar companies.

Although most business valuations are performed for closely held companies, publicly traded companies with established market value may have issues that require additional analysis. For example, the market price at a particular date may have been determined using financial information that was distorted or fraudulent. Additionally, investors look for firms that they believe are undervalued by the market for investment opportunities, and some business appraisals may be done in investment research situations.

¶ 17,031 STANDARDS OF VALUE[4]

The standard of value used in a business valuation is critical because it establishes the guidelines under which the valuation will be performed. The use of different standards may produce vastly different values for the same company; therefore, the valuator must know the standards under which he or she should proceed. In many valuation situations, statutory or case law dictates the standard of value.

The following six standards of value and their common uses are explained in more detail next.

- Fair market value (commonly used for gift and estate tax, purchase or sale, buy-sell agreements, and divorce valuations)
- Fair value—100 percent controlling interest value (commonly used in dissenting minority shareholder valuations)
- Fair value—minority interest and marketable value (commonly used in dissenting minority shareholder valuations)
- Fair value—minority interest but nonmarketable value (commonly used in dissenting minority shareholder valuations)
- Investment value (sometimes used in the purchase of businesses in examining the value to a specific buyer)
- Intrinsic value (commonly used in equitable distribution valuations)

Fair Market Value

The IRS defines *fair market value* as the amount at which property would change hands between a willing seller and a willing buyer when neither is acting under compulsion and when both have knowledge of the relevant facts. Fair market value is usually the governing standard for gift and estate tax valuations, asset purchase or sale, divorce, and many other situations calling for a valuation.

Fair Value

Fair value is used most commonly in conjunction with dissenting minority shareholder situations. Fair value is generally a judicially determined concept of value that can vary widely in interpretation in each state. "Fair value" can be interpreted in at least three different ways:

- *Minority shareholder's pro-rata share of the 100-percent controlling interest value.* This view of fair value is perceived as favoring the minority shareholder because it affords the maximum protection to the dissenting minority shareholder and does the most damage to the remaining shareholders in the business, as well as to the business itself.
- *Fair market value of the minority shareholder's specific shares, discounted for minority interest status only, without discounts for lack of marketability.* This approach is a compromise view that tries to give some value to the shares of the dissenting minority shareholder without unfairly penalizing the business and its remaining shareholders.
- *Fair market value of the minority shareholder's specific shares, ordinarily discounted for minority interest status and lack of marketability.* This view of fair value is perceived as favoring the company at the expense of the minority shareholder, because it does not give the minority shareholder anything more than he or she already has.

Investment Value

Investment value is the value to a specific buyer of a business. Investment value incorporates all of the synergies and other factors that arise from a particular purchase of a business. The value may be that a business is far more attractive to a particular buyer due to various advantages that the purchase of that business brings to the buyer. Examples include a beverage distributor trying to purchase a fellow distributor to fill in its geographic territory or a manufacturer/wholesaler trying to purchase a retailer in order to form a completely integrated company.

In order to accurately estimate investment value, a valuator must analyze and predict what the particular benefits of ownership will be to the potential purchaser. In many situations, investment value may be above fair market value. In these instances, "backward-looking" valuation techniques, such as capitalization of income method, may be of little use in arriving at an accurate value. "Forward-looking" valuation techniques, such as a discounted future income method, are likely to be more suitable. The advantage to a forward-looking valuation model is its ability to capture the anticipated competitive advantages and synergies expected by a potential buyer.

Intrinsic Value

Intrinsic value is the value to a specific individual. Intrinsic value commonly arises in the divorce context where the sale of a business may not be possible, however, the court still finds that the business has value to its owner or owners. Although this may be an appealing concept, in reality, the ability to support a logical conclusion of value under the intrinsic value standard can be quite difficult.

Size of Ownership Interest Impacts Final Value

The percentage of ownership interest being valued is of crucial importance to an interest's ultimate value. The key issue is control:

- How much power and influence does the ownership interest have by virtue of its size and its relationship to the overall distribution of ownership?
- Can the ownership interest force the sale or liquidation of all or a part of the company's assets?
- Can the ownership interest declare and pay dividends?

If so, the ownership interest is able to potentially receive some value (i.e., immediate cash) from the interest. If the ownership interest does not have such power, the owner has fewer and more difficult avenues to realize immediate value for the interest.

Shareholder value can be segregated along three levels of value, ranging from 100-percent control to minority interest status.

The middle level is called "minority marketable" because the price-earnings multiples or capitalization rates applied to the private company's earnings are derived from the returns on public company stocks. The public company stocks are fully marketable and represent small minority interests (e.g., one share of IBM).

Business Enterprise, or 100-Percent Controlling Interest Value

The owner of a 100-percent controlling interest has unilateral control of all the decisions that affect the company. This includes the sale and liquidation of the company and the declaration and payment of dividends.

The 100-percent controlling interest value often includes a premium for control. Some data suggests that the premium may be about 30 percent to 40 percent above the value afforded to freely traded minority interests. One excellent source of control premium data is MERGERSTAT® Review. Control premium data is developed by comparing the market price per share before any takeover offer has been made (a minority value) to the price later paid in the takeover (a 100-percent controlling interest value). The increase in price represents the premium for control.

EYEWITNESS

In 1988, R.J. Reynolds was trading at about $55 per share before any takeover rumors surfaced. The company was ultimately sold for about $110 per share, representing a control premium of 100 percent.

Control, But Less Than 100-Percent Interest

In some situations an ownership interest of less than 100 percent may still be able to exercise a significant amount of control over a business, therefore warranting a control premium adjustment to the minority, marketable value.

51-Percent Ownership Interest

For instance, a 51-percent ownership block in a company where the corporate bylaws and relevant state law call only for a majority vote for all corporate action has the same force and impact as a 100-percent owner. Because of the power and influence held by the 51-percent owner under this scenario, a premium for control may be appropriate. However, clearly a 51-percent interest is not as valuable as the 100-percent interest on a pro-rata basis. Whereas the 100-percent owner has unfettered control over the company and can do as he or she wishes, a 51-percent owner still must deal with the rights and concerns of minority shareholders. This factor may limit the 51-percent owner from specific actions that a 100-percent owner could do.

50-Percent to 100-Percent Ownership Interest

There are situations where ownership of interests between 50 percent and 100 percent does not carry all the benefits of full, 100-percent control of the business. For example, a greater-than-50-percent interest may not give an owner full control of the business if bylaw provisions or state laws require a greater-than-majority vote for various corporate actions. Although a 51-percent-and-above interest is often called a "controlling interest," this may not actually be the case if, for example, the corporate bylaws call for a two-thirds majority to effect various corporate actions. In this instance, the 51-percent block may be effectively powerless if at least 34 percent of the other shares oppose the action desired by the 51-percent holder.

Minority Interest: Technically Less Than 50 Percent

The value of a minority holder's interest might be worth less (and perhaps substantially less) than a pro-rata share of the total 100-percent value. The main factor influencing the value of a minority interest is the amount of control that the minority interest can exert over the corporation. Those minority interests that are limited in their power to influence corporate action are worth less than the pro-rata share of the total 100-percent value because they generally cannot force the corporation to allow the minority interest holder to realize any value from his or her interest (primarily through the payment of dividends or salaries; the implementation of business strategy and plans; or the merger, sale, or liquidation of the company).

The influence of a minority interest may be limited by a combination of statute, case law, and the governing corporate documents. A minority interest does not necessarily have to be as small as one percent or less to lack the ability to influence corporate action.

If the corporate bylaws call for a supermajority voting approval of 80 percent for various corporate actions, a 79-percent interest is essentially a minority interest, because its holder cannot by himself or herself affect corporate action.

"Swing Vote" Interests

Conversely, there may be times when a miniscule minority interest is worth more than a pro-rata share of the total 100-percent value. A small minority share may be the "swing vote" in a business.

EXAMPLE 17.1 There are two 49-percent ownership interests and one 2-percent ownership interest. Assuming that the relative statutes and corporate bylaws call for a simple majority for approval of various corporate action, the 2-percent interest becomes much more valuable because without its vote, the 49-percent interests are powerless to direct the corporation. The 2-percent interest thus becomes extremely valuable to the 49-percent interest holders who would be willing to pay a premium (i.e., a value greater than its pro-rata share of the total 100-percent value) to acquire the 2-percent interest.

Analyzing the Distribution of Ownership

In determining the proper discount (if any) for a minority interest, one must analyze the distribution of ownership. There may be other situations in which the dynamics of share ownership call for a smaller or larger discount for minority interest than would be considered "normal."

EXAMPLE 17.2 One shareholder of Public Corporation A owns a 30-percent interest, with all other shareholders owning less-than-1-percent interests. If the other minority shareholders cannot consolidate their stock for a vote, conceivably, this factor justifies a lower minority interest discount for the 30-percent block.

Buy-Sell Agreements May Impact Value

Another situation influencing the value of a minority interest to become equal to or greater than its pro-rata share of the total 100-percent value occurs when a buy-sell agreement governs the disposition of a departing or dying shareholder's interest. In this situation, a "formula" calculation of value may be required that yields a value equal to or greater than the pro-rata share of the total 100-percent value. Alternatively, the buy-sell agreement may specifically dictate that the departing minority shareholder be paid his or her pro-rata share of the total 100-percent value of the company.

¶ 17,041 PURPOSE OF THE VALUATION AFFECTS THE VALUATION METHODS USED[5]

The purpose of the valuation impacts the standards of value employed and the valuation methods used. There are numerous reasons for private company valuations, including, but not limited to, gift and estate tax planning, dissenting minority shareholder actions, equitable distribution (divorce), employee stock ownership plans (ESOPs), asset purchases and sales, buy-sell agreements, bankruptcies, and business damages. Applicable standards, statutes, regulations, and specific case law govern several of these areas. It is crucial for the valuation expert to understand the relevant governing authority and make sure the business valuation complies with the required guidelines.

Business valuators are supposed to be totally unbiased about the outcome of their valuation. Under this premise, the business valuator is supposed to select those methods he or she feels are most applicable and reasonable in a particular case. However, in some instances, there may be a controlling standard or case law that dictates a particular method or methods to use that may result in an estimate of value that is different from that obtained under "normal" circumstances. Following are some examples of how purposes affect the choice of methods.

Gift and Estate Tax Planning

Certain IRS revenue rulings and relevant case law may contain standards that dictate the appropriate method of valuation.

Revenue Ruling 59-60[6]

The controlling authority on gift and estate tax valuations is Revenue Ruling 59-60 and subsequent rulings. Promulgated in 1959, this revenue ruling lists eight broad factors requiring careful analysis for the valuation of closely held stocks for gift and estate tax purposes. The eight factors are as follows:

1. The nature of the business and the history of the enterprise from its inception
2. The economic outlook in general and for the specific industry in particular
3. The book value of the stock and the financial condition of the business
4. The earnings capacity of the company
5. The dividend-paying capacity of the company
6. Whether or not the enterprise has goodwill or other intangible value
7. Sales of the stock and the size of the block of stock to be valued
8. The market price of stocks of corporations engaged in the same or similar line of business having their stocks actively traded in a free and open market, either on an exchange or over-the-counter

Dissenting Minority Shareholder Actions

Owners of closely held businesses may not get along. Unlike a public corporation where disgruntled shareholders can sell their stock and move on, a minority shareholder in a closely held company often does not have such an option and is forced to hold his or her shares despite a conflict with other owners. Often, the only redress a minority shareholder has is to file a dissenting minority shareholder action. Generally, this type of action is governed by the laws of the state in which the company is incorporated. Although the laws vary from state to state, one recurring provision allows for dissenting minority shareholders to be paid the "fair value" of their stock upon selling their shares. Unfortunately, in many states, "fair value" is not a defined, objective term and, therefore, is subject to interpretation. Ultimately, the decision on "fair value" may rest with a business valuation or through the determination of value by state courts and applicable state law.

Equitable Distribution (Divorce): Impact of State Statutes and Case Law

Another area of business valuation in which the valuator must be aware of controlling law is in equitable distribution or divorce valuations. All states have statutory requirements applying to this area, and a valuation expert must know the ground rules before starting a valuation.

Relevant Valuation Date—A Key Issue

State laws vary as to how long couples must wait before they can be divorced. Some states allow an immediate divorce; others require a period of separation before the actual divorce is granted. Some states requiring a separation period before the divorce require the valuation to be the fair market value as of the date of separation.

Marital Versus Separate Property and Related Appreciation Issues

A business valuator must understand state guidelines as to the differences between marital and separate property. Suppose a man owns a business worth $1 million on his wedding day. Twenty years later, when the couple divorces, the company is worth $3 million. Many states will consider the $1 million to be separate property that was brought to the marriage. However, the $2 million in appreciation that occurred during the marriage may be considered marital property and, thus, subject to equitable distribution. Under this hypothetical situation, $1 million of the business value remains the sole property of the husband, but the $2 million of appreciated business value can be divided between the husband and wife. The original $1 million can also become "tainted" and turn into community property.

DIVORCE SITUATION VALUATIONS.[7] Divorce is an emotional event for those involved. Because the emotions are typically negative—anxiety, anger, mistrust—it is common for one spouse to suspect the other is hiding or undervaluing significant assets in an attempt to keep them out of the divorce settlement. This suspicion often arises when a family-owned business is at stake. Here, determining whether one spouse has hidden assets requires that a valuation professional investigate the business's financial records and documents. The valuator then can understand the location of assets, track any significant changes in spending habits of either spouse prior to the date of separation, and look for patterns or breaks in patterns that may point to suspicious activity.

Unearthing hidden assets can be a painstaking process because the spouse involved in the business may have taken steps to cover his or her tracks in anticipation of the increased level of scrutiny. Careful investigation of the company and the industry (as well as consideration of other factors, such as the individuals involved) can often reveal the trends that will show an investigator how and where assets have been moved.[8]

The valuation issue does not end there, however, because there may be an issue as to whether the $2 million appreciation noted above is "active" or "passive." In some states, if the appreciation is considered to be "passive," the $1 million remains the separate property of the husband. If the appreciation is considered to be "active," the $1 million is marital property and, thus, subject to division. In general, "passive" appreciation is appreciation that happens regardless of the actions of the owners (e.g., stocks or bonds). In contrast, "active" appreciation is appreciation that is the result of the action and hard work undertaken by the owners (e.g., a business).

Under the passive appreciation argument, the husband's attorney will argue that, at an average historical annual inflation rate of five percent, the husband's original $1 million business value grew to $2.65 million. Given the total business value of $3 million on the date of separation, only $350,000 ($3 million less $2.65 million) of the $2 million appreciation is "active" and, thus, subject to division. The remaining $2.65 million is the separate property of the husband.

The wife's attorney will argue that this inflation argument makes no sense, and the entire $2 million appreciation in the value of the business is active and, thus, subject to division. Her attorney will argue that, unlike a piece of raw land that appreciates passively over time, a closely held business is an entity that requires constant care and attention. No owner can leave a business alone for 20 years and expect to come back to a value that has increased at the rate of inflation—the business will have been long dead.

Increases in company values result from factors such as the development and production of a product superior to those of competitors (Microsoft), filling a niche in the market that previously had been unsatisfied (Home Depot), consolidating similar operations and achieving economies of scale (Bank of America), or providing a consistently excellent and popular product year after year (Coca-Cola). Inflation has little, if anything, to do with the rise or fall of corporate value. In fact, some studies indicate that inflation actually has a negative correlation to the value of a business. Indeed, much of the tremendous bull market of the '80s and '90s was arguably the result of a low-inflation environment.

Lack of Case Guidance as Typical Issue

As just evidenced, the resolution of the separate/marital and active/passive issues are key to a valuator reaching a correct estimate of value in an equitable distribution dispute. Unfortunately, in many states these issues have not been heavily litigated, and there is a paucity of case law for guidance. Alternatively, many court decisions are never appealed, making a determination of judicial valuation trends and their application to a specific situation difficult to ascertain. A business valuator must work closely with the family law attorney to be sure the valuator understands the relevant standards.

Professional Practices Valuations in Equitable Distributions

Even if the relevant statute mandates that the measure of value for the valuation of professional practices is "fair market value," this concept may be interpreted differently for equitable distributions than in an estate or dissenting minority shareholder situation. In some states, the value of a professional practice may not be what a willing buyer would pay a willing seller for the practice. Instead, some state equitable distribution statutes direct that the value of the professional practice be measured by its worth to the owner.

A husband with a lucrative law practice might not be allowed to sell the goodwill to a buyer. Under the fair market value standard, the practice may have little value; however, in an equitable distribution context, the practice may have a significant value.

Again, a valuator must work closely with qualified legal advisors to determine the proper valuation standard to apply in equitable distribution cases.

Personal Versus Practice Goodwill Issues

A related issue to consider in the valuation of professional practices is the treatment of "personal" versus "practice" goodwill. *Goodwill* is that portion of practice value that is beyond the hard assets (including accounts receivable) of the practice. If a medical practice has a total value of $300,000, with $50,000 in fixed assets and $50,000 in accounts receivable, that practice is said to have a goodwill value of $200,000. Goodwill is that intangible asset that keeps existing patients coming back for treatment and attracts new patients to the practice. Goodwill includes, but is not limited to, reputation, name recognition, employees, location, years in the community, and even telephone number.

Personal goodwill is the goodwill that attaches to a particular individual or individuals. *Practice goodwill,* on the other hand, is the goodwill that attaches to a particular entity. In reality, the two can be difficult to isolate and quantify. Do patients go to a particular medical practice because it is a long-standing, well-respected practice in their community? Or do they go to see a particular physician whom they really like? If a physician left practice A and joined practice B, would practice A suffer a drop-off in business because a number of patients followed the departing doctor to practice B? Or would practice A continue to thrive as the patients continued to come to the practice with different physicians? These can be very difficult issues to deal with in a valuation context.

The reason it is so important to understand and be able to segregate personal versus practice goodwill is that state law may dictate whether one qualifies as a marital asset. In a situation where one or both spouses have a lucrative professional practice, this issue becomes pivotal in valuing the marital estate for an equitable distribution case.

Employee Stock Ownership Plans (ESOPs)

Employee stock ownership plans (ESOPs) represent another fertile field for business valuation. In general, ESOPs are tax-favored devices that encourage employee ownership of businesses. By giving employees an equity stake in the company, the hope is that they will work harder to improve the value of the company. Furthermore, by allowing employees to annually add to their shares held in the ESOP, it is hoped that employees will have additional resources upon their retirement. ESOPs are encouraged by means of various tax advantages. Some of these advantages include tax deferral for the owner selling more than 30 percent of the company's stock to the ESOP and company deduction of both the interest and principal of the ESOP loan.

Valuation issues arise in the ESOP context in several areas. First, if the ESOP is leveraged (i.e., if the company must borrow money to fund the ESOP), the newly created ESOP trust will be the primary source of repayment. However, the company, in effect, is the ultimate source of repayment for the loan. This debt service must be a key part of any discount cash flow forecast done as a part of the company valuation.

Another key issue to consider in the valuation of the ESOP shares is the mandatory put option required under the Employee Retirement Income Security Act (ERISA). ERISA requires that an ESOP must provide a market for an employee's company shares upon the employee's retirement or termination of employment. This share repurchase liability of the company ensures that employees will have some degree of liquidity to their investment and will not be forced to sell their company shares in what otherwise would be an illiquid market.

Indeed, the ERISA-mandated put option is why most business valuations are prepared in the ESOP context. A put option creates another issue to be considered in the valuation because it provides a degree of liquidity to the closely held shares that would not exist without the ESOP. Therefore, a smaller discount for lack of marketability of the stock may be appropriate, given that the ESOP does create some market, albeit limited, for the shares.

Asset Purchase or Sale

The key issue to consider in a valuation done in the context of a purchase or sale is the value of the subject company to the specific buyer. A specific buyer may place a value on a subject company that is substantially different from the normal concept of fair market value. Reasons for this difference include synergies or competitive advantages gained from the purchase of the subject company that otherwise are not present or available to the normal "willing buyer." Indeed, in the public company realm, company values are often bid to ever-higher levels as buyers seek to supplement their businesses by purchasing complementary operations, as opposed to having to develop competing operations. This concept is discussed later in this chapter; however, the business valuator needs to be cognizant of the buyer's perspective in a purchase or sale valuation.

Buy-Sell Agreements

Buy-sell agreements are common in many closely held companies. A buy-sell agreement can serve several purposes, including ensuring the continuity of management and ownership, providing liquidity to deceased or withdrawing owners, and (in some cases) establishing company values for estate tax purposes. Buy-sell agreements may be drafted in several ways; however, the most common valuation provision calls for either a formula provision to calculate value or the appointment of a third-party valuator or valuators to determine company value.

Formula provisions, although usually easy to calculate, run the risk of severely over- or undervaluing the business. Many buy-sell agreements calling for formula calculations of value have been in place for many years, and the company and its industry may have undergone changes in the interim that render the company unrecognizable from the day the document was drafted. As an example, a formula buy-sell calculation at "accounting book value" for a real estate holding company may grossly understate the value of the business if the land is in an area that has experienced rapid development over the years.

In addition to antiquated formulas, some buy-sell agreements may suffer from vague or ambiguous language that renders them all but unusable. A valuation professional hired to help an attorney draft a buy-sell agreement must consider these potential risks and pitfalls. The most efficient way to derive an accurate company value for a buy-sell agreement is to provide for a current valuation at the time the buy-sell is activated. However, the owners may want to keep the buy-sell simple and peg the price at an easily calculated figure. Some owners may be happy with the formula after enacted, but this still does not mean it is necessarily a valid indicator of the current "real world" fair market value of the shares.

Another problem occurs when the buy-sell agreement value is an artificially low price to minimize the potential exposure of the shareholder's spouse in a divorce. For example, professional practice buy-sell agreements will sometimes establish a value based on accounting book value per share measures, ignoring the inclusion of any goodwill value, even though other valuation techniques clearly demonstrate the existence of goodwill value. The family law attorney will vigorously argue on behalf of the shareholder spouse that book value is all he or she can receive and that goodwill value is irrelevant. This view is not necessarily universally accepted by the courts. Whether a buy-sell value will prevail in a family law setting that is at odds with other valuation methods varies from state to state. Therefore, a valuator should address this issue with the attorney involved.

Problems can arise, however, when either the buying or selling party is upset with a formula-derived value that does not accurately reflect the true value of the business. Problems also arise if the buying and selling parties cannot agree on how the buy-sell specifies that the value be calculated. All of these issues make the buy-sell agreement a potentially contentious issue for a business valuator.

Bankruptcies

Business valuators are often used when private companies become bankrupt. Potential valuation services include the valuation of a business to determine an allocation to creditors or as part of a proposed reorganization plan. In valuing businesses within these scenarios, the valuator must consider the value of the business from the perspective of the creditor(s). For companies that are troubled financially, the valuator may appropriately place more emphasis on the cost approach to valuation as opposed to the income or market approach. Because creditors generally have the option of looking to collateral as a secondary source of repayment for their loan, they may possess many of the same attributes of control as the majority or 100-percent owner of a business. Given this power possessed by the creditors, one may appropriately value the business on a 100-percent control basis.

Bankruptcy valuations also can view fair market value in a hypothetical vacuum. For example, the court might direct that the valuation ignore a company's crushing debt load and value it as if the company had a normal level of debt. This approach enables a court to decide how to allocate the going concern value to the various classes of creditors.

Business Damages

Business damages cases generally arise in a litigation context. A typical case involves a plaintiff business owner who alleges that someone or something caused a diminution in his or her private company's value. Generally, the plaintiff asks for business damages measured by the difference between what the company would have been worth without the damages and what the company is actually worth. Business damages disputes call for creative valuation solutions because of the difficulty of estimating the difference between a business's actual value and its hypothetical value.

Common methodologies include the extrapolation of company performance from the before-damages period throughout the period of damages. This process may be as simple as forecasting lost revenue that resulted from the damages; however, the valuation also may require a forecast of the alleged damages' effect on the operating structure and margins of the company. Alternative valuation methods include the comparative analysis of the damaged company to companies in the same or similar industries.

In any case, valuations involving business damages unavoidably involve some subjective degree of analysis and/or forecasting. A business valuator must be able to logically support his or her conclusions. This support is particularly true for valuators engaged by the plaintiff because they shoulder the burden of proof on business damages. See Chapter 10 for more information about commercial damages.

Medical Practice Acquisitions by Tax-exempt Entities

One field in valuation that has seen explosive growth over the past decade is medical practice acquisition by hospitals. This acquisition activity is driven by several forces, including the continued consolidation of healthcare providers in the country, as well as continued private and public pressure to control ever-increasing health care costs. In many situations, the acquiring hospitals are not-for-profit organizations that must follow strict federal and regulatory guidelines to preserve their tax-exempt status. Failure to follow these guidelines can generate serious tax and legal ramifications for both the selling and acquiring parties.

The Three Valuation Approaches

Like the valuation of real estate, business valuation boils down to three basic approaches: income, market, and cost.

¶ 17,051   **INCOME APPROACH**[9]

There are numerous methods within the income approach category, including capitalization of income, excess earnings, discounted future income, discounted future cash flow, and others.

Capitalization of Income Method

All capitalization methods estimate value by converting a company's estimated future income stream into value. This conversion is accomplished through application of an appropriate capitalization rate, which incorporates both an investor's required rate of return for risk, and a factor for future growth in income. The resulting value is ultimately based on the present worth, today, of anticipated benefits the buyer will receive in the future (in the form of income, cash flow, or dividends). An offshoot of the Gordon-Shapiro dividend discount valuation model, the capitalization of an income stream is a single-period valuation approach.[10]

Discounted Future Income Method

Discounted projected future income methods involve projecting the possible future income streams (e.g., earnings, cash flow) on a year-by-year basis, usually for five or seven years. Future income streams are then discounted at an appropriate discount rate (required rate of return on investment for risk) required by a buyer, back to a present value. For the final projection year, a terminal value is determined that represents the estimated value for the sale of the company at that time. This terminal value is then discounted back (at the discount rate) to its present value. The summation of the present value of both the income streams and the terminal value yields a fair market value estimate of the company.

When an "invested capital" approach is employed, the income streams are discounted to present value at a "weighted average cost of capital," a measure incorporating the costs of debt and equity. The resulting value represents the value for the total capitalization of the company, including debt and equity. From this value, the total present value of debt is subtracted in order to obtain the fair market value of equity in the company benefiting common shareholders.

The value is the sum of the present values of the annual income streams and the capitalized future sale (or *terminal value*) of the company.

If a company's income or cash flow is growing at a constant rate into perpetuity, the previous method does not need to be employed because the formula is then mathematically equivalent to the results achieved by the capitalization approach discussed earlier. However, when a company is experiencing a near-term rate of growth that is above a sustainable long-term trend, or when there are cyclical or unusual near-term factors that are influencing results (and which can be reasonably predicted), this method can more reliably capture the impact of those changes on valuation than a capitalization approach.

Discounted Future Cash Flow Method

The discounted future cash flow method is nearly identical to the discounted future income method described earlier. The essential difference between the two methods is that the discounted future cash flow method requires the estimation and projection of a company's future cash flows. This process requires the consideration of a company's noncash charges (such as depreciation and amortization), a company's working capital needs, anticipated capital expenditures and related depreciation schedules, the retirement or assumption of debt, and other associated calls on company cash flows. After this process, the methodology and procedure are identical to the future earnings method. One important adjustment the valuator must make is to be sure the discount rate employed is applicable to cash flows (as opposed to earnings or some other income measure).

Capitalization of Excess Earnings Method

The excess earnings (formula) method is really a hybrid of the cost and income approaches because it involves the determination of the portion of the earnings that may be attributed separately to the tangible and intangible assets of a company. This method is available to estimate intangible value.

This method involves the following steps:

1. Multiply the net tangible assets of the company by the rate of return such assets might reasonably be required to earn.
2. Deduct this estimate of earnings from the total earnings to derive that portion of the earnings that might be attributed to the intangible assets.
3. Divide the earnings attributed to intangibles by a capitalization rate for intangibles to estimate the total value attributed to the intangibles.
4. Sum the value attributed to intangibles and the market value of the net tangible assets of the firm to estimate an overall fair market value.

EYEWITNESS

Michael Paschall from Banister Financial, Inc., a business valuation firm, states, "The IRS indicates that this method should only be used as a last resort when better methods are not available. In practice, this method has a significant number of logical flaws and inconsistencies in its application. This method has been heavily criticized by the IRS and the business valuation community and is rarely, if ever, used any more. In fact, the use of this method is usually a strong indication of an unsophisticated business appraiser who is out of touch with current valuation methodologies."

¶ 17,061   MARKET APPROACH[11]

Some of the numerous market approaches include the identification of comparable publicly traded companies whose securities sell on a free and open market, the examination of definitive and verifiable transaction data available on actual sales of similar privately held concerns, the existence of actual or potential markets for a security, such as buy-sell or shareholder agreements, and past transactions in the shares or other interests in the business itself.

Guideline (Public Company) Method

Under the guideline (public company) method, the valuator seeks to identify publicly traded companies in the same or a similar line of business as the subject private company. The assumption is that a private company in the same line of business as public companies is influenced by the same economic, industry, and market conditions. Therefore, one may reasonably assume that a public company's prices and multiples should be a reasonable proxy of a private company's prices. This comparison, however, is not done on a *pari passu* basis because there likely are numerous differences between the public comparables and the private company that the valuator must take into consideration. Some of these considerations include size differences (assets and revenues) between the public comparables and the private company, differences in accounting methods used, the degree of marketability of the public shares, the size and control features of the private shares being valued, differences in company operations, and many more.

Market Data Method

Another useful method under the market valuation approach is to analyze recent sales of entire companies that are in the same line of business as the subject private company. As with the public market for trades of very small minority interests (the guideline method just described), market data on what 100-percent controlling interests of companies are selling for can also lend insight into the value of the subject private company. As with the guideline method, however, direct application of sale multiples is probably not appropriate to the subject private company due to the considerations mentioned earlier. Detailed analysis is required by the valuator to ensure that differences between the company sale data and the subject private company are properly accounted for in the valuation estimate.

Past Transactions Method

A third useful method under the market valuation approach is to examine past transactions in the shares of the private company. Share liquidity is a spectrum that ranges from companies whose shares have not, do not, and are not expected to trade at all to companies whose shares trade daily by the hundreds of thousands on national, public exchanges. Some "privately held" companies do experience some trading activity among their shares. Other "public company" shares trade quite infrequently through local market makers or as noted in such publications as the "pink sheets." Some private companies may create their own "market" for the shares by offering to match up willing sellers with willing buyers.

Past transactions in the shares of a company can be useful indicators of value if the trades were recent enough, were under a true arm's length relationship, and were not forced, coerced, or dictated by a prearranged formula. In using past trade data, a valuator must be careful to inquire into and analyze the circumstances surrounding each prior trade. Many times in the private company context, trades among shareholders are intrafamily transfers, distress sales by financially strapped shareholders, or forced sales dictated by a formula. Shares trading under these and similar circumstances may not meet the appropriate criteria (such as fair market value) for valuation of the subject private company's shares.

¶ 17,071   COST APPROACH[12]

The cost approach involves adjusting a company's assets and liabilities up or down to reflect their "fair market value." This method considers tangible and intangible assets and any contingent liabilities. Although tangible assets can be appraised and their actual balance sheet values adjusted to reflect those results accordingly, the major problem with this method is dealing with the valuation of the intangible assets, such as the company's name, reputation, trained workforce, and other factors.

The cost approach is a suitable approach for valuation only in the context of a liquidation of a company. The implication of a cost approach that generates a value higher than values generated by the income or market approaches is that the company may be worth more "dead" than "alive." In other words, the economically logical course of action to take to maximize value would be to sell the assets of the company, pay off the liabilities, and distribute the proceeds to the shareholders. To continue to operate the business under this scenario is an inefficient and illogical use of economic resources.

Book Value: Not Really a Valuation Method

In accounting terms, *book value* is the difference between total assets and total liabilities. Alternatively, book value is known as "net worth" or "equity." Although book value may be of some use when used in conjunction with other valuation measures (such as the "price to book value" of public comparables), as a stand-alone measure, book value is generally of little use in valuing a business. The primary reason for its uselessness is that book value is basically an accounting convention that has little or nothing to do with the actual value of a company. Many companies may have had significant land and improvements on their balance sheet for many years. Over time, the land value remains unchanged on the company's balance sheet while the value of the improvements is depreciated to zero. If the land and improvements have appreciated over time and are in fact quite valuable, the book value significantly understates the value of the company. Similar problems arise with potential differences between actual and book values of other assets and liabilities.

Adjusted Book Value (Adjusted Net Asset Value)

If a cost method approach to valuation is appropriate, adjusted book value provides a much more accurate method of valuation. In its most basic sense, the adjusted book value method calls for an item-by-item adjustment of each balance sheet component (both assets and liabilities). In addition, the estimation or reservation for anticipated windfalls or liabilities is an integral part of adjusted book value.

Tangible Assets

Tangible assets include physical assets and liabilities that can actually be seen or touched (such as inventory and fixed assets) or can be evidenced by documentation that verifies their existence (such as investments, receivables, payables, and bank debt). Adjustment of tangible assets can take several forms. As previously mentioned, some tangible assets (such as land or fixed assets) can be adjusted from their book value to their appraised value. Other tangible assets, such as accounts receivable, can be valued based on their estimated collectibility. Assets such as corporate debt can be valued based on their existing interest rate and repayment schedule, as compared to the similarly risky publicly traded debt instruments on the market.

Intangible Assets

Intangible assets are those assets of a company that cannot be verified in a physical sense, yet still add value to a business. Examples of intangible assets include:

- Name
- Company reputation
- The existence of a skilled and trained workforce
- Customer base
- Patents and trademarks

As compared to tangible assets, intangible assets can be far more difficult to value for the business valuator. Challenges arise with the analysis of such issues as:

- What would the company be worth with a different name?
- What would the value be without this particular patent?

Valuation techniques for intangible assets vary widely. One technique is the capitalization of estimated value derived from the intangible asset. Another is "what-if" analysis, where the company is valued as it exists today, and compared to its estimated value as if a certain intangible asset had never been associated with the business.

Gathering Initial Information[13]

The two most important parts of any valuation assignment are the preparation before the company interview and the focus and depth of the interview itself. Every company is unique. Although corporations, partnerships, and limited liability companies (LLCs) are merely legal creations, each business is its own mix of management, people, customers, suppliers, competition, industry, regulations, and numerous other internal and external factors. These elements come together in unique ways to make the company what it has been, what it is today, and what it might become in the future. The valuator's job is to identify how these elements are present in a specific company and to discern what each implies about the risks, opportunities, and future of the business from the viewpoint of a buyer.

Unlike the shareholders and management of a company, the business valuator is an outsider looking inside, albeit for a brief amount of time. Therefore, the valuator must quickly identify key risk factors and opportunities and how they impact the company's valuation. Details are important, but a valuator also must not get lost in the minutiae and miss the big picture. The most substantial risks and opportunities facing most businesses usually come down to a handful of critical issues. The ability to identify these issues depends on the thoroughness of the valuation effort.

¶ 17,081   INITIAL INFORMATION REQUEST[14]

Prior to the management interview, a valuator performs an initial analysis to prepare the appropriate questions to be asked. Because every company is different, some of the items might not apply to a specific assignment, and additional items might be added after consideration of the specific issues raised at the time of the initial pre-engagement contact with the client.

Goals of Pre-engagement Phone Contact

In the initial pre-engagement phone contact with a client, the valuator should gain a broad understanding of the company's activities. The information needs list can then be modified with any unique needs before it is transmitted to the client. Pre-engagement phone conversations with the client should be aimed at reaching the following goals:

- *Develop trust and rapport.* Clients are asked to share a substantial amount of confidential information they might not even share with their banker, accountant, or perhaps even their spouse about the business. Proactively assure the client that any information requested will be kept confidential. Additionally, establish a dialogue with clients.

One of the best ways to start is to ask clients how they started the business, since most owners enjoy sharing this information with others.

- *Gain a brief understanding of the business.* In order to ensure that the information needs list is complete, obtain a brief overview of the company. The following questions are helpful:
  - Obtain a brief overview of what the company does and how it is done. Who are its customers and suppliers? Is there any major change about to occur that is different than what gave rise to the firm's historic financial results? (If a major change has just occurred, or is about to occur, the valuator must request additional information on the impact of the change.)
  - How cyclical is the business and why? When was the last downturn experienced? (These questions help in determining how many years of financials to request to see the full industry cycle.)
- *Determine who will be responsible for gathering information.* Because the information needs list is broad and covers a variety of areas (financial, legal, etc.), ask the client who will be responsible for gathering the data (chief financial officer, controller, outside accountant, law firm, etc.). This tells the valuator who to contact if there is a delay in receiving information, and for follow-up purposes to see whether any questions have arisen on the data that is being requested. Information needs lists have a habit of sitting in an in-box somewhere in an organization, and are often low on an individual's "to do" list, because this information is not fun to gather and copy. Knowing who is gathering the data allows follow-up by the valuator to make sure the project does not languish.
- *Explaining the valuation process and timing.* Many clients have never had their company valued, have no clue about the valuation process or timing, and may be intimidated by the process. Explain the nature of the information needs list, its role in gaining a clear picture of the business, and how it will be used to prepare for the company interview. Additionally, because information needs lists are generic, the client should be told not to be surprised to find items on the list that are not applicable. If so, they should not be concerned and should move on to the next item. Additionally, the valuator can tell clients to call once the list is received to go over any questions they might have and to avoid any misunderstanding of what is being requested. Finally, explain the timing of meeting with the client for the interview once the information has been received, and then the expected time for an issuance of a draft valuation report for client review.
- *Methods of corresponding with the client.* A valuation is a confidential matter; therefore, find out how the client wants the valuator to handle correspondence, faxes, e-mail, phone messages, and voicemail messages pertaining to the assignment. For example:
  - *Mail.* Should mail be sent to the business or the individual's home to avoid the possibility that someone at the company might inadvertently open it? If items should be sent to the home, what is the address? Do clients have individuals they wish to receive copies of all correspondence, such as their estate or corporate attorney?
  - *Faxes.* Is it acceptable to fax questions or correspondence to the company? If so, is there a special fax number that should be used? Should the valuator call and receive approval before each fax to ensure that the appropriate person can stand by the fax machine to receive confidential information?
  - *E-mail.* Do clients prefer correspondence by e-mail? Is the e-mail read by others in the company who might not be authorized to see this type of sensitive correspondence? While corresponding by e-mail yields a significant time advantage, unless files of sensitive data are encrypted, there is a risk that unauthorized persons could gain access to the information. Even encryption is not foolproof.
  - *Phone messages.* Is it acceptable to leave detailed phone messages with a secretary, and if so, with whom?
  - *Voicemail messages.* If the client has voicemail, is it acceptable to leave confidential messages on that system?

¶ 17,091   DISCERNING WHAT DATA IS REQUIRED[15]

Request Forecasts of Future Financial Results

One of the items on the information needs list is a request for the client to provide copies of forecasts of a company's future financial results. The larger the company, the greater the likelihood that forecasts have been prepared or that management has the expertise to prepare them. However, many small and mid-sized closely held businesses have never prepared forecasts, and may lack the sophistication or the willingness to do so. This factor means that the burden of developing forecasts may fall on the shoulders of the valuator. Just because there are no forecasts does not absolve the valuator from the responsibility of preparing them. Remember that the income valuation approach is based on the worth, in today's dollars, of a company's expected future income streams. If income streams are expected to be different than a company's past results, forecasts will be crucial in arriving at the value impact through the use of the discounted future income method.

Review Articles on Industry-related Valuation Issues

If the valuator has limited experience with valuations in an industry, articles on the industry-related valuation issues might be reviewed to determine if there are unique factors in the industry that warrant additional information needs. A good place to start would be to review past issues of valuation periodicals, such as *Business Valuation Review*, *Valuation Examiner*, and *Shannon Pratt's Business Valuation Update*, to see if past articles have been written on valuing companies in that industry or profession.

Request Client Information Prior to Company Interviews

Clients are eager to have valuations prepared quickly, and often have unrealistic expectations of the time requirements. Rather than sending information to the valuator for a prior review, clients prefer to give it to the appraiser at the time of the company interview. This is ill advised. Few people can scan through a variety of financial and other documents and then ask appropriate questions. Important issues will be overlooked, the valuator will be unprepared, and the interview will be a waste of everyone's time.

Financial Analysis[16]

A thorough financial analysis is an important aspect of any valuation assignment. Examining the financial condition and performance of a company provides crucial insight into its risks, the factors that impacted its historic results, and what this portends about the future. A purchaser of a company is always looking forward and assessing the risks and rewards associated with owning shares in the business. Although a company's history is not guaranteed to repeat itself, the analysis of past results assists valuators in identifying forces internal and external to the business that may impact future performance.

¶ 17,101   HOW MUCH HISTORY IS ENOUGH?[17]

In order to begin a financial statement analysis, a valuator needs sufficient years of historical financial statements to provide an accurate picture of the business, and to identify positive or negative trends. Valuation firms, banks, and other creditors often request the last five years of financial statements. However, five years is an arbitrary number, and is sometimes insufficient to gain perspective on broad and long-term financial trends.

For example, if a company is in a cyclical industry, five years may not be enough to see all aspects of the cycle, including the peak and the trough. Another problem is that abnormally long economic expansions obscure the presence of cycles.

Homebuilding exemplifies a cyclical industry because it tends to have periods of booms and busts tied to the general economy, interest rates, and other macroeconomic forces. The last few years represent the "boom" part of the cycle. If information only for those years is requested, the valuator might erroneously conclude that the financial trends are always onward and upward. In the next few months, the bust portion of the cycle may occur, devastating the industry and its participants, causing a sharp contraction in revenues and profitability (perhaps even losses), and forcing a significant number of homebuilders to go bankrupt.

Thinking in broad terms about what drives an industry and whether it might be cyclical is helpful in deciding how many years of financial information is enough. In the initial phone contact with a client, valuators should ask whether there are cyclical aspects to the company, and when the current cycle last turned up or down. Then the investigator should request financials going back at least several years prior to those dates to capture the full length of the cycle. A client will often have a good understanding of the typical length of an industry cycle.

¶ 17,111   SPREADING FINANCIAL STATEMENTS[18]

It is difficult to discern broad trends over time or to put the results in perspective by merely looking at a company's printed financial statements. "Spreading" a company's historic financial statements provides an added level of insight in a simple, yet powerful way. Spreading financial statements involves putting the results in a common format that is more easily reviewed and analyzed. Financial spreadsheet reports include:

- Actual and common-sized income statements and balance sheets
- Financial statement ratios
- Trend analyses

Actual and Common-Sized Income Statements

Placing a company's historic annual income statements side-by-side enables the trends and variations over time to be identified. "Common-sized" means that each revenue and expense item is shown in terms of its relationship to the overall revenues of the business (i.e., expressed as a percentage of total annual net revenues). In the common-sized report, revenues, costs of goods sold, and later operating expenses are shown both in dollar terms and as a percentage of net revenues. Then, other income and expense items are detailed, followed by the net profit of the company.

Actual and Common-Sized Balance Sheets

Common-sized balance sheets are much like their income statement counterpart, with the only difference being that each asset, liability, and shareholders' equity dollar item is shown as a percentage of the company's total assets.

Financial Statement Ratios

Financial statement ratios enable the valuator to spot the individual results of the income statement and the balance sheet, both separately and in terms of how the statements are linked together. The ratios help forensic practitioners to assess the company's performance and financial risks, and to identify positive and negative trends.

Trend Statements

Trend statements are an important tool in analyzing the income statements and balance sheet results of a company. Trend statements show the actual dollar amount of changes for key income, expense, and balance sheet items over time, in terms of actual dollars, and on the basis of the annual rate of increase or decrease.

¶ 17,121   ANALYZING FINANCIAL STATEMENTS FOR TRENDS AND RISKS[19]

The purpose of analyzing a company's historic financial statements is to provide information about these factors that are crucial in the preparation of a valid valuation:

- Trends and what they say about the possible future. Although the future might not resemble the past, past trends and actual results provide insight into what the future might look like.
- How well or how poorly a company performs compared to industry peers. Knowing that a client company makes a five-percent pretax profit margin says little about how well or poorly the company is managed if it cannot be compared against some meaningful yardstick. Using financial performance and ratio studies from a company's specific industry allows meaningful comparisons and conclusions concerning a company's performance, and provides insight into its strengths, weaknesses, and risks.
- Key elements of company strategy. Analyzing historic results gives a clearer perspective of how the company operates. Such an analysis provides an indication of the company's financial reliance on customers, suppliers, and banks. Finally, this analysis helps valuators determine whether a company's approach is financially more or less risky than industry peers.

Sources of Industry Financial and Ratio Information

Perhaps the most comprehensive source of information on financial statements and credit analysis by industry is Risk Management Association (RMA), a national banking industry association. Financial statement and credit analysis is the lifeblood of RMA's member banks, which must make daily decisions about which companies to finance, the risks associated with extending credit, and the prospects that loans can be repaid. RMA has an array of publications on credit and financial analysis, including literally hundreds of articles on specific industry analysis.

RMA also produces *Annual Statement Studies,* an annual ratio publication that is a required publication for any valuation practice. Based on data submitted by thousands of member banks, the publication contains financial performance and ratio data on companies in hundreds of industry classifications, with the data stratified by company size (based on either total annual revenues or total assets). Such data is essential as a yardstick to help assess the financial performance and risk of a private company being valued. The study is available in print and electronic formats, and optional regional ratio editions can also be purchased.

An equally valuable part of the *Annual Statement Studies* is an element many business appraisers who use it daily frequently overlook. Near the end of the publication is a detailed, comprehensive list of financial statement ratio and compensation surveys available from literally hundreds of different industry and professional associations, covering different unique industry segments.[20]

Income Statement Profitability Analysis

A company's net profit (or net earnings) on its income statement is the result of revenues, costs of the goods sold (or services provided), and operating expenses. How these elements combine to produce the resulting net income depends on numerous factors, such as management's skill, the impact of competition, industry forces, the economy, pressures from customers and suppliers, and other issues that may affect all companies or are unique to a specific company. Income statement profitability analysis helps valuators determine the following:

- Judgments about the historic performance of the company and the variability of results. This step provides insight into the risks associated with the business and the earnings outlook.
- Results against which to assess management's strengths and weaknesses, and how this would impact an investor's perception of the shares as an investment, and their associated risk.

- An objective basis for comparing a company's performance relative to its industry peers. This step assists valuators in determining the relative attractiveness of the company as an investment.
- Insight into a company's economics and how the business achieves its net profit on a given level of revenues. This step assists valuators in identifying fixed and variable cost components in the company's operating structure. Understanding these elements assists valuators in preparing more reliable forecasts of earnings and cash flow for use in the discounted future income valuation method.
- Clues concerning the internal and external forces that affect the business, and what this suggests about risk, future threats, and opportunities. Spotting trends and changes in the income statement enables the development of questions to pinpoint the causes of observed changes, and to determine their significance to the valuation process.

¶ 17,131   REVENUES[21]

Without revenues there is ultimately no business, no need for employees, and no reason to exist. Additionally, many of a company's expenses are directly or indirectly tied to generating revenues. Given this important role, factors that influence a company's historic actual revenues must be understood, along with what they suggest about the future.

Before one delves into the detail behind a company's actual reported revenue numbers, one should first look at historic trends.

Next, using the common-sized income statement, efforts are made to discern any noticeable trends or issues that might be apparent related to the company's level of returns and allowances, that is, products that were sold to its customers but later returned, or for which allowances were given to the customer. If observations suggest that the company is indeed cyclical, management should be asked whether cyclical forces are present. If so, the valuator must ascertain where the company presently stands in its cycle and ask management what it believes are good indicators of the near and intermediate term outlook, and why. Furthermore, it is important to understand why returns and allowances are increasing in recent years. The forensic practitioner would want to address the following issues with management:

- Is the high level of returns a function of problems with product quality?
- Has the company changed its return policies?
- Is industry and customer demand slowing, forcing the company to accept returns from customers who are themselves experiencing slowing growth? Is this an indicator that the company and its industry are about to enter a cyclical downturn?

Essentially, the analysis of revenues is largely commonsense, involving the consideration of past trends, growth rates, the variability in individual annual results, and overall observed results, and the identification of the appropriate questions. Additionally, revenue analysis raises issues the valuator may need to explore through industry research. What do the answers imply about the company's outlook? Finally, what do these revenue-related issues indicate about the level of risk associated with owning shares in the company?

¶ 17,141   GROSS PROFITS[22]

Gross profits of a business represent the actual profit realized on the sale of a company's goods or services after taking into account the expenses associated with the cost of producing the product or service, but before considering the impact of general and administrative and other types of costs.

Components of Cost of Goods Sold

The components that make up the calculation of cost of goods sold can differ materially, depending upon the type of enterprise. For example, a wholesaler's only cost included may be the product the company purchases from its suppliers. However, in a manufacturing business, cost of goods sold may include the cost of raw materials purchased from others; labor, factory, and other costs incurred to produce the product; and depreciation expense.

Calculating Cost of Goods Sold

The valuator needs to determine how cost of goods sold is calculated, and whether that calculation differs from that used by competitors in the industry. If it differs, comparisons of the company's performance with industry financial ratios become more difficult. Also, what type of inventory accounting method is used: last-in-first-out (LIFO), first-in-first-out (FIFO), or some other method?

Analyzing Gross Profit

As with revenues, the same aims of financial statement analysis are present for assessing a company's gross profit. This involves the consideration of past trends, growth rates, and the variability in individual and overall observed results. The "gross profit margin" is computed by dividing gross profit (net revenues less cost of goods sold) by net revenues, with the margin expressed as a percentage. In beginning the process of analyzing the gross profit margins, it helps to compare the common-sized income statement data of the company against industry peer average results.

Industry data and comparisons studies are used as a general guideline, and not as absolute industry norms. In these industry studies, data is organized by standard industrial classification (SIC) codes; a review of the industry descriptions at the front of the RMA publication suggest the SIC code fit for the company being valued. SIC codes are gradually being replaced by the North American Industrial Classification System (NAICS) codes. Initially developed in 1997, the five-digit NAICS codes offer far more detail and specification of industry classification than the four-digit SIC codes.

¶ 17,151   OPERATING EXPENSES[23]

A company's ability to manage operating expenses can be a critical variable impacting its overall profitability. Even if the company has a strong revenue base and gross profit margins on its sales, if it does not control its operating expenses it will experience poor operating profits, or perhaps even losses.

The company's operating expenses, expressed as a percentage of revenues, will be compared to the industry average.

¶ 17,161   OPERATING PROFITS[24]

Operating profits represent the gross profit of a business, less its operating expenses, but before taking into account other income and expenses, and income taxes. The amount of a company's debt affects its interest expense and reported profits. Because operating profit measures are taken into account before interest and taxes, they allow the company's underlying profitability to be analyzed without respect to how the company is financed.

¶ 17,171   OTHER INCOME AND EXPENSE[25]

The practitioner will also compare the company's net other income (or expense) levels with the industry average.

¶ 17,181   PRETAX PROFITABILITY[26]

The pretax profit margin is a measure of the profitability of a company after taking into account all revenues and expenses except income taxes. This margin is calculated by dividing the company's pretax profit by revenues, and is expressed as a percentage. The higher the pretax profit margin, the more pretax profit the company earns on each dollar of sales, and vice versa.

Practical Illustrations

Virtually all business valuation methods use the company's financial statements over some period of time and/or at some point in time. This section applies concepts, approaches, and methods described throughout the chapter to the valuation of hypothetical businesses, such as the Fenton Trucking Company.

¶ 17,191 EARNINGS HISTORY

To illustrate the process, five years of financial information for the Fenton Trucking Company are presented in Table 17.1, showing income statement data for the five years ending December 31, 2009, through December 31, 2013. Many practitioners believe that income statements provide the most useful information in valuing profitable operating businesses. Indeed, Revenue Ruling 59-60 indicates that earnings should be the most important element in valuing operating businesses.[27] Many practitioners prefer some form of earnings model or discounted cash flow model for purposes of valuing businesses. The common belief is that earnings and cash flow business valuation models are the best methods for predicting future streams of cash inflows to investors. In some circumstances, however, earning data may not be the most appropriate valuation method.

Table 17.1. Fenton Trucking Company Income Statements for the Years Ending 12/31/09 Through 12/31/13

	2009	2010	2011	2012	2013
Revenue	$6,000,000	$5,600,000	$5,800,000	$6,700,000	$7,100,000
Operating exp.					
Vehicle exp.	3,100,000	2,700,000	2,800,000	3,300,000	3,450,000
Other oper exp.	1,400,000	1,420,000	1,320,000	1,550,000	1,700,000
Admin and mark. exp.	1,210,000	1,200,000	1,230,000	1,320,000	1,320,000
Total oper. Exp.	5,710,000	5,320,000	5,350,000	6,170,000	6,470,000
Income from oper.	290,000	280,000	450,000	530,000	630,000
Other rev. or gains:					
Gain on sale of assets	130,000	150,000	0	190,000	110,000
Other exp. or losses:					
Int. on bonds pay	90,000	90,000	90,000	90,000	90,000
Loss on sale of assets			110,000		
Income before taxes	330,000	340,000	250,000	630,000	650,000
Income taxes	130,000	25,000	150,000	170,000	190,000
Net income	$200,000	$315,000	$100,000	$460,000	$460,000

¶ 17,201 INCOME STATEMENT METHODS OF DETERMINING A BUSINESS VALUATION

Earnings measures of valuation are preferred because they are presumed to provide the best surrogate for cash inflows to the business over the life of the business. Although assets clearly play an important role in a business's ability to generate profits and provide cash inflows over the life of the business, many experts argue that a firm's earnings as presented in its income statements are the *real* testament to the effectiveness, or lack thereof, of the use of those assets. But merely stating that earnings are the key factor in business valuation does not immediately provide an answer about the value of the business. By their very nature, earnings only cover a period of time, usually one year.

Table 17.2 presents a five-year earnings history for Fenton Trucking Company. The earnings during the five years vary from a low of $100,000 to a high of $460,000.

Table 17.2. Fenton Trucking Company Income Summary for the Years Ending 12/31/09 Through 12/31/13

Year	Income
2009	$200,000
2010	315,000
2011	100,000
2012	460,000
2013	460,000

Using a series of years' earnings is logical because it gives a more realistic picture of the company's earnings ability over an extended period of time. Using five years of earnings data adjusts or smooths out the effects of an unusual earnings performance. For example, the earnings in the year 2011 are much lower than for the other four years. By using five years of earnings data in the analysis, the valuator can reduce the impact of the lower earnings using four other years whose earnings appear to be more normal for the firm. Some may argue that the $100,000 earnings indicates 2011 was an outlier year for earnings, and that year's income should not be included at all in the analysis. Others might state the opinion that Fenton has some bad years in the normal course of its business and that omitting bad years from the valuation analysis would result in an overstatement of the firm's value.

Calculating Average Earnings

If the valuator uses the firm's five-year earning history to determine the value of the business, sum the earnings from 2009 through 2013 to get total earnings for the period—in this case, $1,535,000 ($200,000 + $315,000 + $100,000 + $460,000 + $460,000). Next the valuator divides the total earnings to find the average earnings for the five-year period, $1,535,000 ÷ 5 years = $307,000.

Capitalizing Earnings

Applying a Discount Rate

Next the valuator determines what discount rate to use to capitalize the earnings. The discount rate is the inverse of the price earnings ratio. Because the valuator is, in effect, looking for the price/value of the company, other similar firms are compared to determine the appropriate price earnings ratio. Assuming that there are six firms that have similar size and operating characteristics to Fenton Trucking Company, their price earnings ratios currently range from 6 to 8 with an average of 7. The valuator then multiplies the average earnings of Fenton ($307,000) by the average price earnings ratio of similar companies, 7, to get a valuation of $2,149,000 ($307,000 × 7). Alternatively, the valuator can divide 7 into 1 to get a capitalization rate of 0.142857143. This rate is used to capitalize earnings as follows: $307,000 ÷ 0.142857143 = $2,149,000. The capitalization rate is often used to determine a percentage rate by which a steady stream of income is divided to find the value of a business. One can capitalize net income, pretax income, income before interest, or any base.

Weighted Values

The valuation approach just used gives equal weight to Fenton's earnings for each of the five years of data. In other words, the amount of earnings in 2009 was given just as much weight in determining the valuation of the business and the earnings of the most recent year. Many practitioners, however, believe that more recent earnings data are more indicative of a business's potential for future earnings and cash flows. In such situations, practitioners may choose to give more recent earnings figures more weight and earlier earnings figures less weight in determining the value of the business. This weighting can be done in a variety of ways. The practitioner can use whatever weighting scale he or she desires, but a very simple and easy way is to give the most recent year a weight of five and the earliest year a weight of one. Table 17.3 presents one weighting scale for the Fenton Trucking Company income for the five years used in the valuation.

Table 17.3. Fenton Trucking Company Weighting Scale for Income for the Years Ending 12/31/09 Through 12/31/13

Year	Income	Weight	Total
2009	$200,000	1	$200,000
2010	315,000	2	630,000
2011	100,000	3	300,000
2012	460,000	4	1,840,000
2013	460,000	5	2,300,000
Total		15	$5,270,000

The calculation is as follows:

Average annual earnings, weighting most recent earnings heavier = $5,270,000 ÷ 15 = $351,333

Using the same average price earnings ratio of 7 to capitalize the average earnings, the valuator gets a valuation of $2,459,333 ($351,333 × 7). The increase in the estimated value of the business is about $300,000 caused by the fact that recent annual earnings were higher than those of earlier years. The computed value of a firm using earnings models usually provides a value that is somewhat different from the book value of the firm at the date of valuation. This result is common because accounting treatments for inventory valuations, fixed asset depreciation, nonpurchased goodwill, and other items often result in differences between accounting book values and fair market value for a business.

In attempting to value a business, a forensic practitioner must consider the nature and quality of the firm's earnings. If management is aggressive in its efforts to earn a desired level of profit, there may be questions about when and how much revenue should be recognized during the period and questions about whether all expenses that have been incurred are actually recorded. If there is some question about the quality of the earnings, the practitioner may need to reflect that in the valuation. In the extreme, exceptionally aggressive accounting practices can result in fraudulent financial reporting. In such cases, the company's financial statements may be less useful for purposes of business valuations.

Another issue is the distinction between operating income and income from other sources. For the Fenton Trucking Company, the firm had a material amount of gains and losses from the sale of assets. Here the gains and losses resulted primarily from the sale of trucks the company used in its business. The company reported gains on the sale of trucks during four years and a loss on the sale of assets during one year. Averaging the amounts of gains and losses over the five years, the average gain is $94,000 per year ($130,000 − $110,000 + $150,000 + $190,000 + $110,000) ÷ 5 years = $94,000. The average annual earnings used for this valuation analysis was net income after taxes, so the average annual pretax gain on the sale of assets of $94,000 should be adjusted to an after-tax basis. For Fenton Trucking, that would translate into about $66,000 per year on an after-tax basis.

What should be done with the $66,000 average after-tax gain on the sale of assets? Some would argue to do nothing because the company experiences gains on the sale of its assets on a regular basis. As a result, these gains should be considered a normal component of bottom-line net income and should be treated like the operating income components of the income statement. Other valuation practitioners might argue that these gains are not as indicative of the firm's ability to sustain earnings during a longer period of time. Thus, the gains and losses on the sale of assets should be discounted or, in the extreme, ignored in the valuation analysis. To ignore the gains and losses altogether would have a significant impact on this valuation of

Fenton Trucking. For example, in the first valuation calculation of Fenton Trucking, the earnings were weighted equally for the five-year period. By ignoring the gains and losses on the sale of assets in making the business valuation calculation, the valuator would average total earnings *minus* the average after-tax gains and losses *times* the price earnings ratio ($307,000 – $66,000) × 7 = $1,687,000. This value is $462,000 less than the original valuation.

¶ 17,211   CASH FLOW METHODS OF DETERMINING THE BUSINESS VALUATION

Discounted Cash Flow Method

The discounted cash flow (DCF) valuation method is a favorite among many practitioners. Typically, the cash flow used in the valuation process is *free cash flow,* the after-tax operating earnings of the company + noncash charges – investments in operating working capital, property, plant, and equipment, and other assets.[28] However, there is no consensus as to the definition of free cash flow or even cash flow.[29]

Palepu, Healy, and Bernard, the authors of *Business Analysis & Valuation Using Financial Statements*, suggest these three steps in calculating discounted cash flow methods:

1. Forecast the free cash flows available over a finite period (e.g., 5–10 years),
2. Forecast the cash flows beyond the terminal period using some simplifying assumption, and
3. Discount the free cash flows.[30]

The discount rate is an amount expressed in a percentage that a buyer will pay to receive some estimated level of cash in the future, given the level of risk of not receiving the future cash flows. The higher the risk, the higher the discount rate, which results in lower current values. Discount rate is the inverse of the price earnings (P/E) ratio. Say six firms have P/E ratios ranging from 6 to 8, with an average of 7. For example, if average earnings are $293,000, valuation is $2,051,000 ($293,000 × 7). Or a capitalization rate of 1/7 = 0.142857143 means $293,000 ÷ 0.142857143 = $2,051,000. If the capitalization rate had been 20 percent, the value would only be $1,465,000 ($293,000 ÷ 20 percent), or, 5 × $293,000 = $1,465,000.

To illustrate this approach, estimate the future free cash flows for some finite time period such as 5 to 10 years. Next, estimate cash flows for the future time period beyond the estimated cash flow period. Of course, forecasting cash flows into the future can be difficult, but often the discounted present value of such cash flow estimates is not that large. Table 17.4 presents estimated free cash flows for the Uptown Company, a real estate venture that builds and operates apartment complexes. Year 10 is called the terminal year.

Table 17.4. Uptown Company Estimated Free Cash Flows for Years 1 to 30

Year	Estimated Free Cash Flows	PV Factor	PV of Free Cash Flows
1	$30,000,000	0.8929	$26,787,000
2	35,000,000	0.7972	27,902,000
3	40,000,000	0.7118	28,472,000
4	40,000,000	0.6355	25,420,000
5	45,000,000	0.5674	25,533,000
6	50,000,000	0.5066	25,330,000
7	50,000,000	0.4524	22,620,000
8	40,000,000	0.4039	16,156,000
9	40,000,000	0.3606	14,424,000
10	30,000,000	0.3220	9,660,000
11-30	25,000,000/yr.	2.4052	60,130,000
Present value using discounted free cash flows			$282,434,000

Beyond the 10-year period, assume a steady free cash flow of $25 million a year. Forecasting is always a difficult process, because there are so many variables that may enter into the determination of earnings and free cash flows. These factors are not easy to estimate more than a few years into the future. The more technological a business's products and services, the harder it is to forecast earnings and free cash flows for long periods into the future. An offsetting variable is that cash flows that are discounted for long periods of time have a low present value. For example, the $25 million per year expected free cash flows for years 11–30 are discounted using an annuity factor at 12 percent, starting in year 11 and going to year 30. To find this factor, which is 2.4052, the valuator goes to the present value of an annuity table for 12 percent and finds the value for 30 periods. From that amount, the valuator subtracts the present value of an annuity at 12 percent for 10 periods. The resulting factor of 2.4052 yields a present value of the 20 years' worth of $25 million annual free cash flows of $60,130,000. The total projected free cash flow for the 20 year period is $500 million, but the present value of those cash flows is only $60,130,000.

Balance Sheet Valuation Methods

Accountants sometimes sacrifice one financial statement for another. For example, using last-in-first-out (LIFO) inventory valuation during periods of rising prices tends to match the current cost of inventory with current revenues. This approach may make the income statement more current and relevant for users, but typically it leaves old, noncurrent values in the inventory account on the balance sheet. Similarly, accelerated depreciation methods and historical cost data may mean long-lived assets are reported in the balance sheet at amounts much lower than their current market value.

When there are difficult choices to make between relevant treatment of accounting items on the balance sheet or the income statement, the income statement tends to win out. This "residual value" problem is one of the reasons that many practitioners do not believe balance sheet or book value valuations are relevant in most valuation situations. In addition, as the argument goes, asset values per se are not good indicators of the ability of a firm to generate future earnings and cash flows. Instead, recent earnings experiences of the firm are viewed as more indicative of the ability to generate future earnings and cash flows. The AICPA's Management Advisors Services Practice Aid, *Valuation of Closely Held Businesses*, indicates that the Internal Revenue Service strongly recommends the use of earnings-based valuation models for valuing businesses.[31]

Nonetheless, there are situations where balance sheets or book value measures are considered relevant in valuing a business. In a closely held business, there may be contract stipulations that state that in the event one owner wants to sell his or her shares to the other owners, the shares will be transferred at book value. As noted earlier in the discussion of the excess earnings model, in the absence of evidence of abnormal earnings, book value may be the appropriate measure of value. Table 17.5 presents the balance sheet of Burt Manufacturing Company. Unlike income statements that cover a period of time, balance sheets capture the financial condition of a company at a point in time. A simple way to use the balance sheet approach is to take the value of the equity at the last balance sheet (in this example, 12/31/13). Here the value of the firm would be $1,900,000 ($500,000 + $300,000 + $1,100,000). Because there are 10,000 shares of common stock issued and outstanding, the per-share value would be $190. This value is adjusted for a variety of issues that are discussed in the next section.

Table 17.5. Burt Manufacturing Company Balance Sheets for the Years Ending 12/31/10 Through 12/31/13

	2010	2011	2012	2013
Current assets:				
Cash	$110,000	$270,000	$340,000	$380,000
Accounts receivables	940,000	880,000	920,000	990,000
Inventory	1,165,000	1,245,000	1,190,000	1,210,000
Prepaid expenses	175,000	125,000	160,000	180,000
Total current assets	2,520,000	2,420,000	2,500,000	2,650,000
Fixed assets:				
Fixed assets	2,200,000	2,000,000	2,400,000	2,600,000
Accumulated Depreciation	1,300,000	1,100,000	1,320,000	1,380,000
Net fixed assets	900,000	900,000	1,080,000	1,220,000
Total assets	$3,420,000	$3,320,000	$3,580,000	$3,870,000
Liabilities and Owners' Equity				
Current liabilities:				
Accounts Payable	$520,000	$480,000	$660,000	$740,000
Accrued payables	80,000	85,000	90,000	100,000
Total current liabilities	600,000	565,000	750,000	840,000
Long-term liabilities	1,500,000	1,500,000	1,500,000	1,500,000
Total liabilities	2,100,000	2,165,000	2,250,000	2,340,000
Stockholders' Equity:				
Common stock	500,000	500,000	500,000	500,000
Add paid in capital	300,000	300,000	300,000	300,000
Retained earnings	420,000	615,000	820,000	1,100,000
Total liabilities and Stock Equity	$3,320,000	$3,580,000	$3,870,000	$4,240,000

Other Factors That May Be Relevant

Level of ownership interest discussed previously is one of the most important factors in valuing a business. Another common issue in the sale of ownership interest in a closely held company is the *loss of a key employee*. Commonly, when two or more people join together to form a business, they bring different supporting skills and knowledge to the business. One person may be excellent at marketing and customer relations, another person might be great with finances and fund raising, and yet another might be good at organization and operations. If one of these individuals leaves the firm and wants to sell his or her interest in the business, there may be much more than the loss of capital at stake. The entire character and competitive nature of the business may change. If so, the value of the business shares must be discounted, perhaps significantly, to reflect the value of the "new business." Here again, the size of the adjustment to the business valuation, however determined, will require skill, experience, and an understanding of the nature of the business.

Another issue that forensic accountants may face is the diversity of results that may arise from using different business valuation approaches. A practitioner may use two or more business valuation models and get different measures of value. Which one is correct? Commonly, a valuation practitioner has a preference for one method depending on the circumstances in the case and the evaluator's own preferences and experiences. If, however, the professional feels there is some merit to using more than one method or approach in the business valuation, he or she may develop a weighting for the various methods and compute a weighted average value.

Suppose that three valuation methods were used in estimating the value of a business. Method A resulted in a value of $3,500,000, Method B found a value of $3,200,000, and Method C resulted in a value of $4,500,000. The practitioner believes that Method A is the most reliable, but the other two methods have some merit as well. Weights are assigned to each of the three valuation approaches as follows. Method A is assigned a weight of 60 percent, and a 20 percent weighting is assigned to each of the other two methods. The final valuation is computed as follows:

Table 17.6. Final Weighted Valuation Computation

Valuation Method	Valuation Amount	Weighting	Value
A	$3,500,000	.60	$2,100,000
B	3,200,000	.20	640,000
C	4,500,000	.20	900,000
Weighted average valuation			$3,640,000

Selling the Results

In most valuation engagements, the practitioner is not the only person performing a valuation of the business. Typically, a practitioner prepares a business valuation for one party in the dispute. The other party has a forensic expert preparing a business valuation as well. The two experts then present their valuation positions at trial, in arbitration, or in some other form of dispute resolution. Why do professionals operating with the same business information not arrive at similar dollar valuation for the business? Business valuation is as much an art as it is a science, and each party is approaching the dispute from a different direction.

To prevail with the judge and/or jury, an expert must present a position in the most effective way possible. Like other areas of forensic accounting practice, communications skills are essential to effectively present a business valuation. The inability to communicate properly is a fatal career flaw in the practice of forensic accounting. Effective communication requires at least three distinct skills in forensic practice. One is the ability to write clearly, concisely, and understandably if you are to persuade your readers. The second communications skill area is speaking. Typically, at trial, one is speaking to a naïve audience. Juries tend to have little or no knowledge of accounting. Even the simplest accounting concepts must be presented in a clear, simple, understandable manner if an accountant is to succeed in persuading jury members that the accountant's position is the correct one. Finally, an expert must have the ability to listen carefully. During deposition testimony and during cross-examination at trial, the expert must be intent on hearing and understanding the questions being asked. The witness must not think about the answer to a previous question, and fail to understand the next question. If one is to be successful in "selling" a position, the expert must listen intently to the questions and then formulate the best possible answer to the questions asked.

¶ 17,221 RULES OF THUMB—VALUATION ON THE CHEAP

Formulas or rules of thumb are sometimes suggested as a way to value a business. These rules have their uses and are fairly common among business brokers, but generally a professionally performed, objective business valuation with supporting data is necessary. There are several books that provide suggested formulas, but the author of one of these books says this about the formula approach:

> No single formula will work for every business. Formula multipliers offer ease of calculation, but they also obscure details. This can be misleading. Net revenue multipliers are particularly troublesome because they are blind to the company's expense and profit history. It is easy to see how two businesses in any given industry group might have the same annual net revenue, yet show very different cash flows. A proper valuation will go beyond formulas and include a full financial analysis whenever possible.[32]

Preparing to Testify

¶ 17,225   STRATEGIES FOR EFFECTIVE TESTIMONY

Many of the strategies that are effective for expert witnesses in other types of cases also work well in valuation cases. The following is a short discussion of many key issues an expert should consider when preparing to testify. One useful approach in preparing to testify is to review a checklist of items that should be addressed before testifying. In a recent *Journal of Accountancy* article "Expert Testimony Guidelines for CPA Valuation Analysts" the author provides a checklist of issues that typically would be useful in preparing for testifying in a valuation case.[33] Below we discuss some guidelines for preparing to testify in valuation cases. Included are:

1. Review and update your resume.
2. Know and understand the facts of the case.
3. Anticipate and prepare answers for expected difficult questions at deposition and cross examination.
4. Understand all information and calculations in the expert report.
5. Carefully prepare for deposition testimony.
6. Be certain there are no conflicts of interest.
7. The expert must testify so that court can clearly understand the issues in the expert's testimony.

Experts should review and update their resume regularly. A forensic accountant should never provide a potential client with a resume that indicates that the expert's resume is not current or completely accurate. Often a favorite strategy of opposing counsel is to scrutinize the resume of an expert looking for items that are not current or not completely accurate. Even if the opposing attorney finds only very minor errors or exaggerations on a resume, the attorney may be use the questionable items on the resume to characterize the opposing expert's testimony as questionable or even untrue. Early in my career as a forensic accountant a wise attorney told me, "You are what you are, and we hired you based on your credentials, do not embellish you qualifications on your resume or during testimony. If you do, it almost always comes back to haunt you." An expert can jeopardize his/her entire testimony by minor errors or exaggerations on the expert's resume.

Every case has many issues and facts related to the case. Although many of the facts may not relate directly to the analyses made by the forensic accountants, the expert should know as much about all the issues in the case as possible. Forensic accountants testify about accounting/financial issues that the court might otherwise not understand, but the expert must demonstrate an understanding of the facts and issues in the case and how they relate to the technical issues about which the expert testified. If it appears that the expert is uniformed about key issues in the case, the technical opinions in the expert's testimony may be discounted or ignored by the court.

Deposition testimony and cross examination testimony require an expert to be able to answer whatever questions the opposing attorney might ask. Many of those questions might be quite challenging to answer in a manner that supports the expert's opinions. If the expert prepares for testimony by anticipating the difficult questions and framing an answer to those questions before testifying, often the expert's testimony is much more effective. Typically an expert knows his/her case-related weak points far better than the opposition. The expert should use this knowledge in advance of testifying to prepare for the tough questioning of the opposing attorney. The attorney for the expert's side in the case usually will have some advice and thoughts about questions relating to challenging issues in the case.

An expert must be well versed in all components of the expert report. To students this may sound self-evident, but in large forensic practices, testifying experts typically have a team of support staff that works on all aspects of the expert report. Although the testifying expert manages all the analysis team, the expert usually does not make all of the calculations and does not assemble all of the relevant materials in the report. Therefore, the testifying expert should carefully review the expert report and as many details in the report as is possible. The report should identify all of the information that was received and reviewed in forming the opinions expressed in the report. The expert does not need to describe the specific impact of each item that was used in forming the opinions in the report, but if there were essential documents or other information that was critical to forming the opinions, the expert should be able to discuss them. If others were involved in making calculations or in other ways supporting the expert report, the expert must be certain that he/she clearly understands all parts of the report.

Effective experts carefully prepare for deposition testimony. Most attorneys will work with their experts to be sure the expert is ready for the deposition. For relatively new experts, the attorney will explain the nature, purpose, process, and expectations of depositions. It is likely the expert's attorney will provide whatever information is required relating to the questioning style and other characteristics of the deposing attorney. Because experts are usually deposed late in the discovery process, the deposing attorney will probably have taken a number of depositions in the case already. It is likely the expert's attorney will have provided the expert with copies of some of the deposing attorney's prior depositions. The expert should read the depositions to see the nature and style of the attorney's questions. Usually the foundation of much of the expert's deposition will be the expert report. Expect to be asked about everything that is in the report. In particular, expect to be asked about the opinions in the report and how they were developed. Near the end of deposition, the expert probably will be asked if at trial the expert expects to render any opinions that are not included in the expert report and what, if any, additional work will be performed between now and the trial.

The expert must be certain that there are no conflicts of interest relating to the case. Experts that are in demand have many opportunities to participate in a wide variety of cases. It is easy to overlook some seemingly innocent relationships with current or former clients or other relationships that might render an expert ineligible for a case because of a conflict of interest. The expert must remain diligent about avoiding potential conflict of interest problems.

Perhaps the final item on the expert's checklist is be certain that the opinions that will be presented at trial are presented so that lay members of a jury will be able to understand the issues presented by the expert. Many accounting/financial concepts in cases are complex and comprehensive. Often the issues are difficult even for professionals, which may be why the case arose in the first place. When these complex technical issues are presented to others who have little or no knowledge of accounting/financial concepts, it is easy to confuse the court. Even judges typically have limited knowledge of accounting issues. Therefore, it is very important that the expert develops and presents the opinions in the expert report in a way that enhances the court's understanding and appreciation of the accounting/financial issues presented in the expert's testimony.

There is no single checklist that serves as an effective guideline for every case in which an expert might testify, but there are many articles, books, and practice guides that provide a wealth of information to guide experts in pursuing their career objectives. One excellent source for practitioners is the "California Society of CPAs Litigation Sections Practice Aid" that is issued by the California Society of Certified Public Accountants.[34] This document is a non-authoritative practice aid designed to assist members in complying with the AICPA's" Statement on Standards for Valuation Services No. 1 (SSVS No. 1). The practice aid does not attempt to interpret SSVS No. 1, but instead it offers a series of detailed checklists to assist practitioners in the field.

Business Valuation Standards

¶ 17,231   UNIFORM STANDARDS OF PROFESSIONAL APPRAISAL PRACTICE (USPAP)[35]

Producing a professional, objective, and supported business valuation should be the objective of any business appraiser. Fortunately, the major national accrediting bodies have issued their own similar sets of business valuation standards, covering required content in a business valuation. All real estate valuations used in connection with any federally related transactions are required to comply with the Uniform Standards of Professional Appraisal Practice (USPAP), issued by the Appraisal Standards Board of The Appraisal Foundation. USPAP is a recognized provider of standards not only for real estate valuations but also for business and personal property valuations.

In the 1980s, the savings and loan industry encountered severe problems, brought on in large part by poor lending practices. Many of the real estate loans in failed institutions were in part the result of substandard—or even fraudulent—real estate appraisals. The Appraisal Foundation was formed in 1987 to implement reforms and develop uniform appraisal standards.

Appraisal society members of the North American Council of Appraisal Organizations, and six nonappraiser special members, including the American Bankers Association and the U.S. League of Savings Institutions, incorporated The Appraisal Foundation. Of the appraisal society incorporators, all were real estate-related except the American Society of Appraisers (ASA), which, in addition to real estate, certifies appraisers in business appraisal, machinery and equipment, personal property, and other disciplines. The Appraisal Standards Board of The Appraisal Foundation develops, interprets, and amends the Uniform Standards of Professional Appraisal Practice (USPAP), which sets appraisal standards to be followed by members of each of the Foundation's incorporators.

In 1989, Congress passed the Financial Institutions Reform, Recovery, and Enforcement Act (FIRREA), which led to the bailout of failed lending institutions. Title XI of the act requires real estate appraisers to become licensed or certified by their respective states and to follow appraisal standards mandated by the Appraisal Standards Board of The Appraisal Foundation. Additionally, USPAP must be followed whenever a real estate appraisal is used for any loan or other transaction involving the federal government, including home loans guaranteed by governmental and quasi-governmental agencies.

Although it clearly pertains to real estate appraisal, there has been some uncertainty about whether or not business appraisers are required to follow USPAP in a valuation with federal government implications (for example, a valuation to be submitted to the IRS with an estate or gift tax return). In many ways, USPAP merely codifies many common sense standards of professionalism that appraisers should have been following anyway, so it seems hard to imagine why a business appraiser would not want to comply with USPAP, required or not. However, given the increasing expectations of federal officials, it would be foolhardy for a business appraiser not to prepare reports in conformity with USPAP.

Obtaining USPAP

The Uniform Standards of Professional Appraisal Practice, which are quite lengthy (almost one hundred pages), are periodically modified and updated. Therefore, new and experienced business valuators alike are encouraged to obtain a copy of USPAP and its periodic updates from the following:

The Appraisal Foundation
1029 Vermont Ave., NW
Suite 900
Washington, DC 20005–3517
Phone: (202) 347–7722
Fax: (202) 347–7727

¶ 17,241 AMERICAN INSTITUTE OF CERTIFIED PUBLIC ACCOUNTANTS (AICPA)[36]

Unlike the appraisal organizations mentioned previously, the AICPA is much more broadly based, and issues standards pertaining to certified public accountants in all types of accounting practices. The AICPA is currently drafting business valuation standards. Other than the general standards to which CPAs must adhere, those providing consulting services are governed by Rule 201 of the AICPA Code of Professional Conduct. A copy of these standards can be obtained by contacting the AICPA as follows:

American Institute of Certified Public Accountants
1211 Avenue of the Americas
New York, NY 10036-8775
Phone: (212) 596–6200
Fax: (212) 596–6213
Internet: www.aicpa.org

¶ 17,246 STATEMENT OF FINANCIAL ACCOUNTING STANDARDS NO. 157

Fair Value Measurements

September 2006

The Financial Accounting Standards Board (FASB) recently issued FASB No. 157 with the following stated *Objective*:

> 1. This statement defines fair value, establishes a framework for measuring fair value, and expands disclosures about fair value measurements. Where applicable, this statement simplifies and codifies related guidance within generally accepted accounting principles (GAAP).[37]

In the opening *Summary* of the document, the document states:

> This Statement defines fair value, establishes a framework for measuring fair value in generally accepted accounting principles (GAAP), and expands disclosures about fair value measurements. This Statement applies under other accounting pronouncements that require or permit fair value measurements, the Board having previously concluded in those accounting pronouncements that fair value is the relevant measurement attribute.[38]

The board states that fair value remains the primary focus of valuation measurements. The Board states:

> The definition of fair value retains the exchange price notion in earlier definitions of fair value. This Statement clarifies that the exchange price is the price in an orderly transaction between market participants to sell the asset or transfer the liability in the market in which the reporting entity would transact for the asset or liability, that is, the principle or most advantageous market for the asset or liability...This Statement emphasizes that fair value is a market-based measurement, not an entity-specific measurement...This Statement emphasizes that market participant assumptions include assumptions about risk, for example, the risk inherent in a particular valuation technique used to measure fair value (such as a pricing model) and/or the risk inherent in the inputs to the valuation technique. A fair value measurement should include an adjustment

for risk if market participants would include one in pricing the related asset or liability, even if the adjustment is difficult to determine.[39]

FASB No. 157 includes a number of specific valuation issues that outline how the conclusions in the statement relate to the FASB's Conceptual Framework. The Statement specifically relates its conclusions to FASB Concepts Statements No. 2, No. 6, and No. 7.[40] FASB No. 157 also carefully describes and defines key issues in valuation activities. Of course, the primary function of the Statement is to provide guidance for GAAP based financial reporting. A complete discussion of FASB No. 157 is beyond the scope of this book. If more specific information about the contents of this Statement is required, one should refer to the Statement itself.

¶ 17,251   COMMON REQUIREMENTS OF BUSINESS VALUATION STANDARDS OF VALUATION SOCIETIES[41]

The three major valuation societies—the American Society of Appraisers (ASA), The Institute of Business Appraisers, Inc. (IBA), and the National Association of Certified Valuation Analysts (NACVA)—each has its own set of rigorous business valuation standards. Each requires its accredited members and candidates to adhere to these strict standards in each business valuation assignment. These standards have led to greater professionalism within the valuation community.

¶ 17,261   FEATURES OF THE STANDARDS[42]

All of the standards are similar in that each requires the following broad elements in any business appraisal.

Independence

The appraiser must be unbiased and independent, and not act in any way as an advocate for the client or any other party. If independence and ethics are abandoned, how can users place any reliance on an appraiser's opinion of value?

Fee Not Contingent on Appraised Value

No appraiser can accept a valuation assignment where the fee paid depends on the finding of value. For example, it is unethical for an appraiser to accept a fee that is contingent on the outcome, such as a fee based on a percentage of the value. Each organization requires valuators to warrant in the report that their fee arrangement is not based on the finding of value.

Limiting Conditions

All reports must set forth key assumptions, conditions, and restrictions that impact the value estimate. This way, the reader is informed of key assumptions. For example, a common limiting condition in valuation reports is the statement that the valuator has not independently verified or audited any of the financial or other information provided by the company being valued. Or, suppose a company has a lawsuit outstanding, which is a material factor that could negatively impact the business, but whose impact cannot be fully known or foreseen. The valuator would clearly want to state in the report that this uncertainty exists and that its impact is unknown.

Professionals Participating in the Assignment

All individuals materially participating in the valuation assignment must be disclosed and must sign the report, including a certification regarding their independence, fee arrangement, and other factors required in each specific society's standards, as well as those required by USPAP. If a participant disagrees with the valuation findings in the report, this must also be stated, along with the nature of the dissent.

Information Sources Used

Valuation reports should be able to be replicated by the reader. Therefore, a sound business appraisal needs to include all key sources relied upon.

Report Content

Although each society's standards requirements differ, all essentially require that a valuation report be fully documented to include detailed discussions of the following items.

Purpose and Scope of the Assignment

Valuation requirements and methodologies can differ depending upon the purpose (e.g., estate tax, gift planning, buy-sell agreement, or purchase or sale). A valuation of a real estate holding corporation, for estate tax purposes, might be required to ignore trapped-in capital gains taxes that would be due by the corporation if it sold its real property. By contrast, in a valuation for a possible purchase of those shares, an adjustment downward in value for trapped-in capital gains taxes would be an important factor impacting value. Therefore, a valuation is only designed to be valid for a specific purpose. Any restrictions on the use of the report should be included in the narrative.

Standard of Value Used

The appropriate standard of value used must be clearly set forth and defined, such as fair market value, fair value, or investment value.

Identification of the Specific Interest Being Valued

The report must clearly delineate the interest that is being valued (e.g., 100 common shares in XYZ Corporation, representing 10 percent of the 1,000 total issued and outstanding common shares). It is not enough to state that the appraiser is valuing a "minority interest in the shares of XYZ Company." Different share holdings, even of minority interests, can have different values depending upon the distribution of a company's ownership, the potential for swing block attributes, and the impact of relevant state law and shareholders' agreements.

Specific Valuation Date Used

The value of any asset is only valid as of a given date because market conditions, the investment climate, and other factors change from one day to the next. For example, for a divorce a company might be valued as of the date of the couple's separation. At that time, the company might have a value of $5 million. Six months later, the company might lose a major customer accounting for 50 percent of its revenues, causing its value to drop to only $1 million. This is why valuations must carry a specific date.

Relevant State Law Governing the Entity

State statutes affect elements of valuations. For example, if a company is incorporated in Maryland, this is important, because Maryland state law may impact the rights of the interest holder, its income taxation, and other factors.

Scope of the Valuation Report

The report should outline the scope of the procedures undertaken in the valuation, and also disclose any way in which they are limited. Note that valuators should carefully read USPAP concerning the scope of a valuation assignment and the restrictions pertaining to limited scope valuations.

Data Collection and Analysis

Nature and History of the Business

A valuation must consider both the nature and the history of a business. Understanding how a business started and has evolved over time tells a great deal about the risks and opportunities that impact it and its value. Additionally, it is important to consider the management of the business, its strengths and weaknesses, products and services offered, customers, supply relationships, sales and marketing, competition, credit relationships, contractual arrangements, facilities, the location of the company's activities, and a variety of other factors that impact the business. The reader of a valuation report should come away with a clear grasp of the who, what, when, where, why, and how of a company's business. This places the valuation findings in context and allows readers to draw their own independent conclusions about whether they believe the valuation findings are reasonable.

By contrast, poorly written reports with little detail leave readers knowing little more about the company than when they started the report. This leaves the reader with no basis on which to judge the report's validity.

Historical Financial Information on the Business

Historical financial results and performance tell a great deal about the investment attributes of a company, the quality of its management, and its risks and opportunities. This history also serves as a clue to the company's possible future outlook. All business appraisals should include a full summary of historic financial results of the business, including income statements and balance sheets for prior years. Business valuation standards are silent on the number of years to be included; however, a commonly held view is that five years is a minimum if the business has been in business that long. However, in cyclical companies, a five-year snapshot may not capture the full view of an industry cycle. Therefore, valuators may conclude that more years of information ought to be included to give an accurate representation of the business.

Financial Analysis

Reports must undertake a thorough financial analysis of the business, including an examination of historic financial trends and key factors impacting results, and compare financial performance and financial statement ratios with industry performance measures (if available). This should also include common-sized income statements (items shown as a percentage of net company revenues) and balance sheets (items shown as a percentage of total company assets). Financial statement ratios typically include measures of profitability, liquidity, working capital, leverage, debt service coverage, asset utilization, and return on equity.

Industry and Economic Conditions, Outlook, and Impact on the Subject Company

Each company is subject to unique industry and economic trends and forces, often over which it has little or no control, but which can heavily impact future financial and investment performance and value. The valuation report should include a discussion of these key factors and how they impact the company. For example, an industry might face a worsening outlook due to a tight supply of a key raw material, which will lead to higher prices and lower demand for the resulting end product. Alternatively, a government agency may be preparing to deregulate the industry, leading to potentially greater competition and downward pressure on prices as new competitors enter the business. From an economic perspective, local, regional, and national economies can impact a company and should be discussed.

Current Investment Climate and Rates of Return for Similar Investments

The investment climate at the valuation date is relevant because it impacts the rates of return buyers require for investing in different types of assets. Similarly, historic rates of return on investments similar to the company being valued may provide indications as to its current value. The valuation should consider and discuss these elements, and define and discuss the specific data used, and why. For example, in using the capitalization of income method (an income valuation approach), the valuation may depend upon a capitalization rate developing using data based on long-run returns from investing in public companies. The report should clearly document the development of the capitalization rate and the specific resources used to develop the rate of return.

Past Transactions in Company Shares and Acquisition or Sale Factors

Past transactions in the shares of the company itself, if they have occurred, can sometimes serve as an indicator of the company's present worth. Such transactions need to be discussed, if they are relevant indicators of present value, and why or why not. Also, plans by the company for a sale or merger, or any past solicitations by potential outside acquirers, could be highly relevant in how an investor might view the present value of the shares. These situations, if present, should be discussed, and their relevance to the value detailed. The valuator should place him- or herself in the shoes of a shareholder who is considering selling shares, and who bases the asking price for the shares in large part on his or her consideration of the valuation report. Suppose four weeks before the valuation date the company entered into preliminary discussions with a possible buyer for a purchase of the whole company, and discussions were continuing. This would certainly be relevant information for the prospective seller and reader of the report to know.

Methodology

Methods Considered and Reasons for Selecting the Ones Used

All business valuations should include consideration of the income, cost, and market approaches to valuation. A report should include a discussion of the methodologies considered, which ones were employed, and why. Equally important is a discussion of why certain methods were *not* employed.

Implementation of the Methods

A valuation report should fully discuss all of the steps used in implementing each valuation method, and any adjustments made to financial statements and why. The reader should be able to fully replicate the process that the valuator went through and understand how the valuator arrived at each finding.

Reconciliation of Findings of Value

A reconciliation is a section of the business valuation that summarizes the findings by each of the respective valuation methods, then gives the rationale for how each was considered, and why, in arriving at a final estimate of value. This reconciliation might be accomplished through an explanation of why various weightings were attached to each method. Alternatively, if mathematical weightings were not employed, the narrative should explain the basis of what led the business appraiser to the ultimate value and why.

Adjustments to Valuation Findings

The report should discuss and consider any possible adjustments to the value that might be relevant. These might include premiums for control and minority, lack of marketability, key persons, and other discounts. If the business or entity has nonoperating or excess assets (e.g., excess cash, investment property, and marketable securities) not needed in the day-to-day business, adjustments to the value should be made and supported. The rationale for these adjustments must be clearly specified. If studies are used as a basis, they should be cited. Many valuation reports fall miserably short in this area, particularly with regard to discounts for lack of marketability. The report spends 40 to 60 pages analyzing the company to arrive at a sound and supported preliminary value. Then, with no supporting rationale, the valuator arbitrarily, and without any stated basis or support, reduces the value by a discount for lack of marketability, often in the 30- to 40-percent range. Readers must have a clear indication of adjustments, their basis, and the valuator's rationale.

Conclusion of Value

This element is straightforward and involves a clear statement of the findings of value.

Business Valuation Reports

¶ 17,271   ## ORGANIZATION OF THE REPORT[43]

The greatest analysis in the world is of little use if the reader cannot follow it. A valuation report must make the analysis undertaken and ultimate results derived easy to understand. A well-organized report will help anyone, even its author, be able to refer to it many years down the road, long after the facts and particulars of the company have faded from memory. A well-organized report is also of great help in court or with an IRS agent when explaining the valuation methods used and the conclusions reached. Trying to explain the valuation work with an obtuse or murky report can lead to confusion on the witness stand or with the IRS agent and, ultimately, can detract from the presentation.

¶ 17,281   ## ATTENTION TO MECHANICS[44]

A well-organized report is also easier to check for mathematical errors because it carefully shows the step-by-step calculations. Nothing is more embarrassing or casts more doubt on a valuator's professional capabilities than a simple math error that is brought to light, especially during a trial or in negotiations with the IRS. The implication the other side will make is that if the "expert" cannot even add, subtract, multiply, or divide, how in the world is he or she qualified to understand and apply advanced business valuation techniques? Professionals should not allow themselves to be put in this position.

Along the same vein, the valuation report should be spell-checked at every stage and examined to make sure that tables are not broken by page, the numbering of sections is sequential, and the format and type makes the information easy to read.

¶ 17,291   ## MAIN SECTIONS OF THE VALUATION REPORT[45]

Seven main sections help to organize the report. Tabbed pages dividing the sections will give the reader quick and accurate access to the information.

1. Front Pages

The first section, immediately following the report's cover, consists of:
1. Cover sheet (with company name and the valuation date),
2. Transmittal letter, and
3. Table of contents.

2. Introduction

This second section provides explanations of the purpose of the appraisal, the summary of the findings, the independence and qualifications of the valuator, the information used in the report, and any legal precedents followed in the report (e.g., Rev. Rul. 59-60).

3. Company Information

Under a tab labeled "Company Information" is an overview that addresses key issues at the company—the history and nature of the business, ownership, management, customers, suppliers, competitors, banking relationships, related-party transactions, legal issues, material factors affecting the company, etc. Also included in the Company Information section are analyses of the company's industry as well as the economic and population outlook.

4. Financial Condition

Under a tab labeled "Financial Condition," source data for comparative financial information is given as well as a thorough financial analysis of the company, both from balance sheet and income statement perspectives.

5. Valuation Methodology

Following a "Valuation Methodology" tab is an explanation of the various valuation approaches considered in the report and those ultimately used. Each approach's effect on value is explained in detail, both mathematically as well as in real-world terms. Step-by-step calculations of each approach used in the report are shown from an objective perspective, leaving nothing out or subject to question (except the reasonable differences of a subjective nature).

6. Valuation Conclusion

Under a tab labeled "Valuation Conclusion," the preliminary values from the prior section are assimilated into one table and then analyzed for the ultimate selection and/or weighting of one or more methodologies. This section also contains the analysis of the application of any minority discount, control premium, discount for lack of marketability, or adjustment for nonoperating or nonessential assets or liabilities. This section concludes with the final estimate of value.

7. Exhibits

The final tab houses the exhibits. In general, the following six exhibits can be consistent and placed first in every report. They include:

1. Limiting conditions
2. Definitions of valuation terms (as promulgated by the ASA)
3. Qualifications of the valuation professionals who worked on the report
4. Common size balance sheets of the company
5. Common size income statements of the company
6. Ratio analysis of the company

Additional exhibits are added as necessary to support the valuation analysis. Examples of additional exhibits commonly included are the following:

- Discounted cash flow analysis with supporting assumptions
- Information on publicly traded comparable companies
- Information on private transactions of similar businesses

The valuator decides where it is best to show financial statement adjustments or spreadsheets based on their complexity and size. Whether they end up in the body of the report or in the exhibits, a good goal for each report is to show as much information as possible in the body without interrupting the reader with large and complex pages of data. Large charts, such as the additional exhibits mentioned above, may be too large to effectively include in the body of the report and, thus, are better shown as an exhibit. When tabbed pages are used in the report, the reader can easily flip to the exhibit section.

¶ 17,301   CONCLUSION

Business valuations are difficult to prepare well. Understanding the different approaches to valuation and the standards of value are critical starting points. This chapter has gone well beyond the concepts and demonstrated much of the real-world processes involved. Valuations may be more art than science, but a great deal of accounting, financial analysis, and even legal discipline has to be built into the process or the valuation will not hold up in court. Although there are at present four standards-setting bodies, they generally agree on the important standards involved in the process. A business valuation report requires rigors of its own. Even if the right data has been gathered and all the right calculations and interpretations have been made, the report must be properly constructed to demonstrate that an objective supportable valuation has been performed. This chapter has described proper report construction as well.

For the accounting student who has a penchant for things forensic and an interest in finance, business valuation is one area that merits career consideration. For more information on business valuation see the *CCH Business Valuation Guide*.[46]

ENDNOTES

1. G.S. Gaffen, "Guidance for the CPA Entering the Business Valuation Profession," THE OHIO CPA JOURNAL (July–September 2002), p. 22.

2. The discussion in this section is adapted from George Hawkins and Michael Paschall, CCH BUSINESS VALUATION GUIDE (Chicago: CCH INCORPORATED, 2003).

3. *Ibid.*

4. *Ibid.*

5. *Ibid.*

6. 1959-1 CB 237, amplified by Rev. Ruls. 83-120, 80-213, and 77-287.

7. The section entitled "Divorce Situation Valuations" does not appear in the CCH BUSINESS VALUATION GUIDE.

8. "Buried Treasure: Looking for Hidden Assets in a Divorce," CBIZ Valuation Group, Inc., *www.cbiz-onesource.com*.

9. The discussion in this section is adapted from George Hawkins and Michael Paschall, CCH BUSINESS VALUATION GUIDE (Chicago: CCH INCORPORATED, 2003).

10. Gordon developed two models using dividends as the income measure of value. The first is a "single stage" model where the anticipated dividends per share for the coming year are divided by a capitalization rate. The second is a multi-stage dividend valuation model that works like the discounted cash flow method, the only difference being that actual anticipated dividends, not free cash flow, is the income measure. *See* Myron J. Gordon, THE INVESTMENT, FINANCING, AND VALUATION OF THE CORPORATION (Homewood, Illinois: Richard D. Irwin, 1962).

11. The discussion in this section is adapted from George Hawkins and Michael Paschall, CCH BUSINESS VALUATION GUIDE (Chicago: CCH INCORPORATED, 2003).

12. *Ibid.*

13. *Ibid.*

14. *Ibid.*

15. *Ibid.*

16. *Ibid.*

17. *Ibid.*

18. *Ibid.*

19. *Ibid.*

20. Information on purchasing *Annual Statement Studies,* as well as RMA's other publications can be obtained at the following address: Risk Management Association, One Liberty Place, Suite 2300, Philadelphia, PA, 19103-7398, phone: 800-677-7621, fax: 215-446-4101, Internet: *www.rmahq.org*.

21. The discussion in this section is adapted from George Hawkins and Michael Paschall, CCH BUSINESS VALUATION GUIDE (Chicago, CCH INCORPORATED, 2003).

22. *Ibid.*

23. *Ibid.*

24. *Ibid.*

25. *Ibid.*

26. *Ibid.*

27. 1959-1 CB 237.

28. Copeland, Koller, and Murrin, VALUATION: MEASURING AND MANAGING THE VALUE OF COMPANIES (New York: John Wiley & Sons Inc., 2000), p. 134.

29. See John Mills, Lynn Bible, and Richard Mason, "Defining Free Cash Flow," THE CPA JOURNAL (January 2002).

30. Palepu, Healy, and Bernard, BUSINESS ANALYSIS & VALUATION USING FINANCIAL STATEMENTS, 2d ed. (South-Western: 2000), p. 11–16.

31. AICPA, *Valuation of Closely Held Businesses,* Management Advisory Services Practice Aid (New York: AICPA, 1897), p. 12.

32. Glen Desmond, HANDBOOK OF SMALL BUSINESS VALUATION FORMULAS AND RULES OF THUMB, 3d ed. (Camden, Maine: Valuation Press, 1993).

33. Robert Reilly, "Expert Testimony Guidelines for CPA Valuation Analysts," JOURNAL OF ACCOUNTANCY (November 2010), p. 20.

34. CalCPA's Litigation Sections, "California Society of CPAs Litigation Sections Practice Aid," California Society of Certified Public Accountants (January 18, 2008), v. 1.01.

35. The discussion in this section is adapted from George Hawkins and Michael Paschall, CCH BUSINESS VALUATION GUIDE (Chicago: CCH INCORPORATED, 2003).

36. *Ibid.*

37. Statement of Financial Accounting Standards No. 157, Financial Accounting Standards Board (September 2006), p. 6.

38. *Ibid*, p. 1.

39. *Ibid*, p. 2.

40. *Ibid*, p. 4.

41. The discussion in this section is adapted from George Hawkins and Michael Paschall, CCH BUSINESS VALUATION GUIDE (Chicago: CCH INCORPORATED, 2003).

42. *Ibid.*

43. *Ibid.*

44. *Ibid.*

45. *Ibid.*

46. George Hawkins and Michael Paschall, CCH BUSINESS VALUATION GUIDE (Chicago: CCH INCORPORATED, 2003).

EXERCISES

1. Why would a forensic accountant need to perform a business valuation? Can people not just look up the value at a particular date on the appropriate stock exchange? Explain.

2. Do you agree that there really are many situations in which closely held companies need to be valued because of a desired or required sale of some portion of the ownership? Explain.

3. If a stock is traded publicly, is there ever a need to secure the services of a forensic accountant to perform a business valuation of the company? Explain.

4. Given the same financial and other relevant information about a particular company, is it not logical that any informed business valuation professional would come to similar valuations? Explain.

5. Describe some situations giving rise to the need for valuations.

6. Valuation methods can be broken into what three types?

7. Group these valuation approaches into asset-based, income approach, and market approach types:
   a. Adjusted book value method
   b. Capitalization of earnings method
   c. Discounted future earnings method
   d. Guideline public company method
   e. Merger and acquisition method
   f. Rules of thumb approach

8. Define these terms:
   a. Historical cost
   b. Replacement cost
   c. Intrinsic value
   d. Fair market value
   e. Discounted future earnings method
   f. Capitalization of earnings method
   g. Capital asset pricing model (CAPM)

9. Identify and describe the most common measure of value used in business valuations.

10. What are the most commonly used methods of business valuation? Are there any reasons to use business valuation methods other than the common ones? Explain.

11. If a forensic accountant decides to use an earnings model to perform a business valuation, should all earnings data be treated in the same way? Explain.

12. Two partners, Jones and Smith, owned and operated a successful dairy business together for 15 years. The business processed dairy products and operated a popular retail ice cream store. During the past year, the two partners have had an increasing number of serious arguments about how to operate the business and about planned future expansion of the business. Both partners have agreed that they no longer can operate the business together. Either partner is willing to sell his share of the business to someone else and to get out of the dairy business altogether. An independent appraiser has valued the total value of the business at $1.5 million. Partner Jones owns 49 percent of the business, and Partner Smith owns 51 percent of the business. What is the value of each partner's share of the business? What was the basis for your evaluation of the partners' share of the business?

13. What would be the effect on free cash flows of each of the following items:
    a. Purchase of $400,000 of fixed assets
    b. Sale of $220,000 of book value fixed assets for a loss of $50,000
    c. A $90,000 increase in net working capital
    d. Issuance of $600,000 of first mortgage bonds

14. E&K Company has a net book value of $220,000. The company has a 10 percent cost of capital. The firm expects to have profits of $45,000, $40,000, and $35,000 respectively for the next three years. The company pays no dividends and depreciation is five percent per year of book value.
    a. Using the excess earnings model, should the firm be valued at more or less than its book value?
    b. What, if anything, are the company's abnormal earnings for the next three years?
    c. What is your best estimate of the firm's value using the excess earnings model?

15. **Earnings valuation models.** Bayview Real Estate Development is a company that owns and operates a number of real estate ventures. The company also engages in real estate acquisitions and sales of properties, some of which are properties the company no longer wishes to operate. Similar real estate firms earn a

15-percent rate of return. Bayview reported the following earnings over the last five years:

Year	Operating Income	Gain (Loss) on Sale of Assets	Net Income
1	$1,500,000	$800,000	$2,300,000
2	1,700,000	900,000	2,600,000
3	1,800,000	200,000	2,000,000
4	1,900,000	(500,000)	1,400,000
5	2,000,000	(200,000)	1,800,000

Prepare a business valuation for the Bayview Real Estate Development Company using an earnings model:

a. Prepare your analysis giving equal weights to the five years of earnings data.

b. Prepare your analysis giving greater weight to the more recent earning periods (where five is more recent).

c. What assumptions or adjustments did you make in your analysis with respect to nonoperating income?

16. **Discounted cash flows valuation model.** Smoothtone Products manufactures sound systems. The company's weighted average cost of capital is 15 percent. The company forecasted the following free cash flows for the next 20 years.

Year	Free Cash Flows
1	$10,000,000
2	15,000,000
3	20,000,000
4	22,000,000
5	25,000,000
6–10	20,000,000 per year
11–20	15,000,000 per year

Use the discounted cash flow approach to value the Smoothtone Products Company.

17. **Business valuation.** The Branson Trucking Company was started by three brothers in Columbus, Ohio in 1977. In 1982, Dave James came into the company primarily for marketing and growth purposes. Soon Dave showed that he was effective at increasing business and making deals that caused the company to grow significantly. Within 10 years, Branson trucking was one of the major regional carriers in the central Midwest.

Over the years, the Branson brothers gave stock options to Dave James to keep him happy with the firm and to reflect his con-

tributions to the firm's growth and general success. Dave exercised these options over time, and by 1995, the three Branson brothers and Dave James each owned 25 percent of the stock of the Branson Trucking Company.

By the late-1990s, two of the Branson brothers wanted to bring children and their spouses into the trucking business. The role that these new family members would play in the business created significant discussions and some strife. Dave James in particular was opposed to bringing in family members. Dave threatened to leave, and some of the Bransons thought that was a good idea. After several months of negotiations, it was agreed that Dave James would receive one year's severance pay, and the three Branson brothers would buy his stock in the company at its fair value. At the end of 2011, Dave James resigned from the trucking company.

Branson Trucking Company is a closely held company that does not trade in any market. The only stock sales have been directly from the company to the original holders of the stock. Below are income statements for the Branson Trucking Company for the years 2007–2011. The Branson Trucking Company financial statements are prepared by the Black & Blue CPA Group directly from Branson's accounting data. This accounting firm also prepares all of the Branson Trucking Company's tax returns. The financial statements are prepared directly from Branson Trucking's accounting data and are not audited by any accounting firm.

Dave James received severance pay of $125,000. He is currently employed in a similar marketing position earning $135,000 a year. During the 2007–2011 time period, the average price earnings ratio for similar trucking firms that were traded in open markets were 9, 11, 12, 10, and 8, respectively, for the five year period. Branson Trucking Company's net income for the years 2012–2013 was $450,000 and $690,000, respectively, for the two year period. Below is an appraisal of the Branson Trucking Company's assets as of December 31, 2011. At that time the firm's total liabilities were $5,100,000.

You are hired as a forensic accounting expert. Prepare a business valuation for the Branson Trucking Company at the time that

Dave James left the business. Determine what the shares of Dave James were worth at the time of his departure from the company. What limitations, if any, will you list in your report in connection with your valuation of this business? Would your valuation of the business or of the value of Dave James's share in the business change depending on whether you were hired as an expert by Dave James or the Branson Family?

Dan Willens, Appraiser
4610 E. Washington Street
Columbus, Ohio 43218

At your request, I have appraised the non-financial assets of the Branson Trucking Company as of December 31, 2011. In arriving at my valuations of these assets I used industry trade data, expert evaluations, and other sources of valuations, as I deemed appropriate under the circumstances. Below is a summary of the results:

Current Assets:

Cash	$218,000	
Accounts Receivable (net)	610,000	
Inventory and Supplies	165,000	
Prepaid Expenses	141,000	$1,134,000

Fixed assets:

Land	650,000	
Building & Fixtures	2,920,000	
Rolling Stock	4,230,000	7,800,000

Investments:

Bond Sinking Fund	340,000	
Common Stock of other firms	650,000	990,000

Total Asset Value		$9,924,000

UNAUDITED

Branson Trucking Company
Income Statement
For the Year Ended December 31, 2007

Sales	$17,281,000	
Less Sales Allowances	562,000	
Net Sales		$16,719,000
Cost of Sales		12,617,000
Gross Profit		4,102,000
Operating Expenses		4,886,000
Operating Income (Loss)		(784,000)
Other Income:		
Gain (Loss) on Sale of Assets		588,000
Income (Loss) Before Taxes		**(196,000)**
Income Taxes		**0**
Net Income (Loss)		**$(196,000)**

Branson Trucking Company
Statement of Retained Earnings
For the Year Ended December 31, 2007

Beginning Retained Earnings	**$1,456,000**
Net Income for the year	**(196,000)**
Retained Earnings	**$1,260,000**

UNAUDITED

Branson Trucking Company
Income Statement
For the Year Ended December 31, 2008

Sales	$20,321,000	
Less Sales Allowances	768,000	
Net Sales		$19,553,000
Cost of Sales		12,977,000
Gross Profit		6,576,000
Operating Expenses		6,894,000
Operating Income (Loss)		(318,000)
Other Income: Gain (Loss) on Sale of Assets		671,000
Income (Loss) Before Taxes		**353,000**
Income Taxes		**15,000**
Net Income (Loss)		**$338,000**

Branson Trucking Company
Statement of Retained Earnings
For the Year Ended December 31, 2008

Retained Earnings	$1,260,000
Net Income	338,000
	1,598,000
Less Dividends	120,000
Retained Earnings	$1,478,000

UNAUDITED

Branson Trucking Company
Income Statement
For the Year Ended December 31, 2009

Sales	$22,149,000	
Less Sales Allowances	883,000	
Net Sales		$21,266,000
Cost of Sales		14,122,000
Gross Profit		7,144,000
Operating Expenses		6,452,000
Operating Income (Loss)		692,000
Other Income: Gain (Loss) on Sale of Assets*		254,000
Income (Loss) Before Taxes		946,000
Income Taxes		286,000
Net Income (Loss)		$660,000

* Switched from ACR (tax) depreciation
to straight-line depreciation.

Branson Trucking Company
Statement of Retained Earnings
For the Year Ended December 31, 2009

Retained Earnings	$1,478,000
Net Income	660,000
	2,138,000
Less Dividends	400,000
Retained Earnings	$1,738,000

UNAUDITED

Branson Trucking Company
Income Statement
For the Year Ended December 31, 2010

Sales	$29,258,000	
Less Sales Allowances	1,186,000	
Net Sales		$28,072,000
Cost of Sales		20,346,000
Gross Profit		7,726,000
Operating Expenses		6,488,000
Operating Income (Loss)		1,238,000
Other Income: Gain (Loss) on Sale of Assets		254,000
Income (Loss) Before Taxes		1,492,000
Income Taxes		665,000
Net Income (Loss)		$827,000

Branson Trucking Company
Statement of Retained Earnings
For the Year Ended December 31, 2010

Retained Earnings	$1,738,000
Net Income	827,000
	2,565,000
Less Dividends	500,000
Retained Earnings	$2,065,000

UNAUDITED

Branson Trucking Company
Income Statement
For the Year Ended December 31, 2011

Sales	$34,610,000	
Less Sales Allowances	2,407,000	
Net Sales		$32,203,000
Cost of Sales		21,677,000
Gross Profit		10,526,000
Operating Expenses		8,738,000
Operating Income (Loss)		1,788,000
Other Income: Gain (Loss) on Sale of Assets		344,000
Income (Loss) Before Taxes		2,132,000
Income Taxes		960,000
Net Income (Loss)		$1,172,000

Branson Trucking Company
Statement of Retained Earnings
For the Year Ended December 31, 2011

Retained Earnings	$2,065,000
Net Income	1,172,000
	3,237000
Less Dividends	**800,000**
Retained Earnings	**$2,437,000**

PART 6
FORENSIC CAPSTONE ILLUSTRATION

chapter

18

FORENSIC ACCOUNTING IN ACTION

Education never ends, Watson. It is a series of lessons with the greatest for the last.

—Sherlock Holmes, *The Adventure of the Red Circle*

OBJECTIVES

After completing Chapter 18, you should be able to:

1. Understand the nature of a forensic engagement.
2. Describe the steps in the investigative process from engagement to conclusion.
3. Outline the investigative process and the types of documents needed.
4. Identify "red flags" among personnel and processes under investigation.
5. Distinguish fraudulent activity from mistakes or incompetence.
6. Explain the essential elements of a fraud investigation.
7. Gain a basic understanding of how data mining software works with data files.

OVERVIEW

The substance of forensic accounting is the real-life encounter with fraud, which can have far-reaching effects. Beyond the financial damage suffered by the particular business attacked, fraud can undermine investor confidence in an entire industry or a large segment of the economy.

In most cases of fraud, a tip-off begins the investigative process. Because those with the intent and means to defraud a company will attempt to hide their crime, a superficial, or pro forma audit, would be unlikely to detect even modestly clever schemes.

Incorporated here is a "capstone" or end-of-course project intended to enhance and test the knowledge of students using the *CCH Forensic and Investigative Accounting* textbook. It is based on two Problem-Based Learning (PBL) cases, which were developed independently for the teaching of principles of forensic accounting and the application of those principles to investigating fraud. Case Number 1, *TruGloss Shanghai JV: Investigating Fraud in an International Joint Venture*, was developed by Brian Ballou, Associate Professor, Miami University; Jennifer Mueller, Assistant Professor, Auburn University; and Paul Zikmund, Director Forensic Audit, Tyco International (US) Inc., and published in the *Journal of Forensic Accounting.*[1] Case Number 2, *Return of the Tallahassee BeanCounters: A Case in Forensic Accounting* was developed by Carol Callaway Dee, Associate Professor at University of Colorado, Denver, and Cindy Durtschi, Associate Professor at DePaul University, and published in *Issues in Accounting Education.*[2]

In addition to the end-of-course project included in this chapter, we have also included additional material that will allow students to work with the Tallahassee Bean Counter problem using the IDEA data mining software for analyzing electronic data (see Chapter 13 for a description of the IDEA software). This interactive exercise will allow students to conduct an audit function of certain elements of the Tallahassee Bean Counter business including: concessions, construction, maintenance and revenue. Please refer to **Appendix 10** in the book for step by step instructions for working with the data files of the Tallahassee Bean Counter problem. In Appendix 10 instructions, you will see a reference to the IDEA version Nine Tutorial and this tutorial can be found in the software download.

To download the demo version of IDEA, go to *http://www.caseware.com/IDEACDBook1*

The book is listed at the bottom. Once installed, students can simply select the option Try IDEA and install it.

We have included digital data files for the Tallahassee Bean Counter problem that will allow students to perform an electronic audit of various data sets to discover fraud or inconsistencies in the data. Once the students import the data they can begin analyzing and mining the data. All steps are retained in History for documentation purposes. Some of the many pre-programmed features included in IDEA are: Summarization, Stratification, Duplicate Detection, Gap Detection, Benford's Law, various Sampling techniques, and Aging.

To download the Data, students can obtain the files at: *http://ideasupport.caseware.com/public/downloads/datafia.zip*

Both cases reinforce principles discussed in the textbook and taught in forensic accounting/auditing courses throughout the United States. As outlined in the beginning of the textbook, "forensic" relates to the use of accounting and investigative techniques not only to uncover illegal activity but also to prove such fraud in a court of law under American rules of evidence and courtroom procedure. If you encounter problems downloading the software or accessing the files you may contact: *ideasupport@caseware.com*

Finally, it is important to note that any engagement by or on behalf of a company being investigated must clearly be set out in an agreement letter or consulting contract that delineates the duties and expectations of the forensic professional and the client with respect to each other. This includes, aside from the fees, the term and nature of the investigation, the amount and purpose of human and other resources committed, and the allocation of costs of obtaining, authenticating, and preserving documentation. The engagement agreement should also memorialize the parties' understanding about the type of report, how and to whom it is presented and shared (i.e. confidentiality, trade secret, and privacy considerations), and whether it is expected that the author will be called as an expert witness in a deposition, hearing or trial in a court of law.

The Elements of Fraud

¶ 18,001   ## EYE ON THE INVESTIGATIVE OUTCOME

"To begin with the end in mind," goes the oft-quoted management and management consulting maxim, means to have a clear understanding, or picture, of the final outcome; in this case, the results of a successful fraud investigation. The success of such an investigation can only be tested in a court of law, so it is critical to be able to clearly articulate results and findings in terms expected and accepted by the legal system. It will be left to lawyers and judges to decide what information is evidence and to judges and juries to decide the ultimate issue of guilt or innocence. Nevertheless, the forensic professional must provide the required information upon which evidentiary and other legal decisions will be made.

Questions Answered by Fraud Investigation

That information, developed through the application of investigative and auditing techniques, must answer the following questions with the best and most comprehensive documentary support possible:

- Who had the opportunity to commit fraudulent activity?
- How and when was the fraud committed?
- What was taken (how much money was lost)?
- Where were the assets moved (how were the assets converted to the benefit of the perpetrator)?
- Why was the activity intentional, rather than accidental, or the result of mistake or misunderstanding ("I thought it would be safer to keep the diamonds in a safe at home rather than a place professional thieves would stake out....")?

As noted, the information needed to answer these questions may not be obvious. Thus, to truly begin at the beginning requires assembling documentation on a company's employees and regular customers—the people who control or supervise the acquisition and distribution of assets (including money), and the basic paper trails (books, ledgers, invoices, and receipts) recording the movement of those assets. Looking for "red flags" involves both financial document and character analysis, getting to the first level of analysis: Who and what is susceptible to fraudulent activity.

No amount of discussing "red flags" will substitute for learning how to recognize red flags and accounting anomalies by comparing documents containing the same information from different sources, even though the information may be presented in the documents using different formats or for different purposes.

For example, a bill of lading, a sales invoice, and a warehouse receipt may look different but the important issue is whether they contain corroborating information (information consistent with other documents) or anomalous information (information that is inconsistent with other documents) about the same transactions and assets. Likewise, just as there is multiple documentation (both inside and outside a company) on transactions and assets, there is usually more than one source of information about employees and customers.

The investigator is almost invariably given a tip to critically inspect some aspect of the business activity leading to the engagement in the first place. Documentation in almost every case is likely quite voluminous, the proverbial needle in a haystack. Therefore, which superficially normal-appearing surfaces to scratch, how deep is the core of the practice, and the amount of experience to be gained is decided on a case-by-case basis.

The following case studies contain fairly obvious discrepancies once the surface is scratched in the direction of a few standout characters, which underscores the nature of the "game's afoot" being about who and what. When and how follow naturally with a little more digging, and finally the all-encompassing Why wraps up the story and satisfies the legal system's need for a motive (in the sense of intentional vs. accidental).

¶18,011   CASE NUMBER 1: TRUGLOSS SHANGHAI JV

The authors of Case Number 1 have laid out succinctly the basic principles and parameters of analysis to be applied in uncovering and proving the fraudulent activity at *TruGloss Shanghai JV*. It is based on an actual and successfully investigated case of fraud involving a United States company with operations in Asia. Though unique in its particulars, the circumstances and business conditions that underlie the illegal activity uncovered are quite common and not just in the context of international business ventures. The issues confronted and described are equally applicable in domestic operations of any size company in America. The *TruGloss* presentation includes a substantial analysis of the case laid out for the student. Understanding the *TruGloss* case will also help the student focus on the type of issues addressed in the *Tallahassee BeanCounters* case No. 2, which follows it and ends the chapter. Unlike the *TruGloss* case, in the *BeanCounters* case the student is asked to perform forensic investigation.

Case Synopsis

TruGloss is a producer of high-quality paints sold to warehouse distributors and warehouse home improvement retailers throughout the United States and Canada. TruGloss recently has begun efforts to expand internationally by forming joint ventures with international distributors to help in managing operations within Europe and Asia. In countries where government restrictions dictate how such joint ventures are structured, TruGloss must alter its typical partnership strategy in order to operate.

TruGloss believes that China possesses significant opportunities for growth and long term viability. With the economic growth of that country, particularly in Shanghai and Hong Kong, the Company believes that many of its product lines, particularly its industrial-duty and commercial-grade products, will thrive for the next 10 – 15 years at a minimum. However, to open operations in China, TruGloss must form a joint venture with a local government—the Shanghai City Government in this case—in which TruGloss is a 49 percent minority owner and the government is a 51 percent majority owner. TruGloss agreed to these terms and formed the TruGloss Shanghai JV.

Each party agreed to several conditions under the joint venture. As part of the agreement, TruGloss agreed to allow the joint venture to use its brand name and supply products for sale at the joint venture under several conditions. TruGloss required that the joint venture conform to all of its corporate policies, such that all business practices conform to United States laws and regulations for conducting business in a foreign country. The practices include internal controls, operating procedures, and external reporting issues. TruGloss also required that it supply several employees for key positions at the joint venture. These employees are employed by TruGloss but seconded (on loan) to the joint venture. The Shanghai City Government agreed to supply office space and warehousing for TruGloss products in Shanghai and several other Chinese cities and enable all TruGloss products to be imported into China. The city also required that several key executive positions be filled with individuals from its offices. The remainder of the employees at TruGloss Shanghai JV was hired locally.

Employees Seconded to TruGloss Shanghai JV

Several key positions at TruGloss Shanghai JV are filled by seconded managers from TruGloss, Alex Richards and Grant Williams, who serve as General Manager and Finance Manager at TruGloss Shanghai JV, respectively. Both Alex and Grant speak fluent Chinese and worked for other companies with Chinese operations prior to joining TruGloss at its Philadelphia headquarters five years before the joint venture was formed. However, neither Alex nor Grant has ever actually worked in China. All employees who work under the seconded managers are from Shanghai. As part of their duties, Alex and Grant are responsible for oversight of their subordinates and are to ensure that TruGloss policies and practices are followed, including ensuring that all internal controls are in place and consistently applied.

Process for Ordering and Shipping Inventory from United States to Joint Venture

Since all paint is purchased from the United States, Alex Richards is responsible for establishing the lowest acceptable prices to charge customers in China. However, he allows his three sales managers, Cheng Xi (Shekou), Hong Wu (Shanghai), and Jueng Chan (Yantian), to negotiate prices above the floor price and schedule delivery of orders. Before Alex will place an order for paint to be shipped from the United States to the joint venture, he complies with company policy that a 20 percent down payment be made by the customer. Also, under TruGloss policy for international sales at joint ventures, all sales are made ex-terminal and therefore require cash payment prior to final "delivery" of products.

In order to receive inventory and release it to customers, the logistics manager at each of the three TruGloss warehouses in China requires an original bill of lading, packing list, and sales invoice. The logistics manager at each plant is also responsible for processing all customs declarations. Once documentation is appropriately handled, customers are responsible for removing their orders from the warehouse. There are three TruGloss warehouses located in Shanghai, Yantian, and Shekou that are managed by Daqing Yang, Marti Chow, and Xong Chae, respectively.

Operations at TruGloss Shanghai JV after Three Years

TruGloss and Shanghai City Officials conduct a review of operations with Alex Richards and Grant Williams at the end of the joint venture's third year of operations. TruGloss Shanghai JV has performed above expectations over its first three years of operations, steadily growing at sales increases of between 30 and 50 percent each year. The Shanghai government has been discussing the possibility of adding three new warehouses in other provinces with TruGloss executives during each of the next few years.

Alex Richards credits much of his success on his reliance on his managers and their knowledge of local customers and customs in developing solid business relationships. Repeat sales to customers have been steadily increasing over the first three years of operations, particularly for customers in the Shanghai sales territory. Richards has been pleased with the ability of the sales managers and logistics managers to work closely to ensure that products are delivered to warehouses and customers in a timely fashion. TruGloss (U.S.) has been pleased that down payments for purchases are made on a timely basis, which enables the supply chain to work effectively.

Alex has been pleased with the volume of sales by each of the sales managers. Hong Wu has been the top sales manager each year with average sales over the three years of $20 million USD per year. Cheng Xi also has performed quite well with average sales over the three years of $14 million USD per year. Wu credits his success to his ability to efficiently work with local customers to ensure timely down payments and Daqing Yang (the Shanghai logistics manager) to quickly process orders and have them available for customers in a faster time than any local competitors. Xi credits his success to the long-term relationships that he has cultivated in Shekou.

Grant Williams attributes some of the success of the joint venture to his ability to effectively hedge currency risk utilizing state-of-the art derivatives that he learned about while at his prior employer, an investment banking firm in Philadelphia. He credits the employees in the joint venture's financial management business process for working well with managers in key operational processes, particularly sales and supply chain management. He has been so impressed with their work ethic and commitment to servicing those processes that he has been able to focus most of his time on the treasury side of the business.

Although pleased with the performance of TruGloss Shanghai JV, the CFO of TruGloss, Jane Urley, (US) is interested in learning more about how the joint venture has been able to perform so well as a new market entrant, particularly in Shanghai, where 45 percent of its sales have been generated. To help explain their success, Alex and Grant ask Hong Wu (the sales representative in charge of Shanghai), Daqing Yang (the logistics manager in charge of the Shangai plant), and Xiang Chu (accounting manager for Shanghai) to attend the meeting with he and Grant Williams.

When asked about why the Shanghai operations were so successful, Wu discussed his ability to tap into the high demand for quality U.S. paints in the Shanghai market because of all of the construction occurring in and around the city. Wu noted that although there were several competitors in the area, the reputation of TruGloss gave him the competitive advantage to sell the paints at prices that were slightly higher than competitors. He noted that receiving timely down payments was the secret in turning over inventory rapidly and shortening sales cycles.

Daqing Yang echoed Wu's explanation by stating that customers were constantly putting pressure on him to get sales cleared through customs and into their hands. He noted that it seemed as if the customers were standing outside the warehouse door looking at their watches, waiting to give him their cash for the inventory.

Xiang Chu added that Wu and Yang were excellent about informing them of customer payments and deliveries so that accounting could update its records on a timely basis. She noted that Wu personally handled sales transactions by placing orders, collecting cash down payments, and getting cash from Yang to match with invoices so that personnel in accounting could perform their duties more efficiently (e.g., deposit cash and record sales).

Chu's only concern was that some customers were not paying for their inventory in full when they were picking up their goods. Wu failed, on more than one occasion, to provide proper supporting documentation for sales made to customers. He was unable to present sales invoices or customs declaration forms to substantiate the sale. He also failed to present customer background check information to show the legitimacy of the customers. However, since they were continuing to buy more merchandise and make down payments, she believed that the customers probably were following up quite well. While the other sales and logistics managers were also performing well, none were doing so as efficiently as the Shanghai sales and logistics managers, according to Chu.

TruGloss' CFO, Jane Urley, was satisfied by the responses of the joint venture managers, but she was a bit concerned about whether internal controls were being followed in a manner consistent with TruGloss policy. Alex Richards assured her that the joint venture was acting in the spirit of the Company's policies but that some controls were not consistently followed because of the volume of sales that had been occurring over the first three years.

Further, the local culture and work practices in Shanghai are different than that of the United States, resulting in a transition period of adapting to controls designed for western cultures and work practices. Both he and Shanghai City officials assured the CFO that no serious policies were being violated (e.g., bribes, etc.); however, Alex noted that often orders were being processed ahead of proper documentation and that internal audits had occurred less often than expected by TruGloss policy. He informed the CFO that he had been so busy putting out fires that he had not been performing due diligence on new customers, but that all were making timely 20 percent down payments prior to shipment. Alex, on one occasion, manually checked a few shipments and was unable to locate the bill of lading and packing slip for the shipment. Xu referenced the fact that some of the records may not be properly documented and/or stored correctly but Xu would research the issue and get back to Alex. Alex became busy with other issues and failed to follow-up with the issue.

Grant Williams is responsible for ensuring that an audit be performed, but he has been so understaffed and preoccupied with treasury operations that he has not been able to complete several audits that he had begun in each of the past two years. He informed the CFO that physical inventories had been completed at the Yantian and Shekou plants the prior year and would be performed the following year at all three plants. The Shanghai inventory was not performed because Daqing Yang's wife was in a car accident and he was unable to be present the day it was scheduled. Since neither party could re-arrange their schedule after that time, they decided to wait until the following year. He assured the CFO that a thorough audit was scheduled for the following year, which also would include a review of all customer accounts to ensure timely payments were occurring for all paint sold and reconciliation of all cash accounts.

¶18,015   PRINCIPLES OF APPLIED FORENSIC ANALYSIS

Culture Consideration

An important component of global business is to consider the influence of diverse cultures. Students can perform research of the Chinese culture using the Internet and library resources to get a sense of how a forensic accountant may prepare for a case involving business outside our culture. The primary theme that students should take away from their research is that in communist China, the government is often a party to business ventures—particularly those concerning non-national companies. Companies outside China go through an "entrance application" process to acquire a license to conduct business. Further, the government has policies concerning the structure of the business (e.g., government ownership interest) and how the business will operate (e.g., workforce must be hired locally).

The case is no different with Shanghai JV. In order for TruGloss to operate in Shanghai, it was required to form a joint venture with the local government. Furthermore, the local government retained majority interest (51 percent). Employees were hired locally and executive positions were held by Shanghai city government officials. TruGloss was able to fill only two key positions with employees from its Philadelphia headquarters (the General Manager and Finance Manager positions).

Students should recognize that from the outset this business structure afforded TruGloss little control over the operation of the business. TruGloss was ultimately dependent on the two seconded employees of its own to oversee and monitor business practices, operations, and accounting. Even though the business transactions and control procedures were designed similarly to TruGloss' US operations, only the two managers seconded by TruGloss were really accountable to headquarters for proper operation.

Accounting Anomalies Often Signal the Presence of Fraud

Examples of accounting anomalies include:

    a. Irregularities in source documents (e.g., missing documents, excessive voids or credits, common names or addresses of customers, increases in past due receivables, increased reconciling of items, etc.)

    b. Faulty journal entries, and

    c. Inaccuracies in ledgers

For each of the accounting anomalies, the discussion below describes conditions from the case that increase concerns that fraudulent activity could be present.

Irregularities in Source Documents

- Shanghai JV sales transactions utilize cash payments at the time the customer takes possession of inventory at the warehouse. Alternatively, corporate sales transactions typically utilize a process of sending invoices and subsequently receiving cash payments.
- The Shanghai warehouse has been allowing sales transactions to customers for cash without documentation required up front by TruGloss. Thus, orders were processed ahead of (or without) documentation to verify new customers.
- Many sales have been attributed to repeat customers in Shanghai. However, the other two locations of the joint venture have had far fewer sales to repeat customers.
- Shanghai JV has experienced failure of customers to pay in full at time of delivery despite documentation showing payment.

Faulty Journal Entries

- Accounting personnel make journal entries based on what they are told to do by the sales representatives and warehouse managers. No supporting documentation is required by the accounting manager.

- Customers are required to make a 20 percent down payment at the time of placing an order and required to pay the remaining amount when picking up purchased inventory at the warehouse. With the sales manager claiming that some customers were not paying for their inventory in full when picking up their goods, it appears that accounting personnel are allowing partial and incomplete payments to be recorded for certain repeat customers even though the policy explicitly states that balances are to be paid in full.

Inaccuracies in Ledgers

- The use of cash transactions and lack of required documentation for each sales transaction reduces the likelihood that the customer account subledger will be accurate.
- Since the accounting department makes entries based on instructions from other personnel, there is a greater likelihood that the general ledger might be inaccurate (unless timely and thorough reconciliation of account balances are performed).

While the case does not include much explicit information on accounting anomalies, it provides the students with information from which they can infer these and possibly other anomalies likely to exist. Rarely would an accounting manager, sales representative, or warehouse manager voluntarily provide explicit information about accounting anomalies. Rather, fraud investigators interpret cues that suggest the existence of such anomalies.

Internal Control Weaknesses Make Fraud Easier to Perpetrate

The following internal control weaknesses can contribute to fraud:

- a. Lack of segregation of duties
- b. Lack of physical safeguards
- c. Lack of independent checks
- d. Lack of proper authorization
- e. Lack of proper documents and records
- f. Overriding of existing controls
- g. Inadequate accounting system

For each of the items in the list, the discussion below describes conditions from the case that increase concerns that fraudulent activity could be present.

Lack of Segregation of Duties

- Sales manager dictates accounting transactions to accounting manager
- Logistics manager dictates accounting transactions to accounting manager
- Finance manager also responsible for conducting internal audits of the joint venture
- Logistics manager releases inventory and collects cash payments from customers at warehouse
- Sales manager handles cash and determines accounting treatment
- Accounting managers handle cash and make deposits

Lack of Physical Safeguards

- Customers take possession of inventory directly from warehouse, which is not designed for separate access for customers
- Cash down payments for orders handled by sales manager before being given to accounting manager
- Cash received from customers at time of order pickup is handled by logistics manager and/or sales manager before being given to accounting manager

Lack of Independent Checks

- No formal reconciliation process appears to exist by accounting personnel before recording a transaction (even though a company policy regarding required documentation exists)

- Finance manager (seconded TruGloss employee) appears to perform little oversight over accounting personnel
- General manager (seconded TruGloss employee) appears to perform little oversight over sales personnel
- Logistics managers appear to be operating under little oversight
- Accounting manager and sales manager have not questioned logistics manager for why less than full payments have been received when releasing inventory to repeat customers

Lack of Proper Authorization
- Sales manager is empowered to sell inventory to customers at any negotiated price above the floor
- Accounting transactions are being dictated by sales and logistics managers

Lack of Proper Documents and Records
- Inventory has been released to customers without proper documentation
- Accounting managers making journal entries based on instructions from sales representatives
- Sales representatives are establishing prices for customers based on negotiation and not a set pricing list
- Down payments and sales of inventory being conducted using cash instead of by using invoices and bank drafts (reducing the audit trail)

Overriding of Existing Controls
- Inventory has been released to customers without proper documentation
- Inventory has been released to customers without receiving the full remaining balance
- Reconciliation of physical inventory to accounting records at the Shaghai warehouse hasn't occurred

Inadequate Accounting System
- Lack of an integrated information system that enables the accounting process to rely on more than the instructions by the sales managers
- System only allows for cash payments by customers
- Accounting system allows for handling of cash received by too many parties
- Reconciliation of ledgers and subledgers does not appear to be adequate, if present at all

Unusual or Unrealistic Procedures and Relationships

Analytical anomalies include transactions or events that appear out of the ordinary or results too unrealistic to be believable. Forensic accountants identify many procedures, relationships and results that appear to be unusual or unrealistic. This categorization can be used to compare and contrast the facts in this case that are/are not related to the organization being an international joint venture. Although the control weakness might be more apparent in an international joint venture, the analytical anomalies are not that different from those often found for fraud involving domestic organizations.

Analytical Anomalies Likely to Occur in Domestic Organizations
- Sales growth exceeding expectations (30–50 percent per year over a three-year period), particularly when driven by one or a few individuals
- High concentrations of repeat customers for certain sales representatives
- Significantly shortened transaction cycle times relative to competition
- Sustained sales growth at prices above competition's in a developing economy
- Higher than average performance across most metrics for only a few individuals

Analytical Anomalies Likely to Occur only in International Organizations

- High percentage of customers purchasing inventory with cash

In many investigations, only a sparse amount of information about the suspected fraud is originally available so that investigator will need to carefully examine the initial facts of the case to identify clues and *make inferences* about what likely took place. Additional inquiries are made and additional facts gathered until the picture of fraud comes to light. The key analysis for TruGloss is highlighted below.

What Was Taken?

- $6 million USD of inventory missing from the Shanghai warehouse
- $6 million USD cash associated with sales to customers
- $5 million USD of accounts receivable (70 percent of which was for sales that were claimed never to have occurred) associated with customers claiming never to have ordered any inventory

Who Had the Opportunity?

- Hong Wu, the sales manager in Shanghai who was responsible for sales
- Daqing Yang, the logistics manager for the Shanghai warehouse
- Xiang Chu, accounting manager who made accounting entries and deposits
- Alex Richards, Wu's and Yang's supervisor
- Grant Williams, Chu's supervisor

How Were the Assets Moved?

- Individuals—likely not actual customers—picked up inventory from the warehouse, sometimes without the need for required documentation
- Logistics manager released inventory to individuals (supposedly customers) for cash
- Cash was transferred from Yang to Wu

How Was the Theft Concealed?

- Wu attributed all/some of cash received by legitimate customers to other customers—some of which would have been used as down payments for other fictitious/improper sales
- Part of cash received from individuals for inventory used to account for actual sales and part of cash withheld by Yang and Wu
- Sales made to future customers could have been made for amounts below those approved by TruGloss Shanghai JV
- Yang and Wu could have involved Chu, Richards, and/or Williams to help ensure that fraud was not detected

How Were the Assets Converted?

- Inventory sold to individuals (who are not actual customers) at below market prices for cash—not possible to trace payments originating from certain customers to accounting transactions (because of the nature of a cash transaction)
- Yang and Wu may have laundered cash
- Lapping of accounts receivable enabled turnover to occur until fraud detected

What Were the Red Flag Symptoms?

- Better than expected growth relative to local competition
- Lack of proper separation of duties for operations, custody, accounting, and monitoring of assets
- Insufficient oversight of operational employees
- Above average performance for one segment of the joint venture, involving only a few individuals
- Sales of inventory for cash at the warehouse, often without necessary documentation
- High concentrations of repeat customers for one segment of the joint venture
- Increase in accounts receivable aging

What Pressures and Rationalization Might Have Motivated the Frauds?

- None—perpetrators could be sociopathic fraud perpetrators—TruGloss Shanghai happens to be the latest victim
- Financial pressures on any individual: Wu, Yang, Chu, Richards, and/or Williams
- Pressure to achieve growth targets in a new market
- Competitive pressure among sales or logistics managers
- Belief that other competitors are conducting business in the same fashion
- Culturally acceptable to conduct sales based on cash transactions at warehouse locations, regardless of internal controls imposed by partner from the United States

What Key Internal Controls Could Have Prevented or Detected the Fraud?

- Background checks of managers at TruGloss Shanghai JV
- Proper oversight by General Manager (Richards) and Finance Manager (Williams)
- Completion of required monitoring mechanism (i.e., internal audits) as required by policy
- Insistence by accounting managers that no transaction be recorded without proper documentation and approval
- Periodic and diligent comparisons of the joint venture to local competition and other international joint ventures—are the results at TruGloss Shanghai "too good to be true"?
- Periodic monitoring and follow-up for aged accounts receivable
- Required physical counts of inventories and mandatory reconciliations
- Periodic analysis of gross margins and any other key ratios based on recorded amounts
- Mandatory vacations for all management positions

¶ 18,021 CASE NUMBER 2: TALLAHASSEE BEANCOUNTERS

Case No. 2 is a problem-based learning (PBL) exercise designed for students to interact with each other in teams and with the instructor, who is intended to act more as a facilitator and gatekeeper of information exchange. Regardless of whether students work alone or in teams, the instructor should be viewed as either a cooperative insider recruited by the client to gather less obvious documents, or as an outside private investigation firm hired for the purpose of following leads to dead-ends or fruitful resources, as the case may be.

After the case synopsis, which follows, a series of basic documents are provided of who and what are involved in the Tallahassee BeanCounter (a minor-league baseball team) company under investigation. Students are then asked to provide preliminary analysis and explicit follow-up questions and information requests.

After the students submit their preliminary analysis, the students will be told by the instructor how to proceed, depending on how much course time the instructor wishes to devote to the exercise. A PBL case like this could be accomplished in as little as one or up to several sessions or weeks, in a course curriculum. Regardless of which option, or options, is chosen, asking pointed questions in the right direction will be required before additional information can be uncovered.

This additional information will take the form of secondary documents that either corroborate and vouchsafe the superficial accounting information initially provided or reveal anomalies and discrepancies pointing to who, what, when, where, how, and why. Again, this can be done over a period of time, or all at once as the instructor chooses and course time allows.

In addition, as explained in the Overview of this chapter, we have also included additional material to accompany this chapter that will allow students to work with the Tallahassee Bean Counter problem using the IDEA data mining software for analyzing electronic data (see Chapter 13). This interactive exercise will allow students to conduct an audit function of certain elements of the business including: concessions, construction, maintenance and revenue. Please refer to **Appendix 10** in the book for step by step instructions for working with the data files of the Tallahassee Bean Counter problem. In Appendix 10 instructions, you will see a reference to the IDEA version Nine Tutorial and this tutorial can be found in the software download.

To download the demo version of IDEA, go to *http://www.caseware.com/IDEACDBook1*

The book is listed at the bottom. Once installed, students can simply select the option Try IDEA and install it.

We have included digital data files for the Tallahassee Bean Counter problem that will allow students to perform electronic audit of various data sets to discover fraud or inconsistencies in the data. Once the students import the data they can begin analyzing and mining the data. All steps are retained in History for documentation purposes. Some of the many pre-programmed features included in IDEA are: Summarization, Stratification, Duplicate Detection, Gap Detection, Benford's Law, various Sampling techniques, and Aging.

To download the Data, students can obtain the file at: *http://ideasupport.caseware.com/public/downloads/datafia.zip.* If there are problems downloading the software or accessing the data files you may contact *ideasupport@caseware.com.*

Case Synopsis

Your firm has been hired to conduct a forensic investigation of the Tallahassee BeanCounters (TBC), a minor league baseball team in Tallahassee, Florida. TBC has never before been audited. Franklin Kennedy, the team's owner, has told employees that the audit is a requirement of the bank, which provided the mortgage loan for the recently completed training facility. However, Mr. Kennedy privately tells your audit team that he received an anonymous note (below) in the mail leading him to suspect that someone within the company is committing fraud. The envelope, addressed to Mr. Kennedy, had a Tallahassee postmark and no return address. Because Mr. Kennedy lives in Boston, he has entrusted the running of this franchise to his long-time associate Phil Ackers. Mr. Kennedy had assumed that things were running efficiently until the note arrived. TBC has no formal procedures to accommodate whistle-blowers and the employees of TBC are unaware of the true nature of your engagement.

Mr. Kennedy:

I think there is something funny going on here at TBC. Numbers that do not add up, lots of whispers in the hallways and closed-door discussions have me suspicious. If I were you I would check it out.

A long-time friend.

The owner has asked you to focus your investigation on the last five months (May through September). This is the time period during which the training facility was constructed. As you familiarize yourself with the company, you note that in addition to revenue from ticket sales, TBC generates funds from parking, fundraising, and sales of concessions and game programs. Franklin Kennedy also gives TBC some start-up money at the beginning of the season to assist with expenses until the team starts earning revenue from games. He withdraws that money over the course of the season. Operating expenses consist primarily of payroll, equipment (bats, balls, etc.), team travel, programs, and concession inventory. Any fees due to the baseball league, such as franchise fees, are paid by the Boston Sox (Franklin Kennedy's major league team) on behalf of TBC. Payroll is processed by an outside service company. Other office expenses are similar to those of most small businesses.

Student Handout (SH)1 provides an organizational chart for TBC. Office manager Ben Hill oversees daily operations of the organization. Michelle Shelton provides support for management and handles most of the bookkeeping, including accounts payable, cash receipts, and equipment purchase orders. Candace (Candie) Larson, receptionist, answers phones and compiles time sheets for processing. Julie Roper, assistant to the president, assists with donor relations and is also responsible for concessions ordering and inventory as well as accounts receivable collections. President Phil Ackers oversees fundraising activities and supervised the building of TBC's newly completed training facility.

To familiarize yourself with TBC, you attend a night game and chat with some of the employees. The three women who work in the ticket booth seem particularly eager to chat. Myrna Myers, their supervisor, tells you the three women have worked together in the booth for 20 years. Their husbands come to every game, and the six often socialize together as well. Myrna is happy to talk to you about the other TBC employees, especially those in the front office. Below is a summary of Myrna's opinions.

Company Overview: Things have changed a lot this last year. Mr. Ackers cut down on excess employees, particularly some of the game-day employees because it's expensive to build a new training facility. I don't mind because this new building is great. It's state-of-the-art and I hope it will help us recruit and keep our players in shape. We've had a great season this year, and all of the ladies here would love to see that continue. A lot of people complained during the building because of the mess and there was some tension because Mr. Ackers was on us to be efficient and cut expenses so we could qualify for a good rate on the mortgage loan, but we qualified and I think it was worth it. Phil brought in food and drinks for all of us the day we got the loan and everything was set. It was a lot of fun.

Phil Ackers Company President : Phil's a nice guy; he oversees the fundraising, and seems to know everyone everywhere. That's probably because he was a professional ballplayer years ago. He was pretty tense during the building of the new training facility, but now that it's completed, he's getting back to his old self. He's really close to his family; in fact, he even hired his niece Julie Roper to take the place of Terri Hughes who had been his assistant forever when she left to go take care of her mother.

Julie Roper Assistant to the President : She's a great change from Terri Hughes, Mr. Acker's former assistant. Terri guarded Mr. Ackers' office to the point it was impossible to get hold of Mr. Ackers to ask even the simplest question. Anyway, Terri's mother got sick and Terri left, then Mr. Ackers hired his niece, Julie. Like I said, she's a welcome change. She works very hard, even has taken over some jobs that Terri wouldn't touch, like the ordering for concessions and group ticket sales. She also took over accounts receivable collections from Michelle, who was thrilled to get rid of that job.

Tucker Johnson General Manager : The players love Tucker. He has an interesting coaching philosophy—never raises his voice to the players or uses foul language. We've sent many players up to the majors, so he still gets the job done even without the four-letter words. Tucker can't stand paperwork, so he has Sam do most of the ordering as well as taking care of all the equipment.

Ben Hill Office Manager : Ben still thinks it's 1979 and disco is king. He dresses like John Travolta in Saturday Night Fever and is always hitting on the women in the office. He has several ex-wives; most of whom he started dating while still married to a previous one. When TBC qualified for its bank loan, Ben got a nice bonus which he blew on a new car. He calls it his "chick magnet." He keeps things running smoothly in the office though, so Mr. Ackers pretty much lets him run day-to-day operations however he wants.

Candace Larson Receptionist : Candie is a sweet young girl. She's good with the phones, and everyone likes her. She's the reigning Queen of the Taylor County Crab Festival. We were all real proud when she won. She's always at the practice field after work—sometimes I think she's more interested in dating players than in doing her job, but overall she's a good worker.

Michelle Shelton A/P Clerk : Michelle is really hard working. She handles all the bookkeeping and paperwork, like the purchase orders and stuff. She's also going to school part time.

To begin your audit, your team does a walk-through of each process at TBC. SH 2 describes your observations of those processes and how employees handle their responsibilities. You also collect a copy of the team game schedule (SH 3) and copies of the last five months of financial information (SH 4 through SH 17).

ASSIGNMENT

Your instructor will divide the class into teams. Working with your team, your assignment is to determine whether fraud has been committed at TBC, and, if so, to gather and present evidence sufficient to prove the guilt of the suspect(s). This is a competitive exercise. It is essential that you keep the information that your team has gathered private. Leaks provide other teams with cheap information, and will put your team at a disadvantage at the time of grading.

Procedure

The first step is to review the background and financial information provided. Then, working with your team, brainstorm.[3] Given the company, its employees, and processes, how could a fraud be committed and concealed? Remember the "fraud triangle:" to commit fraud, a perpetrator must have pressure, opportunity, and a rationalization for his or her behavior (AICPA, para. 33). Are there weaknesses in controls that could be exploited by an unscrupulous employee? Which employees have the incentive to do so? Review the given financial data. Do relationships between financial and non-financial information seem reasonable? Are there any unusual trends, postings, or transactions about which your group is curious?

As in a real audit or forensic investigation, your group is not provided, initially, with all the information needed to solve the case. Once your group has reviewed the materials provided and completed your brainstorming session covering the questions listed above, compile a list of additional information you would like to receive. You will request this information via your instructor. To obtain the additional information you need, send an email to your instructor, but address your request to the appropriate employee of TBC, or the appropriate outside party. For example, "Michelle Shelton: Please provide us with copies of the phone invoices for May."

As this is a forensic investigative exercise, you have greater latitude than in most audit situations to gather information in any legal manner you see fit. For example, you can question TBC employees, their friends, relatives, and business associates. If you have enough evidence to give probable cause, you can obtain a subpoena from a judge enabling you to acquire private information (such as credit reports or bank accounts). If requesting evidence from outside of TBC, be clear in your request. For example, "If I examine public records, what will I learn about cars owned by Sam McCarty?" or "If I attend the TBC fundraising event on April 3, what will I see?" You can also conduct other information gathering exercises—for example, surveillance of TBC employees.

Interviewing Suspects

If time allows, your instructor may provide your team an opportunity to interrogate your suspect(s) near the end of your work on the case. The goal of the interrogation is to obtain a confession from your suspect(s). You can include any confessions you obtain as additional evidence in your final fraud report. You will question any suspects as a team, so think of ways you can use your team effectively. The interviews are generally short (10 to 20 minutes), so consider the following:

1. Be prepared. The more information you have gathered toward solving the case, the higher the likelihood you can induce an admission of guilt from your suspect. For example, if you know who did it, how they did it, why they did it, and can show that they benefited from the crime, you can box your suspect(s) into a corner and obtain a confession.
2. Have a plan. Organize your information and decide on a method of presentation that will best demonstrate to the perpetrator that denial of guilt is futile. However, do not treat your pre-planned questions as a script to which you must adhere. You will want to modify your approach as the interview progresses based upon the responses of the suspect.
3. Have a theme for your interview. How will you behave toward the suspect? Will you be empathetic and understanding, allowing the suspect to rationalize his or her behavior? Or will you act as if resistance to questioning is fruitless, as you have all the information you need and are just letting the suspect state his or her side? Will you team up to play "good-cop, bad-cop"? Make certain that all members of your team are using the same line of reasoning.

Final Fraud Report

Your team will be graded based upon your written final fraud report. Your report should be convincing and include the following for each fraud your group uncovers:

4. The name(s) of the perpetrator(s) of the crime.
5. How the perpetrator(s) committed the fraud.
6. The dollar magnitude of the fraud.
7. The personal gain received by the perpetrator(s) from the fraud.

In your report, you should include evidence to back up your assertions in the four areas above. This evidence might include documentation you have gathered from your emails, information summarized from interviews and other sources such as surveillance, and analysis based on data from the student handouts. Finally, experience has shown that the most successful teams are those that work together. Each team member's point of view is valuable. Divide this case and work alone, at your own peril.

Documents for Analysis

Figures 18.1 through 18.28 provide the immediate information that is available for you to begin your investigation of fraud at the BeanCounters. These include an organizational chart and an analysis based on interviews with the various employees regarding their backgrounds and job functions and how they conduct the company's business on a regular basis. There is a copy of the game schedule and financial files (registers, ledgers, inventory, invoices, payroll records, revenue and expense accounting) for the period April through July where you are told to expect that fraudulent activity is most likely to have occurred.

Figure 18.1. Tallahassee BeanCounters Organizational Chart

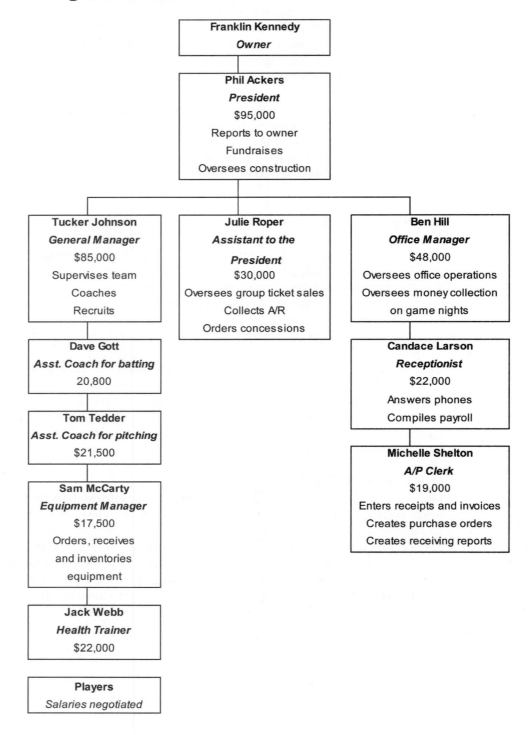

Figure 18.2. Observations of TBC Functions

Concessions:

You arrive an hour before the gates open to observe the concession operation. There is one concession booth. Holly Hope, the supervisor, rushes back and forth between the storeroom under the bleachers and the booth with needed supplies. She is always answering questions and seems to do three things at once. Toward the end of the evening, you make a trip to the storeroom with her and note that Julie Roper is manning the storeroom. She seems very efficient as she hands Holly the supplies she needs to take back upstairs. The storeroom seems to be neatly ordered and though some supplies are low, they do not seem to be in real danger of running out of anything. As you help Holly carry the supplies back to the concession booths, she tells you what a relief it is to have Julie's help, because before Julie took over, she was the one who had to stay after the game to count inventory and prepare the concession order for the next home game. She laughs when she tells you that old habits die hard, because she continued to go into the storeroom the morning after games to take inventory for awhile because it seemed so low. She finally stopped because Julie must be doing a good job, they never run out of anything.

Upstairs in the stadium, you observe three people working in the booth and six college-aged, young people working the bleachers. The bleacher workers come back periodically to refill drinks and trays. You note the bleacher workers are given $50 in small bills at the beginning of the night. When they return with an empty tray, they are required to turn over the money for the tray they sold. For example, if they sold 40 drinks, they turn over $40.00. At the end of the night, each returns $50.00 to the register. Ben Hill is there to observe Holly and the workers as they count cash from the bleacher workers during the night.

The concession booth closes during the ninth inning and the money counting begins. The register report shows the number of items sold and total receipts. Holly and one worker count the cash and compare the numbers with the register-generated receipts. Ben Hill arrives back from observing the money counts in parking and programs before Holly and the worker have finished and makes the two stay until the numbers balance.

Ben then takes the register tape and cash to the office under the protection of an armed security guard. Ben locks the money in the safe, and leaves the register tape on Michelle's (A/P clerk) desk. The next day, Michelle and Ben recount the money to make certain it reconciles with the number of items sold on the register report. Michelle records receipts in the QuickBooks program that automatically adjusts the inventory and creates a deposit slip. Ben Hill takes the sales report summarizing the sales to Phil Ackers then personally takes the deposit to the bank.

Construction of the Training Facility:

A year ago, Franklin Kennedy, owner of TBC, decided to build a new training facility. A complete set of blueprints and related specifications were made available to local contractors. Five different contractors submitted sealed bids. The bids were kept in a safe in Phil Acker's office. Eight months ago, all the contractors assembled and the bids were opened. Larkin Construction had the lowest bid. Construction began six months ago and was completed by the end of the season. Phil acted as the on-site project manager. The construction loan was provided by US Bank, and the construction draws were drafted against it. The mortgage loan was issued upon completion of the construction. Phil and Ben received a bonus from Franklin Kennedy (the team owner) because the profit ratio the company achieved during the testing period was good enough to qualify for a low interest loan, saving the company a considerable amount of money over the life of the loan.

Equipment Purchases:

Equipment orders originate with Tucker Johnson, the general manager, or Sam McCarty, the equipment manager. When new equipment is needed, they take the list of needed equipment to Ben Hill for approval. Ben chooses a vendor and Michelle generates a purchase order in the bookkeeping program. The bookkeeping program also generates a receiving report that Michelle returns to Sam. When the equipment arrives, you observe Sam receive the shipment. He carefully counts the shipment and checks off the appropriate amounts on his receiving report. Sam later takes his receiving report to Michelle. Michelle compares the receiving report, the purchase order and the invoice to make certain all the equipment has arrived, then staples the paperwork together and gives it to Julie who generates a check. She forwards the check and supporting documentation to Ben, or Phil who checks all the paperwork before signing the check. Michelle mails the checks and picks up and opens the mail.

Parking:

You spend an evening watching the parking operation. You notice there are five employees working in addition to the supervisor. Two workers hand out tickets, the other three help direct and park the vehicles. The workers wear carpenter's aprons and collect $2.00 for cars and $3.00 for larger vehicles such as RVs. They put the cash in their aprons, and put a ticket under the windshield wiper of each vehicle. You count 1,500 parking spaces in the lot. The crew quits collecting money an hour after the game begins. The workers turn their aprons and remaining tickets over to the supervisor. The supervisor then takes the aprons and tickets to the ticket booth where he reconciles the number of tickets sold with the cash on hand. Ben supervises the process and verifies the amounts.

Payroll:

Payroll is subcontracted out to ADP Payroll Services. Permanent staff and players are paid bi-monthly. Players and some seasonal office workers have eight-month contracts while five management personnel have 12 month contracts. Salaried employees are paid on the 1st and 15th of each month. Game-day (temporary) employees are paid after each home game series. Candace Larson collects the time cards from the supervisor of each division after each game (concessions, parking, programs, ticket sales, security, and the team mascot). Each employee's time card is signed by his or her supervisor and co-signed by the person from the front office who is responsible for that division. Candace creates a consolidated timesheet after each series showing worker's name, hours worked and rate of pay. Ben Hill verifies her numbers and sends the sheet on to ADP. ADP tabulates the amount owed in payroll including matching FICA taxes, and distributes the payments. Michelle forwards the necessary funds to ADP who distributes the wages to TBC personnel. (TBC does not have a separate payroll bank account.) Salaried workers have their money deposited directly into their bank accounts; checks are written and mailed to the game-day employees. ADP sends a summary receipt to TBC.

Programs:

Before the season begins, and again prior to the playoffs, the team orders a large number of programs, which include player biographies, team statistics, and advertisements. Prior to each game series, TBC orders inserts that contain updated player statistics as well as information on the opposing team. Two people sell programs at each game. One salesperson is near the front gate; one is near the concession stand. The program sellers arrive before the game to stuff the new inserts into the

Programs (continued):

programs. They continue to sell programs until the 7th inning. At that time they return to the ticket booth with their money and count it under the supervision of Ben Hill. The money is taken back to the office safe under armed guard. Ben and Candace determine the number of programs sold by dividing the total receipts by $3.00 (sales price). Julie checks the program inventory once a month to ensure there is no shrinkage. Michelle enters the receipts into the bookkeeping system and prepares a deposit slip. The bookkeeping program keeps a perpetual inventory count. Ben Hill or Phil Ackers deposit the money into the bank and return the deposit slip to Michelle for verification. Later in the season, when the program inventory runs low, they purchase more programs.

Promotions (Fundraising):

Phil Ackers hosts a series of fundraising/promotional activities throughout the Southeastern United States. He makes an occasional trip to Boston, since the TBC is affiliated with the Boston Sox. He rents a hotel conference room, displays team souvenirs, and has a team member or two sign the merchandise and autographs. The merchandise is sold to raise money for the team as well as promote the team. Phil uses Seminole Catering, a catering company staffed by Florida State University students, to provide the non-perishable items, which the caterer ships ahead to the affairs. Perishable snacks are provided by the various hotels. Phil usually drives to events within a few hours driving time of Tallahassee, and flies coach to events which are further away. Phil returns all money and receipts to Michelle. Michelle verifies the receipts, and then forwards the invoices to Julie who writes any necessary checks. Ben Hill usually deposits the promotional receipts.

Tickets Sales:

The ticket booth is a small wooden structure with three windows. There are three women working there—Myrna Myers, Janice Lipponi, and Gerta Child. They have obviously been working together for a long time, since they spend the evening catching up on each other's grandchildren and their activities. The women meet outside the booth two hours before game time and enter the booth together. They accept cash, checks and debit cards. You notice that some of the group tickets have been pre-sold and are picked up at Myrna's window. Myrna tells you that Julie takes orders for group ticket sales over the phone, and provides Myrna with a list of those to be picked up on game day. You note that several sets of will-call tickets are not picked up. When you ask Myrna if this is unusual, she says, "No, it happens sometimes, though it seems people are less responsible these days than they were in the past."

The ladies ring the sales up on simple registers, and the registers number each ticket. Attendance is calculated by the number of tickets collected at the gates. A security officer is posted nearby as tickets are sold. An hour after the opening pitch, the ladies close up the windows and count the money. Janice and Gerta are permitted to leave when Ben Hill and the security officer arrive. Ben and Myrna recount the money and verify it against the computer generated number of tickets sold. Ben takes the ticket log, along with the cash, under guard to his office safe.

The next morning, Ben gives the register receipt to Michelle who enters the sales into the bookkeeping system, generates a deposit slip and adds the money to the post-game deposit. Ben Hill or Phil Ackers then deposits the money. The deposit slip is returned to Michelle for reconciliation.

Figure 18.3. Game Schedule

Tallahassee BeanCounters

Game Schedule May – September		
Date	**Opponent**	**Location**
May		
2 - 4	Dogs	Dothan, AL
13 - 15	Marauders	Home
21 - 22	Kings	Baton Rouge, LA
June		
5- 7	Knights	Home
20 - 21	Gorillas	Gainesville, FL
24 - 26	Dogs	Home
July		
2 - 4	Marauders	Macon, GA
10 - 11	Kings	Home
22 - 24	Knights	Pensacola, FL
August		
3 - 4	Gorillas	Gainesville
7 - 8	Dogs	Home
14 - 15	Marauders	Macon, GA
22	Kings	Home
September (Playoffs)		
5 - 6	Gorillas	Gainesville, FL
11 - 12	Gorillas	Home
19 - 20	Kings	Baton Rouge, LA
26 - 27	Kings	Home

Figure 18.4. General Journal—May

Date	Amount	Debit	Credit	To	Date	Amount	Debit	Credit	To
1-May	10,451.23	2100	1100	Fl Dept of Rev.	14-May	3,016.90	5100	1500	Expense
1-May	2,500.00	6100	1100	Astro Travel	14-May	8,259.00	1100	4100	Revenue
1-May	3,000.00	6300	1100	Expense	14-May	2,354.00	1100	4400	Revenue
1-May	445.78	8180	1100	VISA	14-May	5,400.00	1100	4500	Revenue
1-May	57,848.42	8200	1100	ADP	14-May	21,208.00	1100	4600	Revenue
1-May	29,400.00	1400	2200	Johnson Print.	14-May	7,092.00	1200	4600	Revenue
1-May	75,000.00	1100	4300	Revenue-sharing	15-May	1,615.29	8200	1100	ADP
4-May	3,825.00	6200	1100	Day's Inn	15-May	57,848.42	8200	1100	ADP
5-May	700.00	8130	1100	Freddy's Fix-it	15-May	2,664.00	5100	1400	Expense
6-May	2,500.00	2200	1100	Johnson Print.	15-May	4,973.20	5100	1500	Expense
6-May	400.00	8100	1100	Media Too	15-May	13,595.00	1100	4100	Revenue
6-May	350.00	8110	1100	Merri Maids	15-May	3,285.00	1100	4400	Revenue
6-May	205.21	8115	1100	Danka	15-May	7,992.00	1100	4500	Revenue
6-May	900.00	8120	1100	Allstate	15-May	34,180.00	1100	4600	Revenue
6-May	350.00	8125	1100	Payton Brothers	15-May	9,360.00	1200	4600	Revenue
6-May	75.00	8130	1100	AIA Handyman	17-May	1,500.00	8130	1100	Freddy's Fix-it
6-May	3,000.00	8135	1100	Trimax Properties	19-May	76.88	7100	1100	Bloomberg Ad
6-May	250.00	8140	1100	Helms Extermin.	19-May	320.00	7300	1100	Seminole Cater.
6-May	115.00	8145	1100	US PO	19-May	307.00	7400	1100	Champion
6-May	722.43	8150	1100	City of Tall	19-May	489.00	7500	1100	Marriott-Ft. Laud.
6-May	361.19	8150	1100	Sprint	19-May	864.00	7600	1100	Astro Travel
6-May	387.00	8155	1100	1 Hr. Cleaners	19-May	8,157.00	1100	4200	Revenue
6-May	500.00	8210	1100	ADP	20-May	2,500.00	6100	1100	Astro Travel
7-May	123.75	7100	1100	Bloomberg Ad	20-May	2,250.00	6300	1100	Expense
7-May	307.50	7300	1100	Seminole Cater.	21-May	344.94	8500	1100	Sports Chalet
7-May	495.00	7400	1100	Champion	22-May	2,312.00	6200	1100	Day's Inn
7-May	597.00	7500	1100	Marriott-Boston	29-May	10,716.91	4600	2100	Sales Tax Pay.
7-May	7,371.45	8500	1100	Sports Chalet	30-May	4,677.50	8105	1100	Canopy Roads
7-May	4,950.00	1100	4200	Revenue	30-May	14,402.00	1100	1200	A/R
8-May	486.00	7600	1100	Astro Travel	30-May	2,160.00	5110	1500	Expense
9-May	36.88	7100	1100	Bloomberg Ad	30-May	9,713.00	1100	4700	B. R. Kings
9-May	378.00	7300	1100	Seminole Cater.	30-May	9,800.00	1100	4700	Dothan Dogs
9-May	147.00	7400	1100	Champion	30-May	55,240.47	1600	9000	Larkin Const.
9-May	5,475.00	1100	4200	Revenue	31-May	5,000.00	3100	1100	F. Kennedy
11-May	1,500.00	8165	1100	Johnson Print.	31-May	5,000.00	8600	1350	Acc. Dep.
13-May	2,160.00	5100	1400	Expense	1-Jun	10,716.91	2100	1100	Fl Dept of Rev.
13-May	3,612.00	5100	1500	Expense	1-Jun	1,500.00	8165	1100	Johnson Print.
13-May	9,720.00	1100	4100	Revenue	1-Jun	558.92	8180	1100	VISA
13-May	2,672.00	1100	4400	Revenue	1-Jun	57,848.42	8200	1100	ADP
13-May	6,480.00	1100	4500	Revenue	5-Jun	2,500.00	2200	1100	Johnson Print.
13-May	24,062.00	1100	4600	Revenue	5-Jun	400.00	8100	1100	Media Too
13-May	7,188.00	1200	4600	Revenue	5-Jun	350.00	8110	1100	Merri Maids
14-May	13,280.00	1500	1100	Sysco	5-Jun	205.21	8115	1100	Danka
14-May	1,800.00	5100	1400	Expense	5-Jun	900.00	8120	1100	Allstate

Figure 18.5. General Journal—June

Date	Amount	Debit	Credit	To	Date	Amount	Debit	Credit	To
5-Jun	350.00	8125	1100	Payton Brothers	19-Jun	2,250.00	6300	1100	Expense
5-Jun	75.00	8130	1100	AIA Handyman	21-Jun	2,006.00	6200	1100	Day's Inn
5-Jun	3,000.00	8135	1100	Trimax Properties	21-Jun	250.00	8130	1100	Freddy's Fix-it
5-Jun	250.00	8140	1100	Helms Extermin.	21-Jun	2,299.90	8500	1100	Sports Chalet
5-Jun	100.00	8145	1100	US PO	23-Jun	1,500.00	8165	1100	Johnson Print.
5-Jun	1,311.23	8150	1100	City of Tall	24-Jun	25,500.00	1300	1100	Farmer's Supply
5-Jun	410.27	8150	1100	Sprint	24-Jun	1,826.00	5100	1400	Expense
5-Jun	402.00	8155	1100	1 Hr. Cleaners	24-Jun	2,814.30	5100	1500	Expense
5-Jun	500.00	8210	1100	ADP	24-Jun	7,569.00	1100	4100	Revenue
5-Jun	2,628.00	5100	1400	Expense	24-Jun	2,160.00	1100	4400	Revenue
5-Jun	4,635.85	5100	1500	Expense	24-Jun	5,478.00	1100	4500	Revenue
5-Jun	12,482.00	1100	4100	Revenue	24-Jun	16,880.00	1100	4600	Revenue
5-Jun	3,255.00	1100	4400	Revenue	24-Jun	12,540.00	1200	4600	Revenue
5-Jun	7,884.00	1100	4500	Revenue	25-Jun	1,199.00	5100	1400	Expense
5-Jun	29,800.00	1100	4600	Revenue	25-Jun	1,942.85	5100	1500	Expense
5-Jun	10,500.00	1200	4600	Revenue	25-Jun	5,339.00	1100	4100	Revenue
6-Jun	3,116.00	5100	1400	Expense	25-Jun	1,469.00	1100	4400	Revenue
6-Jun	4,895.90	5100	1500	Expense	25-Jun	3,597.00	1100	4500	Revenue
6-Jun	13,171.00	1100	4100	Revenue	25-Jun	12,396.00	1100	4600	Revenue
6-Jun	3,225.00	1100	4400	Revenue	25-Jun	10,944.00	1200	4600	Revenue
6-Jun	9,348.00	1100	4500	Revenue	26-Jun	9,575.00	1500	1100	Sysco
6-Jun	36,697.00	1100	4600	Revenue	26-Jun	8,474.75	8105	1100	Canopy Roads
6-Jun	9,048.00	1200	4600	Revenue	26-Jun	1,638.03	8200	1100	ADP
7-Jun	1,642.47	8200	1100	ADP	26-Jun	2,184.00	5100	1400	Expense
7-Jun	1,819.44	8500	1100	Sports Chalet	26-Jun	3,564.65	5100	1500	Expense
7-Jun	2,268.00	5100	1400	Expense	26-Jun	9,772.00	1100	4100	Revenue
7-Jun	4,203.60	5100	1500	Expense	26-Jun	2,760.00	1100	4400	Revenue
7-Jun	11,346.00	1100	4100	Revenue	26-Jun	6,552.00	1100	4500	Revenue
7-Jun	3,119.00	1100	4400	Revenue	26-Jun	25,600.00	1100	4600	Revenue
7-Jun	6,804.00	1100	4500	Revenue	26-Jun	16,020.00	1200	4600	Revenue
7-Jun	28,730.00	1100	4600	Revenue	27-Jun	11,628.00	1100	1200	A/R
7-Jun	9,840.00	1200	4600	Revenue	28-Jun	157,148.01	1600	9000	Larkin Const.
8-Jun	15,890.00	1500	1100	Sysco	29-Jun	19,329.63	4100	2100	Sales Tax Pay.
15-Jun	57,848.42	8200	1100	ADP	30-Jun	15,000.00	3100	1100	F. Kennedy
16-Jun	104.36	7100	1100	Bloomberg Ad	30-Jun	33,500.00	8130	1100	Freddy's Fix-it
16-Jun	340.75	7300	1100	Seminole Cater.	30-Jun	6,500.00	8160	1100	Pen. Knights
16-Jun	417.00	7400	1100	Champion	30-Jun	7,000.00	8160	1100	Dothan Dogs
16-Jun	898.00	7500	1100	Marriott-Boston	30-Jun	5,000.00	8600	1350	Acc. Dep.
16-Jun	582.00	7600	1100	Astro Travel	30-Jun	3,445.00	5110	1500	Expense
16-Jun	4,175.00	1100	4200	Revenue	30-Jun	7,400.00	1100	4700	Gsville Gorillas
17-Jun	2,000.00	8130	1100	Freddy's Fix-it	1-Jul	19,329.63	2100	1100	Fl Dept of Rev.
19-Jun	2,500.00	6100	1100	Astro Travel	1-Jul	2,500.00	6100	1100	Astro Travel

Figure 18.6. General Journal—July

Date	Amount	Debit	Credit	To	Date	Amount	Debit	Credit	To
1-Jul	3,000.00	6300	1100	Expense	16-Jul	80.00	7100	1100	Bloomberg Ad
1-Jul	621.02	8180	1100	VISA	16-Jul	653.75	7300	1100	Seminole Cater.
1-Jul	57,848.42	8200	1100	ADP	16-Jul	320.00	7400	1100	Champion
2-Jul	2,500.00	2200	1100	Johnson Print.	16-Jul	876.00	7500	1100	Marriott-Miami
2-Jul	400.00	8100	1100	Media Too	16-Jul	254.00	7600	1100	Astro Travel
2-Jul	350.00	8110	1100	Merri Maids	16-Jul	5,200.00	1100	4200	Revenue
2-Jul	205.21	8115	1100	Danka	18-Jul	35.00	7100	1100	Bloomberg Ad
2-Jul	900.00	8120	1100	Allstate	18-Jul	540.00	7300	1100	Seminole Cater.
2-Jul	350.00	8125	1100	Payton Brothers	18-Jul	140.00	7400	1100	Champion
2-Jul	75.00	8130	1100	AIA Handyman	18-Jul	1,200.00	8130	1100	Freddy's Fix-it
2-Jul	3,000.00	8135	1100	Trimax Properties	18-Jul	6,400.00	1100	4200	Revenue
2-Jul	250.00	8140	1100	Helms Extermin.	21-Jul	2,500.00	6100	1100	Astro Travel
2-Jul	100.00	8145	1100	US PO	21-Jul	3,000.00	6300	1100	Expense
2-Jul	812.33	8150	1100	City of Tall	24-Jul	3,978.00	6200	1100	Day's Inn
2-Jul	404.16	8150	1100	Sprint	29-Jul	8,962.12	4100	2100	Sales Tax Pay.
2-Jul	352.00	8155	1100	1 Hr. Cleaners	30-Jul	4,193.70	8105	1100	Canopy Roads
2-Jul	500.00	8210	1100	ADP	30-Jul	13,130.00	1100	1200	A/R
3-Jul	48.75	7100	1100	Bloomberg Ad	30-Jul	5,000.00	8600	1350	Acc. Dep.
3-Jul	296.25	7300	1100	Seminole Cater.	30-Jul	1,290.00	5110	1500	Expense
3-Jul	195.00	7400	1100	Champion	30-Jul	13,000.00	1100	4700	Macon Marauders
3-Jul	378.00	7500	1100	Marriott-Jacksonville	30-Jul	12,000.00	1100	4700	Pen. Knights
3-Jul	187.50	7600	1100	Phil Ackers	30-Jul	177,136.49	1600	9000	Larkin Const.
3-Jul	10,950.00	1100	4200	Revenue	31-Jul	15,000.00	3100	1100	F. Kennedy
4-Jul	4,335.00	6200	1100	Holiday Inn	1-Aug	8,962.12	2100	1100	Fl Dept of Rev.
4-Jul	1,000.00	8130	1100	Freddy's Fix-it	1-Aug	1,500.00	8120	1100	Allstate
8-Jul	1,500.00	8165	1100	Johnson Print.	1-Aug	667.52	8180	1100	VISA
10-Jul	3,078.00	5100	1400	Expense	1-Aug	57,848.42	8200	1100	ADP
10-Jul	5,307.70	5100	1500	Expense	2-Aug	2,500.00	6100	1100	Astro Travel
10-Jul	14,342.00	1100	4100	Revenue	2-Aug	2,250.00	6300	1100	Expense
10-Jul	3,225.00	1100	4400	Revenue	4-Aug	2,210.00	6200	1100	Day's Inn
10-Jul	9,234.00	1100	4500	Revenue	5-Aug	250.00	8130	1100	Freddy's Fix-it
10-Jul	33,290.00	1100	4600	Revenue	5-Aug	1,500.00	8165	1100	Johnson Print.
10-Jul	13,800.00	1200	4600	Revenue	7-Aug	2,500.00	2200	1100	Johnson Print.
11-Jul	1,037.21	8200	1100	ADP	7-Aug	400.00	8100	1100	Media Too
11-Jul	2,940.00	5100	1400	Expense	7-Aug	350.00	8110	1100	Merri Maids
11-Jul	4,585.70	5100	1500	Expense	7-Aug	205.21	8115	1100	Danka
11-Jul	12,602.00	1100	4100	Revenue	7-Aug	900.00	8120	1100	Allstate
11-Jul	3,270.00	1100	4400	Revenue	7-Aug	350.00	8125	1100	Payton Brothers
11-Jul	8,820.00	1100	4500	Revenue	7-Aug	75.00	8130	1100	AIA Handyman
11-Jul	30,544.00	1100	4600	Revenue	7-Aug	3,000.00	8135	1100	Trimax Properties
11-Jul	14,640.00	1200	4600	Revenue	7-Aug	250.00	8140	1100	Helms Extermin.
15-Jul	57,848.42	8200	1100	ADP	7-Aug	135.00	8145	1100	US PO

Figure 18.7. General Journal—August

Date	Amount	Debit	Credit	To	Date	Amount	Debit	Credit	To
7-Aug	1,432.00	8150	1100	City of Tall	22-Aug	44,788.00	1100	4600	Revenue
7-Aug	386.24	8150	1100	Sprint	22-Aug	26,280.00	1200	4600	Revenue
7-Aug	325.00	8155	1100	1 Hr. Cleaners	23-Aug	13,230.00	1500	1100	Sysco
7-Aug	500.00	8210	1100	ADP	25-Aug	241.88	7100	1100	Bloomberg Ad
7-Aug	2,204.79	8500	1100	Sports Chalet	25-Aug	319.75	7300	1100	Seminole Cater.
7-Aug	3,034.00	5100	1400	Expense	25-Aug	867.00	7400	1100	Champion
7-Aug	5,371.00	5100	1500	Expense	25-Aug	721.00	7500	1100	Marriott-Boston
7-Aug	14,760.00	1100	4100	Revenue	25-Aug	581.00	7600	1100	Astro Travel
7-Aug	3,240.00	1100	4400	Revenue	25-Aug	9,675.00	1100	4200	Revenue
7-Aug	9,102.00	1100	4500	Revenue	29-Aug	16,148.23	4100	2100	Sales Tax Pay.
7-Aug	34,100.00	1100	4600	Revenue	30-Aug	7,261.00	8105	1100	Canopy Roads
7-Aug	23,400.00	1200	4600	Revenue	30-Aug	8,000.00	8160	1100	B. R. Kings
8-Aug	1,188.32	8200	1100	ADP	30-Aug	26,548.00	1100	1200	A/R
8-Aug	3,397.00	5100	1400	Expense	30-Aug	1,430.00	5110	1500	Expense
8-Aug	5,733.00	5100	1500	Expense	30-Aug	9,300.00	1100	4700	Gsville Gorillas
8-Aug	15,480.00	1100	4100	Revenue	30-Aug	9,000.00	1100	4700	Macon Marauders
8-Aug	3,285.00	1100	4400	Revenue	30-Aug	194,902.18	1600	9000	Larkin Const.
8-Aug	10,191.00	1100	4500	Revenue	31-Aug	15,000.00	3100	1100	F. Kennedy
8-Aug	37,580.00	1100	4600	Revenue	1-Sep	16,148.23	2100	1100	Fl. Dept. of Revenue
8-Aug	22,080.00	1200	4600	Revenue	1-Sep	789.29	8180	1100	VISA
9-Aug	10,390.00	1500	1100	Sysco	1-Sep	57,848.42	8200	1100	ADP
13-Aug	2,500.00	6100	1100	Astro Travel	1-Sep	839.72	8500	1100	Sports Chalet
13-Aug	2,250.00	6300	1100	Expense	2-Sep	250.00	8130	1100	Freddy's Fix-it
14-Aug	54.38	7100	1100	Bloomberg Ad	4-Sep	2,500.00	6100	1100	Astro Travel
14-Aug	668.75	7300	1100	Seminole Cater.	4-Sep	2,250.00	6300	1100	Expense
14-Aug	217.00	7400	1100	Champion	4-Sep	3,000.00	8135	1100	Trimax Properties
14-Aug	449.00	7500	1100	LaQuinta-Tampa	4-Sep	27,000.00	1400	2200	Johnson Print.
14-Aug	252.00	7600	1100	Astro Travel	5-Sep	787.52	8150	1100	City of Tall
14-Aug	2,175.00	1100	4200	Revenue	6-Sep	1,938.00	6200	1100	Motor Lodge
15-Aug	2,482.00	6200	1100	Fairfield Inn	6-Sep	392.55	8150	1100	Sprint
15-Aug	57,848.42	8200	1100	ADP	6-Sep	2,589.66	8500	1100	Sports Chalet
20-Aug	1,950.00	8130	1100	Freddy's Fix-it	7-Sep	205.21	8115	1100	Danka
20-Aug	1,500.00	8165	1100	Johnson Print.	7-Sep	7,441.41	8500	1100	Sports Chalet
21-Aug	189.99	8500	1100	Sports Chalet	8-Sep	2,500.00	2200	1100	Johnson Print.
22-Aug	28.13	7100	1100	Bloomberg Ad	8-Sep	900.00	8120	1100	Allstate
22-Aug	497.50	7300	1100	Seminole Cater.	9-Sep	160.00	7100	1100	Bloomberg Ad
22-Aug	112.00	7400	1100	Champion	9-Sep	367.75	7300	1100	Seminole Cater.
22-Aug	739.82	8200	1100	ADP	9-Sep	640.00	7400	1100	Champion
22-Aug	3,990.00	5100	1400	Expense	9-Sep	384.00	7500	1100	LaQuinta-Orlando
22-Aug	6,343.05	5100	1500	Expense	9-Sep	251.00	7600	1100	Astro Travel
22-Aug	17,159.00	1100	4100	Revenue	9-Sep	75.00	8130	1100	AIA Handyman
22-Aug	1,125.00	1100	4200	Revenue	9-Sep	1,500.00	8165	1100	Johnson Print.
22-Aug	3,255.00	1100	4400	Revenue	9-Sep	6,400.00	1100	4200	Revenue
22-Aug	11,970.00	1100	4500	Revenue	10-Sep	115.00	8145	1100	US PO

Figure 18.8. General Journal—September

Date	Amount	Debit	Credit	To	Date	Amount	Debit	Credit	To
11-Sep	6,685.00	1500	1100	Sysco	27-Sep	4,661.00	5100	1400	Expense
11-Sep	500.00	8210	1100	ADP	27-Sep	4,854.10	5100	1500	Expense
11-Sep	3,570.00	5100	1400	Expense	27-Sep	13,376.00	1100	4100	Revenue
11-Sep	5,639.60	5100	1500	Expense	27-Sep	3,150.00	1100	4400	Revenue
11-Sep	15,231.00	1100	4100	Revenue	27-Sep	13,983.00	1100	4500	Revenue
11-Sep	3,225.00	1100	4400	Revenue	27-Sep	53,600.00	1100	4600	Revenue
11-Sep	10,710.00	1100	4500	Revenue	27-Sep	1,080.00	1200	4600	Revenue
11-Sep	37,720.00	1100	4600	Revenue	29-Sep	22,516.41	4100	2100	Sales Tax Pay.
11-Sep	2,400.00	1200	4600	Revenue	30-Sep	43,900.00	2200	1100	Johnson Print.
12-Sep	350.00	8125	1100	Payton Brothers	30-Sep	15,000.00	3100	1100	F. Kennedy
12-Sep	1,029.94	8200	1100	ADP	30-Sep	9,108.90	8105	1100	Canopy Roads
12-Sep	3,652.00	5100	1400	Expense	30-Sep	8,000.00	8130	1100	Freddy's Fix-it
12-Sep	5,821.35	5100	1500	Expense	30-Sep	6,000.00	8160	1100	Macon Marauders
12-Sep	15,717.00	1100	4100	Revenue	30-Sep	10,000.00	8160	1100	Dothan Dogs
12-Sep	3,270.00	1100	4400	Revenue	30-Sep	6,000.00	8160	1100	B. R. Kings
12-Sep	10,956.00	1100	4500	Revenue	30-Sep	10,000.00	8160	1100	Gsville Gorillas
12-Sep	39,776.00	1100	4600	Revenue	30-Sep	6,500.00	8160	1100	B. R. Kings
12-Sep	3,480.00	1200	4600	Revenue	30-Sep	17,352.00	8200	1100	Ben Hill, bonus
13-Sep	250.00	8140	1100	Helms Extermin.	30-Sep	34,704.00	8200	1100	P. Ackers, bonus
14-Sep	400.00	8100	1100	Media Too	30-Sep	27,832.00	1100	1200	A/R
14-Sep	2,000.00	8130	1100	Freddy's Fix-it	30-Sep	5,000.00	8600	1350	Acc. Dep.
15-Sep	387.00	8155	1100	1 Hr. Cleaners	30-Sep	5,000.00	8600	1350	Acc. Dep.
15-Sep	57,848.42	8200	1100	ADP	30-Sep	4,509.00	5110	1400	Expense
16-Sep	350.00	8110	1100	Merri Maids	30-Sep	6,352.50	5110	1500	Expense
16-Sep	10,000.00	8130	1100	Freddy's Fix-it	30-Sep	10,000.00	1100	4700	B. R. Kings
18-Sep	2,500.00	6100	1100	Astro Travel	30-Sep	10,000.00	1100	4700	Gsville Gorillas
18-Sep	2,250.00	6300	1100	Expense	30-Sep	273,765.12	1600	9000	Larkin Const.
20-Sep	1,870.00	6200	1100	Day's Inn					
23-Sep	13,280.00	1500	1100	Sysco					
24-Sep	264.38	7100	1100	Bloomberg Ad					
24-Sep	412.75	7300	1100	Seminole Cater.					
24-Sep	1,057.00	7400	1100	Champion					
24-Sep	798.00	7500	1100	Marriott-Boston					
24-Sep	423.00	7600	1100	Astro Travel					
24-Sep	1,500.00	8165	1100	Johnson Print.					
24-Sep	6,625.00	1100	4200	Revenue					
26-Sep	3,724.00	5100	1400	Expense					
26-Sep	6,316.40	5100	1500	Expense					
26-Sep	17,335.00	1100	4100	Revenue					
26-Sep	3,240.00	1100	4400	Revenue					
26-Sep	11,172.00	1100	4500	Revenue					
26-Sep	42,442.00	1100	4600	Revenue					
26-Sep	1,680.00	1200	4600	Revenue					
27-Sep	633.66	8200	1100	ADP					

Figure 18.9. Chart of Accounts

Account #	Account Name	Type of Account
1100	Cash	Asset
1200	Accounts Receivable	Asset
1300	Equipment	Asset
1350	Accumulated Depreciation	Contra Asset
1400	Inventory: Programs	Asset
1500	Inventory: Concessions	Asset
1600	Construction in Progress	Asset
2100	Sales Tax Payable	Liability
2200	Accounts Payable	Liability
3100	Owner's equity: Owner's Draw	Equity
4100	Revenue: Concessions	Income
4200	Revenue: Fundraising	Income
4300	Revenue: League Revenue Sharing	Income
4400	Revenue: Parking	Income
4500	Revenue: Programs	Income
4600	Revenue: Tickets	Income
4700	Revenue: Visiting Fees (from away games)	Income
5100	Cost of Goods Sold	Expense
5110	Cost of Goods Sold: Spoilage	Expense
6100	Away Game: Bus Rental	Expense
6200	Away Game: Hotel	Expense
6300	Away Game: Per diem	Expense
7100	Fundraising: Advertising	Expense
7300	Fundraising: Catering	Expense
7400	Fundraising: Giveaways	Expense
7500	Fundraising: Lodging & Event Space Rental	Expense
7600	Fundraising: Travel	Expense
8100	Administration: Advertising	Expense
8105	Administration: Arena Rental	Expense
8110	Administration: Cleaning Service	Expense
8115	Administration: Copier Lease	Expense
8120	Administration: Insurance	Expense
8125	Administration: Lawn Care	Expense
8130	Administration: Maintenance	Expense
8135	Administration: Rent	Expense
8140	Administration: Pest Control	Expense
8145	Administration: Postage	Expense
8150	Administration: Utilities	Expense
8155	Administration: Dry Cleaning	Expense
8160	Administration: Revenue Sharing with Visitors	Expense
8165	Administration: Printing	Expense
8180	Administration: Miscellaneous	Expense
8200	Administration: Compensation	Expense
8210	Administration: Payroll Preparation Fee	Expense
8500	Program: Equipment Expense	Expense
8600	Depreciation	Expense
9000	Construction Loan	Liability

Figure 18.10. Recurring Expenses

Vendor	Amount	Expense
ADP Payroll Services	$500	Monthly preparation fee.
ADP Payroll Services		ADP issues payroll checks. 7.65% FICA & Medicare, 15% Federal withholding. No state income tax in Florida.
AIA Handyman	$75	$75 per month for routine maintenance in offices (changing bulbs, etc.), larger repairs will be negotiated.
Allstate Insurance	$900	$900 per month for insurance on buildings, equipment, vehicles.
Boston Sox	$75,000	Franklin Kennedy, owner of the Boston Sox, helps the TBC get started each season with $75,000 seed money for salaries.
Canopy Roads	varies	Arena Rental. Due at end of month. Equals 5% of ticket sales based on attendance
City of Tallahassee	varies	Fees for electricity, water, sewage
Danka	$205	Monthly for copier lease.
Florida Department of Revenue	7.50%	Applies to ticket revenue, program sales, parking revenue and promotional sales.
Franklin Kennedy	varies	Monthly owner's draw (to recover seed money from beginning of season)
Helms Exterminator	$250	Monthly upkeep for pest control
Johnson Printers	$2,500	Monthly payments for the season's programs purchased at the beginning of the year, so only inserts with updated stats have to be purchased for each game series.
Johnson Printers	$1,500	For inserts for each game series.
League Teams	varies	Teams in the league share revenues from games, so all teams benefit from each game played. Amounts are negotiated on a game by game basis.
Media Too	$400	Annual advertising contract
Merri Maids	$350	Monthly fee for cleaning of offices and training center
One Hour Cleaners	varies	Dry cleaning uniforms
Payton Brothers	$350	Monthly lawn maintenance. Includes office, training field, training facilities
Sprint	varies	Fees for telephone service
Sysco Foods	varies	Supplier for concession food.
Trimax Properties	$3,000	Monthly rental payment for office building.
US Post Office	varies	Postage.

Figure 18.11. TBC Pricing Information

Tickets	Cost	Sales Price	Taxable	
Standard	N/A	$12.00	Yes	Tax included in sales price, paid to State monthly.
Disc. Standard	N/A	$9.60	Yes	Some groups, who prepay, get discounted tickets
Disc Balcony	N/A	$5.60	Yes	
Balcony	N/A	$7.00	Yes	

Parking	Cost	Sales Price	Taxable	
Cars	N/A	$2.00	Yes	Tax included in sales price, paid to State monthly.
Oversized Vehicles	N/A	$3.00	Yes	

Programs	Cost	Sales Price	Taxable	
Programs	$1.00	$3.00	Yes	Tax included in sales price, paid to State monthly.
Inserts	$0.50	Included		

Concessions	Cost	Sales Price	Taxable	
Hamburgers	$1.40	$4.00	Yes	Tax included in sales price, paid to State monthly.
Hotdogs	$1.25	$3.00	Yes	
Popcorn	$0.70	$2.00	Yes	
Peanuts	$0.70	$2.00	Yes	
Soda	$0.35	$1.00	Yes	
Beer	$1.35	$4.00	Yes	
Condiments	$0.05	$0.00	No	

Arena Seating Capacity= 5500 (4000 std, 1500 balcony)

Figure 18.12. Away Game Expense Invoices

Cash for Players for food each trip:				
Date Perdiem given to players	Number of days of per diem*	Per diem given per player	Total per diem	Number of players and staff given per diem
May 1	4	$25.00	$3,000.00	30
May 20	3	$25.00	$2,250.00	30
June 19	3	$25.00	$2,250.00	30
July 1	4	$25.00	$3,000.00	30
July 21	4	$25.00	$3,000.00	30
August 2	3	$25.00	$2,250.00	30
August 13	3	$25.00	$2,250.00	30
September 4	3	$25.00	$2,250.00	30
September 18	3	$25.00	$2,250.00	30
*Includes one travel day per away series.				

Figure 18.13. Astro Travel

Astro Travel
Contract for Bus Rental @ $2500.00 per away game trip

Hotel Invoices (Players, coaches and a few lucky staff) for Away Games:				
Dates of Hotel Stay	Number of rooms*	Number of nights	Price per room	Location
May 1 - 4	17	3	$75.00	Day's Inn, Dothan, AL
May 20 - 22	17	2	$68.00	Day's Inn, Baton Rouge, LA
June 19 - 21	17	2	$59.00	Day's Inn, Gainesville, FL
July 1 - 4	17	3	$85.00	Holiday Inn, Macon, GA
July 21 - 24	17	3	$78.00	Day's Inn Pensacola, FL
August 2 - 4	17	2	$65.00	Day's inn Gainesville, FL
August 13 - 15	17	2	$73.00	Fairfield Inn, Macon, GA
September 4 - 6	17	2	$57.00	Motor Lodge, Gainesville, FL
September 18 - 20	17	2	$55.00	Day's Inn Baton Rouge, LA
*Players are required to stay 2 to a room				

Figure 18.14. Equipment Purchase Orders, Invoices, and Receiving Slips

Purchase Order Date	Invoice & delivery date	Items ordered and delivered	Qty	Price per item	Total Price	Shipment verified by Sam or Julie
May 3	May 5	Dry-line marker	1	$429.00	$429.00	May 5
		Men's Jerseys	31	$29.99	$929.69	
		Men's Pants	31	$69.99	$2,169.69	
		Shoes	31	$79.99	$2,479.69	
		Socks	62	$21.99	$1,363.38	
		Total			$7,371.45	
May 18	May 20	Batting gloves	4	$39.99	$159.96	May 20
		Eye black	2	$2.99	$5.98	
		Bases	1	$179.00	$179.00	
		Total			$344.94	
June 3	June 5	Sliding shorts	28	$49.99	$1,399.72	June 5
		Supporters	28	$14.99	$419.72	
		Tape	10	$4.99	$49.90	
		Total			$1,869.34	
June 18	June 20	Game bats	10	$229.99	$2,299.90	June 20
		Total			$2,299.90	
July 3	July 5	Practice balls /36	7	$89.99	$629.93	July 5
		Game balls/dozen	7	$79.99	$559.93	
		Machine balls/doz.	10	$69.99	$699.90	
		Practice bats	10	$69.99	$699.90	
		Total			$2,589.66	
July 18	July 20	Batting helmets	28	$29.99	$839.72	July 20
		Total			$839.72	
August 3	August 5	Baseball mitts	21	$104.99	$2,204.79	August 5
		Total			$2,204.79	
August 18	August 20	First base mitts	1	$189.99	$189.99	August 20
		Total			$189.99	
Sept. 3	Sept. 5	Bases	1	$179.00	$179.00	Sept. 5
		Game balls/dozen	4	$79.99	$319.96	
		Men's Jerseys	31	$29.99	$929.69	
		Men's Pants	31	$69.99	$2,169.69	
		Shoes	31	$79.99	$2,479.69	
		Socks	62	$21.99	$1,363.38	
		Total			$7,441.41	

Figure 18.15. Fundraising Revenue and Expense

Travel, lodging, and food			/------------Billed by Hotel---------/			
Date	Location	Astro Travel	Room	Food	Amenities	Hotel
May 6	Boston	$486.00	$490.00	$92.00	$15.00	Marriott
May 8	Tallahassee	0.00	0.00	0.00	0.00	
May 16 - 19	Ft. Lauderdale	864.00	381.00	83.00	25.00	Marriott
Jun 14 - 15	Boston	582.00	594.00	289.00	15.00	Marriott
Jul 1 - 2	Jacksonville	187.50	254.00	100.00	24.00	Marriott
Jul 13 - 15	Miami	254.00	675.00	188.00	13.00	Marriott
July 17	Tallahassee	0.00	0.00	0.00	0.00	
Aug 12 - 13	Tampa	252.00	170.00	229.00	50.00	La Quinta
Aug 21	Tallahassee	0.00	0.00	0.00	0.00	
Aug 23 - 24	Boston	581.00	450.00	221.00	50.00	Marriott
Sep 6 - 8	Orlando	251.00	381.00	0.00	3.00	La Quinta
Sep 22 - 23	Boston	423.00	378.00	345.00	75.00	Marriott

Advertising Expenses (Invoices from Bloomberg Advertising)					
Date	Radio Ads	Flyers	Print Ads	TV Ads	Total
May 7	$103.75	$20.00	$0.00	$0.00	$123.75
May 9	36.88	0.00	0.00	0.00	36.88
May 19	76.88	0.00	0.00	0.00	76.88
Jun 16	84.36	20.00	0.00	0.00	104.36
Jul 3	48.75	0.00	0.00	0.00	48.75
Jul 16	80.00	0.00	0.00	0.00	80.00
Jul 18	35.00	0.00	0.00	0.00	35.00
Aug 14	54.38	0.00	0.00	0.00	54.38
Aug 22	0.00	0.00	28.13	0.00	28.13
Aug 25	241.88	0.00	0.00	0.00	241.88
Sep 9	160.00	0.00	0.00	0.00	160.00
Sep 24	0.00	50.00	0.00	214.38	264.38

Invoices from Seminole Catering					
Date	TBC Cakes	Centerpieces	Linens	Other	Total
May 7	$150.00	$57.50	$65.00	$35.00	$307.50
May 9	200.00	68.00	65.00	45.00	378.00
May 19	175.00	65.00	55.00	25.00	320.00
Jun 16	175.00	52.00	40.00	73.75	340.75
Jul 3	150.00	60.00	38.00	48.25	296.25
Jul 16	350.00	118.00	110.00	75.75	653.75
Jul 18	325.00	86.00	75.00	54.00	540.00
Aug 14	410.00	95.00	88.00	75.75	668.75
Aug 22	310.00	72.00	82.50	33.00	497.50
Aug 25	150.00	85.00	47.00	37.75	319.75
Sep 9	225.00	57.75	40.00	45.00	367.75
Sep 24	230.00	69.00	73.75	40.00	412.75

Seminole Catering provides items decorated with TBC colors and logos.

Invoices from Champion Sport Novelties

Item	Unit Price	May 7 QTY	May 9 QTY	May 19 QTY	June 16 QTY	July 3 QTY	July 16 QTY
T-shirts	$7	0	11	11	11	10	10
Baseball hats	$15	5	0	10	10	0	0
Pom-poms	$2	0	10	10	5	10	5
Souvenir bats	$3	0	0	10	10	10	10
Bobbing-head doll	$15	0	0	0	10	1	0
TBC gym bags	$20	20	0	0	0	0	10
TBC Blazers	$250	0	0	0	0	0	0
Bumper stickers	$1	20	10	30	0	20	10
TBC flags	$4	0	10	0	0	10	0
Total Invoice		$495.00	$147.00	$307.00	$417.00	$195.00	$320.00

Item	Unit Price	July 18 QTY	Aug 14 QTY	Aug 22 QTY	Aug 25 QTY	Sept 9 QTY	Sept 24 QTY
T-shirts	$7	20	11	0	5	10	1
Baseball hats	$15	0	9	5	5	10	3
Pom-poms	$2	0	1	0	0	10	0
Souvenir bats	$3	0	1	0	0	10	0
Bobbing-head doll	$15	0	0	0	0	10	0
TBC gym bags	$20	0	0	0	0	10	0
TBC Blazers	$250	0	0	0	3	0	4
Bumper stickers	$1	0	0	29	7	0	5
TBC flags	$4	0	0	2	0	5	0
Total Invoice		$140.00	$217.00	$112.00	$867.00	$640.00	$1,057.00

Fundraiser	Donor	Amount	Fundraiser	Donor	Amount
May 6 Boston, MA	Barney Smith	$1,000.00	July 17 Tallahassee, FL	Larry John	$5,700.00
	Nick Antonio	$1,000.00		Julie Harris	$700.00
	Jack Washington	$1,000.00			
	Everett Rosenbaum	$1,000.00	August 12 - 13 Tampa, FL	Hannah Hamilton	$500.00
	Buster Rhimes	$950.00		Harriet Sellers	$500.00
				Mabel Burns	$500.00
May 8 Tallahassee, FL	Harry Roswell	$4,200.00		M. Mendenhall	$500.00
	Oliver Newton	$200.00		Opal Drew	$100.00
	Gerald Lopez	$200.00		Penelope Walker	$75.00
	Flora Fawn	$200.00			
	Bambi Kelly	$200.00	August 21 Tallahassee, FL	Marks & Assoc.	$300.00
	Fontana Rogers	$475.00		Tarpon Electric	$100.00
				Capital Motor Co.	$100.00
May 16 - 18 Ft. Lauderdale, FL	John Yumo	$3,075.00		Wakulla Pools	$300.00
	George Thomas	$357.00		Moody Service	$100.00
	Suzy Lee	$4,725.00		Service Plus	$225.00
June 14 - 15 Boston, MA	Joe Icerman	$2,000.00	August 23 - 24 Boston, MA	Murphy Oil Corp	$7,000.00
	Jerry Jenkins	$2,000.00		Jason Wozniak	$2,000.00
	Terry Redford	$175.00		Cyndi Goodbody	$300.00
				Suzi Cuddle	$375.00
July 1 - 2 Jacksonville, FL	Robert Taylor	$500.00			
	Joe Caldwell	$500.00	Sept. 6 - 8 Orlando, FL	Jose Garcia	$3,000.00
	Lance Cox	$500.00		Eric Menendez	$2,000.00
	Misty Moss	$9,450.00		Robin Egg	$1,400.00
July 13 - 15 Miami, FL	Mitchell Plumbing	$2,500.00	Sept. 22 - 23 Boston, MA	Larry Golf	$4,000.00
	Georgia Drywall	$500.00		Ann Johnson	$750.00
	No. Florida Doors	$500.00		Ted Ramsey	$375.00
	Panhandle Beer	$500.00		Hunter Keaton	$1,500.00
	Hampton Attny	$500.00			
	Precision Paints	$500.00			
	Toni Gams	$100.00			
	Pepper Salsa	$100.00			

Figure 18.16. Payroll

Area	Name	Hourly Wage	Hours May 13-15	Hours June 5-7	Hours June 24-26	Hours July 10-11	Hours Aug 7-8	Hours Aug 22	Hours Sept 11-12	Hours Sept 26-27
Concessions	Tuney, P.	$6.00		10.0	9.5	6.0		3.5	6.3	4.5
Concessions	Hernandez, R.	$6.00	9.5		9.5	6.5	6.3		6.3	4.0
Concessions	Fitzgerald, L.	$6.00	9.5	10.0		6.5	6.0	3.3		4.0
Concessions	Maroney, M	$6.00	9.0	9.5	9.0		6.5	3.0	6.0	
Concessions	Hope, H.	$6.00	10.0	10.0	11.0	7.0	7.5	4.0	7.0	5.0
Bleacher	Garcia, M.	$6.00	9.5	9.5	9.5			3.0		
Bleacher	Newman, T.	$6.00	9.5				6.0	3.3	6.5	4.0
Bleacher	Bennett, M.	$6.00		10.0	10.0	6.0	6.0	3.3	6.3	
Bleacher	Zimmerman, G.	$6.00			9.5	6.5	7.0	4.5	7.0	4.0
Bleacher	Valroy, G.	$6.00				7.0	7.0	3.0	6.5	4.0
Bleacher	Sheffield, K.	$6.00				6.5	7.8	3.0	7.0	4.0
Bleacher	Fuentes, P.	$6.00	9.5	9.5					6.8	4.0
Bleacher	Donaldson, D.	$6.00	12.0	12.0	12.0					5.0
Bleacher	Cook, B.	$6.00	10.0	9.5	10.0	6.0				
Bleacher	Stapleton, A.	$6.00	10.5	10.5	10.0	6.0	7.5			
Parking	Houser, R.	$6.00	9.0	9.0	9.5			3.0	6.0	3.0
Parking	Kelley, D.	$6.00	12.0	12.0	12.0	7.0			7.0	3.5
Parking	Fernandez, H.	$6.00	9.5		10.0		7.5	3.8		4.0
Parking	Johnson, E.	$6.00		10.0	11.0	6.0				3.0
Parking	Kapella, K.	$6.00	11.0			7.0	7.0	3.5	6.5	3.0
Parking	Fusilli, G.	$6.00		11.0		6.0	7.0	5.0	6.0	
Parking	Flanagon, B.	$6.00	12.0	12.0			6.5	3.5	6.5	3.5
Parking	Brighton, Y.	$6.00			11.5	6.0	6.0			
Tickets	Myers, M.	$7.25	10.0	10.0	10.5	6.0	6.0	9.0	6.0	3.5
Tickets	Lipponi, J.	$7.25	10.0	10.5	10.5	6.0	6.0	9.0	6.0	3.5
Tickets	Child, G.	$7.25	10.0	10.0	10.5	6.0	6.0	9.0	6.0	3.5
Programs	Riley, S.	$6.00	6.5	7.0	6.0	4.5	6.5	6.3	5.0	3.0
Programs	Stivers, K.	$6.00	6.5	7.0	6.0	4.5	6.5	6.3	5.0	3.0
Security	Webster, P.	$7.25	14.0	14.0	14.0	9.5	14.0	5.0	8.5	5.0
Security	Evans, B.	$7.25	14.0	14.0	14.0	9.5	14.0	5.0	8.5	5.0
Mascot	Wonka, W.	$7.25	12.0	12.5	13.0	9.0	11.5	4.0	8.0	4.0

Area	Name	Contract Length	Amount
Player	Abelson, B.	8 months	$25,000.00
Player	Bailey, R.	8 months	$24,000.00
Player	Biancalana, B.	8 months	$20,000.00
Player	Brett, J.	8 months	$25,000.00
Player	Bridges, S.	8 months	$22,000.00
Player	Buckner, W.	8 months	$23,000.00
Player	Campbell, L.	8 months	$28,000.00
Player	Chester, B.	8 months	$24,000.00
Player	Curtis, J.	8 months	$25,000.00
Player	Dell, Aaron	8 months	$20,000.00
Player	Fox, V.	8 months	$21,000.00
Player	Holstein, D.	8 months	$22,000.00
Player	Johnson, J.	8 months	$23,000.00
Player	McArthur, M.	8 months	$24,000.00
Player	Merrick, J.	8 months	$25,000.00
Player	Patek, F.	8 months	$26,000.00
Player	Oquindo, I.	8 months	$27,000.00
Player	Ortega, J.	8 months	$20,000.00
Player	Pryor, K.	8 months	$21,000.00
Player	Santiago, J.	8 months	$22,000.00
Player	Stalker, K.	8 months	$23,000.00
Player	Wahlburg, W.	8 months	$24,000.00
Player	Wash, U.R.	8 months	$25,000.00
Player	Ziegler, H.	8 months	$26,000.00
Office	Ackers, P	12 months	$95,000.00
Office	Roper, J.	12 months	$30,000.00
Office	Hill, B	12 months	$48,000.00
Office	Larson, C.	8 months	$22,000.00
Office	Shelton, M.	8 months	$19,000.00
Office	Johnson, T.	12 months	$85,000.00
Office	McCarty, S.	8 months	$17,500.00
Office	Webb, J	8 months	$22,000.00
Office	Tedder, T	8 months	$21,500.00
Office	Gott, D	8 months	$20,800.00

Figure 18.17. Construction Invoices Received by TBC

Larkin Construction Company, Application for Payment, certified for payment Jun 30, Phil Ackers

	Scheduled Value	Previous work complete	Work completed In May	Total completed to date	Pct. comp.	Balance to finish	Retained by General Contractor
General conditions	177,404.70	0.00	17,740.47	17,740.47	0.10	159,664.23	1,774.05
Demolition	16,000.00	0.00	15,500.00	15,500.00	0.97	500.00	1,550.00
Site work	39,994.00	0.00	22,000.00	22,000.00	0.55	17,994.00	2,200.00
Landscape, sod	4,600.00	0.00	0.00	0.00	0.00	4,600.00	0.00
Concrete	54,487.00	0.00	0.00	0.00	0.00	54,487.00	0.00
Masonry	25,000.00	0.00	0.00	0.00	0.00	25,000.00	0.00
Structural steel	152,147.00	0.00	0.00	0.00	0.00	152,147.00	0.00
Carpentry	18,000.00	0.00	0.00	0.00	0.00	18,000.00	0.00
Thermal, moisture	8,319.00	0.00	0.00	0.00	0.00	8,319.00	0.00
Doors, windows, etc	25,000.00	0.00	0.00	0.00	0.00	25,000.00	0.00
Stucco, drywall etc.	28,500.00	0.00	0.00	0.00	0.00	28,500.00	0.00
Floor covering	6,400.00	0.00	0.00	0.00	0.00	6,400.00	0.00
Painting	10,000.00	0.00	0.00	0.00	0.00	10,000.00	0.00
Specialties	7,270.00	0.00	0.00	0.00	0.00	7,270.00	0.00
Toilet, accessories	3,584.00	0.00	0.00	0.00	0.00	3,584.00	0.00
Sign reconst.	645.00	0.00	0.00	0.00	0.00	645.00	0.00
Plumbing etc	13,237.00	0.00	0.00	0.00	0.00	13,237.00	0.00
Heating, a/c	58,407.00	0.00	0.00	0.00	0.00	58,407.00	0.00
Electrical	62,000.00	0.00	0.00	0.00	0.00	62,000.00	0.00
Sound system	4,000.00	0.00	0.00	0.00	0.00	4,000.00	0.00
Total	**714,994.70**	**0.00**	**55,240.47**	**55,240.47**	**0.08**	**659,754.23**	**5,524.05**

Larkin Construction Company, Application for Payment, certified for payment Jun 30, Phil Ackers

	Scheduled Value	Previous work complete	Work completed In June	Total completed to date	Pct. comp.	Balance to finish	Retained by General Contractor
General conditions	177,404.70	17,740.47	15,816.80	33,557.27	0.19	143,847.43	3,355.73
Demolition	16,000.00	15,500.00	500.00	16,000.00	1.00	0.00	1,600.00
Site work	39,994.00	22,000.00	18,000.00	40,000.00	1.00	-6.00	4,000.00
Landscape, sod	4,600.00	0.00	0.00	0.00	0.00	4,600.00	0.00
Concrete	54,487.00	0.00	29,967.85	29,967.85	0.55	24,519.15	2,996.79
Masonry	25,000.00	0.00	0.00	0.00	0.00	25,000.00	0.00
Structural steel	152,147.00	0.00	55,229.36	55,229.36	0.36	96,917.64	5,522.94
Carpentry	18,000.00	0.00	5,000.00	5,000.00	0.28	13,000.00	500.00
Thermal, moisture	8,319.00	0.00	2,000.00	2,000.00	0.24	6,319.00	200.00
Doors, windows, etc	25,000.00	0.00	15,000.00	15,000.00	0.60	10,000.00	1,500.00
Stucco, drywall etc.	28,500.00	0.00	0.00	0.00	0.00	28,500.00	0.00
Floor covering	6,400.00	0.00	0.00	0.00	0.00	6,400.00	0.00
Painting	10,000.00	0.00	0.00	0.00	0.00	10,000.00	0.00
Specialties	7,270.00	0.00	0.00	0.00	0.00	7,270.00	0.00
Toilet, accessories	3,584.00	0.00	0.00	0.00	0.00	3,584.00	0.00
Sign reconst.	645.00	0.00	0.00	0.00	0.00	645.00	0.00
Plumbing etc	13,237.00	0.00	3,500.00	3,500.00	0.26	9,737.00	350.00
Heating, a/c	58,407.00	0.00	10,789.00	10,789.00	0.18	47,618.00	1,078.90
Electrical	62,000.00	0.00	1,345.00	1,345.00	0.02	60,655.00	134.50
Sound system	4,000.00	0.00	0.00	0.00	0.00	4,000.00	0.00
Total	**714,994.70**	**55,240.47**	**157,148.01**	**212,388.48**	**0.30**	**502,606.22**	**21,238.85**

Larkin Construction Company, Application for Payment, certified for payment Jul 31, Phil Ackers							
	Scheduled Value	Previous work complete	Work completed In July	Total completed to date	Pct. comp.	Balance to finish	Retained by General Contractor
General conditions	177,404.70	33,557.27	15,816.80	49,374.07	0.28	128,030.63	4,937.41
Demolition	16,000.00	16,000.00	0.00	16,000.00	1.00	0.00	1,600.00
Site work	39,994.00	40,000.00	0.00	40,000.00	1.00	-6.00	4,000.00
Landscape, sod	4,600.00	0.00	0.00	0.00	0.00	4,600.00	0.00
Concrete	54,487.00	29,967.85	29,967.85	59,935.70	1.10	-5,448.70	5,993.57
Masonry	25,000.00	0.00	0.00	0.00	0.00	25,000.00	0.00
Structural steel	152,147.00	55,229.36	55,229.36	110,458.72	0.73	41,688.28	11,045.87
Carpentry	18,000.00	5,000.00	5,000.00	10,000.00	0.56	8,000.00	1,000.00
Thermal, moisture	8,319.00	2,000.00	3,000.00	5,000.00	0.60	3,319.00	500.00
Doors, windows, etc	25,000.00	15,000.00	2,000.00	17,000.00	0.68	8,000.00	1,700.00
Stucco, drywall etc.	28,500.00	0.00	1,000.00	1,000.00	0.04	27,500.00	100.00
Floor covering	6,400.00	0.00	0.00	0.00	0.00	6,400.00	0.00
Painting	10,000.00	0.00	1,000.00	1,000.00	0.10	9,000.00	100.00
Specialties	7,270.00	0.00	0.00	0.00	0.00	7,270.00	0.00
Toilet, accessories	3,584.00	0.00	0.00	0.00	0.00	3,584.00	0.00
Sign reconst.	645.00	0.00	0.00	0.00	0.00	645.00	0.00
Plumbing etc	13,237.00	3,500.00	4,000.00	7,500.00	0.57	5,737.00	750.00
Heating, a/c	58,407.00	10,789.00	15,000.00	25,789.00	0.44	32,618.00	2,578.90
Electrical	62,000.00	1,345.00	32,550.00	33,895.00	0.55	28,105.00	3,389.50
Sound system	4,000.00	0.00	0.00	0.00	0.00	4,000.00	0.00
Subtotal	**714,994.70**	**212,388.48**	**164,564.01**	**376,952.49**	**0.53**	**338,042.21**	**37,695.25**
Chg Order July							
General conditions	5,586.00	0.00	1,000.00	1,000.00	0.18	4,586.00	100.00
Site work	1,184.00	0.00	689.25	689.25	0.58	494.75	68.93
Thermal, moisture	568.00	0.00	962.40	962.40	1.69	-394.40	96.24
Masonry	1,484.00	0.00	0.00	0.00	0.00	1,484.00	0.00
Carpentry	4,410.00	0.00	1,600.83	1,600.83	0.36	2,809.17	160.08
Doors, windows	11,323.00	0.00	5,320.00	5,320.00	0.47	6,003.00	532.00
Stucco, drywall etc.	30,052.00	0.00	0.00	0.00	0.00	30,052.00	0.00
Specialties	2,000.00	0.00	1,000.00	1,000.00	0.50	1,000.00	100.00
Plumbing etc	4,237.00	0.00	2,000.00	2,000.00	0.47	2,237.00	200.00
Heating a/c	1,000.00	0.00	0.00	0.00	0.00	1,000.00	0.00
Subtotal	**61,844.00**	**0.00**	**12,572.48**	**12,572.48**	**0.20**	**49,271.52**	**1,257.25**
Total	**776,838.70**	**212,388.48**	**177,136.49**	**389,524.97**		**387,313.73**	**38,952.50**

Larkin Construction Company, Application for Payment, certified for payment Aug 31, Phil Ackers							
	Scheduled Value	Previous work complete	Work completed In August	Total completed to date	Pct. comp.	Balance to finish	Retained by General Contractor
General conditions	177,404.70	49,374.07	15,816.80	65,190.87	0.37	112,213.83	6,519.09
Demolition	16,000.00	16,000.00	0.00	16,000.00	1.00	0.00	1,600.00
Site work	39,994.00	40,000.00	0.00	40,000.00	1.00	-6.00	4,000.00
Landscape, sod	4,600.00	0.00	1,000.00	1,000.00	0.22	3,600.00	100.00
Concrete	54,487.00	59,935.70	0.00	59,935.70	1.10	-5,448.70	5,993.57
Masonry	25,000.00	0.00	5,000.00	5,000.00	0.20	20,000.00	500.00
Structural steel	152,147.00	110,458.72	55,229.36	165,688.08	1.09	-13,541.08	16,568.81
Carpentry	18,000.00	10,000.00	5,000.00	15,000.00	0.83	3,000.00	1,500.00
Thermal, moisture	8,319.00	5,000.00	3,000.00	8,000.00	0.96	319.00	800.00
Doors, windows, etc	25,000.00	17,000.00	2,000.00	19,000.00	0.76	6,000.00	1,900.00
Stucco, drywall etc.	28,500.00	1,000.00	10,000.00	11,000.00	0.39	17,500.00	1,100.00
Floor covering	6,400.00	0.00	6,000.00	6,000.00	0.94	400.00	600.00
Painting	10,000.00	1,000.00	8,000.00	9,000.00	0.90	1,000.00	900.00
Specialties	7,270.00	0.00	500.00	500.00	0.07	6,770.00	50.00
Toilet, accessories	3,584.00	0.00	3,621.00	3,621.00	1.01	-37.00	362.10
Sign reconst.	645.00	0.00	640.00	640.00	0.99	5.00	64.00
Plumbing etc	13,237.00	7,500.00	2,000.00	9,500.00	0.72	3,737.00	950.00
Heating, a/c	58,407.00	25,789.00	10,000.00	35,789.00	0.61	22,618.00	3,578.90
Electrical	62,000.00	33,895.00	32,550.00	66,445.00	1.07	-4,445.00	6,644.50
Sound system	4,000.00	0.00	0.00	0.00	0.00	4,000.00	0.00
Subtotal	714,994.70	376,952.49	160,357.16	537,309.65	0.75	177,685.05	53,730.97
Chg Order July							
General conditions	5,586.00	1,000.00	1,000.00	2,000.00	0.36	3,586.00	200.00
Site work	1,184.00	689.25	500.00	1,189.25	1.00	-5.25	118.93
Thermal, moisture	568.00	962.40	0.00	962.40	1.69	-394.40	96.24
Masonry	1,484.00	0.00	200.00	200.00	0.13	1,284.00	20.00
Carpentry	4,410.00	1,600.83	1,600.83	3,201.66	0.73	1,208.34	320.17
Doors, windows	11,323.00	5,320.00	6,000.00	11,320.00	1.00	3.00	1,132.00
Stucco, drywall etc.	30,052.00	0.00	15,000.00	15,000.00	0.50	15,052.00	1,500.00
Specialties	2,000.00	1,000.00	1,000.00	2,000.00	1.00	0.00	200.00
Plumbing etc	4,237.00	2,000.00	0.00	2,000.00	0.47	2,237.00	200.00
Heating a/c	1,000.00	0.00	1,295.18	1,295.18	1.30	-295.18	129.52
Subtotal	61,844.00	12,572.48	26,596.01	39,168.49	8.18	22,675.51	3,916.85
Chg Order August							
General conditions	1,134.00	0.00	134.00	134.00	0.12	1,000.00	13.40
Doors, windows	2,000.00	0.00	1,000.00	1,000.00	0.50	1,000.00	100.00
Carpentry	9,270.00	0.00	5,000.00	5,000.00	0.54	4,270.00	500.00
Heating a/c	2,000.00	0.00	1,000.00	1,000.00	0.50	1,000.00	100.00
Site work	2,000.00	0.00	815.00	815.00	0.41	1,185.00	81.50
Subtotal	16,404.00	0.00	7,949.00	7,949.00	0.48	8,455.00	794.90
Total	793,242.70	389,524.97	194,902.17	584,427.14		208,815.56	58,442.71

Larkin Construction Company, Application for Payment, certified for payment Sep 30, Phil Ackers							
	Scheduled Value	Prior completed	Completed In Sept.	Completed to date	% comp	Bal. to finish	Retained Contractor
General conditions	177,404.70	65,190.87	112,213.83	177,404.70	1.00	0.00	17,740.47
Demolition	16,000.00	16,000.00	0.00	16,000.00	1.00	0.00	1,600.00
Site work	39,994.00	40,000.00	0.00	40,000.00	1.00	-6.00	4,000.00
Landscape, sod	4,600.00	1,000.00	3,600.00	4,600.00	1.00	0.00	460.00
Concrete	54,487.00	59,935.70	0.00	59,935.70	1.10	-5,448.70	5,993.57
Masonry	25,000.00	5,000.00	20,000.00	25,000.00	1.00	0.00	2,500.00
Structural steel	152,147.00	165,688.08	0.00	165,688.08	1.09	-13,541.08	16,568.81
Carpentry	18,000.00	15,000.00	3,150.00	18,150.00	1.01	-150.00	1,815.00
Thermal, moisture	8,319.00	8,000.00	334.95	8,334.95	1.00	-15.95	833.50
Doors, windows, etc	25,000.00	19,000.00	6,300.00	25,300.00	1.01	-300.00	2,530.00
Stucco, drywall etc.	28,500.00	11,000.00	18,375.00	29,375.00	1.03	-875.00	2,937.50
Floor covering	6,400.00	6,000.00	420.00	6,420.00	1.00	-20.00	642.00
Painting	10,000.00	9,000.00	1,000.00	10,000.00	1.00	0.00	1,000.00
Specialties	7,270.00	500.00	7,108.50	7,608.50	1.05	-338.50	760.85
Toilet, accessories	3,584.00	3,621.00	0.00	3,621.00	1.01	-37.00	362.10
Sign reconst.	645.00	640.00	0.00	640.00	0.99	5.00	64.00
Plumbing etc	13,237.00	9,500.00	4,073.33	13,573.33	1.03	-336.33	1,357.33
Heating, a/c	58,407.00	35,789.00	23,748.90	59,537.90	1.02	-1,130.90	5,953.79
Electrical	62,000.00	66,445.00	0.00	66,445.00	1.07	-4,445.00	6,644.50
Sound system	4,000.00	0.00	4,200.00	4,200.00	1.05	-200.00	420.00
Subtotal	714,994.70	537,309.65	204,524.51	741,834.16	1.04	-26,839.46	74,183.42
Chg Order July							
General conditions	5,586.00	2,000.00	3,586.00	5,586.00	1.00	0.00	558.60
Site work	1,184.00	1,189.25	0.00	1,189.25	1.00	-5.25	118.93
Thermal, moisture	568.00	962.40	0.00	962.40	1.69	-394.40	96.24
Masonry	1,484.00	200.00	1,348.20	1,548.20	1.04	-64.20	154.82
Carpentry	4,410.00	3,201.66	1,600.83	4,802.49	1.09	-392.49	480.25
Doors, windows	11,323.00	11,320.00	0.00	11,320.00	1.00	3.00	1,132.00
Stucco, drywall etc.	30,052.00	15,000.00	16,062.40	31,062.40	1.03	-1,010.40	3,106.24
Specialties	2,000.00	2,000.00	295.18	2,295.18	1.15	-295.18	229.52
Plumbing etc	4,237.00	2,000.00	2,500.00	4,500.00	1.06	-263.00	450.00
Heating a/c	1,000.00	1,295.18	1,500.00	2,795.18	2.80	-1,795.18	279.52
Subtotal	61,844.00	39,168.49	26,892.61	66,061.10	1.07	-4,217.10	6,606.11
Chg Order August							
General conditions	1,134.00	134.00	0.00	134.00	0.12	1,000.00	13.40
Doors, windows	2,000.00	1,000.00	1,000.00	2,000.00	1.00	0.00	200.00
Carpentry	9,270.00	5,000.00	5,124.00	10,124.00	1.09	-854.00	1,012.40
Heating a/c	2,000.00	1,000.00	2,000.00	3,000.00	1.50	-1,000.00	300.00
Site work	2,000.00	815.00	1,822.00	2,637.00	1.32	-637.00	263.70
Subtotal	16,404.00	7,949.00	9,946.00	17,895.00	1.09	-1,491.00	1,789.50
Chg Order Sept.							
Sound system	3,543.00	0.00	4,251.60	4,251.60	1.20	-708.60	425.16
Floor covering	19,042.00	0.00	22,250.40	22,250.40	1.17	-3,208.40	2,225.04
Sign reconstruction	400.00	0.00	400.00	400.00	1.00	0.00	40.00
Heating a/c	3,100.00	0.00	3,500.00	3,500.00	1.13	-400.00	350.00
Thermal, moisture	1,454.00	0.00	2,000.00	2,000.00	1.38	-546.00	200.00
Subtotal	27,539.00	0.00	32,402.00	32,402.00	1.18	-4,863.00	3,240.20
Total	820,781.70	584,427.14	273,765.12	858,192.26		-37,410.56	85,819.23

Figure 18.18. Concessions

Date	Hamburgers # sold	Hotdogs # sold	Popcorn # sold	Peanuts # sold	Soda # sold	Beer # sold	Condiments # used*
May 13	540	810	540	405	1080	540	1500
May 14	482	725	475	362	982	375	0
May 15	689	1256	777	548	1521	725	0
Jun 5	722	1108	752	544	1322	589	1500
Jun 6	752	1202	772	571	1523	587	1500
Jun 7	630	945	630	473	1265	630	1500
Jun 24	441	662	445	332	885	345	1000
Jun 25	296	445	298	224	592	296	0
Jun 26	560	842	562	421	1124	479	0
Jul 10	760	1140	658	782	1802	800	2000
Jul 11	700	1050	700	525	1402	700	0
Aug 7	820	1230	820	615	1640	820	0
Aug 8	860	1290	860	645	1720	860	2000
Aug 22	950	1425	950	712	1952	952	2000
Sep 11	840	1260	852	621	1685	865	2000
Sep 12	881	1322	847	569	1875	880	2000
Sep 26	981	1470	987	735	1969	897	0
Sep 27	650	1050	750	800	1526	750	0

*Because it is so tedious, Julie does not count the condiments used after each game. Rather, she counts them on a sporadic basis.

Invoices from Sysco (matches purchase orders)								
Item	Cost	QTY ordered May 12	QTY ordered June 6	QTY ordered June 24	QTY ordered July 9	QTY ordered Aug 7	QTY ordered Aug 22	QTY ordered Sept 9
Hamburgers	1.40	2000	2500	1500	1500	2000	1000	2000
Hotdogs	1.25	3000	3500	2000	2500	3000	1500	3000
Popcorn	0.70	2000	2500	1500	1500	2000	1000	2000
Peanuts	0.70	1400	1200	1000	1200	1400	800	1400
Soda	0.35	4000	5000	3000	3000	4000	2000	4000
Beer	1.35	2000	2500	1500	1500	2000	1000	2000
Condiments	0.05	5000	6000	3000	4000	4000	2000	5000
		Rec'd	Rec'd	Rec'd	Rec'd	Rec'd	Rec'd	Rec'd
		13-May	7-Jun	25-Jun	10-Jul	8-Aug	23-Aug	10-Sep

Perpetual Inventory, Concessions							
	Hamburgers	Hotdogs	Popcorn	Peanuts	Soda	Beer	Condiments
Beg Inventory	3,500	4,000	3,000	3,000	5,500	2,500	5,000
13-May	4,960	6,190	4,460	3,995	8,420	3,960	8,500
14-May	4,478	5,465	3,985	3,633	7,438	3,585	8,500
15-May	3,789	4,209	3,208	3,085	5,917	2,860	8,500
31-May	3,389	3,609	3,208	3,085	5,317	2,460	6,500
5-Jun	2,667	2,501	2,456	2,541	3,995	1,871	5,000
6-Jun	1,915	1,299	1,684	1,970	2,472	1,284	3,500
7-Jun	3,785	3,854	3,554	2,697	6,207	3,154	8,000
24-Jun	4,844	5,192	4,609	3,365	8,322	4,309	10,000
25-Jun	4,548	4,747	4,311	3,141	7,730	4,013	10,000
26-Jun	3,988	3,905	3,749	2,720	6,606	3,534	10,000
30-Jun	3,188	3,105	3,749	2,720	5,806	2,834	8,000
10-Jul	3,928	4,465	4,591	3,138	7,004	3,534	10,000
11-Jul	3,228	3,415	3,891	2,613	5,602	2,834	10,000
31-Jul	2,928	3,115	3,891	2,613	5,102	2,634	9,000
7-Aug	2,108	1,885	3,071	1,998	3,462	1,814	9,000
8-Aug	3,248	3,595	4,211	2,753	5,742	2,954	11,000
22-Aug	3,298	3,670	4,261	2,841	5,790	3,002	11,000
31-Aug	2,898	3,370	4,261	2,841	5,290	2,802	10,000
10-Sep	4,898	6,370	6,261	4,241	9,290	4,802	15,000
11-Sep	4,058	5,110	5,409	3,620	7,605	3,937	13,000
12-Sep	3,177	3,788	4,562	3,051	5,730	3,057	11,000
26-Sep	2,196	2,318	3,575	2,316	3,761	2,160	11,000
27-Sep	1,546	1,268	2,825	1,516	2,235	1,410	11,000
30-Sep	146	68	2,825	1,516	35	60	5,000
Inventory amounts are computed after purchases, sales and end of the month spoilage write-off.							

Figure 18.19. Maintenance Purchase Orders and Invoices

Purchase Orders for Misc Maintenance: To Freddy's Fix-it		
PO Date		**Amount**
May 3	Install office dividers	$700.00
May 15	Maintenance on weightlifting equip	$1,500.00
June 10	Repair flooring in gym	$2,000.00
June 14	Tires, maintenance, painting, logos all vehicles and carts in TBC colors and logos	$33,500.00
June 20	Fix broken screen doors	$250.00
July 3	Fix whirlpool	$1,000.00
July 14	Painting floor of gym	$1,200.00
Aug 5	Repair dryer	$250.00
Aug 17	Repair leaking skylight in training facility	$1,950.00
Sept 2	change shower heads	$250.00
Sept 6	Redo Roof on training facilities	$10,000.00
Sept 13	Carpet cleaning	$2,000.00
Sept 30	Painting offices	$8,000.00

Invoices from Freddy's Fix-it Shop			
Freddy's Fix-it shop 12639 Mission Rd. Tallahassee, FL 32304			
Proprietor: Freddy Harris			
completed	**Item**	**Billed**	**Rec'd by**
May 5	Install office dividers	$700	Julie Roper
May 17	Maintenance for weights	$1,500	Phil Ackers
June 17	Repair flooring in gym	$2,000	Julie Roper
June 21	Fix broken screen doors	$250	Phil Ackers
June 30	Paint and logos all vehicles and carts	$33,500	Phil Ackers
July 4	Fix whirlpool	$1,000	Phil Ackers
July 18	Paint the floor	$1,200	Julie Roper
Aug 5	Fix dryer	$250	Julie Roper
Aug 20	Repair leaky roof	$1,950	Julie Roper
Sept 2	Change shower heads	$250	Julie Roper
Sept 14	Clean carpets	$2,000	Julie Roper
Sept 16	Redo roof	$10,000	Phil Ackers
Sept 30	Repaint offices	$8,000	Julie Roper

Figure 18.20. Ticket Sales, Parking, and Program Sales

	Standard seats sold on game night	Will-call standard	Discounted standard	Balcony	Discounted balcony	Total sold
May 13	1,501	599	200	550	50	2,900
May 14	1,359	591		700		2,650
May 15	2,265	780		1,000		4,045
Jun 5	1,500	875	500	100	1,125	4,100
Jun 6	2,046	754	700	275	625	4,400
Jun 7	1,580	820	500	150	700	3,750
Jun 24	955	1,045	200	100	500	2,800
Jun 25	788	912		180	300	2,180
Jun 26	1,690	1,335		200	700	3,925
Jul 10	2,500	1,150	175	50	225	4,100
Jul 11	2,400	1,220	30	40	210	3,900
Aug 7	2,150	1,950	500	500		5,100
Aug 8	2,360	1,840	600	500		5,300
Aug 22	2,844	2,190	600	700		6,334
Sep 11	2,160	200	150	640	1,050	4,200
Sep 12	2,190	290	336	1,000	584	4,400
Sep 26	1,560	140	1,293	450	1,457	4,900
Sep 27	1,910	90	2,105	300	1,495	5,900

Date	Parking cars	Parking oversized	Sales programs
May 13	1006	220	2160
May 14	916	174	1800
May 15	1215	285	2664
Jun 5	1245	255	2628
Jun 6	1275	225	3116
Jun 7	1174	257	2268
Jun 24	840	160	1826
Jun 25	544	127	1199
Jun 26	1056	216	2184
Jul 10	1275	225	3078
Jul 11	1230	270	2940
Aug 7	1260	240	3034
Aug 8	1215	285	3397
Aug 22	1245	255	3990
Sep 11	1275	225	3570
Sep 12	1230	270	3652
Sep 26	1260	240	3724
Sep 27	1350	150	4661

Figure 18.21. Visa Statements

Visa	PO Box 38571	Previous Balance	$353.27
	Youngstown, OH	Last Payment	$200.00
		Beginning Balance	$153.27
Account 2354 2236 8957 2567		charges	
Date 20-Apr		**Charges**	$97.54
		Publix	$152.08
Due Date 1-May		BP Oil	$42.89
	Balance $445.78	current balance	$445.78
Visa	PO Box 38571	Previous Balance	$445.78
	Youngstown, OH	Last Payment	$445.78
		Beginning Balance	$0.00
Account 2354 2236 8957 2567		**Charges**	
Date 20-May		Home Depot	$397.54
		Sportsman	$252.08
Due Date 1-Jun		Eckerd's	$42.89
		BB Sports	
	Balance $692.51	current balance	$692.51
Visa	PO Box 38571	Previous Balance	$692.51
	Youngstown, OH	Last Payment	$558.92
		Beginning Balance	$133.59
Account 2354 2236 8957 2567		**Charges**	
Date 20-Jun		Wal-Mart	$397.54
		Play it again sports	$252.08
Due Date 1-Jul		Target	$42.89
	Balance $826.10	current balance	$826.10
Visa	PO Box 38571	Previous Balance	$826.10
	Youngstown, OH	Last Payment	$621.02
		Beginning Balance	$205.08
Account 2354 2236 8957 2567		**Charges**	
Date 20-Jul		Havertys	$397.54
		Eckerd's	$252.08
Due Date 1-Aug		Lowes	$42.89
	Balance $897.59	current balance	$897.59
Visa	PO Box 38571	Previous Balance	$897.59
	Youngstown, OH	Last Payment	$667.52
		Beginning Balance	$230.07
Account 2354 2236 8957 2567		**Charges**	
Date 20-Aug		Home Depot	$397.54
		Wal-Mart	$252.08
Due Date 1-Sep		Georgios	$42.89
		Tinos	
	Balance $922.58	current balance	$922.58

Figure 18.22. Monthly Financial Statements

Tallahassee BeanCounters
Statements of Income and Owner's Equity for months ended

	May 31	Jun 30	Jul 31	Aug 31	Sep 30
Revenue					
Game Revenue	$152,130	$314,995	$134,805	$260,522	$281,027
Cost of Goods Sold	(20,386)	(38,723)	(17,201)	(29,298)	(49,100)
Paid to visiting Teams	-	(13,500)	-	(8,000)	(38,500)
Net Home Game Income	131,744	262,772	117,603	223,224	193,427
Fundraising					
Revenue	18,582	4,175	22,550	12,975	13,025
Expenses	(4,628)	(2,342)	(4,004)	(5,009)	(4,758)
Net fundraising Income	13,954	1,833	18,546	7,966	8,267
Other Revenues and Expenses					
League Revenue Sharing	94,513	7,400	25,000	18,300	20,000
Away Game Expenses	(16,387)	(6,756)	(19,313)	(14,192)	(13,308)
Operating Expenses	(138,751)	(180,015)	(137,947)	(140,562)	(220,277)
Game Equipment Exp	(7,716)	(4,119)	-	(2,395)	(10,871)
Net other Rev and Exp	(68,342)	(183,490)	(132,260)	(138,849)	(224,456)
Net Income (Loss)	77,356	81,115	3,889	92,341	(22,762)
Beginning Owner's Equity	96,675	169,032	235,147	224,036	301,376
Net Income (Loss)	77,356	81,115	3,889	92,341	(22,762)
Owner Draws	(5,000)	(15,000)	(15,000)	(15,000)	(15,000)
Ending Owner's Equity	169,032	235,147	224,036	301,376	263,614

Tallahassee BeanCounters
Balance Sheet as of

	May 31	Jun 30	Jul 31	Aug 31	Sep 30
Assets					
Cash	$98,450	$106,172	$89,085	$131,577	$112,111
Accounts Receivable	14,338	71,602	86,912	132,124	112,932
Equipment (net)	51,917	72,417	67,417	67,417	57,417
Programs	22,776	9,555	3,537	-6,884	0
Concessions	19,168	19,131	7,947	12,690	3,671
Construction in Progress	55,240	212,388	389,525	584,427	858,192
Total Assets	261,889	491,265	644,423	921,352	1,144,323
Liabilities					
Accounts Payable	26,900	24,400	21,900	19,400	0
Sales Tax Payable	10,717	19,330	8,962	16,148	22,516
Notes Payable	55,240	212,388	389,525	584,427	858,192
Total Liabilities	92,857	256,118	420,387	619,975	880,709
Owner's Equity	169,032	235,147	224,036	301,376	263,614
Total Liabilities & Owner's Equity	261,889	491,265	644,423	921,352	1,144,323

¶ 18,031   PROBLEM-BASED LEARNING TO ASK THE RIGHT QUESTIONS

At this stage in the case analysis, you should provide a written preliminary analysis of the case to your instructor. See the Comprehensive Problem at the end of this chapter on page 18-41. The analysis should be comprised of four parts. The first part of the analysis should identify red flags and possible suspects, based upon an analysis and understanding of the accounts by type and determine which are the most susceptible to fraudulent activity, such as: sales vs. inventory, hours and wages, and purchase order invoices and receipts. Also, review the employee materials and organizational chart for overlapping job functions (recording sales *and* making deposits; requisitioning *and* receiving merchandise, clerical *and* supervisory functions, etc.). The second part of your analysis should identify where internal business process controls over personnel, material, and accountancy are weak and who is in a position to exploit those weaknesses. The third part of your analysis should discuss how you would exploit such a weakness, knowing what you know about accounting processes, keeping in mind that in order "to catch a thief," at least think like one, or as Wu Tzu put it in *The Art of War*, "know your enemy."

For the fourth part of the analysis, you must determine what additional information is needed and where to get it. For example, ask yourself, "If this were a real-life situation, what evidence do I need to convince someone that a fraud is being committed? Who would I need to talk to, or where do I need to go to gather that evidence? What might I need to see, and how can I see it?"

This part of your report should use the following format:

a. Address correspondence to the person you believe could provide the information you want. Keep in mind that you don't want to "tip off" or offend your suspects.

b. Describe specifically the information you want. For example, "Dear Ms. Hughes, Could you please forward me a copy of the invoices for promotional activities?"

c. Requests for information that would not be made via letter should just be described. For example, for a request outside the company (BeanCounters) you would describe the person, entity, or process you want clearly: "I would like to ask the Accounts Payable person at the phone company for a copy of the bills they sent to TBC." "If I look in the property registration records, what vehicles, homes, boats or recreational vehicles will I find registered to Candie Harris?" or "If I conducted a surveillance of the parking operations on April 30 from 4 p.m. to 10 p.m., what would I see?"

Remember, you may ask for any type of information (other than information that is illegal to obtain). So, investigate from any angle you can imagine. You can communicate with TBC employees, their families or associates, vendors, or anyone else you think might have information you need.

Optimally, the exercise is designed to take advantage of group analysis, or brainstorming. The greater the number of individuals thinking about the potential frauds and suspects, the faster the case will be solved. Although any individual student can resolve the case given enough time and focus, the more investigative minds are engaged in the problem-solving process, the better. Even if only an hour of in-class time is devoted to brainstorming potential leads, the exercise will move forward far more expeditiously than any one student could accomplish alone.

The materials given to the students to this point in the exercise (above) are sufficient to narrow the field to at least one and possibly three fraud schemes that require further investigation. The information given is also sufficient to point in the direction of the sources of that additional information and documentation. Nevertheless, in order to finally and conclusively resolve the case with enough information to warrant prosecution, surveillance will be required in order to ferret out the essential missing link between perpetrator and paper trail to ill-gotten gains.

Identifying the Specific Circumstances of Fraud

In your initial analysis that makes up the first three parts of the assignment described above, you are looking at the BeanCounter processes, the weaknesses in controls, and the personnel issues that might relate to fraud. Once you have some ideas on the potential problems with the company, you formulate questions and those become the fourth part of your initial analysis. As you formulate your questions and even after you receive additional information from your instructor, you will also want to look beyond the existing processes and personnel to the actual circumstances of fraud.

The following questions must be answered with respect to the potential or likely fraud circumstances in the BeanCounter case:

- Who could have committed a fraud?
- How could the fraud have been committed?
- Evidence of intent (which can be shown by repeated instances of taking).
- Economic impact (difference in reported and actual revenue, plus (if negative) under-paid sales tax (to the state) and arena rent (to the stadium owner) must be included as total loss due to theft.
- Evidence of conversion tracing funds to "dummy" (usually bank) account of employee suspect under a different, or possibly assumed, name.

Once the instructor reviews your analysis and the queries, more information will be provided that will allow the ultimate resolution of the case.

¶ 18,041   CONCLUSION

Problem-based learning exercises and capstone case studies are meant to simulate important aspects of a professional practice. First used in medical education (as portrayed in such television shows as *ER*), this educational model has been extended and successfully used in other practice-oriented professions like law and now forensic accounting.

Therefore, the purpose and importance of case studies in a forensic professional education cannot be overstated. The two cases presented here are intended to educate both formatively and summatively, and highlight the application of forensic principles as process-oriented as well as outcome-oriented.

The *TruGloss Shanghai* case directs the student toward the application of a forensic investigative process, rather than the more outcome-oriented *Tallahassee BeanCounters* case. In the *TruGloss Shanghai* case, the questions matter more than the answers, which are more straightforwardly provided so as to focus attention on how the fraud was uncovered as much as if not more than how to uncover it in the first place. On the other hand, the *Tallahassee BeanCounters* case has definite right and wrong answers, and even just guessing the right answer based on a "hunch" is as valid as any exhaustive analysis might reveal.

Another distinction is to view the purpose of the *TruGloss Shanghai* case as a cautionary tale in order to stimulate discussion of how such fraud can be prevented in the future. On the other hand, the type of criminal activity engaged in at *Tallahassee BeanCounters* is essentially prevented only by enforcement and punishment of the guilty.

Both of these cases, as types, are real in the world today and both were chosen to give students a taste of the challenges encountered in any forensic and investigative accounting practice.

ENDNOTES

[1] This discussion is being adapted from the case article with permission of the authors and the JOURNAL OF FORENSIC ACCOUNTING, Vol. V (September 2004), pp. 433-456.

[2] Adapted from, Carol Callaway Dee and Cindy Durtschi, "Return of the Tallahassee BeanCounters: A Case in Forensic Accounting," ISSUES IN ACCOUNTING EDUCATION, Vol. 25, No. 2., pp. 279-321. The American Accounting Association holds the copyright to this article. The full

text of many AAA articles are available online at *http://aaapubs.org/*.

[3] Statement on Auditing Standards (SAS) No.99 requires the audit team to brainstorm "… about how and where they believe the entity's financial statements might be susceptible to material misstatement due to fraud, how management could perpetrate and conceal fraudulent financial reporting, and how assets of the entity could

be misappropriated" (AICPA 2002, para. 14). Generally SAS No. 99 does not apply to forensic investigators unless they are certified public accountants engaged to render an opinion on financial statements.

EXERCISES

1. Why is it so important to be able to clearly articulate the results of a fraud investigation?

2. Who decides what information provided by the forensic accountant can be used as evidence in a court of law?

3. What are the basic questions that the forensic accountant sets out to answer in a fraud investigation?

4. The forensic accountant must not only analyze documents, but investigate the character of individuals who may be involved in fraudulent activities. Based on your reading of the *TruGloss* and *BeanCounters* cases, what are some of the character "red flags" discovered in these studies?

5. What is it that generally sparks a forensic investigation? (It is not clever detective work!)

6. Do you believe the high expectations for the China operation of *TruGloss* may have contributed to the fraudulent activities involved? Why or why not?

7. Are there parallels between *Enron* and *TruGloss*?

8. Please identify at least one, up to three, pieces of documentary information that would corroborate the resolution of questions appearing at the end of the *TruGloss* exercise, namely: "What was taken?"; "Who had the opportunity?"; "How were the assets moved?"; "How was the theft concealed?"; and "How were the assets converted?"

9. Aside from documentary evidence available from a client and from third-parties that do business with the client (banks, vendors, outsourced administrative services, like ADP payroll), what other types of nondocumentary evidence is readily available in a forensic investigation?

10. How might a business valuation-type fraud case differ from the types of fraud cases in this chapter?

COMPREHENSIVE PROBLEM

Write up an analysis of the *Tallahassee BeanCounters* case that is comprised of the following Four Parts:

1. Identify red flags and possible suspects in the case and state your rationale. This discussion should include your analysis of the account by type such as sales versus inventory, wages and hours, purchase orders invoices and receipts along with a discussion of any overlapping job functions such as recording sales and making deposits, requisitioning and receiving merchandise, clerical and supervisory functions, etc.

2. Identify where internal controls over personnel, material and accountancy are weak and who is in a position to exploit those weaknesses.

3. Describe how you might perpetrate fraud based on your understanding of the BeanCounters' processes.

4. Determine what additional information is needed.
    a. Write requests to specific individuals you believe could provide the information you want making sure your letters do not "tip off" any suspects. Be specific in your description.
    b. Write up additional requests that you may want to make outside the BeanCounters for additional information. These might include invoices from the phone company, property registration records or even surveillance data on the parking lot.

Read ¶18,031 carefully before you start this exercise.

APPENDICES

appendix

Reference Materials from the Institute of Internal Auditors

THE INSTITUTE OF INTERNAL AUDITORS
247 Maitland Avenue
Altamonte Springs, Florida 32701-4201 USA

Standards for the Professional Practice of Internal Auditing

2320 – Analysis and Evaluation
Internal auditors should base conclusions and engagement results on appropriate analyses and evaluations.

Practice Advisory

Practice Advisory 2320-1: Analysis and Evaluation
Interpretation of Standard 2320 from the Standards for the Professional Practice of Internal Auditing

Related Standard: 2320 - Analysis and Evaluation
Internal auditors should base conclusions and engagement results on appropriate analyses and evaluations.

Nature of this Practice Advisory
Internal auditors should consider the following suggestions when using analysis and

evaluation to reach conclusions. This guidance is not intended to represent all the considerations that may be necessary during such an evaluation, but simply a recommended set of items that should be addressed. Compliance with Practice Advisories is optional.

1. Analytical auditing procedures provide internal auditors with an efficient and effective means of assessing and evaluating information collected in an engagement. The assessment results from comparing information with expectations identified or developed by the internal auditor. Analytical auditing procedures are useful in identifying, among other things:
    - Differences that are not expected.
    - The absence of differences when they are expected.
    - Potential errors.
    - Potential irregularities or illegal acts.
    - Other unusual or nonrecurring transactions or events.

2. Analytical auditing procedures may include:
    - Comparison of current period information with similar information for prior periods.
    - Comparison of current period information with budgets or forecasts.
    - Study of relationships of financial information with the appropriate nonfinancial information (for example, recorded payroll expense compared to changes in average number of employees).
    - Study of relationships among elements of information (for example, fluctuation in recorded interest expense compared to changes in related debt balances).
    - Comparison of information with similar information for other organizational units.
    - Comparison of information with similar information for the industry in which the organization operates.

3. Analytical auditing procedures may be performed using monetary amounts, physical quantities, ratios, or percentages. Specific analytical auditing procedures include, but are not limited to, ratio, trend and regression analysis, reasonableness tests, period-to-period comparisons, comparisons with budgets, forecasts, and external economic information. Analytical auditing procedures assist internal auditors in identifying conditions which may require subsequent engagement procedures. Internal auditors should use analytical auditing procedures in planning the engagement in accordance with the guidelines contained in Section 2200 of the Standards (Practice Advisory 2210-1).

4. Analytical auditing procedures should also be used during the engagement to examine and evaluate information to support engagement results. Internal auditors should consider the factors listed below in determining the extent to which analytical auditing procedures should be used. After evaluating these factors, internal auditors should consider and use additional auditing procedures, as necessary, to achieve the engagement objective.
    - The significance of the area being examined.
    - The adequacy of the system of internal control.
    - The availability and reliability of financial and nonfinancial information.
    - The precision with which the results of analytical auditing procedures can be predicted.
    - The availability and comparability of information regarding the industry in which the organization operates.
    - The extent to which other engagement procedures provide support for engagement results.

5. When analytical auditing procedures identify unexpected results or relationships, internal auditors should examine and evaluate such results or relationships. The examination and evaluation of unexpected results or relationships from applying analytical auditing procedures should include inquiries of management and the application of other engagement procedures until internal auditors are satisfied that the results or relationships are sufficiently explained. Unexplained results or relationships from applying analytical auditing procedures may be indicative of a significant condition such as a potential error, irregularity, or illegal act. Results or relationships from applying analytical auditing procedures that are not sufficiently explained should be communicated to the appropriate levels of management. Internal auditors may recommend appropriate courses of action, depending on the circumstances.

2

STATEMENT ON AUDITING STANDARDS NO. 99

AU Section 316

Consideration of Fraud in a Financial Statement Audit

(Supersedes SAS No. 82)

Source: SAS No. 99.

Effective for audits of financial statements for periods beginning on or after December 15, 2002.

Introduction and Overview

.01 Section 110, *Responsibilities and Functions of the Independent Auditor*, paragraph .02, states, "The auditor has a responsibility to plan and perform the audit to obtain reasonable assurance about whether the financial statements are free of material misstatement, whether caused by error or fraud. [footnote omitted]"[1] This section establishes standards and provides guidance to auditors in fulfilling that responsibility, as it relates to fraud, in an audit of financial statements conducted in accordance with generally accepted auditing standards (GAAS).[2]

.02 The following is an overview of the organization and content of this section:
- *Description and characteristics of fraud.* This section describes fraud and its characteristics. (See paragraphs .05 through .12.)

- *The importance of exercising professional skepticism.* This section discusses the need for auditors to exercise professional skepticism when considering the possibility that a material misstatement due to fraud could be present. (See paragraph .13.)
- *Discussion among engagement personnel regarding the risks of material misstatement due to fraud.* This section requires, as part of planning the audit, that there be a discussion among the audit team members to consider how and where the entity's financial statements might be susceptible to material misstatement due to fraud and to reinforce the importance of adopting an appropriate mindset of professional skepticism. (See paragraphs .14 through .18.)
- *Obtaining the information needed to identify risks of material misstatement due to fraud.* This section requires the auditor to gather information necessary to identify risks of material misstatement due to fraud, by

  a. Inquiring of management and others within the entity about the risks of fraud. (See paragraphs .20 through .27.)

  b. Considering the results of the analytical procedures performed in planning the audit. (See paragraphs .28 through .30.)

  c. Considering fraud risk factors. (See paragraphs .31 through .33, and the Appendix, "Examples of Fraud Risk Factors" [paragraph .85].)

  d. Considering certain other information. (See paragraph .34.)
- *Identifying risks that may result in a material misstatement due to fraud.* This section requires the auditor to use the information gathered to identify risks that may result in a material misstatement due to fraud. (See paragraphs .35 through .42.)
- *Assessing the identified risks after taking into account an evaluation of the entity's programs and controls.* This section requires the auditor to evaluate the entity's programs and controls that address the identified risks of material misstatement due to fraud, and to assess the risks taking into account this evaluation. (See paragraphs .43 through .45.)
- *Responding to the results of the assessment.* This section emphasizes that the auditor's response to the risks of material misstatement due to fraud involves the application of professional skepticism when gathering and evaluating audit evidence. (See paragraph .46 through .49.) The section requires the auditor to respond to the results of the risk assessment in three ways:

  a. A response that has an overall effect on how the audit is conducted, that is, a response involving more general considerations apart from the specific procedures otherwise planned. (See paragraph .50.)

  b. A response to identified risks that involves the nature, timing, and extent of the auditing procedures to be performed. (See paragraphs .51 through .56.)

  c. A response involving the performance of certain procedures to further address the risk of material misstatement due to fraud involving management override of controls. (See paragraphs .57 through .67.)
- *Evaluating audit evidence.* This section requires the auditor to assess the risks of material misstatement due to fraud throughout the audit and to evaluate at the completion of the audit whether the accumulated results of auditing procedures and other observations affect the assessment. (See paragraphs .68 through .74.) It also requires the auditor to consider whether identified misstatements may be indicative of fraud and, if so, directs the auditor to evaluate their implications. (See paragraphs .75 through .78.)
- *Communicating about fraud to management, the audit committee, and others.* This section provides guidance regarding the auditor's communications about fraud to management, the audit committee, and others. (See paragraphs .79 through .82.)
- *Documenting the auditor's consideration of fraud.* This section describes related documentation requirements. (See paragraph .83.)

.03 The requirements and guidance set forth in this section are intended to be integrated into an overall audit process, in a logical manner that is consistent with the requirements and guidance provided in other sections, including section 311, *Planning and Supervision*; section 312, *Audit Risk and Materiality in Conducting an Audit*; and section 319, *Consideration of Internal Control in a Financial Statement Audit*. Even though some requirements and guidance set forth in this section are presented in a manner that suggests a sequential audit process, auditing in fact involves a continuous process of gathering, updating, and analyzing information throughout the audit. Accordingly the sequence of the requirements and guidance in this section may be implemented differently among audit engagements.

.04 Although this section focuses on the auditor's consideration of fraud in an audit of financial statements, it is management's responsibility to design and implement programs and controls to prevent, deter, and detect fraud.[3] That responsibility is described in section 110.03, which states, "Management is responsible for adopting sound accounting policies and for establishing and maintaining internal control that will, among other things, initiate, record, process, and report transactions (as well as events and conditions) consistent with management's assertions embodied in the financial statements." Management, along with those who have responsibility for oversight of the financial reporting process (such as the audit committee, board of trustees, board of directors, or the owner in owner-managed entities), should set the proper tone; create and maintain a culture of honesty and high ethical standards; and establish appropriate controls to prevent, deter, and detect fraud. When management and those responsible for the oversight of the financial reporting process fulfill those responsibilities, the opportunities to commit fraud can be reduced significantly.

Description and Characteristics of Fraud

.05 Fraud is a broad legal concept and auditors do not make legal determinations of whether fraud has occurred. Rather, the auditor's interest specifically relates to acts that result in a material misstatement of the financial statements. The primary factor that distinguishes fraud from error is whether the underlying action that results in the misstatement of the financial statements is intentional or unintentional. For purposes of the section, *fraud* is an intentional act that results in a material misstatement in financial statements that are the subject of an audit.[4]

.06 Two types of misstatements are relevant to the auditor's consideration of fraud—misstatements arising from fraudulent financial reporting and misstatements arising from misappropriation of assets.

- *Misstatements arising from fraudulent financial reporting* are intentional misstatements or omissions of amounts or disclosures in financial statements designed to deceive financial statement users where the effect causes the financial statements not to be presented, in all material respects, in conformity with generally accepted accounting principles (GAAP).[5] Fraudulent financial reporting may be accomplished by the following:
  — Manipulation, falsification, or alteration of accounting records or supporting documents from which financial statements are prepared
  — Misrepresentation in or intentional omission from the financial statements of events, transactions, or other significant information
  — Intentional misapplication of accounting principles relating to amounts, classification, manner of presentation, or disclosure
  Fraudulent financial reporting need not be the result of a grand plan or conspiracy. It may be that management representatives rationalize the appropriateness of a material misstatement, for example, as an aggressive rather than indefensible interpretation of complex accounting rules, or as a temporary misstatement of financial statements, including interim statements, expected to be corrected later when operational results improve.

- *Misstatements arising from misappropriation of assets* (sometimes referred to as theft or defalcation) involve the theft of an entity's assets where the effect of the theft causes the financial statements not to be presented, in all material respects, in conformity with GAAP. Misappropriation of assets can be accomplished in various ways, including embezzling receipts, stealing assets, or causing an entity to pay for goods or services that have not been received. Misappropriation of assets may be accompanied by false or misleading records or documents, possibly created by circumventing controls. The scope of this section includes only those misappropriations of assets for which the effect of the misappropriation causes the financial statements not to be fairly presented, in all material respects, in conformity with GAAP.

.07 Three conditions generally are present when fraud occurs. First, management or other employees have an *incentive* or are under *pressure*, which provides a reason to commit fraud. Second, circumstances exist—for example, the absence of controls, ineffective controls, or the ability of management to override controls—that provide an *opportunity* for a fraud to be perpetrated. Third, those involved are able to *rationalize* committing a fraudulent act. Some individuals possess an *attitude*, character, or set of ethical values that allow them to knowingly and intentionally commit a dishonest act. However, even otherwise honest individuals can commit fraud in an environment that imposes sufficient pressure on them. The greater the incentive or pressure, the more likely an individual will be able to rationalize the acceptability of committing fraud.

.08 Management has a unique ability to perpetrate fraud because it frequently is in a position to directly or indirectly manipulate accounting records and present fraudulent financial information. Fraudulent financial reporting often involves management override of controls that otherwise may appear to be operating effectively.[6] Management can either direct employees to perpetrate fraud or solicit their help in carrying it out. In addition, management personnel at a component of the entity may be in a position to manipulate the accounting records of the component in a manner that causes a material misstatement in the consolidated financial statements of the entity. Management override of controls can occur in unpredictable ways.

.09 Typically, management and employees engaged in fraud will take steps to conceal the fraud from the auditors and others within and outside the organization. Fraud may be concealed by withholding evidence or misrepresenting information in response to inquiries or by falsifying documentation. For example, management that engages in fraudulent financial reporting might alter shipping documents. Employees or members of management who misappropriate cash might try to conceal their thefts by forging signatures or falsifying electronic approvals on disbursement authorizations. An audit conducted in accordance with GAAS rarely involves the authentication of such documentation, nor are auditors trained as or expected to be experts in such authentication. In addition, an auditor may not discover the existence of a modification of documentation through a side agreement that management or a third party has not disclosed.

.10 Fraud also may be concealed through collusion among management, employees, or third parties. Collusion may cause the auditor who has properly performed the audit to conclude that evidence provided is persuasive when it is, in fact, false. For example, through collusion, false evidence that controls have been operating effectively may be presented to the auditor, or consistent misleading explanations may be given to the auditor by more than one individual within the entity to explain an unexpected result of an analytical procedure. As another example, the auditor may receive a false confirmation from a third party that is in collusion with management.

.11 Although fraud usually is concealed and management's intent is difficult to determine, the presence of certain conditions may suggest to the auditor the possibility that fraud may exist. For example, an important contract may be missing, a subsidiary ledger may not be satisfactorily reconciled to its control account, or the results of an analytical procedure performed during the audit may not be consistent with expectations. However, these conditions may be the result of circumstances other than fraud. Documents may legitimately have been lost or misfiled; the subsidiary ledger may be out of balance with its control account because of an unintentional accounting error; and unexpected analytical relationships may be the result of unanticipated changes in underlying economic factors. Even reports of alleged fraud may not always be reliable because an employee or outsider may be mistaken or may be motivated for unknown reasons to make a false allegation.

.12 As indicated in paragraph .01, the auditor has a responsibility to plan and perform the audit to obtain reasonable assurance about whether the financial statements are free of material misstatement, whether caused by fraud or error.[7] However, absolute assurance is not attainable and thus even a properly planned and performed audit may not detect a material misstatement resulting from fraud. A material misstatement may not be detected because of the nature of audit evidence or because the characteristics of fraud as discussed above may cause the auditor to rely unknowingly on audit evidence that appears to be valid, but is, in fact, false and fraudulent. Furthermore, audit procedures that are effective for detecting an error may be ineffective for detecting fraud.

The Importance of Exercising Professional Skepticism

.13 Due professional care requires the auditor to exercise professional skepticism. See section 230, *Due Professional Care in the Performance of Work*, paragraphs .07 through .09. Because of the characteristics of fraud, the auditor's exercise of professional skepticism is important when considering the risk of material misstatement due to fraud. Professional skepticism is an attitude that includes a questioning mind and a critical assessment of audit evidence. The auditor should conduct the engagement with a mindset that recognizes the possibility that a material misstatement due to fraud could be present, regardless of any past experience with the entity and regardless of the auditor's belief about management's honesty and integrity. Furthermore, professional skepticism requires an ongoing questioning of whether the information and evidence obtained suggests that a material misstatement due to fraud has occurred. In exercising professional skepticism in gathering and evaluating evidence, the auditor should not be satisfied with less-than-persuasive evidence because of a belief that management is honest.

Discussion Among Engagement Personnel Regarding the Risks of Material Misstatement Due to Fraud

.14 Prior to or in conjunction with the information-gathering procedures described in paragraphs .19 through .34 of this section, members of the audit team should discuss the potential for material misstatement due to fraud. The discussion should include:

- An exchange of ideas or "brainstorming" among the audit team members, including the auditor with final responsibility for the audit, about how and where they believe the entity's financial statements might be susceptible to material misstatement due to fraud, how management could perpetrate and conceal fraudulent financial reporting, and how assets of the entity could be misappropriated. (See paragraph .15.)
- An emphasis on the importance of maintaining the proper state of mind throughout the audit regarding the potential for material misstatement due to fraud. (See paragraph .16.)

.15 The discussion among the audit team members about the susceptibility of the entity's financial statements to material misstatement due to fraud should include a consideration of the known external and internal factors affecting the entity that might (a) create incentives/pressures for management and others to commit fraud, (b) provide the opportunity for fraud to be perpetrated, and (c) indicate a culture or environment that enables management to rationalize committing fraud. The discussion should occur with an attitude that includes a questioning mind as described in paragraph .16 and, for this purpose, setting aside any prior beliefs the audit team members may have that management is honest and has integrity. In this regard, the discussion should include a consideration of the risk of management override of controls.[8] Finally, the discussion should include how the auditor might respond to the susceptibility of the entity's financial statements to material misstatement due to fraud.

.16 The discussion among the audit team members should emphasize the need to maintain a questioning mind and to exercise professional skepticism in gathering and evaluating evidence throughout the audit, as described in paragraph .13. This should lead the audit team members to continually be alert for information or other conditions (such as those presented in paragraph .68) that indicate a material misstatement due to fraud may have occurred. It should also lead audit team members to thoroughly probe the issues, acquire additional evidence as necessary, and consult with other team members and, if appropriate, experts in the firm, rather than rationalize or dismiss information or other conditions that indicate a material misstatement due to fraud may have occurred.

.17 Although professional judgment should be used in determining which audit team members should be included in the discussion, the discussion ordinarily should involve the key members of the audit team. A number of factors will influence the extent of the discussion and how it should occur. For example, if the audit involves more than one location, there could be multiple discussions with team members in differing locations. Another factor to consider in planning the discussions is whether to include specialists assigned to the audit team. For example, if the auditor has determined that a professional possessing information technology skills is needed on the audit team (see section 319.32), it may be useful to include that individual in the discussion.

.18 Communication among the audit team members about the risks of material misstatement due to fraud also should continue throughout the audit—for example, in evaluating the risks of material misstatement due to fraud at or near the completion of the field work. (See paragraph .74 and footnote 28).

Obtaining the Information Needed to Identify the Risks of Material Misstatement Due to Fraud

.19 Section 311.06–.08 provides guidance about how the auditor obtains knowledge about the entity's business and the industry in which it operates. In performing that work, information may come to the auditor's attention that should be considered in identifying risks of material misstatement due to fraud. As part of this work, the auditor should perform the following procedures to obtain information that is used (as described in paragraphs .35 through .42) to identify the risks of material misstatement due to fraud:

> *a*. Make inquiries of management and others within the entity to obtain their views about the risks of fraud and how they are addressed. (See paragraphs .20 through .27.)
>
> *b*. Consider any unusual or unexpected relationships that have been identified in performing analytical procedures in planning the audit. (See paragraphs .28 through .30.)
>
> *c*. Consider whether one or more fraud risk factors exist. (See paragraphs .31 through .33, and the Appendix [paragraph .85].)
>
> *d*. Consider other information that may be helpful in the identification of risks of material misstatement due to fraud. (See paragraph .34.)

Making Inquiries of Management and Others Within the Entity About the Risks of Fraud

.20 The auditor should inquire of management about:[9]

- Whether management has knowledge of any fraud or suspected fraud affecting the entity
- Whether management is aware of allegations of fraud or suspected fraud affecting the entity, for example, received in communications from employees, former employees, analysts, regulators, short sellers, or others
- Management's understanding about the risks of fraud in the entity, including any specific fraud risks the entity has identified or account balances or classes of transactions for which a risk of fraud may be likely to exist
- Programs and controls[10] the entity has established to mitigate specific fraud risks the entity has identified, or that otherwise help to prevent, deter, and detect fraud, and how management monitors those programs and controls. For examples of programs and controls an entity may implement to prevent, deter, and detect fraud, see the exhibit titled "Management Antifraud Programs and Controls" [paragraph .88] at the end of this section.
- For an entity with multiple locations, (*a*) the nature and extent of monitoring of operating locations or business segments, and (*b*) whether there are particular operating locations or business segments for which a risk of fraud may be more likely to exist
- Whether and how management communicates to employees its views on business practices and ethical behavior

.21 The inquiries of management also should include whether management has reported to the audit committee or others with equivalent authority and responsibility[11] (hereafter referred to as the audit committee) on how the entity's internal control[12] serves to prevent, deter, or detect material misstatements due to fraud.

.22 The auditor also should inquire directly of the audit committee (or at least its chair) regarding the audit committee's views about the risks of fraud and whether the audit committee has knowledge of any fraud or suspected fraud affecting the entity. An entity's audit committee sometimes assumes an active role in oversight of the entity's assessment of the risks of fraud and the programs and controls the entity has established to mitigate these risks. The auditor should obtain an understanding of how the audit committee exercises oversight activities in that area.

.23 For entities that have an internal audit function, the auditor also should inquire of appropriate internal audit personnel about their views about the risks of fraud, whether they have performed any procedures to identify or detect fraud during the year, whether management has satisfactorily responded to any findings resulting from these procedures, and whether the internal auditors have knowledge of any fraud or suspected fraud.

.24 In addition to the inquiries outlined in paragraphs .20 through .23, the auditor should inquire of others within the entity about the existence or suspicion of fraud. The auditor should use professional judgment to determine those others within the entity to whom inquiries should be directed and the extent of such inquiries. In making this determination, the auditor should consider whether others within the entity may be able to provide information that will be helpful to the auditor in identifying risks of material misstatement due to fraud—for example, others who may have additional knowledge about or be able to corroborate risks of fraud identified in the discussions with management (see paragraph .20) or the audit committee (see paragraph .22).

.25 Examples of others within the entity to whom the auditor may wish to direct these inquiries include:
- Employees with varying levels of authority within the entity, including, for example, entity personnel with whom the auditor comes into contact during the course of the audit in obtaining (*a*) an understanding of the entity's systems and internal control, (*b*) in observing inventory or performing cutoff procedures, or (*c*) in obtaining explanations for fluctuations noted as a result of analytical procedures
- Operating personnel not directly involved in the financial reporting process
- Employees involved in initiating, recording, or processing complex or unusual transactions— for example, a sales transaction with multiple elements, or a significant related party transaction
- In-house legal counsel

.26 The auditor's inquiries of management and others within the entity are important because fraud often is uncovered through information received in response to inquiries. One reason for this is that such inquiries may provide individuals with an opportunity to convey information to the auditor that otherwise might not be communicated. Making inquiries of others within the entity, in addition to management, may be useful in providing the auditor with a perspective that is different from that of individuals involved in the financial reporting process. The responses to these other inquiries might serve to corroborate responses received from management, or alternatively, might provide information regarding the possibility of management override of controls—for example, a response from an employee indicating an unusual change in the way transactions have been processed. In addition, the auditor may obtain information from these inquiries regarding how effectively management has communicated standards of ethical behavior to individuals throughout the organization.

.27 The auditor should be aware when evaluating management's responses to the inquiries discussed in paragraph .20 that management is often in the best position to perpetrate fraud. The auditor should use professional judgment in deciding when it is necessary to corroborate responses to inquiries with other information. However, when responses are inconsistent among inquiries, the auditor should obtain additional audit evidence to resolve the inconsistencies.

Considering the Results of the Analytical Procedures Performed in Planning the Audit

.28 Section 329, *Analytical Procedures*, paragraphs .04 and .06, requires that analytical procedures be performed in planning the audit with an objective of identifying the existence of unusual transactions or events, and amounts, ratios, and trends that might indicate matters that have financial statement and audit planning implications. In performing analytical procedures in planning the audit, the auditor develops expectations about plausible relationships that are reasonably expected to exist, based on the auditor's understanding of the entity and its environment. When comparison of those expectations with recorded amounts or ratios developed from recorded amounts yields unusual or unexpected relationships, the auditor should consider those results in identifying the risks of material misstatement due to fraud.

.29 In planning the audit, the auditor also should perform analytical procedures relating to revenue with the objective of identifying unusual or unexpected relationships involving revenue accounts that may indicate a material misstatement due to fraudulent financial reporting. An example of such an analytical procedure that addresses this objective is a comparison of sales volume, as determined from recorded revenue amounts, with production capacity. An excess of sales volume over production capacity may be indicative of recording fictitious sales. As another example, a trend analysis of revenues by month and sales returns by month during and shortly after the reporting period may indicate the existence of undisclosed side agreements with customers to return goods that would preclude revenue recognition.[13]

.30 Analytical procedures performed during planning may be helpful in identifying the risks of material misstatement due to fraud. However, because such analytical procedures generally use data aggregated at a high level, the results of those analytical procedures provide only a broad initial indication about whether a material misstatement of the financial statements may exist. Accordingly, the results of analytical procedures performed during planning should be considered along with other information gathered by the auditor in identifying the risks of material misstatement due to fraud.

Considering Fraud Risk Factors

.31 Because fraud is usually concealed, material misstatements due to fraud are difficult to detect. Nevertheless, the auditor may identify events or conditions that indicate incentives/pressures to perpetrate fraud, opportunities to carry out the fraud, or attitudes/rationalizations to justify a fraudulent action. Such events or conditions are referred to as "fraud risk factors." Fraud risk factors do not necessarily indicate the existence of fraud; however, they often are present in circumstances where fraud exists.

.32 When obtaining information about the entity and its environment, the auditor should consider whether the information indicates that one or more fraud risk factors are present. The auditor should use professional judgment in determining whether a risk factor is present and should be considered in identifying and assessing the risks of material misstatement due to fraud.

.33 Examples of fraud risk factors related to fraudulent financial reporting and misappropriation of assets are presented in the Appendix [paragraph .85]. These illustrative risk factors are classified based on the three conditions generally present when fraud exists: *incentive/pressure* to perpetrate fraud, an *opportunity* to carry out the fraud, and *attitude/rationalization* to justify the fraudulent action. Although the risk factors cover a broad range of situations, they are only examples and, accordingly, the auditor may wish to consider additional or different risk factors. Not all of these examples are relevant in all circumstances, and some may be of greater or lesser significance in entities of different size or with different ownership characteristics or circumstances. Also, the order of the examples of risk factors provided is not intended to reflect their relative importance or frequency of occurrence.

Considering Other Information That May Be Helpful in Identifying Risks of Material Misstatement Due to Fraud

.34 The auditor should consider other information that may be helpful in identifying risks of material misstatement due to fraud. Specifically, the discussion among the engagement team members (see paragraphs .14 through .18) may provide information helpful in identifying such risks. In addition, the auditor should consider whether information from the results of (*a*) procedures relating to the acceptance and continuance of clients and engagements[14] and (*b*) reviews of interim financial statements may be relevant in the identification of such risks. Finally, as part of the consideration of audit risk at the individual account balance or class of transaction level (see section 312.24 through .33), the auditor should consider whether identified inherent risks would provide useful information in identifying the risks of material misstatement due to fraud (see paragraph .39).

Identifying Risks That May Result in a Material Misstatement Due to Fraud

Using the Information Gathered to Identify Risk of Material Misstatements Due to Fraud

.35 In identifying risks of material misstatement due to fraud, it is helpful for the auditor to consider the information that has been gathered (see paragraphs .19 through .34) in the context of the three conditions present when a material misstatement due to fraud occurs—that is, incentives/pressures, opportunities, and attitudes/rationalizations (see paragraph .07). However, the auditor should not assume that all three conditions must be observed or evident before concluding that there are identified risks. Although the risk of material misstatement due to fraud may be greatest when all three fraud conditions are observed or evident, the auditor cannot assume that the inability to observe one or two of these conditions means there is no risk of material misstatement due to fraud. In fact, observing that individuals have the requisite attitude to commit fraud, or identifying factors that indicate a likelihood that management or other employees will rationalize committing a fraud, is difficult at best.

.36 In addition, the extent to which each of the three conditions referred to above are present when fraud occurs may vary. In some instances the significance of incentives/pressures may result in a risk of material misstatement due to fraud, apart from the significance of the other two conditions. For example, an incentive/pressure to achieve an earnings level to preclude a loan default, or to "trigger" incentive compensation plan awards, may alone result in a risk of material misstatement due to fraud. In other instances, an easy opportunity to commit the fraud because of a lack of controls may be the dominant condition precipitating the risk of fraud, or an individual's attitude or ability to rationalize unethical actions may be sufficient to motivate that individual to engage in fraud, even in the absence of significant incentives/pressures or opportunities.

.37 The auditor's identification of fraud risks also may be influenced by characteristics such as the size, complexity, and ownership attributes of the entity. For example, in the case of a larger entity, the auditor ordinarily considers factors that generally constrain improper conduct by management, such as the effectiveness of the audit committee and the internal audit function, and the existence and enforcement of a formal code of conduct. In the case of a smaller entity, some or all of these considerations may be inapplicable or less important, and management may have developed a culture that emphasizes the importance of integrity and ethical behavior through oral communication and management by example. Also, the risks of material misstatement due to fraud may vary among operating locations or business segments of an entity, requiring an identification of the risks related to specific geographic areas or business segments, as well as for the entity as a whole.[15]

.38 The auditor should evaluate whether identified risks of material misstatement due to fraud can be related to specific financial-statement account balances or classes of transactions and related assertions, or whether they relate more pervasively to the financial statements as a whole. Relating the risks of material misstatement due to fraud to the individual accounts, classes of transactions, and assertions will assist the auditor in subsequently designing appropriate auditing procedures.

.39 Certain accounts, classes of transactions, and assertions that have high inherent risk because they involve a high degree of management judgment and subjectivity also may present risks of material misstatement due to fraud because they are susceptible to manipulation by management. For example, liabilities resulting from a restructuring may be deemed to have high inherent risk because of the high degree of subjectivity and management judgment involved in their estimation. Similarly, revenues for software developers may be deemed to have high inherent risk because of the complex accounting principles applicable to the recognition and measurement of software revenue transactions. Assets resulting from investing activities may be deemed to have high inherent risk because of the subjectivity and management judgment involved in estimating fair values of those investments.

.40 In summary, the identification of a risk of material misstatement due to fraud involves the application of professional judgment and includes the consideration of the attributes of the risk, including:
- The *type* of risk that may exist, that is, whether it involves fraudulent financial reporting or misappropriation of assets
- The *significance* of the risk, that is, whether it is of a magnitude that could lead to result in a possible material misstatement of the financial statements
- The *likelihood* of the risk, that is, the likelihood that it will result in a material misstatement in the financial statements[16]
- The *pervasiveness* of the risk, that is, whether the potential risk is pervasive to the financial statements as a whole or specifically related to a particular assertion, account, or class of transactions.

A Presumption That Improper Revenue Recognition Is a Fraud Risk

.41 Material misstatements due to fraudulent financial reporting often result from an overstatement of revenues (for example, through premature revenue recognition or recording fictitious revenues) or an understatement of revenues (for example, through improperly shifting revenues to a later period). Therefore, the auditor should ordinarily presume that there is a risk of material misstatement due to fraud relating to revenue recognition. (See paragraph .54 for examples of auditing procedures related to the risk of improper revenue recognition.)[17]

A Consideration of the Risk of Management Override of Controls

.42 Even if specific risks of material misstatement due to fraud are not identified by the auditor, there is a possibility that management override of controls could occur, and accordingly, the auditor should address that risk (see paragraph .57) apart from any conclusions regarding the existence of more specifically identifiable risks.

Assessing the Identified Risks After Taking Into Account an Evaluation of the Entity's Programs and Controls That Address the Risks

.43 Section 319 requires the auditor to obtain an understanding of each of the five components of internal control sufficient to plan the audit. It also notes that such knowledge should be used to identify types of potential misstatements, consider factors that affect the risk of material misstatement, design tests of controls when applicable, and design substantive tests. Additionally, section 319 notes that controls, whether manual or automated, can be circumvented by collusion of two or more people or inappropriate management override of internal control.

.44 As part of the understanding of internal control sufficient to plan the audit, the auditor should evaluate whether entity programs and controls that address identified risks of material misstatement due to fraud have been suitably designed and placed in operation.[18] These programs and controls may involve (*a*) specific controls designed to mitigate specific risks of fraud—for example, controls to address specific assets susceptible to misappropriation, and (*b*) broader programs designed to prevent, deter, and detect fraud—for example, programs to promote a culture of honesty and ethical behavior. The auditor should consider whether such programs and controls mitigate the identified risks of material misstatement due to fraud or whether specific control deficiencies may exacerbate the risks (see paragraph .80). The exhibit at the end of this section [paragraph .88] discusses examples of programs and controls an entity might implement to create a culture of honesty and ethical behavior, and that help to prevent, deter, and detect fraud.

.45 After the auditor has evaluated whether the entity's programs and controls that address identified risks of material misstatement due to fraud have been suitably designed and placed in operation, the auditor should assess these risks taking into account that evaluation. This assessment should be considered when developing the auditor's response to the identified risks of material misstatement due to fraud (see paragraphs .46 through .67).[19]

Responding to the Results of the Assessment

.46 The auditor's response to the assessment of the risks of material misstatement due to fraud involves the application of professional skepticism in gathering and evaluating audit evidence. As noted in paragraph .13, professional skepticism is an attitude that includes a critical assessment of the competency and sufficiency of audit evidence. Examples of the application of professional skepticism in response to the risks of material misstatement due to fraud are (*a*) designing additional or different auditing procedures to obtain more reliable evidence in support of specified financial statement account balances, classes of transactions, and related assertions, and (*b*) obtaining additional corroboration of management's explanations or representations concerning material matters, such as through third-party confirmation, the use of a specialist, analytical procedures, examination of documentation from independent sources, or inquiries of others within or outside the entity.

.47 The auditor's response to the assessment of the risks of material misstatement of the financial statements due to fraud is influenced by the nature and significance of the risks identified as being present (paragraphs .35 through .42) and the entity's programs and controls that address these identified risks (paragraphs .43 through .45).

.48 The auditor responds to risks of material misstatement due to fraud in the following three ways:

a. A response that has an overall effect on how the audit is conducted—that is, a response involving more general considerations apart from the specific procedures otherwise planned (see paragraph .50).

b. A response to identified risks involving the nature, timing, and extent of the auditing procedures to be performed (see paragraphs .51 through .56).

c. A response involving the performance of certain procedures to further address the risk of material misstatement due to fraud involving management override of controls, given the unpredictable ways in which such override could occur (see paragraphs .57 through .67).

.49 The auditor may conclude that it would not be practicable to design auditing procedures that sufficiently address the risks of material misstatement due to fraud. In that case, withdrawal from the engagement with communication to the appropriate parties may be an appropriate course of action (see paragraph .78).

Overall Responses to the Risk of Material Misstatement

.50 Judgments about the risk of material misstatement due to fraud have an overall effect on how the audit is conducted in the following ways:

- *Assignment of personnel and supervision.* The knowledge, skill, and ability of personnel assigned significant engagement responsibilities should be commensurate with the auditor's assessment of the risks of material misstatement due to fraud for the engagement (see section 210, *Training and Proficiency of the Independent Auditor*, paragraph .03). For example, the auditor may respond to an identified risk of material misstatement due to fraud by assigning additional persons with specialized skill and knowledge, such as forensic and information technology (IT) specialists, or by assigning more experienced personnel to the engagement. In addition, the extent of supervision should reflect the risks of material misstatement due to fraud (see section 311.11).

- *Accounting principles.* The auditor should consider management's selection and application of significant accounting principles, particularly those related to subjective measurements and complex transactions. In this respect, the auditor may have a greater concern about whether the accounting principles selected and policies adopted are being applied in an inappropriate manner to create a material misstatement of the financial statements. In developing judgments about the quality of such principles (see section 380, *Communication With Audit Committees*, paragraph .11), the auditor should consider whether their collective application indicates a bias that may create such a material misstatement of the financial statements.

- *Predictability of auditing procedures.* The auditor should incorporate an element of unpredictability in the selection from year to year of auditing procedures to be performed—for example, performing substantive tests of selected account balances and assertions not otherwise tested due to their materiality or risk, adjusting the timing of testing from that otherwise expected, using differing sampling methods, and performing procedures at different locations or at locations on an unannounced basis.

Responses Involving the Nature, Timing, and Extent of Procedures to Be Performed to Address the Identified Risks

.51 The auditing procedures performed in response to identified risks of material misstatement due to fraud will vary depending upon the types of risks identified and the account balances, classes of transactions, and related assertions that may be affected. These procedures may involve both substantive tests and tests of the operating effectiveness of the entity's programs and controls. However, because management may have the ability to override controls that otherwise appear to be operating effectively (see paragraph .08), it is unlikely that audit risk can be reduced to an appropriately low level by performing only tests of controls.

.52 The auditor's responses to address specifically identified risks of material misstatement due to fraud may include changing the nature, timing, and extent of auditing procedures in the following ways:

- The *nature* of auditing procedures performed may need to be changed to obtain evidence that is more reliable or to obtain additional corroborative information. For example, more evidential matter may be needed from independent sources outside the entity, such as public-record information about the existence and nature of key customers, vendors, or counterparties in a major transaction. Also, physical observation or inspection of certain assets may become more important (see section 326, *Evidential Matter*, paragraphs .15 through .21). Furthermore, the auditor may choose to employ computer-assisted audit techniques to gather more extensive evidence about data contained in significant accounts or electronic transaction files. Finally, inquiry of additional members of management or others may be helpful in identifying issues and corroborating other evidential matter (see paragraphs .24 through .26 and paragraph .53).

- The *timing* of substantive tests may need to be modified. The auditor might conclude that substantive testing should be performed at or near the end of the reporting period to best address an identified risk of material misstatement due to fraud (see section 313, *Substantive Tests Prior to the Balance-Sheet Date*). That is, the auditor might conclude that, given the risks of intentional misstatement or manipulation, tests to extend audit conclusions from an interim date to the period-end reporting date would not be effective.

  In contrast, because an intentional misstatement—for example, a misstatement involving inappropriate revenue recognition—may have been initiated in an interim period, the auditor might elect to apply substantive tests to transactions occurring earlier in or throughout the reporting period.

- The *extent* of the procedures applied should reflect the assessment of the risks of material misstatement due to fraud. For example, increasing sample sizes or performing analytical procedures at a more detailed level may be appropriate (see section 350, *Audit Sampling*, paragraph .23, and section 329). Also, computer-assisted audit techniques may enable more extensive testing of electronic transactions and account files. Such techniques can be used to select sample transactions from key electronic files, to sort transactions with specific characteristics, or to test an entire population instead of a sample.

.53 The following are examples of modification of the nature, timing, and extent of tests in response to identified risks of material misstatements due to fraud.

- Performing procedures at locations on a surprise or unannounced basis, for example, observing inventory on unexpected dates or at unexpected locations or counting cash on a surprise basis.
- Requesting that inventories be counted at the end of the reporting period or on a date closer to period end to minimize the risk of manipulation of balances in the period between the date of completion of the count and the end of the reporting period.
- Making oral inquiries of major customers and suppliers in addition to sending written confirmations, or sending confirmation requests to a specific party within an organization.
- Performing substantive analytical procedures using disaggregated data, for example, comparing gross profit or operating margins by location, line of business, or month to auditor-developed expectations.[20]
- Interviewing personnel involved in activities in areas where a risk of material misstatement due to fraud has been identified to obtain their insights about the risk and how controls address the risk (also see paragraph .24).
- If other independent auditors are auditing the financial statements of one or more subsidiaries, divisions, or branches, discussing with them the extent of work that needs to be performed to address the risk of material misstatement due to fraud resulting from transactions and activities among these components.

Additional Examples of Responses to Identified Risks of Misstatements Arising From Fraudulent Financial Reporting

.54 The following are additional examples of responses to identified risks of material misstatements relating to fraudulent financial reporting:

- *Revenue recognition.* Because revenue recognition is dependent on the particular facts and circumstances, as well as accounting principles and practices that can vary by industry, the auditor ordinarily will develop auditing procedures based on the auditor's understanding of the entity and its environment, including the composition of revenues, specific attributes of the revenue transactions, and unique industry considerations. If there is an identified risk of material misstatement due to fraud that involves improper revenue recognition, the auditor also may want to consider:

    — Performing substantive analytical procedures relating to revenue using disaggregated data, for example, comparing revenue reported by month and by product line or business segment during the current reporting period with comparable prior periods. Computer-assisted audit techniques may be useful in identifying unusual or unexpected revenue relationships or transactions.

    — Confirming with customers certain relevant contract terms and the absence of side agreements, because the appropriate accounting often is influenced by such terms or agreements.[21] For example, acceptance criteria, delivery and payment terms, the absence of future or continuing vendor obligations, the right to return the product, guaranteed resale amounts, and cancellation or refund provisions often are relevant in such circumstances.

    — Inquiring of the entity's sales and marketing personnel or in-house legal counsel regarding sales or shipments near the end of the period and their knowledge of any unusual terms or conditions associated with these transactions.

    — Being physically present at one or more locations at period end to observe goods being shipped or being readied for shipment (or returns awaiting processing) and performing other appropriate sales and inventory cutoff procedures.

    — For those situations for which revenue transactions are electronically initiated, processed, and recorded, testing controls to determine whether they provide assurance that recorded revenue transactions occurred and are properly recorded.

- *Inventory quantities.* If there is an identified risk of material misstatement due to fraud that affects inventory quantities, examining the entity's inventory records may help identify locations or items that require specific attention during or after the physical inventory count. Such a review may lead to a decision to observe inventory counts at certain locations on an unannounced basis (see paragraph .53) or to conduct inventory counts at all locations on the same date. In addition, it may be appropriate for inventory counts to be conducted at or near the end of the reporting period to minimize the risk of inappropriate manipulation during the period between the count and the end of the reporting period.

It also may be appropriate for the auditor to perform additional procedures during the observation of the count, for example, more rigorously examining the contents of boxed items, the manner in which the goods are stacked (for example, hollow squares) or labeled, and the quality (that is, purity, grade, or concentration) of liquid substances such as perfumes or specialty chemicals. Using the work of a specialist may be helpful in this regard.[22] Furthermore, additional testing of count sheets, tags, or other records, or the retention of copies of these records, may be warranted to minimize the risk of subsequent alteration or inappropriate compilation.

Following the physical inventory count, the auditor may want to employ additional procedures directed at the quantities included in the priced out inventories to further test the reasonableness of the quantities counted—for example, comparison of quantities for the current period with prior periods by class or category of inventory, location or other criteria, or comparison of quantities counted with perpetual records. The auditor also may consider using computer-assisted audit techniques to further test the compilation of the physical inventory counts—for example, sorting by tag number to test tag controls or by item serial number to test the possibility of item omission or duplication.

- *Management estimates.* The auditor may identify a risk of material misstatement due to fraud involving the development of management estimates. This risk may affect a number of accounts and assertions, including asset valuation, estimates relating to specific transactions (such as acquisitions, restructurings, or disposals of a segment of the business), and other significant accrued liabilities (such as pension and other postretirement benefit obligations, or environmental remediation liabilities). The risk may also relate to significant changes in assumptions relating to recurring estimates. As indicated in section 342, *Auditing Accounting Estimates,* estimates are based on subjective as well as objective factors and there is a potential for bias in the subjective factors, even when management's estimation process involves competent personnel using relevant and reliable data.

  In addressing an identified risk of material misstatement due to fraud involving accounting estimates, the auditor may want to supplement the audit evidence otherwise obtained (see section 342.09 through .14). In certain circumstances (for example, evaluating the reasonableness of management's estimate of the fair value of a derivative), it may be appropriate to engage a specialist or develop an independent estimate for comparison to management's estimate. Information gathered about the entity and its environment may help the auditor evaluate the reasonableness of such management estimates and underlying judgments and assumptions.

  A retrospective review of similar management judgments and assumptions applied in prior periods (see paragraphs .63 through .65) may also provide insight about the reasonableness of judgments and assumptions supporting management estimates.

Examples of Responses to Identified Risks of Misstatements Arising From Misappropriations of Assets

.55 The auditor may have identified a risk of material misstatement due to fraud relating to misappropriation of assets. For example, the auditor may conclude that the risk of asset misappropriation at a particular operating location is significant because a large amount of easily accessible cash is maintained at that location, or there are inventory items such as laptop computers at that location that can easily be moved and sold.

.56 The auditor's response to a risk of material misstatement due to fraud relating to misappropriation of assets usually will be directed toward certain account balances. Although some of the audit responses noted in paragraphs .52 through .54 may apply in such circumstances, such as the procedures directed at inventory quantities, the scope of the work should be linked to the specific information about the misappropriation risk that has been identified. For example, if a particular asset is highly susceptible to misappropriation and a potential misstatement would be material to the financial statements, obtaining an understanding of the controls related to the prevention and detection of such misappropriation and testing the operating effectiveness of such controls may be warranted. In certain circumstances, physical inspection of such assets (for example, counting cash or securities) at or near the end of the reporting period may be appropriate. In addition, the use of substantive analytical procedures, such as the development by the auditor of an expected dollar amount at a high level of precision, to be compared with a recorded amount, may be effective in certain circumstances.

Responses to Further Address the Risk of Management Override of Controls

.57 As noted in paragraph .08, management is in a unique position to perpetrate fraud because of its ability to directly or indirectly manipulate accounting records and prepare fraudulent financial statements by overriding established controls that otherwise appear to be operating effectively. By its nature, management override of controls can occur in unpredictable ways. Accordingly, in addition to overall responses (paragraph .50) and responses that address specifically identified risks of material misstatement due to fraud (see paragraphs .51 through .56), the procedures described in paragraphs .58 through .67 should be performed to further address the risk of management override of controls.

.58 *Examining journal entries and other adjustments for evidence of possible material misstatement due to fraud.* Material misstatements of financial statements due to fraud often involve the manipulation of the financial reporting process by (*a*) recording inappropriate or unauthorized journal entries throughout the year or at period end, or (*b*) making adjustments to amounts reported in the financial statements that are not reflected in formal journal entries, such as through consolidating adjustments, report combinations, and reclassifications. Accordingly, the auditor should design procedures to test the appropriateness of journal entries recorded in the general ledger and other adjustments (for example, entries posted directly to financial statement drafts) made in the preparation of the financial statements. More specifically, the auditor should:

> *a.* Obtain an understanding of the entity's financial reporting process[23] and the controls over journal entries and other adjustments. (See paragraphs .59 and .60.)
>
> *b.* Identify and select journal entries and other adjustments for testing. (See paragraph .61.)
>
> *c.* Determine the timing of the testing. (See paragraph .62.)
>
> *d.* Inquire of individuals involved in the financial reporting process about inappropriate or unusual activity relating to the processing of journal entries and other adjustments.

.59 The auditor's understanding of the entity's financial reporting process may help in identifying the type, number, and monetary value of journal entries and other adjustments that typically are made in preparing the financial statements. For example, the auditor's understanding may include the sources of significant debits and credits to an account, who can initiate entries to the general ledger or transaction processing systems, what approvals are required for such entries, and how journal entries are recorded (for example, entries may be initiated and recorded online with no physical evidence, or may be created in paper form and entered in batch mode).

.60 An entity may have implemented specific controls over journal entries and other adjustments. For example, an entity may use journal entries that are preformatted with account numbers and specific user approval criteria, and may have automated controls to generate an exception report for any entries that were unsuccessfully proposed for recording or entries that were recorded and processed outside of established parameters. The auditor should obtain an understanding of the design of such controls over journal entries and other adjustments and determine whether they are suitably designed and have been placed in operation.

.61 The auditor should use professional judgment in determining the nature, timing, and extent of the testing of journal entries and other adjustments. For purposes of identifying and selecting specific entries and other adjustments for testing, and determining the appropriate method of examining the underlying support for the items selected, the auditor should consider:

- *The auditor's assessment of the risk of material misstatement due to fraud.* The presence of fraud risk factors or other conditions may help the auditor to identify specific classes of journal entries for testing and indicate the extent of testing necessary.

- *The effectiveness of controls that have been implemented over journal entries and other adjustments.* Effective controls over the preparation and posting of journal entries and adjustments may affect the extent of substantive testing necessary, provided that the auditor has tested the operating effectiveness of those controls. However, even though controls might be implemented and operating effectively, the auditor's procedures for testing journal entries and other adjustments should include the identification and testing of specific items.

- *The entity's financial reporting process and the nature of the evidence that can be examined.* The auditor's procedures for testing journal entries and other adjustments will vary based on the nature of the financial reporting process. For many entities, routine processing of transactions involves a combination of manual and automated steps and procedures. Similarly, the processing of journal entries and other adjustments might involve both manual and automated procedures and controls. Regardless of the method, the auditor's procedures should include selecting from the general ledger journal entries to be tested and examining support for those items. In addition, the auditor should be aware that journal entries and other adjustments might exist in either electronic or paper form. When information technology (IT) is used in the financial reporting process, journal entries and other adjustments might exist only in electronic form. Electronic evidence often requires extraction of the desired data by an auditor with IT knowledge and skills or the use of an IT specialist. In an IT environment, it may be necessary for the auditor to employ computer-assisted audit techniques (for example, report writers, software or data extraction tools, or other systems-based techniques) to identify the journal entries and other adjustments to be tested.

- *The characteristics of fraudulent entries or adjustments.* Inappropriate journal entries and other adjustments often have certain unique identifying characteristics. Such characteristics may include entries (*a*) made to unrelated, unusual, or seldom-used accounts, (*b*) made by individuals who typically do not make journal entries, (*c*) recorded at the end of the period or as post-closing entries that have little or no explanation or description, (*d*) made either before or during the preparation of the financial statements that do not have account numbers, or (*e*) containing round numbers or a consistent ending number.

- *The nature and complexity of the accounts.* Inappropriate journal entries or adjustments may be applied to accounts that (*a*) contain transactions that are complex or unusual in nature, (*b*) contain significant estimates and period-end adjustments, (*c*) have been prone to errors in the past, (*d*) have not been reconciled on a timely basis or contain unreconciled differences, (*e*) contain intercompany transactions, or (*f*) are otherwise associated with an identified risk of material misstatement due to fraud. The auditor should recognize, however, that inappropriate journal entries and adjustments also might be made to other accounts. In audits of entities that have several locations or components, the auditor should consider the need to select journal entries from locations based on the factors set forth in section 312.18.

- *Journal entries or other adjustments processed outside the normal course of business.* Standard journal entries used on a recurring basis to record transactions such as monthly sales, purchases, and cash disbursements, or to record recurring periodic accounting estimates generally are subject to the entity's internal controls. Nonstandard entries (for example, entries used to record nonrecurring transactions, such as a business combination, or entries used to record a nonrecurring estimate, such as an asset impairment) might not be subject to the same level of internal control. In addition, other adjustments such as consolidating adjustments, report combinations, and reclassifications generally are not reflected in formal journal entries and might not be subject to the entity's internal controls. Accordingly, the auditor should consider placing additional emphasis on identifying and testing items processed outside of the normal course of business.

.62 Because fraudulent journal entries often are made at the end of a reporting period, the auditor's testing ordinarily should focus on the journal entries and other adjustments made at that time. However, because material misstatements in financial statements due to fraud can occur throughout the period and may involve extensive efforts to conceal how it is accomplished, the auditor should consider whether there also is a need to test journal entries throughout the period under audit.

.63 *Reviewing accounting estimates for biases that could result in material misstatement due to fraud.* In preparing financial statements, management is responsible for making a number of judgments or assumptions that affect significant accounting estimates[24] and for monitoring the reasonableness of such estimates on an ongoing basis. Fraudulent financial reporting often is accomplished through intentional misstatement of accounting estimates. As discussed in section 312.36, the auditor should consider whether differences between estimates best supported by the audit evidence and the estimates included in the financial statements, even if they are individually reasonable, indicate a possible bias on the part of the entity's management, in which case the auditor should reconsider the estimates taken as a whole.

.64 The auditor also should perform a retrospective review of significant accounting estimates reflected in the financial statements of the prior year to determine whether management judgments and assumptions relating to the estimates indicate a possible bias on the part of management. The significant accounting estimates selected for testing should include those that are based on highly sensitive assumptions or are otherwise significantly affected by judgments made by management. With the benefit of hindsight, a retrospective review should provide the auditor with additional information about whether there may be a possible bias on the part of management in making the current-year estimates. This review, however, is not intended to call into question the auditor's professional judgments made in the prior year that were based on information available at the time.

.65 If the auditor identifies a possible bias on the part of management in making accounting estimates, the auditor should evaluate whether circumstances producing such a bias represent a risk of a material misstatement due to fraud. For example, information coming to the auditor's attention may indicate a risk that adjustments to the current-year estimates might be recorded at the instruction of management to arbitrarily achieve a specified earnings target.

.66 *Evaluating the business rationale for significant unusual transactions.* During the course of the audit, the auditor may become aware of significant transactions that are outside the normal course of business for the entity, or that otherwise appear to be unusual given the auditor's understanding of the entity and its environment. The auditor should gain an understanding of the business rationale for such transactions and whether that rationale (or the lack thereof) suggests that the transactions may have been entered into to engage in fraudulent financial reporting or conceal misappropriation of assets.

.67 In understanding the business rationale for the transactions, the auditor should consider:
- Whether the form of such transactions is overly complex (for example, involves multiple entities within a consolidated group or unrelated third parties).
- Whether management has discussed the nature of and accounting for such transactions with the audit committee or board of directors.
- Whether management is placing more emphasis on the need for a particular accounting treatment than on the underlying economics of the transaction.
- Whether transactions that involve unconsolidated related parties, including special purpose entities, have been properly reviewed and approved by the audit committee or board of directors.
- Whether the transactions involve previously unidentified related parties[25] or parties that do not have the substance or the financial strength to support the transaction without assistance from the entity under audit.

Evaluating Audit Evidence

.68 *Assessing risks of material misstatement due to fraud throughout the audit.* The auditor's assessment of the risks of material misstatement due to fraud should be ongoing throughout the audit. Conditions may be identified during fieldwork that change or support a judgment regarding the assessment of the risks, such as the following:
- Discrepancies in the accounting records, including:
  — Transactions that are not recorded in a complete or timely manner or are improperly recorded as to amount, accounting period, classification, or entity policy
  — Unsupported or unauthorized balances or transactions
  — Last-minute adjustments that significantly affect financial results
  — Evidence of employees' access to systems and records inconsistent with that necessary to perform their authorized duties
  — Tips or complaints to the auditor about alleged fraud
- Conflicting or missing evidential matter, including:
  — Missing documents
  — Documents that appear to have been altered[26]
  — Unavailability of other than photocopied or electronically transmitted documents when documents in original form are expected to exist
  — Significant unexplained items on reconciliations
  — Inconsistent, vague, or implausible responses from management or employees arising from inquiries or analytical procedures (See paragraph .72.)
  — Unusual discrepancies between the entity's records and confirmation replies
  — Missing inventory or physical assets of significant magnitude
  — Unavailable or missing electronic evidence, inconsistent with the entity's record retention practices or policies

    — Inability to produce evidence of key systems development and program change testing and implementation activities for current-year system changes and deployments

- Problematic or unusual relationships between the auditor and management, including:
  — Denial of access to records, facilities, certain employees, customers, vendors, or others from whom audit evidence might be sought[27]
  — Undue time pressures imposed by management to resolve complex or contentious issues
  — Complaints by management about the conduct of the audit or management intimidation of audit team members, particularly in connection with the auditor's critical assessment of audit evidence or in the resolution of potential disagreements with management
  — Unusual delays by the entity in providing requested information
  — Unwillingness to facilitate auditor access to key electronic files for testing through the use of computer-assisted audit techniques
  — Denial of access to key IT operations staff and facilities, including security, operations, and systems development personnel
  — An unwillingness to add or revise disclosures in the financial statements to make them more complete and transparent

.69 *Evaluating whether analytical procedures performed as substantive tests or in the overall review stage of the audit indicate a previously unrecognized risk of material misstatement due to fraud.* As discussed in paragraphs .28 through .30, the auditor should consider whether analytical procedures performed in planning the audit result in identifying any unusual or unexpected relationships that should be considered in assessing the risks of material misstatement due to fraud. The auditor also should evaluate whether analytical procedures that were performed as substantive tests or in the overall review stage of the audit (see section 329) indicate a previously unrecognized risk of material misstatement due to fraud.

.70 If not already performed during the overall review stage of the audit, the auditor should perform analytical procedures relating to revenue, as discussed in paragraph .29, through the end of the reporting period.

.71 Determining which particular trends and relationships may indicate a risk of material misstatement due to fraud requires professional judgment. Unusual relationships involving year-end revenue and income often are particularly relevant. These might include, for example, (*a*) uncharacteristically large amounts of income being reported in the last week or two of the reporting period from unusual transactions, as well as (*b*) income that is inconsistent with trends in cash flow from operations.

.72 Some unusual or unexpected analytical relationships may have been identified and may indicate a risk of material misstatement due to fraud because management or employees generally are unable to manipulate certain information to create seemingly normal or expected relationships. Some examples are as follows:

- The relationship of net income to cash flows from operations may appear unusual because management recorded fictitious revenues and receivables but was unable to manipulate cash.
- Changes in inventory, accounts payable, sales, or cost of sales from the prior period to the current period may be inconsistent, indicating a possible employee theft of inventory, because the employee was unable to manipulate all of the related accounts.
- A comparison of the entity's profitability to industry trends, which management cannot manipulate, may indicate trends or differences for further consideration when identifying risks of material misstatement due to fraud.
- A comparison of bad debt write-offs to comparable industry data, which employees cannot manipulate, may provide unexplained relationships that could indicate a possible theft of cash receipts.
- An unexpected or unexplained relationship between sales volume as determined from the accounting records and production statistics maintained by operations personnel—which may be more difficult for management to manipulate—may indicate a possible misstatement of sales.

.73 The auditor also should consider whether responses to inquiries throughout the audit about analytical relationships have been vague or implausible, or have produced evidence that is inconsistent with other evidential matter accumulated during the audit.

.74 *Evaluating the risks of material misstatement due to fraud at or near the completion of fieldwork.* At or near the completion of fieldwork, the auditor should evaluate whether the accumulated results of auditing procedures and other observations (for example, conditions and analytical relationships noted in paragraphs .69 through .73) affect the assessment of the risks of material misstatement due to fraud made earlier in the audit. This evaluation primarily is a qualitative matter based on the auditor's judgment. Such an evaluation may provide further insight about the risks of material misstatement due to fraud and whether there is a need to perform additional or different audit procedures. As part of this evaluation, the auditor with final responsibility for the audit should ascertain that there has been appropriate communication with the other audit team members throughout the audit regarding information or conditions indicative of risks of material misstatement due to fraud.[28]

.75 *Responding to misstatements that may be the result of fraud.* When audit test results identify misstatements in the financial statements, the auditor should consider whether such misstatements may be indicative of fraud.[29] That determination affects the auditor's evaluation of materiality and the related responses necessary as a result of that evaluation.[30]

.76 If the auditor believes that misstatements are or may be the result of fraud, but the effect of the misstatements is not material to the financial statements, the auditor nevertheless should evaluate the implications, especially those dealing with the organizational position of the person(s) involved. For example, fraud involving misappropriations of cash from a small petty cash fund normally would be of little significance to the auditor in assessing the risk of material misstatement due to fraud because both the manner of operating the fund and its size would tend to establish a limit on the amount of potential loss, and the custodianship of such funds normally is entrusted to a nonmanagement employee.[31] Conversely, if the matter involves higher-level management, even though the amount itself is not material to the financial statements, it may be indicative of a more pervasive problem, for example, implications about the integrity of management.[32] In such circumstances, the auditor should reevaluate the assessment of the risk of material misstatement due to fraud and its resulting impact on (*a*) the nature, timing, and extent of the tests of balances or transactions and (*b*) the assessment of the effectiveness of controls if control risk was assessed below the maximum.

.77 If the auditor believes that the misstatement is or may be the result of fraud, and either has determined that the effect could be material to the financial statements or has been unable to evaluate whether the effect is material, the auditor should:

> *a.* Attempt to obtain additional evidential matter to determine whether material fraud has occurred or is likely to have occurred, and, if so, its effect on the financial statements and the auditor's report thereon.[33]
>
> *b.* Consider the implications for other aspects of the audit (see paragraph .76).
>
> *c.* Discuss the matter and the approach for further investigation with an appropriate level of management that is at least one level above those involved, and with senior management and the audit committee.[34]
>
> *d.* If appropriate, suggest that the client consult with legal counsel.

.78 The auditor's consideration of the risks of material misstatement and the results of audit tests may indicate such a significant risk of material misstatement due to fraud that the auditor should consider withdrawing from the engagement and communicating the reasons for withdrawal to the audit committee or others with equivalent authority and responsibility.[35] Whether the auditor concludes that withdrawal from the engagement is appropriate may depend on (*a*) the implications about the integrity of management and (*b*) the diligence and cooperation of management or the board of directors in investigating the circumstances and taking appropriate action. Because of the variety of circumstances that may arise, it is not possible to definitively describe when withdrawal is appropriate.[36] The auditor may wish to consult with legal counsel when considering withdrawal from an engagement.

Communicating About Possible Fraud to Management, the Audit Committee, and Others[37]

.79 Whenever the auditor has determined that there is evidence that fraud may exist, that matter should be brought to the attention of an appropriate level of management. This is appropriate even if the matter might be considered inconsequential, such as a minor defalcation by an employee at a low level in the entity's organization. Fraud involving senior management and fraud (whether caused by senior management or other employees) that causes a material misstatement of the financial statements should be reported directly to the audit committee. In addition, the auditor should reach an understanding with the audit committee regarding the nature and extent of communications with the committee about misappropriations perpetrated by lower-level employees.

.80 If the auditor, as a result of the assessment of the risks of material misstatement, has identified risks of material misstatement due to fraud that have continuing control implications (whether or not transactions or adjustments that could be the result of fraud have been detected), the auditor should consider whether these risks represent reportable conditions relating to the entity's internal control that should be communicated to senior management and the audit committee.[38] (See section 325, *Communication of Internal Control Related Matters Noted in an Audit*, paragraph .04). The auditor also should consider whether the absence of or deficiencies in programs and controls to mitigate specific risks of fraud or to otherwise help prevent, deter, and detect fraud (see paragraph .44) represent reportable conditions that should be communicated to senior management and the audit committee.

.81 The auditor also may wish to communicate other risks of fraud identified as a result of the assessment of the risks of material misstatements due to fraud. Such a communication may be a part of an overall communication to the audit committee of business and financial statement risks affecting the entity and/or in conjunction with the auditor communication about the quality of the entity's accounting principles (see section 380.11 INCLUDEPICTURE "http://www.accountingresearchmanager.com/icons/ doclink.gif" * MERGEFORMATINET).

.82 The disclosure of possible fraud to parties other than the client's senior management and its audit committee ordinarily is not part of the auditor's responsibility and ordinarily would be precluded by the auditor's ethical or legal obligations of confidentiality unless the matter is reflected in the auditor's report. The auditor should recognize, however, that in the following circumstances a duty to disclose to parties outside the entity may exist:

> *a.* To comply with certain legal and regulatory requirements[39]
>
> *b.* To a successor auditor when the successor makes inquiries in accordance with section 315, *Communications Between Predecessor and Successor Auditors*[40]
>
> *c.* In response to a subpoena
>
> *d.* To a funding agency or other specified agency in accordance with requirements for the audits of entities that receive governmental financial assistance[41]

Because potential conflicts between the auditor's ethical and legal obligations for confidentiality of client matters may be complex, the auditor may wish to consult with legal counsel before discussing matters covered by paragraphs .79 through .81 with parties outside the client.

Documenting the Auditor's Consideration of Fraud

.83 The auditor should document the following:

- The discussion among engagement personnel in planning the audit regarding the susceptibility of the entity's financial statements to material misstatement due to fraud, including how and when the discussion occurred, the audit team members who participated, and the subject matter discussed (See paragraphs .14 through .17.)
- The procedures performed to obtain information necessary to identify and assess the risks of material misstatement due to fraud (See paragraphs .19 through .34.)
- Specific risks of material misstatement due to fraud that were identified (see paragraphs .35 through .45), and a description of the auditor's response to those risks (See paragraphs .46 through .56.)

- If the auditor has not identified in a particular circumstance, improper revenue recognition as a risk of material misstatement due to fraud, the reasons supporting the auditor's conclusion (See paragraph .41.)
- The results of the procedures performed to further address the risk of management override of controls (See paragraphs .58 through .67.)
- Other conditions and analytical relationships that caused the auditor to believe that additional auditing procedures or other responses were required and any further responses the auditor concluded were appropriate, to address such risks or other conditions (See paragraphs .68 through .73.)
- The nature of the communications about fraud made to management, the audit committee, and others (See paragraphs .79 through .82.)

Effective Date

.84 This section is effective for audits of financial statements for periods beginning on or after December 15, 2002. Early application of the provisions of this section is permissible.

.85

Appendix

Examples of Fraud Risk Factors

A.1 This appendix contains examples of risk factors discussed in paragraphs .31 through .33 of the section. Separately presented are examples relating to the two types of fraud relevant to the auditor's consideration—that is, fraudulent financial reporting and misappropriation of assets. For each of these types of fraud, the risk factors are further classified based on the three conditions generally present when material misstatements due to fraud occur: (*a*) incentives/pressures, (*b*) opportunities, and (*c*) attitudes/rationalizations. Although the risk factors cover a broad range of situations, they are only examples and, accordingly, the auditor may wish to consider additional or different risk factors. Not all of these examples are relevant in all circumstances, and some may be of greater or lesser significance in entities of different size or with different ownership characteristics or circumstances. Also, the order of the examples of risk factors provided is not intended to reflect their relative importance or frequency of occurrence.

Risk Factors Relating to Misstatements Arising From Fraudulent Financial Reporting

A.2 The following are examples of risk factors relating to misstatements arising from fraudulent financial reporting.

Incentives/Pressures

a. Financial stability or profitability is threatened by economic, industry, or entity operating conditions, such as (or as indicated by):

— High degree of competition or market saturation, accompanied by declining margins

— High vulnerability to rapid changes, such as changes in technology, product obsolescence, or interest rates

— Significant declines in customer demand and increasing business failures in either the industry or overall economy

— Operating losses making the threat of bankruptcy, foreclosure, or hostile takeover imminent

— Recurring negative cash flows from operations or an inability to generate cash flows from operations while reporting earnings and earnings growth

— Rapid growth or unusual profitability, especially compared to that of other companies in the same industry

— New accounting, statutory, or regulatory requirements

b. Excessive pressure exists for management to meet the requirements or expectations of third parties due to the following:

— Profitability or trend level expectations of investment analysts, institutional investors, significant creditors, or other external parties (particularly expectations that are unduly aggressive or unrealistic), including expectations created by management in, for example, overly optimistic press releases or annual report messages

— Need to obtain additional debt or equity financing to stay competitive—including financing of major research and development or capital expenditures

— Marginal ability to meet exchange listing requirements or debt repayment or other debt covenant requirements

— Perceived or real adverse effects of reporting poor financial results on significant pending transactions, such as business combinations or contract awards

c. Information available indicates that management or the board of directors' personal financial situation is threatened by the entity's financial performance arising from the following:

— Significant financial interests in the entity

— Significant portions of their compensation (for example, bonuses, stock options, and earn-out arrangements) being contingent upon achieving aggressive targets for stock price, operating results, financial position, or cash flow[42]

— Personal guarantees of debts of the entity

d. There is excessive pressure on management or operating personnel to meet financial targets set up by the board of directors or management, including sales or profitability incentive goals.

Opportunities

a. The nature of the industry or the entity's operations provides opportunities to engage in fraudulent financial reporting that can arise from the following:

— Significant related-party transactions not in the ordinary course of business or with related entities not audited or audited by another firm

— A strong financial presence or ability to dominate a certain industry sector that allows the entity to dictate terms or conditions to suppliers or customers that may result in inappropriate or non-arm's-length transactions

— Assets, liabilities, revenues, or expenses based on significant estimates that involve subjective judgments or uncertainties that are difficult to corroborate

— Significant, unusual, or highly complex transactions, especially those close to period end that pose difficult "substance over form" questions

— Significant operations located or conducted across international borders in jurisdictions where differing business environments and cultures exist

— Significant bank accounts or subsidiary or branch operations in tax-haven jurisdictions for which there appears to be no clear business justification

b. There is ineffective monitoring of management as a result of the following:

— Domination of management by a single person or small group (in a nonowner-managed business) without compensating controls

— Ineffective board of directors or audit committee oversight over the financial reporting process and internal control

c. There is a complex or unstable organizational structure, as evidenced by the following:

— Difficulty in determining the organization or individuals that have controlling interest in the entity

— Overly complex organizational structure involving unusual legal entities or managerial lines of authority

— High turnover of senior management, counsel, or board members

d. Internal control components are deficient as a result of the following:

— Inadequate monitoring of controls, including automated controls and controls over interim financial reporting (where external reporting is required)

— High turnover rates or employment of ineffective accounting, internal audit, or information technology staff

— Ineffective accounting and information systems, including situations involving reportable conditions

Attitudes/Rationalizations

Risk factors reflective of attitudes/rationalizations by board members, management, or employees, that allow them to engage in and/or justify fraudulent financial reporting, may not be susceptible to observation by the auditor. Nevertheless, the auditor who becomes aware of the existence of such information should consider it in identifying the risks of material misstatement arising from fraudulent financial reporting. For example, auditors may become aware of the following information that may indicate a risk factor:

- Ineffective communication, implementation, support, or enforcement of the entity's values or ethical standards by management or the communication of inappropriate values or ethical standards
- Nonfinancial management's excessive participation in or preoccupation with the selection of accounting principles or the determination of significant estimates
- Known history of violations of securities laws or other laws and regulations, or claims against the entity, its senior management, or board members alleging fraud or violations of laws and regulations
- Excessive interest by management in maintaining or increasing the entity's stock price or earnings trend
- A practice by management of committing to analysts, creditors, and other third parties to achieve aggressive or unrealistic forecasts
- Management failing to correct known reportable conditions on a timely basis
- An interest by management in employing inappropriate means to minimize reported earnings for tax-motivated reasons
- Recurring attempts by management to justify marginal or inappropriate accounting on the basis of materiality
- The relationship between management and the current or predecessor auditor is strained, as exhibited by the following:

— Frequent disputes with the current or predecessor auditor on accounting, auditing, or reporting matters

— Unreasonable demands on the auditor, such as unreasonable time constraints regarding the completion of the audit or the issuance of the auditor's report

— Formal or informal restrictions on the auditor that inappropriately limit access to people or information or the ability to communicate effectively with the board of directors or audit committee

— Domineering management behavior in dealing with the auditor, especially involving attempts to influence the scope of the auditor's work or the selection or continuance of personnel assigned to or consulted on the audit engagement

Risk Factors Relating to Misstatements Arising From Misappropriation of Assets

A.3 Risk factors that relate to misstatements arising from misappropriation of assets are also classified according to the three conditions generally present when fraud exists: incentives/pressures, opportunities, and attitudes/rationalizations. Some of the risk factors related to misstatements arising from fraudulent financial reporting also may be present when misstatements arising from misappropriation of assets occur. For example, ineffective monitoring of management and weaknesses in internal control may be present when misstatements due to either fraudulent financial reporting or misappropriation of assets exist. The following are examples of risk factors related to misstatements arising from misappropriation of assets.

Incentives/Pressures

a. Personal financial obligations may create pressure on management or employees with access to cash or other assets susceptible to theft to misappropriate those assets.

b. Adverse relationships between the entity and employees with access to cash or other assets susceptible to theft may motivate those employees to misappropriate those assets. For example, adverse relationships may be created by the following:

— Known or anticipated future employee layoffs

— Recent or anticipated changes to employee compensation or benefit plans

— Promotions, compensation, or other rewards inconsistent with expectations

Opportunities

a. Certain characteristics or circumstances may increase the susceptibility of assets to misappropriation. For example, opportunities to misappropriate assets increase when there are the following:

— Large amounts of cash on hand or processed

— Inventory items that are small in size, of high value, or in high demand

— Easily convertible assets, such as bearer bonds, diamonds, or computer chips

— Fixed assets that are small in size, marketable, or lacking observable identification of ownership

b. Inadequate internal control over assets may increase the susceptibility of misappropriation of those assets. For example, misappropriation of assets may occur because there is the following:

— Inadequate segregation of duties or independent checks

— Inadequate management oversight of employees responsible for assets, for example, inadequate supervision or monitoring of remote locations

— Inadequate job applicant screening of employees with access to assets

— Inadequate recordkeeping with respect to assets

— Inadequate system of authorization and approval of transactions (for example, in purchasing)

— Inadequate physical safeguards over cash, investments, inventory, or fixed assets

— Lack of complete and timely reconciliations of assets

— Lack of timely and appropriate documentation of transactions, for example, credits for merchandise returns

— Lack of mandatory vacations for employees performing key control functions

— Inadequate management understanding of information technology, which enables information technology employees to perpetrate a misappropriation

— Inadequate access controls over automated records, including controls over and review of computer systems event logs.

Attitudes/Rationalizations

Risk factors reflective of employee attitudes/rationalizations that allow them to justify misappropriations of assets, are generally not susceptible to observation by the auditor. Nevertheless, the auditor who becomes aware of the existence of such information should consider it in identifying the risks of material misstatement arising from misappropriation of assets. For example, auditors may become aware of the following attitudes or behavior of employees who have access to assets susceptible to misappropriation:

- Disregard for the need for monitoring or reducing risks related to misappropriations of assets
- Disregard for internal control over misappropriation of assets by overriding existing controls or by failing to correct known internal control deficiencies
- Behavior indicating displeasure or dissatisfaction with the company or its treatment of the employee
- Changes in behavior or lifestyle that may indicate assets have been misappropriated

.86

Amendment to Section 230, *Due Professional Care in the Performance of Work* [Not Reproduced.]

.87

Amendment to Section 333, *Management Representations,* paragraph .06 and Appendix A [paragraph .16] [Not Reproduced.]

.88

Exhibit

Management Antifraud Programs and Controls

Guidance to Help Prevent, Deter, and Detect Fraud

(This exhibit is reprinted for the reader's convenience but is not an integral part of the section.)

This document is being issued jointly by the following organizations:
> American Institute of Certified Public Accountants
> Association of Certified Fraud Examiners
> Financial Executives International
> Information Systems Audit and Control Association
> The Institute of Internal Auditors
> Institute of Management Accountants
> Society for Human Resource Management

In addition, we would also like to acknowledge the American Accounting Association, the Defense Industry Initiative, and the National Association of Corporate Directors for their review of the document and helpful comments and materials.

We gratefully acknowledge the valuable contribution provided by the Anti-Fraud Detection Subgroup:

Daniel D. Montgomery, *Chair*	David L. Landsittel
Toby J.F. Bishop	Carol A. Langelier
Dennis H. Chookaszian	Joseph T. Wells
Susan A. Finn	Janice Wilkins
Dana Hermanson	

Finally, we thank the staff of the American Institute of Certified Public Accountants for their support on this project:

Charles E. Landes	Kim M. Gibson
Director	Senior Technical Manager
Audit and Attest Standards	Audit and Attest Standards
Richard Lanza	Hugh Kelsey
Senior Program Manager	Program Manager
Chief Operating Office	Knowledge Management

This document was commissioned by the Fraud Task Force of the AICPA's Auditing Standards Board. This document has not been adopted, approved, disapproved, or otherwise acted upon by a board, committee, governing body, or membership of the above issuing organizations.

Preface

Some organizations have significantly lower levels of misappropriation of assets and are less susceptible to fraudulent financial reporting than other organizations because these organizations take proactive steps to prevent or deter fraud. It is only those organizations that seriously consider fraud risks and take proactive steps to create the right kind of climate to reduce its occurrence that have success in preventing fraud. This document identifies the key participants in this antifraud effort, including the board of directors, management, internal and independent auditors, and certified fraud examiners.

Management may develop and implement some of these programs and controls in response to specific identified risks of material misstatement of financial statements due to fraud. In other cases, these programs and controls may be a part of the entity's enterprise-wide risk management activities.

Management is responsible for designing and implementing systems and procedures for the prevention and detection of fraud and, along with the board of directors, for ensuring a culture and environment that promotes honesty and ethical behavior. However, because of the characteristics of fraud, a material misstatement of financial statements due to fraud may occur notwithstanding the presence of programs and controls such as those described in this document.

Introduction

Fraud can range from minor employee theft and unproductive behavior to misappropriation of assets and fraudulent financial reporting. Material financial statement fraud can have a significant adverse effect on an entity's market value, reputation, and ability to achieve its strategic objectives. A number of highly publicized cases have heightened the awareness of the effects of fraudulent financial reporting and have led many organizations to be more proactive in taking steps to prevent or deter its occurrence. Misappropriation of assets, though often not material to the financial statements, can nonetheless result in substantial losses to an entity if a dishonest employee has the incentive and opportunity to commit fraud.

The risk of fraud can be reduced through a combination of prevention, deterrence, and detection measures. However, fraud can be difficult to detect because it often involves concealment through falsification of documents or collusion among management, employees, or third parties. Therefore, it is important to place a strong emphasis on fraud prevention, which may reduce opportunities for fraud to take place, and fraud deterrence, which could persuade individuals that they should not commit fraud because of the likelihood of detection and punishment. Moreover, prevention and deterrence measures are much less costly than the time and expense required for fraud detection and investigation.

An entity's management has both the responsibility and the means to implement measures to reduce the incidence of fraud. The measures an organization takes to prevent and deter fraud also can help create a positive workplace environment that can enhance the entity's ability to recruit and retain high-quality employees.

Research suggests that the most effective way to implement measures to reduce wrongdoing is to base them on a set of core values that are embraced by the entity. These values provide an overarching message about the key principles guiding all employees' actions. This provides a platform upon which a more detailed code of conduct can be constructed, giving more specific guidance about permitted and prohibited behavior, based on applicable laws and the organization's values. Management needs to clearly articulate that all employees will be held accountable to act within the organization's code of conduct.

This document identifies measures entities can implement to prevent, deter, and detect fraud. It discusses these measures in the context of three fundamental elements. Broadly stated, these fundamental elements are (1) create and maintain a *culture* of honesty and high ethics; (2) *evaluate* the risks of fraud and implement the processes, procedures, and controls needed to mitigate the risks and reduce the opportunities for fraud; and (3) develop an appropriate *oversight* process. Although the entire management team shares the responsibility for implementing and monitoring these activities, with oversight from the board of directors, the entity's chief executive officer (CEO) should initiate and support such measures. Without the CEO's active support, these measures are less likely to be effective.

The information presented in this document generally is applicable to entities of all sizes. However, the degree to which certain programs and controls are applied in smaller, less-complex entities and the formality of their application are likely to differ from larger organizations. For example, management of a smaller entity (or the owner of an owner-managed entity), along with those charged with governance of the financial reporting process, are responsible for creating a culture of honesty and high ethics. Management also is responsible for implementing a system of internal controls commensurate with the nature and size of the organization, but smaller entities may find that certain types of control activities are not relevant because of the involvement of and controls applied by management. However, all entities must make it clear that unethical or dishonest behavior will not be tolerated.

Creating a Culture of Honesty and High Ethics

It is the organization's responsibility to create a culture of honesty and high ethics and to clearly communicate acceptable behavior and expectations of each employee. Such a culture is rooted in a strong set of core values (or value system) that provides the foundation for employees as to how the organization conducts its business. It also allows an entity to develop an ethical framework that covers (1) fraudulent financial reporting, (2) misappropriation of assets, and (3) corruption as well as other issues.[43]

Setting the Tone at the Top

Directors and officers of corporations set the "tone at the top" for ethical behavior within any organization. Research in moral development strongly suggests that honesty can best be reinforced when a proper example is set—sometimes referred to as the tone at the top. The management of an entity cannot act one way and expect others in the entity to behave differently.

In many cases, particularly in larger organizations, it is necessary for management to both behave ethically and openly communicate its expectations for ethical behavior because most employees are not in a position to observe management's actions. Management must show employees through its words and actions that dishonest or unethical behavior will not be tolerated, even if the result of the action benefits the entity. Moreover, it should be evident that all employees will be treated equally, regardless of their position.

For example, statements by management regarding the absolute need to meet operating and financial targets can create undue pressures that may lead employees to commit fraud to achieve them. Setting unachievable goals for employees can give them two unattractive choices: fail or cheat. In contrast, a statement from management that says, "We are aggressive in pursuing our targets, while requiring truthful financial reporting at all times," clearly indicates to employees that integrity is a requirement. This message also conveys that the entity has "zero tolerance" for unethical behavior, including fraudulent financial reporting.

The cornerstone of an effective antifraud environment is a culture with a strong value system founded on integrity. This value system often is reflected in a code of conduct.[44] The code of conduct should reflect the core values of the entity and guide employees in making appropriate decisions during their workday. The code of conduct might include such topics as ethics, confidentiality, conflicts of interest, intellectual property, sexual harassment, and fraud.[45] For a code of conduct to be effective, it should be communicated to all personnel in an understandable fashion. It also should be developed in a participatory and positive manner that will result in both management and employees taking ownership of its content. Finally, the code of conduct should be included in an employee handbook or policy manual, or in some other formal document or location (for example, the entity's intranet) so it can be referred to when needed.

Senior financial officers hold an important and elevated role in corporate governance. While members of the management team, they are uniquely capable and empowered to ensure that all stakeholders' interests are appropriately balanced, protected, and preserved. For examples of codes of conduct, see Attachment 1, "AICPA 'CPA's Handbook of Fraud and Commercial Crime Prevention,' An Organizational Code of Conduct," and Attachment 2, "Financial Executives International Code of Ethics Statement" provided by Financial Executives International. In addition, visit the Institute of Management Accountant's Ethics Center at http://www.imanet.org/content/About_IMA/EthicsCenter/Code_of_Ethics/Ethical_Standards.asp for their members' standards of ethical conduct.

Creating a Positive Workplace Environment

Research results indicate that wrongdoing occurs less frequently when employees have positive feelings about an entity than when they feel abused, threatened, or ignored. Without a positive workplace environment, there are more opportunities for poor employee morale, which can affect an employee's attitude about committing fraud against an entity. Factors that detract from a positive work environment and may increase the risk of fraud include:
- Top management that does not seem to care about or reward appropriate behavior
- Negative feedback and lack of recognition for job performance
- Perceived inequities in the organization
- Autocratic rather than participative management
- Low organizational loyalty or feelings of ownership
- Unreasonable budget expectations or other financial targets
- Fear of delivering "bad news" to supervisors and/or management
- Less-than-competitive compensation
- Poor training and promotion opportunities
- Lack of clear organizational responsibilities
- Poor communication practices or methods within the organization

The entity's human resources department often is instrumental in helping to build a corporate culture and a positive work environment. Human resource professionals are responsible for implementing specific programs and initiatives, consistent with management's strategies, that can help to mitigate many of the detractors mentioned above. Mitigating factors that help create a positive work environment and reduce the risk of fraud may include:
- Recognition and reward systems that are in tandem with goals and results
- Equal employment opportunities
- Team-oriented, collaborative decision-making policies
- Professionally administered compensation programs
- Professionally administered training programs and an organizational priority of career development

Employees should be empowered to help create a positive workplace environment and support the entity's values and code of conduct. They should be given the opportunity to provide input to the development and updating of the entity's code of conduct, to ensure that it is relevant, clear, and fair. Involving employees in this fashion also may effectively contribute to the oversight of the entity's code of conduct and an environment of ethical behavior (see the section titled "Developing an Appropriate Oversight Process").

Employees should be given the means to obtain advice internally before making decisions that appear to have significant legal or ethical implications. They should also be encouraged and given the means to communicate concerns, anonymously if preferred, about potential violations of the entity's code of conduct, without fear of retribution. Many organizations have implemented a process for employees to report on a confidential basis any actual or suspected wrongdoing, or potential violations of the code of conduct or ethics policy. For example, some organizations use a telephone "hotline" that is directed to or monitored by an ethics officer, fraud officer, general counsel, internal audit director, or another trusted individual responsible for investigating and reporting incidents of fraud or illegal acts.

Hiring and Promoting Appropriate Employees

Each employee has a unique set of values and personal code of ethics. When faced with sufficient pressure and a perceived opportunity, some employees will behave dishonestly rather than face the negative consequences of honest behavior. The threshold at which dishonest behavior starts, however, will vary among individuals. If an entity is to be successful in preventing fraud, it must have effective policies that minimize the chance of hiring or promoting individuals with low levels of honesty, especially for positions of trust.

Proactive hiring and promotion procedures may include:
- Conducting background investigations on individuals being considered for employment or for promotion to a position of trust[46]
- Thoroughly checking a candidate's education, employment history, and personal references
- Periodic training of all employees about the entity's values and code of conduct, (training is addressed in the following section)
- Incorporating into regular performance reviews an evaluation of how each individual has contributed to creating an appropriate workplace environment in line with the entity's values and code of conduct
- Continuous objective evaluation of compliance with the entity's values and code of conduct, with violations being addressed immediately

Training

New employees should be trained at the time of hiring about the entity's values and its code of conduct. This training should explicitly cover expectations of all employees regarding (1) their duty to communicate certain matters; (2) a list of the types of matters, including actual or suspected fraud, to be communicated along with specific examples; and (3) information on how to communicate those matters. There also should be an affirmation from senior management regarding employee expectations and communication responsibilities. Such training should include an element of "fraud awareness," the tone of which should be positive but nonetheless stress that fraud can be costly (and detrimental in other ways) to the entity and its employees.

In addition to training at the time of hiring, employees should receive refresher training periodically thereafter. Some organizations may consider ongoing training for certain positions, such as purchasing agents or employees with financial reporting responsibilities. Training should be specific to an employee's level within the organization, geographic location, and assigned responsibilities. For example, training for senior manager level personnel would normally be different from that of nonsupervisory employees, and training for purchasing agents would be different from that of sales representatives.

Confirmation

Management needs to clearly articulate that all employees will be held accountable to act within the entity's code of conduct. All employees within senior management and the finance function, as well as other employees in areas that might be exposed to unethical behavior (for example, procurement, sales and marketing) should be required to sign a code of conduct statement annually, at a minimum.

Requiring periodic confirmation by employees of their responsibilities will not only reinforce the policy but may also deter individuals from committing fraud and other violations and might identify problems before they become significant. Such confirmation may include statements that the individual understands the entity's expectations, has complied with the code of conduct, and is not aware of any violations of the code of conduct other than those the individual lists in his or her response. Although people with low integrity may not hesitate to sign a false confirmation, most people will want to avoid making a false statement in writing. Honest individuals are more likely to return their confirmations and to disclose what they know (including any conflicts of interest or other personal exceptions to the code of conduct). Thorough follow-up by internal auditors or others regarding nonreplies may uncover significant issues.

Discipline

The way an entity reacts to incidents of alleged or suspected fraud will send a strong deterrent message throughout the entity, helping to reduce the number of future occurrences. The following actions should be taken in response to an alleged incident of fraud:

- A thorough investigation of the incident should be conducted.[47]
- Appropriate and consistent actions should be taken against violators.
- Relevant controls should be assessed and improved.
- Communication and training should occur to reinforce the entity's values, code of conduct, and expectations.

Expectations about the consequences of committing fraud must be clearly communicated throughout the entity. For example, a strong statement from management that dishonest actions will not be tolerated, and that violators may be terminated and referred to the appropriate authorities, clearly establishes consequences and can be a valuable deterrent to wrongdoing. If wrongdoing occurs and an employee is disciplined, it can be helpful to communicate that fact, on a no-name basis, in an employee newsletter or other regular communication to employees. Seeing that other people have been disciplined for wrongdoing can be an effective deterrent, increasing the perceived likelihood of violators being caught and punished. It also can demonstrate that the entity is committed to an environment of high ethical standards and integrity.

Evaluating Antifraud Processes and Controls

Neither fraudulent financial reporting nor misappropriation of assets can occur without a perceived opportunity to commit and conceal the act. Organizations should be proactive in reducing fraud opportunities by (1) identifying and measuring fraud risks, (2) taking steps to mitigate identified risks, and (3) implementing and monitoring appropriate preventive and detective internal controls and other deterrent measures.

Identifying and Measuring Fraud Risks

Management has primary responsibility for establishing and monitoring all aspects of the entity's fraud risk-assessment and prevention activities.[48] Fraud risks often are considered as part of an enterprise-wide risk management program, though they may be addressed separately.[49] The fraud risk-assessment process should consider the vulnerability of the entity to fraudulent activity (fraudulent financial reporting, misappropriation of assets, and corruption) and whether any of those exposures could result in a material misstatement of the financial statements or material loss to the organization. In identifying fraud risks, organizations should consider organizational, industry, and country-specific characteristics that influence the risk of fraud.

The nature and extent of management's risk assessment activities should be commensurate with the size of the entity and complexity of its operations. For example, the risk assessment process is likely to be less formal and less structured in smaller entities. However, management should recognize that fraud can occur in organizations of any size or type, and that almost any employee may be capable of committing fraud given the right set of circumstances. Accordingly, management should develop a heightened "fraud awareness" and an appropriate fraud risk-management program, with oversight from the board of directors or audit committee.

Mitigating Fraud Risks

It may be possible to reduce or eliminate certain fraud risks by making changes to the entity's activities and processes. An entity may choose to sell certain segments of its operations, cease doing business in certain locations, or reorganize its business processes to eliminate unacceptable risks. For example, the risk of misappropriation of funds may be reduced by implementing a central lockbox at a bank to receive payments instead of receiving money at the entity's various locations. The risk of corruption may be reduced by closely monitoring the entity's procurement process. The risk of financial statement fraud may be reduced by implementing shared services centers to provide accounting services to multiple segments, affiliates, or geographic locations of an entity's operations. A shared services center may be less vulnerable to influence by local operations managers and may be able to implement more extensive fraud detection measures cost-effectively.

Implementing and Monitoring Appropriate Internal Controls

Some risks are inherent in the environment of the entity, but most can be addressed with an appropriate system of internal control. Once fraud risk assessment has taken place, the entity can identify the processes, controls, and other procedures that are needed to mitigate the identified risks. Effective internal control will include a well-developed control environment, an effective and secure information system, and appropriate control and monitoring activities.[50] Because of the importance of information technology in supporting operations and the processing of transactions, management also needs to implement and maintain appropriate controls, whether automated or manual, over computer-generated information.

In particular, management should evaluate whether appropriate internal controls have been implemented in any areas management has identified as posing a higher risk of fraudulent activity, as well as controls over the entity's financial reporting process. Because fraudulent financial reporting may begin in an interim period, management also should evaluate the appropriateness of internal controls over interim financial reporting.

Fraudulent financial reporting by upper-level management typically involves override of internal controls within the financial reporting process. Because management has the ability to override controls, or to influence others to perpetrate or conceal fraud, the need for a strong value system and a culture of ethical financial reporting becomes increasingly important. This helps create an environment in which other employees will decline to participate in committing a fraud and will use established communication procedures to report any requests to commit wrongdoing. The potential for management override also increases the need for appropriate oversight measures by the board of directors or audit committee, as discussed in the following section.

Fraudulent financial reporting by lower levels of management and employees may be deterred or detected by appropriate monitoring controls, such as having higher-level managers review and evaluate the financial results reported by individual operating units or subsidiaries. Unusual fluctuations in results of particular reporting units, or the lack of expected fluctuations, may indicate potential manipulation by departmental or operating unit managers or staff.

Developing an Appropriate Oversight Process

To effectively prevent or deter fraud, an entity should have an appropriate oversight function in place. Oversight can take many forms and can be performed by many within and outside the entity, under the overall oversight of the audit committee (or board of directors where no audit committee exists).

Audit Committee or Board of Directors

The audit committee (or the board of directors where no audit committee exists) should evaluate management's identification of fraud risks, implementation of antifraud measures, and creation of the appropriate "tone at the top." Active oversight by the audit committee can help to reinforce management's commitment to creating a culture with "zero tolerance" for fraud. An entity's audit committee also should ensure that senior management (in particular, the CEO) implements appropriate fraud deterrence and prevention measures to better protect investors, employees, and other stakeholders. The audit committee's evaluation and oversight not only helps make sure that senior management fulfills its responsibility, but also can serve as a deterrent to senior management engaging in fraudulent activity (that is, by ensuring an environment is created whereby any attempt by senior management to involve employees in committing or concealing fraud would lead promptly to reports from such employees to appropriate persons, including the audit committee).

The audit committee also plays an important role in helping the board of directors fulfill its oversight responsibilities with respect to the entity's financial reporting process and the system of internal control.[51] In exercising this oversight responsibility, the audit committee should consider the potential for management override of controls or other inappropriate influence over the financial reporting process. For example, the audit committee may obtain from the internal auditors and independent auditors their views on management's involvement in the financial reporting process and, in particular, the ability of management to override information processed by the entity's financial reporting system (for example, the ability for management or others to initiate or record nonstandard journal entries). The audit committee also may consider reviewing the entity's reported information for reasonableness compared with prior or forecasted results, as well as with peers or industry averages. In addition, information received in communications from the independent auditors[52] can assist the audit committee in assessing the strength of the entity's internal control and the potential for fraudulent financial reporting.

As part of its oversight responsibilities, the audit committee should encourage management to provide a mechanism for employees to report concerns about unethical behavior, actual or suspected fraud, or violations of the entity's code of conduct or ethics policy. The committee should then receive periodic reports describing the nature, status, and eventual disposition of any fraud or unethical conduct. A summary of the activity, follow-up and disposition also should be provided to the full board of directors.

If senior management is involved in fraud, the next layer of management may be the most likely to be aware of it. As a result, the audit committee (and other directors) should consider establishing an open line of communication with members of management one or two levels below senior management to assist in identifying fraud at the highest levels of the organization or investigating any fraudulent activity that might occur.[53] The audit committee typically has the ability and authority to investigate any alleged or suspected wrongdoing brought to its attention. Most audit committee charters empower the committee to investigate any matters within the scope of its responsibilities, and to retain legal, accounting, and other professional advisers as needed to advise the committee and assist in its investigation.

All audit committee members should be financially literate, and each committee should have at least one financial expert. The financial expert should possess:

- An understanding of generally accepted accounting principles and audits of financial statements prepared under those principles. Such understanding may have been obtained either through education or experience. It is important for someone on the audit committee to have a working knowledge of those principles and standards.
- Experience in the preparation and/or the auditing of financial statements of an entity of similar size, scope and complexity as the entity on whose board the committee member serves. The experience would generally be as a chief financial officer, chief accounting officer, controller, or auditor of a similar entity. This background will provide a necessary understanding of the transactional and operational environment that produces the issuer's financial statements. It will also bring an understanding of what is involved in, for example, appropriate accounting estimates, accruals, and reserve provisions, and an appreciation of what is necessary to maintain a good internal control environment.
- Experience in internal governance and procedures of audit committees, obtained either as an audit committee member, a senior corporate manager responsible for answering to the audit committee, or an external auditor responsible for reporting on the execution and results of annual audits.

Management

Management is responsible for overseeing the activities carried out by employees, and typically does so by implementing and monitoring processes and controls such as those discussed previously. However, management also may initiate, participate in, or direct the commission and concealment of a fraudulent act. Accordingly, the audit committee (or the board of directors where no audit committee exists) has the responsibility to oversee the activities of senior management and to consider the risk of fraudulent financial reporting involving the override of internal controls or collusion (see discussion on the audit committee and board of directors above).

Public companies should include a statement in the annual report acknowledging management's responsibility for the preparation of the financial statements and for establishing and maintaining an effective system of internal control. This will help improve the public's understanding of the respective roles of management and the auditor. This statement has also been generally referred to as a "Management Report" or "Management Certificate." Such a statement can provide a convenient vehicle for management to describe the nature and manner of preparation of the financial information and the adequacy of the internal accounting controls. Logically, the statement should be presented in close proximity to the formal financial statements. For example, it could appear near the independent auditor's report, or in the financial review or management analysis section.

Internal Auditors

An effective internal audit team can be extremely helpful in performing aspects of the oversight function. Their knowledge about the entity may enable them to identify indicators that suggest fraud has been committed. The *Standards for the Professional Practice of Internal Auditing* (IIA Standards), issued by the Institute of Internal Auditors, state, "The internal auditor should have sufficient knowledge to identify the indicators of fraud but is not expected to have the expertise of a person whose primary responsibility is detecting and investigating fraud." Internal auditors also have the opportunity to evaluate fraud risks and controls and to recommend action to mitigate risks and improve controls. Specifically, the IIA Standards require internal auditors to assess risks facing their organizations. This risk assessment is to serve as the basis from which audit plans are devised and against which internal controls are tested. The IIA Standards require the audit plan to be presented to and approved by the audit committee (or board of directors where no audit committee exists). The work completed as a result of the audit plan provides assurance on which management's assertion about controls can be made.

Internal audits can be both a detection and a deterrence measure. Internal auditors can assist in the deterrence of fraud by examining and evaluating the adequacy and the effectiveness of the system of internal control, commensurate with the extent of the potential exposure or risk in the various segments of the organization's operations. In carrying out this responsibility, internal auditors should, for example, determine whether:
- The organizational environment fosters control consciousness.
- Realistic organizational goals and objectives are set.
- Written policies (for example, a code of conduct) exist that describe prohibited activities and the action required whenever violations are discovered.
- Appropriate authorization policies for transactions are established and maintained.
- Policies, practices, procedures, reports, and other mechanisms are developed to monitor activities and safeguard assets, particularly in high-risk areas.
- Communication channels provide management with adequate and reliable information.
- Recommendations need to be made for the establishment or enhancement of cost-effective controls to help deter fraud.

Internal auditors may conduct proactive auditing to search for corruption, misappropriation of assets, and financial statement fraud. This may include the use of computer-assisted audit techniques to detect particular types of fraud. Internal auditors also can employ analytical and other procedures to isolate anomalies and perform detailed reviews of high-risk accounts and transactions to identify potential financial statement fraud. The internal auditors should have an independent reporting line directly to the audit committee, to enable them to express any concerns about management's commitment to appropriate internal controls or to report suspicions or allegations of fraud involving senior management.

Independent Auditors

Independent auditors can assist management and the board of directors (or audit committee) by providing an assessment of the entity's process for identifying, assessing, and responding to the risks of fraud. The board of directors (or audit committee) should have an open and candid dialogue with the independent auditors regarding management's risk assessment process and the system of internal control. Such a dialogue should include a discussion of the susceptibility of the entity to fraudulent financial reporting and the entity's exposure to misappropriation of assets.

Certified Fraud Examiners

Certified fraud examiners may assist the audit committee and board of directors with aspects of the oversight process either directly or as part of a team of internal auditors or independent auditors. Certified fraud examiners can provide extensive knowledge and experience about fraud that may not be available within a corporation. They can provide more objective input into management's evaluation of the risk of fraud (especially fraud involving senior management, such as financial statement fraud) and the development of appropriate antifraud controls that are less vulnerable to management override. They can assist the audit committee and board of directors in evaluating the fraud risk assessment and fraud prevention measures implemented by management. Certified fraud examiners also conduct examinations to resolve allegations or suspicions of fraud, reporting either to an appropriate level of management or to the audit committee or board of directors, depending upon the nature of the issue and the level of personnel involved.

Other Information

To obtain more information on fraud and implementing antifraud programs and controls, please go to the following Web sites where additional materials, guidance, and tools can be found.

American Institute of Certified Public Accountants	http://www.aicpa.org
Association of Certified Fraud Examiners	http://www.cfenet.com
Financial Executives International	http://www.fei.org
Information Systems Audit and Control Association	http://www.isaca.org
The Institute of Internal Auditors	http://www.theiia.org
Institute of Management Accountants	http://www.imanet.org
National Association of Corporate Directors	http://www.nacdonline.org
Society for Human Resource Management	http://www.shrm.org

Attachment 1: AICPA "CPA's Handbook of Fraud and Commercial Crime Prevention," An Organizational Code of Conduct

The following is an example of an organizational code of conduct, which includes definitions of what is considered unacceptable, and the consequences of any breaches thereof. The specific content and areas addressed in an entity's code of conduct should be specific to that entity.

Organizational Code of Conduct
The Organization and its employees must, at all times, comply with all applicable laws and regulations. The Organization will not condone the activities of employees who achieve results through violation of the law or unethical business dealings. This includes any payments for illegal acts, indirect contributions, rebates, and bribery. The Organization does not permit any activity that fails to stand the closest possible public scrutiny.
All business conduct should be well above the minimum standards required by law.

Accordingly, employees must ensure that their actions cannot be interpreted as being, in any way, in contravention of the laws and regulations governing the Organization's worldwide operations.

Employees uncertain about the application or interpretation of any legal requirements should refer the matter to their superior, who, if necessary, should seek the advice of the legal department.

General Employee Conduct

The Organization expects its employees to conduct themselves in a businesslike manner. Drinking, gambling, fighting, swearing, and similar unprofessional activities are strictly prohibited while on the job.

Employees must not engage in sexual harassment, or conduct themselves in a way that could be construed as such, for example, by using inappropriate language, keeping or posting inappropriate materials in their work area, or accessing inappropriate materials on their computer.

Conflicts of Interest

The Organization expects that employees will perform their duties conscientiously, honestly, and in accordance with the best interests of the Organization. Employees must not use their position or the knowledge gained as a result of their position for private or personal advantage. Regardless of the circumstances, if employees sense that a course of action they have pursued, are presently pursuing, or are contemplating pursuing may involve them in a conflict of interest with their employer, they should immediately communicate all the facts to their superior.

Outside Activities, Employment, and Directorships

All employees share a serious responsibility for the Organization's good public relations, especially at the community level. Their readiness to help with religious, charitable, educational, and civic activities brings credit to the Organization and is encouraged.

Employees must, however, avoid acquiring any business interest or participating in any other activity outside the Organization that would, or would appear to:

- Create an excessive demand upon their time and attention, thus depriving the Organization of their best efforts on the job.
- Create a conflict of interest—an obligation, interest, or distraction—that may interfere with the independent exercise of judgment in the Organization's best interest.

Relationships With Clients and Suppliers

Employees should avoid investing in or acquiring a financial interest for their own accounts in any business organization that has a contractual relationship with the Organization, or that provides goods or services, or both to the Organization, if such investment or interest could influence or create the impression of influencing their decisions in the performance of their duties on behalf of the Organization.

Gifts, Entertainment, and Favors

Employees must not accept entertainment, gifts, or personal favors that could, in any way, influence, or appear to influence, business decisions in favor of any person or organization with whom or with which the Organization has, or is likely to have, business dealings. Similarly, employees must not accept any other preferential treatment under these circumstances because their position with the Organization might be inclined to, or be perceived to, place them under obligation.

Kickbacks and Secret Commissions

Regarding the Organization's business activities, employees may not receive payment or compensation of any kind, except as authorized under the Organization's remuneration policies. In particular, the Organization strictly prohibits the acceptance of kickbacks and secret commissions from suppliers or others. Any breach of this rule will result in immediate termination and prosecution to the fullest extent of the law.

Organization Funds and Other Assets

Employees who have access to Organization funds in any form must follow the prescribed procedures for recording, handling, and protecting money as detailed in the Organization's instructional manuals or other explanatory materials, or both. The Organization imposes strict standards to prevent fraud and dishonesty. If employees become aware of any evidence of fraud and dishonesty, they should immediately advise their superior or the Law Department so that the Organization can promptly investigate further.

When an employee's position requires spending Organization funds or incurring any reimbursable personal expenses, that individual must use good judgment on the Organization's behalf to ensure that good value is received for every expenditure.

Organization funds and all other assets of the Organization are for Organization purposes only and not for personal benefit. This includes the personal use of organizational assets, such as computers.

Organization Records and Communications

Accurate and reliable records of many kinds are necessary to meet the Organization's legal and financial obligations and to manage the affairs of the Organization. The Organization's books and records must reflect in an accurate and timely manner all business transactions. The employees responsible for accounting and recordkeeping must fully disclose and record all assets, liabilities, or both, and must exercise diligence in enforcing these requirements. Employees must not make or engage in any false record or communication of any kind, whether internal or external, including but not limited to:

- False expense, attendance, production, financial, or similar reports and statements
- False advertising, deceptive marketing practices, or other misleading representations

Dealing With Outside People and Organizations

Employees must take care to separate their personal roles from their Organization positions when communicating on matters not involving Organization business. Employees must not use organization identification, stationery, supplies, and equipment for personal or political matters.

When communicating publicly on matters that involve Organization business, employees must not presume to speak for the Organization on any topic, unless they are certain that the views they express are those of the Organization, and it is the Organization's desire that such views be publicly disseminated.

When dealing with anyone outside the Organization, including public officials, employees must take care not to compromise the integrity or damage the reputation of either the Organization, or any outside individual, business, or government body.

Prompt Communications

In all matters relevant to customers, suppliers, government authorities, the public and others in the Organization, all employees must make every effort to achieve complete, accurate, and timely communications—responding promptly and courteously to all proper requests for information and to all complaints.

Privacy and Confidentiality

When handling financial and personal information about customers or others with whom the Organization has dealings, observe the following principles:

1. Collect, use, and retain only the personal information necessary for the Organization's business. Whenever possible, obtain any relevant information directly from the person concerned. Use only reputable and reliable sources to supplement this information.

2. Retain information only for as long as necessary or as required by law. Protect the physical security of this information.

3. Limit internal access to personal information to those with a legitimate business reason for seeking that information. Use only personal information for the purposes for which it was originally obtained. Obtain the consent of the person concerned before externally disclosing any personal information, unless legal process or contractual obligation provides otherwise.

Attachment 2: Financial Executives International Code of Ethics Statement

The mission of Financial Executives International (FEI) includes significant efforts to promote ethical conduct in the practice of financial management throughout the world. Senior financial officers hold an important and elevated role in corporate governance. While members of the management team, they are uniquely capable and empowered to ensure that all stakeholders' interests are appropriately balanced, protected, and preserved. This code provides principles that members are expected to adhere to and advocate. They embody rules regarding individual and peer responsibilities, as well as responsibilities to employers, the public, and other stakeholders.

All members of FEI will:
1. Act with honesty and integrity, avoiding actual or apparent conflicts of interest in personal and professional relationships.
2. Provide constituents with information that is accurate, complete, objective, relevant, timely, and understandable.
3. Comply with rules and regulations of federal, state, provincial, and local governments, and other appropriate private and public regulatory agencies.
4. Act in good faith; responsibly; and with due care, competence, and diligence, without misrepresenting material facts or allowing one's independent judgment to be subordinated.
5. Respect the confidentiality of information acquired in the course of one's work except when authorized or otherwise legally obligated to disclose. Confidential information acquired in the course of one's work will not be used for personal advantage.
6. Share knowledge and maintain skills important and relevant to constituents' needs.
7. Proactively promote ethical behavior as a responsible partner among peers, in the work environment, and in the community.
8. Achieve responsible use of and control over all assets and resources employed or entrusted.

Endnotes

[1] The auditor's consideration of illegal acts and responsibility for detecting misstatements resulting from illegal acts is defined in section 317, *Illegal Acts by Clients*. For those illegal acts that are defined in that section as having a direct and material effect on the determination of financial statement amounts, the auditor's responsibility to detect misstatements resulting from such illegal acts is the same as that for errors (see section 312, *Audit Risk and Materiality in Conducting an Audit*, or fraud).

[2] Auditors are sometimes requested to perform other services related to fraud detection and prevention, for example, special investigations to determine the extent of a suspected or detected fraud. These other services usually include procedures that extend beyond or are different from the procedures ordinarily performed in an audit of financial statements in accordance with generally accepted auditing standards (GAAS). AT section 101, *Attest Engagements*, and CS section 100, *Consulting Services: Definitions and Standards*, provide guidance to accountants relating to the performance of such services.

[3] In its October 1987 report, the National Commission on Fraudulent Financial Reporting, also known as the Treadway Commission, noted, "The responsibility for reliable financial reporting resides first and foremost at the corporate level. Top management, starting with the chief executive officer, sets the tone and establishes the financial reporting environment. Therefore, reducing the risk of fraudulent financial reporting must start with the reporting company."

[4] Intent is often difficult to determine, particularly in matters involving accounting estimates and the application of accounting principles. For example, unreasonable accounting estimates may be unintentional or may be the result of an intentional attempt to misstate the financial statements. Although an audit is not designed to determine intent, the auditor has a responsibility to plan and perform the audit to obtain reasonable assurance about whether the financial statements are free of material misstatement, whether the misstatement is intentional or not.

[5] Reference to generally accepted accounting principles (GAAP) includes, where applicable, a comprehensive basis of accounting other than GAAP as defined in section 623, *Special Reports*, paragraph .04.

[6] Frauds have been committed by management override of existing controls using such techniques as (*a*) recording fictitious journal entries, particularly those recorded close to the end of an accounting period to manipulate operating results, (*b*) intentionally biasing assumptions and judgments used to estimate account balances, and (*c*) altering records and terms related to significant and unusual transactions.

7   For a further discussion of the concept of reasonable assurance, see section 230, *Due Professional Care in the Performance of Work*, paragraphs .10 through .13.

8   See footnote 6.

9   In addition to these inquiries, section 333, *Management Representations*, requires the auditor to obtain selected written representations from management regarding fraud.

10   Section 319, *Consideration of Internal Control in a Financial Statement Audit*, paragraphs .06 and .07, defines internal control and its five interrelated components (the control environment, risk assessment, control activities, information and communication, and monitoring). Entity programs and controls intended to address the risks of fraud may be part of any of the five components discussed in section 319.

11   Examples of "others with equivalent authority and responsibility" may include the board of directors, the board of trustees, or the owner in an owner-managed entity, as appropriate.

12   See footnote 10.

13   See paragraph .70 for a discussion of the need to update these analytical procedures during the overall review stage of the audit.

14   See Statement on Quality Control Standards (SQCS) No. 2, *System of Quality Control for a CPA Firm's Accounting and Auditing Practice* [QC section 20.14–.16], as amended.

15   Section 312.18 provides guidance on the auditor's consideration of the extent to which auditing procedures should be performed at selected locations or components.

16   The occurrence of material misstatements of financial statements due to fraud is relatively infrequent in relation to the total population of published financial statements. However, the auditor should not use this as a basis to conclude that one or more risks of a material misstatement due to fraud are not present in a particular entity.

17   For a discussion of indicators of improper revenue recognition and common techniques for overstating revenue and illustrative audit procedures, see the AICPA Audit Guide *Auditing Revenue in Certain Industries*.

18   See footnote 10.

19   Notwithstanding that the auditor assesses identified risks of material misstatement due to fraud, the assessment need not encompass an overall judgment about whether risk for the entity is classified as *high*, *medium*, or *low* because such a judgment is too broad to be useful in developing the auditor's response described in paragraphs .46 through .67.

20   Section 329, *Analytical Procedures*, provides guidance on performing analytical procedures as substantive tests.

21   Section 330, *The Confirmation Process*, provides guidance about the confirmation process in audits performed in accordance with GAAS.

22   Section 336, *Using the Work of a Specialist*, provides guidance to an auditor who uses the work of a specialist in performing an audit in accordance with GAAS.

23   Section 319 requires the auditor to obtain an understanding of the automated and manual procedures an entity uses to prepare financial statements and related disclosures, and how misstatements may occur. This understanding includes (*a*) the procedures used to enter transaction totals into the general ledger; (*b*) the procedures used to initiate, record, and process journal entries in the general ledger; and (*c*) other procedures used to record recurring and nonrecurring adjustments to the financial statements.

24   See section 342, *Auditing Accounting Estimates*, paragraphs .02 and .16, for a definition of accounting estimates and a listing of examples.

25   Section 334, *Related Parties*, provides guidance with respect to the identification of related-party relationships and transactions, including transactions that may be outside the ordinary course of business (see, in particular, section 334.06).

26   As discussed in paragraph .09, auditors are not trained as or expected to be experts in the authentication of documents; however, if the auditor believes that documents may not be authentic, he or she should investigate further and consider using the work of a specialist to determine the authenticity.

27   Denial of access to information may constitute a limitation on the scope of the audit that may require the auditor to consider qualifying or disclaiming an opinion on the financial statements. (See section 508, *Reports on Audited Financial Statements*, paragraph .24.)

28 To accomplish this communication, the auditor with final responsibility for the audit may want to arrange another discussion among audit team members about the risks of material misstatement due to fraud (see paragraphs .14 through .18).

29 See footnote 4.

30 Section 312.34 states in part, "Qualitative considerations also influence the auditor in reaching a conclusion as to whether misstatements are material." Section 312.11 states, "As a result of the interaction of quantitative and qualitative considerations in materiality judgments, misstatements of relatively small amounts that come to the auditor's attention could have a material effect on the financial statements."

31 However, see paragraphs .79 through .82 of this section for a discussion of the auditor's communication responsibilities.

32 Section 312.08 states that there is a distinction between the auditor's response to detected misstatements due to error and those due to fraud. When fraud is detected, the auditor should consider the implications for the integrity of management or employees and the possible effect on other aspects of the audit.

33 See section 508 for guidance on auditors' reports issued in connection with audits of financial statements.

34 If the auditor believes senior management may be involved, discussion of the matter directly with the audit committee may be appropriate.

35 See footnote 11.

36 If the auditor, subsequent to the date of the report on the audited financial statements, becomes aware that facts existed at that date that might have affected the report had the auditor been aware of such facts, the auditor should refer to section 561, *Subsequent Discovery of Facts Existing at the Date of the Auditor's Report*, for guidance. Furthermore, section 315, *Communications Between Predecessor and Successor Auditors*, paragraphs .21 and .22, provide guidance regarding communication with a predecessor auditor.

37 The requirements to communicate noted in paragraphs .79 through .82 extend to any intentional misstatement of financial statements (see paragraph .03). However, the communication may use terms other than fraud—for example, irregularity, intentional misstatement, misappropriation, or defalcations—if there is possible confusion with a legal definition of fraud or other reason to prefer alternative terms.

38 Alternatively, the auditor may decide to communicate solely with the audit committee.

39 These requirements include reports in connection with the termination of the engagement, such as when the entity reports an auditor change on Form 8-K and the fraud or related risk factors constitute a *reportable event* or is the source of a *disagreement*, as these terms are defined in Item 304 of Regulation S-K. These requirements also include reports that may be required, under certain circumstances, pursuant to Section 10A(b)1 of the Securities Exchange Act of 1934 relating to an illegal act that has a material effect on the financial statements.

40 Section 315 requires the specific permission of the client.

41 For example, *Government Auditing Standards* (the Yellow Book) require auditors to report fraud or illegal acts directly to parties outside the audited entity in certain circumstances.

42 Management incentive plans may be contingent upon achieving targets relating only to certain accounts or selected activities of the entity, even though the related accounts or activities may not be material to the entity as a whole.

43 Corruption includes bribery and other illegal acts.
   Creating a culture of honesty and high ethics should include the following.

44 An entity's value system also could be reflected in an ethics policy, a statement of business principles, or some other concise summary of guiding principles.

45 Although the discussion in this document focuses on fraud, the subject of fraud often is considered in the context of a broader set of principles that govern an organization. Some organizations, however, may elect to develop a fraud policy separate from an ethics policy. Specific examples of topics in a fraud policy might include a requirement to comply with all laws and regulations and explicit guidance regarding making payments to obtain contracts, holding pricing discussions with competitors, environmental discharges, relationships with vendors, and maintenance of accurate books and records.

46 Some organizations also have considered follow-up investigations, particularly for employees in positions of trust, on a periodic basis (for example, every five years) or as circumstances dictate.

47 Many entities of sufficient size are employing antifraud professionals, such as certified fraud examiners, who are responsible for resolving allegations of fraud within the organization and who also assist in the detection and deterrence of fraud. These individuals typically report their findings internally to the corporate security, legal, or internal audit departments. In other instances, such individuals may be empowered directly by the board of directors or its audit committee.

48 Management may elect to have internal audit play an active role in the development, monitoring, and ongoing assessment of the entity's fraud risk-management program. This may include an active role in the development and communication of the entity's code of conduct or ethics policy, as well as in investigating actual or alleged instances of noncompliance.

49 Some organizations may perform a periodic self-assessment using questionnaires or other techniques to identify and measure risks. Self-assessment may be less reliable in identifying the risk of fraud due to a lack of experience with fraud (although many organizations experience some form of fraud and abuse, material financial statement fraud or misappropriation of assets is a rare event for most) and because management may be unwilling to acknowledge openly that they might commit fraud given sufficient pressure and opportunity.

50 The report of the Committee of Sponsoring Organizations (COSO) of the Treadway Commission, *Internal Control—Integrated Framework*, provides reasonable criteria for management to use in evaluating the effectiveness of the entity's system of internal control.

51 See the Report of the NACD Blue Ribbon Commission on the Audit Committee, (Washington, D.C.: National Association of Corporate Directors, 2000). For the board's role in the oversight of risk management, see Report of the NACD Blue Ribbon Commission on Risk Oversight, (Washington, D.C.: National Association of Corporate Directors, 2002).

52 See section 325, *Communication of Internal Control Related Matters Noted in an Audit*, and section 380, *Communications With Audit Committees*.

53 *Report of the NACD Best Practices Council: Coping with Fraud and Other Illegal Activity, A Guide for Directors, CEOs, and Senior Managers* (1998) sets forth "basic principles" and "implementation approaches" for dealing with fraud and other illegal activity.

Council of Europe Convention on Cybercrime

Excerpt from the Council of Europe Convention on Cybercrime, November 23, 2001, Budapest, Hungary. Excerpt contains the first 28 of 48 articles.

Convention on Cybercrime

Preamble

The member States of the Council of Europe and the other States signatory hereto, Considering that the aim of the Council of Europe is to achieve a greater unity between its members; Recognising the value of fostering co-operation with the other States parties to this Convention; Convinced of the need to pursue, as a matter of priority, a common criminal policy aimed at the protection of society against cybercrime, *inter alia* by adopting appropriate legislation and fostering international co-operation; Conscious of the profound changes brought about by the digitalisation, convergence and continuing globalisation of computer networks; Concerned at the risk that computer networks and electronic information may also be used for committing criminal offences and that evidence relating to such offences may be stored and transferred by these networks; Recognising the need for co-operation between States and private industry in combating cybercrime and the need to protect legitimate interests in the use and development of information technologies; Believing that an effective fight against cybercrime requires increased, rapid and well-functioning international co-operation in criminal matters; Convinced that the present Convention is necessary to deter actions directed against the confidentiality, integrity and availability of computer systems, networks and computer data, as well as the misuse of such systems, networks and data, by providing for the criminalisation of such conduct, as described in this Convention, and the adoption of powers sufficient for effectively combating such criminal offences, by facilitating the detection, investigation and prosecution of such criminal offences at both the domestic and international level, and by providing arrangements for fast and reliable international co-operation; Mindful of the need to ensure a proper balance between the interests of law enforcement and respect for fundamental human rights, as enshrined in the 1950 Council of Europe Convention for the Protection of Human Rights and Fundamental Freedoms, the 1966 United Nations International Covenant on Civil and Political Rights, as well as other applicable international human rights treaties, which reaffirm the right of everyone to hold opinions without interference, as well as the right to freedom of expression, including the freedom to seek, receive, and impart information and ideas of all kinds, regardless of frontiers, and the rights concerning the respect for privacy;

Mindful also of the protection of personal data, as conferred e.g. by the 1981 Council of Europe Convention for the Protection of Individuals with Regard to Automatic Processing of Personal Data; Considering the 1989 United Nations Convention on the Rights of the Child and the 1999 International Labour Organization Worst Forms of Child Labour Convention; Taking into account the existing Council of Europe conventions on co-operation in the penal field as well as similar treaties which exist between Council of Europe member States and other States and stressing that the present Convention is intended to supplement those conventions in order to make criminal investigations and proceedings concerning criminal offences related to computer systems and data more effective and to enable the collection of evidence in electronic form of a criminal offence.

Have agreed as follows:

Chapter I – Use of terms

Article 1 – Definitions

For the purposes of this Convention:

a.   "computer system" means any device or a group of inter-connected or related devices, one or more of which, pursuant to a program, performs automatic processing of data;

b.   "computer data" means any representation of facts, information or concepts in a form suitable for processing in a computer system, including a program suitable to cause a computer system to perform a function;

c.   "service provider" means:

i.   any public or private entity that provides to users of its service the ability to communicate by means of a computer system, and

ii.   any other entity that processes or stores computer data on behalf of such communication service or users of such service.

d.   "traffic data" means any computer data relating to a communication by means of a computer system, generated by a computer system that formed a part in the chain of communication, indicating the communication's origin, destination, route, time, date, size, duration, or type of underlying service.

Chapter II – Measures to be taken at the national level

Section 1 – Substantive criminal law

Title 1 – Offences against the confidentiality, integrity and availability of computer data and systems

Article 2 – Illegal access

Each Party shall adopt such legislative and other measures as may be necessary to establish as criminal offences under its domestic law, when committed intentionally, the access to the whole or any part of a computer system without right. A Party may require that the offence be committed by infringing security measures, with the intent of obtaining computer data or other dishonest intent, or in relation to a computer system that is connected to another computer system.

Article 3 – Illegal interception

Each Party shall adopt such legislative and other measures as may be necessary to establish as criminal offences under its domestic law, when committed intentionally, the interception without right, made by technical means, of non-public transmissions of computer data to, from or within a computer system, including electromagnetic emissions from a computer system carrying such computer data. A Party may require that the offence be committed with dishonest intent, or in relation to a computer system that is connected to another computer system.

Article 4 – Data interference
1. Each Party shall adopt such legislative and other measures as may be necessary to establish as criminal offences under its domestic law, when committed intentionally, the damaging, deletion, deterioration, alteration or suppression of computer data without right.
2. A Party may reserve the right to require that the conduct described in paragraph 1 result in serious harm.

Article 5 – System interference
Each Party shall adopt such legislative and other measures as may be necessary to establish as criminal offences under its domestic law, when committed intentionally, the serious hindering without right of the functioning of a computer system by inputting, transmitting, damaging, deleting, deteriorating, altering or suppressing computer data.

Article 6 – Misuse of devices
1. Each Party shall adopt such legislative and other measures as may be necessary to establish as criminal offences under its domestic law, when committed intentionally and without right:
a.   the production, sale, procurement for use, import, distribution or otherwise making available of:
i.   a device, including a computer program, designed or adapted primarily for the purpose of committing any of the offences established in accordance with Article 2 – 5;
ii.   a computer password, access code, or similar data by which the whole or any part of a computer system is capable of being accessed
with intent that it be used for the purpose of committing any of the   offences established in Articles 2 - 5; and
b.   the possession of an item referred to in paragraphs (a)(1) or (2) above, with intent that it be used for the purpose of committing any of the offences established in Articles 2 – 5. A Party may require by law that a number of such items be possessed before criminal liability attaches.
2. This article shall not be interpreted as imposing criminal liability where the production, sale, procurement for use, import, distribution or otherwise making available or possession referred to in paragraph 1 of this Article is not for the purpose of committing an offence established in accordance with articles 2 through 5 of this Convention, such as for the authorised testing or protection of a computer system.
3. Each Party may reserve the right not to apply paragraph 1 of this Article, provided that the reservation does not concern the sale, distribution or otherwise making available of the items referred to in paragraph 1 (a) (2).

Title 2 – Computer-related offences

Article 7 – Computer-related forgery
Each Party shall adopt such legislative and other measures as may be necessary to establish as criminal offences under its domestic law, when committed intentionally and without right, the input, alteration, deletion, or suppression of computer data, resulting in inauthentic data with the intent that it be considered or acted upon for legal purposes as if it were authentic, regardless whether or not the data is directly readable and intelligible. A Party may require an intent to defraud, or similar dishonest intent, before criminal liability attaches.

Article 8 – Computer-related fraud
Each Party shall adopt such legislative and other measures as may be necessary to establish as criminal offences under its domestic law, when committed intentionally and without right, the causing of a loss of property to another by:
a.   any input, alteration, deletion or suppression of computer data,
b.   any interference with the functioning of a computer system,
with fraudulent or dishonest intent of procuring, without right, an economic benefit for oneself or for another.

Title 3 – Content-related offences

Article 9 – Offences related to child pornography
1. Each Party shall adopt such legislative and other measures as may be necessary to establish as criminal offences under its domestic law, when committed intentionally and without right, the following conduct:
a.   producing child pornography for the purpose of its distribution through a computer system;

b.   offering or making available child pornography through a computer system;

c.   distributing or transmitting child pornography through a computer system;

d.   procuring child pornography through a computer system for oneself or for another;

e.   possessing child pornography in a computer system or on a computer-data storage medium.

2. For the purpose of paragraph 1 above "child pornography" shall include pornographic material that visually depicts:

a.   a minor engaged in sexually explicit conduct;

b.   a person appearing to be a minor engaged in sexually explicit conduct;

c.   realistic images representing a minor engaged in sexually explicit conduct.

3. For the purpose of paragraph 2 above, the term "minor" shall include all persons under 18 years of age. A Party may, however, require a lower age-limit, which shall be not less than 16 years.

4. Each Party may reserve the right not to apply, in whole or in part, paragraph 1(d) and 1(e), and 2(b) and 2(c).

*Title 4 – Offences related to infringements of copyright
and related rights*

Article 10 – Offences related to infringements of copyright and related rights

1. Each Party shall adopt such legislative and other measures as may be necessary to establish as criminal offences under its domestic law the infringement of copyright, as defined under the law of that Party pursuant to the obligations it has undertaken under the Paris Act of 24 July 1971 of the Bern Convention for the Protection of Literary and Artistic Works, the Agreement on Trade-Related Aspects of Intellectual Property Rights and the WIPO Copyright Treaty, with the exception of any moral rights conferred by such Conventions, where such acts are committed wilfully, on a commercial scale and by means of a computer system.

2. Each Party shall adopt such legislative and other measures as may be necessary to establish as criminal offences under its domestic law the infringement of related rights, as defined under the law of that Party, pursuant to the obligations it has undertaken under the International Convention for the Protection of Performers, Producers of Phonograms and Broadcasting Organisations done in Rome (Rome Convention), the Agreement on Trade-Related Aspects of Intellectual Property Rights and the WIPO Performances and Phonograms Treaty, with the exception of any moral rights conferred by such Conventions, where such acts are committed wilfully, on a commercial scale and by means of a computer system.

3. A Party may reserve the right not to impose criminal liability under paragraphs 1 and 2 of this article in limited circumstances, provided that other effective remedies are available and that such reservation does not derogate from the Party's international obligations set forth in the international instruments referred to in paragraphs 1 and 2 of this article.

Title 5 – Ancillary liability and sanctions

Article 11 – Attempt and aiding or abetting

1. Each Party shall adopt such legislative and other measures as may be necessary to establish as criminal offences under its domestic law, when committed intentionally, aiding or abetting the commission of any of the offences established in accordance with Articles 2 – 10 of the present Convention with intent that such offence be committed.

2. Each Party shall adopt such legislative and other measures as may be necessary to establish as criminal offences under its domestic law, when committed intentionally, an attempt to commit any of the offences established in accordance with Articles 3 through 5, 7, 8, 9 (1) a and 9 (1) c of this Convention.

3. Each Party may reserve the right not to apply, in whole or in part, paragraph 2 of this article.

Article 12 – Corporate liability

1. Each Party shall adopt such legislative and other measures as may be necessary to ensure that a legal person can be held liable for a criminal offence established in accordance with this Convention, committed for its benefit by any natural person, acting either individually or as part of an organ of the legal person, who has a leading position within the legal person, based on:

a.   a power of representation of the legal person;

b.   an authority to take decisions on behalf of the legal person;

c.   an authority to exercise control within the legal person.

2. Apart from the cases already provided for in paragraph 1, each Party shall take the measures necessary to ensure that a legal person can be held liable where the lack of supervision or control by a natural person referred to in paragraph 1 has made possible the commission of a criminal offence established in accordance with this Convention for the benefit of that legal person by a natural person acting under its authority.

3. Subject to the legal principles of the Party, the liability of a legal person may be criminal, civil or administrative.

4. Such liability shall be without prejudice to the criminal liability of the natural persons who have committed the offence.

Article 13 – Sanctions and measures

1. Each Party shall adopt such legislative and other measures as may be necessary to ensure that the criminal offences established in accordance with Articles 2 – 11 are punishable by effective, proportionate and dissuasive sanctions, which include deprivation of liberty.

2. Each Party shall ensure that legal persons held liable in accordance with Article 12 shall be subject to effective, proportionate and dissuasive criminal or non-criminal sanctions or measures, including monetary sanctions.

Section 2 – Procedural law

Title 1 – Common provisions

Article 14 – Scope of procedural provisions

1. Each Party shall adopt such legislative and other measures as may be necessary to establish the powers and procedures provided for in this Section for the purpose of specific criminal investigations or proceedings.

2. Except as specifically otherwise provided in Article 21, each Party shall apply the powers and procedures referred to in paragraph 1 to:

a.   the criminal offences established in accordance with articles 2-11 of this Convention;

b.   other criminal offences committed by means of a computer system; and

c.   the collection of evidence in electronic form of a criminal offence.

3.   a.   Each Party may reserve the right to apply the measures referred to in Article 20 only to offences or categories of offences specified in the reservation, provided that the range of such offences or categories of offences is not more restricted than the range of offences to which it applies the measures referred to in Article 21. Each Party shall consider restricting such a reservation to enable the broadest application of the measure referred to in Article 20.

b.   Where a Party, due to limitations in its legislation in force at the time of the adoption of the present Convention, is not able to apply the measures referred to in Articles 20 and 21 to communications being transmitted within a computer system of a service provider, which system

i.   is being operated for the benefit of a closed group of users, and

ii.   does not employ public communications networks and is not connected with another computer system, whether public or private,

that Party may reserve the right not to apply these measures to such communications. Each Party shall consider restricting such a reservation to enable the broadest application of the measures referred to in Articles 20 and 21.

Article 15 – Conditions and safeguards

1. Each Party shall ensure that the establishment, implementation and application of the powers and procedures provided for in this Section are subject to conditions and safeguards provided for under its domestic law, which shall provide for the adequate protection of human rights and liberties, including rights arising pursuant to obligations it has undertaken under the 1950 Council of Europe Convention for the Protection of Human Rights and Fundamental Freedoms, the 1966 United Nations International Covenant on Civil and Political Rights, and other applicable international human rights instruments, and which shall incorporate the principle of proportionality.

2. Such conditions and safeguards shall, as appropriate in view of the nature of the power or procedure concerned, inter alia, include judicial or other independent supervision, grounds justifying application, and limitation on the scope and the duration of such power or procedure.

3. To the extent that it is consistent with the public interest, in particular the sound administration of justice, a Party shall consider the impact of the powers and procedures in this Section upon the rights, responsibilities and legitimate interests of third parties.

Title 2 - Expedited preservation of stored computer data

Article 16 – Expedited preservation of stored computer data

1. Each Party shall adopt such legislative and other measures as may be necessary to enable its competent authorities to order or similarly obtain the expeditious preservation of specified computer data, including traffic data, that has been stored by means of a computer system, in particular where there are grounds to believe that the computer data is particularly vulnerable to loss or modification.

2. Where a Party gives effect to paragraph 1 above by means of an order to a person to preserve specified stored computer data in the person's possession or control, the Party shall adopt such legislative and other measures as may be necessary to oblige that person to preserve and maintain the integrity of that computer data for a period of time as long as necessary, up to a maximum of 90 days, to enable the competent authorities to seek its disclosure. A Party may provide for such an order to be subsequently renewed.

3. Each Party shall adopt such legislative or other measures as may be necessary to oblige the custodian or other person who is to preserve the computer data to keep confidential the undertaking of such procedures for the period of time provided for by its domestic law.

4. The powers and procedures referred to in this article shall be subject to Articles 14 and 15.

Article 17 – Expedited preservation and partial disclosure of traffic data

1. Each Party shall adopt, in respect of traffic data that is to be preserved under Article 16, such legislative and other measures as may be necessary to:

a.   ensure that such expeditious preservation of traffic data is available regardless of whether one or more service providers were involved in the transmission of that communication; and

b.   ensure the expeditious disclosure to the Party's competent authority, or a person designated by that authority, of a sufficient amount of traffic data to enable the Party to identify the service providers and the path through which the communication was transmitted.

2. The powers and procedures referred to in this article shall be subject to Articles 14 and 15.

Title 3 – Production order

Article 18 – Production order

1. Each Party shall adopt such legislative and other measures as may be necessary to empower its competent authorities to order:

a.   a person in its territory to submit specified computer data in that person's possession or control, which is stored in a computer system or a computer-data storage medium; and

b.   a service provider offering its services in the territory of the Party to submit subscriber information relating to such services in that service provider's possession or control;

2. The powers and procedures referred to in this article shall be subject to Articles 14 and 15.

3. For the purpose of this article, "subscriber information" means any information, contained in the form of computer data or any other form, that is held by a service provider, relating to subscribers of its services, other than traffic or content data, by which can be established:

a.   the type of the communication service used, the technical provisions taken thereto and the period of service;

b.   the subscriber's identity, postal or geographic address, telephone and other access number, billing and payment information, available on the basis of the service agreement or arrangement;

c.   any other information on the site of the installation of communication equipment available on the basis of the service agreement or arrangement.

Title 4 – Search and seizure of stored computer data

Article 19 – Search and seizure of stored computer data

1. Each Party shall adopt such legislative and other measures as may be necessary to empower its competent authorities to search or similarly access:

a.   a computer system or part of it and computer data stored therein; and

b.   computer-data storage medium in which computer data may be stored in its territory.

2. Each Party shall adopt such legislative and other measures as may be necessary to ensure that where its authorities search or similarly access a specific computer system or part of it, pursuant to paragraph 1 (a), and have grounds to believe that the data sought is stored in another computer system or part of it in its territory, and such data is lawfully accessible from or available to the initial system, such authorities shall be able to expeditiously extend the search or similar accessing to the other system.

3. Each Party shall adopt such legislative and other measures as may be necessary to empower its competent authorities to seize or similarly secure computer data accessed according to paragraphs 1 or 2. These measures shall include the power to :

a.   seize or similarly secure a computer system or part of it or a computer-data storage medium;

b.   make and retain a copy of those computer data;

c.   maintain the integrity of the relevant stored computer data; and

d.   render inaccessible or remove those computer data in the accessed computer system.

4. Each Party shall adopt such legislative and other measures as may be necessary to empower its competent authorities to order any person who has knowledge about the functioning of the computer system or measures applied to protect the computer data therein to provide, as is reasonable, the necessary information, to enable the undertaking of the measures referred to in paragraphs 1 and 2.

5. The powers and procedures referred to in this article shall be subject to Articles 14 and 15.

Title 5 – Real-time collection of computer data

Article 20 – Real-time collection of traffic data

1. Each Party shall adopt such legislative and other measures as may be necessary to empower its competent authorities to:

a.   collect or record through application of technical means on the territory of that Party, and

b.   compel a service provider, within its existing technical capability, to:

i. collect or record through application of technical means on the territory of that Party, or

ii. co-operate and assist the competent authorities in the collection or recording of,

traffic data, in real-time, associated with specified communications in its territory transmitted by means of a computer system.

2. Where a Party, due to the established principles of its domestic legal system, cannot adopt the measures referred to in paragraph 1 (a), it may instead adopt legislative and other measures as may be necessary to ensure the real-time collection or recording of traffic data associated with specified communications in its territory through application of technical means on that territory.

3. Each Party shall adopt such legislative and other measures as may be necessary to oblige a service provider to keep confidential the fact of and any information about the execution of any power provided for in this Article.

4. The powers and procedures referred to in this article shall be subject to Articles 14 and 15.

Article 21 – Interception of content data

1. Each Party shall adopt such legislative and other measures as may be necessary, in relation to a range of serious offences to be determined by domestic law, to empower its competent authorities to:

a.   collect or record through application of technical means on the territory of that Party, and

b.   compel a service provider, within its existing technical capability, to:

i.   collect or record through application of technical means on the territory of that Party, or

ii.   co-operate and assist the competent authorities in the collection or recording of,

content data, in real-time, of specified communications in its territory transmitted by means of a computer system.

2. Where a Party, due to the established principles of its domestic legal system, cannot adopt the measures referred to in paragraph 1 (a), it may instead adopt legislative and other measures as may be necessary to ensure the real-time collection or recording of content data of specified communications in its territory through application of technical means on that territory.

3. Each Party shall adopt such legislative and other measures as may be necessary to oblige a service provider to keep confidential the fact of and any information about the execution of any power provided for in this Article.

4. The powers and procedures referred to in this article shall be subject to Articles 14 and 15.

Section 3 – Jurisdiction
Article 22 – Jurisdiction

1. Each Party shall adopt such legislative and other measures as may be necessary to establish jurisdiction over any offence established in accordance with Articles 2 – 11 of this Convention, when the offence is committed :

a.   in its territory; or

b.   on board a ship flying the flag of that Party; or

c.   on board an aircraft registered under the laws of that Party; or

d.   by one of its nationals, if the offence is punishable under criminal law where it was committed or if the offence is committed outside the territorial jurisdiction of any State.

2. Each Party may reserve the right not to apply or to apply only in specific cases or conditions the jurisdiction rules laid down in paragraphs (1) b – (1) d of this article or any part thereof.

3. Each Party shall adopt such measures as may be necessary to establish jurisdiction over the offences referred to in Article 24, paragraph (1) of this Convention, in cases where an alleged offender is present in its territory and it does not extradite him/her to another Party, solely on the basis of his/her nationality, after a request for extradition.

4. This Convention does not exclude any criminal jurisdiction exercised in accordance with domestic law.

5. When more than one Party claims jurisdiction over an alleged offence established in accordance with this Convention, the Parties involved shall, where appropriate, consult with a view to determining the most appropriate jurisdiction for prosecution.

Chapter III – International co-operation
Section 1 – General principles

Title 1 – General principles relating to international co-operation

Article 23 – General principles relating to international co-operation

The Parties shall co-operate with each other, in accordance with the provisions of this chapter, and through application of relevant international instruments on international co-operation in criminal matters, arrangements agreed on the basis of uniform or reciprocal legislation, and domestic laws, to the widest extent possible for the purposes of investigations or proceedings concerning criminal offences related to computer systems and data, or for the collection of evidence in electronic form of a criminal offence.

Title 2 – Principles relating to extradition

Article 24 – Extradition

1.   a.   This article applies to extradition between Parties for the criminal offences established in accordance with Articles 2 – 11 of this Convention, provided that they are punishable under the laws of both Parties concerned by deprivation of liberty for a maximum period of at least one year, or by a more severe penalty.

     b.   Where a different minimum penalty is to be applied under an arrangement agreed on the basis of uniform or reciprocal legislation or an extradition treaty, including the European Convention on Extradition (ETS No. 24), applicable between two or more parties, the minimum penalty provided for under such arrangement or treaty shall apply.

2. The criminal offences described in paragraph 1 of this Article shall be deemed to be included as extraditable offences in any extradition treaty existing between or among the Parties. The Parties undertake to include such offences as extraditable offences in any extradition treaty to be concluded between or among them.

3. If a Party that makes extradition conditional on the existence of a treaty receives a request for extradition from another Party with which it does not have an extradition treaty, it may consider this Convention as the legal basis for extradition with respect to any criminal offence referred to in paragraph 1 of this article.

4. Parties that do not make extradition conditional on the existence of a treaty shall recognise the criminal offences referred to in paragraph 1 of this article as extraditable offences between themselves.

5. Extradition shall be subject to the conditions provided for by the law of the requested Party or by applicable extradition treaties, including the grounds on which the requested Party may refuse extradition.

6. If extradition for a criminal offence referred to in paragraph 1 of this article is refused solely on the basis of the nationality of the person sought, or because the requested Party deems that it has jurisdiction over the offence, the requested Party shall submit the case at the request of the requesting Party to its competent authorities for the purpose of prosecution and shall report the final outcome to the requesting Party in due course. Those authorities shall take their decision and conduct their investigations and proceedings in the same manner as in the case of any other offence of a comparable nature under the law of that Party.

7.   a.   Each Party shall, at the time of signature or when depositing its instrument of ratification, acceptance, approval or accession, communicate to the Secretary General of the Council of Europe the name and addresses of each authority responsible for the making to or receipt of a request for extradition or provisional arrest in the absence of a treaty.

b.   The Secretary General of the Council of Europe shall set up and keep updated a register of authorities so designated by the Parties. Each Party shall ensure that the details held on the register are correct at all times.

Title 3 – General principles relating to mutual assistance

Article 25 – General principles relating to mutual assistance

1. The Parties shall afford one another mutual assistance to the widest extent possible for the purpose of investigations or proceedings concerning criminal offences related to computer systems and data, or for the collection of evidence in electronic form of a criminal offence.

2. Each Party shall also adopt such legislative and other measures as may be necessary to carry out the obligations set forth in Articles 27 - 35.

3. Each Party may, in urgent circumstances, make requests for mutual assistance or communications related thereto by expedited means of communications, including fax or e-mail, to the extent that such means provide appropriate levels of security and authentication (including the use of encryption, where necessary), with formal confirmation to follow, where required by the requested Party. The requested Party shall accept and respond to the request by any such expedited means of communication.

4. Except as otherwise specifically provided in Articles in this Chapter, mutual assistance shall be subject to the conditions provided for by the law of the requested Party or by applicable mutual assistance treaties, including the grounds on which the requested Party may refuse co-operation. The requested Party shall not exercise the right to refuse mutual assistance in relation to the offences referred to in Articles 2 to 11 solely on the ground that the request concerns an offence which it considers a fiscal offence.

5. Where, in accordance with the provisions of this chapter, the requested Party is permitted to make mutual assistance conditional upon the existence of dual criminality, that condition shall be deemed fulfilled, irrespective of whether its laws place the offence within the same category of offence or denominates the offence by the same terminology as the requesting Party, if the conduct underlying the offence for which assistance is sought is a criminal offence under its laws.

Article 26 – Spontaneous information

1. A Party may, within the limits of its domestic law, without prior request, forward to another Party information obtained within the framework of its own investigations when it considers that the disclosure of such information might assist the receiving Party in initiating or carrying out investigations or proceedings concerning criminal offences established in accordance with this Convention or might lead to a request for co-operation by that Party under this chapter.

2. Prior to providing such information, the providing Party may request that it be kept confidential or used subject to conditions. If the receiving Party cannot comply with such request, it shall notify the providing Party, which shall then determine whether the information should nevertheless be provided. If the receiving Party accepts the information subject to the conditions, it shall be bound by them.

Title 4 – Procedures pertaining to mutual assistance requests in the absence of applicable international agreements

Article 27 – Procedures pertaining to mutual assistance requests in the absence of applicable international agreements

1. Where there is no mutual assistance treaty or arrangement on the basis of uniform or reciprocal legislation in force between the requesting and requested Parties, the provisions of

paragraphs 2 through 9 of this article shall apply. The provisions of this article shall not apply where such treaty, arrangement or legislation is available, unless the Parties concerned agree to apply any or all of the remainder of this article in lieu thereof.

2.   a.   Each Party shall designate a central authority or authorities that shall be responsible for sending and answering requests for mutual assistance, the execution of such requests, or the transmission of them to the authorities competent for their execution.

b.   The central authorities shall communicate directly with each other.

c.   Each Party shall, at the time of signature or when depositing its instrument of ratification, acceptance, approval or accession, communicate to the Secretary General of the Council of Europe the names and addresses of the authorities designated in pursuance of this paragraph.

d.   The Secretary General of the Council of Europe shall set up and keep updated a register of central authorities so designated by the Parties. Each Party shall ensure that the details held on the register are correct at all times.

3. Mutual assistance requests under this Article shall be executed in accordance with the procedures specified by the requesting Party except where incompatible with the law of the requested Party.

4. The requested Party may, in addition to grounds for refusal available under Article 25, paragraph (4), refuse assistance if:

a. the request concerns an offence which the requested Party considers a political offence or an offence connected with a political offence; or

b. it considers that execution of the request is likely to prejudice its sovereignty, security, *ordre public* or other essential interests.

5. The requested Party may postpone action on a request if such action would prejudice criminal investigations or proceedings conducted by its authorities.

6. Before refusing or postponing assistance, the requested Party shall, where appropriate after having consulted with the requesting Party, consider whether the request may be granted partially or subject to such conditions as it deems necessary.

7. The requested Party shall promptly inform the requesting Party of the outcome of the execution of a request for assistance. If the request is refused or postponed, reasons shall be given for the refusal or postponement. The requested Party shall also inform the requesting Party of any reasons that render impossible the execution of the request or are likely to delay it significantly.

8. The requesting Party may request that the requested Party keep confidential the fact and substance of any request made under this Chapter except to the extent necessary to execute the request. If the requested Party cannot comply with the request for confidentiality, it shall promptly inform the requesting Party, which shall then determine whether the request should nevertheless be executed.

9.   a.   In the event of urgency, requests for mutual assistance or communications related thereto may be sent directly by judicial authorities of the requesting Party to such authorities of the requested Party. In any such cases a copy shall be sent at the same time to the central authority of the requested Party through the central authority of the requesting Party.

b.   Any request or communication under this paragraph may be made through the International Criminal Police Organisation (Interpol).

c.   Where a request is made pursuant to subparagraph (a) and the authority is not competent to deal with the request, it shall refer the request to the competent national authority and inform directly the requesting Party that it has done so.

d.   Requests or communications made under this paragraph that do not involve coercive action may be directly transmitted by the competent authorities of the requesting Party to the competent authorities of the requested Party.

e.   Each Party may, at the time of signature or when depositing its instrument of ratification, acceptance, approval or accession inform the Secretary General of the Council of Europe that, for reasons of efficiency, requests made under this paragraph are to be addressed to its central authority.

Article 28 – Confidentiality and limitation on use

1. When there is no mutual assistance treaty or arrangement on the basis of uniform or reciprocal legislation in force between the requesting and the requested Parties, the provisions

of this article shall apply. The provisions of this article shall not apply where such treaty, arrangement or legislation, is available unless the Parties concerned agree to apply any or all of the remainder of this article in lieu thereof.

2. The requested Party may make the furnishing of information or material in response to a request dependent on the condition that it is:

a. kept confidential where the request for mutual legal assistance could not be complied with in the absence of such condition, or

b. not used for investigations or proceedings other than those stated in the request.

3. If the requesting Party cannot comply with a condition referred to in paragraph 2, it shall promptly inform the other Party, which shall then determine whether the information is nevertheless provided. When the requesting Party accepts the condition, it shall be bound by it.

4. Any Party that furnishes information or material subject to a condition referred to in paragraph 2 may require the other Party to explain, in relation to that condition, the use made of such information or material.

FRAUD RISK ASSESSMENT FRAMEWORK EXAMPLE

NOTE: This example is for illustrative purposes and focuses solely on potential revenue recognition risks within financial reporting. A full fraud risk assessment would consider fraudulent financial reporting in other areas relevant to the organization, such as accounts subject to estimation, related-party transactions, and inventory accounting. In addition, the risk of misappropriation of assets, corruption, and other misconduct would be assessed in the same manner.

Identified Fraud Risks and Schemes (1)	Likelihood (2)	Significance (3)	People and/or Department (4)	Existing Anti-fraud Controls (5)	Controls Effectiveness Assessment (6)	Residual Risks (7)	Fraud Risk Response (8)
Financial Reporting Revenue recognition • Backdating agreements	Reasonably possible	Material	Sales personnel	Controlled contract administration system	Tested by IA	N/A	Periodic testing by IA
• Channel stuffing	Remote	Insignificant	N/A	N/A	N/A	N/A	N/A
• Holding books open	Reasonably possible	Material	Accounting	Standard monthly close process	Tested by IA	Risk of management override	Testing of late journal entries
				Reconciliation of invoice register to general ledger	Tested by management		Cut off testing by IA
				Established procedures for shipping, invoicing, and revenue recognition	Tested by IA		
				Established process for consolidation	Tested by IA		

Identified Fraud Risks and Schemes (1)	Likelihood (2)	Significance (3)	People and/or Department (4)	Existing Anti-fraud Controls (5)	Controls Effectiveness Assessment (6)	Residual Risks (7)	Fraud Risk Response (8)
• Late shipments	Reasonably possible	Significant	Shipping dept.	Integrated shipping system, linked to invoicing and sales register Daily reconciliation of shipping log to invoice register Required management approval of manual invoices	Tested by IA Tested by management Tested by IA	Risk of management override	Cut off testing by IA
• Side letters/ agreements	Probable	Material	Sales personnel	Annual training of sales and finance personnel on revenue recognition practices Quarterly signed attestation of sales personnel concerning extra contractual agreements Internal audit confirming with customers that there are no other agreements, written or oral, that would modify the terms of the written agreement	Tested by management Tested by management	Risk of override	Disaggregated analysis of sales, sales returns, and adjustments by salesperson
• Inappropriate journal entries	Reasonably possible	Material	Accounting & Finance	Established process for consolidation Established, systematic access controls to the general ledger Standard monthly and quarterly journal entry log maintained. Review process in place for standard entries, and nonstandard entries subject to two levels of review	Tested by IA Tested by IA Tested by management	Risk of override	Data mining of journal entry population by IA for: • Unusual Dr/CR combinations • Late entries to accounts subject to estimation
• Roundtrip transactions	Remote	Insignificant	N/A	N/A	N/A	N/A	N/A
• Manipulation of bill and hold arrangements	Remote	Insignificant	N/A	N/A	N/A	N/A	N/A
• Early delivery of product	Reasonably possible	Significant	Sales and shipping	Systematic matching of sales order to shipping documentation; exception reports generated.	Tested by management	Adequately mitigated by controls	N/A
• Partial shipments	Reasonably possible	Significant	Sales and shipping	Systematic shipping documents manually checked against every shipment. Systematic matching of sales order to shipping documentation; exception reports generated. Customer approval of partial shipment required prior to revenue recognition.	Tested by management	Adequately mitigated by controls	N/A
• Additional revenue risks				Systematic shipping documents manually checked against every shipment.			

1. Identified Fraud Risks and Schemes: This column should include a full list of the potential fraud risks and schemes that may face the organization. This list will be different for different organizations and should be informed by (a) industry research, (b) interviews of employees and other stakeholders, (c) brainstorming sessions, and (d) activity on the whistleblower hotline.

2. Likelihood of Occurrence: To design an efficient fraud risk management program, it is important to assess the likelihood of the identified fraud risks so that the organization establishes proper anti-fraud controls for the risks that are deemed most likely. For purposes of the assessment, it should be adequate to evaluate the likelihood of risks as remote, reasonably possible, and probable.

3. Significance to the Organization: Quantitative and qualitative factors should be considered when assessing the significance of fraud risks to an organization. For example, certain fraud risks may only pose an immaterial direct financial risk to the organization, but could greatly impact its reputation, and therefore, would be deemed to be a more significant risk to the organization. For purposes of the assessment, it should be adequate to evaluate the significance of risks as immaterial, significant, and material.

4. People and/or Department Subject to the Risk: As fraud risks are identified and assessed, it is important to evaluate which people inside and outside the organization are subject to the risk. This knowledge will assist the organization in tailoring its fraud risk response, including establishing appropriate segregation of duties, proper review and approval chains of authority, and proactive fraud auditing procedures.

5. Existing Anti-fraud Internal Controls: Map pre-existing controls to the relevant fraud risks identified. Note that this occurs after fraud risks are identified and assessed for likelihood and significance. By progressing in this order, this framework intends for the organization to assess identified fraud risks on an inherent basis, without consideration of internal controls.

6. Assessment of Internal Controls Effectiveness: The organization should have a process in place to evaluate whether the identified controls are operating effectively and mitigating fraud risks as intended. Companies subject to the provisions of The U.S. Sarbanes-Oxley Act of 2002 Section 404 will have a process such as this in place. Organizations not subject to Sarbanes-Oxley should consider what review and monitoring procedures would be appropriate to implement to gain assurance that their internal control structure is operating as intended.

APPENDIX 4

7. Residual Risks: After consideration of the internal control structure, it may be determined that certain fraud risks may not be mitigated adequately due to several factors, including (a) properly designed controls are not in place to address certain fraud risks or (b) controls identified are not operating effectively. These residual risks should be evaluated by the organization in the development of the fraud risk response.

8. Fraud Risk Response: Residual risks should be evaluated by the organization and fraud risk responses should be designed to address such remaining risk. The fraud risk response could be one or a combination of the following: (a) implementing additional controls, (b) designing proactive fraud auditing techniques, and/or (c) reducing the risk by exiting the activity.

Adapted from *Managing the Business Risk of Fraud: A Practical Guide*, IIA, AICPA, ACFE; http://www.acfe.com/ documents/managing-business-risk.pdf, 2008, pp. 55-56.

5

FRAUD RISK EXPOSURE

NOTE: This appendix is a sample from another entity.[1] As such, no adjustment has been made to this material. The information may or may not agree with all the concepts noted within this paper. The material is being provided as an example that may be used as a tool, reference, or starting point.

The following illustrates the types of frauds an organization might encounter. This listing is not meant to be all-inclusive but to provide a starting point for an organization to identify which areas are vulnerable to fraud. More attention will be needed to identify specific industry, location, and cultural factors that can influence fraudulent behavior. Once identified, the fraud risk assessment framework shown in Appendix D could be used.[2]

1) Intentional manipulation of financial statements can lead to:
    a) Inappropriately reported revenues
        (1) Fictitious revenues
        (2) Premature revenue recognition
        (3) Contract revenue and expense recognition
    b) Inappropriately reported expenses
        (1) Period recognition of expenses
    c) Inappropriately reflected balance sheet amounts, including reserves
        (1) Improper asset valuation
            (a) Inventory
            (b) Accounts receivable
            (c) Mergers and acquisitions
            (d) Capitalization of intangible items
        (2) Misclassification of assets
        (3) Inappropriate depreciation methods

      (4) Concealed liabilities and expenses
         (a) Omission
         (b) Sales returns and allowances and warranties
         (c) Capitalization of expenses
         (d) Tax liability
    d) Inappropriately improved and/or masked disclosures
      (1) Liabilities omissions
      (2) Subsequent events
      (3) Related-party transactions
      (4) Accounting changes
      (5) Management frauds uncovered
      (6) Backdating transactions
    e) Concealing misappropriation of assets
    f) Concealing unauthorized receipts and expenditures
    g) Concealing unauthorized acquisition, disposition, and use of assets
2) Misappropriation of:
    a) Tangible assets by
      (1) Cash theft
         (a) Sales register manipulation
         (b) Skimming
         (c) Collection procedures
         (d) Understated sales
         (e) Theft of checks received
         (f) Check for currency substitution
         (g) Lapping accounts
         (h) False entries to sales account
         (i) Inventory padding
         (j) Theft of cash from register
         (k) Deposit lapping
      (l) Deposits in transit
      (2) Fraudulent disbursements
         (a) False refunds
         (b) False voids
         (c) Small disbursements
         (d) Check tampering
         (e) Billing schemes
         (f) Personal purchases with company funds
         (g) Returning merchandise for cash
      (3) Payroll fraud
         (a) Ghost employees
         (b) Falsified hours and salary
         (c) Commission sales
      (4) Expense reimbursement
         (a) Mischaracterized expenses
         (b) Overstated expenses
         (c) Fictitious expenses
         (d) Multiple reimbursements
      (5) Loans
         (a) Loans to nonexistent borrowers
         (b) Double pledged collateral
         (c) False application information
         (d) Construction loans

          (6) Real estate
               (a) Appraisal value
               (b) Fraudulent appraisal
          (7) Wire transfer
               (a) System password compromise
               (b) Forged authorizations
               (c) Unauthorized transfer account
               (d) ATM59
          (8) Check and credit card fraud
               (a) Counterfeiting checks
               (b) Check theft
               (c) Stop payment orders
               (d) Unauthorized or lost credit cards
               (e) Counterfeit credit cards
               (f) Mail theft
          (9) Insurance fraud
               (a) Dividend checks
               (b) Settlement checks
               (c) Premium
               (d) Fictitious payee
               (e) Fictitious death claim
               (f) Underwriting misrepresentation
               (g) Vehicle insurance — staged accidents
               (h) Inflated damages
               (i) Rental car fraud
        (10) Inventory
               (a) Misuse of inventory
               (b) Theft of inventory
               (c) Purchasing and receiving falsification
               (d) False shipments
               (e) Concealing inventory shrinkage
      b) Intangible assets
          (1) Theft of intellectual property
               (a) Espionage
               (b) Loss of information
               (c) Spying
               (d) Infiltration
               (e) Informants
               (f) Trash and waste disposal
               (g) Surveillance
          (2) Customers
          (3) Vendors
    c) Proprietary business opportunities
3) Corruption including:
    a) Bribery and gratuities to
          (1) Companies
          (2) Private individuals
          (3) Public officials 60
    b) Embezzlement
          (1) False accounting entries
          (2) Unauthorized withdrawals
          (3) Unauthorized disbursements
          (4) Paying personal expenses from bank funds

     (5) Unrecorded cash payments
     (6) Theft of physical property
     (7) Moving money from dormant accounts
   c) Receipt of bribes, kickbacks, and gratuities
     (1) Bid rigging
     (2) Kickbacks
       (a) Diverted business to vendors
       (b) Over billing
     (3) Illegal payments
       (a) Gifts
       (b) Travel
       (c) Entertainment
       (d) Loans
       (e) Credit card payments for personal items
       (f) Transfers for other than fair value
       (g) Favorable treatment
     (4) Conflicts of interest
       (a) Purchases
       (b) Sales
       (c) Business diversion
       (d) Resourcing
       (e) Financial disclosure of interest in vendors
       (f) Ownership interest in suppliers
  d) FCPA violations
     (1) Anti-bribery provisions
     (2) Books and records violations
     (3) Internal control weaknesses
  e) Money laundering
  f) Aiding and abetting fraud by other parties (customers, vendors)

    Adapted from Managing the Business Risk of Fraud: A Practical Guide, IIA, AICPA, ACFE; http://www.acfe.com/documents/managing-business-risk.pdf, 2008, pp. 57, 58, 59, 60.

[1] *The Fraud Risk Manual* issued by the ACFE, 2007.

[2] For a sample list of fraud schemes and potential controls to be installed to combat the fraud, see Appendix 8 of MANAGING THE RISK OF FRAUD: A GUIDE FOR MANAGERS by HM Treasury, in Appendix A of this paper.

6

FRAUD PREVENTION SCORECARD

To assess the strength of the organization's fraud prevention system, carefully assess each area below and score the area, factor, or consideration as:

- **Red:** indicating that the area, factor, or consideration needs substantial strengthening and improvement to bring fraud risk down to an acceptable level.
- **Yellow:** indicating that the area, factor, or consideration needs some strengthening and improvement to bring fraud risk down to an acceptable level.
- **Green:** indicating that the area, factor, or consideration is strong and fraud risk has been reduced — at least — to a minimally acceptable level.

Each area, factor, or consideration scored either red or yellow should have a note associated with it that describes the action plan for bringing it to green on the next scorecard.

Fraud Prevention Area, Factor, or Consideration	Score	Notes
Our organizational culture — tone at the top — is as strong as it can possibly be and establishes a zero-tolerance environment with respect to fraud.		
Our organization's top management consistently displays the appropriate attitude regarding fraud prevention and encourages free and open communication regarding ethical behavior.		
Our Code of Organizational Conduct has specific provisions that address and prohibit inappropriate relationships whereby members of our board or members of management could use their positions for personal gain or other inappropriate purposes.		

Fraud Prevention Area, Factor, or Consideration	Score	Notes
We have done a rigorous fraud risk assessment using the COSO Enterprise Risk Management–Integrated Framework and have taken specific actions to strengthen our prevention mechanisms as necessary.		
We have assessed fraud risk for our organization adequately based on evaluations of similar organizations in our industry, known frauds that have occurred in similar organizations, in-house fraud brainstorming, and periodic reassessments of risk.		
We have addressed the strengths and weaknesses of our internal control environment adequately and have taken specific steps to strengthen the internal control structure to help prevent the occurrences of fraud.		
Our organizational structure contains no unnecessary entities that might be used for inappropriate purposes or that might enable less-than-arms-length transactions or relationships.		
We have assessed all overseas and decentralized operations carefully and have taken proactive steps to ensure that they have fraud preventive controls in place to conform with the strictest legal standards and highest ethical principles.		
We have divested our organization of all unnecessary third-party and related-party relationships.		
For any remaining third-party and related-party relationships, we have taken positive measures to ensure that such relationships do not allow opportunities for frauds to occur without detection.		
We have assessed the alignment of authorities and responsibilities at all levels of organization management and are not aware of any misalignments that might represent vulnerabilities to fraud.		
Our audit committee has taken a very proactive posture with respect to fraud prevention.		
Our audit committee is composed only of independent directors and includes persons with financial accounting and reporting expertise.		
Our audit committee meets at least quarterly and devotes substantial time to assessing fraud risk and proactively implementing fraud preventive mechanisms.		
We have a strong internal audit department (if applicable) that functions independently of management. The charter of our internal audit department expressly states that the internal audit team will help prevent and detect fraud and misconduct.		
We have designated an individual with the authority and responsibility for overseeing and maintaining our fraud prevention programs, and have given this individual the resources needed to manage our fraud prevention programs effectively. This individual has direct access to the audit committee.		
Our human resources department conducts background investigations with the specific objective of assuring that persons with inappropriate records or characters inconsistent with our corporate culture and ethics are identified and eliminated from the hiring process.		
Our human resources department conducts background investigations with respect to promotions or transfers into positions of responsibility.		
Personnel involved in the financial reporting process have been assessed with regard to their competencies and integrity and have been found to be of the highest caliber.		

Fraud Prevention Area, Factor, or Consideration	Score	Notes
All of our employees, vendors, contractors, and business partners have been made aware of our zero-tolerance policies related to fraud and are aware of the appropriate steps to take in the event that any evidence of possible fraud comes to their attention.		
We have a rigorous program for communicating our fraud prevention policies and procedures to all employees, vendors, contractors, and business partners.		
We have policies and procedures in place for authorization and approvals of certain types of transactions and for certain values of transactions to help prevent and detect the occurrences of fraud.		
Our performance measurement and evaluation process includes an element specifically addressing ethics and integrity as well as adherence to the Code of Organizational Conduct.		
All new hires must undergo rigorous ethics and fraud awareness and fraud prevention training.		
All employees must attend periodic (at least annual) ethics and fraud awareness and fraud prevention training, and the effectiveness of this training is affirmed through testing.		
Terminated, resigning, or retiring employees participate in an exit interview process designed to identify potential fraud and vulnerabilities to fraud that may be taking place in our organization. A specific focus of these interviews is an assessment of management's integrity and adherence to the Code of Organizational Conduct. All concerns resulting from these interviews are communicated to our audit committee.		
We have an effective whistleblower protection program and fraud hotline in place, and its existence and procedures are known to all employees, vendors, contractors, and business partners.		
We review the above fraud preventive mechanisms on an ongoing basis and document these reviews as well as the communication with the audit committee regarding areas that need improvement.		
We have a fraud response plan in place and know how to respond if a fraud allegation is made. The fraud response plan considers: • Who should perform the investigation. • How the investigation should be performed. • When a voluntary disclosure to the government should be made. • How to determine the remedial action. • How to remedy control deficiencies identified. • How to administer disciplinary action.		

Adapted from *Managing the Business Risk of Fraud: A Practical Guide*, IIA, AICPA, ACFE; http://www.acfe.com/documents/managing-business-risk.pdf, 2008, pp. 61-64.

SAMPLE ENGAGEMENT LETTERS

Exhibit 70A-1

Sample Engagement Letter 1—Litigation Services

CPA & Company
Anytown, USA

September 4, 200X

John A. Smith, Esq.
Smith, Smith & Jones
100 Courthouse Way
Anytown, USA

Dear Mr. Smith:

You have asked me to read and analyze certain documents relating to a lawsuit brought against your client, XYZ Company. You have also asked that I be available to testify at the time of trial should you decide to use me as an expert witness. Any written reports or other documents that I prepare are to be used only for the purpose of this litigation and may not be published or used for any other purpose without my written consent.

Irrespective of the outcome of this matter, I understand that you will compensate me at my standard hourly rate (currently $____) for all time spent, including travel, whether or not the engagement is completed or its results are used. You will also compensate me for any out-of-pocket costs that I may incur. I will submit bills monthly, which are due and payable on receipt and in all events prior to the commencement of my testimony.

[*Optional sentence: Before commencing work on this engagement, I would like a retainer of $____ which will be applied to final billing on this engagement or refunded to the extent that it exceeds such billing.*]

Any controversy or claim arising out of or relating to this contract, or the breach thereof, shall be settled by binding arbitration, in [*insert desired venue*], in accordance with the Commercial Arbitration Rules of the American Arbitration Association, and judgment upon the award rendered by the arbitrator may be entered in any court having jurisdiction thereof.

I look forward to assisting you in this matter and hope that my services will be beneficial. If you approve of the engagement terms described above, I would appreciate your signing the enclosed copy of this letter and returning it to me.

Sincerely yours,   Accepted:

John Jones, CPA   Name of attorney's firm

Exhibit 70A-2

Sample Engagement Letter 2—Litigation Services
[Optional additions are bracketed]

CPA & Company
Anytown, USA

September 4, 200X

John A. Smith, Esq.
Smith, Smith & Jones
100 Courthouse Way
Anytown, USA

Dear Mr. Smith:

The purpose of this letter is to summarize our understanding of the assistance that CPA & Company will provide to you and your client, XYZ, Inc. in the matter of XYZ, Inc. v. ABC Corporation et al. before the Superior Court of the State of California, County of Los Angeles, which matter is Case. No. XXXXXX.

You have requested that we assist you with analysis and consultation with regard to the XYZ litigation matter as you may direct. I would also be prepared to provide testimony at deposition and trial should you decide that to be appropriate.

I will be responsible for the performance of our engagement with you and your client. My hourly billing rate is $XXX. From time to time, if necessary, other professionals may also assist when appropriate and needed. The hourly rates for our professionals are in the following ranges: Senior managers and managers — $XXX to $XXX; senior accountants and senior consultants — $XXX to $XXX; and consultants — $XXX to $XXX. [*Our hourly rates are subject to change from time to time. We will advise you immediately if the rates are being adjusted by our firm.*]

Fees for our services are based upon the actual time expended on the engagement at the standard hourly rates for the individuals assigned. In addition to our professional fees, we are reimbursed at cost for any travel and out-of-pocket expenses. Bills are rendered and are payable monthly as work progresses. [*We reserve the right to defer rendering further services until payment is received on past due invoices.*]

[*Our normal practice is to obtain a retainer, and we herewith request such a retainer in the amount of $XX,XXX. This retainer is not intended to represent an estimate of the total cost of the work to be performed. The retainer will be held against the final invoice for the engagement; any unused retainer will be refunded.*]

Sample Engagement Letter 3—Litigation Services

We are certain that you recognize that it is difficult to estimate the amount of time that this engagement may require. The time involved depends upon the extent and nature of available information, as well as the developments that may occur as work progresses. It is our intention to work closely with you to structure our work so that the appropriate personnel from our staff are assigned to the various tasks in order to keep fees at a minimum.

[*Furthermore, you, your client and I, all agree that any dispute over fees charged by our firm in this engagement will be submitted for resolution by arbitration in accordance with the rules of the American Arbitration Association. Such arbitration is limited only to the issue of fees charged and shall be binding and final. In agreeing to arbitration, we each acknowledge that in the event of a dispute over fees, each of us is giving up the right to have the dispute decided in a court of law before a judge or jury and instead are accepting the use of arbitration for resolution.*]

[*You or your law firm or the court itself will advise us (with sufficient notice) of the work to be performed by us and the requirement for appearance in court. If there is a substitution or change in the association of attorneys involved in this litigation, we reserve the right to withdraw from this engagement.*]

If the arrangements described in this letter are acceptable to you and the services outlined are in accordance with your requirements, please sign and return a copy of this letter. We look forward to working with you in this matter. If I can provide you with any additional information, please do not hesitate to call me at (555) 123-4567.

The proposed terms of this letter are subject to change if not accepted within 60 days of the date of this letter.

Very truly yours,

_____
(Name and Title)
CPA & Company

The services described in this letter are in accordance with our requirements and are acceptable to me and my client.

Accepted:

_____
John A. Smith, Esq.   Date
Smith, Smith & Jones

appendix

8

ProSystem fx® ActiveData™

We are pleased to provide access to the fraud-detection software, ProSystem fx ActiveData. ActiveData (AD) is a data mining program for extracting data from a financial accounting database, and it is useful in uncovering financial frauds. It is similar to IDEA and ACL, which are other data mining systems, but unlike those products, AD acts as a plug-in for MS Excel. As a result, data does not have to be imported into AD; although that feature is available. If the data can be recognized by MS Excel, it can be analyzed by AD. There are over 70 functions in AD that can be used to analyze and manipulate financial data.

To install the software, first go to: http://support.cch.com/updates/ActiveData/

From there, the application can be downloaded (in either 32-bit or 64-bit, depending on the version of Microsoft Office/Excel you are using) and installed as a custom tab within Excel. In order to verify which version of Office you have installed, simply open up a Word or Excel file. Then, depending on your version, you will need to look either under File -> Help (if you are in Office 2010 or newer, as highlighted in the screenshot below) or simply under Help -> About Microsoft Word/Excel (for older versions of Office):

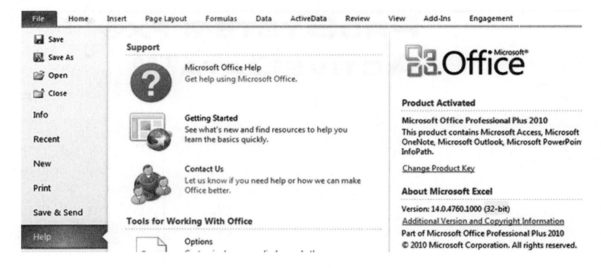

Once you have determined the version you need and have downloaded the appropriate one, run the downloaded file and it will install ActiveData as an Add-On to Excel. The application requires Excel 2003 or newer as well as the .NET 4.0 Framework and the installer will check for those requirements automatically.

Inside Excel, it looks like this below – note the ActiveData tab and the pop-up which is accessed from the Help menu showing the 30-day evaluation period:

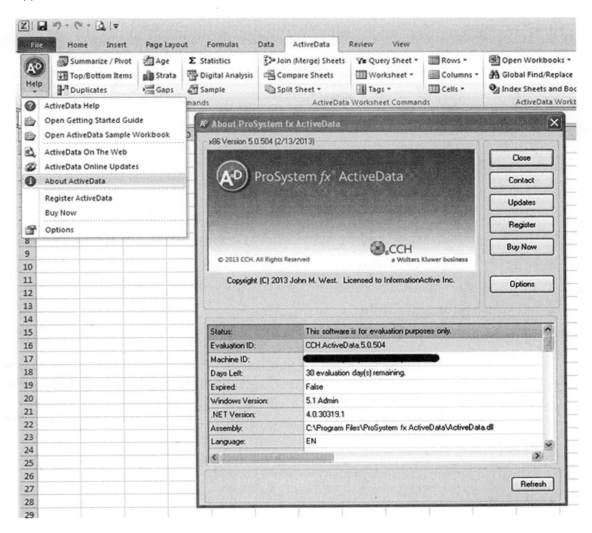

To unlock the software:
- Make sure that you have an internet connection and then start Excel
- Go to ActiveData -> Help -> Register ActiveData
- Click on the Get Registration Key button
- Enter your account # (999999) and software license # (10111445) in the obtain registration key dialog and then click the Get Key button
- Once you have the key, click the Register button
- You now have an unlocked version

If you are behind a firewall you may receive an error message. If this is the case, simply copy and paste the information in the bottom section of the screen into an email addressed to activedata@wolterskluwer.com. You will receive your key via email.

Unauthorized use of the test bank questions and answers, textbook solutions, Classroom Navigator and ProSystem fx ActiveData is prohibited. Please refer to License Agreement.

Help is just a phone call away!

If you'd prefer to talk directly to a support representative, please call Customer Support at 1-800-PFX-9998 (1-800-739-9998), option 6, followed by option 6.

Additionally, from within the Help menu, there are also two links to note – Open Getting Started Guide and Open ActiveData Sample Workbook – see the image below:

- The <u>Getting Started Guide</u> includes examples and instructions for the commands and references the <u>ActiveData Sample Workbook</u> so someone would be able to work with data hands-on while they are reading through the Getting Started Guide
- The overall <u>ActiveData Help</u> files also reference the Sample Workbook so there are lots of opportunities to learn the program through the Help menu

9

SAMPLE IDEA PROJECT

IDEA Payroll Project Introduction

Appendix 9 presents the step-by-step procedures for working with IDEA and two data files related to the Spotlight problem that follows the introduction to IDEA software, which is found in Chapter 13. To learn how to use IDEA and get started on the IDEA Project visit *www.caseware. com/IDEACDBook1*. The Tutorial is available to be downloaded at the install screen. If you experience problems with downloading the software or accessing the data files, you may contact: *ideasupport@caseware.com*. Appendix 9 instructs students on how to download data files from the caseware site that contain payroll information for over 700 employees. The payroll and human resources (HR) databases contain information on the employee's name, social security numbers, hire and termination dates, home address, payroll dates, pay rate, deduction percent, overtime hours, gross pay, dollar amount of total deductions (not each deduction), and net pay. The payroll and HR data for the IDEA fraud analysis is available as a zip file at: *http:// ideasupport.caseware.com/public/downloads/datafia.zip*. For assistance with download problems or data files you may contact *ideasupport@caseware.com*.

The zip file contains two Excel folders: (1)HR_Master.xlsx and (2) Payroll_Extract.xlsx. The step-by-step instructions in Appendix 9 explain how to use these files and where to save them on your computer. Please check the instruction under "Load Data" as to where to save these files. If you have an older computer, WinZip or 7-Zip (free) can be used to open a compressed zip file. As each of the databases on the website is an Excel file, you will also need MS Excel to open them.

IDEA can provide a check on these examples of payroll fraud. IDEA has the ability to review hundreds of payroll records for duplicate address, names, Social Security numbers, account deposits numbers, post office box addresses, suspicious overtime charges, and find ghost employees. Usually the implementation of these procedures begins after there is a fraud, a suspicion of fraud, or as a periodic check.

As you go through the procedures outlined in Appendix 9, it is important to try to determine if the reports provide any indication of possible payroll fraud and if they do what is the type of fraud that may be occurring.

Remember classroom versions of the software and a tutorial are available at: *http://www. caseware.com/IDEACDBook1*

Create a New Project

To facilitate housekeeping, it is recommended that a separate **Project** be used for each audit or investigation. All information relating to the audit, including data files, equations, views or report definitions, import definitions, etc. may be stored in the **Project**.

This exercise will explain how to create a **Project** and enter client information that will be printed on all reports. Note that once a **Project** is set, it remains the active folder until changed.

There are two alternatives when creating a new **Project**: **Managed Project** and **External Project.**

Managed Projects are stored in the following location on your computer: **C:\Users\[UserID]\ Documents\My IDEA Documents\IDEA Projects**

External Projects can be stored at other locations on your computer.

After creating a project you will see that IDEA has created the following project structure:

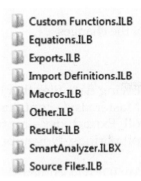

Custom Functions.ILB
Equations.ILB
Exports.ILB
Import Definitions.ILB
Macros.ILB
Other.ILB
Results.ILB
SmartAnalyzer.ILBX
Source Files.ILB

1. From the IDEA Ribbon, make sure the **Home** tab has been selected and then click
   Create.

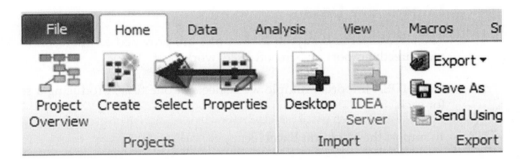

2. Select the **Managed project** option and enter **CCH Sample IDEA Project** as the
   Project Name.

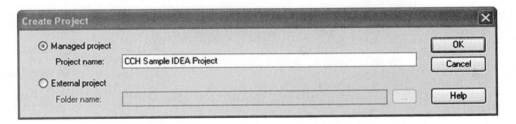

Once you click on **OK,** IDEA will create a new folder called:

C:\Users\[UserID]\Documents\My IDEA Documents\IDEA Projects\Sample IDEA Project

3. From the **Home** tab, in the **Projects** group, click **Properties** to change the **Project
   Properties**.
4. In the **Project Properties** dialog enter the following information:
   - **Report name:** Sample IDEA Project
   - **Report period:** Nov 16, 2012 – Dec 28, 2012

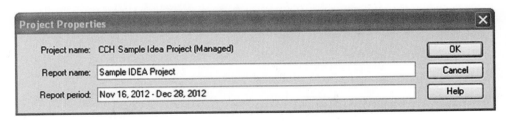

Click on **OK** to accept the changes.

Load Data

1. Copy the following data files that came with the Workbook:
   - HR_Master.xlsx – contains 201 employees
   - Payroll_Extract.xlsx – contains 774 records and consists of four by-weekly payroll periods. November 16, 2012 through December 28, 2012

to
C:\Users\[UserID]\My IDEA Documents\IDEA Projects\CCH Sample IDEA Project\Source Files.ILB

This is the default location within a Project to store any source files.

Import the Data

The HR Master and Payroll Extract files are provided as Microsoft Excel worksheets. IDEA will directly import a Microsoft Excel worksheet.

Note: IDEA imports multiple worksheets at one time, producing a separate IDEA database for each.

To import the Microsoft Excel file:

1. From the **Home** tab, in the **Import** group, click **Desktop**.

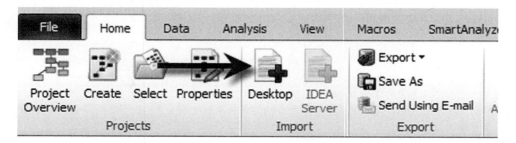

2. Select **Microsoft Excel** and click the **Browse** button to navigate to and select the file.

3. Select **C:\Users\[UserID]\Documents\My IDEA Documents\IDEA Project\ CCH Sample IDEA Project\Source Files.ILB\HR_Master.xlsx.**

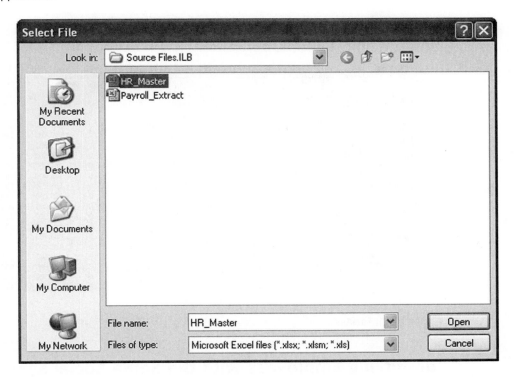

4. Click **Next**.
5. The **Import Assistant** will display a preview of the data and a list of any worksheets defined within the file. Select the **HR_Master** worksheet in the **Select sheets to import** box.
6. Select the **First row is field names** option. In the **Output file name** box, accept the default file name.
7. Click **OK**.

Note: IDEA will name the new database with the prefix that has been supplied during the import followed by the name of the worksheet. For this example, the new database will be called **HR_Master – HR_Master**.

The **HR_Master – HR_Master** database will be imported, opened, and selected as the active database.

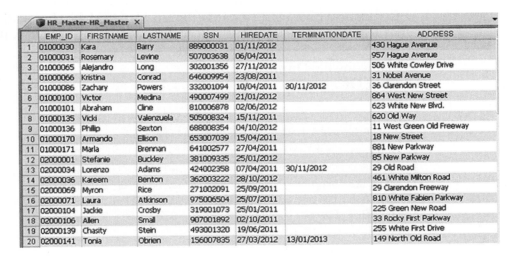

Follow the above steps to import the Payroll Extract file.

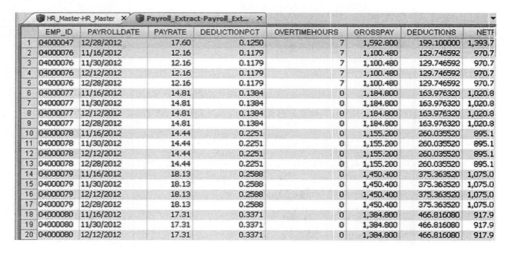

Close all databases.

Identifying Employees with the Same Social Security Numbers

1. Open the **HR_Master** database.
2. From the **Analysis** tab, click **Duplicate Key** and then **Detection.**

3. There are two options for duplicate testing: **Output duplicate records** or **Output records without duplicates**. For this test, select **Output duplicate records** to get a database containing any records that are duplicated.
4. Consider which field or fields should be tested for duplication (a maximum of 8 fields may be selected). In this case, duplicate SS#s. Click the **Key** button and select **SSN – Ascending**. Click **OK**.
5. Name the file **Duplicate SSNs**.
6. Click **OK**.

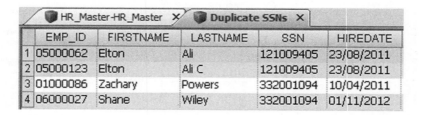

7. Close all databases.

Identifying Employees with the Same Telephone Numbers

1. Open the **HR_Master** database.
2. From the **Analysis** tab, click **Duplicate Key** and then **Detection.**
3. When the **Duplicate Key** Detection dialog box opens, select **Output duplicate records** to get a database containing any records that are duplicated.
4. Consider which field or fields should be tested for duplication (a maximum of 8 fields may be selected). In this case, duplicate telephone #s. Click the **Key** button and select **TELEPHONE - Ascending.** Click **OK.**

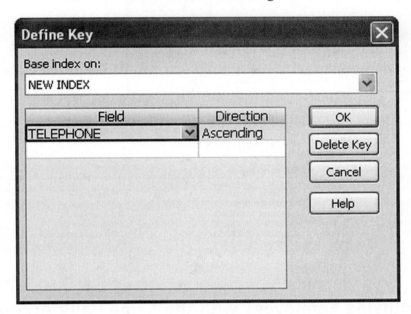

5. Name the file **Duplicate Telephone Nbr.**
6. Click **OK.**

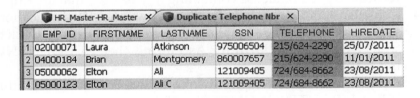

7. Close all databases.

Identifying Employees with the Same Address

1. Open the **HR_Master** database.
2. From the **Analysis** tab, click **Duplicate Key** and then **Detection.**
3. When the **Duplicate Key** Detection dialog box opens, select **Output duplicate records** to get a database containing any records that are duplicated.
4. Consider which field or fields should be tested for duplication (a maximum of 8 fields may be selected). In this case, duplicate addresses. Click the **Key** button and select **ADDRESS – Ascending,** then **CITY – Ascending,** and then **STATE - Ascending.** Click **OK.**

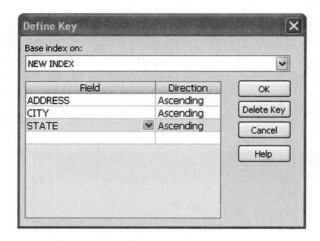

5. Name the file **Duplicate Address**.
6. Click **OK**.

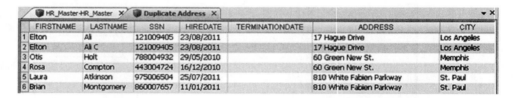

7. Close all databases.

Identifying Employees with the Same Bank Account

1. Open the **HR_Master** database.
2. From the **Analysis** tab, click **Duplicate Key** and then **Detection.**
3. When the **Duplicate Key** Detection dialog box opens, select **Output duplicate records** to get a database containing any records that are duplicated.
4. Consider which field or fields should be tested for duplication (a maximum of 8 fields may be selected). In this case, duplicate addresses. Click the **Key** button and select **ROUTINGNUMBER – Ascending**, then **ACCOUNTNUMBER – Ascending.** Click **OK**.
5. Add **Criteria** by clicking on the **Equation Editor** and inputting the formula "@ **ISBlank(ROUTINGNUMBER) = 0**".

6. Name the file **Duplicate Bank Account**.
7. Click **OK**.

8. Close all databases.

Identifying Employees without Deductions

1. Open the **HR_Master** database.
2. Select the **Direct Extraction** task by clicking on the relevant button on the **Analysis** tab.

The **Direct Extraction** dialog box appears.

3. In the **File Name** field, enter **Zero Deductions**
4. Click the **Equation Editor** button.

The Equation Editor will appear and is used to enter the required equation:

"DEDUCTIONPCT = 0".

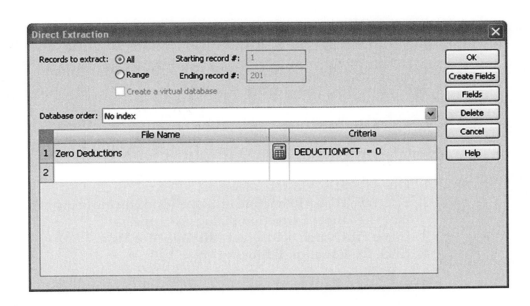

5. Click **OK**.

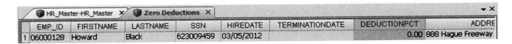

6. Close all databases.

Identifying Employees without or Incomplete Telephone Numbers

1. Open the **HR_Master** database.
2. Select the **Direct Extraction** task by clicking on the relevant button on the **Analysis** tab. The **Direct Extraction** dialog box appears.
3. In the **File Name** field, enter **Incomplete Telephone Nbr**
4. Click the **Equation Editor** button.

The Equation Editor will appear and is used to enter the required equation:

"@Len(TELEPHONE) < 12".

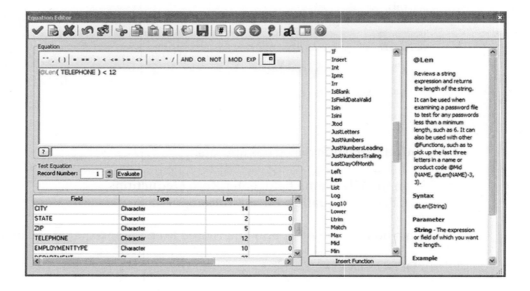

5. Click **OK**.

6. Close all databases.

Identifying Employees without a Hire Date

1. Open the **HR_Master** database.
2. Select the **Direct Extraction** task by clicking on the relevant button on the **Analysis** tab. The **Direct Extraction** dialog box appears.
3. In the **File Name** field, enter **Missing Hire Date**.
4. Click the **Equation Editor** button.

The Equation Editor will appear and is used to enter the required equation:
" HIREDATE = """.

5. Click **OK**.

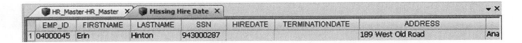

6. Close all databases.

Identifying Employees Having a PO Box for an Address

1. Open the **HR_Master** database.
2. From the **Data** tab, in the **Search** group, click **Search**.
3. Fill in the **Search dialog box** as follows:
   - Search: PO or P.O. or Box
   - Match case sensitivity: Do not check
   - Whole word: Do not check
   - Use advanced searching techniques: Check off
   - Fields to look in: "HR Master – ADDRESS"
   - Create an extraction database: Check off and name file **Employee Address is a PO Box**
4. Click **OK**.

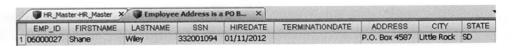

5. Close all databases.

Joining Payroll with HR Master

1. Open the **Payroll Extract** database.
2. From the **Analysis** tab, in the **Relate** group, click **Join**.

3. The **Join Databases** dialog box appears with the details of the **Primary database** in the top section.
4. Specify the **Secondary database** as follows: click **Select**. The **Select Database** dialog box appears. Select the **HR Master** database and then click **OK**.
5. Change the **File name** in the lower section of the **Join databases** dialog box to **Join Payroll with HR Master**.
6. Specify the common match key by clicking on **Match** to display the **Match Key Fields** dialog box.
7. Click the **Primary** text box and select **EMP ID** from the list of fields. Note the **Order** text box and accept the default, **Ascending**. Click the **Secondary** text box and select **EMP ID** from the list of fields. Click **OK**.

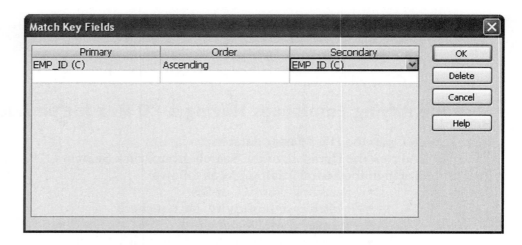

8. There are 5 join options at the bottom of the screen. Select the option: **Matches Only**.

The **Join Databases** dialog box should appear as in the screen below.

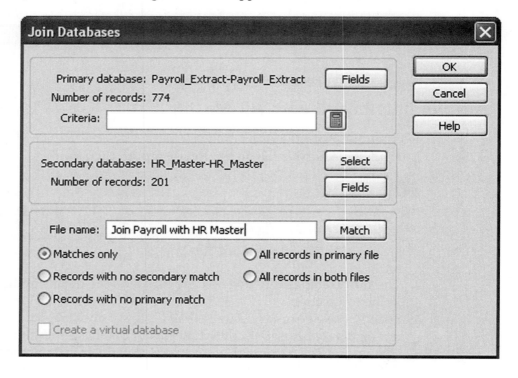

9. Click **OK**.

	EMP_ID	PAYROLLDATE	PAYRATE	DEDUCTIONPCT	OVERTIMEHOURS	GROSSPAY	DEDUCTIONS	NETF
1	01000030	11/16/2012	17.70	0.1890	0	1,416.000	267.624000	1,148.3
2	01000030	11/30/2012	17.70	0.1890	0	1,416.000	267.624000	1,148.3
3	01000030	12/12/2012	17.70	0.1890	0	1,416.000	267.624000	1,148.3
4	01000030	12/28/2012	17.70	0.1890	0	1,416.000	267.624000	1,148.3
5	01000031	11/16/2012	19.87	0.1889	0	1,589.600	300.275440	1,289.3
6	01000031	11/30/2012	19.87	0.1889	0	1,589.600	300.275440	1,289.3
7	01000031	12/12/2012	19.87	0.1889	0	1,589.600	300.275440	1,289.3
8	01000031	12/28/2012	19.87	0.1889	0	1,589.600	300.275440	1,289.3
9	01000065	11/16/2012	15.80	0.1201	0	1,264.000	151.806400	1,112.1
10	01000065	11/30/2012	15.80	0.1201	0	1,264.000	151.806400	1,112.1

10. Close all databases.

Identifying Exempt Employees with Overtime

1. Open the **Join Payroll with HR Master** database.
2. Select the **Direct Extraction** task by clicking on the relevant button on the **Analysis** tab. The **Direct Extraction** dialog box appears.
3. In the **File Name** field, enter **Exempt Employees Receiving Non-Exempt Pay**.
4. Click the **Equation Editor** button.

The Equation Editor will appear and is used to enter the required equation:
"EMPLOYMENTTYPE = "Exempt" .AND. OVERTIMEHOURS > 0"

5. Click **OK**.

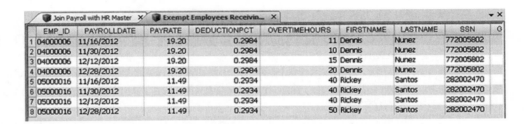

6. Close all databases.

Identifying Employees Where the Payroll Date is Post Termination Date

1. Open the **Join Payroll with HR Master** database.
2. First we have to make sure our date fields have the same field type. Since TERMINATIONDATE is a character field, we need to append it to a Date field to match the PAYROLLDATE.
3. Double-click anywhere on the database to open the **Field Manipulation dialog box**. Change the field type of **TERMINATIONDATE** to **Date** with a mask of **"DD/MM/YYYY"**.

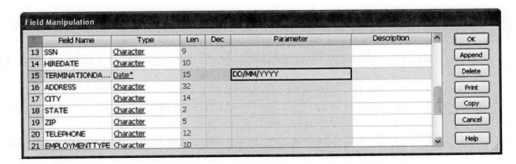

4. Now we can proceed with the extraction. Select the **Direct Extraction** task by clicking on the relevant button on the **Analysis** tab. The **Direct Extraction** dialog box appears.
5. In the **File Name** field, enter **Employee Payment after Termination**.
6. Click the **Equation Editor** button.

The Equation Editor will appear and is used to enter the required equation:

"@Dtoc(TERMINATIONDATE , "DD/MM/YYYY") <> "00/00/0000" .AND. PAYROLLDATE > TERMINATIONDATE".

7. Click **OK**.

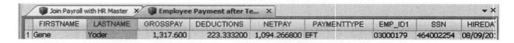

8. Close all databases.

Consolidating Indicators with Multiple Results per Employee

1. Open the **Exempt Employees Receiving Non-Exempt Pay** database.
2. First we need to append the field type of the TERMINATIONDATE from Character to Date.
3. Double-click anywhere on the database to open the **Field Manipulation dialog box**. Change the field type of **TERMINATIONDATE** to **Date** with a mask of **"DD/MM/YYYY"**.
4. Now we can proceed to Appending this database with the **Employee Payment after Termination** database.
5. From the **Analysis** tab, in the **Relate** group, click **Append**.
6. The **Append Databases dialog box** opens. Name the file: **Multiple Results per Employee** and select **Employee Payment after Termination** from the Desktop Project list and then click **add.** Click **OK**.

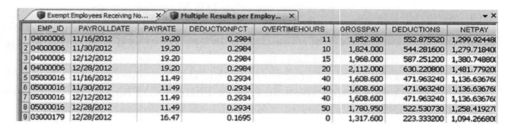

7. Close all databases.

Summarizing the Multiple Results per Employee Database

1. Open the **Multiple Results per Employee** database.
2. From the **Analysis** tab, in the **Categorize** group, click **Summarization**.
3. In the **Fields to summarize** area, select **EMP_ID**.
4. Accept the option to **Create database**, but do **not** check **Create result** (i.e., report). Name the file: **Multiple Results per Employee Summarization** and then click **OK**.

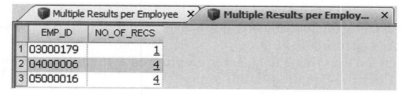

5. View the resultant database and note the **NO_OF_RECS** field (i.e., number of results per employee).
6. You can view the individual results per employee by clicking on the **NO_OF_RECS**.

10

Tallahassee Bean Counter Problem: IDEA Interactive Exercise

TBC II – Audit of Concessions

OBTAINING THE DATA

Having thought about the possible audit tests the following data files have been made available for the audit of the concessions:

- Concessions Sold
- Perpetual Inventory

However, these documents may not be the only files required to complete the concessions audit. Additional information regarding this area can be obtained upon request of the client in a Microsoft Excel format.

A demo version of IDEA can be downloaded for free at: *www.caseware.com/IDEACDBook1* To learn how to use IDEA and get started on the IDEA Project the Tutorial is available to be downloaded at the install screen. If you have problems downloading the software or accessing the data files, you may contact *ideasupport@caseware.com*. Data files for the Tallahassee Bean Counter Problem are available as a zip file at: *http://ideasupport.caseware.com/public/downloads/datafia.zip*.

AUDIT SET-UP

In order to begin the audit of the Tallahassee Bean Counters concessions it will be necessary to set up a **Managed Project** to facilitate file management. Use the steps found on page 17 of the IDEA Version Nine Tutorial , which is available to be downloaded at the install screen at *www.caseware.com/IDEACDBook1*, as a reference for creating a **Managed Project** using the following information:

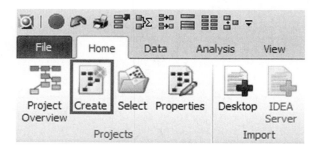

- **Project Name:** Concessions Audit

IMPORTING THE FILES

Prior to importing the necessary files it is important to ensure that the date format in the **Concessions Sold** file has been input properly. In the **Microsoft Excel** document ensure that dates are formatted as follows.

- June 5 should be input as June 05 (not June 5)

It is necessary to input the data in this format to allow IDEA to compare information across multiple databases. It is necessary to complete this step because IDEA does not insert zeros in non-numeric dates.

Next, follow the steps found on page 17 of the IDEA Version Nine Tutorial to import the **Concessions Sold** file into IDEA. Follow the specific steps below to ensure the files are correctly imported into IDEA:

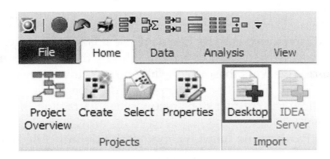

1. At the **Import Assistant** dialog box select **Microsoft Excel** and click the **Browse** button to navigate to and select the correct file.
2. Check off the "First row is field names" option.

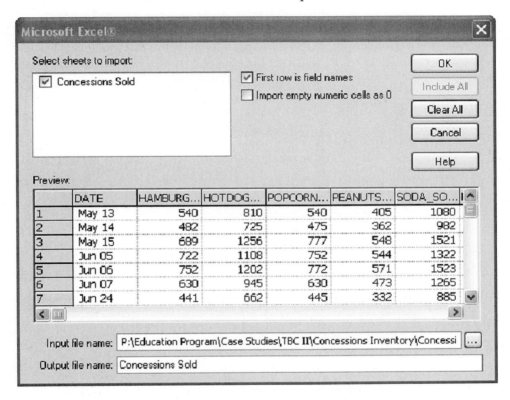

3. In the **Output file name** box ensure that **Concessions Sold** is displayed.
4. Next, follow the steps above to import the file **Perpetual Inventory** into IDEA. In the **Output file name** box, allow the default name.

	DATE	HAMBURGERS	HOTDOGS	POPCORN	PEANUTS	SODA	BEER	CONDIMENTS
1	5/1/2009	3500	4000	3000	3000	5500	2500	5000
2	5/13/2009	4960	6190	4460	3995	8420	3960	8500
3	5/14/2009	4478	5465	3985	3633	7438	3585	8500
4	5/15/2009	3789	4209	3208	3085	5917	2860	8500
5	5/31/2009	3389	3609	3208	3085	5317	2460	6500
6	6/5/2009	2667	2501	2456	2541	3995	1871	5000
7	6/6/2009	1915	1299	1684	1970	2472	1284	3500
8	6/7/2009	3785	3854	3554	2697	6207	3154	8000
9	6/24/2009	4844	5192	4609	3365	8322	4309	10000
10	6/25/2009	4548	4747	4311	3141	7730	4013	10000
11	6/26/2009	3988	3905	3749	2720	6606	3534	10000

EXTRACING THE INDIVIDUAL INVENTORY ITEM INFORMATION

Next, with **Perpetual Inventory** as the active database it is helpful to generate a separate database for each inventory item in order to facilitate joining the databases in later steps. For the purposes of this exercise we want to isolate the hamburgers inventory information in order to explain the functionality of IDEA. Use the steps found on pages 24 - 25 of the IDEA Version Nine Tutorial and follow the specific steps below when extracting the information for your databases:

1. At the **Direct Extractions** window change the default **File Name** provided from EXTRACTION1 to **Hamburgers Database**.
2. Next, click **Fields** to select the fields to extract located in the *Fields to Include* list.
3. First, click **Clear All** to deselect the *Fields to Include* list. Click DATE and HAMBURGERS in the *Fields to Include* list.

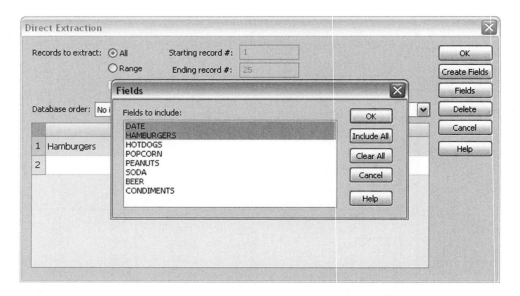

DETERMINE THE CHANGE IN INVENTORY ACCORDING TO THE PERPTUAL INVENTORY LIST

Ensure that the **Hamburgers Database** is the active database and use the steps found on pages 40-41 of the IDEA Version Nine Tutorial, found at the install screen, and the specific steps below to calculate the change in inventory levels from the previous date:

1. Prior to entering the equation below, ensure that the data is listed in the proper chronological order. Once this appended field is created the database cannot be sorted due to the nature of the equation.

2. Double-click to open the **Field Manipulation** window and click **Append** and enter the following details:
   a. **Field Name:** CHANGES_HB
   b. **Field Type:** Virtual Numeric
   c. **Field Length:** Do not enter
   d. **Decimals:** 0
   e. **Description:** The change in inventory level from the previous date.
3. Click the **Parameter** box to load the **Equation Editor** for building the equation. Enter the equation **HAMBURGERS-@GetPreviousValue("HAMBURGERS")**
   a. Note that this equation is case sensitive
   b. Starting at the first value for the specified field, the **@GetPreviousValue** function returns the preceding value.

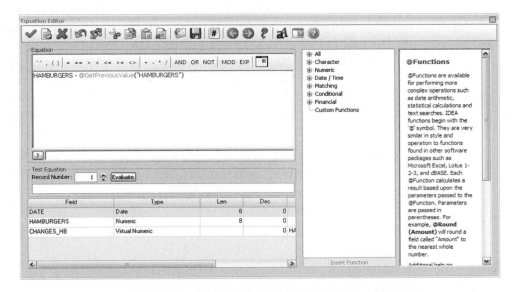

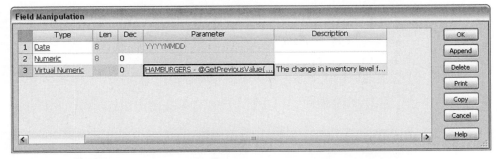

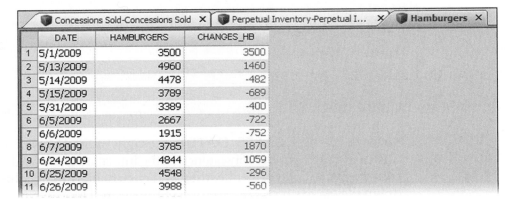

Close all of the database windows before proceeding to the next step.

ALTERING THE DATABASE TO ENABLE DATA EXTRACTION

Open the **Concessions Sold** database before proceeding with the audit testing of the Tallahassee Bean Counters concessions inventory. Use the steps found on pages 40-41 of the IDEA Version Nine Tutorial, available at the install screen, and the specific steps below to append the **DATE** column type from character to date.

1. At the **Field Manipulation** dialog box click **Append** and enter the following details:
    a. **Field Name:** SALES_DATE
    b. **Field Type:** Virtual Date
    c. **Field Length:** 8
    d. **Decimals:** 0
2. Click the **Parameter** box to load the **Equation Editor** for building the equation. Enter the equation **@Ctod(DATE + "2009", "MMM DDYYYY")**
    a. The function **@Ctod** converts a field containing dates stored as a Character field type to a Date field using the IDEA Date format (MMM DDYYYY)
    b. **DATE + "2009"** in this function will add the year 2009 to these fields
    c. The **"MMM DDYYYY"** is the **Mask**, which is the format the date is currently stored as. This **Mask** will return the date **May 13** as **5/13/2009**
    d. **Description:** Formatted sales date for joining databases

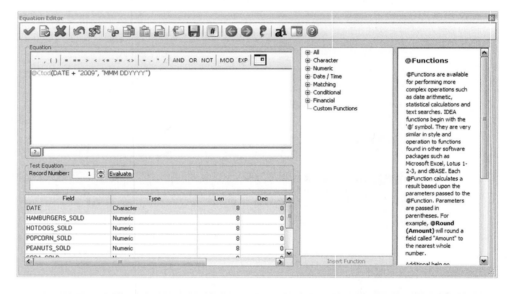

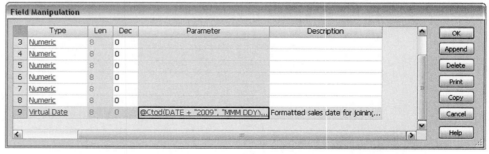

3. Move the column **SALES_DATE** to the right of the **DATE** field. Moving this column will help with the consistency of the information in the databases. To move a column, place cursor over heading and click to high-light column. While holding down the cursor, move the column to the desired location, noting that the column will be placed to the right of the red line.

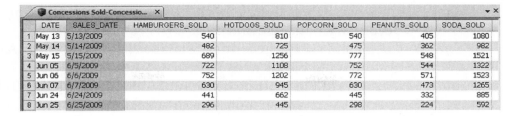

EXTRACTING THE HAMBURGERS SOLD INFORMATION

With the appended **Concessions Sold** database as the active database, use the steps found on pages 24 - 25 of the IDEA Version Nine Tutorial and the specific steps below when extracting the data for your databases:

1. At the **Direct Extractions** window change the default **File Name** provided from EXTRACTION1 to **Hamburgers Sold**.
2. Next, click **Fields** to select the fields to extract located in the *Fields to Include* list.
3. Click **Clear All** to deselect the *Fields to Include* list. Click SALES_DATE and HAMBURGERS_SOLD in the *Fields to Include* list.

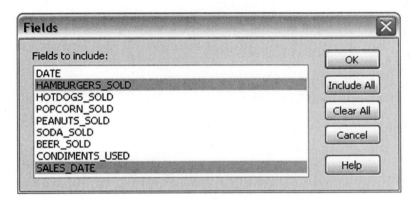

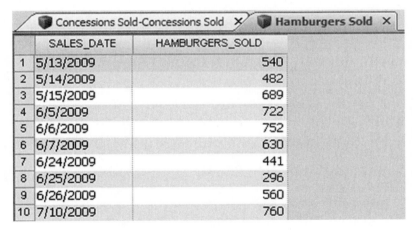

Close all of the database windows before proceeding to the next step.

JOIN THE DATABASES FOR COMPARISON

Use the steps found beginning at the bottom of page 36 - 37 of the IDEA Version Nine Tutorial and follow the specific steps listed below in order to complete this task:

1. Open the **Hamburgers Database**.
2. Click the **Join Databases** icon on the **Relate** section under the **Analysis** tab.

3. Click the **Select** button to choose the **Hamburgers Sold** database as the **Secondary database** and click **OK.**
4. Click **Fields** in the **Secondary Database** window, **Clear All** to deselect each option in the **Fields to include** list.
5. In the **Fields to include** list select **HAMBURGERS_SOLD** and click **OK**
6. Specify the common match key by clicking the **Match** button to display the **Match Key Fields** dialog box:
   a. Click the **Primary** text box and select **DATE** from the list of fields.
   b. Note the **Order** text box and accept the default, **Ascending.**
   c. Click the **Secondary** text box and select **SALES DATE** from the list of fields and the click **OK**
7. Select: **All records in primary file**
8. In the **File name** field, enter **Hamburgers Join Database**
9. Click **OK**

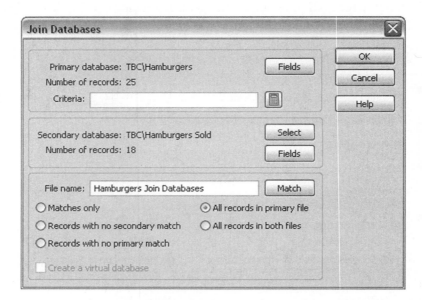

	DATE	HAMBURGERS	CHANGES_HB	HAMBURGERS_SOLD
1	5/1/2009	3500	3500	0
2	5/13/2009	4960	1460	540
3	5/14/2009	4478	-482	482
4	5/15/2009	3789	-689	689
5	5/31/2009	3389	-400	0
6	6/5/2009	2667	-722	722
7	6/6/2009	1915	-752	752
8	6/7/2009	3785	1870	630
9	6/24/2009	4844	1059	441
10	6/25/2009	4548	-296	296
11	6/26/2009	3988	-560	560
12	6/30/2009	3188	-800	0

CREATING THE COLUMNS MONTH & LAST DAY

Ensure **Hamburgers Join Database** is the active database and use the steps found on pages 40-41 of the IDEA Version Nine Tutorial and the specific steps below to create the column **MONTH** and **LAST_DAY**:

1. At the **Field Manipulation** dialog box click **Append** and enter the following details:
   a. **Field Name:** MONTH
   b. **Field Type:** Virtual Character
   c. **Field Length:** 3
   d. **Decimals:** 0
   e. **Description:** The corresponding month for the date
2. Click the **Parameter** box to load the **Equation Editor** for building the equation. Enter the equation **@Dtoc(DATE, "MMM")**
   a. Converts a Date field which is stored in Date format into a Character field with the format of the specified date mask. This is the reverse of **@Ctod**. **"MMM"** is the mask, which will be the formatting IDEA will use for the date.

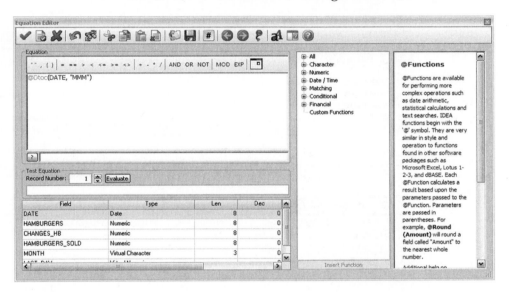

3. Click **Append** once more and enter the following details:
   a. **Field Name:** LAST_DAY
   b. **Field Type:** Virtual Numeric
   c. **Field Length:** Do not enter
   d. **Decimals:** 0
   e. **Description:** The last day for this month
4. Click the **Parameter** box to load the **Equation Editor** for building the equation. Enter the equation **@LastDayOfMonth(@Month(DATE), @Year(DATE))**
   a. The function **@LastDayOfMonth** returns the last day of a given month.
   b. The function **@Month** returns the month, in numeric format, from a date.
   c. The function **@Year** returns the year, in numeric format, from a date.

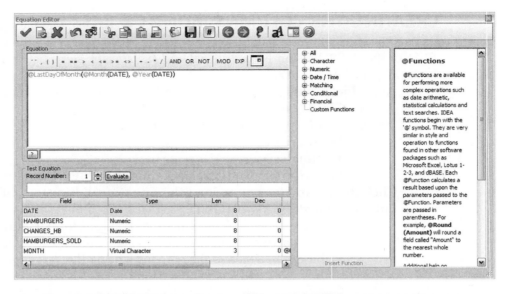

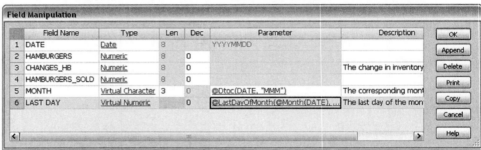

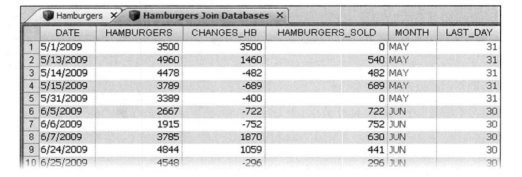

COMPLETING THE AUDIT

In order to finish the audit of the Tallahassee Bean Counters payroll there are additional documents and tests that must be completed. When using IDEA to complete this audit use the steps above as a guide to input and manipulate the data as necessary.

USEFUL RESOURCES

Use the following pages from the IDEA Version Nine Tutorial as a reference to aid in the completion of the audit for the Tallahassee Bean Counters:

- **Data Extraction:** pages 24 – 25
    - The formula @Day(DATE) = LAST_DAY may be useful when completing this operation.

TBC II – Audit of Construction Bids

OBTAINING THE DATA

Having thought about the possible audit tests the following data files have been made available for the audit of equipment purchases:

- Larkin Invoices September 30
- Change Order July
- Change Order August
- Change Order September

However, these documents may not be the only files required to complete the audit of construction bids. Additional information regarding this area can be obtained upon request of the client in a Microsoft Excel format.

AUDIT SET-UP

In order to begin the audit of the Tallahassee Bean Counters construction bids it will be necessary to set up a **Managed Project** to facilitate file management. Page 17 describes how to create a **Managed Project**.

To create a **Managed Project**, Select the **Create** icon in the menu ribbon at the top

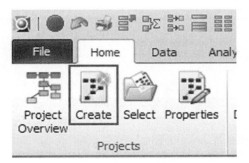

IMPORTING THE DATA FILES

Import the **Larkin Invoices** file into IDEA.

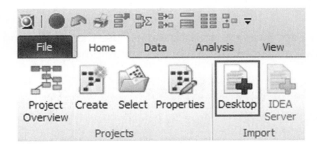

Follow the steps below to ensure you will import the files correctly:

1. At the **Import Assistant** dialog box select **Microsoft Excel** and click the **Browse** button to navigate to and select the correct file.
2. Check off the "First row is field names" and "Import empty numeric cells as 0" options.
3. In the **Output file name** box ensure that **Larkin Invoices Sept 30** is displayed.

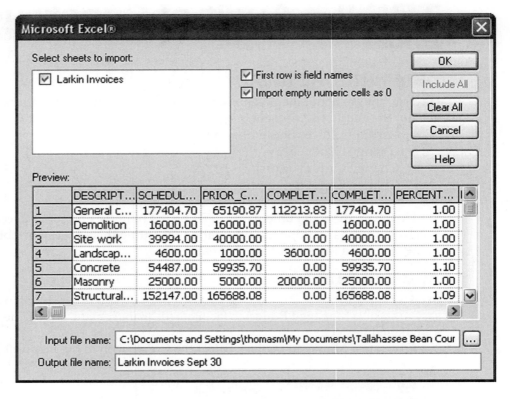

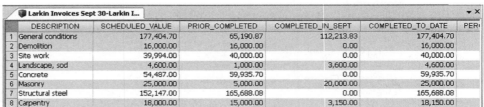

Next, follow the steps above to import **Change Order July, Change Order August** and **Change Order September** into IDEA. In the **Output file name** box, allow the default name for each file.

Close all of the database windows before proceeding to the next step.

EXTRACTING THE SCHEDULED VALUE INFORMATION

With **Larkin Invoices Sept 30** as the active database use the steps found on pages 24 – 25 of the IDEA Version Nine Tutorial as guide when extracting the data.

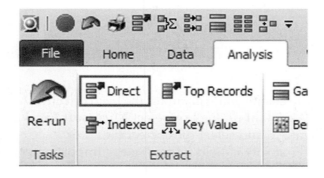

Follow the specific steps below when extracting the data:
1. At the **Direct Extractions** window change the default **File Name** provided from EXTRACTION1 to **Larkin Invoice Amounts**.
2. Next, click **Fields** to select the fields to extract located in the *Fields to Include* list.
3. Click **Clear All** to deselect the *Fields to Include* list. Click DESCRIPTION and SCHEDULED_VALUE in the *Fields to Include* list.

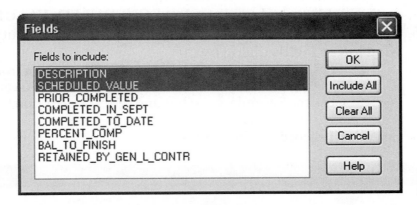

Close all databases.

Then, using the guidelines for data extraction outlined above, extract the change order amounts for July, August and September from each of the corresponding change order databases. Additionally, for each data extraction use the respective file name **Change Order July, Change Order August** and **Change Order September.**

Close all of the database windows before proceeding to the next step.

APPEND ALL DATABASES

Open **Larkin Invoice Amounts** and ensure this is the active database in order to join the file with the database **Change Order July**.

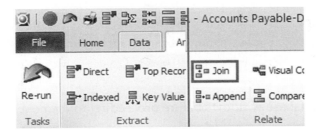

Follow the specific steps listed below in order to complete this task:
1. Click the **Join** icon under Relate in the **Analysis** tab.
2. Click the **Select** button to choose the **Change Order July** database as the **Secondary database** and click **OK.**
3. Click **Fields** in the **Secondary Database** window, **Clear All** to deselect each option in the **Fields to include** list.
4. In the **Fields to include** list select **SCHEDULED_VALUE** and click **OK**
5. Specify the common match key by clicking the **Match** button to display the **Match Key Fields** dialog box:
   a.   Click the **Primary** text box and select **Description** from the list of fields.
   b.   Note the **Order** text box and accept the default, **Ascending.**
   c.   Click the **Secondary** text box and select **Description** from the list of fields and the click **OK**
6. Select: **All records in both files**

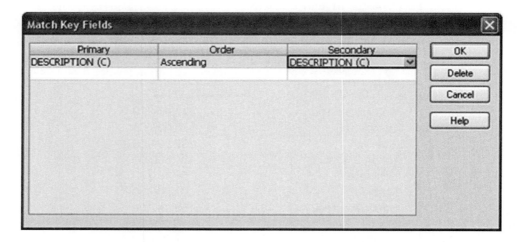

7. In the **File name** field, enter **Joined Invoices and Change Order July.**
8. Click **OK**

   While **Joined Invoices and Change Order July** is the active database, use the steps listed above to join this file with **Change Order August** and use the file name **Joined Invoices and Change Order August.** Then while the **Joined Invoices and Change Order August** is the active database, join this file with **Change Order September** and use the file name **Joined Invoices and All Change Orders.**

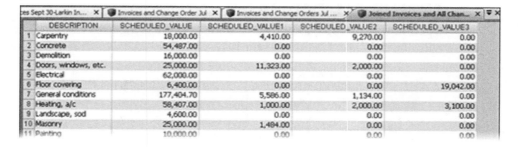

   Close all of the database windows before proceeding to the next step.

RENAMING THE COLUMN TITLES AND TOTALING CHANGE ORDERS

Open **Joined Invoices and All Change Orders** and ensure that this is the active database before proceeding with the audit testing of the Tallahassee Bean Counters construction bids. Use the steps below to change the field name **Scheduled_Value** to **Larkin Bid** and the July, August and September change order columns to **Change Order Jul, Change Order Aug** and **Change Order Sep**, respectively.

1. At the **Field Manipulation** dialog box change the following column field names.
   a. **SCHEDULED_VALUE:** LARKIN_BID
   b. **SCHEDULED_VALUE1:** CHG_ORDER_JUL
   c. **SCHEDULED_VALUE2:** CHG_ORDER_AUG
   d. **SCHEDULED_VALUE 3:** CHG_ORDER_SEP

Once the field names have been adjusted, append the column to add the field **TOT_CHG_ORDER.** Follow the specific steps below to append this column.

1. At the **Field Manipulation** dialog box click **Append** and enter the following details:
   a. **Field Name:** TOT_CHG_ORDER
   b. **Field Type:** Virtual Numeric
   c. **Field Length:** Do Not Enter
   d. **Decimals:** 0
   e. **Description:** Total change order amount for the corresponding item.
2. Click the **Parameter** box to load the **Equation Editor** for building the equation. Enter the equation **CHG_ORDER_JUL + CHG_ORDER_AUG + CHG_ORDER_SEP.**

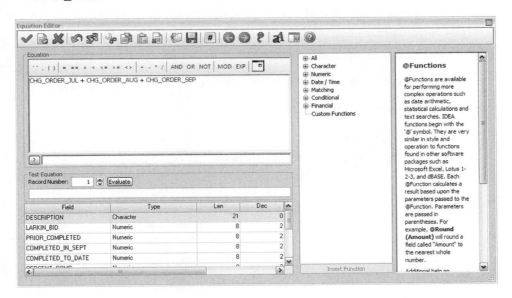

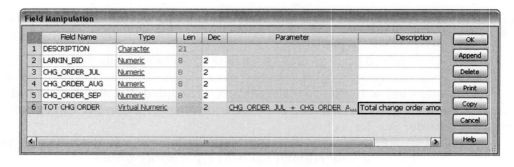

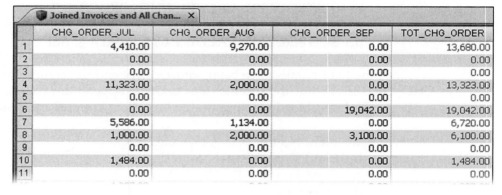

TOTALING THE COLUMN AMOUNTS

Once **Joined Invoices and All Change Orders** has been created and TOT_CHG_ORDER appended, view the total amounts listed for each column using **Field Statistics**. Use the steps found on pages 21 and 22 of the IDEA Version Nine Tutorial as guide when completing this task.

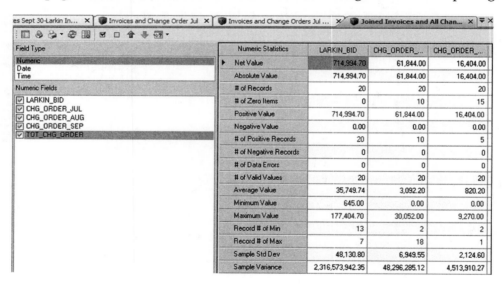

COMPLETING THE AUDIT

In order to finish the audit of the Tallahassee Bean Counters payroll there are additional documents and tests that must be completed. When using IDEA to complete this audit use the steps above as a guide to input and manipulate the data as necessary.

TBC II – Audit of Maintenance Account

OBTAINING THE DATA

Having thought about the possible audit tests the following data files have been made available for the audit of the maintenance account:

- Maintenance POs
- Maintenance Invoices

However, these documents may not be the only files required to complete the audit of the maintenance account. Additional information regarding this area can be obtained upon request of the client in a Microsoft Excel format.

AUDIT SET-UP

In order to begin the audit of the Tallahassee Bean Counters maintenance account will be necessary to set up a **Managed Project** to facilitate file management. Use the steps found on pages 17 of the IDEA Version Nine Tutorial as a reference for creating a **Project** using the following information:

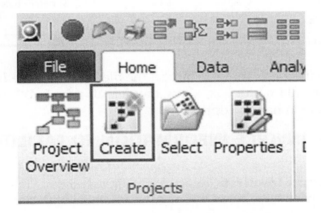

Project Name: Audit of the Maintenance Account

IMPORTING THE FILES

Next, follow the steps found on page 17 of the IDEA Version Nine Tutorial to import the **Maintenance POs** file into IDEA. Follow the steps below to ensure you will import the files correctly:

1. At the **Import Assistant** dialog box select **Microsoft Excel** and click the **Browse** button to navigate to and select the correct file.
2. Check off the "First row is field names" option.
3. In the **Output file name** box ensure that **Maintenance POs** is displayed.

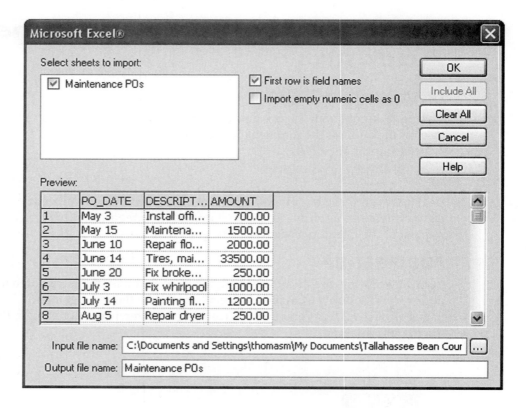

4. Next, follow the steps above to import the file **Maintenance Invoices** into IDEA. In the **Output file name** box, allow the default name. Be sure to check off the "First row is field names" option.

ALTERING THE INVOICE INFORMATION TO FACILITATE JOINING DATABASES

Ensure that **Maintenance Invoices** is the active database. Reference the steps found on pages 40-41 of the IDEA Version Nine Tutorial to adjust the number of Decimals in the **BILLED** column and append the database using the following information:

1. Click **Field Manipulation** and change the Decimals in the **BILLED** column from **0** to **2** and click **OK**.
2. Click **Field Manipulation** again and then click **Append** and enter the following details:
   a. **Field Name:** RECORD_NO
   b. **Field Type:** Editable Numeric
   c. **Field Length:** Do not enter
   d. **Decimals:** 0
   e. **Parameter:** 0
   f. **Description:** Record number used to facilitate joining databases

Once the **RECORD_NO** column has been created, move **RECORD_NO** to the right of the **DATE_COMPLETED** column. Editable columns make it possible to enter record numbers for each date. The creation of the **RECORD_NO** column will facilitate joining databases in a later step.

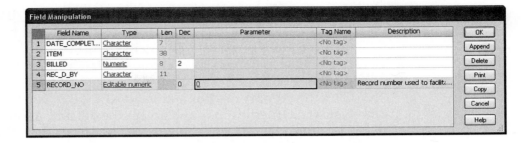

3. At the **Maintenance Invoices** database enter record numbers in ascending order for the dates listed in chronological order:
   a. **May 5:**   1
   b. **May 17:** 2
   c. **June 17:** 3
   d. **Sept 30:** 13

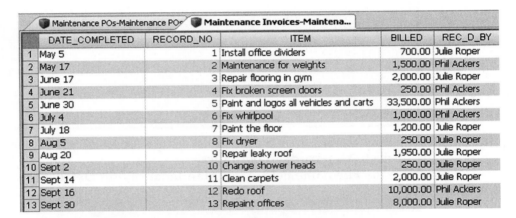

4. Open **Maintenance POs** and ensure this is the active database. Follow the steps described above to append the **Maintenance POs** database adding the column **RECORD_NO**. In ascending order input the record numbers with the corresponding chronological date as follows:
   a. **May 3:**   1
   b. **May 15:** 2
   c. **June 10:** 3
   d. **Sept 30:** 13

Close all of the database windows before proceeding to the next step.

JOINING INFORMATION FROM MULTIPLE DATABASES

Use the steps found beginning on pages 36-37 of the IDEA Version Nine Tutorial to complete the following test. Joining these databases will allow you to compare the purchase order amounts to the amounts listed on the invoice for each date. Additionally, follow the specific steps listed below in order to complete this task:

1. Open the **Maintenance POs** database.
2. Click the **Join Databases** icon on the **Operations** toolbar.
3. Click the **Select** button to choose the **Maintenance Invoices** database as the **Secondary database** and click **OK.**
4. Click **Fields** in the **Secondary Database** window, **Clear All** to deselect each option in the **Fields to include** list.

5. In the **Fields to include** list select BILLED and REC_D_BY and click **OK**
   a. This will allow for the comparison of the amount billed with amount invoiced and also show who received the invoice.
6. Specify the common match key by clicking the **Match** button to display the **Match Key Fields** dialog box:
   a. Click the **Primary** text box and select **RECORD_NO** from the list of fields.
   b. Note the **Order** text box and accept the default, **Ascending.**
   c. Click the **Secondary** text box and select **RECORD_NO** from the list of fields and the click **OK**

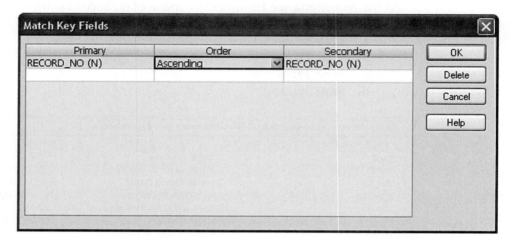

7. Select: **All records in both files**
8. In the **File name** field, enter **Maintenance Join Database**

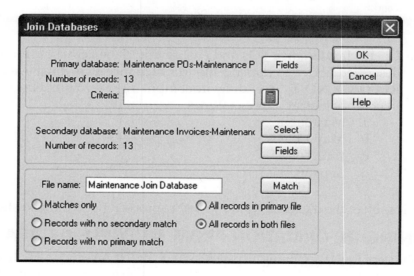

9. Click **OK**
10. Finally, click and drag the **RECORD_NO** column to the right of the **PO_DATE** column.

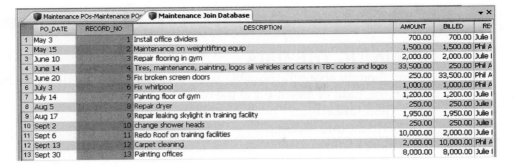

	PO_DATE	RECORD_NO	DESCRIPTION	AMOUNT	BILLED	RE
1	May 3	1	Install office dividers	700.00	700.00	Julie I
2	May 15	2	Maintenance on weightlifting equip	1,500.00	1,500.00	Phil A
3	June 10	3	Repair flooring in gym	2,000.00	2,000.00	Julie I
4	June 14	4	Tires, maintenance, painting, logos all vehicles and carts in TBC colors and logos	33,500.00	250.00	Phil A
5	June 20	5	Fix broken screen doors	250.00	33,500.00	Phil A
6	July 3	6	Fix whirlpool	1,000.00	1,000.00	Phil A
7	July 14	7	Painting floor of gym	1,200.00	1,200.00	Julie I
8	Aug 5	8	Repair dryer	250.00	250.00	Julie I
9	Aug 17	9	Repair leaking skylight in training facility	1,950.00	1,950.00	Julie I
10	Sept 2	10	change shower heads	250.00	250.00	Julie I
11	Sept 6	11	Redo Roof on training facilities	10,000.00	2,000.00	Julie I
12	Sept 13	12	Carpet cleaning	2,000.00	10,000.00	Phil A
13	Sept 30	13	Painting offices	8,000.00	8,000.00	Julie I

COMPLETING THE AUDIT

In order to finish the audit of the Tallahassee Bean Counters equipment purchases there are additional documents and tests that must be completed. When using IDEA to complete this audit use the steps above as a guide to input and manipulate the data as necessary.

TBC II – Audit of Revenue

OBTAINING THE DATA

Having thought about the possible audit tests the following data files have been made available for the audit of revenue and the related accounts:

- General Ledger
- Pricing Info Tickets
- Ticket Sales

However, these documents may not be the only files required to complete the audit of revenue. Additional information regarding this area can be obtained upon request of the client in a Microsoft Excel format.

AUDIT SET-UP

In order to begin the audit of the Tallahassee Bean Counters revenue it is necessary to set up a **Managed Project** to facilitate file management. Use the steps found on page 17 of the IDEA Version Nine Tutorial as a reference for creating a **Managed Project** using the following information:

- **Project Name:** Audit of Revenue

IMPORTING THE FILES

Prior to importing the necessary files it is important to ensure that the date format in the **Ticket Sales** file has been input properly. In the **Microsoft Excel** document ensure that dates are formatted as follows.

- June 5th should be input as June 05 (not June 5)

It is necessary to input the data in this format to allow IDEA to compare information across multiple databases. It is necessary to complete this step because IDEA does not insert zeros in non-numeric dates.

Next, follow import the **General Ledger** file into IDEA.

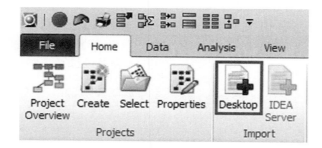

Follow the steps below to ensure you will import the files correctly:
1. At the **Import Assistant** dialog box select **Microsoft Excel** and click the **Browse** button to navigate to and select the correct file.
2. Check off the "First row is field names" and "Import empty numeric cells as 0" options.
3. In the **Output file name** box ensure that **General Ledger** is displayed.

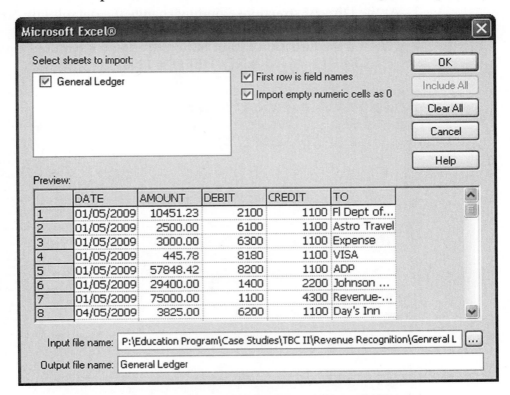

Next, follow the steps above to import the file **Pricing Info Tickets** and **Ticket Sales** into IDEA. *Be sure to check off "First row is field names" and "Import empty numeric cells as 0" options.* In the **Output file name** box, allow the default name for each file.

Close all of the database windows before proceeding to the next step.

EXTRACING THE ACCOUNTS RECEIVABLE INFORMATION

With the **General Ledger** as the active database it is helpful to generate a separate database for the entries debiting accounts receivable and debiting revenue. This extraction will allow you to focus on revenue and accounts receivable. Use the steps found on pages 24 - 25 of the IDEA Version Nine Tutorial as a guide when extracting the data. Follow the specific steps below when extracting the information for your database:

1. At the **Direct Extractions** window change the default **File Name** provided from EXTRACTION1 to **Accounts Receivable Entries.**
2. Click on the **Equation Editor** button to enter the required equation as follows:
   CREDIT = 4600 .AND. DEBIT = 1200

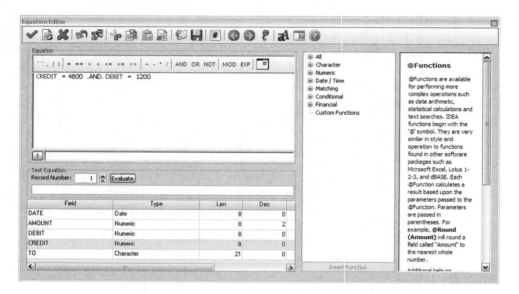

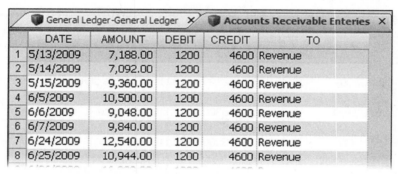

EXTRACTING THE TICKET SALES INFORMATION

With **Accounts Receivable Entries** as the active database use the steps found on pages 24 – 25 of the IDEA Version Nine Tutorial as guide when extracting the data. Extracting this data will make joining the database easier in a later step. Follow the specific steps below when extracting the data:

1. At the **Direct Extractions** window change the default **File Name** provided from EXTRACTION1 to **Sales Revenue Extraction**.
2. Next, click **Fields** to select the fields to extract located in the *Fields to Include* list.
3. Click **Clear All** to deselect the *Fields to Include* list. Click DATE and AMOUNT in the *Fields to Include* list.

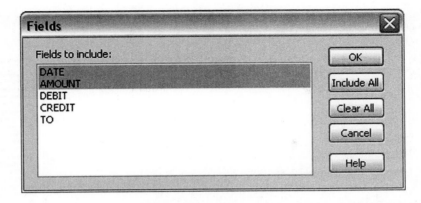

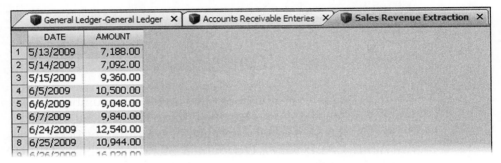

Close all of the database windows before proceeding to the next step.

CALCULATING THE TOTAL TICKET SALES REVENUE

Open the **Ticket Sales** file and ensure it is the active database. The next step will be to calculate the total ticket sales revenue for each ticket type using the **Ticket Sales** database and information found on the **Pricing Info Tickets** database. In addition to the steps listed below, at the **Field Manipulation** dialog box ensure that each of the various ticket types display the field type **Numeric.** Calculate the total ticket sales revenue for each ticket type by date using the following information:

1. At the **Field Manipulation** dialog box click **Append** and enter the following details:
    a. **Field Name:** STD_REV
    b. **Field Type:** Virtual Numeric
    c. **Field Length:** Do not enter
    d. **Parameter:** STANDARD_SEATS_SOLD * 12
    e. **Decimals:** 0
    f. **Description:** Total standard ticket sales revenue.

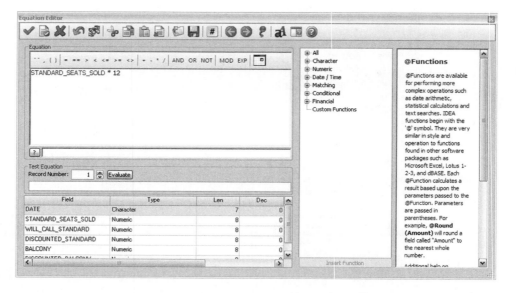

For this equation, the number following the total number of tickets sold will be the corresponding ticket price located on the **Pricing Info Tickets** database.

2. Repeat the above steps for each of the different ticket types: Will Call Standard (WILL_CALL_REV), Discounted Standard (DISC_STD_REV), Balcony (BALC_REV), and Discounted Balcony (DISC_BALC_REV).

For each ticket type click the **Parameter** box and enter an equation multiplying the total number of tickets sold by their corresponding sales price from the **Pricing Info Tickets**

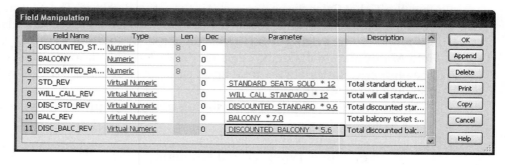

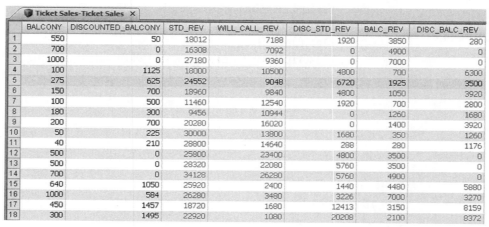

	BALCONY	DISCOUNTED_BALCONY	STD_REV	WILL_CALL_REV	DISC_STD_REV	BALC_REV	DISC_BALC_REV
1	550	50	18012	7188	1920	3850	280
2	700	0	16308	7092	0	4900	0
3	1000	0	27180	9360	0	7000	0
4	100	1125	18000	10500	4800	700	6300
5	275	625	24552	9048	6720	1925	3500
6	150	700	18960	9840	4800	1050	3920
7	100	500	11460	12540	1920	700	2800
8	180	300	9456	10944	0	1260	1680
9	200	700	20280	16020	0	1400	3920
10	50	225	30000	13800	1680	350	1260
11	40	210	28800	14640	288	280	1176
12	500	0	25800	23400	4800	3500	0
13	500	0	28320	22080	5760	3500	0
14	700	0	34128	26280	5760	4900	0
15	640	1050	25920	2400	1440	4480	5880
16	1000	584	26280	3480	3226	7000	3270
17	450	1457	18720	1680	12413	3150	8159
18	300	1495	22920	1080	20208	2100	8372

ALTERING THE DATABASE TO ENABLE DATA EXTRACTION

Ensure **Ticket Sales** is the active database before proceeding with the audit testing of the Tallahassee Bean Counters revenue. Use steps below to change the **DATE** column type from character to date.

1. At the **Field Manipulation** dialog box click **Append** and enter the following details:
   a. **Field Name:** SALES_DATE
   b. **Field Type:** Virtual Date
   c. **Field Length:** 8
   d. **Decimals:** 0
   e. **Description:** Formatted sales date for joining databases
2. Click the **Parameter** box to load the **Equation Editor** for building the equation. Enter the equation **@Ctod(DATE + "2009", "MMDDYYYY")**
   a. The function **@Ctod** coverts a field containing dates stored as a Character field type with the IDEA Date format (MMM DDYYYY)
   b. **DATE + "2009"** in this function will add the year 2009 to these fields
   c. **"MMDDYYYY"** is the **Mask**, which is the format the date is currently stored as. This **Mask** will return the date **May 13** as **5/13/2009**

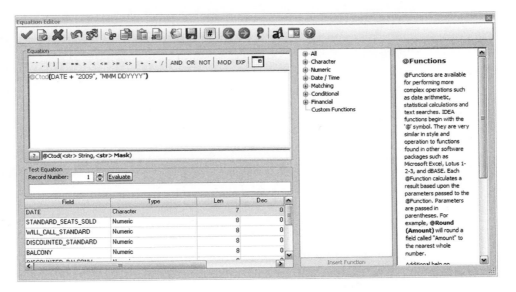

Move the column **SALES_DATE** to the right of the date field. Moving this column will help with the consistency of the information in the databases.

	DATE	SALES_DATE	STANDARD_SEATS_SOLD	WILL_CALL_STANDARD	DISCOUNTED_STANDARD	BALCONY	
1	May 13	5/13/2009	1501	599	200	550	
2	May 14	5/14/2009	1359	591	0	700	
3	May 15	5/15/2009	2265	780	0	1000	
4	Jun 05	6/5/2009	1500	875	500	100	
5	Jun 06	6/6/2009	2046	754	700	275	
6	Jun 07	6/7/2009	1580	820	500	150	
7	Jun 24	6/24/2009	955	1045	200	100	
8	Jun 25	6/25/2009	788	912	0	180	
9	Jun 26	6/26/2009	1690	1335	0	200	
10	Jul 10	7/10/2009	2500	1150	175	50	

Using the guidelines for data extraction outlined above, extract the will call sales revenue information and sales dates from the appended **Ticket Sales** database and create a file using the file name **Will Call Sales Revenue.**

Close all of the database windows before proceeding to the next step.

JOIN THE DATABASES FOR COMPARISON

Open **Sales Revenue Extraction** and ensure this is the active database in order to join the file with the **Will Call Sales Revenue** information. Use the steps found beginning at the bottom of pages 36 - 37 of the IDEA Version Nine Tutorial to complete the following test. Additionally, follow the specific steps listed below in order to complete this task:

1. On the **Analysis** tab, in the **Relate** group, click **Join**.
2. Click the **Select** button to choose the **Will Call Ticket Sales Revenue** database as the **Secondary database** and click **OK**.
3. Click **Fields** in the **Secondary Database** window, **Clear All** to deselect each option in the **Fields to include** list.
4. In the **Fields to include** list select WILL_CALL_REV and click **OK**
5. Specify the common match key by clicking the **Match** button to display the **Match Key Fields** dialog box:
    a. Click the **Primary** text box and select **DATE** from the list of fields.
    b. Note the **Order** text box and accept the default, **Ascending.**
    c. Click the **Secondary** text box and select **SALES_DATE** from the list of fields and the click **OK**

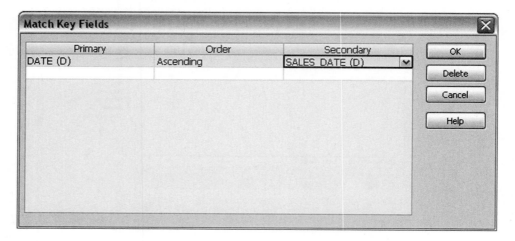

6. Select: **All records in both files**
7. In the **File name** field, enter **Ticket Revenue Join Database**
8. Click **OK**

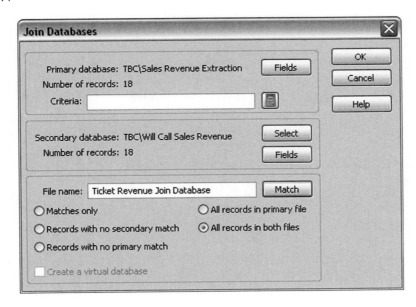

9. Next, double-click on the **DATE** column to display the database in ascending, chronological order.

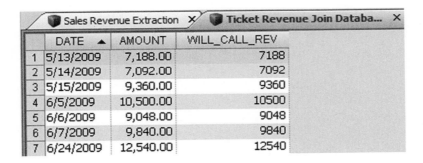

COMPLETING THE AUDIT

In order to finish the audit of the Tallahassee Bean Counters payroll there are additional documents and tests that must be completed. When using IDEA to complete this audit use the steps above as a guide to input and manipulate the data as necessary.

Glossary of Terms

A

Abusive earnings management.
According to the SEC, an intentional and material misrepresentation of results.

Ad hoc.
For a single particular or special purpose (e.g., an ad hoc commission).

Ad valorem.
According to value (e.g., tax assessment based on property value).

Adjusted book value method.
A method within the asset approach in which all assets and liabilities (off-balance sheet, intangible, and contingent) are adjusted to their fair market values (Note: In Canada on a going concern basis).

Adjusted net asset method. See Adjusted book value method.

Affirm (Aff'd; Aff'g).
To ratify or approve (e.g., to uphold a lower court's judgment).

Alter ego.
"Second self." Under the doctrine of alter ego, the owners of the corporation are held responsible for corporate acts, disregarding the corporate entity.

Amicus curiae.
A "friend of the court." A party who is not directly involved with a dispute and is allowed to file an amicus curiae brief on behalf of one of the parties.

Answer.
The formal response by a defendant to a plaintiff's complaint.

Appellant.
The party who makes an appeal to another court to review a lower court's decision.

Appraisal. See Valuation.

Appraisal approach. See Valuation approach.

Appraisal date. See Valuation date.

Appraisal method. See Valuation method.

Appraisal procedure. See Valuation procedure.

Arbitrage pricing theory.
A multivariate model for estimating the cost of equity capital, which incorporates several systematic risk factors.

Asset (asset-based) approach.
A general way of determining a value indication of a business, business ownership interest, or security using methods based on the value of the assets net of their liabilities.

Authentication.
The process of making a written document admissible as evidence.

B

Backdating stock options.
Management intentionally selects a pricing date that precedes the corporate action resulting in the employee stock option grant.

Benefit-of-the bargain rule.
A rule permitting a defrauded purchaser to recover the difference between the actual value received and what the purchaser expected to receive.

Best evidence rule.
The rule requiring that the best evidence available (i.e., an original document or object) be presented unless it is shown that the original has been lost, destroyed, or not subject to the jurisdiction of the court. Today, the application of the rule is influenced by practicality and governed by statutes.

Beta.
A measure of systematic risk of a stock price; the tendency of the stock's price to correlate with increases or declines in a specific index.

Bid rigging.
A scheme in which a vendor is given an unfair advantage in an open competition for a certain contract.

Bitcoins.
Digital coins are a form of encrypted currency, in a highly controlled market, and an alternative to national currencies. They can be exchanged for various national currencies., and its value is based on trades taking place in an online market.

Blockage discount.
An amount or percentage deducted from the current market price of a publicly traded stock, reflecting the lower per share value of a block of shares that is not of a size that could be sold in a reasonable period of time assuming normal trading volume.

Bona fide.
In good faith; without fraud or deceit.

Book value. See Net book value.

Bots.
(Shorthand for robots.) Electronic robots that act as agents for a person to help make decisions based on information the bots collect.

Business. See Business enterprise.

Business enterprise.
A commercial, industrial, service, or investment entity (or combination thereof) that pursues an economic activity.

Business risk.
The amount of uncertainty in realizing expected future returns of the business resulting from other factors than financial leverage. *See also* Financial risk.

Business valuation.
The act or process of determining the value of a business enterprise or ownership interest.

C

Capital asset pricing model (CAPM).
A stock or portfolio pricing model in which the cost of capital equals a risk-free rate plus a risk premium that is proportionate to the systematic risk of those stocks or portfolios.

Capital structure.
The makeup of the invested capital within a business enterprise; the mix of debt and equity financing.

Capitalization.
A conversion of economic benefits from a single period into value.

Capitalization factor.
A multiple or divisor used in converting anticipated economic benefits from a single period into value.

Capitalization of earnings method.
A method within the income approach in which economic benefits for a representative single period are converted to value by division using a capitalization rate.

Capitalization rate.
Any divisor (usually a percentage) used in converting anticipated economic benefits from a single period into value.

Cash flow.
Cash that is generated over a period of time by an asset, group of assets, or business enterprise. It may be used generally to encompass various levels of specifically defined cash flows. The term should be supplemented by a qualifier (for example, "discretionary" or "operating") and a definition for a particular valuation context.

Cash hoard.
Money that is not in a bank account or other readily verifiable location that the taxpayer alleges should be in the beginning cash balance.

Cash T.
An analysis of all of the cash received by the taxpayer and all of the cash spent by the taxpayer over a period of time. The theory of the cash T is that if a taxpayer's expenditures during a given year exceed reported income, and the source of the funds for such expenditures is unexplained, such excess amount represents unreported income.

Cert. den.
An appellate court's denial of a request for a writ of certiorari; a refusal by the appellate court to review a lower court's decision.

Cert. granted.
An appellate court's grant of a request for a writ of certiorari; an agreement by the appellate court to review a lower court's decision.

Chaffing.
An Internet-based methodology for sending hidden messages.

Channel stuffing.
Various schemes that stuff the distribution channel with revenue that may be fraudulent (e.g., bill-and-hold schemes).

Circumstantial evidence.
Evidence from which the truth or validity of an issue may be proved indirectly.

Class action.
A suit brought on behalf of a class of persons by one or more persons with claims that are typical of and fairly represent the claims.

Cloud computing.
Instead of placing software on each individual computer. Cloud computing puts all software and files on a webserver that is remotely accessed from the employee's work computer, but none of the application software or any files are stored on their work computer. Rather, they are stored somewhere in the Internet "cloud."

Coefficient of correlation (r).
A measure of the strength of the association between the dependent and the independent variable.

Coefficient of determination.
A measure of the amount of explained variance.

Coefficient of nondetermination.
The portion of the relationship between two variables that is not explained by the coefficient of determination.

Collateral estoppel.
The rule that a prior judgment in a case involving the same parties (or persons privy to those parties) bars retrial of issues decided in the prior judgment.

Common size statements.
Financial statements in which each line is expressed as a percentage of the total. On the balance sheet, each line item is shown as a percentage of total assets; on the income statement, as a percentage of sales.

Compensatory damages.
Damages to recompense an injured party for an injury and restore the injured party to his or her position prior to the injury.

Complaint.
The formal written pleading expressing a plaintiff's claim for relief and initiating a court action.

Computer forensics.
The procedures applied to computers and peripherals for gathering evidence that may be used in civil and criminal courts of law.

Concentration account.
A suspense account that banks use to temporarily commingle their funds until they are transferred out or otherwise assigned. See also Suspense account.

Concurring opinion.
A separate opinion by one or more judges that agrees with the court's ruling, but for a different reason.

Consequential damages.
Damages that do not result directly and immediately from an act but instead result from the consequences or results of that act.

Control.
The power to direct a business enterprise through management actions and policies.

Control premium.
An amount or a percentage reflecting the power of control by which the pro rata value of a controlling interest exceeds the pro rata value of a noncontrolling interest in a business enterprise.

Control risk.
The risk that a material error in the balance or transaction class will not be prevented or detected, which rises with weaknesses in the internal controls.

Correspondent banking.
A situation in which one bank provides services to another bank to move funds, exchange currencies, and access investment services such as money market accounts, overnight investment accounts, CDs, trading accounts, and computer software for making wire transfers and instant updates on account balances.

Cost approach.
A general means of determining an individual asset's value by quantifying the amount of money required to replace the future service capability of that asset.

Cost of capital.
The expected rate of return required by the market to attract funds for a particular investment.

Covenant.
A promise to do or not do something.

Cross-examination.
Questioning of a witness by the attorney for the opposing party.

Crowdfunding.
The new Jumpstart Our Business Startups Act signed in 2012 allows for companies to raise up to $1M in equity over the Internet on Securities and Exchange registered websites. The Act eliminates many of the previous legal safeguards on selling stock over the Internet.

Cut-off bank statement.
A bank balance report similar to a normal bank statement except that it covers a shorter period of time (10 to 20 days).

CUT

Cybersmear.
Bashing a stock, causing the stock price to decline.

D

Data mining.
A technique that uses mathematical algorithms to seek hidden patterns or associations in data.

Datagram.
Layers of computer information needed to verify the packet and get the information from the sender's to the receiver's locations following traffic control guidelines.

De facto.
In fact; actually.

De jure.
In law; lawful.

Debt-free.
The use of this term is discouraged. *See* Invested capital.

Demonstrative evidence.
Objects or documents (photos, videos, models, charts, etc.) that illustrate points of testimony but possess no probative intrinsic value.

Demurrer.
A defendant's allegation that the issues alleged in a complaint are insufficient to require the defendant to respond to them.

Denial of Service Attack.
A DOS is an attack that floods a target, usually a website, with so many data packets that the website is unusable and either has to shut down or crashes.

Deposition.
The testimony given under oath by a witness outside of court. The person deposed is the *deponent*.

Detection risk.
The risk that audit procedures will not turn up material error when it exists, which rises with smaller quantities and less competence of audit evidence.

Dictum.
(pl., dicta). A court's opinion that exceeds the facts before the court and does not bind subsequent courts as legal precedent.

Direct evidence.
Evidence that directly proves a fact at issue, without the need for any inference or presumption, usually based on personal knowledge of the witness.

Direct examination.
Questioning of a witness by the attorney for the party for whom the witness is testifying.

Discount for lack of control.
An amount or percentage deducted from the pro rata share of value of 100 percent equity interest in a business reflecting the absence of some or all powers of control.

Discount for lack of marketability.
An amount or percentage deducted from the value of an ownership interest reflecting the relative absence of marketability of the interest.

Discount for lack of voting rights.
An amount or percentage deducted from the per share value of a minority interest voting share to reflect the absence of voting rights of the shares.

Discount rate.
A rate of return used to convert a future sum into its present monetary value.

Discounted cash flow method.
A method within the income approach in which the present value of future expected net cash flows is determined using a discount rate.

Discounted future earnings method.
A method within the income approach in which the present value of future expected economic benefits is determined using a discount rate.

Discovery.
The pretrial process in which information from a party helps the other party prepare for trial.

Discovery sampling.
The use of random-number-generating software to select the checks or other items that an auditor is auditing.

Dissenting opinion.
A judge's opinion disagreeing with the majority decision of the judges.

Drill-down functionality.
A feature of software that enables financial managers and forensic accountants to go below the surface of a statement and uncover the source of any number and how it was calculated.

Dynamic IP address.
A changing IP address that is assigned to an Internet user each time he or she dials into the ISP connection with a dial phone connection.

E

Earnings management.
The purposeful intervention in the external financial reporting process, with the intent of obtaining some private gain.

Economic benefits.
Inflows such as revenues, net income, and net cash flows.

Economic life.
The time period during which property may generate economic benefits.

Effective date. See Valuation date.

Embezzlement.
The fraudulent appropriation of money or property lawfully in one's possession to be used personally by the embezzler. An embezzler steals from his or her employer.

Employee fraud.
The use of fraudulent means to take money or other property from an employer, usually involving some kind of falsification (e.g., false documents, lying, exceeding authority, or violating employer policies).

En banc.
The full court.

Enjoin.
To command or instruct with authority (e.g., a judge enjoins someone to do or not to take an action).

Enterprise. See Business enterprise.

Equity.
The owner's interest in property after all liabilities have been deducted.

Equity net cash flows.
The cash flows available to distribute to equity holders as dividends after funding operations of the business enterprise, making necessary capital investments, and increasing or decreasing debt financing.

Equity risk premium.
A rate of return added to the risk-free rate to reflect the additional risk of equity instruments compared with risk free instruments; a component of the cost of equity capital or equity discount rate.

Evidence.
The testimony, writings, and material objects offered in court to prove an alleged fact or proposition. *See also* Circumstantial evidence, Demonstrative evidence, *and* Direct evidence.

Excess earnings.
The amount of anticipated economic benefits exceeding an appropriate rate of return on the value of a selected asset base (commonly, net tangible assets) used to create those anticipated economic benefits.

Excess earnings method.
A specific way of determining a business valuation, business ownership interest, or security value by summing the value of the assets derived by capitalizing excess earnings and the value of the selected asset base. The method also is frequently used in valuing intangible assets. *See also* Excess earnings.

Exemplary damages.
Synonymous with punitive damages.

Expert report.
A written report prepared about a dispute by an expert witness.

Expert witness.
A person who, because of specialized training or experience, testifies in court to enable the judge or jurors to understand complicated and technical subjects.

F

Fact witness.
A witness who testifies as to facts.

Fair market value.
The price, expressed as cash equivalents, at which property would change hands between a hypothetical willing and able buyer and a hypothetical willing and able seller, acting at arm's length in an open, unrestricted market, when neither buyer or seller is under compulsion to buy or sell and when both parties have knowledge of the relevant facts. [Note: In Canada, "price" should be replaced with the term "highest price".]

Fairness opinion.
An opinion from a financial point of view about whether the consideration in a transaction is fair.

Fictitious receivables.
Payments due invented to cover a phony sale, which may eventually be written off.

Financial risk.
The degree of uncertainty of realizing expected future returns of the business resulting from financial leverage. *See* Business Risk.

Flags.
Computer data used to signal the connection state of the data exchange.

Forced liquidation value.
Liquidation value, at which the asset or assets are sold as quickly as possible, such as at an auction.

Foreign Corrupt Practices Act (FCPA).
Prohibits corrupt payments to foreign officials for the purpose of obtaining or keeping business.

Forensic.
An item used in debate or argument; items used in public debate or forum. In commerce or business, things forensic are generally ones that relate to a legal forum or court.

Forensic accounting.
The use of intelligence-gathering techniques and accounting/business skills to develop information and opinion for use by attorneys involved in civil litigation and give trial testimony if called upon; the action of identifying, recording, settling, extracting, sorting, reporting, and verifying past financial data or other accounting activities for settling current or prospective legal disputes or using such past financial data for projecting future financial data to settle legal disputes.

Free cash flow.
The use of this term is discouraged. *See* Net cash flow.

Full Faith and Credit Clause.
The U.S. Constitution clause that requires states to recognize other states' legislative acts and judicial decisions.

G

Going concern.
A currently ongoing and operating business enterprise.

Going concern value.
The value of a business enterprise that is expected to continue to operate into the future. The intangible elements of this value result from factors such as having an operational plant; trained staff; and the necessary licenses, systems, and procedures in place.

Goodwill.
That intangible asset created as a result of name, reputation, customer loyalty, location, product loyalty, and similar factors not separately identified.

Goodwill value.
The value of an asset that is attributable to goodwill.

Grand jury.
A panel of 16–23 sworn people, often retired people or people with flexible work schedules, that meets biweekly or monthly and hands down indictments when at least 12 votes favor them, without the prosecutor present. A grand jury has the power to accuse but not the power to convict.

Guideline public company method.
A method within the market approach in which market multiples are derived from market prices of shares of companies engaged in the same or similar lines of business, and that are actively traded in a free and open market.

H

Habeas corpus
(writ of). A writ requesting a court to release a prisoner from unlawful imprisonment.

Hacker.
An individual or group whose intent is to gain access to a computer network for malicious purposes.

Hearsay.
An out-of-court statement of another party offered during a court proceeding to prove the truth of the matter asserted.

High-low method.
An approach that identifies the highest and lowest costs, along with their related activity levels. The difference is calculated between the two costs and the two activity levels. The difference in costs is then divided by the difference in activity levels to determine an estimate of the variable cost per unit.

I

Impeachment of witness.
The attempt to cast doubt on the veracity of a witness through evidence that the witness is not trustworthy. An expert witness might be impeached by showing that he or she is unfamiliar with authoritative publications, has stated inconsistent opinions, or has shown bias.

Income (income-based) approach.
A general way of determining a business valuation, business ownership interest, security value, or worth of an intangible asset using one or more methods that convert anticipated economic benefits into a present single amount.

Intangible assets.
Nonphysical property such as franchises, trademarks, patents copyrights, goodwill, equities, mineral rights, securities, or contracts (as distinguished from physical assets) that grant rights and privileges, and possess value for the owner.

Intent or mens rea.
State of someone's mind.

Internal rate of return.
A discount rate at which the present value of the investment's future cash flows equals the cost of the investment.

Interrogation.
The process of questioning an individual suspected of being involved in a crime.

Interview.
The informal questioning of an individual.

Intrinsic value.
The value that an investor considers, after evaluation or consideration of available facts, to be the "true" or "real" value that will become the market value when other investors reach the same conclusion. When the term applies to options, it connotes the difference between the exercise price or strike price of an option and the market value of the underlying security.

Invested capital.
The sum of equity and debt in a business enterprise. Debt is typically all interest-bearing debt or long-term interest-bearing debt. The term should be supplemented by a specific definition in the given valuation context.

Invested capital net cash flows.
Those cash flows available to distribute to equity holders as dividends and debt investors as principal and interest after funding operations of the business enterprise and making necessary capital investments.

Investment risk.
The degree of investors' uncertainty about the realization of an investment's expected returns.

Investment value.
The value of an investment for a particular investor based on individual investment requirements and expectations. (Note: In Canada, the term used is "Value to the Owner".)

IP address.
A 32-bit number (four bytes) that identifies the sender and recipient who is sending or receiving a packet of information over the Internet. The IP address acts as the phone number for the Internet.

IPv6.
Version six is the new 64 bit protocol to be followed in assigning Internet addresses. It is replacing IPv4.

IRS Form 8300.
This is a form that must be filed with the IRS by businesses receiving more than $10,000 in cash on a sale of services or merchandise in a single transaction or a series of related transactions.

J

Judicial precedent.
A court decision establishing a legal principle that subsequently is followed in cases having similar or identical facts.

K

Key person discount.
An amount or percentage deducted from the value of an ownership interest that reflects the reduced value resulting from the actual or potential loss of a key person in a business enterprise.

Kiting.
Building up balances in bank accounts by floating checks drawn against similar accounts in other banks.

L

Land flip.
A situation in which a company decides to purchase land for a project, and a person or group finds the land and buys it using a front name or company. The fraudster then increases the price of the land before selling it to the company.

Lapping.
The recording of payment on a customer's account some time after the receipt of the payment, so that cash is taken to be covered with the receipt from another customer.

Larceny of cash.
The theft of cash after the cash has been recorded on the books, such as directly from a cash register or petty cash.

Law of the case.
The principle that, once an appellate court decides a legal issue, that decision will govern the case through subsequent appeals.

Layering transactions.
Creation of a set of complex transfers to disguise the original source for the money and to hide the audit trail.

Least squares regression line.
(Line of best fit.) The line that does the best job of minimizing the squared distance between the regression line and the individual data observations used in computing the regression line.

Levered beta.
The beta reflecting a capital structure, including debt.

Limited appraisal.
The act or process of determining a business valuation, business ownership interest, security value, or intangible asset worth with limitations in analyses, procedures, or scope.

Liquidated damages clause.
A contract clause that specifies a dollar amount that a party will pay if that party breaches the contract.

Liquidation value.
The net amount that would be realized if a business terminates and its assets are sold piecemeal. Liquidation can be either "orderly" or "forced."

Liquidity.
A property of an investment that enables it to be quickly converted to cash or payment for a liability.

Litigation services.
According to AICPA, services that involve pending or potential formal legal or regulatory proceedings before a trier of fact in connection with the resolution of a dispute between two or more parties.

Logs.
Logs are electronic records of the activities that have occurred within a program, a computer, or other electronic media.

M

Majority control.
The degree of control provided by a majority interest.

Majority interest.
An ownership interest greater than 50 percent but less than 100 percent of the voting interest in a business enterprise.

Mala prohibita.
An act or omission that is made criminal under a statute without proof of intent (mens rea).

Manipulation.
The falsification or alteration of accounting records or supporting documents from which financial statements are prepared.

Market (market-based) approach.
A general way of determining a business valuation, value of a business ownership interest, security price, or intangible asset's value by using one or more methods that compare the asset to similar (comparable) businesses, business ownership interests, securities, or intangible assets that have been sold.

Market capitalization of equity.
The amount determined by multiplying the share price of a publicly traded stock by the number of outstanding shares.

Market capitalization of invested capital.
The market capitalization of equity summed with the market value of the debt component of invested capital.

Market multiple.
The market value of a company's stock or invested capital divided by a company measure (e.g., economic benefits or number of customers).

Marketability.
The capacity to quickly convert property to cash at minimal cost.

Marketability discount. See Discount for lack of marketability.

Materiality.
The measure of whether something is significant enough to change an investor's investment decision.

Merger and acquisition method.
A method within the market approach in which pricing multiples are derived from transactions of significant interests in other companies engaged in the same or similar lines of business.

Message authentication codes (MACs).
Computer codes used to identify all real information in the packets, but only the recipient can separate the real packets from random packets using the authentication codes.

Message encapsulation.
A computer process in which each layer of information in the sent packet is interpreted by the same layer at the receiving end of the transmission. Additionally, each layer can only communicate with the one directly above or below it.

Midyear discounting.
A convention used in the discounted future earnings method that reflects economic benefits being generated at midyear by approximating the effect of economic benefits being generated evenly throughout the year.

Minority discount.
A discount for lack of control applied to the value of a minority interest.

Minority interest.
A business ownership interest of less than 50 percent of the voting interest.

Misappropriation.
Fraud; obtaining something of value or avoiding an obligation by deception.

Misrepresentation.
The intentional omission from the financial statements of events, transactions, or other significant information.

Mitigate.
To take actions to minimize the damages suffered.

Money laundering.
The use of techniques to take money coming from one source, hide that source, and make the funds available in another setting so that the funds can be used without incurring legal restrictions or penalties.

Motion.
A request to a court for a rule or order in the applicant's favor.

Motion in limine.
A pretrial motion requesting a court to prohibit opposing counsel from offering certain evidence.

Multiple.
The opposite of the capitalization rate.

N

Net book value.
The difference between total assets (net of accumulated depreciation, depletion, and amortization) and total liabilities as they appear on the balance sheet of a business enterprise.

Net cash flows.
A term used to describe income that should be supplemented by a qualifier. *See* Equity net cash flows *and* Invested capital net cash flows.

Net fraud.
A scheme to ensnare unsuspecting Internet users into giving up their resources to an online criminal.

Net present value.
The value of future cash inflows less all cash outflows (including the cost of investment) calculated as of a specified date using an appropriate discount rate.

Net tangible asset value.
The value of the tangible assets of a business enterprise (excluding excess assets and nonoperating assets) minus the value of its liabilities.

Nolo contendere.
A defendant's plea in a criminal case that does not admit or deny the charges but instead says that the defendant does not contest the charges; it has a similar legal effect to a guilty plea.

Nonoperating assets.
Assets unnecessary to the ongoing operations of a business enterprise. (Note: In Canada, the term used is "redundant assets").

Normalized earnings.
Economic benefits adjusted for nonrecurring, noneconomic, or other unusual items in order to eliminate anomalies (outliers) and/or facilitate comparisons.

Normalized financial statements.
Financial statements adjusted for nonoperating assets and liabilities and/or for nonrecurring, noneconomic, or other unusual items (outliers) in order to eliminate anomalies and/or facilitate comparisons.

O

Official Reporter.
A publication of court decisions that is sanctioned by statute, such as the United States Supreme Court Reports.

Opinion report.
A report by an expert, such as a valuation report, that is more subjective and relies more on the professional judgment of the expert than does a fact-oriented report.

Orderly liquidation value.
Liquidation value at which assets are sold over a reasonable period of time to maximize their proceeds.

OSI Model.
The Open Systems Interconnection Model is a communication system composed of seven protocol layers that allow different Internet platforms to interact with each other. The OSI Model allows Internet communications to be standardized.

Out-of-pocket loss.
Damages measured as the difference between the actual value received and the actual value conveyed.

Outliers.
Data that is not usual.

Overrule.
To reverse or invalidate.

P

Parol evidence.
Oral evidence.

Payable-through account.
A bank account enabling the respondent bank's clients within the country where the bank is registered to write checks that are drawn directly on the respondent bank's correspondent account in the United States.

Per curiam.
A decision reached by the whole court.

Pleadings.
The formal, written allegations of the parties in a suit--complaint and answer--expressing their respective claims and defenses.

Point estimates.
Single estimates made using regression parameters.

Portfolio discount.
A monetary amount or percentage deducted from the value of a business enterprise to reflect the fact that the enterprise owns dissimilar operations or assets that do not fit well together.

Predatory pricing.
The act of pricing a product so low that the only logical explanation is that the pricing is designed to drive competitors out of business.

Premise of value.
An assumption regarding the most likely set of transactional circumstances that may apply to the asset's valuation, such as going concern or liquidation.

Present value.
The value, as of a specified date, of future economic benefits and/or proceeds from sale, determined using an applicable discount rate.

Price/earnings multiple.
The price of a stock share divided by the stock's earnings per share.

Privileged communications.
Statements made between individuals within certain protected relationships (e.g., attorney–client, priest–penitent).

Pro se.
Appearing for oneself.

Productivity losses.
Business losses that arise from the reduction of efficient, "normal" production of work due to an event such as a cyber attack.

Protocols.
Those rules allowing different computer operating systems and machines to communicate with one another over the Internet.

Pump and dump.
A spam computer trading scheme causing thinly traded stock to move up rapidly in price, after which the perpetrator sells the stock at a huge gain.

Punitive damages.
Damages awarded in excess of actual damages sustained in order to punish reprehensible conduct and deter future wrongdoers.

Q

Qui tam suit.
A lawsuit filed by a whistle-blower under the Federal False Claims Act against a company or contractor on behalf of the federal government.

R

Rate of return.
An amount of an investment's income, loss, or change in value, either realized or anticipated, expressed as a percentage of that investment.

Ratio decidendi.
The reason for a ruling.

Real options.
Strategic options that include value placed on both the developmental costs and the option.

Rebutter.
A defendant's response to a plaintiff's surrejoinder.

Redirect examination.
Testimony in which the direct examiner gives the witness the opportunity to clear up any confusion that may have been caused by the cross-examination and complete any answers that the witness could not complete during cross-examination.

Redundant assets. See Nonoperating assets.

Regression or correlation analysis.
A statistical technique for measuring the nature and strength of the relationship between two variables.

Rejoinder.
A defendant's pleading in answer to a plaintiff's reply.

Remailers.
Services that send anonymous e-mail messages. The remailer strips away the mail headers from the original e-mail and substitutes its own mail headers to make the message untraceable.

Remand.
To return a case to a lower court for further consideration.

Replacement cost new.
The current cost of a similar new property that has the nearest equivalent use to the property being valued.

Reply.
A plaintiff's pleading that is required or permitted to respond to a defendant's setoff or counterclaim.

Report date.
The date stated conclusions are transmitted to a client.

Reproduction cost new.
The current cost of an identical new asset.

Required rate of return.
The minimum rate of return investors will accept before they will commit money to an investment having a given level of risk.

Residual value.
The value at the conclusion of the discrete projection period in a discounted future earnings model.

Residuum rule.
A rule (generally not upheld by the federal courts) that a decision by an administrative board may not be confirmed if it is supported solely by hearsay evidence.

Res ipsa loquitur.
The circumstantial evidence is overwhelming.

Res judicata.
The rule that a final judgment by a court of competent jurisdiction on the merits of a case is conclusive as to the rights and facts at issue that bars any subsequent action involving the same cause of action brought by the same parties (or persons privy to those parties).

Respondent.
The person against whom an appeal is made to a higher court.

Return on equity.
A percentage amount earned on a company's common equity for a given period.

Return on investment. See Return on invested capital and Return on equity.

Return on invested capital.
A percentage amount earned on a company's total capital for a given period.

Reverse (rev'd; rev'g).
To set aside or reject a decision of a lower court.

RICO laws.
(Racketeer Influenced and Corrupt Organization laws) Laws designed to control illegal acts by organized crime.

Risk premium.
A rate of return added to a risk-free rate to incorporate the degree of risk.

Risk-free rate.
The rate of return the market makes available for an investment that is free of default risk.

Rule of thumb.
A mathematical formula developed from the relationship between price and certain variables based on experience, observation, hearsay, or a combination of such factors, usually industry specific.

Rules of evidence.
In a legal action, the rules governing the admissibility of evidence and the weight that evidence is given.

S

Scanner.
As used here, a scanner is a port scanner like Nmap. It is used to identify activity on the ports of a web server.

Scienter.
The guilty knowledge of the defendant.

Shell banks.
High-risk banks that exist without any physical presence in any legal jurisdiction.

Shell company.
A company formed that has no any real business operations. In many cases, it is used as a conduit for transferring money or hiding and obscuring accounting transactions.

Shodan (http://www.shodanhq.com).
The Shodan search engine interrogates the ports on webservers to determine the locations and character of specific equipment and software tied to the Internet. Attackers use it to find vulnerable networks.

Skimming.
An "off-book" technique to remove cash before a company records the receipts.

Side agreement.
After a business enters into an arrangement, there may be an oral or written agreement that allows important changes.

Smurfing.
A money laundering technique in which confederates of the money launderer deposit random amounts of less than $10,000 into variously named accounts at a number of different banks. Due diligence procedures such as CTR and SAR filings usually are not triggered by such transactions.

Sniffer.
A program used to secretly capture datagrams moving across a network and disclose the information contained in the datagram's network protocols. Sniffers are used to analyze the data packets traveling across a network. The data is captured by the sniffer for later analysis. It is not a port scanner.

Social engineering.
Any technique that is used to deceive an employee into revealing a password or access code.

Source and application of funds method.
(Also called the *expenditure method*) a technique approved for IRS use by the Supreme Court in 1942 that shows increases and decreases in a taxpayer's accounts at the end of the year.

Special interest purchasers.
Acquirers who believe they can attain postacquisition economies of scale, synergies, or strategic advantages by combining the purchased business interest with their own.

Special master.
A court-appointed representative of the court.

Spoofing.
The misappropriation of one's identity when the entity whose identity is stolen does not know misappropriation has occurred. On the Internet, one purpose of the spoof is to gain unauthorized access to a network by assuming the identity of a trusted site.

Standard error of the estimate.
A measure indicating the variability of the data used in regression calculations.

Standard of value.
The identification of the type of value that is used within a specific engagement, such as fair market value, fair value, or investment value.

Stare decisis.
The policy of courts to adhere to legal principles that are established by other courts.

Static IP address.
An Internet address that does not change, usually given to a user who is continually connected to the Internet with a cable modem.

Steganography.
A technique for hiding an unencrypted computer file in a digital photo or wave file.

Stipulation.
A voluntary agreement between opposing parties in an action concerning the disposition of certain points and/or facts to avoid the need for proof or to narrow the issues under consideration.

Subpoena.
A command presented to a witness to appear at a specified time and place in order to testify.

Subpoena ad testificandum.
A command presented to a witness to appear at a specified time and place in order to testify; a technical term for an ordinary subpoena.

Subpoena duces tecum.
A command to produce specified documents or other items to the court.

Summary judgment.
A judge's disposition of a controversy without a trial when there is no dispute about a material fact and the case involves only a question of law.

Surrebutter.
A plaintiff's reply to a defendant's rebutter.

Surrejoinder.
The plaintiff's response to a defendant's rejoinder.

Suspense account.
A temporary ledger account that can be used to "store" dollar amounts until the organization decides how to record the transaction. The balance in the account is closed prior to preparing the financial statements and its use is never disclosed.

Sustaining capital reinvestment.
The periodic outlay of funds required to maintain business operations at existing levels, net of the tax shield available from such monetary outlays.

Systematic risk.
The risk common to all risky securities that cannot be eliminated through diversification. For stock, systematic risk is measured using the beta coefficient.

T

Tangible assets.
Physical assets (such as cash, accounts receivable, inventory, property, and plant and equipment).

Terminal value. See Residual value.

Time to live (TTL).
The time a datagram is allowed to be active on the Internet.

Tort.
A private wrong or injury committed upon a person or property independent of contract.

Transaction method. See Merger and acquisition method.

Trier of fact.
Per AICPA, a court, regulatory body, or government authority; its agents; a grand jury; or an arbitrator or mediator of a dispute.

Trust.
A legal relationship that is established by one person when assets have been placed under the control of another person for the benefit of the beneficiary for a specific purpose.

U

Unlevered beta.
The beta reflecting a capital structure not having debt.

Unsystematic risk.
The risk specific to an individual security that diversification can avoid.

V

Valuation.
The process of determining the worth of a business, business ownership interest, security, or intangible asset.

Valuation approach.

A general way of calculating a value indication of a business, business ownership interest, security, or intangible asset that uses one or more valuation methods.

Valuation date.

The specific point in time as of which the valuator's report of value applies (also referred to as *effective date* or *appraisal date*).

Valuation method.

Within valuation approaches, a specific way of determining an asset's value.

Valuation procedure.

The act, manner, and technique of completing steps of an appraisal method.

Valuation ratio.

A fraction in which the numerator is a value or price and the denominator is financial, operating, or physical data.

Value to the owner. See Investment value.

Venue.

The specific county in which a court will hear and decide a case.

Vertical analysis.

The approach, often referred to as common-size statements, that presents every item in a statement as a percentage of the largest item in the statement.

Voir dire examination.

The preliminary questioning by an attorney (or court) of juror candidates (or expert witness) to determine whether they are qualified to serve as jurors.

Voting control.

De jure control of a business enterprise.

W

Wardialer.

A downloadable software program that allows a modem attacker to rapidly dial and check all phone numbers within a given range.

Wardriving.

Wardriving got its name from the procedure used to identify WiFi networks from a moving vehicle. Once identified, these wireless networks can be accessed without authorization.

Washing checks.

Chemically removing the payee and the amount from checks in order to substitute another payee or amount.

Weighted average cost of capital (WACC).

The cost of capital (discount rate) determined by the weighted average, using market value, of the cost of all financing sources in the business enterprise's capital structure.

Work product rule.

Rule that protects personal memoranda, written statements of witnesses, and other materials prepared by an attorney in anticipation of litigation from disclosure to other parties involved in litigation. The work product rule was developed to prevent an attorney's work product from being used against a client and undermining the attorney–client privilege.

Writ of certiorari.

An appellate court's order requiring a lower court to certify the record and send it for review by the higher court.

Z

Zipf's Law.

A natural phenomena that uses the frequency distribution of words as a means of identifying anomalies that may be an indication of fraud risks. Similar to Benford's Law.

Zone transfer.

A request for a zone transfer will provide all the connectivity information that is available about a domain name. Zone transfers allow for updated connectivity information about new web hosts being added to a network or the Internet. A zone transfer provides a blueprint on the trusted IP addresses used by a website

Topical Index

All references are to paragraph (¶) numbers.

References are to paragraph (¶) numbers

References are to paragraph (¶) numbers

B

Backdoor entry created for unauthorized computer system access...15,021

Balance sheet accounts
manipulation of...4151
reserve estimates for...4171

Balance sheet approach, net worth method as indirect...6061

Balance sheet valuation methods...17,211

Balance sheets, actual and common sized...17,111

Bank accounts, paying to use other people's...5061

Bank deposit method of reconstructing income...6071

Bank deposit slips, lapping uncovered by comparing customer credits with...5041

Bank deposits
direct deposits to minimize employee fraud with...5061
employee fraud in misappropriating...5031
kiting involving large...5031
online account information to track...5031

Bank fraud as type of net fraud cybercrime...15,001

Bank of Credit and Commerce International, The, money laundering in...7141

Bank personnel filings of SARs and CTRs...7041

Bank reports
as difficult to falsify...7091
identification of money laundering schemes through...7091

Bank Secrecy Act, CTR rules under...7091

Bank statements
cut-off...5031
revealing check tampering schemes by reconciling...5031

Banking institutions
due diligence laws for...7051
identity confirmations by...7101
tools used for uncovering money laundering by...7041

Bankruptcies
business valuations in cases of...17,041
governmental...5111

Baptist Foundation of Arizona (BFA), employee fraud at...5091

Barter deals, revenues increased using...4191

Bearer shares, formation of company using...7111

Before-and-after lost profits method...10,061

Behavioral approaches...4236

Beneficiaries of trust, letters of confirmation proving...7121

Benefit-of-the-bargain damages approach...10,051

Benford's Law analysis to identify fraud...9121

Best evidence (original writing) rule...9071

Beta software destruction as example of real options...16,031

Big bath of write-offs directly against earnings...4141

Bid rigging
in construction projects...6081
operation and detection of...5061

Bill-and-hold transactions, fraudulent...3021

Binomial tree to map changes in future profits...16,031

Birth certificate database searches...14,071

Black's Law Dictionary, fraud as defined by...4001

Board of directors' role in financial fraud detection...4026; 14,065

Book value as valuation measure in cost approach...17,071

Borrowing against accounts receivable...5041

Bots (robots), websites searched by...15,031

Brainstorming
by audit team about fraud during audit process...4005; 4041
types of...4041

Breach of contract
civil trials for, study of...8001
by expert witnesses...8221
as type of harm...10,031

Bribes
global examples of...6081
in bid rigging...5061
money laundering for...7021

Budget deficit, governmental...5111

Bulletin boards, staff assigned to monitor Internet...5061

Business associations used by money launderers...7101

Business damages
commercial. See Commercial damages
methodologies for measuring...17,041
three outcomes of...10,091

Business ethics policy, sample...5071

Business expenses, reimbursement of nonexistent, as type of misappropriation of assets by employees...5021

Business options, loss of, as intangible loss...16,031

Business records exception from hearsay rule...9051

Business risk, fraud and assessment of company's...5071

Business valuations...17,001–17,301
accreditations for practitioners preparing...17,001
conflicts giving rise to...17,021
data collection and analysis for...17,261
data required for, discerning...17,091
disputed...17,211
engagement agreement for...17,011
expert witnesses in court examining appraisal for...17,021
financial analysis in...17,101–17,181
fundamentals of...17,001–17,041
gathering initial information for...17,081–17,091
illustration of process of...17,191–17,221
methodology considered and selection for...17,261; 17,291
publications helpful for...17,091
purposes for obtaining...17,021; 17,041
report of. See Valuation report
rules of thumb used in...17,221
size of ownership interest as affecting final value in...17,031
standards of professional appraisal applied to...17,231–17,261

References are to paragraph (¶) numbers

References are to paragraph (¶) numbers

Clearing House for Interbank Payments System (CHIPS)...**7091**

Client information for business valuation, requesting...**17,091**

Closely held businesses, valuation of...**17,211**

Closely held stocks, valuation of...**17,041**

Cluster analysis...**13,061**

"Code Red" virus, losses from...**16,001**

Coefficient of correlation...**11,041**

Coefficient of determination...**11,041**

Coefficient of nondetermination...**11,041**

Cohen Commission. See Treadway Commission

College curricula in forensic accounting...**2001–2021**

Collusion
    discovery of...2041
    in inventory fraud...5051
    in money laundering schemes by purchasing department employees...5061

Combination method in lost profits calculation...**10,061**

Commercial damages...**10,001–10,231**
    after-trial, discounting...10,091; 10,221
    amounts of awards and settlements in major cases of...10,061
    analyses used in projecting...10,081
    approaches to estimating...10,051–10,081
    basics of litigation for...10,021–10,041
    components of...10,101; 10,121
    damages period for...10,221
    defendant's estimate of, example of calculations for...10,111
    expert report for, defending...10,181
    expert report for, sample...10,161
    expert witnesses for cases of...10,001–10,011
    forensic analyses in...10,041
    measuring loss for...10,091–10,161
    plaintiff's estimate of, example of components in...10,121–10,151
    proof required to win...10,021
    recovery rules for...10,091
    types of...10,041

Commercial measures in employee fraud prevention...**5081**

Commissions, fictitious sales to pump up salesperson's...**5061**

Committee on Sponsoring Organizations (COSO)
    comprehensive risk assessment...5071
    listing of internal control variables...4031
    overview...1131

Company susceptibility to employee fraud...**5001**

Company-specific analysis in damages projections...**10,081**

Comparables in land valuations...**5061**

Compensation packages of CEOs, correlation of SEC indictments and...**4191**

Computer access, unauthorized...**15,021**

Computer and Security Survey, financial losses and incidence of security breaches described in...**16,001**

Computer Assisted Audit Tools (CAATs), auditor's use of...**13,041**

Computer crimes, listing by state of statutes pertaining to...**15,071**

Computer data. See also Cyber attacks, Cybercrime, and Electronic evidence
    copying files from outside media as...13,041
    recovery of deleted...13,061
    seizure of...13,051–13,061
    virtual presence of cybercriminal gaining unauthorized access to...15,031

Computer forensics...**9131; 13,001–13,071.** See also Electronic evidence
    auditor's job for...13,011
    auditor's skill set for...13,031
    data mining combined with...13,061

Confidential client information, use by expert witnesses of...**8041; 8131**

Conflicts of interest of accountants performing litigation services...**8041–8051**

Consultant, accountant's litigation services as...**8011; 9041**

Consulting fees for independent forensic accounting contractors...**2031**

Continuous monitoring...**5126**

Contract fraud...**6081**

Contractor disputes with government under Federal False Claims Act...**11,061**

Control of Business Information Technology (COBIT) model...**13,011**

Control risk inversely correlated with strength of internal controls...**4005**

Controlling interest, valuation of 100 percent...**17,031**

Converse Technology, stock options fraud at...**14,065**

Cookie-jar accounting using reserves...**4171**

Cooper, Cynthia, discovery of WorldCom's questionable transfers in capital accounts by...**4011**

Corporate investigation...**1131**

Correlation analysis...**11,041**

Correspondent bank accounts, MLAA regulations for...**7151**

Correspondent banking...**7031; 7091**

Corruption Perception Index (CPI)...**3001**

Corruption risks...**3061**

COSO cube...**4031**

COSO report, Fraudulent Financial Reporting: 1987–1997...**4011**

COSO report, fraudulent financial reporting (1998–2007)...**3011**
    internal control framework developed in...13,001
    motives for fraud listed in...3041

Cost analysis in defense against predatory pricing claim...**11,051**

Cost behavior
    assumptions about, relevant range and time...10,211
    defined...10,191
    types of, common...10,201
    ways of estimating...10,211

Cost behavior estimates, basis of...**10,211**

Cost behavior patterns, estimating...**10,211; 11,031–11,041**

Cost increases factored into damages calculations, material, labor, shipping, and advertising...**10,141**

References are to paragraph (¶) numbers

References are to paragraph (¶) numbers

References are to paragraph (¶) numbers

References are to paragraph (¶) numbers

References are to paragraph (¶) numbers

References are to paragraph (¶) numbers

References are to paragraph (¶) numbers

References are to paragraph (¶) numbers

References are to paragraph (¶) numbers

References are to paragraph (¶) numbers

References are to paragraph (¶) numbers

References are to paragraph (¶) numbers

References are to paragraph (¶) numbers

S

References are to paragraph (¶) numbers

References are to paragraph (¶) numbers

References are to paragraph (¶) numbers

References are to paragraph (¶) numbers

References are to paragraph (¶) numbers